CHILTON®

CHRYSLER
SERVICE MANUAL
2008 EDITION
VOLUME I

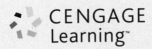
CENGAGE
Learning™

Australia • Brazil • Japan • Korea • Mexico • Singapore • Spain • United Kingdom • United States

CHILTON®
Chrysler Service Manual
2008 Edition
Volume I

Vice President,
Technology Professional Business Unit:
Gregory L. Clayton

Publisher,
Technology Professional Business Unit:
David Koontz

Director of Marketing:
Beth A. Lutz

Production Director:
Patty Stephan

Editorial Assistant:
Jason Yager

Production Manager:
Andrew Crouth

Marketing Specialist:
Jennifer Stall

Marketing Assistant:
Rachael Conover

Publishing Coordinator:
Paula Baillie

Sr. Content Project Manager:
Elizabeth C. Hough

Managing Editor:
Terry L. Blomquist

Editors:
Nick D'Andrea
Eugene F. Hannon Jr.
Will Kesseler
David G. Olson
Christine Sheeky
Jon Wallace

Graphical Designer:
Melinda Possinger

For more information contact:
Cengage Learning
Executive Woods
5 Maxwell Drive, PO Box 8007,
Clifton Park, NY 12065-8007
Visit us at **www.chiltonsonline.com**
For more learning solutions, visit **www.cengage.com**
For permission to use material from
the text or product, contact us by
Tel. (800) 730-2214
Fax (800) 730-2215
www.cengage.com/permissions

Cengage Learning products are represented in Canada by Nelson Education, Ltd.

ISBN10: 1-4283-2205-1
ISSN 13: 978-14283-2205-9
ISSN: 1939-621X

NOTICE TO THE READER

Publisher does not warrant or guarantee any of the products described herein or perform any independent analysis in connection with any of the product information contained herein. Publisher does not assume, and expressly disclaims, any obligation to obtain and include information other than that provided to it by the manufacturer.

The reader is expressly warned to consider and adopt all safety precautions that might be indicated by the activities herein and to avoid all potential hazards. By following the instructions contained herein, the reader willingly assumes all risks in connection with such instructions.

The publisher makes no representation or warranties of any kind, including but not limited to, the warranties of fitness for particular purpose or merchantability, nor are any such representations implied with respect to the material set forth herein, and the publisher takes no responsibility with respect to such material. The publisher shall not be liable for any special, consequential, or exemplary damages resulting, in whole or part, from the readers' use of, or reliance upon, this material.

Printed in the United States of America
1 2 3 4 5 xx12 11 10 09 08 07

Table of Contents

Model Index

USING THIS INFORMATION

Organization

To find where a particular model section or procedure is located, look in the Table of Contents. Main topics are listed with the page number on which they may be found. Following the main topics is an alphabetical listing of all of the procedures within the section and their page numbers.

Manufacturer and Model Coverage

This product covers 2005–2008 Chrysler models that are produced in sufficient quantities to warrant coverage, and which have technical content available from the vehicle manufacturers before our publication date. Although this information is as complete as possible at the time of publication, some manufacturers may make changes which cannot be included here. While striving for total accuracy, the publisher cannot assume responsibility for any errors, changes, or omissions that may occur in the compilation of this data.

Part Numbers & Special Tools

Part numbers and special tools are recommended by the publisher and vehicle manufacturer to perform specific jobs. Before substituting any part or tool for the one recommended, you must be completely satisfied that neither your personal safety, nor the performance of the vehicle will be endangered.

ACKNOWLEDGEMENT

The publisher would like to express appreciation to Chrysler LLC for its assistance in producing this publication. No further reproduction or distribution of the material in this manual is allowed without the expressed written permission of Chrysler LLC and the publisher.

PRECAUTIONS

Before servicing any vehicle, please be sure to read all of the following precautions, which deal with personal safety, prevention of component damage, and important points to take into consideration when servicing a motor vehicle:

- Always wear safety glasses or goggles when drilling, cutting, grinding or prying.
- Steel-toed work shoes should be worn when working with heavy parts. Pockets should not be used for carrying tools. A slip or fall can drive a screwdriver into your body.
- Work surfaces, including tools and the floor should be kept clean of grease, oil or other slippery material.
- When working around moving parts, don't wear loose clothing. Long hair should be tied back under a hat or cap, or in a hair net.
- Always use tools only for the purpose for which they were designed. Never pry with a screwdriver.
- Keep a fire extinguisher and first aid kit handy.
- Always properly support the vehicle with approved stands or lift.
- Always have adequate ventilation when working with chemicals or hazardous material.
- Carbon monoxide is colorless, odorless and dangerous. If it is necessary to operate the engine with vehicle in a closed area such as a garage, always use an exhaust collector to vent the exhaust gases outside the closed area.
- When draining coolant, keep in mind that small children and some pets are attracted by ethylene glycol antifreeze, and

are quite likely to drink any left in an open container, or in puddles on the ground. This will prove fatal in sufficient quantity. Always drain the coolant into a sealable container.

- To avoid personal injury, do not remove the coolant pressure relief cap while the engine is operating or hot. The cooling system is under pressure; steam and hot liquid can come out forcefully when the cap is loosened slightly. Failure to follow these instructions may result in personal injury. The coolant must be recovered in a suitable, clean container for reuse. If the coolant is contaminated it must be recycled or disposed of correctly.
- When carrying out maintenance on the starting system be aware that heavy gauge leads are connected directly to the battery. Make sure the protective caps are in place when maintenance is completed. Failure to follow these instructions may result in personal injury.
- Do not remove any part of the engine emission control system. Operating the engine without the engine emission control system will reduce fuel economy and engine ventilation. This will weaken engine performance and shorten engine life. It is also a violation of Federal law.
- Due to environmental concerns, when the air conditioning system is drained, the refrigerant must be collected using refrigerant recovery/recycling equipment. Federal law requires that refrigerant be recovered into appropriate recovery equipment and the process be conducted by qualified technicians who have been certified by an approved organization, such as MACS, ASI,

etc. Use of a recovery machine dedicated to the appropriate refrigerant is necessary to reduce the possibility of oil and refrigerant incompatibility concerns. Refer to the instructions provided by the equipment manufacturer when removing refrigerant from or charging the air conditioning system.

- Always disconnect the battery ground when working on or around the electrical system.
- Batteries contain sulfuric acid. Avoid contact with skin, eyes, or clothing. Also, shield your eyes when working near batteries to protect against possible splashing of the acid solution. In case of acid contact with skin or eyes, flush immediately with water for a minimum of 15 minutes and get prompt medical attention. If acid is swallowed, call a physician immediately. Failure to follow these instructions may result in personal injury.
- Batteries normally produce explosive gases. Therefore, do not allow flames, sparks or lighted substances to come near the battery. When charging or working near a battery, always shield your face and protect your eyes. Always provide ventilation. Failure to follow these instructions may result in personal injury.
- When lifting a battery, excessive pressure on the end walls could cause acid to spew through the vent caps, resulting in personal injury, damage to the vehicle or battery. Lift with a battery carrier or with your hands on opposite corners. Failure to follow these instructions may result in personal injury.
- Observe all applicable safety precautions when working around fuel. Whenever

servicing the fuel system, always work in a well-ventilated area. Do not allow fuel spray or vapors to come in contact with a spark, open flame, or excessive heat (a hot drop light, for example). Keep a dry chemical fire extinguisher near the work area. Always keep fuel in a container specifically designed for fuel storage; also, always properly seal fuel containers to avoid the possibility of fire or explosion. Do not smoke or carry lighted tobacco or open flame of any type when working on or near any fuel-related components.

• Fuel injection systems often remain pressurized, even after the engine has been turned OFF. The fuel system pressure must be relieved before disconnecting any fuel lines. Failure to do so may result in fire and/or personal injury.

• The evaporative emissions system contains fuel vapor and condensed fuel vapor. Although not present in large quantities, it still presents the danger of explosion or fire. Disconnect the battery ground cable from the battery to minimize the possibility of an electrical spark occurring, possibly causing a fire or explosion if fuel vapor or liquid fuel is present in the area. Failure to follow these instructions can result in personal injury.

• The EPA warns that prolonged contact with used engine oil may cause a number of skin disorders, including cancer! You should make every effort to minimize your exposure to used engine oil. Protective gloves should be worn when changing oil. Wash your hands and any other exposed skin areas as soon as possible after exposure to used engine oil. Soap and water, or waterless hand cleaner should be used.

• Some vehicles are equipped with an air bag system, often referred to as a Supple-mental Restraint System (SRS) or Supple-mental Inflatable Restraint (SIR) system. The system must be disabled before performing service on or around system components, steering column, instrument panel components, wiring and sensors. Failure to follow safety and disabling procedures could result in accidental air bag deployment, possible personal injury and unnecessary system repairs.

• Always wear safety goggles when working with, or around, the air bag system. When carrying a non-deployed air bag, be sure the bag and trim cover are pointed away from your body. When placing a non-deployed air bag on a work surface, always face the bag and trim cover upward, away from the surface. This will reduce the motion of the module if it is accidentally deployed.

• Electronic modules are sensitive to electrical charges. The ABS module can be damaged if exposed to these charges.

• Brake pads and shoes may contain asbestos, which has been determined to be a cancer-causing agent. Never clean brake surfaces with compressed air. Avoid inhaling brake dust. Clean all brake surfaces with a commercially available brake cleaning fluid.

• When replacing brake pads, shoes, discs or drums, replace them as complete axle sets.

• When servicing drum brakes, disassemble and assemble one side at a time, leaving the remaining side intact for reference.

• Brake fluid often contains polyglycol ethers and polyglycols. Avoid contact with the eyes and wash your hands thoroughly after handling brake fluid. If you do get brake fluid in your eyes, flush your eyes with clean, running water for 15 minutes. If eye irritation persists, or if you have taken brake fluid internally, immediately seek medical assistance.

• Clean, high quality brake fluid from a sealed container is essential to the safe and proper operation of the brake system. You should always buy the correct type of brake fluid for your vehicle. If the brake fluid becomes contaminated, completely flush the system with new fluid. Never reuse any brake fluid. Any brake fluid that is removed from the system should be discarded. Also, do not allow any brake fluid to come in contact with a painted or plastic surface; it will damage the paint.

• Never operate the engine without the proper amount and type of engine oil; doing so will result in severe engine damage.

• Timing belt maintenance is extremely important! Many models utilize an interference-type, non-freewheeling engine. If the timing belt breaks, the valves in the cylinder head may strike the pistons, causing potentially serious (also time-consuming and expensive) engine damage.

• Disconnecting the negative battery cable on some vehicles may interfere with the functions of the on-board computer system (s) and may require the computer to undergo a relearning process once the negative battery cable is reconnected.

• Steering and suspension fasteners are critical parts because they affect performance of vital components and systems and their failure can result in major service expense. They must be replaced with the same grade or part number or an equivalent part if replacement is necessary. Do not use a replacement part of lesser quality or substitute design. Torque values must be used as specified during reassembly to ensure proper retention of these parts.

CHRYSLER AND DODGE

300 • 300C • Charger • Magnum

1

SPECIFICATIONS AND MAINTENANCE CHARTS

ENGINE AND VEHICLE IDENTIFICATION

	Engine							Model Year	
Code ①	Liters (cc)	Cu. In.	Cyl.	Fuel Sys.	Engine Type	Eng. Mfg.		Code ②	Year
R	2.7 (2736)	167	6	SMFI	DOHC	DaimlerChrysler		5	2005
T	2.7 (2736)	167	6	SMFI	DOHC	DaimlerChrysler		6	2006
G	3.5 (3507)	214	6	SMFI	SOHC	DaimlerChrysler		7	2007
V	3.5 (3507)	214	6	SMFI	SOHC	DaimlerChrysler		8	2008
H	5.7 (5654)	345	8	SMFI	OHV	DaimlerChrysler			
2	5.7 (5654)	345	8	SMFI	OHV	DaimlerChrysler			

SMFI: Sequential Multi-port Fuel Injection

① 8th position of VIN

② 10th position of VIN

22043_300C_C0001

GENERAL ENGINE SPECIFICATIONS

Year	Model	Engine Displacement Liters	Engine Series VIN	Net Horsepower @ rpm	Net Torque @ rpm (ft. lbs.)	Bore x Stroke (in.)	Compression Ratio	Oil Pressure @ rpm
2005	300, 300C, Magnum	2.7	R	190@6400	190@4000	3.386x3.091	9.67:1	45-105@3000
		3.5	G	250@6400	250@3800	3.780x3.189	10:01	45-105@3000
		5.7	H	340@5000	390@4000	3.910x3.580	9.6:1	25-110@3000
2006	300, 300C, Charger Magnum	2.7	R, T	190@6400	190@4000	3.386x3.091	9.67:1	45-105@3000
		3.5	G, V	250@6400	250@3800	3.780x3.189	10:01	45-105@3000
		5.7	H, 2	340@5000	390@4000	3.910x3.580	9.6:1	25-110@3000
2007	300, 300C, Charger Magnum	2.7	R, T	190@6400	190@4000	3.386x3.091	9.67:1	45-105@3000
		3.5	G, V	250@6400	250@3800	3.780x3.189	10:01	45-105@3000
		5.7	H, 2	340@5000	390@4000	3.910x3.580	9.6:1	25-110@3000
2008	300, 300C, Charger Magnum	2.7	R, T	190@6400	190@4000	3.386x3.091	9.67:1	45-105@3000
		3.5	G, V	250@6400	250@3800	3.780x3.189	10:01	45-105@3000
		5.7	H, 2	340@5000	390@4000	3.910x3.580	9.6:1	25-110@3000

22043_300C_C0002

GASOLINE ENGINE TUNE-UP SPECIFICATIONS

Year	Engine Displacement Liters	Engine VIN	Spark Plug Gap (in.)	Ignition Timing (deg.)	Fuel Pump (psi)	Idle Speed (rpm)	Valve Clearance	
							Intake	Exhaust
2005	2.7	R	0.048-0.058	①	53-63	②	HYD	HYD
	3.5	G	0.048-0.058	①	53-63	②	HYD	HYD
	5.7	H	0.045	①	53-63	②	HYD	HYD
2006	2.7	R	0.048-0.058	①	53-63	②	HYD	HYD
	3.5	G	0.048-0.058	①	53-63	②	HYD	HYD
	5.7	H	0.045	①	53-63	②	HYD	HYD
2007	2.7	R	0.048-0.058	①	53-63	②	HYD	HYD
	3.5	G	0.048-0.058	①	53-63	②	HYD	HYD
	5.7	H	0.045	①	53-63	②	HYD	HYD
2008	2.7	R	0.048-0.058	①	53-63	②	HYD	HYD
	3.5	G	0.048-0.058	①	53-63	②	HYD	HYD
	5.7	H	0.045	①	53-63	②	HYD	HYD

NOTE: The Vehicle Emission Control Information (VECI) label often reflects specification changes made during production.

The label figures must be used if they differ from those in this chart.

HYD: Hydraulic

① Ignition timing is controlled by the PCM and is not adjustable.

② Idle speed is controlled by the PCM and is not adjustable

22043_300C_C0003

CAPACITIES

Year	Engine Displacement Liters	Engine VIN	Engine Oil with Filter (qts.)	Transmission pts. ①	Transfer Case (pts.)	Front Axle (pts.)	Rear Axle (pts.)	Fuel Tank (gal.)	Cooling System (qts.)
2005	2.7	R	6.0	②	1.3	1.26	③	18.0	9.7
	3.5	G	6.0	②	1.3	1.26	③	18.0	10.6
	5.7	H	7.0	②	1.3	1.26	③	19.0	14.6
2006	2.7	R, T	6.0	②	1.3	1.26	③	18.0	9.7
	3.5	G, V	6.0	②	1.3	1.26	③	18.0	10.6
	5.7	H, 2	7.0	②	1.3	1.26	③	19.0	14.6
2007	2.7	R, T	6.0	②	1.3	1.26	③	18.0	9.7
	3.5	G, V	6.0	②	1.3	1.26	③	18.0	10.6
	5.7	H, 2	7.0	②	1.3	1.26	③	19.0	14.6
2008	2.7	R, T	6.0	②	1.3	1.26	③	18.0	9.7
	3.5	G, V	6.0	②	1.3	1.26	③	18.0	10.6
	5.7	H, 2	7.0	②	1.3	1.26	③	19.0	14.6

NOTE: All capacities are approximate. Add fluid gradually and check to be sure a proper fluid level is obtained.

① For fluid drain and filter replacement only.

② NAG1: 10.6 pts.

  42RLE: 8.0 pts.

③ 198mm axle: 3.0 pts.

  210 and 215mm axle: 3.4 pts.

22043_300C_C0004

FLUID SPECIFICATIONS

Year	Model	Engine Displacement Liters (cc)	Engine ID/VIN	Engine Oil	Auto. Trans.	Drive Axle ①	Transfer Case	Power Steering Fluid	Brake Master Cylinder	Engine Coolant
2005	300, 300C, Magnum	2.7 (2736)	R	5W-20	ATF+4	75W-90	②	ATF+4	DOT 3	Mopar® (HOAT)
		3.5 (3507)	G	10W-30	ATF+4	75W-90	②	ATF+4	DOT 3	Mopar® (HOAT)
		5.7 (5654)	H	5W-20	ATF+4	75W-90	②	ATF+4	DOT 3	Mopar® (HOAT)
2006	300, 300C, Charger, Magnum	2.7 (2736)	R, T	5W-20	ATF+4	75W-90	②	ATF+4	DOT 3	Mopar® (HOAT)
		3.5 (3507)	G, V	10W-30	ATF+4	75W-90	②	ATF+4	DOT 3	Mopar® (HOAT)
		5.7 (5654)	H, 2	5W-20	ATF+4	75W-90	②	ATF+4	DOT 3	Mopar® (HOAT)
2007	300, 300C, Charger, Magnum	2.7 (2736)	R, T	5W-20	ATF+4	75W-90	②	ATF+4	DOT 3	Mopar® (HOAT)
		3.5 (3507)	G, V	10W-30	ATF+4	75W-90	②	ATF+4	DOT 3	Mopar® (HOAT)
		5.7 (5654)	H, 2	5W-20	ATF+4	75W-90	②	ATF+4	DOT 3	Mopar® (HOAT)
2008	300, 300C, Charger, Magnum	2.7 (2736)	R, T	5W-20	ATF+4	75W-90	②	ATF+4	DOT 3	Mopar® (HOAT)
		3.5 (3507)	G, V	10W-30	ATF+4	75W-90	②	ATF+4	DOT 3	Mopar® (HOAT)
		5.7 (5654)	H, 2	5W-20	ATF+4	75W-90	②	ATF+4	DOT 3	Mopar® (HOAT)

NOTE: Check the engines oil cap or owners manual for specific engine oil grade variations.

DOT: Department Of Transpotation

① Rear axle: 75W140 Synthetic gear lubricant

② Mopar® P/N-05170055EA

22043_300C_C0005

VALVE SPECIFICATIONS

Year	Engine Displacement Liters	Engine VIN	Seat Angle (deg.)	Face Angle (deg.)	Spring Test Pressure (lbs. @ in.)	Spring Installed Height (in.)	Stem-to-Guide Clearance (in.) Intake	Stem-to-Guide Clearance (in.) Exhaust	Stem Diameter (in.) Intake	Stem Diameter (in.) Exhaust
2005	2.7	R	45-45.5	44.5-45.5	①	1.496	0.0009-0.0026	0.0020-0.0037	0.2337-0.2344	0.2326-0.2333
	3.5	G	45-45.5	44.5-45	②	1.496	0.0009-0.0026	0.0020-0.0037	0.2730-0.2737	0.2719-0.2726
	5.7	H	44.5-45	45-45.5	242@1.322	1.811	0.0008-0.0025	0.0019-0.0037	0.3120-0.3130	0.3110-0.3120
2006	2.7	R, T	45-45.5	44.5-45.5	①	1.496	0.0009-0.0026	0.0020-0.0037	0.2337-0.2344	0.2326-0.2333
	3.5	G, V	45-45.5	44.5-45	②	1.496	0.0009-0.0026	0.0020-0.0037	0.2730-0.2737	0.2719-0.2726
	5.7	H, 2	44.5-45	45-45.5	242@1.322	1.811	0.0008-0.0025	0.0019-0.0037	0.3120-0.3130	0.3110-0.3120
2007	2.7	R, T	45-45.5	44.5-45.5	①	1.496	0.0009-0.0026	0.0020-0.0037	0.2337-0.2344	0.2326-0.2333
	3.5	G, V	45-45.5	44.5-45	②	1.496	0.0009-0.0026	0.0020-0.0037	0.2730-0.2737	0.2719-0.2726
	5.7	H, 2	44.5-45	45-45.5	242@1.322	1.811	0.0008-0.0025	0.0019-0.0037	0.3120-0.3130	0.3110-0.3120
2008	2.7	R, T	45-45.5	44.5-45.5	①	1.496	0.0009-0.0026	0.0020-0.0037	0.2337-0.2344	0.2326-0.2333
	3.5	G, V	45-45.5	44.5-45	②	1.496	0.0009-0.0026	0.0020-0.0037	0.2730-0.2737	0.2719-0.2726
	5.7	H, 2	44.5-45	45-45.5	242@1.322	1.811	0.0008-0.0025	0.0019-0.0037	0.3120-0.3130	0.3110-0.3120

① Intake: 148-162@1.1417

Exhaust: 138-151@1.1811

② Intake: 130-144@1.239

Exhaust: 140-155@1.239

22043_300C_C0006

CAMSHAFT AND BEARING SPECIFICATIONS CHART
All measurements are given in inches.

Year	Engine Displ. Liters	Engine ID/VIN	Journal Dia.	Brg. Oil Clearance	Shaft End-play	Runout	Journal Bore	Lobe Height Intake	Lobe Height Exhaust
2005	2.7	R	0.9449 0.9441	0.0020- 0.0035	0.0051 0.0110	N/A	0.9469 0.0948	N/A	N/A
	3.5	G	1.6905- 1.6913	0.003- 0.0047	0.001- 0.0140	N/A	1.6944 1.6953	N/A	N/A
	5.7	H	①	②	0.0031- 0.0114	N/A	NA	N/A	N/A
2006	2.7	R, T	0.9449 0.9441	0.0020- 0.0035	0.0051 0.0110	N/A	0.9469 0.0948	N/A	N/A
	3.5	G, V	1.6905- 1.6913	0.003- 0.0047	0.001- 0.0140	N/A	1.6944 1.6953	N/A	N/A
	5.7	H, 2	①	②	0.0031- 0.0114	N/A	NA	N/A	N/A
2007	2.7	R, T	0.9449 0.9441	0.0020- 0.0035	0.0051 0.0110	N/A	0.9469 0.0948	N/A	N/A
	3.5	G, V	1.6905- 1.6913	0.003- 0.0047	0.001- 0.0140	N/A	1.6944 1.6953	N/A	N/A
	5.7	H, 2	①	②	0.0031- 0.0114	N/A	NA	N/A	N/A
2008	2.7	R, T	0.9449 0.9441	0.0020- 0.0035	0.0051 0.0110	N/A	0.9469 0.0948	N/A	N/A
	3.5	G, V	1.6905- 1.6913	0.003- 0.0047	0.001- 0.0140	N/A	1.6944 1.6953	N/A	N/A
	5.7	H, 2	①	②	0.0031- 0.0114	N/A	NA	N/A	N/A

N/A: Not Available

① No.1: 2.29
No.2: 2.27
No.3: 2.26
No.4: 2.24
No.5: 1.72

② No.1: .0015-.003
No.2: 0.0019-.0035
No.3: .0015-.003
No.4: 0.0019-.0035
No.5: .0015-.003

22043_300C_C0007

CRANKSHAFT AND CONNECTING ROD SPECIFICATIONS
All measurements are given in inches.

Year	Engine Displacement Liters	Engine VIN	Crankshaft				Connecting Rod		
			Main Brg. Journal Dia.	Main Brg. Oil Clearance	Shaft End-play	Thrust on No.	Journal Diameter	Oil Clearance	Side Clearance
2005	2.7	R	2.4997-2.5004	0.0012-0.0022	0.0019-0.0108	3	2.1060-2.1067	0.0013-0.0027	0.0052-0.0150
	3.5	G	2.5190-2.5120	0.0014-0.0026	0.0040-0.0120	3	2.2282-2.2283	0.0010-0.0030	0.0153 max.
	5.7	H	2.5585-2.5595	0.0009-0.0020	0.0020-0.0110	3	2.1250-2.1260	0.0007-0.0023	0.0030-0.0137
2006	2.7	R, T	2.4997-2.5004	0.0012-0.0022	0.0019-0.0108	3	2.1060-2.1067	0.0013-0.0027	0.0052-0.0150
	3.5	G, V	2.5190-2.5120	0.0014-0.0026	0.0040-0.0120	3	2.2282-2.2283	0.0010-0.0030	0.0153 max.
	5.7	H, 2	2.5585-2.5595	0.0009-0.0020	0.0020-0.0110	3	2.1250-2.1260	0.0007-0.0023	0.0030-0.0137
2007	2.7	R, T	2.4997-2.5004	0.0012-0.0022	0.0019-0.0108	3	2.1060-2.1067	0.0013-0.0027	0.0052-0.0150
	3.5	G, V	2.5190-2.5120	0.0014-0.0026	0.0040-0.0120	3	2.2282-2.2283	0.0010-0.0030	0.0153 max.
	5.7	H, 2	2.5585-2.5595	0.0009-0.0020	0.0020-0.0110	3	2.1250-2.1260	0.0007-0.0023	0.0030-0.0137
2008	2.7	R, T	2.4997-2.5004	0.0012-0.0022	0.0019-0.0108	3	2.1060-2.1067	0.0013-0.0027	0.0052-0.0150
	3.5	G, V	2.5190-2.5120	0.0014-0.0026	0.0040-0.0120	3	2.2282-2.2283	0.0010-0.0030	0.0153 max.
	5.7	H, 2	2.5585-2.5595	0.0009-0.0020	0.0020-0.0110	3	2.1250-2.1260	0.0007-0.0023	0.0030-0.0137

22043_300C_C0008

PISTON AND RING SPECIFICATIONS
All measurements are given in inches.

Year	Engine Displacement Liters	Engine VIN	Piston Clearance	Ring Gap			Ring Side Clearance		
				Top Compression	Bottom Compression	Oil Control	Top Compression	Bottom Compression	Oil Control
2005	2.7	R	0-0.0016	0.0080-0.0140	0.0146-0.0249	0.010-0.030	0.0013-0.0032	0.0016-0.0031	0.0022-0.0080
	3.5	G	0-0.0018	0.0080-0.0140	0.0078-0.0157	0.010-0.030	0.0016-0.0031	0.0016-0.0031	0.0015-0.0073
	5.7	H	0.0008-0.0019	0.0090-0.0149	0.0137-0.0236	0.006-0.026	0.0007-0.0026	0.0007-0.0022	0.0007-0.0091
2006	2.7	R, T	0-0.0016	0.0080-0.0140	0.0146-0.0249	0.010-0.030	0.0013-0.0032	0.0016-0.0031	0.0022-0.0080
	3.5	G, V	0-0.0018	0.0080-0.0140	0.0078-0.0157	0.010-0.030	0.0016-0.0031	0.0016-0.0031	0.0015-0.0073
	5.7	H, 2	0.0008-0.0019	0.0090-0.0149	0.0137-0.0236	0.006-0.026	0.0007-0.0026	0.0007-0.0022	0.0007-0.0091
2007	2.7	R, T	0-0.0016	0.0080-0.0140	0.0146-0.0249	0.010-0.030	0.0013-0.0032	0.0016-0.0031	0.0022-0.0080
	3.5	G, V	0-0.0018	0.0080-0.0140	0.0078-0.0157	0.010-0.030	0.0016-0.0031	0.0016-0.0031	0.0015-0.0073
	5.7	H, 2	0.0008-0.0019	0.0090-0.0149	0.0137-0.0236	0.006-0.026	0.0007-0.0026	0.0007-0.0022	0.0007-0.0091
2008	2.7	R, T	0-0.0016	0.0080-0.0140	0.0146-0.0249	0.010-0.030	0.0013-0.0032	0.0016-0.0031	0.0022-0.0080
	3.5	G, V	0-0.0018	0.0080-0.0140	0.0078-0.0157	0.010-0.030	0.0016-0.0031	0.0016-0.0031	0.0015-0.0073
	5.7	H, 2	0.0008-0.0019	0.0090-0.0149	0.0137-0.0236	0.006-0.026	0.0007-0.0026	0.0007-0.0022	0.0007-0.0091

22043_300C_C0009

TORQUE SPECIFICATIONS

All readings in ft. lbs.

Year	Engine Displacement Liters	Engine VIN	Cylinder Head Bolts	Main Bearing Bolts	Rod Bearing Bolts	Crankshaft Damper Bolts	Flywheel Bolts	Manifold Intake	Manifold Exhaust	Spark Plugs	Oil Pan Drain Plug
2005	2.7	R	①	②	③	125	70	④	16	15	20
	3.5	G	⑤	②	③	70	70	⑥	16	20	20
	5.7	H	①	⑦	⑧	129	70	⑨	18	13	20
2006	2.7	R, T	①	②	③	125	70	④	16	15	20
	3.5	G, V	⑤	②	③	70	70	⑥	16	20	20
	5.7	H, 2	①	⑦	⑧	129	70	⑨	18	13	20
2007	2.7	R, T	①	②	③	125	70	④	16	15	20
	3.5	G, V	⑤	②	③	70	70	⑥	16	20	20
	5.7	H, 2	①	⑦	⑧	129	70	⑨	18	13	20
2008	2.7	R, T	①	②	③	125	70	④	16	15	20
	3.5	G, V	⑤	②	③	70	70	⑥	16	20	20
	5.7	H, 2	①	⑦	⑧	129	70	⑨	18	13	20

① See the text section

② First, tighten the main cap bolts to 15 ft. lbs. +90 degrees
Second, tighten the windasge tray bolts to 20 ft. lbs. +90 degrees
Third, tighten the tie (horizontal) bolts to 250 inch lbs.

③ 20 ft. lbs. + 90 degrees

④ Upper and Lower: 105 inch lbs.

⑤ Step 1: 45 ft. lbs.
Step 2: 65 ft. lbs.
Step 3: Verify 65 ft. lbs.
Step 4: + 90 degrees

⑥ Upper: 105 inch lbs.
Lower: 250 inch lbs.

⑦ First, install the main bearing cap bolts, and torque them, in sequence, to:
Step 1: 20 ft. lbs.
Step 2: +90 degrees
Then, install the crossbolts and torque them, in sequence, to 21 ft. lbs.

⑧ 15 ft. lbs. +90 degrees

⑨ 105 inch lbs.

22043_300C_C0010

WHEEL ALIGNMENT

Year	Model		Caster Range (+/-Deg.)	Caster Preferred Setting (Deg.)	Camber Range (+/-Deg.)	Camber Preferred Setting (Deg.)	Toe-in (in.)
2005	AWD	F	1.0	①	0.50	②	0.00
		R	—	—	0.50	-0.75	③
	RWD	F	1.5	①	0.50	②	0.00
		R	—	—	0.50	-0.75	③
2006	AWD	F	1.0	①	0.50	②	0.00
		R	—	—	0.50	-0.75	③
	RWD	F	1.5	①	0.50	②	0.00
		R	—	—	0.50	-0.75	③
2007	AWD	F	1.0	①	0.50	②	0.00
		R	—	—	0.50	-0.75	③
	RWD	F	1.5	①	0.50	②	0.00
		R	—	—	0.50	-0.75	③
2008	AWD	F	1.0	①	0.50	②	0.00
		R	—	—	0.50	-0.75	③
	RWD	F	1.5	①	0.50	②	0.00
		R	—	—	0.50	-0.75	③

① Left: +4.50
   Right: +5.10
② Left: 0.00
   Right: -0.30
③ Left: 0.02-0.32
   Right: 0.08-0.22

22043_300C_C0013

TIRE, WHEEL AND BALL JOINT SPECIFICATIONS

Year	Model	OEM Tires Standard	OEM Tires Optional	Tire Pressures (psi) Front	Tire Pressures (psi) Rear	Wheel Size	Ball Joint Play	Wheel Lug Nut Torque
2005	300	P215/65TR17	P225/60HR18	①	①	std.: 7.0 opt: 7.5	0.059 in. max.	110
	300C	P225/60HR18	none	①	①	7.5	0.059 in. max.	110
	Magnum SE	P215/65TR17	none	①	①	7.0	0.059 in. max.	110
	Magnum SXT	P225/60HR18	none	①	①	7.5	0.059 in. max.	110
	Magnum RT	P225/60HR18	none	①	①	7.5	0.059 in. max.	110
2006	300	P215/65TR17	P225/60HR18	①	①	std.: 7.0 opt: 7.5	0.059 in. max.	110
	300C	P225/60HR18	none	①	①	7.5	0.059 in. max.	110
	Magnum SE	P215/65TR17	none	①	①	7.0	0.059 in. max.	110
	Magnum SXT	P225/60HR18	none	①	①	7.5	0.059 in. max.	110
	Magnum RT	P225/60HR18	none	①	①	7.5	0.059 in. max.	110
	Charger SE	P215/65TR17	none	①	①	7.0	0.059 in. max.	110
	Charger RT	225/60HR18	235/55HR18	①	①	7.5	0.059 in. max.	110
2007	300	P215/65TR17	P225/60HR18	①	①	std.: 7.0 opt: 7.5	0.059 in. max.	110
	300C	P225/60HR18	none	①	①	7.5	0.059 in. max.	110
	Magnum SE	P215/65TR17	none	①	①	7.0	0.059 in. max.	110
	Magnum SXT	P225/60HR18	none	①	①	7.5	0.059 in. max.	110
	Magnum RT	P225/60HR18	none	①	①	7.5	0.059 in. max.	110
	Charger SE	P215/65TR17	none	①	①	7.0	0.059 in. max.	110
	Charger RT	225/60HR18	235/55HR18	①	①	7.5	0.059 in. max.	110
2008	300	P215/65TR17	P225/60HR18	①	①	std.: 7.0 opt: 7.5	0.059 in. max.	110
	300C	P225/60HR18	none	①	①	7.5	0.059 in. max.	110
	Magnum SE	P215/65TR17	none	①	①	7.0	0.059 in. max.	110
	Magnum SXT	P225/60HR18	none	①	①	7.5	0.059 in. max.	110
	Magnum RT	P225/60HR18	none	①	①	7.5	0.059 in. max.	110
	Charger SE	P215/65TR17	none	①	①	7.0	0.059 in. max.	110
	Charger RT	225/60HR18	235/55HR18	①	①	7.5	0.059 in. max.	110

NA: Information not available

OEM: Original Equipment Manufacturer

PSI: Pounds Per Square Inch

STD: Standard

OPT: Optional

① See placard on the vehicle

22043_300C_C0012

BRAKE SPECIFICATIONS
All measurements in inches unless noted

Year	Model		Brake Disc Original Thickness	Brake Disc Minimum Thickness	Brake Disc Maximum Run-out	Minimum Lining Thickness	Brake Caliper Bracket Bolts (ft. lbs.)	Brake Caliper Mounting Pins (ft. lbs.)
2005	300, 300C	F	1.097-1.107	1.040	0.0014	NA	70	44
	Magnum,	R	①	②	0.0014	NA	85	23
2006	300, 300C	F	1.097-1.107	1.040	0.0014	NA	70	44
	Charger, Magnum	R	①	②	0.0014	NA	85	23
2007	300, 300C	F	1.097-1.107	1.040	0.0014	NA	70	44
	Charger, Magnum	R	①	②	0.0014	NA	85	23
2008	300, 300C	F	1.097-1.107	1.040	0.0014	NA	70	44
	Charger, Magnum	R	①	②	0.0014	NA	85	23

NA: Information not available

① 17 inch brakes: 0.389-0.399
  18 inch brakes: 0.861-0.871

② 17 inch brakes: 0.335
  18 inch brakes: 0.807

22043_300C_C0011

SCHEDULED MAINTENANCE INTERVALS
2005-08 Chrysler 300, 300C, Dodge Magnum and Charger

TO BE SERVICED	TYPE OF SERVICE	VEHICLE MILEAGE INTERVAL (x1000)												
		3	6	9	12	15	18	21	24	27	30	33	36	39
Engine oil & filter	R	✓	✓	✓	✓	✓	✓	✓	✓	✓	✓	✓	✓	✓
Tires	Rotate		✓		✓		✓		✓		✓		✓	
A/C filter	R					✓					✓			
Brake linings	I			✓			✓			✓			✓	
Engine air filter	S/I	✓	✓	✓	✓	✓	✓	✓	✓	✓	✓	✓	✓	✓
Engine air filter	R					✓					✓			
Spark plugs (5.7L)	R										✓			
PCV valve	S/I										✓			
Rear axle fluid	R	Every 48,000 miles												
Transfer case fluid	R	Every 48,000 miles												
Power steering fluid	R	Every 60,000 miles												
Auto. trans. fluid and filter	R	Every 60,000 miles												
Accessory drive belt	I/R	Every 72,000 miles												
Spark plugs (2.7L and 3.5L)	R	Every 100,000 miles												
Engine coolant	R	Every 102,000 miles												
Timing belt (3.5L)	R	Every 105,000 miles												

R: Replace   S: Service   I: Inspect   Adj: Adjust

The above schedule is to be used if you drive under any of the following conditions:

Driving in temperatures under 32 degrees F

Stop and go traffic

Extensive engine idling

Driving in dusty conditions

Frequent trips under 10 miles

More than 50 % of your driving is in hot weather (90 deg. F) above 50 miles per hour

Trailer towing

Taxi, police or delivery service

If none of these conditions is met, double the maintenance intervals

22043_300C_C0014

PRECAUTIONS

Before servicing any vehicle, please be sure to read all of the following precautions, which deal with personal safety, prevention of component damage, and important points to take into consideration when servicing a motor vehicle:

• Never open, service or drain the radiator or cooling system when the engine is hot; serious burns can occur from the steam and hot coolant.

• Observe all applicable safety precautions when working around fuel. Whenever servicing the fuel system, always work in a well-ventilated area. Do not allow fuel spray or vapors to come in contact with a spark, open flame, or excessive heat (a hot drop light, for example). Keep a dry chemical fire extinguisher near the work area. Always keep fuel in a container specifically designed for fuel storage; also, always properly seal fuel containers to avoid the possibility of fire or explosion. Refer to the additional fuel system precautions later in this section.

• Fuel injection systems often remain pressurized, even after the engine has been turned **OFF**. The fuel system pressure must be relieved before disconnecting any fuel lines. Failure to do so may result in fire and/or personal injury.

• Brake fluid often contains polyglycol ethers and polyglycols. Avoid contact with the eyes and wash your hands thoroughly after handling brake fluid. If you do get brake fluid in your eyes, flush your eyes with clean, running water for 15 minutes. If eye irritation persists, or if you have taken

brake fluid internally, IMMEDIATELY seek medical assistance.

• The EPA warns that prolonged contact with used engine oil may cause a number of skin disorders, including cancer. You should make every effort to minimize your exposure to used engine oil. Protective gloves should be worn when changing oil. Wash your hands and any other exposed skin areas as soon as possible after exposure to used engine oil. Soap and water, or waterless hand cleaner should be used.

• All new vehicles are now equipped with an air bag system, often referred to as a Supplemental Restraint System (SRS) or Supplemental Inflatable Restraint (SIR) system. The system must be disabled before performing service on or around system components, steering column, instrument panel components, wiring and sensors. Failure to follow safety and disabling procedures could result in accidental air bag deployment, possible personal injury and unnecessary system repairs.

• Always wear safety goggles when working with, or around, the air bag system. When carrying a non-deployed air bag, be sure the bag and trim cover are pointed away from your body. When placing a non-deployed air bag on a work surface, always face the bag and trim cover upward, away from the surface. This will reduce the motion of the module if it is accidentally deployed. Refer to the additional air bag system precautions later in this section.

• Clean, high quality brake fluid from a sealed container is essential to the safe and

proper operation of the brake system. You should always buy the correct type of brake fluid for your vehicle. If the brake fluid becomes contaminated, completely flush the system with new fluid. Never reuse any brake fluid. Any brake fluid that is removed from the system should be discarded. Also, do not allow any brake fluid to come in contact with a painted surface; it will damage the paint.

• Never operate the engine without the proper amount and type of engine oil; doing so WILL result in severe engine damage.

• Timing belt maintenance is extremely important. Many models utilize an interference-type, non-freewheeling engine. If the timing belt breaks, the valves in the cylinder head may strike the pistons, causing potentially serious (also time-consuming and expensive) engine damage. Refer to the maintenance interval charts for the recommended replacement interval for the timing belt, and to the timing belt section for belt replacement and inspection.

• Disconnecting the negative battery cable on some vehicles may interfere with the functions of the on-board computer system(s) and may require the computer to undergo a relearning process once the negative battery cable is reconnected.

• When servicing drum brakes, only disassemble and assemble one side at a time, leaving the remaining side intact for reference.

• Only an MVAC-trained, EPA-certified automotive technician should service the air conditioning system or its components.

BRAKES

GENERAL INFORMATION

PRECAUTIONS

• Certain components within the ABS system are not intended to be serviced or repaired individually.

• Do not use rubber hoses or other parts not specifically specified for and ABS system. When using repair kits, replace all parts included in the kit. Partial or incorrect repair may lead to functional problems and require the replacement of components.

• Lubricate rubber parts with clean, fresh brake fluid to ease assembly. Do not use shop air to clean parts; damage to rubber components may result.

• Use only DOT 3 brake fluid from an unopened container.

• If any hydraulic component or line is

removed or replaced, it may be necessary to bleed the entire system.

• A clean repair area is essential. Always clean the reservoir and cap thoroughly before removing the cap. The slightest amount of dirt in the fluid may plug an orifice and impair the system function. Perform repairs after components have been thoroughly cleaned; use only denatured alcohol to clean components. Do not allow ABS components to come into contact with any substance containing mineral oil; this includes used shop rags.

• The Anti-Lock control unit is a microprocessor similar to other computer units in the vehicle. Ensure that the ignition switch is **OFF** before removing or installing controller harnesses. Avoid static electricity discharge at or near the controller.

ANTI-LOCK BRAKE SYSTEM (ABS)

• If any arc welding is to be done on the vehicle, the control unit should be unplugged before welding operations begin.

SPEED SENSORS

REMOVAL & INSTALLATION

Front Sensor

One wheel speed sensor is mounted to each knuckle. The wheel speed sensor, using a tone wheel attached to the hub and bearing (RWD) or front half shaft (AWD) as a trigger mechanism, communicates with the Antilock Brake Module, informing it of that wheel's speed.

The head of the front wheel speed sensor used on Rear-Wheel-Drive (RWD) vehicles mounts to the inside of the knuckle.

The head of the front wheel speed sensor used on All-Wheel-Drive (AWD) vehicles mounts to the rear of the knuckle.

Vehicles without antilock brakes are equipped with one front wheel speed sensor. It is attached to the right front knuckle and is used to provide wheel speed sense to various vehicle systems.

RWD Vehicles

See Figure 1.

1. Raise and support the vehicle.
2. Remove the sensor cable routing clip from brake hose bracket.

➡ **To release the sensor connector from the body wiring harness connector, move retaining clip and pull sensor connector outward.**

3. Remove the sensor connector from body wiring harness connector.
4. Remove the screw fastening the wheel speed sensor to knuckle. Pull sensor head out of knuckle.
5. Remove the wheel speed sensor cable routing clip from brake hose routing bracket.

To install:

6. Install the wheel speed sensor head into knuckle and install mounting screw. Tighten screw to 95 inch lbs. (11 Nm).
7. Attach the wheel speed sensor cable and routing clip to brake hose routing bracket.
8. Attach the sensor cable routing clip to brake hose bracket.
9. Attach the sensor connector to body

wiring harness connector. When installing connector, make sure retaining clip on body connector is properly in place and sensor connect cannot be pulled out.

10. Lower the vehicle.
11. Perform Verification Test and clear any diagnostic trouble code faults.

AWD Vehicles

See Figure 2.

1. Raise and support the vehicle.

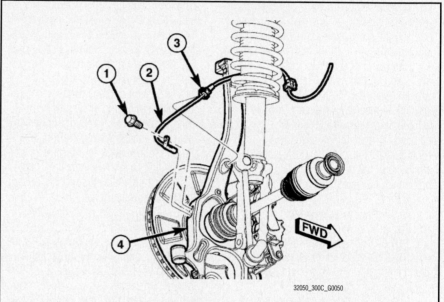

Fig. 2 Remove screw (1) fastening wheel speed sensor (2) to knuckle (4). Pull sensor head out of knuckle. Remove wheel speed sensor cable routing clip (3) from knuckle (4)

➡ **To remove the sensor connector from body wiring harness connector, move retaining clip and pull sensor connector outward.**

2. Remove the sensor cable routing clip from brake hose bracket.
3. Remove the sensor connector from body wiring harness connector.
4. Remove the screw fastening wheel speed sensor to knuckle. Pull sensor head out of knuckle.

5. Remove the wheel speed sensor cable routing clip from knuckle.
6. Remove the wheel speed sensor.

To install:

7. Install the wheel speed sensor head into knuckle and install mounting screw. Tighten screw to 95 inch lbs. (11 Nm).
8. Attach the wheel speed sensor cable and routing clip to knuckle.
9. Attach the sensor cable routing clip to brake hose bracket.
10. Connect the sensor connector to body wiring harness connector. When installing connector, make sure retaining clip on body connector is properly in place and sensor connect cannot be pulled out.
11. Lower the vehicle.
12. Perform Verification Test and clear any diagnostic trouble code faults.

Rear Sensor

1. Raise and support the vehicle.

➡ **To remove the sensor connector from body wiring harness connector, move**

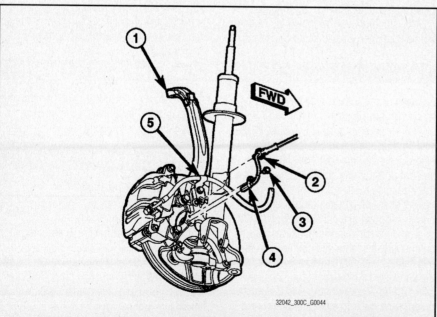

Fig. 1 Remove the retaining screw (3) holding the wheel speed sensor to the knuckle (1). Pull the sensor head (4) from the knuckle, then remove the sensor cable routing clip (2) from the brake hose routing bracket (5)

retaining clip and pull sensor connector outward.

2. Remove the sensor connectors from body wiring harness connector located in luggage compartment floor pan.

3. Separate the left sensor connector from right sensor connector.

4. If removing the left sensor, unclip sensor cable from routing clip near body connector.

5. If removing the left sensor, unclip sensor cable from routing clips along rear of crossmember near rear differential.

6. If removing the left sensor, unclip sensor cable from routing clip above toe link mount on rear crossmember.

7. Unclip the sensor cable from routing clips along toe link.

8. Unclip the sensor cable at rear brake rotor shield.

9. Remove the screw fastening sensor head to rear knuckle.

10. Remove the wheel speed sensor.

To install:

11. Insert the wheel speed sensor head into mounting hole in rear of knuckle.

12. Install the screw fastening sensor head to rear knuckle. Tighten the screw to 100 inch lbs. (11 Nm).

13. Install the sensor cable at rear brake rotor shield.

14. Clip the sensor cable to routing clips along toe link.

15. If installing the left sensor, clip sensor cable to routing clip above toe link mount on rear crossmember.

16. If installing the left sensor, clip sensor cable to routing clips along rear of crossmember near rear differential.

17. If installing the left sensor, clip sensor cable to routing clip near body connector.

18. Match the left sensor connector to right sensor connector to make one connector.

19. Insert the sensor connectors into body wiring harness connector located in luggage compartment floor pan. When installing connector, make sure retaining clip on body connector is properly in place and sensor connector cannot be pulled out.

20. Lower the vehicle.

BRAKES

BLEEDING THE BRAKE SYSTEM

BLEEDING PROCEDURE

BLEEDING PROCEDURE

1. Before servicing the vehicle, refer to the precautions in the beginning of this section.

➡ **To bleed the base brake system manually, an assistant's help is required. To ensure all air is bled from the ICU or junction block in a timely manner, it is recommended to raise the rear of the vehicle approximately 10–12 inches as measured at the rear bumper.**

2. Raise and support vehicle placing rear of vehicle approximately 10–12 inches above level. It will be necessary to add extra support stands under vehicle to support this angle.

3. Remove rubber duct caps from all 4 bleeder screws.

4. Attach a clear hose to the bleeder screw at one wheel and feed the other end of the hose into a clear jar containing fresh brake fluid.

5. Have an assistant pump the brake pedal three or four times and hold it down before the bleeder screw is opened.

❋❋ WARNING

Open the bleeder screw at least one full turn when instructed. Some air may be trapped in the brake lines or valves far upstream, as far as ten feet or more from the bleeder screw. If the bleeder screw is not opened sufficiently, fluid flow is restricted causing a slow, weak fluid discharge. This will NOT get all the air out.

Therefore, it is essential to open the bleeder screw at least one full turn to allow a fast, large volume discharge of brake fluid.

6. While the pedal is being held down, open the bleeder screw at least 1 full turn. When the bleeder screw opens the brake pedal will drop all the way to the floor. Continue to hold the pedal all the way down.

7. Once the brake pedal has dropped, close the bleeder screw. The pedal can then be released.

8. Repeat steps 1 through 5 until all trapped air is removed from that wheel circuit (usually four or five times). This should pass a sufficient amount of fluid to expel all the trapped air from the brakes hydraulic system. Be sure to monitor brake fluid level in master cylinder fluid reservoir making sure it stays at a proper level. This will ensure air does not reenter brake hydraulic system through master cylinder.

➡ **Monitor the brake fluid level in the fluid reservoir periodically to make sure it does not go too low. This will ensure that air does not reenter the brake hydraulic system.**

9. Bleed the remaining wheel circuits in the same manner until all air is removed from the brake hydraulic system.

10. Check brake pedal travel. If pedal travel is excessive or has not improved, some air may still be trapped in the hydraulic system. Re-bleed the brake system as necessary.

11. If equipped with antilock brakes, the hydraulic control unit may need to be bled, then re-bleed base brakes.

12. Reinstall all 4 bleeder screw dust caps.

13. Test drive vehicle to ensure brakes are operating properly and pedal feel is correct.

PRESSURE BLEEDING METHOD

➡ **Follow the pressure bleeder manufacturer's instructions for use of pressure bleeding equipment.**

1. Remove filler cap from the top of fluid reservoir on master cylinder

2. Install the adapter special tool 6921, in the caps place on the reservoir.

3. Attach the bleeder tank, special tool C—3496—B, or equivalent, to adapter 6921.

❋❋ WARNING

Pressurize the system following the pressure bleeder manufacturer's instructions.

4. Raise and support vehicle placing rear of vehicle approximately 5° higher than the front or if measured at the rear bumper , approximately 10—12 inches above level. It will be necessary to add extra support stands under vehicle to support this angle.

5. If installed, remove rubber dust caps from all four bleeder screws on calipers.

6. Starting at the first wheel circuit as listed earlier, attach a clear hose to the bleeder screw at that wheels brake caliper and feed the other end of hose into a clear jar containing enough fresh brake fluid to submerge the end of the hose.

✳✳ WARNING

Open the bleeder screw at least one full turn when instructed. Some air may be trapped in the brake lines or valves far upstream, as far as ten feet or more from the bleeder screw. If the bleeder screw is not opened sufficiently, fluid flow is restricted causing a slow, weak fluid discharge. This will NOT get all the air out. Therefore, it is essential to open the bleeder screw at least one full turn to allow a fast, large volume discharge of brake fluid.

7. Open bleeder screw at least one full turn or more to obtain an adequate flow of brake fluid.

8. After 4 to 8 ounces of brake fluid has been bled through the brake hydraulic circuit, and an air—free flow (no bubbles) is maintained in the clear plastic hose and jar, close the bleeder screw.

9. Bleed the remaining wheel circuits in the same manner until all air is removed from the brake hydraulic system.

10. Check brake pedal travel. If pedal travel is excessive or has not improved, some air may still be trapped in the hydraulic system. Rebleed the brake system as necessary.

11. If equipped with antilock brakes, the hydraulic control unit may need to be bled, then rebleed base brakes.

12. Reinstall all 4 bleeder screw dust caps.

13. Test drive vehicle to ensure brakes are operating properly and pedal feel is correct.

BLEEDING THE ABS SYSTEM

1. Before servicing the vehicle, refer to the precautions in the beginning of this section.

The base brake's hydraulic system must be bled anytime air enters the hydraulic system. The ABS must always be bled anytime it is suspected that the HCU has ingested air.

Brake systems with ABS must be bled as two independent braking systems. The non-ABS portion of the brake system with ABS is to be bled the same as any non-ABS system.

The ABS portion of the brake system must be bled separately. Use the following procedure to properly bleed the brake hydraulic system including the ABS.

➡**During the brake bleeding procedure, be sure the brake fluid level remains close to the FULL level in the master cylinder fluid reservoir. Check the fluid level periodically during the bleeding procedure and add Mopar® DOT 3 brake fluid as required.**

When bleeding the ABS system, the following bleeding sequence must be followed to insure complete and adequate bleeding.

2. Make sure all hydraulic fluid lines are installed and properly torqued.

3. Connect the scan tool to the diagnostics connector. The diagnostic connector is located under the lower steering column cover to the left of the steering column.

4. Using the scan tool, check to make sure the ABM does not have any fault codes stored. If it does, clear them.

✳✳ CAUTION

When bleeding the brake system wear safety glasses. A clear bleed tube must be attached to the bleeder screws and submerged in a clear container filled part way with clean brake fluid. Direct the flow of brake fluid away from yourself and the painted surfaces of the vehicle. Brake fluid at high pressure may come out of the bleeder screws when opened.

5. Bleed the base brake system.

6. Using a scan tool, select ECU VIEW, followed by ABS MISCELLANEOUS FUNCTIONS to access bleeding. Follow the instructions displayed. When finished, disconnect the scan tool and proceed.

7. Bleed the base brake system a second time. Check brake fluid level in the reservoir periodically to prevent emptying, causing air to enter the hydraulic system.

8. Fill the master cylinder fluid reservoir to the MAX level.

9. Test drive the vehicle to be sure the brakes are operating correctly and that the brake pedal does not feel spongy.

BRAKES

✳✳ CAUTION

Dust and dirt accumulating on brake parts during normal use may contain asbestos fibers from production or aftermarket brake linings. Breathing excessive concentrations of asbestos fibers can cause serious bodily harm. Exercise care when servicing brake parts. Do not sand or grind brake lining unless equipment used is designed to contain the dust residue. Do not clean brake parts with compressed air or by dry brushing. Cleaning should be done by dampening the brake components with a fine mist of water, then wiping the brake components clean with a dampened cloth. Dispose of cloth and all residue containing asbestos fibers in an impermeable container with the appropriate label. Follow practices prescribed by the Occupational Safety and Health Administration (OSHA) and the Environmental Protection Agency (EPA) for the handling, processing, and disposing of dust or debris that may contain asbestos fibers.

BRAKE CALIPER

REMOVAL & INSTALLATION

Single Piston

See Figure 3.

1. Before servicing the vehicle, refer to the precautions in the beginning of this section.

2. Disconnect and isolate battery negative cable from battery post.

FRONT DISC BRAKES

3. Using a brake pedal holding tool, depress brake pedal past its first inch of travel and hold it in this position. Holding pedal in this position will isolate master cylinder from hydraulic brake system and will not allow brake fluid to drain out of brake fluid reservoir while brake lines are open.

4. Raise and support vehicle.

5. Remove wheel mounting nuts, then tire and wheel assembly.

6. Remove banjo bolt connecting flexible brake hose to caliper. There are two sealing washers (one on each side of hose fitting) that will come off when bolt is removed. Discard these washers; install NEW washers on installation.

7. While holding guide pins from turning, remove caliper guide pin bolts.

8. Remove brake caliper from brake adapter and pads.

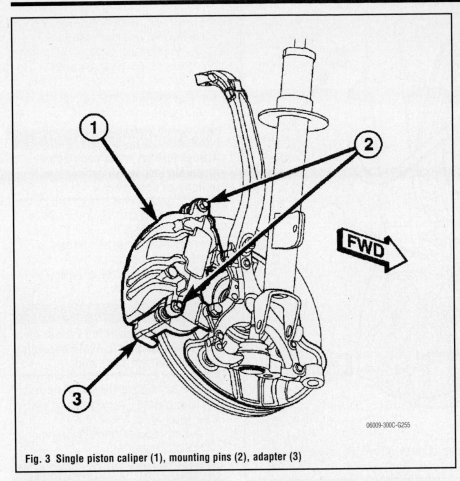

06009-300C-G255

Fig. 3 Single piston caliper (1), mounting pins (2), adapter (3)

To install:

⁂ WARNING

Always inspect brake pads before installing disc brake caliper and replace as necessary.

9. Completely retract caliper piston back into bore of caliper. Use hand pressure or a C-clamp may be used to retract piston, first placing a wood block over piston before installing C-clamp to avoid damaging piston.

⁂ WARNING

Use care when installing caliper onto disc brake adapter to avoid damaging boots on caliper guide pins.

10. Push caliper guide pins into caliper adapter to clear caliper mounting bosses when installing.
11. Slide caliper over brake pads and onto caliper adapter.

⁂ WARNING

Extreme caution should be taken not to cross-thread caliper guide pin bolts when they are installed.

12. Align caliper mounting holes with guide pins, then install guide pin bolts. While holding guide pins from turning, tighten bolts to 44 ft. lbs. (60 Nm) torque.
13. Install banjo bolt attaching brake hose to caliper. Install NEW washers on each side of hose fitting as banjo bolt is placed through fitting. Thread banjo bolt into caliper and tighten to 32 ft. lbs. (43 Nm) torque.
14. Install tire and wheel assembly. Tighten wheel mounting nuts to 110 ft. lbs. (150 Nm) torque.
15. Lower vehicle.
16. Remove brake pedal holding tool.
17. Connect battery negative cable to battery post. It is important that this is performed properly.
18. Bleed base brake hydraulic system as necessary.
19. Road test vehicle making several stops to wear off any foreign material on brakes and to seat brake shoes.

Dual Piston

2WD

See Figure 4.

1. Before servicing the vehicle, refer to the precautions in the beginning of this section.

2. Disconnect and isolate battery negative cable from battery post.
3. Using a brake pedal holding tool, depress brake pedal past its first inch of travel and hold it in this position. Holding pedal in this position will isolate master cylinder from hydraulic brake system and will not allow brake fluid to drain out of brake fluid reservoir while brake lines are open.
4. Raise and support vehicle.
5. Remove wheel mounting nuts, then tire and wheel assembly.
6. Remove banjo bolt connecting flexible brake hose to caliper. There are two sealing washers (one on each side of hose fitting) that will come off when bolt is removed. Discard these washers; install NEW washers on installation.
7. While holding guide pins from turning, remove caliper guide pin bolts.
8. Remove brake caliper from brake adapter and pads.

To install:

⁂ WARNING

Always inspect brake pads before installing disc brake caliper and replace as necessary.

9. Completely retract caliper pistons back into bores of caliper. Use hand pressure or a C-clamp may also be used to retract pistons, first placing a wood block over piston before installing C-clamp to avoid damaging piston.

⁂ WARNING

Use care when installing caliper onto disc brake adapter to avoid damaging boots on caliper guide pins.

10. Push caliper guide pins into caliper adapter to clear caliper mounting bosses when installing.
11. Slide caliper over brake pads and onto caliper adapter.

⁂ WARNING

Extreme caution should be taken not to cross-thread caliper guide pin bolts when they are installed.

12. Align caliper mounting holes with guide pins, then install guide pin bolts. While holding guide pins from turning, tighten bolts to 44 ft. lbs. (60 Nm) torque.
13. Install banjo bolt attaching brake hose to caliper. Install NEW washers on each side of hose fitting as banjo bolt is placed through fitting. Thread banjo bolt into caliper and tighten to 32 ft. lbs. (43 Nm) torque.

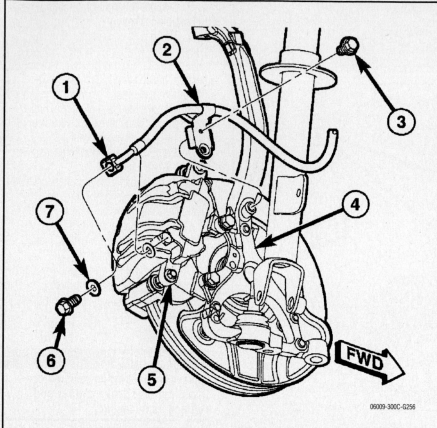

Fig. 4 Dual piston caliper mounting. (1) banjo fitting, (2) hose, (3) bolt, (4) adapter, (5) caliper pin, (6) banjo bolt, (7) washer

bolt is removed. Discard these washers; install NEW washers on installation.

7. While holding guide pins from turning, remove caliper guide pin bolts.

8. Remove brake caliper from brake adapter and pads.

To install:

> ※ **WARNING**
>
> **Always inspect brake pads before installing disc brake caliper and replace as necessary.**

9. Completely retract caliper pistons back into bores of caliper. Use hand pressure or a C-clamp may also be used to retract pistons, first placing a wood block over piston before installing C-clamp to avoid damaging piston.

> ※ **WARNING**
>
> **Use care when installing caliper onto disc brake adapter to avoid damaging boots on caliper guide pins.**

10. Push caliper guide pins into caliper adapter to clear caliper mounting bosses when installing.

11. Slide caliper over brake pads and onto caliper adapter.

> ※ **WARNING**
>
> **Extreme caution should be taken not to cross-thread caliper guide pin bolts when they are installed.**

12. Align caliper mounting holes with guide pins, then install guide pin bolts. While holding guide pins from turning, tighten bolts to 44 ft. lbs. (60 Nm) torque.

14. Install tire and wheel assembly. Tighten wheel mounting nuts to 110 ft. lbs. (150 Nm).

15. Lower vehicle.

16. Remove brake pedal holding tool.

17. Connect battery negative cable to battery post. It is important that this is performed properly.

18. Bleed base brake hydraulic system as necessary.

19. Road test vehicle making several stops to wear off any foreign material on brakes and to seat brake shoes.

AWD

See Figures 5 and 6.

1. Before servicing the vehicle, refer to the precautions in the beginning of this section.

2. Disconnect and isolate battery negative cable from battery post.

3. Using a brake pedal holding tool, depress brake pedal past its first inch of travel and hold it in this position. Holding pedal in this position will isolate master cylinder from hydraulic brake system and will not allow brake fluid to drain out of brake fluid reservoir while brake lines are open.

4. Raise and support vehicle.

5. Remove wheel mounting nuts, then tire and wheel assembly.

6. Remove banjo bolt (3) connecting flexible brake hose (1) to caliper (4). There are two sealing washers (2) (one on each side of hose fitting) that will come off when

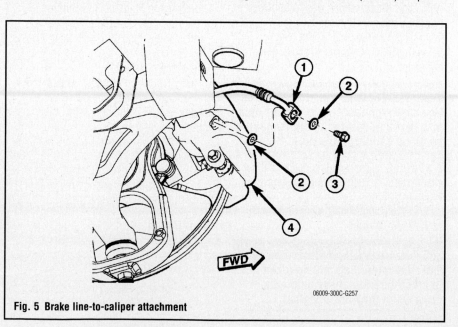

Fig. 5 Brake line-to-caliper attachment

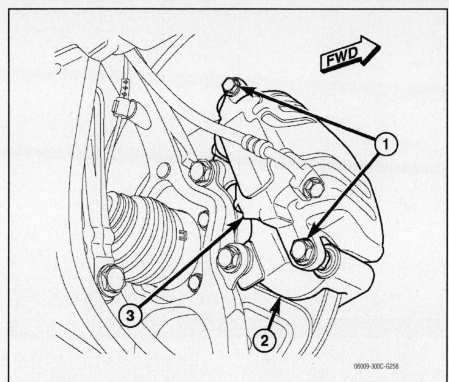

Fig. 6 Caliper attachment. (1) caliper pins, (2) anchor plate, (3) caliper—dual piston caliper with AWD

06009-300C-G258

13. Install banjo bolt attaching brake hose to caliper. Install NEW washers on each side of hose fitting as banjo bolt is placed through fitting. Thread banjo bolt into caliper and tighten to 32 ft. lbs. (43 Nm) torque.

14. Install tire and wheel assembly. Tighten wheel mounting nuts to 110 ft. lbs. (150 Nm) torque.

15. Lower vehicle.

16. Remove brake pedal holding tool.

17. Connect battery negative cable to battery post. It is important that this is performed properly.

18. Bleed base brake hydraulic system as necessary.

19. Road test vehicle making several stops to wear off any foreign material on brakes and to seat brake shoes.

DISC BRAKE PADS

REMOVAL & INSTALLATION

See Figures 7 and 8.

1. Before servicing the vehicle, refer to the precautions in the beginning of this section.

2. Raise and support vehicle.

3. Remove wheel mounting nuts, then tire and wheel assembly.

➡In some cases, it may be necessary to retract caliper piston in its bore

a small amount in order to provide sufficient clearance between shoes and rotor to easily remove caliper from knuckle. This can usually be accomplished before guide pin bolts are

removed by grasping rear of caliper and pulling outward working with guide pins, thus retracting piston. Never push on piston directly as it may get damaged.

4. Remove Lower caliper guide pin bolt. To do so, hold the guide pin (3) stationary while turning bolt (1).

5. Rotate caliper upward (1), exposing brake pads (2 and 5). Use care not to overextend brake hose when doing this or damage may occur.

6. Remove inboard (2) and outboard (5) brake pads from caliper adapter (4).

7. If necessary, remove anti-rattle clips (3) from upper and lower abutments of adapter (4).

To install:

8. Completely retract caliper piston(s) back into bore(s) of caliper. To do so:

    a. Remove fluid reservoir cap.

    b. Use hand pressure or a C-clamp may be used to retract piston, first placing a wood block over piston(s) before installing C-clamp to avoid damaging piston(s).

    c. Install fluid reservoir cap.

9. If removed, attach anti-rattle clips to upper and lower abutments of adapter.

10. Install inboard and outboard brake pads on caliper adapter. Inboard and outboard pads are interchangeable.

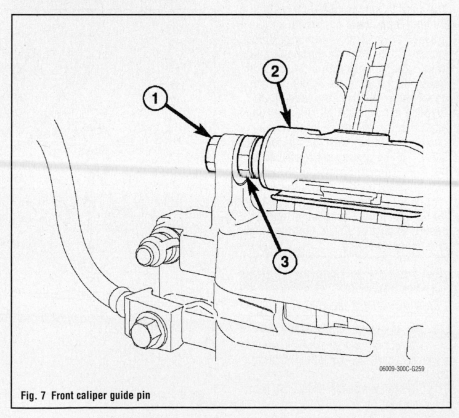

Fig. 7 Front caliper guide pin

06009-300C-G259

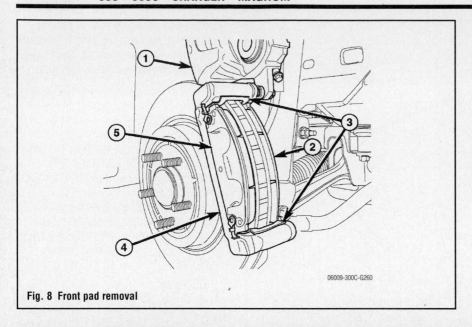

Fig. 8 Front pad removal

06009-300C-G260

11. Push caliper guide pins into caliper adapter to clear caliper mounting bosses when installing.

12. Rotate caliper downward, aligning upper mounting boss with lower guide pin.

13. Install upper caliper guide pin bolt. While holding guide pin stationary tighten bolt to 44 ft. lbs. (60 Nm) torque.

14. Install tire and wheel assembly. Tighten wheel mounting nuts to 110 ft. lbs. (150 Nm) torque.

15. Lower vehicle.

16. Pump brake pedal several times to set pads to caliper and brake rotor.

17. Check and adjust brake fluid level in reservoir.

18. Road test vehicle making several stops to wear off any foreign material on brakes and to seat brake shoes.

BRAKES

REAR DISC BRAKES

✳✳ CAUTION

Dust and dirt accumulating on brake parts during normal use may contain asbestos fibers from production or aftermarket brake linings. Breathing excessive concentrations of asbestos fibers can cause serious bodily harm. Exercise care when servicing brake parts. Do not sand or grind brake lining unless equipment used is designed to contain the dust residue. Do not clean brake parts with compressed air or by dry brushing. Cleaning should be done by dampening the brake components with a fine mist of water, then wiping the brake components clean with a dampened cloth. Dispose of cloth and all residue containing asbestos fibers in an impermeable container with the appropriate label. Follow practices prescribed by the Occupational Safety and Health Administration (OSHA) and the Environmental Protection Agency (EPA) for the handling, processing, and disposing of dust or debris that may contain asbestos fibers.

BRAKE CALIPER

REMOVAL & INSTALLATION

See Figures 9 and 10.

1. Before servicing the vehicle, refer to the precautions in the beginning of this section.

2. Disconnect and isolate battery negative cable from battery post.

3. Using a brake pedal holding tool, depress brake pedal past its first inch of travel and hold it in this position. Holding pedal in this position will isolate master cylinder from hydraulic brake system and will not allow brake fluid to drain out of brake fluid reservoir while brake lines are open.

4. Raise and support vehicle.

5. Remove wheel mounting nuts, then tire and wheel assembly.

6. Remove banjo bolt connecting flexible brake hose to caliper. There are two sealing washers (one on each side of hose fitting) that will come off when bolt is removed. Discard these washers; install NEW washers on installation.

7. While holding guide pins from turning, remove caliper guide pin bolts.

8. Remove brake caliper from brake adapter and pads.

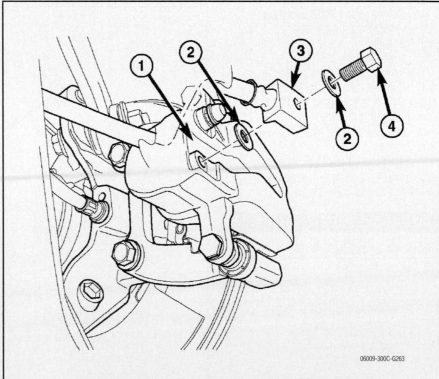

06009-300C-G263

Fig. 9 Rear brake line (3) connection. (1) caliper, (2) washers, (4) banjo bolt

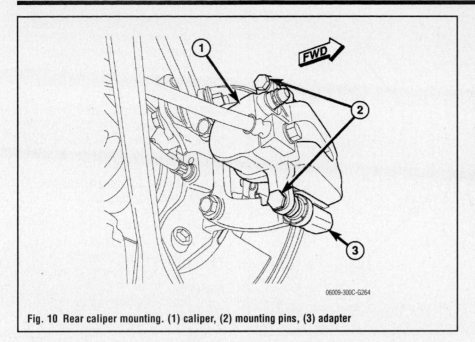

Fig. 10 Rear caliper mounting. (1) caliper, (2) mounting pins, (3) adapter

To install:

9. Completely retract caliper piston back into bore of caliper. Use hand pressure or a C-clamp may be used to retract piston, first placing a wood block over piston before installing C-clamp to avoid damaging piston.

❊❊ WARNING

Use care when installing caliper onto disc brake adapter to avoid damaging boots on caliper guide pins.

10. Push caliper guide pins into caliper adapter to clear caliper mounting bosses when installing.

11. Slide caliper over brake pads and onto caliper adapter.

❊❊ WARNING

Extreme caution should be taken not to cross-thread caliper guide pin bolts when they are installed.

12. Align caliper mounting holes with guide pins, then install guide pin bolts. While holding guide pins from turning, tighten bolts to 44 ft. lbs. (60 Nm) torque.

13. Install banjo bolt attaching brake hose to caliper. Install NEW washers on each side of hose fitting as banjo bolt is placed through fitting. Thread banjo bolt into caliper and tighten to 32 ft. lbs. (43 Nm).

14. Install tire and wheel assembly. Tighten wheel mounting nuts to 110 ft. lbs. (150 Nm).

15. Lower vehicle.

16. Remove brake pedal holding tool.

17. Connect battery negative cable to battery post. It is important that this is performed properly.

18. Bleed base brake hydraulic system as necessary.

19. Road test vehicle making several stops to wear off any foreign material on brakes and to seat brake shoes.

DISC BRAKE PADS

REMOVAL & INSTALLATION

See Figures 11 and 12.

1. Before servicing the vehicle, refer to the precautions in the beginning of this section.

2. Raise and support vehicle.

3. Remove wheel mounting nuts, then tire and wheel assembly.

➡**In some cases, it may be necessary to retract caliper piston in its bore a small amount in order to provide sufficient clearance between shoes and rotor to easily remove caliper from knuckle. This can usually be accomplished before guide pin bolts are removed by grasping rear of caliper and pulling outward working with guide pins, thus retracting piston. Never push on piston directly as it may get damaged.**

4. Remove upper caliper guide pin bolt. To do so, hold the guide pin stationary while turning bolt.

5. Rotate caliper downward, exposing brake pads. Use care not to overextend brake hose when doing this or damage may occur.

6. Remove inboard and outboard brake pads from caliper adapter.

7. If necessary, remove anti-rattle clips from upper and lower abutments of adapter.

To install:

8. Completely retract caliper piston back into bore of caliper. To do so:

   a. Remove fluid reservoir cap.

   b. Use hand pressure or a C-clamp may be used to retract piston, first placing a wood block over piston before installing C-clamp to avoid damaging piston.

   c. Install fluid reservoir cap.

9. If removed, attach anti-rattle clips to upper and lower abutments of adapter.

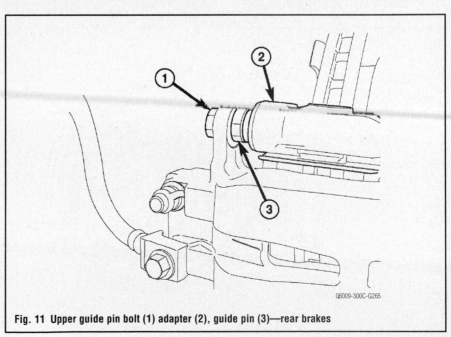

Fig. 11 Upper guide pin bolt (1) adapter (2), guide pin (3)—rear brakes

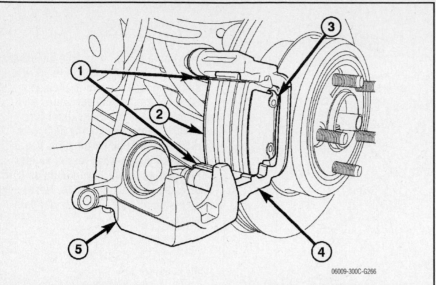

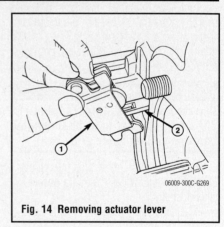

Fig. 12 Rear brake pad removal/installation. (1) anti-rattle clips, (2, 3) brake pads, (4) adapter, (5) caliper

06009-300C-G266

10. Install NEW inboard and outboard brake pads on caliper adapter. NEW Inboard and outboard pads are interchangeable.

11. Push caliper guide pins into caliper adapter to clear caliper mounting bosses when installing.

12. Rotate caliper upward, aligning upper mounting boss with upper guide pin.

13. Install Upper caliper guide pin bolt. While holding guide pin stationary tighten bolt to 44 ft. lbs. (60 Nm) torque.

14. Install tire and wheel assembly. Tighten wheel mounting nuts to 110 ft. lbs. (150 Nm) torque.

15. Lower vehicle.

16. Pump brake pedal several times to set pads to caliper and brake rotor.

17. Check and adjust brake fluid level in reservoir.

18. Road test vehicle making several stops to wear off any foreign material on brakes and to seat brake shoes.

BRAKES

PARKING BRAKE

PARKING BRAKE SHOES

REMOVAL & INSTALLATION

See Figures 13 through 16.

1. Before servicing the vehicle, refer to the precautions in the beginning of this section.

➡**The following procedure may be used to remove shoes on either side of the vehicle.**

2. Raise and support vehicle.

3. Remove rear hub and bearing.

4. Completely back off parking brake shoe adjustment.

5. Remove parking brake shoe adjuster spring.

6. Remove shoe adjuster.

7. Remove upper brake shoe hold-down clip and pin.

8. Remove upper shoe from return spring and shoe actuator lever.

9. Remove return spring from lower shoe.

10. Remove shoe actuator lever from end of cable.

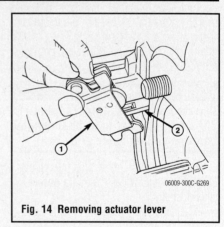

Fig. 14 Removing actuator lever

06009-300C-G269

11. Remove lower brake shoe hold-down clip and pin.

12. Remove lower shoe.

13. Inspect springs, adjuster, lever and aluminum shoe anchor pin for wear or damage. Replace as necessary.

To install:

➡**The following procedure may be used to install shoes on either side of the vehicle.**

➡**Inspect springs, adjuster, lever and aluminum shoe anchor pin for wear or damage prior to installation. Replace as necessary.**

14. Install lower brake shoe hold-down pin through rear of support.

15. Install lower shoe against support plate.

16. Install lower brake shoe hold-down clip.

1. Shoe actuator lever
2. Backing plate
3. Adjuster spring
4. Return spring
5. Adapter
6. Brake shoes
7. Hold-down pins
8. Adjuster

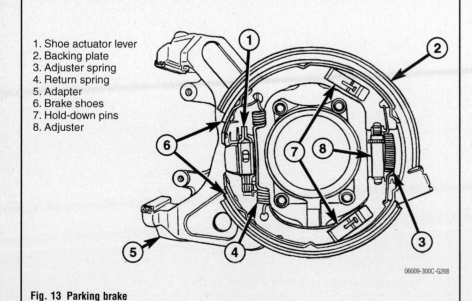

Fig. 13 Parking brake

06009-300C-G268

17. Install shoe actuator lever on end of parking brake cable. Make sure actuator lever is positioned with word "UP" facing outward.

18. Install return spring to lower shoe.

19. Install upper shoe against support plate and onto shoe actuator lever.

20. Install upper brake shoe hold-down pin through rear of support and upper shoe.

21. Install upper brake shoe hold-down clip.

22. Attach return spring to upper shoe.

23. Install shoe adjuster. Place end of adjuster with star wheel upward.

24. Install parking brake shoe adjuster spring.

25. Using Brake Shoe Gauge, Special Tool C-3919, or equivalent, measure inside diameter of parking brake drum portion of rotor.

26. Place Gauge over parking brake shoes at widest point.

27. Using adjuster star wheel, adjust parking brake shoes until linings on both park brake shoes just touch jaws on gauge. This will give a good preliminary adjustment of parking brake shoes, before a final adjustment is made at end of this procedure.

28. Install hub and bearing with wheel speed sensor as well as all components necessary to access it.

29. Lower vehicle.

30. Perform final adjustment of parking brake shoes.

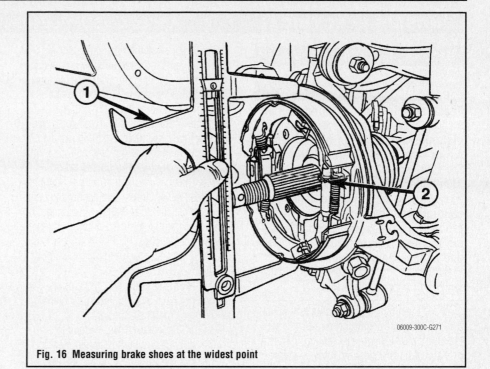

Fig. 16 Measuring brake shoes at the widest point

ADJUSTMENT
See Figure 17.

1. Place parking brake lever in "full released" position.

2. Raise and support vehicle.

3. Remove plug in parking brake shoe support to access adjuster star-wheel.

➡ **Through the access hole, rotate the adjuster star wheel in the following direction to expand the shoes outward against the drum. Left brake: rotate**

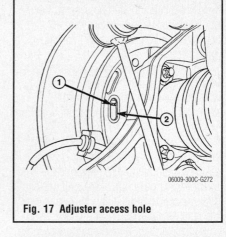

Fig. 17 Adjuster access hole

star-wheel toward rear of vehicle. Right brake: rotate starwheel toward front of vehicle.

4. Using an appropriate tool, turn adjuster starwheel until wheel will not rotate.

5. Back off adjuster six detents (teeth).

6. Rotate wheel, checking for light drag. If drag is too heavy, continue to back off adjuster one detent at a time until light drag is present. Do not back off star-wheel more than 17 detents from wheel lock.

7. Install access plug.

8. Adjust opposite wheel parking brake shoes using same method.

9. Lower vehicle.

10. Apply and release parking brake lever once to ensure proper operation of parking brakes.

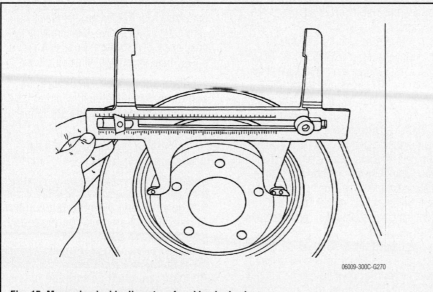

Fig. 15 Measuring inside diameter of parking brake drum

CHASSIS ELECTRICAL

AIR BAG (SUPPLEMENTAL RESTRAINT SYSTEM)

GENERAL INFORMATION

✷✷ CAUTION

These vehicles are equipped with an air bag system. The system must be disarmed before performing service on, or around, system components, the steering column, instrument panel components, wiring and sensors. Failure to follow the safety precautions and the disarming procedure could result in accidental air bag deployment, possible injury and unnecessary system repairs.

SERVICE PRECAUTIONS

Disconnect and isolate the battery negative cable before beginning any airbag system component diagnosis, testing, removal, or installation procedures. Allow system capacitor to discharge for two minutes before beginning any component service. This will disable the airbag system. Failure to disable the airbag system may result in accidental airbag deployment, personal injury, or death.

Do not place an intact undeployed airbag face down on a solid surface. The airbag will propel into the air if accidentally deployed and may result in personal injury or death.

When carrying or handling an undeployed airbag, the trim side (face) of the airbag should be pointing towards the body to minimize possibility of injury if accidental deployment occurs. Failure to do this may result in personal injury or death.

Replace airbag system components with OEM replacement parts. Substitute parts may appear interchangeable, but internal differences may result in inferior occupant protection. Failure to do so may result in occupant personal injury or death.

Wear safety glasses, rubber gloves, and long sleeved clothing when cleaning powder residue from vehicle after an airbag deployment. Powder residue emitted from a deployed airbag can cause skin irritation. Flush affected area with cool water if irritation is experienced. If nasal or throat irritation is experienced, exit the vehicle for fresh air until the irritation ceases. If irritation continues, see a physician.

Do not use a replacement airbag that is not in the original packaging. This may result in improper deployment, personal injury, or death.

The factory installed fasteners, screws and bolts used to fasten airbag components have a special coating and are specifically designed for the airbag system. Do not use substitute fasteners. Use only original equipment fasteners listed in the parts catalog when fastener replacement is required.

During, and following, any child restraint anchor service, due to impact event or vehicle repair, carefully inspect all mounting hardware, tether straps, and anchors for proper installation, operation, or damage. If a child restraint anchor is found damaged in any way, the anchor must be replaced. Failure to do this may result in personal injury or death.

Deployed and non-deployed airbags may or may not have live pyrotechnic material within the airbag inflator.

Do not dispose of driver/passenger/curtain airbags or seat belt tensioners unless you are sure of complete deployment. Refer to the Hazardous Substance Control System for proper disposal.

Dispose of deployed airbags and tensioners consistent with state, provincial, local, and federal regulations.

After any airbag component testing or service, do not connect the battery negative cable. Personal injury or death may result if the system test is not performed first.

If the vehicle is equipped with the Occupant Classification System (OCS), do not connect the battery negative cable before performing the OCS Verification Test using the scan tool and the appropriate diagnostic information. Personal injury or death may result if the system test is not performed properly.

Never replace both the Occupant Restraint Controller (ORC) and the Occupant Classification Module (OCM) at the same time. If both require replacement, replace one, then perform the Airbag System test before replacing the other.

Both the ORC and the OCM store Occupant Classification System (OCS) calibration data, which they transfer to one another when one of them is replaced. If both are replaced at the same time, an irreversible fault will be set in both modules and the OCS may malfunction and cause personal injury or death.

If equipped with OCS, the Seat Weight Sensor is a sensitive, calibrated unit and must be handled carefully. Do not drop or handle roughly. If dropped or damaged, replace with another sensor. Failure to do so may result in occupant injury or death.

If equipped with OCS, the front passenger seat must be handled carefully as well. When removing the seat, be careful when setting on floor not to drop. If dropped, the sensor may be inoperative, could result in occupant injury, or possibly death.

If equipped with OCS, when the passenger front seat is on the floor, no one should sit in the front passenger seat. This uneven force may damage the sensing ability of the seat weight sensors. If sat on and damaged, the sensor may be inoperative, could result in occupant injury, or possibly death.

DISARMING THE SYSTEM

1. Before servicing the vehicle, refer to the precautions in the beginning of this section.

Disconnect and isolate the negative battery cable. Wait 2 minutes for the system capacitor to discharge before performing any service.

ARMING THE SYSTEM

1. Before servicing the vehicle, refer to the precautions in the beginning of this section.

To arm the system, connect the negative battery cable.

CLOCKSPRING CENTERING

1. Before servicing the vehicle, refer to the precautions in the beginning of this section.

If the rotating tape (wire coil) in the clockspring is not positioned properly with the steering wheel and the front wheels, the clockspring may fail. The following procedure MUST BE USED to center the clockspring if it is not known to be properly positioned, or if the front wheels were moved from the straight ahead position.

➡**Before starting this procedure, be certain to turn the steering wheel until the front wheels are in the straight-ahead position.**

2. Position steering wheel and front wheels straight-ahead.

✷✷ CAUTION

Before servicing the steering column the airbag system must be disarmed.

✷✷ WARNING

All fasteners must be torqued to specification to ensure proper operation of the steering column.

3. Position the front wheels straight-ahead.

4. Fully extend or pull out adjustable steering column.

5. Disconnect the negative (ground) cable from the battery.

6. From behind the steering wheel, remove the two screw covers and screws to the driver airbag.

✳✳ WARNING

Do not pull on the horn switch feed pigtail wire to disengage the connector from the driver's airbag or to disconnect the horn switch to steering wheel wire harness connection. Improper pulling on this pigtail wire or connection can result in damage to the horn switch membrane or feed circuit.

7. Carefully pull airbag rearward just far enough to disconnect the two airbag squib connectors and the horn connector.

8. Separate driver airbag from steering column.

➡The driver's airbag trim cover is available for service separately. If the horn switch is faulty or the trim cover is damaged, the airbag cushion assembly may be transferred to a new trim cover. If the airbag is defective, the entire driver airbag and driver airbag trim cover must be replaced as an assembly.

9. Remove the steering wheel retaining bolt, then slide the steering wheel off the shaft.

10. Remove at least one clockspring screw. This will help keep the clockspring from un-centering itself.

11. Back out the set screw through the access hole in the bottom of the Steering Column Control Module (SCCM).

12. Pull the SCCM off the steering column shaft.

13. Remove the three clockspring screws.

14. Carefully pull straight up on clockspring to remove.

15. The clockspring can rotate approximately 5¾ turns from lock to lock. To be properly centered, rotate the clockspring rotor clockwise until the rotor stops. Do not apply excessive force.

16. From the end of travel, rotate the rotor counterclockwise two turns and then keep going a little more until the wires end up on the right side of the column shaft (at the 3 o'clock position).

17. Tighten the set screw securing the SCCM.

18. Tighten clockspring screws that were backed out to keep the clockspring from unwinding.

19. Align the spline on the steering wheel hub to shaft and install the steering wheel.

20. Install a NEW retaining bolt. Torque the bolt to 52 ft. lbs. (70 Nm).

21. Install the driver's airbag.

22. Connect the battery negative cable. If equipped with Electronic Stability Program (ESP), the steering angle sensor must be calibrated.

23. Install the steering column control module.

✳✳ CAUTION

Do not connect the battery negative cable. Personal injury or death may result if the following system test is not performed properly:

d. With the battery negative cable disconnected, connect the scan tool to the Data Link Connector (DLC).

e. Turn the ignition key to the ON position, then exit vehicle with the scan tool.

f. After checking that no one is inside the vehicle, connect the battery negative remote terminal.

g. Read and record the ACTIVE Diagnostic Trouble Code (DTC) data.

h. Read and record any STORED DTCs.

i. Refer to the proper diagnostic information if any DTCs are found in Step 4 and Step 5.

j. If the airbag warning lamp either fails to light, or goes ON and stays ON, there is a system malfunction.

24. Position driver airbag in steering wheel near mounting location.

25. Connect the two airbag squib connectors and the horn connector.

26. Position the driver's airbag mounting screws into the driver airbag. From behind the steering wheel install the two screws to the driver airbag. Torque the two screws to 89 inch lbs. (10 Nm).

DRIVETRAIN

AUTOMATIC TRANSMISSION ASSEMBLY

REMOVAL & INSTALLATION

NAG1

See Figures 18 through 20.

1. Before servicing the vehicle, refer to the precautions in the beginning of this section.

➡If the transmission is being reconditioned (clutch/seal replacement) or replaced, it is necessary to perform the TCM Adaptation Procedure using the scan tool.

2. Disconnect the negative battery cable.

3. Raise and support the vehicle.

4. Mark driveshaft and the transmission flange for assembly alignment.

5. Remove the bolts holding the rear driveshaft coupler to the transmission flange.

6. Slide the driveshaft rearward until the coupler clears the driveshaft pilot on the transmission output shaft.

7. Remove the bolts holding the starter motor to the transmission.

8. Remove the starter from the transmission starter pocket and safely relocate.

9. Remove the bolt holding the torque converter access cover to the transmission.

10. Remove the torque converter access cover from the transmission.

11. Rotate crankshaft in clockwise direction until converter bolts are accessible. Then remove bolts one at a time. Rotate crankshaft with socket wrench on dampener bolt.

12. Disconnect the gearshift cable) from the transmission manual valve lever.

13. Loosen the bolts holding the shift cable retaining strap to the transmission.

14. Remove the shift cable from the transmission.

15. Remove bolt and screw holding the heat shield to the transmission.

16. Remove the heat shield from the transmission.

17. Disconnect 13-pin plug connector. Turn bayonet lock of guide bushing counterclockwise.

18. Remove the 13-pin connector from the transmission.

19. Disconnect transmission fluid cooler lines at transmission fittings and clips.

20. Disconnect the transmission vent hose from the transmission.

21. Support rear of engine with safety stand or jack.

22. Raise transmission slightly with service jack to relieve load on crossmember and supports.

23. Remove bolts securing rear support and cushion to transmission crossmember.

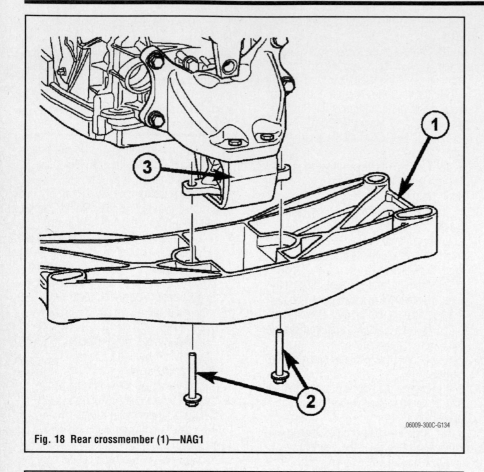

Fig. 18 Rear crossmember (1)—NAG1

.06009-300C-G134

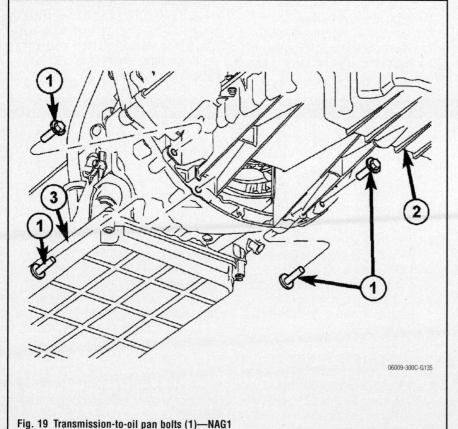

Fig. 19 Transmission-to-oil pan bolts (1)—NAG1

06009-300C-G135

24. Remove the bolts holding the engine oil pan to the transmission.

25. Remove all remaining bolts holding the engine to the transmission.

26. Carefully work transmission and torque converter assembly rearward off engine block dowels.

27. Hold torque converter in place during transmission removal.

28. Lower transmission and remove assembly from under the vehicle.

29. To remove torque converter, carefully slide torque converter out of the transmission.

To install:

30. Check torque converter hub and hub drive flats for sharp edges burrs, scratches, or nicks. Polish the hub and flats with 320/400 grit paper and crocus cloth if necessary. The hub must be smooth to avoid damaging pump seal at installation.

31. If a replacement transmission is being installed, transfer any components necessary, such as the manual shift lever and shift cable bracket, from the original transmission onto the replacement transmission.

32. Lubricate oil pump seal lip with transmission fluid.

33. Place torque converter in position in transmission.

✳✳ WARNING

Do not damage oil pump seal or converter hub while inserting torque converter into the front of the transmission.

34. Align torque converter to oil pump seal opening.

35. Insert torque converter hub into oil pump.

36. While pushing torque converter inward, rotate converter until converter is fully seated in the oil pump gears.

37. Check converter seating with a scale and straight-edge at "A". Surface of converter lugs should be at least 1

38. mm (¾ in.) to rear of straight-edge when converter is fully seated.

39. If necessary, temporarily secure converter with C-clamp attached to the converter housing.

40. Check condition of converter driveplate. Replace the plate if cracked, distorted or damaged. Also be sure transmission dowel pins are seated in engine block and protrude far enough to hold transmission in alignment.

41. Apply a light coating of Mopar° High Temp Grease, or equivalent, to the torque

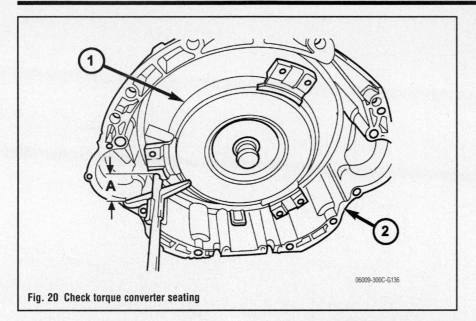

06009-300C-G136

Fig. 20 Check torque converter seating

converter hub pocket in the rear pocket of the engine's crankshaft.

42. Raise transmission and align the torque converter with the drive plate and the transmission converter housing with the engine block.

43. Move transmission forward. Then raise, lower, or tilt transmission to align the converter housing with the engine block dowels.

44. Carefully work transmission forward and over engine block dowels until converter hub is seated in crankshaft. Verify that no wires, or the transmission vent hose, have become trapped between the engine block and the transmission.

45. Install two bolts to attach the transmission to the engine.

46. Install remaining torque converter housing to engine bolts. Tighten to 29 ft. lbs. (39 Nm).

47. Install rear transmission crossmember. Tighten crossmember to frame bolts to 50 ft. lbs. (68 Nm).

48. Install rear support to transmission. Tighten bolts to 35 ft. lbs. (47 Nm).

49. Lower transmission onto crossmember and install bolts attaching transmission mount to crossmember. Tighten clevis bracket to crossmember bolts to 35 ft. lbs. (47 Nm).

50. Remove engine support fixture.

51. Install the transmission to engine oil pan bolts. Tighten to 29 ft. lbs. (39 Nm).

52. Connect the gearshift cable to the transmission manual shift lever.

53. Check O-ring on plug connector, and replace if necessary.

54. Install the plug connector into the guide bushing. Turn bayonet lock of guide bushing clockwise to connect plug connector.

55. Position the heat shield onto the transmission housing and install the screw and bolt to hold the shield in place.

❉❉ WARNING

It is essential that correct length bolts be used to attach the converter to the driveplate. Bolts that are too long will damage the clutch surface inside the converter.

56. Install all torque converter-to-driveplate bolts by hand.

57. Verify that the torque converter is pulled flush to the driveplate. Tighten bolts to 31 ft. lbs. (42 Nm).

58. Install the torque converter bolt access cover onto the transmission. Install the access cover bolt and tighten to 96 inch lbs. (11 Nm).

59. Install starter motor.

60. Connect the cooler line fittings and cooler lines to the transmission.

➡Inspect the fill tube grommet to determine if the grommet is new or used. If a new fill tube grommet is in the transmission case, pierce the center of the grommet with a ballpoint pen, or similar instrument, to prepare the grommet for the fill tube installation.

61. Install transmission fill tube.
62. Install exhaust components.
63. Align and connect the driveshaft.
64. Adjust gearshift cable if necessary.
65. Lower vehicle.
66. Connect negative battery cable.
67. Fill the transmission with the appropriate transmission fluid.
68. Verify proper operation.

42RLE

See Figures 21 and 22.

1. Before servicing the vehicle, refer to the precautions in the beginning of this section.

2. Disconnect the negative battery cable.

3. Raise and support the vehicle.

4. Mark driveshaft and the transmission flange for assembly alignment.

5. Remove the bolts holding the rear driveshaft coupler to the transmission flange.

6. Slide the driveshaft rearward until the coupler clears the driveshaft pilot on the transmission output shaft.

7. Remove the bolts holding the starter motor to the transmission.

8. Remove the starter from the transmission starter pocket and safely relocate.

9. Remove the bolt holding the torque converter access cover to the transmission, 3.5L engines.

10. Remove the torque converter access cover from the transmission.

11. Remove the structural collar bolts and structural collar on vehicles equipped with 2.7L engines.

12. Rotate crankshaft in clockwise direction until converter bolts are accessible. Then remove bolts one at a time. Rotate crankshaft with socket wrench on dampener bolt.

13. Disconnect the gearshift cable from the transmission manual valve lever.

14. Loosen the bolts holding the shift cable retaining strap to the transmission.

15. Remove the shift cable from the transmission.

16. Disconnect wires from the input and output speed sensors.

17. Disconnect wires from the transmission range sensor.

18. Disconnect wires from the solenoid/pressure switch assembly.

19. Remove the crankshaft position sensor.

20. Remove the bolt holding the transmission fill tube to the transmission.

21. Remove the transmission fill tube.

22. Disconnect transmission fluid cooler lines at transmission fittings and clips.

23. Disconnect the transmission vent hose from the transmission.

24. Support rear of engine with safety stand or jack.

25. Raise transmission slightly with service jack to relieve load on crossmember and supports.

26. Remove bolts securing rear support and cushion to transmission crossmember.

27. Remove bolts attaching crossmember to frame and remove crossmember.

28. Remove the bolts holding the engine oil pan to the transmission.

29. Remove all remaining bolts holding the engine to the transmission.

30. Carefully work transmission and torque converter assembly rearward off engine block dowels.

31. Hold torque converter in place during transmission removal.

32. Lower transmission and remove assembly from under the vehicle.

33. To remove torque converter, carefully slide torque converter out of the transmission.

To install:

34. Check torque converter hub and hub drive flats for sharp edges burrs, scratches, or nicks. Polish the hub and flats with 320/400 grit paper and crocus cloth if necessary. The hub must be smooth to avoid damaging pump seal at installation.

35. If a replacement transmission is being installed, transfer any components necessary, such as the manual shift lever and shift cable bracket, from the original transmission onto the replacement transmission.

36. Lubricate oil pump seal lip with transmission fluid.

37. Place torque converter in position in transmission.

✵✵ WARNING

Do not damage oil pump seal or converter hub while inserting torque converter into the front of the transmission.

38. Align torque converter to oil pump seal opening.

39. Insert torque converter hub into oil pump.

40. While pushing torque converter inward, rotate converter until converter is fully seated in the oil pump gears.

41. Check converter seating with a scale and straight-edge at "A". Surface of converter lugs should be at least 19 mm (¾ in.) to rear of straight-edge when converter is fully seated.

42. If necessary, temporarily secure converter with C-clamp attached to the converter housing.

43. Check condition of converter drive-plate. Replace the plate if cracked, distorted or damaged. Also be sure transmission dowel pins are seated in engine block and protrude far enough to hold transmission in alignment.

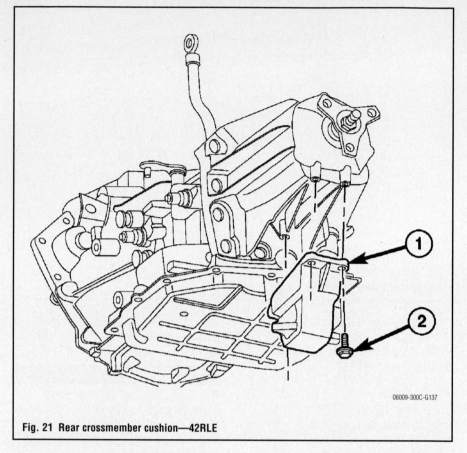

06009-300C-G137

Fig. 21 Rear crossmember cushion—42RLE

44. Apply a light coating of Mopar° High Temp Grease to the torque converter hub pocket in the rear pocket of the engine's crankshaft.

45. Raise transmission and align the torque converter with the drive plate and the transmission converter housing with the engine block.

46. Move transmission forward. Then raise, lower, or tilt transmission to align the converter housing with the engine block dowels.

47. Carefully work transmission forward and over engine block dowels until converter hub is seated in crankshaft. Verify that no wires, or the transmission vent hose,

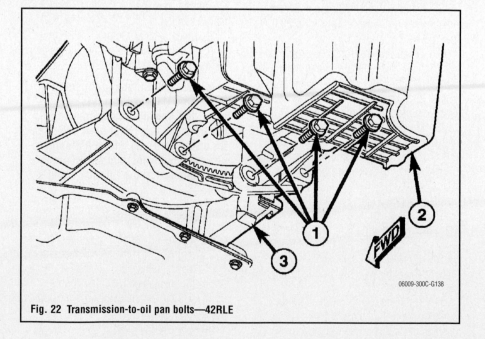

06009-300C-G138

Fig. 22 Transmission-to-oil pan bolts—42RLE

have become trapped between the engine block and the transmission.

48. Install two bolts to attach the transmission to the engine.

49. Install remaining torque converter housing to engine bolts. Tighten to 29 ft. lbs. (39 Nm).

50. Install rear transmission crossmember. Tighten crossmember to frame bolts to 50 ft. lbs. (68 Nm).

51. Install rear support to transmission. Tighten bolts to 35 ft. lbs. (47 Nm).

52. Lower transmission onto crossmember and install bolts attaching transmission mount to crossmember. Tighten clevis bracket to crossmember bolts to 39 ft. lbs. (47 Nm).

53. Remove engine support fixture.

54. Install the transmission to engine oil pan bolts. Tighten to 29 ft. lbs. (39 Nm).

55. Connect input and output speed sensor wires and the transmission range sensor.

56. Connect wires to the solenoid/pressure switch assembly.

57. Install the crankshaft position sensor.

58. Connect the gearshift cable to the transmission manual shift lever.

⁕⁕ WARNING

It is essential that correct length bolts be used to attach the converter to the driveplate. Bolts that are too long will damage the clutch surface inside the converter.

59. Install all torque converter-to-driveplate bolts by hand.

60. Verify that the torque converter is pulled flush to the driveplate. Tighten bolts to 31 ft. lbs. (42 Nm).

61. Install the torque converter bolt access cover onto the transmission, for vehicles equipped with 3.5L engines. Install the access cover bolt and tighten to 96 inch lbs. (11 Nm).

62. Install the structural collar and bolts for vehicles equipped with a 2.7L engine.

63. Install starter motor.

64. Connect the cooler line fittings and cooler lines to the transmission.

➥**Inspect the fill tube grommet to determine if the grommet is new or used. If a new fill tube grommet is in the transmission case, pierce the center of the grommet with a ballpoint pen, or similar instrument, to prepare the grommet for the fill tube installation.**

65. Install the transmission fill tube.

66. Install exhaust components.

67. Align and connect the driveshaft.

68. Adjust gearshift cable if necessary.

69. Lower vehicle.

70. Connect negative battery cable.

71. Fill transmission with appropriate transmission fluid.

72. Verify proper operation.

TRANSFER CASE ASSEMBLY

REMOVAL & INSTALLATION

See Figures 23 through 25.

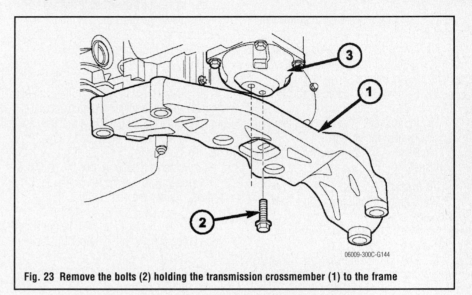

Fig. 23 Remove the bolts (2) holding the transmission crossmember (1) to the frame

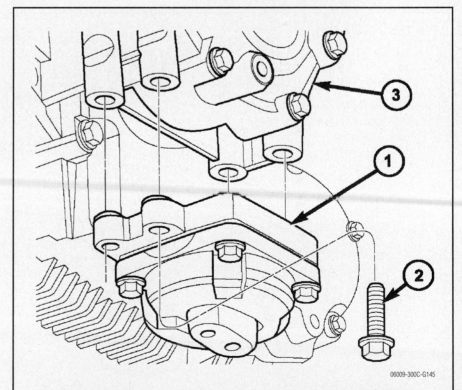

Fig. 24 Remove the bolts (2) holding the transmission mount (1) to the transfer case (3)— 5.7L engine

1. Before servicing the vehicle, refer to the precautions in the beginning of this section.

2. Raise support vehicle.

3. Disconnect the front and rear driveshafts from the transfer case.

4. Support transmission with jackstand.

5. Remove the bolts holding the transmission crossmember to the frame.

6. Remove the bolts holding the transmission crossmember to the transmission mount.

7. Remove the bolts holding the transmission mount to the transfer case, 5.7L engine, and remove the transmission mount.

8. Remove the bolts holding the transmission mount assembly to the transfer case, 3.5L engine, and remove the transmission mount assembly.

9. Remove the transfer case damper.

10. Remove the transfer case drain plug and drain transfer case lubricant.

11. Support transfer case with transmission jack.

12. Secure transfer case to jack with chains.

13. Lower the transmission and transfer case slightly, to improve access to the upper transfer case to transmission fasteners.

14. Remove nuts and bolts attaching transfer case to transmission.

15. Pull transfer case and jack rearward to disengage transfer case.

16. Remove transfer case from under vehicle.

To install:

17. Support transfer case on a transmission jack.

18. Secure transfer case to jack with chains.

19. Position the transfer case under the vehicle and align the input shaft with the transmission output shaft.

20. Move the transfer case and jack forward to engage transfer case to the transmission.

21. Install the nuts and bolts to attach transfer case to transmission. Tighten the 120mm bolts to 25 Nm (18 ft. lbs.), the 30mm bolts to 20 ft. lbs. (27 Nm), and the nuts to15 ft. lbs. (20 Nm)

22. Raise the transmission and transfer case into their normal position.

23. Fill the transfer case with the appropriate fluid.

24. Install the transfer case damper.

25. Install the transmission mount assembly to the transfer case and install the bolts to hold the transmission mount assembly to the transfer case, 3.5L engine. Tighten the bolts to 41 ft. lbs. (55 Nm).

26. Install the transmission mount to the transfer case and install the bolts to hold the transmission mount to the transfer case, 5.7L engine. Tighten the bolts to 50 ft. lbs. (68 Nm).

27. Install the bolts to hold the transmission crossmember to the transmission mount. Tighten the bolts to 48 ft. lbs. (65 Nm).

28. Install the bolts to hold the transmission crossmember to the frame. Tighten the bolts to 50 ft. lbs. (68 Nm).

29. Install the front and rear driveshafts to the transfer case.

FRONT DRIVESHAFT

REMOVAL & INSTALLATION

See Figure 26.

1. Before servicing the vehicle, refer to the precautions in the beginning of this section.

2. Place gearshift lever in NEUTRAL and raise vehicle on hoist.

3. Remove driveshaft heat shield.

4. Apply alignment index marks on the driveshaft and front axle flanges.

5. Remove four front driveshaft-to-axle flange bolts.

6. Apply alignment index marks on the driveshaft and transfer case flanges.

7. Remove four front driveshaft-to-transfer case flange bolts.

8. Remove the driveshaft assembly.

To install:

9. Install the driveshaft into position.

10. Starting at transfer case end, align index marks. Install driveshaft-to-transfer case flange bolts.

11. Align index marks at front axle end of shaft, and loose-install driveshaft-to-front axle flange bolts.

12. Torque driveshaft-to-transfer case and axle flange bolts to 22 ft. lbs. (30 Nm).

13. Install driveshaft heat shield.

14. Lower the vehicle.

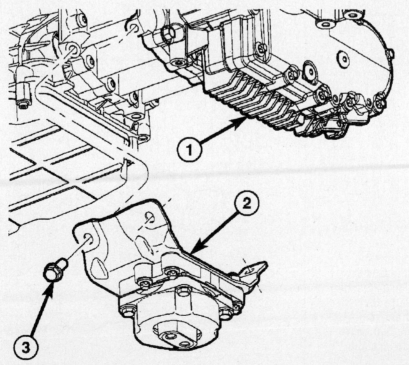

06009-300C-G146

Fig. 25 Remove the bolts (3) holding the transmission mount assembly (2) to the transfer case (1)—3.5L engine

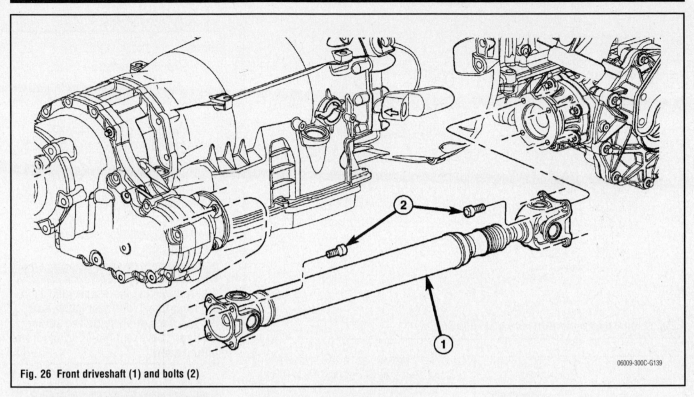

Fig. 26 Front driveshaft (1) and bolts (2)

06009-300C-G139

FRONT HALFSHAFT

REMOVAL & INSTALLATION

See Figures 27 through 29.

1. Before servicing the vehicle, refer to the precautions in the beginning of this section.
2. Raise and support vehicle.
3. Remove wheel mounting nuts, then tire and wheel assembly.
4. While holding link ball joint stem from rotating, remove nut fastening stabilizer link to shock clevis bracket. Slide link ball joint stem from clevis bracket.
5. Remove nut and pinch bolt fastening clevis bracket to bottom of shock assembly.
6. Remove nut and bolt attaching shock clevis bracket to lower control arm.
7. Pull lower end of clevis bracket outward away from lower control arm bushing, then slide it off shock assembly. It may be necessary to use an appropriate prying tool to spread clamp area of clevis bracket allowing removal from shock assembly.
8. While a helper applies brakes to keep hub from rotating, remove hub nut from axle halfshaft.

➡In some cases, it may be necessary to retract caliper piston in its bore a small amount in order to provide sufficient clearance between shoes and rotor to easily remove caliper from knuckle. This can usually be accomplished before mounting bolts are removed, by grasping rear of caliper and pulling outward working with guide pins, thus retracting piston. Never push on piston directly as it may get damaged.

9. Remove two bolts securing disc brake caliper and adapter to knuckle.
10. Remove disc brake caliper and adapter from knuckle as an assembly. Hang assembly out of way using wire or a bungee cord. Use care not to overextend brake hose when doing this.
11. Remove any clips retaining brake rotor to wheel studs.
12. Slide brake rotor off hub and bearing.

⁂ WARNING

In following step, use care not to damage ball joint seal boot while sliding the puller into place past seal boot.

13. Separate upper ball joint stud from knuckle.
14. Remove tool.
15. Remove nut from end of upper ball joint stud.
16. Remove clip fastening wheel speed sensor to knuckle.
17. Disengage right halfshaft from axle and remove from vehicle.
18. Remove left halfshaft from vehicle.

To install:

19. Install left halfshaft assembly.
20. Using Tool C-4193-A, install new axle seal.
21. Install right halfshaft assembly.

➡Before installing halfshafts into hub/bearing assemblies, ensure isolation washer is present on end of halfshaft. Inspect washer making sure it is not worn or damaged. Washer is bidirectional and can be installed in either direction on shaft.

22. Install halfshaft isolation washer.
23. Install halfshaft into hub/bearing assembly.
24. Loosely install halfshaft hub nut, and do not tighten at this time.

⁂ WARNING

It is important to tighten nut as described in following step to avoid damaging ball stud joint.

25. Place upper ball joint stud through hole in top of knuckle and install nut. Tighten nut by holding ball joint stud with a hex wrench while turning nut with a wrench. Tighten nut using crow foot wrench on torque wrench to 47 Nm + 90° turn (35 ft. lbs. + 90° turn) torque.

➡Inspect brake shoes (pads) before installation.

26. Clean hub face to remove any dirt or corrosion where rotor mounts.

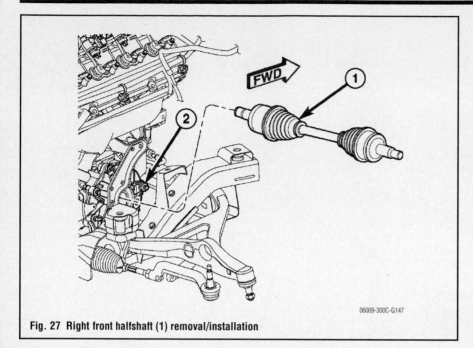

Fig. 27 Right front halfshaft (1) removal/installation

06009-300C-G147

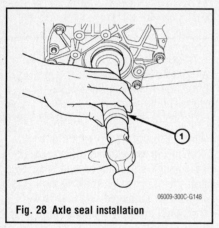

Fig. 28 Axle seal installation

06009-300C-G148

27. Install brake rotor over studs on hub and bearing.

28. Install disc brake caliper and adapter assembly over brake rotor.

29. Install mounting bolts securing caliper adapter to knuckle. Tighten bolts to 125 ft. lbs. (169 Nm) torque.

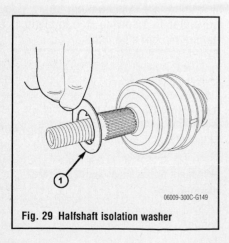

Fig. 29 Halfshaft isolation washer

06009-300C-G149

30. Pull lower end of shock assembly outward, then slide clevis bracket onto lower end. Slide clevis bracket onto shock assembly until bracket contacts collar on shock housing.

31. Install pinch bolt and nut fastening clevis bracket to bottom of shock assembly. Install pinch bolt from rear. Do not tighten at this time.

32. Slide clevis bracket over bushing mounted in lower control arm.

33. Install bolt and nut attaching shock clevis bracket to lower control arm. Do not tighten at this time.

34. Tighten pinch bolt attaching clevis bracket to shock assembly to 45 ft. lbs. (61 Nm) torque.

35. Slide stabilizer link ball joint stem into clevis bracket. Install nut fastening link to clevis bracket. Tighten nut by holding ball joint stud while turning nut. Tighten nut using crow foot wrench on torque wrench to 108 ft. lbs. (146 Nm) torque.

36. Attach wheel speed sensor cable routing clip at knuckle.

37. Install hub nut on end of axle halfshaft. While a helper applies brakes to keep hub from turning, tighten hub nut to 157 ft. lbs. (213 Nm) torque.

38. Install tire and wheel assembly. Tighten wheel mounting nuts to 110 ft. lbs. (150 Nm) torque.

39. Lower vehicle.

➡ **When tightening lower shock clevis mounting bolt, do not attempt rotating bolt. Bolt shaft is serrated. Turn nut only.**

40. Tighten lower shock clevis bracket bolt nut to 128 ft. lbs. (174 Nm) torque.

CV-JOINTS OVERHAUL

Inner

See Figures 30 through 37.

1. Before servicing the vehicle, refer to the precautions in the beginning of this section.

2. Remove large boot clamp which retains inner tripod joint sealing boot to tripod joint housing and discard.

3. Remove small clamp which retains inner tripod joint sealing boot to interconnecting shaft and discard.

4. Remove the sealing boot from the tripod housing and slide it down the interconnecting shaft.

✳✳ WARNING

When removing the tripod joint housing from the spider assembly, hold the bearings in place on the spider trunions to prevent the bearings from falling away.

5. Slide the tripod joint housing off the spider assembly and the interconnecting shaft.

6. Remove snapring which retains spider assembly to interconnecting shaft. Do not hit the outer tripod bearings in an

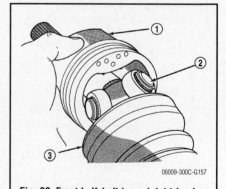

Fig. 30 Front halfshaft inner joint tripod housing (1), spider (2), boot (3)

06009-300C-G157

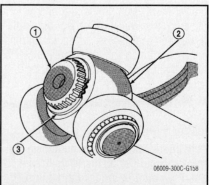

Fig. 31 Front shaft inner joint (1) shaft, (2) spider, (3) snapring

06009-300C-G158

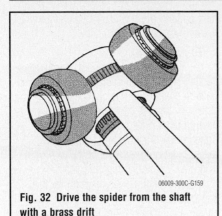

Fig. 32 Drive the spider from the shaft with a brass drift

06009-300C-G159

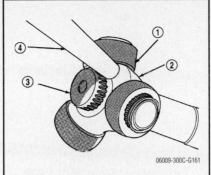

Fig. 34 Drive the spider (2) into place with a brass drift (4)

06009-300C-G161

attempt to remove spider assembly from interconnecting shaft.

7. Remove the spider assembly from interconnecting shaft. If spider assembly will not come off interconnecting shaft by hand, it can be removed by tapping spider assembly with a brass drift.

8. Slide sealing boot off interconnecting shaft.

9. Thoroughly clean and inspect spider assembly, tripod joint housing, and interconnecting shaft for any signs of excessive wear. If any parts show signs of excessive wear, the driveshaft assembly will require replacement. Component parts of these driveshaft assemblies are not serviceable.

To assemble:

10. Slide inner tripod joint seal boot retaining clamp, onto interconnecting shaft. Then, slide the replacement inner tripod joint sealing boot onto the interconnecting shaft. Inner tripod joint seal boot MUST be positioned on interconnecting shaft, so the raised bead on the inside of the seal boot is in groove on interconnecting shaft.

11. Install spider assembly onto interconnecting shaft. Spider assembly must be installed on interconnecting shaft far enough to fully install spider retaining snapring.

12. If spider assembly will not fully install on interconnecting shaft by hand, it can be installed by tapping the spider body with a brass drift. Do not hit the outer tripod bearings in an attempt to install spider assembly on interconnecting shaft.

13. Install the spider assembly to interconnecting shaft retaining snapring into groove on end of interconnecting shaft. Be sure the snapring is fully seated into groove on interconnecting shaft.

14. Distribute ½ the amount of grease provided in the seal boot service package (DO NOT USE ANY OTHER TYPE OF GREASE) into tripod housing. Put the remaining amount into the sealing boot.

15. Align tripod housing with spider assembly and then slide tripod housing over spider assembly and interconnecting shaft.

16. Install inner tripod joint seal boot to interconnecting shaft clamp evenly on sealing boot.

17. Clamp sealing boot onto interconnecting shaft using crimper, Special Tool C-4975-A and the following procedure. Place crimping tool C-4975-A over bridge of clamp. Tighten nut on crimping tool C-4975-A until jaws on tool are closed completely together, face to face.

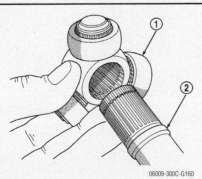

Fig. 33 Install spider assembly (1) onto interconnecting shaft (2)

06009-300C-G160

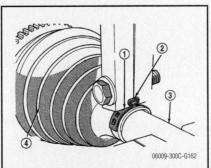

Fig. 35 Clamp type band tool. (1) clamp, (2) crimp completely closed, (3) shaft, boot (4)

06009-300C-G162

✳✳ WARNING

Seal must not be dimpled, stretched or out of shape in any way. If seal is NOT shaped correctly, equalize pressure in seal and shape it by hand.

18. Position sealing boot into the tripod housing retaining groove. Install seal boot retaining clamp evenly on sealing boot.

✳✳ WARNING

The following positioning procedure determines the correct air pressure inside the inner tripod joint assembly prior to clamping the sealing boot to inner tripod joint housing. If this procedure is not done prior to clamping sealing boot to tripod joint housing sealing boot durability can be adversely affected.

✳✳ WARNING

When venting the inner tripod joint assembly, use care so inner tripod sealing boot does not get punctured, or in any other way damaged. If sealing boot is punctured, or damaged in any way while being vented, the sealing boot can not be used.

19. Insert a trim stick between the tripod joint and the sealing boot to vent inner tripod joint assembly. When inserting trim stick between tripod housing and sealing boot ensure trim stick is held flat and firmly against the tripod housing. If this is not done damage to the sealing boot can occur. If inner tripod joint has a Hytrel (hard plastic) sealing boot, be sure trim stick is inserted between soft rubber insert and tripod housing not the hard plastic sealing boot and soft rubber insert.

20. With trim stick inserted between sealing boot and tripod joint housing, position the interconnecting shaft so it is at the center of its travel in the tripod joint housing. Remove the trim stick from between the sealing boot and the tripod joint housing. This procedure will equalize the air pressure in the tripod joint, preventing premature sealing boot failure.

21. Position trilobal boot to interface with the tripod housing. The lobes of the boot must be properly aligned with the recesses of the tripod housing.

22. Clamp sealing boot (3) onto tripod housing using clamp locking tool, Snap-On YA3050 (2) or an equivalent.

23. Place prongs of clamp locking tool in the holes of the clamp (1).

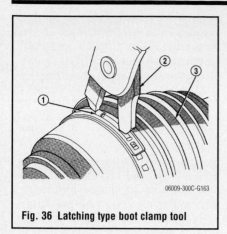

Fig. 36 Latching type boot clamp tool

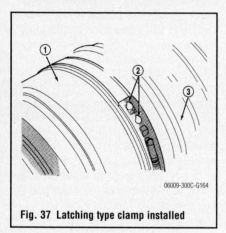

Fig. 37 Latching type clamp installed

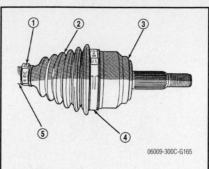

Fig. 38 Outer CV-joint. (1) small clamp, (2) boot, (3) joint housing, (4) large clamp, (5) shaft

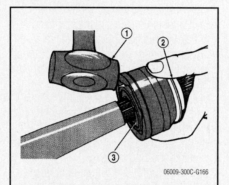

Fig. 39 Outer CV-joint removal. (1) soft-faced hammer, (2) joint, (3) circlip

24. Squeeze tool together until top band of clamp is latched behind the two tabs on lower band of clamp (2).

Outer

See Figures 38 through 42.

1. Before servicing the vehicle, refer to the precautions in the beginning of this section.

2. Remove large boot clamp retaining CV-joint sealing boot to CV-joint housing and discard.

3. Remove small clamp that retains outer CV-joint sealing boot to interconnecting shaft and discard.

4. Remove sealing boot from outer CV-joint housing and slide it down interconnecting shaft.

5. Wipe away grease to expose outer CV-joint and interconnecting shaft.

6. Remove outer CV-joint from interconnecting shaft using the following procedure:

   a. Support interconnecting shaft in a vise equipped with protective caps on jaws of vise to prevent damage to interconnecting shaft.

   b. Then, using a soft-faced hammer, sharply hit the end of the CV-joint housing to dislodge housing from internal circlip on interconnecting shaft.

   c. Then slide outer CV-joint off end of interconnecting shaft, joint may have to be tapped off shaft using a soft-faced hammer.

7. Remove large circlip from the interconnecting shaft before attempting to remove outer CV-joint sealing boot.

8. Slide failed sealing boot off interconnecting shaft.

9. Thoroughly clean and inspect outer CV-joint assembly and interconnecting joint for any signs of excessive wear. If any parts show signs of excessive wear, the driveshaft assembly will require replacement. Compo-

nent parts of these driveshaft assemblies are not serviceable.

To assemble:

10. Slide new sealing boot to interconnecting shaft retaining clamp onto interconnecting shaft. Slide the outer CV-joint assembly sealing boot onto the interconnecting shaft. Seal boot MUST be positioned on interconnecting shaft so the raised bead on the inside of the seal boot is in groove on interconnecting shaft.

11. Align splines on interconnecting shaft with splines on cross of outer CV-joint assembly and start outer CV-joint onto interconnecting shaft.

12. Install outer CV-joint assembly (3) onto interconnecting shaft by using a soft-faced hammer (1) and tapping end of stub axle (2), with nut (4) installed, until outer CV-joint is fully seated on interconnecting shaft.

13. Outer CV-joint assembly must be installed on interconnecting shaft until cross of outer CV-joint assembly is seated against circlip on interconnecting shaft.

14. Distribute ½ the amount of grease provided in seal boot service package (DO NOT USE ANY OTHER TYPE OF GREASE) into outer CV-joint assembly housing. Put the remaining amount into the sealing boot.

15. Install outer CV-joint sealing boot to interconnecting shaft clamp evenly on sealing boot.

16. Clamp sealing boot onto interconnecting shaft using crimper, Special Tool C-4975-A and the following procedure. Place crimping tool C-4975-A over bridge of clamp. Tighten nut on crimping tool C-4975-A until jaws on tool are closed completely together, face to face.

✷✷ WARNING

Seal must not be dimpled, stretched, or out-of-shape in any way. If seal is NOT shaped correctly, equalize pressure in seal and shape it by hand.

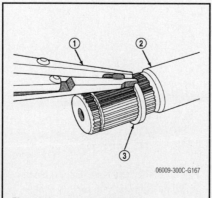

Fig. 40 Large circlip removal

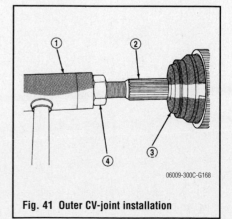

Fig. 41 Outer CV-joint installation

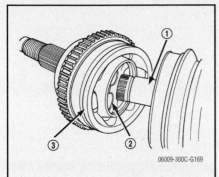

Fig. 42 Outer CV-joint assembly (3) must be installed on interconnecting shaft (1) until cross of outer CV-joint assembly (2) is seated against circlip on interconnecting shaft

17. Position outer CV-joint sealing boot into its retaining groove on outer CV-joint housing. Install sealing boot to outer CV-joint retaining clamp evenly on sealing boot.

18. Clamp sealing boot onto outer CV-joint housing using Crimper, Special Tool C-4975-A and the following procedure. Place crimping tool C-4975-A over bridge of clamp. Tighten nut on crimping tool C-4975-A until jaws on tool are closed completely together, face to face.

INTERMEDIATE SHAFT

REMOVAL & INSTALLATION

See Figure 43.

➡The intermediate shaft assembly is serviced only as an assembly.

1. Before servicing the vehicle, refer to the precautions in the beginning of this section.
2. Remove four intermediate shaft assembly-to-oil pan bolts.
3. Remove intermediate shaft assembly from engine oil pan.

To install:

4. If previously removed, install intermediate shaft assembly.
5. Install four intermediate shaft-to-oil pan bolts and torque to 18 ft. lbs. (25 Nm).

FRONT AXLE HOUSING

REMOVAL & INSTALLATION

See Figures 44 through 47.

1. Before servicing the vehicle, refer to the precautions in the beginning of this section.
2. Raise and support vehicle.
3. Remove both front halfshafts.
4. Remove front intermediate shaft assembly.
5. Remove front driveshaft.

✳✳ CAUTION

The normal operating temperature of the exhaust system is very high. therefore, never work around or attempt to service any part of the exhaust system until it is cooled. special care should be taken when working near the catalytic converter. The temperature of the converter rises to a high level after a short period of engine operation time.

6. Disconnect negative battery cable.
7. Raise and safely support the vehicle.
8. Disconnect downstream oxygen sensor connectors.
9. Remove muffler and resonator.
10. On 2.7L or 3.5L engine, remove nuts and cross-brace.
11. Remove catalytic converter to ball flange nuts.
12. Remove catalytic converter.
13. Remove nuts and tunnel reinforcement.
14. With a 5.7L engine, remove left side resonator and tailpipe assembly.
15. Remove isolators.
16. Remove muffler and tailpipe assembly by twisting/turning while pulling assembly out of catalytic converters.
17. Separate power steering return line from cradle by unfastening clips.
18. Remove front axle housing support bracket (1).
19. Remove seven front axle assembly-to-oil pan bolts.
20. Remove axle assembly (1) from vehicle.

To install:

21. Install front axle assembly) into position. Install and torque seven bolts to 48 ft. lbs. (65 Nm).

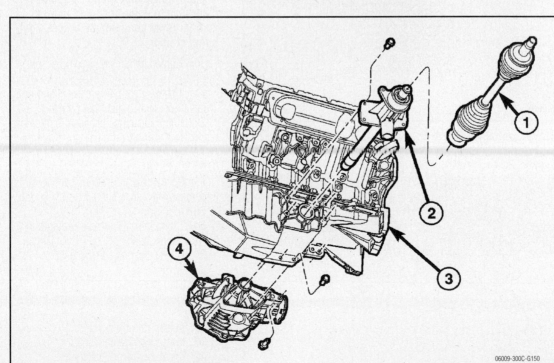

Fig. 43 Intermediate shaft removal/installation

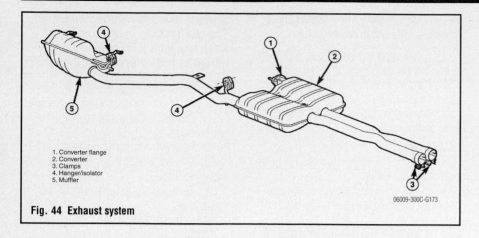

1. Converter flange
2. Converter
3. Clamps
4. Hanger/isolator
5. Muffler

06009-300C-G173

Fig. 44 Exhaust system

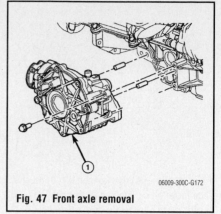

06009-300C-G172

Fig. 47 Front axle removal

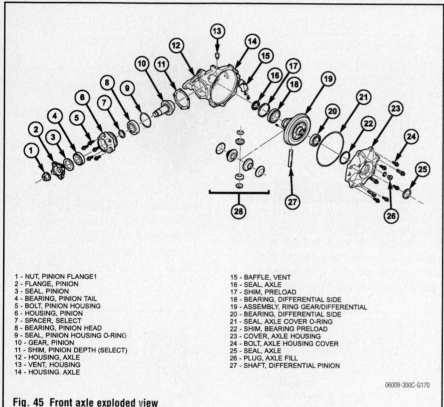

1 - NUT, PINION FLANGE1	15 - BAFFLE, VENT
2 - FLANGE, PINION	16 - SEAL, AXLE
3 - SEAL, PINION	17 - SHIM, PRELOAD
4 - BEARING, PINION TAIL	18 - BEARING, DIFFERENTIAL SIDE
5 - BOLT, PINION HOUSING	19 - ASSEMBLY, RING GEAR/DIFFERENTIAL
6 - HOUSING, PINION	20 - BEARING, DIFFERENTIAL SIDE
7 - SPACER, SELECT	21 - SEAL, AXLE COVER O-RING
8 - BEARING, PINION HEAD	22 - SHIM, BEARING PRELOAD
9 - SEAL, PINION HOUSING O-RING	23 - COVER, AXLE HOUSING
10 - GEAR, PINION	24 - BOLT, AXLE HOUSING COVER
11 - SHIM, PINION DEPTH (SELECT)	25 - SEAL, AXLE
12 - HOUSING, AXLE	26 - PLUG, AXLE FILL
13 - VENT, HOUSING	27 - SHAFT, DIFFERENTIAL PINION
14 - HOUSING. AXLE	

06009-300C-G170

Fig. 45 Front axle exploded view

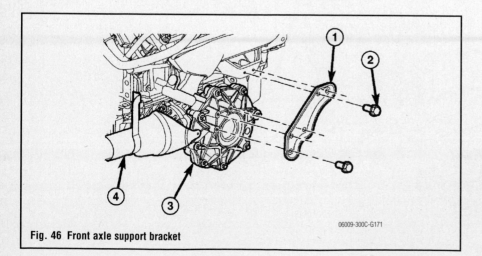

06009-300C-G171

Fig. 46 Front axle support bracket

22. Install power steering return line to cradle by fastening clips.

23. Install axle assembly support bracket and torque bolts to 21 ft. lbs. (28 Nm).

24. Install catalytic converter onto exhaust manifold ball flange. Only finger tighten nuts at this time.

25. Install muffler and resonator assembly.

26. Position front exhaust pipe module clamps on exhaust pipe assembly.

27. Install exhaust pipe assembly into catalytic converters.

➡**Isolators will have an approximately 10° forward angle when installed.**

28. Install isolators.

29. With a 5.7L engine, install left side rear resonator and tailpipe assembly.

➡**Check for proper alignment and clearance to underbody and engine compartment components before tightening clamps.**

30. Tighten band clamps to 45 ft. lbs. (61 Nm).

31. Install tunnel reinforcement and nuts. Tighten nuts to 215 inch lbs. (25 Nm)

32. Check clearance between muffler and resonator assembly and fuel tank. Clearance is 14mm (0.55 in.) for V8 engine and 16mm (0.62 in.) for V6 engine.

33. Check clearance at rear tunnel reinforcement. Clearance should be 15–20mm (0.59–0.78 in.).

34. The tailpipe should be centered in the rear fascia opening.

35. Adjust clearance as necessary.

36. Lower vehicle.

37. Start the engine and inspect for exhaust leaks. Repair exhaust leaks as necessary.

38. Install front driveshaft.

39. Install intermediate shaft.

40. Install both front halfshafts.

41. Fill axle with 600ml (0.64 qts.)

of Mopar® 75W-90 Synthetic Gear Lubricant. Fluid level should be at or near bottom of fill hole. Torque fill plug to 22 ft. lbs. (30 Nm).

42. Lower vehicle.

FRONT PINION SEAL

REMOVAL & INSTALLATION

See Figures 48 and 49.

1. Before servicing the vehicle, refer to the precautions in the beginning of this section.

2. Remove driveshaft and heat shield.

3. Using Tool 6958 (2), remove pinion flange nut.

4. Using Puller 1026 (1), remove pinion flange.

5. Remove pinion flange seal with suitable screwdriver and discard.

To install:

6. Using a seal driver, install new pinion flange seal.

7. Lightly tap pinion flange onto the shaft, just enough to start flange nut by hand.

8. Install pinion flange nut and torque to 350 ft. lbs. (475 Nm).

9. Install driveshaft and heat shield.

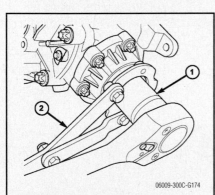

Fig. 48 Remove the pinion flange nut—Front drive axle

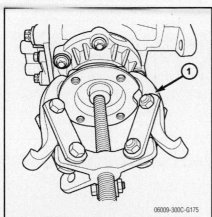

Fig. 49 Remove the pinion flange—Front drive axle

REAR AXLE HOUSING

REMOVAL & INSTALLATION

198 RII Axle

1. Before servicing the vehicle, refer to the precautions in the beginning of this section.

➡This procedure requires the compression of the rear suspension to ride height. A drive-on hoist should be used. If a drive-on hoist is not used, screw-style under-hoist jackstands are required to compress the rear suspension, facilitating rear halfshaft removal.

❊❊ WARNING

Never grasp halfshaft assembly by the inner or outer boots. Doing so may cause the boot to pucker or crease, reducing the service life of the boot and joint. Avoid over angling or stroking the CV-joints when handling the halfshaft.

2. With vehicle in neutral, position and raise vehicle on hoist.

3. Using 14mm hex, remove axle drain plug and drain rear axle fluid into container suitable for fluid reuse.

4. Install drain plug and torque to 44 ft. lbs. (60 Nm) torque.

5. Remove rear exhaust system on dual-outlet exhaust models, otherwise, lower exhaust system at rear hanger(s) to provide adequate clearance.

6. Remove the driveshaft.

7. Remove the halfshafts.

8. Remove two rear axle-to-crossmember bolts.

9. Carefully lower rear axle. While lowering axle, separate driveshaft from axle and support with suitable rope or wire.

10. Remove axle assembly from vehicle and transfer to bench.

11. Using suitable screwdriver, remove axle seals and discard.

To install:

12. Install new axle seal(s).

➡Use care when installing halfshaft to axle assembly. The halfshaft installation angle should be minimized to avoid damage to seal upon installation.

13. Install the halfshafts.

14. Raise rear axle assembly into position. Align driveshaft index marks and start driveshaft coupler-to-axle bolt/nuts by hand.

15. Install two rear axle-to-crossmember bolts and torque to 162 ft. lbs. (220 Nm).

16. Install rear axle front mount isolator and torque bolt/nut to 48 ft. lbs. (65 Nm).

17. Again verify halfshaft inner joints are fully engaged to axle assembly.

18. Remove transmission jack.

19. If used, remove screw-type under-hoist jackstands.

20. Torque driveshaft coupler-to-axle flange bolt/nuts to 43 ft. lbs. (58 Nm).

21. Using a 14mm hex, remove rear axle fill plug. Fill axle with 1.4L (1.5 qts.) of Mopar® 75W-140 Synthetic Gear & Axle Lubricant. Install fill plug and torque to 44 ft. lbs. (60 Nm).

210RII

1. Before servicing the vehicle, refer to the precautions in the beginning of this section.

➡This procedure requires the compression of the rear suspension to ride height. A drive-on hoist should be used. If a drive-on hoist is not used, screw-style under-hoist jackstands are required to compress the rear suspension, facilitating rear halfshaft removal.

❊❊ WARNING

Never grasp halfshaft assembly by the inner or outer boots. Doing so may cause the boot to pucker or crease, reducing the service life of the boot and joint. Avoid over angling or stroking the CV-joints when handling the halfshaft.

2. With vehicle in neutral, position and raise vehicle on hoist.

3. Using 14mm hex, remove axle drain plug and drain rear axle fluid into container suitable for fluid reuse.

4. Install drain plug and torque to 37 ft. lbs. (50 Nm) torque.

5. Remove rear exhaust system on dual-outlet exhaust models, otherwise, lower exhaust system at rear hanger.

6. Remove the rear driveshaft.

7. Remove the halfshafts.

8. Remove two rear axle-to-crossmember bolts.

9. Carefully lower rear axle. While lowering axle, separate driveshaft from axle and support with suitable rope or wire.

10. Remove axle assembly from vehicle and transfer to bench.

11. Using suitable screwdriver, remove axle seals and discard.

To install:

12. Install new axle seal(s) using Tool 9223.

➡Use care when installing halfshaft to axle assembly. The halfshaft installation angle should be minimized to avoid damage to seal upon installation.

13. Install the halfshafts.

14. Raise rear axle assembly into position. Align driveshaft index marks and start driveshaft coupler-to-axle bolt/nuts by hand.

15. Install two rear axle-to-crossmember bolts and torque to 162 ft. lbs. (220 Nm).

16. Install rear axle front mount isolator and torque bolt/nut to 48 ft. lbs. (65 Nm).

17. Again verify halfshaft inner joints are fully engaged to axle assembly.

18. Remove transmission jack.

19. If used, remove screw-type underhoist jackstands.

20. Torque driveshaft coupler-to-axle flange bolt/nuts to 43 ft. lbs. (58 Nm).

21. Using a 14mm hex, remove rear axle fill plug. Fill axle with 1.6L (1.7 qts.) of Mopar® 75W-140 synthetic gear and axle lubricant. Install fill plug and torque to 37 ft. lbs. (50 Nm).

REAR DRIVESHAFT

REMOVAL & INSTALLATION

See Figures 50 through 53.

1. Before servicing the vehicle, refer to the precautions in the beginning of this section.

✳✳ WARNING

Driveshaft removal is a 2-person operation. Never allow driveshaft to hang from the center bearing, or while only connected to the transmission or rear axle flanges. A helper is required. If a driveshaft section is hung unsupported, damage may occur to the shaft, coupler, and/or center bearing from over-angulations. This may result in driveline vibrations and/or component failure.

2. With vehicle in neutral, position on hoist.

3. Apply alignment index marks on the transmission and axle flanges and rubber couplers.

4. Remove crossmember.

5. Remove rear exhaust system.

6. Remove heat shield.

7. Remove driveshaft front coupler-to-flange bolts.

8. Remove driveshaft rear coupler-to-flange bolts.

9. Remove center bearing mounting bolts.

10. With the aid of a helper, remove driveshaft assembly.

11. Remove three coupler-to-driveshaft bolt/nuts.

12. Separate coupler and damper (if equipped) from driveshaft. Note orientation and direction of components. It is imperative that they are properly reinstalled.

To install:

13. If coupler and/or damper (V6 Models) were removed, align index marks and reinstall. Make sure protruding sleeve is properly seated into driveshaft or damper counter bores.

14. Install three bolts with washers and nuts and torque to 43 ft. lbs. (58 Nm) torque.

15. Obtain helper and install driveshaft into position at axle. Align index marks placed upon removal. Install driveshaft rear coupler-to-axle flange bolt/nuts by hand. Do not torque at this time.

16. Install driveshaft into position at transmission flange. Align index marks placed upon removal. Install driveshaft front coupler-to-transmission flange bolt/nuts by hand. Do not torque at this time.

17. Loosely install center bearing-to-body bolts. Do not torque at this time.

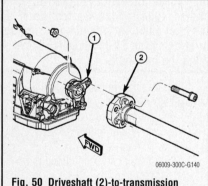

Fig. 50 Driveshaft (2)-to-transmission flange (1) attachment

06009-300C-G140

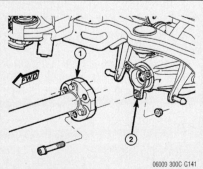

Fig. 51 Driveshaft (1)-to-rear axle flange (2) attachment

06009 300C G141

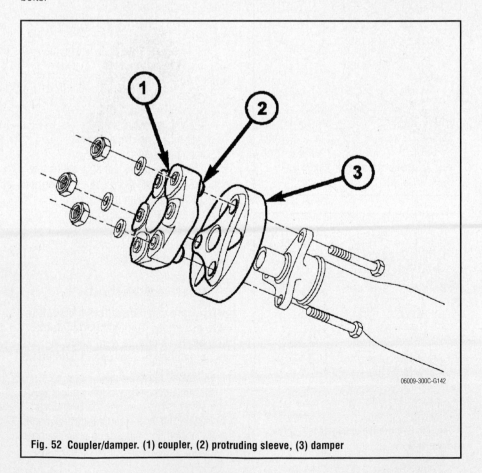

Fig. 52 Coupler/damper. (1) coupler, (2) protruding sleeve, (3) damper

06009-300C-G142

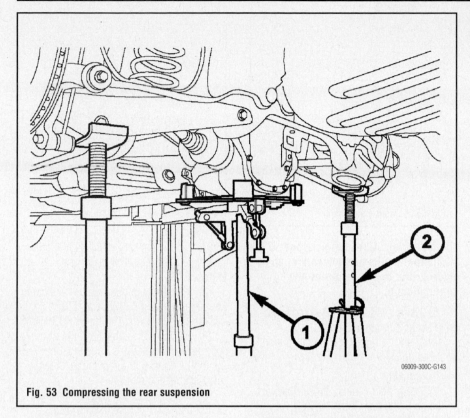
Fig. 53 Compressing the rear suspension

18. Torque driveshaft front coupler-to-transmission flange bolt/nuts to 43 ft. lbs. (58 Nm)

19. Torque driveshaft rear coupler-to-axle flange bolt/nuts to 43 ft. lbs. (58 Nm)

➡Note: It is necessary to compress rear suspension to ride height before securing center bearing to body. Failure to compress suspension may result in objectionable noise and premature bearing wear.

20. Compress rear suspension with suitable jackstands.
21. Torque center bearing-to-body bolts to 20 ft. lbs. (27 Nm).
22. Install heat shield.
23. Install rear exhaust system.
24. Install the crossmember.

REAR HALFSHAFT

REMOVAL & INSTALLATION

1. Before servicing the vehicle, refer to the precautions in the beginning of this section.

➡This procedure requires the compression of the rear suspension to ride height. A drive-on hoist should be used. If a drive-on hoist is not used, screw-style under-hoist jack stands are required to compress the rear suspension, facilitating rear halfshaft

removal. Halfshaft inner and outer boots are not serviceable separately. Boot replacement requires entire shaft assembly replacement.

✳✳ WARNING

Unequal-length halfshafts are used. The left halfshaft is shorter than the right, and it is necessary to identify and tag halfshafts upon removal to ensure proper installation.

2. With vehicle in neutral, position and raise vehicle on hoist.
3. Using 14mm hex, remove axle drain plug and drain rear axle fluid into container suitable for fluid reuse.
4. Install drain plug and torque to:
   • 198 Axle: 44 ft. lbs. (60 Nm).
   • 210 Axle: 37 ft. lbs. (50 Nm).
5. Remove rear exhaust system on V8—equipped models.
6. Remove wheel/tire assembly from sides that shaft is to be removed.
7. Remove wheel hub nut and discard.
8. Apply alignment index marks to the propeller shaft rubber coupler and axle flange.
9. Remove three propeller shaft coupler-to-axle flange bolt/nuts.
10. Using suitable screwdriver, partially disengage halfshaft(s) from axle assembly.
11. If a drive—on hoist is used, position transmission jack to rear axle assembly. If a drive—on hoist is not used, compress rear

suspension using screw-style under—hoist jack stands, then position transmission jack to rear axle assembly.

12. Remove rear axle forward mount isolator bolt/nut.

➡Access to rear axle-to-crossmember bolts is best achieved by use of short socket and a flexible-head ratchet.

13. Remove two rear axle-to-crossmember bolts.
14. Carefully lower the rear axle. While lowering axle, separate propeller shaft from axle and support with suitable rope or wire.
15. Lower the axle just enough to remove halfshafts one at a time. Shift axle assembly in one direction, compressing one halfshaft while removing the other. Use caution to protect axle seal and journal.

To install:

16. Install new axle seals using the seal driver tool 9223 or equivalent.
17. Install halfshaft isolation washer. Washer is bi—directional, and can be installed in either direction.
18. Install halfshaft to wheel hub/knuckle assembly. Install new hub nut by hand.
19. Inspect slinger(s) for handling damage. Straighten as necessary to avoid contact with axle seal.
20. Lubricate halfshaft inner joint bearing journal with Mopar® gear and axle lubricant (75W–140). Using new circlip(s), install halfshaft to rear axle assembly. Use care not to damage axle seals. Verify proper installation by pulling outward on joint by hand.
21. Raise rear axle assembly into position. Align propeller shaft index marks (3) and start propeller shaft coupler-to-axle bolt/nuts by hand.
22. Install two rear axle-to-crossmember bolts and torque to 162 ft. lbs. (220 Nm).
23. Install rear axle front mount isolator as shown and torque bolt/nut to 48 ft. lbs. (65 Nm).
24. Again verify halfshaft inner joints are fully engaged to axle assembly.
25. Remove the transmission jack.
26. If used, remove screw-type under-hoist jack stands (2).
27. Torque the propeller shaft coupler-to-axle flange bolt/nuts to 43 ft. lbs. (58 Nm).
28. Using a 14mm hex, remove rear axle fill plug . Fill axle with Mopar®75W-140 synthetic gear and axle lubricant in the following quantities:
   • 198 Axle: 1.5 qts. (1.4L)
   • 210 Axle: 1.7 qts. (1.6L)
29. Install and torque fill plug to:
   • 198 Axle: 44 ft. lbs. (60 Nm).
   • 210 Axle: 37 ft. lbs. (50 Nm).

30. For V8 models install exhaust system. Tighten band clamps to 45 ft. lbs. (61 Nm).

31. Lower the vehicle. Tighten halfshaft hub nut to 157 ft. lbs. (213 Nm) and install wheel center cap.

32. Install wheel/tire assembly and torque lug nuts to 110 ft. lbs. (150 Nm).

CV-JOINT OVERHAUL

These joints are not serviced separately. If they are defective, the entire shaft must be replaced.

REAR PINION SEAL

REMOVAL & INSTALLATION

See Figures 54 through 57.

1. Before servicing the vehicle, refer to the precautions in the beginning of this section.

2. Remove rear axle assembly from vehicle.

3. Measure axle assembly rotating torque and record measurement for reuse on assembly.

4. Using flange holder C-3281(1) and 41mm socket, remove pinion flange nut and discard.

➡ **Due to axle imbalance concerns, it is necessary to make sure pinion flange-**

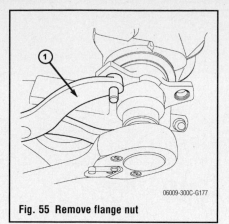
Fig. 55 Remove flange nut

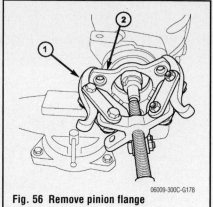
Fig. 56 Remove pinion flange

to-shaft orientation is maintained. If alignment marks are not visible, apply appropriate marks before removing pinion flange.

5. Using puller 1026 (1), remove pinion flange (2) from pinion shaft.

6. Using suitable tool, remove pinion seal and discard.

To install:

7. Apply light coating of gear lubricant to the lip of the pinion seal.

8. Using a seal driver, install pinion seal until tool bottoms on carrier.

9. Install pinion flange into position. Align index marks to maintain assembly balance.

10. Lightly tap on pinion flange until adequate pinion shaft threads are exposed.

11. Install new pinion flange nut. Using flange holder tool C-3281and 41mm socket, torque nut to 100 ft. lbs. (136 Nm).

12. Measure assembly turning torque. Axle assembly rotating torque must be should be equal to the reading recorded upon seal/flange removal.

13. If rotating torque is low, increase pinion flange nut torque in 60 inch lbs. (7 Nm) increments. Repeat until proper rotating torque is received.

14. Stake pinion flange nut (1) as shown.

15. Install rear axle assembly.

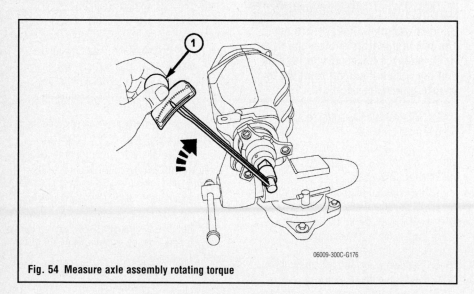
Fig. 54 Measure axle assembly rotating torque

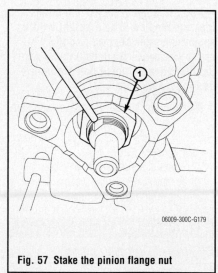
Fig. 57 Stake the pinion flange nut

ENGINE COOLING

ENGINE FAN

REMOVAL & INSTALLATION

1. Disconnect the negative battery cable.
2. Partially drain the cooling system.
3. Remove the upper radiator hose.
4. Detach the cooling fan electrical connector.
5. Remove the cooling fan mounting bolts.
6. Remove radiator cooling fan assembly from vehicle.

To install:

7. Position the radiator cooling fan assembly in the vehicle.
8. Install the cooling fan mounting bolts and tighten them to 50 inch lbs. (6 Nm)
9. Attach the cooling fan electrical connector.
10. Install upper radiator hose.
11. Fill the cooling system.
12. Operate the engine until it reaches normal operating temperature. Check cooling system and automatic transmission for correct fluid levels

RADIATOR

REMOVAL & INSTALLATION

See Figures 58 and 59.

1. Disconnect the negative battery cable.
2. Drain the cooling system.
3. Disconnect the upper radiator hose.
4. Remove the upper radiator closure panels.
5. Remove the radiator fan assembly.
6. Raise and safely support the vehicle.
7. Remove the lower splash shield.
8. Disconnect the lower radiator hose.
9. Remove the lower condenser mount bolts.
10. Lower the vehicle.
11. Remove the upper radiator hose.

➡**Bolts have a thread locker on them, use hand tools to remove the upper radiator mounting bolts.**

12. Remove the upper radiator mounting brackets and bolts.
13. Remove the upper condenser mounting bolts.
14. Separate the condenser assembly from radiator.
15. Tilt the radiator toward engine and remove radiator from vehicle.

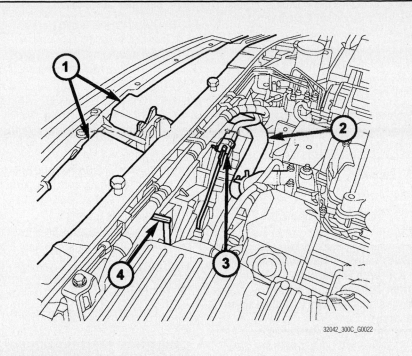

Fig. 58 View of the upper radiator closure panels (1), upper radiator hose (2), fan electrical connector (3) and fan assembly (4)

To install:

16. Position the radiator into the engine compartment. Seat the radiator assembly lower rubber isolators into the mounting holes in radiator lower support .
17. Install radiator mounting bracket and bolts. Tighten the bolts to 106 inch lbs. (12 Nm).
18. Position the condenser on the radiator and install upper mounting bolts. Tighten bolts to 50 inch lbs. (6 Nm).

19. Install the lower condenser mounting bolts. Tighten bolts to 88 inch lbs. (10 Nm)
20. Install the lower radiator hose and clamp.
21. Install the radiator fan.
22. Install the upper radiator upper hose. Align the hose so it does not interfere with the accessory drive belt or engine. Position hose clamp so it will not interfere with the hood.

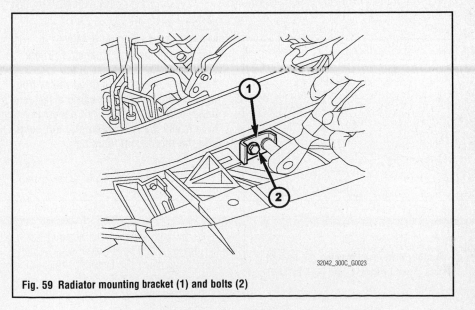

Fig. 59 Radiator mounting bracket (1) and bolts (2)

23. Install the upper radiator closure panels.

24. Connect the negative battery cable.

25. Fill the cooling system with coolant.

26. Operate the engine until it reaches normal operating temperature. Check cooling system and automatic transmission for correct fluid levels.

THERMOSTAT

REMOVAL & INSTALLATION

2.7L Engine

See Figure 60.

1. Disconnect the negative battery cable.

> ✳✳ **CAUTION**
>
> **Do not remove pressure cap with the system hot and under pressure because serious burns from coolant can occur.**

2. Drain the cooling system into a suitable container

3. Disconnect the radiator lower hose from thermostat housing.

4. Remove nuts from the heater tube flange studs.

5. Loosen the starter bolt at heater tube bracket.

6. Pull the heater tube out of thermostat housing and position out of the way.

7. Remove the thermostat housing (1), O-ring (2) and thermostat (4).

8. Remove the thermostat housing bolts (3).

To install:

9. Thoroughly clean the gasket sealing surfaces.

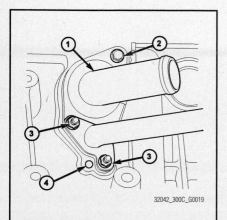

Fig. 60 Thermostat housing (1), bolt (2), nuts (3) and weeping hole (4)—2.7L engine

➡**Install the thermostat with the bleed valve located at the 12 o'clock position, between tabs on seal.**

10. Install the thermostat and seal (2) into thermostat housing (1).

11. If removed, install the two studs.

12. Lubricate a new heater return tube O-ring with coolant.

13. Position the heater return tube flange over the two studs. Install the 3 retaining nuts and torque to 53 inch lbs. (6 Nm).

14. Tighten the starter bolt to 40 ft. lbs. (54 Nm).

15. Connect the lower radiator hose to the thermostat housing. Install the hose clamps.

16. Refill cooling system

17. Connect the negative battery cable. Start and warm the engine. Check for leaks.

3.5L Engine

See Figure 61.

1. Disconnect the negative battery cable.

> ✳✳ **WARNING**
>
> **Do not remove pressure cap with the system hot and under pressure because serious burns from coolant can occur.**

2. Drain the cooling system.

3. Raise and safely support the vehicle.

4. Detach the electrical connectors from the engine oil and power steering pressure switches.

5. Disconnect the radiator and heater hoses from thermostat housing.

6. Remove the thermostat housing bolts.

7. Remove the housing, thermostat, and gasket.

➡**The OEM thermostat is staked in place at the factory. To ensure proper seating of the replacement thermostat, carefully remove the bulged metal from the thermostat housing using a suitable hand held grinder. It is not necessary to re-stake the replacement thermostat into the thermostat housing.**

To install:

8. Thoroughly clean the gasket mating surfaces.

9. Position a new gasket on the thermostat and housing.

10. Install the thermostat housing, gasket and mounting bolts onto block. Tighten attaching bolts to 105 inch lbs. (12 Nm).

11. Install the radiator hose.

12. Install the bypass hose.

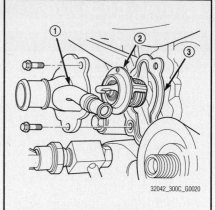

Fig. 61 Thermostat housing/coolant inlet (1), thermostat (2) and gasket (3)—3.5L engine

13. Connect the negative battery cable.

14. Fill the cooling system. Start and warm the engine. Check for leaks.

5.7L Engine

See Figure 62.

1. Disconnect the negative battery cable.

2. Drain the cooling system.

3. Disconnect the radiator hose from the thermostat housing.

➡**The thermostat o-ring is part of thermostat and is not serviced separately.**

4. Remove the thermostat housing mounting bolts, thermostat housing and thermostat.

To install:

5. Clean the mating areas of timing chain cover and thermostat housing (1).

➡**Install the thermostat with the bleed valve located at the 12 o'clock position.**

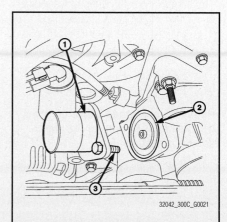

Fig. 62 Thermostat housing (1), thermostat (2) and retaining bolt (3)—5.7L engine

6. Install thermostat (spring side down) into recessed machined groove on timing chain cover with bleed valve located at the 12 o'clock position.

7. Position the thermostat housing on timing chain cover.

8. Install the two housing-to-timing chain cover bolts (3). Tighten bolts to 112 inch lbs. (13 Nm) torque.

❊❊ WARNING

The thermostat housing must be tightened evenly and the thermostat must be centered into recessed groove in timing chain cover. If not, it may result in a cracked thermostat housing, damaged timing chain cover threads or coolant leaks.

9. Attach the lower radiator hose to the thermostat housing.

10. Carefully lower the vehicle.

11. Fill the cooling system.

12. Connect the negative battery cable. Start and warm the engine. Check for leaks.

WATER PUMP

REMOVAL & INSTALLATION

2.7L Engine

See Figure 63.

1. Before servicing the vehicle, refer to the precautions in the beginning of this section.

❊❊ CAUTION

Do not remove pressure cap with the system hot and pressurized. Serious burns from coolant can result.

2. Drain the cooling system.

3. Disconnect negative battery cable.

4. Remove upper radiator hose.

5. Disconnect the cooling fan electrical connector.

6. Remove cooling fan mounting bolts.

7. Remove radiator cooling fan assembly from vehicle.

8. Remove the radiator fan assembly.

9. Remove the accessory drive belt.

➡The water pump is driven by the primary timing chain.

10. Remove the timing chain and all chain guides.

11. Remove bolts attaching water pump to block.

12. Remove water pump and gasket.

To install:

13. Clean all sealing surfaces.

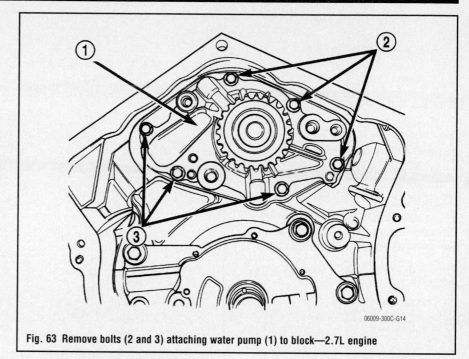

Fig. 63 Remove bolts (2 and 3) attaching water pump (1) to block—2.7L engine

14. Install water pump and gasket. Tighten mounting bolts to 105 inch lbs. (12 Nm).

15. Install the timing chain guides and timing chain.

16. Install the accessory drive belts.

17. Position radiator cooling fan assembly in vehicle.

18. Install cooling fan mounting bolts. Tighten to 50 inch lbs. (6 Nm)

19. Connect the cooling fan electrical connector.

20. Install the upper radiator hose.

21. Fill cooling system.

22. Operate engine until it reaches normal operating temperature. Check cooling system and automatic transmission for correct fluid levels.

3.5L Engine

See Figure 64.

1. Before servicing the vehicle, refer to the precautions in the beginning of this section.

❊❊ CAUTION

Do not remove pressure cap with the system hot and under pressure because serious burns from coolant can occur.

2. Drain the cooling system.

3. Remove the accessory drive belts.

➡The water pump is driven by the timing belt.

4. Remove engine timing belt.

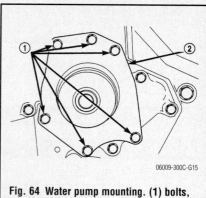

Fig. 64 Water pump mounting. (1) bolts, (2) pump—3.5L engine

5. Remove water pump mounting bolts. Note position of longer bolts for proper installation.

6. Remove water pump body from engine.

To install:

7. Clean all O-ring surfaces on front cover.

8. Position water pump and O-ring to engine.

9. Install the mounting bolts. Tighten to 105 inch lbs. (12 Nm).

10. Install the timing belt.

11. Install the accessory drive belts.

12. Fill the cooling system.

5.7L Engine

See Figure 65.

1. Before servicing the vehicle, refer to the precautions in the beginning of this section.

2. Disconnect negative battery cable.

3. Drain the cooling system.

4. Disconnect negative battery cable.

5. Remove the upper radiator hose.

6. Disconnect cooling fan electrical connector.

7. Remove cooling fan mounting bolts.

8. Remove the radiator cooling fan assembly from vehicle.

9. Remove the radiator fan assembly.

10. Remove accessory drive belt.

11. Remove the thermostat.

➡**The water pump mounting bolts are different lengths. Note the location of the water pump mounting bolts.**

12. Remove water pump mounting bolts and remove water pump.

To install:

13. Install water pump and mounting bolts. Tighten mounting bolts to 20 ft. lbs. (28 Nm).

14. Make sure double ended bolt is in the proper location. Tighten double ended bolt to 20 ft. lbs. (28 Nm).

15. Position the radiator cooling fan assembly in vehicle.

16. Install cooling fan mounting bolts. Tighten to 50 inch lbs. (6 Nm)

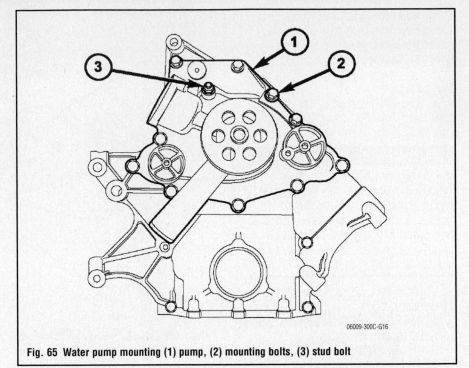

Fig. 65 Water pump mounting (1) pump, (2) mounting bolts, (3) stud bolt

17. Connect the cooling fan electrical connector.

18. Install the upper radiator hose.

19. Install the thermostat.

20. Install the accessory drive belt.

21. Install the radiator fan assembly.

22. Connect negative battery cable.

23. Fill the cooling system.

24. Pressure test cooling system.

ENGINE ELECTRICAL

ALTERNATOR

REMOVAL & INSTALLATION

❈❈ WARNING

Disconnect negative cable from battery before removing battery output wire (b+ wire) from alternator. Failure to do so can result in injury or damage to electrical system.

2.7L Engine

1. Before servicing the vehicle, refer to the precautions in the beginning of this section.

2. Disconnect negative battery cable.

3. Remove alternator drive belt.

4. Disconnect alternator field circuit plug.

5. Remove the B+ terminal nut and wire.

6. Remove 2 lower mounting bolts.

7. Remove the alternator.

To install:

8. Install the alternator.

9. Install upper bolt mounting bolt.

10. Install 2 lower mounting bolts.

11. Tighten bolts to 48 ft. lbs. (65 Nm).

12. Install the B+ terminal nut and wire. Tighten nut to 115 inch lbs. (13 Nm).

13. Connect alternator field circuit plug.

14. Install the alternator drive belt.

15. Connect negative battery cable.

3.5L Engine

1. Before servicing the vehicle, refer to the precautions in the beginning of this section.

2. Disconnect negative battery cable.

3. Remove the alternator drive belt.

4. Remove bracket bolts.

5. Remove the upper mounting bolt.

6. Raise and support vehicle.

7. Remove middle splash pan.

8. Disconnect alternator field circuit plug.

9. Remove the B+ terminal nut and wire.

10. Remove lower mounting bolts.

11. Remove the alternator.

To install:

12. Install the alternator.

13. Install lower mounting bolts. Loosen install the upper mounting bolt.

14. Tighten lower mounting bolts to 48 ft. lbs. (65 Nm).

CHARGING SYSTEM

15. Connect alternator field circuit plug.

16. Install B+ terminal nut and wire. Tighten nut to 115 inch lbs. (13 Nm).

17. Install middle splash pan.

18. Lower the vehicle.

19. Remove loose installed upper bolt.

20. Install bracket and bracket bolt.

21. Install upper mounting bolt and bracket.

22. Tighten the upper mounting bolt to 48 ft. lbs. (65 Nm).

23. Tighten the bracket bolt to 40 ft. lbs. (54 Nm).

24. Install the alternator drive belt.

25. Connect negative battery cable.

5.7L Engine

See Figures 66 and 67.

1. Before servicing the vehicle, refer to the precautions in the beginning of this section.

2. Disconnect negative battery cable at battery.

3. Remove the alternator drive belt.

4. Raise and support vehicle.

5. Unsnap plastic insulator cap from B+ output terminal.

6. Remove B+ terminal mounting nut at

rear of alternator. Disconnect terminal from alternator.

7. Disconnect field wire connector at rear of alternator by pushing on connector tab.

8. Remove the alternator support bracket nut and bolt. Remove support bracket.

9. Remove the 2 alternator mounting bolts.

10. Remove the alternator from vehicle.

To install:

11. Position alternator to engine and install 2 mounting bolts.

12. Tighten bolts to 48 ft. lbs. (65 Nm).

13. Position support bracket to alternator and install bolt and nut. Tighten bolt/nut to 48 ft. lbs. (65 Nm).

14. Snap field wire connector into rear of alternator.

15. Install B+ terminal eyelet to alternator output stud.

16. Lower the vehicle.

✳✳ WARNING

Never force a belt over a pulley rim using a screwdriver. The synthetic fiber of the belt can be damaged. When installing a serpentine acces-

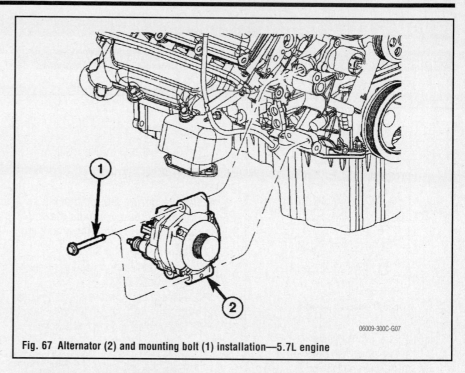

Fig. 67 Alternator (2) and mounting bolt (1) installation—5.7L engine

sory drive belt, the belt MUST be routed correctly. The water pump may be rotating in the wrong direction if the belt is installed incorrectly, causing the engine to overheat. Refer

to belt routing label in engine compartment.

17. Install the alternator drive belt.
18. Install negative battery cable to battery.

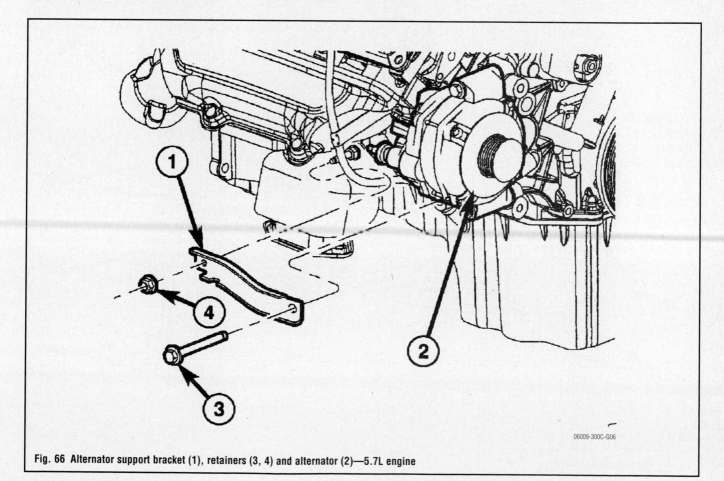

Fig. 66 Alternator support bracket (1), retainers (3, 4) and alternator (2)—5.7L engine

ENGINE ELECTRICAL **IGNITION SYSTEM**

FIRING ORDER

See Figures 68 and 69.

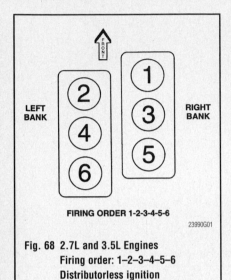

Fig. 68 2.7L and 3.5L Engines
Firing order: 1–2–3–4–5–6
Distributorless ignition

IGNITION COIL

REMOVAL & INSTALLATION

2.7L Engine

See Figure 70.

1. Disconnect the negative battery cable.
2. Remove the intake manifold.

➡ Before removing the ignition coils, spray compressed air around the coil area and spark plug to remove any dirt or debris.

3. Detach the electrical connector from the ignition coil.
4. Remove the 2 fasteners from ignition coil assembly.
5. Remove the ignition coil assembly.

To install:

6. Install the ignition coil assembly to the spark plug.

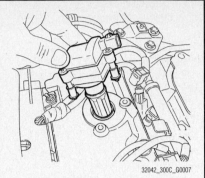

Fig. 70 Removing the ignition coil—2.7L engine shown, 3.5L engine similar

7. Install the coil screws and tighten to 55 inch lbs. (6.2 Nm.
8. Attach the electrical connector and lock.
9. Install the intake manifold.
10. Connect the negative battery cable.

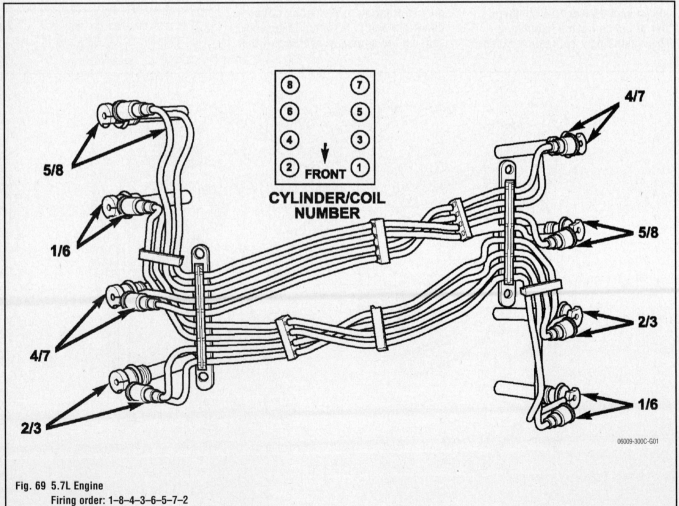

Fig. 69 5.7L Engine
Firing order: 1–8–4–3–6–5–7–2
Distributorless ignition

3.5L Engine

See Figure 70.

1. Disconnect the negative battery cable.
2. Remove the intake manifold.

➡**Before removing the ignition coils, spray compressed air around the coil area and spark plug to remove any dirt or debris.**

3. Unlock and remove the electrical connector from the ignition coil.

➡**On 3.5L engines, it is necessary to loosen the screws by alternating back and forth. Do not lose the spacers under the coil when loosening the screws.**

4. Remove the 2 fasteners from the ignition coil assembly.
5. Remove the ignition coil assembly.

To install:

➡**On 3.5L engines, it is necessary to tighten the screws by alternating back and forth. Do not lose the spacers under the coil when installing ignition coils.**

6. Install the ignition coil assembly to the spark plug.
7. Install the coil screws and tighten them to 60 inch lbs. (6.7 Nm.
8. Connect the electrical connector and lock.
9. Install the intake manifold.
10. Connect the negative battery cable.

5.7L Engine

See Figures 71 and 72.

➡**Before removing or disconnecting any spark plug cables, note their original position. Remove cables one-at-a-time. To prevent ignition crossfire, spark plug cables MUST be placed in cable tray (routing loom) into their original position.**

An individual ignition coil is used at each cylinder. The coil mounts to the top of the valve cover with two bolts. The bottom of the coil is equipped with a rubber boot to seal the spark plug to the coil. Inside each rubber boot is a spring. The spring is used for a mechanical contact between the coil and the top of the spark plug.

Depending on which coil is being removed, the throttle body air intake tube or intake box may need to be removed to gain access to coil.

1. Disconnect the negative battery cable.

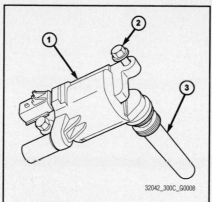

Fig. 71 View of the ignition coil (1), mounting bolts (2), and rubber boot (3)—5.7L engine

2. Unlock the electrical connector by moving the slide lock first. Press on release lock while pulling the electrical connector from coil.
3. Disconnect the secondary high-voltage cable from coil with a twisting action.

➡**Clean the area at the base of the ignition coil with compressed air before removal.**

4. Remove the 2 ignition coil mounting bolts (note that the mounting bolts are secured to the coil).
5. Carefully pull the coil up from the cylinder head opening with a slight twisting action.
6. Remove the ignition coil from vehicle.

Before installing spark plug cables to either the spark plugs or coils, or before installing a coil to a spark plug, apply dielectric grease to inside of boots.

To install:

7. Position the ignition coil into cylinder head opening and push the boot onto the spark plug. Twist coil into position.
8. Install the 2 coil mounting bolts and tighten to 105 inch lbs. (12 Nm)
9. Attach the electrical connector to the coil, then lock the connector.
10. Install the cable to the coil. To prevent ignition crossfire, the spark plug cables MUST be placed in cable tray (routing loom) into their original position.
11. If necessary, install throttle body air tube.
12. Connect the negative battery cable.

IGNITION COIL CAPACITOR

REMOVAL & INSTALLATION

2.7L and 3.5L Engines

See Figure 73.

1. Disconnect the negative battery cable.
2. Detach the electrical connector.
3. Remove the retaining nut and capacitor.

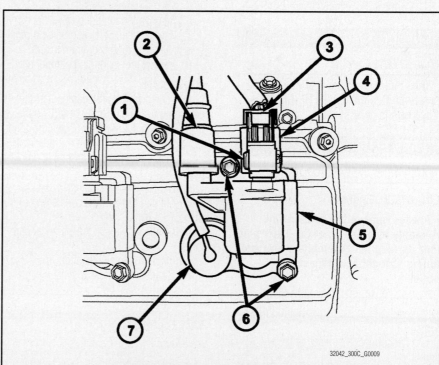

Fig. 72 Ignition coil (5) components—slide lock (1), secondary high-voltage cable (2), release lock (3), electrical connector (4), mounting bolts (6)

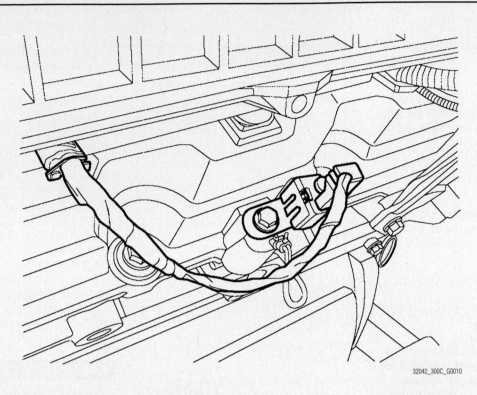

Fig. 73 View of the ignition coil capacitor—2.7L and 3.5L engines

To install:

4. Install capacitor and tighten the nut securely.

5. Attach the electrical connector to capacitor.

6. Connect the negative battery cable.

IGNITION TIMING

ADJUSTMENT

The ignition timing is controlled by the Powertrain Control Module (PCM). No adjustment is necessary or possible.

SPARK PLUGS

REMOVAL & INSTALLATION

2.7L & 3.5L Engines

➡**Always remove the ignition coil assembly by grasping at the spark plug boot, turning the assembly ½ turn and pulling straight back in a steady motion.**

1. Before servicing the vehicle, refer to the precautions in the beginning of this section.

2. Disconnect the negative battery cable.

3. Remove the intake manifold.

4. Prior to removing the ignition coils, spray compressed air around the coil area

and spark plug to remove contaminates from around spark plug tube.

5. On 3.5L engines, it is necessary to loosen the screws by alternating back and forth. Do not lose the spacers under the coil when loosening the screws.

6. Remove the ignitions coil.

7. Remove the spark plug using a quality socket with a rubber or foam insert.

8. Inspect the spark plug condition.

To install:

9. To avoid cross threading, start the spark plug into the cylinder head by hand.

10. Tighten spark plugs. Tighten to 20 ft. lbs. (28 Nm).

11. Install ignition coil assembly onto spark plug.

12. Hand tighten the coil screws.

13. Tighten the ignition coil screws to 60 in. lbs. (6.7 Nm).

14. Connect and lock the electrical connector.

15. Install the intake manifold.

16. Connect the negative battery cable.

5.7L Engine

2005 Engines

See Figure 74.

1. Before servicing the vehicle, refer to the precautions in the beginning of this section.

✳✳ WARNING

Before removing or disconnecting any spark plug cables, note their original position. Remove cables one-at-a-time. To prevent ignition crossfire, spark plug cables MUST be placed in cable tray (routing loom) into their original position.

2. Disconnect the negative battery cable.

3. Remove necessary air filter tubing at throttle body.

4. Unlock the electrical connector by moving the slide lock first. Press on release lock while pulling the electrical connector from coil.

5. Disconnect the secondary high-voltage cable from coil with a twisting action.

➡**Clean the area at the base of the ignition coil with compressed air before removal.**

6. Remove the 2 ignition coil mounting bolts (note that the mounting bolts are secured to the coil).

7. Carefully pull the coil up from the cylinder head opening with a slight twisting action.

8. Remove the ignition coil from vehicle.

9. Remove the spark plug from cylinder head using a quality socket with a rubber or

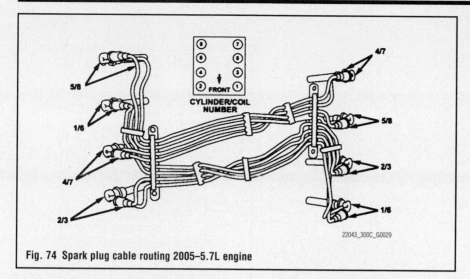

Fig. 74 Spark plug cable routing 2005–5.7L engine

foam insert. Also check condition of ignition coil O-ring and replace as necessary.

10. Inspect spark plug condition.

To install:

✳✳ WARNING

Special care should be taken when installing spark plugs into the cylinder head spark plug wells. Be sure the plugs do not drop into the plug wells as electrodes can be damaged. Always tighten spark plugs to the specified torque. Over tightening can cause distortion resulting in a change in the spark plug gap or a cracked porcelain insulator.

11. Start the spark plug into the cylinder head by hand to avoid cross threading.

12. Tighten spark plugs to 13 ft. lbs. (18 Nm).

13. Before installing ignition coil(s), check condition of coil o-ring and replace as necessary. To aid in coil installation, apply silicone to coil o-ring.

2006–08 Engines
See Figure 75.

A separate ignition coil, mounted to the valve cover is used for each cylinder. Each coil fires the two spark plugs at times predetermined by the Powertrain Control Module (PCM).

1. Before servicing the vehicle, refer to the precautions in the beginning of this section.

2. Unlock the electrical connector by pressing on tab while pulling electrical connector from the coil.

3. Remove two coil mounting bolts.

4. Carefully pull up coil from cylinder head opening with a slight twisting action. Twisting will help break loose boots from spark plugs.

To install:

5. Before installing coil(s), apply dielectric grease to inside of spark plug boots.

6. Position ignition coil into valve cover and push both spark plug boots onto each spark plug.

7. Install two coil mounting bolts and tighten to 106 in. lbs. (12 Nm).

8. Connect the electrical connector to the ignition coil and lock connector.

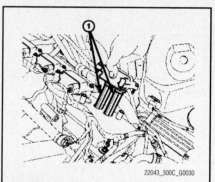

Fig. 75 Ignition coil removal with boots (1) shown

ENGINE ELECTRICAL

STARTER

REMOVAL & INSTALLATION

2.7L and 3.5L Engines
See Figures 76 through 81.

1. Before servicing the vehicle, refer to the precautions in the beginning of this section.

2. Disconnect the negative battery cable

3. Install a suitable steering wheel holder to lock the steering wheel in straight-ahead position.

4. Raise and safely support the vehicle.

5. Remove the underbody splash shield.

6. Remove the intermediate steering shaft center bolt.

7. Separate the intermediate steering shaft upper and lower shaft.

8. Disconnect the electrical connection from the starter.

STARTING SYSTEM

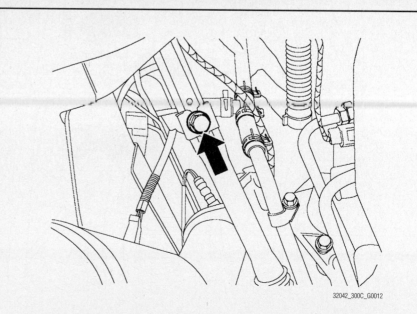

Fig. 76 Remove the intermediate steering shaft center bolt—2.7L and 3.5L engines

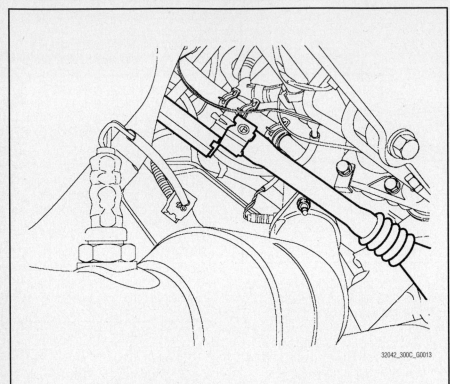

Fig. 77 Separate the intermediate steering shaft upper and lower shaft—2.7L and 3.5L engines

9. Remove the 3 starter mounting bolts and wiring clip.

10. Pull the starter forward and down.

11. Maneuver the starter up and around exhaust.

12. Work starter past the intermediate steering shaft, then remove the starter from vehicle.

To install:

13. Work the starter up and past the transmission and exhaust.

14. Maneuver the starter up and past the intermediate shafts.

15. Angle the starter up toward engine.

16. Install the plastic retainer into starter dust shield. The dust shield has TOP marked on it and the plastic retainer goes in the hole.

17. Install the dust shield to the engine block using the plastic retainer to hold dust shield in place.

18. Install the starter and secure with the retaining bolts. Torque the bolts to 40 ft. lbs. (54 Nm).

19. Attach the electrical connection to starter.

20. Match flats inside the intermediate shaft with that in the intermediate shaft

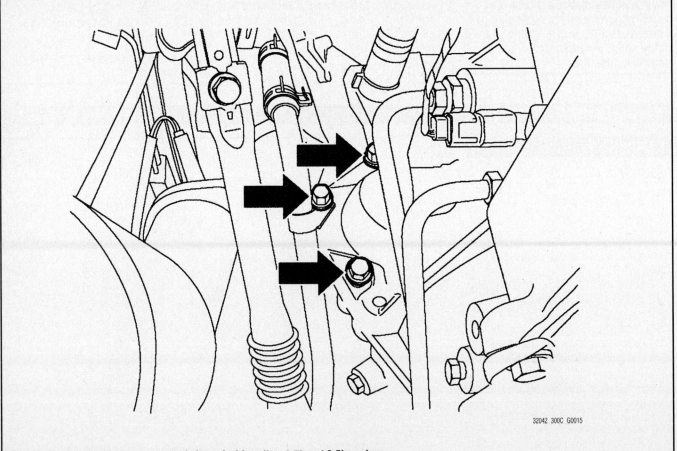

Fig. 78 Remove the 3 starter mounting bolts and wiring clip—2.7L and 3.5L engines

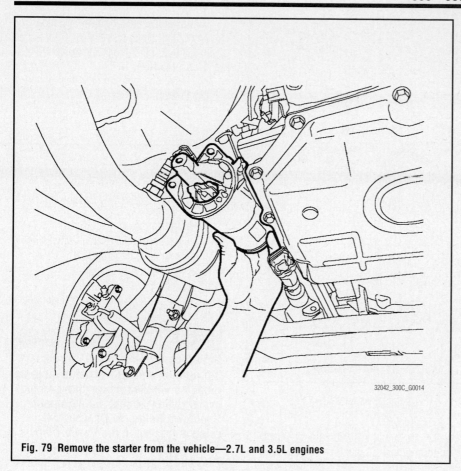

Fig. 79 Remove the starter from the vehicle—2.7L and 3.5L engines

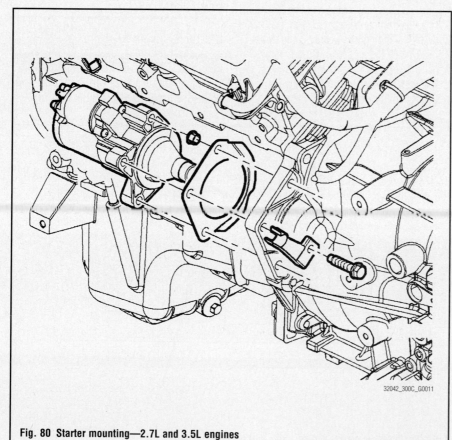

Fig. 80 Starter mounting—2.7L and 3.5L engines

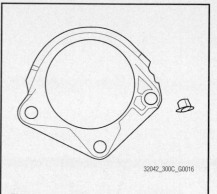

Fig. 81 Install the plastic retainer into starter dust shield. The dust shield has TOP marked on it and the plastic retainer goes in the hole—2.7L and 3.5L engines

extension, then slide the intermediate shaft onto extension.

21. Align the hole in the shafts.

22. Install the pinch bolt fastening intermediate shaft to intermediate shaft extension. Tighten the bolt to 32 ft. lbs. (43 Nm).

23. Install the underbody splash shield.

24. Carefully lower the vehicle.

25. Remove the steering wheel holder, then connect the negative battery cable.

5.7L Engine

Rear Wheel Drive (RWD) Models

See Figure 82.

1. Before servicing the vehicle, refer to the precautions in the beginning of this section.

2. Disconnect and isolate the negative battery cable.

3. Raise and safely support the vehicle.

4. Remove the 3 starter mounting bolts.

5. Move the starter motor towards front of vehicle far enough for nose of starter to clear. Always support the starter motor during this process. Never let starter motor hang from wire harness.

6. Remove the battery cable-to-solenoid nut.

7. Remove the solenoid wire from solenoid stud.

8. Remove the starter motor from the vehicle.

To install:

9. Position the starter (2) into transmission but do not install bolts.

10. Connect solenoid wire to starter motor. The wire snaps onto the starter.

11. Position the battery cable to solenoid stud. Install and tighten battery cable eyelet nut to 97 inch lbs. (11 Nm). Do not allow starter motor to hang from wire harness.

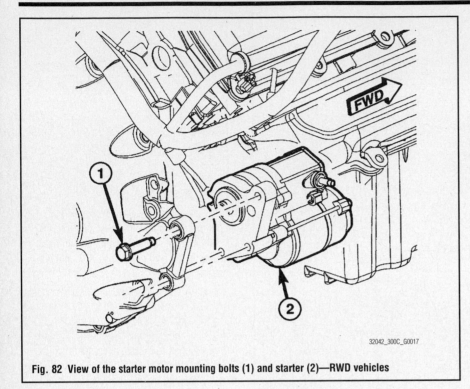

Fig. 82 View of the starter motor mounting bolts (1) and starter (2)—RWD vehicles

12. Install and tighten the three mounting bolts to 40 ft. lbs. (54 Nm).

13. Lower the vehicle.

14. Connect negative battery cable.

All Wheel Drive (AWD) Models

See Figure 83.

1. Before servicing the vehicle, refer to the precautions in the beginning of this section.

2. Disconnect and isolate the negative battery cable.

3. Raise and safely support the vehicle.

➡ **The steering gear assembly must be partially lowered to gain access to starter. Do not disconnect any hydraulic hoses or remove any steering linkage.**

4. Remove the coupling bolt (pinch bolt) securing steering gear to steering column.

5. Remove the three steering gear mounting bolts and slightly lower the gear. Temporarily support the steering gear.

6. Remove the steering gear heat-shield.

7. Remove the 2 starter mounting bolts.

8. Move the starter motor towards front of vehicle far enough for nose of starter to clear. Always support the starter motor during this process. Do not let starter motor hang from wire harness.

9. Remove the battery cable-to-solenoid nut.

10. Remove the solenoid wire from solenoid stud.

11. Remove the starter motor.

To install:

12. Position the starter into transmission but do not install bolts.

13. Connect the solenoid wire to starter motor. The wire snaps onto the starter.

14. Position the battery cable to solenoid stud. Install and tighten battery cable eyelet nut to 97 inch lbs. (11 Nm). Do not allow starter motor to hang from wire harness.

15. Install and tighten both starter mounting bolts to 40 ft. lbs. (54 Nm)

16. Install the steering gear assembly and mounting bolts. Install steering column coupling bolt (pinch bolt) and tighten to 32 ft. lbs. (43 Nm).

17. Install the steering gear heat-shield.

18. Lower the vehicle.

19. Connect the negative battery cable.

TESTING

Control Circuit Test

The starter control circuit has:

- Starter motor with integral solenoid
- Starter relay
- Transmission range sensor, or Park/Neutral Position switch with automatic transmissions
- Ignition switch
- Battery
- All related wiring and connections
- Powertrain Control Module (PCM)

> ※※ **CAUTION**
>
> **Before performing any starter tests, the ignition and fuel systems must be disabled. To disable ignition and fuel systems, disconnect the Automatic Shutdown Relay (ASD). The ASD relay is located in the Power Distribution Center (PDC). Refer to the PDC cover for the proper relay location.**

Starter Solenoid

> ※※ **CAUTION**
>
> **Check to ensure that the transmission is in the park position with the park-**

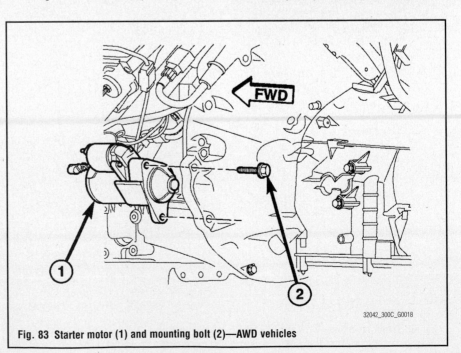

Fig. 83 Starter motor (1) and mounting bolt (2)—AWD vehicles

ing brake applied. This may result in personal injury or death.

1. Verify the battery condition. Battery must be in good condition with a full charge before performing any starter tests.

2. Perform Starter Solenoid test BEFORE performing the starter relay test.

3. Perform a visual inspection of the starter/starter solenoid for corrosion, loose connections or faulty wiring.

4. Locate and remove the starter relay from the Power Distribution Center (PDC). Refer to the PDC label for relay identification and location.

5. Connect a remote starter switch or a jumper wire between the remote battery positive post and terminal 87 of the starter relay connector.

6. If engine cranks, starter/starter solenoid is good. Go to the Starter Relay Test.

7. If engine does not crank or solenoid chatters, check wiring and connectors from starter relay to starter solenoid and from the battery positive terminal to starter post for loose or corroded connections particularly at starter terminals.

8. Repeat test. If engine still fails to crank properly, trouble is within starter or starter mounted solenoid, and replace starter. Inspect the ring gear teeth.

Starter Relay

The starter relay is located in the Power Distribution Center (PDC) in the engine compartment. Refer to the PDC label for relay identification and location.

Remove the starter relay from the PDC to perform the following tests:

1. A relay in the de-energized position should have continuity between terminals 87A and 30, and no continuity between terminals 87 and 30. If OK, go to Step 2. If not OK, replace the faulty relay. Resistance between terminals 85 and 86 (electromagnet) should be 75 ±5 ohms. If OK, go to Step 3. If not OK, replace the faulty relay.

2. Connect a battery B+ lead to terminals 85 and a ground lead to terminal 86 to energize the relay. The relay should click. Also test for continuity between terminals 30 and 87, and no continuity between terminals 87A and 30. If OK, refer to Relay

Circuit Test procedure. If not OK, replace the faulty relay.

Relay Circuit Test

1. The relay common feed terminal cavity (30) is connected to battery voltage and should be hot at all times. If OK, go to Step 2. If not OK, repair the open circuit to the PDC fuse as required.

2. The relay normally closed terminal (87A) is connected to terminal 30 in the de-energized position, but is not used for this application. Go to Step 3.

3. The relay normally open terminal (87) is connected to the common feed terminal (30) in the energized position. This terminal supplies battery voltage to the starter solenoid field coils. There should be continuity between the cavity for relay terminal 87 and the starter solenoid terminal at all times. If OK, go to Step 4. If not OK, repair the open circuit to the starter solenoid as required.

4. The coil battery terminal (85) is connected to the electromagnet in the relay. It is energized when the ignition switch is held in the Start position and the clutch pedal is depressed (manual trans). Check for battery voltage at the cavity for relay terminal 86 with the ignition switch in the Start position and the clutch pedal is depressed (manual trans), and no voltage when the ignition switch is released to the On position. If OK, go to Step 5. If not OK, check for an open or short circuit to the ignition switch and repair, if required. If the circuit to the ignition switch is OK, see the Ignition Switch Test procedure in this group.

5. The coil ground terminal (86) is connected to the electromagnet in the relay. It is grounded by the PCM if the conditions are right to start the car. For automatic trans. cars the PCM must see Park Neutral switch low and near zero engine speed (rpm). For manual trans. cars the PCM only needs to see near zero engine speed (rpm) and low clutch interlock input and see near zero engine speed (rpm). To diagnose the Park Neutral switch of the trans range sensor refer to the transaxle section. Check for continuity to ground while the ignition switch is in the start position and if equipped the clutch pedal depressed. If not OK and the vehicle has an automatic trans. verify Park Neutral switch operation. If that checks OK check for continuity between PCM and the terminal 86. Repair open circuit as required. Also check the clutch interlock switch operation if equipped with a manual transmission. If OK, the PCM may be defective.

Feed Circuit Resistance Test

Before proceeding with this operation, review Diagnostic Preparation and Starter Feed Circuit Tests. The following operation will require a voltmeter, accurate to 1/10 of a volt.

To disable the Ignition and Fuel systems, disconnect the Automatic Shutdown Relay (ASD). The ASD relay is located in the Power Distribution Center (PDC). Refer to the PDC cover for proper relay location. Gain access to battery terminals.

1. With all wiring harnesses and components properly connected, perform the following:

2. Connect the negative lead of the voltmeter to the battery negative post, and positive lead to the battery negative cable clamp. Rotate and hold the ignition switch in the START position. Observe the voltmeter. If voltage is detected, correct poor contact between cable clamp and post.

3. Connect positive lead of the voltmeter to the battery positive post, and negative lead to the battery positive cable clamp. Rotate and hold the ignition switch key in the START position. Observe the voltmeter. If voltage is detected, correct poor contact between the cable clamp and post.

4. Connect negative lead of voltmeter to battery negative terminal, and positive lead to engine block near the battery cable attaching point. Rotate and hold the ignition switch in the START position. If voltage reads above 0.2 volt, correct poor contact at ground cable attaching point. If voltage reading is still above 0.2 volt after correcting poor contacts, replace ground cable.

5. Connect positive voltmeter lead to the starter motor housing and the negative lead to the battery negative terminal. Hold the ignition switch key in the START position. If voltage reads above 0.2 volt, correct poor starter to engine ground.

6. Connect the positive voltmeter lead to the battery positive terminal, and negative lead to battery cable terminal on starter solenoid. Rotate and hold the ignition switch in the START position. If voltage reads above 0.2 volt, correct poor contact at battery cable to solenoid connection. If reading is still above 0.2 volt after correcting poor contacts, replace battery positive cable.

7. If resistance tests do not detect feed circuit failures, replace the starter motor.

ENGINE MECHANICAL

➡Disconnecting the negative battery cable may interfere with the functions of the on board computer systems and may require the computer to undergo a relearning process, once the negative battery cable is reconnected.

ACCESSORY DRIVE BELTS

ACCESSORY BELT ROUTING

See Figures 84 through 86.

INSPECTION

Inspect the serpentine drive belt for signs of glazing or cracking. A glazed belt will be perfectly smooth from slippage, while a good belt will have a slight texture of fabric visible. Cracks will usually start at the inner

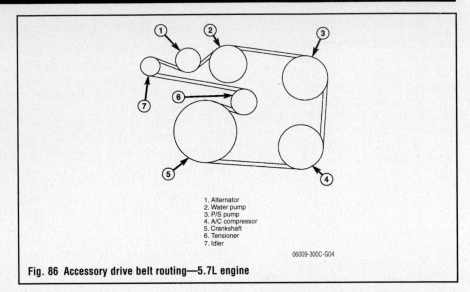

1. Alternator
2. Water pump
3. P/S pump
4. A/C compressor
5. Crankshaft
6. Tensioner
7. Idler

06009-300C-G04

Fig. 86 Accessory drive belt routing—5.7L engine

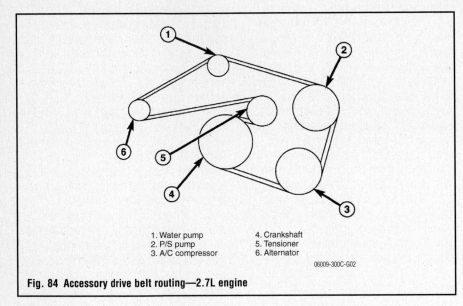

1. Water pump   4. Crankshaft
2. P/S pump   5. Tensioner
3. A/C compressor 6. Alternator

06009-300C-G02

Fig. 84 Accessory drive belt routing—2.7L engine

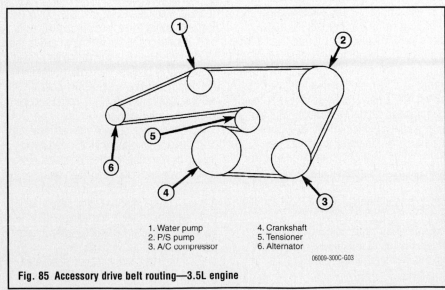

1. Water pump   4. Crankshaft
2. P/S pump   5. Tensioner
3. A/C compressor 6. Alternator

06009-300C-G03

Fig. 85 Accessory drive belt routing—3.5L engine

edge of the belt and run outward. All worn or damaged drive belts should be replaced immediately.

ADJUSTMENT

The belts used on these vehicle are equipped with automatic tensioners which maintain tension. No adjustment is necessary or possible.

REMOVAL & INSTALLATION

✷✷ WARNING

Do not let tensioner arm snap back to the freearm position. This may severely damage the tensioner.

1. Disconnect the negative battery cable from battery.
2. Rotate the belt tensioner counterclockwise until it contacts its stop. Remove belt, then slowly rotate the tensioner into the freearm position.

To install:
3. Check condition of all pulleys.

✷✷ WARNING

When installing the serpentine accessory drive belt, the belt MUST be routed correctly. If not, the engine may overheat due to the water pump rotating in the wrong direction.

4. Install a new belt. Route the belt around all pulleys except the idler pulley. Rotate the tensioner arm until it contacts its stop position. Route the belt around the idler and slowly let the tensioner rotate into the belt. Make sure the belt is seated onto all pulleys. The tensioner is equipped

with an indexing tang on the back of the tensioner and an indexing stop on the tensioner housing. If a new belt is being installed, the tang must be within approximately 0.24–0.32 in. (6–8mm) of indexing stop (i.e. tang is approximately between the two indexing stops). A belt is considered new if it has been used 15 minutes or less.

5. With the drive belt installed, inspect the belt wear indicator.

6. Connect the negative battery cable.

CAMSHAFT AND VALVE LIFTERS

INSPECTION

See Figure 87.

1. Inspect the camshaft bearing journals (4) for damage and binding. If journals are binding, check the cylinder head for damage. Also check cylinder head oil holes for clogging.

2. Check the cam lobe (5) and bearing surfaces for abnormal wear and damage. Replace camshaft if defective.

➡**If camshaft is replaced due to lobe wear or damage, always replace the rocker arms.**

3. Measure the lobe actual wear and replace camshaft if out of limit. Standard value is 0.001 in. (0.0254mm), wear limit is 0.010 (0.254mm).

REMOVAL & INSTALLATION

2.7L Engine

See Figures 88 through 93.

1. Before servicing the vehicle, refer to the precautions in the beginning of this section.

2. Remove the primary timing chain.

3. Remove secondary chain tensioner mounting bolts.

➡**Camshaft bearing caps have been marked during engine manufacturing. For example, number one exhaust camshaft bearing is marked "1E"**

4. Slowly loosen camshaft bearing cap bolts in the order shown.

5. Remove the camshaft bearing caps.

6. Remove intake camshaft, exhaust camshaft, secondary timing chain, and secondary timing chain tensioner together as an assembly.

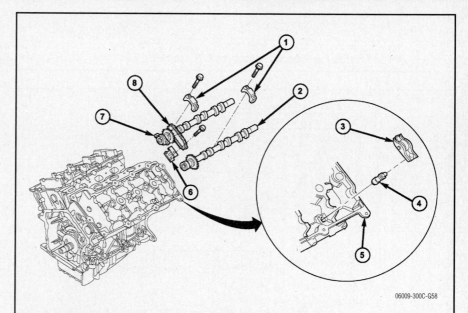

06009-300C-G58

Fig. 88 Camshafts and related parts (1) bearing caps, (2) exhaust camshaft (3) rocker arm, (4) lash adjuster, (5) head, (6) secondary timing chain tensioner, (7) intake camshaft—2.7L engine

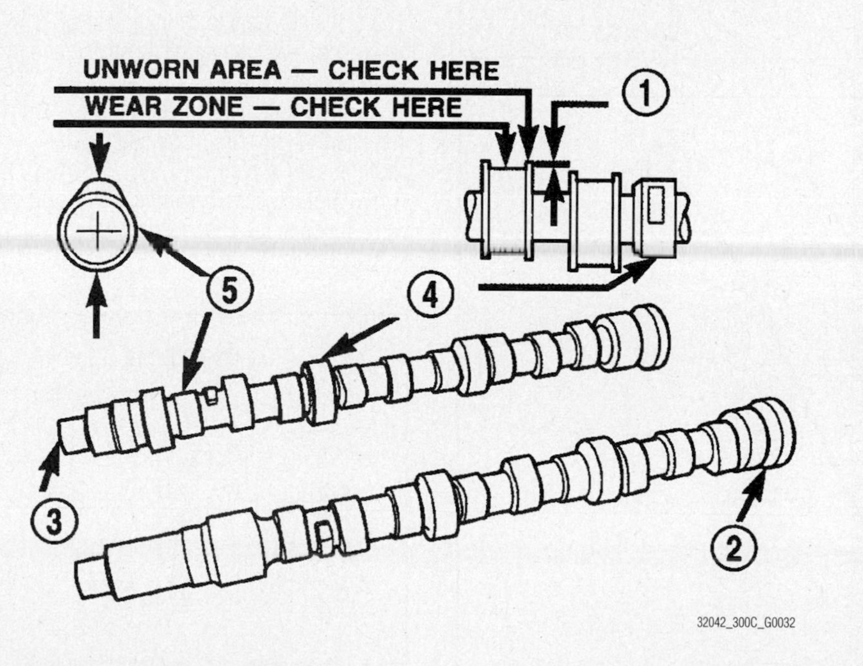

7. Remove secondary timing chain tensioner and secondary timing chain from camshafts.

8. Remove rocker arms.

➡**If lash adjusters and rocker arms are to be reused, always mark position for reassembly in their original positions.**

9. Remove lash adjuster(s).

To install:

10. Inspect camshaft bearing journals for damage and binding. If journals are binding, check the cylinder head for damage. Also check cylinder head oil holes for clogging.

11. Inspect camshaft sprockets for excessive wear. Replace camshafts if necessary.

12. Check the cam lobe surfaces for abnormal wear and damage. Replace camshaft if defective. Measure the actual wear and replace, if out of limits—standard value is 0.0254 mm (0.001 in.); wear limit is 0.254 mm (0.010 in.).

UNWORN AREA — CHECK HERE
WEAR ZONE — CHECK HERE

32042_300C_G0032

Fig. 87 Inspecting the camshaft

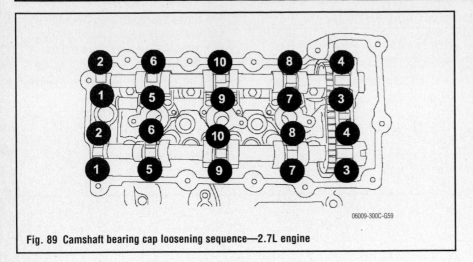

Fig. 89 Camshaft bearing cap loosening sequence—2.7L engine

06009-300C-G59

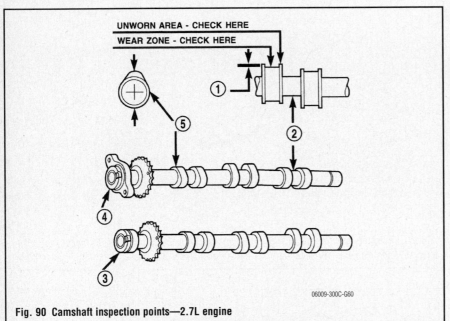

UNWORN AREA - CHECK HERE
WEAR ZONE - CHECK HERE

06009-300C-G60

Fig. 90 Camshaft inspection points—2.7L engine

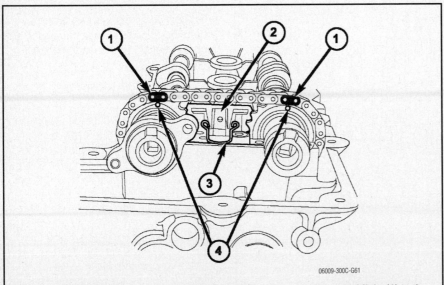

06009-300C-G61

Fig. 91 Verify that plated links (1) are facing toward the front. Align the plated links (1) to the dots (4) on the camshaft sprockets—2.7L engine

✳✳ WARNING

When the timing chain is removed and the cylinder heads are installed, DO NOT rotate the camshafts or crankshaft without first locating the proper crankshaft position. Failure to do so will result in valve and/or piston damage.

13. Install hydraulic lash adjuster making sure adjusters are at least partially full of oil. This can be verified by little or no plunger travel when lash adjuster is depressed.

14. Install rocker arm(s) and cylinder head covers.

15. Assemble camshaft chain on the cams. Verify that plated links are facing toward the front. Align the plated links to the dots on the camshaft sprockets.

16. If camshaft chain tensioner is already in the compressed and locked position, skip the next step.

17. When the camshaft chain tensioner is removed, it is necessary to compress and lock the tensioner using the following procedures:

  a. Place tensioner into a soft jaw vise.

  b. SLOWLY compress tensioner until fabricated lock pin or the equivalent can be inserted into the locking holes.

  c. Remove compressed and locked tensioner from the vise.

18. Insert the compressed and locked camshaft chain tensioner in-between the camshafts and chain.

19. Rotate the cams so that the plated links and dots are facing the 12:00 o'clock position.

20. Install cams to cylinder head. Verify that rocker arms are correctly seated and in proper positions.

21. Install camshaft bearing caps. Verify that bearing caps are installed in same position as removed.

22. Tighten cam bearing cap bolts gradually in sequence shown in to 105 inch lbs. (12 Nm).

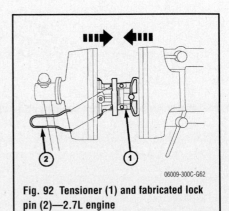

06009-300C-G62

Fig. 92 Tensioner (1) and fabricated lock pin (2)—2.7L engine

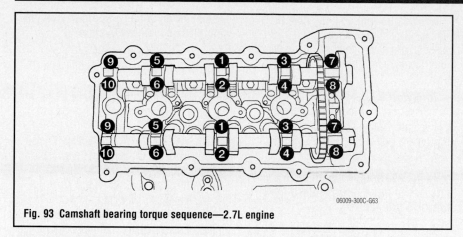

Fig. 93 Camshaft bearing torque sequence—2.7L engine

To install:

4. Inspect camshaft bearing journals for damage and binding. If journals are binding, check the cylinder head for damage. Also check cylinder head oil holes for clogging.

5. Check the cam lobe and bearing surfaces for abnormal wear and damage. Replace camshaft if defective.

➡If camshaft is replaced due to lobe wear or damage, always replace the rocker arms.

6. Measure the lobe actual wear and replace camshaft if out of limit. Standard

23. Install secondary chain tensioner (2) bolts and tighten to 105 inch lbs. (12 Nm).
24. Remove locking pin from secondary tensioners.
25. Measure camshafts end play.
26. Install the primary timing chain.

3.5L Engine

See Figures 94 and 95.

1. Before servicing the vehicle, refer to the precautions in the beginning of this section.

➡Camshafts are removed from the rear of each cylinder head.

2. Remove the cylinder head.

⁕⁕ WARNING

Care must be taken not to nick or scratch the journals when removing the camshaft.

3. Carefully remove the camshaft from the rear of the cylinder head.

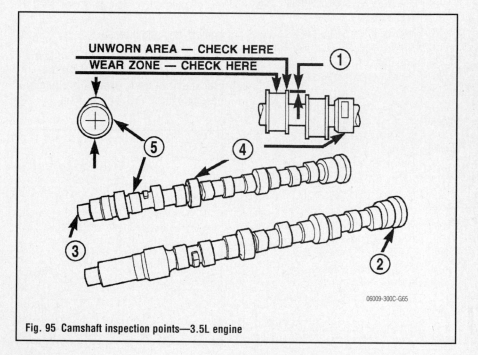

Fig. 95 Camshaft inspection points—3.5L engine

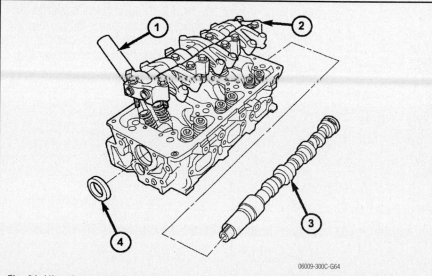

Fig. 94 (1) rocker arm tool, (2) rocker arm assembly, (3) camshaft, (4) thrust collar—3.5L engine

value is 0.0254 mm (0.001 in.), wear limit is 0.254 mm (0.010 in.).

➡Care must be taken not to scrape or nick the camshaft journals when installing the camshaft into position.

7. Lubricate camshaft bearing journals, camshaft lobes and camshaft seal with clean engine oil and install camshaft into cylinder head.

8. Install the cylinder head.

5.7L Engine

See Figures 96 and 97.

1. Before servicing the vehicle, refer to the precautions in the beginning of this section.
2. Remove the battery negative cable.
3. Remove the air cleaner assembly.
4. Drain the coolant.
5. Remove the accessory drive belt.

6. Remove the alternator.

7. Remove the air conditioning compressor, and set aside. Do not disconnect the lines.

8. Remove upper radiator hose.

9. Remove upper radiator closure panels.

10. Disconnect cooling fan electrical connector.

11. Remove cooling fan mounting bolts.

12. Remove radiator cooling fan assembly from vehicle.

13. Raise vehicle.

14. Remove lower splash shield.

15. Remove lower radiator hose.

16. Remove lower condenser mount bolts.

17. Lower vehicle.

18. Remove upper radiator hose.

19. Remove upper radiator mounting brackets and bolts.

20. Remove upper condenser mounting bolts.

21. Separate condenser assembly from radiator.

22. Tilt radiator toward engine and remove radiator from vehicle.

23. Remove the intake manifold.

24. Remove cylinder head covers.

25. Remove both left and right cylinder heads.

26. Remove the oil pan.

27. Remove timing case cover.

28. Remove the oil pick up tube.

29. Remove the oil pump.

30. Remove timing chain.

31. Remove camshaft tensioner/thrust plate assembly.

32. Remove the tappets and retainer assembly.

33. Install a long bolt into front of camshaft to aid in removal of the camshaft. Remove camshaft, being careful not to damage cam bearings with the cam lobes.

To install:

34. The cam bearings are not serviceable. Do not attempt to replace cam bearings for any reason.

35. Clean core hole in block.

➡ **Do not apply adhesive to the new core hole plug. A new plug will have adhesive pre-applied.**

36. Install a new core hole plug at the rear of camshaft, using suitable flat faced tool. The plug must be fully seated on the cylinder block shoulder.

➡ **The 5.7L LX engine uses a unique camshaft for use with the Multi Displacement System. When installing a new camshaft, the replacement**

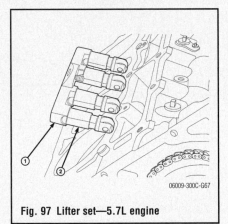

06009-300C-G67

Fig. 97 Lifter set—5.7L engine

camshaft must be compatible with the Multi Displacement System.

37. Lubricate camshaft lobes and camshaft bearing journals and insert the camshaft.

38. Install camshaft Tensioner plate assembly. Tighten bolts to 21 ft. lbs. (28 Nm) torque.

39. Install timing chain and sprockets.

40. Measure camshaft end play. If not within limits (0.0031–0.0114 in.) install a new thrust plate.

41. Install the oil pump.

42. Install the oil pick up tube.

43. Each tappet reused must be installed in the same position from which it was removed. When camshaft is replaced, all of the tappets must be replaced.

➡ **The 5.7L LX engine uses both standard roller tappets and deactivating roller tappets, for use with the Multi Displacement System. The deactivating roller tappets must be used in cylinders 1, 4, 6, 8. The deactivating tappets can be identified by the two holes in the side of the tappet body, for the latching pins.**

44. Install tappets and retaining yoke assembly.

45. Install both left and right cylinder heads.

46. Install pushrods.

47. Install rocker arms.

48. Install timing case cover.

49. Install the oil pan.

50. Install cylinder head covers.

51. Install intake manifold.

52. Position the air conditioning compressor on the engine.

53. Install the bolts that secure the air conditioning compressor and the automatic transmission cooler line bracket to the cylinder block. Tighten the bolts to 41 ft. lbs. (55 Nm).

54. Install the air conditioning compressor.

55. Install the alternator.

56. Install the accessory drive belt.

57. Position radiator into engine compartment. Seat the radiator assembly lower rubber isolators into the mounting holes in radiator lower support.

58. Install radiator mounting bracket and bolts. Tighten to 106 inch lbs. (12 Nm).

59. Position condenser on radiator and install upper mounting bolts. Tighten bolts to 50 inch lbs. (6 Nm).

60. Raise vehicle.

61. Install lower condenser mounting bolts. Tighten bolts to 88 inch lbs. (10 Nm).

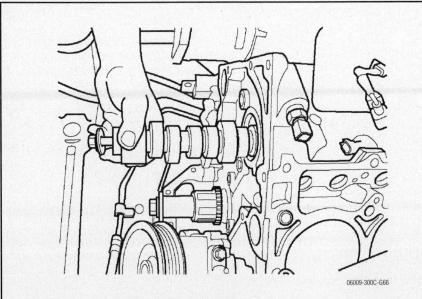

06009-300C-G66

Fig. 96 Camshaft removal/installation—5.7L engine

62. Install lower radiator hose and clamp.

63. Lower vehicle.

64. Position radiator cooling fan assembly in vehicle.

65. Install cooling fan mounting bolts. Tighten to 50 inch lbs. (6 Nm).

66. Connect cooling fan electrical connector.

67. Install upper radiator upper hose. Align hose so it does not interfere with the accessory drive belt or engine. Position hose clamp so it will not interfere with the hood.

68. Install the air cleaner assembly.

69. Install the battery negative cable.

70. Refill coolant.

71. Refill engine oil.

72. Start engine and check for leaks.

CRANKSHAFT FRONT SEAL

REMOVAL & INSTALLATION

3.5L Engine

See Figures 98 through 100.

For front seal service on the 2.7L and 5.7L engines, see Timing Chain Cover and Seal.

1. Before servicing the vehicle, refer to the precautions in the beginning of this section.

2. Remove the crankshaft sprocket.

3. Tap the dowel pin out of the crankshaft.

4. Remove crankshaft seal using Special Tool 6341A.

➡**Do not nick shaft seal surface or seal bore.**

5. Shaft seal lip surface must be free of varnish, dirt or nicks. Polish with 400 grit paper if necessary.

To install:

6. Install the crankshaft seal using Special Tool 6342.

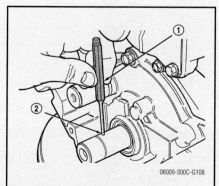

Fig. 98 Tap the dowel pin (2) out of the crankshaft—3.5L engine

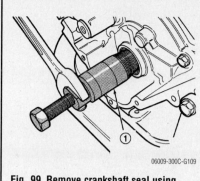

Fig. 99 Remove crankshaft seal using Special Tool 6341A (1)—3.5L engine

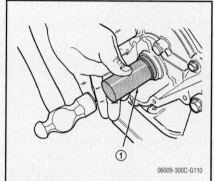

Fig. 100 Install crankshaft seal using Special Tool 6342 (1)—3.5L engine

7. Install the dowel pin into the crankshaft to 1.2 mm (0.047 in.) protrusion.

8. Install the crankshaft sprocket.

CYLINDER HEAD

REMOVAL & INSTALLATION

2.7L Engine

See Figures 101 through 108.

1. Before servicing the vehicle, refer to the precautions in the beginning of this section.

2. Perform fuel pressure release procedure before attempting any repairs.

3. Disconnect negative cable from battery.

4. Raise and safely support the vehicle.

5. Drain cooling system.

6. Remove accessory drive belt.

7. Remove the vibration damper.

8. Disconnect camshaft position sensor, and coolant temperature sensor connectors.

9. Remove upper intake manifold.

10. Disconnect coils, capacitors, and injector connectors.

11. Reposition harness out of the way.

12. Disconnect fuel feed line.

13. Remove lower intake manifold.

14. Remove the cylinder head cover.

15. Remove upper radiator hose.

16. Remove upper radiator closure panels.

17. Disconnect cooling fan electrical connector.

18. Remove cooling fan mounting bolts.

19. Remove radiator cooling fan assembly from vehicle.

20. Raise vehicle.

21. Remove lower splash shield.

22. Remove lower radiator hose.

23. Remove lower condenser mount bolts.

24. Lower vehicle.

25. Remove upper radiator mounting brackets and bolts.

26. Remove upper condenser mounting bolts.

27. Separate condenser assembly from radiator.

28. Tilt radiator toward engine and remove radiator from vehicle.

29. Disconnect engine coolant temperature sensor connector.

30. Remove radiator upper hose at tube.

31. Remove heater hose from heater tube at rear of engine.

32. Disconnect heater tube from retaining clip at rear of engine.

33. Disconnect electrical connector from coolant temperature sensor.

34. Remove screws attaching heater tube to outlet connector.

35. Disengage heater tube from outlet connector. To remove heater tube, move forward until the tube clears cylinder heads.

36. Remove coolant outlet.

37. Remove timing chain cover.

38. Rotate crankshaft until crankshaft sprocket timing mark aligns with timing mark on oil pump housing.

39. Remove primary timing chain.

40. Remove upper primary timing chain guides.

41. Remove camshaft bearing caps gradually in the sequence shown.

42. Remove camshafts and valvetrain components from cylinder head. Note component locations for reinstallation in original locations.

43. For left cylinder head removal:

    a. Remove fastener securing engine oil dipstick tube to cylinder head. Remove engine oil dipstick tube.

    b. Remove alternator.

44. For right cylinder head removal:

    a. Remove cylinder head ground strap.

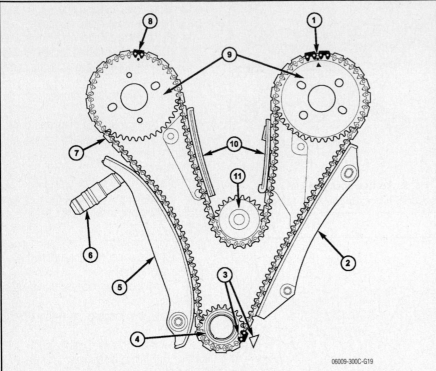

Fig. 101 Rotate crankshaft until crankshaft sprocket timing mark aligns with timing mark on oil pump housing—2.7L engine

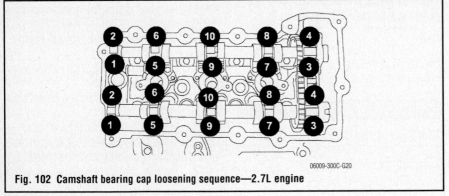

Fig. 102 Camshaft bearing cap loosening sequence—2.7L engine

b. Disconnect EGR valve electrical connector and remove EGR valve from head.

✳✳ WARNING

Ensure cylinder head bolts 1–3 are removed before attempting the removal of cylinder head, as damage to cylinder head and/or block may occur.

45. Remove cylinder left head bolts and right head bolts in sequence shown.
46. Remove cylinder head(s).
47. Remove and discard cylinder head gasket.

To install:

To ensure engine gasket sealing, proper surface preparation must be performed,

especially with the use of aluminum engine components and multi-layer steel cylinder head gaskets.

➡ **Multi-Layer Steel (MLS) head gaskets require a scratch free sealing surface. Remove all gasket material from cylinder head and block. Be careful not to gouge or scratch the aluminum head sealing surface. Clean all engine oil passages.**

48. Before cleaning, check for leaks, damage and cracks.
49. Clean cylinder head and oil passages.
50. Check cylinder head for flatness.
51. Cylinder head must be flat within:
- Standard dimension = less than 0.05 mm (0.002 inch.)
- Service Limit = 0.2 mm (0.008 inch.)
- Grinding Limit = Maximum of 0.2 mm (0.008 inch.) is permitted.

✳✳ WARNING

0.20 mm (0.008 in.) MAX is a combined total dimension of the stock removal limit from cylinder head and block top surface (deck) together.

➡ **The cylinder head bolts are tightened using a torque plus angle procedure. The bolts must be examined BEFORE reuse. If the threads are necked down the bolts must be replaced**

Necking can be checked by holding a straight-edge against the threads. If all the threads do not contact the scale, the bolt must be replaced.

✳✳ WARNING

When cleaning cylinder head and cylinder block surfaces, DO NOT use

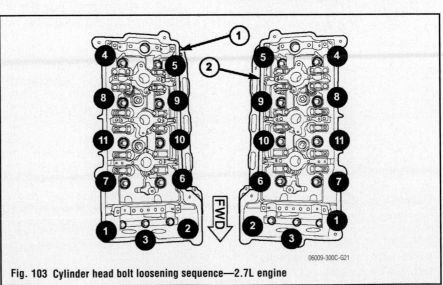

Fig. 103 Cylinder head bolt loosening sequence—2.7L engine

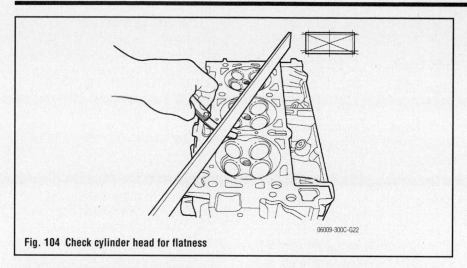

Fig. 104 Check cylinder head for flatness

a metal scraper because the surfaces could be cut or ground. Use ONLY a wooden or plastic scraper.

52. Clean sealing surfaces of cylinder head and block.

53. Install new head gasket over locating dowels.

54. Install cylinder head to block, assuring head is properly positioned over locating dowels.

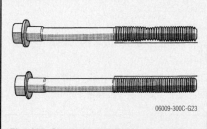

Fig. 105 Check the head bolts for necking

55. Lubricate bolt threads with clean engine oil and install bolts.

56. Tighten bolts in sequence shown for left head and right head, using the following steps and torque values:
- Step 1: Bolts 1–8 to 35 ft. lbs. (48 Nm)
- Step 2: Bolts 1–8 to 55 ft. lbs. (75 Nm)
- Step 3: Bolts 1–8 to 55 ft. lbs. (75 Nm)
- Step 4: Bolts 1–8 to +90° turn. Do not use a torque wrench for this step.
- Step 5: Bolts 9–11 to 21 ft. lbs. (28 Nm)

57. For left cylinder head installation:
- Install engine oil dipstick tube.
- Install alternator.

58. For right cylinder head installation:
a. Install cylinder head ground strap.

b. Clean mounting surface and install EGR valve.

c. Install the EGR valve mounting bolts.

d. Inspect rubber silicone seals on intake manifold end of EGR tube.

e. Install upper tube into the intake manifold, being careful that the silicone rubber seals are correctly installed and undamaged.

f. Install new gasket between the EGR valve and upper tube and install bolts.

g. Install the lower tube to exhaust manifold.

h. Install new gasket between the EGR valve and lower tube and install bolts.

i. Tighten the lower tube to EGR valve bolts to 95 inch lbs. (11 Nm) torque.

j. Tighten the lower tube to exhaust manifold bolts to 275 inch lbs. (31 Nm) torque.

k. Tighten the upper tube to EGR valve bolts to 95 inch lbs. (11 Nm) torque.

l. Tighten EGR valve to cylinder head bolts to 275 inch lbs. (31 Nm) torque.

59. Install all valve train components and camshafts. Tighten camshaft bearing caps in sequence shown to 105 inch lbs. (12 Nm).

60. Install primary timing chain, guides and sprockets.

61. Inspect heater tube O-ring. Replace as necessary.

62. Lubricate O-ring with silicone type grease such as Mopar® dielectric grease.

63. Install the heater tube by inserting tube in between cylinder heads. Insert tube into outlet connector.

64. Attach heater tube to the retaining clip at rear of engine.

65. Install coolant outlet. Install attaching screws and tighten to 30 inch lbs. (3 Nm).

66. Position radiator into engine compartment. Seat the radiator assembly lower

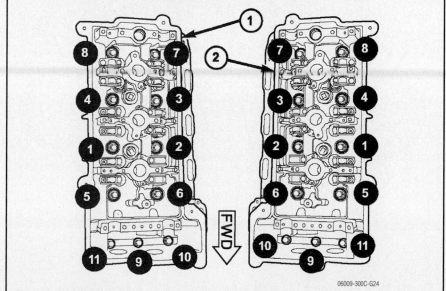

Fig. 106 Cylinder head bolt torque sequence—2.7L engine

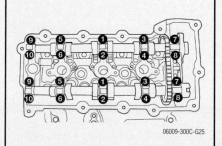

Fig. 107 Camshaft bearing cap bolt torque sequence—2.7L engine

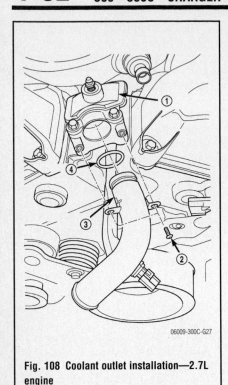

Fig. 108 Coolant outlet installation—2.7L engine

06009-300C-G27

rubber isolators into the mounting holes in radiator lower support.

67. Install radiator mounting bracket and bolts. Tighten to 106 inch lbs. (12 Nm).

68. Position condenser on radiator and install upper mounting bolts. Tighten bolts to 50 inch lbs. (6 Nm).

69. Raise vehicle.

70. Install lower condenser mounting bolts. Tighten bolts to 88 inch lbs. (10 Nm).

71. Install lower radiator hose and clamp.

72. Lower vehicle.

73. Position radiator cooling fan assembly in vehicle.

74. Install cooling fan mounting bolts. Tighten to 50 inch lbs. (6 Nm).

75. Connect cooling fan electrical connector.

76. Install upper radiator upper hose. Align hose so it does not interfere with the accessory drive belt or engine. Position hose clamp so it will not interfere with the hood.

77. Install lower intake manifold.

78. Install the cylinder head cover.

79. Connect camshaft position sensor and coolant temperature sensor connectors.

80. Install timing chain cover.

81. Install crankshaft vibration damper.

82. Install upper intake manifold.

83. Connect oil pressure sensor connector.

84. Install accessory drive belt.

85. Fill the cooling system.

86. Connect negative battery cable.

87. Start engine and check for leaks.

3.5L Engine

Right Side

See Figures 109 and 110.

1. Before servicing the vehicle, refer to the precautions in the beginning of this section.

2. Perform the fuel relief procedure.

3. Disconnect the negative battery cable.

4. Drain cooling system.

5. Remove the upper intake manifold.

6. Remove the lower intake manifold.

7. Remove accessory drive belt.

8. Remove accessory drive belt idler pulley.

9. Remove the power steering mounting bolts and set the pump aside.

10. Raise the vehicle.

11. Remove crankshaft damper.

12. Remove lower outer timing belt cover bolts.

13. Remove front exhaust pipe to exhaust manifold mounting nuts.

14. Disconnect both oxygen sensor harness connectors on each side.

15. Lower vehicle.

16. Remove the remaining outer timing belt cover bolts and cover.

17. Rotate the engine to TDC and align timing belt marks.

18. Remove the timing belt tensioner and reset the tensioner.

19. Remove the timing belt.

20. Remove the right cylinder head cover to cylinder head ground strap and capacitor.

21. Remove the EGR valve and tube assembly.

22. Remove the right cylinder head cover.

23. Remove the right rocker arm assembly.

24. Remove the right rear camshaft thrust plate.

25. Counterhold the cam gear and remove the right cam gear retaining bolt.

26. Push the camshaft out of the back of the cylinder head approximately 3.5 inches and remove the right cam gear.

27. Remove the inner timing cover to cylinder head retaining bolts.

28. Remove the cylinder head bolts in REVERSE of tightening sequence.

29. Remove the cylinder head.

30. Clean and inspect all mating surfaces.

To install:

To ensure engine gasket sealing, proper surface preparation must be performed, especially with the use of aluminum engine components and multi-layer steel cylinder head gaskets.

➡**Multi-Layer Steel (MLS) head gaskets require a scratch free sealing surface.**

Remove all gasket material from cylinder head and block. Be careful not to gouge or

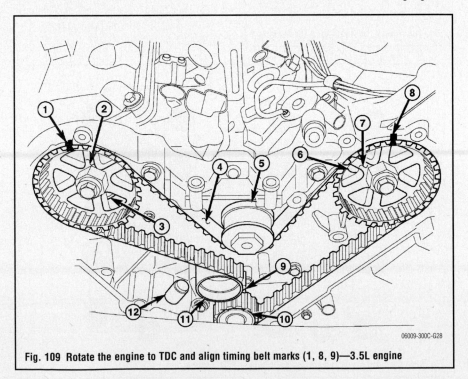

Fig. 109 Rotate the engine to TDC and align timing belt marks (1, 8, 9)—3.5L engine

06009-300C-G28

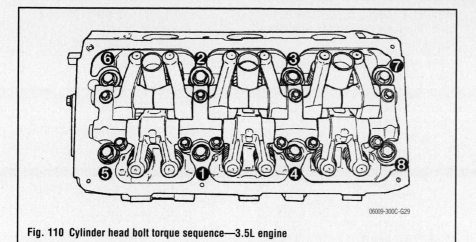

Fig. 110 Cylinder head bolt torque sequence—3.5L engine

scratch the aluminum head sealing surface. Clean all engine oil passages.

31. Before cleaning, check for leaks, damage and cracks.

32. Clean cylinder head and oil passages.

33. Check cylinder head for flatness.

34. Cylinder head must be flat within:
- Standard dimension = less than 0.05 mm (0.002 inch.)
- Service Limit = 0.2 mm (0.008 inch.)
- Grinding Limit = Maximum of 0.2 mm (0.008 inch.) is permitted.

✳✳ WARNING

0.20 mm (0.008 in.) MAX is a combined total dimension of the stock removal limit from cylinder head and block top surface (deck) together.

✳✳ WARNING

The cylinder head gaskets are not interchangeable between cylinder heads and are clearly marked right or left.

➡The cylinder head bolts are tightened using a torque plus angle procedure. The bolts must be examined BEFORE reuse. If the threads are necked down the bolts must be replaced.

Necking can be checked by holding a scale or straight-edge against the threads. If all the threads do not contact the scale the bolt must be replaced.

✳✳ WARNING

When cleaning cylinder head and cylinder block surfaces, DO NOT use a metal scraper because the surfaces could be cut or ground. Use ONLY a wooden or plastic scraper.

35. Clean sealing surfaces of cylinder head and block.

✳✳ WARNING

Ensure that the correct head gaskets are used and are oriented correctly on cylinder block.

➡Before installing the cylinder head bolts, lubricate the threads with clean engine oil.

36. Install the cylinder head over locating dowels and finger tighten the head bolts.

37. Tighten the cylinder head bolts in the following sequence, using the 4 step torque-turn method. Tighten according to the following torque values:
- Step 1: All to 45 ft. lbs. (61 Nm)
- Step 2: All to 65 ft. lbs. (88 Nm)
- Step 3: All (again) to 65 ft. lbs. (88 Nm)
- Step 4: + 90° turn. Do not use a torque wrench for this step.

38. Bolt torque after 90° turn should be over 90 ft. lbs. (122 Nm) in the tightening direction. If not, replace the bolt.

39. Install the inner timing cover to cylinder head bolts. Tighten bolts to 40 ft. lbs. (54 Nm).

40. Install camshaft sprocket. Counterhold the camshaft sprocket gear and tighten the camshaft sprocket bolt to 75 ft. lbs. plus a 90° turn (102 Nm plus a 90° turn).

41. Install the rear camshaft thrust plate and seal and the EGR valve.

42. Rotate the camshaft gear to its alignment mark and check the left camshaft gear and crankshaft gear timing alignment marks.

43. Install the timing belt and tensioner.

44. Install the timing belt outer cover.

45. Install the power steering reservoir.

46. Install the vibration damper.

47. Install the accessory drive belt tensioner.

48. Install the accessory drive belt idler pulley.

49. Install the right exhaust manifold.

50. Raise and support the vehicle.

51. Install the front exhaust pipe and connect the oxygen sensors.

52. Lower the vehicle.

53. Install the right rocker arm assembly.

54. Clean cylinder head and cover mating surfaces. Inspect and replace gasket and seals as necessary.

55. Install cylinder head cover bolts and tighten to 105 inch lbs. (12 Nm).

56. Install the ground strap retaining bolt to the cylinder head cover.

57. Install the wire harness track.

58. Install the ignition coils. Tighten mounting screws to 60 inch lbs. (6.7 Nm).

59. Connect the ignition coil electrical connectors.

60. Install the right cylinder head cover, ground strap and insulator.

61. Install lower intake manifold.

62. Install the fuel rail.

63. Install the upper intake manifold.

64. Connect the air cleaner element housing.

65. Fill the coolant system.

66. Connect the negative battery cable.

Left Side

1. Before servicing the vehicle, refer to the precautions in the beginning of this section.

2. Perform the fuel relief procedure.

3. Disconnect the negative battery cable.

4. Drain cooling system.

5. Remove the upper intake manifold.

6. Remove the lower intake manifold

7. Remove the accessory drive belt.

8. Remove the belt tensioner.

9. Remove the accessory drive idler pulley.

10. Remove the power steering mounting bolts and set pump aside.

11. Remove the crankshaft damper.

12. Remove the lower outer timing belt cover.

13. Raise and support the vehicle.

14. Remove the front exhaust pipe to exhaust manifold mounting nuts.

15. Disconnect both oxygen sensor harness connectors.

16. Lower the vehicle.

17. Remove the outer timing belt cover.

18. Rotate the engine to TDC and align the timing marks.

19. Remove the timing belt tensioner, timing belt, then reset tensioner.

20. Remove the left cylinder head cover to cylinder head ground strap.

21. Remove the left cylinder head cover.

22. Remove the left rocker arm assembly.

23. Remove the left camshaft thrust plate.

24. Counterhold the left cam gear and remove the cam gear retaining bolt.

25. Push the camshaft out of the back of the cylinder head approximately 3.5 inches and remove the cam gear. Remove the front timing belt housing to cylinder head bolts.

26. Remove the cylinder head bolts in REVERSE of tightening sequence.

27. Remove the cylinder head.

28. Clean and inspect all mating surfaces.

To install:

To ensure engine gasket sealing, proper surface preparation must be performed, especially with the use of aluminum engine components and multi-layer steel cylinder head gaskets.

➡**Multi-Layer Steel (MLS) head gaskets require a scratch free sealing surface.**

Remove all gasket material from cylinder head and block. Be careful not to gouge or scratch the aluminum head sealing surface. Clean all engine oil passages.

❋❋ WARNING

The cylinder head gaskets are not interchangeable between cylinder heads and are clearly marked right or left.

➡**The cylinder head bolts are tightened using a torque plus angle procedure. The bolts must be examined BEFORE reuse. If the threads are necked down the bolts must be replaced.**

Necking can be checked by holding a scale or straight-edge against the threads. If all the threads do not contact the scale the bolt must be replaced.

❋❋ WARNING

When cleaning cylinder head and cylinder block surfaces, DO NOT use a metal scraper because the surfaces could be cut or ground. Use ONLY a wooden or plastic scraper.

29. Clean sealing surfaces of cylinder head and block.

❋❋ WARNING

Ensure that the correct head gaskets are used and are oriented correctly on cylinder block.

➡**Before installing the cylinder head bolts, lubricate the threads with clean engine oil.**

30. Install the cylinder head over locating dowels and finger tighten the head bolts.

31. Tighten the cylinder head bolts in the following sequence, using the 4 step torque-turn method. Tighten according to the following torque values:

- Step 1: All to 45 ft. lbs. (61 Nm)
- Step 2: All to 65 ft. lbs. (88 Nm)
- Step 3: All (again) to 65 ft. lbs. (88 Nm)
- Step 4: + 90° turn. Do not use a torque wrench for this step.

32. Bolt torque after 90° turn should be over 90 ft. lbs. (122 Nm) in the tightening direction. If not, replace the bolt.

33. Install the inner timing cover to cylinder head bolts. Tighten bolts to 54 N. (40 ft. lbs.).

34. Install camshaft sprocket. Counter-hold the camshaft sprocket gear and tighten the camshaft sprocket bolt to 102 Nm plus a 90° turn (75 lbs. ft. plus a 90° turn).

35. Install the rear camshaft thrust plate and seal and the EGR valve.

36. Rotate the camshaft gear to its alignment mark and check the left camshaft gear and crankshaft gear timing alignment marks.

37. Install the timing belt and tensioner.

38. Install the timing belt outer cover.

39. Install the power steering reservoir.

40. Install the vibration damper.

41. Install the accessory drive belt tensioner.

42. Install the accessory drive belt idler pulley.

43. Install the right exhaust manifold.

44. Raise and support the vehicle.

45. Install the front exhaust pipe and connect the oxygen sensors.

46. Lower the vehicle.

47. Install the right rocker arm assembly.

48. Install the right cylinder head cover, ground strap and insulator.

49. Install lower intake manifold.

50. Install the fuel rail.

51. Install the upper intake manifold.

52. Connect the air cleaner element housing.

53. Fill the coolant system.

54. Connect the negative battery cable.

5.7L Engine

See Figures 111 and 112.

1. Before servicing the vehicle, refer to the precautions in the beginning of this section.

2. Perform the fuel system pressure release procedure.

3. Disconnect the fuel supply line.

4. Disconnect the battery negative cable.

5. Drain cooling system.

6. Remove the air cleaner resonator and duct work.

7. Remove closed crankcase ventilation system.

8. Disconnect the exhaust at the exhaust manifolds.

9. Disconnect the evaporation control system.

10. Disconnect heater hoses.

11. Remove the power steering pump.

12. Disconnect coil on plug connectors.

❋❋ WARNING

The ground straps must be installed in the same location as removed. The covers are machined to accept the ground straps in those locations only.

13. Remove cylinder head cover.

➡**The gasket may be used again, provided no cuts, tears, or deformation has occurred.**

14. Remove intake manifold and throttle body as an assembly.

15. Remove rocker arm assemblies and push rods. Identify to ensure installation in original locations.

16. Remove the head bolts from each cylinder head, using the sequence provided, and remove cylinder heads. Discard the cylinder head gasket.

To install:

17. Clean all surfaces of cylinder block and cylinder heads.

18. Clean cylinder block front and rear gasket surfaces using a suitable solvent.

19. Inspect the cylinder head for out-of-flatness, using a straight-edge and a feeler gauge. If tolerances exceed 0.0508mm (0.002 in.), replace the cylinder head.

20. Inspect the valve seats for damage. Service the valve seats as necessary.

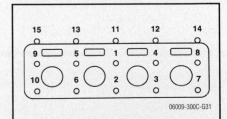

06009-300C-G31

Fig. 111 Cylinder head bolt removal/tightening sequence—5.7L engine

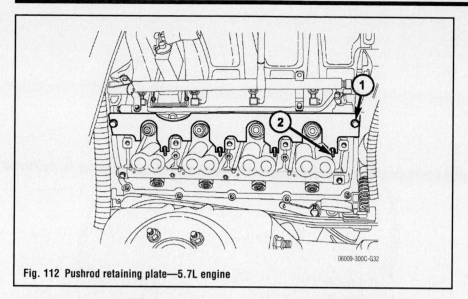

Fig. 112 Pushrod retaining plate—5.7L engine

06009-300C-G32

21. Inspect the valve guides for wear, cracks or looseness. If either condition exists, replace the cylinder head.

22. Inspect pushrods. Replace worn or bent pushrods.

23. Clean all surfaces of cylinder block and cylinder heads.

24. Clean cylinder block front and rear gasket surfaces using a suitable solvent.

✳✳ WARNING

The head gaskets are not inter-changeable between left and right sides. They are marked "L" and "R" to indicate left and right sides.

✳✳ WARNING

The head gaskets are marked "TOP" to indicate which side goes up.

25. Position new cylinder head gaskets onto the cylinder block.

26. Position cylinder heads onto head gaskets and cylinder block.

27. Tighten the cylinder head bolts in three steps using the sequence provided:

- Step 1: Snug tighten M12 cylinder head bolts, in sequence, to 25 ft. lbs. (34 Nm) and M8 bolts to 15 ft. lbs. (20 Nm) torque.
- Step 2: Tighten M12 cylinder head bolts, in sequence, to 40 ft. lbs. (54 Nm) and verify M8 bolts to 15 ft. lbs. (20 Nm) torque.
- Step 3: Turn M12 cylinder head bolts, in sequence, 90 degrees and tighten M8 bolts to 25 ft. lbs. (34 Nm) torque.

28. Install pushrods and rocker arm assemblies in their original position, using pushrod retaining plate special tool 9070.

29. Install the intake manifold and throttle body assembly.

30. If required, adjust spark plugs to specifications. Install the plugs.

31. Connect the heater hoses.

32. Install the fuel supply line.

33. Install the power steering pump.

34. Install the drive belt.

35. Install the cylinder head cover.

36. Install ignition coil on plug, and torque fasteners to 105 inch lbs. (12 Nm)

37. Connect, ignition coil electrical connectors.

38. Install PCV hose.

39. Connect the evaporation control system.

40. Install the air cleaner.

41. Fill cooling system.

42. Connect the negative cable to the battery.

43. Start engine check for leaks.

ENGINE ASSEMBLY

REMOVAL & INSTALLATION

2.7L Engine

See Figures 113 and 114.

1. Before servicing the vehicle, refer to the precautions in the beginning of this section.

2. Remove hood.

3. Release fuel pressure.

4. Disconnect negative battery cable located in the trunk.

5. Disconnect intake air temperature sensor electrical connector.

6. Remove air cleaner housing assembly.

7. Remove accessory drive belt.

8. Disconnect lines from power steering pump.

9. Remove power steering pump attaching bolts and set pump aside.

10. Recover air conditioning system using a suitable refrigerant recovery machine.

11. Disconnect the wire harness connector from the air conditioning compressor clutch coil connector.

12. Remove the nuts that secure the air conditioning suction line and air conditioning discharge line to the air conditioning compressor.

13. Disconnect the suction and discharge lines from the air conditioning compressor and remove and discard the dual plane seals.

14. Install plugs in, or tape over all of the opened refrigerant line fittings and the compressor ports.

15. Raise and support the vehicle.

16. Remove the front end splash shield.

17. Remove the bolts that secure the automatic transmission cooler line bracket and the air conditioning compressor to the cylinder block.

18. Position the cooler lines out of the way and remove the air conditioning compressor from the engine compartment.

19. Disconnect air conditioning compressor electrical connectors.

20. Remove air conditioning compressor.

21. Raise vehicle.

22. Remove lower splash shield bolts and remove splash shield.

23. Drain cooling system.

24. Drain the engine oil and remove the oil filter.

25. Disconnect down stream oxygen sensor connectors.

26. Disconnect exhaust pipes at the manifolds.

27. Disconnect starter electrical connectors.

28. Remove starter bolts and set starter aside.

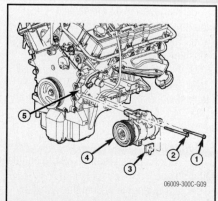

06009-300C-G09

Fig. 113 A/C compressor (4) mounting—2.7L engine

29. Disconnect coolant pipe near starter from hose.

30. Disconnect crankshaft position sensor electrical connector and remove sensor.

31. Disconnect ground strap.

32. Disconnect oil pressure sensor electrical connector.

33. Remove 4 engine mount nuts.

34. Remove engine mount studs from mount.

35. Remove steering gear mounting bolts and lower steering gear for clearance.

36. Using a block of wood and a suitable lifting device under the oil pan, raise the engine.

37. Remove structural collar bolts.

38. Remove structural collar.

39. Remove lower bell housing bolts.

40. Lower engine and remove jackstand.

41. Mark flex plate to torque converter location.

42. Remove torque converter bolts.

43. Lower the vehicle.

44. Remove the wiper arms.

45. Remove the wiper cowl.

46. Remove strut tower support.

47. Reposition purge solenoid.

48. Remove the intake manifold.

49. Disconnect all the vacuum lines and electrical connectors.

50. Disconnect all ground straps attaching to the engine.

51. Disconnect fuel line at fuel rail.

52. Disconnect coil, injector, capacitor, and knock sensor connectors.

53. Remove purge solenoid from bracket.

54. Remove the bolts from the EGR tube to exhaust manifold.

55. Remove the lower tube bolts to EGR valve and remove tube.

56. Remove upper tube bolts to EGR valve.

57. Remove the EGR valve mounting bolts.

58. Remove valve from vehicle. Clean mounting surface.

59. Remove upper bellhousing bolts and reposition electrical harness.

60. Attach the lifting tool 8342A.

61. Support the transmission with a block of wood and floor jack.

62. Hoist engine from engine compartment.

To install:

63. Attach special tool no. 8342A engine lifting fixture.

64. Lower engine into engine compartment.

65. Remove special tool no. 8342A.

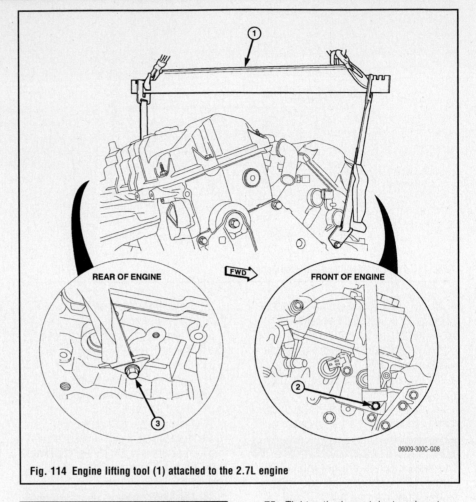

Fig. 114 Engine lifting tool (1) attached to the 2.7L engine

06009-300C-G08

⁂ WARNING

Do not tighten the transmission case to engine block bolts until all bolts have been hand started, and the two mating surfaces are completely joined together, as damage to cylinder block or transmission could occur.

66. Install bellhousing to cylinder block bolts and tighten to 50 ft. lbs. (68 Nm).

67. Install the EGR valve.

68. Install the EGR valve mounting bolts.

69. Inspect the rubber silicone seals on intake manifold end of EGR tube.

70. Install upper tube into the intake manifold, being careful that the silicone rubber seals are correctly installed and undamaged.

71. Install new gasket between the EGR valve and upper tube and install bolts.

72. Install the lower tube to exhaust manifold.

73. Install new gasket between the EGR valve and lower tube and install bolts.

74. Tighten the lower tube to EGR valve bolts to 95 inch lbs. (11 Nm) torque.

75. Tighten the lower tube to exhaust manifold bolts to 23 ft. lbs. (31 Nm) torque.

76. Tighten the upper tube to EGR valve bolts to 95 inch lbs. (11 Nm) torque.

77. Tighten EGR valve to cylinder head bolts to 23 ft. lbs. (31 Nm) torque.

78. Connect the electrical connector to EGR valve and lock.

79. Relocate the purge solenoid.

80. Install purge solenoid to bracket.

81. Connect coil, injector, capacitor, and knock sensor connectors.

82. Connect the fuel line.

83. Install upper intake manifold.

84. Install purge solenoid.

85. Connect all ground straps.

86. Connect all vacuum lines and electrical connectors.

87. Raise the vehicle.

88. Align flexplate and torque converter.

➡**Make sure all four bolts are installed finger tight before torquing bolts.**

89. Tighten torque converter bolts to 55 ft. lbs. (75 Nm).

90. Using a block of wood and a suitable lifting device under the oil pan, raise the engine.

91. Install the structural collar and position in place.

➡**Make sure that structural collar is flush with the oil pan and the transmission bell housing.**

92. Finger tighten all bolts.
93. Tighten the structural collar to oil pan bolts to 40 ft. lbs. (55 Nm).
94. Tighten structural collar to transmission bolts to 40 ft. lbs. (55 Nm).
95. Align power steering pump with mounting holes on engine bracket.
96. Install three pump mounting bolts through access holes in pulley and engine bracket. Tighten bolts to 21 ft. lbs. (28 Nm) torque.

➡**Always use a NEW O-ring on the end of the pressure hose.**

97. Lubricate NEW O-ring on end of pressure hose with clean power steering fluid.
98. Install pressure hose to pump. Tighten pressure hose tube nut to 35 ft. lbs. (47 Nm) torque.
99. Install supply hose on pump. Install clamp securing hose in place.
100. Install serpentine drive belt.
101. Install air cleaner housing and inlet tube.

➡**Be certain to check the refrigerant oil level if the air conditioning compressor is being replaced. Use only refrigerant oil of the type recommended for the air conditioning compressor in the vehicle.**

102. Position the air conditioning compressor into the engine compartment.
103. Install the bolts that secure the air conditioning compressor and the automatic transmission cooler line bracket to the cylinder block. Tighten the bolts to 41 ft. lbs. (55 Nm).
104. Install the front end splash shields.
105. Lower the vehicle.
106. Remove the tape or plugs from the opened fittings on the air conditioning suction line and the air conditioning discharge line and the compressor ports.
107. Lubricate the new dual plane seals with clean refrigerant oil and install them onto the suction and the discharge line fittings. Use only the specified seals as they are made of a special material for the R-134a system. Use only refrigerant oil of the type recommended for the air conditioning compressor in the vehicle.
108. Install the suction and discharge lines onto the air conditioning compressor.
109. Install the nuts that secure the suction and discharge lines to the air condi-

tioning compressor. Tighten the nuts to 17 ft. lbs. (23 Nm).
110. Connect the wire harness connector to the air conditioning compressor clutch coil connector.
111. Install the crankshaft position sensor and connect electrical connector.
112. Connect oil pressure sensor electrical connector.
113. Install starter, tighten bolts to 30 ft. lbs. (41 Nm).
114. Connect electrical connectors at starter.
115. Connect the coolant pipe to coolant hose.
116. Connect the exhaust pipes to the manifolds.
117. Connect the down stream oxygen sensor connectors.
118. Connect air conditioning compressor electrical connectors.
119. Install new oil filter.
120. Install lower splash shield and tighten retaining bolts.
121. Lower vehicle.
122. Install power steering pump.
123. Connect lines to power steering pump.
124. Install accessory drive belt.
125. Install air cleaner housing assembly.
126. Connect intake air temperature sensor connector.
127. Connect negative battery cable.
128. Fill coolant system.
129. Fill engine with correct grade of oil.
130. Install strut tower support.
131. Install cowl screen.
132. Install wiper arms.
133. Install the hood.
134. Fill the pump fluid reservoir to the proper level and let the fluid settle for at least two minutes.
135. Evacuate and charge air conditioning system
136. Start engine and check for leaks.
137. Turn steering wheel all the way to the left.
138. Raise the front wheels off the ground.
139. Slowly turn the steering wheel lock-to-lock 20 times with the engine off while checking the fluid level.

➡**Vehicles with long return lines or oil coolers turn wheel 40 times.**

140. Start the engine. With the engine idling maintain the fluid level.
141. Lower the front wheels and let the engine idle for two minutes.
142. Turn the steering wheel in both direction and verify power assist and quiet operation of the pump.

➡**If the fluid is extremely foamy or milky looking, allow the vehicle to stand a few minutes and repeat the procedure.**

3.5L Engine

1. Before servicing the vehicle, refer to the precautions in the beginning of this section.

➡**Capture and store any residual fluid drainage, or leakage from ancillary components, in the appropriately marked containers.**

2. Perform the fuel pressure release procedure.
3. Center and secure the steering wheel.
4. Disconnect negative battery cable.
5. Evacuate the air conditioning system.
6. Remove the hood.
7. Remove the windshield cowl assembly.
8. Raise and support the vehicle.
9. Remove the power steering pump and set it aside without disconnecting the lines.
10. Remove the lower engine close out panel.
11. Drain the cooling system.
12. Disconnect the lower radiator hose.
13. Remove the front drive axles and housing (if equipped with AWD).
14. Disconnect the alternator electrical connectors.
15. Separate the steering column coupling from the steering gear.
16. Remove the starter and spacer plate.
17. Disconnect the oil cooler hose at the oil cooler and remove the cooler hose retainer at the transmission.
18. Disconnect the transmission line bracket at the air conditioning compressor and allow the bolt to rest on the cradle.
19. Disconnect the ground strap at the right transmission housing.
20. Disconnect the engine block heater wiring connector and set aside (if equipped).
21. Remove the crankshaft position sensor.
22. Disconnect the left No.2 oxygen sensor electrical connector and separate the exhaust manifold from the left exhaust pipe.
23. Disconnect the right No.2 oxygen senior electrical connector and separate the exhaust manifold from the right exhaust pipe.
24. Remove the flex plate inspection cover and torque converter bolts.
25. Remove the transmission housing to engine mounting bolts accessible.

26. Remove the engine mounting to cradle fasteners.

27. Lower the vehicle.

28. Remove the upper intake manifold.

29. Disconnect the heater hose and coolant reservoir hose from the rear coolant pipe.

30. Disconnect the oxygen sensor connector and the ground wire on the left cylinder head cover.

31. Disconnect the coolant temperature, cam position, oil pressure sensor electrical connectors.

32. Disconnect the left ignition coil and fuel injector harness connectors and position the wiring harness aside

33. Remove the right intake manifold support braces.

34. Disconnect the capacitor and ground strap from the right cylinder head cover.

35. Disconnect the oxygen sensor, knock, EGR, injector and ignition coil harness connectors and position the wiring harness aside.

36. Disconnect the engine wiring harness from the transmission housing and remove the remaining transmission housing bolts.

37. Connect the engine lifting bracket from special tool kit 8534B to the right rear of the cylinder head outer most bolt access hole.

38. Install a bolt into the inner most bolt access hole next to the engine lift bracket to assure lifting bracket positioning.

39. Connect an engine hoisting chain to the left timing chain cover engine lifting point and engine lift bracket.

✳ WARNING

While slowly separating the engine from the vehicle, constant checks must be made to assure proper positioning and that no damage to other components or wiring harnesses occur during separation.

➡ **As the engine is hoisted from the engine bay area, remove the loosened air conditioning compressor bolt retaining the transmission cooler lines and direct the lines aside.**

40. Carefully remove the engine from the engine bay area.

To install:

✳ WARNING

Care must be taken when installing the engine to prevent pinching the power steering rack sensor with the left engine mount.

41. Install special tool 8534B, engine lifting bracket to the right rear of the cylinder head and install a bolt into the inner most bolt hole next to the bracket.

42. Connect an engine hoisting chain to the left timing chain cover lifting point and the engine lifting bracket.

✳✳ WARNING

Care must be taken when installing the engine to prevent pinching the power steering rack sensor with the left engine mount. Constantly check to assure proper positioning and no damage occurs to other components or harnesses until union is made.

➡ **As the engine is lowered into the engine bay area, install and hand tighten the air conditioning compressor bolts.**

43. Carefully install the engine into the engine bay area and complete the union with the transmission.

44. Properly route the engine wiring harness behind the engine and tighten the accessible transmission bolts to 50 ft. lbs. (68 Nm).

45. Properly position the right engine harness and connect the oxygen sensor, knock sensor, EGR, fuel injector and ignition coil harness connectors.

46. Connect the capacitor and ground strap to the right cylinder head cover.

47. Install the right intake manifold support braces.

48. Properly position the left engine harness and connect the ignition coil and fuel injector harness connectors.

49. Connect the coolant temperature, cam position, oil pressure sensor harness connectors.

50. Connect the oxygen sensor, and the ground wire, to the left cylinder head cover.

51. Connect the heater hose and coolant reservoir hose to the rear coolant pipe.

52. Install the upper intake manifold.

53. Install the power steering pump. Install three pump mounting bolts through access holes in pulley and engine bracket. Tighten bolts to 21 ft. lbs. (28 Nm) torque.

54. Connect the upper radiator hose.

55. Raise and support the vehicle.

56. Install the engine mounting nuts and tighten to 75 ft. lbs. (101 Nm).

57. Install the remaining transmission housing bolts and tighten to 50 ft. lbs. (68 Nm).

58. Install the torque converter bolts. Tighten bolts to 55 ft. lbs. (75 Nm).

59. Install the torque converter inspection cover. Tighten bolts to 105 inch lbs. (12 Nm)

60. Connect the right exhaust pipe to the exhaust manifold and connect the oxygen sensor.

61. Install the front drive axle housing and front axle shafts (if equipped with AWD).

62. Connect the left exhaust pipe to the exhaust manifold and connect the oxygen sensor.

63. Install the crankshaft position sensor. Torque to 106 inch lbs. (12 Nm).

64. Connect the engine block heater (if equipped).

65. Connect the ground strap at the right transmission housing.

66. Tighten the air conditioning compressor bolts to 41 ft. lbs. (55 Nm).

67. Connect the oil cooler hose at the cooler and secure the cooler hose retainer at the transmission.

68. Connect the lower radiator hose.

69. Install the starter and spacer plate.

70. Align and connect the steering column coupler to the steering gear.

71. Connect the alternator electrical connectors.

72. Install new oil filter.

73. Install the lower engine close out panel.

74. Lower the vehicle.

75. Fill the cooling system to the proper level using the appropriate coolant.

76. Fill engine crankcase with proper oil to correct level.

77. Evacuate and recharge air conditioning.

78. Install the windshield wiper cowl assembly.

79. Install the hood.

80. Connect the negative battery cable.

81. Start engine and run until operating temperature is reached and radiator fans cycle.

82. Check all fluid levels and properly fill.

5.7L Engine

See Figures 115 through 118.

1. Before servicing the vehicle, refer to the precautions in the beginning of this section.

2. Remove the engine cover.

3. Perform the fuel system pressure release procedure.

4. Disconnect the battery negative cable.

5. Remove the air cleaner resonator and duct work as an assembly.

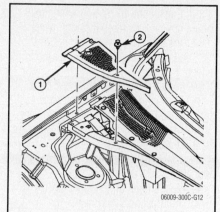

Fig. 115 Remove the two push pins (2) that secure the front cowl top panel (1) to the right rear corner of the engine compartment

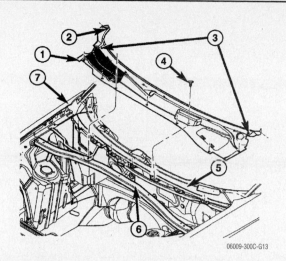

Fig. 116 Remove the push-pin (2) that secures each end of the cowl top panel (1) to each front fender (7). Disengage the two ¼ turn fasteners that secure the cowl top panel to the dash panel. Remove the six push-pins (4) that secure the cowl top panel to the strut tower support (6)

6. Remove the two push pins that secure the front cowl top panel to the right rear corner of the engine compartment.

7. Remove the front cowl top panel.

8. Remove the windshield wiper arms.

9. Remove the push-pin that secures each end of the cowl top panel to each front fender.

10. Disengage the two ¼ turn fasteners that secure the cowl top panel to the dash panel.

11. Remove the six push-pins that secure the cowl top panel to the strut tower support.

12. Disengage the integral retaining clips that secure the cowl top panel to the dash panel and remove the cowl panel from the engine compartment.

13. Drain cooling system.

14. Remove the accessory drive belt.

15. Remove upper radiator hose.

16. Disconnect cooling fan electrical connector.

17. Remove cooling fan mounting bolts.

18. Remove radiator cooling fan assembly from vehicle.

19. Remove the air conditioning compressor with the lines attached. Secure compressor out of the way.

20. Remove the alternator support bracket.

21. Remove alternator.

22. Remove the intake manifold and IAFM as an assembly.

23. Remove the ground wires from the rear of each cylinder head.

24. Disconnect the heater hoses.

➡It is not necessary to disconnect power steering hoses from pump, for power steering pump removal.

25. Remove the power steering pump and set aside.

26. Disconnect the fuel supply line.

27. Raise and support the vehicle on a hoist and drain the engine oil.

28. Remove the belly pan.

29. Remove engine front mount to frame nuts.

30. For AWD only: Mark the front driveshaft to the flange at both ends to ensure correct installation.

31. For AWD only: Remove front drive shaft fasteners from the differential and transfer case. Remove the driveshaft from the vehicle.

32. For AWD only: Remove the left and right front drive axles.

33. For AWD only: Remove the differential support bracket from the differential to the engine block.

34. For AWD only: Unbolt the differential from the oil pan.

35. For AWD only: Rotate the differential so the drive flange is facing forward and the oil pan side is facing up. Remove the differential out through the opening at the rear of the cradle.

36. For AWD only: Remove the intermediate shaft from the oil pan.

37. Disconnect the transmission oil cooler lines from their retainers at the oil pan bolts.

38. Disconnect exhaust pipe at manifolds.

39. Disconnect the starter wires. Remove starter motor.

40. Remove the torque converter access cover.

41. Remove drive plate to converter bolts.

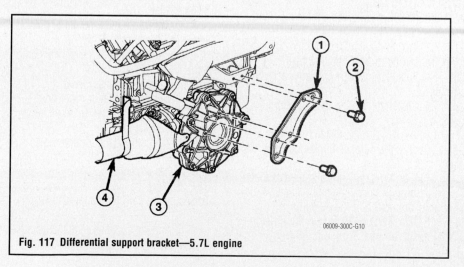

Fig. 117 Differential support bracket—5.7L engine

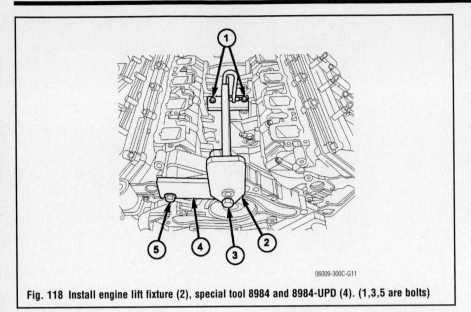

Fig. 118 Install engine lift fixture (2), special tool 8984 and 8984-UPD (4). (1,3,5 are bolts)

06009-300C-G11

42. Remove transmission bellhousing to engine block bolts.

43. Lower the vehicle.

44. Install engine lift fixture, special tool 8984 and 8984-UPD.

45. Separate engine from transmission, remove engine from vehicle, and install engine assembly on a repair stand.

To install:

46. Install engine lift fixture Special tool 8984 and 8984-UPD.

47. Position the engine in the engine compartment.

48. Lower engine into compartment and align engine with transmission.

49. Mate engine and transmission and install two transmission-to-engine block mounting bolts finger tight.

50. Lower engine assembly until engine mount studs rest in frame perches.

51. Install remaining transmission to engine block mounting bolts and tighten to 29 ft. lbs. (39 Nm).

52. Install and tighten engine mount to frame nuts.

53. Install drive plate to torque converter bolts. Torque to 31 ft. lbs. (42 Nm).

54. Install the torque converter access cover.

55. Install the starter and connect the starter wires.

56. For AWD only: Install the intermediate shaft to the oil pan. Torque fasteners to 21 ft. lbs. (28 Nm).

57. For AWD only: Install the front differential through the opening at the rear of the cradle, and attach to the oil pan.

58. For AWD only: Fasten the differential to the oil pan. Torque to 48 ft. lbs. (65 Nm).

59. For AWD only: Install the differential support bracket to the differential and the engine block.

60. For AWD only: Install the left and right front drive axles.

61. For AWD only: Install front drive shaft into the differential and transfer case.

62. Install exhaust pipe to manifold.

63. Lower the vehicle.

64. Remove engine lift fixture, special tool 8984 and 8984-UPD.

65. Connect the fuel supply line.

66. Install the power steering pump. Torque to 21 ft. lbs. (28 Nm).

67. Connect the heater hoses.

68. Reconnect the ground wires to the rear of each cylinder head.

69. Install the intake manifold.

70. Install the alternator, alternator support bracket, and wire connections.

71. Install air conditioning compressor.

72. Install the accessory drive belt.

73. Position radiator cooling fan assembly in vehicle.

74. Install cooling fan mounting bolts. Tighten to 50 inch lbs. (6 Nm)

75. Connect cooling fan electrical connector.

76. Install upper radiator hose.

77. Connect the radiator lower hose.

78. Connect the transmission oil cooler lines to the radiator.

79. Connect the radiator upper hose.

80. Position the cowl top panel into the engine compartment.

81. Engage the integral retaining clips that secure the cowl top panel to the dash panel.

82. Install the six push-pins that secure the cowl top panel to the strut tower support.

83. Engage the ¼ turn fasteners that secure cowl top panel to the dash panel.

84. Install the push-pin that secures each end of the cowl top panel to each front fender.

85. Install the windshield wiper arms.

86. Position the front cowl top panel to the right rear corner of the engine compartment.

87. Install the two push-pins that secure the front cowl top panel.

88. Install the air cleaner resonator and duct work.

89. Add engine oil to crankcase.

90. Fill the cooling system.

91. Install the engine cover.

92. Connect the negative battery cable.

93. Start engine and inspect for leaks.

94. Install the belly pan.

95. Road test the vehicle.

EXHAUST MANIFOLD

REMOVAL & INSTALLATION

2.7L Engine

Left Side

See Figure 119.

1. Before servicing the vehicle, refer to the precautions in the beginning of this section.

2. Disconnect negative battery cable located in trunk.

3. Disconnect intake air temperature sensor connector.

4. Remove air cleaner housing assembly.

5. Remove oil dipstick tube.

6. Disconnect and remove oxygen sensor.

7. Remove upper heat shield and lower heat shield.

8. Raise and safely support the vehicle.

9. Disconnect down stream oxygen sensor connector.

10. Remove exhaust pipe from manifold.

11. Remove exhaust manifold attaching bolts and remove manifold.

To install:

12. Inspect exhaust manifolds for damage or cracks.

13. Check manifold flatness.

14. Inspect the exhaust manifold gasket for obvious discoloration or distortion.

15. Check distortion of the cylinder head mounting surface with a straight-edge and thickness gauge.

16. Install exhaust manifold gasket and manifold. Tighten bolts starting at the center working outward to 200 inch lbs. (23 Nm).

17. Install manifold lower heat shield and upper heat shield. Tighten fasteners to 21 ft. lbs. (28 Nm).

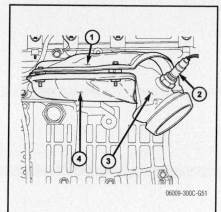

Fig. 119 Left side exhaust manifold. (1) upper heat shield, (2) oxygen sensor, (3) manifold, (4) lower heat shield—3.5L engine

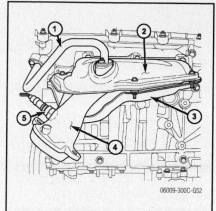

Fig. 120 Right side exhaust manifold. (1) EGR tube, (2) upper heat shield, (3) lower heat shield, (4) manifold, (5) oxygen sensor—2.7L engine

18. If removed, install the exhaust pipe bolts and cross brace. Tighten bolts to 40 ft. lbs. (55 Nm).

19. Tighten manifold ball flange nut to 106 inch lbs. (12 Nm).

20. Check clearance between exhaust module and fuel tank. Clearance should be 16mm (0.62 in.).

21. Check clearance at rear tunnel reinforcement. Clearance should be 15–20mm (0.59–0.78 in.).

22. Adjust clearance as necessary.

23. Tighten ball flange nuts to 25 ft. lbs. (34 Nm).

24. Connect down stream oxygen sensor connectors.

25. Lower vehicle.

26. Install oxygen sensor and connect electrical connector.

27. Connect negative battery cable.

Right Side

See Figure 120.

1. Before servicing the vehicle, refer to the precautions in the beginning of this section

2. Disconnect negative battery cable located in trunk.

3. Disconnect and remove upstream oxygen sensor.

4. Raise vehicle.

5. Remove EGR tube at EGR valve.

6. Remove EGR tube at manifold.

7. Disconnect down stream oxygen sensor electrical connector.

8. Disconnect exhaust pipe from manifold.

9. Remove upper heat shield and lower heat shield.

10. Remove manifold attaching bolts and remove manifold.

To install:

11. Inspect exhaust manifolds for damage or cracks.

12. Check manifold flatness.

13. Inspect the exhaust manifold gasket for obvious discoloration or distortion.

14. Check distortion of the cylinder head mounting surface with a straight-edge and thickness gauge.

15. Install exhaust manifold gasket and manifold. Tighten bolts working from center outwards to 200 inch lbs. (23 Nm).

16. If removed, install bolts and cross brace. Tighten bolts to 40 ft. lbs. (55 Nm).

17. Tighten manifold ball flange nut to 106 inch lbs. (12 Nm).

18. Check clearance between exhaust module and fuel tank. Clearance should be 16mm (0.62 in.).

19. Check clearance at rear tunnel reinforcement. Clearance should be 15–20mm (0.59–0.78 in.).

20. Adjust clearance as necessary.

21. Tighten ball flange nuts to 25 ft. lbs. (34 Nm).

22. Connect oxygen sensor connectors.

23. Install lower heat shield and upper heat shield.

24. Install oxygen sensor and connect electrical connector.

25. Connect down stream oxygen sensor electrical connector.

26. Lower vehicle.

27. Install EGR tube using new gaskets. Tighten screws to 95 inch lbs. (11 Nm).

28. Connect negative battery cable.

3.5L Engine

Left Side

See Figure 121.

1. Before servicing the vehicle, refer to

the precautions in the beginning of this section.

2. Disconnect and isolate the negative battery cable.

3. Raise and support the vehicle.

4. Separate the front exhaust pipe to manifold union.

5. Lower the vehicle.

6. Disconnect and remove the oxygen sensor from the exhaust manifold.

7. Remove the exhaust manifold shield retaining bolts, exhaust manifold, and discard gasket.

To install:

8. Inspect exhaust manifolds for damage or cracks.

9. Check manifold flatness.

10. Inspect the exhaust manifold gasket for obvious discoloration or distortion.

11. Check distortion of the cylinder head mounting surface with a straight-edge and thickness gauge.

➡**If replacing the exhaust manifold, tighten the exhaust outlet studs to manifold to 29 ft. lbs. (40 Nm).**

12. Position the exhaust manifold and gasket. Install the retaining bolts. Tighten 4 bolts starting at the center working outward to 17 ft. lbs. (23 Nm).

13. Install the exhaust manifold heat shields. Tighten the bolts to 105 inch lbs. (12 Nm).

14. Tighten the out most stud nuts to 73 inch lbs. (8 Nm).

15. Connect the oxygen sensor.

16. Raise and support the vehicle.

17. Connect the exhaust pipe to manifold union. Tighten the exhaust stud nuts to 25 ft. lbs. (34 Nm).

18. Connect the negative battery cable.

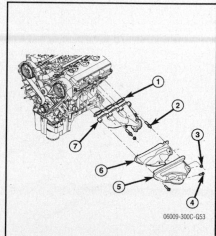

Fig. 121 Left side exhaust manifold (7) and related components—3.5L engine

Right Side

See Figure 122.

1. Before servicing the vehicle, refer to the precautions in the beginning of this section.
2. Disconnect the negative battery cable.
3. Disconnect the upstream oxygen sensor electrical connector.
4. Raise and support the vehicle.
5. Remove the exhaust manifold to exhaust pipe flange retaining bolts.
6. Lower the vehicle.
7. Remove the exhaust manifold heat shield and manifold.
8. Remove the oxygen sensor from the exhaust manifold.

To install:

9. Clean gasket surfaces.

➡ **If replacing the exhaust manifold, tighten the exhaust outlet studs to 29 ft. lbs. (39 Nm).**

10. Position the exhaust manifold and gasket. Install the retaining bolts. Tighten 4 bolts starting at the center working outward to 17 ft. lbs. (23 Nm).
11. Install the heat shields. Tighten the heat shield fasteners to 105 inch lbs. (12 Nm).
12. Tighten the 2 out most nuts to 73 inch lbs. (8 Nm).
13. Connect the oxygen sensor.
14. Raise and support the vehicle.
15. Connect the front exhaust pipe to exhaust manifold. Tighten the fasteners to 25 ft. lbs. (34 Nm).
16. Connect the negative battery cable.

5.7L Engine

See Figures 123 and 124.

1. Before servicing the vehicle, refer to the precautions in the beginning of this section.
2. Disconnect negative battery cable.
3. Raise vehicle.
4. Remove exhaust pipe to manifold bolts.
5. Remove engine mount to frame fasteners.
6. Using suitable jack, raise engine enough to remove manifolds.

✳✳ WARNING

Do not damage engine harness while raising the engine.

7. Remove the engine mount.
8. Remove heat shield.
9. Remove manifold bolts using sequence provided.
10. Remove manifold and gasket.

To install:

11. Clean mating surfaces on cylinder head and manifold. Wash with solvent and blow dry with compressed air.
12. Inspect manifold for cracks.
13. Inspect mating surfaces of manifold for flatness with a straight-edge. Gasket surfaces must be flat within 0.2 mm per 300 mm (0.008 inch per foot).
14. Install manifold gasket and manifold.
15. Install manifold bolts and tighten to 18 ft. lbs. (25 Nm).
16. Install heat shield and tighten nuts to 70 inch lbs. (8 Nm).
17. Install engine mounts. Torque to 70 ft. lbs. (95 Nm).

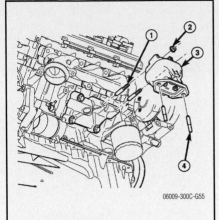

Fig. 123 Engine mount. (1) stud bolts, (2) nuts, (3) mount, (4) stud bolts—5.7L engine

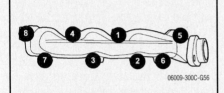

Fig. 124 Exhaust manifold loosening/tightening sequence—5.7L engine

18. Lower engine.

✳✳ WARNING

Do not damage engine harness while lowering the engine.

19. Install and tighten right and left side engine mount to frame fasteners. Torque to 70 ft. lbs. (95 Nm).
20. Install exhaust flange to pipe bolts.
21. Lower vehicle.
22. Connect negative battery cable.

INTAKE MANIFOLD

REMOVAL & INSTALLATION

2.7L Engine

Upper Manifold

See Figure 125.

1. Before servicing the vehicle, refer to the precautions in the beginning of this section.
2. Disconnect negative battery cable.
3. Remove throttle body air inlet hose and air cleaner housing assembly.
4. Disconnect electrical connectors from the following components:
   • Manifold Absolute Pressure (MAP) Sensor

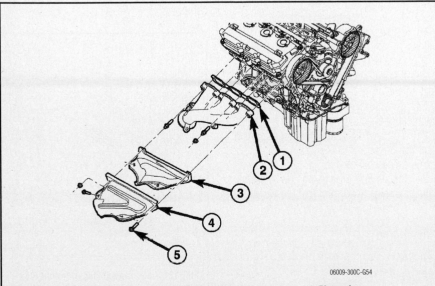

Fig. 122 Right side exhaust manifold (2) and related components—3.5L engine

- Electronic Throttle Control
- Manifold Tuning Valve

5. Disconnect vapor purge hose, brake booster hose, positive crankcase ventilation (PCV) hose.

6. Remove manifold support brackets.

7. Remove manifold attaching bolts.

8. Remove the upper manifold.

9. Remove foam insulator.

10. Check manifold for:
- Damage and cracks
- Gasket surface damage or warpage
- Damaged or clogged EGR ports

11. If the manifold exhibits any damaged or warped conditions, replace the manifold. Clean EGR ports as necessary.

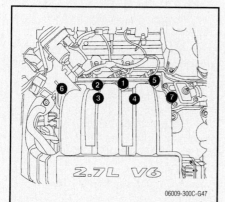

Fig. 125 Upper intake manifold loosening/ tightening sequence—2.7L engine

To install:

12. Clean and inspect sealing surfaces. Gaskets can be reused, if free of cuts or tears.

➡**Make sure fuel injectors and wiring harnesses are in correct position to not interfere with upper manifold installation.**

13. Install the upper manifold gasket.

14. Position the upper manifold onto lower manifold.

15. Install manifold attaching bolts and tighten in sequence shown in to 105 inch lbs. (12 Nm).

16. Connect PCV, brake booster, and vapor purge hoses.

17. Connect electrical connectors to the following components:
- Manifold Absolute Pressure (MAP) Sensor
- Electronic Throttle Control
- Manifold Tuning Valve

18. Install throttle body air inlet hose and air cleaner housing assembly.

Lower Manifold

See Figure 126.

1. Before servicing the vehicle, refer to the precautions in the beginning of this section.

2. Release fuel system pressure.

3. Disconnect negative battery cable located in trunk.

4. Remove upper intake manifold.

5. Disconnect injector electrical connectors.

6. Disconnect fuel supply hose from fuel rail.

7. Remove bolts attaching fuel rail.

8. Remove fuel rail and injectors as an assembly.

9. Remove manifold attaching bolts.

10. Remove lower manifold.

To install:

11. Check manifold for:
- Damage and cracks
- Gasket surface damage or warpage
- Damaged fuel injector ports

If the manifold exhibits any of these conditions, replace the manifold.

12. Clean and inspect sealing surfaces of cylinder head and manifold. Gaskets can be reused provided they are free of cuts or tears.

13. Install lower manifold gasket.

14. Position manifold on cylinder head surfaces.

➡**For ease of installing upper intake manifold, install a bolt 2–3 turns to the rearmost attaching hole of intake. This will properly position lower manifold.**

15. Install fuel rail with injectors and start bolts.

16. Install manifold attaching bolts and tighten in sequence shown in to 105 inch lbs. (12 Nm). Remove bolt used for aligning manifold.

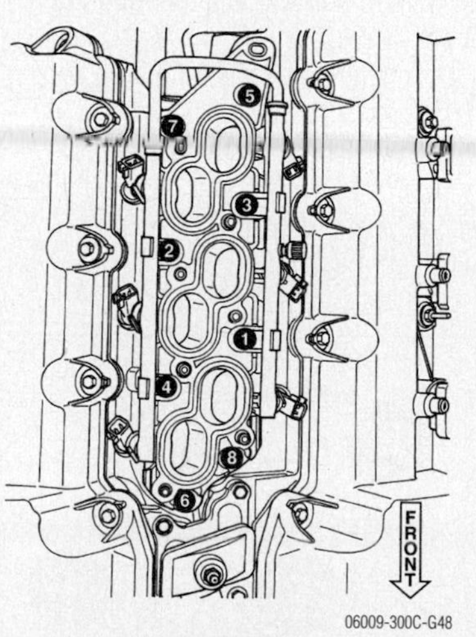

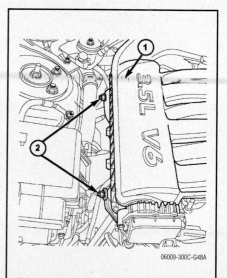

Fig. 126 Lower intake manifold loosening/ tightening sequence—2.7L engine

17. Connect the fuel injector electrical connectors.

➡**Make sure fuel injectors are located in the correct location and position, as upper intake manifold interference could occur.**

18. Connect fuel supply hose to fuel rail.

19. Install upper intake manifold.

3.5L Engine

Upper Manifold

See Figure 127.

1. Before servicing the vehicle, refer to the precautions in the beginning of this section.

2. Disconnect negative battery cable.

3. Disconnect the IAT sensor electrical connector.

4. Remove air inlet hose from the throttle body.

5. Disconnect the MAP sensor electrical connector.

6. Separate the engine electrical harness connectors from the intake manifold.

7. Disconnect the EGR tube, PCV, purge and power brake booster vacuum hoses from the upper intake manifold.

8. Disconnect the electronic throttle control electrical connector.

9. Remove the throttle bracket fasteners from the throttle body and cylinder head.

10. Disconnect electrical connectors from the Manifold Tuning Valve (MTV) and Short Runner Valve.

11. Remove the right intake manifold support brackets.

12. Remove the upper intake manifold retaining bolts, insulation foam pad and

Fig. 127 Right upper intake manifold (1) support brackets (2)—3.5L engine

manifold. Clean all gasket sealing surfaces.

To install:

13. Clean and inspect gasket sealing surfaces.

14. Position new gasket.

15. Install the upper intake manifold insulator foam.

16. Install the upper intake manifold. Tighten bolts to 105 inch lbs. (12 Nm) starting in the center working outward in a cross sequence pattern.

17. Install the right manifold support brackets. Tighten fasteners to 105 inch lbs. (12 Nm).

18. Install the throttle bracket. Tighten fasteners to 105 inch lbs. (12 Nm) at the throttle body and 28Nm (259 inch lbs.) at the cylinder head.

19. Connect the manifold tuning valve and short runner valve electrical connectors.

20. Connect the electronic throttle control harness connector.

21. Connect the engine electrical connectors to the intake manifold.

22. Connect the EGR tube, PCV, purge and power brake booster vacuum hoses to the intake manifold.

23. Connect the MAP sensor harness connector.

24. Install the inlet hose and connect the IAT sensor harness connector.

25. Connect negative battery cable.

Lower Manifold

See Figures 128 and 129.

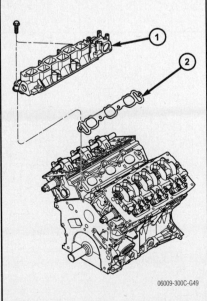

Fig. 128 Lower intake manifold (1) and gasket (2)—3.5L engine

1. Before servicing the vehicle, refer to the precautions in the beginning of this section.

2. Perform fuel pressure release procedure.

3. Drain the cooling system.

4. Disconnect the upper radiator hose from the thermostat housing.

5. Remove the upper intake manifold.

6. Reposition power steering fluid reservoir and bracket.

7. Disconnect the electrical connectors to fuel injectors and coolant temperature sensor.

8. Disconnect heater hose from the rear intake manifold.

9. Disconnect the coolant container hose at the rear intake manifold.

10. Disconnect the fuel supply hose from fuel rail.

11. Remove the bolts attaching fuel rail.

12. Remove fuel rail and injectors as an assembly.

13. Remove bolts attaching lower intake and remove intake manifold.

To install:

14. Clean all sealing surfaces.

15. Position new gaskets and intake manifold on cylinder head surfaces.

16. Install intake manifold bolts and gradually tighten in sequence shown until a torque of 21 ft. lbs. (28 Nm is obtained.

17. Install fuel rail and injectors as an assembly.

18. Connect fuel supply hose to fuel rail.

19. Connect heater hose to rear lower intake manifold.

20. Connect coolant container hose to the rear lower intake manifold.

21. Connect electrical connectors to fuel injectors and coolant temperature sensor.

22. Install power steering fluid reservoir and bracket.

23. Install upper intake manifold.

24. Connect the upper radiator hose to the thermostat housing.

25. Fill the cooling system.

5.7L Engine

1. Before servicing the vehicle, refer to the precautions in the beginning of this section.

2. Remove engine cover.

3. Bleed fuel system.

4. Disconnect negative cable from battery.

5. Remove air inlet hose.

6. Remove ignition wires from on top of intake manifold.

7. Disconnect electrical connectors for the following components:

- Manifold Absolute Pressure (MAP) Sensor
- Fuel Injectors
- ETC (Electric Throttle Control)

8. Remove wire harness from intake manifold.

9. Disconnect brake booster hose, purge hose, and MUA hose (Make Up Air Hose).

10. Remove EGR tube from intake manifold.

11. Remove intake manifold retaining fasteners in a crisscross pattern starting from the outside bolts and ending at the middle bolts.

12. Remove intake manifold as an assembly.

To install:

➡There is no approved repair procedure for the intake manifold. If severe damage is found during inspection, the intake manifold must be replaced.

Before installing the intake manifold thoroughly clean the mating surfaces. Use a suitable cleaning solvent, then air dry.

13. Inspect the intake sealing surface for cracks, nicks and distortion.

14. Inspect the intake manifold vacuum hose fittings for looseness or blockage.

15. Position intake manifold.

16. Install intake manifold retaining bolts, and tighten in sequence from the middle bolts towards the outside in a crisscross pattern. Torque fasteners to 105 inch lbs. (12 Nm).

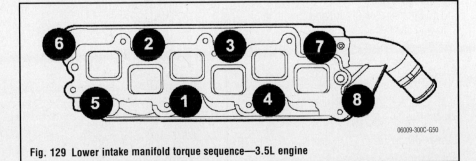

Fig. 129 Lower intake manifold torque sequence—3.5L engine

17. Install EGR tube.

18. Install wire harness on intake mani-fold.

19. Connect electrical connectors for the following components:
- Manifold Absolute Pressure (MAP) Sensor
- Fuel Injectors
- ETC (Electronic Throttle Control)

20. Install ignition wires.

21. Connect Brake booster hose, purge hose, and MUA hose (Make Up Air hose).

22. Install air inlet hose.

23. Connect negative cable to battery.

24. Install engine cover.

OIL PAN

REMOVAL & INSTALLATION

2.7L Engine

See Figures 130 and 131.

1. Before servicing the vehicle, refer to the precautions in the beginning of this sec-tion.

2. Disconnect negative battery cable located in trunk.

3. Remove engine oil indicator.

4. Raise and safely support the vehicle.

5. Remove lower splash shield retain-ing bolts and splash shield.

6. Drain engine oil and remove oil filter.

7. Remove the steering coupler bolt and separate coupler from rack.

8. Disconnect power steering pressure switch electrical connector.

9. Remove steering rack mounting bolts.

10. Remove power steering line support from frame.

11. Reposition rack out of the way.

12. Remove structural collar.

13. Remove alternator mounting bracket to oil pan lower bolt.

14. Remove air conditioning compressor bracket to oil pan lower bolt.

15. Remove lower timing chain cover to oil pan bolts.

✳✳ WARNING

Assure removal of the four lower tim-ing cover bolts, as damage to the timing cover and/or oil pan may occur.

16. Remove oil pan attaching bolts. Remove oil pan and gasket.

To install:

17. Clean oil pan and sealing surfaces. Inspect timing chain cover gaskets. Replace as necessary.

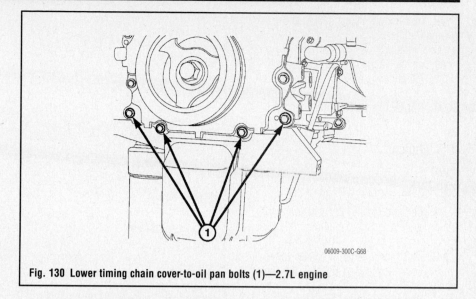

Fig. 130 Lower timing chain cover-to-oil pan bolts (1)—2.7L engine

06009-300C-G68

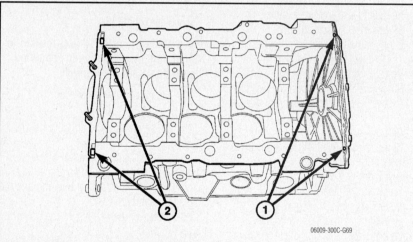

Fig. 131 Apply a ⅛ inch bead of Mopar® Engine RTV GEN II, or equivalent, to the front T-joints (1) and the rear T-joints (2)—2.7L engine

06009-300C-G69

18. Apply a ⅛ inch bead of Mopar® Engine RTV GEN II, or equivalent, to the front T-joints (oil pan gasket to timing cover gasket interface) and the rear T-joints (oil pan gasket to crankshaft rear oil seal retainer gasket interface).

19. Install oil pan gasket to block.

➡**To prevent oil leaks at oil pan to tim-ing chain cover, the following tighten-ing sequence procedure must be performed.**

20. Install oil pan and fasteners using the following tightening sequence:

a. Install oil pan bolts and nuts finger tight only—just tight enough to com-press the gasket's rubber seal. Line up front of oil pan to be flush with front face of block.

b. Install lower timing chain cover bolts (1) and tighten to 105 inch lbs. (12 Nm).

c. Tighten oil pan bolts to 21 ft. lbs. (28 Nm).

d. Tighten oil pan nuts to 105 inch lbs. (12 Nm).

21. Install lower bolt attaching the air conditioning compressor to oil pan. Tighten bolt to 21 ft. lbs. (28 Nm).

22. Install lower bolt attaching the alter-nator bracket to oil pan. Tighten bolt to 21 ft. lbs. (28 Nm).

23. Install oil filter and drain plug.

24. Install structural collar.

25. Position steering gear in place and install mounting bolts. Tighten bolts to 70 ft. lbs. (95 Nm).

26. Install the steering coupling lower pinch bolt at the gear using a new bolt. Tighten to 22 ft. lbs. (30 Nm).

27. Connect electrical connector to steering gear.

28. Install power steering line support and tighten.

29. Install lower splash shield and retaining bolts.

30. Lower vehicle.

31. Install engine oil level indicator.

32. Fill engine crankcase with proper oil to correct level.

33. Connect negative battery cable.

34. Start engine and check for leaks.

3.5L Engine

2WD

See Figures 132 through 136.

1. Before servicing the vehicle, refer to the precautions in the beginning of this section.

2. Disconnect negative battery cable.

3. Lock the steering wheel in the center position.

4. Remove engine oil indicator.

5. Raise and support the vehicle.

6. Remove the splash shield.

7. Drain engine oil and remove the oil filter.

8. Drain cooling system.

9. Raise and safely support the vehicle.

10. Disconnect coolant hoses from oil cooler.

11. Remove oil filter.

12. Remove oil cooler attaching fastener from center of oil cooler.

13. Remove oil cooler.

14. Separate the steering column coupler from the steering gear.

15. Remove steering gear to cradle mounting bolts and suspend steering gear aside

16. Remove the flex plate access cover.

17. Remove the rear oil pan to transmission bolts.

18. Remove the two rear oil pan bolts.

19. Remove the remaining oil pan bolts.

20. Loosen the engine mount bolts at the cradle.

21. Raise and support the engine using a suitable floor jack with a block of wood at the transmission housing.

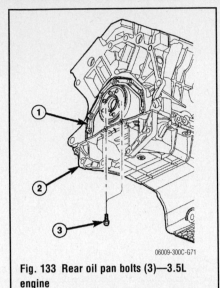

Fig. 133 Rear oil pan bolts (3)—3.5L engine

06009-300C-G71

22. Remove the oil pan.

➡A small amount of oil will remain in the oil pan. Use care when removing the oil pan from the engine.

23. Clean all mating surfaces.

To install:

24. Clean oil pan and all gasket surfaces.

25. Apply a ⅛ inch bead of Mopar® Engine RTV GEN II, or equivalent, at the parting line of the oil pump housing and the rear seal retainer.

26. Install oil pan gasket to the engine block.

27. Install the oil pan while aligning the oil level indicator tube and attach fasteners finger tight.

➡Assure that the rear face of the oil pan is flush to the transmission bell housing when installing the oil pan.

28. Pre-torque the horizontal rear oil

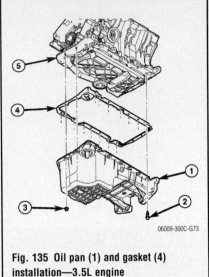

Fig. 135 Oil pan (1) and gasket (4) installation—3.5L engine

06009-300C-G73

pan to transmission bolts to 12 inch lbs. (1.4 Nm).

29. First tighten the M8 oil pan alignment bolt to 21 ft. lbs. (28 Nm), then tighten bolt to 21 ft. lbs. (28 Nm).

30. Tighten the remaining M8 bolts and M8 nuts to 21 ft. lbs. (28 Nm), and the M6 bolts to 105 inch lbs. (12 Nm).

31. Tighten the four M10 oil pan to transmission bolts to 40 ft. lbs. (55 Nm).

32. Lower the engine and remove the lifting fixture. Tighten the engine mount to cradle fasteners to 55 ft. lbs. (75 Nm).

33. Install the flex plate inspection cover and tighten the fastener to 97 inch lbs. (11 Nm)

34. Position oil cooler to fitting on oil pan.

➡Remove all oil and debris from the seal retainer surface. The cut out section of the oil cooler seal retainer flange (top) must be aligned with the tab on the oil pan. The oil cooler must

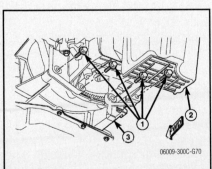

Fig. 132 Rear oil pan (2) to transmission (3) bolts (1)—3.5L engine

06009-300C-G70

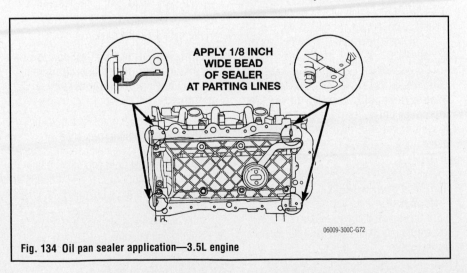

APPLY 1/8 INCH WIDE BEAD OF SEALER AT PARTING LINES

Fig. 134 Oil pan sealer application—3.5L engine

06009-300C-G72

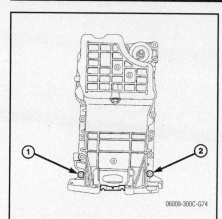

Fig. 136 First tighten the M8 (1) oil pan alignment bolt to 21 ft. lbs. (28 Nm), then tighten bolt (2) to 21 ft. lbs. (28 Nm) (250 inch lbs.)—3.5L engine

06009-300C-G74

be prevented from turning during the tightening sequence.

35. Install oil cooler attaching fastener and tighten to 55 ft. lbs. (75 Nm).

36. Install oil filter and tighten to 106 inch lbs. (12 Nm).

37. Connect coolant hoses to oil cooler.

38. Fill cooling system.

39. Install the engine oil filter.

40. Install the steering gear to cradle bolts and tighten the fasteners to 70 ft. lbs. (95 Nm).

41. Connect the steering gear coupler and tighten the fastener to 22 ft. lbs. (30 Nm)

42. Attach the splash shield.

43. Lower the vehicle.

44. Install the engine oil indicator.

45. Fill engine crankcase with proper oil to correct level.

46. Connect negative battery cable.

AWD

1. Before servicing the vehicle, refer to the precautions in the beginning of this section.

2. Disconnect the negative battery cable.

3. Drain the cooling system.

4. Remove the oil level indicator tube fastener at the right exhaust manifold.

5. Raise and support the vehicle.

6. Drain engine oil and remove the oil filter.

7. Remove the left axle shaft.

8. Disconnect the power steering hoses from the power steering rack.

9. Remove the left front axle intermediate shaft support bracket and housing.

10. Remove the front drive shaft heat shield.

11. Paint mark and remove the front driveshaft.

12. Remove the right catalytic converter.

13. Separate the power steering hose from cradle hold down and position the hose aside.

14. Remove the lower engine mount to cradle fasteners.

15. Remove the front sway bar.

16. Raise and support the engine with a jackstand.

17. Remove the front axle housing support bracket.

18. Remove the front axle housing fasteners, rotate the housing position and remove the axle housing.

19. Lower the engine and remove the jackstand.

20. Disconnect coolant hoses from oil cooler.

21. Remove oil filter.

22. Remove oil cooler attaching fastener from center of oil cooler.

23. Remove oil cooler.

24. Separate the oil level indicator tube from the oil pan.

25. Remove the torque converter access cover.

26. Remove the oil pan.

To install:

27. Clean oil pan and all mating surfaces.

28. Replace the oil level indicator tube seal.

29. Apply a ⅛ inch bead of Mopar® Engine RTV GEN II, or equivalent, at the parting line of the oil pump housing and the rear seal retainer.

30. Install the oil pan gasket to the engine block.

31. Install the oil pan while aligning the oil level indicator tube and attach the fasteners finger tight.

➡**Assure that the rear face of the oil pan is flush to the transmission bell housing when installing the oil pan.**

32. Pre-torque the horizontal rear oil pan to transmission bolts to 12 inch lbs. (1.4 Nm)

33. First tighten the M8 oil pan alignment bolt to 21 ft. lbs. (28 Nm), then tighten bolt to 21 ft. lbs. (28 Nm).

34. Tighten the remaining M8 bolts and M8 nuts to 21 ft. lbs. (28 Nm), and the M6 bolts to 105 inch lbs. (12 Nm).

35. Tighten the four M10 oil pan to transmission bolts to 40 ft. lbs. (55 Nm).

36. Install the torque converter access cover and tighten the fastener to 97 inch lbs. (11 Nm).

37. Position oil cooler to fitting on oil pan.

➡**Remove all oil and debris from the seal retainer surface. The cut out section of the oil cooler seal retainer flange (top) must be aligned with the tab on the oil pan. The oil cooler must be prevented from turning during the tightening sequence.**

38. Install oil cooler attaching fastener and tighten to 55 ft. lbs. (75 Nm).

39. Install oil filter and tighten to 106 inch lbs. (12 Nm).

40. Connect coolant hoses to oil cooler.

41. Support the engine with a jackstand.

42. Install the front drive axle housing. Tighten mounting bolts to oil pan to 48 ft. lbs. (65 Nm).

43. Remove the jackstand.

44. Install the front drive axle housing support.

45. Install the front suspension sway bar to cradle.

46. Install the engine mount to front cradle fasteners. Tighten the fasteners to 55 ft. lbs. (75 Nm).

47. Position and install the power steering hose to cradle hold downs.

48. Install the right catalytic converter.

49. Align the paint marks and install the front drive shaft.

50. Install the front drive shaft heat shield.

51. Install the left front drive axle intermediate shaft housing and support bracket. Tighten fasteners to 19 ft. lbs. (25 Nm).

52. Connect the power steering hoses to the steering rack.

53. Install the left front drive axle.

54. Install the right front drive axle.

55. Lower the vehicle.

56. Install the oil level indicator tube fastener to the right exhaust manifold.

57. Fill engine crankcase with the proper oil to the correct level.

58. Fill the cooling system.

59. Fill the power steering.

60. Connect the negative battery cable.

5.7L Engine

2WD

See Figures 137 and 138.

1. Before servicing the vehicle, refer to the precautions in the beginning of this section.

2. Disconnect the negative battery cable.

3. Remove the intake manifold.

4. Install engine lift fixture special tool 8984 and adapter 8984-UPD. See the Engine Removal & Installation procedure.

✳✳ WARNING

Never use air tools when installing fasteners to engine.

5. Raise vehicle.
6. Remove the belly pan.
7. Drain engine oil and remove the oil filter.
8. Unbolt and lower the steering rack from the mounts. Do not remove power steering hoses, tie rod ends or disconnect steering column.
9. Remove both left and right side engine hydromount to frame nuts, and studs.
10. Remove the engine oil dipstick and tube from the oil pan.
11. Lower the vehicle.
12. Install engine support fixture special tool 8534. Do not use the third leg. See the Engine Removal & Installation procedure.
13. Raise engine using special tool 8534 and 8984 to provide clearance to remove oil pan.

➡ **Do not pry on oil pan or oil pan gasket. Gasket is integral to engine windage tray and does not come out with oil pan.**

➡ **The horizontal M10 fasteners are 5 mm longer in length, and must be reinstalled in original locations.**

14. Remove the M10 fasteners (vertical and horizontal) from the rear of the oil pan to the transmission and engine.
15. Remove the oil pan mounting bolts and oil pan.

➡ **When the oil pan is removed, a new oil pan gasket/windage tray assembly must be installed. The old gasket cannot be reused.**

16. Discard the integral windage tray and gasket and replace.

To install:

17. Clean the oil pan gasket mating surface of the block and oil pan.

➡ **Mopar® Engine RTV must be applied to the 4 T-joints, (area where front cover, rear retainer, block, and oil pan gasket meet). The bead of RTV should cover the bottom of the gasket. This area is approximately 4.5 mm x 25 mm in each of the 4 T-joint locations.**

18. Apply Mopar® Engine RTV at the 4 T-joints.

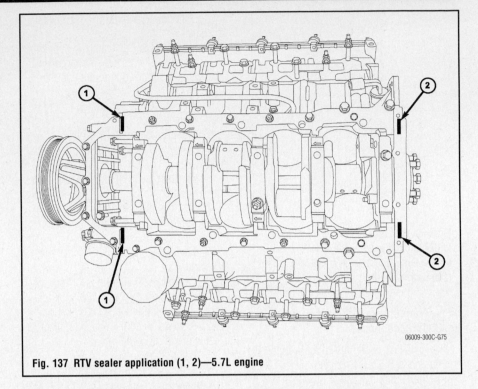

Fig. 137 RTV sealer application (1, 2)—5.7L engine

06009-300C-G75

➡ **When the oil pan is removed, a new oil pan gasket/windage tray assembly must be installed. The old gasket cannot be reused.**

19. Install a new oil pan gasket/windage tray assembly.
20. If removed, reinstall the oil pump pickup tube with new O-ring. Tighten tube to pump fasteners to 21 ft. lbs. (28 Nm).

➡ **The horizontal M10 fasteners are 5 mm longer in length, and must be reinstalled in original locations.**

21. Align the rear of the oil pan with the rear face of the engine block, and install the M10 and M6 oil pan fasteners finger tight. Using the accompanying torque sequence, torque the M6 mounting bolts to 44 inch lbs. (5 Nm).
22. Using the accompanying torque sequence, torque the M10 oil pan fasteners to 39 ft. lbs. (54 Nm).
23. Using the accompanying torque sequence, torque the M6 oil pan fasteners to 106 inch lbs. (12 Nm).
24. Lower the engine into mounts using special tool 8534.
25. Install both the left and right side engine mount studs and nuts. Torque the studs and nuts to 70 ft. lbs. (95 Nm).
26. Install the engine oil dipstick and tube.
27. Install the steering rack.
28. Remove special tool 8534.

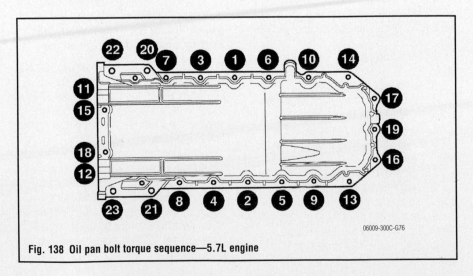

06009-300C-G76

Fig. 138 Oil pan bolt torque sequence—5.7L engine

29. Remove special tool 8984.
30. Install the intake manifold.
31. Fill engine oil.
32. Install oil filter, if removed.
33. Reconnect the negative battery cable.
34. Start engine and check for leaks.
35. Install the belly pan.

AWD

1. Before servicing the vehicle, refer to the precautions in the beginning of this section.
2. Disconnect the negative battery cable.
3. Remove the engine cover.
4. Remove the intake manifold.
5. Install engine lift fixture special tool 8984 and adapter 8984-UPD. See the Engine Removal & Installation procedure.

➡ **Never use air tools when installing fasteners to engine.**

6. Raise vehicle.
7. Remove the belly pan.
8. Remove both left and right side engine mount to frame fasteners.
9. Drain engine oil and remove the oil filter.
10. Unbolt and lower the steering rack from the mounts. Do not remove power steering hoses, tie rod ends or disconnect steering column.
11. Remove the engine oil dipstick and tube from the oil pan.
12. Remove the left and right side exhaust at the manifolds.
13. Mark the front driveshaft to the flange at both ends to ensure correct installation.
14. Remove front driveshaft fasteners from the differential and transfer case. Remove the driveshaft from the vehicle.
15. Remove the left and right front drive axles.
16. Remove the differential support bracket from the differential to the engine block.
17. Unbolt the differential from the oil pan.
18. Rotate the differential so the drive flange is facing forward and the oil pan side is facing up. Remove the differential out through the opening at the rear of the cradle.
19. Remove the intermediate shaft from the oil pan.
20. Lower the vehicle.
21. Install engine support fixture special tool 8534. Do not attempt to fasten fixture to vehicle body, or attach the third support leg to the radiator support. See the Engine Removal & Installation procedure.

22. Raise engine using special tool 8534 and 8984 to provide clearance to remove oil pan.
23. Raise vehicle.

➡ **Do not pry on oil pan or oil pan gasket. Gasket is integral to engine windage tray and does not come out with oil pan.**

➡ **The horizontal M10 fasteners are 5 mm longer in length, and must be reinstalled in original locations.**

24. Remove the M10 fasteners (vertical and horizontal) from the rear of the oil pan to the transmission and engine.
25. Remove the oil pan mounting bolts and oil pan.

➡ **When the oil pan is removed, a new oil pan gasket/windage tray assembly must be installed. The old gasket cannot be reused.**

26. Discard the integral windage tray and gasket and replace.

To install:
27. Clean the oil pan gasket mating surface of the block and oil pan.

➡ **Mopar® Engine RTV must be applied to the 4 T-joints, (area where front cover, rear retainer, block, and oil pan gasket meet). The bead of RTV should cover the bottom of the gasket. This area is approximately 4.5 mm x 25 mm in each of the 4 T-joint locations.**

28. Apply Mopar® Engine RTV at the 4 T-joints.

➡ **When the oil pan is removed, a new oil pan gasket/windage tray assembly must be installed. The old gasket cannot be reused.**

29. Install a new oil pan gasket/windage tray assembly.
30. If removed, reinstall the oil pump pickup tube with new O-ring. Tighten tube to pump fasteners to 21 ft. lbs. (28 Nm).

➡ **The horizontal M10 fasteners are 5 mm longer in length, and must be reinstalled in original locations.**

31. Align the rear of the oil pan with the rear face of the engine block, and install the M10 and M6 oil pan fasteners finger tight. Using the following torque sequence, torque the M6 mounting bolts to 44 inch lbs. (5 Nm).
32. Using the following torque sequence, torque the M10 oil pan fasteners to 39 ft. lbs. (54 Nm).
33. Using the following torque sequence,

torque the M6 oil pan fasteners to 106 inch lbs. (12 Nm).
34. Install the intermediate shaft to the oil pan. Torque fasteners to 21 ft. lbs. (28 Nm).
35. Install the front differential through the opening at the rear of the cradle, and attach to the oil pan.
36. Fasten the differential to the oil pan. Torque to 48 ft. lbs. (65 Nm).
37. Install the differential support bracket to the differential and the engine block.
38. Install the left and right front drive axles.
39. Install front driveshaft into the differential and transfer case.
40. Install the engine oil dipstick and tube.
41. Install the steering gear.
42. Lower the engine into mounts using special tool 8534.
43. Install both the left and right side engine mount studs and nuts. Torque to 70 ft. lbs. (95 Nm).
44. Remove special tool 8534.
45. Remove special tool 8984.
46. Install the intake manifold.
47. Install the left and right side exhaust at the manifolds.
48. Fill engine oil.
49. Install oil filter, if removed.
50. Reconnect the negative battery cable.
51. Start engine and check for leaks.
52. Install the engine cover.

OIL PUMP

REMOVAL & INSTALLATION

2.7L Engine
See Figures 139 and 140.

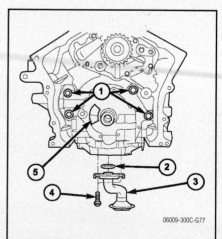

06009-300C-G77

Fig. 139 Oil pump bolts (1), O-ring (2), pick-up tube (3), bolts (4), oil pump (5)—2.7L engine

1. Before servicing the vehicle, refer to the precautions in the beginning of this section.

2. Remove the crankshaft vibration damper.

3. Remove timing chain cover.

4. Remove the timing chain and sprockets.

5. Remove oil pan.

6. Remove oil pick-up tube and O-ring.

7. Ensure that crankshaft position is at 60° ATDC of No.1 cylinder, or crankshaft sprocket mark aligns with mark on oil pump. This position will properly locate oil pump upon installation.

8. Remove oil pump attaching bolts.

9. Remove oil pump.

To install:

✳✳ WARNING

Crankshaft position must be at 60° ATDC of No.1 cylinder before installing oil pump. This position will properly locate oil pump. If not properly located, severe damage to oil pump can occur.

10. Prime oil pump before installation by filling rotor cavity with engine oil.

11. If crankshaft has been rotated, it must be repositioned to 60° ATDC of No.1 cylinder prior to oil pump installation.

12. Install oil pump carefully over crankshaft and into position.

13. Install oil pump attaching bolts. Tighten bolts to 21 ft. lbs. (28 Nm).

14. Install oil pick-up tube with new O-ring. Lubricate O-ring with clean engine oil before installation. Tighten attaching bolts to 21 ft. lbs. (28 Nm).

15. Install oil pan.

16. Install the timing chain and sprockets.

17. Install timing chain cover.

18. Install the crankshaft vibration damper.

19. Fill the crankcase with engine oil to correct level.

3.5L Engine

See Figure 141.

1. Before servicing the vehicle, refer to the precautions in the beginning of this section.

2. Drain the cooling system.

3. Remove the timing belt.

4. Remove the crankshaft sprocket.

5. Remove the oil pan.

6. Remove the oil pickup tube.

7. Remove the oil pump fasteners. Remove the oil pump and gasket from engine.

To install:

8. Prime oil pump before installation by filling rotor cavity with clean engine oil.

9. Install oil pump and gasket carefully over the crankshaft. Position pump onto block and tighten bolts to 21 ft. lbs. (28 Nm).

10. Install new O-ring on oil pickup tube.

11. Install oil pickup tube.

12. Install oil pan.

13. Install crankshaft sprocket.

14. Install timing belt.

15. Install the timing belt covers.

16. Install the crankshaft vibration damper. Torque to 70 ft. lbs. (95 Nm).

17. Install the accessory drive belt.

18. Fill the cooling system.

19. Fill engine crankcase with proper oil to the correct level.

5.7L Engine

See Figures 142 through 145.

1. Before servicing the vehicle, refer to the precautions in the beginning of this section.

2. Remove the oil pan and pick-up tube.

3. Remove the timing chain cover.

4. Remove the four bolts, and the oil pump.

5. Wash all parts in a suitable solvent.

➡**Oil pump pressure relief valve and spring should not be removed from the oil pump. If these components are disassembled and or removed from the pump the entire oil pump assembly must be replaced.**

6. Remove the pump cover.

7. Clean all parts thoroughly. Mating surface of the oil pump housing should be smooth. If the pump cover is scratched or grooved the oil pump assembly should be replaced.

8. Slide outer rotor into the body of the oil pump. Press the outer rotor to one side of the oil pump body and measure clearance between the outer rotor and the body. If the measurement is 0.235mm (0.009 in.) or more the oil pump assembly must be replaced.

9. Install the inner rotor in the into the oil pump body. Measure the clearance between the inner and outer rotors. If the clearance between the rotors is 0.150 mm (0.006 in.) or more the oil pump assembly must be replaced.

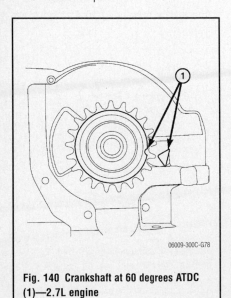

06009-300C-G78

Fig. 140 Crankshaft at 60 degrees ATDC (1)—2.7L engine

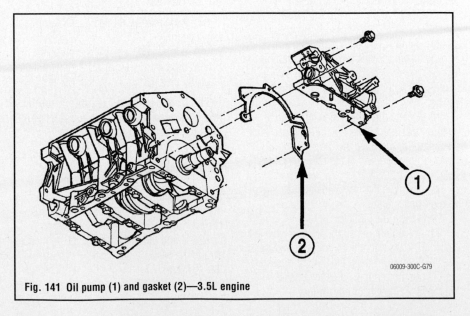

06009-300C-G79

Fig. 141 Oil pump (1) and gasket (2)—3.5L engine

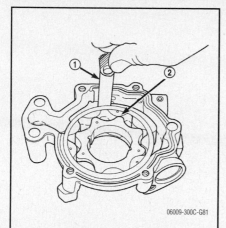

Fig. 142 Press the outer rotor to one side of the oil pump body and measure clearance between the outer rotor (2) and the body—5.7L engine

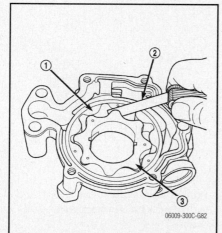

Fig. 143 Measure the clearance between the inner (3) and outer rotors (1)—5.7L engine

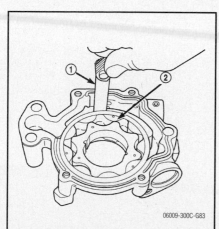

Fig. 144 If a feeler gauge (2) of 0.095 mm (0.0038 in.) or greater can be inserted between the straightedge and the rotors, the pump must be replaced—5.7L engine

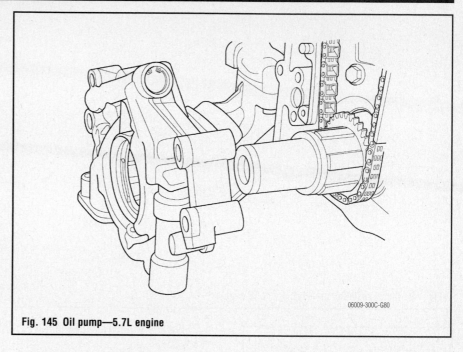

Fig. 145 Oil pump—5.7L engine

10. Place a straight-edge across the body of the oil pump (between the bolt holes), if a feeler gauge of 0.095 mm (0.0038 in.) or greater can be inserted between the straight-edge and the rotors, the pump must be replaced.

11. Reinstall the pump cover. Torque fasteners to 132 inch lbs. (15 Nm).

To install:

12. Position the oil pump onto the crankshaft and install the 4 oil pump retaining bolts.

13. Tighten the oil pump retaining bolts to 21 ft. lbs. (28 Nm).

14. Install the timing chain cover.

15. Install the pick-up tube and oil pan.

INSPECTION

➡ DO NOT inspect the oil relief valve assembly. If the oil relief valve is suspect, replace the oil pump.

1. Disassemble oil pump.

2. Clean all parts thoroughly. Mating surface of the oil pump housing should be smooth. Replace pump cover if scratched or grooved.

3. Lay a straightedge across the pump cover surface. If a 0.001 in. (0.025mm) feeler gauge can be inserted between cover and straight edge, cover should be replaced.

4. Measure the thickness and diameter of outer rotor. If outer rotor thickness measures 0.563 in. (14.299mm) or less, or if the diameter is 3.141 in. (79.78mm) or less, replace outer rotor.

5. If inner rotor measures 0.563 in. (14.299mm) or less replace inner rotor .

6. Slide outer rotor into body, press to one side with fingers and measure clearance between rotor and body . If measurement is 0.015 in. (0.39mm) or more, replace body only if outer rotor is in specifications.

7. Install inner rotor into body. If clearance between inner and outer rotors is 0.008 in. (0.20mm) or more, replace both rotors.

8. Place a straightedge across the face of the body, between bolt holes. If a feeler gauge of 0.003 in. (0.077mm) or more can be inserted between rotors and the straight-edge, replace pump assembly ONLY if rotors are in specs.

9. Assemble oil pump.

PISTON AND RING

POSITIONING

See Figures 146 through 148.

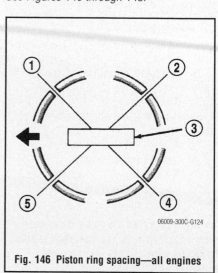

Fig. 146 Piston ring spacing—all engines

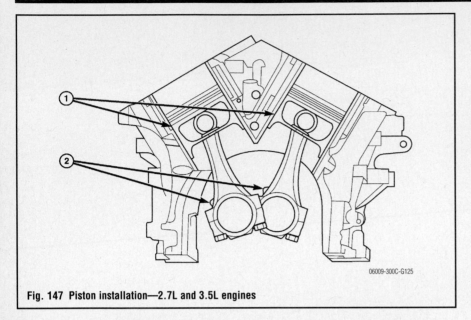

Fig. 147 Piston installation—2.7L and 3.5L engines

Fig. 150 Install seal assembly (2) using special tool 6926-1(1)—2.7L engine

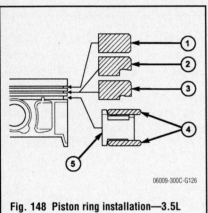

Fig. 148 Piston ring installation—3.5L engine

REAR MAIN SEAL

REMOVAL & INSTALLATION

2.7L and 3.5L Engines

See Figures 149 through 151.

1. Before servicing the vehicle, refer to the precautions in the beginning of this section.
2. Disconnect negative battery cable.
3. Raise the vehicle.
4. Remove splash shield retaining bolts and splash shield.
5. Remove the structural collar.
6. Remove transmission
7. Remove flex plate attaching bolts, backing plate and flex plate.
8. Remove oil pan.

➡**The integrated stamped steel rear crankshaft seal is not interchangeable with the cast aluminum rear seal adapter and seal assembly.**

9. Remove seal retainer attaching screws.
10. Remove the crankshaft rear oil seal/adapter.

To install:

➡**The integrated rear crankshaft seal is not interchangeable with the cast aluminum rear seal adapter and seal assembly.**

11. Clean all sealing surfaces.
12. Install seal assembly using special tool 6926-1.
13. Install seal retaining bolts finger tight.

➡**The following steps must be performed to prevent oil leaks at sealing joints.**

14. Attach Special Tools 8225 to pan rail using the oil pan fasteners.

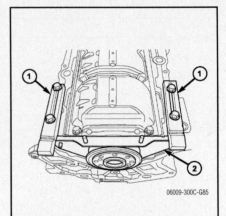

Fig. 151 Attach Special Tools 8225 (1) to pan rail using the oil pan fasteners—2.7L engine

➡**Make sure that the "2.7L" stamped on the special tool is facing the cylinder block (flat side of tools against pan rail).**

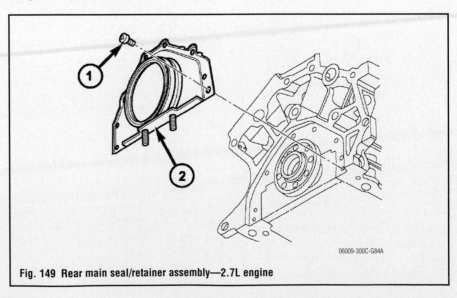

Fig. 149 Rear main seal/retainer assembly—2.7L engine

15. While applying firm pressure to the seal assembly against Special Tools 8225, tighten seal assembly screws to 105 inch lbs. (12 Nm).

16. Remove special tool 8225.

17. Install oil pan.

18. Install flex plate, backing plate, and attaching bolts.

19. Install transmission.

20. Install lower splash shield retaining bolts and splash shield.

21. Lower vehicle.

22. Fill with oil.

5.7L Engine

See Figures 152 and 153.

1. Before servicing the vehicle, refer to the precautions in the beginning of this section.

➡**This procedure can be performed in vehicle.**

2. If being performed in vehicle, remove the transmission.

3. Remove the flexplate.

➡**The crankshaft oil seal can not be reused after removal.**

➡**The crankshaft rear oil seal remover Special Tool 8506 must be installed deeply into the seal. Continue to tighten the removal tool into the seal until the tool can not be turned farther. Failure to install tool correctly the first time will cause tool to pull free of seal without removing seal from engine.**

4. Using Special Tool 8506 (1), remove the crankshaft rear oil seal (2).

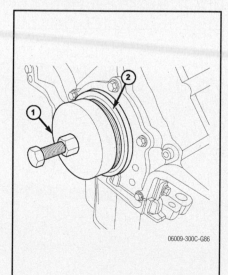

Fig. 152 Rear main seal removal—5.7L engine

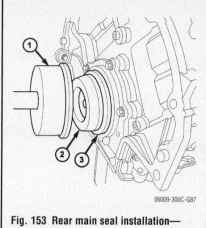

Fig. 153 Rear main seal installation—5.7L engine

To install:

⁂ WARNING

The rear seal must be installed dry for proper operation. Do not lubricate the seal lip or outer edge.

5. Position the plastic seal guide (2) onto the crankshaft rear face. Then position the crankshaft rear oil seal (3) onto the guide.

6. Using Special Tools 8349 Crankshaft Rear Oil Seal Installer (1) and C-4171 Driver Handle, with a hammer, tap the seal (3) into place. Continue to tap on the driver handle until the seal installer seats against the cylinder block crankshaft bore.

7. Install the flexplate.

8. Install the transmission.

TIMING CHAIN FRONT COVER AND SEAL

REMOVAL & INSTALLATION

2.7L Engine

See Figures 154 through 160.

1. Before servicing the vehicle, refer to the precautions in the beginning of this section.

2. Disconnect negative battery cable.

3. Drain cooling system.

4. Remove coolant recovery bottle.

5. Raise and safely support the vehicle.

6. Remove lower splash shield retaining bolts and splash shield.

7. Remove accessory drive belts.

8. Use special tool 9365 Damper Holder to hold damper while removing attaching bolt.

9. Remove damper by using Special Tools 8194 Insert and 8454 Puller.

10. Lower vehicle.

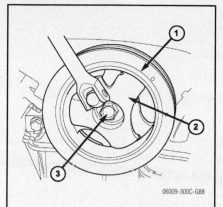

Fig. 154 Use special tool 9365 Damper Holder (2) to hold damper (1) while removing attaching bolt (3)—2.7L engine

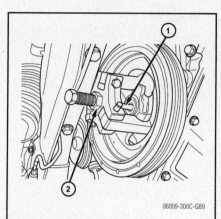

Fig. 155 Remove damper by using Special Tools 8194 Insert (1) and 8454 Puller (2)—2.7L engine

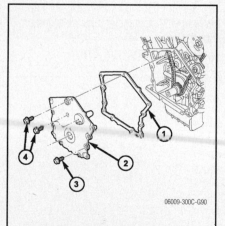

Fig. 156 Timing chain cover gasket (1), cover (2), and bolts (3 & 4)—2.7L engine

11. Remove timing chain cover bolts.

12. Remove timing chain cover.

13. Discard timing chain cover gasket.

14. Install Special Tool 8194, insert into crankshaft nose. Remove seal using Special Tool 6771, Remover.

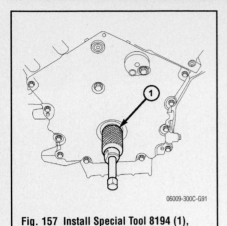

Fig. 157 Install Special Tool 8194 (1), Insert into crankshaft nose to remove the seal—2.7L engine

To install:

15. Inspect and clean timing chain cover sealing surfaces.

16. Before installing timing cover gasket apply a ⅛ inch bead of Mopar® Engine RTV GEN II, or equivalent, to the parting lines between the oil pan and cylinder block.

17. Install timing cover and gasket. Tighten M10 cover bolts to 40 ft. lbs. (54 Nm) and M6 bolts to 105 inch lbs. (12 Nm).

18. Install new seal using Special Tools 6780-2 Sleeve, 6780-1 Installer, and 8179 Stud.

19. Install damper using Special Tools 8179 Screw, with Nut and Thrust Bearing from 6792, and 6792-1 Installer.

20. Install damper attaching bolt. Use special tool 9365 damper holder to hold damper while tightening attaching bolt to 125 ft. lbs. (170 Nm).

21. Install accessory drive belts.

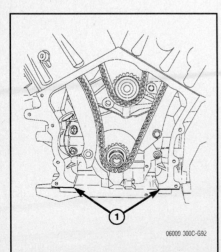

Fig. 158 RTV application points at parting lines between the oil pan and cylinder block—2.7L engine

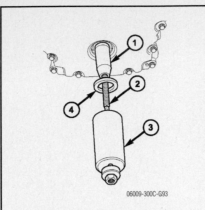

Fig. 159 Install new seal (4) using Special Tools 6780-2 Sleeve (1), 6780-1 Installer (3), and 8179 Stud (2)—2.7L engine

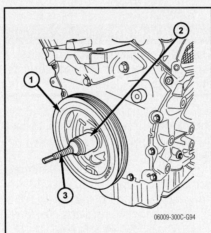

Fig. 160 Install damper (1) using Special Tools 8179 Screw (3), with Nut and Thrust Bearing from 6792, and 6792-1 Installer (2)—2.7L engine

22. Install lower splash shield and retaining bolts.

23. Lower vehicle.

24. Fill cooling system.

25. Connect negative battery cable.

5.7L Engine

See Figures 161 through 165.

1. Before servicing the vehicle, refer to the precautions in the beginning of this section.

2. Disconnect the battery negative cable.

3. Remove the engine cover.

4. Remove air cleaner assembly.

5. Drain cooling system.

6. Remove accessory drive belt.

7. Disconnect cooling fan electrical connector.

8. Remove cooling fan mounting bolts.

9. Remove radiator cooling fan assembly from vehicle.

10. Remove coolant bottle and washer bottle.

11. Remove fan shroud.

➡It is not necessary to disconnect air conditioning lines or discharge refrigerant.

12. Remove air conditioning compressor and set aside.

13. Remove the alternator.

14. Remove upper radiator hose.

15. Disconnect both heater hoses at timing cover.

16. Disconnect lower radiator hose at engine.

17. Remove accessory drive belt tensioner and both idler pulleys.

18. Remove crankshaft damper bolt and remove the damper (2) with a puller (1).

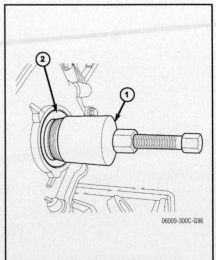

Fig. 161 Removing the damper—5.7L engine

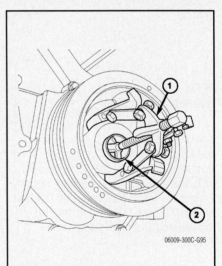

Fig. 162 Removing the front seal—5.7L engine

19. Using Special Tool 9071 (1), remove crankshaft front seal (2).

➡**Do not remove the hoses from the power steering pump.**

20. Remove power steering pump and set aside.
21. Remove the dipstick support bolt.
22. Drain the engine oil.
23. Remove the oil pan and pick up tube.

➡**It is not necessary to remove water pump for timing cover removal.**

24. Remove timing cover bolts and remove cover.
25. Verify that timing cover slide bushings (1) are located in timing cover.

To install:

26. Clean timing chain cover and block surface.

➡**Always install a new gasket on timing cover.**

27. Verify that the slide bushings are installed in timing cover.
28. Install cover and new gasket. Tighten fasteners to 21 ft. lbs. (28 Nm).

➡**The large lifting stud is torqued to 40 ft. lbs. (55 Nm).**

29. Install the oil pan and pick up tube.
30. Install the air conditioning compressor.
31. Install the alternator.
32. Install power steering pump.
33. Install the dipstick support bolt.
34. Install the thermostat housing.

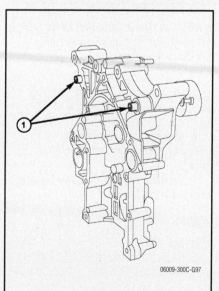

Fig. 163 Timing cover slide bushings in place (1)—5.7L engine

---

✳✳ WARNING

The front crankshaft seal must be installed dry. Do not apply lubricant to sealing lip or to outer edge.

35. Using Special Tool 8348 (1) and 8512A (2), install crankshaft front seal.

✳✳ WARNING

To prevent severe damage to the crankshaft, damper or Special Tool 8512-A, thoroughly clean the damper bore and the crankshaft nose before installing damper.

36. Slide damper onto crankshaft slightly.

✳✳ WARNING

Special Tool 8512-A, is assembled in a specific sequence. Failure to assemble this tool in this sequence can result in tool failure and severe damage to either the tool or the crankshaft.

37. Assemble Special Tool 8512-A as follows, the nut is threaded onto the shaft first (2). Then, the roller bearing (1) is placed onto the threaded rod (3). The hardened bearing surface of the bearing (1) MUST face the nut (2). Then, the hardened washer (5) slides onto the threaded rod (3). Once assembled coat the threaded rod's threads with Mopar® Nickel Anti-Seize or (Loctite® No. 771).
38. Using Special Tool 8512-A, press damper onto crankshaft.
39. Install then tighten crankshaft damper bolt to 129 ft. lbs. (176 Nm).
40. Install accessory drive belt tensioner assembly and both idler pulleys.

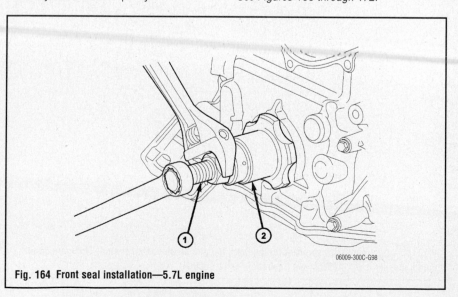

Fig. 164 Front seal installation—5.7L engine

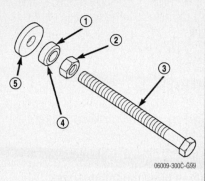

Fig. 165 Crankshaft damper installation tool—5.7L engine

41. Install radiator lower hose.
42. Install both heater hoses.
43. Position radiator cooling fan assembly in vehicle.
44. Install cooling fan mounting bolts. Tighten to 50 inch lbs. (6 Nm)
45. Connect cooling fan electrical connector.
46. Install the fan and fan drive assembly
47. Install the accessory drive belt.
48. Install the coolant bottle and washer bottle.
49. Install the upper radiator hose.
50. Install the air cleaner assembly.
51. Fill cooling system.
52. Refill engine oil.
53. Connect the battery negative cable.
54. Install the engine cover.

TIMING CHAIN AND SPROCKETS

REMOVAL & INSTALLATION

2.7L Engine

See Figures 166 through 172.

1. Before servicing the vehicle, refer to the precautions in the beginning of this section.

2. Disconnect negative battery cable.

3. Drain cooling system.

4. Remove upper intake manifold.

5. Remove cylinder head covers, crankshaft vibration damper, and timing chain cover.

✳✳ WARNING

When aligning timing marks, always rotate engine by turning the crankshaft. Failure to do so will result in valve and/or piston damage.

6. Align crankshaft sprocket timing mark to mark on oil pump housing. The mark on oil pump housing is 60° ATDC of no.1 cylinder.

✳✳ WARNING

When the timing chain is removed and the cylinder heads are still installed, DO NOT rotate the camshafts or crankshaft without first locating the proper crankshaft position. Failure to do so will result in valve and/or piston damage.

7. Remove primary timing chain tensioner retainer cap and tensioner from right cylinder head.

8. Disconnect and remove camshaft position sensor (4) from left cylinder head.

9. Remove timing chain guide access plugs (3) from cylinder heads.

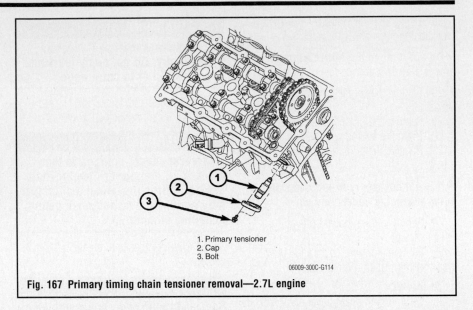

1. Primary tensioner
2. Cap
3. Bolt

06009-300C-G114

Fig. 167 Primary timing chain tensioner removal—2.7L engine

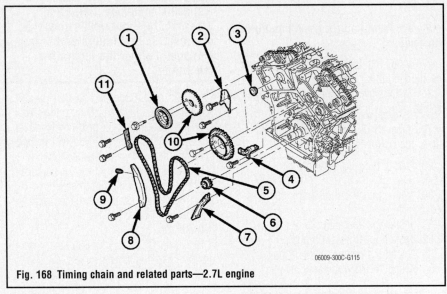

06009-300C-G115

Fig. 168 Timing chain and related parts—2.7L engine

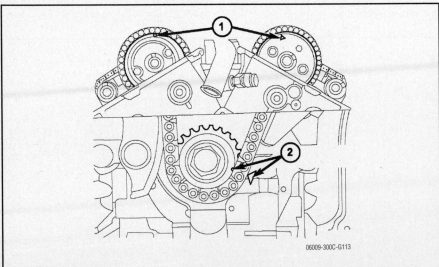

06009-300C-G113

Fig. 166 Align crankshaft sprocket timing mark to mark on oil pump housing. The mark on oil pump housing is 60° ATDC of no.1 cylinder—2.7L engine

➡ **When camshaft sprocket bolts are removed, the camshafts will rotate in a clockwise direction.**

10. Starting with the right camshaft sprocket, remove the sprocket attaching bolts. Remove camshaft damper (1) (if equipped) and sprocket.

11. Remove left side camshaft sprocket attaching bolts and remove sprocket.

12. Remove lower chain guide (7) and tensioner arm (8).

13. Remove the primary timing chain (5).

14. Remove crankshaft sprocket (6).

To install:

15. Inspect all sprockets (4, 9, and 11) and chain guides (2, 5, and 10). Replace if worn.

16. Install crankshaft sprocket.

17. If removed, install right and left side

short chain guides (10). Tighten attaching bolts to 21 ft. lbs. (28 Nm).

18. Align crankshaft sprocket timing mark to the mark on oil pump housing (3).

➡ **Lubricate timing chain and guides with engine oil before installation.**

19. Place left side primary chain sprocket onto the chain so that the timing mark is located in-between the two (plated) timing links (1).

20. Lower the primary chain with left side sprocket through the left cylinder head opening.

➡ **The camshaft sprockets can be allowed to float on the camshaft hub during installation.**

21. Loosely position left side camshaft sprocket over camshaft hub.

22. Align timing (plated) link to the crankshaft sprocket timing mark (3).

23. Position primary chain onto water pump drive sprocket (11).

24. Align right camshaft sprocket timing mark to the timing (plated) link on the timing chain (8) and loosely position over camshaft hub.

25. Verify that all chain timing (plated) links are properly aligned to the timing marks on all sprockets.

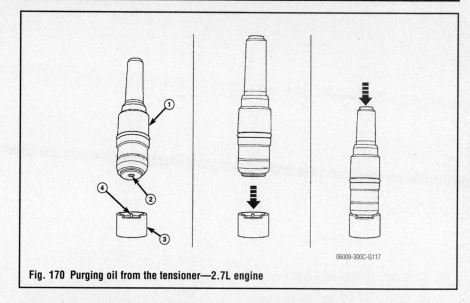

Fig. 170 Purging oil from the tensioner—2.7L engine

06009-300C-G117

26. Install left side lower chain guide (2) and tensioner arm (5). Tighten attaching bolts to 21 ft. lbs. (28 Nm).

➡ **Inspect O-ring on chain guide access plugs before installing. Replace O-ring as necessary.**

27. Install chain guide access plugs to cylinder heads. Tighten plugs to 15 ft. lbs. (20 Nm).

➡ **To reset the primary timing chain tensioner, engine oil will first need to be purged from the tensioner.**

28. Purge oil from timing chain tensioner using the following procedure:

a. Place the check ball (2) end of tensioner into the shallow end of Special Tool 8186 (3).

b. Using hand pressure, slowly depress tensioner until oil is purged from tensioner.

29. Reset timing chain tensioner using the following procedure:

a. Position cylinder plunger (4) into the deeper end of Special Tool 8186 (3).

b. Apply a downward force until tensioner is reset.

➡ **If oil was not first purged from the tensioner, use slight finger pressure to assist the center arm pin of Special Tool 8186 to unseat the tensioner's check ball.**

⚙ WARNING

Ensure the tensioner is properly reset. The tensioner body (4) must bottom against the top edge of Special Tool 8186 (3). Failure to properly perform the resetting procedure may cause tensioner jamming.

➡ **Inspect the tensioner O-ring (2) for nicks or cuts and make sure the snapring (1) is correctly installed, replace as necessary.**

30. Install the reset chain tensioner into the right cylinder head.

31. Position tensioner retaining plate and tighten bolts to 105 inch lbs. (12 Nm).

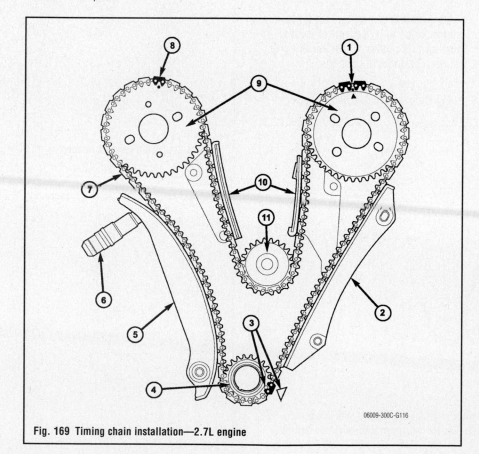

Fig. 169 Timing chain installation—2.7L engine

06009-300C-G116

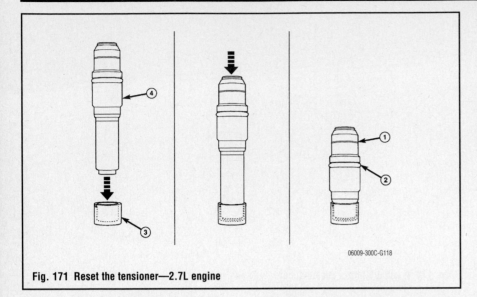

Fig. 171 Reset the tensioner—2.7L engine

32. Starting at the right cylinder bank, first position the camshaft damper (if equipped) on camshaft hub, then insert a ⅜ in. square drive extension with a breaker bar into intake camshaft drive hub.

33. Rotate camshaft until the camshaft hub aligns to the camshaft sprocket and damper attaching holes. Install the sprocket attaching bolts and tighten to 21 ft. lbs. (28 Nm).

34. Turn the left side camshaft by inserting a ⅜ in. square drive extension with a breaker bar into intake camshaft drive hub and rotate camshaft until the sprocket attaching bolts can be installed. Tighten sprocket bolts to 21 ft. lbs. (28 Nm).

35. Rotate engine slightly clockwise to remove timing chain slack, if necessary.

36. Activate the timing chain tensioner by using a flat bladed pry tool to gently pry tensioner arm towards the tensioner slightly. Then release the tensioner arm. Verify the tensioner is activated (extends).

37. Install camshaft position sensor and connect electrical connector.

38. Install the timing chain cover, crankshaft vibration damper, and cylinder head covers.

39. Install upper intake manifold.

➡ **After installation of a reset tensioner, engine noise will occur after initial start-up. This noise will normally disappear within 5–10 seconds.**

40. Fill cooling system.
41. Connect negative battery cable.

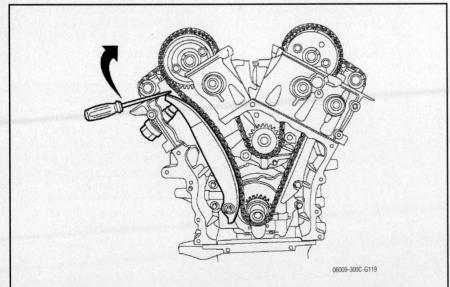

Fig. 172 Activate the timing chain tensioner by using a flat bladed pry tool to gently pry tensioner arm towards the tensioner slightly. Then release the tensioner arm. Verify the tensioner is activated (extends)—2.7L engine

2.7L—Engine Crankshaft Sprocket

See Figures 173 and 174.

1. Before servicing the vehicle, refer to the precautions in the beginning of this section.

2. Remove primary timing chain.

❊❊ WARNING

Use care not to turn crankshaft while removing crankshaft sprocket, as damage to valves and or pistons could occur.

3. Remove crankshaft sprocket by first installing the crankshaft damper bolt. Apply grease or equivalent to damper bolt head and position Special Tools 5048-1(3), 5048-6 (2), and 8539 (1) on sprocket and crankshaft nose. Remove sprocket using care not to rotate the crankshaft.

To install:

4. Install crankshaft sprocket using Special Tools 6780-1(1) and 8179 (2)

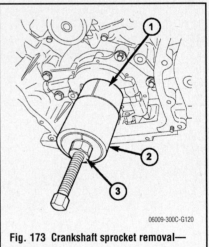

Fig. 173 Crankshaft sprocket removal—2.7L engine

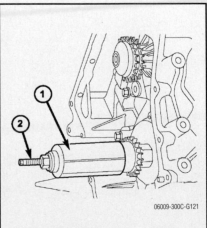

Fig. 174 Crankshaft sprocket installation—2.7L engine

until sprocket bottoms against crankshaft step flange. Use care not to rotate crankshaft.

5. Verify that crankshaft sprocket is installed to proper depth by measuring from sprocket outer face to end of crankshaft. Measurement should read: 39.05 ± 0.50 mm (1.5374 ± 0.020 in.).

6. Install primary timing chain.

5.7L Engine

See Figures 175 and 176.

1. Before servicing the vehicle, refer to the precautions in the beginning of this section.

2. Disconnect battery negative cable.

3. Drain cooling system.

4. Remove timing chain cover.

5. Re-install the vibration damper bolt finger tight. Using a suitable socket and breaker bar, rotate the crankshaft to align timing chain sprockets and keyways as shown.

> ### ✳✳ WARNING
> **The camshaft pin and the slot in the cam sprocket must be positioned at 12:00 (2). The crankshaft keyway must be positioned at 2:00 (3). The crankshaft sprocket must be installed so that the dots and or paint marking is at 6:00.**

6. Retract tensioner shoe until hole in shoe lines up with hole in bracket.

7. Slide a suitable pin into the holes.

8. Remove camshaft sprocket attaching bolt and remove timing chain with crankshaft and camshaft sprockets.

9. If tensioner assembly is to be replaced, remove the tensioner to block bolts and remove tensioner assembly.

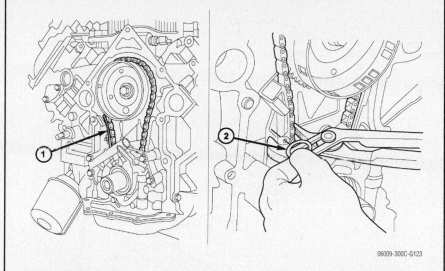

Fig. 176 Retract tensioner shoe (1) until hole in shoe lines up with hole in bracket. Slide a suitable pin (2) into the holes—5.7L engine

06009-300C-G123

To install:

10. If tensioner assembly is being replaced, install tensioner and mounting bolts. Torque bolts to 21 ft. lbs. (28 Nm).

11. Retract tensioner if required.

> ### ✳✳ WARNING
> **The timing chain must be installed with the single plated link aligned with the dot and or paint marking on the camshaft sprocket. The crankshaft sprocket is aligned with the dot and or paint marking on the sprocket between two plated timing chain links.**

> ### ✳✳ WARNING
> **The camshaft pin and the slot in the cam sprocket must be clocked at 12:00. The crankshaft keyway must be clocked at 2:00. The crankshaft sprocket must be installed so that the dots and or paint marking Is at 6:00.**

12. Place both camshaft sprocket and crankshaft sprocket on the bench with timing marks on exact imaginary center line through both camshaft and crankshaft bores.

13. Place timing chain around both sprockets.

14. Lift sprockets and chain. Keep sprockets tight against the chain.

15. Slide both sprockets evenly over their respective shafts and check alignment of timing marks.

16. Install the camshaft bolt. Tighten the bolt to 90 ft. lbs. (122 Nm) torque.

17. Remove tensioner pin. Again, verify alignment of timing marks.

18. Install the oil pump.

19. Install the oil pan and pick up.

20. Install the timing chain cover

21. Refill engine oil.

22. Fill cooling system.

23. Connect battery negative cable.

24. Start engine and check for oil and coolant leaks.

TIMING BELT FRONT COVER

REMOVAL & INSTALLATION

3.5L Engine

See Figures 177 and 178.

1. Before servicing the vehicle, refer to the precautions in the beginning of this section.

2. Perform fuel pressure release procedure.

3. Disconnect negative battery cable.

4. Remove accessory drive belt.

5. Remove accessory drive belt tensioner.

6. Remove bolts for power steering pump. Reposition power steering pump aside.

7. Raise and safely support the vehicle.

8. Remove crankshaft damper bolt and remove the damper with a puller.

9. Remove the lower front timing belt cover fasteners.

10. Lower the vehicle.

11. Remove the upper timing belt cover bolts and remove front timing belt cover.

To install:

12. Exchange the accessory drive belt pulley if necessary. Tighten bolt to 45 ft. lbs. (61 Nm).

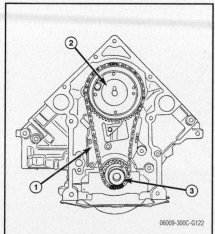

Fig. 175 Timing mark alignment—5.7L engine

06009-300C-G122

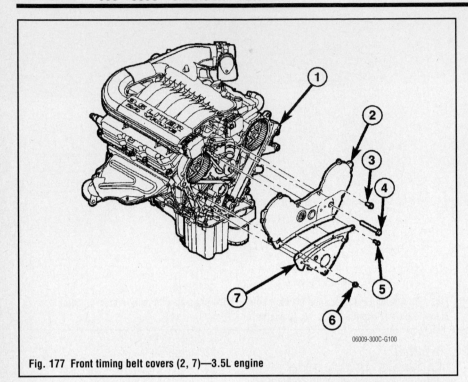

Fig. 177 Front timing belt covers (2, 7)—3.5L engine

13. Install upper front timing belt cover.

14. Install lower timing belt front cover.

15. Tighten the timing cover bolts as follows:
- M6 bolts: 105 inch lbs. (12 Nm)
- M8 bolts: 21 ft. lbs. (28 Nm)
- M10 bolts: 40 ft. lbs. (54 Nm)

16. Install power steering pump fasteners. Tighten bolts to 200 inch lbs. (23 Nm).

17. Install crankshaft damper. Torque to 70 ft. lbs. (95 Nm).

18. Install accessory drive belt tensioner. Torque fastener to 21 ft. lbs. (28 Nm).

19. Install accessory drive belt.

20. Lower vehicle.

21. Connect negative battery cable.

TIMING BELT REAR COVER

REMOVAL & INSTALLATION

3.5L Engine

See Figures 179 and 180.

1. Before servicing the vehicle, refer to the precautions in the beginning of this section.

➡ **The rear timing belt cover has O-rings to seal the water pump passages to cylinder block. Do not reuse the O-rings.**

2. Perform fuel pressure release procedure.

3. Disconnect the negative battery cable.

4. Remove timing belt.

5. Remove camshaft sprockets.

6. Remove rear timing belt cover bolts (1, 2, and 3).

7. Remove the rear cover.

To install:

8. Clean rear timing belt cover O-ring sealing surfaces and grooves. Lubricate new O-rings with Mopar° Dielectric Grease, or equivalent, to facilitate assembly.

9. Position NEW O-rings on cover.

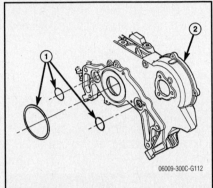

Fig. 180 Rear timing belt cover (2) O-rings (1)—3.5L engine

10. Install rear timing belt cover. Tighten bolts to the following specified torque:
- M10 (2, 4): 40 ft. lbs. (54 Nm)
- M8 (1): 20 ft. lbs. (28 Nm)
- M6 (3): 105 inch lbs. (12 Nm)

11. Install the camshaft sprockets.

12. Install the timing belt.

TIMING BELT AND SPROCKETS

REMOVAL & INSTALLATION

3.5L Engine

See Figures 181 through 183.

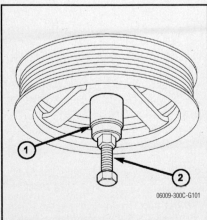

Fig. 178 Damper installation—3.5L engine

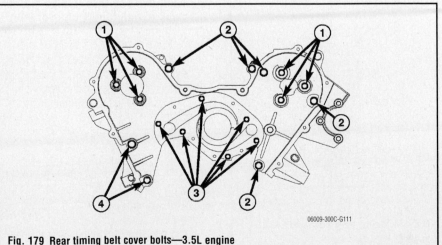

Fig. 179 Rear timing belt cover bolts—3.5L engine

1. Before servicing the vehicle, refer to the precautions in the beginning of this section.

⁂ WARNING

The 3.5L is NOT a freewheeling engine. Therefore, loosen the valve train rocker assemblies before servicing the timing drive.

2. Perform fuel pressure release procedure.

3. Disconnect negative battery cable.

4. Remove both cylinder head covers and loosen the rocker arm assemblies.

5. Remove the front timing belt cover.

6. Mark belt running direction, if timing belt is to be reused.

⁂ WARNING

When aligning timing marks, always rotate engine by turning the crankshaft. Failure to do so will result in valve and/or piston damage.

7. Rotate engine clockwise until crankshaft (10) mark aligns with the TDC mark on oil pump housing (9) and the camshaft sprocket (2, 7) timing marks (1, 8) are aligned with the marks on the rear cover.

8. Remove the timing belt tensioner (12) and remove timing belt.

9. Inspect the tensioner for fluid leakage.

10. Inspect the pivot and bolt for free movement, bearing grease leakage, and smooth rotation. If not rotating freely, replace the arm and pulley assembly.

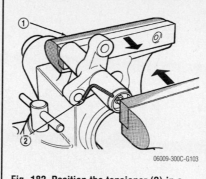

Fig. 182 Position the tensioner (2) in a vise (1)—3.5L engine

11. When tensioner is removed from the engine it is necessary to compress the plunger into the tensioner body.

➡**Index the tensioner in the vise the same way it is installed on the engine. This ensures proper pin orientation when tensioner is installed on the engine.**

c. Place the tensioner into a vise and SLOWLY compress the plunger. Total bleed down of tensioner should take about 5 minutes.

d. When plunger is compressed into the tensioner body install a pin through the body and plunger to retain plunger in place until tensioner is installed.

12. Inspect both sides of the timing belt. Replace belt if any of the following conditions exist:

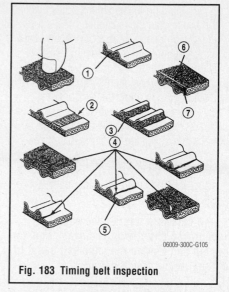

Fig. 183 Timing belt inspection

a. Hardening of back rubber back side is glossy without resilience and leaves no indent when pressed with fingernail.

b. Cracks (4) on rubber back.

c. Cracks or peeling (1) of canvas.

d. Cracks on rib root.

e. Cracks on belt sides.

f. Missing teeth (2).

g. Abnormal wear (7) of belt sides. The sides are normal if they are sharp as if cut by a knife.

h. Vehicle mileage or time at component maintenance requirement.

13. If none of the above conditions are seen on the belt, the front timing belt cover can be installed.

To install:

⁂ WARNING

If camshafts have moved from the timing marks, always rotate camshaft towards the direction nearest to the timing marks. Do not turn camshafts a full revolution or damage to valves and/or pistons could result.

14. Align the crankshaft sprocket with the TDC mark on oil pump cover.

15. Align the camshaft sprockets timing reference marks with the marks on the rear cover.

16. Install the timing belt starting at the crankshaft sprocket going in a counterclockwise direction. Install the belt around the last sprocket. Maintain tension on the belt as it is positioned around the tensioner pulley.

➡**If the camshaft gears have been removed it is only necessary to have the camshaft gear retaining bolts installed to a snug torque at this time.**

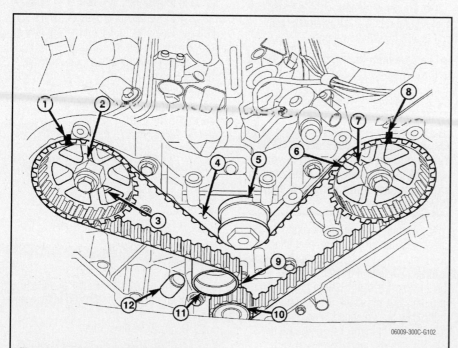

Fig. 181 Timing mark alignment—3.5L engine

17. Holding the tensioner pulley against the belt, install the tensioner into the housing and tighten to 21 ft. lbs. (28 Nm). Each camshaft sprocket mark should remain aligned the cover marks.

18. When tensioner is in place pull retaining pin to allow the tensioner to extend to the pulley bracket.

19. Rotate crankshaft sprocket 2 revolutions and check the timing marks on the camshafts and crankshaft. The marks should line up within their respective locations. If marks do not line up, repeat procedure.

➡If camshaft gears have been removed and timing is correct, counterhold and tighten the camshaft gears to final torque specification.

20. Install the front timing belt cover.
21. Tighten the rocker arm assemblies and install the cylinder head covers.
22. Connect negative battery cable.

Camshaft Sprockets

See Figure 184.

1. Before servicing the vehicle, refer to the precautions in the beginning of this section.

※※ WARNING

The 3.5L engine is not a free-wheeling design. Therefore, care should be taken not to rotate the camshafts or crankshaft with the timing belt removed.

➡The camshaft timing gears are keyed to the camshaft.

2. Perform fuel pressure release procedure.

3. Remove front timing belt cover.

4. Position crankshaft sprocket to the TDC mark on the oil pump housing by turning crankshaft in the clockwise direction.

5. Install a dial indicator in number 1 cylinder to check TDC of the piston. Rotate the crankshaft until the piston is at exactly TDC.

6. Remove camshaft retainer/thrust plate from rear of right cylinder head.

7. Remove the right cylinder head cover.

8. Remove the right rocker arm assembly.

9. Remove the timing belt tensioner and timing belt.

10. Hold left camshaft sprocket with a 36 mm (1⁷⁄₁₆ in.) box end wrench.

11. Loosen and remove the camshaft gear retaining bolt and washer. The left bolt is 255 mm (10.0 in.) long.

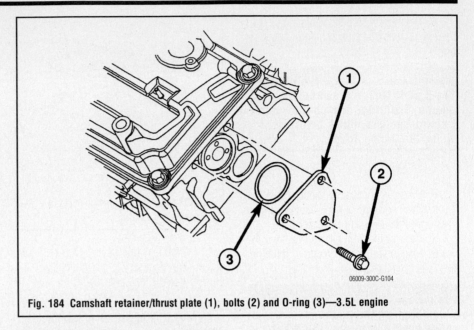

Fig. 184 Camshaft retainer/thrust plate (1), bolts (2) and O-ring (3)—3.5L engine

06009-300C-G104

➡The camshaft timing gears are keyed to the camshaft.

12. Remove the camshaft sprocket.

※※ WARNING

The right camshaft must be pushed rearward approximately 3½ inches to remove the camshaft gear retaining bolt and gear. Care must be taken not to scratch or nick the camshaft or cylinder head journals when moving camshaft.

13. Hold right camshaft sprocket with a 36 mm (1⁷⁄₁₆ in.) box end wrench.

14. Loosen and remove the camshaft gear retaining bolt and washer. The right bolt is 213 mm (8⅜ in.) long.

➡The camshaft timing gears are keyed to the camshaft.

15. Remove the camshaft sprocket.

To install:

※※ WARNING

The camshaft sprockets are keyed and not interchangeable from side to side because of the camshaft position sensor pick-up.

16. Install camshaft sprockets onto the camshafts. Install NEW sprocket attaching bolts into place. The 255 mm (10 in.) bolt is to be installed in the left camshaft and the 213 mm (8⅜ in.) bolt is to be installed into the right camshaft. Do not tighten the bolts; they are tightened later. Camshaft sprocket (2, 7) marks (1, 8) should be aligned with the marks on the cover at both sprockets.

17. Install the camshaft thrust plates and O-ring. Tighten bolts to 21 ft. lbs. (28 Nm).

18. Install the timing belt starting first at the crankshaft sprocket, then to remaining components in a counterclockwise direction.

19. Install the belt around the last sprocket. Maintain tension on the belt as it is positioned around the tensioner pulley. Each camshaft sprockets mark should still be aligned with the rear cover marks.

20. Hold the tensioner pulley against the belt and install the reset (pinned) timing belt tensioner into the housing. Tighten attaching bolts to 21 ft. lbs. (28 Nm).

21. Remove tensioner retaining pin to allow the tensioner to extend to the pulley bracket.

22. Using a dial indicator, position the number 1 piston at TDC.

23. Hold the camshaft sprocket hex with a 36 mm (1⁷⁄₁₆ in.) wrench and tighten the camshaft bolts to the following:
   - Right side: 75 ft. lbs. (102 Nm) +90° turn
   - Left side: 75 ft. lbs. (102 Nm) +90° turn

24. Remove dial indicator and install spark plug.

25. Install front timing belt cover.

Crankshaft Sprocket

See Figures 185 and 186.

1. Before servicing the vehicle, refer to thc precautions in the beginning of this section.

2. Remove the timing belt.

3. Remove crankshaft sprocket using a gear puller.

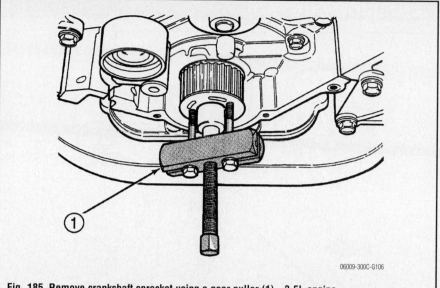

Fig. 185 Remove crankshaft sprocket using a gear puller (1)—3.5L engine

To install:

✳✳ WARNING

To ensure proper installation depth of crankshaft sprocket, Special Tool 6641 must be used.

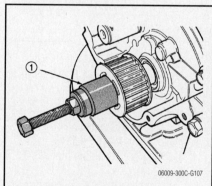

Fig. 186 To ensure proper installation depth of crankshaft sprocket, Special Tool 6641 (1) must be used—3.5L engine

4. Install crankshaft sprocket using Special Tools 6641 (1) and C-4685-C1.
5. Install the timing belt.

3.5L Engine

See Figures 187 and 188.

1. Before servicing the vehicle, refer to the precautions in the beginning of this section.

➡The rear timing belt cover has O-rings to seal the water pump passages to cylinder block. Do not reuse the O-rings.

2. Perform fuel pressure release procedure.
3. Disconnect the negative battery cable.
4. Remove the timing belt.
5. Remove the camshaft sprockets.
6. Remove rear timing belt cover bolts (1, 2, and 3).
7. Remove the rear cover.

To install:

8. Clean rear timing belt cover O-ring sealing surfaces and grooves. Lubricate new

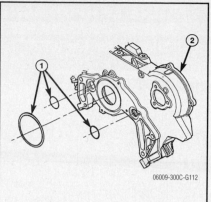

Fig. 188 Rear timing belt cover (2) O-rings (1)—3.5L engine

O-rings with Mopar° Dielectric Grease, or equivalent, to facilitate assembly.

9. Position NEW O-rings on cover.
10. Install rear timing belt cover. Tighten bolts to the following specified torque:

- M10 (2, 4): 40 ft. lbs. (54 Nm)
- M8 (1): 20 ft. lbs. (28 Nm)
- M6 (3): 105 inch lbs. (12 Nm)

11. Install the camshaft sprockets.
12. Install the timing belt.

VALVE LASH

ADJUSTMENT

These engines use hydraulic lifters to take up the free-play in the valve train system, therefore no lash adjustments are necessary.

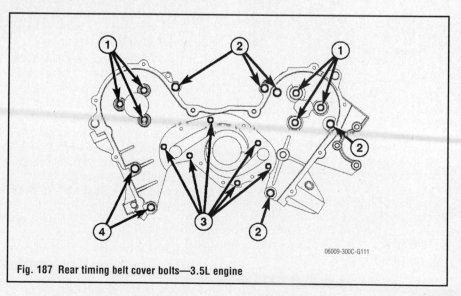

Fig. 187 Rear timing belt cover bolts—3.5L engine

ENGINE PERFORMANCE & EMISSION CONTROL

CAMSHAFT POSITION (CMP) SENSOR

LOCATION

2.7L Engine

See Figure 189.

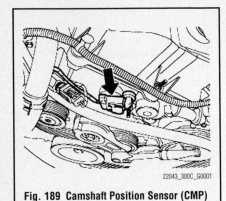

Fig. 189 Camshaft Position Sensor (CMP) 2.7L Engine

The Camshaft Position Sensor (CMP) is located just above the drive belt tensioner.

3.5L Engine

See Figure 190.

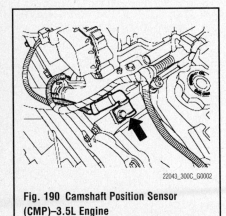

Fig. 190 Camshaft Position Sensor (CMP)–3.5L Engine

The Camshaft Position Sensor (CMP) is located just below the oil fill cap.

5.7L Engine

See Figure 191.

The Camshaft Position Sensor (CMP) on the 5.7L engine is bolted to the front/top of the timing chain cover.

OPERATION

The Camshaft Position sensor (CMP) is

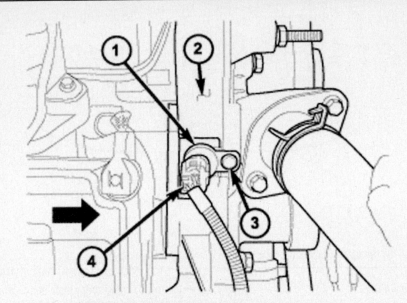

1. Camshaft position sensor
2. Timing chain cover
3. Mounting bolt
4. Electrical connector

Fig. 191 Camshaft Position Sensor (CMP)–5.7L Engine

used in conjunction with the crankshaft position sensor to differentiate between fuel injection and spark events. It is also used to synchronize the fuel injectors with their respective cylinders. The sensor generates electrical pulses. These pulses (signals) are sent to the Powertrain Control Module (PCM). The PCM will then determine crankshaft position from both the camshaft position sensor and crankshaft position sensor.

The tonewheel is located at the front of the camshaft. As the tonewheel rotates, notches pass through the sync signal generator.

When the cam gear is rotating, the sensor will detect the notches. Input voltage from the sensor to the PCM will then switch from a low (approximately 0.3 volts) to a high (approximately 5 volts). When the sensor detects a notch has passed, the input voltage switches back low to approximately 0.3 volts.

REMOVAL & INSTALLATION

2.7L & 3.5L Engines

1. Disconnect negative battery cable.
2. Unlock and disconnect electrical connector.

3. Remove the mounting bolt.
4. Remove the Camshaft Position Sensor (CMP).

To install:
5. Install the CMP sensor.
6. Install the mounting bolt.
7. Tighten CMP mounting bolt to 105 inch lbs. (12 Nm).
8. Connect the electrical connector and lock.
9. Connect negative battery cable.

5.7L Engine

1. Disconnect the electrical connector at CMP sensor.
2. Remove the CMP sensor mounting bolt.
3. Carefully twist sensor from timing chain cover.
4. Check condition of the sensor O-ring.

To install:
5. Clean out the machined hole in the timing chain cover.
6. Apply a small amount of engine oil to sensor o-ring.
7. Install the CMP sensor into timing chain cover with a slight rocking action.

Do not twist sensor into position as damage to o-ring may result.

⁂ WARNING

Before tightening sensor mounting bolt, be sure sensor is completely flush to timing chain cover. If sensor is not flush, damage to sensor mounting tang may result.

8. Install mounting bolt and tighten to 105 inch lbs. (12 Nm).
9. Connect the electrical connector to sensor.

TESTING

2.7L, 3.5L & 5.7L Engines

See Figures 192 and 193.

1. Disconnect the CMP Sensor connector.
2. Ignition on, engine not running.
3. Measure the voltage on the (F856) 5-volt Supply circuit in the CMP harness connector.
4. If the voltage is not between 4.5–5.2 volts. Repair the open or short to ground in the (F856) 5-volt Supply circuit.

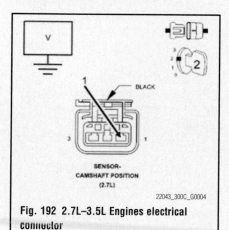

Fig. 192 2.7L–3.5L Engines electrical connector

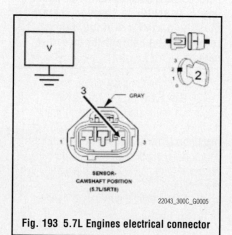

Fig. 193 5.7L Engines electrical connector

CRANKSHAFT POSITION (CKP) SENSOR

LOCATION

2.7L & 3.5L Engines

See Figure 194.

Fig. 194 The Crankshaft Position (CKP) sensor location—2.7L & 3.5L engines

The Crankshaft Position (CKP) sensor is located at the right rear side of the engine cylinder block.

5.7L Engine

See Figure 195.

The Crankshaft Position (CKP) sensor is located at the right rear side of the engine cylinder block. It is positioned and bolted into a machined hole in the engine block.

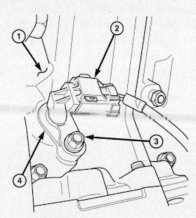

1. Engine block
2. Electrical connector
3. Mounting bolt
4. Crankshaft Position Sensor (CKP)

Fig. 195 Crankshaft Position (CKP) sensor view 5.7L engine

OPERATION

The crankshaft position and engine speed are detected contactless signal (hall effect). The distance between the crankshaft position sensor and the gaps of the tone wheel is fixed by the installation position.

When the crankshaft rotates, an alternating voltage is generated in the crankshaft position sensor by the gaps of the tone wheel located behind the flex plate.

In this case, the metal portion of the tone wheel generates a positive voltage pulse and the gap in the tone wheel a negative voltage pulse. The distance from the positive to the negative voltage peak equals the length of the gap. The gap created by 3 missing teeth has the effect that no voltage is generated in the crankshaft position sensor. This gap, or time without a signal from the crankshaft sensor, is analyzed by the ECM in order to detect the TDC position of cylinder 1

REMOVAL & INSTALLATION

2.7L & 3.5L Engines

1. Disconnect negative battery cable.
2. Raise and support the vehicle.
3. Unlock and disconnect the electrical connector.
4. Remove the Crankshaft Position Sensor (CKP) mounting bolt.
5. Remove the CKP sensor.

To install:
6. Install the CKP sensor.
7. Install the mounting bolt and tighten to 105 inch lbs. (12 Nm).
8. Connect the electrical connector and lock.
9. Lower the vehicle.
10. Connect negative battery cable.

5.7L Engine

1. If equipped with All Wheel Drive (AWD) disconnect and isolate negative battery cable.
2. Raise and support the vehicle.
3. If equipped with AWD remove the starter motor.
4. Disconnect the CKP electrical connector at the sensor.
5. Remove CKP mounting bolt.
6. Carefully twist sensor from the cylinder block.
7. Remove the CKP sensor from the vehicle.
8. Check condition of the sensor O-ring.

To install:
9. Clean out the machined hole in the engine block.

10. Apply a small amount of engine oil to the sensor O-ring.

11. Install the CKP sensor into the engine block with a slight rocking and twisting action.

12. Before tightening the sensor mounting bolt, be sure sensor is completely flush to cylinder block. If sensor is not flush, damage to the sensor mounting tang may result.

13. Install CKP mounting bolt and tighten to 105 inch lbs. (12 Nm).

TESTING

2.7L, 3.5L & 5.7L Engines

1. Turn the ignition off.

2. Disconnect the Crankshaft Position Sensor (CKP) sensor harness connector.

3. Check connectors and clean or repair as necessary.

4. Turn the ignition on.

5. Measure the voltage of the (F855) 5 volt supply circuit in the CKP harness connector.

6. The voltage should be between 4.7–5.1 volts.

7. If the reading is not as stated check and repair open or high resistance in 5 volt supply circuit.

ENGINE COOLANT TEMPERATURE (ECT) SENSOR

LOCATION

2.7L Engine

See Figure 196.

The Engine Coolant Temperature Sensor (ECT) is located at the front of the engine and is mounted in the coolant outlet tube.

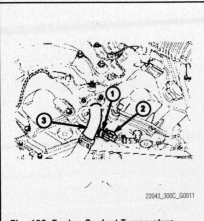

22043_300C_G0011

Fig. 196 Engine Coolant Temperature Sensor (ECT) 2.7L engine location view

3.5L Engine

The Engine Coolant Temperature (ECT) sensor is located just below the upper radiator hose and is installed into the lower intake manifold.

5.7L Engine

See Figure 197.

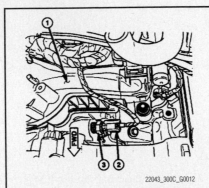

22043_300C_G0012

Fig. 197 Engine Coolant Temperature Sensor (ECT) (3) 5.7L engine location view

The Engine Coolant Temperature (ECT) sensor is located under the air conditioning compressor. It is installed into a water jacket at the front of the cylinder block.

OPERATION

The Engine Coolant Temperature (ECT) sensor is used to sense engine coolant temperature. The sensor protrudes into an engine water jacket.

The ECT sensor is a two-wire Negative Thermal Coefficient (NTC) sensor. Meaning, as engine coolant temperature increases, resistance (voltage) in the sensor decreases. As temperature decreases, resistance (voltage) in the sensor increases.

The PCM compares the ECT, Intake Air Temperature (IAT), and Ambient Air Temperature (AAT) under cold start conditions. Following a start to run delay time, the sensor values are compared. If the one sensor value is not within a specified range of the other two sensors, the value is determined to be irrational.

REMOVAL & INSTALLATION

2.7L Engine

✳✳ WARNING

Hot, pressurized coolant can cause injury by scalding. Cooling system must be partially drained before removing the coolant temperature sensor.

1. Disconnect negative battery cable.

2. Partially drain cooling system.

3. Disconnect the Engine Coolant Temperature Sensor (ECT) electrical connector.

4. Remove engine coolant sensor from coolant outlet tube.

5. Apply thread sealant to sensor threads.

To install:

6. Install engine coolant temperature sensor into coolant outlet tube.

7. Tighten the sensor to 20 ft. lbs. (28 Nm).

8. Connect the electrical connector to ECT sensor.

3.5L Engine

✳✳ WARNING

Hot, pressurized coolant can cause injury by scalding. Cooling system must be partially drained before removing the coolant temperature sensor.

1. Disconnect the negative battery cable.

2. Partially drain the cooling system

3. With the engine cold, disconnect coolant sensor electrical connector.

4. Remove the Engine Coolant Temperature Sensor (ECT).

To install:

5. Install engine coolant temperature sensor. Tighten sensor to 20 ft. lbs. (28 Nm).

6. Attach the electrical connector to ECT sensor.

7. Connect negative battery cable.

5.7L Engine

✳✳ WARNING

Hot, pressurized coolant can cause injury by scalding. Cooling system must be partially drained before removing the coolant temperature sensor.

1. Partially drain the cooling system.

2. Remove accessory drive belt

3. Carefully unbolt air conditioning compressor from front of engine. Do not disconnect any A/C hoses from compressor. Temporarily support compressor to gain access to Engine Coolant Temperature Sensor (ECT).

4. Disconnect the electrical connector from ECT sensor.

5. Remove the ECT sensor from cylinder block.

To install:

6. Apply thread sealant to sensor threads.

7. Install the ECT sensor to engine cylinder block.

8. Tighten the sensor to 97.3 inch lbs. (11 Nm).

9. Connect the electrical connector to ECT sensor.

10. Install air conditioning compressor.

11. Install the drive belt.

12. Fill the cooling system.

TESTING

2.7L, 3.5L & 5.7L Engines

See Figure 198.

1. Turn the ignition off.

2. Disconnect the Engine Coolant Temperature Sensor (ECT) harness connector.

3. Turn the ignition on.

4. With a scan tool, read the ECT sensor voltage.

5. The sensor voltage should be approximately 5.0 volts (plus or minus .1 volt) with the connector disconnected.

6. Turn the ignition off.

7. Connect a jumper wire between the (K2) Engine Coolant Temperature Sensor (ECT) signal circuit and the (K900) sensor ground circuit in the ECT harness connector.

8. Turn the ignition on.

9. With a scan tool, read the voltage.

10. The sensor voltage should be approximately 0.0 volts (plus or minus .1 volt) with the jumper wire in place.

11. If voltage is present as stated suspect faulty ECT sensor.

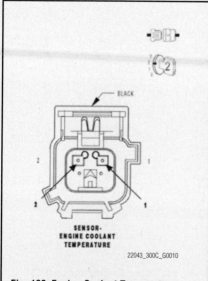

Fig. 198 Engine Coolant Temperature Sensor (ECT) electrical connector

HEATED OXYGEN (HO2S) SENSOR

LOCATION

2.7L, 3.5L & 5.7L Engines

See Figure 199.

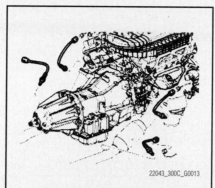

Fig. 199 Heated Oxygen (HO2S) Sensors location view

The engines uses two Heated Oxygen (HO2S) Sensors, one in each exhaust manifold. Refer to the illustration for typical HO2S locations if equipped with four oxygen sensors.

OPERATION

The HO2S detects the presence of oxygen in the exhaust and produces a variable voltage according to the amount of oxygen detected. A high concentration of oxygen (lean air/fuel ratio) in the exhaust produces a voltage signal less than 0.4 volt. A low concentration of oxygen (rich air/fuel ratio) produces a voltage signal greater than 0.6 volt. The HO2S provides feedback to the PCM indicating air/fuel ratio in order to achieve a near stoichiometric air/fuel ratio of 14.7:1during closed loop engine operation. The HO2S generates a voltage between 0.0 and 1.1 volts.

Embedded with the sensing element is the HO2S heater. The heating element heats the sensor to a temperature of 800°C (1,472°F). At approximately 300°C (572°F) the engine can enter closed loop operation. The PCM turns the heater on by providing the ground when the correct conditions occur. The heater allows the engine to enter closed loop operation sooner.

REMOVAL & INSTALLATION

2.7L, 3.5L & 5.7L Engines

❋❋ WARNING

Never apply any type of grease to the Heated Oxygen (HO2S) Sensors electrical connector, or attempt any soldering of the sensor wiring harness.

1. Raise and support vehicle.

2. Disconnect wire connector from HO2S sensor.

➡**When disconnecting sensor electrical connector, do not pull directly on wire going into sensor.**

3. Remove the HO2S sensor with an oxygen sensor removal and installation tool.

4. Clean threads in exhaust pipe using appropriate tap.

To install:

5. Install the HO2S sensor and tighten to 30 ft. lbs. (41 Nm).

6. Connect the HO2S sensor wire connector.

7. Lower the vehicle.

TESTING

2.7L, 3.5L & 5.7L Engines

See Figure 200.

This procedure checks the heater circuit of the HO2S.

1. Warm up the engine until operating temperature is reached.

2. Turn the ignition off.

3. Wait a minimum of 8 minutes to allow the O2 Sensor to cool down before continuing the test. Allow the O2 Sensor voltage to stabilize between 4.6–5.0 volts.

4. With the ignition on, engine not running.

5. Install a scan tool, actuate the HO2S heater test.

6. With the scan tool, monitor O2 Sensor voltage for at least 2 minutes.

7. If the voltage stays above 4.5 volts, turn the ignition off. (If not problem maybe intermittent).

8. Allow the O2 sensor to cool down to room temperature.

9. Disconnect the HO2S sensor harness connector.

10. Measure the resistance of the O2 heater element, between the HO2S heater control terminal and the O2 heater ground terminal in the HO2S sensor connector.

11. HO2S heater element resistance values should be measured at 21.1°C (70°F). The resistance value will vary with different temperature values.

12. The resistance of the HO2S sensor heater element should be between 2.0–30.0 ohms.

13. If the resistance is not as stated replace the HO2S sensor.

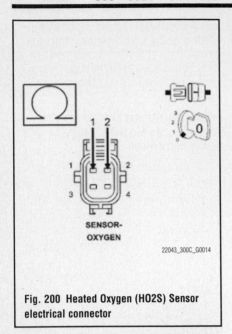

Fig. 200 Heated Oxygen (HO2S) Sensor electrical connector

INTAKE AIR TEMPERATURE (IAT) SENSOR

LOCATION

2.7L, 3.5L & 5.7L Engines

See Figure 201.

The Inlet Manifold Air Temperature (IAT) sensor is installed into the rubber air intake hose.

OPERATION

The Intake Air Temperature (IAT) Sensor provides an input voltage to the Powertrain Control Module (PCM) indicating the density of the air entering the intake manifold based upon intake manifold temperature. At key-on, a 5-volt power circuit is supplied to the sensor from the PCM. The sensor is grounded at the PCM through a low-noise, sensor-return circuit. The resistance values of the IAT sensor are the same as for the Engine Coolant Temperature (ECT) sensor.

The PCM uses this input to calculate the following:

• Injector pulse-width
• Adjustment of spark timing (to help prevent spark knock with high intake manifold air-charge temperatures).

REMOVAL & INSTALLATION

2.7L, 3.5L & 5.7L Engines

1. Disconnect negative battery cable.
2. Unlock the Inlet Manifold Air Temperature (IAT) sensor electrical connector.
3. Remove electrical connector from sensor
4. Note the orientation of the sensor.
5. Remove the sensor from air inlet hose.

To install:

6. Install the IAT sensor. Rotate for proper orientation of sensor.

7. Install the electrical connector and lock.
8. Connect negative battery cable.

TESTING

2.7L, 3.5L & 5.7L Engines

See Figure 202.

1. If possible, allow the vehicle to sit with the ignition off for more than 480 minutes in an environment where the temperature is consistent and above 19.4°F (-7°C).
2. With a scan tool, select View DTCs.
3. If an Intake Air Temperature (IAT) Sensor code is present, turn the ignition off.
4. Disconnect the Intake Air Temperature Sensor harness connector.
5. Turn the ignition on.
6. With a scan tool, read the IAT sensor voltage.
7. The sensor voltage should be approximately 5.0 volts (plus or minus .1 volt) with the connector disconnected. If not check the signal circuit for an open or high resistance.
8. If the sensor voltage was approximately 5.0 volts (plus or minus .1 volt), turn the ignition off.
9. Connect a jumper wire between the (K21) IAT Signal circuit and the (K900) Sensor Ground circuit in the Intake Air Temperature Sensor harness connector.
10. Turn the ignition on.
11. With a scan tool, read the IAT sensor voltage.
12. The sensor voltage should be approximately 0.0 volts (plus or minus .1 volt) with the jumper wire in place.

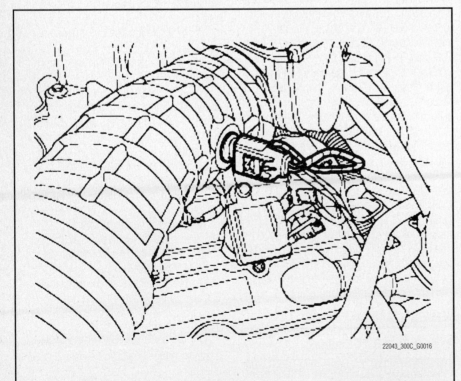

Fig. 201 Inlet Manifold Air Temperature (IAT) sensor location 2.7L engine; other engines similar

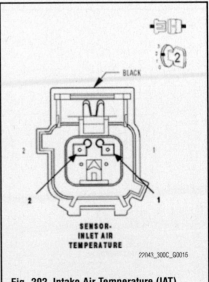

Fig. 202 Intake Air Temperature (IAT) Sensor harness connector

13. If the scan tool displays the voltage as described above suspect faulty IAT sensor.

KNOCK SENSOR (KS)

LOCATION

2.7L & 3.5L Engine

The Knock Sensor (KS) screws into the cylinder block, directly below the intake manifold.

5.7L Engine

See Figure 203.

Two sensors are used. Each sensor is bolted to the outside of cylinder block below the exhaust manifold.

OPERATION

Two knock sensors are used; one for each cylinder bank. When the knock sensor detects a knock in one of the cylinders on the corresponding bank, it sends an input signal to the Powertrain Control Module (PCM). In response, the PCM retards ignition timing for all cylinders by a scheduled amount.

Knock sensors contain a piezoelectric material which constantly vibrates and sends an input voltage (signal) to the PCM while the engine operates. As the intensity of the crystal's vibration increases, the knock sensor output voltage also increases.

The voltage signal produced by the knock sensor increases with the amplitude of vibration. The PCM receives the knock sensor voltage signal as an input. If the signal rises above a predetermined level, the PCM will store that value in memory and retard ignition timing to reduce engine knock. If the knock sensor voltage exceeds a preset value, the PCM retards ignition timing for all cylinders. It is not a selective cylinder retard.

The PCM ignores knock sensor input during engine idle conditions. Once the engine speed exceeds a specified value, knock retard is allowed.

Knock retard uses its own short term and long term memory program. Long term memory stores previous detonation information in its battery—backed RAM. The maximum authority that long term memory has over timing retard can be calibrated.

Short term memory is allowed to retard timing up to a preset amount under all operating conditions (as long as rpm is above the minimum rpm) except at Wide Open Throttle (WOT). The PCM, using short term memory, can respond quickly to retard timing when engine knock is detected. Short term memory is lost any time the ignition key is turned off.

REMOVAL & INSTALLATION

2.7L Engine

1. Disconnect negative battery cable.
2. Remove the intake manifold.
3. Remove the passenger side cylinder head, refer to the engine section.
4. Disconnect the electrical connector from knock sensor.
5. Use a crow's foot socket to remove the knock sensor.

To install:

6. Install the knock sensor. Tighten sensor to 7 ft. lbs. (10 Nm).

✳✳ WARNING

Over or under tightening effects knock sensor performance resulting in possible improper spark control.

7. Attach the electrical connector to knock sensor.
8. Install the passenger side cylinder head, refer to the engine section.
9. Install the intake manifold.
10. Connect the negative battery cable.

3.5L Engine

1. Disconnect the negative battery cable.
2. Remove the upper intake manifold.
3. Disconnect the electrical connector.
4. Remove the knock sensor.

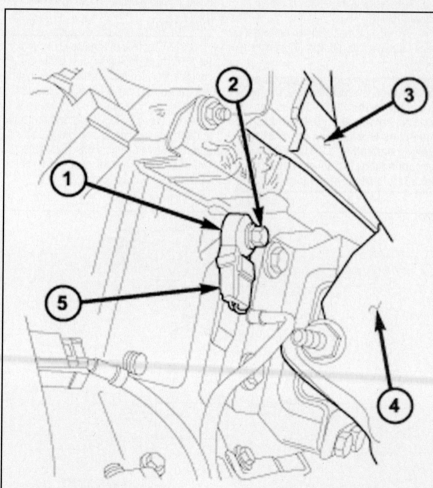

1. Knock Sensor
2. Mounting bolt
3. Exhaust manifold
4. Heat shield

22043_300C_G0017

Fig. 203 Knock Sensor (KS) location 5.7L engine

To install:

5. Install knock sensor. Tighten knock sensor to 15 ft. lbs. (20 Nm).

✳✳ WARNING

Over or under tightening effects knock sensor performance resulting in possible improper spark control.

6. Route the knock sensor wire in the proper location.

7. Install the intake manifold.

8. Reconnect knock sensor electrical connector.

9. Connect the negative battery cable.

5.7L Engine

1. Raise and support the vehicle.

2. Disconnect knock sensor electrical connector.

3. Remove the sensor mounting bolt. Note foam strip on bolt threads. This foam is used only to retain the bolts to sensors for plant assembly. It is not used as a sealant. Do not apply any adhesive, sealant or thread locking compound to these bolts.

4. Remove knock sensor from the engine block.

To install:

5. Thoroughly clean the knock sensor mounting hole.

6. Install knock sensor into cylinder block.

✳✳ WARNING

Over or under tightening the sensor mounting bolts will affect knock sensor performance, possibly causing improper spark control. Always use the specified torque when installing the knock sensors. The torque for the knock sensor bolt is relatively light for an 8mm bolt.

7. Install and tighten mounting bolt to 15 ft. lbs. (20 Nm).

8. Install the knock sensor electrical connector.

TESTING

2.7L, 3.5L & 5.7L Engines

See Figure 204.

1. Start the engine and allow it to reach normal operating temperature.

2. With the scan tool, select view DTCs.

➡ **It may be necessary to test drive the vehicle within the DTC monitoring conditions in order for this DTC to reset.**

3. If the DTC is Active or Pending at this time. Turn the ignition off.

4. Disconnect the Knock Sensor (KS) harness connector.

5. Disconnect the PCM harness connector.

6. With the ignition on, engine not running.

7. Measure the voltage on the (K42) KS number (1) signal circuit in the KS harness connector.

8. If there is any voltage present repair the short to voltage in the (K42) KS number (1) signal circuit.

9. If voltage was not present measure the resistance of the (K42) KS number (1) signal circuit from the KS harness connector to the appropriate terminal of pin out box tool 8815.

10. The resistance reading should be below 5.0 ohms.

11. If reading is not as stated repair the open in the (K42) KS number (1) signal circuit.

✳✳ WARNING

Do not probe the PCM harness connectors. Probing the PCM harness connectors will damage the PCM terminals resulting in poor terminal to pin connection. Install pin out box tool 8815 to perform diagnosis.

MANIFOLD ABSOLUTE PRESSURE (MAP) SENSOR

LOCATION

2.7L Engine

The Manifold Absolute Pressure (MAP) sensor is mounted to the rear of the throttle body into the top of the intake manifold.

3.5L Engine

The Manifold Absolute Pressure (MAP) sensor is mounted to the left of the throttle body into the top of the intake manifold.

5.7L Engine

The Manifold Absolute Pressure (MAP) sensor is mounted into the top rear of the intake manifold near the cowl hood seal.

OPERATION

The MAP sensor is used as an input to the Powertrain Control Module (PCM). It contains a silicon based sensing unit to provide data on the manifold vacuum that draws the air/fuel mixture into the combustion chamber. The PCM requires this information to determine injector pulse width and spark advance. When Manifold Absolute Pressure (MAP) equals Barometric pressure, the pulse width will be at maximum.

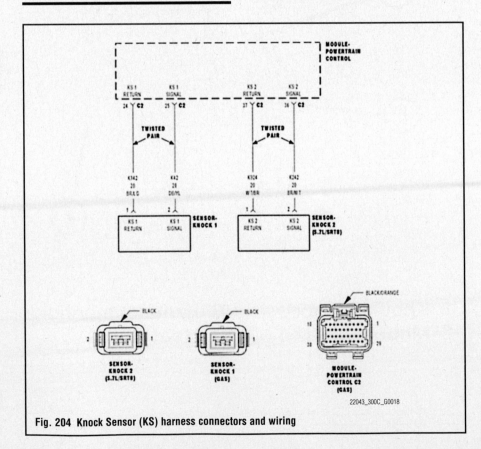

Fig. 204 Knock Sensor (KS) harness connectors and wiring

22043_300C_G0018

A 5 volt reference is supplied from the PCM and returns a voltage signal to the PCM that reflects manifold pressure. The zero pressure reading is 0.5V and full scale is 4.5V. For a pressure swing of 0-15 psi, the voltage changes 4.0V. To operate the sensor, it is supplied a regulated 4.8 to 5.1 volts. Ground is provided through the low-noise, sensor return circuit at the PCM.

The MAP sensor input is the number one contributor to fuel injector pulse width. The most important function of the MAP sensor is to determine barometric pressure. The PCM needs to know if the vehicle is at sea level or at a higher altitude, because the air density changes with altitude. It will also help to correct for varying barometric pressure. Barometric pressure and altitude have a direct inverse correlation; as altitude goes up, barometric goes down. At key-on, the PCM powers up and looks at MAP voltage, and based upon the voltage it sees, it knows the current barometric pressure (relative to altitude). Once the engine starts, the PCM looks at the voltage again, continuously every 12 milliseconds, and compares the current voltage to what it was at key-on. The difference between current voltage and what it was at key-on, is manifold vacuum.

As the altitude increases, the air becomes thinner (less oxygen). If a vehicle is started and driven to a very different altitude than where it was at key-on, the barometric pressure needs to be updated. Any time the PCM sees Wide Open Throttle (WOT), based upon Throttle Position Sensor (TPS) angle and RPM, it will update barometric pressure in the MAP memory cell. With periodic updates, the PCM can make its calculations more effectively.

The MAP sensor signal is provided from a single piezoresistive element located in the center of a diaphragm. The element and diaphragm are both made of silicone. As manifold pressure changes, the diaphragm moves causing the element to deflect, which stresses the silicone. When silicone is exposed to stress, its resistance changes. As manifold vacuum increases, the MAP sensor input voltage decreases proportionally. The sensor also contains electronics that condition the signal and provide temperature compensation.

The PCM recognizes a decrease in manifold pressure by monitoring a decrease in voltage from the reading stored in the barometric pressure memory cell. The MAP sensor is a linear sensor; meaning as pressure changes, voltage changes proportionately. The range of voltage output from the sensor is usually between 4.6 volts at sea level to as low as 0.3 volts at 26 in. of Hg. Barometric pressure is the pressure exerted by the atmosphere upon an object. At sea level on a standard day, no storm, barometric pressure is approximately 29.92 in Hg. For every 100 feet of altitude, barometric pressure drops 0.10 in. Hg. If a storm goes through, it can change barometric pressure from what should be present for that altitude. You should know what the average pressure and corresponding barometric pressure is for your area.

REMOVAL & INSTALLATION

2.7L, 3.5L & 5.7L Engines

1. Disconnect the negative battery cable.
2. Unlock the Manifold Absolute Pressure (MAP) Sensor electrical connector.
3. Disconnect the MAP sensor electrical connector.
4. Rotate the MAP sensor ¼ turn clockwise.
5. Pull up on the MAP sensor and remove from the intake manifold.

To install:

6. Clean the MAP sensor mounting hole at intake manifold.
7. Check the MAP sensor O-ring seal for cuts or tears.
8. Position the MAP sensor into intake manifold.
9. Rotate the MAP sensor ¼ turn clockwise for installation.
10. Connect the electrical connector to the MAP sensor.

TESTING

2.7L, 3.5L & 5.7L Engines

See Figure 205.

1. Scan for pending Manifold Absolute Pressure (MAP) Sensor codes, if codes are present turn off the ignition.
2. Disconnect the MAP Sensor harness connector.

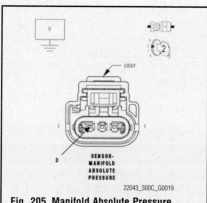

Fig. 205 Manifold Absolute Pressure (MAP) Sensor harness connector

3. Turn the ignition switch on, engine off.
4. Check pin (3) of the Map sensor harness connector for voltage supply.
5. The sensor voltage should be approximately 5.0 volts (plus or minus .1 volt) with the connector disconnected.
6. If the voltage was not as stated above repair open or high resistance in circuit (F856).

POWER CONTROL MODULE (PCM)

LOCATION

2.7L, 3.5L & 5.7L Engines
See Figure 206.

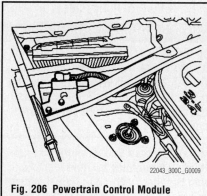

Fig. 206 Powertrain Control Module (PCM) location view

The Powertrain Control Module (PCM) is located in the engine compartment. The PCM is referred to as NGC.

OPERATION

The Powertrain Control Module (PCM) operates the fuel system. The PCM is a pre-programmed, triple microprocessor digital computer. It regulates ignition timing, air-fuel ratio, emission control devices, charging system, certain transmission features, speed control, air conditioning compressor clutch engagement and idle speed. The PCM can adapt its programming to meet changing operating conditions

The PCM receives input signals from various switches and sensors. Based on these inputs, the PCM regulates various engine and vehicle operations through different system components. These components are referred to as Powertrain Control Module (PCM) Outputs. The sensors and switches that provide inputs to the PCM are considered Powertrain Control Module (PCM) Inputs.

The PCM adjusts ignition timing based

upon inputs it receives from sensors that react to: engine rpm, manifold absolute pressure, engine coolant temperature, throttle position, transmission gear selection (automatic transmission), vehicle speed, power steering pump pressure, and the brake switch.

The PCM adjusts idle speed based on inputs it receives from sensors that react to: throttle position, vehicle speed, transmission gear selection, engine coolant temperature and from inputs it receives from the air conditioning clutch switch and brake switch.

Based on inputs that it receives, the PCM adjusts ignition coil dwell. The PCM also adjusts the generator charge rate through control of the generator field and provides speed control operation.

REMOVAL & INSTALLATION

2.7L, 3.5L & 5.7L Engines

> ❊❊ **WARNING**
>
> **To avoid possible voltage spike damage to Powertrain Control Module (PCM), ignition key must be off, and negative battery cable must be disconnected before unplugging PCM connectors.**

➡ Use the scan tool to reprogram new PCM with vehicles original Identification Number (VIN) and original vehicle mileage.

1. Disconnect the negative battery cable.
2. Remove the PCM bracket-to-body mounting bolt.
3. Lift up the PCM assembly.
4. Unlock and disconnect the electrical connectors from PCM.
5. Remove the assembly from vehicle.
6. Remove bracket from PCM.
7. Remove the rubber bumper from PCM.

To install:
8. Install rubber bumper to PCM back.
9. Check pins in electrical connectors for damage.
10. Repair pins as necessary.
11. Install the electrical connectors to PCM.
12. Install the mounting bracket to PCM.
13. Install the assembly to body.
14. Tighten mounting bolt to 80 inch lbs. (9 Nm).
15. Connect negative cable to battery.

TESTING

2.7L, 3.5L & 5.7L Engines

Service of the Powertrain Control Module (PCM) should consist of either replacement of the PCM or programming. If the diagnostic procedures call for the PCM to be replaced, the replacement PCM should be checked to ensure that the correct part is being used. If the correct part is being used, remove the faulty PCM and install the new service PCM.

1. Check for possible causes before replacement of PCM as follows:
   - (A209) Fused B (+) circuit open or shorted
   - (Z904) ground circuit open
   - (F202) Fused ignition switch output circuit open or shorted
   - (D65) Can C Bus (+) circuit open
   - (D64) Can C Bus (-) circuit open

THROTTLE POSITION SENSOR (TPS)

LOCATION

2.7L, 3.5L & 5.7L Engines

The Throttle Position Sensors (TPS) are integral to the throttle body assembly.

OPERATION

The PCM supplies approximately 5 volts to the TPS. The TPS output voltage (input signal to the PCM) represents the throttle blade position. The PCM receives an input signal voltage from the TPS. This will vary in an approximate range of from .26 volts at minimum throttle opening (idle), to 4.49 volts at wide open throttle. Along with inputs from other sensors, the PCM uses the TPS input to determine current engine operating conditions. In response to engine operating conditions, the PCM will adjust fuel injector pulse width and ignition timing.

REMOVAL & INSTALLATION

2.7L Engine

1. Disconnect negative cable from battery
2. Disconnect the inlet hose from the throttle body.
3. Disconnect the electrical connectors.
4. Disconnect vacuum hose.
5. Remove the 3 throttle body bolts.
6. Remove the throttle body.
7. Remove the throttle body gasket.
8. Clean the mating surfaces.

To install:

> ❊❊ **WARNING**
>
> **Do not use spray (carb) cleaners on any part of the throttle body. Do not apply silicone lubricants to any part of the throttle body.**

9. Install new throttle body gasket.
10. Install the throttle body and bolts.
11. Tighten bolts to 105 inch lbs. (11.9 Nm).
12. Connect the electrical connectors.
13. Connect all vacuum hoses.
14. Install inlet hose and tighten clamp.
15. Connect negative cable to battery.
16. A Scan Tool may be used to learn electrical parameters. Go to the miscellaneous menu, and then select ETC relearn. If the relearn is not preformed, a Diagnostic Trouble Code (DTC) will be set. If necessary, use a scan tool to erase any Diagnostic Trouble Codes (DTC's) from PCM.

3.5L Engine

1. Disconnect negative cable from battery
2. Remove the inlet hose from throttle body.
3. Disconnect all electrical connectors.
4. Disconnect vacuum hose.
5. Remove the throttle body support bracket.
6. Remove the throttle body and bolts.
7. Remove the throttle body gasket.
8. Clean the mating surfaces.

To install:

> ❊❊ **WARNING**
>
> **Do not use spray (carb) cleaners on any part of the throttle body. Do not apply silicone lubricants to any part of the throttle body.**

9. Install new throttle body gasket.
10. Install throttle body and bolts.
11. Tighten bolts to 105 inch lbs. (11.9 Nm).
12. Install the throttle body support bracket to the bottom of the throttle body. Tighten the bolts to 20 ft. lbs. (27.1 Nm).
13. Install inlet hose and tighten clamp.
14. Connect negative cable to battery.
15. A Scan Tool may be used to learn electrical parameters. Go to the miscellaneous menu, and then select ETC relearn. If the relearn is not preformed, a Diagnostic Trouble Code (DTC) will be set. If necessary, use a scan tool to erase any Diagnostic Trouble Codes (DTC's) from PCM.

5.7L Engine

> ❊❊ **WARNING**
>
> **Do not use spray (carb) cleaners on any part of the throttle body. Do not apply silicone lubricants to any part of the throttle body.**

1. Remove the rubber air duct at front of throttle body.

2. Disconnect the electrical connector at throttle body.

3. Remove four throttle body mounting bolts .

4. Remove throttle body from intake manifold.

5. Remove the throttle body gasket.

To install:

6. Clean mating surfaces of throttle body and intake manifold.

7. Install new throttle body gasket.

8. Install throttle body to intake manifold by positioning throttle body to manifold alignment pins.

9. Install and tighten four mounting bolts. Refer to Torque Specifications

10. Install the electrical connector.

11. Install the rubber air hose to throttle body.

12. A Scan Tool may be used to learn electrical parameters. Go to the miscellaneous menu, and then select ETC relearn. If the relearn is not preformed, a Diagnostic Trouble Code (DTC) will be set. If necessary, use a scan tool to erase any Diagnostic Trouble Codes (DTC's) from PCM.

TESTING

2.7L, 3.5L & 5.7L Engines
See Figure 207.

1. Scan for pending Throttle Position Sensor (TPS) codes, if codes are present turn off the ignition.

2. Disconnect the throttle body harness connector.

3. Turn the ignition switch on, engine off.

4. Measure the voltage of the (F855) 5 Volt Supply circuit in the Throttle Body harness connector pin (2).

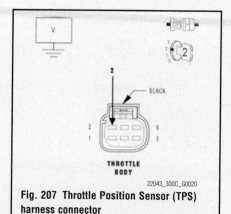

Fig. 207 Throttle Position Sensor (TPS) harness connector

5. If the voltage reading is not above 4.5 volts check and repair circuit (F855) for an open or high resistance problem.

VEHICLE SPEED SENSOR (VSS)

➡The Vehicle Speed Sensor (VSS) is also known as the Output Shaft Speed (OSS) sensor.

LOCATION
See Figure 208.

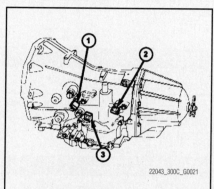

Fig. 208 Input (1) and Output (2) Speed Sensor (OSS) location

The Input and Output Speed Sensors are two-wire magnetic pickup devices that generate AC signals as rotation occurs. They are mounted in the left side of the transmission case and are considered primary inputs to the Transmission Control Module (TCM).

OPERATION

The Output Speed Sensor is a two—wire magnetic pickup devices that generate AC signals as rotation occurs. The Output Speed Sensor generates an AC signal in a similar fashion, though its coil is excited by rotation of the rear planetary carrier lugs. The TCM interprets this information as output shaft rpm.

REMOVAL & INSTALLATION

1. Raise the vehicle.

2. Place a suitable fluid catch pan under the transmission.

3. Remove the wiring connector from the output speed sensor.

➡The speed sensor bolt has a sealing patch applied from the factory. Be sure to reuse the same bolt.

4. Remove the bolt holding the output speed sensor to the transmission case.

5. Remove the output speed sensor from the transmission case.

To install:

6. Install the output speed sensor into the transmission case.

7. Install the bolt to hold the output speed sensor into the transmission case. Tighten the bolt to 80 inch lbs. (9 Nm).

8. Install the wiring connector onto the output speed sensor.

9. Lower the vehicle.

10. Verify the transmission fluid level. Add fluid as necessary.

TESTING

1. Start the engine in park.

2. Raise the drive wheels off of the ground.

✳✳ CAUTION

Properly support the vehicle. Be sure to keep hands and feet clear of rotating wheels. Firmly apply the brakes and place the transmission selector in drive.

3. Release the brakes and allow the drive wheels to spin freely.

4. With the scan tool, read the output rpm.

5. Is the Output rpm below 100.

6. Turn the ignition off to the lock position.

7. Remove the Ignition Switch Feed fuse from the TIPM.

➡Removal of the Ignition Switch Feed fuse from the TIPM will prevent the vehicle from being started in gear.

✳✳ CAUTION

The Ignition Switch Feed fuse must be removed from the TIPM. Failure to do so can result in personal injury or death.

8. Install the Transmission Simulator, Miller tool number 8333 and the Electronic Transmission Adapter kit.

9. Ignition on, engine not running

10. With the Transmission Simulator, set the "Input/Output Speed" switch to "ON" and the rotary switch to the "3000/1250" position.

11. With the scan tool , read the Input and Output rpm.

12. If the input rpm reads 3000 and the output rpm reads 1250 (within 50 rpm). Replace the Output Speed Sensor (OSS)

FUEL SYSTEM SERVICE PRECAUTIONS

Safety is the most important factor when performing not only fuel system maintenance but any type of maintenance. Failure to conduct maintenance and repairs in a safe manner may result in serious personal injury or death. Maintenance and testing of the vehicle's fuel system components can be accomplished safely and effectively by adhering to the following rules and guidelines.

• To avoid the possibility of fire and personal injury, always disconnect the negative battery cable unless the repair or test procedure requires that battery voltage be applied.

• Always relieve the fuel system pressure prior to disconnecting any fuel system component (injector, fuel rail, pressure regulator, etc.), fitting or fuel line connection. Exercise extreme caution whenever relieving fuel system pressure to avoid exposing skin, face and eyes to fuel spray. Please be advised that fuel under pressure may penetrate the skin or any part of the body that it contacts.

• Always place a shop towel or cloth around the fitting or connection prior to loosening to absorb any excess fuel due to spillage. Ensure that all fuel spillage (should it occur) is quickly removed from engine surfaces. Ensure that all fuel soaked cloths or towels are deposited into a suitable waste container.

• Always keep a dry chemical (Class B) fire extinguisher near the work area.

• Do not allow fuel spray or fuel vapors to come into contact with a spark or open flame.

• Always use a back-up wrench when loosening and tightening fuel line connection fittings. This will prevent unnecessary stress and torsion to fuel line piping.

• Always replace worn fuel fitting O-rings with new Do not substitute fuel hose or equivalent where fuel pipe is installed.

Before servicing the vehicle, make sure to also refer to the precautions in the beginning of this section as well.

RELIEVING FUEL SYSTEM PRESSURE

1. Before servicing the vehicle, refer to the precautions in the beginning of this section.
2. Remove fuel pump relay from Power Distribution Center (PDC). For location of relay, refer to label on underside of PDC cover.
3. Start and run engine until it stalls.
4. Attempt restarting engine until it will no longer run.
5. Turn the ignition key to OFF position.
6. Return fuel pump relay to PDC.
7. One or more Diagnostic Trouble Codes (DTC's) may have been stored in PCM memory due to fuel pump relay removal. A scan tool must be used to erase a DTC.

FUEL FILTER

REMOVAL & INSTALLATION

The fuel filter is replaceable only as part of the fuel pump module. Refer to that procedure for more information.

FUEL INJECTORS

REMOVAL & INSTALLATION

2.7L and 3.5L Engine

See Figure 209.

1. Before servicing the vehicle, refer to the precautions in the beginning of this section.

✳✳ CAUTION

The fuel system is under constant pressure even with engine off. Before servicing fuel injector(s), fuel system pressure must be released.

2. Release fuel system pressure.
3. Disconnect negative cable to battery.
4. Remove intake manifold plenum.
5. Lift Plenum up off of engine. Cover intake manifold to prevent foreign material from entering engine.
6. Disconnect fuel supply tube quick connect fittings at the rear of intake manifold.

➡**If the injector connectors are not tagged with their cylinder number, tag them to identify the correct cylinder.**

7. Disconnect electrical connectors at fuel injectors. Push red colored slider away from injector (1). While pushing slider, depress tab (2) and remove connector (3) from injector. The factory fuel injection wiring harness is numerically tagged (INJ 1, INJ 2, etc.) for injector position identification. If harness is not tagged, note wiring location before removal.
8. Remove fuel rail mounting bolts.
9. Lift fuel rail straight up off of the cylinder head.

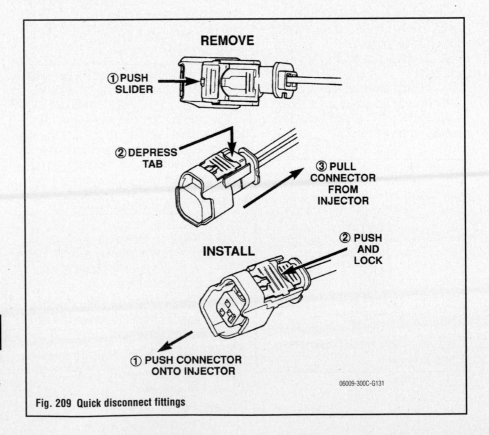

Fig. 209 Quick disconnect fittings

06009-300C-G131

10. Remove retaining clips from fuel injectors at fuel rail.

11. Remove fuel injectors.

12. Repeat for remaining injectors.

13. Check injector O-ring for damage. If O-ring is damaged, it must be replaced. Replace the injector clip if it is damaged.

To install:

14. Lightly lubricate the fuel injector O-rings with a couple drops of clean engine oil.

15. Install retaining clips on fuel injectors.

16. Push injectors into fuel injector rail until clips are in the correct position.

17. Position fuel rail over cylinder head, and push rail into place. Tighten fuel rail mounting bolts to 100 inch lbs. (11 Nm) torque.

18. Connect fuel supply tube quick connect fittings at the rear of intake manifold.

19. Connect electrical connectors to fuel injectors.

20. Install intake manifold plenum.

21. Connect negative cable to battery.

22. Use a scan tool to pressurize the fuel system. Check for leaks.

5.7L Engine

See Figures 210 and 211.

1. Before servicing the vehicle, refer to the precautions in the beginning of this section.

❋❋ CAUTION

The fuel system is under constant pressure even with engine off. Before servicing fuel rail, fuel system pressure must be released.

❋❋ WARNING

The left and right fuel rails are replaced as an assembly. Do not attempt to separate rail halves at connector tube. Due to design of tube, it does not use any clamps. Never attempt to install a clamping device of any kind to tube. When removing fuel rail assembly for any reason, be careful not to bend or kink tube.

2. Remove fuel tank filler tube cap.

3. Perform fuel system pressure release procedure.

4. Remove negative battery cable at battery.

5. Remove flex tube (air cleaner housing to engine).

6. Remove air resonator box at throttle body.

7. Disconnect all spark plug cables from all spark plugs and ignition coils. Do not remove cables from cable routing tray. Note original cable positions while removing.

8. Remove spark plug cable tray from engine by releasing 4 retaining clips. Remove tray and cables from engine as an assembly.

➡**Before removing or disconnecting any spark plug cables, note their original position. Remove cables one-at-a-time. To prevent ignition crossfire, spark plug cables must be placed in cable tray (routing loom) into their original position.**

An individual ignition coil is used at each cylinder. The coil mounts to the top of the valve cover with two bolts. The bottom of the coil is equipped with a rubber boot to seal the spark plug to the coil. Inside each rubber boot is a spring. The spring is used for a mechanical contact between the coil and the top of the spark plug.

9. Depending on which coil is being removed, the throttle body air intake tube or intake box may need to be removed to gain access to coil.

10. Unlock electrical connector by moving slide lock first. Press on release lock while pulling electrical connector from coil.

11. Disconnect secondary high-voltage cable from coil with a twisting action.

12. Clean area at base of coil with compressed air before removal.

13. Remove two mounting bolts (note that mounting bolts are retained to coil).

14. Carefully pull up coil from cylinder head opening with a slight twisting action.

15. Remove coil from vehicle.

16. Before installing spark plug cables to either the spark plugs or coils, or before installing a coil to a spark plug, apply dielectric grease to inside of boots.

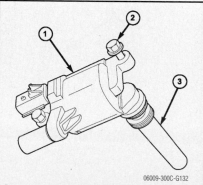

Fig. 210 Ignition coil (1), bolt (2), spark plug boot (3)—5.7L engine

06009-300C-G132

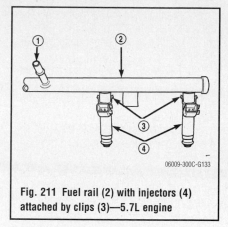

06009-300C-G133

Fig. 211 Fuel rail (2) with injectors (4) attached by clips (3)—5.7L engine

17. Disconnect fuel line latch clip and fuel line at fuel rail. A special tool will be necessary for fuel line disconnection.

18. Disconnect electrical connectors at all 8 fuel injectors. Push red colored slider away from injector (1). While pushing slider, depress tab (2) and remove connector (3) from injector. The factory fuel injection wiring harness is numerically tagged (INJ 1, INJ 2, etc.) for injector position identification. If harness is not tagged, note wiring location before removal.

19. Disconnect electrical connectors at all throttle body sensors.

20. Remove four fuel rail mounting bolts and hold-down clamps.

21. Gently rock and pull left side of fuel rail until fuel injectors just start to clear machined holes in intake manifold. Gently rock and pull right side of rail until injectors just start to clear intake manifold head holes. Repeat this procedure (left/right) until all injectors have cleared machined holes.

22. Remove fuel rail (with injectors attached) from engine.

23. Remove clip(s) retaining injector(s) to fuel rail.

24. Remove injector(s) from fuel rail.

To install:

25. Clean out fuel injector machined bores in intake manifold.

26. Apply a small amount of engine oil to each fuel injector O-ring. This will help in fuel rail installation.

27. Position fuel rail/fuel injector assembly to machined injector openings in intake manifold.

28. Guide each injector into intake manifold. Be careful not to tear injector O-rings.

29. Push right side of fuel rail down until fuel injectors have bottomed on shoulders. Push left fuel rail down until injectors have bottomed on shoulders.

30. Install 4 fuel rail hold-down clamps and 4 mounting bolts and. Torque to 100 inch lbs. (11 Nm).

31. Position spark plug cable tray (7) and cable assembly to intake manifold. Snap 4 cable tray retaining clips into intake manifold.

32. Install all cables to spark plugs and ignition coils.

33. Connect the electrical connector to throttle body.

34. Using compressed air, blow out any dirt or contaminants from around top of spark plug.

35. Before installing spark plug cables to either the spark plugs or coils, or before installing a coil to a spark plug, apply dielectric grease to inside of boots.

36. Position ignition coil into cylinder head opening and push boot onto spark plug. Twist coil into position.

37. Install two coil mounting bolts and tighten to 105 inch lbs. (12 Nm).

38. Connect electrical connector to coil and lock connector.

39. Install spark plug cables to coils. To prevent ignition crossfire, spark plug cables MUST be placed in cable tray (routing loom) into their original position. See the Specifications section of this chapter, following the Tune-up Chart, for correct wiring.

40. If necessary, install throttle body air tube.

41. Connect the electrical connector to throttle body.

42. Connect electrical connectors at all fuel injectors. Push connector onto injector and then push and lock red colored slider. Verify connector is locked to injector by lightly tugging on connector.

43. Connect fuel line latch clip and fuel line to fuel rail.

44. Install air resonator to throttle body (2 bolts).

45. Install flexible air duct to air box.

46. Connect the negative battery cable.

47. Start engine and check for leaks.

FUEL PUMP

REMOVAL & INSTALLATION

See Figures 212 through 215.

1. Before servicing the vehicle, refer to the precautions in the beginning of this section.

2. Release the fuel pressure.

3. Disconnect negative battery cable.

➡**The fuel level of the vehicle must be below ⅝ of a tank before you remove the module lock-rings. If it is above that you can spill fuel in the vehicle.**

4. Drain partial fuel from fuel tank through the filler tube. Use a hard nylon

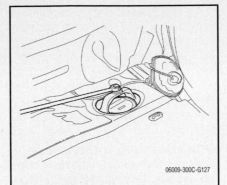

Fig. 212 Use special tool 9340 to remove left side module lock ring

06009-300C-G127

tube, with a 30° cut on the end, to push the check valve open to drain fuel from tank.

5. Remove the rear lower seat cushion.

6. Push seat back and up to remove seat cushion.

7. Fold back the foam pad covering access cover for modules.

8. Disconnect the electrical connector from left side module.

9. Mark the module orientation.

10. Use special tool 9340 to remove left side module lockring.

11. Drain fuel from left side of fuel tank. Lift module up enough to push hose into tank and drain. Do not spill fuel in interior of vehicle.

12. Disconnect the electrical connectors from the module top.

13. Remove the module top half.

14. Press in the fuel line release tab and pull up on fuel line.

15. Remove fuel line.

16. Remove fuel return line.

17. Tip module on its side to drain remaining fuel from reservoir and remove module from vehicle.

To install:

18. Install pump module into tank.

19. Connect fuel return lines to module.

20. Lines connected.

21. Connect fuel supply line to module and make sure it is locked in place.

22. Connect electrical connectors to bottom of module top, Install module top to module bottom.

23. Install module and align marks on the module for proper orientation.

24. Install module lockring.

25. Use special tool 9340 to tighten left side module lock ring.

26. Connect the electrical connector to left side module.

27. Install plastic access cover.

28. Fold the foam pad covering access cover for modules back into place.

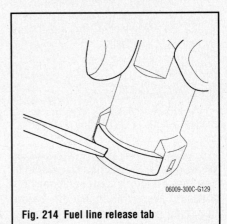

Fig. 214 Fuel line release tab

06009-300C-G129

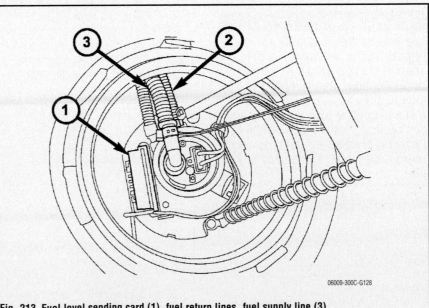

Fig. 213 Fuel level sending card (1), fuel return lines, fuel supply line (3)

06009-300C-G128

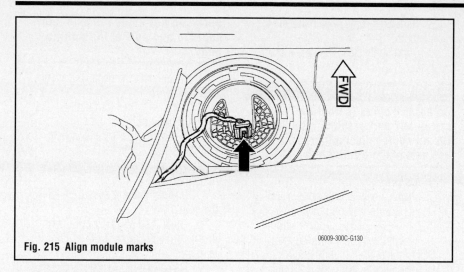

Fig. 215 Align module marks

06009-300C-G130

29. Install rear lower seat cushion
30. Fill fuel tank.
31. Connect negative battery cable.
32. Fill fuel tank. Use the scan tool to pressurize the fuel system. Check for leaks.

FUEL TANK

REMOVAL & INSTALLATION

1. Before servicing the vehicle, refer to the precautions in the beginning of this section.
2. Release the fuel pressure, refer to the (Fuel Pressure Release Procedure) in this section.
3. Disconnect negative battery cable.

➡**The fuel level of the vehicle must be below ⅝ of a tank before you remove the module lock-rings. If it is above that you can spill fuel in the vehicle.**

4. Drain the partial fuel from fuel tank through the filler tube. Use a hard nylon tube, with a 30° cut on the end, to push the check valve open to drain fuel from tank.
5. Remove the rear lower seat cushion.
6. Push seat back and up to remove seat cushion.
7. Fold back the foam pad covering access cover for modules.
8. Remove plastic access covers from floor pan right side.
9. Disconnect the fuel supply line from module.
10. Mark the module orientation.
11. Use the special tool number 9340 to remove right side module lock ring.
12. Drain fuel from right side of fuel tank. Lift module up enough to push hose into tank and drain. Do not spill fuel in interior of vehicle.
13. Disconnect the electrical connector from left side module.

14. Mark the module orientation.
15. Use special tool 9340 to remove left side module lock ring.
16. Drain fuel from left side of fuel tank. Lift module up enough to push hose into tank and drain. Do not spill fuel in interior of vehicle.
17. Install both module temporally, hand tighten the lock ring to hold modules in place.
18. Raise and support the vehicle.
19. Remove left rear tire.
20. Remove the inner splash shield.
21. Disconnect the filler tube vent line.
22. Remove clamp from filler tube.
23. Remove metal filler tube from rubber tube on fuel tank.
24. Remove the exhaust system.
25. Remove the drive shaft.
26. Remove the left underbody splash shield.
27. Remove the right underbody splash shield.
28. Disconnect the EVAP line in the right rear wheel well.
29. Disconnect vapor line.
30. Disconnect the fuel supply line.
31. Support fuel tank with transmission jack.
32. Fuel tank strap bolt locations.
33. Remove bolt for fuel tank strap.
34. Remove bolt for fuel tank strap.
35. Lower tank and pull filler tube vent line through bracket.
36. Lower Fuel tank and remove from vehicle.
37. If fuel tank is being replaced remove modules, control valve and lines.

To install:

38. If fuel tank was replaced install modules, control valve and lines.
39. Support fuel tank with transmission jack.
40. Raise tank and push filler tube vent line through bracket.

41. Install the bolts for fuel tank straps and tighten.
42. Connect vapor line.
43. Connect the fuel supply line.
44. Connect the EVAP line in the right rear wheel well.
45. Install the drive shaft.
46. Install the exhaust system.
47. Install metal filler tube to rubber tube on fuel tank.
48. Install clamp to filler tube and tighten
49. Connect the filler tube vent line.
50. Install the inner splash shield.
51. Install the left underbody splash shield.
52. Install the right underbody splash shield.
53. Install left rear tire.
54. Lower the vehicle.
55. Install module and align marks on the module for proper orientation.
56. Install the module lock-ring.
57. Use the special tool number 9340 to tighten left side module lock ring.
58. Connect the electrical connector to left side module and install plastic access cover.
59. Install module and align marks on the module for proper orientation.
60. Install the module lock-ring.
61. Use then special tool number 9340 to tighten right side module lock ring.
62. Connect the fuel supply line to module.
63. Install plastic access covers to floor pan right side.
64. Fold the foam pad covering access cover for modules back into place.
65. Install rear lower seat cushion
66. Fill the fuel tank.
67. Connect negative battery cable.
68. Fill fuel tank. Use the scan tool to pressurize the fuel system. Check for leaks.

IDLE SPEED

ADJUSTMENT

Idle speed is maintained by the Powertrain Control Module (PCM). No adjustment is necessary or possible.

THROTTLE BODY

REMOVAL & INSTALLATION

2.7L Engine

1. Disconnect the negative battery cable.
2. Disconnect inlet hose from the throttle body.
3. Label and detach all electrical connectors and vacuum hose(s).

4. Remove 3 throttle body bolts, then remove throttle body.

5. Thoroughly clean the gasket mating surfaces.

✳✳ WARNING

Do not use spray (carburetor) cleaners on any part of the throttle body. Do not apply silicone lubricants to any part of the throttle body.

To install:

6. Install a new throttle body gasket.

7. Install throttle body and bolts. Torque the bolts to 105 inch lbs. (11.9 Nm).

8. Connect the electrical connectors.

9. Connect vacuum hoses.

10. Install inlet hose and tighten clamp.

11. Connect negative cable to battery.

➡ **A Scan Tool may be used to learn electrical parameters. Go to the Miscellaneous menu, and then select ETC Relearn. If the relearn is not preformed, a Diagnostic Trouble Code (DTC) will be set. If necessary, use a scan tool to erase any Diagnostic Trouble Codes (DTC's) from PCM.**

3.5L Engine

1. Disconnect the negative battery cable.

2. Disconnect inlet hose from the throttle body.

3. Label and detach all electrical connectors and vacuum hose(s).

4. Remove the throttle body support bracket.

5. Remove throttle body bolts and the throttle body.

6. Thoroughly clean the gasket mating surfaces.

✳✳ WARNING

Do not use spray (carburetor) cleaners on any part of the throttle body. Do not apply silicone lubricants to any part of the throttle body.

To install:

7. Install a new throttle body gasket.

8. Install the throttle body and torque the bolts to 105 inch lbs. (11.9 Nm).

9. Install the throttle body support bracket to the bottom of the throttle body. Tighten the bolts to 20 ft. lbs. (27 Nm).

10. Connect the vacuum hoses and electrical connectors.

11. Install inlet hose and tighten clamp.

12. Connect negative cable to battery.

➡ **A Scan Tool may be used to learn electrical parameters. Go to the Miscellaneous menu, and then select ETC Relearn. If the relearn is not preformed, a Diagnostic Trouble Code (DTC) will be set. If necessary, use a scan tool to erase any Diagnostic Trouble Codes (DTC's) from PCM.**

5.7L Engine

✳✳ WARNING

Do not use spray (carburetor) cleaners on any part of the throttle

body. Do not apply silicone lubricants to any part of the throttle body.

1. Disconnect the negative battery cable.

2. Remove rubber air duct from the front of throttle body.

3. Detach the electrical connector from the throttle body.

4. Remove the four throttle body mounting bolts.

5. Remove throttle body from intake manifold.

6. Clean and check condition of throttle body O-ring at front of intake manifold.

7. Clean mating surfaces of throttle body and intake manifold (1).

To install:

8. Install throttle body to intake manifold by positioning throttle body to manifold alignment pins.

9. Install and tighten four mounting bolts to 105 inch lbs. (11.9 Nm).

10. Attach the electrical connector.

11. Install the rubber air hose to throttle body.

➡ **A Scan Tool may be used to learn electrical parameters. Go to the Miscellaneous menu, and then select ETC Relearn. If the relearn is not preformed, a Diagnostic Trouble Code (DTC) will be set. If necessary, use a scan tool to erase any Diagnostic Trouble Codes (DTC's) from PCM.**

HEATING & AIR CONDITIONING SYSTEM

BLOWER MOTOR

REMOVAL & INSTALLATION
See Figures 216 and 217.

✳✳ CAUTION

On vehicles equipped with airbags, disable the airbag system before attempting any steering wheel, steering column, or instrument panel component diagnosis or service. Disconnect and isolate the negative battery (ground) cable, then wait two minutes for the airbag system capacitor to discharge before performing further diagnosis or service. This is the only sure way to disable the airbag system. Failure to take the proper precautions could result in accidental airbag deploy-

ment and possible personal injury or death.

1. Disconnect and isolate the negative battery cable.

2. Remove the instrument panel silencer from the passenger side of the instrument panel, as follows:

　a. Remove the two push-pins that secure the instrument panel silencer to the instrument panel.

　b. Pull the instrument panel silencer rearward to disengage it from the brackets located near the dash panel.

　c. Remove the instrument panel silencer from the vehicle.

3. Disengage the wire harness connector locking tab and disconnect the wire harness connector and wire harness retainers from the blower motor.

4. Remove the four screws that secure the blower motor to the HVAC housing.

5. Remove the blower motor from HVAC housing.

To install:

6. Position the blower motor into the HVAC housing.

7. Install the four screws that secure the blower motor to the HVAC housing. Tighten the screws to 20 inch lbs. (2.2 Nm).

8. Attach the wire harness connector to the blower motor and engage the wire harness connector locking tab.

9. Install the HVAC wire harness retainers onto the blower motor.

10. Install the instrument panel silencer onto the passenger side of the instrument panel, as follows:

　a. Position the instrument panel silencer into the vehicle.

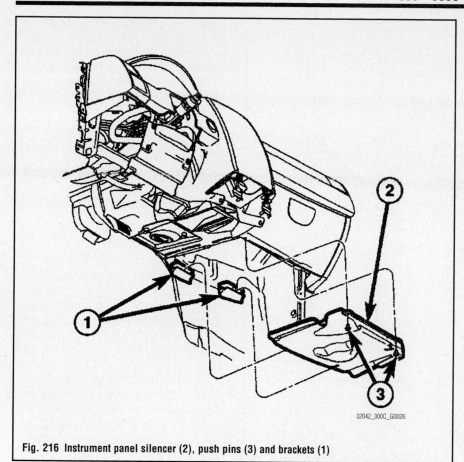

Fig. 216 Instrument panel silencer (2), push pins (3) and brackets (1)

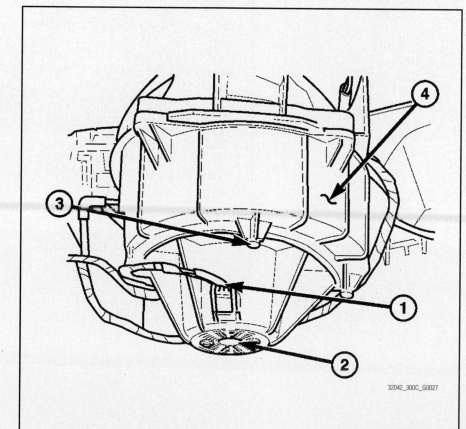

Fig. 217 Blower motor (2), harness connector (1), retaining screws (3) and HVAC housing (4)

b. Install the instrument panel silencer above the brackets located near the dash panel.

c. Install the two push-pins that secure the instrument panel silencer to the instrument panel.

11. Reconnect the negative battery cable.

HEATER CORE

REMOVAL & INSTALLATION

See Figures 218 and 219.

The heater core is mounted into the driver's side of HVAC air distribution housing, located behind the instrument panel.

✳✳ CAUTION

On vehicles equipped with airbags, disable the airbag system before attempting any steering wheel, steering column, or instrument panel component diagnosis or service. Disconnect and isolate the negative battery (ground) cable, then wait two minutes for the airbag system capacitor to discharge before performing further diagnosis or service. This is the only sure way to disable the airbag system. Failure to take the proper precautions could result in accidental airbag deployment and possible personal injury or death.

1. Before servicing the vehicle, refer to the precautions in the beginning of this section.

2. Drain the engine cooling system

3. Disconnect and isolate the negative battery cable.

4. Carefully disconnect the heater hoses from the heater core tubes.

5. Remove the two push-pins (4) that secure the instrument panel silencer (1) to the instrument panel bracket (2).

6. Pull the instrument panel silencer rearward to disengage it from the brackets (3) located near the dash panel.

7. Remove the instrument panel silencer from the vehicle.

8. Remove the blend door actuator from the driver's side of the HVAC air distribution housing.

9. Remove the two screws that secure the flange to the front of the HVAC housing near the dash panel.

10. Remove the flange from the HVAC housing.

➡Take proper precautions to protect the carpeting from spilled engine coolant. Have absorbent toweling readily available to clean up any spills.

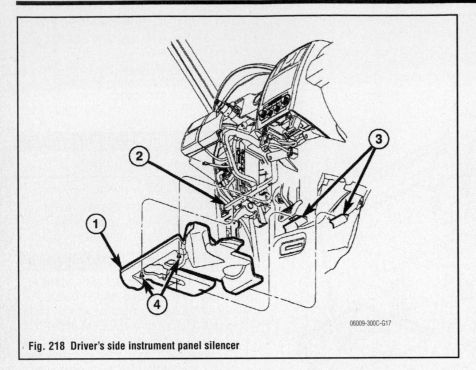

Fig. 218 Driver's side instrument panel silencer

06009-300C-G17

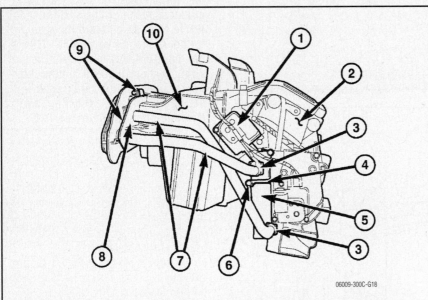

06009-300C-G18

Fig. 219 HVAC unit: (1) blend door actuator, (2) air distribution unit, (3) heater core tube retaining clamps, (4) heater core retaining bracket, (5) heater core, (6) screw, (7) heater core tubes, (8) flange, (9) screws (10) HVAC unit

11. Remove the retaining clamps that secure the heater core tubes to the heater core.

12. Disconnect the heater core tubes from the heater core and remove and discard the O-ring seals.

13. Carefully pull the heater core tubes through the dash panel.

14. Install plugs in, or tape over the opened heater core ports.

15. Remove the screw that secures the heater core retaining bracket to the driver's side of the HVAC air distribution housing.

16. Remove the heater core retaining bracket from the air distribution housing.

17. Carefully pull the heater core out of the air distribution housing.

To install:

18. Carefully install the heater core into the driver's side of the HVAC air distribution housing.

19. Install heater core retaining bracket onto the air distribution housing.

20. Install the screw that secures the heater core retaining bracket onto the air distribution housing. Tighten the screw to 20 inch lbs. (2.2 Nm).

21. Remove the tape or plugs from the heater core ports.

22. Lubricate new rubber O-ring seals with clean engine coolant and install them onto the heater core tube fittings. Use only the specified O-rings as they are made of a special material for the engine cooling system.

23. Install the heater core tubes through the dash panel and onto the heater core.

24. Install the two retaining clamps that secure the heater core tubes to the heater core. Make sure that the clamps are installed correctly and securely.

25. Install the flange over the heater core tubes and onto the HVAC housing near the dash panel.

26. Install the two screws that secure the flange to the HVAC housing. Tighten the screws to 20 inch lbs. (2.2 Nm).

27. Install the blend door actuator to the driver's side of the air distribution housing.

28. Position the instrument panel silencer into the vehicle.

29. Install the instrument panel silencer above the brackets located near the dash panel.

30. Install the two push-pins that secure the instrument panel silencer to the instrument panel bracket.

31. Connect the heater hoses to the heater core tubes.

32. Connect the negative battery cable.

33. If the heater core is being replaced, flush the cooling system.

34. Refill the engine cooling system.

STEERING

POWER STEERING GEAR

REMOVAL & INSTALLATION

2WD

See Figures 220 through 223.

1. Before servicing the vehicle, refer to the precautions in the beginning of this section.

2. Disconnect and isolate battery negative cable from battery post.

3. Siphon power steering fluid from pump reservoir.

4. Raise and support vehicle.

5. Remove wheel mounting nuts, then both front tire and wheel assemblies.

❋ WARNING

When loosening jam nut and rotating inner tie rod, use care not to twist bellows at inner tie rod. Remove clamp at inner tie rod and make sure bellows moves freely before rotating inner tie rod.

6. Loosen tie rod jam nut (3) at each outer tie rod (5).

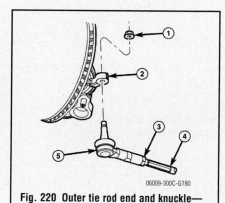

Fig. 220 Outer tie rod end and knuckle— 2WD

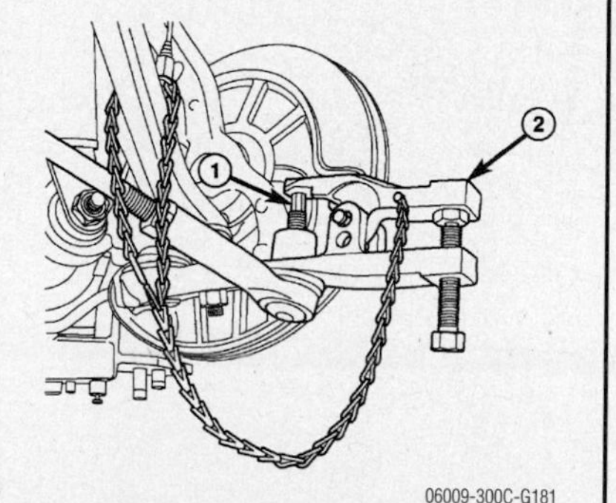

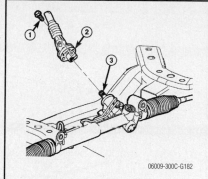

06009-300C-G182

Fig. 222 Remove the steering coupling from the gear—2WD

7. Remove outer tie rod nut (1) at each knuckle (2).

8. Using Remover (2), Special Tool 9630, separate outer tie rod (1) from each knuckle.

9. Remove steering coupling (2) pinch bolt (1) at steering gear (3).

10. Unthread pressure hose tube nut from steering gear. Remove pressure hose from steering gear.

11. Unthread return hose tube nut from steering gear. Remove return hose from steering gear.

12. Remove steering gear mounting bolts.

13. If necessary, remove outer tie rods from gear. Count number of revolutions off for each tie rod for reference upon installation to replacement gear.

To install:

14. If necessary, install outer tie rods from original gear to replacement inner tie rods. Install each outer tie rod same amount of threads as it was installed on original gear.

This will get toe setting close, saving some time when toe is set later in this procedure.

15. Lift steering gear into mounted position and install steering gear mounting bolts. Tighten bolts to 70 ft. lbs. (95 Nm) torque.

➡**Always use a new O-ring on the ends of the steering hoses.**

16. Lubricate new O-ring on end of return hose with clean power steering fluid.

17. Install return hose to steering gear. Tighten tube nut to 35 ft. lbs. (47 Nm) torque.

18. Lubricate new O-ring on end of pressure hose with clean power steering fluid.

19. Install pressure hose to steering gear. Tighten tube nut to 35 ft. lbs. (47 Nm) torque.

❋❋ WARNING

Prior to coupling installation, make sure gear is centered in its travel to match clockspring centering in steering column.

20. Align coupling with input shaft and install steering coupling. Install new pinch bolt. Tighten bolt to 40 ft. lbs. (54 Nm) torque.

21. Install each outer tie rod end to its knuckle. Install nuts and tighten to 63 ft. lbs. (85 Nm) torque.

22. Install tire and wheel assemblies. Tighten wheel mounting nuts to 110 ft. lbs. (150 Nm) torque.

23. Lower vehicle.

24. Connect battery negative cable to battery post. It is important that this is performed properly.

06009-300C-G181

Fig. 221 Removing outer tie rod end from the knuckle with tool 9630

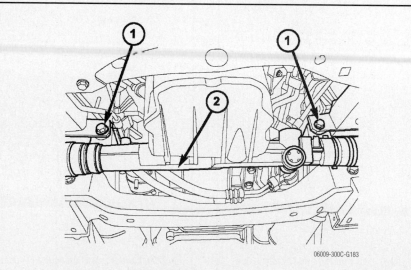

06009-300C-G183

Fig. 223 Steering gear (2) mounting bolts (1) —2WD

25. Fill pump reservoir with fluid and perform pump initial operation procedure.

26. Perform wheel alignment setting toe to specifications.

AWD

See Figures 224 through 227.

1. Before servicing the vehicle, refer to the precautions in the beginning of this section.

2. Disconnect and isolate battery negative cable from battery post.

3. Siphon power steering fluid from pump reservoir.

4. Raise and support vehicle.

5. Remove wheel mounting nuts, then both front tire and wheel assemblies.

✳✳ WARNING

When loosening jam nut and rotating inner tie rod, use care not to twist bellows at inner tie rod.

6. Remove clamp (2) at inner tie rod (3) and make sure bellows moves freely before rotating inner tie rod.

7. Loosen tie rod jam nut (1) at each outer tie rod (4).

8. Remove outer tie rod end nut at each knuckle.

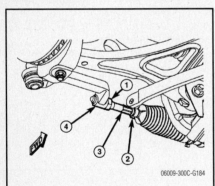

Fig. 224 Inner-to-outer tie rod connection—AWD

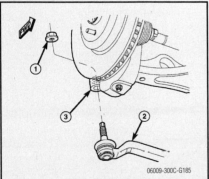

Fig. 225 Outer tie rod end (2) to knuckle (3) connection—AWD

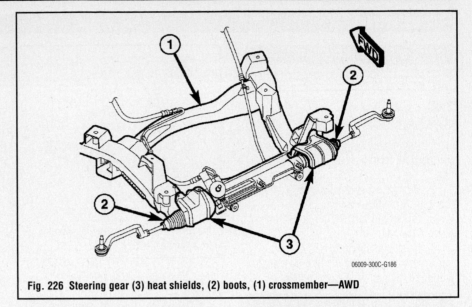

Fig. 226 Steering gear (3) heat shields, (2) boots, (1) crossmember—AWD

9. Using Remover, Special Tool 9630, separate outer tie rod from each knuckle.

10. Remove steering coupling pinch bolt at steering gear.

11. Unthread return hose tube nut from steering gear. Remove return hose from steering gear.

12. Unthread pressure hose tube nut from steering gear. Remove pressure hose from steering gear.

13. Remove mounting screws, then heat shield above each inner tie rod bellows.

14. Remove steering gear upper mounting bolt and nut.

15. Remove steering gear lower mounting bolts.

16. Remove steering gear.

17. If necessary, remove outer tie rods from gear. Count number of revolutions off for each tie rod for reference upon installation to replacement gear.

To install:

18. If necessary, install outer tie rods from original gear to replacement inner tie rods. Install each outer tie rod same amount of threads as it was installed on original gear. This will get toe setting close, saving some time when toe is set later in this procedure.

19. Lift steering gear into mounted position and install steering gear lower mounting bolts. Install upper mounting bolt and nut. Tighten all bolts to 75 ft. lbs. (102 Nm) torque.

20. Install heat shield above each inner tie rod bellows. Tighten screws to 89 inch lbs. (10 Nm) torque.

➡**Always use a NEW O-ring on the ends of the steering hoses.**

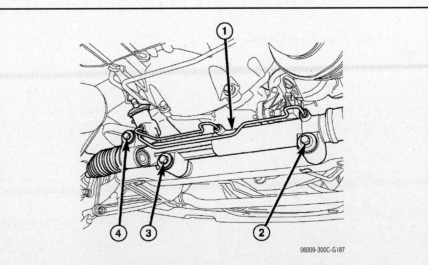

Fig. 227 Steering gear mounting (1) gear, (2, 3) lower mounting bolts, (4) upper mounting bolt—AWD

21. Lubricate NEW O-ring on end of pressure hose with clean power steering fluid.

22. Install pressure hose to steering gear. Tighten tube nut to 35 ft. lbs. (47 Nm) torque.

23. Lubricate NEW O-ring on end of return hose with clean power steering fluid.

24. Install return hose to steering gear. Tighten tube nut to 35 ft. lbs. (47 Nm) torque.

25. Align splines and install steering coupling to steering gear shaft. Install NEW pinch bolt. Tighten bolt to 40 ft. lbs. (54 Nm) torque.

26. Install each outer tie rod end to its knuckle. Install nut and tighten to 63 ft. lbs. (85 Nm) torque.

27. Install tire and wheel assemblies. Tighten wheel mounting nuts to 110 ft. lbs. (150 Nm) torque.

28. Lower vehicle.

POWER STEERING PUMP

REMOVAL & INSTALLATION

2.7L & 3.5L Engines

See Figures 228 through 231.

1. Disconnect and isolate battery negative cable (2) from battery post.

2. Siphon power steering fluid from pump reservoir.

3. Remove the air cleaner housing and inlet tube to throttle body.

4. Remove the serpentine drive belt.

5. Remove the hose clamp, then the supply hose from pump.

6. Unthread the tube nut, then remove pressure hose from pump.

7. Remove three pump mounting bolts through access holes in pulley.

8. Remove pump from engine bracket.

⁂ WARNING

Do not hammer on power steering pump pulley or shaft to remove power steering pump pulley. This will damage pulley and power steering pump.

9. If necessary, remove the pulley as follows:

a. Mount Puller, Special Tool C-4333, on power steering pump pulley.

b. Mount Puller (with power steering pump) in a vise as shown; Do not mount pump in vise. Placing Puller in vise will keep shaft of pump from turning while removing pulley and help keep tension on Puller and pulley hub.

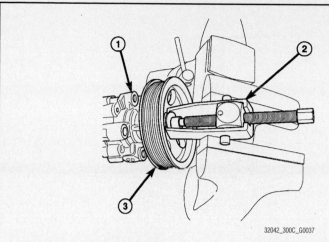

Fig. 228 View of the puller (2) installed on the power steering pump pulley. Mount the puller with the pump (1) in the vise as shown

c. Tighten Puller and remove pulley from shaft of power steering pump.

➡ **Inspect pulley. Replace if pulley is bent, cracked, or loose.**

To install:

⁂ WARNING

Do not hammer on power steering pump pulley or pump shaft to install pulley. This action will damage pulley and power steering pump.

10. If the pulley was removed, perform the following:

a. Place power steering pump pulley squarely on end of power steering pump shaft.

b. Place Installation Spacer, Special Tool 6936, on top of pump pulley.

➡ **Later build pumps (vehicles built on or after 1/3/05) feature a shaft with internal threads that are not as deep as earlier production, thus requiring a stack of washers, approximately 0.5 in. (13mm) thickness, placed over Spacer 6936, before mounting Installer C-4063C on the pump. To know if a replacement pump requires the stack of washers, measure the depth of the shaft hole. A later build pump will have a depth of 0.78 in. (20mm) while an earlier build pump will have a depth of 1.25 in. (32mm).**

c. Thread Installer, Special Tool C-4063C, completely into internal threads of power steering pump shaft, then rotate Installer Nut down against Spacer on pump pulley.

d. Ensuring that special tools and pulley remain aligned with pump shaft,

tighten Installer Nut, forcing pulley onto power steering pump shaft until Spacer comes in contact with end of pump shaft. When Spacer is against shaft of power steering pump, Installer Nut will no longer rotate.

e. Remove special tools from power steering pump.

11. Align the power steering pump with mounting holes on engine bracket.

12. Install three pump mounting bolts through access holes in pulley and engine bracket. Tighten bolts to 21 ft. lbs. (28 Nm).

➡ **Always use a NEW O-ring on the end of the pressure hose.**

13. Lubricate NEW O-ring on end of pressure hose with clean power steering fluid.

14. Connect the pressure hose to pump. Tighten the pressure hose tube nut to 35 ft. lbs. (47 Nm) torque.

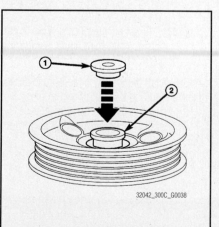

Fig. 229 Place Installation Spacer (1), Special Tool 6936, on top of pump pulley (2)

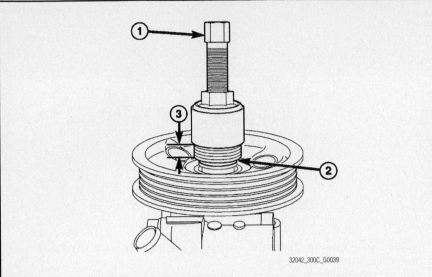

Fig. 230 Later build pumps have a shaft with internal threads that are not as deep as earlier production, thus requiring a stack of washers, approximately 0.5 in. (13mm) thickness (3), placed over Spacer 6936 (2), before mounting Installer C-4063C (1) on the pump

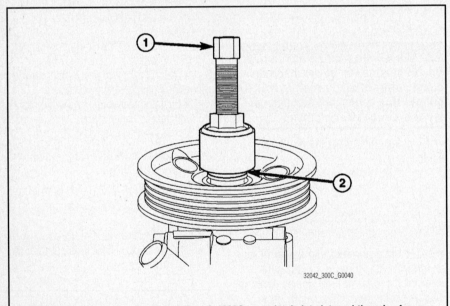

Fig. 231 Thread Installer (1), Special Tool C-4063C, completely into internal threads of power steering pump shaft, then rotate Installer Nut down against Spacer (2) on pump pulley

15. Install the supply hose on the pump. Install the clamp securing hose in place.

16. Install serpentine drive belt.

17. Install air cleaner housing and inlet tube.

18. Connect battery negative cable to battery post. It is important that this is performed properly.

19. Fill the power steering pump reservoir with fluid and perform pump initial operation procedure.

5.7L Engine
See Figures 228 through 232.

1. Disconnect and isolate the negative battery cable from battery post.

2. Siphon power steering fluid from pump reservoir.

3. Remove the air cleaner housing and inlet tube to throttle body.

4. Remove the serpentine drive belt, as outlined in the Engine Mechanical Section.

5. Remove the hose clamp, then the supply hose from pump.

6. Unthread the tube nut, then remove pressure hose from pump.

7. Remove three pump mounting bolts through access holes in pulley.

8. Remove the power steering pump from the engine.

    f. Mount Puller, Special Tool C-4333, on power steering pump pulley.

    g. Mount Puller (with power steering pump) in a vise as shown; Do not mount pump in vise. Placing Puller in vise will keep shaft of pump from turning while removing pulley and help keep tension on Puller and pulley hub.

    h. Tighten Puller and remove pulley from shaft of power steering pump.

➡**Inspect pulley. Replace if pulley is bent, cracked, or loose.**

To install:

✳✳ WARNING

Do not hammer on power steering pump pulley or pump shaft to install pulley. This action will damage pulley and power steering pump.

9. If the pulley was removed, perform the following:

    a. Place power steering pump pulley squarely on end of power steering pump shaft.

    b. Place Installation Spacer, Special Tool 6936, on top of pump pulley.

➡**Later build pumps (vehicles built on or after 1/3/05) feature a shaft with internal threads that are not as deep as earlier production, thus requiring a stack of washers, approximately 0.5 in. (13mm) thickness, placed over Spacer 6936, before mounting Installer C-4063C on the pump. To know if a replacement pump requires the stack of washers, measure the depth of the shaft hole. A later build pump will have a depth of 0.78 in. (20mm) while an earlier build pump will have a depth of 1.25 in. (32mm).**

    c. Thread Installer, Special Tool C-4063C, completely into internal threads of power steering pump shaft, then rotate Installer Nut down against Spacer on pump pulley.

    d. Ensuring that special tools and pulley remain aligned with pump shaft, tighten Installer Nut, forcing pulley onto power steering pump shaft until Spacer comes in contact with end of pump shaft. When Spacer is against shaft of power steering pump, Installer Nut will no longer rotate.

    e. Remove special tools from power steering pump.

10. Align the power steering pump with mounting holes on engine.

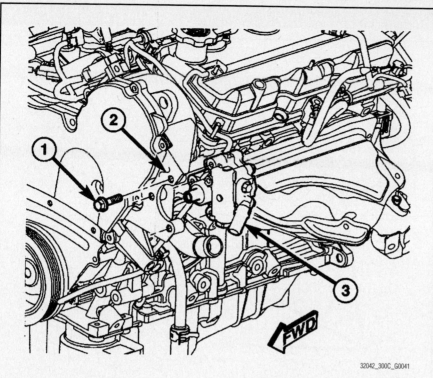

Fig. 232 To remove the power steering pump (1), first remove the mounting bolts (2) through the access holes in the pulley

11. Install the three pump mounting bolts through access holes in pulley. Tighten the bolts to 21 ft. lbs. (28 Nm).

➡Always use a NEW O-ring on the end of the pressure hose.

12. Lubricate NEW O-ring on end of pressure hose with clean power steering fluid.

13. Connect the pressure hose to the pump. Tighten pressure hose tube nut to 35 ft. lbs. (47 Nm).

14. Install the supply hose on the pump. Install clamp securing hose in place.

15. Install the serpentine drive belt.

16. Install the air cleaner housing and inlet tube.

17. Connect battery negative cable to battery post. It is important that this is performed properly.

18. Fill the power steering pump reservoir with fluid and perform pump initial operation procedure

BLEEDING

✳✳ WARNING

The fluid level should be checked with engine off to prevent injury from moving components.

✳✳ WARNING

Only MOPAR® ATF+4 is to be used in the power steering system. No other power steering or automatic transmission fluid is to be used in the system. Damage may result to the power steering pump and system if any other fluid is used, and do not overfill.

1. Wipe filler cap clean, then check the fluid level. The dipstick should indicate COLD when the fluid is at normal temperature.

2. Turn steering wheel all the way to the left.

3. Fill the pump fluid reservoir to the proper level and let the fluid settle for at least two (2) minutes.

4. Raise the front wheels off the ground.

5. Slowly turn the steering wheel lock-to-lock 20 times with the engine off while checking the fluid level.

➡For vehicles with long return lines or oil coolers, you must turn the wheel 40 times.

6. Start the engine. With the engine idling maintain the fluid level.

7. Lower the front wheels and let the engine idle for two minutes.

8. Turn the steering wheel in both direction and verify power assist and quiet operation of the pump.

9. If the fluid is extremely foamy or milky looking, allow the vehicle to stand a few minutes and repeat the procedure.

✳✳ WARNING

Do not run a vehicle with foamy fluid for an extended period. This may cause pump damage.

➡Suspension components with rubber/urethane bushings should be tightened with the vehicle at normal ride height. It is important to have the springs supporting the weight of the vehicle when the fasteners are torqued. If springs are not at their normal ride position, vehicle ride comfort could be affected and premature bushing wear may occur.

COIL SPRING

REMOVAL & INSTALLATION
See Figures 233 through 239.

1. Before servicing the vehicle, refer to the precautions in the beginning of this section.

The strut assembly must be removed from vehicle for it to be disassembled and assembled. For strut assembly disassembly and assembly, use of strut Spring Compressor, Pentastar Service Equipment (PSE) tool W-7200, or equivalent, is recommended to compress coil spring. Follow manufacturer's instructions closely.

❊ CAUTION

Do not remove strut shaft nut before coil spring is compressed. Coil spring is held under pressure and must be compressed, removing spring tension from upper and lower mounts, before strut removal.

2. Position strut assembly coil spring on hooks of compressor following manufac-

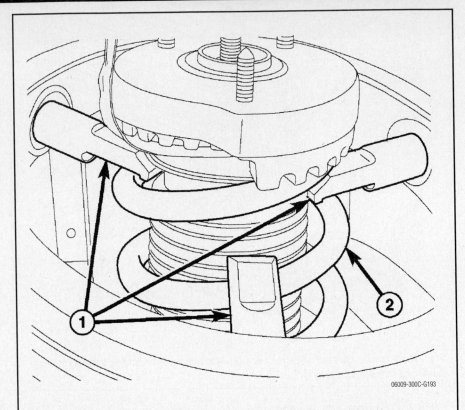

Fig. 234 Position compressor upper hooks (1) on upper coil spring (2) following manufacturer's instructions

turer's instructions. Install clamp securing strut to lower spring coil.

3. Position compressor upper hooks on upper coil spring following manufacturer's instructions. To ease installation, rotate strut as necessary positioning strut in compressor so that upper spring coil ends (step in upper mount) at straight outward position from compressor.

4. Compress coil spring until all spring tension is removed from upper mount.

5. Position Wrench (2), Special Tool 9362, on strut shaft (1) retaining nut. Next,

insert 8mm socket though wrench onto hex located on end of strut shaft. While holding strut shaft from turning, remove nut from strut shaft using wrench.

6. Remove clamp from bottom of coil spring and remove strut and lower isolator out through bottom of coil spring.

7. Remove upper mount from strut shaft and coil spring.

➡Prior to removing spring from compressor, note location of lower spring coil end in relationship to compressor to ease assembly of components later.

Fig. 233 Position strut assembly coil spring (1) on hooks (2) of compressor following manufacturer's instructions. Install clamp securing strut to lower spring Coil

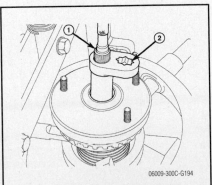

Fig. 235 Position Wrench (2), Special Tool 9362, on strut shaft (1) retaining nut

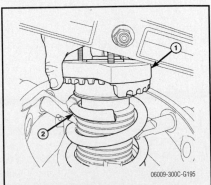

Fig. 236 Remove upper mount (1) from strut shaft and coil spring (2)

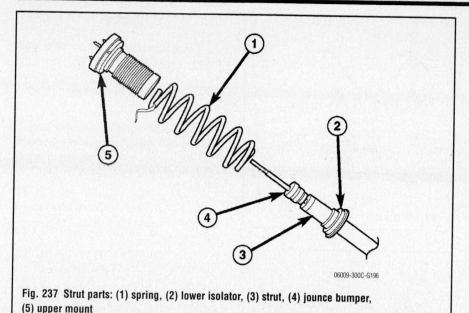

Fig. 237 Strut parts: (1) spring, (2) lower isolator, (3) strut, (4) jounce bumper, (5) upper mount

8. Back off compressor drive, releasing tension from coil spring. Push back compressor upper hooks and remove coil spring from compressor.

9. Remove jounce bumper from strut shaft by pulling straight up and off.

10. Remove lower isolator from strut body by pulling straight up and off strut shaft.

11. Inspect strut assembly components for following and replace as necessary:
- Inspect strut for any condition of shaft binding over full stroke of shaft.
- Inspect upper mount for cracks and distortion and its retaining studs for any sign of damage.
- Inspect upper spring isolator for severe deterioration.
- Inspect lower spring isolator for severe deterioration.
- Inspect dust shield for tears and deterioration.
- Inspect coil spring for cracks in the coating and corrosion.
- Inspect jounce bumper for cracks and signs of deterioration.

To assemble:

❋❋ WARNING

Use care not to damage coil spring coating during spring assembly. Damage to coating will jeopardize its corrosion protection.

➡**Left and right springs must not be interchanged.**

12. Place coil spring (part number tag end upward) in compressor lower hooks

following manufacturer's instructions. To ease strut reassembly, rotate coil spring around until upper coil ends at straight outward position from compressor. Proper orientation of spring to upper mount (once installed) is necessary.

13. Position compressor upper hooks over coil spring following manufacturer's instructions.

14. Compress coil spring far enough to allow strut installation.

15. If separated, install upper mount onto coil spring. Match step in upper isolator to end of spring coil.

16. Install lower spring isolator on strut body.

17. Install jounce bumper on strut shaft, small end first.

18. Install strut through bottom of coil spring until lower spring isolator (on strut) contacts lower end of coil spring. Match step built into isolator to lower coil end. Once in this position, stabilizer bar bracket, or clevis key on AWD models, should point straight inward toward compressor body. If not, rotate isolator on strut body until alignment is achieved when isolator is correctly positioned with lower spring coil.

19. Install clamp to hold strut and coil spring together.

20. Install retaining nut on strut shaft as far as possible by hand. Make sure nut is installed far enough for 8mm socket to grasp hex on end of shaft for tightening.

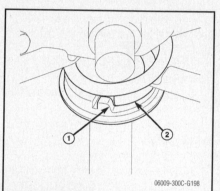

Fig. 239 Match step built into isolator (1) to lower coil end (2)

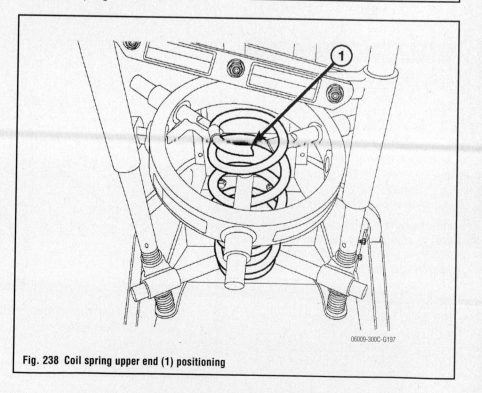

Fig. 238 Coil spring upper end (1) positioning

21. Install Wrench (on end of a torque wrench), Special Tool 9362, on strut shaft retaining nut. Next, insert 8mm socket though wrench onto hex located on end of strut shaft. While holding strut shaft from turning, tighten nut using wrench to 66 ft. lbs. (90 Nm) torque.

22. Slowly release tension from coil spring by backing off compressor drive fully. As tension is relieved, make sure strut components are properly in place.

23. Remove clamp from lower end of coil spring and strut. Push back spring compressor upper and lower hooks, then remove strut assembly from spring compressor.

24. Install strut assembly on vehicle.

CONTROL LINKS

REMOVAL & INSTALLATION

1. Before servicing the vehicle, refer to the precautions in the beginning of this section.

2. Raise and support the vehicle.

3. Remove belly pan.

4. Remove the upper and lower stabilizer link mounting nuts.

5. Remove the stabilizer link.

To install:

6. Install the stabilizer link.

7. While holding the stem from rotating at hex or flat tighten the upper and lower stabilizer link mounting nuts to 95 ft. lbs. (128 Nm).

8. Install belly pan.

9. Lower the vehicle.

LOWER BALL JOINT

REMOVAL & INSTALLATION

2WD

See Figures 240 through 243.

1. Before servicing the vehicle, refer to the precautions in the beginning of this section.

2. Remove steering knuckle, refer to the steering knuckle removal and installation.

➡ **To perform this procedure it works best to mount press, special tool C—4212F, in a vise and hold the component in your hands.**

3. Place Receiver (1), Special Tool 9320—5, into cup area of Press (3), Special Tool C—4212F, as shown and tighten set screw.

4. Place Remover (2), Special Tool 9320-3, onto end of screw—drive of Press (3), Special Tool C—4212F, as shown.

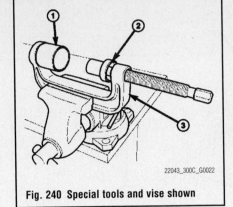
Fig. 240 Special tools and vise shown

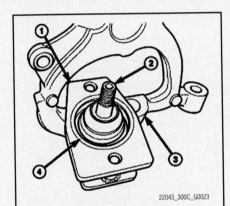
Fig. 241 Halves of support clamps

5. Using a pair of snap-ring pliers, remove snap-ring from bottom of ball joint.

6. Install halves of Support Clamp (1), Special Tool 9320—1, over ball joint (2) and around knuckle surface (3) as shown.

Install and snug Support Clamp (1) screws from underside.

7. Position knuckle (1) over tools guiding top of ball joint inside of Receiver (6), then hand tighten. Press screw—drive (4) until Remover (3) comes into contact with bottom of ball joint (2).

➡ **When positioning the knuckle over tools, make sure the Receiver, Special Tool 9320—5, sets into recessed area (4) of Support Clamp, Special Tool 9320—1.**

8. Tighten Press screw-drive (4) forcing ball joint out of knuckle (1) and into Receiver (6).

9. Loosen screw-drive (4) and remove knuckle (1) from Press. Remove ball joint from Receiver (6).

10. Remove Support Clamp (1) from knuckle.

To install:

11. Place Installer (1), Special Tool 9320—4, into cup area of Press (3), Special Tool C—4212F, as shown and tighten set screw.

12. Place Remover (2), Special Tool 9320—3, onto end of screw—drive of Press (3), Special Tool C—4212F, as shown.

➡ **This is the reverse of how the remover is installed on the screw—drive for removal.**

13. Start new ball joint (1) into bore of knuckle (2).

14. Position knuckle (1) over tools guiding top of ball joint inside of Installer (5) until

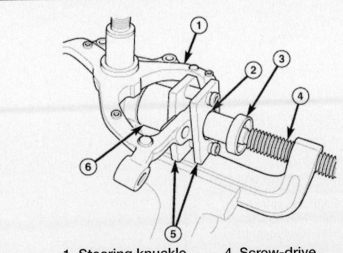

1. Steering knuckle
2. Bottom of ball joint
3. Remover
4. Screw-drive
5. Support clamps
6. Receiver

Fig. 242 Lower ball joint removal with special tools

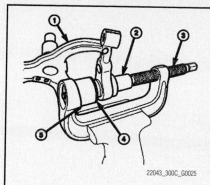

Fig. 243 Lower ball joint installation with special tools

outside flange of ball joint (4) comes into contact with Installer, then hand tighten Press screw-drive (3) until Remover (2) comes into contact with bottom of knuckle (1).

15. Using hand tools, tighten screw—drive (3), pressing ball joint into knuckle until flange (4) comes to a stop against the knuckle.

16. Loosen screw—drive and remove knuckle from Press.

17. Install the snap ring into groove on bottom of ball joint.

18. Inspect ball joint for proper fit. Make sure seal boot is uniform and wire rings are in place

19. Install knuckle on vehicle, refer to the steering knuckle removal and installation.

LOWER CONTROL ARM

2WD

See Figures 244 and 245.

1. Before servicing the vehicle, refer to the precautions in the beginning of this section.

2. Raise and support vehicle.

3. Remove wheel mounting nuts, then tire and wheel assembly.

4. Remove belly pan.

5. Remove screws fastening stabilizer bar heat shield on side of control arm repair.

6. Remove bolts fastening stabilizer bar bushing retainer in place on side of control arm repair.

7. Remove retainer halves from around stabilizer bar bushing.

8. Utilizing slit, remove bushing from stabilizer bar.

➡In the following step, the lower control arm cradle bolt is accessed through the opening created by removal of the bushing from the stabilizer bar.

✳✳ WARNING

If the lower control arm bolt at the engine cradle has a lengthwise grooved shaft, it is a special wheel alignment adjustment bolt and the bolt head must not be rotated in the vehicle or damage to the bolt and engine cradle will result. While holding the bolt in place with a wrench, remove the nut, then slide the bolt out of the bushing and cradle taking note of bolt positioning in engine cradle for reassembly purposes. The bolt needs to be installed in the same position as removed to make sure wheel camber and caster return to adjusted position.

9. Remove bolt and nut securing lower control arm to engine cradle. If bolt has a lengthwise grooved shaft (see above note), remove bolt and nut by holding the bolt in place with a wrench, removing nut, then sliding bolt out of bushing and cradle while taking note of bolt positioning in lower control arm bushing for reassembly purposes.

10. Remove bolt securing shock assembly to lower control arm.

11. Remove screw fastening wheel speed sensor to knuckle. Pull sensor head out of knuckle.

12. Remove wheel speed sensor cable routing clip from brake flex hose routing bracket.

13. Loosen nut attaching ball joint stud to lower control arm. Back nut off until nut is even with end of stud. Keeping nut on at

this location will help keep end of stud from distorting while using Puller in next step.

➡In following step, use care not to damage ball joint seal boot.

14. Using Puller, Special Tool 9360, separate ball joint stud from lower control arm.

15. Remove nut from end of ball joint stud attaching lower control arm to knuckle.

16. Pry knuckle downward and slide ball joint stud out of lower control arm. Position knuckle outward, away from lower control arm.

17. Slide lower control arm out of engine cradle and remove from vehicle.

To install:

➡If installing a lower control arm engine cradle bolt that is a wheel alignment adjustment bolt (lengthwise grooved shaft), make sure to install it in the same position which it was in upon removal.

18. Slide lower control arm into position in engine cradle and install mounting bolt from rear.

19. Install nut on lower control arm cradle bolt, but do not tighten at this time.

✳✳ WARNING

Before installing knuckle to lower control arm, measure height of ball joint seal boot mounted on knuckle. If seal boot height is above 25.5 mm, any air inside seal boot must be expelled. To do so, follow these steps:

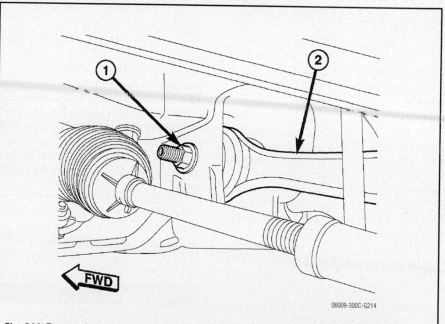

Fig. 244 Remove bolt and nut (1) securing lower control arm (2) to engine cradle—2WD

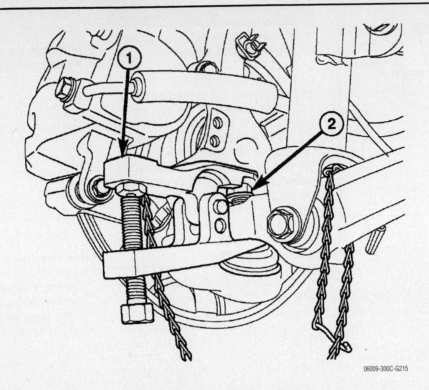

Fig. 245 Using Puller (1), Special Tool 9360, separate ball joint stud (2) from lower control arm—2WD

06009-300C-G215

- Tip ball joint stud completely to one side.
- Using thumb and index finger, gently squeeze seal boot together at center expelling any air. Do not allow grease to be release.
- Push down very top of seal boot.
- Return ball joint stud to original "centered" position.
- Measure ball joint seal boot height making sure it is within specification.
- Wipe any grease from ball joint stud.

20. Pull knuckle downward and position lower control arm over ball joint stud. Release knuckle, guiding stud into lower control arm. Install NEW nut on ball joint stud attaching lower control arm to knuckle. Tighten nut by holding ball joint stud with a hex wrench while turning nut with a wrench. Tighten nut using crow foot wrench on torque wrench to 50 ft. lbs. (68 Nm) + 90°.

21. Install wheel speed sensor head into knuckle and install mounting screw. Tighten screw to 95 inch lbs. (11 Nm) torque.

22. Attach wheel speed sensor cable and routing clip to brake flex hose routing bracket.

23. Install lower shock mounting bolt attaching shock assembly to lower control arm. Do not tighten bolt at this time.

24. Install tire and wheel assembly.

Tighten wheel mounting nuts to 110 ft. lbs. (150 Nm) torque.

25. Lower vehicle.

❊❊ WARNING

Because stabilizer bar is disconnected at cradle it is important to use extra care while moving vehicle to alignment rack/drive-on lift.

26. Position vehicle on an alignment rack/drive-on lift.

27. Tighten lower shock mounting bolt to 128 ft. lbs. (174 Nm).

28. Perform wheel alignment.

❊❊ WARNING

If the control arm engine cradle bolt is a wheel alignment adjustment bolt (lengthwise grooved shaft), be sure to only tighten the nut. Do not rotate the bolt head or damage to the bushing will occur.

29. Once camber is found to be within specifications, using a crowfoot wrench, tighten lower control arm cradle bolt nut to 130 ft. lbs. (176 Nm) torque while holding the bolt stationary.

❊❊ WARNING

Because of stabilizer bushing outer shape, it is very important to install

bushings in position discussed in following step.

30. Utilizing slit in bushing, install stabilizer bar bushing against locating collar on stabilizer. Make sure slit in bushing is positioned toward rear of vehicle.

31. Install stabilizer bar bushing retainer halves around bushing.

32. Install bolts securing stabilizer bar bushing retainer halves to cradle. Tighten bolts to 44 ft. lbs. (60 Nm) torque.

33. Install stabilizer bar heat shield over stabilizer bar bushing retainer. Install mounting screws.

34. Install belly pan.

AWD

See Figures 246 through 249.

1. Before servicing the vehicle, refer to the precautions in the beginning of this section.

2. Raise and support vehicle.

3. Remove wheel mounting nuts, then tire and wheel assembly.

4. While a helper applies brakes to keep hub from rotating, remove hub nut from the axle halfshaft.

5. Remove belly pan.

6. Loosen nut attaching lower control arm ball joint stud to knuckle. Back nut off until nut is even with end of stud. Keeping nut on at this location will help keep end of

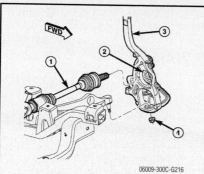

Fig. 246 Knuckle-to-lower control arm attachment. (1) halfshaft, (2) hub/bearing, (3) knuckle, (4) lower control arm stud nut—AWD

stud from distorting while using Puller in next step.

✳✳ WARNING

In following step, use care not to damage ball joint seal boot.

7. Using Special Tool 9360, separate ball joint stud from knuckle.

8. Remove tool.

9. Remove nut from end of ball joint stud.

10. Back off nut from bolt attaching shock clevis bracket to lower control arm until it is flush with end of bolt.

11. Using a brass drift punch, tap the bolt out of the clevis bracket until bolt serrations clear bracket.

12. Remove nut and bolt for clevis bracket and control arm.

13. Remove mounting screws, then heat shields above both inner tie rod bellows.

✳✳ WARNING

While steering gear bolts are removed, it important to avoid

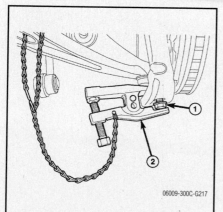

Fig. 247 Separating the lower ball joint from the knuckle with special tool 9360—AWD

putting downward force on steering gear.

14. See the accompanying illustration, and remove steering gear mounting bolts as follows:

- Left side arm: Remove bolts (3) and (4). Loosen, but do not remove, bolt (2). It is important leave bolt (2) installed to avoid dropping gear too far, putting excessive force on steering coupling.
- Right side arm: Remove bolts (2) and (3). Loosen, but do not remove, bolt (4). It is important to leave bolt (4) installed to avoid dropping gear too far, putting excessive force on steering coupling.

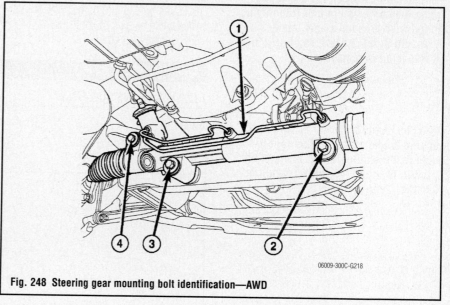

Fig. 248 Steering gear mounting bolt identification—AWD

➡If the lower control arm bolt at the engine cradle has a lengthwise grooved shaft, it is a special wheel alignment adjustment bolt and the bolt head must not be rotated in the vehicle or damage to the bolt and engine cradle will result. While holding the bolt in place with a wrench, remove the nut, then slide the bolt out of the bushing and cradle taking note of bolt positioning in engine cradle for reassembly purposes. The bolt needs to be installed in the same position as removed to make sure wheel camber and caster return to adjusted position.

15. Remove bolt (3) and nut securing forward end of lower control arm (1) to engine cradle (2). If bolt has a lengthwise grooved shaft (see above note), remove bolt

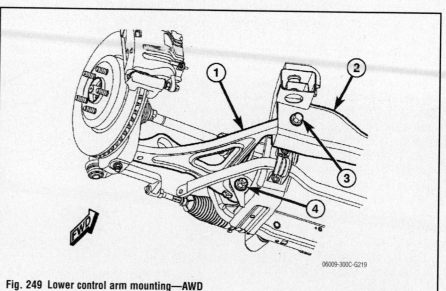

Fig. 249 Lower control arm mounting—AWD

and nut by holding bolt stationary with a wrench, removing nut, then sliding bolt out of bushing and cradle while taking note of bolt positioning in engine cradle for reassembly purposes.

16. Remove bolt and nut (4) securing rearward end of lower control arm (1) to engine cradle (2). If bolt has a lengthwise grooved shaft (see above note), remove bolt and nut by holding bolt stationary with a wrench, removing nut, then sliding bolt out of bushing and cradle while taking note of bolt positioning in engine cradle for reassembly purposes.

17. Slide lower control arm (1) from engine cradle (2) and knuckle, and remove from vehicle.

To install:

➡ If installing a lower control arm engine cradle bolt that is a wheel alignment adjustment bolt (identifying lengthwise grooved shaft), make sure to install it in the same position which it was in upon removal.

18. Slide lower control arm into position in engine cradle and place ball joint stem into mounting hole in knuckle.

➡ When installing lower control arm engine cradle bolts, it important to note that the forward bolt is installed front-to-rear and the rearward bolt is installed rear-to-front.

19. Install lower control arm mounting bolts and nuts. Do not tighten bolts at this time.

20. Raise steering gear to mounted position and install lower mounting bolts. Install upper mounting bolt and nut. Tighten all mounting bolts to 90 ft. lbs. (122 Nm) torque.

21. Install heat shields above both inner tie rod bellows. Tighten mounting screws to 62 inch lbs. (7 Nm).

22. Pull downward on control arm and guide ball joint stud into knuckle. Install NEW nut on ball joint stud. Tighten nut by holding ball joint stud with a hex wrench while turning nut with a wrench. Tighten nut using crow foot wrench on torque wrench to 90 ft. lbs. (122 Nm) torque.

23. Align shock clevis bracket with lower control arm bushing and install mounting bolt and nut. Do not tighten nut at this time.

24. Install hub nut on end of axle half-shaft. While a helper applies brakes to keep hub from turning, tighten hub nut to 157 ft. lbs. (213 Nm).

25. Install tire and wheel assembly. Tighten wheel mounting nuts to 110 ft. lbs. (150 Nm) torque.

26. Lower vehicle.
27. Position vehicle on an alignment rack/drive-on lift.

➡ When tightening lower shock clevis mounting bolt, do not attempt rotating bolt. Bolt shaft is serrated. Turn nut only.

28. Tighten lower shock clevis bracket bolt nut to 128 ft. lbs. (174 Nm) torque.
29. Perform wheel alignment.

✳✳ WARNING

If lower control arm engine cradle bolt is a wheel alignment adjustment bolt (lengthwise grooved shaft), be sure to only tighten nut. Do not rotate bolt or damage to cradle will occur.

30. Once camber is found to be within specifications, tighten lower control arm cradle bolt nuts to 130 ft. lbs. (176 Nm) torque while holding the bolts stationary.
31. Install belly pan.

MACPHERSON STRUT

REMOVAL & INSTALLATION

2WD

See Figures 250 through 253.

1. Before servicing the vehicle, refer to the precautions in the beginning of this section.
2. If equipped, remove front strut tower cap from top of strut assembly.
3. Remove three nuts fastening strut assembly to strut tower.
4. Raise and support vehicle.
5. Remove wheel mounting nuts, then tire and wheel assembly.
6. Remove nut (2) fastening stabilizer link (3) to strut assembly (1). Slide link ball joint stem from strut assembly.
7. Remove bolt securing strut assembly to lower control arm.
8. Disconnect wheel speed sensor cable routing clip at brake tube bracket.
9. Loosen nut attaching upper ball joint stud to knuckle. Back nut off until nut is even with end of stud. Keeping nut on at this location will help keep end of stud from distorting while using Puller in next step.

✳✳ WARNING

In following step, use care not to damage ball joint seal boot while sliding Puller, Special Tool 9360, into place past seal boot.

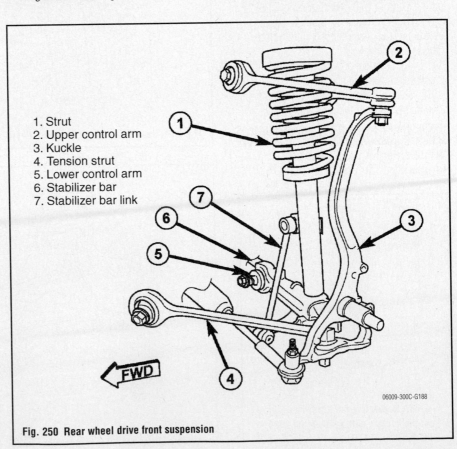

1. Strut
2. Upper control arm
3. Kuckle
4. Tension strut
5. Lower control arm
6. Stabilizer bar
7. Stabilizer bar link

06009-300C-G188

Fig. 250 Rear wheel drive front suspension

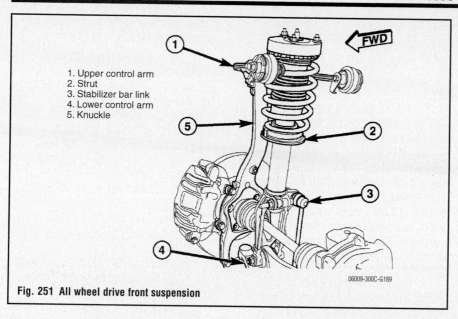

1. Upper control arm
2. Strut
3. Stabilizer bar link
4. Lower control arm
5. Knuckle

Fig. 251 All wheel drive front suspension

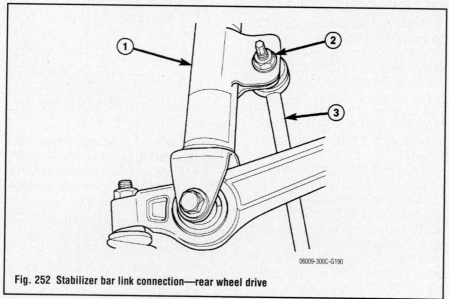

Fig. 252 Stabilizer bar link connection—rear wheel drive

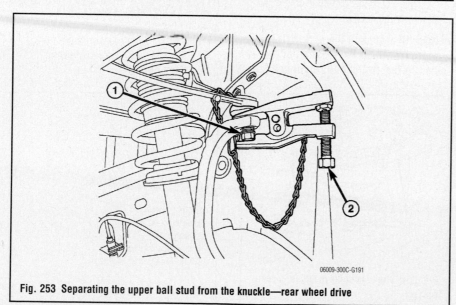

Fig. 253 Separating the upper ball stud from the knuckle—rear wheel drive

10. Using Puller (2), Special Tool 9360, separate the upper ball joint stud (1) from knuckle.

11. Remove nut from end of upper ball joint stud.

12. Tip top of knuckle outward using care not to overextend bake flex hose.

13. Remove strut assembly from vehicle.

To install:

14. Place strut assembly into front suspension using reverse direction in which it was removed.

✳ WARNING

It is important to tighten nut as described in following step to avoid damaging ball stud joint.

15. Place upper ball joint stud through hole in top of knuckle and install nut. Tighten nut by holding ball joint stud with a hex wrench while turning nut with a wrench. Tighten nut using crow foot wrench on torque wrench to 35 ft. lbs. (47 Nm) + 90° turn torque.

16. Connect wheel speed sensor cable routing clip at brake tube bracket.

17. Install lower strut mounting bolt attaching strut assembly to lower control arm. Do not tighten bolt at this time.

18. Slide stabilizer link ball joint stem into strut assembly from front. Install nut fastening link to strut assembly. Tighten nut by holding ball joint stud while turning nut. Tighten nut using crow foot wrench on torque wrench to 95 ft. lbs. (128 Nm) torque.

19. Install tire and wheel assembly. Tighten wheel mounting nuts to 110 ft. lbs. (150 Nm) torque.

20. Lower vehicle.

21. Install three nuts fastening strut assembly to strut tower. Tighten nuts to 20 ft. lbs. (27 Nm) torque.

22. If equipped, align strut tower cap with strut mounting nuts and snap into place.

AWD

1. Before servicing the vehicle, refer to the precautions in the beginning of this section.

2. Raise and support vehicle.

3. Remove wheel mounting nuts, then tire and wheel assembly.

4. While holding link ball joint stem from rotating, remove nut fastening stabilizer link to strut clevis bracket. Slide link ball joint stem from clevis bracket.

5. Remove nut and pinch bolt fastening clevis bracket to bottom of strut assembly.

6. Remove nut and bolt attaching strut clevis bracket to lower control arm.

7. Pull lower end of clevis bracket outward away from lower control arm bushing, then slide it off strut assembly. It may be necessary to use an appropriate prying tool to spread clamp area of clevis bracket allowing removal from strut assembly.

8. Lower vehicle just enough to access upper strut assembly mounting nuts.

9. If equipped, remove strut tower cap from top of strut assembly.

10. Remove three nuts fastening strut assembly to strut tower.

11. Remove strut assembly from vehicle.

To install:

12. Guide strut assembly up into strut tower and into mounting holes.

13. Install three nuts fastening strut assembly to strut tower. Tighten nuts to 20 ft. lbs. (27 Nm) torque.

14. If equipped, align strut tower cap with strut mounting nuts and snap into place.

15. Raise and support vehicle.

16. Pull lower end of strut assembly outward, then slide clevis bracket onto lower end. Slide clevis bracket onto strut assembly until bracket contacts collar on strut housing.

17. Install pinch bolt and nut fastening clevis bracket to bottom of strut assembly. Install pinch bolt from rear. Do not tighten at this time.

18. Slide clevis bracket over bushing mounted in lower control arm.

19. Install bolt and nut attaching strut clevis bracket to lower control arm. Do not tighten at this time.

20. Tighten pinch bolt attaching clevis bracket to strut assembly to 45 ft. lbs. (61 Nm) torque.

21. Slide stabilizer link ball joint stem into clevis bracket. Install nut fastening link to clevis bracket. Tighten nut by holding ball joint stud while turning nut. Tighten nut using crow foot wrench on torque wrench to 95 ft. lbs. (128 Nm) torque.

22. Install tire and wheel assembly. Tighten wheel mounting nuts to 110 ft. lbs. (150 Nm) torque.

23. Lower vehicle.

➡**When tightening lower strut clevis mounting bolt, do not attempt rotating bolt. Bolt shaft is serrated. Turn nut only.**

24. Tighten the lower strut clevis bracket bolt nut to 128 ft. lbs. (174 Nm) torque.

OVERHAUL

See Figures 254 and 255.

1. Before servicing the vehicle, refer to the precautions in the beginning of this section.

2. Remove the Strut assembly from vehicle, refer to MacPherson Strut removal and installation section.

❊❊ **WARNING**

Do not remove strut shaft nut before coil spring is compressed. Coil spring is held under pressure and must be compressed, removing spring tension from upper and lower mounts, before strut removal.

3. Position the strut assembly coil spring on hooks of Compressor following manufacturer's instructions. Install clamp securing strut to lower spring coil.

4. Position Compressor upper hooks on upper coil spring following manufacturers instructions. To ease installation, rotate strut as necessary positioning strut in compressor so that upper spring coil ends (step in upper mount) at straight outward position from Compressor.

5. Compress coil spring until all spring tension is removed from upper mount.

6. Position wrench, special tool 9362, on shock shaft retaining nut. Next, insert 8 mm socket though wrench onto hex located on end of strut shaft. While holding strut shaft from turning, remove nut from strut shaft using wrench.

7. Remove clamp from bottom of coil spring and remove strut and lower isolator out through bottom of coil spring.

8. Remove upper mount from shock shaft and coil spring.

➡**Prior to removing the spring from the compressor, note the location of the lower spring coil end in relationship to**

the compressor to ease assembly of components later.

9. Back off Compressor drive, releasing tension from coil spring. Push back compressor upper hooks and remove coil spring from Compressor.

10. Remove jounce bumper from shock shaft by pulling straight up and off.

11. Remove the lower isolator from shock body by pulling straight up and off shock shaft.

12. Inspect strut assembly components for following and replace as necessary:

- Inspect strut for any condition of shaft binding over full stroke of shaft.
- Inspect upper mount for cracks and distortion and its retaining studs for any sign of damage.
- Inspect upper spring isolator for severe deterioration.
- Inspect lower spring isolator for severe deterioration.
- Inspect dust shield for tears and deterioration.
- Inspect coil spring for cracks in the coating and corrosion.
- Inspect jounce bumper for cracks and signs of deterioration.

➡**Use care not to damage coil spring coating during spring assembly. Damage to coating will jeopardize its corrosion protection. Left and right springs must not be interchanged.**

13. Place coil spring (part number tag end upward) in compressor lower hooks following manufacturer's instructions. To ease strut reassembly, rotate coil spring around until upper coil ends at straight outward position from Compressor. Proper orientation of spring to upper mount (once installed) is necessary.

14. Position compressor upper hooks over coil spring following manufacturers instructions.

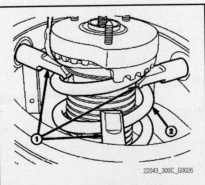

Fig. 254 Strut assembly mounted in compressor

22043_300C_G0026

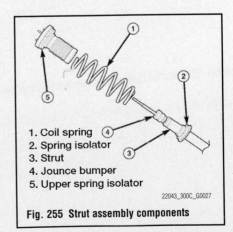

1. Coil spring
2. Spring isolator
3. Strut
4. Jounce bumper
5. Upper spring isolator

22043_300C_G0027

Fig. 255 Strut assembly components

15. Compress the coil spring far enough to allow strut installation.

16. If separated, install upper mount onto coil spring. Match step in upper isolator to end of spring coil.

17. Install the lower spring isolator on shock body.

18. Install the jounce bumper on shock shaft, small end first.

19. Install strut through bottom of coil spring until lower spring isolator (on strut) contacts lower end of coil spring. Match step built into isolator to lower coil end. Once in this position, stabilizer bar bracket, or clevis key on AWD models, should point straight inward toward Compressor body. If not, rotate isolator on strut body until alignment is achieved when isolator is correctly positioned with lower spring coil.

20. Install clamp to hold shock and coil spring together.

21. Install the retaining nut on strut shaft as far as possible by hand. Make sure nut is installed far enough for 8 mm socket to grasp hex on end of the shaft for tightening.

22. Install the wrench (on end of a torque wrench), special tool 9362, on strut shaft retaining nut. Next, insert 8 mm socket though wrench onto hex located on end of shock shaft. While holding the strut shaft from turning, tighten nut using the wrench to 66 ft. lbs. (90 Nm).

23. Slowly release tension from coil spring by backing off Compressor drive fully. As tension is relieved, make sure the strut components are properly in place.

24. Remove clamp from lower end of coil spring and shock. Push back spring compressor upper and lower hooks, then remove shock assembly from spring compressor.

25. Install shock assembly on the vehicle.

TENSION STRUT

REMOVAL & INSTALLATION

See Figures 256 through 259.

1. Before servicing the vehicle, refer to the precautions in the beginning of this section.

2. Raise and support vehicle.

3. Remove wheel mounting nuts, then tire and wheel assembly.

4. Remove belly pan.

5. Loosen nut attaching tension strut ball joint stud to knuckle. Back nut off until nut is even with end of stud. Keeping nut on at this location will help keep end of stud from distorting while using puller in next step.

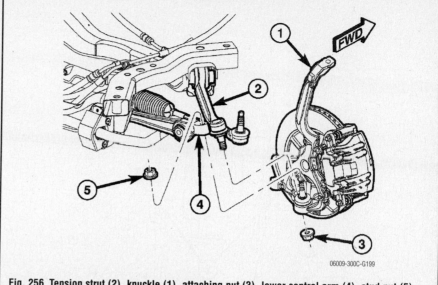

Fig. 256 Tension strut (2), knuckle (1), attaching nut (3), lower control arm (4), stud nut (5)

❊❊ WARNING

In following step, use care not to damage ball joint seal boot while sliding Puller, Special Tool 9360, into place past seal boot.

6. Using a Puller, Special Tool 9360, separate tension strut ball joint stud from knuckle.

7. Remove nut from end of tension strut ball joint stud.

8. Rotate knuckle outward and push ball joint upward, out of knuckle.

❊❊ WARNING

If the tension strut bolt at the engine cradle has a lengthwise grooved shaft (2), it is a special wheel alignment adjustment bolt and the bolt head (1) must not be rotated in the vehicle or damage to the bolt and engine cradle will result. While

holding the bolt in place with a wrench, remove the nut, then slide the bolt out of the bushing and cradle taking note of bolt positioning in engine cradle for reassembly purposes. The bolt needs to be installed in the same position as removed to make sure wheel camber and caster return to adjusted position.

9. Remove nut and bolt securing tension strut to engine cradle.

10. Slide tension strut out of cradle bracket and remove from vehicle.

To install:

➡If installing a tension strut engine cradle bolt that is a wheel alignment adjustment bolt (lengthwise grooved shaft), make sure to install it in the same position which it was in upon removal.

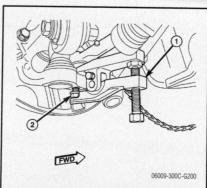

Fig. 257 Using Puller (1), Special Tool 9360, separate tension strut ball joint stud (2) from knuckle

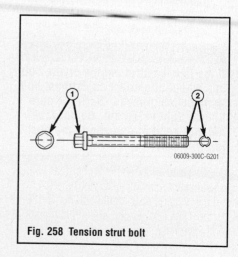

Fig. 258 Tension strut bolt

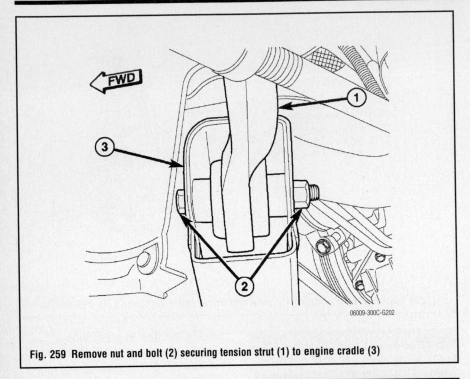

Fig. 259 Remove nut and bolt (2) securing tension strut (1) to engine cradle (3)

11. Slide bushing end of tension strut into cradle bracket.

12. Install mounting bolt from front through cradle and bushing.

13. Install nut, but do not tighten at this time.

14. Insert tension strut ball joint stud downward, into knuckle hole.

15. Completely install NEW nut on ball joint stud attaching tension strut to knuckle. Tighten nut by holding ball joint stud with a hex wrench while turning nut with a wrench. Tighten nut using crow foot wrench on torque wrench to 50 ft. lbs. (68 Nm) + 90° turn.

16. Install tire and wheel assembly. Tighten wheel mounting nuts to 110 ft. lbs. (150 Nm).

17. Lower the vehicle.

18. Position the vehicle on an alignment rack/drive-on lift.

19. Perform wheel alignment.

✷✷ WARNING

If the tension strut engine cradle bolt is a wheel alignment adjustment bolt (lengthwise grooved shaft), be sure to only tighten the nut. Do not rotate the bolt head or damage to the bushing will occur.

20. Once alignment is found to be within specifications, using a crowfoot wrench, tighten tension strut cradle bolt nut to 130 ft. lbs. (176 Nm) torque while holding the bolt stationary.

21. Install belly pan.

STABILIZER BAR

REMOVAL & INSTALLATION

2WD

See Figures 260 through 264.

1. Before servicing the vehicle, refer to the precautions in the beginning of this section.

2. Raise and support vehicle.

3. Remove belly pan.

4. On each side of vehicle, remove screws fastening stabilizer bar heat shield. Remove heat shield.

5. On each side of vehicle, remove bolts fastening stabilizer bar isolator retainer in place.

6. On each side of vehicle, remove retainer halves from around stabilizer bar isolator.

7. Utilizing slit, remove each isolator from stabilizer bar.

8. On each side of vehicle, remove nut (5) fastening stabilizer link (3) to stabilizer bar (4). Slide link ball joint stem (1) from bar, then remove bar from vehicle.

To install:

➡ **When attaching stabilizer link to stabilizer bar, make sure link ball joint stem is pointed inboard toward engine cradle.**

9. On each side of vehicle, raise stabilizer bar to stabilizer link and slide link ball

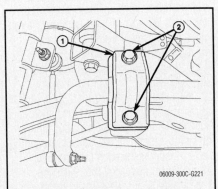

Fig. 261 Isolator retainer (1) and bolts (2)—2-wheel drive

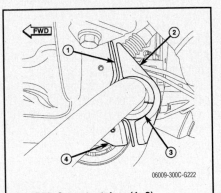

Fig. 262 Correct retainer (1, 2) positioning—2-wheel drive

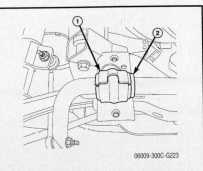

Fig. 263 Utilizing slit, remove each isolator (1) from stabilizer bar (2)—2-wheel drive

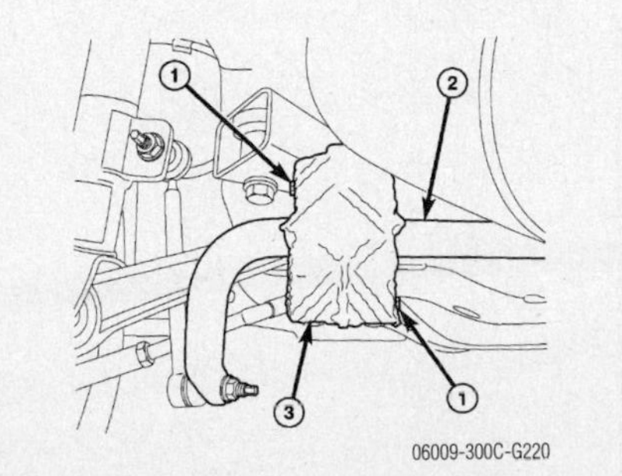

Fig. 260 Stabilizer bat heat shield (3), stabilizer bar (2), heat shield screws (1)—2-wheel drive

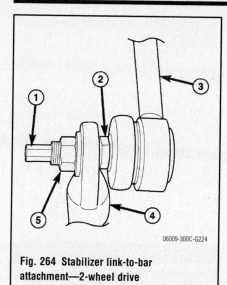

Fig. 264 Stabilizer link-to-bar attachment—2-wheel drive

06009-300C-G224

joint stem through mounting hole in bar. Loosely install nut at this time.

✳✳ WARNING

Because of stabilizer isolator outer shape, it is very important to install isolators in position discussed in following step.

10. Utilizing slit in isolator, install each stabilizer bar isolator on bar resting against locating collar as shown. Make sure slit in isolator is positioned toward rear of vehicle.

11. On each side of vehicle, install stabilizer bar isolator retainer halves around isolator.

12. On each side of vehicle, install bolts securing stabilizer bar isolator retainer halves to cradle. Tighten bolts to 44 ft. lbs. (60 Nm) torque.

13. On each side of vehicle, install stabilizer bar heat shield over stabilizer bar isolator retainer. Install mounting screws.

14. While holding stem from rotating at hex or flat tighten stabilizer link nuts at each end of stabilizer bar to 95 ft. lbs. (128 Nm) torque.

15. Install belly pan.

16. Lower vehicle.

AWD

1. Before servicing the vehicle, refer to the precautions in the beginning of this section.

2. Raise and support vehicle.

3. Remove belly pan.

4. On each side of vehicle, remove nut fastening stabilizer link to stabilizer bar. Slide link ball joint stem from bar.

5. On each side of vehicle, remove bolts fastening stabilizer bar isolator retainer in place.

6. Remove stabilizer bar with isolators and retainers from vehicle.

7. On each side of bar, remove retainers from around stabilizer bar isolators.

8. Utilizing slit, remove each isolator from stabilizer bar.

To install:

9. Utilizing slit in isolator, install each stabilizer bar isolator on bar. Make sure slit in isolator is positioned toward rear of vehicle once installed on vehicle.

10. Install stabilizer bar isolator retainer over each isolator.

➡**When attaching stabilizer link to stabilizer bar, make sure link ball joint stem is pointed inboard toward engine cradle.**

11. Install stabilizer bar ends to each stabilizer link. Slide link ball joint stem through mounting hole in bar. Loosely install nuts at this time.

12. Raise stabilizer bar to engine cradle, placing bushings into mounted position.

13. Install bolts securing each stabilizer bar isolator retainer to cradle. Tighten bolts to 44 ft. lbs. (60 Nm) torque.

14. While holding stem from rotating at hex or flat tighten stabilizer link nuts at each end of stabilizer bar to 95 ft. lbs. (128 Nm).

15. Install belly pan.

16. Lower the vehicle.

STEERING KNUCKLE

REMOVAL & INSTALLATION

2WD

See Figure 265.

1. Before servicing the vehicle, refer to the precautions in the beginning of this section.

2. Raise and support vehicle.

3. Remove wheel mounting nuts, then tire and wheel assembly.

4. Remove screw fastening wheel speed sensor to knuckle. Pull sensor head out of knuckle.

5. Remove wheel speed sensor cable routing clip from brake flex hose routing bracket.

6. Remove screw fastening brake flex hose routing bracket to knuckle.

7. Access and remove front brake rotor.

8. Remove nut from outer tie rod end stud.

9. Using a separator, separate tie rod stud from knuckle.

10. Loosen nut attaching upper ball joint stud to knuckle. Back nut off until nut is even with end of stud. Keeping nut on at

this location will help keep end of stud from distorting in next step.

✳✳ WARNING

In following step, use care not to damage ball joint seal boot while sliding the separator into place past seal boot.

11. Separate upper ball joint stud from knuckle.

12. Remove nut from end of upper ball joint stud.

13. Loosen nut attaching tension strut ball joint stud to knuckle. Back nut off until nut is even with end of stud. Keeping nut on at this location will help keep end of stud from distorting while using Puller in next step.

✳✳ WARNING

In following step, use care not to damage ball joint seal boot.

14. Separate tension strut ball joint stud from knuckle.

15. Remove nut from end of tension strut ball joint stud.

16. Loosen nut attaching ball joint stud to lower control arm. Back nut off until nut is even with end of stud. Keeping nut on at this location will help keep end of stud from distorting while using Puller in next step.

✳✳ WARNING

In following step, use care not to damage ball joint seal boot.

17. Separate ball joint stud from lower control arm.

18. Remove nut from end of ball joint stud attaching lower control arm to knuckle.

19. Remove knuckle from vehicle.

To install:

20. Before installing knuckle on lower control arm, measure height of ball joint seal boot mounted on knuckle. If seal boot height is above 25.5 mm, any air inside seal boot must be expelled. To do so, follow these steps.

   a. Tip ball joint stud completely to one side.

   b. Using thumb and index finger, gently squeeze seal boot together at center expelling any air. Do not allow grease to be release.

   c. Push down very top of seal boot.

   d. Return ball joint stud to original "centered" position.

   e. Measure ball joint seal boot height (1) making sure it is within specification.

   f. Wipe any grease from ball joint stud.

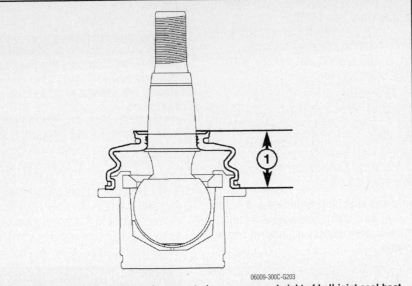

Fig. 265 Before installing knuckle on lower control arm, measure height of ball joint seal boot (1) mounted on knuckle

06009-300C-G203

21. Place knuckle over lower ball joint studs on vehicle and loosely install NEW nuts by hand.

> **⁕ WARNING**
>
> **It is important to tighten nuts as described in following steps to avoid damaging ball stud joints.**

22. Completely install NEW nut on ball joint stud attaching lower control arm to knuckle. Tighten nut by holding ball joint stud with a hex wrench while turning nut with a wrench. Tighten nut using crow foot wrench on torque wrench to 50 ft. lbs. (68 Nm) + 90°.

23. Completely install NEW nut on ball joint stud attaching tension strut to knuckle. Tighten nut by holding ball joint stud with a hex wrench while turning nut with a wrench. Tighten nut using crow foot wrench on torque wrench to 50 ft. lbs. (68 Nm) + 90°.

> **⁕ WARNING**
>
> **It is important to tighten nut as described in following step to avoid damaging ball stud joint.**

24. Place upper ball joint stud through hole in top of knuckle and install nut. Tighten nut by holding ball joint stud with a hex wrench while turning nut with a wrench. Tighten nut using crow foot wrench on torque wrench to 35 ft. lbs. (47 Nm) + 90°.

> **⁕ WARNING**
>
> **It is important to tighten nut as described in following step to avoid damaging ball stud joint.**

25. Place outer tie rod stud through hole in knuckle and install nut. Tighten nut by holding stud with a wrench while turning nut with another wrench. Tighten nut using crow foot wrench on torque wrench to 63 ft. lbs. (85 Nm) torque.

26. Install brake rotor, then disc brake caliper and adapter assembly.

27. Install screw fastening brake flex hose routing bracket to knuckle. Tighten screw to 106 inch lbs. (12 Nm) torque.

28. Install wheel speed sensor head into knuckle and install mounting screw. Tighten screw to 95 inch lbs. (11 Nm) torque.

29. Attach wheel speed sensor cable and routing clip to brake flex hose routing bracket.

30. Install tire and wheel assembly. Tighten wheel mounting nuts to 110 ft. lbs. (150 Nm) torque.

31. Lower vehicle.

32. Pump brake pedal several times to ensure vehicle has a firm brake pedal before moving vehicle.

33. Check and adjust brake fluid level in reservoir as necessary.

34. Perform wheel alignment.

AWD

1. Before servicing the vehicle, refer to the precautions in the beginning of this section.

2. Raise and support vehicle.

3. Remove wheel mounting nuts, then tire and wheel assembly.

4. While a helper applies brakes to keep hub from rotating, remove hub nut from axle halfshaft.

5. Remove clip fastening wheel speed sensor to knuckle.

6. Remove screw fastening wheel speed sensor to knuckle. Pull sensor head out of knuckle.

7. Access and remove front brake rotor.

8. Remove nut from outer tie rod end stud.

9. Separate tie rod stud from knuckle.

10. Loosen nut attaching lower control arm ball joint stud to knuckle. Back nut off until nut is even with end of stud. Keeping nut on at this location will help keep end of stud from distorting while using puller in next step.

> **⁕⁕ WARNING**
>
> **In following step, use care not to damage ball joint seal boot.**

11. Separate ball joint stud from knuckle.

12. Remove tool.

13. Remove nut from end of ball joint stud.

14. Loosen nut attaching upper ball joint stud to knuckle. Back nut off until nut is even with end of stud. Keeping nut on at this location will help keep end of stud from distorting while using Puller in next step.

> **⁕⁕ WARNING**
>
> **In following step, use care not to damage ball joint seal boot.**

15. Separate upper ball joint stud from knuckle.

16. Remove tool.

17. Remove nut from end of upper ball joint stud.

18. Slide knuckle off halfshaft and remove from vehicle.

To install:

19. Place knuckle over lower ball joint stud and guide hub and bearing onto axle halfshaft.

20. Start NEW nut on lower ball joint stud. Do not tighten at this time.

> **⁕⁕ WARNING**
>
> **It is important to tighten nut as described in following step to avoid damaging ball stud joint.**

21. Place upper ball joint stud through hole in top of knuckle and install nut. Tighten nut by holding ball joint stud with a hex wrench while turning nut with a wrench. Tighten nut using crow foot wrench on torque wrench to 35 ft. lbs. (47 Nm) +90°.

⁂ WARNING

It is important to tighten nut as described in following step to avoid damaging ball stud joint.

22. Tighten lower ball joint nut by holding ball joint stud with a hex wrench while turning nut with a wrench. Tighten nut using crow foot wrench on torque wrench to 50 ft. lbs. (68 Nm) +90°.

⁂ WARNING

It is important to tighten nut as described in following step to avoid damaging ball stud joint.

23. Place outer tie rod stud through hole in knuckle and install nut. Tighten nut by holding stud with a wrench while turning nut with another wrench. Tighten nut using crow foot wrench on torque wrench to 63 ft. lbs. (85 Nm).

24. Install brake rotor, then disc brake caliper and adapter assembly.

25. Install hub nut on end of axle halfshaft. While a helper applies brakes to keep hub from turning, tighten hub nut to 157 ft. lbs. (213 Nm) torque.

26. Install wheel speed sensor head into knuckle and install mounting screw. Tighten screw to 95 inch lbs. (11 Nm) torque.

27. Attach wheel speed sensor cable routing clip at knuckle.

28. Install tire and wheel assembly. Tighten wheel mounting nuts to 110 ft. lbs. (150 Nm) torque.

29. Lower vehicle.

30. Pump brake pedal several times to ensure vehicle has a firm brake pedal before moving vehicle.

31. Check and adjust brake fluid level in reservoir as necessary.

32. Perform wheel alignment.

UPPER BALL JOINT

REMOVAL & INSTALLATION

The upper ball joint is not replaceable. If defective, the control arm assembly must be replaced.

UPPER CONTROL ARM

REMOVAL & INSTALLATION

See Figures 266 through 268.

1. Before servicing the vehicle, refer to the precautions in the beginning of this section.

2. If removing left upper control arm,

remove and reposition coolant recovery container.

3. If removing right upper control arm, remove IPM from mount and reposition.

4. If equipped, remove front shock tower cap from top of shock assembly.

5. Remove three nuts fastening shock assembly to shock tower.

6. Remove nuts from upper control arm mounting bolts.

7. Raise and support vehicle.

8. Remove wheel mounting nuts, then tire and wheel assembly.

9. Disconnect the wheel speed sensor cable routing clip at brake tube bracket.

10. Loosen nut attaching upper ball joint stud to knuckle. Back nut off until nut is even with end of stud. Keeping nut on at this location will help keep end of stud from distorting while using puller in next step.

⁂ WARNING

In following step, use care not to damage ball joint seal boot.

11. Using Puller, Special Tool 9360, separate upper ball joint stud from knuckle.

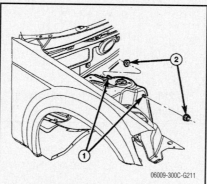

Fig. 266 Upper control arm mounting bolts (1) and nuts (2)

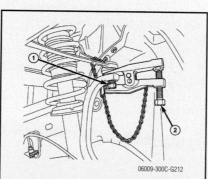

Fig. 267 Using Puller (2), Special Tool 9360, separate upper ball joint stud (1) from knuckle

12. Remove nut from end of upper ball joint stud.

13. Pull shock assembly downward until studs clear shock tower, then pull it outward allowing access to upper control arm mounting bolts.

14. Remove upper control arm mounting (flag) bolts.

15. Remove upper control arm (2) from bracket (3) in shock tower (4).

To install:

➡Although AWD and RWD upper control arms are similar in appearance, they are not interchangeable.

16. Slide upper control arm into bracket located in shock tower.

17. Install upper control arm mounting (flag) bolts through bracket, arm and tower. Position flags on bolt heads outward, toward wheel opening.

18. Move shock assembly allowing studs to be inserted through shock tower mounting holes.

19. Place upper ball joint stud (1) through hole in top of knuckle and install nut. Tighten nut by holding ball joint stud with a hex wrench while turning nut with a wrench. Tighten nut using crow foot wrench on torque wrench to 35 ft. lbs. (47 Nm) +90°.

20. Connect wheel speed sensor cable routing clip at brake tube bracket.

21. Install tire and wheel assembly. Tighten wheel mounting nuts to 110 ft. lbs. (150 Nm) torque.

22. Lower vehicle to curb position.

23. Install nuts on upper control arm body mounting bolts. Tighten nuts to 55 ft. lbs. (75 Nm).

24. Install three nuts fastening shock assembly to shock tower. Tighten nuts to 20 ft. lbs. (27 Nm) torque.

25. If equipped, align shock tower cap with shock mounting nuts and snap into place.

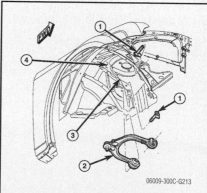

Fig. 268 Upper control arm (3) removal

26. If installing left upper control arm, install coolant recovery container.

27. If installing the right upper control arm, install the IPM.

WHEEL BEARINGS

REMOVAL & INSTALLATION

2WD

See Figure 269.

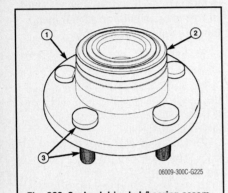

Fig. 269 2-wheel drive hub/bearing assembly (1), magnetic encoder (2), stud (3)

1. Before servicing the vehicle, refer to the precautions in the beginning of this section.

2. Raise and support vehicle.

3. Remove wheel mounting nuts, then tire and wheel assembly.

4. Access and remove front brake rotor.

5. Remove dust cap. When doing this, avoid damaging internal bore of hub to preserve seal integrity.

6. Remove hub nut.

7. Slide hub and bearing off knuckle spindle.

To install:

➡**Prior to installation, inspect magnetic encoder (for wheel speed sensor) for any damage and make sure any metal debris sticking to it is removed.**

8. Slide hub and bearing onto knuckle spindle.

9. Install hub nut on end of spindle. Tighten hub nut to 184 ft. lbs. (250 Nm) torque.

10. Install brake rotor, then disc brake caliper and adapter assembly.

➡**Install a new dust cap to preserve seal integrity.**

11. Install NEW dust cap on hub and bearing.

12. Install tire and wheel assembly. Tighten wheel mounting nuts to 110 ft. lbs. (150 Nm) torque.

13. Lower vehicle.

14. Pump brake pedal several times to ensure vehicle has a firm brake pedal before moving vehicle.

15. Check and adjust brake fluid level in reservoir as necessary.

16. Road test vehicle and make several stops to wear off any foreign material on brakes and to seat brake pads.

AWD

See Figures 270 and 271.

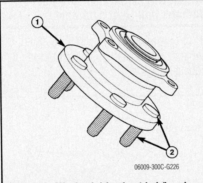

Fig. 270 All wheel drive front hub/bearing (1), studs (2)

1. Before servicing the vehicle, refer to the precautions in the beginning of this section.

2. Raise and support vehicle.

3. Remove wheel mounting nuts, then tire and wheel assembly.

4. While a helper applies brakes to keep hub from rotating, remove hub nut from the axle halfshaft.

5. Access and remove front brake rotor.

6. Remove four bolts fastening hub and bearing to knuckle.

7. Slide hub and bearing off axle halfshaft and knuckle.

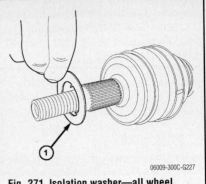

Fig. 271 Isolation washer—all wheel drive

To install:

➡**Before installing hub and bearing on end of axle halfshaft, ensure isolation washer is present on end of halfshaft. Inspect washer making sure it is not worn or damaged. Washer can be installed in either direction on shaft.**

8. Slide hub and bearing onto axle halfshaft. Position hub and bearing onto knuckle, lining up mounting bolt holes.

9. Install four bolts fastening hub and bearing in place. Tighten mounting bolts to 50 ft. lbs. (68 Nm) torque.

10. Install brake rotor, then disc brake caliper and adapter assembly.

11. Install hub nut on end of axle halfshaft. While a helper applies brakes to keep hub from turning, tighten hub nut to 157 ft. lbs. (213 Nm).

12. Install tire and wheel assembly. Tighten wheel mounting nuts to 110 ft. lbs. (150 Nm) torque.

13. Lower vehicle.

14. Pump brake pedal several times to ensure vehicle has a firm brake pedal before moving vehicle.

15. Check and adjust brake fluid level in reservoir as necessary.

16. Road test vehicle and make several stops to wear off any foreign material on brakes and to seat brake pads.

ADJUSTMENT

The front wheel bearing and wheel hub of this vehicle are a one piece sealed unit or hub and bearing unit type assembly. No adjustment is possible.

SUSPENSION

COIL SPRING

REMOVAL & INSTALLATION

See Figure 272.

1. Before servicing the vehicle, refer to the precautions in the beginning of this section.
2. Raise and support vehicle.
3. On both sides of vehicle, remove wheel mounting nuts, then rear tire and wheel assembly.

✳✳ CAUTION

Before opening fuel system, review all warnings and cautions under Fuel System.

4. On the left side, remove fuel filler tube:

   a. Disconnect negative battery cable.
   b. Drain fuel from tank.
   c. Fuel filler tube assembly.
   d. Open filler tube door.
   e. Remove retaining wire from inside filler tube rubber.
   f. Start removing rubber from body sheet metal.
   g. Remove retaining wire from inside filler tube rubber.
   h. Start removing rubber from body sheet metal.
   i. Filler tube and rubber removed from body sheet metal.
   j. Remove the left inner splash shield.
   k. Disconnect the filler tube vent line.
   l. Remove the filler tube mounting bolt.
   m. Remove the under body splash shield.
   n. Loosen the filler tube hose clamp. Leave the clamp tight on the hose and fuel tank location.
   o. Move clamp toward the fuel tank.
   p. Remove the filler tube assembly from the vehicle.

5. Position an extra pair of jackstands under and support forward end of engine cradle to help stabilize vehicle during rear suspension removal/installation.
6. Perform following if vehicle is equipped with dual exhaust or are servicing right side on vehicle with single exhaust:

   a. Position under-hoist utility jack or stand several inches below exhaust at muffler.
   b. Disconnect exhaust isolators at muffler and resonators hangers.
   c. Lower exhaust down to rest upon top of jack or stand placed below muffler.

7. Position under-hoist utility jack or transmission jack (3) under center of rear axle differential (1). Raise jack head to contact differential and secure in place. When securing crossmember to jack, be sure not to secure stabilizer bar.
8. Remove shock absorber upper mounting screws.
9. Remove shock absorber lower mounting bolt and nut.

➡When removing crossmember mounting bolts in following step, be sure to not to misplace spacers between crossmember mounts and body.

✳✳ WARNING

If equipped with AWD, when removing crossmember mounting bolts it is important NOT to loosen or remove crossmember mounting bolts on opposite side of vehicle. Doing so will require rear wheel alignment following reinstallation to ensure proper thrust angle.

10. Remove both front and rear crossmember mounting bolts on side of vehicle being serviced.

✳✳ WARNING

To avoid damaging other components of vehicle, do not lower crossmember any further than necessary to remove shock absorber.

11. Slowly lower jack allowing repair-side of crossmember to drop. Do not lower jack at a fast rate. Lower jack just enough to allow top of shock absorber to clear body flange.
12. Remove shock absorber by tipping top outward and lifting lower end out of pocket in spring link.
13. Disconnect brake hose at bracket mounted to body to allow to avoid overextending hose, damaging it, during following step.
14. Slowly lower jack until crossmember is low enough to remove coil spring. Do not lower jack any further than necessary to remove spring.
15. Remove coil spring and isolators (1, 2 and 5).

To install:

16. Install upper and lower isolators on coil spring.

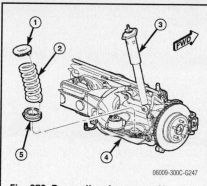

Fig. 272 Rear coil spring removal/ installation

➡Before installing coil spring, make sure isolators are completely installed on ends of spring.

17. Install coil spring with isolators into spring pocket of spring link fitting lower isolator to shape of pocket, then align top of spring with body mount.
18. Install shock absorber by setting lower end into pocket in spring link, then tipping top inward until aligned with upper mounting holes.
19. Install lower shock mounting bolt and nut. Do not tighten at this time.
20. Make sure spacers on top of crossmember mount bushings on side of repair are in position.
21. Carefully raise jack, guiding coil spring and upper end of shock absorber into mounted positions.
22. Install shock absorber upper mounting bolts. Tighten upper mounting bolts to 38 ft. lbs. (52 Nm).

➡Rear crossmember mounting bolts are longer than front mounting bolts. Do not interchange mounting bolts.

23. Install crossmember mounting bolts. Snug, but do not fully tighten bolts at this time.
24. Measure distance between from tension link to body weld flange directly in front of it, just outboard of front mount bushing. This distance must be at least 12mm to allow proper clearance for suspension movement. If distance is less than 12mm, shift that side of rear crossmember directly rearward until distance is 12mm or greater. To do so, loosen 3 mounting bolts slightly, leaving one on opposite side shifted, snugged to pivot off of. Shift crossmember rearward and snug loosened bolts. Measure opposite side to be sure it also maintains minimum 12mm distance.

25. Tighten all crossmember mounting bolts to 133 ft. lbs. (180 Nm) torque.

26. Remove jack from under rear axle differential.

27. If previously lowered, raise rear exhaust back to mounted position and connect exhaust isolators at muffler and resonators hangers. Remove jack or stand below exhaust muffler.

28. If removed, install fuel filler tube:

　a. Insert filler tube into the fuel tank rubber hose.

　b. Slide hose clamp into place and tighten.

　c. Hose clamp in place and tighten.

　d. Install filler tube mounting bolt.

　e. Install filler tube vent line.

　f. Install the underbody splash shield.

　g. Install the left inner splash shield.

29. Install tire and wheel assemblies. Tighten wheel mounting nuts to 110 ft. lbs. (150 Nm) torque.

30. Lower vehicle.

31. Position vehicle on alignment rack/drive-on lift. Raise lift as necessary to access lower mounting bolt.

32. Tighten shock absorber lower mounting bolt nut to 53 ft. lbs. (72 Nm).

CAMBER LINK

REMOVAL & INSTALLATION

See Figures 273 and 274.

1. Before servicing the vehicle, refer to the precautions in the beginning of this section.

2. Raise and support vehicle.

3. On both sides of vehicle, remove wheel mounting nuts, then rear tire and wheel assembly.

✳✳ CAUTION

Before opening fuel system, review all warnings and cautions under Fuel System.

4. If servicing left side shock absorber, remove fuel filler tube:

　a. Disconnect negative battery cable.

　b. Drain fuel from tank.

　c. Fuel filler tube assembly.

　d. Open filler tube door.

　e. Remove retaining wire from inside filler tube rubber.

　f. Start removing rubber from body sheet metal.

　g. Remove retaining wire from inside filler tube rubber.

　h. Start removing rubber from body sheet metal.

　i. Filler tube and rubber removed from body sheet metal.

　j. Remove the left inner splash shield.

　k. Disconnect the filler tube vent line.

　l. Remove the filler tube mounting bolt.

　m. Remove the under body splash shield.

　n. Loosen the filler tube hose clamp. Leave the clamp tight on the hose and fuel tank location.

　o. Move clamp toward the fuel tank.

　p. Remove the filler tube assembly from the vehicle.

5. Position an extra pair of jackstands under and support forward end of engine cradle to help stabilize vehicle during rear suspension removal/installation.

6. Perform following if vehicle is equipped with dual exhaust or are servicing right side on vehicle with single exhaust:

　a. Position under-hoist utility jack or stand several inches below exhaust at muffler.

　b. Disconnect exhaust isolators at muffler and resonators hangers.

　c. Lower exhaust down to rest upon top of jack or stand placed below muffler.

7. Position under-hoist utility jack or transmission jack under center of rear axle differential. Raise jack head to contact differential and secure in place. When securing crossmember to jack, be sure not to secure stabilizer bar.

8. Remove shock absorber upper mounting screws.

9. Remove shock absorber lower mounting bolt and nut.

➡**If equipped with AWD, when removing crossmember mounting bolts in following step, be sure to not to misplace spacers between crossmember mounts and body.**

✳✳ WARNING

When removing crossmember mounting bolts it is important NOT to loosen or remove crossmember mounting bolts on opposite side of vehicle. Doing so will require rear wheel alignment following reinstallation to ensure proper thrust angle.

10. Remove both front and rear crossmember mounting bolts on repair-side of vehicle.

✳✳ WARNING

To avoid damaging other components of vehicle, do not lower crossmem-

ber any further than necessary to remove shock absorber.

11. Slowly lower jack allowing repair-side of crossmember to drop. Do not lower jack at a fast rate. Lower jack just enough to allow top of shock absorber to clear body flange.

12. Remove shock absorber by tipping top outward and lifting lower end out of pocket in spring link.

➡**Do not lower side of crossmember any further than necessary to gain access to link mounting bolts at crossmember.**

13. Remove nut (4) and bolt (2) mounting link to knuckle (3).

14. Remove nut (4) and bolt (2) mounting link to crossmember (1).

15. Remove link.

To install:

16. When installing link, note the following:

- Heavier, thicker end goes toward crossmember.
- Fore-or-aft bow faces forward (curves around coil spring).
- Up-or-down bow faces downward.

17. Place link in bracket on crossmember. Install bolt and nut at crossmember. Do not tighten bolt at this time.

18. Install bolt and nut mounting link to knuckle. Do not tighten bolt at this time.

19. Install shock absorber by setting lower end into pocket in spring link, then tipping top inward until aligned with upper mounting holes.

20. Install lower shock mounting bolt and nut. Do not tighten at this time.

21. If vehicle is equipped with AWD, make sure spacers on top of crossmember mount bushings on side of repair are in position.

22. Carefully raise jack, guiding coil spring and upper end of shock absorber into mounted positions.

23. Install shock absorber upper mounting screws. Tighten upper mounting screws to 38 ft. lbs. (52 Nm) torque.

➡**Rear crossmember mounting bolts are longer than front mounting bolts. Do not interchange mounting bolts.**

24. Install crossmember mounting bolts. Snug, but do not fully tighten bolts at this time.

25. Measure distance between from tension link to body weld flange directly in front of it, just outboard of front mount bushing. This distance must be at least 12mm to allow proper clearance for sus-

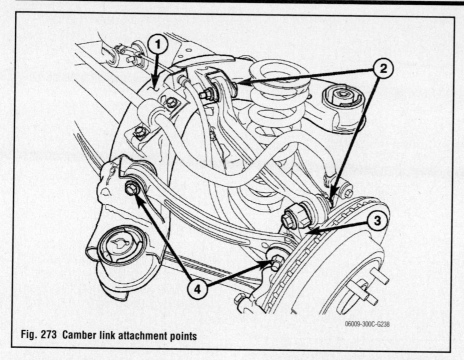

Fig. 273 Camber link attachment points

pension movement. If distance is less than 12mm, shift that side of rear crossmember directly rearward until distance is 12mm or greater. To do so, loosen 3 mounting bolts slightly, leaving one on opposite side shifted, snugged to pivot off of. Shift crossmember rearward and snug loosened bolts. Measure opposite side to be sure it also maintains minimum 12mm distance.

26. Tighten all crossmember mounting bolts to 133 ft. lbs. (180 Nm) torque.

27. Remove jack from under rear axle differential.

28. If previously lowered, raise rear exhaust back to mounted position and connect exhaust isolators at muffler and resonators hangers. Remove jack or stand below exhaust muffler.

29. If removed, install fuel filler tube:

a. Insert filler tube into the fuel tank rubber hose.

b. Slide hose clamp into place and tighten.

c. Hose clamp in place and tighten.

d. Install filler tube mounting bolt.

e. Install Filler tube vent line.

f. Install the underbody splash shield.

g. Install the left inner splash shield.

30. Lower vehicle until front tires contact floor but rear is still suspended. Place jackstands under each rear suspension spring link. Place an appropriate wooden block between stand and link to avoid damaging spring link, then lower vehicle until full vehicle weight is supported by suspension.

31. Tighten camber link fasteners to:
- Bolt at crossmember: 63 ft. lbs. (85 Nm) torque.
- Bolt nut at knuckle: 72 ft. lbs. (98 Nm) torque.

32. Tighten shock absorber lower mounting bolt nut to 53 ft. lbs. (72 Nm) torque.

33. Raise vehicle and remove jackstands.

34. Install tire and wheel assemblies.

Tighten wheel mounting nuts to 110 ft. lbs. (150 Nm) torque.

35. Lower vehicle.

36. Perform wheel alignment.

COMPRESSION LINK

REMOVAL & INSTALLATION

See Figure 275.

1. Before servicing the vehicle, refer to the precautions in the beginning of this section.

2. Raise and support vehicle.

3. Remove wheel mounting nuts, then rear tire and wheel assembly.

4. Remove bolt and nut mounting link at knuckle.

5. Remove bolt and nut mounting link at crossmember.

6. Remove link.

To install:

➡ **Although the compression link is different end-to-end, there is no top and bottom.**

7. Position link and install bolt and nut mounting link at crossmember. Do not tighten bolt at this time.

8. Install bolt and nut mounting link at knuckle. Do not tighten bolt at this time.

9. Install tire and wheel assembly. Tighten wheel mounting nuts to 110 ft. lbs. (150 Nm).

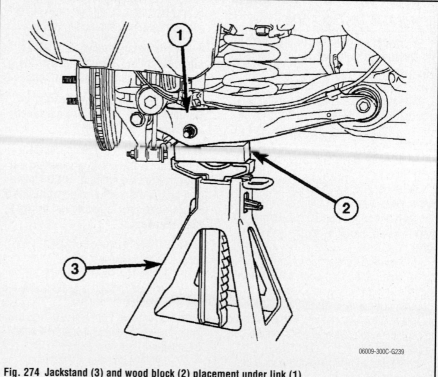

Fig. 274 Jackstand (3) and wood block (2) placement under link (1)

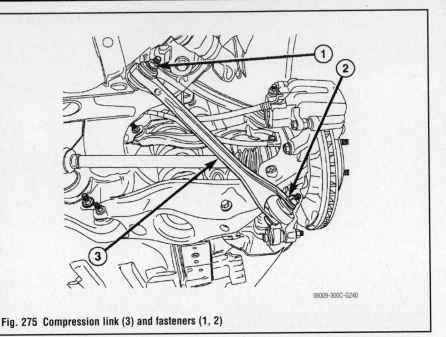

Fig. 275 Compression link (3) and fasteners (1, 2)

06009-300C-G240

10. Lower vehicle.

11. Position vehicle on alignment rack/drive-on lift. Raise vehicle as necessary to access link fasteners.

12. Tighten compression link fasteners to:
- Bolt at crossmember: 63 ft. lbs. (85 Nm) torque.
- Bolt at knuckle: 60 ft. lbs. (81 Nm) torque.

13. Perform wheel alignment.

KNUCKLE

REMOVAL & INSTALLATION

1. Before servicing the vehicle, refer to the precautions in the beginning of this section.

2. Raise and support vehicle.

3. Unclip wheel speed sensor cable at rear brake rotor shield.

4. Remove screw fastening sensor head to rear knuckle.

5. Remove wheel speed sensor head from knuckle.

6. Remove rear hub and bearing.

7. Remove parking brake shoes.

8. If not removed, remove parking brake shoe actuator lever from end of cable.

9. Remove shoe support from knuckle.

10. Remove parking brake cable screw at knuckle and pull cable out of knuckle.

11. Position under-hoist utility jack or jackstand under spring link. Raise jack head to contact spring link at shock mount secure in place.

12. Remove spring link-to-knuckle nut and bolt.

❋❋ WARNING

It important to use Guide, Special Tool 9361-2, when tapping sleeve in knuckle to help keep Tap, Special Tool 9361-1, straight during use or damage to Tap may occur.

13. Place Guide 9361-2 against sleeve in knuckle to keep Tap 9361-1 straight. Using Tap with an appropriate handle, cut threads approximately halfway through bushing (or about six complete threads). It is important to back tap out, clean out burrs and lubricate Tap often during process.

➡Prior to using Special Tool 9361, lubricate Bolt (1) threads to provide ease of use and promote tool longevity.

➡When installing thrust bearing on Remover, be sure to place hardened side against nut.

➡It is important to use appropriate Sleeve on Remover to provide proper Tool-to-Knuckle contact. RWD sleeve can be used on either side while AWD knuckles require specific left or right side Sleeves.

14. Thread Remover Bolt 9361-3 into tapped knuckle sleeve.

15. Rotate Nut down, matching Sleeve angled end with angled face of knuckle.

16. Continue to rotate Nut until knuckle sleeve is removed from knuckle. Discard knuckle sleeve; replace it with new upon installation.

17. Remove bolt and nut fastening compression link to knuckle.

18. Remove bolt fastening toe link to knuckle.

19. Remove nut and bolt fastening stabilizer link to knuckle.

20. Remove nut and bolt fastening tension link to knuckle.

21. Remove nut and bolt fastening camber link to knuckle.

22. Remove knuckle.

23. Remove hub mounting bolts from knuckle.

To install:

24. Install four hub mounting bolts through knuckle from inboard side allowing ends to protrude from opposite side.

25. Position knuckle on vehicle and install bolt and nut fastening camber link to knuckle. Do not tighten bolt at this time.

26. Install bolt and nut fastening tension link to knuckle. Do not tighten bolt at this time.

27. Install bolt and nut fastening stabilizer link to knuckle. Do not tighten bolt at this time.

28. Install bolt fastening toe link to knuckle. Do not tighten bolt at this time.

29. Install bolt and nut fastening compression link to knuckle. Do not tighten bolt at this time.

➡Prior to using Special Tool 9361, lubricate bolt threads to provide ease of use and promote tool longevity.

30. Place NEW knuckle sleeve onto Installer Bolt 9361-7, and slide it up to Bolt's head.

31. Slide Bolt 9361-7 with sleeve through knuckle and spring link ball joint starting from knuckle forward end.

32. Install thrust bearing and nut on end of Bolt.

33. While holding Bolt head stationary, rotate Nut (using hand tools) installing sleeve in knuckle. Install sleeve until Nut stops turning. Do not over tighten Nut.

34. Remove special tool.

35. Install spring link-to-knuckle bolt front-to-rear through knuckle and link, then install nut. While holding bolt head stationary, tighten nut to 102 ft. lbs. (138 Nm) torque.

36. Remove under-hoist utility jack or jackstand from under spring link.

37. Insert end of cable through rear knuckle and install mounting screw. Tighten screw to 71 inch lbs. (8 Nm).

38. Install parking brake shoe support over hub and bearing mounting screws and onto face of knuckle.

39. Install shoe actuator lever on end of parking brake cable. Make sure actuator

lever is positioned with word "UP" facing outward.

40. Install parking brake shoes.

➡**Before installing hub and bearing on end of axle halfshaft, ensure isolation washer is present on end of halfshaft. Inspect washer making sure it is not worn or damaged. Washer can be installed in either direction on shaft.**

41. Install hub and bearing.

42. Insert wheel speed sensor head into mounting hole in rear of knuckle.

43. Install screw fastening sensor head to rear knuckle. Tighten Screw to 97 inch lbs. (11 Nm) torque.

44. Install sensor cable at rear brake rotor shield.

45. Lower vehicle.

46. Adjust parking brake shoes as necessary.

47. Position vehicle on alignment rack/drive-on hoist. Raise vehicle as necessary to access mounting bolts.

48. Tighten fasteners at knuckle (vehicle at curb height) as follows:
- Camber Link: 72 ft. lbs. (98 Nm).
- Compression Link: 60 ft. lbs. (81 Nm).
- Stabilizer Link: 45 ft. lbs. (61 Nm).
- Tension Link: 72 ft. lbs. (98 Nm).
- Toe Link: 60 ft. lbs. (81 Nm).

49. Perform wheel alignment.

SHOCK ABSORBER

REMOVAL & INSTALLATION

With Load Leveling

See Figures 276 and 277.

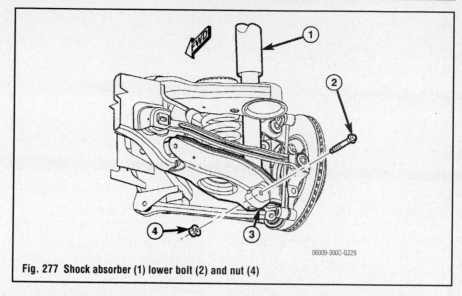

Fig. 277 Shock absorber (1) lower bolt (2) and nut (4)

06009-300C-G229

1. Before servicing the vehicle, refer to the precautions in the beginning of this section.

2. Raise and support vehicle.

3. Remove wheel mounting nuts, then tire and wheel assembly.

4. Position under-hoist utility jack or jackstand under outer spring link adding just enough support to keep suspension from going into full-rebound when shock absorber mounting bolts are removed.

5. Remove shock absorber lower mounting bolt and nut.

6. Remove shock absorber upper mounting bolts.

7. Remove shock absorber.

To install:

8. Insert lower end of shock absorber into well of spring link.

9. Raise upper end of shock absorber up into mounted position on body and install upper mounting screws. Tighten upper mounting screws to 38 ft. lbs. (52 Nm) torque.

10. Install lower shock mounting bolt and nut. Do not tighten at this time.

11. Remove under-hoist utility jack or jackstand from under spring link.

12. Install tire and wheel assembly. Tighten wheel mounting nuts to 110 ft. lbs. (150 Nm) torque.

13. Lower vehicle.

14. Position vehicle on alignment rack/drive-on hoist. Raise vehicle as necessary to access lower mounting bolt.

15. Tighten shock absorber lower mounting bolt nut to 53 ft. lbs. (72 Nm) torque.

Without Load Leveling

See Figures 278 through 285.

1. Before servicing the vehicle, refer to the precautions in the beginning of this section.

2. Raise and support vehicle.

3. On both sides of vehicle, remove wheel mounting nuts, then rear tire and wheel assembly.

✳✳ CAUTION

Before opening fuel system, review all warnings and cautions under Fuel System.

4. If servicing left side shock absorber, remove fuel filler tube:
  a. Disconnect negative battery cable.
  b. Drain fuel from tank.
  c. Fuel filler tube assembly.
  d. Open filler tube door.
  e. Remove retaining wire from inside filler tube rubber.

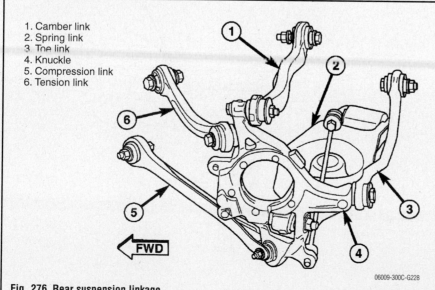

1. Camber link
2. Spring link
3. Toe link
4. Knuckle
5. Compression link
6. Tension link

FWD

06009-300C-G228

Fig. 276 Rear suspension linkage

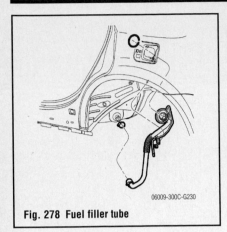

Fig. 278 Fuel filler tube

06009-300C-G230

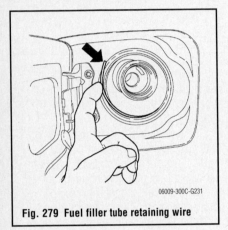

Fig. 279 Fuel filler tube retaining wire

06009-300C-G231

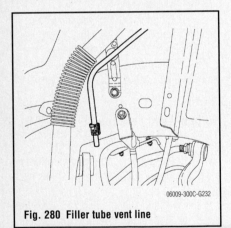

Fig. 280 Filler tube vent line

06009-300C-G232

f. Start removing rubber from body sheet metal.

g. Remove retaining wire from inside filler tube rubber.

h. Start removing rubber from body sheet metal.

i. Filler tube and rubber removed from body sheet metal.

j. Remove the left inner splash shield.

k. Disconnect the filler tube vent line.

l. Remove the filler tube mounting bolt.

m. Remove the under body splash shield.

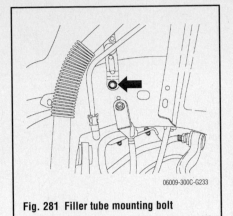

Fig. 281 Filler tube mounting bolt

06009-300C-G233

n. Loosen the filler tube hose clamp. Leave the clamp tight on the hose and fuel tank location.

o. Move clamp toward the fuel tank.

p. Remove the filler tube assembly from the vehicle.

5. Position an extra pair of jackstands under and support forward end of engine cradle to help stabilize vehicle during rear suspension removal/installation.

6. Perform following if vehicle is equipped with dual exhaust or are servicing right side on vehicle with single exhaust:

q. Position under-hoist utility jack or stand several inches below exhaust at muffler.

r. Disconnect exhaust isolators at muffler and resonators hangers.

s. Lower exhaust down to rest upon top of jack or stand placed below muffler.

7. Position under-hoist utility jack or

transmission jack (3) under center of rear axle differential (1). Raise jack head to contact differential and secure in place. When securing crossmember to jack, be sure not to secure stabilizer bar.

8. Remove shock absorber upper mounting screws.

9. Remove shock absorber lower mounting bolt and nut.

➡When removing crossmember mounting bolts in following step, be sure to not to misplace spacers between crossmember mounts and body.

✳✳ WARNING

If equipped with AWD, when removing crossmember mounting bolts it is important NOT to loosen or remove crossmember mounting bolts on opposite side of vehicle. Doing so will require rear wheel alignment following reinstallation to ensure proper thrust angle.

10. Remove both front and rear crossmember mounting bolts on side of vehicle being serviced.

✳✳ WARNING

To avoid damaging other components of vehicle, do not lower crossmember any further than necessary to remove shock absorber.

11. Slowly lower jack allowing repair-side of crossmember to drop. Do not lower jack at a fast rate. Lower jack just enough to

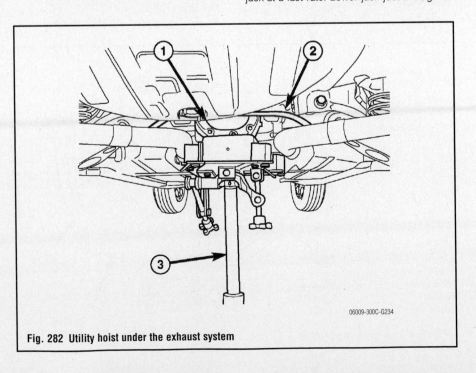

Fig. 282 Utility hoist under the exhaust system

06009-300C-G234

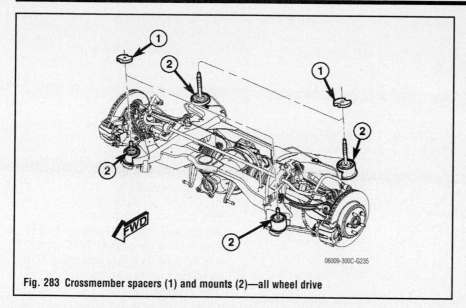

Fig. 283 Crossmember spacers (1) and mounts (2)—all wheel drive

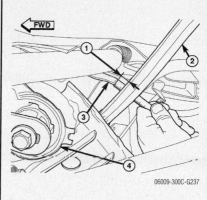

Fig. 285 Measure distance (1) between from tension link (2) to body weld flange (3) directly in front of it, just outboard of front mount bushing (4)

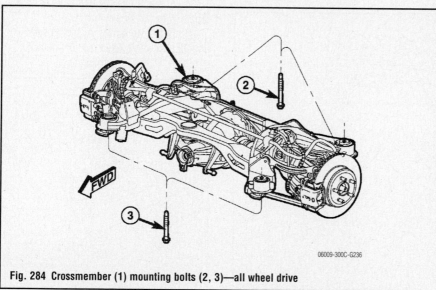

Fig. 284 Crossmember (1) mounting bolts (2, 3)—all wheel drive

allow top of shock absorber to clear body flange.

12. Remove shock absorber by tipping top outward and lifting lower end out of pocket in spring link.

To install:

13. Install shock absorber by setting lower end into pocket in spring link, then tipping top inward until aligned with upper mounting holes.

14. Install lower shock mounting bolt and nut. Do not tighten at this time.

15. Make sure spacers on top of crossmember mount bushings on side of repair are in position.

16. Carefully raise jack, guiding coil spring and upper end of shock absorber into mounted positions.

17. Install shock absorber upper mounting bolts. Tighten upper mounting bolts to 38 ft. lbs. (52 Nm).

➡**Rear crossmember mounting bolts are longer than front mounting bolts. Do not interchange mounting bolts.**

18. Install crossmember mounting bolts. Snug, but do not fully tighten bolts at this time.

19. Measure distance between from tension link to body weld flange directly in front of it, just outboard of front mount bushing. This distance must be at least 12mm to allow proper clearance for suspension movement. If distance is less than 12mm, shift that side of rear crossmember directly rearward until distance is 12mm or greater. To do so, loosen 3 mounting bolts slightly, leaving one on opposite side shifted, snugged to pivot off of. Shift crossmember rearward and snug loosened bolts. Measure opposite side to be sure it also maintains minimum 12mm distance.

20. Tighten all crossmember mounting bolts to 133 ft. lbs. (180 Nm) torque.

21. Remove jack from under rear axle differential.

22. If previously lowered, raise rear exhaust back to mounted position and connect exhaust isolators at muffler and resonators hangers. Remove jack or stand below exhaust muffler.

23. If removed, install fuel filler tube:

   a. Insert filler tube into the fuel tank rubber hose.

   b. Slide hose clamp into place and tighten.

   c. Hose clamp in place and tighten.

   d. Install filler tube mounting bolt.

   e. Install Filler tube vent line.

   f. Install the underbody splash shield.

   g. Install the left inner splash shield.

24. Install tire and wheel assemblies. Tighten wheel mounting nuts to 110 ft. lbs. (150 Nm) torque.

25. Lower vehicle.

26. Position vehicle on alignment rack/drive-on lift. Raise lift as necessary to access lower mounting bolt.

27. Tighten shock absorber lower mounting bolt nut to 53 ft. lbs. (72 Nm).

SPRING LINK

REMOVAL & INSTALLATION

See Figures 286 through 291.

1. Before servicing the vehicle, refer to the precautions in the beginning of this section.

2. Raise and support vehicle.

3. Remove rear spring.

4. Remove spring link-to-knuckle nut and bolt.

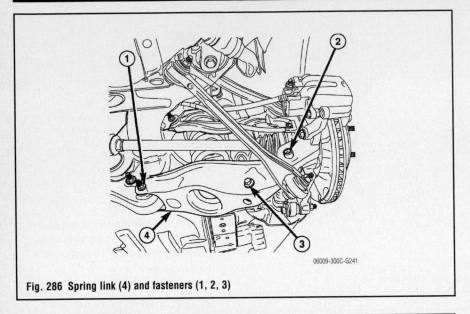

Fig. 286 Spring link (4) and fasteners (1, 2, 3)

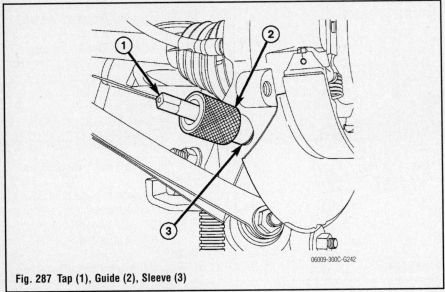

Fig. 287 Tap (1), Guide (2), Sleeve (3)

- 1. Bolt 9361-3
- 2. Nut
- 3. Spherical Washer
- 4. Thrust Bearing
- 5. Sleeve 9361-4 (RWD)
- 5. Sleeve 9361-5 (AWD—Left Side)
- 5. Sleeve 9361-6 (AWD—Right Side)

➡ **When installing thrust bearing on remover, be sure to place hardened side against nut.**

➡ **It is important to use appropriate Sleeve on Remover to provide proper Tool-to-Knuckle contact. RWD sleeve can be used on either side while AWD knuckles require specific left or right side Sleeves.**

7. Thread Remover Bolt 9361-3 into tapped knuckle sleeve.

8. Rotate nut down, matching sleeve angled end with angled face of knuckle.

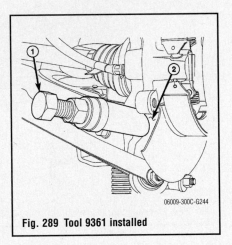

Fig. 289 Tool 9361 installed

⁂ WARNING

It important to use Guide, Special Tool 9361-2, when tapping sleeve in knuckle to help keep Tap, Special Tool 9361-1, straight during use or damage to Tap may occur.

5. Place Guide 9361-2 against sleeve in knuckle to keep Tap 9361-1 straight. Using Tap with an appropriate handle, cut threads approximately halfway through bushing (or about six complete threads). It is important to back tap out, clean out burrs and lubricate Tap often during process.

➡ **Prior to using Special Tool 9361, lubricate bolt threads to provide ease of use and promote tool longevity.**

6. Assemble Remover, Special Tool 9361, as shown.

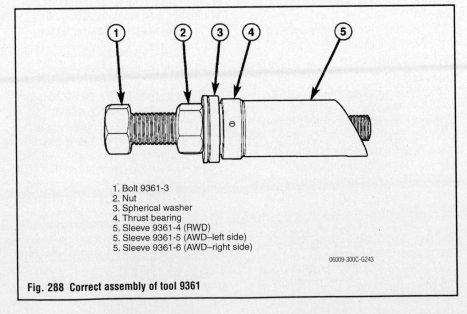

1. Bolt 9361-3
2. Nut
3. Spherical washer
4. Thrust bearing
5. Sleeve 9361-4 (RWD)
5. Sleeve 9361-5 (AWD–left side)
5. Sleeve 9361-6 (AWD–right side)

Fig. 288 Correct assembly of tool 9361

9. Continue to rotate Nut until knuckle sleeve is removed from knuckle. Discard knuckle sleeve; replace it with new upon installation.

10. Remove bolt and nut fastening spring link to crossmember.

11. Remove spring link.

To install:

12. Guide ball joint end of spring link into mounting pocket of knuckle, then swing opposite end up to bushing in crossmember and install bolt and nut fastening spring link to crossmember. Do not tighten bolt at this time.

➡**Prior to using Special Tool 9361, lubricate bolt threads to provide ease of use and promote tool longevity.**

13. Place new knuckle sleeve onto Installer Bolt 9361-7, and slide it up to bolt's head.

14. Slide Bolt 9361-7 with sleeve through knuckle and spring link ball joint starting from knuckle forward end.

15. Install thrust bearing and nut on end of bolt.

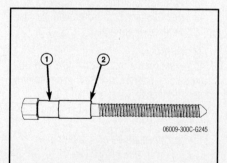

06009-300C-G245

Fig. 290 Place new knuckle sleeve (2) onto Installer Bolt 9361-7 (1), and slide it up to bolt's head

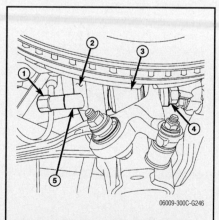

06009-300C-G246

Fig. 291 Slide Bolt 9361-7 (1) with sleeve (5) through knuckle (2) and spring link ball joint (3) starting from knuckle forward end

16. While holding bolt head stationary, rotate nut (using hand tools) installing sleeve in knuckle. Install sleeve until nut stops turning. Do not over tighten nut.

17. Remove special tool.

18. Install spring link-to-knuckle bolt front-to-rear through knuckle and link, then install nut. While holding bolt head stationary, tighten nut to 102 ft. lbs. (138 Nm) torque.

19. Install rear spring.

20. Lower vehicle.

21. Position vehicle on alignment rack/drive-on lift. Raise vehicle as necessary to access mounting bolt.

22. Tighten spring link bolt at crossmember to 80 ft. lbs. (108 Nm) torque.

23. Perform wheel alignment.

STABILIZER BAR

REMOVAL & INSTALLATION

See Figures 292 through 294.

1. Before servicing the vehicle, refer to the precautions in the beginning of this section.

2. Disconnect and isolate battery negative cable from battery post.

3. Raise and support vehicle.

4. On each side of vehicle rear, remove wheel mounting nuts, then tire and wheel assembly.

5. Remove rear exhaust system.

6. Apply alignment index marks to the driveshaft rubber coupler and axle flange.

7. Remove three driveshaft coupler-to-axle flange bolts and nuts.

8. Support driveshaft using a bungee cord. Attach ends of cord to fuel tank straps as shown.

➡**Due to short travel and low spring tension, it is not necessary to lock-out parking brake lever to service parking brake components.**

9. Disconnect front parking brake cable at connector to right rear parking brake cable.

10. Remove front parking brake cable from equalizer.

11. On each rear disc brake:

a. While holding guide pins from turning, remove disc brake caliper guide pin bolts.

b. Remove brake caliper from brake adapter and pads.

c. Guide brake caliper up through suspension, following brake hose path. Support caliper above rear suspension using with bungee cord or wire to keep caliper from overextending brake hose when crossmember is lowered.

➡**To remove wheel speed sensor connector from body wiring harness connector, move retaining clip and pull sensor connector outward.**

12. Remove wheel speed sensor connectors from body wiring harness connector located in luggage compartment floor pan.

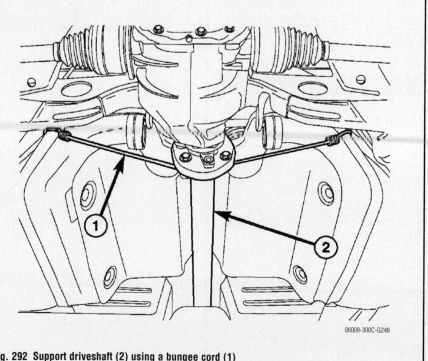

06009-300C-G248

Fig. 292 Support driveshaft (2) using a bungee cord (1)

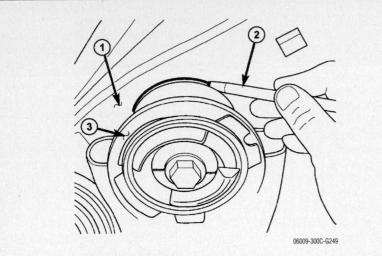

Fig. 293 Carefully mark location of rear crossmember on body at all four mount (bushing) locations using a marker

13. Unclip left wheel speed sensor cable from routing clip near body connector.

14. On each side of vehicle, remove shock absorber lower mounting bolt and nut.

15. Carefully mark location of rear crossmember on body at all four mount (bushing) locations using a marker or crayon. Do not use a scratch awl to mark location.

16. Position an extra pair of jackstands under and support forward end of engine cradle to help stabilize vehicle during rear suspension removal/installation.

17. Position under-hoist utility jack or transmission jack under center of rear axle differential. Raise jack head to contact differential and secure in place. When securing crossmember to jack, be sure not to secure stabilizer bar.

❋❋ CAUTION

Before opening fuel system, review all warnings and cautions under Fuel System.

18. Disconnect negative battery cable.
19. Drain fuel from tank.
20. Fuel filler tube assembly.
21. Open filler tube door.
22. Remove retaining wire from inside filler tube rubber.
23. Start removing rubber from body sheet metal.
24. Remove retaining wire from inside filler tube rubber.
25. Start removing rubber from body sheet metal.
26. Filler tube and rubber removed from body sheet metal.
27. Remove the left inner splash shield.

28. Disconnect the filler tube vent line.
29. Remove the filler tube mounting bolt.
30. Remove the under body splash shield.
31. Loosen the filler tube hose clamp. Leave the clamp tight on the hose and fuel tank location.
32. Move clamp toward the fuel tank.
33. Remove the filler tube assembly from the vehicle.

➡If equipped with AWD, when removing crossmember mounting bolts in following step, be sure to not to misplace spacers between crossmember mounts and body.

34. Remove both front and both rear mounting bolts fastening crossmember in place.

35. Slowly lower crossmember using jack. Do not lower jack at a fast rate. Lower just enough to allow driveshaft removal from rear axle differential. Do not lower jack any further than necessary. Slide driveshaft out of rear axle differential and allow bungee cord previously installed to support.

36. Slowly lower crossmember several inches.

37. Remove screw fastening front parking brake cable routing bracket to rear crossmember.

38. Continue to lower jack until crossmember is at a comfortable working level to access stabilizer bar fasteners.

39. On each end, remove bolt (3) and nut fastening stabilizer bar (4) to stabilizer link (2).

40. Remove bolts (1) fastening each stabilizer bar isolator retainer to crossmember.

41. Remove stabilizer bar (4) with isolators and retainers.

42. Remove retainers from isolators.

43. Remove isolators from stabilizer bar utilizing slits in bushings.

To install:

44. Install isolators on stabilizer bar utilizing slits in bushings. Install each isolator so its slit faces forward and flat side is positioned toward crossmember once installed.

45. Install retainers on isolators.

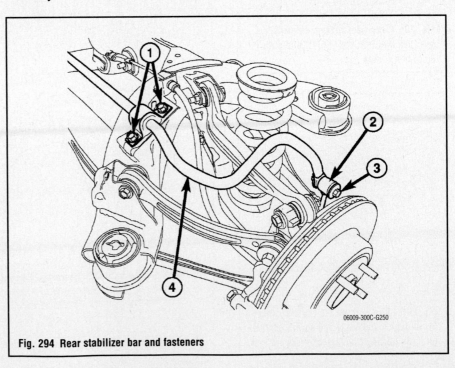

Fig. 294 Rear stabilizer bar and fasteners

46. Install stabilizer bar with isolators and retainers on crossmember.

47. Install isolator retainer mounting bolts. Do not tighten at this time.

48. Install bolt and nut fastening stabilizer bar ends to each stabilizer links. Do not tighten at this time.

49. Tighten isolator retainer mounting bolts to 45 ft. lbs. (61 Nm) torque.

50. Remove coil springs with isolators from spring links.

51. Raise crossmember using jack until there is about 10 inches clearance to the to body mounting points.

52. Install screw fastening front parking brake cable routing bracket to rear cross-member.

53. Raise crossmember to body mounting points. As crossmember is raised, slide driveshaft onto rear axle differential flange and align shocks with pockets in spring links.

➡ There are four crossmember mounting bolts. Rear mounting bolts are longer than front mounting bolts. Do not interchange mounting bolts.

54. Continue to raise crossmember with jack until crossmember mounting bolts can be installed. Install left side crossmember mounting bolts, but not the right side bolts. It is not necessary to tighten bolts at this point.

✳✳ WARNING

To avoid damaging other components of vehicle, do not lower crossmember any further than necessary to install coil spring.

55. Slowly lower jack allowing right side of crossmember to drop. Do not lower jack at a fast rate. Lower jack just enough to allow spring Installation. Do not lower jack any further than necessary.

➡ Before installing coil spring, make sure isolators are completely installed on ends of spring.

56. Install coil spring with isolators into spring pocket of spring link fitting the lower isolator to the shape of the pocket, then align top of spring with body mount.

57. Carefully raise jack, guiding coil spring and lower end of shock absorber into mounted positions. Once shock absorber lower mounting hole lines up with hole in spring link, stop jacking.

58. Install lower shock mounting bolt and nut. Do not tighten at this time.

59. If vehicle is equipped with AWD, insert spacers on top of right crossmember mount bushings before crossmember is raised into place.

➡ There are four crossmember mounting bolts. Rear mounting bolts are longer than front mounting bolts. Do not interchange mounting bolts.

60. Raise right side of crossmember into mounted position. Install right side crossmember mounting bolts. Snug, but do not fully tighten bolts at this time.

61. Remove both front and rear crossmember mounting bolts on left side of vehicle.

✳✳ WARNING

To avoid damaging other components of vehicle, do not lower crossmember any further than necessary to install coil spring.

62. Slowly lower jack allowing left side of crossmember to drop. Do not lower jack at a fast rate. Lower jack just enough to allow spring installation. Do not lower jack any further than necessary.

➡ Before installing coil spring, make sure isolators are completely installed on ends of spring.

63. Install coil spring with isolators into spring pocket of spring link fitting the lower isolator to the shape of the pocket, then align top of spring with body mount.

64. Carefully raise jack, guiding coil spring and lower end of shock absorber into mounted positions. Once shock absorber lower mounting hole lines up with hole in spring link, stop jacking.

65. Install lower shock mounting bolt and nut. Do not tighten at this time.

66. If vehicle is equipped with AWD, insert spacers on top of left crossmember mount bushings before crossmember is raised into place.

➡ There are four crossmember mounting bolts. Rear mounting bolts are longer than front mounting bolts. Do not interchange mounting bolts.

67. Raise left side of crossmember into mounted position. Install left side crossmember mounting bolts. Snug, but do not fully tighten bolts at this time.

68. Shift crossmember as necessary to line up mounts with location marks drawn on body before removal.

69. Once mounts are lined up with location marks, on both sides of vehicle, measure distance between the tension link and weld flange on body directly in front of it, just outboard of the front mount bushing.

This distance must be at least 12mm to allow proper clearance for suspension movement. If distance is less than 12mm on either side of vehicle, shift that side of rear crossmember directly rearward until distance is 12mm or greater. To do so, loosen 3 mounting bolts slightly, leaving one on opposite side of shift snugged to pivot off of. Shift crossmember rearward and snug loosened bolts. Re-measure opposite side to be sure it still maintains minimum 12mm distance.

70. Tighten all four crossmember mounting bolts to 133 ft. lbs. (180 Nm) torque.

71. Remove jack from under rear axle differential.

72. Remove bungee cord supporting driveshaft.

73. Align driveshaft index marks placed upon removal. Install driveshaft rear coupler-to-axle flange bolts and nuts by hand. Tighten driveshaft rear coupler-to-axle flange bolts to 60 ft. lbs. (81 Nm) torque.

74. Insert filler tube into the fuel tank rubber hose.

75. Slide hose clamp into place and tighten.

76. Hose clamp in place and tighten.

77. Install filler tube mounting bolt.

78. Install filler tube vent line.

79. Install the underbody splash shield.

80. Install the left inner splash shield.

81. Clip left rear wheel speed sensor cable to routing clip near body connector.

82. Match left rear wheel speed sensor connector to right sensor connector to make one connector.

83. Insert speed sensor connectors into body wiring harness connector located in luggage compartment floor pan. When installing connector, make sure retaining clip on body connector is properly in place and sensor connector cannot be pulled out.

84. On each rear disc brake:

   a. Push caliper guide pins into caliper adaptor to clear caliper mounting bosses when installing.

   b. Guide caliper and brake hose down through rear suspension, then slide caliper over brake pads and onto caliper adapter.

✳✳ WARNING

Extreme caution should be taken not to cross-thread caliper guide pin bolts when they are installed. Align caliper mounting holes with guide pins, then install guide pin bolts. While holding guide pins from turning, tighten bolts to 44 ft. lbs. (60 Nm).

c. Make sure brake hose is properly routed and will not come in contact with suspension components.

85. Route parking brake cable above rear crossmember, then slide cable through equalizer above rear differential.

➡ **Due to short travel and low spring tension, it is not necessary to lock-out parking brake lever to service parking brake components.**

86. Connect front parking brake cable at connector to right rear parking brake cable.

87. Install rear exhaust system.

88. Install tire and wheel assemblies. Tighten wheel mounting nuts to 110 ft. lbs. (150 Nm) torque.

89. Lower vehicle until rear wheels are just above floor level.

90. Apply parking brake lever. Release lever, then reapply.

91. Check to make sure rear wheels will not rotate with lever applied.

92. Lower vehicle.

93. Connect battery negative cable to battery post. It is important that this is performed properly.

94. Pump brake pedal several times to ensure vehicle has a firm brake pedal before moving vehicle.

95. Position vehicle on alignment rack/drive-on hoist. Raise vehicle as necessary to access mounting bolts.

96. Tighten shock absorber lower mounting bolt nuts to 53 ft. lbs. (72 Nm) torque.

97. Tighten stabilizer link fasteners to 45 ft. lbs. (61 Nm).

98. Perform wheel alignment.

TENSION LINK

REMOVAL & INSTALLATION

1. Before servicing the vehicle, refer to the precautions in the beginning of this section.

2. Raise and support vehicle.

3. On both sides of vehicle, remove wheel mounting nuts, then rear tire and wheel assembly.

❊❊ CAUTION

Before opening fuel system, review all warnings and cautions under Fuel System.

4. If servicing left side shock absorber, remove fuel filler tube:

   a. Disconnect negative battery cable.

   b. Drain fuel from tank.

c. Fuel filler tube assembly.

d. Open filler tube door.

e. Remove retaining wire from inside filler tube rubber.

f. Start removing rubber from body sheet metal.

g. Remove retaining wire from inside filler tube rubber.

h. Start removing rubber from body sheet metal.

i. Filler tube and rubber removed from body sheet metal.

j. Remove the left inner splash shield.

k. Disconnect the filler tube vent line.

l. Remove the filler tube mounting bolt.

m. Remove the under body splash shield.

n. Loosen the filler tube hose clamp. Leave the clamp tight on the hose and fuel tank location.

o. Move clamp toward the fuel tank.

p. Remove the filler tube assembly from the vehicle.

5. Position an extra pair of jackstands under and support forward end of engine cradle to help stabilize vehicle during rear suspension removal/installation.

6. Perform following if vehicle is equipped with dual exhaust or are servicing right side on vehicle with single exhaust:

   a. Position under-hoist utility jack or stand several inches below exhaust at muffler.

   b. Disconnect exhaust isolators at muffler and resonators hangers.

   c. Lower exhaust down to rest upon top of jack or stand placed below muffler.

7. Position under-hoist utility jack or transmission jack under center of rear axle differential. Raise jack head to contact differential and secure in place. When securing crossmember to jack, be sure not to secure stabilizer bar.

8. Remove shock absorber upper mounting screws.

9. Remove shock absorber lower mounting bolt and nut.

➡ **If equipped with AWD, when removing crossmember mounting bolts in following step, be sure to not to misplace spacers between crossmember mounts and body.**

❊❊ WARNING

When removing crossmember mounting bolts it is important NOT to loosen or remove crossmember mounting bolts on opposite side of

vehicle. Doing so will require rear wheel alignment following reinstallation to ensure proper thrust angle.

10. Remove both front and rear crossmember mounting bolts on repair-side of vehicle.

❊❊ WARNING

To avoid damaging other components of vehicle, do not lower crossmember any further than necessary to remove shock absorber.

11. Slowly lower jack allowing repair-side of crossmember to drop. Do not lower jack at a fast rate. Lower jack just enough to allow top of shock absorber to clear body flange.

12. Remove shock absorber by tipping top outward and lifting lower end out of pocket in spring link.

➡ **Do not lower side of crossmember any further than necessary to gain access to link mounting bolts at crossmember.**

13. Remove nut and bolt mounting link to knuckle.

14. Remove nut and bolt mounting link to crossmember.

15. Remove link.

To install:

➡ **When installing tension link, although link is same end-to-end, make sure that center bow is facing downward.**

16. Place link in bracket on crossmember. Install bolt and nut at crossmember. Do not tighten bolt at this time.

17. Install bolt and nut mounting link to knuckle. Do not tighten bolt at this time.

18. Install shock absorber by setting lower end into pocket in spring link, then tipping top inward until aligned with upper mounting holes.

19. Install lower shock mounting bolt and nut. Do not tighten at this time.

20. If vehicle is equipped with AWD, make sure spacers on top of crossmember mount bushings on side of repair are in position.

21. Carefully raise jack, guiding coil spring and upper end of shock absorber into mounted positions.

22. Install shock absorber upper mounting screws. Tighten upper mounting screws to 38 ft. lbs. (52 Nm) torque.

➡ **Rear crossmember mounting bolts are longer than front mounting bolts. Do not interchange mounting bolts.**

23. Install crossmember mounting bolts. Snug, but do not fully tighten bolts at this time.

24. Measure distance between from tension link to body weld flange directly in front of it, just outboard of front mount bushing. This distance must be at least 12mm to allow proper clearance for suspension movement. If distance is less than 12mm, shift that side of rear crossmember directly rearward until distance is 12mm or greater. To do so, loosen 3 mounting bolts slightly, leaving one on opposite side shifted, snugged to pivot off of. Shift crossmember rearward and snug loosened bolts. Measure opposite side to be sure it also maintains minimum 12mm distance.

25. Tighten all crossmember mounting bolts to 133 ft. lbs. (180 Nm) torque.

26. Remove jack from under rear axle differential.

27. If previously lowered, raise rear exhaust back to mounted position and connect exhaust isolators at muffler and resonators hangers. Remove jack or stand below exhaust muffler.

28. If removed, install fuel filler tube:

  a. Insert filler tube into the fuel tank rubber hose.

  b. Slide hose clamp into place and tighten.

  c. Hose clamp in place and tighten.

  d. Install filler tube mounting bolt.

  e. Install Filler tube vent line.

  f. Install the underbody splash shield.

  g. Install the left inner splash shield.

29. Lower vehicle until front tires contact floor but rear is still suspended. Place jackstands under each rear suspension spring link. Place an appropriate wooden block between stand and link to avoid damaging spring link, then lower vehicle until full vehicle weight is supported by suspension.

30. Tighten camber link fasteners to:

  • Bolt at crossmember: 63 ft. lbs. (85 Nm) torque.

  • Bolt nut at knuckle: 72 ft. lbs. (98 Nm) torque.

31. Tighten shock absorber lower mounting bolt nut to 53 ft. lbs. (72 Nm) torque.

32. Raise vehicle and remove jackstands.

33. Install tire and wheel assemblies. Tighten wheel mounting nuts to 110 ft. lbs. (150 Nm) torque.

34. Lower vehicle.

35. Perform wheel alignment.

TOE LINK

REMOVAL & INSTALLATION

Left Side

See Figures 295 and 296.

1. Before servicing the vehicle, refer to the precautions in the beginning of this section.

2. Raise and support vehicle.

3. On both sides of vehicle, remove wheel mounting nuts, and then rear tire and wheel assembly.

✳✳ CAUTION

Before opening fuel system, review all warnings and cautions.

4. Disconnect negative battery cable.

5. Drain fuel from tank.

6. Fuel filler tube assembly.

7. Open filler tube door.

8. Remove retaining wire from inside filler tube rubber.

9. Start removing rubber from body sheet metal.

10. Remove retaining wire from inside filler tube rubber.

11. Start removing rubber from body sheet metal.

12. Filler tube and rubber removed from body sheet metal.

13. Remove the left inner splash shield.

14. Disconnect the filler tube vent line.

15. Remove the filler tube mounting bolt.

16. Remove the under body splash shield.

17. Loosen the filler tube hose clamp. Leave the clamp tight on the hose and fuel tank location.

18. Move clamp toward the fuel tank.

19. Remove the filler tube assembly from the vehicle.

20. Position an extra pair of jackstands under and support forward end of engine cradle to help stabilize vehicle during rear suspension removal/installation.

21. Perform following if vehicle is equipped with dual exhaust:

  a. Position under-hoist utility jack or stand several inches below exhaust at muffler.

  b. Disconnect exhaust isolators at muffler and resonators hangers.

  c. Lower exhaust down to rest upon top of jack or stand placed below muffler.

22. Position under-hoist utility jack or transmission jack under center of rear axle differential. Raise jack head to contact differential and secure in place.

23. Remove shock absorber lower mounting bolt and nut.

✳✳ WARNING

When removing crossmember mounting bolts it is important NOT to loosen or remove crossmember mounting bolts on opposite side of vehicle. Doing so will require rear wheel alignment following reinstallation to ensure proper thrust angle.

24. Remove both front and rear crossmember mounting bolts on repair-side of vehicle. If equipped with AWD, be sure to not to misplace spacers between crossmember mounts and body.

✳✳ WARNING

To avoid damaging other components of the vehicle do not lower crossmember any further than necessary to remove shock absorber.

25. Slowly lower jack allowing repair-side of crossmember to drop. Do not lower jack at a fast rate. Lower jack just enough to allow toe link mounting bolt at crossmember.

26. If equipped, remove wheel speed sensor cable from toe link.

27. While holding toe adjustment cam bolt from rotating, remove nut (3) securing toe link at crossmember (1).

28. Slide cam bolt rearward out of crossmember and link.

29. Remove mounting bolt and nut at knuckle.

30. Remove toe link.

To install:

31. Slide crossmember end of toe link into box bracket on crossmember. Slide cam bolt through bracket and link from rear.

32. Install bolt and nut securing link to knuckle. Do not tighten bolt at this time.

33. While holding toe adjustment cam bolt from rotating (cam facing upward), Install cam washer and nut securing toe link at crossmember. Do not tighten nut at this time.

34. If equipped, attach wheel speed sensor cable to toe link.

35. Carefully raise jack, guiding coil spring and lower end of shock absorber into mounted positions.

36. When lower shock mounting bolt holes line up install bolt and nut. Do not tighten at this time.

➡Rear crossmember mounting bolts are longer than front mounting bolts. Do not interchange mounting bolts.

37. Continue to raise crossmember in not already in mounted position, then install

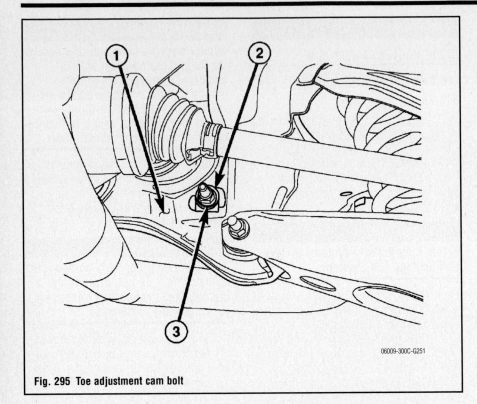

Fig. 295 Toe adjustment cam bolt

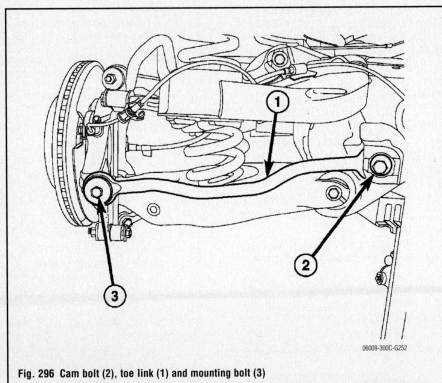

Fig. 296 Cam bolt (2), toe link (1) and mounting bolt (3)

crossmember mounting bolts. Snug, but do not fully tighten bolts at this time.

38. Measure distance between from tension link to body weld flange directly in front of it, just outboard of front mount bushing. This distance must be at least 12mm to allow proper clearance for suspension movement. If distance is less than 12mm, shift that side of rear crossmember directly rearward until distance is 12mm or greater. To do so, loosen 3 mounting bolts slightly, leaving one on opposite side of shift snugged to pivot off of. Shift crossmember rearward and snug loosened bolts. Measure opposite side to be sure it also maintains minimum 12mm distance.

39. Tighten all crossmember mounting bolts to 133 ft. lbs. (180 Nm) torque.

40. Remove jack from under rear axle differential.

41. If previously lowered, raise rear exhaust back to mounted position and connect exhaust isolators at muffler and resonators hangers. Remove jack or stand below exhaust muffler.

42. Insert filler tube into the fuel tank rubber hose.

43. Slide hose clamp into place and tighten.

44. Hose clamp in place and tighten.

45. Install filler tube mounting bolt.

46. Install filler tube vent line.

47. Install the underbody splash shield.

48. Install the left inner splash shield.

49. Install tire and wheel assemblies. Tighten wheel mounting nuts to 110 ft. lbs. (150 Nm) torque.

50. Lower vehicle.

51. Position vehicle on alignment rack/drive-on lift. Raise vehicle as necessary to access mounting bolts.

52. Tighten shock absorber lower mounting bolt nut to 53 ft. lbs. (72 Nm) torque.

53. Tighten toe link fasteners to:
- Nut at crossmember: 80 ft. lbs. (108 Nm) torque (This nut may be tightened after rear wheel alignment toe is set. Do not tighten from bolt head end.).
- Bolt at knuckle: 60 ft. lbs. (81 Nm).

54. Perform wheel alignment.

Right Side

1. Before servicing the vehicle, refer to the precautions in the beginning of this section.

2. Raise and support vehicle.

3. Remove wheel mounting nuts, then rear tire and wheel assembly.

4. If equipped, remove wheel speed sensor cable from toe link.

5. While holding toe adjustment cam bolt from rotating, remove nut securing toe link at crossmember.

6. Slide cam bolt rearward out of crossmember and link.

7. Remove mounting bolt and nut at knuckle.

8. Remove toe link.

To install:

9. Slide crossmember end of toe link into box bracket on crossmember. Slide cam bolt through bracket and link from rear of vehicle.

10. Install bolt and nut securing link to knuckle. Do not tighten bolt at this time.

11. While holding toe adjustment cam bolt from rotating (cam facing upward), Install cam washer and nut securing toe link at crossmember. Do not tighten nut at this time.

12. If equipped, Attach wheel speed sensor cable to toe link.

13. Raise rear exhaust back to mounted position and connect exhaust isolators at muffler and resonators hangers. Remove jack or stand below exhaust muffler.

14. Install tire and wheel assembly. Tighten wheel mounting nuts to 110 ft. lbs. (150 Nm) torque.

15. Lower vehicle.

16. Position vehicle on alignment rack/drive-on lift. Raise vehicle as necessary to access mounting bolts.

17. Tighten toe link fasteners to:
- Nut at crossmember: 80 ft. lbs. (108 Nm). (This nut may be tightened after rear wheel alignment toe is set. Do not tighten from bolt head end.).
- Bolt at knuckle: 60 ft. lbs. (81 Nm) torque.

18. Perform wheel alignment.

WHEEL BEARINGS

REMOVAL & INSTALLATION

See Figures 297 and 298.

1. Before servicing the vehicle, refer to the precautions in the beginning of this section.

2. Raise and support vehicle.

3. Remove wheel mounting nuts, then tire and wheel assembly.

4. While a helper applies brakes to keep hub from rotating, remove hub nut from the halfshaft.

➡ **In some cases, it may be necessary to retract caliper piston in its bore a small amount in order to provide sufficient clearance between shoes and rotor to easily remove caliper from knuckle. This can usually be accomplished before guide pin bolts are removed, by grasping rear of caliper and pulling outward working with guide pins, thus retracting piston. Never push on piston directly as it may get damaged.**

5. Remove two bolts securing disc brake caliper adapter to knuckle.

6. Remove disc brake caliper and adapter from knuckle as an assembly. Hang assembly out of way using wire or a bungee cord. Use care not to overextend brake hose when doing this.

7. Remove any clips retaining brake rotor to wheel mounting studs.

8. Slide brake rotor off hub and bearing.

9. Loosen each hub and bearing mounting bolt a turn or two at a time while pulling outward on hub and bearing to avoid bolt contact with halfshaft outer joint. Once removed from threads in hub and

bearing (but not knuckle), allow bolts to stay in and protrude through knuckle and brake support plate to keep brake support plate in place when hub and bearing is removed.

10. Slide hub and bearing off knuckle and halfshaft.

To install:

➡ **Before installing hub and bearing on end of axle halfshaft, ensure isolation washer is present on end of halfshaft. Inspect washer making sure it is not worn or damaged. Washer can be installed in either direction on shaft.**

11. Position hub and bearing bolts though rear of knuckle and parking brake support just enough to hold support in place as hub and bearing is installed.

12. Slide hub and bearing onto halfshaft. Place hub and bearing through brake support, onto knuckle, lining up mounting bolt holes with bolts.

13. Install four bolts fastening hub and bearing in place. Tighten mounting bolts to 50 ft. lbs. (68 Nm) torque.

➡ **Inspect disc brake pads and parking brake shoes before brake rotor installation.**

14. Install brake rotor over wheel mounting studs and onto hub.

15. Install disc brake caliper and adapter assembly over brake rotor.

16. Install mounting bolts securing

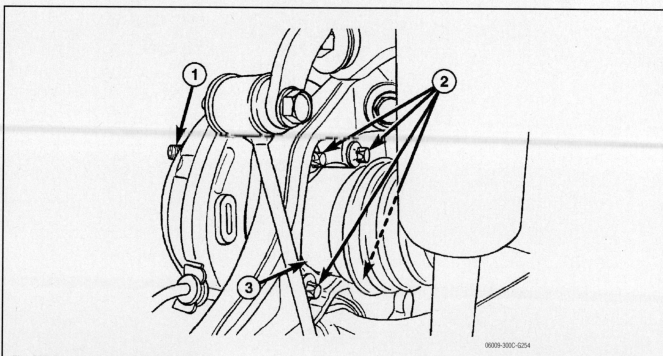

Fig. 298 Rear hub/bearing mounting bolts (2)

06009-300C-G254

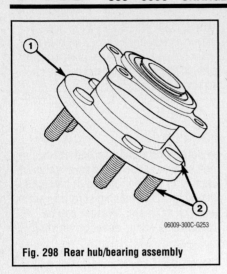

Fig. 298 Rear hub/bearing assembly

06009-300C-G253

caliper adapter to knuckle. Tighten bolts to 70 ft. lbs. (95 Nm) torque.

17. Install hub nut on end of halfshaft. While a helper applies brakes to keep hub from turning, tighten hub nut to 157 ft. lbs. (213 Nm) torque.

18. Verify proper adjustment of the parking brake shoes and adjust as necessary.

19. Install tire and wheel assembly. Tighten wheel mounting nuts to 110 ft. lbs. (150 Nm) torque.

20. Lower vehicle.

21. Pump brake pedal several times to ensure vehicle has a firm brake pedal before moving vehicle.

22. Check and adjust brake fluid level in reservoir as necessary.

23. Road test vehicle and make several stops to wear off any foreign material on brakes and to seat brake pads.

ADJUSTMENT

The rear wheel bearing and wheel hub of this vehicle are a one piece sealed unit or hub and bearing unit type assembly. No adjustments are possible.

The center of the hub and bearing is splined to match the axle halfshaft.

The wheel mounting studs used to mount the tire and wheel to the vehicle are the only replaceable components of the hub and bearing. Otherwise, the hub and bearing is serviced only as a complete assembly.

SPECIFICATIONS AND MAINTENANCE CHARTS

ENGINE AND VEHICLE IDENTIFICATION

			Engine						Model Year	
Code	Liters (cc)	Cu. In.	Cyl.	Fuel Sys.	Engine Type	Eng. Mfg.			Code	Year
K	3.7 (3701)	226	6	MFI	SOHC	Chrysler			5	2005
N	4.7 (4701)	287	8	MFI	SOHC	Chrysler			6	2006
P	4.7 (4701)	287	8	FFV	SOHC	Chrysler			7	2007
D	5.7 (5653)	345	8	MFI	OHV	Chrysler				
2	5.7 (5654)	345	8	MFI	OHV	Chrysler				

SOHC: Single overhead camshaft

OHV: Overhead Valve

MFI: Multi-port Fuel Injection

FFV: Flex Fuel Vehicle

22043_DURA_C0001

GENERAL ENGINE SPECIFICATIONS

Year	Model	Engine Displ. Liters	Engine VIN	Net Horsepower @ rpm	Net Torque @ rpm (ft. lbs.)	Bore x Stroke (in.)	Com- pression Ratio	Oil Pressure @ rpm
2005	Durango	3.7	K	210@5200	225@4200	3.66x3.40	9.1:1	25-110@3000
		4.7	N	235@4800	295@3200	3.66x3.40	9.0:1	25-110@3000
		5.7	D	335@5200	370@4200	3.91x3.58	9.6:1	25-110@3000
2006	Durango	3.7	K	210@5200	225@4200	3.66x3.40	9.1:1	25-110@3000
		4.7	N	235@4800	295@3200	3.66x3.40	9.0:1	25-110@3000
		4.7	P	235@4800	295@3200	3.66x3.40	9.0:1	25-110@3000
		5.7	2	335@5200	370@4200	3.91x3.58	9.6:1	25-110@3000
2007	Aspen	4.7	N	235@4800	295@3200	3.66x3.40	9.0:1	25-110@3000
		4.7	P	235@4800	295@3200	3.66x3.40	9.0:1	25-110@3000
		5.7	2	345@5400	375@4200	3.91x3.58	9.6:1	25-110@3000
	Durango	3.7	K	210@5200	225@4200	3.66x3.40	9.1:1	25-110@3000
		4.7	N	235@4800	295@3200	3.66x3.40	9.0:1	25-110@3000
		4.7	P	235@4800	295@3200	3.66x3.40	9.0:1	25-110@3000
		5.7	2	335@5200	370@4200	3.91x3.58	9.6:1	25-110@3000

22043_DURA_C0002

GASOLINE ENGINE TUNE-UP SPECIFICATIONS

Year	Engine Displacement Liters	Engine VIN	Spark Plug Gap (in.)	Ignition Timing (deg.)	Fuel Pump (psi)	Idle Speed (rpm)	Valve Clearance Intake	Exhaust
2005	3.7	K	0.042	①	44-54	②	HYD	HYD
	4.7	N	0.040	①	47-51	②	HYD	HYD
	5.7	D	0.045	①	49.0-49.4	②	HYD	HYD
2006	3.7	K	0.042	①	44-54	②	HYD	HYD
	4.7	N	0.040	①	47-51	②	HYD	HYD
	4.7	P	0.040	①	47-51	②	HYD	HYD
	5.7	2	0.045	①	49.0-49.4	②	HYD	HYD
2007	3.7	K	0.042	①	44-54	②	HYD	HYD
	4.7	N	0.040	①	47-51	②	HYD	HYD
	4.7	P	0.040	①	47-51	②	HYD	HYD
	5.7	2	0.045	①	49.0-49.4	②	HYD	HYD

NOTE: The Vehicle Emission Control Information (VECI) label often reflects specification changes made during production.

The label figures must be used if they differ from those in this chart.

HYD: Hydraulic

① Ignition timing is controlled by the PCM and is not adjustable.

② Idle speed is controlled by the PCM and is not adjustable

22043_DURA_C0003

CAPACITIES

Year	Model	Engine Displ. Liters	Engine VIN	Engine Oil with Filter (qts.)	Transmission (pts.)	Transfer Case (pts.)	Drive Axle Front (pts.)	Rear (pts.)	Fuel Tank (gal.)	Cooling System (qts.)
2005	Durango	3.7	K	5.0	①	②	3.4	③	27.0	16.2
		4.7	N	6.0	①	②	3.4	③	27.0	16.2
		5.7	D	7.0	①	②	3.4	③	27.0	16.2
2006	Durango	3.7	K	5.0	①	②	3.4	③	27.0	16.2
		4.7	N	6.0	①	②	3.4	③	27.0	16.2
		4.7	P	6.0	①	②	3.4	③	27.0	16.2
		5.7	2	7.0	①	②	3.4	③	27.0	16.2
2007	Aspen	4.7	N	6.0	①	②	3.4	③	27.0	16.2
		4.7	P	6.0	①	②	3.4	③	27.0	16.2
		5.7	2	7.0	①	②	3.4	③	27.0	16.2
	Durango	3.7	K	5.0	①	②	3.4	③	27.0	16.2
		4.7	N	6.0	①	②	3.4	③	27.0	16.2
		4.7	P	6.0	①	②	3.4	③	27.0	16.2
		5.7	2	7.0	①	②	3.4	③	27.0	16.2

NOTE: All capacities are approximate. Add fluid gradually and check to be sure a proper fluid level is obtained.

① 42RLE Fluid drain/filter service: 8pts.; Overhaul: 17.6 pts.

545RFE Fluid drain/filter service, 2wd: 11 pts.; 4wd: 13 pts.; Overhaul: 28 pts.

② NV144: 1.8 pts.; NV244 GEN II: 3.4 pts.

③ The following values include 0.25 pt. of friction
modifier for LSD axles.

8.25 axle: 4.4 pts.

9.25 axle: 4.9 pts.

22043_DURA_C0004

FLUID SPECIFICATIONS

Year	Model	Engine Displacement Liters (cc)	Engine ID/VIN	Engine Oil	Auto. Trans.	Drive Axle	Power Steering Fluid	Brake Master Cylinder
2005	Durango	3.7	K	5W-30	Mopar ATF+4	①	Mopar ATF+4	DOT-3
		4.7	N	5W-30	Mopar ATF+4	①	Mopar ATF+4	DOT-3
		5.7	D	5W-20	Mopar ATF+4	①	Mopar ATF+4	DOT-3
2006	Durango	3.7	K	5W-30	Mopar ATF+4	①	Mopar ATF+4	DOT-3
		4.7	N	5W-30	Mopar ATF+4	①	Mopar ATF+4	DOT-3
		4.7	P	5W-30	Mopar ATF+4	①	Mopar ATF+4	DOT-3
		5.7	2	5W-20	Mopar ATF+4	①	Mopar ATF+4	DOT-3
2007	Aspen	4.7	N	5W-20	Mopar ATF+4	①	Mopar ATF+4	DOT-3
		4.7	P	5W-20	Mopar ATF+4	①	Mopar ATF+4	DOT-3
		5.7	2	5W-20	Mopar ATF+4	①	Mopar ATF+4	DOT-3
	Durango	3.7	K	5W-20	Mopar ATF+4	①	Mopar ATF+4	DOT-3
		4.7	N	5W-20	Mopar ATF+4	①	Mopar ATF+4	DOT-3
		4.7	P	5W-20	Mopar ATF+4	①	Mopar ATF+4	DOT-3
		5.7	2	5W-20	Mopar ATF+4	①	Mopar ATF+4	DOT-3

DOT: Department Of Transpotation

NA: Not Applicable

① Mopar Synthetic Gear Lube 75W-140

22043_DURA_C0005

VALVE SPECIFICATIONS

Year	Engine Displ. Liters	Engine VIN	Seat Angle (deg.)	Face Angle (deg.)	Spring Test Pressure (lbs. @ in.)	Spring Installed Height (in.)	Stem-to-Guide Clearance (in.) Intake	Exhaust	Stem Diameter (in.) Intake	Exhaust
2005	3.7	K	44.5-45	45-45.5	221-242@ 1.107	1.619	0.0008-0.0028	0.0019-0.0039	0.2729-0.2739	0.2717-0.2728
	4.7	N	44.5-45	45-45.5	176.7-193.3 @1.1670	1.601	0.0008-0.0028	0.0019-0.0039	0.2729-0.2739	0.2717-0.2728
	5.7	D	44.5-45	45-45.5	95@1.81	1.81	0.0008-0.0025	0.0019-0.0037	0.3120-0.3130	0.3110-0.3120
2006	3.7	K	44.5-45	45-45.5	221-242@ 1.107	1.619	0.0008-0.0028	0.0019-0.0039	0.2729-0.2739	0.2717-0.2728
	4.7	N	44.5-45	45-45.5	176.7-193.3 @1.1670	1.601	0.0008-0.0028	0.0019-0.0039	0.2729-0.2739	0.2717-0.2728
	4.7	P	44.5-45	45-45.5	176.7-193.3 @1.1670	1.601	0.0008-0.0028	0.0019-0.0039	0.2729-0.2739	0.2717-0.2728
	5.7	2	44.5-45	45-45.5	95@1.81	1.81	0.0008-0.0025	0.0019-0.0037	0.3120-0.3130	0.3110-0.3120
2007	3.7	K	44.5-45	45-45.5	221-242@ 1.107	1.619	0.0008-0.0028	0.0019-0.0039	0.2729-0.2739	0.2717-0.2728
	4.7	N	44.5-45	45-45.5	176.7-193.3 @1.1670	1.601	0.0008-0.0028	0.0019-0.0039	0.2729-0.2739	0.2717-0.2728
	4.7	P	44.5-45	45-45.5	176.7-193.3 @1.1670	1.601	0.0008-0.0028	0.0019-0.0039	0.2729-0.2739	0.2717-0.2728
	5.7	2	44.5-45	45-45.5	95@1.81	1.81	0.0008-0.0025	0.0019-0.0037	0.3120-0.3130	0.3110-0.3120

22043_DURA_C0006

CAMSHAFT AND BEARING SPECIFICATIONS CHART
All measurements are given in inches.

Year	Engine Displacement Liters	Engine VIN	Journal Diameter	Brg. Oil Clearance	Shaft End-play	Runout	Journal Bore	Lobe Lift	
								Intake	Exhaust
2005	3.7	K	1.0227-1.0235	0.0010-0.0026	0.0030-0.0079	NA	NA	NA	NA
	4.7	N	1.0227-1.0235	0.0010-0.0026	0.0030-0.0079	NA	NA	NA	NA
	5.7	D	①	②	0.0031-0.0114	NA	NA	0.2830	0.2830
2006	3.7	K	1.0227-1.0235	0.0010-0.0026	0.0030-0.0079	NA	NA	NA	NA
	4.7	N	1.0227-1.0235	0.0010-0.0026	0.0030-0.0079	NA	NA	NA	NA
	4.7	P	1.0227-1.0235	0.0010-0.0026	0.0039-0.0079	NA	NA	NA	NA
	5.7	2	①	②	0.0031-0.0114	NA	NA	0.2830	0.2830
2007	3.7	K	1.0227-1.0235	0.0010-0.0026	0.0030-0.0079	NA	NA	NA	NA
	4.7	N	1.0227-1.0235	0.0010-0.0026	0.0030-0.0079	NA	NA	NA	NA
	4.7	P	1.0227-1.0235	0.0010-0.0026	0.0039-0.0079	NA	NA	NA	NA
	5.7	2	①	②	0.0031-0.0114	NA	NA	0.2830	0.2830

NA: Not Available

① No. 1: 2.29 in. ② No. 1: 0.0015-0.0030 in.
   No. 2: 2.27 in.   No. 2: 0.0019-0.0035 in.
   No. 3: 2.26 in.   No. 3: 0.0015-0.0030 in.
   No. 4: 2.24 in.   No. 4: 0.0019-0.0035 in.
   No. 5: 1.72 in.   No. 5: 0.0015-0.0030 in.
                    No. 5: 0.0031-0.0114 in.

22043_DURA_C0007

CRANKSHAFT AND CONNECTING ROD SPECIFICATIONS

All measurements are given in inches.

Year	Engine Displ. Liters	Engine VIN	Crankshaft			Thrust on No.	Connecting Rod		
			Main Brg. Journal Dia.	Main Brg. Oil Clearance	Shaft End-play		Journal Diameter	Oil Clearance	Side Clearance
2005	3.7	K	2.4996-2.5005	0.0020-0.0034	0.0021-0.0112	2	2.2794-2.2797	0.0004-0.0019	0.0040-0.0138
	4.7	N	2.4996-2.5005	0.0008-0.0021	0.0021-0.0112	2	2.0076-2.0082	0.0006-0.0022	0.0040-0.0138
	5.7	D	2.5585-2.5595	0.0009-0.0020	0.0020-0.0110	3	2.1250-2.1260	0.0007-0.0023	0.0030-0.0137
2006	3.7	K	2.4996-2.5005	0.0020-0.0034	0.0021-0.0112	2	2.2794-2.2797	0.0004-0.0019	0.0040-0.0138
	4.7	N	2.4996-2.5005	0.0008-0.0021	0.0021-0.0112	2	2.0076-2.0082	0.0006-0.0022	0.0040-0.0138
	4.7	P	2.4996-2.5005	0.0008-0.0021	0.0021-0.0112	2	2.0076-2.0082	0.0006-0.0022	0.0040-0.0138
	5.7	2	2.5585-2.5595	0.0009-0.0020	0.0020-0.0110	3	2.1250-2.1260	0.0007-0.0023	0.0030-0.0137
2007	3.7	K	2.4996-2.5005	0.0020-0.0034	0.0021-0.0112	2	2.2794-2.2797	0.0004-0.0019	0.0040-0.0138
	4.7	N	2.4996-2.5005	0.0008-0.0021	0.0021-0.0112	2	2.0076-2.0082	0.0006-0.0022	0.0040-0.0138
	4.7	P	2.4996-2.5005	0.0008-0.0021	0.0021-0.0112	2	2.0076-2.0082	0.0006-0.0022	0.0040-0.0138
	5.7	2	2.5585-2.5595	0.0009-0.0020	0.0020-0.0110	3	2.1250-2.1260	0.0007-0.0023	0.0030-0.0137

22043_DURA_C0008

PISTON AND RING SPECIFICATIONS

All measurements are given in inches.

Year	Engine Displ. Liters	Engine VIN	Piston Clearance	Ring Gap Top Comp.	Ring Gap Bottom Comp.	Ring Gap Oil Control	Ring Side Clearance Top Comp.	Ring Side Clearance Bottom Comp.	Ring Side Clearance Oil Control
2005	3.7	K	0.0014	0.0146-0.0249	0.0146-0.0249	0.0100-0.0300	0.0020-0.0037	0.0016-0.0031	0.0007-0.0091
	4.7	N	0.0014	0.0146-0.0249	0.0146-0.0249	0.0099-0.0300	0.0020-0.0037	0.0016-0.0031	0.0175-0.0185
	5.7	D	0.0008-0.0019	0.0090-0.0149	0.0137-0.0236	0.0059-0.0259	0.0007-0.0026	0.0007-0.0022	0.0007-0.0091
2006	3.7	K	0.0014	0.0146-0.0249	0.0146-0.0249	0.0100-0.0300	0.0020-0.0037	0.0016-0.0031	0.0007-0.0091
	4.7	N	0.0014	0.0146-0.0249	0.0146-0.0249	0.0099-0.0300	0.0020-0.0037	0.0016-0.0031	0.0175-0.0185
	4.7	P	0.0014	0.0146-0.0249	0.0146-0.0249	0.0099-0.0300	0.0020-0.0037	0.0016-0.0031	0.0175-0.0185
	5.7	2	0.0008-0.0019	0.0090-0.0149	0.0137-0.0236	0.0059-0.0259	0.0007-0.0026	0.0007-0.0022	0.0007-0.0091
2007	3.7	K	0.0014	0.0146-0.0249	0.0146-0.0249	0.0100-0.0300	0.0020-0.0037	0.0016-0.0031	0.0007-0.0091
	4.7	N	0.0014	0.0146-0.0249	0.0146-0.0249	0.0099-0.0300	0.0020-0.0037	0.0016-0.0031	0.0175-0.0185
	4.7	P	0.0014	0.0146-0.0249	0.0146-0.0249	0.0099-0.0300	0.0020-0.0037	0.0016-0.0031	0.0175-0.0185
	5.7	2	0.0008-0.0019	0.0090-0.0149	0.0137-0.0236	0.0059-0.0259	0.0007-0.0026	0.0007-0.0022	0.0007-0.0091

22043_DURA_C0009

TORQUE SPECIFICATIONS

All readings in ft. lbs.

Year	Engine Displ. Liters	Engine VIN	Cylinder Head Bolts	Main Bearing Bolts	Rod Bearing Bolts	Crankshaft Damper Bolts	Flexplate Bolts	Manifold Intake	Manifold Exhaust	Spark Plugs	Oil Pan Drain Plug
2005	3.7	K	①	②	③	130	70	④	18	20	25
	4.7	N	①	⑤	③	130	45	④	18	20	25
	5.7	D	⑥	⑦	⑧	90	70	④	18	13	25
2006	3.7	K	①	②	③	130	70	④	18	20	25
	4.7	N	①	⑤	③	130	45	④	18	20	25
	4.7	P	①	⑤	③	130	45	④	18	20	25
	5.7	2	⑥	⑦	⑧	90	70	④	18	13	25
2007	3.7	K	①	②	③	130	70	④	18	20	25
	4.7	N	①	⑤	③	130	45	④	18	20	25
	4.7	P	①	⑤	③	130	45	④	18	20	25
	5.7	2	⑥	⑦	⑧	90	70	④	18	13	25

① See text

② See the illustration

Step 1: Hand tighten bolts 1D, 1G and 1F until bedplate contacts the block

Step 2: tighten bolts 1A-1J to 40 ft. lbs.

Step 3: Tighten bolts 1-8 to 60 inch lbs.

Step 4: Tighten bolts 1-8 an additional 90 degrees

Step 5: Tighten bolts A-E to 20 ft. lbs.

③ 20 ft. lbs. plus 90 degrees

④ 105 inch lbs.

⑤ Bed plate bolt sequence. Refer to illustration

Step 1: Bolts A-L to 40 ft. lbs.

Step 2: Bolts 1-10 25 inch lbs.

Step 3: Bolts 1-10 plus 90 degrees

Step 4: Bolts A1-A6 20 ft. lbs.

⑥ M8

Step 1: 15 ft. lbs.

Step 2: 25 ft. lbs.

M12

Step 1: 25 ft. lbs.

Step 2: 40 ft. lbs.

Step 3: plus 90 degree turn

⑦ See the illustration

Step 1: Bolts 1-10 to 20 ft. lbs.

Step 2: bolts 1-10 an additional 90 degrees

Step 3: Bolts (cross bolts) A-J to 21 ft. lbs.

⑧ 15 ft. lbs. Plus 90 degrees

22043_DURA_C0010

WHEEL ALIGNMENT

Year	Model		Caster Range (+/-Deg.)	Caster Preferred Setting (Deg.)	Camber Range (+/-Deg.)	Camber Preferred Setting (Deg.)	Toe-in (Deg.)
2005	Durango 4x2	LF	0.50	+3.20	0.50	0	0.10+/-0.05
		RF	0.50	+3.50	0.50	0	0.10+/-0.05
		R	—	—	0.35	-0.10	0.30+/-0.35
	Durango 4x4	LF	0.50	+3.50	0.50	0.15	0.10+/-0.05
		RF	0.50	+3.50	0.50	-0.15	0.10+/-0.05
		R			0.35	-0.10	0.30+/-0.35
2006	Durango 4x2	LF	0.50	+3.20	0.50	0	0.10+/-0.05
		RF	0.50	+3.50	0.50	0	0.10+/-0.05
		R	—	—	0.35	-0.10	0.30+/-0.35
	Durango 4x4	LF	0.50	+3.50	0.50	0.15	0.10+/-0.05
		RF	0.50	+3.50	0.50	-0.15	0.10+/-0.05
		R	—	—	0.35	-0.10	0.30+/-0.35
2007	Aspen 4x2	LF	0.50	+3.20	0.50	0	0.10+/-0.05
		RF	0.50	+3.50	0.50	0	0.10+/-0.05
		R	—	—	0.35	-0.10	0.30+/-0.35
	Aspen 4x4	LF	0.50	+3.50	0.50	0.15	0.10+/-0.05
		RF	0.50	+3.50	0.50	-0.15	0.10+/-0.05
		R	—	—	0.35	-0.10	0.30+/-0.35
	Durango 4x2	LF	0.50	+3.20	0.50	0	0.10+/-0.05
		RF	0.50	+3.50	0.50	0	0.10+/-0.05
		R	—	—	0.35	-0.10	0.30+/-0.35
	Durango 4x4	LF	0.50	+3.50	0.50	0.15	0.10+/-0.05
		RF	0.50	+3.50	0.50	-0.15	0.10+/-0.05
		R	—	—	0.35	-0.10	0.30+/-0.35

22043_DURA_C0011

TIRE, WHEEL AND BALL JOINT SPECIFICATIONS

Year	Model	OEM Tires Standard	OEM Tires Optional	Tire Pressures (psi) Front	Tire Pressures (psi) Rear	Wheel Size	Ball Joint Inspection	Lug Nut Torque (ft. lbs.)
2005	Durango	P245/70R17	P265/65R17	①	①	std: 7 opt: 8	0.020 in. ②	100
2006	Durango	P245/70R17	P265/65R17 P275/60R17	①	①	std: 7 opt: 8	0.020 in. ②	135
2007	Aspen	P265/80R18	P265/60R18 P265/50R20	①	①	std: 7 opt: 8	0.020 in. ②	135
	Durango	P245/70R17	P265/65R17 P275/60R17	①	①	std: 7 opt: 8	0.020 in. ②	135

NA: Information not available

OEM: Original Equipment Manufacturer

PSI: Pounds Per Square Inch

STD: Standard

OPT: Optional

① See placard on vehicle

② Both upper and lower

22043_DURA_C0012

BRAKE SPECIFICATIONS

All measurements in inches unless noted

Year	Model		Brake Disc			Brake Drum			Minimum Lining Thickness	Brake Caliper	
			Original Thickness	Minimum Thickness	Maximum Run-out	Original Inside Diameter	Max. Wear Limit	Maximum Machine Diameter		Bracket Bolts (ft. lbs.)	Mounting Bolts (ft. lbs.)
2005	Durango	F	1.100	1.039	0.0009	—	—	—	NA	①	24
		R	0.866	0.811	0.0009	—	—	—	NA	①	11
2006	Durango	F	1.100	1.039	0.0009	—	—	—	NA	①	24
		R	0.866	0.811	0.0009	—	—	—	NA	①	11
2007	Aspen	F	1.100	1.039	0.0009	—	—	—	NA	①	24
		R	0.866	0.811	0.0009	—	—	—	NA	①	11
	Durango	F	1.100	1.039	0.0009	—	—	—	NA	①	24
		R	0.866	0.811	0.0009	—	—	—	NA	①	11

NA: Not Available

① Adapter plate: front 130 ft. lbs.; rear 100 ft. lbs.
   Support plate: 47 ft. lbs.

22043_DURA_C0013

SCHEDULED MAINTENANCE INTERVALS
CHRYSLER ASPEN - DODGE DURANGO

TO BE SERVICED	TYPE OF SERVICE	VEHICLE MILEAGE INTERVAL (x1000)																
		6	12	18	24	30	36	42	48	54	60	66	72	78	84	90	96	102
Engine oil & filter	R	✓	✓	✓	✓	✓	✓	✓	✓	✓	✓	✓	✓	✓	✓	✓	✓	✓
Tires	Rotate	✓	✓	✓	✓	✓	✓	✓	✓	✓	✓	✓	✓	✓	✓	✓	✓	✓
Brake linings	S/I			✓			✓			✓			✓					
Air cleaner element	R					✓					✓					✓		
Spark plugs	R					✓					✓					✓		
Transfer case fluid	I					✓					✓							
Engine coolant	R	Replace every 60 months regardless of mileage																
Spark plug wires (5.7L)	R								✓									
PCV valve	S/I										✓							
Drive belt tensioner	S/I										✓							
Automatic transmission fluid ①	R																	✓
Transfer case fluid	R	Drain the fluid every 120,000 miles																

R: Replace   S/I: Service or Inspect

① On 4.7L and 5.7L, change the filter, if equipped

FREQUENT OPERATION MAINTENANCE (SEVERE SERVICE)

If a vehicle is operated under any of the following conditions it is considered severe service:

- Extremely dusty areas.

- Day or night time temperatures below 0°C (32°F).

- Prolonged idling (vehicle operation in stop and go traffic.)

- Frequent short running periods (engine does not warm to normal operating temperatures).

- Police, taxi, delivery usage or trailer towing usage.

- Off road or desert operation

- 50% or more of your driving is done in temperatures above 90 degrees F (32 deg. C)

Oil & oil filter change: change every 3000 miles.

Air filter: change every 15,000 miles and change as necessary.

Drive belts: check and replace as necessary every 60,000 miles.

Automatic transmission fluid, filter every 30,000 miles 4.7L and 5.7L.

Automatic transmission fluid, filter every 60,000 miles 3.7L.

Front and rear axle fluid: change every 15,000 miles.

Inspect PCV valve every 30,000 miles

22043_DURA_C0014

PRECAUTIONS

Before servicing any vehicle, please be sure to read all of the following precautions, which deal with personal safety, prevention of component damage, and important points to take into consideration when servicing a motor vehicle:

• Never open, service or drain the radiator or cooling system when the engine is hot; serious burns can occur from the steam and hot coolant.

• Observe all applicable safety precautions when working around fuel. Whenever servicing the fuel system, always work in a well-ventilated area. Do not allow fuel spray or vapors to come in contact with a spark, open flame, or excessive heat (a hot drop light, for example). Keep a dry chemical fire extinguisher near the work area. Always keep fuel in a container specifically designed for fuel storage; also, always properly seal fuel containers to avoid the possibility of fire or explosion. Refer to the additional fuel system precautions later in this section.

• Fuel injection systems often remain pressurized, even after the engine has been turned **OFF**. The fuel system pressure must be relieved before disconnecting any fuel lines. Failure to do so may result in fire and/or personal injury.

• Brake fluid often contains polyglycol ethers and polyglycols. Avoid contact with the eyes and wash your hands thoroughly after handling brake fluid. If you do get brake fluid in your eyes, flush your eyes with clean, running water for 15 minutes. If eye irritation persists, or if you have taken brake fluid internally, IMMEDIATELY seek medical assistance.

• The EPA warns that prolonged contact with used engine oil may cause a number of skin disorders, including cancer. You should make every effort to minimize your exposure to used engine oil. Protective gloves should be worn when changing oil. Wash your hands and any other exposed skin areas as soon as possible after exposure to used engine oil. Soap and water, or waterless hand cleaner should be used.

• All new vehicles are now equipped with an air bag system, often referred to as a Supplemental Restraint System (SRS) or Supplemental Inflatable Restraint (SIR) system. The system must be disabled before performing service on or around system components, steering column, instrument panel components, wiring and sensors. Failure to follow safety and disabling procedures could result in accidental air bag deployment, possible personal injury and unnecessary system repairs.

• Always wear safety goggles when working with, or around, the air bag system. When carrying a non-deployed air bag, be sure the bag and trim cover are pointed away from your body. When placing a non-deployed air bag on a work surface, always face the bag and trim cover upward, away from the surface. This will reduce the motion of the module if it is accidentally deployed. Refer to the additional air bag system precautions later in this section.

• Clean, high quality brake fluid from a sealed container is essential to the safe and proper operation of the brake system. You should always buy the correct type of brake fluid for your vehicle. If the brake fluid becomes contaminated, completely flush the system with new fluid. Never reuse any brake fluid. Any brake fluid that is removed from the system should be discarded. Also, do not allow any brake fluid to come in contact with a painted surface; it will damage the paint.

• Never operate the engine without the proper amount and type of engine oil; doing so WILL result in severe engine damage.

• Timing belt maintenance is extremely important. Many models utilize an interference-type, non-freewheeling engine. If the timing belt breaks, the valves in the cylinder head may strike the pistons, causing potentially serious (also time-consuming and expensive) engine damage. Refer to the maintenance interval charts for the recommended replacement interval for the timing belt, and to the timing belt section for belt replacement and inspection.

• Disconnecting the negative battery cable on some vehicles may interfere with the functions of the on-board computer system(s) and may require the computer to undergo a relearning process once the negative battery cable is reconnected.

• When servicing drum brakes, only disassemble and assemble one side at a time, leaving the remaining side intact for reference.

• Only an MVAC-trained, EPA-certified automotive technician should service the air conditioning system or its components.

BRAKES

GENERAL INFORMATION

PRECAUTIONS

• Certain components within the ABS system are not intended to be serviced or repaired individually.

• Do not use rubber hoses or other parts not specifically specified for and ABS system. When using repair kits, replace all parts included in the kit. Partial or incorrect repair may lead to functional problems and require the replacement of components.

• Lubricate rubber parts with clean, fresh brake fluid to ease assembly. Do not use shop air to clean parts; damage to rubber components may result.

• Use only DOT 3 brake fluid from an unopened container.

• If any hydraulic component or line is removed or replaced, it may be necessary to bleed the entire system.

• A clean repair area is essential. Always clean the reservoir and cap thoroughly before removing the cap. The slightest amount of dirt in the fluid may plug an orifice and impair the system function. Perform repairs after components have been thoroughly cleaned; use only denatured alcohol to clean components. Do not allow ABS components to come into contact with any substance containing mineral oil; this includes used shop rags.

• The Anti-Lock control unit is a microprocessor similar to other computer units in the vehicle. Ensure that the ignition switch is **OFF** before removing or installing controller harnesses. Avoid static electricity discharge at or near the controller.

ANTI-LOCK BRAKE SYSTEM (ABS)

• If any arc welding is to be done on the vehicle, the control unit should be unplugged before welding operations begin.

SPEED SENSORS

REMOVAL & INSTALLATION

Front Wheel Speed Sensor
See Figure 1.

1. Raise and support the vehicle.
2. Remove the front rotor.
3. Remove the wheel speed sensor mounting bolt from the hub.
4. Remove the wheel speed sensor from the hub.
5. Remove the wiring from the clips and disconnect the electrical connector.

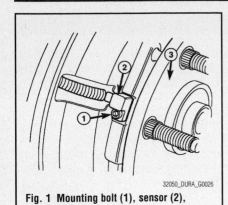

Fig. 1 Mounting bolt (1), sensor (2), front hub (3)

32050_DURA_G0026

To install:

6. Install the wiring to the clips and reconnect the electrical connector.

7. Install the wheel speed sensor to the hub.

8. Install the wheel speed sensor mounting bolt to the hub. Tighten the bolt to 190 inch lbs. (21 Nm).

9. Install the front rotor and brake caliper assembly.

10. Remove support and lower the vehicle.

Rear Wheel Speed Sensor

Without Traction Control

See Figure 2.

1. Raise the vehicle on a hoist.

2. Disconnect the sensor wire harness.

3. Remove the brake line mounting nut

and remove the brake line from the sensor stud.

4. Remove the mounting stud from the sensor and shield.

5. Remove the sensor and shield from the differential housing.

To install:

6. Install the O–ring on the sensor (if removed).

7. Insert the sensor in the differential housing.

8. Install the sensor shield.

9. Install the sensor mounting stud and tighten to 200 inch lbs. (24 Nm).

10. Install the brake line on the sensor stud and install the nut.

11. Connect the harness to the sensor.

➡**Be sure the seal is securely in place between the sensor and the wiring connector.**

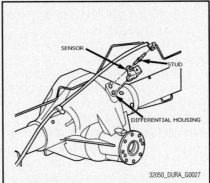

Fig. 2 Rear wheel speed sensor—without traction control

32050_DURA_G0027

12. Lower the vehicle.

With Traction Control

See Figure 3.

1. Raise the vehicle on a hoist.

2. Disconnect the wheel speed sensor electrical connector.

3. Remove the mounting bolt from the sensor.

4. Remove the sensor from the brake caliper adapter.

To install:

5. Insert the wheel speed sensor in the brake caliper adapter.

6. Install the sensor mounting bolt and tighten to 200 inch lbs. (24 Nm).

7. Reconnect the electrical wiring connector to the sensor.

8. Lower the vehicle.

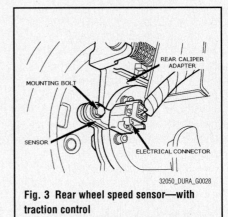

Fig. 3 Rear wheel speed sensor—with traction control

32050_DURA_G0028

BRAKES

BLEEDING THE BRAKE SYSTEM

BLEEDING PROCEDURE

BLEEDING PROCEDURE

➡**Add only fresh, clean brake fluid from a sealed container when bleeding the brakes. If pressure bleeding equipment is used, the front brake metering valve will have to be held open to bleed the front brakes. The valve stem is located in the forward end or top of the combination valve. The stem must either be pressed inward or held outward slightly. Follow equipment manufacturer's instructions carefully when using pressure equipment. Do not exceed the maker's pressure recommendations. Generally, a tank pressure of 15—20 psi is sufficient. Do not pressure bleed without the proper master cylinder adapter.**

When any part of the hydraulic system

has been disconnected for repair or replacement, air may get into the lines and cause spongy pedal action (because air can be compressed and brake fluid cannot). To correct this condition, it is necessary to bleed the hydraulic system so to be sure all air is purged.

Bleeding must start where the lines were disconnected. If lines were disconnected at the master cylinder, for example, bleeding must be done at that point before proceeding downstream.

When bleeding the brake system, bleed one brake bleeder point at a time. Failure to do so may result in more air being drawn into the lines.

If the existing system fluid seems dirty or if the vehicle has covered considerable mileage, it is recommended that the system be completely purged and refilled with fresh, clean fluid. The best way to start is to siphon the old fluid out of the master cylin-

der reservoir and fill it completely with fresh fluid.

Brake fluid tends to darken over time. This does not necessarily indicate contamination. Examine fluid closely for foreign matter.

The primary and secondary hydraulic brake systems are separate and are bled independently. During the bleeding operation, do not allow the reservoir to run dry. Keep the master cylinder reservoir filled with brake fluid. Never use brake fluid that has been drained from the hydraulic system, no matter how clean it seems.

1. Clean all dirt from around the master cylinder fill cap, remove the cap and fill the master cylinder with brake fluid until the level is within ¼ in. (6mm) of the top edge of the reservoir.

2. Clean the bleeder screws at all 4 wheels. The bleeder screws are located on the back of the brake calipers.

3. Bleeder screws should be protected with rubber caps. If they are missing, the orifice may easily become clogged with road dirt. If the screw refuses to bleed when loosened, remove it and blow clear. Aftermarket caps are readily available.

Manual Bleeding
See Figure 4.

Manual bleeding requires two people and a degree of patience and cooperation. Bleeding should be performed in this order: (1) Right rear, (2) Left rear, (3) Right front, (4) Left front

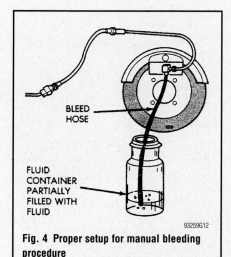

Fig. 4 Proper setup for manual bleeding procedure

1. Follow the preparatory steps, above.
2. Attach a length of rubber hose over the bleeder screw and place the other end of the hose in a glass jar, submerged in brake fluid.
3. Have your assistant press down on the brake pedal, then open the bleeder screw ½–¾ turn.
4. The brake pedal will go to the floor.
5. Close the bleeder screw—preferably before the pedal reaches the floor. Tell your assistant to allow the brake pedal to return slowly.
6. Repeat these steps to purge all air from the system.
7. When bubbles cease to appear at the end of the bleeder hose, close the bleeder screw and remove the hose. Check that the pedal is firm or at least more firm than it was when you started. If not, continue the procedure.
8. Check the master cylinder fluid level and add fluid accordingly. Do this after bleeding each wheel.
9. Repeat the bleeding operation at the remaining three wheels, ending with the one closet to the master cylinder.

10. Fill the master cylinder reservoir to the proper level.

➡If there is excessive air in the system, it is possible that the stroke of the brake pedal will be insufficient to purge the lines. In this case a pressure bleeder or vacuum bleeder is the easiest solution.

Vacuum Bleeding

Vacuum bleeding can be carried out by one person. Since a good vacuum bleeder will normally move more fluid than a brake pedal stroke, this procedure is preferred. These tools are inexpensive and readily available at auto parts outlets. Bleeding should be performed in this order: (1) Right rear, (2) Left rear, (3) Right front, (4) Left front.
1. Follow the preparatory steps, above.
2. Attach the vacuum bleeder according to the manufacturer's recommendations.
3. Pump up the unit until maximum vacuum is reached. Loosen the bleeder screw slightly until bubbles and fluid issue forth. Close the screw before the vacuum is equalized.
4. Repeat the procedure until fluid without bubbles issues from the bleeder screw.
5. Keep a close check on master cylinder fluid level during this procedure as vacuum bleeders move considerable amounts of fluid.

MASTER CYLINDER BLEEDING
See Figure 5.

❋❋ CAUTION

When clamping the master cylinder in a vise, only clamp the master cylinder by its mounting flange. Do not clamp the master cylinder piston rod, reservoir, seal or body.

1. Clamp the master cylinder in a vise.

➡Master cylinder outlet ports vary in size and type depending on whether master cylinder is for a vehicle equipped with ABS or not. ABS equipped master cylinders require the additional use of ISO style flare adapters supplied in Special Tool Package 8822 to be used in conjunction with the bleeder tubes in Special Tool Package 8358.

2. Attach special tools for bleeding master cylinder in the following fashion:
   a. For non–ABS control equipped master cylinders, thread bleeder tube

Special Tool 8358–1, into each outlet port. Tighten each tube to 145 inch lbs. (17 Nm). Flex the bleeder tubes and place the open ends into the mouth of the fluid reservoir as far down as possible.
   b. For ABS equipped master cylinders, thread one adapter Special Tool 8822–2 in each outlet port. Tighten the adapters to 145 inch lbs. (17 Nm). Next, thread a bleeder tube Special Tool 8358–1 into each adapter. Flex the bleeder tubes and place the open ends into the mouth of the fluid reservoir as far down as possible .

➡Make sure open ends of bleeder tubes stay below surface of brake fluid once reservoir is filled to proper level.

3. Fill brake fluid reservoir with brake fluid meeting DOT 3 (DOT 4 and DOT 4+ are acceptable) specifications. Make sure fluid level is above tips of bleeder tubes in reservoir to ensure no air is ingested during bleeding.
4. Using a wooden dowel as a pushrod, slowly depress the master cylinder pistons, then release pressure, allowing the pistons to return to the released position.
5. Repeat several times until all air bubbles are expelled. Make sure the fluid level stays above the tips of the bleeder tubes in the reservoir while bleeding.
6. Remove the bleeder tubes from the master cylinder outlet ports, then plug the outlet ports and install the fill cap on the reservoir.
7. Install the master cylinder on vehicle then follow the brake bleeding procedure.

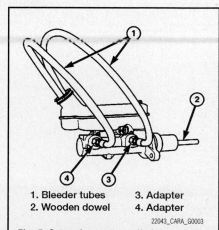

1. Bleeder tubes   3. Adapter
2. Wooden dowel   4. Adapter

Fig. 5 Setup the master cylinder as shown to bleed it

BLEEDING THE ABS SYSTEM

ABS system bleeding requires conventional bleeding methods plus use of the DRB scan tool. The procedure involves performing a base brake bleeding, followed by use of the scan tool to cycle and bleed the HCU pump and solenoids. A second base brake bleeding procedure is then required to remove any air remaining in the system.

1. Perform base brake bleeding. Refer to the appropriate section.
2. Connect the scan tool to the data link connector beneath the dashboard.
3. Select "Anti-lock Brakes" followed by "Miscellaneous", then "Bleed Brakes". Follow the instructions displayed until the unit displays "Test Complete", then disconnect the scan tool and proceed.
4. Perform a base brake bleeding a second time.
5. Top up the master cylinder.

BRAKES

✳✳ CAUTION

Dust and dirt accumulating on brake parts during normal use may contain asbestos fibers from production or aftermarket brake linings. Breathing excessive concentrations of asbestos fibers can cause serious bodily harm. Exercise care when servicing brake parts. Do not sand or grind brake lining unless equipment used is designed to contain the dust residue. Do not clean brake parts with compressed air or by dry brushing. Cleaning should be done by dampening the brake components with a fine mist of water, then wiping the brake components clean with a dampened cloth. Dispose of cloth and all residue containing asbestos fibers in an impermeable container with the appropriate label. Follow practices prescribed by the Occupational Safety and Health Administration (OSHA) and the Environmental Protection Agency (EPA) for the handling, processing, and disposing of dust or debris that may contain asbestos fibers.

BRAKE CALIPER

REMOVAL & INSTALLATION

1. Before servicing the vehicle, refer to the precautions section.
2. Install prop rod on the brake pedal to keep pressure on the brake system.
3. Raise and support the vehicle.
4. Remove the tire and wheel assembly.
5. Compress the disc brake caliper.
6. Remove the banjo bolt and discard the copper washers.
7. Remove the caliper slide pin bolts.
8. Remove the disc brake caliper from the caliper adapter.

To install:

➡Install a new copper washers on the banjo bolt when installing

9. Install the disc brake caliper on the brake caliper adapter.

✳✳ CAUTION

Verify brake hose is not twisted or kinked before tightening fitting bolt.

10. Install the banjo bolt with new copper washers on the caliper. Tighten to 21 ft. lbs. (28 Nm)
11. Install the caliper slide pin bolts. Tighten to 24 ft. lbs. (32 Nm).
12. Remove the prop rod.
13. Bleed the base brake system.
14. Install the tire and wheel assembly.

DISC BRAKE PADS

REMOVAL & INSTALLATION

See Figure 6.

1. Before servicing the vehicle, refer to the precautions section.
2. Raise and support vehicle.
3. Remove the wheel and tire assemblies.
4. Compress the caliper.
5. Remove the caliper.
6. Remove the caliper by tilting the top up and off the caliper adapter.

➡Do not allow brake hose to support caliper assembly.

7. Support and hang the caliper.
8. Remove the inboard brake shoe from the caliper adapter.
9. Remove the outboard brake shoe from the caliper adapter.

➡Anti-rattle springs are not interchangeable.

10. Remove the top anti-rattle springs from the caliper adapter.

FRONT DISC BRAKES

11. Remove the bottom anti-rattle springs from the caliper adapter.

To install:

12. Bottom pistons in caliper bore with C-clamp. Place an old brake shoe between a C-clamp and caliper piston.
13. Clean caliper mounting adapter and anti-rattle springs.
14. Lubricate anti-rattle springs with brake grease.

➡Anti-rattle springs are not interchangeable.

15. Install the bottom anti-rattle springs.
16. Install the top anti-rattle springs.
17. Install inboard brake shoe in adapter.
18. Install outboard brake shoe in adapter.
19. Tilt the top of the caliper over rotor and under adapter. Then push the bottom of the caliper down onto the adapter.
20. Install caliper.
21. Install wheel and tire assemblies and lower vehicle.
22. Apply brakes several times to seat caliper pistons and brake shoes and obtain firm pedal.
23. Top off master cylinder fluid level.

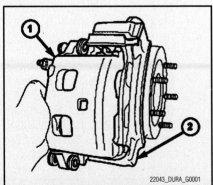

22043_DURA_G0001

Fig. 6 Remove the brake caliper by rotating the top (1) away from the mount (2)

BRAKES

✳✳ CAUTION

Dust and dirt accumulating on brake parts during normal use may contain asbestos fibers from production or aftermarket brake linings. Breathing excessive concentrations of asbestos fibers can cause serious bodily harm. Exercise care when servicing brake parts. Do not sand or grind brake lining unless equipment used is designed to contain the dust residue. Do not clean brake parts with compressed air or by dry brushing. Cleaning should be done by dampening the brake components with a fine mist of water, then wiping the brake components clean with a dampened cloth. Dispose of cloth and all residue containing asbestos fibers in an impermeable container with the appropriate label. Follow practices prescribed by the Occupational Safety and Health Administration (OSHA) and the Environmental Protection Agency (EPA) for the handling, processing, and disposing of dust or debris that may contain asbestos fibers.

BRAKE CALIPER

REMOVAL & INSTALLATION

1. Before servicing the vehicle, refer to the precautions section.
2. Install prop rod on the brake pedal to keep pressure on the brake system.
3. Raise and support vehicle.
4. Remove the wheel and tire assembly.
5. Drain small amount of fluid from master cylinder brake reservoir with suction gun.

6. Remove the brake hose banjo bolt if replacing caliper.
7. Remove the caliper mounting slide pin bolts.
8. Remove the caliper from vehicle.

To install:

9. Install caliper to the caliper adapter.
10. Coat the caliper mounting slide pin bolts with silicone grease. Then install and tighten the bolts to 11 ft. lbs. (15 Nm).
11. Install the brake hose banjo bolt and new copper seal washers if caliper was removed.
12. Install the brake hose to the caliper with and tighten fitting bolt to 21 ft. lbs. (28 Nm).

✳✳ CAUTION

Verify brake hose is not twisted or kinked before tightening fitting bolt.

13. Remove the prop rod from the vehicle.
14. Bleed the base brake system.
15. Install the wheel and tire assemblies.
16. Remove the supports and lower the vehicle.
17. Verify a firm pedal before moving the vehicle.

DISC BRAKE PADS

REMOVAL & INSTALLATION

1. Before servicing the vehicle, refer to the precautions section.
2. Raise and support vehicle.
3. Remove the wheel and tire assemblies.
4. Compress the caliper.
5. Remove the caliper.
6. Remove the caliper by tilting the top up and off the caliper adapter.

➡ Do not allow brake hose to support caliper assembly.

7. Support and hang the caliper.
8. Remove the inboard brake shoe from the caliper adapter.
9. Remove the outboard brake shoe from the caliper adapter.

➡ Anti-rattle springs are not interchangeable.

10. Remove the top anti-rattle springs from the caliper adapter.
11. Remove the bottom anti-rattle springs from the caliper adapter.

To install:

12. Bottom pistons in caliper bore with C-clamp. Place an old brake shoe between a C-clamp and caliper piston.
13. Clean caliper mounting adapter and anti-rattle springs.
14. Lubricate anti-rattle springs with brake grease.

➡ Anti-rattle springs are not interchangeable.

15. Install the bottom anti-rattle springs.
16. Install the top anti-rattle springs.
17. Install inboard brake shoe in adapter.
18. Install outboard brake shoe in adapter.
19. Tilt the top of the caliper over rotor and under adapter. Then push the bottom of the caliper down onto the adapter.
20. Install caliper.
21. Install wheel and tire assemblies and lower vehicle.
22. Apply brakes several times to seat caliper pistons and brake shoes and obtain firm pedal.
23. Top off master cylinder fluid level.

BRAKES   **PARKING BRAKE**

PARKING BRAKE CABLES

ADJUSTMENT

➡Tensioner adjustment is only necessary when the tensioner, or a cable has been replaced or disconnected for service. When adjustment is necessary, perform adjustment only as described in the following procedure. This is necessary to avoid faulty park brake operation.

1. Before servicing the vehicle, refer to the precautions section.
2. Raise and support vehicle.
3. Remove the wheel and tire assemblies.
4. Back off the cable tensioner adjusting nut to create slack in the cables.
5. Remove the brake rotors.
6. Verify the brakes are in good condition and operating properly.
7. Verify the park brake cables operate freely and are not binding, or seized.
8. Install the rotors. Adjust the shoes until the rotors just begin to drag, then back it off slightly until the rotors rotate freely without drag.
9. Install the wheel/tire assemblies.
10. Lower the vehicle enough for access to the park brake foot pedal. Then fully apply the park brakes.

➡Leave park brakes applied until adjustment is complete.

11. Raise the vehicle again.
12. Mark the tensioner rod 0.25 in. (6.35 mm) from edge of the tensioner.
13. Tighten the adjusting nut on the tensioner rod until the mark is no longer visible.

❋❋ WARNING

Do not loosen, or tighten the tensioner adjusting nut for any reason after completing adjustment.

14. Lower the vehicle until the rear wheels are a few inches off the floor.
15. Release the park brake foot pedal and verify that rear wheels rotate freely without drag. Then lower the vehicle.

PARKING BRAKE SHOES

REMOVAL & INSTALLATION

See Figure 7.

The cross-section of the rear disc rotor resembles a top hat; the center section is actually a small brake drum. This assembly is often referred to as "drum in hat". Drum in hat parking brakes are dual shoe, internal expanding units with an external adjusting mechanism and are mechanically operated via a cable attached to the parking brake pedal.

1. Raise and support the vehicle.
2. Remove the wheel.
3. Remove the disc brake caliper.
4. Remove the caliper adapter.
5. Remove the disc brake rotor.
6. Disengage the park brake cable from behind the rotor assembly to allow easier disassembly of the park brake shoes.
7. Remove the axleshaft.
8. Disassemble the rear park brake shoes.

To install:

➡On a new vehicle or after parking brake lining replacement, it is recommended that the parking brake system be conditioned prior to use. This is done by making one stop from 25 mph on dry pavement or concrete using light to moderate force on the parking brake foot pedal.

9. Reassemble the rear park brake shoes.
10. Install the axleshaft.
11. Install park brake cable to the lever behind the support plate.
12. Adjust the rear brake shoes.
13. Install the disc brake rotor.
14. Install the disc brake caliper adapter.
15. Install the disc brake caliper.
16. Install the wheel.
17. Remove support and lower the vehicle.

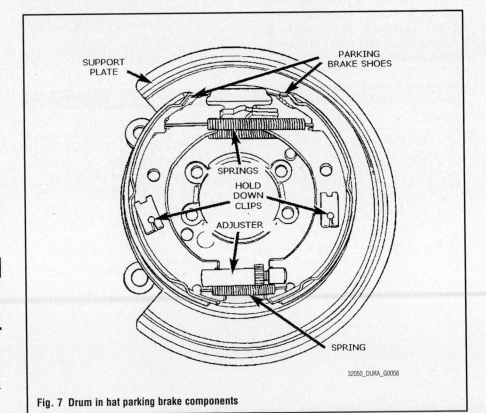

32050_DURA_G0058

Fig. 7 Drum in hat parking brake components

CHASSIS ELECTRICAL   AIR BAG (SUPPLEMENTAL RESTRAINT SYSTEM)

GENERAL INFORMATION

✳✳ CAUTION

These vehicles are equipped with an air bag system. The system must be disarmed before performing service on, or around, system components, the steering column, instrument panel components, wiring and sensors. Failure to follow the safety precautions and the disarming procedure could result in accidental air bag deployment, possible injury and unnecessary system repairs.

SERVICE PRECAUTIONS

Disconnect and isolate the battery negative cable before beginning any airbag system component diagnosis, testing, removal, or installation procedures. Allow system capacitor to discharge for two minutes before beginning any component service. This will disable the airbag system. Failure to disable the airbag system may result in accidental airbag deployment, personal injury, or death.

Do not place an intact undeployed airbag face down on a solid surface. The airbag will propel into the air if accidentally deployed and may result in personal injury or death.

When carrying or handling an undeployed airbag, the trim side (face) of the airbag should be pointing towards the body to minimize possibility of injury if accidental deployment occurs. Failure to do this may result in personal injury or death.

Replace airbag system components with OEM replacement parts. Substitute parts may appear interchangeable, but internal differences may result in inferior occupant protection. Failure to do so may result in occupant personal injury or death.

Wear safety glasses, rubber gloves, and long sleeved clothing when cleaning powder residue from vehicle after an airbag deployment. Powder residue emitted from a deployed airbag can cause skin irritation. Flush affected area with cool water if irritation is experienced. If nasal or throat irritation is experienced, exit the vehicle for fresh air until the irritation ceases. If irritation continues, see a physician.

Do not use a replacement airbag that is not in the original packaging. This may result in improper deployment, personal injury, or death.

The factory installed fasteners, screws and bolts used to fasten airbag components have a special coating and are specifically designed for the airbag system. Do not use substitute fasteners. Use only original equipment fasteners listed in the parts catalog when fastener replacement is required.

During, and following, any child restraint anchor service, due to impact event or vehicle repair, carefully inspect all mounting hardware, tether straps, and anchors for proper installation, operation, or damage. If a child restraint anchor is found damaged in any way, the anchor must be replaced. Failure to do this may result in personal injury or death.

Deployed and non-deployed airbags may or may not have live pyrotechnic material within the airbag inflator.

Do not dispose of driver/passenger/curtain airbags or seat belt tensioners unless you are sure of complete deployment. Refer to the Hazardous Substance Control System for proper disposal.

Dispose of deployed airbags and tensioners consistent with state, provincial, local, and federal regulations.

After any airbag component testing or service, do not connect the battery negative cable. Personal injury or death may result if the system test is not performed first.

If the vehicle is equipped with the Occupant Classification System (OCS), do not connect the battery negative cable before performing the OCS Verification Test using the scan tool and the appropriate diagnostic information. Personal injury or death may result if the system test is not performed properly.

Never replace both the Occupant Restraint Controller (ORC) and the Occupant Classification Module (OCM) at the same time. If both require replacement, replace one, then perform the Airbag System test before replacing the other.

Both the ORC and the OCM store Occupant Classification System (OCS) calibration data, which they transfer to one another when one of them is replaced. If both are replaced at the same time, an irreversible fault will be set in both modules and the OCS may malfunction and cause personal injury or death.

If equipped with OCS, the Seat Weight Sensor is a sensitive, calibrated unit and must be handled carefully. Do not drop or handle roughly. If dropped or damaged, replace with another sensor. Failure to do so may result in occupant injury or death.

If equipped with OCS, the front passenger seat must be handled carefully as well.

When removing the seat, be careful when setting on floor not to drop. If dropped, the sensor may be inoperative, could result in occupant injury, or possibly death.

If equipped with OCS, when the passenger front seat is on the floor, no one should sit in the front passenger seat. This uneven force may damage the sensing ability of the seat weight sensors. If sat on and damaged, the sensor may be inoperative, could result in occupant injury, or possibly death.

DISARMING THE SYSTEM

1. Disconnect and isolate the negative battery cable. Wait 2 minutes for the system capacitor to discharge before performing any service.
2. When repairs are completed, connect the negative battery cable.

ARMING THE SYSTEM

Assuming that the system components (air bag control module, sensors, air bag, etc.) are installed correctly and are in good working order, the system is armed whenever the battery's positive and negative battery cables are connected.

✳✳ WARNING

If you have disarmed the air bag system for any reason, and are re-arming the system, make sure no one is in the vehicle (as an added safety measure), then connect the negative battery cable.

CLOCKSPRING CENTERING
See Figure 8.

Disconnect and isolate the battery negative cable before beginning any airbag system component diagnosis, testing, removal, or installation procedures. Allow system capacitor to discharge for two minutes before beginning any component service. This will disable the airbag system. Failure to disable the airbag system may result in accidental airbag deployment, personal injury, or death.

The clockspring is mounted on the steering column behind the steering wheel. Its purpose is to maintain a continuous electrical circuit between the wiring harness and the driver's side air bag module. This assembly consists of a flat, ribbon-like electrically conductive tape that winds and unwinds with the steering wheel rotation.

Service replacement clocksprings are shipped pre-centered and with a molded plastic locking pin that snaps into a receptacle on the rotor and is engaged between two tabs on the upper surface of the rotor case. The locking pin secures the centered clockspring rotor to the clockspring case during shipment, but the locking pin must be removed from the clockspring after it is installed on the steering column. This locking pin should not be removed until the clockspring has been installed on the steering column. If the locking pin is removed before the clockspring is installed on a steering column, the clockspring centering procedure must be performed.

➡ **The clockspring cannot be repaired. If the clockspring is faulty, damaged, or if the driver airbag has been deployed, the clockspring must be replaced.**

Before starting this procedure, be certain to turn the steering wheel until the front wheels are in the straight-ahead position.

1. Place the front wheels in the straight-ahead position.
2. Remove the clockspring from the steering column.
3. Rotate the clockspring rotor clockwise to the end of its travel. Do not apply excessive torque.
4. From the end of the clockwise travel, rotate the rotor about two and one-half turns counterclockwise.
5. The engagement dowel and yellow rubber boot should end up at the bottom, and the arrows on the clockspring rotor and case should be in alignment. The clockspring is now centered.
6. The front wheels should still be in the straight-ahead position. Reinstall the clockspring onto the steering column.

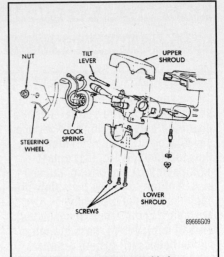

Fig. 8 The clockspring assembly is mounted to the end of the column, behind the steering wheel

DRIVETRAIN

AUTOMATIC TRANSMISSION ASSEMBLY

REMOVAL & INSTALLATION

42RLE Transmission

1. Before servicing the vehicle, refer to the precautions section.
2. Disconnect the negative battery cable.
3. Raise and support the vehicle
4. Remove any necessary skid plates.
5. Mark propeller shaft and axle companion flanges for assembly alignment.
6. Remove the rear propeller shaft.
7. Remove the front propeller shaft, if necessary.
8. Disconnect wires from the input and output speed sensors.
9. Disconnect wires from the transmission range sensor.
10. Disconnect wires from the solenoid/pressure switch assembly.
11. Remove the bolts holding the exhaust crossover pipe to the pre-catalytic converter pipe flanges.
12. Remove the bolts holding the exhaust crossover pipe to the catalytic converter flange.
13. Disconnect gearshift cable from transmission manual valve lever.
14. Disengage the shift cable from the cable support bracket.
15. Remove the starter motor.
16. Remove the engine to transmission collar.
17. Rotate crankshaft in clockwise direction until converter bolts are accessible. Then

remove bolts one at a time. Rotate crankshaft with socket wrench on dampener bolt.
18. Disconnect the transmission vent hose from the transmission.
19. Remove transfer case.
20. Support rear of engine with safety stand or jack.
21. Raise transmission slightly with service jack to relieve load on crossmember and supports.
22. Remove bolts securing rear support and cushion to transmission and crossmember.
23. Remove bolts attaching crossmember to frame and remove crossmember.
24. Disconnect transmission fluid cooler lines at transmission fittings and clips.
25. Remove all remaining converter housing bolts.
26. Carefully work transmission and torque converter assembly rearward off engine block dowels.
27. Hold torque converter in place during transmission removal.
28. Lower transmission and remove assembly from under the vehicle.
29. To remove torque converter, carefully slide torque converter out of the transmission.

To install:

➡ **Check torque converter hub and hub drive flats for sharp edges burrs, scratches, or nicks. Polish the hub and flats with 320/400 grit paper and crocus cloth if necessary. The hub must be smooth to avoid damaging pump seal at installation.**

30. If a replacement transmission is being installed, transfer any components necessary, such as the manual shift lever and shift cable bracket, from the original transmission onto the replacement transmission.
31. Lubricate oil pump seal lip with transmission fluid.
32. Align converter and oil pump.
33. Carefully insert converter in oil pump. Then rotate converter back and forth until fully seated in pump gears.
34. Check converter seating with steel scale and straightedge. Surface of converter lugs should be at least 13mm to rear of straightedge when converter is fully seated.
35. Temporarily secure converter with C-clamp.
36. Position transmission on jack and secure it with chains.
37. Check condition of converter driveplate. Replace the plate if cracked, distorted or damaged. Also be sure transmission dowel pins are seated in engine block and protrude far enough to hold transmission in alignment.
38. Apply a light coating of high temperature grease to the torque converter hub pocket in the rear pocket of the engine's crankshaft.
39. Raise transmission and align the torque converter with the drive plate and transmission converter housing with the engine block.
40. Move transmission forward. Then raise, lower or tilt transmission to align the converter housing with engine block dowels.

41. Carefully work transmission forward and over engine block dowels until converter hub is seated in crankshaft. Verify that no wires, or the transmission vent hose, have become trapped between the engine block and the transmission.

42. Install two bolts to attach the transmission to the engine.

43. Install remaining torque converter housing to engine bolts. Tighten to 50 ft. lbs. (68 Nm).

44. Install transfer case, if equipped. Tighten transfer case nuts to 26 ft. lbs. (35 Nm).

45. Install rear transmission crossmember. Tighten crossmember to frame bolts to 50 ft. lbs. (68 Nm).

46. Install rear support to transmission. Tighten bolts to 35 ft. lbs. (47 Nm).

47. Lower transmission onto crossmember and install bolts attaching transmission mount to crossmember. Tighten clevis bracket to crossmember bolts to 35 ft. lbs. (47 Nm). Tighten the clevis bracket to rear support bolt to 50 ft. lbs. (68 Nm).

48. Connect gearshift cable to support bracket and transmission manual lever.

49. Connect input and output speed sensor wires and the transmission range sensor.

50. Connect wires to the solenoid/pressure switch assembly.

✳✳ CAUTION

It is essential that correct length bolts be used to attach the converter to the driveplate. Bolts that are too long will damage the clutch surface inside the converter.

51. Install torque converter-to-driveplate bolts. Tighten bolts to 65 ft. lbs. (88 Nm).

52. Install starter motor and cooler line bracket.

53. Connect cooler lines to transmission.

54. Install transmission fill tube.

55. Install exhaust components.

56. Align and connect propeller shaft(s).

57. Adjust gearshift cable if necessary.

58. Install any skid plates removed previously.

59. Lower vehicle.

60. Fill transmission with Mopar® ATF +4, Automatic Transmission Fluid or equivalent.

545RFE Transmission

1. Before servicing the vehicle, refer to the precautions section.

2. Disconnect the negative battery cable.

3. Raise and support the vehicle

4. Remove any necessary skid plates.

5. Mark propeller shaft and axle companion flanges for assembly alignment.

6. Remove the rear propeller shaft.

7. Remove the front propeller shaft, if necessary.

8. Remove the engine to transmission collar.

9. Remove the exhaust support bracket from the rear of the transmission.

10. Disconnect and lower or remove any necessary exhaust components.

11. Remove the starter motor.

12. Rotate crankshaft in clockwise direction until converter bolts are accessible. Then remove bolts one at a time. Rotate crankshaft with socket wrench on dampener bolt.

13. Disengage the output speed sensor connector from the output speed sensor.

14. Disengage the input speed sensor connector from the input speed sensor.

15. Disengage the transmission solenoid/TRS assembly connector from the transmission solenoid/TRS assembly.

16. Disengage the line pressure sensor connector from the line pressure sensor.

17. Disconnect gearshift cable from transmission manual valve lever.

18. Remove the gearshift cable from the shift cable support bracket.

19. Disconnect transmission fluid cooler lines at transmission fittings and clips.

20. Support rear of engine with safety stand or jack.

21. Raise transmission slightly with service jack to relieve load on crossmember and supports.

22. Remove bolts securing rear support and cushion to transmission and crossmember.

23. Remove bolts attaching crossmember to frame and remove crossmember.

24. Remove transfer case.

25. Remove all remaining converter housing bolts.

26. Carefully work transmission and torque converter assembly rearward off engine block dowels.

27. Hold torque converter in place during transmission removal.

28. Lower transmission and remove assembly from under the vehicle.

29. To remove torque converter, carefully slide torque converter out of the transmission.

To install:

➡ Check torque converter hub and hub drive flats for sharp edges burrs, scratches, or nicks. Polish the hub and

flats with 320/400 grit paper and crocus cloth if necessary. Verify that the converter hub O-ring is properly installed and is free of any debris. The hub must be smooth to avoid damaging pump seal at installation.

30. If a replacement transmission is being installed, transfer any components necessary, such as the manual shift lever and shift cable bracket, from the original transmission onto the replacement transmission.

31. Lubricate oil pump seal lip with transmission fluid.

32. Align converter and oil pump.

33. Carefully insert converter in oil pump. Then rotate converter back and forth until fully seated in pump gears.

34. Check converter seating with steel scale and straightedge. Surface of converter lugs should be at least 13mm to rear of straightedge when converter is fully seated.

35. Temporarily secure converter with C-clamp.

36. Position transmission on jack and secure it with chains.

37. Check condition of converter driveplate. Replace the plate if cracked, distorted or damaged. Also be sure transmission dowel pins are seated in engine block and protrude far enough to hold transmission in alignment.

38. Apply a light coating of high temperature grease to the torque converter hub pocket in the rear pocket of the engine's crankshaft.

39. Raise transmission and align the torque converter with the drive plate and transmission converter housing with the engine block.

40. Move transmission forward. Then raise, lower or tilt transmission to align the converter housing with engine block dowels.

41. Carefully work transmission forward and over engine block dowels until converter hub is seated in crankshaft. Verify that no wires, or the transmission vent hose, have become trapped between the engine block and the transmission.

42. Install two bolts to attach the transmission to the engine.

43. Install remaining torque converter housing to engine bolts. Tighten to 50 ft. lbs. (68 Nm).

44. Install transfer case, if equipped. Tighten transfer case nuts to 26 ft. lbs. (35 Nm).

45. Install rear transmission crossmember. Tighten crossmember to frame bolts to 50 ft. lbs. (68 Nm).

46. Install rear support to transmission. Tighten bolts to 35 ft. lbs. (47 Nm).

47. Lower transmission onto crossmember and install bolts attaching transmission mount to crossmember. Tighten clevis bracket to crossmember bolts to 35 ft. lbs. (47 Nm). Tighten the clevis bracket to rear support bolt to 50 ft. lbs. (68 Nm).

48. Remove engine support fixture.

49. Connect gearshift cable to transmission.

50. Connect the wiring harness connector to the solenoid and pressure switch assembly connector. Be sure transmission harnesses are properly routed.

51. Connect the wiring harness connector to the input speed sensor.

52. Connect the wiring harness connector to the output speed sensor.

53. Connect the wiring harness connector to the line pressure sensor.

❊❊ CAUTION

It is essential that correct length bolts be used to attach the converter to the driveplate. Bolts that are too long will damage the clutch surface inside the converter.

54. Install torque converter-to-driveplate bolts. Tighten bolts to 270 inch lbs. (31 Nm).

55. Install starter motor and cooler line bracket.

56. Connect cooler lines to transmission.

57. Install transmission fill tube.

58. Install exhaust components.

59. Install the structural dust cover onto the transmission and the engine.

60. Align and install the front propeller shaft, if necessary.

61. Align and install the rear propeller shaft.

62. Adjust gearshift cable if necessary.

63. Install any skid plates removed previously.

64. Lower vehicle.

65. Fill transmission with Mopar® ATF +4, Automatic Transmission Fluid.

TRANSFER CASE ASSEMBLY

REMOVAL & INSTALLATION

NV144

1. Before servicing the vehicle, refer to the precautions section.

2. Shift transfer case into AWD.

3. Raise vehicle.

4. Drain transfer case lubricant.

5. Mark front and rear propeller shafts for alignment reference.

6. Support transmission with jack stand.

7. Remove the transfer case skid plate, if equipped.

8. Disconnect front and rear propeller shafts at transfer case.

9. Disconnect transfer case shift motor and mode sensor wire connectors.

10. Disconnect transfer case vent hose.

11. Support transfer case with transmission jack.

12. Secure transfer case to jack with chains.

13. Remove nuts attaching transfer case to transmission.

14. Pull transfer case and jack rearward to disengage transfer case.

15. Remove transfer case from under vehicle.

To install:

16. Mount transfer case on a transmission jack.

17. Secure transfer case to jack with chains.

18. Position transfer case under vehicle.

19. Align transfer case and transmission shafts and install transfer case onto the transmission.

20. Install and tighten transfer case attaching nuts to 20–25 ft. lbs. (27–34 Nm) torque.

21. Connect the vent hose.

22. Connect the shift motor and mode sensor assembly wiring connector. Secure wire harness to clips on transfer case.

23. Align and connect the propeller shafts.

24. Fill transfer case with correct fluid.

25. Install skid plate, if equipped.

26. Remove transmission jack and support stand.

27. Lower vehicle and verify transfer case shift operation.

NV244

1. Before servicing the vehicle, refer to the precautions section.

2. Shift transfer case into AWD.

3. Raise vehicle.

4. Drain transfer case lubricant.

5. Mark front and rear propeller shafts for alignment reference.

6. Support transmission with jack stand.

7. Remove the transfer case skid plate, if equipped.

8. Disconnect front and rear propeller shafts at transfer case.

9. Disconnect transfer case shift motor and mode sensor wire connectors.

10. Disconnect transfer case vent hose.

11. Support transfer case with transmission jack.

12. Secure transfer case to jack with chains.

13. Remove nuts attaching transfer case to transmission.

14. Pull transfer case and jack rearward to disengage transfer case.

15. Remove transfer case from under vehicle.

To install:

16. Mount transfer case on a transmission jack.

17. Secure transfer case to jack with chains.

18. Position transfer case under vehicle.

19. Align transfer case and transmission shafts and install transfer case onto the transmission.

20. Install and tighten transfer case attaching nuts to 20–25 ft. lbs. (27–34 Nm) torque.

21. Connect the vent hose.

22. Connect the shift motor and mode sensor assembly wiring connector. Secure wire harness to clips on transfer case.

23. Align and connect the propeller shafts.

24. Fill transfer case with correct fluid.

25. Install skid plate, if equipped.

26. Remove transmission jack and support stand.

27. Lower vehicle and verify transfer case shift operation.

FRONT DRIVESHAFT

REMOVAL & INSTALLATION

See Figure 9.

1. Before servicing the vehicle, refer to the precautions section.

2. Mark propeller shaft and pinion flange for installation reference.

3. Remove front propeller shaft.

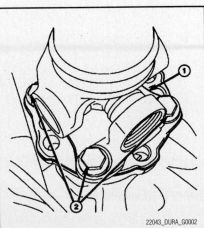

22043_DURA_G0002

Fig. 9 Shaft flange (1) and mounting bolts (2)

To install:

4. Install propeller shaft with reference marks aligned.

5. Using new bolts, tighten them to 85 ft. lbs. (115 Nm).

FRONT HALFSHAFT

REMOVAL & INSTALLATION

See Figure 10.

1. Before servicing the vehicle, refer to the precautions section.

2. With vehicle in neutral, position vehicle on hoist.

3. Remove skid plate, if equipped.

4. Remove hub nut from the halfshaft.

5. Remove brake caliper and rotor.

6. Remove wheel speed sensor if equipped.

7. Remove hub bearing bolts from the knuckle.

8. Remove hub bearing and brake shield from knuckle.

9. Support halfshaft at the CV-joint housings.

10. Position two pry bars behind the inner C/V housing and disengage the CV-joint from the axle.

11. Remove halfshaft through the knuckle.

To install:

12. Apply a light coating of wheel bearing grease on the axle splines.

13. Insert halfshaft through the steering knuckle and onto the axle. Verify shaft snapring engages with the groove on the inside of the joint housing.

14. Clean hub bearing bore and hub bearing mating surface. Lightly coat mating surfaces with grease.

15. Install hub bearing onto the axle halfshaft and into steering knuckle. Tighten hub bearing bolts to 120 ft. lbs. (163 Nm).

16. Install wheel speed sensor, if equipped.

17. Install brake rotor and caliper adapter with caliper.

18. Install halfshaft nut. Apply brakes and tighten shaft nut to 185 ft. lbs. (251 Nm).

19. Install skid plate, if equipped.

CV-JOINTS OVERHAUL

Outer CV-Joint

See Figures 11 through 16.

1. Before servicing the vehicle, refer to the precautions section.

2. Place shaft in vise with soft jaws and support CV-joint.

✳✳ CAUTION

Do not damage CV-joint housing or halfshaft.

3. Remove clamps with a cut-off wheel or grinder.

4. Slide the boot down the shaft.

5. Remove lubricant to expose the CV-joint snapring.

6. Spread snapring and slide the joint off the shaft.

7. Slide boot off the shaft and discard old boot.

8. Mark alignment marks on the inner race/hub, bearing cage and housing with dabs of paint.

9. Clamp CV-joint in a vertical position in a soft jawed vise.

10. Press down one side of the bearing cage to gain access to the ball at the opposite side.

➡ **If joint is tight, use a hammer and brass drift to loosen the bearing hub. Do not contact the bearing cage with the drift.**

11. Remove ball from the bearing cage.

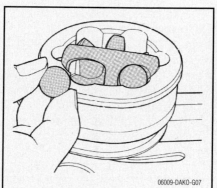
06009-DAKO-G07

Fig. 13 Removing the balls from the bearing cage

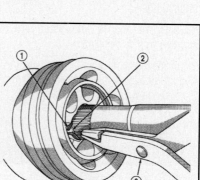
06009-DAKO-G05

Fig. 11 Removing the snapring (1) from the shaft (2) with snapring pliers (3)

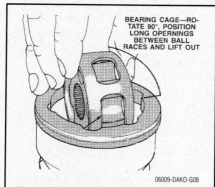
06009-DAKO-G08

Fig. 14 Removing the cage and inner race from the housing

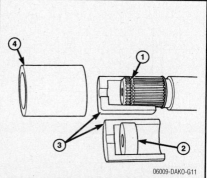
06009-DAKO-G11

Fig. 10 Assembling the axle shaft removal tool 8420A

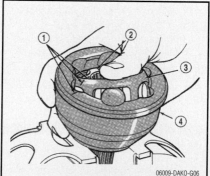
06009-DAKO-G06

Fig. 12 Make alignment marks (1) on the inner race/hub (2) and cage (3)

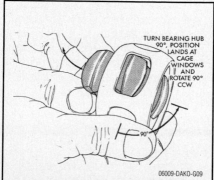
06009-DAKO-G09

Fig. 15 Removing the inner race/hub from the cage

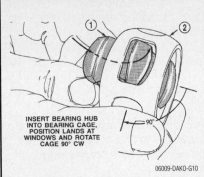

Fig. 16 Assembling the inner race cage and housing

12. Repeat step above until all six balls are removed from the bearing cage.

13. Lift cage and inner race upward and out from the housing.

14. Turn inner race 90° in the cage and rotate the inner race/hub out of the cage.

To Install:

15. Apply a light coat of grease to the CV-joint components before assembling them.

16. Align inner race, cage and housing according to the alignment reference marks.

17. Insert inner race into the cage and rotate race into the cage.

18. Rotate inner race/hub in the cage.

19. Insert cage into the housing.

20. Rotate cage 90° into the housing.

21. Apply lubricant included with replacement boot/joint to the ball races. Spread lubricant equally among all the races.

22. Tilt inner race/hub and cage and install the balls.

23. Place new clamps onto new boot and slide boot onto the shaft to its original position.

24. Apply the rest of lubricant to the CV-joint and boot.

25. Push the joint onto the shaft until the snapring seats in the groove. Pull on the joint to verify the span ring has engaged.

26. Position boot on the joint in its original position. Ensure boot is not twisted and remove any excess air.

27. Secure both boot clamps with Clamp Installer C-4975A, or equivalent. Place tool on clamp bridge and tighten tool until the jaws of the tool are closed.

Inner Tripod Joint

1. Before servicing the vehicle, refer to the precautions section.

2. Clamp the shaft in a vise with soft jaws and support the CV joint.

3. Remove the clamps with a cut-off wheel or grinder.

✳✳ WARNING
Do not damage the CV housing or half shaft with the cut-off wheel or grinder.

4. Remove the housing from the half shaft and slide the boot down shaft.

5. Remove the housing bushing from the housing.

6. Remove the tripod snapring.

7. Remove the tripod and boot from the halfshaft.

8. Clean and inspect the CV components for excessive wear and damage. Replace the tripod as a unit only if necessary.

To install:

9. Slide a new boot down the halfshaft.

10. Install the tripod and tripod snapring on the halfshaft.

11. Pack the grease supplied with the joint/boot into the housing and boot.

12. Coat the tripod with the supplied grease.

13. Install new bushing onto the housing.

14. Insert the tripod and shaft in the housing.

15. Position the boot on the joint in its original position.

➡ **Verify the boot is not twisted and remove any excess air.**

16. Secure both boot clamps with Clamp Installer C-4975A, or equivalent. Place the tool on the clamp bridge and tighten the tool until the jaws of the tool are closed.

FRONT PINION SEAL

REMOVAL & INSTALLATION
See Figures 17 through 20.

1. Before servicing the vehicle, refer to the precautions section.

2. Remove both half shafts.

3. Mark propeller shaft and pinion flange for installation reference.

4. Remove front propeller shaft.

5. Rotate pinion gear three to four times, to verify pinion rotates smoothly.

6. Record pinion flange rotating torque with an inch pound torque wrench for installation reference.

7. Hold flange with Holder 6719 and four bolts and washers.

8. Remove pinion nut.

9. Remove flange with Remover C-452.

10. Remove pinion seal with a pry tool.

To install:

11. Apply a light coating of gear lubricant on the lip of pinion seal.

12. Install seal with Installer C-3972-A and Handle C-4171.

13. Install pinion flange onto the pinion with Installer C-3718 and holder.

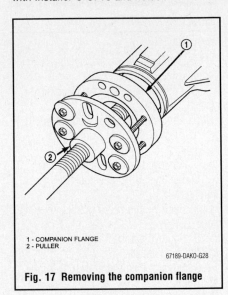

Fig. 17 Removing the companion flange

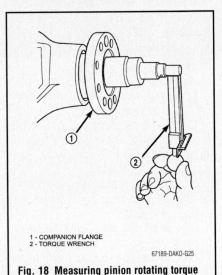

Fig. 18 Measuring pinion rotating torque

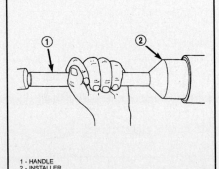

Fig. 19 Pinion seal installer

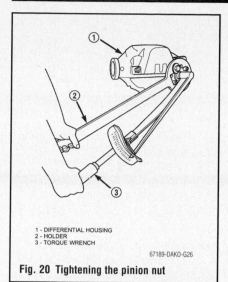

1 - DIFFERENTIAL HOUSING
2 - HOLDER
3 - TORQUE WRENCH

67189-DAK0-G26

Fig. 20 Tightening the pinion nut

14. Hold pinion flange with Holder 6719A.

15. Install new pinion nut and tighten nut until there is zero bearing end-play.

⁂ CAUTION

Do not exceed the minimum tightening torque when installing the companion flange at this point. Damage to the collapsible spacer or bearings may result.

16. Tighten pinion nut to 200 ft. lbs. (271 Nm).

⁂ CAUTION

Never loosen pinion nut to decrease pinion bearing rotating torque and never exceed specified preload torque. If preload torque or rotating torque is exceeded a new collapsible spacer must be installed.

17. Record pinion flange rotating torque, with a torque wrench. Rotating torque should be equal to the reading recorded during removal plus an additional 5 inch lbs. (0.56 Nm).

18. If rotating torque is low, tighten pinion nut in 5 ft. lbs. (6.8 Nm) increments until rotating torque is achieved.

⁂ CAUTION

If maximum tightening torque is reached prior to reaching the required rotating torque, the collapsible spacer may have been damaged. Replace the collapsible spacer.

19. Install propeller shaft with reference marks aligned.
20. Install half shafts.

REAR AXLE HOUSING

REMOVAL & INSTALLATION

See Figure 21.

1. Before servicing the vehicle, refer to the precautions section.

2. With vehicle in neutral, position it on a hoist.

3. Position a lift under axle and secure lift to axle.

4. Remove brake components from the axle.

5. Remove wheel speed sensors.

6. Remove vent hose from the axle shaft tube.

7. Remove the propeller shaft.

8. Remove the stabilizer bar clamps bolts from the axle.

9. Remove the watts link bell crank bolt from differential cover.

10. Remove shock absorbers from axle bracket.

11. Remove upper control arms from axle brackets.

12. Lower axle and remove coil springs and spring isolators.

13. Remove lower control arms from axle brackets.

14. Lower axle and remove from vehicle.

To install:

15. Raise the axle and align lower control arms. Install control arm bolts loose at this time.

16. Install the coil springs.

17. Raise axle and align upper control arms. Install control arm bolts loose at this time.

➡The bell crank bolt has a Loctite patch, a new bolt should be used. If a new bolt is not available, clean the bolt and apply Loctite 242® to the threads.

18. Install watts link bell crank bolt and tighten to 160 ft. lbs. (217 Nm).

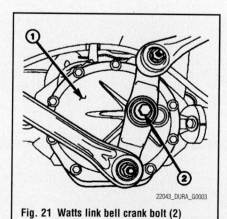

22043_DURA_G0003

Fig. 21 Watts link bell crank bolt (2)

19. Install shock absorbers and tighten the nuts to 75 ft. lbs. (102 Nm).

20. Install the parking brake and brake components.

21. Install the wheel speed sensors.

22. Install the axle vent hose.

23. Install the stabilizer bar and center it with equal spacing on both sides. Tighten bolts to 45 ft. lbs. (61 Nm).

24. Install the propeller shaft.

25. With the vehicle on the ground, tighten the upper control arm bolts to 125 ft. lbs. (170 Nm). Tighten the lower control arm nuts to 170 ft. lbs. (230 Nm).

REAR AXLE SHAFT, BEARING & SEAL

REMOVAL & INSTALLATION

8¼ Inch Axle

Axle Shaft

See Figures 22 and 23.

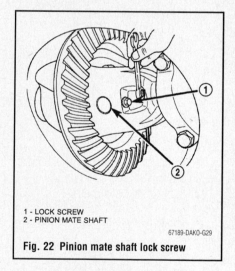

1 - LOCK SCREW
2 - PINION MATE SHAFT

67189-DAK0-G29

Fig. 22 Pinion mate shaft lock screw

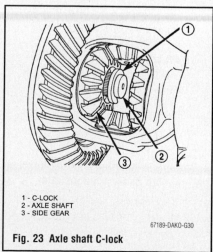

1 - C-LOCK
2 - AXLE SHAFT
3 - SIDE GEAR

67189-DAK0-G30

Fig. 23 Axle shaft C-lock

1. Before servicing the vehicle, refer to the precautions section.

2. With vehicle in neutral, position it on a hoist.

3. Remove brake caliper adapter with caliper and remove rotor.

4. Remove differential housing cover and drain lubricant.

5. Rotate differential case, to access pinion mate shaft lock screw. Remove screw and pinion mate shaft from differential case.

6. Push axle shaft inward and remove axle shaft C-lock.

7. Remove axle shaft.

To install:

8. Lubricate bearing bore and seal lip with gear lubricant.

9. Insert axle shaft through seal and engage into side gear splines.

10. Insert C-lock in end of axle shaft then push axle shaft outward to seat C-lock in side gear.

11. Insert pinion shaft into differential case and through thrust washers and differential pinions.

12. Align hole in shaft with hole in differential case and install lock screw with Loctite® on the threads. Tighten lock screw to 220 inch lbs. (25 Nm).

13. Install differential cover and fill with gear lubricant.

14. Install brake rotor and caliper adapter with caliper.

Bearing and Seal

See Figures 24 and 25.

1. Before servicing the vehicle, refer to the precautions section.

2. Remove axle shaft.

3. Remove axle seal with pry bar.

4. Position bearing Receiver 9338 on axle tube.

5. Insert bearing Remover 6310 with Foot 6310-9 through receiver and bearing.

6. Tighten Remove 6310 nut to pull bearing into the receiver.

To install:

7. Remove any old sealer/burrs from axle tube.

8. Install axle shaft bearing with Installer 9337 and Handle. Drive bearing in until tool contacts the axle tube.

➡Bearing is installed with the bearing part number against the installer.

9. Coat new axle seal lip with axle lubricant and install with Installer 9337 and Handle C-4171.

10. Install axle shaft.

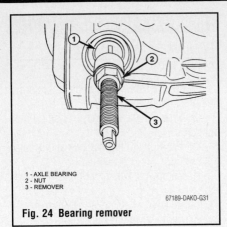

1 - AXLE BEARING
2 - NUT
3 - REMOVER

67189-DAK0-G31

Fig. 24 Bearing remover

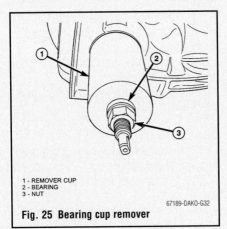

1 - REMOVER CUP
2 - BEARING
3 - NUT

67189-DAK0-G32

Fig. 25 Bearing cup remover

9¼ Inch Axle

Axle Shaft

1. Before servicing the vehicle, refer to the precautions section.

2. With vehicle in neutral, position it on a hoist.

3. Remove brake caliper adapter with caliper and remove rotor.

4. Remove differential housing cover and drain lubricant.

5. Rotate differential case, to access pinion mate shaft lock screw. Remove screw and pinion mate shaft from differential case.

6. Push axle shaft inward and remove axle shaft C-lock.

7. Remove axle shaft.

To install:

8. Lubricate bearing bore and seal lip with gear lubricant.

9. Insert axle shaft (1) through seal (2) and engage into side gear splines.

10. Insert C-lock in end of axle shaft then push axle shaft outward to seat C-lock in side gear.

11. Insert pinion shaft into differential case and through thrust washers and differential pinions.

12. Align hole in shaft with hole in differential case and install lock screw (4) with

Loctite® on the threads. Tighten lock screw to 220 inch lbs. (25 Nm).

13. Install differential cover and fill with gear lubricant.

14. Install brake rotor and caliper adapter with caliper.

Seal

1. Before servicing the vehicle, refer to the precautions section.

2. Remove axle shaft.

3. Remove axle shaft seal from end of the axle tube with a pry bar.

To install:

4. Remove any old sealer/burrs from axle tube.

5. Coat new seal lip with axle lubricant and install seal with Installer 9337 and Handle C-4171.

6. Install axle shaft.

Bearing

1. Before servicing the vehicle, refer to the precautions section.

2. Remove axle shaft.

3. Remove axle seal with pry bar.

4. Position bearing Receiver 9338 on axle tube.

5. Insert bearing Remover 6310 with Foot 6310-9 through receiver and bearing.

6. Tighten Remove 6310 nut to pull bearing into the receiver.

To install:

7. Remove any old sealer/burrs from axle tube.

8. Install axle shaft bearing with Installer 9337 and Handle C-417.

9. Drive bearing in until tool contacts the axle tube.

➡Bearing is installed with the bearing part number against the installer.

10. Coat new axle seal lip with axle lubricant and install with Installer 9337 and Handle C-4171.

11. Install axle shaft.

REAR DRIVESHAFT

REMOVAL & INSTALLATION

1. Before servicing the vehicle, refer to the precautions section.

2. Mark propeller shaft and pinion flange for installation reference.

3. Remove the front propeller shaft.

To install:

4. Install the propeller shaft with reference marks aligned.

5. Using new bolts, tighten them to 80 ft. lbs. (108 Nm).

REAR PINION SEAL

REMOVAL & INSTALLATION

8¼ Inch Axle

1. Before servicing the vehicle, refer to the precautions section.
2. With vehicle in neutral, position vehicle on hoist.
3. Mark a reference line across the axle flange and propeller shaft flange.
4. Remove propeller shaft.
5. Remove brake calipers and rotors to prevent any drag.
6. Rotate flange three or four times and verify flange rotates smoothly.
7. Measure torque to rotating pinion flange with an inch pound torque wrench. Record reading for installation reference.
8. Install bolts into two of the threaded holes in the flange 180° apart.
9. Position Holder 6719 against the flange and install a bolt and washer into one of the remaining threaded holes. Tighten the bolts so the Holder 6719 is held to the flange.
10. Remove pinion nut and washer.
11. Remove flange with Remover C-452.
12. Remove pinion seal with a pry tool or slide-hammer mounted screw.

To install:

13. Apply a light coating of gear lubricant on the lip of pinion seal.
14. Install new pinion seal with Installer C-4076-B and Handle C-4735.
15. Install flange on the end of the shaft with the reference marks aligned.
16. Install bolts into two of the threaded holes in the flange 180° apart.
17. Position Holder 6719 against flange. Install a bolt and washer into one of the remaining threaded holes. Tighten bolts so Holder 6719 is held to the flange.
18. Install flange on pinion shaft with Installer C-3718 and Holder 6719.
19. Install pinion washer and a new pinion nut. The convex side of the washer must face outward.

✳✳ CAUTION

Do not exceed the minimum tightening torque when installing the companion flange retaining nut at this point. Failure to follow these instructions can damage the collapsible spacer or bearings.

20. Hold flange with Holder 6719 and tighten pinion nut to 210 ft. lbs. (285 Nm). Rotate pinion several revolutions to ensure bearing rollers are seated.

21. Rotate pinion flange with an inch pound torque wrench. Rotating torque should be equal to the reading recorded during removal plus an additional 5 inch lbs. (0.56 Nm).

✳✳ CAUTION

Never loosen pinion nut to decrease pinion bearing rotating torque and never exceed specified preload torque. If rotating torque is exceeded, a new collapsible spacer must be installed. Failure to follow these instructions can damage the collapsible spacer or bearings.

22. If rotating torque is low use Holder 6719, to hold flange and tighten pinion nut in 5 ft. lbs. (6.8 Nm) increments until proper rotating torque is achieved.

➡The seal replacement is unacceptable if final pinion nut torque is less than 210 ft. lbs. (285 Nm).

➡The bearing rotating torque should be constant during a complete revolution of the pinion. If the rotating torque varies, this indicates a binding condition.

23. Install propeller shaft.
24. Install rear brake rotors components.

9¼ Inch Axle

1. Before servicing the vehicle, refer to the precautions section.
2. With vehicle in neutral, position it on a hoist.
3. Mark an installation reference line across the pinion flange and driveshaft flange.
4. Remove driveshaft.
5. Remove brake calipers and rotors to prevent any drag.
6. Rotate pinion flange three or four times and verify flange rotates smoothly.
7. Measure rotating torque of the pinion with an inch pound torque wrench and record reading.
8. Install two bolts into the pinion flange threaded holes, 180° apart. Position Holder 6719A, or equivalent, against the flange and install and tighten two bolts and washers into the remaining holes.
9. Hold the flange with Holder 6719A, or equivalent, and remove pinion nut and washer.
10. Remove companion flange with Remover C-452, or equivalent.
11. Remove pinion seal with pry tool or slide-hammer mounted screw.

To install:

12. Apply a light coating of gear lubricant on the lip of pinion seal.
13. Install new pinion seal with Installer C-4076-B and Handle C-4735, or equivalent.
14. Install pinion flange on pinion shaft with Installer C-3718, or equivalent.
15. Install two bolts into the threaded holes in the flange, 180° apart.
16. Position Holder 6719 against the flange and install a bolt and washer into one of the remaining threaded holes. Tighten the bolts so holder is held to the flange.
17. Install pinion washer and a new pinion nut. The convex side of the washer must face outward.

✳✳ CAUTION

Never exceed the minimum tightening torque 210 ft. lbs. (285 Nm) when installing the companion flange retaining nut at this point. Failure to follow these instructions will result in damage to collapsible spacer or bearings.

18. Hold companion flange with Holder 6719, or equivalent, and tighten pinion nut with a torque set to 210 ft. lbs. (285 Nm). Rotate pinion several revolutions to ensure the bearing rollers are seated.
19. Rotate pinion with an inch pound torque wrench. Rotating torque should be equal to the reading recorded during removal plus an additional 5 inch lbs. (0.56 Nm).

✳✳ CAUTION

Never loosen pinion nut to decrease pinion bearing rotating torque and never exceed specified preload torque. If rotating torque is exceeded, a new collapsible spacer must be installed. Failure to follow these instructions will result in damage to the collapsible spacer

20. If rotating torque is low, use Holder 6719, or equivalent, to hold the companion flange and tighten pinion nut in 5 ft. lbs. (6.8 Nm) increments until proper rotating torque is achieved.

➡The bearing rotating torque should be constant during a complete revolution of the pinion. If the rotating torque varies, this indicates a binding condition.

➡The seal replacement is unacceptable if the final pinion nut torque is less than 210 ft. lbs. (285 Nm).

21. Install driveshaft.

ENGINE COOLING

ENGINE FAN

REMOVAL & INSTALLATION

See Figure 26.

1. Partially drain the cooling system.
2. Remove the upper radiator hose.
3. Remove the air filter housing assembly.
4. Stop the water pump from turning with a special tool or prybar on the nuts. Loosen the fan nut (36mm). Turn CCW to loosen.
5. Position the fan/fan drive assembly in the radiator shroud.
6. Remove the two shroud mounting screws.
7. Remove the radiator shroud and fan drive assembly.

➡**After removing fan blade/viscous fan drive assembly, do not place viscous fan drive in horizontal position. If stored horizontally, silicone fluid in the viscous fan drive could drain into its bearing assembly and contaminate lubricant.**

8. Remove four bolts securing fan blade assembly to viscous fan drive.

To install:

9. If drive and fan were separated, tighten the bolts to 17 ft. lbs. (23 Nm).
10. The remainder of the installation procedure is the reverse of removal.
11. If a new viscous drive has been fitted, start and run the engine at 2,000 rpm for about 2 minutes to distribute fluid within the drive.

RADIATOR

REMOVAL & INSTALLATION

3.7L and 4.7L Engines

See Figures 27, 28 and 29.

1. Disconnect the battery negative cable.
2. Drain the radiator.
3. Remove any cables or lines clipped to the radiator or shrouds.
4. Remove the upper and lower heater hoses.

✳✳ WARNING

Most cooling system hoses use "constant tension" hose clamps. When removing or installing, use a tool designed for servicing this type of clamp. The clamps are stamped with a letter or number on the tongue. If replacement is necessary, use only an OEM clamp with a matching ID.

✳✳ CAUTION

Always wear safety glasses when servicing constant tension clamps.

5. If coolant overflow and windshield washer fluid bottles are fitted to the fan shroud, disconnect the lines and remove them. Pull straight up to remove the bottles from shroud.
6. Remove the upper fan shroud. Disconnect the electric fan wiring.
7. Remove the fan shroud hardware and reposition the shroud towards the engine for access to the radiator.
8. Label, then disconnect the automatic transmission lines if the fluid cooler is incorporated into the radiator. Plug the lines to prevent spillage. Be sure to note which line goes to which fitting.
9. Check for rubber shields on the sides of the radiator. Remove them if fitted. These are normally secured with non-reusable plastic pins.
10. Remove the radiator bolts (usually two at the top). Lift the radiator up and out of the vehicle, being careful that the cooling fins do not bang against anything. They are easily damaged.
11. Some vehicles may have an auxiliary automatic transmission fluid cooler which will come away with the radiator.

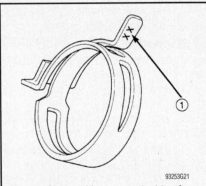

Fig. 27 Size marking on constant tension clamps (1)

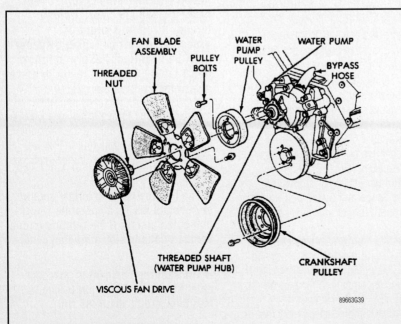

Fig. 26 Typical engine fan assembly

FAN BLADE ASSEMBLY
PULLEY BOLTS
WATER PUMP PULLEY
WATER PUMP
BYPASS HOSE
THREADED NUT
THREADED SHAFT (WATER PUMP HUB)
CRANKSHAFT PULLEY
VISCOUS FAN DRIVE

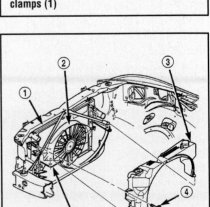

Fig. 28 Shroud assembly (4.7L): Radiator (1), Fan (2), Upper Shroud (3), Bolts (4), Lower Shroud (5).

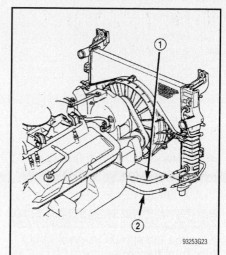

Fig. 29 Mark automatic transmission oil cooler lines before disconnecting. Supply (1) and return (2) lines in this illustration for the 4.7L engine

To install:

12. Lower the radiator into place. There are two alignment pins at the bottom which fit into holes in the lower support.

13. Tighten radiator mounting bolts to 17 ft. lbs. (23 Nm).

14. The remainder of the procedure is the reverse of removal. Double-check the connection of all hoses and lines before adding fluids or operating the vehicle.

5.7L Engine

See Figure 30.

1. Disconnect the battery negative cable.
2. Drain the radiator.
3. Remove any cables or lines clipped to the radiator or shrouds.
4. Remove pushpins and the upper condenser/radiator seal.
5. Remove air filer housing assembly.
6. Remove upper radiator hose.
7. Remove overflow tube.
8. Remove radiator fan shroud from the radiator and position over the radiator fan.
9. Remove the upper radiator support.
10. Raise vehicle.
11. Disconnect the power steering cooler lines.
12. Disconnect the transmission cooler lines.
13. Remove the lower radiator hose.
14. Lower vehicle.
15. Remove upper radiator mount.
16. Remove LH and RH radiator side seals.
17. Remove radiator.
18. Remove power steering cooler form the radiator, if necessary.

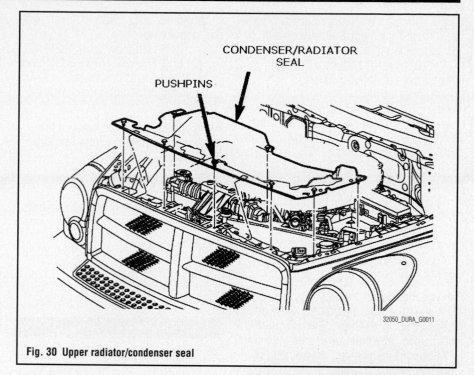

Fig. 30 Upper radiator/condenser seal

19. Remove transmission cooler from radiator, if necessary.

To install:

20. Install power steering cooler, if removed.
21. Install transmission oil cooler, if removed.
22. Install the upper radiator mount
23. Position isolator pins into alignment holes in radiator lower support.

➡The radiator has two isolator pins on bottom of both tanks. These fit into alignment holes in radiator lower support.

24. Install upper radiator support. Tighten bolts to 200 inch lbs. (23 Nm).
25. Install LH and RH radiator side seals.
26. Install upper radiator hose.
27. Install overflow tube.
28. Install radiator shroud.
29. Raise vehicle.
30. Install power steering cooler lines.
31. Install transmission cooler lines.
32. Install lower radiator hose.
33. Lower vehicle.
34. Install air filter housing assembly.
35. Install upper radiator/condenser seal.
36. Fill radiator.
37. Connect battery negative cable.
38. Start and warm the engine; check for leaks.

THERMOSTAT

REMOVAL & INSTALLATION
See Figures 31 and 32.

✳✳ WARNING

Most cooling system hoses use "constant tension" hose clamps. When removing or installing, use a tool designed for servicing this type of clamp. The clamps are stamped with a letter or number on the tongue. If replacement is necessary, use only an OEM clamp with a matching ID.

✳✳ CAUTION

Always wear safety glasses when servicing contact tension clamps.

1. Locate the thermostat. This is located in a housing on the engine side of the upper radiator hose for the 5.7L engines. On the 3.7L and 4.7L engines, the thermostat is located on the engine side of the lower radiator hose.
2. Disconnect the negative battery cable.
3. Drain the engine coolant from the block until the level is below the thermostat.
4. On most models the alternator must be removed or repositioned for access to the thermostat housing.
5. Remove the radiator hose from the thermostat housing.
6. Disconnect any sensors fitted to the thermostat housing.

7. Remove the retaining bolts from the thermostat housing. Note lengths of each for ease of installation.

8. Remove the thermostat housing, thermostat, and gasket, if fitted.

9. Note the relative positions of all components, especially gaskets and seals. Note the orientation of the thermostat in the housing.

To install:

10. Be sure the new thermostat is the correct one for your engine.

11. Clean the gasket or seal mating surfaces.

12. Paper gaskets must be replaced.

13. Install the thermostat, gasket or seals.

14. Install the thermostat housing on the engine.

➡The thermostat housing may have the word the word FRONT stamped on housing (5.7L engines). For adequate clearance, this must be placed towards the front of the vehicle; the housing is slightly angled forward.

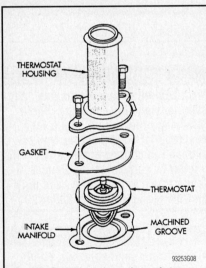

Fig. 31 On 5.7L engines, the gasket goes above the thermostat

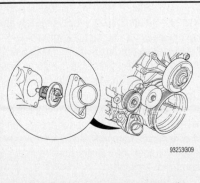

Fig. 32 On the 3.7L and 4.7L engine, the thermostat is at the bottom of the engine

15. Be sure all components are properly seated before tightening.

16. Tighten the housing bolts to 18 ft. lbs. (24 Nm). Fasteners should be tightened evenly to avoid leaks or damage.

17. Reinstall the radiator hose onto the housing.

➡Ensure that you have secured the system drain plug(s) before refilling with coolant.

18. Refill the radiator with a proper coolant mixture.

19. Connect the negative battery cable(s).

20. Start the engine and bleed the cooling system.

21. Ensure that the thermostat is operational (by checking the upper radiator hose for warmth), and that there are no leaks.

WATER PUMP

REMOVAL & INSTALLATION

3.7L Engine

See Figure 33.

1. Before servicing the vehicle, refer to the precautions section.

2. Drain the cooling system.

3. Remove or disconnect the following:
   - Negative battery cable
   - Fan and clutch assembly from the pump
   - Fan shroud and fan assembly. If you're reusing the fan clutch, keep it upright to avoid silicone fluid loss!
   - Lower hose
   - Water pump (8 bolts)

4. Installation is the reverse of removal. Tighten the bolts, in sequence, to 40 ft. lbs. (54 Nm).

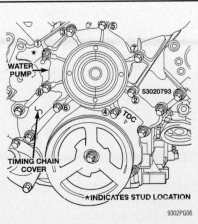

Fig. 33 Water pump torque sequence—3.7L and 4.7L engine

4.7L Engine

1. Before servicing the vehicle, refer to the precautions section.

2. Drain the cooling system.

3. Remove or disconnect the following:
   - Negative battery cable
   - Fan and fan drive assembly from the pump. Don't attempt to remove it from the vehicle, yet.

➡If a new pump is being installed; don't separate the fan from the drive.

   - Shroud and fan

✳✳ WARNING

Keep the fan upright to avoid fluid loss from the drive.

   - Accessory drive belt
   - Lower radiator hose
   - Water pump

4. Installation is the reverse of removal. Tighten the bolts in sequence to 40 ft. lbs. (54 Nm).

5.7L Engine

1. Before servicing the vehicle, refer to the precautions section.

2. Drain the cooling system.

3. Remove or disconnect the following:
   - Negative battery cable
   - Accessory drive belt
   - Engine cooling fan
   - Coolant recovery bottle
   - Washer bottle
   - Fan shroud
   - A/C compressor and alternator brace
   - Idler pulleys
   - Belt tensioner
   - Radiator hoses
   - Heater hoses
   - Water pump

To install:

4. Install or connect the following:
   - Water pump. Tighten the bolts to 18 ft. lbs. (24 Nm).
   - Heater hoses
   - Radiator hoses
   - Idler pulleys
   - A/C compressor and alternator brace
   - Fan shroud
   - Washer bottle
   - Coolant recovery bottle
   - Accessory drive belt
   - Negative battery cable
   - Negative battery cable

5. Fill the cooling system.

6. Start the engine and check for leaks.

ENGINE ELECTRICAL

ALTERNATOR

REMOVAL & INSTALLATION

3.7L and 4.7L Engines

See Figure 34.

1. Before servicing the vehicle, refer to the precautions section.
2. Remove or disconnect the following:
   - Negative battery cable
   - Accessory drive belt
   - Alternator harness connectors
   - Mounting bolts and alternator

➡ **There are 1 vertical and 2 horizontal bolts.**

To install:

3. Before servicing the vehicle, refer to the precautions section.
4. Install the alternator and tighten the bolts to the following specifications:
   - Short horizontal bolt to 55 ft. lbs. (74 Nm)
   - Vertical bolt and long horizontal bolt to 40 ft. lbs. (55 Nm)
5. Install or connect the following:

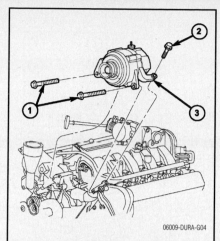

06009-DURA-G04

Fig. 34 Alternator mounting on 3.7L and 4.7L engines. (1) horizontal bolts, (2) vertical bolt, (3) alternator

   - Alternator harness connectors
   - Accessory drive belt
   - Negative battery cable

5.7L Engines

See Figure 35.

CHARGING SYSTEM

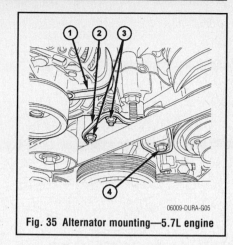

06009-DURA-G05

Fig. 35 Alternator mounting—5.7L engine

1. Before servicing the vehicle, refer to the precautions section.
2. Remove or disconnect the following:
   - Negative battery cable
   - Accessory drive belt
   - Alternator harness connectors
   - Support bracket nuts and bolt
   - Mounting bolts and alternator
3. Installation is the reverse of removal. Torque the bolts to 30 ft. lbs. (41 Nm).

ENGINE ELECTRICAL

FIRING ORDER

See Figures 36 through 38.

IGNITION SYSTEM

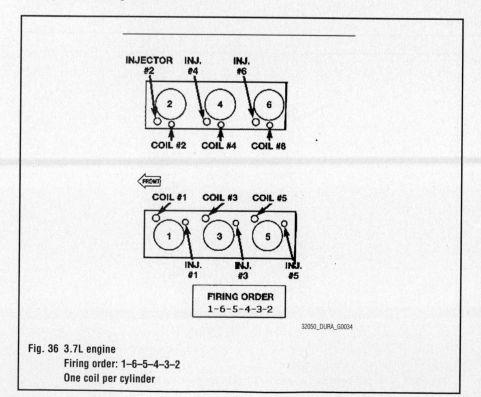

FIRING ORDER
1–6–5–4–3–2

32050_DURA_G0034

Fig. 36 3.7L engine
   Firing order: 1–6–5–4–3–2
   One coil per cylinder

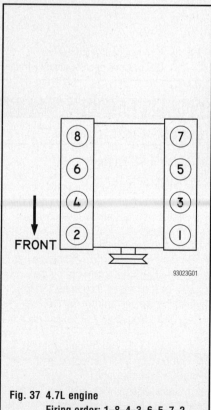

93023G01

Fig. 37 4.7L engine
   Firing order: 1–8–4–3–6–5–7–2
   One coil per cylinder

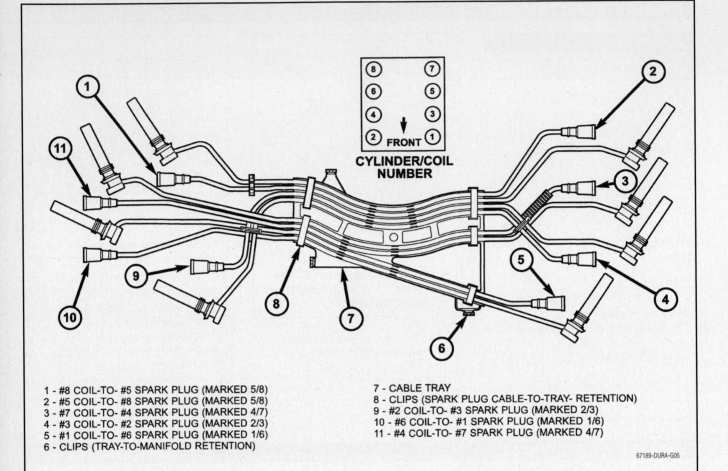

CYLINDER/COIL
NUMBER

1 - #8 COIL-TO- #5 SPARK PLUG (MARKED 5/8)
2 - #5 COIL-TO- #8 SPARK PLUG (MARKED 5/8)
3 - #7 COIL-TO- #4 SPARK PLUG (MARKED 4/7)
4 - #3 COIL-TO- #2 SPARK PLUG (MARKED 2/3)
5 - #1 COIL-TO- #6 SPARK PLUG (MARKED 1/6)
6 - CLIPS (TRAY-TO-MANIFOLD RETENTION)

7 - CABLE TRAY
8 - CLIPS (SPARK PLUG CABLE-TO-TRAY- RETENTION)
9 - #2 COIL-TO- #3 SPARK PLUG (MARKED 2/3)
10 - #6 COIL-TO- #1 SPARK PLUG (MARKED 1/6)
11 - #4 COIL-TO- #7 SPARK PLUG (MARKED 4/7)

67189-DURA-G05

Fig. 38 5.7L engine firing order
One coil and one secondary wire per cylinder

IGNITION COIL

REMOVAL & INSTALLATION

3.7L and 4.7L Engines

See Figures 39 and 40.

1. Certain coils may require removal of the throttle body air intake tube or intake box for access.

2. Disconnect the negative battery cable.

3. Detach the electrical connector from the coil by pushing downward on the release lock on top of the connector and pulling the connector from the coil.

4. Clean the area at the base of each coil with compressed air.

5. Remove the coil mounting nut(s). Pull the coil up with a slight twisting action and remove it from the vehicle.

6. Installation is the reverse of removal. Smear the coil O-ring with silicone grease. Tighten the mounting nut to 70 inch lbs. (8 Nm). Connect the wiring.

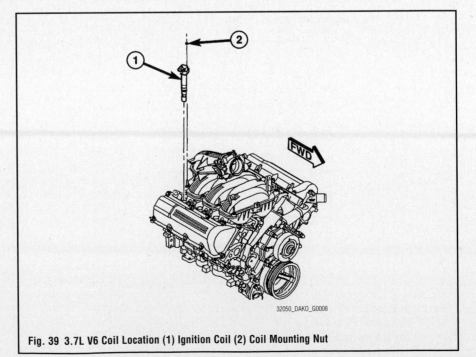

32050_DAKO_G0008

Fig. 39 3.7L V6 Coil Location (1) Ignition Coil (2) Coil Mounting Nut

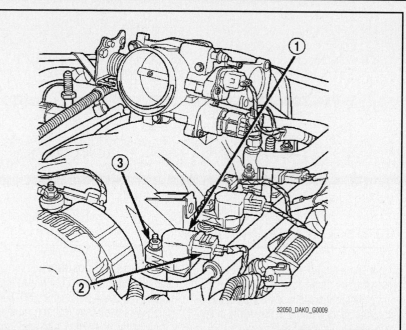

Fig. 40 4.7L V8 Coil Location (1) Ignition Coil (2) Coil Electrical Connector (3) Coil Mounting Stud/Nut

5.7L Engines

See Figure 41.

1. Certain coils may require removal of the throttle body air intake tube or intake box for access.

2. Disconnect the negative battery cable.

3. Unlock connector by first releasing slide lock and pressing on lock release while pulling connector from coil.

4. Remove secondary high—voltage wire with a twisting motion.

5. Loosen coil mounting bolts; the mounting bolts are retained by the coil body.

6. Pull the coil up with a slight twisting action.

7. Installation is the reverse of removal. Smear the coil O–ring with silicone grease. Tighten the mounting nut to 9 ft. lbs. (12 Nm). Connect the wiring.

➡ **To prevent ignition crossfire, spark plug cables MUST be placed in cable**

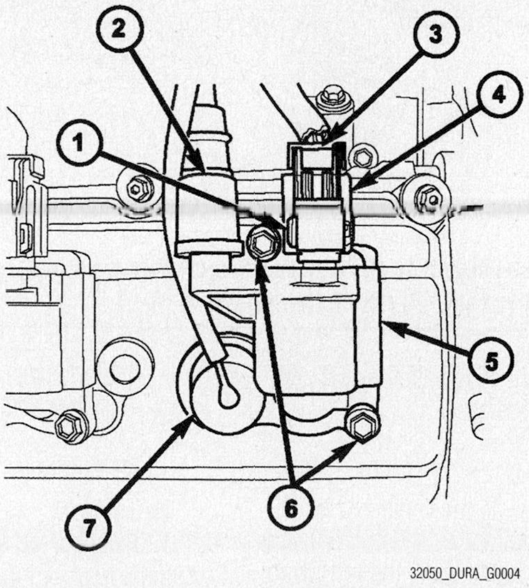

Fig. 41 5.7L Coil location on valve cover. (1) Slide lock (2) Secondary wire (3) Lock release (4) Coil electrical connector (5) Ignition coil (6) Mounting bolts (7) Secondary wire

tray (routing loom) into their original position.

IGNITION TIMING

ADJUSTMENT

The ignition timing is controlled by the Powertrain Control Module (PCM). No adjustment is necessary or possible.

SPARK PLUGS

REMOVAL & INSTALLATION

3.7L and 4.7L Engines

Each individual spark plug is located under each ignition coil. Each individual ignition coil must be removed to gain access to each spark plug. Refer to Ignition Coil Removal/Installation. Prior to removing a spark plug, spray compressed air around base of the ignition coil at cylinder head. This will help prevent foreign material from entering combustion chamber.

1. Remove spark plug from cylinder head using a quality socket with a rubber or foam insert.

2. Inspect spark plug condition.

To install:

3. Start the spark plug into the cylinder head by hand to avoid cross threading.

4. Before installing coil(s), check condition of coil O–ring and replace as necessary. To aid in coil installation, apply silicone to coil O–ring.

5. Tighten spark plugs to 20 ft. lbs. (27 Nm) torque.

6. Install ignition coil(s). Refer to Ignition Coil Removal/Installation.

5.7L Engines

See Figure 42.

Sixteen spark plugs (2 per cylinder) are used with 5.7L V8 engines.

Eight of the 16 spark plugs are located under an ignition coil; the other 8 are not. If the spark plug being removed is under a coil, the coil must be removed to gain access to the spark plug. Refer to Ignition Coil Removal/Installation.

Before removing or disconnecting any spark plug cables, note their original position. Remove cables one at a time. To prevent ignition crossfire, spark plug cables **MUST** be placed in cable tray (routing loom) into their original position. Refer to Spark Plug Cable Removal for proper routing.

Before installing spark plug cables to either the spark plugs or coils, apply dielectric grease to inside of boots.

1. Remove necessary air filter tubing at throttle body.

2. Prior to removing an ignition coil (if necessary), spray compressed air around the coil base at cylinder head cover.

3. Prior to removing a spark plug, spray compressed air into cylinder head opening. This will help prevent foreign material from entering combustion chamber.

4. Remove spark plug from cylinder head using a quality socket with a rubber or foam insert.

5. Inspect spark plug condition.

To install:

✳ WARNING

The 5.7L V8 is equipped with torque critical design spark plugs. Do not exceed 15 ft. lbs. (20 Nm) torque during installation. Special care should be taken when installing spark plugs into the cylinder head spark plug wells; be sure the plugs do not drop into the plug wells as electrodes can be damaged.

6. Start the spark plug into cylinder head by hand to avoid cross threading aluminum threads. To aid in installation, attach

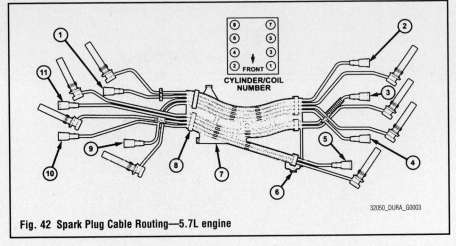

Fig. 42 Spark Plug Cable Routing—5.7L engine

an old spark plug boot or a piece of rubber hose to spark plug.

7. Before installing spark plug cables to either the spark plugs or coils, apply dielectric grease to inside of boots.

8. To prevent ignition crossfire, spark plug cables **MUST** be placed in cable tray (routing loom) into their original position.

9. Spark plug cables on the 5.7L engine are paired on cylinders 1 & 6, 2 & 3, 4 & 7 and 5 & 8. Before removing or disconnecting any spark plug cables, **note**

their original position and remove cables one at a time. To prevent ignition crossfire, spark plug cables **MUST** be placed in cable tray (routing loom) into their original position. The cable retention clips must also be securely locked.

10. Install ignition coil(s) to necessary spark plugs. Refer to Ignition Coil Installation.

11. Install spark plug cables to remaining spark plugs. Remember to apply dielectric grease to inside of boots.

12. Tighten spark plugs.

ENGINE ELECTRICAL   STARTING SYSTEM

STARTER

REMOVAL & INSTALLATION

3.7L and 4.7L Engines

See Figure 43.

1. Before servicing the vehicle, refer to the precautions section.

➡**If equipped with 4WD and certain transmissions, a support bracket is used between front axle and side of transmission. Remove 2 support bracket bolts at transmission. Pry support bracket slightly to gain access to lower starter mounting bolt.**

2. Remove or disconnect the following:
   • Negative battery cable
   • Starter mounting bolts

➡**The left side exhaust pipe and front driveshaft must be disconnected.**

   • Starter solenoid harness connections
   • Starter

To install:

3. Connect the starter solenoid wiring connectors.

4. Install the starter and torque the bolts to 40 ft. lbs. (54 Nm).

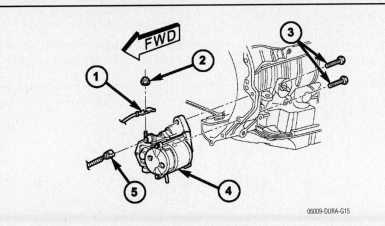

Fig. 43 Starter mounting, 3.7L and 4.7L engines. (1) battery positive cable, (2) nut, (3) starter mounting bolts, (4) starter, (5) wiring harness

5. Install the negative battery cable and check for proper operation.

5.7L Engines

1. Before servicing the vehicle, refer to the precautions section.

2. Remove or disconnect the following:
   • Negative battery cable

➡**Depending on drivetrain configuration, a support bracket may be used.**

   • Starter mounting bolts
   • Starter solenoid harness connections
   • Starter

To install:

3. Connect the starter solenoid wiring connectors.

4. Install the starter and torque the bolts to 50 ft. lbs. (68 Nm).

5. Install the negative battery cable and check for proper operation.

ENGINE MECHANICAL

➡Disconnecting the negative battery cable may interfere with the functions of the on board computer systems and may require the computer to undergo a relearning process, once the negative battery cable is reconnected.

ACCESSORY DRIVE BELTS

ACCESSORY BELT ROUTING

See Figure 44.

INSPECTION

Inspect the drive belt for signs of glazing or cracking. A glazed belt will be perfectly smooth from slippage, while a good belt will have a slight texture of fabric visible. Cracks will usually start at the inner edge of the belt and run outward. All worn or damaged drive belts should be replaced immediately.

ADJUSTMENT

It is not necessary to adjust belt tension on the 3.7L, 4.7L or 5.7L engines. These engines are equipped with an automatic belt tensioner. The tensioner maintains correct belt tension at all times; consequently, do not attempt to use a belt tension gauge on these engines.

REMOVAL & INSTALLATION

See Figure 45.

1. Disconnect negative battery cable.
2. Rotate belt tensioner until it contacts its stop. Remove belt, then slowly rotate the tensioner into the freearm position.

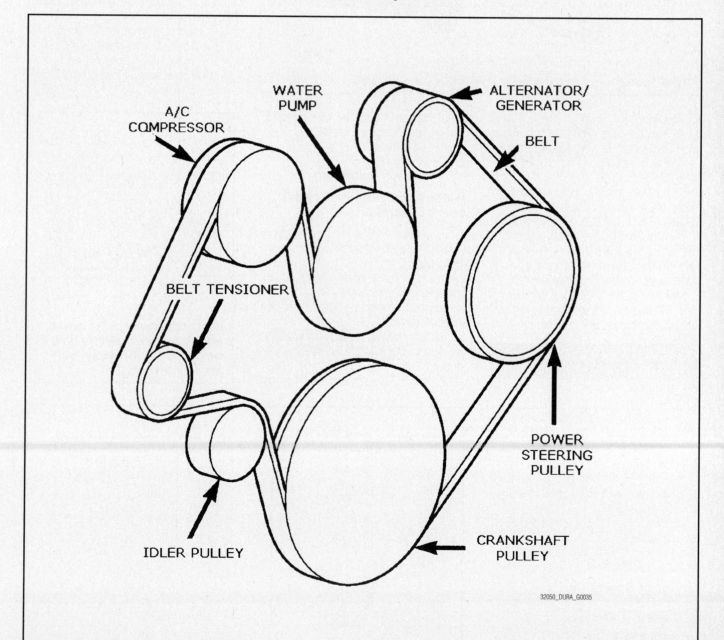

32050_DURA_G0035

Fig. 44 Belt routing—3.7L, 4.7L and 5.7L engines

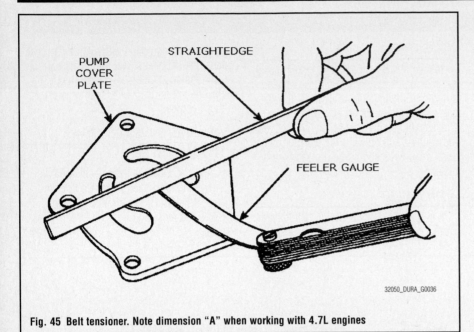

PUMP COVER PLATE

STRAIGHTEDGE

FEELER GAUGE

32050_DURA_G0036

Fig. 45 Belt tensioner. Note dimension "A" when working with 4.7L engines

To install:

3. Install new belt. Route the belt around all pulleys except the idler pulley.

4. Rotate the tensioner arm until it contacts its stop position.

5. Route the belt around the idler and slowly let the tensioner rotate into the belt. Make sure the belt is seated onto all pulleys.

6. With the drive belt installed, inspect the belt wear indicator. On 4.7L Engines only, the gap between the tang and the housing stop (measurement A) must not exceed 0.94 inches (24 mm). If the measurement exceeds this specification replace the serpentine accessory drive belt.

CAMSHAFT AND VALVE LIFTERS

INSPECTION

1. Inspect the camshaft bearing journals for wear or damage.

2. Inspect the cylinder head and check oil return holes.

3. Check the tooth surface of the distributor drive gear teeth of the right camshaft for wear or damage.

4. Check both camshaft surfaces for wear or damage.

5. Check camshaft lobe height and replace if out of limit.

REMOVAL & INSTALLATION

3.7L and 4.7L Engines

See Figures 46 through 49.

1. Before servicing the vehicle, refer to the precautions section.

2. Remove or disconnect the following:
- Negative battery cable
- Valve covers
- Rocker arms
- Hydraulic lash adjusters

➡**Keep all valvetrain components in order for assembly.**

3. Set the engine at Top Dead Center (TDC) of the compression stroke for the No. 1 cylinder.

4. Install Timing Chain Wedge 8350 to retain the chain tensioners.

5. Matchmark the timing chains to the camshaft sprockets.

6. Install Camshaft Holding Tool 6958 and Adapter Pins 8346 to the left camshaft sprocket.

7. Remove or disconnect the following:

- Right camshaft timing sprocket and target wheel
- Left camshaft sprocket
- Camshaft bearing caps, by reversing the tightening sequence
- Camshafts

To install:

8. Install or connect the following:
- Camshafts. Tighten the bearing cap bolts in ½ turn increments, in sequence, to 100 inch lbs. (11 Nm).
- Target wheel to the right camshaft
- Camshaft timing sprockets and chains, by aligning the matchmarks

9. Remove the tensioner wedges and tighten the camshaft sprocket bolts to 90 ft. lbs. (122 Nm).

10. Install or connect the following:
- Hydraulic lash adjusters in their original locations
- Rocker arms in their original locations

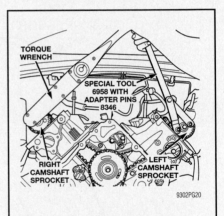

TORQUE WRENCH

SPECIAL TOOL 6958 WITH ADAPTER PINS 8346

RIGHT CAMSHAFT SPROCKET

LEFT CAMSHAFT SPROCKET

9302PG20

Fig. 47 Hold the left camshaft sprocket with a spanner wrench while removing or installing the camshaft sprocket bolts—3.7L and 4.7L engine

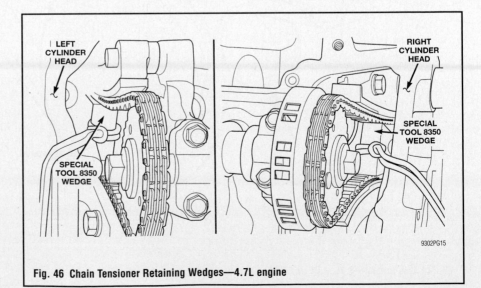

LEFT CYLINDER HEAD

SPECIAL TOOL 8350 WEDGE

RIGHT CYLINDER HEAD

SPECIAL TOOL 8350 WEDGE

9302PG15

Fig. 46 Chain Tensioner Retaining Wedges—4.7L engine

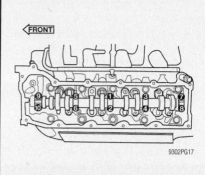

Fig. 48 Camshaft bearing cap bolt tightening sequence—3.7L and 4.7L engines

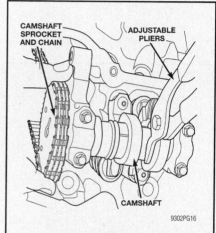

Fig. 49 Turn the camshaft with pliers, if needed, to align the dowel in the sprocket—4.7L engine

- Valve covers
- Negative battery cable

5.7L Engine

See Figure 50.

1. Before servicing the vehicle, refer to the precautions section.
2. Drain the cooling system.
3. Recover the A/C refrigerant, if equipped with air conditioning.
4. Set the crankshaft to Top Dead Center (TDC) of the compression stroke for the No. 1 cylinder.
5. Remove or disconnect the following:
   - Negative battery cable
   - Camshaft rear cam bearing core plug
   - Air cleaner
   - Accessory drive belt
   - Alternator
   - A/C compressor
   - Radiator
   - Intake manifold
   - Valve covers
   - Cylinder heads

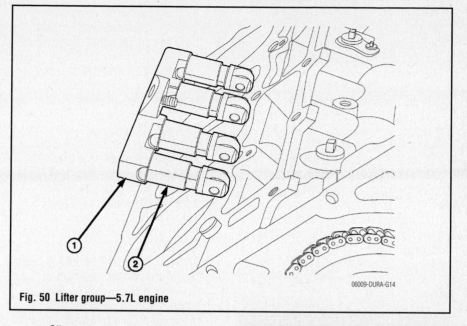

Fig. 50 Lifter group—5.7L engine

- Oil pan
- Front cover
- Oil pickup tube
- Oil pump
- Timing chain and sprockets
- Camshaft thrust plate
- Hydraulic lifters
- Camshaft

To install:

6. Install or connect the following:
   - Camshaft
   - Camshaft thrust plate. Tighten the bolts to 21 ft. lbs. (28 Nm).
   - Timing chain and sprockets
   - Oil pump
   - Oil pickup tube

➡**Lifters must be replaced in their original positions.**

   - Hydraulic lifters
   - Cylinder heads
   - Pushrods
   - Rocker arms
   - Front cover
   - Oil pan
   - Valve covers
   - Intake manifold
   - A/C compressor
   - Alternator
   - Accessory drive belt
   - Radiator
   - Air cleaner
   - Camshaft rear cam bearing core plug
   - Negative battery cable
7. Fill the cooling system.
8. Recharge the A/C system, if equipped.
9. Start the engine and check for leaks.

CRANKSHAFT FRONT SEAL

REMOVAL & INSTALLATION

3.7L and 4.7L Engines

See Figure 51.

1. Disconnect the negative battery cable.
2. Drain the cooling system.
3. Remove the accessory drive belt.
4. Remove the A/C compressor mounting bolts and set the compressor aside.

➡**It is not necessary to disconnect the A/C lines from the compressor.**

5. Remove the upper radiator hose.
6. Disconnect the engine fan electrical connector, located inside the radiator shroud.
7. Remove the engine fan.
8. Remove the camshaft damper bolt.
9. Using Special Tool 8513 Insert and 1026 three-jaw puller, remove the crankshaft damper.
10. Remove the seal using Special Tool 8511.

To install:

11. Using Special Tools 8348 and 8512, install the crankshaft front seal.
12. Install the crankshaft damper as follows:

   a. Align the crankshaft damper slot with the key in the crankshaft. Slide the damper onto the crankshaft.

   b. Assemble Special Tool 8512-A. The nut is threaded onto the threaded rod first. Then the roller bearing is placed onto the threaded rod (The hardened bearing surface of the bearing MUST face the nut). Then the hardened washer slides onto the threaded rod. Once assembled coat the threaded rod's threads with Mopar® Nickel Anti-Seize or equivalent.

c. Using Special Tool 8512-A, press the damper onto the crankshaft.

13. Install the crankshaft damper bolt and tighten to 130 ft. lbs. (175 Nm).

14. Install the engine fan.

15. Install the upper radiator hose.

16. Install the A/C compressor and tighten the mounting bolts to 40 ft. lbs. (54 Nm).

17. Install the accessory drive belt.

18. Refill the cooling system to the correct level.

19. Connect the negative battery cable.

20. Start the engine and check for leaks.

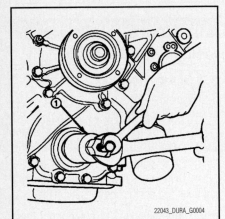

Fig. 51 A special tool is required to remove and install the seal without removing the front timing cover

5.7L Engines

1. Disconnect the negative battery cable.

2. Drain the cooling system.

3. Remove the accessory drive belt.

4. Remove the upper radiator hose.

5. Remove the engine fan.

6. Remove the crankshaft damper bolt.

7. Using Special Tool 8513 Insert and 1026 three-jaw puller, remove the crankshaft damper.

8. Using Special Tool 9071, remove the crankshaft front seal.

To install:

❊❊ WARNING

The front crankshaft seal must be installed dry, without any lubricant applied to the sealing lip or outer edge.

9. Using Special Tools 9072 and 8512-A, install the crankshaft front seal.

10. Install the crankshaft damper as follows:

a. Align the crankshaft damper slot with the key in the crankshaft. Slide the damper onto the crankshaft.

b. Assemble Special Tool 8512-A. The nut is threaded onto the threaded rod first. Then the roller bearing is placed onto the threaded rod (The hardened bearing surface of the bearing MUST face the nut). Then the hardened washer slides onto the threaded rod. Once assembled coat the threaded rod's threads with Mopar® Nickel Anti-Seize or equivalent.

c. Using Special Tool 8512-A, press the damper onto the crankshaft.

11. Install the crankshaft damper bolt and tighten to 129 ft. lbs. (176 Nm).

12. Install the engine fan.

13. Install the upper radiator hose.

14. Install the accessory drive belt.

15. Refill the cooling system to the correct level.

16. Connect the negative battery cable.

17. Start the engine and check for leaks.

CYLINDER HEAD

REMOVAL & INSTALLATION

3.7L Engine

Left Side

See Figures 52 through 55.

1. Before servicing the vehicle, refer to the precautions section.

2. Drain the cooling system.

3. Properly relieve the fuel system pressure.

4. Remove or disconnect the following:

- Negative battery cable
- Exhaust Y-pipe
- Intake manifold
- Cylinder head cover
- Engine cooling fan and shroud
- Accessory drive belt
- Power steering pump

5. Rotate the crankshaft so that the crankshaft timing mark aligns with the Top Dead Center (TDC) mark on the front cover, and the **V6** marks on the camshaft sprockets are at 12 o'clock as shown.

- Crankshaft damper
- Front cover

6. Lock the secondary timing chain to

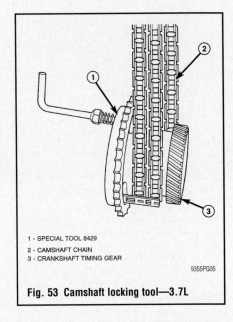

1 - SPECIAL TOOL 8429
2 - CAMSHAFT CHAIN
3 - CRANKSHAFT TIMING GEAR

Fig. 53 Camshaft locking tool—3.7L

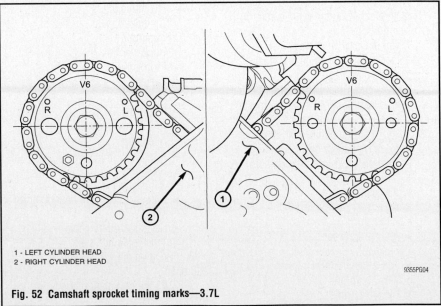

1 - LEFT CYLINDER HEAD
2 - RIGHT CYLINDER HEAD

Fig. 52 Camshaft sprocket timing marks—3.7L

the idler sprocket with Timing Chain Locking tool 8429.

7. Matchmark the secondary timing chain one link on each side of the V6 mark to the camshaft sprocket.
- Left secondary timing chain tensioner
- Cylinder head access plug
- Secondary timing chain guide
- Camshaft sprocket
- Cylinder head

➡The cylinder head is retained by twelve bolts. Four of the bolts are smaller and are at the front of the head.

To install:

8. Check the cylinder head bolts for signs of stretching and replace as necessary.

9. Lubricate the threads of the 11mm bolts with clean engine oil.

10. Coat the threads of the 8mm bolts with Mopar® Lock and Seal Adhesive, or equivalent.

11. Install the cylinder heads. Use new gaskets and tighten the bolts, in sequence, as follows:
   a. Step 1: Bolts 1–8 to 20 ft. lbs. (27 Nm)
   b. Step 2: Bolts 1–10 verify torque without loosening
   c. Step 3: Bolts 9–12 to 10 ft. lbs. (14 Nm)
   d. Step 4: Bolts 1–8 plus ¼ (90 degree) turn
   e. Step 5: Bolts 1–8 plus ¼ (90 degree) turn again
   f. Step 6: Bolts 9–12 to 19 ft. lbs. (26 Nm)

12. Install or connect the following:
- Camshaft sprocket. Align the secondary chain matchmarks and tighten the bolt to 90 ft. lbs. (122 Nm).
- Secondary timing chain guide
- Cylinder head access plug

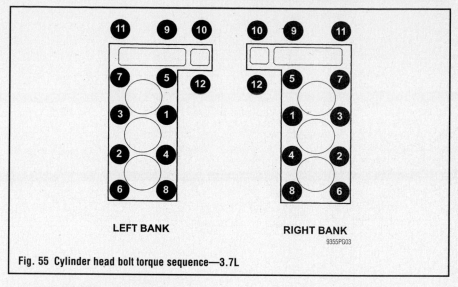

Fig. 55 Cylinder head bolt torque sequence—3.7L

- Secondary timing chain tensioner. Refer to the timing chain procedure in this section.

13. Remove the Timing Chain Locking tool.

14. Install or connect the following:
- Front cover
- Crankshaft damper. Torque the bolt to 130 ft. lbs. (175 Nm).
- Power steering pump
- Accessory drive belt
- Engine cooling fan and shroud
- Cover
- Intake manifold
- Exhaust Y-pipe
- Negative battery cable

15. Fill and bleed the cooling system.

16. Start the engine, check for leaks and repair if necessary.

Right Side

See Figures 56 and 57.

1. Before servicing the vehicle, refer to the precautions section.

2. Drain the cooling system.

3. Properly relieve the fuel system pressure.

4. Remove or disconnect the following:
- Negative battery cable
- Exhaust Y-pipe
- Intake manifold
- Valve cover
- Engine cooling fan and shroud
- Accessory drive belt
- Oil fill housing
- Power steering pump

5. Rotate the crankshaft so that the crankshaft timing mark aligns with the Top Dead Center (TDC) mark on the front cover, and the **V6** marks on the camshaft sprockets are at 12 o'clock as shown.

6. Remove or disconnect the following:
- Crankshaft damper
- Front cover

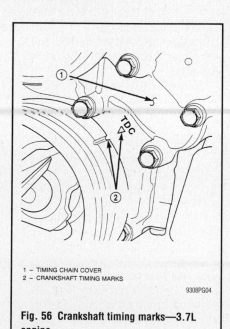

Fig. 56 Crankshaft timing marks—3.7L engine

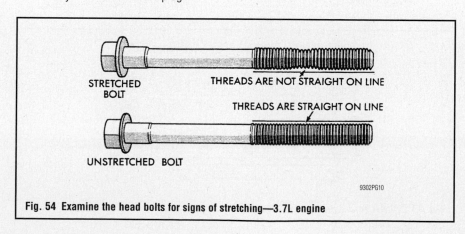

Fig. 54 Examine the head bolts for signs of stretching—3.7L engine

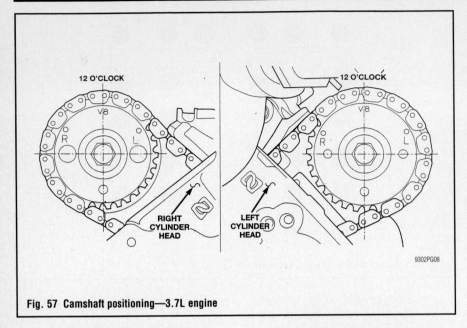

Fig. 57 Camshaft positioning—3.7L engine

7. Lock the secondary timing chains to the idler sprocket with Timing Chain Locking tool 8429.

8. Matchmark the secondary timing chains to the camshaft sprockets.

9. Remove or disconnect the following:
- Secondary timing chain tensioners
- Cylinder head access plugs
- Secondary timing chain guides
- Camshaft sprockets
- Cylinder heads

➡**Each cylinder head is retained by eight 11mm bolts and four 8mm bolts.**

To install:

10. Check the cylinder head bolts for signs of stretching and replace as necessary.

11. Lubricate the threads of the 11mm bolts with clean engine oil.

12. Coat the threads of the 8mm bolts with Mopar® Lock and Seal Adhesive, or equivalent.

13. Install the cylinder heads. Use new gaskets and tighten the bolts, in sequence, as follows:

  a. Step 1: Bolts 1–8 to 20 ft. lbs. (27 Nm)

  b. Step 2: Bolts 1–10 verify torque without loosening

  c. Step 3: Bolts 9–12 to 10 ft. lbs. (14 Nm)

  d. Step 4: Bolts 1–8 plus ¼ (90 degree) turn

  e. Step 5: Bolts 9–12 to 19 ft. lbs. (26 Nm)

14. Install or connect the following:
- Camshaft sprockets. Align the secondary chain matchmarks and tighten the bolts to 90 ft. lbs. (122 Nm).

- Secondary timing chain guides
- Cylinder head access plugs
- Secondary timing chain tensioners. Refer to the timing chain procedure in this section.

15. Remove the Timing Chain Locking tool.

16. Install or connect the following:
- Front cover
- Crankshaft damper. Torque the bolt to 130 ft. lbs. (175 Nm).
- Rocker arms
- Power steering pump
- Oil fill housing
- Accessory drive belt
- Engine cooling fan and shroud
- Valve covers
- Intake manifold
- Exhaust Y-pipe
- Negative battery cable

17. Fill and bleed the cooling system.

18. Start the engine, check for leaks and repair if necessary.

4.7L Engine

See Figure 58.

Left Side

1. Before servicing the vehicle, refer to the precautions section.

2. Drain the cooling system.

3. Remove or disconnect the following:
- Negative battery cable
- Exhaust pipe
- Intake manifold
- Cylinder head cover
- Fan shroud and fan
- Accessory drive belt
- Power steering pump

4. Rotate the crankshaft until the damper mark is aligned with the TDC mark. Verify that the V8 mark on the camshaft sprocket is at the 12 o'clock position.

5. Remove or disconnect the following:
- Vibration damper
- Timing chain cover

6. Lock the secondary timing chains to the idler sprocket with tool 8515, or equivalent.

7. Mark the secondary timing chain, on link on either side of the V8 mark on the cam sprocket.

8. Remove the left side secondary chain tensioner.

9. Remove the cylinder head access plug.

10. Remove the chain guide.

11. Remove the camshaft sprocket.

➡**There are 4 smaller bolts at the front of the head. Don't overlook these.**

12. Remove the head bolts and head.

✳✳ WARNING

Don't lay the head on its sealing surface. Due to the design of the head gasket, any distortion to the head sealing surface will result in leaks.

13. Installation is the reverse of removal. Observe the following:
- Check the head bolts. If any necking is observed, replace the bolt.

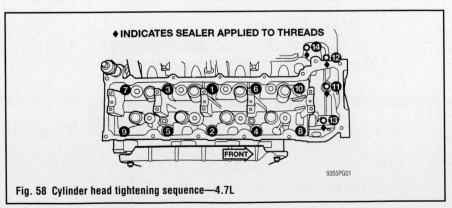

◆ INDICATES SEALER APPLIED TO THREADS

Fig. 58 Cylinder head tightening sequence—4.7L

- The 4 small bolts must be coated with sealer.
- The head bolts are tightened in the following sequence:

Step 1: Bolts 1-10 to 15 ft. lbs. (20 Nm)
Step 2: Bolts 1-10 to 35 ft. lbs. (47 Nm)
Step 3: Bolts 11-14 to 18 ft. lbs. (25 Nm)
Step 4: Bolts 1-10 90 degrees
Step 5: Bolts 11-14 to 22 ft. lbs.

Right Side

1. Before servicing the vehicle, refer to the precautions section.
2. Drain the cooling system.
3. Remove or disconnect the following:
   - Negative battery cable
   - Exhaust pipe
   - Intake manifold
   - Cylinder head cover
   - Fan shroud and fan
   - Oil filler housing
   - Accessory drive belt
4. Rotate the crankshaft until the damper mark is aligned with the TDC mark. Verify that the V8 mark on the camshaft sprocket is at the 12 o'clock position.
5. Remove or disconnect the following:
   - Vibration damper
   - Timing chain cover
6. Lock the secondary timing chains to the idler sprocket with tool 8515, or equivalent.
7. Mark the secondary timing chain, on link on either side of the V8 mark on the cam sprocket.
8. Remove the left side secondary chain tensioner.
9. Remove the cylinder head access plug.
10. Remove the chain guide.
11. Remove the camshaft sprocket.

✳✳ WARNING

Do not pry on the target wheel for any reason!

➡**There are 4 smaller bolts at the front of the head. Don't overlook these.**

12. Remove the head bolts and head.

✳✳ WARNING

Do not lay the head on its sealing surface. Due to the design of the head gasket, any distortion to the head sealing surface will result in leaks.

13. Installation is the reverse of removal. Observe the following:
   - Check the head bolts. If any necking is observed, replace the bolt.

- The 4 small bolts must be coated with sealer.
- The head bolts are tightened in the following sequence:

Step 1: Bolts 1-10 to 15 ft. lbs. (20 Nm)
Step 2: Bolts 1-10 to 35 ft. lbs. (47 Nm)
Step 3: Bolts 11-14 to 18 ft. lbs. (25 Nm)
Step 4: Bolts 1-10 90 degrees
Step 5: Bolts 11-14 to 22 ft. lbs.

5.7L Engine

See Figures 59 and 60.

1. Before servicing the vehicle, refer to the precautions section.
2. Drain the cooling system.
3. Properly relieve the fuel system pressure.
4. Remove or disconnect the following:
   - Negative battery cable
   - Air cleaner resonator and ducts
   - Alternator
   - Closed crankcase ventilation system
   - EVAP control system
   - Heater hoses
   - Cylinder head covers
   - Intake manifold
   - Rocker arms and pushrods
   - Cylinder heads

To install:

➡**The head gaskets are not interchangeable. They are marked "L" and "R".**

5. Install the cylinder heads. Use new gaskets and tighten the bolts, in sequence, as follows:
   a. Step 1: 12 mm bolts–25 ft. lbs. (34 Nm); 8mm bolts–15 ft. lbs. (20 Nm)
   b. Step 2: 12mm bolts–40 ft. lbs. (54 Nm); 8mm bolts retorque–15 ft. lbs. (20 Nm)
   c. Step 3: 12mm bolts–plus 90 degrees; 8mm bolts–25 ft. lbs. (34 Nm)
6. Install or connect the following:
   - Rocker arms and pushrods
   - Intake manifold
   - Heater hoses
   - Alternator
   - Cylinder head covers. Torque the studs and bolts to 70 inch lbs.
   - Air cleaner resonator and ducts
   - Negative battery cable

ENGINE ASSEMBLY

REMOVAL & INSTALLATION

3.7L Engine

See Figure 61.

1. Before servicing the vehicle, refer to the precautions section.
2. Discharge the A/C system.
3. Drain the cooling system.
4. Release the fuel system pressure.
5. Remove the air cleaner assembly.
6. Disconnect the battery.

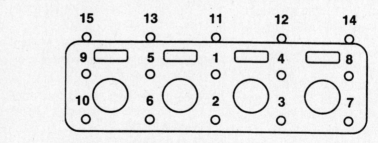

Fig. 59 Cylinder head torque sequence — 5.7L engine

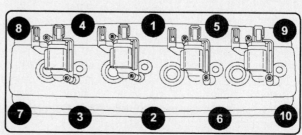

Fig. 60 Cylinder head cover torque sequence—5.7L engine

7. Remove the accessory drive belt.

8. Remove the viscous fan.

9. Remove the A/C compressor.

10. Remove the generator and secure away from engine.

➡Do not remove the phenolic pulley from the P/S pump. It is not required for P/S pump removal.

11. Remove the power steering pump with lines attached and secure away from engine.

12. Disconnect the heater hoses from the engine.

13. Disconnect the heater hoses from heater core and remove hose assembly.

14. Remove the upper radiator hose from engine.

15. Remove the lower radiator hose from engine.

16. Disconnect the transmission oil cooler lines at the radiator.

17. Disconnect the power steering cooler lines.

18. Remove the radiator assembly.

19. Disconnect the throttle and speed control cables.

20. Disconnect the engine to body ground straps at the left side of cowl.

21. Disconnect the engine wiring harness at the following points:

- Intake air temperature (IAT) sensor
- Fuel Injectors
- Throttle Position (TPS) Switch
- Idle Air Control (IAC) Motor
- Engine Oil Pressure Switch
- Engine Coolant Temperature (ECT) Sensor
- Manifold Absolute Pressure MAP) Sensor
- Camshaft Position (CMP) Sensor
- Coil Over Plugs
- Crankshaft Position Sensor

22. Remove the coil over plugs.

23. Remove fuel rail and secure away from engine.

➡It is not necessary to release the quick connect fitting from the fuel supply line for engine removal.

24. Remove the PCV hose.

25. Remove the breather hoses.

26. Remove the vacuum hose for the power brake booster.

27. Disconnect the knock sensors.

28. Remove the engine oil dipstick tube.

29. Remove intake manifold.

30. Install an engine lifting fixture, Tool 8247, using the original fasteners from the removed intake manifold, and fuel rail.

31. Raise the vehicle on hoist.

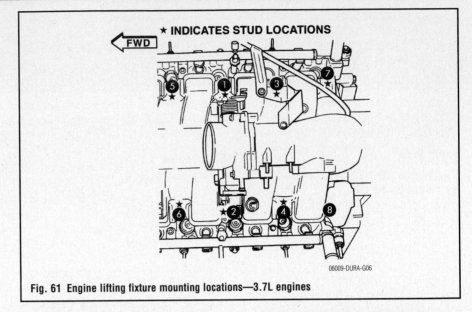

Fig. 61 Engine lifting fixture mounting locations—3.7L engines

★ INDICATES STUD LOCATIONS

FWD

06009-DURA-G06

32. Disconnect the exhaust pipes from exhaust manifolds.

33. On 4WD vehicles disconnect axle vent tube from left side engine mount.

34. Remove the through bolt retaining nut and bolt from both the left and right side engine mounts.

35. On 4WD vehicles Remove locknut from left and right side engine mount brackets.

36. Disconnect two ground straps from the lower left hand side and one ground strap from the lower right hand side of the engine.

37. Disconnect the crankshaft position sensor.

➡The following step applies to 4WD vehicles equipped with automatic transmission only.

38. On 4WD vehicles, remove the axle isolator bracket from the engine, transmission and the axle.

39. Remove the structural cover.

40. Remove the starter.

41. Remove the torque converter bolts (automatic transmission only).

42. Remove the transmission to engine mounting bolts.

43. Disconnect the engine block heater power cable from the block heater, if equipped.

44. Lower the vehicle.

45. Remove throttle body resonator assembly and air inlet hose.

46. Disconnect throttle and speed control cables.

47. Disconnect the tube from both the left and right side crankcase breathers. Remove the breathers.

48. Remove the generator.

49. Disconnect the two heater hoses from the timing chain cover and heater core.

50. Unclip and remove the heater hoses and tubes from the intake manifold.

51. Disconnect engine harness at the following points:

- Intake air temperature (IAT) sensor
- Fuel Injectors
- Throttle Position (TPS) Switch
- Idle Air Control (IAC) Motor
- Engine Oil Pressure Switch
- Engine Coolant Temperature (ECT) Sensor
- Manifold absolute pressure (MAP) Sensor
- Camshaft Position (CMP) Sensor
- Coil Over Plugs

52. Disconnect the vacuum lines at the throttle body and intake manifold.

53. Remove power steering pump and position out of the way.

54. Disconnect body ground strap at the right side cowl.

55. Disconnect body ground strap at the left side cowl.

➡It will be necessary to support the transmission in order to remove the engine.

56. Position a suitable jack under the transmission.

57. Remove engine from the vehicle.

To install:

58. Position engine in the vehicle.

59. Position both the left and right side engine mount brackets and install the through bolts and nuts. Tighten nuts to 70 ft. lbs. (95 Nm) on 2wd vehicles; 75 ft. lbs. (102 Nm) on 4WD vehicles.

60. On 4WD vehicles, install locknuts

onto the engine mount brackets. Tighten locknuts to 30 ft. lbs. (41 Nm).

61. Remove jack from under the transmission.

62. Remove Engine Lifting Fixture Special Tool.

63. Remove Special Tools 8400 Lifting Studs.

64. Position generator wiring behind the oil dipstick tube, then install the oil dipstick tube upper mounting bolt.

65. Connect both left and right side body ground straps.

66. Install power steering pump.

67. Connect fuel supply line quick connect fitting.

68. Connect the vacuum lines at the throttle body and intake manifold.

69. Connect engine harness at the following points:
   • Intake Air Temperature (IAT) Sensor
   • Idle Air Control (IAC) Motor
   • Fuel Injectors
   • Throttle Position (TPS) Switch
   • Engine Oil Pressure Switch
   • Engine Coolant Temperature (ECT) Sensor
   • Manifold Absolute Pressure (MAP) Sensor
   • Camshaft Position (CMP) Sensor
   • Coil Over Plugs

70. Position and install heater hoses and tubes (1) onto intake manifold.

71. Install the heater hoses onto the heater core and the engine front cover.

72. Install generator.

73. Install radiator assembly.

74. Connect radiator upper and lower hoses.

75. Connect power steering cooler lines.

76. Connect the transmission oil cooler lines to the radiator.

77. Install accessory drive belt.

78. Install A/C compressor.

79. Install both breathers. Connect tube to both crankcase breathers.

80. Connect throttle and speed control cables.

81. Install throttle body resonator assembly and air inlet hose. Tighten clamps 35 inch lbs. (4 Nm).

82. Raise vehicle.

83. Install transmission to engine mounting bolts. Tighten the bolts to 30 ft. lbs. (41 Nm).

84. Install torque converter bolts (Automatic Transmission Only).

85. Connect crankshaft position sensor.

86. On 4WD vehicles, position and install the axle isolator bracket onto the axle, transmission and engine block. Tighten bolts to specification.

87. Install starter.

> **⁂ CAUTION**
>
> **The structural cover requires a specific torque sequence. Failure to follow this sequence may cause severe damage to the cover.**

88. Install structural cover.

89. Install exhaust crossover pipe.

90. Install engine block heater power cable, if equipped.

91. On 4WD vehicles, connect axle vent tube to left side engine mount.

92. Lower vehicle.

93. Check and fill engine oil.

94. Recharge the A/C system.

95. Refill the engine cooling system.

96. Install the battery tray and battery.

97. Connect the battery positive and negative cables.

98. Start the engine and check for leaks.

4.7L Engine
See Figures 62 and 63.

1. Before servicing the vehicle, refer to the precautions section.

2. Drain the cooling system and engine oil.

3. Remove or disconnect the following:
   • Negative battery cable
   • Battery and tray
   • Exhaust crossover pipe
   • On 4WD, the axle vent tube
   • Left and right engine mount through bolts
   • On 4WD, the left and right engine mount bracket locknuts
   • Ground straps
   • CKP sensor
   • On 4WD, the axle isolator bracket
   • Structural cover
   • Starter
   • Torque converter bolts
   • Transmission-to-engine bolts
   • Engine block heater
   • Resonator and air inlet
   • Throttle and speed control cables
   • Crankcase breathers
   • A/C compressor
   • Shroud and fan assemblies
   • Transmission cooler lines
   • Radiator hoses

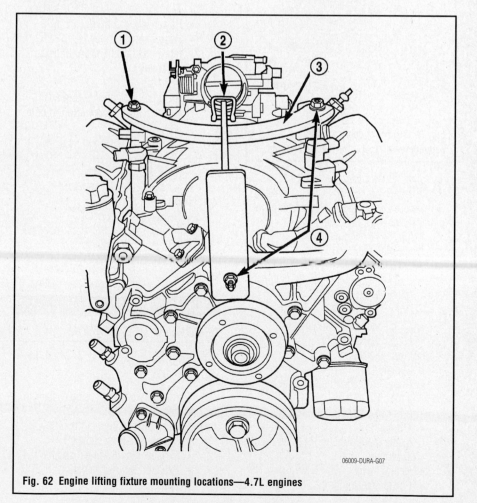

Fig. 62 Engine lifting fixture mounting locations—4.7L engines

- Radiator
- Alternator
- Heater hoses
- Engine harness
- Vacuum lines
- Fuel system pressure
- Fuel line at the rail
- Power steering pump

4. Install lifting eyes and take up the weight of the engine with a crane.

5. Support the transmission with a jack.

6. Remove the engine.

7. Installation is the reverse of removal. Observe the following:

- Left and right engine mount through bolts: 2wd 70 ft. lbs. (95 Nm); 4WD 75 ft. lbs. (102 Nm)
- On 4WD, the bracket locknuts: 30 ft. lbs. (41 Nm)
- Transmission-to-engine bolts: 30 ft. lbs. (41 Nm)

➡The structural cover has a specific torque sequence.

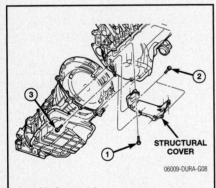

Fig. 63 Structural cover torque sequence—3.7L, 4.7L and 5.7L engines

5.7L Engine

1. Before servicing the vehicle, refer to the precautions section.

2. Drain the cooling system.

3. Drain the engine oil.

4. Relieve the fuel system pressure.

5. Remove or disconnect the following:

- Negative battery cable
- Hood
- Air cleaner and resonator
- Accessory drive belt
- Engine fan
- Radiator
- Upper crossmember and top core support
- A/C compressor, if equipped
- Alternator
- Intake manifold and IAFM as an assembly
- Heater hoses
- Power steering pump

- Fuel line
- Engine front mount thru-bolt nuts
- Transmission oil cooler lines, if equipped
- Exhaust pipes at the manifolds
- Starter motor
- Structural dust cover and transmission inspection cover
- Torque converter-to-flexplate bolts
- Transmission flange bolts. Support the transmission.
- Engine

To install:

6. Install or connect the following:

- Engine. Tighten the engine mount thru-bolt finger tight.
- Transmission flange bolts. Tighten the bolts to 40–45 ft. lbs. (54–61 Nm). Then, tighten the mount bolt nuts to 70 ft. lbs. (95 Nm)
- Transmission oil cooler lines, if equipped
- Torque converter, if equipped. Tighten the bolts to 23 ft. lbs. (31 Nm).
- Structural dust cover and transmission inspection cover
- Starter motor
- Fuel line
- Power steering pump
- Heater hoses
- Intake manifold and IAFM as an assembly
- Alternator
- A/C compressor, if equipped
- Upper crossmember and top core support
- Radiator
- Engine fan
- Accessory drive belt
- Air cleaner and resonator
- Hood
- Negative battery cable

7. Fill the crankcase to the correct level.

8. Fill the cooling system.

9. Start the engine and check for leaks.

EXHAUST MANIFOLD

REMOVAL & INSTALLATION

3.7L Engine

See Figure 64.

1. Before servicing the vehicle, refer to the precautions section.

2. Remove or disconnect the following:

- Negative battery cable
- Exhaust manifold heat shields
- Exhaust Gas Recirculation (EGR) tube

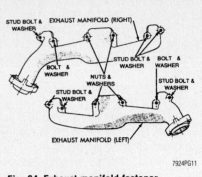

Fig. 64 Exhaust manifold fastener locations—3.7L engines

- Exhaust Y-pipe
- Exhaust manifolds

To install:

➡If the exhaust manifold studs came out with the nuts when removing the exhaust manifolds, replace them with new studs.

3. Install or connect the following:

- Exhaust manifolds. Torque the fasteners to 20 ft. lbs. (27 Nm), starting with the center nuts and work out to the ends.
- Exhaust Y-pipe
- EGR tube
- Exhaust manifold heat shields
- Negative battery cable

4. Start the engine, check for leaks and repair if necessary.

4.7L Engine

See Figure 65.

1. Before servicing the vehicle, refer to the precautions section.

2. Drain the cooling system.

3. Remove or disconnect the following:

- Battery
- Power distribution center
- Battery tray
- Windshield washer fluid bottle
- Air cleaner assembly
- Accessory drive belt
- A/C compressor
- A/C accumulator bracket
- Heater hoses
- Exhaust manifold heat shields
- Exhaust Y-pipe
- Starter motor
- Exhaust manifolds

To install:

4. Install or connect the following:

- Exhaust manifolds, using new gaskets. Tighten the bolts to 18 ft. lbs. (25 Nm), starting with the inner bolts and work out to the ends.

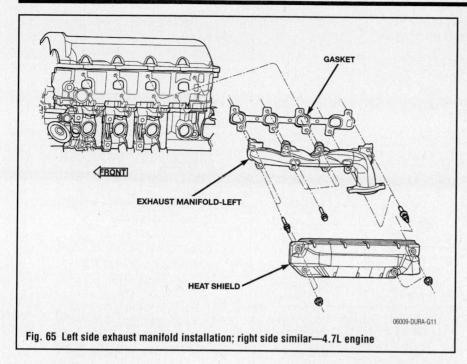

Fig. 65 Left side exhaust manifold installation; right side similar—4.7L engine

- Starter motor
- Exhaust Y-pipe
- Exhaust manifold heat shields
- Heater hoses
- A/C accumulator bracket
- A/C compressor
- Accessory drive belt
- Air cleaner assembly
- Windshield washer fluid bottle
- Battery tray
- Power distribution center
- Battery
5. Fill the cooling system.
6. Start the engine and check for leaks.

5.7L Engine
See Figure 66.

1. Before servicing the vehicle, refer to the precautions section.
2. Drain the cooling system.
3. Remove or disconnect the following:

- Battery
- Exhaust pipe-to-manifold bolts
4. Install an engine crane. Remove the right and left mount through bolts. Raise the engine just enough to provide clearance for manifold removal.
5. Remove or disconnect the following:
- Exhaust manifold heat shields
- Exhaust manifolds

To install:
6. Install or connect the following:
- Exhaust manifolds, using new gaskets. Tighten the bolts to 18 ft. lbs. (25 Nm), starting with the inner bolts and work out to the ends.
- Exhaust manifold heat shields
7. Install the right and left mount through bolts. Remove the crane.
8. Install or connect the following:
- Exhaust pipe-to-manifold bolts
- Battery

INTAKE MANIFOLD

REMOVAL & INSTALLATION

3.7L and 4.7L Engine
See Figure 67.

1. Before servicing the vehicle, refer to the precautions section.
2. Drain the cooling system.
3. Remove or disconnect the following:
- Negative battery cable
- Air cleaner assembly
- Accelerator cable
- Cruise control cable
- Manifold Absolute Pressure (MAP) sensor connector
- Intake Air Temperature (IAT) sensor connector
- Throttle Position (TP) sensor connector
- Idle Air Control (IAC) valve connector
- Engine Coolant Temperature (ECT) sensor
- Positive Crankcase Ventilation (PCV) valve and hose
- Canister purge vacuum line
- Brake booster vacuum line
- Cruise control servo hose
- Accessory drive belt
- Alternator
- A/C compressor
- Engine ground straps
- Ignition coil towers
- Oil dipstick tube
- Fuel line
- Fuel supply manifold
- Throttle body and mounting bracket
- Cowl seal
- Right engine lifting stud
- Intake manifold. Remove the fasteners in reverse of the tightening sequence.

To install:
4. Install or connect the following:
- Intake manifold using new gaskets. Tighten the bolts, in sequence, to 105 inch lbs. (12 Nm).
- Right engine lifting stud
- Cowl seal
- Throttle body and mounting bracket
- Fuel supply manifold
- Fuel line
- Oil dipstick tube
- Ignition coil towers
- Engine ground straps
- A/C compressor
- Alternator
- Accessory drive belt
- Cruise control servo hose
- Brake booster vacuum line

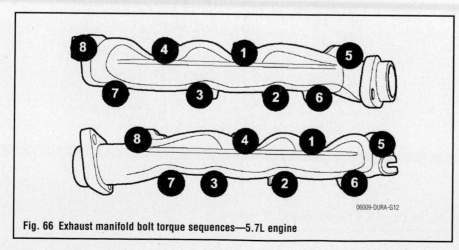

Fig. 66 Exhaust manifold bolt torque sequences—5.7L engine

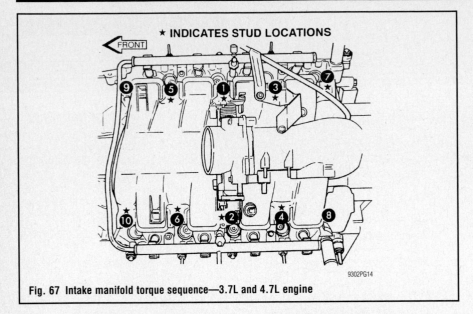

Fig. 67 Intake manifold torque sequence—3.7L and 4.7L engine

- Canister purge vacuum line
- PCV valve and hose
- ECT sensor
- IAC valve connector
- TP sensor connector
- IAT sensor connector
- MAP sensor connector
- Cruise control cable
- Accelerator cable
- Air cleaner assembly
- Negative battery cable

5. Fill the cooling system.
6. Start the engine and check for leaks.

5.7L Engines

1. Before servicing the vehicle, refer to the precautions section.
2. Drain the cooling system.
3. Relieve the fuel system pressure.
4. Remove or disconnect the following:
- Negative battery cable
- Air cleaner assembly
- Accessory drive belt
- MAP connector
- IAT connector
- TPS connector
- CTS connector
- Brake booster hose
- PCV hose
- Alternator
- A/C compressor
- Intake manifold bolts, in a criss-cross pattern, from the outside to the center
- Intake manifold/IAFM

To install:

5. Position new intake manifold seals.
6. Install the intake manifold. Tighten the bolts in sequence from the center outwards, to 105 inch lbs. (12 Nm).

7. Install or connect the following:
- Electrical connectors
- Alternator
- A/C compressor
- Brake booster hose
- PCV hose
- Accessory drive belt
- Negative battery cable
- Air cleaner assembly

OIL PAN

REMOVAL & INSTALLATION

3.7L Engine

See Figure 68.

1. Before servicing the vehicle, refer to the precautions section.

2. Remove or disconnect the following:
- Engine from the vehicle
- Oil pan
- Oil pump pickup tube
- Oil pan gasket

3. Installation is the reverse of removal. Torque the bolts, in sequence, to 11 ft. lbs. (15 Nm).

4.7L Engine

See Figures 69 and 70.

1. Before servicing the vehicle, refer to the precautions section.
2. Drain the engine oil.
3. Remove or disconnect the following:
- Negative battery cable
- Structural cover
- Exhaust Y-pipe
- Starter motor
- Transmission oil cooler lines
- Oil pan
- Oil pump pickup tube
- Oil pan gasket

To install:

4. Install or connect the following:
- Oil pan gasket
- Oil pump pickup tube, using a new O-ring. Tighten the tube bolts to 20 ft. lbs. (28 Nm); tighten the O-ring end bolt first.
- Oil pan. Tighten the bolts, in sequence, to 11 ft. lbs. (15 Nm).
- Transmission oil cooler lines
- Starter motor
- Exhaust Y-pipe
- Structural cover
- Negative battery cable

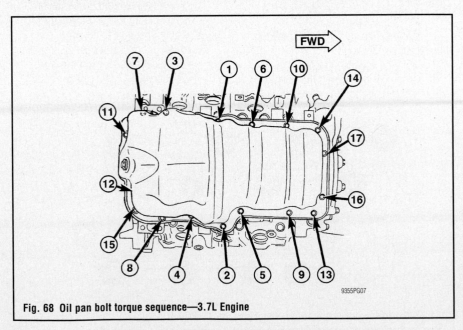

Fig. 68 Oil pan bolt torque sequence—3.7L Engine

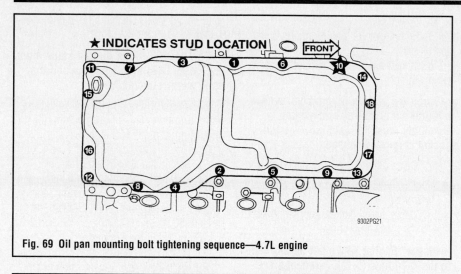

Fig. 69 Oil pan mounting bolt tightening sequence—4.7L engine

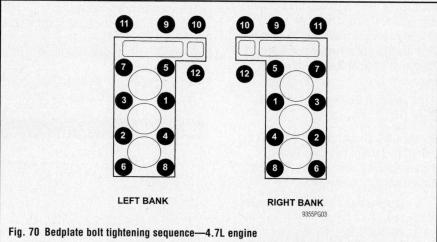

Fig. 70 Bedplate bolt tightening sequence—4.7L engine

5. Fill the crankcase to the proper level with engine oil.

6. Start the engine and check for leaks.

5.7L Engine

2-Wheel Drive

See Figure 71.

1. Before servicing the vehicle, refer to the precautions section.

2. Disconnect the negative battery cable.

3. Loosen both left and right side engine mount through bolts. Do not remove bolts.

4. Install an engine support fixture tool. Do not raise engine at this time.

5. Remove the structural dust cover.

6. Remove fan and fan shroud.

7. Drain engine oil.

8. Remove the front crossmember

9. Raise engine to provide clearance to remove oil pan.

➡Do not pry on oil pan or oil pan gasket. Gasket is integral to engine windage tray and does not come out with oil pan.

➡If more clearance is needed to remove oil pan, the transmission mount can be removed, and the transmission raised to gain clearance.

➡The double ended oil pan studs must be installed in the same location that they were removed from.

10. Remove the oil pan mounting bolts using the sequence provided.

11. Unbolt oil pump pickup tube and remove tube.

➡When the oil pan is removed, a new integral windage tray and gasket assembly must be installed. The old gasket cannot be reused.

12. Discard the integral windage tray and gasket and replace.

To install:

13. Clean the oil pan gasket mating surface of the block and oil pan.

➡Mopar® Engine RTV must be applied to the 4 T-joints (1, 2), (area where front cover, rear retainer, block, and oil pan gasket meet). The bead of RTV should cover the bottom of the gasket. This area is approximately 4.5 mm x 25 mm in each of the 4 T-joint locations.

14. Apply Mopar® Engine RTV at the 4 T- joints.

➡When the oil pan is removed, a new integral windage tray and gasket assembly must be installed. The old gasket cannot be reused.

15. Install a new integral windage tray and gasket.

16. Reinstall the oil pump pickup tube with new O–ring. Tighten tube to pump fasteners to 21 ft. lbs. (28 Nm).

➡The double ended oil pan studs must be installed in the same location that they were removed from.

17. Position the oil pan and install the mounting bolts and studs. Tighten the mounting bolts to 105 inch lbs. (12 Nm).

18. Install the structural cover.

19. Lower the engine into mounts.

20. Install both the left and right side engine mount through bolts. Tighten the nuts to 50 ft. lbs. (68 Nm).

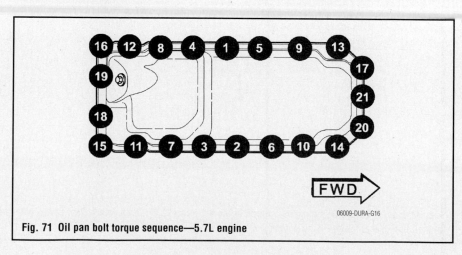

Fig. 71 Oil pan bolt torque sequence—5.7L engine

21. Remove the lifting fixture.
22. Install the front crossmember. Torque to 75 ft. lbs. (102 Nm).
23. Install the fan shroud and fan.
24. Fill engine oil.
25. Reconnect the negative battery cable.
26. Start engine and check for leaks.

4-Wheel Drive

See Figure 72.

1. Before servicing the vehicle, refer to the precautions section.
2. Disconnect the negative battery cable.
3. Loosen both left and right side engine mount through bolts. Do not remove bolts.
4. Install an engine support fixture tool. Do not raise engine at this time.
5. Remove the structural dust cover.
6. Remove fan and fan shroud.
7. Drain engine oil.
8. Remove the front crossmember.
9. Raise engine to provide clearance to remove oil pan.
10. Unbolt and lower the steering rack, without disconnecting the lines.

➡ **The front axle must be lowered to remove the oil pan.**

11. Remove the front driveshaft at the axle. Mark for reassembly.
12. Support the front axle.
13. Remove the right and left axle to mount, bolts.

14. Lower axle.
15. Remove the oil pan mounting bolts and oil pan.
16. Unbolt oil pump pickup tube and remove tube.

➡ **When the oil pan is removed, a new integral windage tray and gasket assembly must be installed. The old gasket cannot be reused.**

17. Discard the integral windage tray and gasket and replace.

To install:

18. Clean the oil pan gasket mating surface of the block and oil pan.

➡ **Mopar® Engine RTV must be applied to the 4 T-joints (1, 2), (area where front cover, rear retainer, block, and oil pan gasket meet). The bead of RTV should cover the bottom of the gasket. This area is approximately 4.5 mm x 25 mm in each of the 4 T-joint locations.**

19. Apply Mopar® Engine RTV at the 4 T-joints.

➡ **When the oil pan is removed, a new integral windage tray and gasket assembly must be installed. The old gasket cannot be reused.**

20. Install a new integral windage tray and gasket.
21. Reinstall the oil pump pickup tube

with new O-ring. Tighten tube to pump fasteners to 21 ft. lbs. (28 Nm).

➡ **The double ended oil pan studs must be installed in the same location that they were removed from.**

22. Position the oil pan and install the mounting bolts and studs.. Tighten the mounting bolts to 105 inch lbs. (12 Nm).
23. Install the structural cover.
24. Lower the engine into mounts.
25. Install both the left and right side engine mount through bolts. Tighten the nuts to 50 ft. lbs. (68 Nm).
26. Reinstall the front axle.
27. Install the steering rack.
28. Install the rear transmission mount.
29. Remove lifting fixture.
30. Install the front crossmember. Torque to 75 ft. lbs. (102 Nm).
31. Install the fan shroud and fan.
32. Fill engine oil.
33. Reconnect the negative battery cable.
34. Start engine and check for leaks.

OIL PUMP

REMOVAL & INSTALLATION

3.7L Engine

See Figure 73.

1. Before servicing the vehicle, refer to the precautions section.

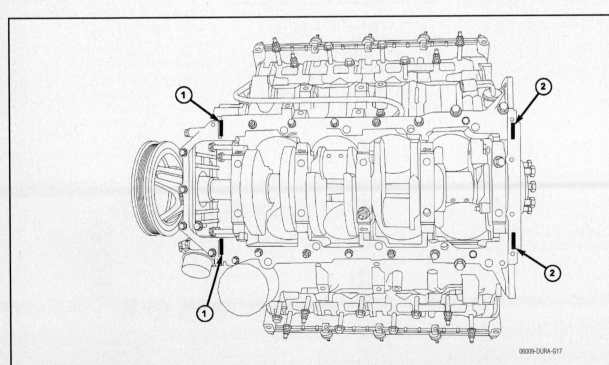

Fig. 72 Mopar® Engine RTV must be applied to the 4 T-joints (1,2), (area where front cover, rear retainer, block, and oil pan gasket meet)—5.7L engine

06009-DURA-G17

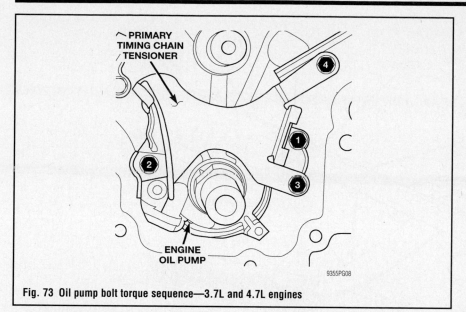

Fig. 73 Oil pump bolt torque sequence—3.7L and 4.7L engines

2. Remove or disconnect the following:
   - Oil Pan
   - Timing chain cover
   - Timing chains and tensioners
   - Oil pump
3. Installation is the reverse of removal. Torque the pump bolts, in sequence, to 21 ft. lbs. (28 Nm),

4.7L Engine

1. Before servicing the vehicle, refer to the precautions section.
2. Drain the engine oil.
3. Remove or disconnect the following:
   - Negative battery cable
   - Oil pan
   - Oil pump pick-up tube
   - Timing chains and tensioners
   - Oil pump

To install:
4. Install or connect the following:
   - Oil pump. Tighten the bolts to 21 ft. lbs. (28 Nm).
   - Timing chains and tensioners
   - Oil pump pick-up tube
   - Oil pan
   - Negative battery cable
5. Fill the crankcase to the correct level.
6. Start the engine and check for leaks.

5.7L Engine

See Figure 74.

1. Before servicing the vehicle, refer to the precautions section.
2. Drain the engine oil.
3. Remove or disconnect the following:
   - Negative battery cable
   - Oil pan
   - Oil pump pick-up tube
   - Timing chains and tensioners
   - Oil pump

To install:
4. Install or connect the following:
   - Oil pump. Tighten the bolts to 21 ft. lbs. (28 Nm).
   - Timing chains and tensioners
   - Oil pump pick-up tube
   - Oil pan
   - Negative battery cable
5. Fill the crankcase to the correct level.
6. Start the engine and check for leaks.

INSPECTION

3.7L and 4.7L Engine

See Figures 75 through 80.

✳✳ WARNING

Oil pump pressure relief valve and spring should not be removed from the oil pump. If these components are disassembled and or removed from the pump the entire oil pump assembly must be replaced.

1. Clean all parts thoroughly. Mating surface of the oil pump housing should be smooth. If the pump cover is scratched or grooved the oil pump assembly should be replaced.
2. Lay a straight edge across the pump cover surface. If a 0.025 mm (0.001 in.) feeler gauge can be inserted between the cover and the straight edge the oil pump assembly should be replaced.
3. Measure the thickness of the outer rotor. If the outer rotor thickness measures at 12.005 mm (0.472 in.) or less the oil pump assembly must be replaced.
4. Measure the diameter of the outer rotor. If the outer rotor diameter measures at 85.925 mm (3.382 in.) or less the oil pump assembly must be replaced.
5. Measure the thickness of the inner rotor. If the inner rotor thickness measures at 12.005 mm (0.472 in.) or less then the oil pump assembly must be replaced.
6. Slide outer rotor into the body of the oil pump. Press the outer rotor to one side of the oil pump body and measure clearance between the outer rotor and the body. If the measurement is 0.235mm (0.009 in.) or more the oil pump assembly must be replaced.
7. Install the inner rotor in the into the oil pump body. Measure the clearance

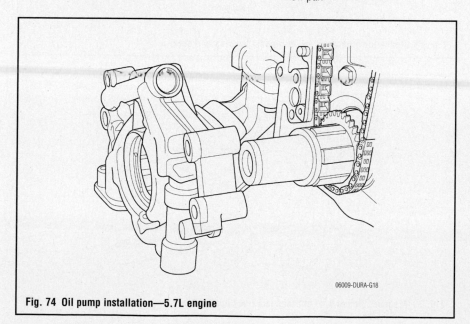

Fig. 74 Oil pump installation—5.7L engine

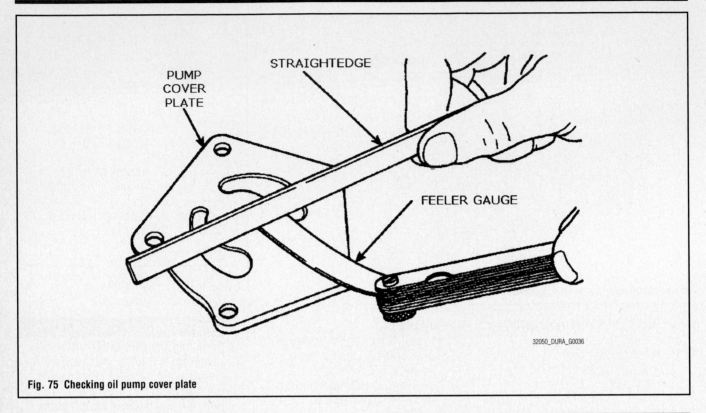

Fig. 75 Checking oil pump cover plate

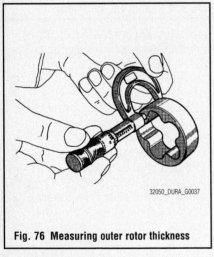

Fig. 76 Measuring outer rotor thickness

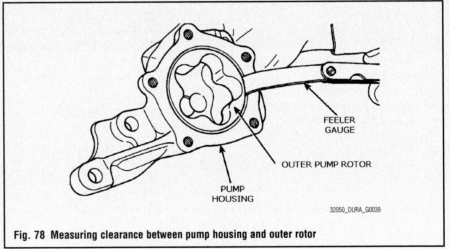

Fig. 78 Measuring clearance between pump housing and outer rotor

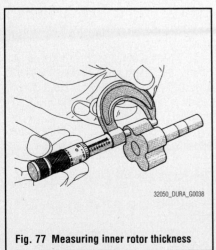

Fig. 77 Measuring inner rotor thickness

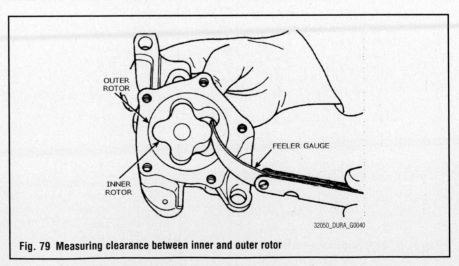

Fig. 79 Measuring clearance between inner and outer rotor

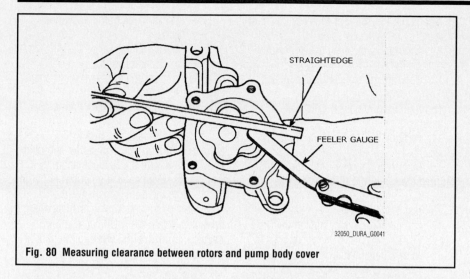

Fig. 80 Measuring clearance between rotors and pump body cover

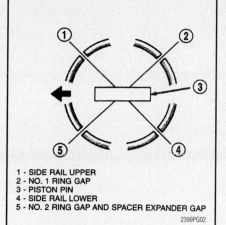

1 - SIDE RAIL UPPER
2 - NO. 1 RING GAP
3 - PISTON PIN
4 - SIDE RAIL LOWER
5 - NO. 2 RING GAP AND SPACER EXPANDER GAP

Fig. 82 Piston ring end-gap spacing—
5.7L engines

between the inner and outer rotors. If the clearance between the rotors is .150 mm (0.006 in.) or more the oil pump assembly must be replaced.

8. Place a straight edge across the body of the oil pump (between the bolt holes); if a feeler gauge of .095 mm (0.0038 in.) or greater can be inserted between the straightedge and the rotors, the pump must be replaced.

➡The 3.7L/4.7L oil pump is released as an assembly; there are no subassembly components. In the event the oil pump is not functioning or out of specification it must be replaced as an assembly.

5.7L Engine

1. Remove the pump cover.
2. Clean all parts thoroughly. Mating surface of the oil pump housing should be smooth. If the pump cover is scratched or grooved the oil pump assembly should be replaced.
3. Slide outer rotor into the body of the oil pump. Press the outer rotor to one side of the oil pump body and measure clearance between the outer rotor and the body. If the measurement is 0.235mm (0.009 in.) or more the oil pump assembly must be replaced.
4. Install the inner rotor in the into the oil pump body. Measure the clearance between the inner and outer rotors. If the clearance between the rotors is 0.150 mm (0.006 in.) or more the oil pump assembly must be replaced.
5. Place a straight edge across the body of the oil pump (between the bolt holes); if a feeler gauge of 0.095 mm (0.0038 in.) or greater can be inserted between the straightedge and the rotors, the pump must be replaced.

6. Reinstall the pump cover. Torque fasteners to 132 inch lbs. (15 Nm).

➡The 5.7 oil pump is released as an assembly. There are no Chrysler part numbers for Sub-Assembly components. In the event the oil pump is not functioning or out of specification it must be replaced as an assembly.

PISTON AND RING

POSITIONING

See Figures 81 and 82.

REAR MAIN SEAL

REMOVAL & INSTALLATION

3.7L and 4.7L Engines

1. Before servicing the vehicle, refer to the precautions section.
2. Remove or disconnect the following:
   • Transmission
   • Flexplate

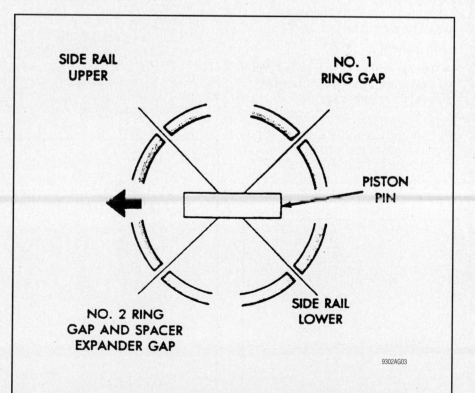

Fig. 81 Piston ring end-gap spacing. Position raised "F" on piston towards front of engine—3.7L and 4.7L engine

3. Thread Oil Seal Remover 8506 into the rear main seal as far as possible and remove the rear main seal.

To install:

4. Install or connect the following:
- Seal Guide 8349-2 onto the crankshaft
- Rear main seal on the seal guide
- Rear main seal, using the Crankshaft Rear Oil Seal Installer 8349 and Driver Handle C-4171; tap it into place until the installer is flush with the cylinder block
- Flexplate. Tighten the bolts to 45 ft. lbs. (60 Nm) for 4.7L; 70 ft. lbs. (95 Nm) for the 3.7L engine.
- Transmission

5. Start the engine and check for leaks.

5.7L Engine

See Figure 83.

1. Before servicing the vehicle, refer to the precautions section.
2. Disconnect negative cable from battery.
3. Remove the transmission.
4. Remove the flexplate.
5. Remove the oil pan.
6. Remove the rear oil seal retainer mounting bolts.
7. Carefully remove the retainer from the engine block.
8. Using a seal puller, remove the crankshaft rear oil seal.

To install:

➡**The rear seal must be installed dry for proper operation. Do not lubricate the seal lip or outer edge.**

9. Position the plastic seal guide onto the crankshaft rear face. Then position the crankshaft rear oil seal onto the guide.
10. Using a seal driver and hammer, tap the seal into place. Continue to tap on the driver handle until the seal installer

seats against the cylinder block crankshaft bore.

11. Thoroughly clean all gasket residue from the engine block.
12. Use extreme care and clean all gasket residue from the retainer.
13. Position the gasket onto the retainer.
14. Position the retainer onto the engine block.
15. Install the retainer mounting bolts. Tighten the bolts to 132 inch lbs. (15 Nm).
16. Install the oil pan.
17. Install the flexplate. Tighten to 70 ft. lbs. (95 Nm).
18. Install the transmission.
19. Check and verify engine oil level.
20. Start engine and check for leaks.

TIMING CHAIN, SPROCKETS, FRONT COVER AND SEAL

REMOVAL & INSTALLATION

3.7L Engines

See Figures 84 through 94.

1. Before servicing the vehicle, refer to the precautions section.
2. Drain the cooling system.
3. Remove or disconnect the following:
- Negative battery cable
- Valve covers
- Radiator fan

4. Rotate the crankshaft so that the crankshaft timing mark aligns with the Top Dead Center (TDC) mark on the front cover, and the **V6** marks on the camshaft sprockets are at 12 o'clock.
- Power steering pump

- Access plugs from the cylinder heads
- Oil fill housing
- Crankshaft damper

5. Compress the primary timing chain tensioner and install a lockpin.
6. Remove the secondary timing chain tensioners.
7. Hold the left camshaft with adjustable pliers and remove the sprocket and chain. Rotate the **left** camshaft 15 degrees **clockwise** to the neutral position.
8. Hold the right camshaft with adjustable pliers and remove the camshaft sprocket. Rotate the **right** camshaft 45 degrees **counterclockwise** to the neutral position.
9. Remove the primary timing chain and sprockets.

To install:

10. Use a small prytool to hold the ratchet pawl and compress the secondary timing chain tensioners in a vise and install locking pins.

➡**The black bolts fasten the guide to the engine block and the silver bolts fasten the guide to the cylinder head.**

11. Install or connect the following:
- Secondary timing chain guides. Tighten the bolts to 21 ft. lbs. (28 Nm).
- Secondary timing chains to the idler sprocket so that the double plated links on each chain are visible through the slots in the primary idler sprocket

12. Lock the secondary timing chains to the idler sprocket with Timing Chain Locking tool as shown.

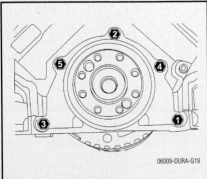

06009-DURA-G19

Fig. 83 Rear seal retainer torque sequence—5.7L engine

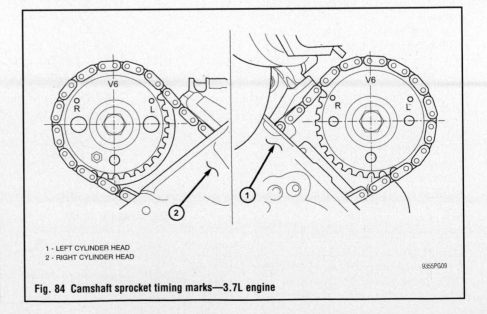

1 - LEFT CYLINDER HEAD
2 - RIGHT CYLINDER HEAD

9355PG09

Fig. 84 Camshaft sprocket timing marks—3.7L engine

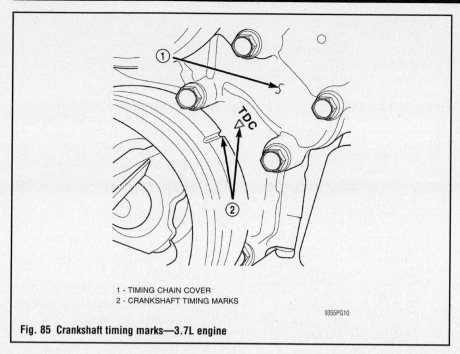

1 - TIMING CHAIN COVER
2 - CRANKSHAFT TIMING MARKS

9355PG10

Fig. 85 Crankshaft timing marks—3.7L engine

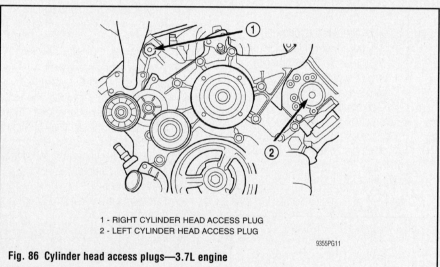

1 - RIGHT CYLINDER HEAD ACCESS PLUG
2 - LEFT CYLINDER HEAD ACCESS PLUG

9355PG11

Fig. 86 Cylinder head access plugs—3.7L engine

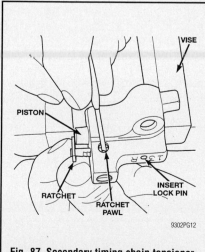

9302PG12

Fig. 87 Secondary timing chain tensioner preparation—3.7L and 4.7L engines

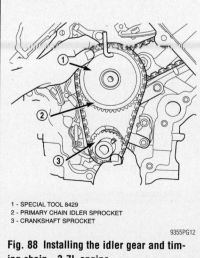

1 - SPECIAL TOOL 8429
2 - PRIMARY CHAIN IDLER SPROCKET
3 - CRANKSHAFT SPROCKET

9355PG12

Fig. 88 Installing the idler gear and timing chain—3.7L engine

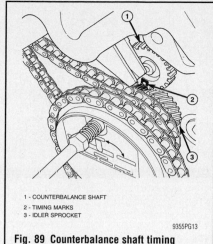

1 - COUNTERBALANCE SHAFT
2 - TIMING MARKS
3 - IDLER SPROCKET

9355PG13

Fig. 89 Counterbalance shaft timing marks—3.7L engine

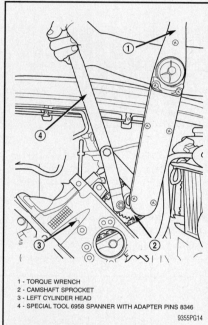

1 - TORQUE WRENCH
2 - CAMSHAFT SPROCKET
3 - LEFT CYLINDER HEAD
4 - SPECIAL TOOL 6958 SPANNER WITH ADAPTER PINS 8346

9355PG14

Fig. 90 Tightening the left side camshaft sprocket—3.7L engine

13. Align the primary chain double plated links with the idler sprocket timing mark and the single plated link with the crankshaft sprocket timing mark.

14. Install the primary chain and sprockets. Tighten the idler sprocket bolt to 25 ft. lbs. (34 Nm).

15. Align the secondary chain single plated links with the timing marks on the secondary sprockets. Align the dot at the **L** mark on the left sprocket with the plated link on the left chain and the dot at the **R** mark on the right sprocket with the plated link on the right chain.

16. Rotate the camshafts back from the neutral position and install the camshaft sprockets.

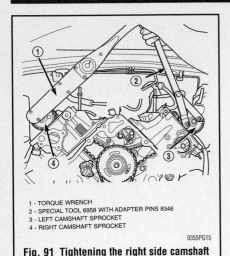

1 - TORQUE WRENCH
2 - SPECIAL TOOL 6958 WITH ADAPTER PINS 8346
3 - LEFT CAMSHAFT SPROCKET
4 - RIGHT CAMSHAFT SPROCKET

9355PG15

Fig. 91 Tightening the right side camshaft sprocket—3.7L engine

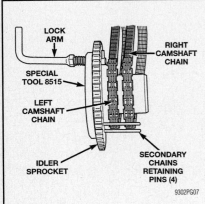

9302PG07

Fig. 92 Use the Timing Chain Locking tool to lock the timing chains on the idler gear—3.7L engine

17. Remove the secondary chain locking tool.

18. Remove the primary and secondary timing chain tensioner locking pins.

19. Hold the camshaft sprockets with a spanner wrench and tighten the retaining bolts to 90 ft. lbs. (122 Nm).

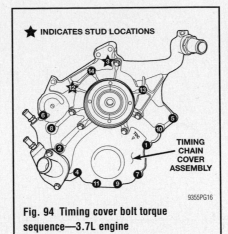

★ INDICATES STUD LOCATIONS

TIMING CHAIN COVER ASSEMBLY

9355PG16

Fig. 94 Timing cover bolt torque sequence—3.7L engine

20. Install or connect the following:
- Front cover. Tighten the bolts, in sequence, to 40 ft. lbs. (54 Nm).
- Front crankshaft seal
- Cylinder head access plugs
- A/C compressor
- Alternator
- Accessory drive belt tensioner. Tighten the bolt to 40 ft. lbs. (54 Nm).
- Oil fill housing

- Crankshaft damper. Tighten the bolt to 130 ft. lbs. (175 Nm).
- Power steering pump
- Lower radiator hose
- Heater hoses
- Accessory drive belt
- Engine cooling fan and shroud
- Camshaft Position (CMP) sensor
- Valve covers
- Negative battery cable

21. Fill and bleed the cooling system.

22. Start the engine, check for leaks and repair if necessary.

4.7L Engine

See Figures 87, 93 and 95 through 100.

1. Before servicing the vehicle, refer to the precautions section.

2. Drain the cooling system.

3. Remove or disconnect the following:
- Negative battery cable
- Valve covers
- Camshaft Position (CMP) sensor
- Engine cooling fan and shroud
- Accessory drive belt
- Heater hoses
- Lower radiator hose
- Power steering pump

4. Rotate the crankshaft so that the crankshaft timing mark aligns with the Top Dead Center (TDC) mark on the front cover, and the **V8** marks on the camshaft sprockets are at 12 o'clock.

5. Remove or disconnect the following:
- Crankshaft damper
- Oil fill housing
- Accessory drive belt tensioner
- Alternator
- A/C compressor
- Front cover
- Front crankshaft seal

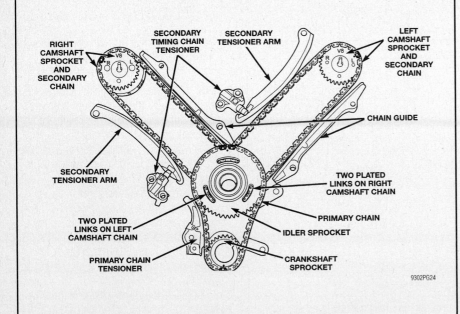

9302PG24

Fig. 93 Timing chain system and alignment marks—3.7L and 4.7L engines

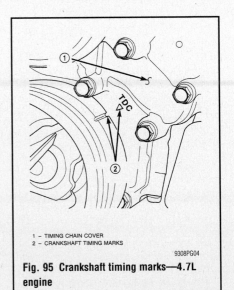

1 – TIMING CHAIN COVER
2 – CRANKSHAFT TIMING MARKS

9308PG04

Fig. 95 Crankshaft timing marks—4.7L engine

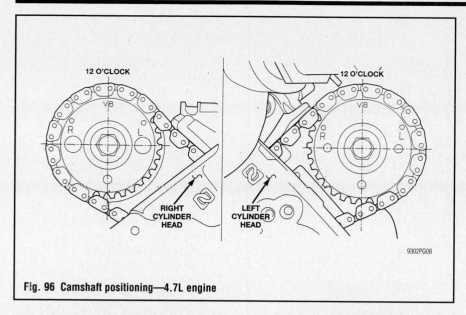

Fig. 96 Camshaft positioning—4.7L engine

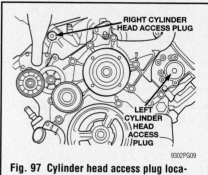

Fig. 97 Cylinder head access plug locations—4.7L engine

- Cylinder head access plugs
- Secondary timing chain guides

6. Compress the primary timing chain tensioner and install a lockpin.

7. Remove the secondary timing chain tensioners.

8. Hold the left camshaft with adjustable pliers and remove the sprocket and chain. Rotate the **left** camshaft 15 degrees **clockwise** to the neutral position.

9. Hold the right camshaft with adjustable pliers and remove the camshaft sprocket. Rotate the **right** camshaft 45 degrees **counterclockwise** to the neutral position.

10. Remove the primary timing chain and sprockets.

To install:

11. Use a small prytool to hold the ratchet pawl and compress the secondary timing chain tensioners in a vise and install locking pins.

➡ **The black bolts fasten the guide to the engine block and the silver bolts fasten the guide to the cylinder head.**

12. Install or connect the following:
- Secondary timing chain guides. Tighten the bolts to 21 ft. lbs. (28 Nm).
- Secondary timing chains to the idler sprocket so that the double plated links on each chain are visible through the slots in the primary idler sprocket

13. Lock the secondary timing chains to the idler sprocket with Timing Chain Locking tool 8515 as shown.

14. Align the primary chain double plated links with the idler sprocket timing mark and the single plated link with the crankshaft sprocket timing mark.

15. Install the primary chain and sprockets. Tighten the idler sprocket bolt to 25 ft. lbs. (34 Nm).

16. Align the secondary chain single plated links with the timing marks on the secondary sprockets. Align the dot at the **L** mark on the left sprocket with the plated link on the left chain and the dot at the **R** mark on the right sprocket with the plated link on the right chain.

17. Rotate the camshafts back from the neutral position and install the camshaft sprockets.

18. Remove the secondary chain locking tool.

19. Remove the primary and secondary timing chain tensioner locking pins.

20. Hold the camshaft sprockets with a spanner wrench and tighten the retaining bolts to 90 ft. lbs. (122 Nm).

21. Install or connect the following:
- Front cover. Tighten the bolts, in sequence, to 40 ft. lbs. (54 Nm).
- Front crankshaft seal
- Cylinder head access plugs
- A/C compressor
- Alternator
- Accessory drive belt tensioner.

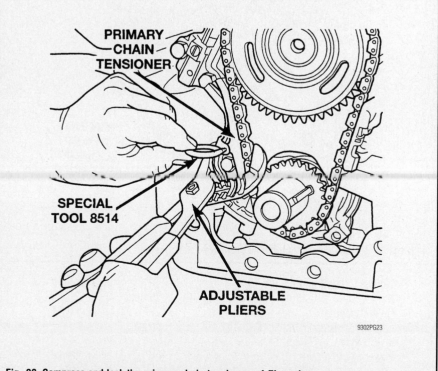

Fig. 98 Compress and lock the primary chain tensioner—4.7L engine

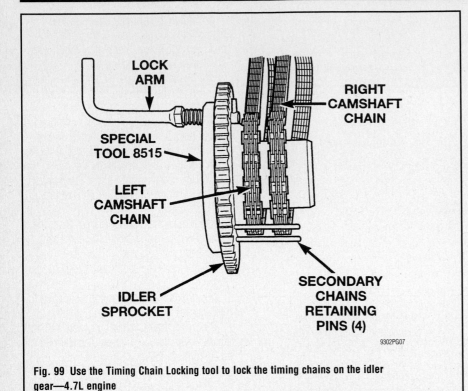

Fig. 99 Use the Timing Chain Locking tool to lock the timing chains on the idler gear—4.7L engine

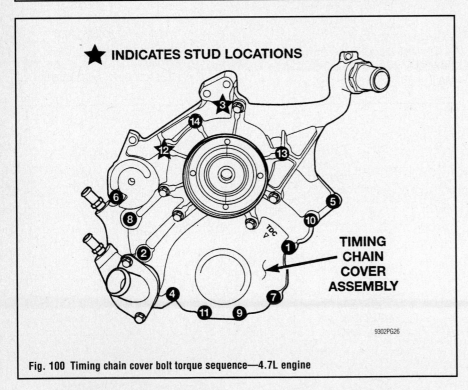

Fig. 100 Timing chain cover bolt torque sequence—4.7L engine

Tighten the bolt to 40 ft. lbs. (54 Nm).
- Oil fill housing
- Crankshaft damper. Tighten the bolt to 130 ft. lbs. (175 Nm).
- Power steering pump
- Lower radiator hose
- Heater hoses
- Accessory drive belt

- Engine cooling fan and shroud
- Camshaft Position (CMP) sensor
- Valve covers
- Negative battery cable
22. Fill the cooling system.
23. Start the engine and check for leaks.

5.7L Engine

See Figure 101.

1. Before servicing the vehicle, refer to the precautions section.
2. Drain the cooling system.
3. Remove or disconnect the following:
   - Negative battery cable
   - Drive belt
   - Radiator fan
   - Coolant and washer bottles
   - Fan shroud
   - A/C compressor
   - Alternator
   - Radiator and heater hoses
   - Tensioner and idler pulleys
   - Crankshaft damper
   - Power steering pump
   - Oil pan and pickup tube
   - Timing cover
   - Re-install the damper
4. Rotate the crankshaft so that the camshaft sprocket and crankshaft sprocket timing marks are aligned.

➡ The camshaft pin and slot in the cam sprocket must be a 12 o'clock, the crankshaft keyway must be at 2 o'clock, and the dots or paint on the crank sprocket must be at 6 o'clock.

5. Pin back the tensioner shoe.
6. Remove the timing chain and sprockets.

To install:

7. With the timing marks aligned, wrap the chain around the sprockets. The chain must be installed with the single plated link aligned with the dot or paint on the cam sprocket. The dot or paint on the crank sprocket should be aligned between the 2 plated links.

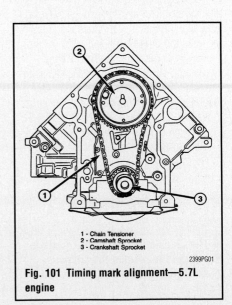

1 - Chain Tensioner
2 - Camshaft Sprocket
3 - Crankshaft Sprocket

Fig. 101 Timing mark alignment—5.7L engine

8. Install the assembly and torque the cam sprocket bolt to 90 ft. lbs. (122 Nm).

9. Unpin the tensioner and verify the alignment.

10. Install or connect the following:
- Timing cover. Torque all fasteners to 21 ft. lbs. (28 Nm). Torque the large lifting lug to 40 ft. lbs. (55 Nm)
- Oil pan and pickup tube

- Power steering pump
- Crankshaft damper
- Tensioner and idler pulleys
- Radiator and heater hoses
- Alternator
- A/C compressor
- Fan shroud
- Coolant and washer bottles
- Radiator fan

- Drive belt
- Negative battery cable

VALVE LASH

ADJUSTMENT

These engines use hydraulic lifters. No maintenance or periodic adjustment is required.

ENGINE PERFORMANCE & EMISSION CONTROL

CAMSHAFT POSITION (CMP) SENSOR

LOCATION

See Figure 102.

The Camshaft Position (CMP) sensor is bolted to the right-front side of the right cylinder head on 3.7L and 4.7L engines. On 5.7L engines, it is located below the alternator on the timing chain cover.

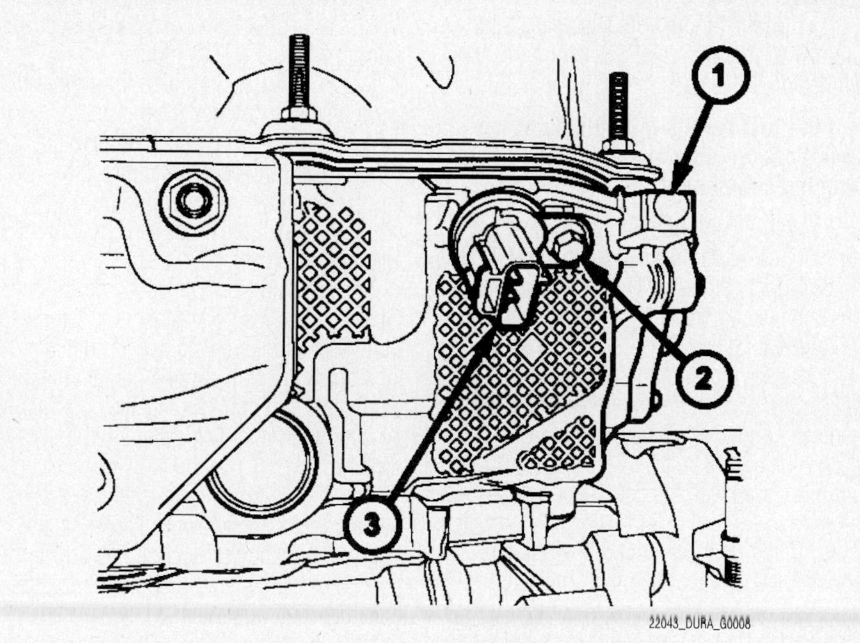

tion Sensor (CKP) to differentiate between fuel injection and spark events. It is also used to synchronize the fuel injectors with their respective cylinders.

When the leading edge of the target wheel notch enters the tip of the CMP, the interruption of magnetic field causes the voltage to switch high, resulting in a sync signal of approximately 5 volts. When the trailing edge of the target wheel notch leaves the tip of the CMP, the change of the

To install:

5. Check the condition of the sensor O-ring.

6. Clean out the machined hole in the cylinder head.

7. Apply a small amount of clean engine oil to the sensor O-ring.

8. Install the CMP sensor into the cylinder head with a slight rocking and twisting action.

9. Install the mounting bolt and tighten to 106 inch lbs. (12 Nm).

10. Connect the electrical connector.

11. Lower the vehicle.

TESTING

1. Using a diagnostic scan tool, check for the presence of any Diagnostic Trouble Codes (DTCs). Record and address these codes as necessary.

2. Turn the ignition **OFF** and disconnect the Camshaft Position (CMP) Sensor harness connector.

➡ **If any of the test results fall outside of the specification, stop and repair the affected component.**

3. With the Ignition on, and engine not running, measure the voltage on the (F856) 5-volt Supply circuit in the CMP Sensor harness connector. Is the voltage between 4.5 and 5.2 volts?

4. If it is, measure the voltage on the (K44) CMP Signal circuit in the CMP Sensor harness connector.

5. The voltage should be between 4.5 and 5.0 volts.

6. If it is, turn the ignition off and disconnect the C2 ECM harness connector.

Fig. 102 CMP sensor mounting on 3.7L and 4.7L engines

OPERATION

The Camshaft Position (CMP) sensor contains a hall effect device referred to as a sync signal generator. A rotating target wheel (tone wheel) for the CMP is located at the front of the camshaft for the right cylinder head. This sync signal generator detects notches located on a tone wheel. As the tone wheel rotates, the notches pass through the sync signal generator. The signal from the CMP sensor is used in conjunction with the Crankshaft Posi-

magnetic field causes the sync signal voltage to switch to 0 volts.

REMOVAL & INSTALLATION

1. Raise and safely support the vehicle.

2. Disconnect the CMP electrical connector.

3. Remove the CMP sensor mounting bolts.

4. Carefully twist the sensor from the cylinder.

✳✳ CAUTION

Do not probe the ECM harness connectors. Probing the ECM harness connectors will damage the ECM terminals resulting in poor terminal to pin connection. Install Miller Special Tool #8815 to perform diagnosis.

7. Measure the resistance of the (K900) Sensor ground circuit from the CMP Sensor harness connector to the appropriate terminal of special tool #8815. If the resistance is below 5.0 ohms, proceed to the next step, otherwise repair the open ground in the K900 sensor.

8. Measure the resistance between the (K44) CMP Signal circuit and the (F856) 5-volt Supply circuit in the CMP Sensor harness connector. If the resistance is below 5.0 ohms, repair the short between the (K44) CMP Signal circuit and the (F856) 5-volt Supply circuit.

➡Inspect the Camshaft sprocket for damage per the Service Information. If a problem is found repair as necessary.

CRANKSHAFT POSITION (CKP) SENSOR

LOCATION

See Figure 103.

The Crankshaft Position (CKP) sensor is mounted into the right rear side of the cylinder block.

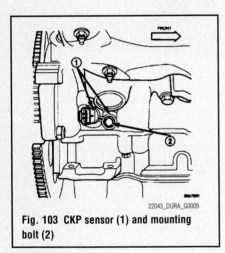

Fig. 103 CKP sensor (1) and mounting bolt (2)

OPERATION

The sensor generates pulses that are the input sent to the Electronic Control Module (ECM). The ECM interprets the sensor input to determine the crankshaft position and engine speed.

The sensor is a hall effect device combined with an internal magnet. It is also sensitive to steel within a certain distance from it. A tonewheel is bolted to the engine crankshaft. The tonewheel has notches that cause a pulse to be generated when they pass under the sensor.

REMOVAL & INSTALLATION

1. Raise and safely support the vehicle.

2. Disconnect the sensor electrical connector.

3. Remove the crankshaft position (CKP) sensor mounting bolt.

4. Carefully twist the CKP sensor from the cylinder block.

To install:

5. Check the condition of the O-ring.

6. Clean out the machined hole in the engine block.

7. Apply a small amount of clean engine oil to the sensor O-ring.

8. Install the CKP sensor into the engine block with a slight rocking and twisting action.

9. Install the mounting bolt and tighten to 21 ft. lbs. (28 Nm).

10. Connect the electrical connector.

11. Lower the vehicle.

TESTING

1. Using a diagnostic scan tool, check for the presence of any Diagnostic Trouble Codes (DTCs). Record and address these codes as necessary.

2. Turn the ignition off. Disconnect the Crankshaft Position (CKP) Sensor harness connector.

➡If the test results fall outside of the specification, stop and repair the affected component.

3. With the Ignition on, and engine not running, measure the voltage on the (F855) 5-volt Supply circuit in the CKP Sensor harness connector. Voltage should be between 4.5 and 5.2 volts.

4. If it is, measure the voltage on the (K24) CKP Signal circuit in the CKP Sensor harness connector. The sensor voltage should be approximately 5.0 volts (plus or minus .1 volt) with the connector disconnected.

5. If it is, turn the ignition off and disconnect the C2 ECM harness connector.

✳✳ CAUTION

Do not probe the ECM harness connectors. Probing the ECM harness connectors will damage the ECM terminals resulting in poor terminal to pin connection. Install Miller Special Tool #8815 to perform diagnosis.

6. Measure the resistance of the (K900) Sensor ground circuit from the CKP Sensor harness connector to the appropriate terminal of special tool #8815. Resistance should be below 5.0 ohms.

7. If it is, measure the resistance between the (K24) CKP Signal circuit and the (F855) 5-volt Supply circuit in the CKP Sensor harness connector. If the resistance below 5.0 ohms, repair the short between the (K24) CKP Signal circuit and the (F855) 5-volt Supply circuit.

8. If not, replace the crankshaft position sensor.

ELECTRONIC CONTROL MODULE (ECM)

LOCATION

The Electronic Control Module (ECM) is attached to the inner fender located in the engine compartment

OPERATION

The Electronic Control Module (ECM) receives input signals from various switches and sensors. Based on these inputs, the ECM regulates various engine and vehicle operations through different system components. These components are referred to as Electronic Control Module (ECM) Outputs. The sensors and switches that provide inputs to the ECM are considered Electronic Control Module (ECM) Inputs.

The ECM adjusts ignition timing based upon inputs it receives from sensors that react to: engine rpm, manifold absolute pressure, engine coolant temperature, throttle position, transmission gear selection (automatic transmission), vehicle speed and the brake switch.

The ECM adjusts idle speed based on inputs it receives from sensors that react to: throttle position, vehicle speed, transmission gear selection, engine coolant temperature and from inputs it receives from the air conditioning clutch switch and brake switch.

Based on inputs that it receives, the ECM adjusts ignition coil dwell. The ECM also adjusts the generator charge rate through control of the generator field and provides speed control operation.

REMOVAL & INSTALLATION

✳✳ WARNING

The use of a diagnostic scan tool is required the Electronic Control Module (ECM) is being in order to reprogram the new ECM.

1. Disconnect the negative battery cable.

2. Unplug the 38-way connectors from the ECM.

➡A locating pin is used in place of one of the mounting bolts.

3. Pry the clip from the locating pin.

4. Remove the two remaining mounting bolts.

5. Remove the ECM from the vehicle.

To install:

6. Position the ECM to the body and install the two mounting bolts.

➡ **Position the ground strap in place before tightening the mounting bolts.**

7. Install the clip to the locating pin.

8. Tighten the mounting bolts to 35 inch lbs. (4 Nm).

9. Carefully plug in the 38-way connectors to the ECM.

10. Connect the negative battery cable.

11. Use a diagnostic scan tool to reprogram the ECM with the VIN and original mileage if ECM has been replaced.

TESTING

1. Start the engine and allow it to reach normal operating temperature. Using a diagnostic scan tool, check for the presence of any Diagnostic Trouble Codes (DTCs). Record and address these codes as necessary.

2. Refer to any Technical Service Bulletins (TSBs) that may apply.

3. Review the scan tool Freeze Frame information. If possible, try to duplicate the conditions under which the DTC set.

4. With the engine running at normal operating temperature, monitor the scan tool parameters related to the DTC while wiggling the wire harness. Look for parameter values to change and/or a DTC to set. Turn the ignition off.

5. Visually inspect the related wire harness. Disconnect all the related harness connectors. Look for any chafed, pierced, pinched, partially broken wires and broken, bent, pushed out, or corroded terminals.

6. Perform a voltage drop test on the related circuits between the suspected inoperative component and the ECM.

✳✳ CAUTION

Do not probe the ECM harness connectors. Probing the ECM harness connectors will damage the ECM terminals resulting in poor terminal to pin connection. Install Miller Special Tool #8815 to perform diagnosis.

7. Inspect and clean all ECM, engine, and chassis grounds that are related to the most current DTC.

8. If numerous trouble codes were set, use a wire schematic and look for any common ground or supply circuits.

9. For any Relay DTCs, actuate the Relay with the scan tool and wiggle the related wire harness to try to interrupt the actuation.

10. For intermittent Evaporative Emission trouble codes perform a visual and physical inspection of the related parts including hoses and the Fuel Filler cap.

11. Use the scan tool to perform a System Test if one applies to failing component. A co-pilot, data recorder, and/or lab scope should be used to help diagnose intermittent conditions.

ENGINE COOLANT TEMPERATURE (ECT) SENSOR

LOCATION

3.7 and 4.7L Engines

The Engine Coolant Temperature (ECT) sensor is installed into a water jacket at the front of the intake manifold.

5.7L Engine

See Figure 104.

The Engine Coolant Temperature (ECT) sensor is located under the air conditioning compressor. It is installed into a water jack at the front of the cylinder block.

OPERATION

The sensor provides an input to the Electronic Control Module (ECM). As coolant temperature varies, the sensor resistance changes, resulting in a different input voltage to the ECM. When the engine is cold, the ECM will demand slightly richer air-fuel mixtures and higher idle speeds until normal operating temperatures are reached.

The engine coolant sensor input also determines operation of the low and high speed cooling fans.

REMOVAL & INSTALLATION

3.7 and 4.7L Engines

1. Drain the cooling system.

2. Disconnect the sensor electrical connector.

3. Remove the ECT sensor.

To install:

4. Apply thread sealant to the sensor threads.

5. Install the ECT sensor into the engine block and tighten the mounting bolt to 8 ft. lbs. (11 Nm).

6. Connect the electrical connector.

7. Refill the cooling system to the correct level.

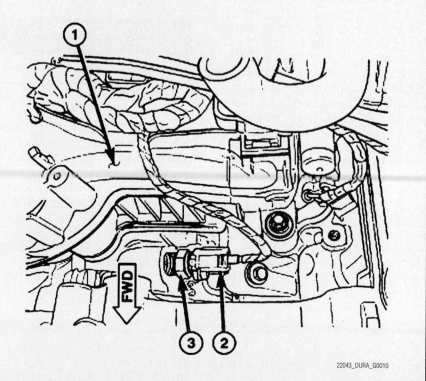

22043_DURA_G0010

Fig. 104 ECT sensor mounting used on 5.7L engines

5.7L Engine

1. Drain the cooling system.
2. Remove the accessory drive belt.
3. Carefully unbolt the A/C compressor. Temporarily support the compressor to access the engine coolant temperature (ECT) sensor.

➡It is not necessary to disconnect the A/C lines from the compressor.

4. Disconnect the sensor electrical connector.
5. Remove the ECT sensor from the engine block.

To install:

6. Apply thread sealant to the sensor threads.
7. Install the sensor into the engine block and tighten the mounting bolt to 8 ft. lbs. (11 Nm).
8. Connect the electrical connector.
9. Position the A/C compressor into place and tighten the mounting bolts.
10. Install the accessory drive belt.
11. Refill the cooling system to the correct level.

TESTING

1. Turn the ignition **OFF**. If possible, allow the vehicle to sit with the ignition off for more than 8 hours in an environment where the temperature is consistent and above 20°F (-7°C).
2. Test drive the vehicle. The vehicle must exceed 30 mph (48 km/h) during the test drive. Do not cycle the ignition off when the test drive is completed.
3. With a scan tool, select View DTCs.
4. Turn the ignition off. Allow the vehicle to sit with the ignition off in an environment where the temperature is consistent and above 20°F (-7°C) until the engine coolant temperature is equal to ambient temperature. Turn the ignition on. With a scan tool, compare the AAT, ECT, and IAT sensor values.
5. If the ECT sensor value is not within 18°F (10°C) of the other two sensor values , perform the following:
6. Refer to any Technical Service Bulletins (TSBs) that may apply.
7. Review the scan tool Freeze Frame information. If possible, try to duplicate the conditions under which the DTC set.
8. With the engine running at normal operating temperature, monitor the scan tool parameters related to the DTC while wiggling the wire harness. Look for parameter values to change and/or a DTC to set. Turn the ignition off.
9. Visually inspect the related wire har-

ness. Disconnect all the related harness connectors. Look for any chafed, pierced, pinched, partially broken wires and broken, bent, pushed out, or corroded terminals.

10. Perform a voltage drop test on the related circuits between the suspected inoperative component and the ECM.

❋❋ CAUTION

Do not probe the ECM harness connectors. Probing the ECM harness connectors will damage the ECM terminals resulting in poor terminal to pin connection. Install Miller Special Tool #8815 to perform diagnosis.

11. Inspect and clean all ECM, engine, and chassis grounds that are related to the most current DTC.
12. If numerous trouble codes were set, use a wire schematic and look for any common ground or supply circuits.
13. For any Relay DTCs, actuate the Relay with the scan tool and wiggle the related wire harness to try to interrupt the actuation.
14. For intermittent Evaporative Emission trouble codes perform a visual and physical inspection of the related parts including hoses and the Fuel Filler cap.
15. Use the scan tool to perform a System Test if one applies to failing component. A co-pilot, data recorder, and/or lab scope should be used to help diagnose intermittent conditions.

HEATED OXYGEN (HO2S) SENSOR

LOCATION

See Figure 105.

If equipped with a Federal Emission Package, two sensors are used: upstream (referred to as 1/1) and downstream (referred to as 1/2). With this emission package, the upstream sensor (1/1) is located just before the main catalytic converter. The downstream sensor (1/2) is located just after the main catalytic converter.

If equipped with a California Emission Package, 4 sensors are used: 2 upstream (referred to as 1/1 and 2/1) and 2 downstream (referred to as 1/2 and 2/2). With this emission package, the right upstream sensor (2/1) is located in the right exhaust downpipe just before the mini-catalytic converter. The left upstream sensor (1/1) is located in the left exhaust downpipe just before the mini-catalytic converter. The right downstream sensor (2/2) is located in the

right exhaust downpipe just after the mini-catalytic converter, and before the main catalytic converter. The left downstream sensor (1/2) is located in the left exhaust downpipe just after the mini-catalytic converter, and before the main catalytic converter.

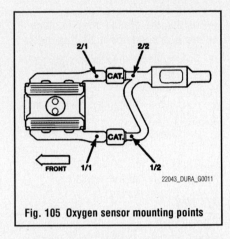

Fig. 105 Oxygen sensor mounting points

OPERATION

An O2 sensor is a galvanic battery that provides the ECM with a voltage signal (0-1 volt) inversely proportional to the amount of oxygen in the exhaust. In other words, if the oxygen content is low, the voltage output is high; if the oxygen content is high the output voltage is low. The ECM uses this information to adjust injector pulse-width to achieve the 14.7to1 air/fuel ratio necessary for proper engine operation and to control emissions.

The O2 sensor must have a source of oxygen from outside of the exhaust stream for comparison. Current O2 sensors receive their fresh oxygen (outside air) supply through the O2 sensor case housing.

Four wires (circuits) are used on each O2 sensor: a 12volt feed circuit for the sensor heating element; a ground circuit for the heater element; a low-noise sensor return circuit to the ECM, and an input circuit from the sensor back to the ECM to detect sensor operation.

REMOVAL & INSTALLATION

1. Raise and safely support the vehicle.
2. Disconnect the wire connector from oxygen sensor.

❋❋ WARNING

When disconnecting sensor electrical connector, do not pull directly on wire going into sensor.

3. Remove the sensor with an oxygen sensor removal and installation tool.

4. Clean threads in exhaust pipe using appropriate tap.

To install:

➡Threads of new oxygen sensors are factory coated with anti-seize compound.

5. Install the oxygen sensor and tighten to 22 ft. lbs. (30 Nm).
6. Connect the electrical connector.
7. Lower the vehicle.

TESTING

1. Start the engine and allow it to idle for at least 60 seconds. Using a diagnostic scan tool, check for the presence of any Diagnostic Trouble Codes (DTCs). Record and address these codes as necessary.
2. Turn the ignition off, allow the sensor to cool down to room temperature disconnect the oxygen sensor wiring harness. Measure the resistance across the sensor heater control terminal and ground terminal. If resistance is not between 2 and 30 ohms, replace the sensor.
3. Refer to any Technical Service Bulletins (TSBs) that may apply.
4. Review the scan tool Freeze Frame information. If possible, try to duplicate the conditions under which the DTC set.
5. With the engine running at normal operating temperature, monitor the scan tool parameters related to the DTC while wiggling the wire harness. Look for parameter values to change and/or a DTC to set. Turn the ignition off.
6. Visually inspect the related wire harness. Disconnect all the related harness connectors. Look for any chafed, pierced, pinched, partially broken wires and broken, bent, pushed out, or corroded terminals.
7. Perform a voltage drop test on the related circuits between the suspected inoperative component and the PCM.

8. Inspect and clean all PCM, engine, and chassis grounds that are related to the most current DTC.

9. If numerous trouble codes were set, use a wire schematic and look for any common ground or supply circuits.
10. For any Relay DTCs, actuate the Relay with the scan tool and wiggle the related wire harness to try to interrupt the actuation.
11. For intermittent Evaporative Emission trouble codes perform a visual and physical inspection of the related parts including hoses and the Fuel Filler cap.
12. Use the scan tool to perform a System Test if one applies to failing component. A co-pilot, data recorder, and/or lab scope should be used to help diagnose intermittent conditions.

INTAKE AIR TEMPERATURE (IAT) SENSOR

LOCATION

The Intake Manifold Air Temperature (IAT) sensor is installed in the air inlet tube.

OPERATION

The IAT sensor is a two-wire Negative Thermal Coefficient (NTC) sensor. Meaning, as inlet air temperatures increase, resistance (voltage) in the sensor decreases. As temperature decreases, resistance (voltage) in the sensor increases.

The IAT sensor provides an input voltage to the Electronic Control Module (ECM) indicating the density of the air entering the intake manifold based upon intake manifold temperature. At key-on, a 5volt power circuit is supplied to the sensor from the ECM. The sensor is grounded at the ECM through a low-noise, sensor-return circuit.

REMOVAL & INSTALLATION

See Figure 106.

1. Disconnect the electrical connector form the Intake Air Temperature (IAT) sensor.
2. Clean any dirt from the air inlet tube at the sensor base.
3. Gently lift the small plastic release tab and rotate the sensor about ¼ turn counterclockwise to remove.

To install:
4. Check the condition of the sensor O-ring.
5. Clean the sensor mounting hole.
6. Position the sensor into the intake air tube and rotate clockwise until the release tab clicks into place.
7. Install the electrical connector.

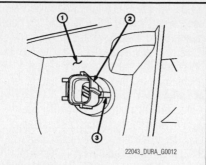

22043_DURA_G0012

Fig. 106 The IAT sensor (2) is located in the air inlet (1). Lift the tab (3) to remove it

TESTING

1. Turn the ignition off. If possible, allow the vehicle to sit with the ignition off for more than 8 hours in an environment where the temperature is consistent and above 20°F (-7°C).
2. Test drive the vehicle. The vehicle must exceed 30 mph (48 km/h) during the test drive. Do not cycle the ignition off when the test drive is completed.
3. With a scan tool, select View DTCs.
4. If a DTC is not active, perform the following:
5. Refer to any Technical Service Bulletins (TSBs) that may apply.
6. Review the scan tool Freeze Frame information. If possible, try to duplicate the conditions under which the DTC set.
7. With the engine running at normal operating temperature, monitor the scan tool parameters related to the DTC while wiggling the wire harness. Look for parameter values to change and/or a DTC to set. Turn the ignition off.
8. Visually inspect the related wire harness. Disconnect all the related harness connectors. Look for any chafed, pierced, pinched, partially broken wires and broken, bent, pushed out, or corroded terminals.
9. Perform a voltage drop test on the related circuits between the suspected inoperative component and the ECM.

10. Inspect and clean all ECM, engine, and chassis grounds that are related to the most current DTC.

11. If numerous trouble codes were set, use a wire schematic and look for any common ground or supply circuits.

12. For any Relay DTCs, actuate the Relay with the scan tool and wiggle the related wire harness to try to interrupt the actuation.

13. For intermittent Evaporative Emission trouble codes perform a visual and physical inspection of the related parts including hoses and the Fuel Filler cap.

14. Use the scan tool to perform a System Test if one applies to failing component. A co-pilot, data recorder, and/or lab scope should be used to help diagnose intermittent conditions.

KNOCK SENSOR (KS)

LOCATION

3.7L and 4.7L Engines

Two knock sensors are bolted into the engine block under the intake manifold.

5.7L Engine

Two knock sensors are bolted into each side of the engine block under the exhaust manifolds.

OPERATION

Two knock sensors are used; one for each cylinder bank. When the knock sensor detects a knock in one of the cylinders on the corresponding bank, it sends an input signal to the Electronic Control Module (ECM). In response, the ECM retards ignition timing for all cylinders by a scheduled amount.

Knock sensors contain a piezoelectric material which constantly vibrates and sends an input voltage (signal) to the ECM while the engine operates. As the intensity of the crystal's vibration increases, the knock sensor output voltage also increases.

REMOVAL & INSTALLATION

3.7L and 4.7L Engines

1. Disconnect the knock sensor dual pigtail harness from engine wiring harness. This connection is made near rear of engine.

2. Remove the intake manifold

3. Remove the Knock Sensor (KS) mounting bolts.

4. Remove the sensors from engine.

To install:

5. Thoroughly clean the KS mounting holes.

6. Install the sensors into the engine

block. Tighten the mounting bolts to 15 ft. lbs. (20 Nm).

7. Install the intake manifold.

8. Connect the KS wiring harness to the engine wiring harness at the rear of the engine.

5.7L Engine

1. Raise and safely support the vehicle.

2. Disconnect the Knock Sensor (KS) electrical connector.

3. Remove the KS mounting bolt.

4. Remove the sensor from the engine.

To install:

5. Thoroughly clean the KS mounting holes.

6. Install the sensors into the engine block. Tighten the mounting bolts to 15 ft. lbs. (20 Nm).

7. Connect the KS electrical connectors.

8. Lower the vehicle.

TESTING

1. Start the engine and allow it to reach normal operating temperature. Using a diagnostic scan tool, check for the presence of any Diagnostic Trouble Codes (DTCs). Record and address these codes as necessary.

2. Refer to any Technical Service Bulletins (TSBs) that may apply.

3. Review the scan tool Freeze Frame information. If possible, try to duplicate the conditions under which the DTC set.

4. With the engine running at normal operating temperature, monitor the scan tool parameters related to the DTC while wiggling the wire harness. Look for parameter values to change and/or a DTC to set. Turn the ignition off.

5. Visually inspect the related wire harness. Disconnect all the related harness connectors. Look for any chafed, pierced, pinched, partially broken wires and broken, bent, pushed out, or corroded terminals.

6. Perform a voltage drop test on the related circuits between the suspected inoperative component and the ECM.

⁂ CAUTION

Do not probe the ECM harness connectors. Probing the ECM harness connectors will damage the ECM terminals resulting in poor terminal to pin connection. Install Miller Special Tool #8815 to perform diagnosis.

7. Inspect and clean all ECM, engine, and chassis grounds that are related to the most current DTC.

8. If numerous trouble codes were set, use a wire schematic and look for any common ground or supply circuits.

9. For any Relay DTCs, actuate the Relay with the scan tool and wiggle the related wire harness to try to interrupt the actuation.

10. For intermittent Evaporative Emission trouble codes perform a visual and physical inspection of the related parts including hoses and the Fuel Filler cap.

11. Use the scan tool to perform a System Test if one applies to failing component. A co-pilot, data recorder, and/or lab scope should be used to help diagnose intermittent conditions.

MANIFOLD ABSOLUTE PRESSURE (MAP) SENSOR

LOCATION

3.7L and 4.7L Engines

The Manifold Absolute Pressure (MAP) sensor is mounted to the front of the intake manifold with two bolts.

5.7L Engine

The Manifold Absolute Pressure (MAP) sensor is mounted to the back of the intake manifold by a quarter turn fastener.

OPERATION

The MAP sensor is used as an input to the Electronic Control Module (ECM). It contains a silicon based sensing unit to provide data on the manifold vacuum that draws the air/fuel mixture into the combustion chamber. The ECM requires this information to determine injector pulse width and spark advance. When manifold absolute pressure (MAP) equals Barometric pressure, the pulse width will be at maximum.

A 5-volt reference is supplied from the ECM and returns a voltage signal to the ECM that reflects manifold pressure. The zero pressure reading is 0.5V and full scale is 4.5V. For a pressure swing of 015 psi, the voltage changes 4.0V. To operate the sensor, it is supplied a regulated 4.8 to 5.1 volts. Ground is provided through the low-noise, sensor return circuit at the ECM.

The MAP sensor input is the number one contributor to fuel injector pulse width. The most important function of the MAP sensor is to determine barometric pressure. The ECM needs to know if the vehicle is at sea level or at a higher altitude, because the air density changes with altitude. It will also help to correct for varying barometric pressure. Barometric pressure and altitude have a direct inverse correlation; as altitude goes up, barometric goes down. At key-on, the ECM powers up and looks at MAP voltage, and based upon the voltage it sees, it knows the current barometric pressure (relative to altitude). Once the engine starts, the ECM looks at the voltage again, continuously every 12 milliseconds, and compares the current voltage to what it was at key-on. The difference between current voltage and what it was at Key On is the manifold vacuum.

During key-on (engine not running) the sensor reads (updates) barometric pressure. A normal range can be obtained by monitoring a known good sensor.

As the altitude increases, the air becomes thinner (less oxygen). If a vehicle is started and driven to a very different altitude than where it was at key-on, the barometric pressure needs to be updated. Any time the ECM sees Wide Open Throttle (WOT), based upon Throttle Position Sensor (TPS) angle and RPM, it will update barometric pressure in the MAP memory cell. With periodic updates, the ECM can make its calculations more effectively.

REMOVAL & INSTALLATION

3.7L and 4.7L Engines

See Figure 107.

1. Disconnect the sensor electrical connector.
2. Clean the area around the Manifold Absolute Pressure (MAP) sensor.
3. Remove the two mounting screws.
4. Remove the MAP sensor from the intake manifold.

To install:

5. Inspect the condition of the sensor O-ring and replace if necessary.
6. Position the MAP sensor into the manifold and install the two mounting screws.
7. Connect the electrical connector.

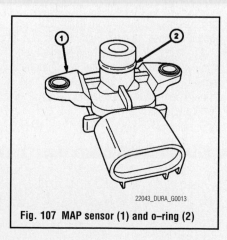

Fig. 107 MAP sensor (1) and o–ring (2)

22043_DURA_G0013

5.7L Engine

1. Disconnect the electrical connector at the Manifold Absolute Pressure (MAP) sensor by sliding the release lock out. Then press down on the lock tab.
2. Rotate the MAP sensor ¼ turn counter-clockwise to remove.

To install:

3. Inspect the condition of the sensor O-ring and replace if necessary.
4. Position the MAP sensor into the intake manifold and rotate ¼ turn clockwise.
5. Connect the electrical connector to the MAP sensor until it clicks into place.

TESTING

1. Start the engine and allow it to reach normal operating temperature. Using a diagnostic scan tool, check for the presence of any Diagnostic Trouble Codes (DTCs). Record and address these codes as necessary.
2. Refer to any Technical Service Bulletins (TSBs) that may apply.
3. Review the scan tool Freeze Frame information. If possible, try to duplicate the conditions under which the DTC set.
4. With the engine running at normal operating temperature, monitor the scan tool parameters related to the DTC while wiggling the wire harness. Look for parameter values to change and/or a DTC to set. Turn the ignition off.
5. Visually inspect the related wire harness. Disconnect all the related harness connectors. Look for any chafed, pierced, pinched, partially broken wires and broken, bent, pushed out, or corroded terminals.
6. Perform a voltage drop test on the related circuits between the suspected inoperative component and the ECM.

✳✳ CAUTION

Do not probe the ECM harness connectors. Probing the ECM harness connectors will damage the ECM terminals resulting in poor terminal to pin connection. Install Miller Special Tool #8815 to perform diagnosis.

7. Inspect and clean all ECM, engine, and chassis grounds that are related to the most current DTC.
8. If numerous trouble codes were set, use a wire schematic and look for any common ground or supply circuits.
9. For any Relay DTCs, actuate the Relay with the scan tool and wiggle the related wire harness to try to interrupt the actuation.

10. For intermittent Evaporative Emission trouble codes perform a visual and physical inspection of the related parts including hoses and the Fuel Filler cap.
11. Use the scan tool to perform a System Test if one applies to failing component. A co-pilot, data recorder, and/or lab scope should be used to help diagnose intermittent conditions.

THROTTLE POSITION SENSOR (TPS)

LOCATION

3.7L and 4.7L Engines

The Throttle Position Sensor (TPS) is mounted on the throttle body and connected to the throttle blade shaft.

5.7L Engine

The 5.7L engine does not use a separate Throttle Position Sensor (TPS) on the throttle body. If it is determined, that the TPS signal is bad, the throttle body assembly must be replaced.

OPERATION

The Throttle Position Sensor (TPS) is a 3-wire variable resistor that provides the Electronic Control Module (ECM) with an input signal (voltage) that represents the throttle blade position of the throttle body. The sensor is connected to the throttle blade shaft. As the position of the throttle blade changes, the resistance (output voltage) of the TPS changes.

The ECM supplies approximately 5 volts to the TPS. The TPS output voltage (input signal to the ECM) represents the throttle blade position. The ECM receives an input signal voltage from the TPS. This will vary in an approximate range of from .26 volts at minimum throttle opening (idle), to 4.49 volts at wide-open throttle. Along with inputs from other sensors, the ECM uses the TPS input to determine current engine operating conditions. In response to engine operating conditions, the ECM will adjust fuel injector pulse width and ignition timing.

REMOVAL & INSTALLATION

1. Remove the air intake tube.
2. Disconnect the Throttle Position Sensor (TPS) electrical connector.
3. Remove the TPS mounting screws.
4. Remove the TPS.

To install:

➡ **The throttle shaft end of throttle body slides into a socket in TPS. The TPS must be installed so that it can be rotated a few degrees. If sensor will not rotate, install the sensor with throttle shaft on other side of socket tangs. The TPS will be under slight tension when rotated.**

5. Install the TPS and tighten the mounting screws to 60 inch lbs. (7 Nm).
6. Connect the TPS electrical connector.
7. Manually operate the throttle by hand to check for any TPS binding before starting the engine.
8. Install the air intake tube.

TESTING

1. Start the engine and allow it to reach normal operating temperature. Using a diagnostic scan tool, check for the presence of any Diagnostic Trouble Codes (DTCs). Record and address these codes as necessary.
2. Refer to any Technical Service Bulletins (TSBs) that may apply.
3. Review the scan tool Freeze Frame information. If possible, try to duplicate the conditions under which the DTC set.
4. With the engine running at normal operating temperature, monitor the scan tool parameters related to the DTC while wiggling the wire harness. Look for parameter values to change and/or a DTC to set. Turn the ignition off.
5. Visually inspect the related wire harness. Disconnect all the related harness connectors. Look for any chafed, pierced, pinched, partially broken wires and broken, bent, pushed out, or corroded terminals.
6. Perform a voltage drop test on the related circuits between the suspected inoperative component and the ECM.

✳✳ CAUTION

Do not probe the ECM harness connectors. Probing the ECM harness connectors will damage the ECM terminals resulting in poor terminal to pin connection. Install Miller Special Tool #8815 to perform diagnosis.

7. Inspect and clean all ECM, engine, and chassis grounds that are related to the most current DTC.
8. If numerous trouble codes were set, use a wire schematic and look for any common ground or supply circuits.
9. For any Relay DTCs, actuate the Relay with the scan tool and wiggle the related wire harness to try to interrupt the actuation.
10. For intermittent Evaporative Emission trouble codes perform a visual and physical inspection of the related parts including hoses and the Fuel Filler cap.
11. Use the scan tool to perform a System Test if one applies to failing component. A co-pilot, data recorder, and/or lab scope should be used to help diagnose intermittent conditions.

VEHICLE SPEED SENSOR (VSS)

LOCATION

The Vehicle Speed Sensor (VSS) is located on the left side of the transmission case.

OPERATION

The Vehicle Speed Sensor (VSS) generates an AC signal as its coil is excited by rotation of the rear planetary carrier lugs. The Transmission Control Module (TCM) interprets this information as output shaft RPM.

REMOVAL & INSTALLATION

1. Raise and safely support the vehicle.
2. Place a suitable catch pan under the transmission for any fluid.
3. Remove the wiring connector from the output speed sensor.
4. Remove the mounting bolt and remove the speed sensor from the transmission case.

To install:

5. Install the speed sensor into the transmission case and tighten the bolt to 105 inch lbs. (12 Nm).
6. Install the wiring connector to the speed sensor.
7. Verify the proper transmission fluid level and refill as necessary.
8. Lower the vehicle.

TESTING

1. Start the engine and allow it to reach normal operating temperature. Using a diagnostic scan tool, check for the presence of any Diagnostic Trouble Codes (DTCs). Record and address these codes as necessary.
2. Refer to any Technical Service Bulletins (TSBs) that may apply.
3. Review the scan tool Freeze Frame information. If possible, try to duplicate the conditions under which the DTC set.
4. With the engine running at normal operating temperature, monitor the scan tool parameters related to the DTC while wiggling the wire harness. Look for parameter values to change and/or a DTC to set. Turn the ignition off.
5. Visually inspect the related wire harness. Disconnect all the related harness connectors. Look for any chafed, pierced, pinched, partially broken wires and broken, bent, pushed out, or corroded terminals.
6. Perform a voltage drop test on the related circuits between the suspected inoperative component and the ECM.

✳✳ CAUTION

Do not probe the ECM harness connectors. Probing the PCM harness connectors will damage the PCM terminals resulting in poor terminal to pin connection. Install Miller Special Tool #8815 to perform diagnosis.

7. Inspect and clean all ECM, engine, and chassis grounds that are related to the most current DTC.
8. If numerous trouble codes were set, use a wire schematic and look for any common ground or supply circuits.
9. For any Relay DTCs, actuate the Relay with the scan tool and wiggle the related wire harness to try to interrupt the actuation.
10. For intermittent Evaporative Emission trouble codes perform a visual and physical inspection of the related parts including hoses and the Fuel Filler cap.
11. Use the scan tool to perform a System Test if one applies to failing component. A co-pilot, data recorder, and/or lab scope should be used to help diagnose intermittent conditions.

FUEL   **GASOLINE FUEL INJECTION SYSTEM**

FUEL SYSTEM SERVICE PRECAUTIONS

Safety is the most important factor when performing not only fuel system maintenance but any type of maintenance. Failure to conduct maintenance and repairs in a safe manner may result in serious personal injury or death. Maintenance and testing of the vehicle's fuel system components can be accomplished safely and effectively by adhering to the following rules and guidelines.

• To avoid the possibility of fire and personal injury, always disconnect the negative battery cable unless the repair or test procedure requires that battery voltage be applied.

• Always relieve the fuel system pressure prior to disconnecting any fuel system component (injector, fuel rail, pressure regulator, etc.), fitting or fuel line connection. Exercise extreme caution whenever relieving fuel system pressure to avoid exposing skin, face and eyes to fuel spray. Please be advised that fuel under pressure may penetrate the skin or any part of the body that it contacts.

• Always place a shop towel or cloth around the fitting or connection prior to loosening to absorb any excess fuel due to spillage. Ensure that all fuel spillage (should it occur) is quickly removed from engine surfaces. Ensure that all fuel soaked cloths or towels are deposited into a suitable waste container.

• Always keep a dry chemical (Class B) fire extinguisher near the work area.

• Do not allow fuel spray or fuel vapors to come into contact with a spark or open flame.

• Always use a back-up wrench when loosening and tightening fuel line connection fittings. This will prevent unnecessary stress and torsion to fuel line piping.

• Always replace worn fuel fitting O-rings with new Do not substitute fuel hose or equivalent where fuel pipe is installed.

Before servicing the vehicle, make sure to also refer to the precautions in the beginning of this section as well.

RELIEVING FUEL SYSTEM PRESSURE

1. Before servicing the vehicle, refer to the precautions section.
2. Remove the fuel tank filler cap to release any fuel tank pressure.
3. Remove the fuel pump relay from the power distribution center (PDC).
4. Start and run the engine until it stops.

5. Continue to restart the engine until it will not run.
6. Turn the key to **OFF**.
7. Unplug the connector from any injector and connect a jumper wire from either injector terminal to the positive battery terminal. Connect another jumper wire to the other terminal and momentarily touch the other end to the negative battery terminal.

✷✷ WARNING

Just touch the jumper to the battery. Powering the injector for more than a few seconds will permanently damage it.

8. Place a rag below the quick-disconnect coupling at the fuel rail and disconnect it.

FUEL FILTER

REMOVAL & INSTALLATION
See Figure 108.

These vehicles incorporate the use of a fuel pump module which comprises:
• An internal fuel filter
• A separate fuel pick-up, or inlet filter
• A fuel pressure regulator
• An electric fuel pump
• A fuel gauge sending unit (fuel level sensor)

If the filter(s), regulator, pump or sending unit requires service, the fuel pump module must be replaced.

FUEL INJECTORS

REMOVAL & INSTALLATION

3.7L Engine

1. Before servicing the vehicle, refer to the precautions section.

✷✷ CAUTION

The left and right fuel rails are replaced as an assembly. Do not attempt to separate rail halves at connector tubes. Due to design of tubes, it does not use any clamps. Never attempt to install a clamping device of any kind to tubes. When removing fuel rail assembly for any reason, be careful not to bend or kink tubes.

2. Remove fuel tank filler tube cap.
3. Perform Fuel System Pressure Release Procedure.
4. Remove negative battery cable at battery.
5. Remove air duct at throttle body air box.
6. Remove air box at throttle body.
7. Remove air resonator mounting bracket at front of throttle body (2 bolts).
8. Disconnect fuel line latch clip and fuel line at fuel rail. A special tool will be necessary for fuel line disconnection.
9. Remove necessary vacuum lines at throttle body.

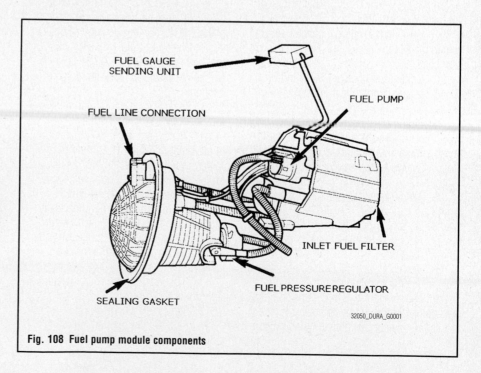

Fig. 108 Fuel pump module components

32050_DURA_G0001

10. Disconnect electrical connectors at all 6 fuel injectors. Push red colored slider away from injector. While pushing slider, depress tab and remove connector from injector. The factory fuel injection wiring harness is numerically tagged (INJ 1, INJ 2, etc.) for injector position identification. If harness is not tagged, note wiring location before removal.

11. Disconnect electrical connectors at all throttle body sensors.

12. Remove 6 ignition coils.

13. Remove four fuel rail mounting bolts.

14. Gently rock and pull left side of fuel rail until fuel injectors just start to clear machined holes in cylinder head. Gently rock and pull right side of rail until injectors just start to clear cylinder head holes. Repeat this procedure (left/right) until all injectors have cleared cylinder head holes.

15. Remove fuel rail (with injectors attached) from engine.

16. Disconnect clip(s) that retain fuel injector(s) to fuel rail.

To install:

17. Install fuel injector(s) into fuel rail assembly and install retaining clip(s).

18. If same injector(s) is being reinstalled, install new O–ring(s).

19. Apply a small amount of clean engine oil to each injector O–ring. This will aid in installation.

20. Clean out fuel injector machined bores in intake manifold.

21. Apply a small amount of engine oil to each fuel injector O–ring. This will help in fuel rail installation.

22. Position fuel rail/fuel injector assembly to machined injector openings in cylinder head.

23. Guide each injector into cylinder head. Be careful not to tear injector O–rings.

24. Push right side of fuel rail down until fuel injectors have bottomed on cylinder head shoulder. Push left fuel rail down until injectors have bottomed on cylinder head shoulder.

25. Install 4 fuel rail mounting bolts and tighten.

26. Install 6 ignition coils.

27. Connect electrical connectors to throttle body.

28. Connect electrical connectors at all fuel injectors. Refer to graphic. Push connector onto injector and then push and lock red colored slider. Verify connector is locked to injector by lightly tugging on connector.

29. Connect necessary vacuum lines to throttle body.

30. Install air resonator mounting bracket near front of throttle body (2 bolts).

31. Connect fuel line latch clip and fuel line to fuel rail.

32. Install air box to throttle body.

33. Install air duct to air box.

34. Connect battery cable to battery.

35. Start engine and check for leaks.

4.7L Engine

See Figure 109.

1. Before servicing the vehicle, refer to the precautions section.

✳✳ CAUTION

The left and right fuel rails are replaced as an assembly. Do not attempt to separate rail halves at connector tubes. Due to design of tubes, it does not use any clamps. Never attempt to install a clamping device of any kind to tubes. When removing fuel rail assembly for any reason, be careful not to bend or kink tubes.

2. Remove fuel tank filler tube cap.

3. Perform Fuel System Pressure Release Procedure.

4. Remove negative battery cable at battery.

5. Remove air duct at throttle body air box.

6. Remove air box at throttle body.

7. Remove air resonator mounting bracket at front of throttle body (2 bolts).

8. Disconnect fuel line latch clip and fuel line at fuel rail. A special tool will be necessary for fuel line disconnection.

9. Remove necessary vacuum lines at throttle body.

10. Disconnect electrical connectors at all 8 fuel injectors. Push red colored slider away from injector. While pushing slider, depress tab and remove connector from injector. The factory fuel injection wiring harness is numerically tagged (INJ 1, INJ 2, etc.) for injector position identification. If harness is not tagged, note wiring location before removal.

11. Disconnect electrical connectors at all throttle body sensors.

12. Remove 8 ignition coils.

13. Remove four fuel rail mounting bolts.

14. Gently rock and pull left side of fuel rail until fuel injectors just start to clear machined holes in cylinder head. Gently rock and pull right side of rail until injectors just start to clear cylinder head holes. Repeat this procedure (left/right) until all injectors have cleared cylinder head holes.

15. Remove fuel rail (with injectors attached) from engine.

16. Disconnect clip(s) that retain fuel injector(s) to fuel rail.

To install:

17. Install fuel injector(s) into fuel rail assembly and install retaining clip(s).

18. If same injector(s) is being reinstalled, install new O–ring(s).

19. Apply a small amount of clean engine oil to each injector O–ring. This will aid in installation.

20. Clean out fuel injector machined bores in intake manifold.

21. Apply a small amount of engine oil to each fuel injector O–ring. This will help in fuel rail installation.

22. Position fuel rail/fuel injector assembly to machined injector openings in cylinder head.

23. Guide each injector into cylinder head. Be careful not to tear injector O–rings.

24. Push right side of fuel rail down until fuel injectors have bottomed on cylinder head shoulder. Push left fuel rail down until injectors have bottomed on cylinder head shoulder.

25. Install 4 fuel rail mounting bolts and tighten.

26. Install 8 ignition coils.

27. Connect electrical connectors to throttle body.

28. Connect electrical connectors at all fuel injectors. Refer to graphic. Push connector onto injector and then push and lock red colored slider. Verify connector is locked to injector by lightly tugging on connector.

29. Connect necessary vacuum lines to throttle body.

30. Install air resonator mounting bracket near front of throttle body (2 bolts).

31. Connect fuel line latch clip and fuel line to fuel rail.

32. Install air box to throttle body.

33. Install air duct to air box.

34. Connect battery cable to battery.

35. Start engine and check for leaks.

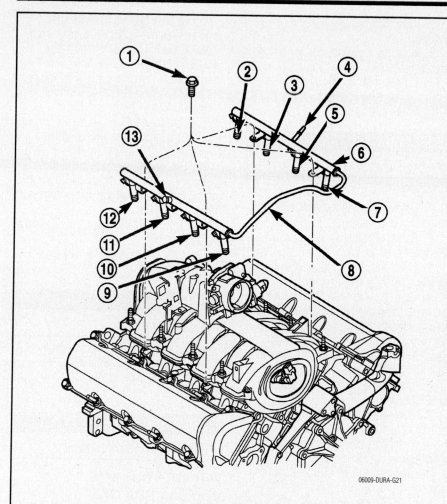

Fig. 109 Fuel rail removal, 4.7L shown; 3.7L and 5.7L similar—(1) retaining bolts (2, 3, 5, 7, 9, 10, 11, and 12) injectors. (6) rail, (4 and 13) fuel fee and return line connections, (8) crossover line

06009-DURA-G21

5.7L Engine

1. Before servicing the vehicle, refer to the precautions section.

⁕⁕ CAUTION

The left and right fuel rails are replaced as an assembly. Do not attempt to separate rail halves at connector tube. Due to design of tube, it does not use any clamps. Never attempt to install a clamping device of any kind to tube. When removing fuel rail assembly for any reason, be careful not to bend or kink tube.

2. Remove fuel tank filler tube cap.
3. Perform Fuel System Pressure Release Procedure.
4. Remove negative battery cable at battery.
5. Remove flex tube (air cleaner housing to engine).

6. Remove air resonator box at throttle body.
7. Disconnect all spark plug cables from all spark plugs and ignition coils. Do not remove cables from cable routing tray. Note original cable positions while removing.
0. Remove spark plug cable tray from engine by releasing 4 retaining clips. Remove tray and cables from engine as an assembly.
9. Disconnect electrical connectors at all 8 ignition coils.
10. Disconnect fuel line latch clip and fuel line at fuel rail. A special tool will be necessary for fuel line disconnection.
11. Disconnect electrical connectors at all 8 fuel injectors. Refer to graphic. Push red colored slider away from injector. While pushing slider, depress tab and remove connector from injector. The factory fuel injection wiring harness is numerically tagged (INJ 1, INJ 2, etc.) for injector position identification. If harness

is not tagged, note wiring location before removal.
12. Disconnect electrical connectors at all throttle body sensors.
13. Remove four fuel rail mounting bolts (2) and hold-down clamps.
14. Gently rock and pull left side of fuel rail until fuel injectors just start to clear machined holes in intake manifold. Gently rock and pull right side of rail until injectors just start to clear intake manifold head holes. Repeat this procedure (left/right) until all injectors have cleared machined holes.
15. Remove fuel rail (with injectors attached) from engine.
16. Disconnect clip(s) that retain fuel injector(s) to fuel rail (2).

To install:

17. Install fuel injector(s) into fuel rail assembly and install retaining clip(s).
18. If same injector(s) is being reinstalled, install new O-ring(s).
19. Clean out fuel injector machined bores in intake manifold.
20. Apply a small amount of engine oil to each fuel injector O-ring. This will help in fuel rail installation.
21. Position fuel rail/fuel injector assembly to machined injector openings in intake manifold.
22. Guide each injector into intake manifold. Be careful not to tear injector O-rings.
23. Push right side of fuel rail down until fuel injectors have bottomed on shoulders. Push left fuel rail down until injectors have bottomed on shoulders.
24. Install 4 fuel rail hold-down clamps and 4 mounting bolts.
25. Position spark plug cable tray and cable assembly to intake manifold. Snap 4 cable tray retaining clips into intake manifold.
26. Install all cables to spark plugs and ignition coils.
27. Connect electrical connector to throttle body.
28. Install electrical connectors to all 8 ignition coils.
29. Connect electrical connector to throttle body.
30. Connect electrical connectors at all fuel injectors. Refer to graphic. Push connector onto injector and then push and lock red colored slider. Verify connector is locked to injector by lightly tugging on connector.
31. Connect fuel line latch clip and fuel line to fuel rail.
32. Install air resonator to throttle body (2 bolts).
33. Install flexible air duct to air box.
34. Connect battery cable to battery.
35. Start engine and check for leaks.

FUEL PUMP

REMOVAL & INSTALLATION

See Figure 110.

1. Before servicing the vehicle, refer to the precautions section.
2. Drain and remove fuel tank.
3. Note rotational position of module before attempting removal. An indexing arrow is located on top of module for this purpose.
4. Position Special Tool 9340 into notches on outside edge of lockring.
5. Install ½ inch drive breaker bar to tool 9340.
6. Rotate breaker bar counter-clockwise to remove lockring.
7. Remove lockring. The module will spring up slightly when lockring is removed.
8. Remove module from fuel tank. Be careful not to bend float arm while removing.

To install:

❊❊ CAUTION

Whenever the fuel pump module is serviced, the rubber seal (gasket) must be replaced.

9. Using a new seal (gasket), position fuel pump module into opening in fuel tank.
10. Position lockring over top of fuel pump module.
11. Rotate module until embossed alignment arrow points to center alignment mark. This step must be performed to prevent float from contacting side of fuel tank. Also be sure fuel fitting on top of pump module is pointed to driver's side of vehicle.

12. Install Special Tool 9340 to lockring.
13. Install ½ inch drive breaker (1) into Special Tool 9340.
14. Tighten lockring (clockwise) until all seven notches have engaged.
15. Install fuel tank.

FUEL TANK

REMOVAL & INSTALLATION

See Figure 111.

1. Before servicing the vehicle, refer to the precautions section.
2. Release the fuel system pressure.
3. Raise and safely support the vehicle.
4. Drain the fuel tank. This is done by removing the clamp and hose from the fuel tank fill fitting at the rear of the tank. Position a draining hose from an approved gasoline draining station into the open fuel tank fill fitting.
5. Unplug the electrical connector from the ESIM switch.
6. Disconnect the quick connect fittings at front of fuel tank.
7. Disconnect the quick connect fitting at the rear of the fuel tank.
8. Support the tank with a hydraulic jack.

9. Remove the two fuel tank strap bolts and remove both tank support straps.
10. Carefully lower the tank a few inches and disconnect the fuel pump module electrical connector at the top of the tank. To disconnect the electrical connector, push upward on the red colored tab to unlock. Push on the black colored tab while removing the connector.
11. Disconnect the fuel line at the fuel pump module fitting by pressing on the tabs at the side of the quick connect fitting.
12. Disconnect the remaining lines from the tank.
13. Continue to lower the tank for removal.

IDLE SPEED

ADJUSTMENT

Idle speed/mixture is maintained by the Electronic Control Module (ECM). No adjustment is necessary or possible.

THROTTLE BODY

REMOVAL & INSTALLATION

3.7L and 4.7L Engines

See Figures 112 and 113.

1. Remove the air cleaner assembly.
2. Perform the fuel system depressurization procedure.
3. Disconnect the battery negative cable.
4. Disconnect all vacuum lines and electrical connectors from the throttle body. Tag for location, if necessary. Electrical connectors include TPS, MAP and IAC motor.
5. Disconnect cables: throttle, cruise control and others fitted.
6. Remove the throttle body bolts.
7. Lift the throttle body from the intake manifold.
8. Put a clean rag into the intake manifold to prevent the entry of foreign matter.

To install:

9. Always use a new gasket. Inspect the O-ring between the throttle body and intake manifold.
10. Reverse the removal procedure.
11. Tighten the throttle body bolts to 9 ft. lbs. (12 Nm).

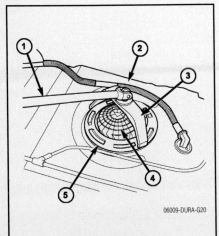

Fig. 110 Module lockring removal. (1) breaker bar, (2) fuel return line, (3) lockring tool, (4) module, (5) lockring

06009-DURA-G20

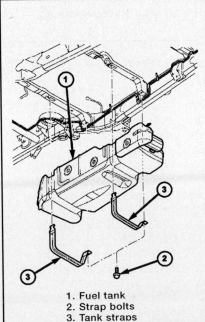

1. Fuel tank
2. Strap bolts
3. Tank straps

22043_DURA_G0005

Fig. 111 Exploded view of the fuel tank mounting

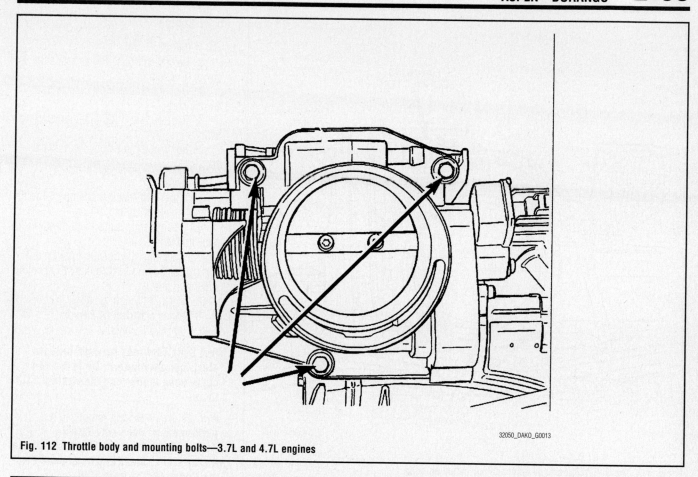

Fig. 112 Throttle body and mounting bolts—3.7L and 4.7L engines

32050_DAKO_G0013

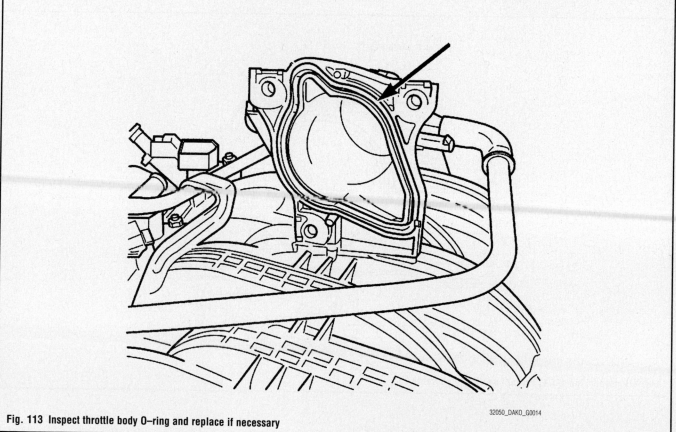

Fig. 113 Inspect throttle body O—ring and replace if necessary

32050_DAKO_G0014

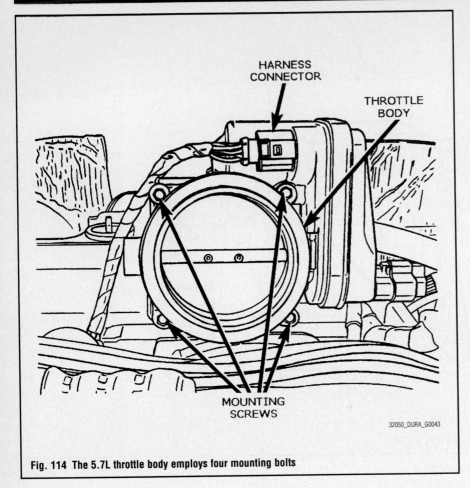

Fig. 114 The 5.7L throttle body employs four mounting bolts

5.7L Engine

See Figures 114 and 115.

1. Remove air duct and air resonator box at throttle body.
2. Disconnect electrical connector at throttle body.
3. Remove four throttle body mounting bolts.
4. Remove throttle body from intake manifold.

To install:

5. Clean and check condition of throttle body-to-intake manifold o-ring.
6. Clean mating surfaces of throttle body and intake manifold.
7. Install throttle body to intake manifold by positioning throttle body to manifold alignment pins.
8. Install 4 mounting bolts.
9. Install electrical connector.
10. Install air plenum.

➡ **A Scan Tool may be used to learn electrical parameters. Go to the Miscellaneous menu, and then select ETC Learn.**

➡ **If the previous step is not performed, a Diagnostic Trouble Code (DTC) will be set. If necessary, use a scan tool to erase any Diagnostic Trouble Codes (DTCs) from ECM.**

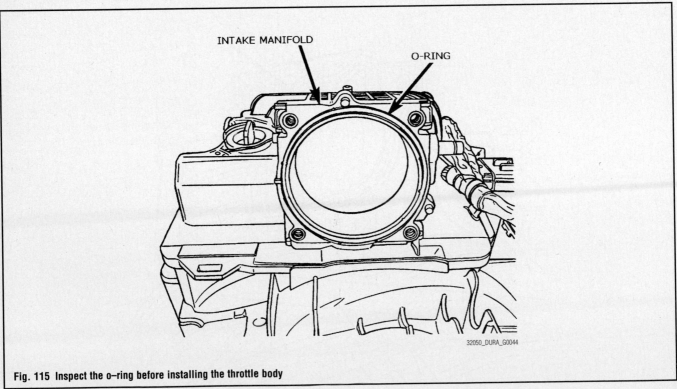

Fig. 115 Inspect the o-ring before installing the throttle body

HEATING & AIR CONDITIONING SYSTEM

BLOWER MOTOR

REMOVAL & INSTALLATION

1. Disconnect and isolate the negative battery cable.
2. Remove the right front door sill trim panel.
3. Remove the right side interior cowl trim cover.
4. Disconnect the wire harness connector from the blower motor.
5. Remove the three screws that secure the blower motor and blower wheel assembly to the HVAC (Heater, Ventilation and Air Conditioning) housing.
6. Remove the blower motor and blower wheel assembly from the HVAC housing.

To install:

7. Position the blower motor and blower wheel assembly into the HVAC housing.
8. Install the three screws that secure the blower motor and blower wheel assembly to the HVAC housing. Tighten the screws to 20 inch lbs. (2.2 Nm).
9. Connect the wire harness connector to the blower motor.
10. Install the right side interior cowl trim cover.
11. Install the right front door sill trim panel.
12. Reconnect the negative battery cable.

HEATER CORE

REMOVAL & INSTALLATION

See Figure 116.

1. Before servicing the vehicle, refer to the precautions section.
2. Drain the engine cooling system.
3. Raise and support the vehicle.
4. Remove the right front wheelhouse splash shield.
5. Remove the heater hoses from the heater core tubes in the engine compartment.
6. Lower the vehicle.

❋❋ WARNING

To avoid personal injury or death, on vehicles equipped with airbags, disable the Supplemental Restraint System (SRS) before attempting any steering wheel, steering column, airbag, occupant classification system, seat belt tensioner, impact sensor, or Instrument panel component

diagnosis or service. Disconnect and isolate the battery negative (ground) cable, then wait two minutes for the system capacitor to discharge before performing further diagnosis or service. This is the only sure way to disable the Supplemental Restraint System (SRS). Failure to take the proper precautions could result in accidental airbag deployment.

7. Before proceeding with the following repair procedure, review all warnings and cautions at the beginning of this chapter.
8. Disconnect and isolate battery negative cable.
9. Using a trim stick C-4755 or equivalent, remove the left door sill trim cover.
10. Remove the screw and remove the left cowl trim cover.
11. Remove the left instrument panel end cap.
12. Remove the two screws and remove the steering column opening cover.
13. Remove the screws and position aside the hood release handle.
14. Remove the four screws and remove the steering column opening reinforcement.
15. Remove the steering column tilt lever.
16. Remove the upper and lower column shrouds.
17. Disconnect the wiring harness connectors to the column.
18. Remove the shift cable from the column shift lever actuator.
19. Release the shift cable from the column bracket and remove it from the bracket.
20. Remove the SKIM module in order to disconnect the electrical connector.
21. Remove the upper steering shaft coupler bolt and slide the shaft down.
22. Remove the brake light switch and discard.
23. Remove the four steering column mounting nuts.
24. Lower the column from the mounting studs.
25. Remove the steering column assembly from the vehicle.
26. Remove the pedal support bracket bolts.
27. Disengage the release rod from the arm on the pedal assembly.
28. Disconnect the electrical connectors from the fuse block.
29. Remove the bolt and remove the ground wire.
30. Open the trim covers in the drivers side a-pillar grab handle and remove the bolts.

31. Remove the a-pillar trim panel.
32. Remove the floor console.
33. Disconnect the two body wire harness connectors from the Occupant Restraint Controller (ORC) connector receptacles located on the forward facing side of the module. To disconnect the wire harness connectors from the ORC, depress the release tab and lift the lever arm on each connector.
34. Position the carpet aside and remove the center harness screws. Pull instrument panel wiring harness from under the carpet.
35. Remove the center support bolts.
36. Remove the driver's seat.
37. Remove the drivers side floor duct.
38. Remove the drivers side support bolts.
39. Remove the right instrument panel end cap.
40. Remove the passenger side support bolts.
41. Using a trim stick C-4755 or equivalent, remove the right door sill trim cover.
42. Remove the screw and remove the right cowl trim cover.
43. Remove the bolts and remove the amplifier.
44. Disconnect the amplifier and antenna electrical connectors.
45. Remove the harness bolt and the ground wire bolt.
46. Remove the passenger side rear floor duct.
47. Open the trim covers in the passenger side a-pillar grab handle and remove the bolts.
48. Remove the a-pillar trim panel.
49. Using a trim stick C-4755 or equivalent, remove the instrument panel defroster grille.
50. Disconnect the sensor electrical connector.
51. Remove the four fenceline bolts.
52. Lift the instrument panel assembly off the side support pins and remove assembly through the driver's door.
53. Remove the bolt that secures the HVAC housing bracket to the dash panel.
54. Remove the two screws that secure the HVAC housing bracket to the top of the HVAC housing.
55. Remove the HVAC housing bracket from the vehicle.
56. Remove the screw that secures the heater core tube retaining bracket to the top of the HVAC housing.
57. Remove the heater core tube retaining bracket from the HVAC housing.

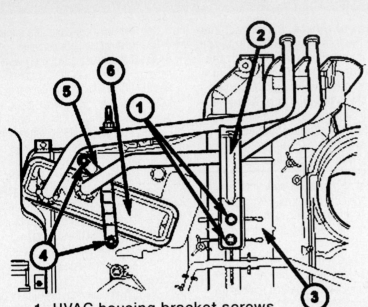

1. HVAC housing bracket screws
2. HVAC housing bracket
3. HVAC housing
4. Heater core retaining bracket screws
5. Heater core retaining bracket
6. Heater core

22043_DURA_G0006

Fig. 116 Heater core and related components

58. Remove the screw that secures the heater core tubes to the heater core.

59. Remove the heater core tubes from the heater core and the dash panel. Remove the O-ring seals from the heater core tube fittings and discard.

60. Remove the two screws that secure the heater core retaining bracket to the top of the HVAC housing.

61. Remove the heater core retaining bracket from the top of the HVAC housing.

62. Carefully lift the heater core out of the HVAC housing.

To install:

63. Carefully install the heater core and the heater core retaining bracket to the top of the HVAC housing. Make sure that the heater core insulator is properly positioned.

64. Install the two screws that secure the heater core and retaining bracket to the HVAC housing. Tighten the screws to 20 inch lbs. (2.2 Nm).

65. Lubricate new rubber O-ring seals with clean engine coolant and install them onto the heater core tube fittings. Use only the specified O-ring as it is made of a special material for the engine cooling system.

66. Install the heater core tubes through the dash panel and to the heater core.

67. Install the screw that secures the heater core tubes to the heater core. Tighten the screw securely.

68. Install the heater core tube retaining bracket to the top of the HVAC housing.

69. Install the screw that secures the heater core tube retaining bracket to the HVAC housing. Tighten the screw to 20 inch lbs. (2.2 Nm).

70. Install the HVAC housing bracket to the top of HVAC housing and to the dash panel.

71. Install the two screws that secure the HVAC housing bracket to the HVAC housing. Tighten the screws to 20 inch lbs. (2.2 Nm).

72. Install the bolt that secures the HVAC housing bracket to the dash panel. Tighten the bolt to 26 inch lbs. (3 Nm).

73. Position the instrument panel assembly into the vehicle through the driver's side door and install onto the side support pins.

74. Install the four fenceline bolts and tighten to 70 inch lbs. (8 Nm).

75. Connect the sensor electrical connector.

76. Install the instrument panel defroster grille and seat fully.

77. Position the passenger side a-pillar trim panel into place and seat fully.

78. Install the bolts and tighten to 55 inch lbs. (6 Nm).

79. Install the passenger side rear floor duct.

80. Install the screws for the ground wire and passenger side wire harness.

81. Tighten the ground wire and harness bolts to 10 ft. lbs. (14 Nm).

82. Connect the amplifier and antenna electrical connectors.

83. Install the amplifier and install the bolts.

84. Tighten the bolts to 50 inch lbs. (6 Nm).

85. Install the right cowl trim cover and install the screw.

86. Install the right door sill trim cover.

87. Install the passenger side support bolts and tighten to 20 ft. lbs. (27 Nm).

88. Install the right instrument panel end cap.

89. Install the drivers side support bolts and tighten to 20 ft. lbs. (27 Nm).

90. Install the drivers side floor duct.

91. Install the driver's seat.

92. Install the center support bolts and tighten to 95 inch lbs. (11 Nm).

93. Position the center instrument panel wiring harness under the carpet and install the bolts.

⁂ CAUTION

The lever arms of the wire harness connectors for the ORC MUST be in the unlatched position before they are inserted into their connector receptacles on the ORC or they may become damaged.

94. Reconnect the two body wire harness connectors to the ORC connector receptacles located on the forward facing side of the module. Be certain that the latches on both connectors are each fully engaged.

95. Install the floor console.

96. Position the driver's side a-pillar trim into place and seat the retaining clips fully.

97. Install the bolts and tighten to 55 inch lbs. (6 Nm).

98. Install the ground wire and install the bolt.

99. Tighten the ground wire bolts to 10 ft. lbs. (14 Nm).

100. Connect the electrical connectors at the fuse block.

101. Connect the brake release rod to the arm on the pedal assembly.

102. Install the pedal support bolts and tighten to 10 ft. lbs. (14 Nm).

⁂ CAUTION

All fasteners must be torqued to specification to ensure proper operation of the steering column.

103. Position the steering column on the dash panel support and loosely install the mounting nuts.

104. Firmly slide the steering column upward against the studs in dash panel and hand tighten the nuts.

105. Install the steering shaft coupler on the steering shaft and loosely install a new bolt.

106. Center steering column in dash opening and tighten mounting nuts to 21 ft. lbs. (28 Nm).

➡**Torque the upper left nut first then the lower right nut. Then torque** the lower left nut then the upper right nut.

➡**A new bolt must be used for reinstallation.**

107. Tighten the coupler bolt to 28 ft. lbs. (38 Nm).

108. Install a new brake light switch.

109. Install the shifter cable.

110. Connect the wiring harness to the column.

111. Install the SKIM module.

112. Install the upper and lower column shrouds and install the screws.

113. Install the column tilt lever.

114. Install the steering column opening reinforcement and install the four screws.

115. Install the hood release handle and install the screws.

116. Install the steering column opening cover and install the two screws.

117. Install the left instrument panel end cap.

118. Install the left cowl trim cover and install the screw.

119. Install the left door sill trim cover and seat fully.

120. Do not reconnect the battery negative cable at this time. The supplemental restraint system verification test procedure should be performed following service of any supplemental restraint system component.

121. Raise the vehicle and install the heater hoses to the heater core tubes in the engine compartment.

122. Install the right front wheelhouse splash shield.

123. Lower the vehicle.

124. Refill the engine cooling system.

STEERING

POWER STEERING GEAR

REMOVAL & INSTALLATION

1. Before servicing the vehicle, refer to the precautions section.
2. Siphon out as much power steering fluid as possible from the pump.
3. Lock the steering wheel.
4. Raise and support the vehicle.
5. Remove the front tires.
6. Remove the nuts from the tie rod ends.
7. Separate tie rod ends from the knuckles.
8. Remove the steering gear pinch bolt.
9. Remove the lower steering coupling from the steering gear.
10. Turn the steering gear to the full right position.
11. Remove the exhaust Y-pipe (3.7L & 4.7L engines only).
12. Remove the power steering lines from the gear.
13. Remove the front crossmember.
14. Remove the steering gear mounting bolts, washers and nuts.
15. Tip the gear forward to allow clearance and move to the right then tip the gear downward on the left side to remove from the vehicle.

To install:

➡**Before installing gear inspect the bushings and replace if worn or damaged, also use new gear mounting bolts and nuts.**

16. Install gear to the vehicle and tighten mounting nuts and bolts to 190 ft. lbs. (258 Nm).

17. Install power steering lines to steering gear and tighten the pressure hose to 28 ft. lbs. (38 Nm) and tighten the return hose to 48 ft. lbs. (65 Nm).

18. Slide the shaft coupler onto gear. Install new bolt and tighten to 36 ft. lbs. (49 Nm).

19. Clean tie rod end studs and knuckle tapers.

20. Install tie rod ends into the steering knuckles and tighten the nuts to 55 ft. lbs. (75 Nm).

21. Install the Y-pipe (3.7L & 4.7L engines only).

22. Install the front crossmember.

23. Install the front tires.

24. Remove the support and lower the vehicle.

25. Unlock the steering wheel.

26. Fill system with fluid.

27. Adjust the toe position.

POWER STEERING PUMP

REMOVAL & INSTALLATION

See Figure 117.

1. Drain and siphon the power steering fluid from the pump.
2. Remove the serpentine drive belt.

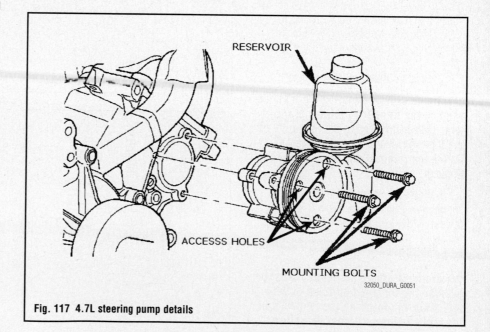

Fig. 117 4.7L steering pump details

3. Remove the reservoir return hose at the reservoir.

4. Remove the pressure hose from the pump.

5. Remove the three pump mounting bolts through pulley access holes.

6. Remove the pump from the engine.

To install:

7. Align the pump with the mounting holes on the engine.

8. Install the three pump mounting bolts through the pulley access holes. Tighten the bolts to 21 ft. lbs. (28 Nm).

9. Install the pressure hose to the pump. Tighten the pressure line to 23 ft. lbs. (31 Nm).

10. Install reservoir return hose to the reservoir.

11. Install the serpentine drive belt.

12. Fill the power steering pump.

BLEEDING

> ✳✳ **CAUTION**
>
> The fluid level should be checked with engine OFF to prevent injury from moving components.

> ✳✳ **WARNING**
>
> MOPAR® ATF+4 is to be used in the power steering system. No other power steering or automatic transmission fluid is to be used in the system. Damage may result to the power steering pump and system if any other fluid is used. Do not overfill.

1. Wipe filler cap clean, then check the fluid level. The dipstick should indicate COLD when the fluid is at normal temperature (before engine has been operated).

2. Turn steering wheel all the way to the left

3. Fill the pump fluid reservoir to the proper level and let the fluid settle for at least two (2) minutes.

4. Raise the front wheels off the ground.

5. Slowly turn the steering wheel lock-to-lock 20 times with the engine OFF while checking the fluid level.

➡Vehicles with long return lines or oil coolers turn wheel 40 times.

6. Start the engine. With the engine idling maintain the fluid level.

7. Lower the front wheels and let the engine idle for two minutes.

8. Turn the steering wheel in both direction and verify power assist and quiet operation of the pump.

9. If the fluid is extremely foamy or milky looking, allow the vehicle to stand a few minutes and repeat the procedure.

> ✳✳ **WARNING**
>
> Do not run a vehicle with foamy fluid for an extended period. This may cause pump damage.

SUSPENSION

FRONT SUSPENSION

LOWER BALL JOINT

REMOVAL & INSTALLATION

See Figures 118 and 119.

1. Before servicing the vehicle, refer to the precautions section.

2. Remove the tire and wheel assembly.

3. Remove the brake caliper and rotor.

4. Disconnect the tie rod from the steering knuckle.

5. Separate the lower ball joint from the steering knuckle.

6. Remove the steering knuckle.

7. Move the halfshaft to the side and support the halfshaft out of the way (4WD only).

8. Chisel out the ball joint stakes.

➡Extreme pressure lubrication must be used on the threaded portions of the tool. This will increase the longevity of the tool and insure proper operation during the removal and installation process.

9. Press the ball joint from the lower control arm using special tools C-4212-F (press), 9331-1 (driver) and 9331-2 (receiver).

To install:

➡Extreme pressure lubrication must be used on the threaded portions of the tool. This will increase the longevity of the tool and insure proper operation

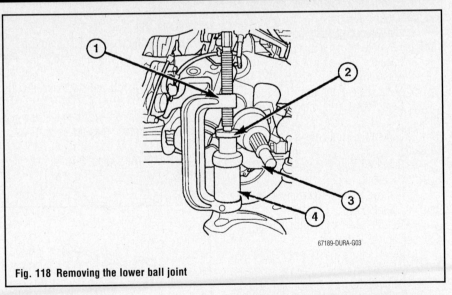

Fig. 118 Removing the lower ball joint

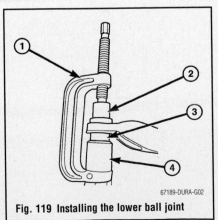

Fig. 119 Installing the lower ball joint

during the removal and installation process.

10. Install the ball joint into the control arm and press in using special tools C-4212-F (press), 9331-1 (receiver) and 9331-3 (driver).

11. Stake the ball joint flange in four evenly spaced places around the ball joint flange, using a chisel and hammer.

12. Remove the support for the halfshaft and install into position (4WD only).

13. Install the steering knuckle.

14. Install the tie rod end into the steering knuckle.

15. Install and tighten the halfshaft nut to 185 ft. lbs. (251 Nm).

16. Install the brake caliper and rotor.

17. Install the tire and wheel assembly.

18. Check the vehicle ride height.

19. Perform a wheel alignment.

LOWER CONTROL ARM

REMOVAL & INSTALLATION

1. Before servicing the vehicle, refer to the precautions section.

2. Raise and support the vehicle.

3. Remove the wheel and tire assembly.

4. Remove the disc brake caliper assembly.

5. Remove the disc brake rotor.

6. Disconnect the wheel speed sensor at the wheel well.

7. Disconnect the tie rod from the knuckle.

8. Remove the front halfshaft nut on 4WD models.

9. Remove the upper ball joint nut. Separate the upper ball joint from the steering knuckle.

10. Remove the lower ball joint nut. Separate the lower ball joint from the steering knuckle.

11. Remove the steering knuckle.

12. Unload the torsion bar using special tool 8686 (1).

13. Remove the torsion bar from the vehicle.

14. Remove the stabilizer bar link.

15. Remove the shock absorber lower bolt.

16. Remove the front and rear pivot bolts.

17. Remove the lower control arm from the vehicle.

To install:

18. Position the lower control arm at the frame rail brackets. Install the pivot bolts and nuts. Tighten the nuts finger-tight.

➡ The ball joint stud taper must be CLEAN and DRY before installing the knuckle. Clean the stud taper with mineral spirits to remove dirt and grease.

19. Install the steering knuckle.

20. Insert the lower ball joint into the steering knuckle. Install and tighten the retaining nut to 70 ft. lbs. (95 Nm).

21. Install the torsion bar.

22. Install shock absorber lower bolt and tighten to 60 ft. lbs. (81 Nm).

23. Install the front halfshaft nut (4WD models).

24. Insert the upper ball joint into the steering knuckle. Install and tighten the retaining nut to 55 ft. lbs. (75 Nm).

25. Install the stabilizer bar link and tighten to 125 ft. lbs. (69 Nm).

26. Tighten the lower control arm pivot nut and bolts to 180 ft. lbs. (244 Nm).

27. Insert the outer tie rod end into the steering knuckle. Install and tighten the retaining nut to 55 ft. lbs. (75 Nm).

28. Install the disc brake rotor.

29. Install the disc brake caliper and adapter assembly and tighten to 100 ft. lbs. (135 Nm).

30. Install the wheel and tire assembly.

31. Remove the support and lower the vehicle.

32. Adjust the front suspension height and perform a wheel alignment.

CONTROL ARM BUSHING REPLACEMENT

See Figure 120.

1. Remove the lower control arm.

2. Secure the control arm in a vise.

3. Install the bushing tools C4212-F (Press), (9334-4 (Driver), 9334-6 (Spacer) and 9334-5 (Receiver) for the replacement of the large bushing.

4. Install bushing remover tools C4212-F (Press), 9334-4 (Driver), 9334-6 (Spacer) and 9334-5 (Receiver) for the small bushing removal.

5. After replacing the bushings, install the control arm in the vehicle.

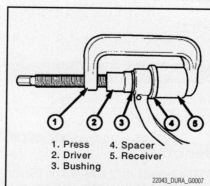

1. Press   4. Spacer
2. Driver   5. Receiver
3. Bushing

22043_DURA_G0007

Fig. 120 The bushings can be pressed in and out of the control arm as shown

STABILIZER BAR

REMOVAL & INSTALLATION

Links

See Figure 121.

➡ 4-wheel drive vehicles do not utilize stabilizer links; the ends of the stabilizer bar fasten directly to the front lower control arm.

1. Raise and support the vehicle.

2. Remove the lower nut.

3. Remove the upper nut, retainers and grommets from the stabilizer bar.

4. Remove the stabilizer link from the vehicle.

To install:

5. Install the stabilizer link to the vehicle.

6. Install the retainers, grommets and upper nut to the stabilizer bar and Tighten to 45 ft. lbs. (61 Nm).

7. Install the lower nut and tighten to 125 ft. lbs. (169 Nm).

8. Remove the support and lower the vehicle.

Bar

➡ To service the stabilizer bar the vehicle should be on a drive on hoist. The vehicle suspension must be at curb height for stabilizer bar installation.

1. Remove the stabilizer link upper nut and remove the retainers and grommets.

2. Remove the stabilizer bar retainer bolts and nuts also remove the retainers from the frame sway bar and remove the bar.

3. If necessary, remove the bushings from the stabilizer bar.

To install:

4. If removed, install the bushings on the stabilizer bar.

5. Position the stabilizer bar on the frame crossmember brackets and install the bracket and bolts finger-tight.

➡ Check the alignment of the bar to ensure there is no interference with the either frame rail or chassis component. Spacing should be equal on both sides.

6. Install the stabilizer bar to the stabilizer link and install the grommets and retainers and tighten to 45 ft. lbs. (61 Nm).

7. Tighten the brackets to the frame and tighten to 45 ft. lbs. (61 Nm).

8. Install the nuts to the stabilizer link and tighten to 125 ft. lbs. (169 Nm).

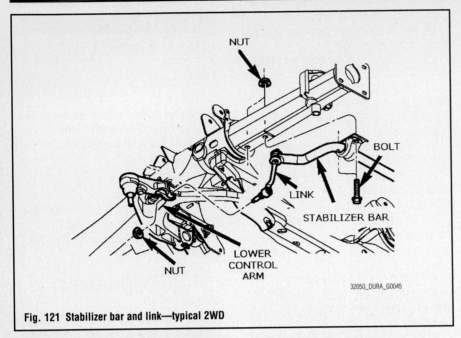

Fig. 121 Stabilizer bar and link—typical 2WD

STEERING KNUCKLE

REMOVAL & INSTALLATION

1. Raise and support the vehicle.
2. Remove the wheel.
3. Remove the brake caliper, rotor, shield and ABS wheel speed sensor if equipped.
4. Remove the front halfshaft nut (4WD only).
5. Remove the tie rod end nut. Separate the tie rod from the knuckle with Remover 8677 or equivalent.

❊ WARNING

Be careful not to damage the ball joint seal.

6. Remove the upper ball joint nut. Separate the ball joint from the knuckle with Remover 8677 or equivalent.
7. Install a hydraulic jack to support the lower control arm.
8. Remove the lower ball joint nut. Separate the ball joint from the knuckle with Remover 8677 or equivalent and remove the knuckle.
9. Remove the hub/bearing bolts from the knuckle.
10. Remove the hub/bearing from the steering knuckle
11. Remove the steering knuckle.

To install:

❊ WARNING

The ball joint stud tapers must be CLEAN and DRY before installing the knuckle. Clean the stud tapers with

mineral spirits to remove dirt and grease.

12. Install the hub/bearing to the steering knuckle and tighten the bolts to 120 ft. lbs. (163 Nm).
13. Install the knuckle onto the upper and lower ball joints.
14. Install the upper ball joint nut. Tighten the nut to 55 ft. lbs. (75 Nm).
15. Install the lower ball joint nut. Tighten the nut to 70 ft. lbs. (95 Nm).
16. Remove the hydraulic jack from the lower suspension arm.
17. Install the tie rod end and tighten the nut to 55 ft. lbs. (75 Nm).
18. Install the front halfshaft into the hub/bearing (4WD only).
19. Install the halfshaft nut and tighten to 185 ft. lbs. (251 Nm) (4X4 only).
20. Install the ABS wheel speed sensor if equipped and brake shield, rotor and caliper.
21. Install the wheel
22. Remove the support and lower the vehicle.
23. Perform a wheel alignment.

TORSION BAR

REMOVAL & INSTALLATION

See Figures 122 and 123.

1. Before servicing the vehicle, refer to the precautions section.

➡ **The left and right side torsion bars are NOT interchangeable. The bars are identified and stamped R or L, for right or left. The bars do not have a front or**

rear end and can be installed with either end facing forward.

2. Raise and support the vehicle with the front suspension hanging.
3. Remove the transfer case skid plate.

➡ **Count and record the number of turns for installation reference.**

4. Mark the adjustment bolt setting.
5. Install Special Tool 8686 or equivalent to the anchor arm and the cross member.
6. Increase the tension on the anchor arm tool 8686 or equivalent until the load is removed from the adjustment bolt and the adjuster nut.
7. Turn the adjustment bolt counterclockwise to remove the bolt and the adjuster nut.
8. Remove the Special Tool 8686 or equivalent, allowing the torsion bar to unload.

To install:

➡ **The left and right side torsion bars are NOT interchangeable. The bars are identified and stamped R or L, for right or left. The bars do not have a front or rear end and can be installed with either end facing forward.**

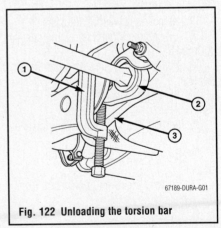

Fig. 122 Unloading the torsion bar

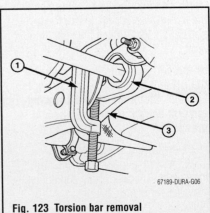

Fig. 123 Torsion bar removal

9. Insert torsion bar ends into anchor and suspension arm.

10. Position the anchor in the cross-member frame.

11. Install Special Tool 8686 or equivalent to the anchor and the crossmember.

12. Increase the tension on the anchor in order to load the torsion bar.

13. Install the adjustment bolt and the adjuster nut.

14. Turn adjustment bolt clockwise the recorded amount of turns.

15. Remove tool 8686 or equivalent from the torsion bar crossmember.

16. Install the transfer case skid plate.

17. Lower vehicle and adjust the front suspension height.

18. Perform a wheel alignment.

UPPER BALL JOINT

REMOVAL & INSTALLATION

These models utilize an upper control arm with an integral ball joint. If the ball joint is damaged or worn, the upper control arm must be replaced.

UPPER CONTROL ARM

REMOVAL & INSTALLATION

1. Before servicing the vehicle, refer to the precautions section.

2. Raise and support vehicle.

3. Remove wheel and tire assembly.

4. Remove the nut from upper ball joint.

5. Separate upper ball joint from the steering knuckle.

➡ **When installing the tool to separate the ball joint, be careful not to damage the ball joint seal.**

6. Remove the control arm pivot bolts and remove control arm.

To install:

7. Position the control arm into the frame brackets. Install bolts and tighten to 75 ft. lbs. (102 Nm).

8. Insert ball joint in steering knuckle and tighten ball joint nut to 55 ft. lbs. (75 Nm).

9. Install the wheel and tire assembly.

10. Remove the support and lower vehicle.

11. Perform a wheel alignment.

WHEEL BEARINGS

REMOVAL & INSTALLATION

See Figure 124.

1. Before servicing the vehicle, refer to the precautions section.

2. Raise and support the vehicle.

3. Remove the wheel and tire assembly.

4. Remove the brake caliper and rotor.

5. Remove the ABS wheel speed sensor if equipped,

6. Remove the halfshaft nut, (4WD only).

➡ **Do not strike the knuckle with a hammer to remove the tie rod end or the ball joint. Damage to the steering knuckle will occur.**

7. Remove the tie rod end nut and separate the tie rod from the knuckle.

8. Remove the upper ball joint nut and separate the upper ball joint from the knuckle.

9. Pull down on the steering knuckle to separate the halfshaft from the hub/bearing, (4WD).

10. Remove the three hub/bearing mounting bolts from the steering knuckle.

11. Slide the hub/bearing out of the steering knuckle.

12. Remove the brake dust shield.

To install:

13. Install the brake dust shield.

14. Install the hub/bearing into the steering knuckle and tighten the bolts to 120 ft. lbs. (163 Nm).

15. Install the brake rotor and caliper.

16. Install the ABS wheel speed sensor if equipped.

17. Install the upper ball joint nut to the steering knuckle and tighten to 55 ft. lbs. (75 Nm).

18. Install the tie rod end nut to the steering knuckle and tighten to 60 ft. lbs. (81 Nm).

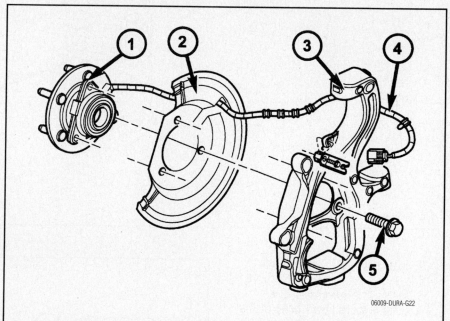

Fig. 124 Hub/bearing installation. (1) hub/bearing, (2) dust shield, (3) knuckle, (4) ABS harness, (5) hub bolt

06009-DURA-G22

19. Install the halfshaft nut and tighten to 185 ft. lbs. (251 Nm) (4WD only).

20. Install the wheel and tire assembly.

21. Remove the support and lower vehicle.

ADJUSTMENT

These models utilize a hub/bearing assembly which is not adjustable.

COIL SPRING

REMOVAL & INSTALLATION

See Figure 125.

➡Before servicing the vehicle, refer to the precautions in the beginning of this section.

11. Remove the holding fixture for the rear axle.

LOWER CONTROL ARM

REMOVAL & INSTALLATION

See Figures 126 and 127.

1. Raise and support the rear axle.
2. Remove the lower control arm bolt and flag nut at the axle.
3. Remove the lower control arm bolt and flag nut at the frame.
4. Remove the lower control arm from the vehicle.

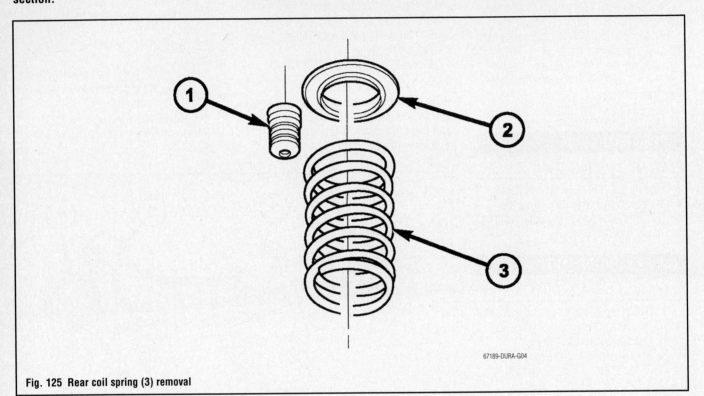

67189-DURA-G04

Fig. 125 Rear coil spring (3) removal

1. Raise and support the vehicle.
2. Support the axle with a suitable holding fixture.
3. Remove the lower shock bolt.
4. Remove the bell crank bolt from the rear axle.
5. Lower the jack to remove the spring and isolator from the vehicle.

To install:

➡All fastener tightening should be made with the full vehicle weight on the ground being supported by the tires.

6. Position spring to the vehicle on top of the isolator.
7. Align the springs to the spring pockets.
8. Raise the rear axle into place.
9. Install the bell crank bolt to the rear axle. Tighten to 185 ft. lbs. (251 Nm).
10. Install the lower shock bolts to the rear axle. Tighten to 75 ft. lbs. (102 Nm).

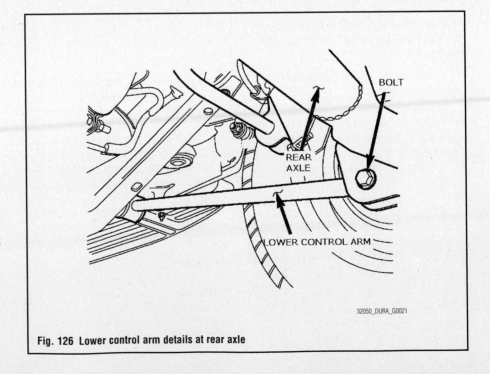

32050_DURA_G0021

Fig. 126 Lower control arm details at rear axle

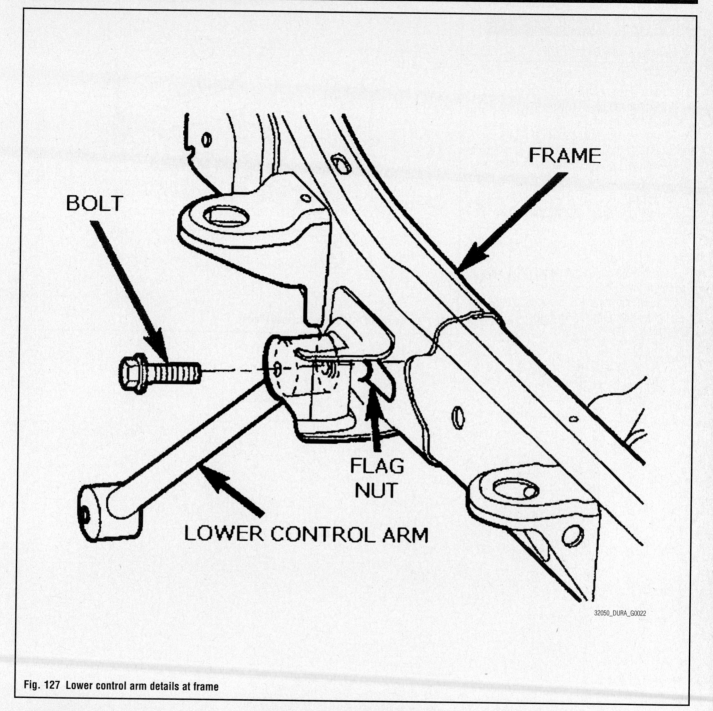

Fig. 127 Lower control arm details at frame

To install:

5. Install the lower control arm to the vehicle.

6. Install the lower control arm bolt and flag nut at the frame.

7. Install the lower control arm bolt and flag nut at the axle.

8. Lower the vehicle to the ground and then tighten the bolts to 185 ft. lbs. (251 Nm).

SHOCK ABSORBER

REMOVAL & INSTALLATION

➡**Before servicing the vehicle, refer to the precautions in the beginning of this section.**

1. Raise vehicle and support the axle.
2. Lower the spare tire.

➡**This step must be done if replacing the left side shock.**

3. Remove the upper shock bolt and flag nut.

4. Remove the lower shock bolt and nut.

5. Remove the rear shock absorber from the vehicle.

To install:

6. Position the shock absorber in the brackets.

7. Install the bolts through the brackets and the shock. Install the flag nut on the top bolt and nut on lower bolt.

8. Tighten the upper and lower bolt/nuts to 75 ft. lbs. (102 Nm)

9. Raise the spare tire back in place, if lowered for the left shock.

10. Remove the support and lower the vehicle.

UPPER CONTROL ARM

REMOVAL & INSTALLATION

See Figure 128.

1. Raise and support the rear axle.
2. Remove the upper control arm bolt and flag nut at the axle.
3. Remove the upper control arm bolt and flag nut at the frame side.
4. Remove the upper control arm from the vehicle.

To install:

5. Install the upper control arm to the vehicle.
6. Install the upper control arm bolt and flag nut at the frame.
7. Install the upper control arm bolt and flag nut at the axle.
8. Lower the vehicle to the ground and then tighten the bolts to 115 ft. lbs. (156 Nm).

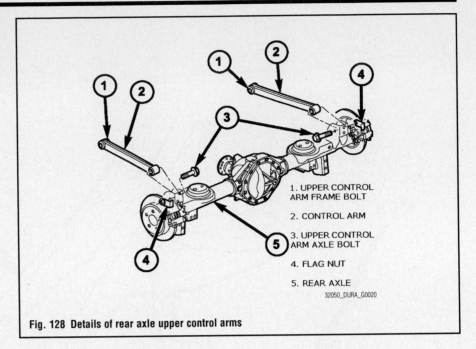

1. UPPER CONTROL ARM FRAME BOLT

2. CONTROL ARM

3. UPPER CONTROL ARM AXLE BOLT

4. FLAG NUT

5. REAR AXLE

32050_DURA_G0020

Fig. 128 Details of rear axle upper control arms

SPECIFICATIONS AND MAINTENANCE CHARTS

ENGINE AND VEHICLE IDENTIFICATION

Engine							Model Year	
Code ①	Liters (cc)	Cu. In.	Cyl.	Fuel Sys.	Engine Type	Eng. Mfg.	Code ②	Year
C	1.8 (1798)	110	4	MFI	DOHC	GEMA	7	2007
B	2.0 (1998)	122	4	MFI	DOHC	GEMA		
K	2.4 (2360)	146.5	4	MFI	DOHC	GEMA		

MFI: Multi-port Fuel Injection

DOHC: Dual Overhead Camshaft

① 8th position of VIN

② 10th position of VIN

22043_CALI_C0001

GENERAL ENGINE SPECIFICATIONS

Year	Model	Engine Displ. Liters	Engine VIN	Net Horsepower @ rpm	Net Torque @ rpm (ft. lbs.)	Bore x Stroke (in.)	Comp. Ratio	Oil Pressure @ rpm
2007	Caliber	1.8	C	148@6500	125@5200	3.39x3.05	10.5:1	25-80@3000
		2.0	B	158@6400	141@5000	3.39x3.39	10.5:1	25-80@3000
		2.4	K	172@6000	165@4400	3.47x3.82	10.5:1	25-80@3000

22043_CALI_C0002

GASOLINE ENGINE TUNE-UP SPECIFICATIONS

Year	Engine Displ. Liters	Engine VIN	Spark Plug Gap (in.)	Ignition Timing (deg.)	Fuel Pump (psi)	Idle Speed (rpm)	Valve Clearance	
							Intake	Exhaust
2007	1.8	C	0.038-0.043	①	NA	①	0.006-0.009	0.010-0.012
	2.0	B	0.038-0.043	①	NA	①	0.006-0.009	0.010-0.012
	2.4	K	0.038-0.043	①	NA	①	0.006-0.009	0.010-0.012

Note: The information on the Vehicle Emission Control label must be used, if different from the figures in this chart.

NA: Not Available

① Ignition timing and idle speed are controlled by the PCM. No adjustment is necessary.

22043_CALI_C0003

CAPACITIES

Year	Model	Engine Displ. Liters	Engine VIN	Engine Oil with Filter	Transmission (pts.) Man.	Transmission (pts.) Auto.**	Transfer Case (pts.)	Drive Axle Front (pts.)	Drive Axle Rear (pts.)	Fuel Tank (gal.)	Cooling System (qts.)
2007	Caliber	1.8	C	4.5	5.0-5.4	17.4	2.2	-	2.0-2.2	13.5	7.2
		2.0	B	4.5	5.0-5.4	17.4	2.2	-	2.0-2.2	13.5	7.2
		2.4	K	4.5	5.0-5.4	17.4	2.2	-	2.0-2.2	13.5	7.2

**Overhaul

22043_CALI_C0004

FLUID SPECIFICATIONS

Year	Model	Engine Displacement Liters	Engine ID/VIN	Engine Oil	Manual Trans.	Auto. Trans.	Front & Rear Axle	Power Steering Fluid	Brake Master Cylinder
2007	Caliber	1.8	C	5W-20	Mopar® ATF +4	Mopar® CVT +4	Mopar® Gear & Axle Lube 80W-90 API GL 5	Mopar® Power Steering Fluid +4 or Mopar® ATF +4	DOT 3
		2.0	B	5W-20	Mopar® ATF +4	Mopar® CVT +4	Mopar® Gear & Axle Lube 80W-90 API GL 5	Mopar® Power Steering Fluid +4 or Mopar® ATF +4	DOT 3
		2.4	K	5W-20	Mopar® ATF +4	Mopar® CVT +4	Mopar® Gear & Axle Lube 80W-90 API GL 5	Mopar® Power Steering Fluid +4 or Mopar® ATF +4	DOT 3

DOT: Department Of Transpotation

22043_CALI_C0005

VALVE SPECIFICATIONS

Year	Engine Displ. Liters	Engine VIN	Seat Angle (deg.)	Face Angle (deg.)	Spring Test Pressure (lbs. @ in.)	Spring Installed Height (in.)	Stem-to-Guide Clearance (in.) Intake	Stem-to-Guide Clearance (in.) Exhaust	Stem Diameter (in.) Intake	Stem Diameter (in.) Exhaust
2007	1.8	C	44.75-45.10	45.25-45.75	78.2-85.8@1.152	1.378	0.0018-0.0025	0.0029-0.0037	0.2151-0.2157	0.2148-0.2153
	2.0	B	44.75-45.10	45.25-45.75	78.2-85.8@1.152	1.378	0.0018-0.0025	0.0029-0.0037	0.2151-0.2157	0.2148-0.2153
	2.4	K	44.75-45.10	45.25-45.75	78.2-85.8@1.152	1.378	0.0018-0.0025	0.0029-0.0037	0.2151-0.2157	0.2148-0.2153

22043_CALI_C0006

CAMSHAFT AND BEARING SPECIFICATIONS CHART
All measurements are given in inches.

Year	Engine Displacement Liters	Engine VIN	Journal Diameter	Brg. Oil Clearance	Shaft End-play	Runout	Journal Bore	Lobe Lift Intake	Lobe Lift Exhaust
2007	1.8	C	0.9430-0.9440	①	0.0040-0.0090	NA	NA	0.3620	0.3310
	2.0	B	0.9430-0.9440	①	0.0040-0.0090	NA	NA	0.3620	0.3310
	2.4	K	0.9430-0.9440	①	0.0040-0.0090	NA	NA	0.3620	0.3310

NA: Not Available
① Front Intake Journal: 0.0008-0.0022 in.
Front Exhaust Journal: 0.0007-0.0020 in.
All Others: 0.0011-0.0026 in.

22043_CALI_C0007

CRANKSHAFT AND CONNECTING ROD SPECIFICATIONS
All measurements are given in inches.

Year	Engine Displ. Liters	Engine VIN	Main Brg. Journal Dia.	Main Brg. Oil Clearance	Shaft End-play	Thrust on No.	Journal Diameter	Oil Clearance	Side Clearance
2007	1.8	C	①	0.0007-0.0024	0.0035-0.0094	3	NA	0.0009-0.0027	0.0050-0.0150
	2.0	B	①	0.0011-0.0018	0.0019-0.0098	3	2.0078-2.0084	0.0010-0.0020	0.0039-0.0098
	2.4	K	①	0.0011-0.0018	0.0019-0.0098	3	2.0078-2.0084	0.0012-0.0023	0.0039-0.0098

NA: Not Available
① 0: 2.0466-2.0467 in.
1: 2.0465-2.0466 in.
2: 2.0464-2.0465 in.
3: 2.0462-2.0464 in.
4: 2.0461-2.0462 in.

22043_CALI_C0008

PISTON AND RING SPECIFICATIONS
All measurements are given in inches.

Year	Engine Displ. Liters	Engine VIN	Piston Clearance	Ring Gap Top Compression	Ring Gap Bottom Compression	Ring Gap Oil Control	Ring Side Clearance Top Compression	Ring Side Clearance Bottom Compression	Ring Side Clearance Oil Control
2007	1.8	C	(-0.0006)-0.0006	0.0059-0.0118	0.0118-0.0177	0.0079-0.0276	0.0012-0.0028	0.0012-0.0028	0.0024-0.0059
	2.0	B	(-0.0006)-0.0006	0.0059-0.0118	0.0118-0.0177	0.0079-0.0276	0.0012-0.0028	0.0012-0.0028	0.0024-0.0059
	2.4	K	(-0.0006)-0.0006	0.0059-0.0118	0.0118-0.0177	0.0079-0.0276	0.0012-0.0028	0.0012-0.0028	0.0024-0.0059

22043_CALI_C0009

TORQUE SPECIFICATIONS

All readings in ft. lbs.

Year	Engine Displ. Liters	Engine VIN	Cylinder Head Bolts	Main Bearing Bolts	Rod Bearing Bolts	Crankshaft Damper Bolts	Flywheel Bolts	Manifold Intake	Manifold Exhaust	Spark Plugs	Oil Pan Drain Plug
2007	1.8	C	①	②	③	155	70	18	25	20	30
	2.0	B	①	②	③	155	70	18	25	20	30
	2.4	K	①	②	③	155	70	18	25	20	30

① Refer to procedure for illustration
   Step 1: Tighten bolts to 25 ft. lbs. (30 Nm)
   Step 2: Tighten bolts to 45 ft. lbs. (61 Nm)
   Step 3: Verify all bolts at 45 ft. lbs. (60 Nm)
   Step 4: Tighten bolts an addt'l 90 degrees

② Refer to procedure for illustration
   Step 1: Tighten all bolts to 20 ft. lbs.
   Step 2: Tighten bolts an addt'l 45 degrees

③ Step 1: Tighten all bolts to 15 ft. lbs. (20 Nm)
   Step 2: Tighten bolts an addt'l 90 degrees

22043_CALI_C0010

WHEEL ALIGNMENT

Year	Model ①		Caster Range (+/-Deg.)	Caster Preferred Setting (Deg.)	Camber Range (+/-Deg.)	Camber Preferred Setting (Deg.)	Toe-in (deg.)
2007	Caliber	F	1.00	②	0.40	-0.50	0.10+/-0.10
	15 inch wheels	R	—	—	0.40	-0.40	0.10+/-0.10
	Caliber	F	1.00	③	0.40	-0.70	0.10+/-0.10
	17 inch wheels	R	—	—	0.40	-0.60	0.10+/-0.10
	Caliber	F	1.00	④	0.40	-0.70	0.10+/-0.10
	18 inch wheels	R	—	—	0.40	-0.70	0.10+/-0.10

① Wheel size refers to OEM wheels only

② Left: +2.90
   Right: +2.60

③ Left: +2.90
   Right: +2.60

④ Left: +3.00
   Right: +2.70

22043_CALI_C0011

TIRE, WHEEL AND BALL JOINT SPECIFICATIONS

Year	Model	OEM Tires Standard	OEM Tires Optional	Tire Pressures (psi) Front	Tire Pressures (psi) Rear	Wheel Size	Ball Joint Inspection	Lug Nut Torque (ft. lbs.)
2007	Caliber SE	P205/70R15	-	①	①	①	②	100
	Caliber SXT	P215/60R17	-	①	①	①	②	100
	Caliber Sport	P215/60R17	-	①	①	①	②	100
	Caliber R/T	P215/55R18	-	①	①	①	②	100

OEM: Original Equipment Manufacturer

STD: Standard

OPT: Optional

① See placard on vehicle

② The ball joint is not servicable. The entire lower control arm must be replaced.

22043_CALI_C0012

BRAKE SPECIFICATIONS
All measurements in inches unless noted

Year	Model		Brake Disc			Brake Drum Diameter			Minimum Lining Thickness	Brake Caliper	
			Original Thickness	Minimum Thickness	Maximum Runout	Original Inside Diameter	Max. Wear Limit	Maximum Machine Diameter		Bracket Bolts (ft. lbs.)	Mounting Bolts (ft. lbs.)
2007	Caliber	F	①	0.961	0.0020	—	—	—	0.040	70	20
		R	①	0.331	0.0016	①	①	①	0.040	-	-

① Not available

22043_CALI_C0013

SCHEDULED MAINTENANCE INTERVALS
2007 Caliber

TO BE SERVICED	TYPE OF SERVICE	VEHICLE MILEAGE INTERVAL (x1000)												
		3	6	9	12	15	18	21	24	27	30	33	36	39
Engine oil & filter	R	✓	✓	✓	✓	✓	✓	✓	✓	✓	✓	✓	✓	✓
Tires	Rotate		✓		✓		✓		✓		✓		✓	
Spare Tire - proper inflation	S/I		✓		✓		✓		✓		✓		✓	
Brake hoses & linings	S/I						✓						✓	
Lubricate steering and suspension ball joints	C/L		✓		✓		✓		✓		✓		✓	
Brake caliper pins	C/L				✓				✓				✓	
Air filter	R					✓					✓			
Cabin air filter	R				✓				✓				✓	
Spark plugs	R										✓			
Drive axle lubricant	R	Every 60,000 miles												
Power Transfer Unit fluid	R	Every 60,000 miles												
PCV valve	I/R										✓			
Rear drive axle fluid	R	Every 60,000 miles												
Accessory drive belt	R										✓			
Manual trans fluid	R	Every 48,000 miles												
Automatic trans. fluid and filter	R	Every 60,000 miles												
Engine coolant	R	Every 60,000 miles												

R: Replace   S/I: Service or Inspect   C/L: Clean and lubricate   I/R: Inspect and rerplace if necessary

The above schedule is to be used if you drive under any of the following conditions:

Driving in temperatures under 32 degrees F

Stop and go traffic

Extensive engine idling

Driving in dusty conditions

Frequent trips under 10 miles

More than 50 % of your driving is in hot weather (90 deg. F) above 50 miles per hour

Trailer towing

Taxi, police or delivery service

Off-road driving

The vehicle is equipped for and operated with E85 (ethonol) fuel

If none of these conditions is met, double the maintenance intervals

22043_CALI_C0014

PRECAUTIONS

Before servicing any vehicle, please be sure to read all of the following precautions, which deal with personal safety, prevention of component damage, and important points to take into consideration when servicing a motor vehicle:

• Never open, service or drain the radiator or cooling system when the engine is hot; serious burns can occur from the steam and hot coolant.

• Observe all applicable safety precautions when working around fuel. Whenever servicing the fuel system, always work in a well-ventilated area. Do not allow fuel spray or vapors to come in contact with a spark, open flame, or excessive heat (a hot drop light, for example). Keep a dry chemical fire extinguisher near the work area. Always keep fuel in a container specifically designed for fuel storage; also, always properly seal fuel containers to avoid the possibility of fire or explosion. Refer to the additional fuel system precautions later in this section.

• Fuel injection systems often remain pressurized, even after the engine has been turned **OFF**. The fuel system pressure must be relieved before disconnecting any fuel lines. Failure to do so may result in fire and/or personal injury.

• Brake fluid often contains polyglycol ethers and polyglycols. Avoid contact with the eyes and wash your hands thoroughly after handling brake fluid. If you do get brake fluid in your eyes, flush your eyes with clean, running water for 15 minutes. If eye irritation persists, or if you have taken brake fluid internally, IMMEDIATELY seek medical assistance.

• The EPA warns that prolonged contact with used engine oil may cause a number of skin disorders, including cancer. You should make every effort to minimize your exposure to used engine oil. Protective gloves should be worn when changing oil. Wash your hands and any other exposed skin areas as soon as possible after exposure to used engine oil. Soap and water, or waterless hand cleaner should be used.

• All new vehicles are now equipped with an air bag system, often referred to as a Supplemental Restraint System (SRS) or Supplemental Inflatable Restraint (SIR) system. The system must be disabled before performing service on or around system components, steering column, instrument panel components, wiring and sensors. Failure to follow safety and disabling procedures could result in accidental air bag deployment, possible personal injury and unnecessary system repairs.

• Always wear safety goggles when working with, or around, the air bag system. When carrying a non-deployed air bag, be sure the bag and trim cover are pointed away from your body. When placing a non-deployed air bag on a work surface, always face the bag and trim cover upward, away from the surface. This will reduce the motion of the module if it is accidentally deployed. Refer to the additional air bag system precautions later in this section.

• Clean, high quality brake fluid from a sealed container is essential to the safe and proper operation of the brake system. You should always buy the correct type of brake fluid for your vehicle. If the brake fluid becomes contaminated, completely flush the system with new fluid. Never reuse any brake fluid. Any brake fluid that is removed from the system should be discarded. Also, do not allow any brake fluid to come in contact with a painted surface; it will damage the paint.

• Never operate the engine without the proper amount and type of engine oil; doing so WILL result in severe engine damage.

• Timing belt maintenance is extremely important. Many models utilize an interference-type, non-freewheeling engine. If the timing belt breaks, the valves in the cylinder head may strike the pistons, causing potentially serious (also time-consuming and expensive) engine damage. Refer to the maintenance interval charts for the recommended replacement interval for the timing belt, and to the timing belt section for belt replacement and inspection.

• Disconnecting the negative battery cable on some vehicles may interfere with the functions of the on-board computer system(s) and may require the computer to undergo a relearning process once the negative battery cable is reconnected.

• When servicing drum brakes, only disassemble and assemble one side at a time, leaving the remaining side intact for reference.

• Only an MVAC-trained, EPA-certified automotive technician should service the air conditioning system or its components.

BRAKES

GENERAL INFORMATION

PRECAUTIONS

• Certain components within the ABS system are not intended to be serviced or repaired individually.

• Do not use rubber hoses or other parts not specifically specified for and ABS system. When using repair kits, replace all parts included in the kit. Partial or incorrect repair may lead to functional problems and require the replacement of components.

• Lubricate rubber parts with clean, fresh brake fluid to ease assembly. Do not use shop air to clean parts; damage to rubber components may result.

• Use only DOT 3 brake fluid from an unopened container.

• If any hydraulic component or line is removed or replaced, it may be necessary to bleed the entire system.

• A clean repair area is essential. Always clean the reservoir and cap thoroughly before removing the cap. The slightest amount of dirt in the fluid may plug an orifice and impair the system function. Perform repairs after components have been thoroughly cleaned; use only denatured alcohol to clean components. Do not allow ABS components to come into contact with any substance containing mineral oil; this includes used shop rags.

• The Anti-Lock control unit is a microprocessor similar to other computer units in the vehicle. Ensure that the ignition switch is **OFF** before removing or installing controller harnesses. Avoid static electricity discharge at or near the controller.

• If any arc welding is to be done on the

ANTI-LOCK BRAKE SYSTEM (ABS)

vehicle, the control unit should be unplugged before welding operations begin.

SPEED SENSORS

REMOVAL & INSTALLATION

Front

See Figures 1 and 2.

1. Disconnect the wheel speed sensor cable connector from the wiring harness connector, located on top of the frame rail just inside the strut tower.
2. Raise and safely support the vehicle.
3. Remove the grommet from the hole in the body and pull the wheel speed sensor cable out of the hole.
4. Remove the speed sensor cable routing clip from the outside frame rail.

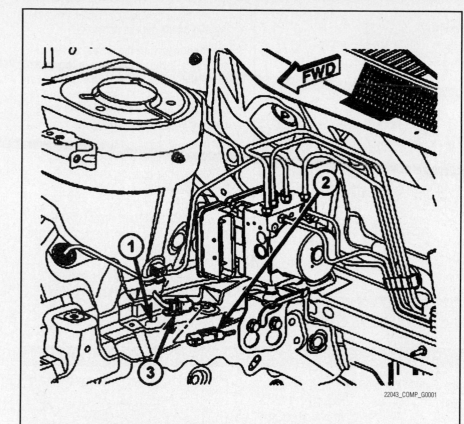

Fig. 1 Disconnect the speed sensor connector (2) from the wiring harness (3) on top of the frame rail (1)—Front speed sensor

5. Remove the screw fastening the cable routing clamp to the outside frame rail.

6. Remove the screw securing the wheel speed sensor routing bracket to the brake flex hose bracket.

7. Remove the mounting screws holding the speed sensor head to the steering knuckle.

8. Remove the routing clip and remove the speed sensor.

To install:

9. Install the wheel speed sensor head into the knuckle. Install the routing clip and mounting screw and tighten it to 106 inch lbs. (12 Nm).

10. Position the wheel speed sensor routing bracket on the brake flex hose bracket and tighten the mounting screw to 13 ft. lbs. (18 Nm).

11. Position the wheel speed sensor cable routing clamp on the outside frame rail and tighten the mounting screw to 13 ft. lbs. (18 Nm).

12. Install the speed sensor cable routing clip on the outside frame rail.

13. Insert the wheel speed sensor cable through the hole in the body and install the grommet in the hole.

14. Lower the vehicle.

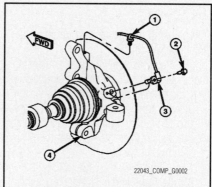

Fig. 2 Remove the screw (2) and routing clip (1) holding the speed sensor (3) to the steering knuckle (4)—Front speed sensor

15. Connect the wheel speed sensor cable connector to the wiring harness connector on top of the frame rail.

16. Using a Diagnostic Scan Tool, clear any faults

Rear

All-Wheel Drive

See Figure 3.

1. Remove the cargo floor cover.

2. Remove the rear floor pan silencer.

3. If equipped, remove the nuts mounting the satellite receiver or amplifier to the rear floor pan. Move the component aside to allow access to the wheel speed sensor wiring connector through the opening in bottom of the quarter trim panel.

4. Through the opening in the bottom of the quarter trim panel, disconnect the wheel speed sensor cable connector at the body wiring harness connector.

5. Raise and safely support the vehicle.

6. Remove the rear wheel.

7. Remove the grommet from the hole in the body and pull the wheel speed sensor cable out through the hole.

8. Remove the speed sensor cable routing clip from the outside frame rail.

9. Remove the screw fastening the cable routing clamp to the rear suspension crossmember.

10. Remove the speed sensor cable routing clip from the trailing link.

11. Remove the screw fastening the cable routing clamp to the trailing link.

12. Unclip the wheel speed sensor head from the spring-loaded retainer on the rear of the hub and bearing. Remove the sensor from the vehicle.

To install:

❊❊ CAUTION

Be sure that cables are installed, routed, and clipped properly. Failure to install speed sensor cables properly may result in contact with moving parts or an over extension of cables causing an open circuit.

➡ When installing the sensor head to the spring-loaded retainer on the hub and bearing, make sure the head is held snug in the retainer. If there is any play, the clip is deformed and the hub and bearing must be replaced. The retainer is not serviced separately.

13. Clip the wheel speed sensor head (flat side to bearing rear face) into the spring-loaded retainer on the rear of the hub and bearing.

14. Position the wheel speed sensor on the trailing link and install the screw securing it in place. Tighten the mounting screw to 13 ft. lbs. (18 Nm).

15. Position the wheel speed sensor and install the routing clip fastening the sensor to the trailing link.

16. Position the wheel speed sensor cable routing clamp on the rear suspension crossmember and install the mounting screw. Tighten the mounting screw to 13 ft. lbs. (18 Nm).

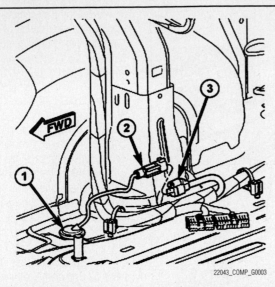

Fig. 3 Disconnect the speed sensor connector (2) from the body wiring harness (3)—Rear speed sensor

17. Install the speed sensor cable routing clip on the outside frame rail.

➡ **When inserting the wheel speed sensor cable through the hole in the body, route the cable toward the shock tower to make it easier to grasp the cable to connect it to the body wiring harness connector in a later step.**

18. Insert the wheel speed sensor cable through the hole in the body and install the grommet in the hole.
19. Install the rear wheel.
20. Lower the vehicle.
21. Through the opening in the bottom of the quarter trim panel, connect the wheel speed sensor cable connector to the body wiring harness connector.
22. If equipped, install the satellite receiver or amplifier to rear floor pan.
23. Install the rear floor pan silencer.
24. Install the cargo floor cover.

BRAKES

BLEEDING THE BRAKE SYSTEM

BLEEDING PROCEDURE

BLEEDING PROCEDURE

1. The following wheel sequence for bleeding the brake hydraulic system should be used to ensure adequate removal of all trapped air from the hydraulic system:
   - Left rear wheel
   - Right front wheel
   - Right rear wheel
   - Left front wheel
2. Attach a clear plastic hose (1) to the bleeder screw and feed the hose into a clear jar (2) containing enough fresh brake fluid to submerge the end of the hose.
3. Have a helper pump the brake pedal three or four times and hold it in the down position.
4. With the pedal in the down position, open the bleeder screw at least one full turn.
5. Once the brake pedal has dropped, close the bleeder screw. After the bleeder screw is closed, release the brake pedal.
6. Repeat the above steps until all trapped air is removed from that wheel circuit (usually four or five times).
7. Bleed the remaining wheel circuits in the same manner until all air is removed from the brake system. Monitor the fluid level in the master cylinder reservoir (2) to make sure it does not go dry.
8. Check and adjust brake fluid level to the FULL mark.
9. Check the brake pedal travel. If pedal travel is excessive or has not improved, some air may still be trapped in

the system. Re-bleed the brakes as necessary.
10. Test drive the vehicle to verify the brakes are operating properly and pedal feel is correct.

MASTER CYLINDER BLEEDING

See Figure 4.

1. Clamp the master cylinder in a vise with soft-jaw caps.
2. Attach the special tools for bleeding the master cylinder in the following fashion:
   a. Thread Special Tool 8822-2 Bleeder Tube Adapters into the primary and secondary outlet ports of the master cylinder. Tighten the Adapters to 150 inch lbs. (17 Nm).
   b. Thread Special Tool 8358-1 Bleeder Tube into each Adapter. Tighten tube nuts to 150 inch lbs. (17 Nm).
   c. Flex each Bleeder Tube and place the open ends into the neck of the master cylinder reservoir. Position the open ends of the tubes into the reservoir so their outlets are below the surface of the brake fluid in the reservoir when filled.

➡ **Make sure the ends of the Bleeder Tubes stay below the surface of the brake fluid in the reservoir at all times during the bleeding procedure.**

3. Fill the brake fluid reservoir with fresh Mopar® Brake Fluid DOT 3 Motor Vehicle, or equivalent.
4. Using an appropriately sized wooden dowel as a pushrod, slowly press the pis-

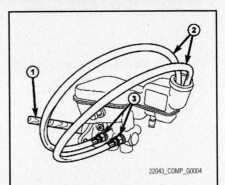

Fig. 4 The master cylinder shown with Bleeder Tube Adapters (3) and Bleeder Tubes (2) installed when bleeding the master cylinder.

tons inward discharging brake fluid through the Bleeder Tubes, then release the pressure, allowing the pistons to return to the released position. Repeat this several times until all air bubbles are expelled from the master cylinder bore and Bleeder Tubes.

5. Remove the Bleeder Tubes and Adapters from the master cylinder and plug the master cylinder outlet ports.
6. Install the fill cap on the reservoir.
7. Remove the master cylinder from the vise.
8. Install the master cylinder on the vehicle.

BLEEDING THE ABS SYSTEM

The ABS must always be bled anytime it is suspected that the Hydraulic Control Unit has ingested air.

1. Make sure all hydraulic fluid lines are installed and properly torqued.

2. Connect the scan tool to the diagnostics connector. The diagnostic connector is located under the lower steering column cover to the left of the steering column.

3. Using the scan tool, check to make sure the ABM does not have any fault codes stored. If it does, clear them.

4. Follow the standard brake bleeding procedure listed above.

5. Using the diagnostic scan tool, select ECU VIEW, followed by ABS MISCELLANEOUS FUNCTIONS to access bleeding. Follow the instructions displayed. When finished, disconnect the scan tool and proceed.

6. Bleed the brake system a second time. Check brake fluid level in the reservoir periodically to prevent emptying, causing air to enter the hydraulic system.

7. Fill the master cylinder fluid reservoir to the FULL level.

8. Test drive the vehicle to be sure the brakes are operating correctly and that the brake pedal does not feel spongy.

BRAKES

✳✳ CAUTION

Dust and dirt accumulating on brake parts during normal use may contain asbestos fibers from production or aftermarket brake linings. Breathing excessive concentrations of asbestos fibers can cause serious bodily harm. Exercise care when servicing brake parts. Do not sand or grind brake lining unless equipment used is designed to contain the dust residue. Do not clean brake parts with compressed air or by dry brushing. Cleaning should be done by dampening the brake components with a fine mist of water, then wiping the brake components clean with a dampened cloth. Dispose of cloth and all residue containing asbestos fibers in an impermeable container with the appropriate label. Follow practices prescribed by the Occupational Safety and Health Administration (OSHA) and the Environmental Protection Agency (EPA) for the handling, processing, and disposing of dust or debris that may contain asbestos fibers.

BRAKE CALIPER

REMOVAL & INSTALLATION

See Figures 5 and 6.

1. Using a brake pedal holding tool as shown, depress the brake pedal past its first 1 inch (25 mm) of travel and hold it in this position. This will isolate the master cylinder from the brake hydraulic system and will not allow the brake fluid to drain out of the master cylinder reservoir when the lines are opened.

2. Raise and safely support the vehicle.

3. Remove the front wheel.

4. Remove the banjo bolt holding the brake hose to the brake caliper.

➡There are two washers that will come off with the banjo bolt. Discard the washers.

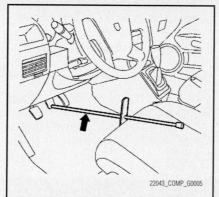

Fig. 5 Use a brake pedal holding tool to depress the brake pedal when disconnecting brake hoses.

5. Remove the caliper guide pin bolts.

6. Slide the caliper assembly from the adapter bracket and brake pads to remove.

To install:

7. Using a C-clamp, completely retract the caliper piston back into the bore of the caliper.

FRONT DISC BRAKES

✳✳ WARNING

Place a block of wood over the piston before using the C-clamp to prevent damage to the piston.

➡When installing the caliper guide pin bolts, ensure the one with the special sleeve on the end is installed in the upper mounting hole.

8. Install the caliper assembly over the brake pads on the caliper adapter bracket.

9. Align the guide pin bolt hose with the adapter bracket. Install the guide pin bolts and tighten to 32 ft. lbs. (43 Nm).

10. Reconnect the brake hose using the banjo bolt and two **new** washers. Tighten the banjo bolt to 18 ft. lbs. (24 Nm).

11. Install the front wheel.

12. Lower the vehicle.

13. Remove the brake pedal holding tool.

14. Bleed the brake system if necessary.

15. Test drive the vehicle to ensure proper brake operation.

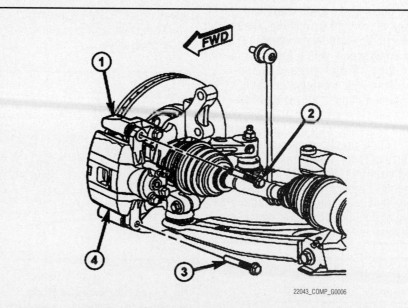

Fig. 6 Remove the guide pins (2,3) to remove the caliper (4) from the adapter bracket (1)—Front caliper assembly

DISC BRAKE PADS

REMOVAL & INSTALLATION

See Figure 7.

1. Raise and safely support the vehicle.
2. Remove the front tire.
3. Remove the two brake caliper guide pin bolts.
4. Remove the brake caliper from the adapter brake and secure with mechanics wire or equivalent.

✳✳ WARNING

Do not let the caliper hang by the brake hose.

5. Remove the brake pads from the caliper bracket.

To install:

6. Install the brake pads in the brake shims clipped into the caliper adapter

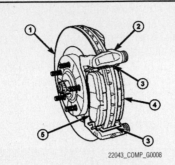

22043_COMP_G0008

Fig. 7 Install the brake pads (4,5) into the brake shims (3) in the adapter bracket (2). Place the wear indicator (4) pad on the inboard side—Front brake assembly shown

bracket. Place the pad with the wear indicator on the inboard side.

7. Using a C-clamp, completely retract the caliper piston back into the bore of the caliper.

✳✳ WARNING

Place a block of wood over the piston before using the C-clamp to prevent damage to the piston.

8. Install the caliper over the brake pads on the caliper adapter bracket.

➡ **When installing the caliper guide pin bolts, ensure the one with the special sleeve on the end is installed in the upper mounting hole.**

9. Align the guide pin bolt hose with the adapter bracket. Install the guide pin bolts and tighten to 32 ft. lbs. (43 Nm).
10. Install the front wheel.
11. Lower the vehicle.
12. Pump the pedal several times to set the pads to the brake rotor.
13. Test drive the vehicle to ensure proper brake operation.

BRAKES

✳✳ CAUTION

Dust and dirt accumulating on brake parts during normal use may contain asbestos fibers from production or aftermarket brake linings. Breathing excessive concentrations of asbestos fibers can cause serious bodily harm. Exercise care when servicing brake parts. Do not sand or grind brake lining unless equipment used is designed to contain the dust residue. Do not clean brake parts with compressed air or by dry brushing. Cleaning should be done by dampening the brake components with a fine mist of water, then wiping the brake components clean with a dampened cloth. Dispose of cloth and all residue containing asbestos fibers in an impermeable container with the appropriate label. Follow practices prescribed by the Occupational Safety and Health Administration (OSHA) and the Environmental Protection Agency (EPA) for the handling, processing, and disposing of dust or debris that may contain asbestos fibers.

BRAKE CALIPER

REMOVAL & INSTALLATION

See Figures 5 and 8.

1. Using a brake pedal holding tool as shown, depress the brake pedal past its first

1 inch (25 mm) of travel and hold it in this position. This will isolate the master cylinder from the brake hydraulic system and will not allow the brake fluid to drain out of the master cylinder reservoir when the lines are opened.

2. Raise and safely support the vehicle.
3. Remove the front wheel.
4. Loosen the brake tube nut at the rear brake hose.
5. Remove the clip holding the rear brake hose to the trailing link bracket, and remove the brake hose from the bracket.
6. Loosen and remove the brake hose from the brake caliper.

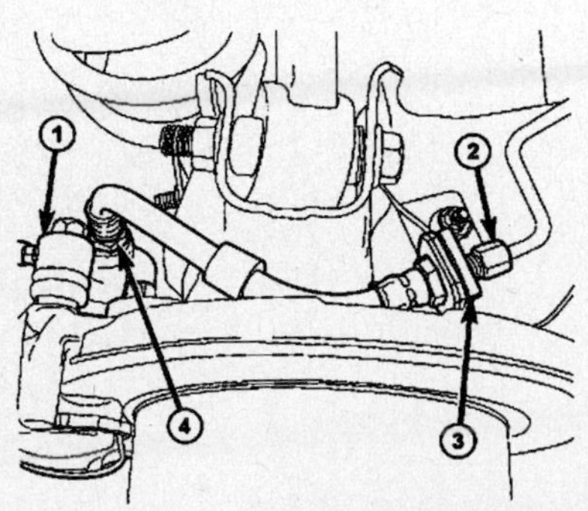

22043_COMP_G0007

Fig. 8 Loosen the brake tube nut (2), remove the clip (3), and loosen the brake hose connection (4) to disconnect it from the caliper (1)—Rear brake caliper

REAR DISC BRAKES

➡ **When removing the caliper guide pin bolts, note the location of the bolt with the special sleeve on the tip. Depending on the build date, this special sleeve bolt can be located in either the top or bottom location. It must be reinstalled in its original position.**

7. Remove the caliper guide pin bolts.
8. Slide and remove the caliper assembly with the outboard brake pad attached.
9. Remove the outboard brake pad from the caliper by prying the pad retaining clip over the raised area on the caliper.

To install:

10. Using a C-clamp, completely retract the caliper piston back into the bore of the caliper.

✳✳ WARNING

Place a block of wood over the piston before using the C-clamp to prevent damage to the piston.

11. Slide the outboard brake pad onto the caliper. Be sure the retaining clip is squarely seated in the depressed areas on the caliper beyond the raised retaining bead.
12. Install the caliper with outboard brake pad attached over the inboard brake pad and rotor, onto the brake caliper adapter bracket.

➡ **When installing the caliper guide pin bolts, make sure the bolts are put back in the same locations as when removed.**

13. Align the caliper guide pin bolt holes with the adapter bracket. Install the caliper guide pin bolts and tighten to 32 ft. lbs. (43 Nm).

14. Inspect the outboard brake pad to make sure it is correctly positioned. The retaining clip must be squarely seated in the depressed areas on the caliper fingers. Also, the nubs on the pad's steel backing plate must be fully seated in the depressions formed into the inside of the caliper fingers. There should be no gap between the pad backing plate and the caliper fingers.

15. Thread the brake hose connection into the brake caliper. Tighten the hose fitting at the caliper to 133 inch lbs. (15 Nm).

16. Route and install the brake hose into the trailing link mounted bracket and install the clip to secure it.

17. Thread the brake tube nut into brake hose and tighten to 150 inch lbs. (17 Nm).

18. Install the rear wheel.
19. Lower the vehicle.
20. Remove the brake pedal holding tool.
21. Bleed the brake system if necessary.
22. Test drive the vehicle to ensure proper brake operation.

DISC BRAKE PADS

REMOVAL & INSTALLATION

See Figure 9.

1. Raise and safely support the vehicle.
2. Remove the rear wheel.
3. Remove the brake caliper lower guide pin bolt.
4. Rotate the caliper upward, using the top guide bolt as a hinge. Hang the caliper assembly with mechanics wire or equivalent.

✳✳ WARNING

Do not let the caliper hang by the brake hose.

5. Remove the inboard brake pad from the caliper adapter bracket.
6. Remove the outboard brake pad from the caliper by prying the retaining clip over the raised area on the caliper.

To install:

7. Using a C-clamp, completely retract the caliper piston back into the bore of the caliper.

✳✳ WARNING

Place a block of wood over the piston before using the C-clamp to prevent damage to the piston.

➡The brake pad with the wear indicator should be installed on the inboard side. The wear indicator should be positioned at the bottom when installed.

8. Slide the outboard pad onto the caliper. Ensure the retaining clip is seated properly in the depressed areas of the caliper.

9. Place the inboard pad in the brake shims clipped into the caliper adapter bracket.

10. Rotate the caliper assembly downward over the rotor into the caliper adapter bracket.

11. Install the lower guide pin bolt and tighten to 32 ft. lbs. (43 Nm).

12. Inspect the outboard brake pad to make sure it is correctly positioned. The retaining clip must be squarely seated in the depressed areas on the caliper fingers. Also, the nubs on the pad's steel backing plate must be fully seated in the depressions formed into the inside of the caliper fingers. There should be no gap between the pad backing plate and the caliper fingers.

13. Install the rear wheel.
14. Lower the vehicle.
15. Pump the pedal several times to set the pads to the brake rotor.
16. Test drive the vehicle to ensure proper brake operation.

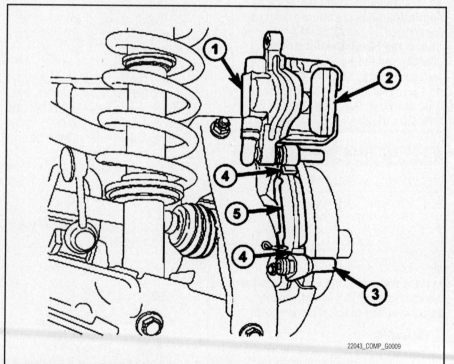

22043_COMP_G0009

Fig. 9 Remove the inboard pad (5) from the adapter bracket (3) and remove the outboard pad (2) from the caliper (1)—Rear brake assembly

✳✳ CAUTION

Dust and dirt accumulating on brake parts during normal use may contain asbestos fibers from production or aftermarket brake linings. Breathing excessive concentrations of asbestos fibers can cause serious bodily harm. Exercise care when servicing brake parts. Do not sand or grind brake lining unless equipment used is designed to contain the dust residue. Do not clean brake parts with compressed air or by dry brushing. Cleaning should be done by dampening the brake components with a fine mist of water, then wiping the brake components clean with a dampened cloth. Dispose of cloth and all residue containing asbestos fibers in an impermeable container with the appropriate label. Follow practices prescribed by the Occupational Safety and Health Administration (OSHA) and the Environmental Protection Agency (EPA) for the handling, processing, and disposing of dust or debris that may contain asbestos fibers.

BRAKE DRUM

REMOVAL & INSTALLATION

1. Raise and safely support the vehicle.
2. Remove the rear wheel.
3. Slide the brake drum off the wheel mounting studs of the hub and bearing and remove it from the vehicle.

➡ If the drum does not come off, further brake clearance can be obtained by backing off the brake adjuster screw.

To install:

4. Remove any building formed along the outer edge of the drum's braking surface.
5. Slide the brake drum on the wheel mounting studs.
6. Install the rear wheel.
7. Lower the vehicle.
8. Test drive the vehicle, stopping in both forward and reverse directions.

➡ The automatic-adjuster will continue to adjust the brakes as necessary during the road test.

BRAKE SHOES

REMOVAL & INSTALLATION

See Figures 10 through 13.

1. Raise and safely support the vehicle.
2. Remove the rear wheel.
3. Remove the brake drum. For additional information, refer to the following section, "Brake Drum, Removal & Installation."
4. Remove the lower shoe spring.
5. Compress and remove the hold-down spring retaining the rear shoe to the support plate.
6. Pull the rear shoe away from the anchor allowing better access to the parking brake cable connection at the lever.
7. Compress the cable return spring, then remove the parking brake cable from the parking brake lever.
8. Compress and remove the hold-down spring retaining the front shoe to the support plate.
9. Remove both brake shoes from the wheel cylinder.
10. Remove both shoes and remaining parts as an assembly through the opening between the wheel cylinder and support plate hub and bearing.
11. Place the shoe assembly outboard-side-up on a flat surface.
12. Remove the adjuster spring from the leading shoe and the lever pawl.
13. Remove the lever pawl from the pivot on the rear shoe.
14. Flip the shoe assembly over to show the inboard side.
15. Remove the upper shoe return spring.
16. Remove the adjuster from the shoes and parking brake lever.

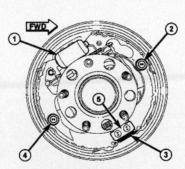

1. Wheel Cylinder
2. Front Shoe Hold-down Spring
3. Lower shoe spring
4. Rear Shoe Hold-down Spring

22043_CALI_G0001

Fig. 10 Rear Drum Brake Components—Wheel Cylinder (1), Front Shoe Hold-down Spring (2), Lower shoe spring (3), Rear Shoe Hold-down Spring (4)

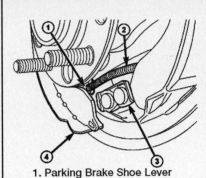

1. Parking Brake Shoe Lever
2. Parking Brake Cable
3. Anchor
4. Rear Shoe

22043_CALI_G0002

Fig. 11 Rear Drum Brake Components—Parking Brake Shoe Lever (1), Parking Brake Cable (2), Anchor (3), Rear Shoe (4)

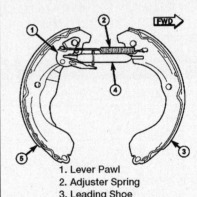

1. Lever Pawl
2. Adjuster Spring
3. Leading Shoe
4. Adjuster
5. Rear Shoe

22043_CALI_G0003

Fig. 12 Rear Drum Brake Components—Lever Pawl (1), Adjuster Spring (2), Leading Shoe (3), Adjuster (4), Rear Shoe (5)

To install:

17. Lubricate shoe contact areas on support plate and anchor using Mopar® Brake Lubricant or equivalent.
18. Lubricate the adjuster screw threads with Mopar® Brake Lubricant or equivalent. Turn adjuster wheel in until it is completely seated.
19. Place one front shoe and one rear shoe inboard-side-up on a flat surface. (rear shoe has parking brake lever attached to it).
20. Install the adjuster, adjuster wheel toward the rear, between the two brake shoes. Make sure the wide notch in the rear fork aligns with the parking brake lever.
21. Install the upper return spring.

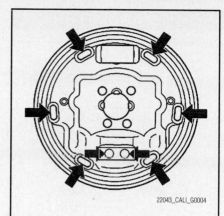

Fig. 13 Lubricate the areas indicated with Mopar®Brake Lubricant or equivalent—Rear drum brakes

22. Flip the shoe assembly over to show the outboard side.

23. Install the lever pawl onto the pivot located on the rear shoe.

24. Install the adjuster spring between the front shoe and the lever pawl.

25. Install the pre-assembled brake shoe assembly through the opening between the wheel cylinder and support plate hub and bearing.

26. Insert the upper tips of the brake shoes into the grooves of the wheel cylinder pistons.

27. Position the bottom of the front shoe against the anchor pin.

28. Install a shoe hold-down pin from the rear, through the support plate and the front shoe.

29. Compress and install the hold-down spring retaining the front shoe to the support plate.

30. Compress the parking brake cable return spring, then carefully install the cable onto the parking brake lever. Release the spring guiding it beneath the retaining tab on the lever.

31. Position the bottom of the rear shoe against the anchor pin.

32. Install a shoe hold-down pin from the rear, through the support plate and the rear shoe.

33. Compress and install the hold-down spring retaining the rear shoe to the support plate.

34. Install the lower shoe spring.

35. Adjust the brake shoes to the drum diameter using a brake shoe gauge.

36. Install the brake drum.

37. Install the rear wheel.

38. Slowly rotate both rear wheels and verify that the brake drums lightly drag on the shoes. Further adjustments may be done using the adjustment procedure as necessary.

39. Lower the vehicle.

40. Test drive the vehicle, stopping in both forward and reverse directions.

➡The automatic-adjuster will continue to adjust the brakes as necessary during the road test.

ADJUSTMENT

See Figures 14 and 15.

1. Verify the parking brake lever is fully released.

2. Raise and safely support the vehicle.

3. Remove the rear wheel.

4. Remove the brake drum.

5. Using Special Tool C-3919 or equivalent brake shoe gauge, measure the inside diameter of the brake drum at the center of the shoe contact area. Tighten the Gauge setscrew at this measurement.

6. Place the opposite side of the brake shoe gauge over the brake shoes as shown.

7. Adjust the shoe diameter to the setting on the gauge. To adjust the shoe diameter, turn the adjuster wheel using a screwdriver inserted through the adjusting hole in the rear of the shoe support plate. Once the tip of the screwdriver contacts the adjuster wheel teeth, move the handle of tool upward using the support plate as a pivot to adjust the shoes outward.

8. If at any time the adjustment needs to be backed off, perform the following:

  a. Remove the plug from the rear of the support plate below the wheel cylinder.

  b. Insert a small screwdriver through the access hole in the support plate, under the adjuster, against the lever pawl. The pawl is attached to and pivots from the rear brake shoe.

  c. While pushing on the pawl with the screwdriver to disengage it from the

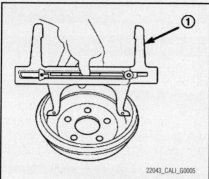

Fig. 14 Measure the inside diameter of the brake drum using a brake shoe gauge (1)

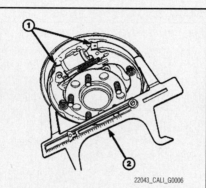

Fig. 15 Place the opposite side of the brake shoe gauge (2) over the brake shoes

adjuster wheel teeth, rotate the wheel upward to back off the adjustment using another screwdriver or a brake adjuster tool.

9. Once the shoe diameter is set, remove the tool and install the brake drum.

10. Turn the brake drum. A slight drag should be felt while rotating the drum. If not, repeat the above procedure.

11. Install the rear wheel.

12. Lower the vehicle.

13. Apply and release the parking brake lever one time after the adjustment process is completed checking parking brake operation.

14. Test drive the vehicle, stopping in both forward and reverse directions.

➡The automatic-adjuster will continue to adjust the brakes as necessary during the road test.

PARKING BRAKE CABLES

ADJUSTMENT

Parking brake cable adjustment is controlled by an automatic tensioner mechanism. The only adjustment possible is to the parking brake shoes using the star wheel adjuster. For additional information, refer to the following section, "Parking Brake Shoes, Removal & Installation."

PARKING BRAKE SHOES

REMOVAL & INSTALLATION

See Figures 16 through 18.

1. Raise and safely support the vehicle.
2. Remove the rear wheel.
3. Remove the caliper assembly. For additional information, refer to the following section, "Rear Disc Brakes, Brake Caliper, Removal & Installation."
4. Remove any clips from the wheels studs and remove the brake rotor.
5. Turn the brake shoe adjuster wheel until the adjuster is at the shortest length.
6. Remove the upper return spring from the anchor pin and rear brake shoe.
7. Remove the second upper return spring from the anchor pin and front brake shoe.
8. Remove the brake shoe hold-down springs and pins. Rotate the pins 90° to disengage and remove.
9. Remove the parking brake cable from the lever on the rear parking brake shoe.
10. Remove the brake shoes, adjuster and lower return spring as an assembly from the support plate.
11. If necessary, remove the strut.
12. Remove the lower return spring and adjuster from the shoes.

To install:

13. Install the lower return spring and adjuster between the parking brake shoes. The rear shoe will have the lever mounted on the inside. Make sure the threaded portion of the adjuster is mounted to the left on both right and left side parking brake assemblies.

14. If necessary, place the strut above the hub on the vehicle. The curved end of the strut is positioned to the rear.
15. Install the assembled brake shoes, adjuster and lower return spring over the hub and onto the support plate and anchor. Be sure to install the strut between the front shoe and the lever on the rear shoe.
16. Install the parking brake cable onto the lever on the parking brake shoe.
17. Install the brake hold-down springs and pins. Rotate the pins 90° to engage.

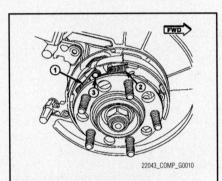

Fig. 16 Remove the upper return springs (1,2) from the anchor pin (3) and brake shoes—Parking brake assembly

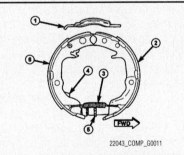

Fig. 17 Exploded view of the LEFT side parking brake assembly—Strut (1), Brake shoes (2,6), Lower return spring (3), Adjuster (5)

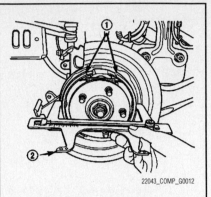

Fig. 18 Adjust the parking brake shoes (1) until linings touch the jaws of the gauge, set to the measurement (2) of the inside of the brake drum portion of the rotor— Parking brake adjustment

18. Install the front upper return spring hooking the front brake shoe and over the anchor pin.
19. Install the front upper return spring hooking the rear brake shoe and over the anchor pin.
20. Adjust the parking brake shows as follows:

   a. Using Special Tool C-3919 Brake Shoe Gauge or equivalent, measure the inside diameter of parking brake drum portion of rotor. Set the Gauge.

   b. Place the gauge over the parking brake shoes at their widest point.

   c. Using the adjuster wheel, adjust the parking brake shoes until the linings on both parking brake shoes just touch the jaws on the gauge.

21. Install the rotor.
22. Install the caliper assembly. Tighten the lower guide pin bolt to 32 ft. lbs. (43 Nm).
23. Install the rear wheel.
24. Lower the vehicle.
25. Verify proper operation of the parking brake.

CHASSIS ELECTRICAL   AIR BAG (SUPPLEMENTAL RESTRAINT SYSTEM)

GENERAL INFORMATION

✳✳ CAUTION

These vehicles are equipped with an air bag system. The system must be disarmed before performing service on, or around, system components, the steering column, instrument panel components, wiring and sensors. Failure to follow the safety precautions and the disarming procedure could result in accidental air bag deployment, possible injury and unnecessary system repairs.

SERVICE PRECAUTIONS

Disconnect and isolate the battery negative cable before beginning any airbag system component diagnosis, testing, removal, or installation procedures. Allow system capacitor to discharge for two minutes before beginning any component service. This will disable the airbag system. Failure to disable the airbag system may result in accidental airbag deployment, personal injury, or death.

Do not place an intact undeployed airbag face down on a solid surface. The airbag will propel into the air if accidentally deployed and may result in personal injury or death.

When carrying or handling an undeployed airbag, the trim side (face) of the airbag should be pointing towards the body to minimize possibility of injury if accidental deployment occurs. Failure to do this may result in personal injury or death.

Replace airbag system components with OEM replacement parts. Substitute parts may appear interchangeable, but internal differences may result in inferior occupant protection. Failure to do so may result in occupant personal injury or death.

Wear safety glasses, rubber gloves, and long sleeved clothing when cleaning powder residue from vehicle after an airbag deployment. Powder residue emitted from a deployed airbag can cause skin irritation. Flush affected area with cool water if irritation is experienced. If nasal or throat irritation is experienced, exit the vehicle for fresh air until the irritation ceases. If irritation continues, see a physician.

Do not use a replacement airbag that is not in the original packaging. This may result in improper deployment, personal injury, or death.

The factory installed fasteners, screws and bolts used to fasten airbag components have a special coating and are specifically designed for the airbag system. Do not use substitute fasteners. Use only original equipment fasteners listed in the parts catalog when fastener replacement is required.

During, and following, any child restraint anchor service, due to impact event or vehicle repair, carefully inspect all mounting hardware, tether straps, and anchors for proper installation, operation, or damage. If a child restraint anchor is found damaged in any way, the anchor must be replaced. Failure to do this may result in personal injury or death.

Deployed and non-deployed airbags may or may not have live pyrotechnic material within the airbag inflator.

Do not dispose of driver/passenger/curtain airbags or seat belt tensioners unless you are sure of complete deployment. Refer to the Hazardous Substance Control System for proper disposal.

Dispose of deployed airbags and tensioners consistent with state, provincial, local, and federal regulations.

After any airbag component testing or service, do not connect the battery negative cable. Personal injury or death may result if the system test is not performed first.

If the vehicle is equipped with the Occupant Classification System (OCS), do not connect the battery negative cable before performing the OCS Verification Test using the scan tool and the appropriate diagnostic information. Personal injury or death may result if the system test is not performed properly.

Never replace both the Occupant Restraint Controller (ORC) and the Occupant Classification Module (OCM) at the same time. If both require replacement, replace one, then perform the Airbag System test before replacing the other.

Both the ORC and the OCM store Occupant Classification System (OCS) calibration data, which they transfer to one another when one of them is replaced. If both are replaced at the same time, an irreversible fault will be set in both modules and the OCS may malfunction and cause personal injury or death.

If equipped with OCS, the Seat Weight Sensor is a sensitive, calibrated unit and must be handled carefully. Do not drop or handle roughly. If dropped or damaged, replace with another sensor. Failure to do so may result in occupant injury or death.

If equipped with OCS, the front passenger seat must be handled carefully as well. When removing the seat, be careful when setting on floor not to drop. If dropped, the sensor may be inoperative, could result in occupant injury, or possibly death.

If equipped with OCS, when the passenger front seat is on the floor, no one should sit in the front passenger seat. This uneven force may damage the sensing ability of the seat weight sensors. If sat on and damaged, the sensor may be inoperative, could result in occupant injury, or possibly death.

DISARMING THE SYSTEM

Disconnect and isolate the negative battery cable. Wait two minutes to allow the system capacitor to discharge before servicing the vehicle.

ARMING THE SYSTEM

Reconnect the negative battery cable.

CLOCKSPRING CENTERING

See Figure 19.

1. Place the front wheels in the straight-ahead position and inhibit the steering column shaft from rotation.
2. Remove the steering wheel from the steering shaft.
3. Rotate the clockspring rotor clockwise to the end of its travel. Do not apply excessive torque.
4. From the end of the clockwise travel, rotate the rotor about two and one-half turns counterclockwise. Turn the rotor slightly clockwise or counterclockwise as necessary so that the clockspring airbag pigtail wires and connector receptacle are at the top and the dowel pin is at the bottom.
5. The clockspring is now centered. Secure the clockspring rotor to the clockspring case using a locking pin or some similar device to maintain clockspring centering until the steering wheel is reinstalled on the steering column.

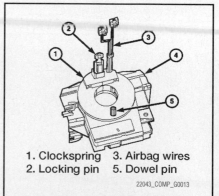

1. Clockspring   3. Airbag wires
2. Locking pin   5. Dowel pin

22043_COMP_G0013

Fig. 19 Rotate the clockspring (1) so the airbag wires (3) is at the top and dowel pin (5) is at the bottom. Secure the clockspring with a locking pin (2).

DRIVETRAIN

AUTOMATIC TRANSAXLE ASSEMBLY

REMOVAL & INSTALLATION

See Figures 20 through 23.

1. Disconnect the negative battery cable.
2. Drain the cooling system.
3. Drain the automatic transaxle.
4. Remove the air intake assembly.
5. Remove the battery.
6. Remove the battery tray.
7. Remove the air intake tube and vacuum supply lines.
8. Remove the shifter cable and mounting bracket.
9. Remove the coolant lines from the CVT fluid cooler.
10. Remove the heater hose from the CVT fluid cooler.
11. Remove the speed sensor connector.
12. Disconnect and remove the wiring harness from the top of the transaxle.
13. Remove the transmission vent tube.
14. Remove the throttle body support bracket.
15. Remove the upper bell housing bolts.
16. Remove the upper transmission mounting bolts, the upper transmission mount through-bolt and upper transmission bolt.
17. Raise and safely support the vehicle.
18. Remove the left and right front lower splash shield.
19. Remove the lower splash shield, if equipped.
20. Support the transaxle assembly with a suitable jack.
21. Remove the starter. For additional information, refer to the following section, "Starter, Removal & Installation."

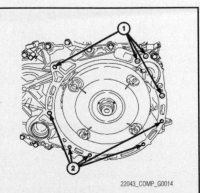

Fig. 20 View of the upper (1) and lower (2) bell housing bolts—Automatic Transaxle

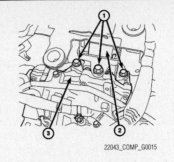

22043_COMP_G0015

Fig. 21 View of the transaxle (3) upper mounting bolts (1) and upper mount (2)— Automatic Transaxle

22. Remove the transaxle fill tube by removing the two mounting bolts.
23. Remove the both front wheels.
24. Remove the left and right halfshafts. For additional information, refer to the following section, "Front halfshafts, Removal & Installation."
25. Remove the torque converter inspection cover.
26. Matchmark the torque converter to the flexplate for the correct alignment during installation.
27. Remove the torque converter bolts and discard the bolts.
28. Support the engine with a suitable jack.
29. Remove the front transaxle mount through-bolt.
30. Remove the transaxle crossmember mounting bolts and remove the crossmember.
31. Remove the transaxle rear mount through-bolt.
32. Remove the rear mount-to-transaxle bolts.
33. Remove the transfer case, if equipped. For additional information, refer to Transfer Case.
34. Remove the lower transaxle bell housing bolts.
35. Carefully lower the transaxle assembly from the vehicle.

To install:

➡**Ensure that both alignment pins are present into the engine before installing the transaxle.**

36. Raise the transaxle assembly in the vehicle using a suitable jack.
37. Install the lower transaxle bell housing bolts and tighten to 35 ft. lbs. (48 Nm).
38. Connect the transaxle cooler lines.
39. Install the transaxle crossmember

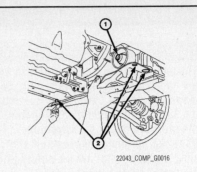

22043_COMP_G0016

Fig. 22 Location of the front transaxle mount through-bolt and transaxle crossmember bolts—Automatic Transaxle

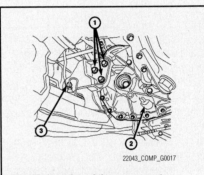

22043_COMP_G0017

Fig. 23 Location of the rear mount through-bolt (3) and rear mount-to-transaxle bolts (1)—Automatic Transaxle

and tighten the mounting bolts to 55 ft. lbs. (75 Nm).
40. Install the through bolt at the front transaxle mount and tighten to 55 ft. lbs. (75 Nm).
41. Install the rear mount through-bolt and tighten to 55 ft. lbs. (75 Nm).
42. Install the rear mount-to-transaxle and tighten to 55 ft. lbs. (75 Nm).
43. Install new torque converter bolts and tighten to 35 ft. lbs. (48 Nm).
44. Install the torque converter inspection cover.
45. Install the transfer case, if equipped.
46. Install the splash shields.
47. Install the halfshafts.
48. Install the front wheels.
49. Lower the vehicle.
50. Install the upper bell housing bolts and tighten to 35 ft. lbs. (48 Nm).
51. Install the upper mount bolts and tighten to 55 ft. lbs. (75 Nm).
52. Install the upper mount through-bolt and tighten to 55 ft. lbs. (75 Nm).
53. Install the throttle body support bracket and tighten the bolts to 105 inch lbs. (11 Nm).

54. The remainder of the installation is the reverse order of removal.

55. Tighten the transaxle fill tube bolts to 79 inch lbs. (9 Nm).

56. Refill the transaxle with fluid to the correct level.

57. Refill the cooling system to the correct level.

58. Test drive the vehicle for proper operation and check for leaks.

MANUAL TRANSAXLE ASSEMBLY

REMOVAL & INSTALLATION

See Figures 24 through 27.

1. Remove the splash shields and drain the transaxle fluid.
2. Disconnect the negative battery cable.
3. Remove the engine appearance cover.
4. Remove the air intake assembly.
5. Unplug the speed sensor connector.
6. Disconnect the back-up lamp switch.
7. Remove the shift cables from the bracket clips.
8. Disconnect the shift selector and crossover cable from the levers. Remove the cables and secure them out of the way.
9. Remove the slave cylinder hose from the bracket.
10. Remove the air inlet tube from the throttle body.
11. Remove the throttle body support bracket.
12. Remove the upper bell housing bolts.
13. Remove the starter mounting bolts and secure the starter out of the way.
14. Support the transaxle with a suitable jack.
15. Loosen the left-upper transaxle mount through-bolt.
16. Remove the transaxle mount bolts.
17. Raise and safely support the vehicle.
18. Remove the halfshafts. For additional information, see Front Halfshaft
19. Remove the transfer case, if equipped.
20. Support the engine with a suitable jack.
21. Support the transaxle with a suitable transmission jack.
22. Remove the bell housing dust cover.
23. Remove four modular clutch-to-drive plate bolts. While removing bolts, one tight-tolerance (slotted) drive plate hole will be encountered. When this bolt is removed, mark drive plate and modular clutch assem-

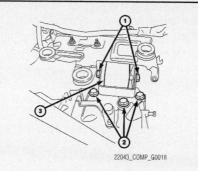

Fig. 24 Location of the left-upper transaxle mount through-bolt (1) and transaxle mount bolts (2)—Manual Transaxle

bly at this location, and be sure to align marks upon reassembly.

24. Remove the front transaxle mount through-bolt.
25. Remove the transaxle crossmember mounting bolts and remove the crossmember.
26. Remove the rear transaxle through-bolt.
27. Remove the rear transaxle mount bolts and mount from the frame.
28. Remove the rear transaxle mount bracket bolts and bracket from the transaxle.
29. Remove the remaining transaxle bell housing bolts.
30. Carefully lower the engine/transaxle assembly on the two jacks until the enough clearance is obtained to remove the transaxle.
31. Obtain a helper to assist in holding transaxle assembly while removing transaxle-to-engine mounting bolts.
32. Remove the transaxle from the vehicle.

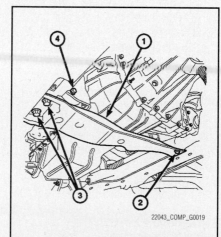

Fig. 25 Location of the front transaxle through-bolt (4) and transaxle crossmember mounting bolts (2,3) and crossmember (1)—Manual Transaxle

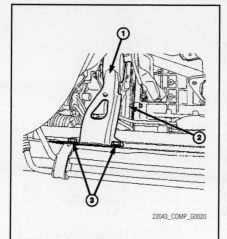

Fig. 26 Location of the rear transaxle mount (1), mount bracket (2), and transaxle mount bolts (3)—Manual Transaxle

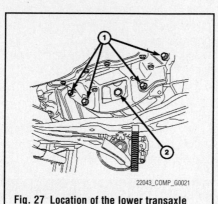

Fig. 27 Location of the lower transaxle bell housing bolts—Manual Transaxle

To install:

33. Using a suitable transmission jack, raise the transaxle assembly into position.
34. Install the transaxle bell housing bolts and tighten to 35 ft. lbs. (48 Nm).
35. Install the transfer case, if equipped.
36. Install the rear transaxle mount bracket and tighten the mounting bolts to 50 ft. lbs. (68 Nm)
37. Install the rear transaxle mount and tighten the bolts to 50 ft. lbs. (68 Nm).
38. Install the rear transaxle mount through-bolt and tighten to 50 ft. lbs. (68 Nm).
39. Install the front mount bracket to the transaxle and tighten the bolts to 50 ft. lbs. (68 Nm).
40. Install the transaxle crossmember and tighten the mounting bolts to 50 ft. lbs. (68 Nm).
41. Lower the vehicle slightly, and raise the engine/transaxle assembly until the upper mount bracket aligns with the upper mount. Tighten the upper mount bolts to 50 ft. lbs. (68 Nm).

42. Tighten the upper mount through-bolt to 50 ft. lbs. (68 Nm).

43. Remove the transaxle jack.

44. Raise and safely support the vehicle.

45. Install the four modular clutch-to-driveplate bolts. Align the driveplate and modular clutch alignment matchmarks made during the removal process. Start with the tight-tolerance (slotted) hole and install the torque bolts to 65 ft. lbs. (88 Nm).

46. Install the starter.

47. Install the bell housing dust cover.

48. Install the axle shafts.

49. Fill the transaxle with fluid to the correct level.

50. Install the splash shields.

51. Lower the vehicle.

52. Install the top remaining bell housing bolts and tighten to 35 ft. lbs. (48 Nm).

53. Connect the hydraulic clutch slave cylinder.

54. Connect the shift and selector cables to shift lever. Install the cables to the bracket clips.

55. Connector the back-up lamp connector.

56. Connect the vehicle speed sensor.

57. Install the air intake tube and air intake assembly.

58. Connect the negative battery cable.

59. Test drive the vehicle for proper operation and check for leaks.

CLUTCH

REMOVAL & INSTALLATION

1. Remove the transaxle assembly from the vehicle.

2. Remove the clutch assembly from the transaxle input shaft.

To install:

3. Install the clutch assembly onto the input shaft of the transaxle.

4. Install the transaxle assembly.

BLEEDING

1. Verify the fluid level in the brake master cylinder. Top off with DOT 3 brake fluid as necessary. Leave cap off.

2. Raise and safely support the vehicle.

3. Remove the bleed port protective cap and install suitable size and length of clear hose to monitor and divert fluid into suitable container.

4. Open up the bleed circuit by turning the thumb screw counter clockwise this will start the air purge and fluid fill process.

5. Lower the vehicle, but only enough to gain access to and fill the brake master cylinder.

➡**Do not allow the clutch master cylinder to run dry while fluid exits bleed port.**

6. Top off the brake master cylinder fluid level while air is being purged and fluid drains from the bleed port. Continue this until no air bubbles are seen and a solid column of fluid exists.

7. Close hydraulic bleed circuit, remove drain hose and replace dust cap on bleed port.

8. From driver's seat, actuate clutch pedal 60-100 times.

9. Apply the parking brake. Start engine and verify clutch operation and pedal feel. If pedal feels fine and clutch operates as designed, stop here. If pedal still feels spongy or clutch does not fully disengage, excessive air is still trapped within the system, most likely at the master cylinder.

10. Top off the brake master cylinder fluid level with DOT 3 brake fluid as necessary.

TRANSFER CASE ASSEMBLY

REMOVAL & INSTALLATION

See Figures 28 through 32.

➡**Dodge refers to the transfer case in this vehicle as the Power Transfer Unit (PTU)**

1. Disconnect the negative battery cable.

2. Remove the engine appearance cover.

3. Remove the air intake assembly.

4. Remove the Power Distribution Center (PDC) from the mounting bracket.

5. Raise and safely support the vehicle.

6. Remove the front halfshafts. For additional information, refer to following section, "Front Halfshaft, Removal & Installation."

7. Drain the transfer case fluid and reinstall the drain plug.

8. Remove the driveshaft.

9. Remove the two exhaust flange mounting bolts and disconnect the downstream O_2 sensor to separate the exhaust system.

10. Lower the vehicle.

11. Unplug the upstream O_2 sensor connector.

12. Remove the upstream O_2 sensor from the exhaust manifold.

13. Remove the exhaust manifold top and side heat shields.

14. Remove the exhaust manifold retaining bolts. Slide the exhaust manifold up and

to the right, and support the exhaust manifold with a bungee cord or equivalent.

15. Raise and safely support the vehicle.

16. Remove the engine-to-exhaust manifold bracket bolts.

17. Remove the rear engine mount through-bolt.

18. Remove the three front engine mount-to-frame bolts and mount through-bolt.

19. Remove the transfer case mounting bolts.

20. Using a suitable jack, support the engine on the front mount bracket.

21. Raise the front of the engine until the rear mount as dropped.

22. Separate the transfer case from the transaxle. Remove and discard the O-ring.

23. Roll the transfer case forward and down to remove.

To install:

24. Roll the transfer in, moving from front to back.

25. Rest the transfer case on the frame while the engine/transaxle assembly is raised into position.

26. Lower the jack on the front engine mount bracket until the rear mount through-bolt can be installed. Tighten the bolt to 55 ft. lbs. (75 Nm).

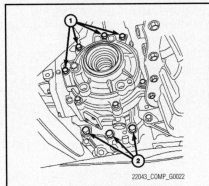

Fig. 28 Location of the upper (1) and lower (2) transfer case mounting bolts.

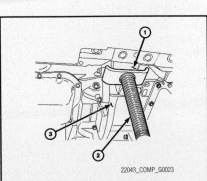

Fig. 29 Support the engine (3) using a suitable jack (2) by the front mount bracket (1)—Transfer case removal

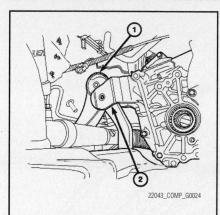

Fig. 30 Raise the front of the engine until the rear mount (1,2) has dropped—Transfer case removal

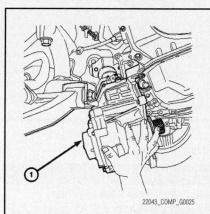

Fig. 31 Roll the transfer case (1) forward and down to remove—Transfer case removal

27. Install the transaxle crossmember and tighten the bolts to 55 ft. lbs. (75 Nm).

28. Install the front transaxle mount through-bolt and tighten to 55 ft. lbs. (75 Nm).

29. Install a new O-ring between the transfer case and transaxle.

➡Coat the O-ring in Vaseline or transaxle assembly grease.

30. Slide the transfer completely into position. Tighten the mounting bolts to 43 ft. lbs. (58 Nm).

31. Lower the vehicle.
32. Install the exhaust manifold.
33. Install the air intake assembly.
34. Install the engine appearance cover.
35. Raise and safely support the vehicle.
36. Reconnect the exhaust system.
37. Install the rear driveshaft.
38. Install the axleshaft.
39. Refill the transfer case with fluid to the correct level.
40. Lower the vehicle.
41. Connect the negative battery cable.

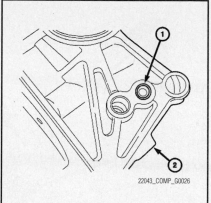

Fig. 32 Ensure the O-ring (1) between the transaxle and transfer case (2) is correct installed.

42. Refill the transaxle with fluid to the correct level if necessary.

43. Test drive the vehicle to ensure proper operation and check for leaks.

FRONT HALFSHAFT

REMOVAL & INSTALLATION

See Figures 33 through 37.

1. Place the automatic transaxle, if equipped, in PARK.
2. Disconnect the negative battery cable.
3. Raise and safely support the vehicle.
4. Remove the front wheel.
5. Remove the cotter pin, nut lock, spring washer and hub nut from the outer axle.
6. If equipped with ABS, disconnect the front speed sensor.

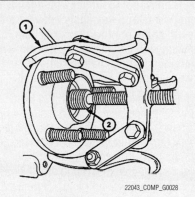

Fig. 34 If it is difficult to remove the halfshaft (2), use Special Tool 1026 (1) to pull the halfshaft out

7. Remove the ball joint retaining bolt and nut.

8. Carefully separate the ball joint stud from the steering knuckle by prying down on the lower control arm.

9. Remove the halfshaft from the steering knuckle by pulling outward on knuckle while pressing in on halfshaft. Support the outer end of halfshaft assembly. If you have difficulty in separating halfshaft from hub is encountered, do not strike shaft with hammer, instead use Special Tool 1026 Puller to separate.

10. If equipped with 2WD:
   a. Remove the halfshaft bracket from the engine lower mounting bolt.
   b. Remove the halfshaft bracket from the upper engine mounting bolts.

11. Support the outer end of the halfshaft assembly.

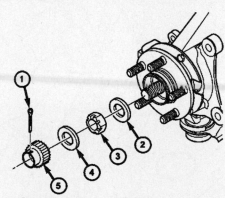

1. Cotter pin 4. Spring washer
2. Washer 5. Nut lock
3. Hub nut

Fig. 33 Exploded view of the halfshaft retaining hardware—Cotter pin (1), nut lock (5), spring washer (4) and hub nut (3) and washer (2)—Front halfshaft

➡Removal of the inner tripod joints is made easier if you apply outward pressure on the joint as you strike the punch with a hammer. Do not pull on interconnecting shaft to remove, as the inner joint will become separated.

12. Remove the inner tripod joints from the side gears of the transaxle using a punch to dislodge the inner tripod joint retaining ring from the transaxle side gear. If removing the right side inner tripod joint, position the punch to the inner tripod joint extraction groove, if equipped. Strike the punch sharply with a hammer to dislodge the right inner joint from the side gear. If removing the left side inner tripod joint, position the punch to the inner tripod joint extraction groove. Strike the punch sharply with a hammer to dislodge the left inner tripod joint from the side gear.

13. Hold the inner tripod joint and interconnecting shaft of halfshaft assembly. Remove inner tripod joint from transaxle by pulling it straight out of transaxle side gear and transaxle oil seal.

❋❋ WARNING

When removing the tripod joint, do not let spline or snap ring drag across sealing lip of the transaxle to tripod joint oil seal. When tripod joint is removed from transaxle, some fluid will leak out.

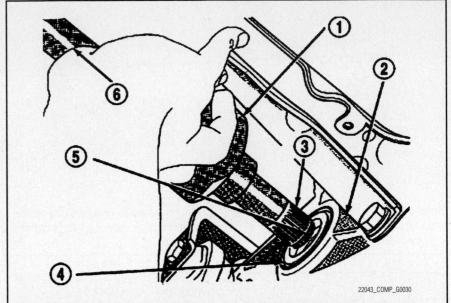

Fig. 36 Hold the inner tripod joint (1) and interconnecting shaft (6) and remove the joint by pulling it straight out of the transaxle oil seal (4)

To install:

❋❋ WARNING

The halfshaft, when installed, acts as a bolt and secures the front hub/bearing assembly. If vehicle is to be supported or moved on its wheels with a halfshaft removed, install a PROPER-SIZED BOLT AND NUT through front hub. Tighten the bolt and nut to 180 ft. lbs. (244 Nm).

This will ensure that the hub bearing cannot loosen.

14. Clean all debris from the steering knuckle opening.

❋❋ WARNING

Boot sealing is vital to retain special lubricants and to prevent foreign contaminants from entering the CV joint. Mishandling, such as allowing the assemblies to dangle unsupported, or pulling or pushing the ends can cut boots or damage CV joints. During removal and installation procedures, always support both ends of the halfshaft to prevent damage.

15. Thoroughly clean the spline and oil seal sealing surfaces on the tripod joint. Lightly lubricate the oil seal sealing surface on the tripod joint with clean transmission fluid.

16. Holding the halfshaft assembly by the tripod joint and interconnecting shaft, install the tripod joint into transaxle side gear as far as possible by hand.

17. Carefully align the tripod joint with the transaxle side gears. Then grasp the halfshaft interconnecting shaft and push tripod joint into the transaxle side gear until fully seated. Test that the snap ring is fully engaged with the side gear by attempting to remove tripod joint from transaxle by hand. If the snap ring is fully engaged with side gear, the tripod joint will not be removable by hand.

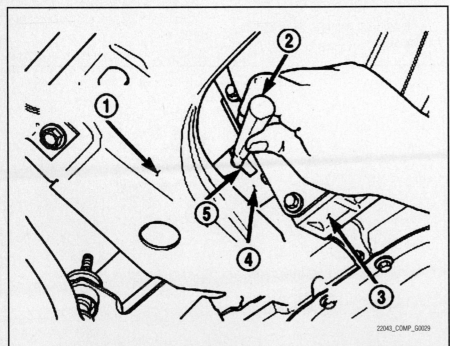

Fig. 35 Position a punch (2) to joint extraction groove (5) to remove the inner tripod joints (4) from the transaxle—Right side front halfshaft removal

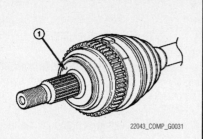

Fig. 37 Apply a light coating of Mopar® multipurpose wheel bearing grease on the facing flat surface (1) of the outer CV-joint

18. If equipped with 2WD:

a. Install the intermediate shaft bracket to the lower engine block and tighten to 55 ft. lbs. (75 Nm).

b. Install the intermediate shaft bracket to the upper engine mounting bolts and tighten to 55 ft. lbs. (75 Nm).

19. Apply a light coating of Mopar® multipurpose wheel bearing grease on the facing flat surface of the outer CV-joint.

20. Install the steering knuckle onto the ball joint stud.

➡ **At this point, the outer joint will not seat completely into the front hub. The outer joint will be pulled into hub and seated when the hub nut is installed and tightened.**

21. Install a **NEW** ball joint bolt and nut and tighten to 70 ft. lbs. (95 Nm).

22. Install the washer and hub nut and tighten the hub nut to 180 ft. lbs. (244 Nm).

23. Install the spring washer, nut lock and cotter pin.

24. Install the front wheel.

25. Inspect the transaxle fluid level.

26. Lower the vehicle.

27. Connect the negative battery cable.

CV-JOINTS OVERHAUL

Inner Joint

See Figures 38 through 42.

1. Remove the halfshaft from the vehicle.

2. Remove large boot clamp that retains inner tripod joint sealing boot to tripod joint housing and discard. Then remove small clamp that retains inner tripod joint sealing boot to interconnecting shaft and discard. Remove the sealing boot from the tripod housing and slide it down the interconnecting shaft.

✳ WARNING

When removing the spider joint from the tripod joint housing, hold the rollers in place on the spider trunions to prevent the rollers and needle bearings from falling away.

3. Slide the interconnecting shaft and spider assembly out of the tripod joint housing.

4. Remove snap ring that retains spider assembly to interconnecting shaft.

5. Remove the spider assembly from interconnecting shaft. If spider assembly will not come off interconnecting shaft by hand, it can be removed by tapping spider assembly with a brass drift. Do not hit the outer tripod bearings in an attempt to remove spider assembly from interconnecting shaft.

6. Slide the sealing boot off the interconnecting shaft.

7. Thoroughly clean and inspect the spider assembly, tripod joint housing, and interconnecting shaft for any signs of excessive wear. If any parts show signs of excessive wear, the halfshaft assembly will require replacement.

➡**Component parts of these halfshaft assemblies are not serviceable.**

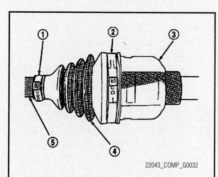

Fig. 38 Small clamp (1), Large boot clamp (2), tripod joint housing (3), sealing boot (4) and interconnecting shaft (5)

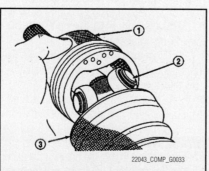

Fig. 39 Slide the interconnecting shaft and spider assembly (2) out of the tripod joint housing

---

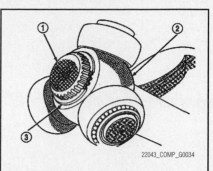

Fig. 40 Remove the snap ring (3) that holds the spider assembly (2) to the shaft (1)

To install:

➡ **The inner tripod joint sealing boots are made from two different types of material. High-temperature applications (close to exhaust system) use silicone rubber whereas standard temperature applications use Hytrel plastic. The silicone sealing boots are soft and pliable. The Hytrel sealing boots are stiff and rigid. The replacement sealing boot MUST BE the same type of material as the sealing boot that was removed.**

8. Slide the inner tripod joint seal boot retaining clamp onto the interconnecting shaft. Then slide the replacement inner tripod joint sealing boot onto interconnecting shaft. Inner tripod joint seal boot MUST be positioned on interconnecting shaft, so the raised bead on the inside of the seal boot is in groove on interconnecting shaft.

✳ WARNING

The rollers can fall off, use caution when installing the tripod

9. Install the spider assembly onto the interconnecting shaft with chamfer on the spider assembly toward the interconnecting shaft.

10. The spider assembly must be installed on the interconnecting shaft far enough to fully install spider retaining snap ring. If spider assembly will not fully install on interconnecting shaft by hand, it can be installed by tapping the spider body with a brass drift. Do not hit the outer tripod bearings in an attempt to install spider assembly on interconnecting shaft.

11. Install the spider assembly-to-interconnecting shaft retaining snap ring into the groove on end of the interconnecting shaft. Be sure the snap ring is fully seated into groove on interconnecting shaft.

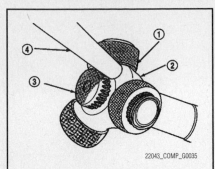

Fig. 41 If necessary, the spider assembly (2) can be installed on the shaft (3) using a brass drift (4)

12. Distribute ½ the amount of grease provided in the seal boot service package into tripod housing. Put the remaining amount into the sealing boot.

✳✳ **WARNING**

Use only the grease provided in the seal boot service package.

13. Align tripod housing with the spider assembly and then slide tripod housing over spider assembly and interconnecting shaft.

14. Install the inner tripod joint seal boot-to-interconnecting shaft clamp evenly on the sealing boot.

15. Clamp the sealing boot onto the interconnecting shaft using Special Tool C-4975-A Clamp and the following procedure. Place Clamp C-4975-A over bridge of clamp.

16. Tighten the nut on Clamp C-4975-A until jaws on the tool are closed completely together, face to face.

➡ **Seal must not be dimpled, stretched, or out-of-shape in any way. If seal is NOT shaped correctly, equalize pressure in seal and shape it by hand.**

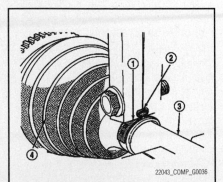

Fig. 42 Tighten the nut on Clamp C-4975-A (1) until completely closed to tighten the boot seal (2)

17. Position the sealing boot into the tripod retaining groove. Install seal boot retaining clamp evenly on sealing boot.

✳✳ **WARNING**

The following positioning procedure determines the correct air pressure inside the inner tripod joint assembly prior to clamping the sealing boot to inner tripod joint housing. If this procedure is not done prior to clamping sealing boot to tripod joint housing, boot durability can be adversely affected.

✳✳ **WARNING**

When venting the inner tripod joint assembly, use care so inner tripod sealing boot does not get punctured or, in any other way, damaged. If sealing boot is punctured or damaged while being vented, the sealing boot can not be used.

18. Insert a trim stick between the tripod and the sealing boot to vent inner tripod joint assembly. When inserting trim stick between tripod housing and sealing boot, ensure trim stick is held flat and firmly against the tripod housing. If this is not done, damage to the sealing boot can occur. If inner tripod joint has a Hytrel (hard plastic) sealing boot, be sure the trim stick is inserted between soft rubber insert and tripod housing, and not the hard plastic sealing boot and soft rubber insert.

19. With the trim stick inserted between the sealing boot and tripod joint housing, position the inner tripod joint on halfshaft until correct sealing boot edge to edge length is obtained for type of sealing boot material being used. Then remove the trim stick.

20. Clamp the tripod joint sealing boot to tripod joint using required procedure for type of boot clamp application. If seal boot uses crimp type boot clamp, clamp sealing boot onto tripod housing using Special Tool C-4975-A Clamp. Place Clamp C-4975-A over bridge of clamp.

21. Tighten the nut on Clamp C-4975-A until jaws on tool are closed completely together, face-to-face.

22. If seal boot uses low profile latching type boot clamp, clamp sealing boot onto tripod housing using Clamping Tool, Snap-On® YA3050, or equivalent. Place the prongs of Clamp Locking Tool in the holes of the clamp.

23. Squeeze tool together until top band of clamp is latched behind the two tabs on lower band of clamp.

24. Install the halfshaft onto the vehicle.

Outer Joint

See Figures 43 through 46.

1. Remove the halfshaft from the vehicle.

2. Remove the large boot clamp retaining CV-joint sealing boot to CV-joint housing and discard.

3. Remove small clamp that retains outer CV-joint sealing boot to interconnecting shaft and discard.

4. Remove sealing boot from outer CV-joint housing and slide it down interconnecting shaft.

5. Wipe away the grease to expose outer CV-joint and interconnecting shaft.

6. Remove outer CV-joint from interconnecting shaft using the following procedure: Support interconnecting shaft in a vise equipped with protective caps on jaws of vise to prevent damage to interconnecting shaft. Then, using a soft-faced hammer, sharply hit the end of the CV-joint housing to dislodge housing from internal circlip on interconnecting shaft. Then slide outer CV-joint off end of interconnecting shaft, joint may have to be tapped off shaft using a soft-faced hammer.

7. Remove large circlip from the interconnecting shaft before attempting to remove outer CV-joint sealing boot.

8. Slide the sealing boot off interconnecting shaft.

9. Thoroughly clean and inspect outer CV-joint assembly and interconnecting joint for any signs of excessive wear.

➡ **If any parts show signs of excessive wear, the halfshaft assembly will require replacement. Component parts of these halfshaft assemblies are not serviceable.**

To install:

10. Slide the new sealing boot clamp onto the interconnecting shaft. Slide the

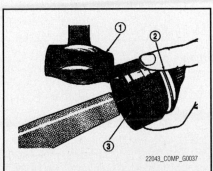

Fig. 43 Use a soft-faced hammer (1) to sharply hit the end of the CV-joint to dislodge the housing from the internal circlip (3)

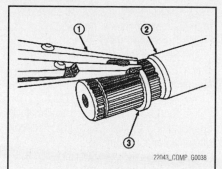

Fig. 44 Remove the large circlip (3) from the interconnecting shaft (2) using a suitable snapring pliers (1)

outer CV-joint assembly sealing boot onto the interconnecting shaft.

✱✱ WARNING

Seal boot MUST be positioned on the interconnecting shaft so the raised bead on the inside of the seal boot is in groove on the interconnecting shaft.

11. Align the splines on the interconnecting shaft with the splines on the cross of the outer CV-joint assembly and start the outer CV-joint onto interconnecting shaft.

12. Install outer CV-joint assembly onto interconnecting shaft by using a soft-faced hammer and tapping end of stub axle (with hub nut installed) until outer CV-joint is fully seated on interconnecting shaft.

13. Outer CV-joint assembly must be installed on interconnecting shaft until cross of outer CV-joint assembly is seated against circlip on interconnecting shaft.

14. Distribute ½ the amount of grease provided in the seal boot service package into tripod housing. Put the remaining amount into the sealing boot.

15. Install the outer CV-joint sealing boot-to-interconnecting shaft clamp evenly on sealing boot.

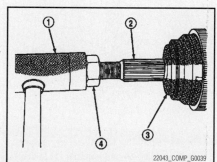

Fig. 45 Use a soft-face hammer (1) to tap the end of the stab axle (2) with the hub nut (4) installed until the CV-joint (3) is fully seated

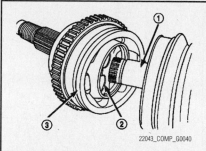

Fig. 46 Press the joint assembly (3) on the shaft until the cross (2) is seated against the circlip on the interconnecting shaft (1)

16. Clamp the sealing boot onto the interconnecting shaft using crimper, Special Tool Clamp C-4975-A and the following procedure. Place Clamp C-4975-A over bridge of clamp.

17. Tighten nut on Clamp C-4975-A until jaws on tool are closed completely together, face to face.

✱✱ CAUTION

Seal must not be dimpled, stretched, or out-of-shape in any way. If seal is NOT shaped correctly, equalize pressure in seal and shape it by hand.

18. Position the outer CV-joint sealing boot into its retaining groove on outer CV-joint housing. Install sealing boot-to-outer CV-joint retaining clamp evenly on sealing boot.

19. Clamp the sealing boot onto outer CV-joint housing using Clamp C-4975-A and the following procedure. Place Clamp C-4975-A over bridge of clamp.

20. Tighten nut on Clamp C-4975-A until jaws on tool are closed completely together, face to face.

21. Install the halfshaft onto the vehicle.

FRONT PINION SEAL

REMOVAL & INSTALLATION

➡ Since no front differential is used, the equivalent of the front pinion seal is the output flange seal on the transfer case.

1. Remove the driveshaft.
2. Using a suitable pry tool, remove the output seal.

To install:

3. Using Special Tool 9851 Installer and C-4171 Handle, drive the output shaft seal into the transfer case.
4. Install the driveshaft.

REAR DRIVESHAFT

REMOVAL & INSTALLATION

See Figures 47 and 48.

1. Raise and safely support the vehicle.
2. Matchmark the driveshaft and differential for alignment during reinstallation.

✱✱ CAUTION

Never allow driveshaft to hang while connected to transfer case, rear differential module flanges or center bearings. If propeller shaft section is hung unsupported, damage may occur to joint, boot and/or center bearing from over-angulation. This may result in vibration/balance issues.

3. Remove the rear driveshaft-to-rear axle retaining nuts.
4. Remove the three bolts from the center support heat shield.
5. Remove the heat shield.
6. Remove the two center support mounting bolts.
7. Remove the driveshaft.

To install:

8. Make sure transaxle is in Neutral (N) position.
9. Obtain a helper if needed and lift driveshaft assembly into position. Install driveshaft spline into transfer case.
10. Align marks on driveshaft with marks on rear axle flange. Slide driveshaft over studs on rear axle flange.
11. Install the four retaining nuts.
12. Raise the center support into position.
13. Install center support bolts and tighten to 30 ft. lbs. (41 Nm).
14. Install driveshaft nuts and tighten to 43 ft. lbs. (58 Nm).

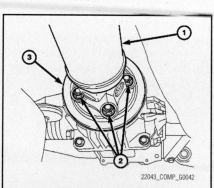

Fig. 47 Remove the driveshaft (1)-to-rear axle (3) retaining nuts (2)—Rear driveshaft

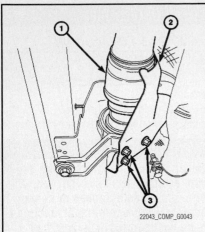

Fig. 48 Remove the mounting bolts (3) to remove the heat shield (2) from the driveshaft (1)—Rear driveshaft

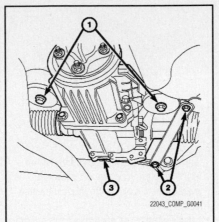

Fig. 49 Location of the two side bolts and left side stay bracket bolts (2) for the rear differential module (2)—Left side rear halfshaft removal

15. Install heat shield nuts and tighten to 15 ft. lbs. (21 Nm).

16. Check all fluid levels starting with transfer case.

REAR HALFSHAFT

REMOVAL & INSTALLATION

See Figure 49.

1. Raise and safely support the vehicle.

2. Remove the rear wheel.

3. Drain the fluid from the rear differential.

4. Remove the rear driveshaft.

5. Remove the sway bar connecting nuts and roll the sway bar down and out of the way, if equipped.

6. Remove the left and right rear halfshaft stay bracket bolts.

7. Remove the exhaust system up to the catalytic converter.

8. Support the rear differential module with a suitable jack.

9. Remove the rear bolt supporting the rear differential module.

10. Remove the two side bolts supporting the rear differential module.

11. Using the jack, lower the differential module enough to gain access to the electrical connector and bracket.

12. Remove the routing bracket bolt and unplug the electrical connector.

13. Lower the rear axle assembly.

14. Disengage the axle shaft.

15. Remove the nut and washer connecting the halfshaft to left rear hub.

16. Remove the halfshaft from the

vehicle. If it's hard to remove, use a punch and hammer to tap it out.

To install:

17. Lift the rear axle assembly as the halfshaft is being installed.

18. Install the nut and washer connecting halfshaft to the left rear hub and tighten to 180 ft. lbs. (244 Nm).

19. Connect the electrical connector, route the wiring harness into the bracket. Tighten the bracket bolts to 89 inch lbs. (10 Nm).

20. Lift the rear axle assembly completely into place.

21. Install the two differential module side bolts and tighten to 75 ft. lbs. (102 Nm).

22. Install the rear differential module rear bolt and tighten to 75 ft. lbs. (102 Nm).

23. Install the halfshaft stay bracket and tighten the bolts to 45 ft. lbs. (61 Nm).

24. Install the driveshaft.

25. Refill the rear differential module to the correct level.

26. If equipped, roll the sway bar into place and tighten the nuts to 45 ft. lbs. (61 Nm).

27. Install any exhaust components removed.

28. Install the wheel.

REAR PINION SEAL

REMOVAL & INSTALLATION

See Figures 50 and 51.

1. Raise and safely support the vehicle.

2. Remove the driveshaft.

3. Disconnect the electrical connector from the rear differential module.

4. Disconnect the breather tube.

5. Remove the electronically control clutch (ECC)-to-rear differential module mounting bolts.

6. Separate and lower the ECC.

7. Remove all of the old gasket material on the mating surfaces of the ECC and rear differential mating surfaces.

8. Remove the wave washer.

9. Remove the flange seal.

To install:

10. Coat the edge face of the seal with liquid gasket and place over the input shaft.

11. Install the wave washer.

12. Install the pinion seal using Special Tool 9931 Installer tool.

13. The remainder of the installation is the reverse order of removal. Tighten the ECC-to-rear differential to 58 ft. lbs. (78 Nm).

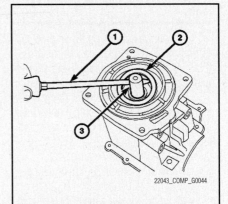

Fig. 50 Use a suitable pry tool (1) to remove the flange seal (2) from the input shaft (3).

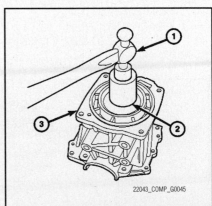

Fig. 51 Install the pinion seal using Special Tool 9931 (2) and hammer (1) to the ECC (3).

ENGINE COOLING

ENGINE FAN

REMOVAL & INSTALLATION

✳✳ CAUTION

Do not open the radiator draincock with the system hot and under pressure because serious burns from coolant can occur.

1. Disconnect the negative battery cable.
2. Drain the cooling system.
3. Remove the radiator crossmember.
4. Disconnect the upper radiator hose from the radiator.
5. Remove the wiring harness bracket from the fan.
6. Disconnect the radiator fan electrical connector.
7. Detach the radiator fan assembly from the retaining clips.
8. Remove the radiator fan by lifting up and out of the engine compartment.

To install:

9. Install the radiator fan assembly into the J-clips.
10. Install the radiator fan fasteners. Tighten the screws to 55 inch lbs. (6 Nm).
11. Install the radiator crossmember.
12. Install the wiring harness bracket and connector the fan electrical connector.
13. Install the upper radiator hose.
14. Refill the cooling system to the correct level.
15. Connect the negative battery cable.

RADIATOR

REMOVAL & INSTALLATION

1. Drain the cooling system.
2. Remove the engine fan.
3. Disconnect the radiator hoses.
4. Remove the fasteners attaching the A/C condenser to the radiator. Reposition the A/C condenser out of the way.
5. Remove the radiator assembly by lifting it up and out of the engine compartment.
6. Installation is the reverse order of removal.
7. Refill the cooling system to the correct level.

THERMOSTAT

REMOVAL & INSTALLATION

These engines contain two thermostats. The primary thermostat is located on the front of the water plenum in the thermostat housing. The secondary thermostat is located in the cylinder head under the water plenum.

Primary Thermostat

See Figure 52.

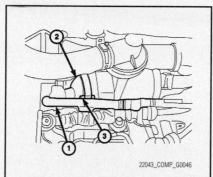

Fig. 52 Remove the coolant hose (1) and mounting bolts (3) from the thermostat housing (2)—Primary thermostat

1. Drain the cooling system.
2. Remove the air intake assembly.
3. Disconnect the coolant hose from the thermostat housing.
4. Remove the housing mounting bolts.
5. Remove the thermostat assembly and clean the sealing surfaces.

To install:

6. Position the thermostat into the water plenum. Align the air bleed hole with the location notch on the thermostat housing.

7. Install the thermostat housing onto the coolant adapter and tighten the bolts to 79 inch lbs. (9 Nm).
8. Connect the coolant hose.
9. Install the air intake assembly.
10. Refill the cooling system to the correct level.

Secondary Thermostat

See Figure 53.

1. Drain the cooling system.
2. Remove the air intake assembly.
3. Disconnect the coolant hoses from the rear of the coolant adapter.
4. Remove the radiator hoses.
5. Remove the coolant adapter mounting bolts.
6. Carefully slide the coolant adapter off the water pump inlet tube to remove the coolant adapter and secondary thermostat.

To install:

7. Position the thermostat into the cylinder head.
8. Inspect the water pump inlet tube O-rings for damage before installing the tube in the coolant adapter. Replace O-ring as necessary.
9. Lubricate the O-rings with soapy water.
10. Position the coolant adapter on water pump inlet tube and cylinder head.
11. Install the coolant adapter mounting bolts and tighten to 159 inch lbs. (18 Nm).

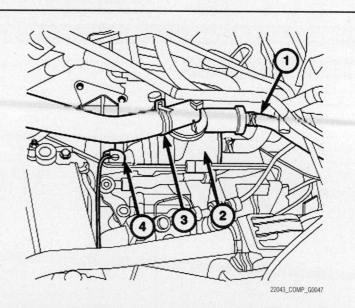

Fig. 53 Location of the coolant hose (1), radiator hoses (3,4) and coolant adapter (2)—Secondary thermostat

12. Connect the front coolant hose.
13. Connect the two rear coolant hoses.
14. Connect the radiator hose.
15. Install the air intake assembly.
16. Refill the cooling system to the correct level.

WATER PUMP

REMOVAL & INSTALLATION

1. Disconnect the negative battery cable.

ENGINE ELECTRICAL

ALTERNATOR

REMOVAL & INSTALLATION

1. Disconnect the negative battery cable.
2. Raise and safely support the vehicle.
3. Remove the right front wheel.
4. Remove the engine splash shield.
5. Remove the accessory drive belt splash shield.
6. Remove the accessory drive belt.
7. Remove the idler pulley.
8. Loosen the alternator lower mounting bolt.
9. Remove the A/C compressor and secure out of the way.

➡**Do not disconnect the A/C lines.**

10. Unplug the ground wiring harness from the alternator.
11. Remove the battery positive terminal nut and wire.
12. Remove the upper and lower mounting bolts.

2. Drain the cooling system.
3. Remove the accessory drive belt.
4. Raise and safely support the vehicle.
5. Remove the accessory drive belt splash shield.
6. Remove the bolts securing the water pump pulley and remove the pulley.
7. Remove the water pump mounting bolts and remove the water pump.

To install:
8. Install the water pump and tighten the mounting bolts to 18 ft. lbs. (24 Nm).

13. Move the A/C line to the other side of the battery terminal stud of the alternator.
14. Pull the alternator down and slide it out of the vehicle.

To install:
15. Slide the alternator up and rotate into place.
16. Move the A/C line back behind the battery terminal stud of the alternator.
17. Loosely install the lower mounting bolt.
18. Install the upper mounting bolt and tighten both mounting bolts to 40 ft. lbs. (54 Nm).
19. Install the battery positive cable and tighten the terminal nut to 89 inch lbs. (10 Nm).
20. Plug in the ground wiring harness.
21. Install the idler pulley.
22. Install the accessory drive belt.
23. Install the accessory drive belt splash shield.
24. Install the engine splash shield.

9. Install the water pump pulley and tighten the pulley bolts to 79 inch lbs. (9 Nm).
10. Install the accessory drive belt splash shield.
11. Lower the vehicle.
12. Install the accessory drive belt.
13. Refill the cooling system to the correct level.
14. Connect the negative battery cable.

CHARGING SYSTEM

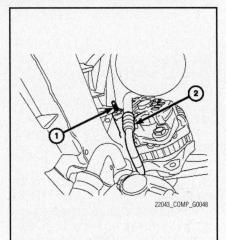

22043_COMP_G0048

Fig. 54 When reinstalling, ensure the battery terminal stud (1) is in front of the A/C line (2).

25. Install the right front wheel.
26. Lower the vehicle.
27. Connect the negative battery cable.

ENGINE ELECTRICAL

IGNITION COIL

REMOVAL & INSTALLATION
See Figures 55 and 56.

1. Disconnect the negative battery cable.
2. Disconnect the electrical connector from the ignition coil.

IGNITION SYSTEM

3. Remove the ignition coil mounting bolts.
4. Twist the ignition coil and then pull straight up.
5. Installation is the reverse order of removal. Tighten the mounting bolts to 80 inch lbs. (9 Nm).

IGNITION TIMING

ADJUSTMENT

Ignition timing is controlled by the Powertrain Control Module (PCM). No adjustment is possible.

SPARK PLUGS

REMOVAL & INSTALLATION
See Figure 57.

22043_COMP_G0049

Fig. 55 There is an ignition coil mounted on the valve cover for each spark plug

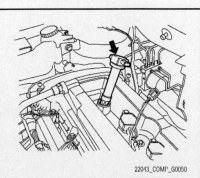

22043_COMP_G0050

Fig. 56 Twist and pull straight up to remove the ignition coil.

Each individual spark plug is located under each ignition coil. The ignition coil must be removed in order to access the spark plug.

1. Remove the ignition coil.
2. Remove the spark plug using a suitable spark plug socket with a rubber or foam insert.

To install:

3. Inspect the condition of the spark plug. Replace if necessary.

☀ **WARNING**

Special care should be used when installing spark plugs in the cylinder head spark plug wells. Be sure the plugs do not drop into the wells, damage to the electrodes can occur.

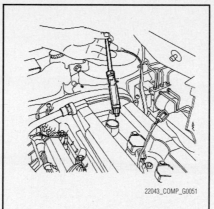

22043_COMP_G0051

Fig. 57 Using a suitable spark plug socket and socket extension to remove each spark plug.

☀ **WARNING**

Always tighten spark plugs to the specified torque. Over tightening can cause distortion resulting in a change in the spark plug gap. Over tightening can also damage the cylinder head.

4. Install the spark plug and start threading it by hand. Tighten the spark plugs to 11–15 ft. lbs. (16–20 Nm).
5. Install the ignition coil to the spark plug. Tighten the mounting bolts to 80 inch lbs. (9 Nm).
6. Connect the negative battery cable.

ENGINE ELECTRICAL

STARTER

REMOVAL & INSTALLATION

1. Disconnect the negative battery cable.
2. Remove the air intake assembly.
3. Remove the starter mounting bolt.
4. Disconnect the throttle body electrical connector.
5. Remove the throttle body.

6. Push the starter under the intake manifold.
7. Tip the nose of the starter toward the cooling module.
8. Pull the starter up and out of the vehicle.
9. Disconnect the starter wiring.

To install:

10. Connect the starter wiring. Tighten the battery cable nut to 89 inch lbs. (10 Nm).

STARTING SYSTEM

11. Install the starter in the vehicle engine compartment and loosely place the starter into position.
12. Install the throttle body and throttle body bracket.
13. Install the starter mounting bolts and tighten to 40 ft. lbs. (54 Nm).
14. Connect the throttle body electrical connector.
15. Install the air intake assembly.
16. Connect the negative battery cable.

ENGINE MECHANICAL

➡**Disconnecting the negative battery cable may interfere with the functions of the on board computer systems and may require the computer to undergo a relearning process, once the negative battery cable is reconnected.**

ACCESSORY DRIVE BELTS

ACCESSORY BELT ROUTING

See Figure 58.

INSPECTION

See Figure 59.

Although many manufacturers recommend that the drive belt(s) be inspected every 30,000 miles (48,000 km) or more, it is really a good idea to check them at least once a year, or at every major fluid change. Whichever interval you choose, the belts should be checked for wear or damage. Obviously, a damaged drive belt can cause problems should it give way while the vehicle is in operation. But, improper length belts (too short or long), as well as exces-

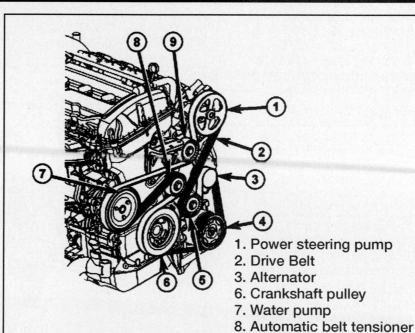

1. Power steering pump
2. Drive Belt
3. Alternator
6. Crankshaft pulley
7. Water pump
8. Automatic belt tensioner

22043_COMP_G0052

Fig. 58 Drive belt (2) components: Power steering pump (1), Alternator (3), Crankshaft pulley (6), Water pump (7), Automatic belt tensioner (8)—1.8L, 2.0L & 2.4L Engines

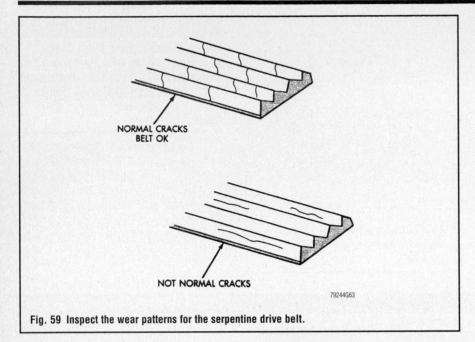

Fig. 59 Inspect the wear patterns for the serpentine drive belt.

sively worn belts, can also cause problems. Loose accessory drive belts can lead to poor engine cooling and diminished output from the alternator, air conditioning compressor or power steering pump. A belt that is too tight places a severe strain on the driven unit and can wear out bearings quickly.

Serpentine drive belts should be inspected for rib chunking (pieces of the ribs breaking off), severe glazing, frayed cords or other visible damage. Any belt which is missing sections of 2 or more adjacent ribs which are ½ in. (13mm) or longer must be replaced. You might want to note that serpentine belts do tend to form small cracks across the backing. If the only wear you find is in the form of one or more cracks are across the backing and NOT parallel to the ribs, the belt is still good and does not need to be replaced.

ADJUSTMENT

Periodic drive belt tensioning is not necessary, because an automatic spring-loaded tensioner is used with these belts to maintain proper adjustment at all times.

REMOVAL & INSTALLATION

1. Using a wrench, rotate the accessory drive belt tensioner counterclockwise until the belt can be removed from the pulleys.
2. Remove the accessory drive belt.

To install:
3. Install the accessory drive belt around all of the pulleys except for the alternator.
4. Using a wrench, rotate the accessory drive belt tensioner counterclockwise until the belt can be installed over the alternator pulley.

5. Release the spring tensioner onto the accessory drive belt.

CAMSHAFT AND VALVE LIFTERS

INSPECTION

See Figure 60.

1. Inspect the camshaft bearing journals for damage. If journals are damaged, check the cylinder head for damage. Also check the cylinder head oil holes for clogging.
2. Check the cam lobe and bearing surfaces for abnormal wear and damage. Replace camshaft if defective.

3. Measure the camshaft end play as follows:
   a. Using a suitable tool, move camshaft as far rearward as it will go.
   b. Zero out the dial indicator.
   c. Move the camshaft as far forward as it will go.
   d. Record the reading on the dial indicator.
   e. If end play is exceeds the specification, check cylinder head and camshaft for wear; replace as necessary

REMOVAL & INSTALLATION

See Figures 61 through 74.

1. Remove the engine appearance cover.
2. Disconnect the negative battery cable.
3. Drain the cooling system.
4. Drain the engine oil.
5. Disconnect the ignition coil electrical connector.
6. Disconnect the Positive Crankcase Valve (PCV) and make-up air hoses from the cylinder head cover.
7. Remove the cylinder head cover bolts and cylinder head cover.
8. Remove the right side engine splash shield.
9. Rotate the engine to Top Dead Center (TDC).
10. Make sure camshaft timing marks are aligned.
11. Mark the chain link corresponding to timing marks with a paint marker.
12. Remove the timing tensioner plug from the front cover.

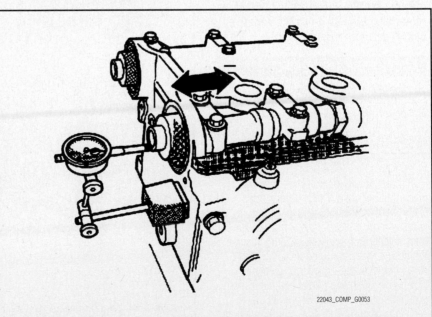

Fig. 60 Measure the endplay of the camshaft with a dial indicator—2.0L & 2.4L engines

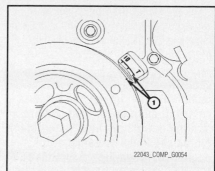

Fig. 61 Align the timing mark (1) on the crankshaft with the reference line to ensure the engine is at TDC

13. Insert a small Allen wrench through the timing tensioner plug hole and lift the ratchet upward to release the tensioner and push the Allen wrench inward. Leave the Allen wrench installed during the remainder of this procedure.

14. Insert Special Tool 9701 Locking Wedge between the camshaft phasers.

15. Lightly tap Special Tool 9701 into place with a suitable tool until it will no longer sink down.

16. Remove the camshaft front bearing cap.

17. Slowly remove the remaining intake and exhaust camshafts cap bolts one turn at a time.

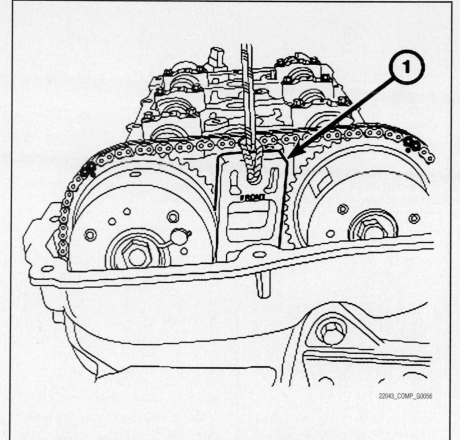

Fig. 63 Insert Special Tool 9701 Locking Wedge (1) between the camshaft phasers

➡**Keep all of the valvetrain components in order for reassembly.**

18. Remove the intake camshaft by lifting the rear of the camshaft upward.

19. Rotate the camshaft while lifting it out of the front bearing cradle.

20. Lift the timing chain off of the sprocket.

21. Remove the exhaust camshaft.

22. Secure the timing chain with wire so it does not fall into the timing chain cover.

23. Remove the valve lifters.

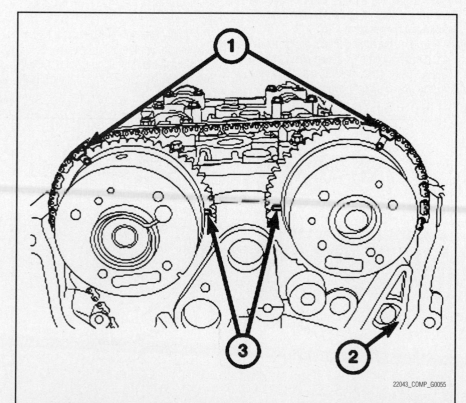

Fig. 62 Make sure camshaft timing marks (3) are aligned and mark the chain link (1) corresponding to the timing marks with a paint marker

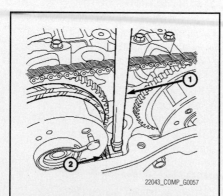

Fig. 64 Lightly tap Special Tool 9701 (2) into place with a suitable tool (1) until it will no longer sink down

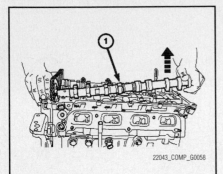

Fig. 65 Remove the intake camshaft (1) by lifting the rear of the camshaft upward

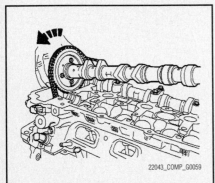

Fig. 66 Rotate the camshaft while lifting it out of the front bearing cradle

➤Keep all of the valvetrain components in order for reassembly.

To install:

24. Apply a light coat of clean engine oil to the valve lifters.

25. Install the lifters into their original positions in the cylinder head.

26. The camshaft cap is numbered 1, 2, or 3. This corresponds to the select fit bearing to use.

27. Install the corresponding select fit bearing.

28. Apply a light coat of clean engine oil to all of the camshaft journals.

29. Install the camshaft phasers on the camshafts, if removed.

   a. Install camshaft phaser making sure that the dowel is in the correct hole.

   b. Install camshaft phaser bolt and hand tighten.

30. Install the timing chain onto exhaust camshaft sprocket, making sure that the timing marks on the sprocket and the painted chain link are aligned.

31. Position the exhaust camshaft on the bearing journals in the cylinder head.

32. Align exhaust camshaft timing mark so it is parallel to the cylinder head as shown.

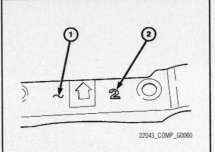

Fig. 67 The camshaft bearing cap (1) is numbered (2) to correspond to the select fit bearing

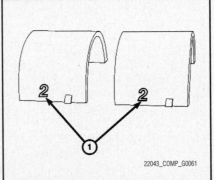

Fig. 68 Install the corresponding select fit bearing (1)

33. Install intake camshaft by raising the rear of the camshaft upward and roll the sprocket into the chain.

34. Align the timing marks on the intake cam sprocket with the painted chain link.

35. Position the intake camshaft into the bearing journals in the cylinder head.

36. Verify that the timing marks are aligned on both camshafts and that the timing marks are parallel with the cylinder head.

⁂ WARNING

Install the front intake and exhaust camshaft bearing cap last. Ensure that the dowels are seated and follow torque sequence or damage to engine could result.

➤If the front camshaft bearing cap is broken, the cylinder head MUST be replaced.

➤Verify that the exhaust bearing shells are correctly installed, and the dowels are seated in the head, prior to tightening bolts.

37. Install intake and exhaust camshaft bearing caps and slowly tighten bolts to 97 inch lbs. (11 Nm) in the sequence shown.

38. Install the front intake and exhaust bearing cap and tighten bolts to 18 ft. lbs. (25 Nm). in the sequence shown.

39. Verify that all of the timing marks are aligned.

40. Remove the Allen wrench from the timing chain tensioner.

41. Remove Special Tool 9701 Locking Wedge by pulling straight up on the pull rope.

42. Apply Mopar® thread sealant to the timing tensioner plug and install.

43. Install the right engine splash shield.

44. Clean any old RTV from the cylinder head cover gasket.

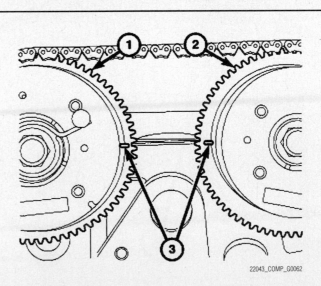

Fig. 69 When installing the exhaust (1) and intake (2) camshafts, make sure the timing marks (3) are aligned and parallel with the cylinder head.

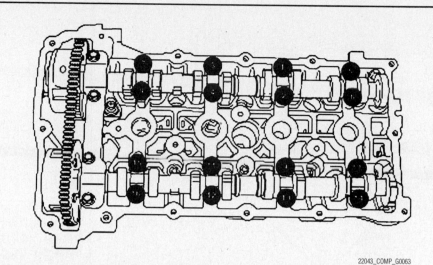

Fig. 70 Camshaft bearing cap torque sequence—2.0L & 2.4L engines

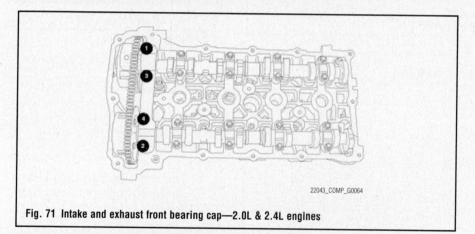

Fig. 71 Intake and exhaust front bearing cap—2.0L & 2.4L engines

48. Apply a dot of Mopar® engine sealant RTV or equivalent to the cylinder head front cover T-joint.

49. Install the cylinder head cover and tighten the bolts in sequence as follows:

  a. Tighten all bolts in sequence to 44 inch lbs. (5 Nm).

50. Tighten all bolts in sequence to 90 inch lbs. (10 Nm).

51. Connect the ignition coil electrical connectors.

52. Connect the PCV and make-up air hoses

53. Refill the cooling system to the correct level.

45. Inspect the cylinder head cover gaskets for damage. If they are not damaged, they may be reinstalled. Otherwise they must be replaced.

46. Install the studs in the cylinder head cover as shown.

47. Clean all RTV from the cylinder head.

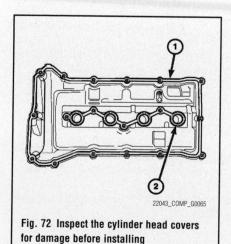

Fig. 72 Inspect the cylinder head covers for damage before installing

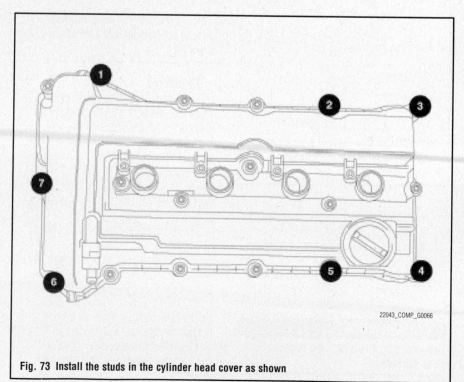

Fig. 73 Install the studs in the cylinder head cover as shown

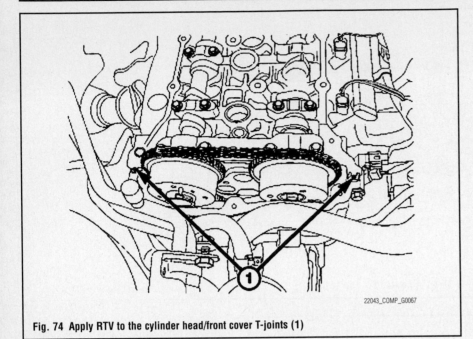

Fig. 74 Apply RTV to the cylinder head/front cover T-joints (1)

54. Refill the engine with oil to the correct level.

55. Install the engine appearance cover.

56. Connect the negative battery cable.

CRANKSHAFT FRONT SEAL

REMOVAL & INSTALLATION

See Figures 75 through 77.

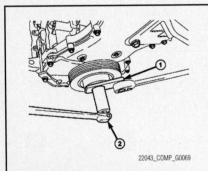

Fig. 75 Install Special Tool 9707 Damper Holder (1) to remove the crankshaft damper bolt.

1. Remove the accessory drive belt.

2. Install Special Tool 9707 Damper Holder to remove the crankshaft damper bolt.

3. Pull the damper off of the crankshaft.

4. Remove the crankshaft front seal by prying it out with a suitable pry tool.

✳✳ WARNING

Take care not to damage the cover seal surface.

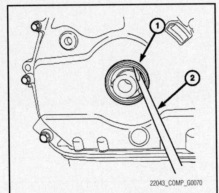

Fig. 76 Remove the crankshaft front seal (1) by prying it out with a suitable pry tool (2).

To install:

5. Place the new seal onto Special Tool 9506 Seal Installer with the seal spring towards the inside of the engine.

6. Install the new crankshaft front seal using the Seal Installer tool and the crankshaft damper bolt.

7. Tighten the crankshaft bolt until the Seal Installer tool seats flush against the timing chain cover.

8. Remove the crankshaft bolt and Installer Tool.

9. Install the crankshaft damper. Oil the bolt threads between the bolt head and washer.

10. Using Special Tool 9707 Damper Holder told on the crankshaft damper and tighten the bolt to 155 ft. lbs. (210 Nm).

11. Install the accessory drive belt.

12. Start the engine and check for leaks.

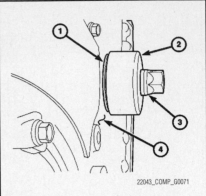

Fig. 77 Install the new seal (1) by tightening the crankshaft bolt (3) until the Seal Installer Tool (2) seats against the timing chain cover (4).

CYLINDER HEAD

REMOVAL & INSTALLATION

See Figures 78 through 81.

1. Properly relieve the fuel system pressure.

2. Disconnect the negative battery cable.

3. Drain the cooling system.

4. Remove the air intake assembly.

5. Remove the engine appearance cover.

6. Remove the coolant recovery bottle.

7. Disconnect the power steering pump and reposition out of the way.

➡**Do not disconnect the power steering lines.**

8. Remove the windshield washer bottle.

9. Disconnect the following:
   - Breather hose
   - Positive Crankcase Valve (PCV) hose
   - Ignition coil electrical connectors

10. Remove the cylinder head cover.

11. Raise and safely support the vehicle.

12. Remove the right engine splash shield.

13. Rotate the engine to Top Dead Center (TDC).

14. Remove the accessory drive belt.

15. Remove the lower A/C compressor mounting bolts and lower mount.

16. Remove the lower idler pulley.

17. Remove the crankshaft damper.

18. Remove the water pump pulley.

19. Remove the right side engine mount bracket lower bolt.

20. Remove the timing chain cover lower bolts.

21. Disconnect the oxygen sensor electrical connector.

22. Remove exhaust pipe at manifold nuts and remove pipe.

23. Lower the vehicle.

24. Support the engine with suitable jack.

25. Remove right engine mount through bolt.

26. Remove right engine mount to mount bracket bolts.

27. Remove right engine mount adapter.

28. Remove accessory drive upper idler pulley.

29. Remove right upper engine mount bracket.

30. Remove the accessory drive belt tensioner.

31. Remove the upper timing chain cover retaining bolts.

32. Remove the timing chain cover.

➡**If the timing chain plated links can no longer be seen, the timing chain links corresponding to the timing marks must be marked prior to removal if the chain is to be reused.**

33. Mark chain link corresponding to camshaft timing mark.

34. Mark chain link corresponding to crankshaft timing mark.

35. Remove the timing chain tensioner.

36. Remove the timing chain.

37. Remove the timing chain guides.

38. Disconnect the fuel line at the fuel rail.

39. Disconnect the fuel injector electrical connectors.

40. Disconnect the top engine electrical connectors and reposition harness.

41. Remove the fuel rail.

42. Remove the throttle body support bracket retaining bolt.

43. Disconnect the electronic throttle control electrical connector.

44. Disconnect the MAP sensor electrical connector.

45. Disconnect the vacuum lines at intake.

46. Remove the intake manifold retaining bolts.

47. Remove the upper radiator hose retaining bolt.

48. Remove the intake manifold.

49. Remove the coolant outlet manifold and set aside.

50. Remove the ground strap at right rear of cylinder head.

51. Remove the exhaust manifold. For additional information, refer to the following section, "Exhaust Manifold, Removal & Installation."

52. Remove the camshafts.

➡**All of the cylinder head bolts have captured washers EXCEPT the front two.**

53. Remove the cylinder head bolts.

54. Remove the cylinder head from engine block.

To install:

55. Replace the variable valve timing filter screen.

❋❋ WARNING

Always replace the variable valve timing filter screen when servicing the head gasket or engine damage could result.

56. Place two pea size dots of Mopar® engine sealant RTV or equivalent (1) on cylinder block as shown.

57. Position the new cylinder head gasket on engine block with the part number facing up. Ensure gasket is seated over the locating dowels in block.

58. Place two pea size dots of Mopar® engine sealant RTV or equivalent (1) on cylinder head gasket as shown.

59. Position the cylinder head onto the engine block.

60. Install washers for the front two cylinder head bolts.

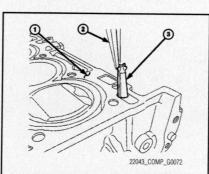
Fig. 78 Always replace the variable valve timing filter screen (3) in the cylinder head (1)

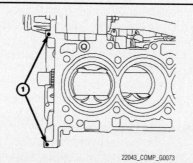
22043_COMP_G0073
Fig. 79 Before installing the head gasket, place two dots of RTV (1) on the cylinder block as shown

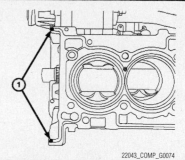
22043_COMP_G0074
Fig. 80 After installing head gasket, place two more dots of RTV (1) on the cylinder block as shown

61. Lightly coat the cylinder head bolts with clean engine oil.

62. Install the cylinder head bolts and tighten in sequence as follows:

a. Tighten all bolts to 25 ft. lbs. (30 Nm).

b. Tighten all bolts to 45 ft. lbs. (61 Nm).

c. Tighten all bolts a second time to 45 ft. lbs. (61 Nm).

d. Tighten all bolts an additional 90°

❋❋ WARNING

Do not use a torque wrench for last torque step.

63. Install the exhaust manifold.

64. Install the ground strap at the right rear of the cylinder head.

65. Install the coolant adapter with new seals.

66. Connect the coolant hoses.

67. Connect the purge hose.

68. Install the intake manifold and tighten to 18 ft. lbs. (24 Nm).

69. Install the upper radiator hose retaining bracket bolt.

70. Install the timing chain.

71. Install the timing chain cover.

72. Remove the ignition coils from cylinder head cover.

73. Install the cylinder head cover.

74. Connect the cam sensor wiring connector.

75. Install the spark plugs and tighten to 20 ft. lbs. (27 Nm).

76. Install ignition coils and tighten to 70 inch lbs. (8 Nm).

77. Install the power steering pump reservoir.

78. Install the windshield washer reservoir.

79. Install the coolant recovery reservoir.

80. Install the accessory drive belt.

81. Connect the engine coolant temperature sensor connector.

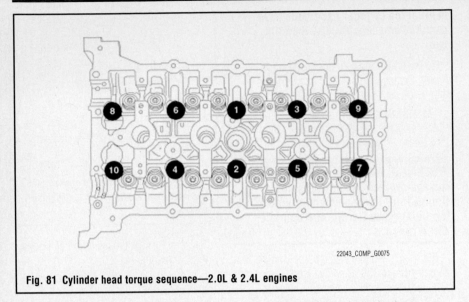

Fig. 81 Cylinder head torque sequence—2.0L & 2.4L engines

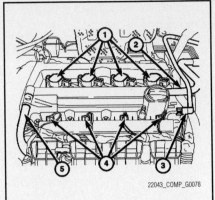

Fig. 82 Location of the Ignition Coil electrical connectors (1), make-up air hose (2), fuel line (3), fuel injector electrical connectors (4), and PCV hose (5)—2.0L & 2.4L engines

82. Connect the coolant hoses to coolant adapter. Connect heater hoses to coolant adapter.

83. Connect the coolant temperature sensor and capacitor electrical connectors.

84. Install the heater tube support bracket to cylinder head.

85. Install the fastener attaching dipstick tube to lower intake manifold.

86. Connect the ignition coil and injector electrical connectors.

87. Install the fuel rail.

88. Connect fuel supply line quick-connect at the fuel rail assembly.

89. Install the air intake assembly.

90. Install the engine appearance cover.

91. Refill the cooling system to the correct level.

92. Refill the engine with oil to the correct level.

93. Connect the negative battery cable.

94. Start the engine and check for leaks.

ENGINE ASSEMBLY

REMOVAL & INSTALLATION

See Figures 82 through 85.

1. Drain the engine oil.
2. Drain the cooling system.
3. Properly relieve the fuel system pressure.
4. Remove the hood.
5. Remove the engine appearance cover.
6. Remove the air intake assembly.
7. Disconnect both cables from the battery.
8. Remove the battery and battery tray.
9. Remove the coolant reservoir.
10. Remove the power steering reservoir.

11. Remove the windshield washer reservoir.

12. Remove the coolant hoses from coolant adapter.

13. Remove the grill closure panel.

14. Remove the upper radiator hose support.

15. Disconnect the engine electrical connectors and reposition harness.

16. Remove the air intake tube from throttle body.

17. Disconnect the fuel line from fuel rail.

18. Remove the vacuum lines from throttle body and intake manifold.

19. Remove the wiring harness from the intake.

20. Remove the throttle body support bracket.

21. Disconnect the electronic throttle control and manifold flow control valve electrical connectors.

22. Remove the PCV hose, and make-up air hose from valve cover.

23. Remove the dipstick.

24. Remove the intake manifold mounting bolts and remove the intake manifold. For additional information, refer to the following section, "Intake Manifold, Removal & Installation."

25. Disconnect electrical connectors and reposition harness.

26. Remove the accessory drive belt. For additional information, refer to the following section, "Accessory Drive Belt, Removal & Installation."

27. Remove the power steering line support at engine mount and exhaust manifold.

28. Remove the power steering pump and set aside.

29. Remove the upper idler pulley.

30. Remove the ground strap near right tower.

31. Raise and safely support the vehicle.

32. Remove the right front wheel.

33. Remove the engine splash shield.

34. Remove the torque converter inspection cover and matchmark the torque converter to the flywheel.

35. Remove the torque converter bolts.

36. Remove the lower bellhousing mounting bolts.

37. Remove the A/C compressor mounting bolts.

38. Remove the alternator and lower idler pulley.

39. Disconnect the crankshaft position (CKP) sensor electrical connector and remove the sensor.

40. Remove the exhaust variable valve timing solenoid.

41. Install an engine lift chain as shown to cylinder head.

42. Connect the chain to the rear engine lift hook.

43. Install engine lifting crane.

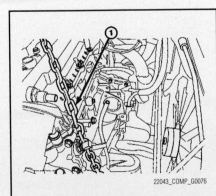

Fig. 83 Install an engine lift chain (1) to the cylinder head as shown.

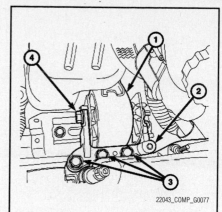

Fig. 84 Remove the right engine mount through-bolt (4), mount adapter retaining bolts (3) and mount adapter (2)—2.0L & 2.4L Engine removal

44. Remove the right engine mount through-bolt.

45. Remove the engine mount adapter retaining bolts and the mount adapter.

46. Carefully lift the engine from engine compartment.

To install:

47. Position the engine assembly over the vehicle and slowly lower the engine into place.

48. Continue lowering engine until the engine/transaxle assembly are aligned to the mounting locations.

49. Install the engine mount adapter and tighten bolts. Install the mount through-bolt and tighten all bolts to 87 ft. lbs. (118 Nm).

50. Remove the engine lift chain.

51. Install the oil control valve.

52. Raise and safely support the vehicle.

53. Install the A/C compressor.

54. Install the exhaust manifold and heat shields.

55. Install the oxygen sensor and connect the electrical connector.

56. Install the crankshaft position sensor and connect connector.

57. Install the manifold to exhaust pipe bolts and tighten bolts.

58. Install the alternator.

59. Install lower bell housing bolts and tighten bolts.

60. Align the torque converter and flex plate matchmark. Install torque converter bolts and tighten.

61. Install the torque converter inspection cover.

62. Install the crankshaft damper, using Special Tool 9707 Damper holder. Apply clean engine oil to the crankshaft damper bolt threads and between bolt head and washer. Tighten bolt to 155 ft. (210 Nm).

63. Install the right engine splash shield.

64. Install the wheel.

65. Install the coolant hose to the oil cooler.

66. Install a new oil filter.

67. Lower the vehicle.

68. Install the upper idler pulley.

69. Install the coolant adapter assembly.

70. Install the ground strap near the right strut tower.

71. Install the power steering line support bracket and install the power steering pump.

72. Install the accessory drive belt.

73. Connect the electrical connectors at block ground, starter, A/C compressor, knock sensor, oil pressure sensor, generator, coolant temperature sensor at block, and block heater (if equipped).

74. Install the intake manifold.

75. Install the throttle body support bracket and wiring harness retainer.

76. Install the dipstick.

77. Install the PCV hose to valve cover and make-up air hose.

78. Connect the manifold flow control valve and electronic throttle control electrical connectors.

79. Install the vacuum lines to the throttle body and intake manifold.

80. Install the intake air tube to the throttle body.

81. Connect the ignition coil electrical connectors.

82. Connect the injector electrical connectors.

83. Connect the fuel line to fuel rail.

84. Connect the intake and exhaust oil control valve electrical connectors.

85. Install the grill trim panel.

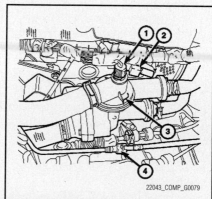

Fig. 85 Location of the coolant temperature sensor (1), capacitor electrical connector (2) and coolant hoses connected to the coolant adapter (3)—2.0L & 2.4L Engines

86. Install the upper radiator support bracket.

87. Connect the coolant temperature sensor.

88. Connect the capacitor electrical connector.

89. Install the coolant hoses at coolant adapter.

90. Install the coolant reservoir and connect hose.

91. Install the battery tray and battery.

92. Connect the battery cables.

93. Install the air intake assembly.

94. Refill the cooling system to the correct level.

95. Refill the engine with oil to the correct level.

96. Install the engine appearance cover.

97. Install the hood.

98. Start the engine and check for leaks.

EXHAUST MANIFOLD

REMOVAL & INSTALLATION

Front Wheel Drive Models

See Figures 86 through 88.

1. Disconnect the negative battery cable.

2. Remove the engine appearance cover.

3. Remove the upper heat shields mounting bolts.

4. Remove the upper heat shield.

5. Disconnect the exhaust pipe from the exhaust manifold.

6. Remove the exhaust manifold support bracket.

7. Disconnect the Oxygen sensor electrical connector.

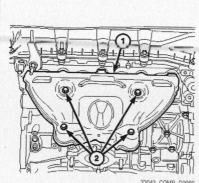

Fig. 86 Remove the upper heat shield mounting bolts (2) to remove the upper heat shield (1)–FWD vehicles

Fig. 87 Remove the bracket mounting bolts (1) and remove the exhaust manifold support bracket (2)—FWD vehicles

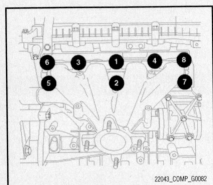

Fig. 88 Exhaust manifold torque sequence—FWD vehicles

8. Remove the exhaust manifold mounting bolts.

9. Remove the exhaust manifold and gasket.

To install:

10. Install the exhaust manifold with a new gasket. Tighten the bolts in sequence to 25 ft. lbs. (34 Nm).

11. Install the exhaust manifold heat shield. Tighten the bolts to 105 inch lbs. (12 Nm).

12. Install the exhaust manifold support bracket.

13. Install a new catalytic converter gasket and connect the exhaust pipe to the exhaust manifold. Tighten the flange bolts to 21 ft. lbs. (28 Nm).

14. Connect the oxygen sensor electrical connector.

15. Install the engine appearance cover.

16. Connect the negative battery cable.

All Wheel Drive Models

See Figure 89.

1. Remove the under floor catalytic converter as follows:

a. Raise and safely support the vehicle.

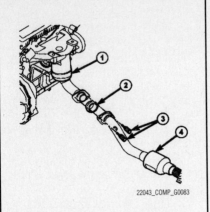

Fig. 89 Exploded view of the exhaust system—Maniverter (1), spherical gasket (2), flange bolts (3), under-floor catalytic converter (4)—AWD vehicles

b. Remove the muffler assembly.

c. Disconnect the oxygen sensor electrical connectors.

d. Remove the flange bolts, springs and spherical gasket.

e. Remove the under floor catalytic converter.

2. Lower the vehicle.

3. Remove the secondary thermostat.

4. Remove the maniverter mounting bolts.

5. Remove the maniverter and gasket.

To install:

6. Using a new flange gasket, install the maniverter to the engine. Tighten the mounting bolts to 21 ft. lbs. (28 Nm).

7. Install the secondary thermostat.

8. Install the under floor catalytic converter as follows:

a. Install the under floor catalytic converter and the isolator supports to the underbody.

9. Position the spherical gasket with white side facing rear of vehicle, and install springs and tighten the bolts to 24 ft. lbs. (33 Nm).

10. Install the muffler assembly.

11. Working from the front of system; align each component to maintain position and proper clearance with underbody parts. Tighten all band clamps to 40 ft. lbs. (55 Nm).

12. Start the engine and check for exhaust leaks.

13. Check the exhaust system for contact with any of the body panels.

INTAKE MANIFOLD

REMOVAL & INSTALLATION

See Figures 90 through 93.

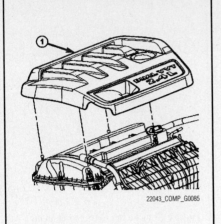

Fig. 90 Remove the engine appearance cover (1) by pulling upward—2.0L & 2.4L engines

1. Properly relieve the fuel system pressure.

2. Drain the cooling system.

3. Disconnect the negative battery cable.

4. Remove the engine appearance cover.

5. Remove the air intake assembly.

6. Disconnect the fuel line from the fuel rail.

7. Disconnect the fuel injector electrical connectors.

8. Remove the fuel rail. For additional information, refer to the following section, "Fuel Injectors, Removal & Installation."

9. Disconnect the electrical connectors for:

- Oil temperature sensor
- Variable valve timing solenoid
- Intake camshaft position sensor

10. Position the wiring harness out of the way.

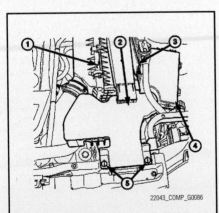

Fig. 91 Air intake components—Air cleaner housing (1), fresh air inlet (2), heat shield (3), retainers (5)—2.0L & 2.4L engines

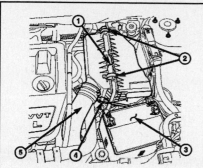

1. Air cleaner housing
2. Housing clasps
3. Battery
4. Intake Air Temperature (IAT) sensor electrical connector
5. Air inlet tube

22043_COMP_G0087

Fig. 92 Air intake components—Air cleaner housing (1), housing clasps (2), battery (3), Intake Air Temperature (IAT) sensor electrical connector (4), Air inlet tube (5)—2.0L & 2.4L engines

11. Remove the throttle body support bracket.
12. Disconnect the electronic throttle control electrical connector.
13. Remove the wiring harness retainer from the intake manifold.
14. Disconnect the manifold absolute pressure (MAP) sensor electrical connector.
15. Disconnect the vacuum lines from the intake manifold.
16. Remove the upper radiator hose retaining bracket.
17. Remove the intake manifold retaining bolts.
18. Remove the intake manifold and gasket.

To install:
19. Clean all of the gasket surfaces.
20. Using a new gasket, install the intake manifold bolts in sequence to 18 ft. lbs. (25 Nm).
21. Install the upper radiator hose support bracket.
22. Connect the vacuum lines to the intake manifold.
23. Install the fuel rail assembly and tighten the mounting bolts to 17 ft. lbs. (23 Nm).
24. Connect the fuel injector electrical connectors.
25. Connect the fuel supply hose.
26. Reconnect the electrical connectors previously removed.
27. Install the air intake assembly.
28. Refill the cooling system to the correct level.
29. Install the engine appearance cover.

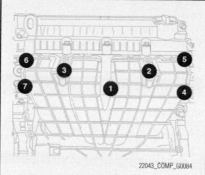

Fig. 93 Intake manifold torque sequence—2.0L & 2.4L engines

OIL PAN

REMOVAL & INSTALLATION
See Figures 94 through 96.

1. Raise and safely support the vehicle.
2. Drain the engine oil.
3. Remove the accessory drive belt splash shield.
4. Remove the lower A/C compressor mounting bolt and remove the A/C mounting bracket.
5. Remove the oil pan mounting bolts.
6. Using a putty knife, loosen the seal around the oil pan.

⁂ WARNING

Do not use the pry points in the engine block to remove the oil pan.

To install:
7. Remove the oil pan.
8. Clean any old gasket material from the mating surfaces.
9. Apply Mopar® Engine RTV GEN II at the front cover-to-engine block parting lines.
10. Apply a 2 mm bead of Mopar®

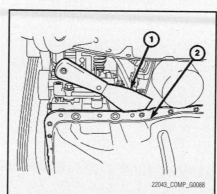

Fig. 94 Use a putty knife (1) to the loose the seal around the oil pan (2)—2.0L & 2.4L Engine

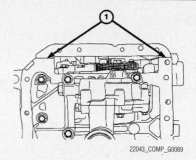

Fig. 95 Apply Mopar® Engine RTV GEN II to the front cover-to-engine block parting lines(1) as shown—Oil pan installation

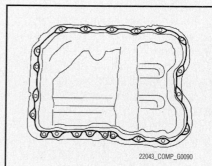

Fig. 96 Apply a 2 mm bead of Mopar® Engine RTV GEN II on the oil pan mating surface as shown—Oil pan installation

Engine RTV GEN II around the oil pan mating surface as shown in the illustration.
11. Install the oil pan into position and tighten the bolts as follows:
• The two long bolts to 16 ft. lbs. (22 Nm).
• All other bolts to 105 ft. lbs. (12 Nm).
12. Install the oil drain plug.
13. Install the A/C compressor mounting bracket and A/C compressor lower mounting bolt.
14. Lower the vehicle.
15. Refill the engine with oil to the correct level.
16. Start the engine and check for leaks.

OIL PUMP

REMOVAL & INSTALLATION
See Figure 97.

1. Rotate the engine to put cylinder #1 at Top Dead Center (TDC).
2. Remove the oil pan. For additional information, refer to the following section, "Oil Pan, Removal & Installation."
3. Matchmark the position of the timing chain to the crankshaft sprocket and the timing chain on the oil pump sprocket.

4. Push the tensioner piston back into the tensioner body.

5. With the piston held back, insert Special Tool 9703 Tensioner Pin into the tensioner body to hold the piston in the retracted position.

6. Remove the balance shaft module (BSM) mounting bolts and discard the bolts.

7. Lower the back of the BSM and remove the timing chain from the oil pump sprocket.

8. Remove the BSM from the engine.

To install:

9. Clean the BSM mounting holes with brake cleaner.

10. If removed, position the timing chain over the sprocket, aligning the matchmarks.

11. Align the matchmarks and install the chain over the oil pump sprocket.

12. Pivot the BSM assembly upwards and position on the ladder frame.

13. Using new bolts, install them first only finger tight. Then tighten as follows:

　a. Tighten the bolts in the sequence shown to 11 ft. lbs. (15 Nm).

　b. Then tighten them to 22 ft. lbs. (29 Nm) in sequence.

　c. Rotate each bolt an additional 90° in the sequence shown

14. Remove the tensioner pin.

15. Install the oil pan.

16. Refill the engine with oil to the correct level.

17. Start the engine and check for leaks.

INSPECTION

The oil pump is integral to the balance shaft module. The oil pump cannot be disassembled for inspection

PISTON AND RING

POSITIONING

See Figure 98.

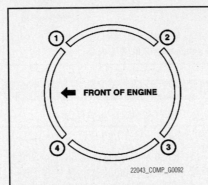

Fig. 98 Position the piston ring end gaps as shown—Top compression ring gap (1), Upper oil ring side rail gap (2), Second compression ring gap (3), Lower oil ring side rail gap (4)—2.0L & 2.4L Engines

REAR MAIN SEAL

REMOVAL & INSTALLATION

See Figure 99.

1. Remove the transaxle assembly.
2. Remove the flexplate.

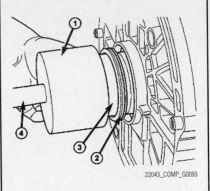

Fig. 99 Install a new seal (2) using Special Tools 9509 (3), 9706 (1) and C-4171 (4)—2.0L & 2.4L Engines

3. Insert a suitable pry tool between the dust lip and metal case of the crankshaft seal. Angle the pry tool through the dust lip against the metal case and pry out the seal.

To install:

4. Lightly coat Special Tool 9509 Seal Guide with clean engine oil. Place the seal guide on the crankshaft.

5. Position a new rear seal over the seal guide. Ensure the lip of the seal is facing towards the crankcase during installation.

6. Drive the seal into the block using Special Tool 9706 Seal Driver and Handle C-4171. When the seal driver bottoms out against the block, the seal is installed.

7. Install the flexplate. Tighten the new bolts to 70 ft. lbs. (95 Nm).

8. Install the transaxle assembly.

TIMING CHAIN, SPROCKETS, FRONT COVER AND SEAL

REMOVAL & INSTALLATION

See Figures 100 through 108.

1. Disconnect the negative battery cable.

2. Turn the crankshaft until cylinder #1 is at Top Dead Center (TDC).

3. Remove the engine appearance cover.

4. Properly relieve the fuel system pressure.

5. Drain the cooling system.

6. Drain the engine oil.

7. Remove the coolant recovery bottle.

8. Remove the power steering reservoir mounting bolts and secure it aside.

➡**Do not disconnect the power steering lines.**

9. Disconnect the fuel, make-up air hose, PCV hose and ignition coil electrical connectors.

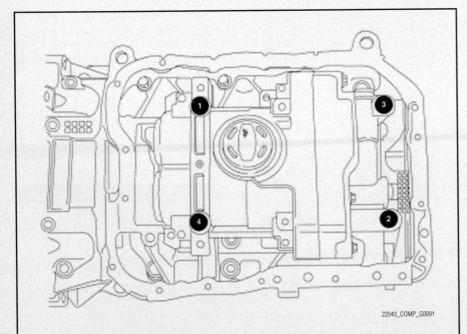

Fig. 97 Balance shaft module (with oil pump) torque sequence—2.0L & 2.4L Engines

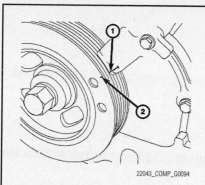

Fig. 100 The timing mark on the crank-shaft (2) should align with the reference mark (1) to indicate that cylinder #1 is at TDC—2.0L & 2.4L Engines

10. Remove the cylinder head cover. For additional information, refer to the following section, "Cylinder Head, Removal & Installation."

11. Raise and safely support the vehicle.

12. Remove the lower right engine splash shield.

13. Remove the accessory drive belt.

14. Remove the lower A/C compressor mounting bolt and remove the A/C compressor lower bracket.

15. Remove the lower idler pulley and crankshaft pulley.

16. Remove the front crankshaft oil seal by prying it out with a suitable pry tool.

17. Remove the water pump pulley.

18. Remove the engine mount bracket lower mounting bolt.

19. Remove the timing chain cover lower mounting bolts.

20. Lower the vehicle.

21. Remove the power steering line support, then remove the power steering pump mounting bolts and secure it out of the way.

➡ **Do not disconnect the power steering lines.**

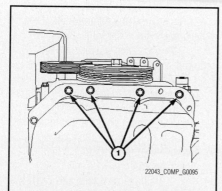

Fig. 101 Lower timing chain cover mounting bolts (1) (looking from the bottom up)—2.0L & 2.4L Engines

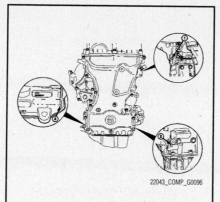

Fig. 102 Location of the timing chain cover mounting bolts and pry points (1,2,3)—2.0L & 2.4L Engines

22. Support the engine with a suitable jack.

➡ **When support the engine, use a block a wood between the jack and oil pan to avoid damage to the engine.**

23. Remove the remaining right engine mount-to-mount bracket bolts.

24. Remove the upper idler pulley.

25. Remove the right engine mount bracket.

26. Remove the accessory drive belt tensioner.

27. Remove the timing chain cover mounting bolts.

28. Using the pry points indicated, remove the timing chain cover out through the bottom of the vehicle.

29. Matchmark the chain links corresponding to the camshaft timing marks.

30. Match mark the chain link corresponding to the crankshaft timing mark.

31. Remove the timing chain tensioner.

32. Remove the timing chain.

33. Remove the oil pump drive chain tensioner and oil pump drive chain. For additional information, refer to the following section, "Oil Pump, Removal & Installation."

34. Remove the crankshaft sprocket.

35. Hold the camshaft in place on the camshaft flats using a wrench.

36. Remove the camshaft phaser assembly from the camshaft.

❊❊ **WARNING**

The camshaft phasers and camshaft sprockets are supplied as an assembly and should not be disassembled.

To install:

37. Using a wrench to hold the camshaft in place, install the phaser assembly to the camshaft.

➡ **Ensure the dowel is seated in the dowel hose and not in an oil feed hole. The dowel hole is larger than the four oil feed holes.**

38. Install the crankshaft sprocket onto the crankshaft.

39. Install the oil pump drive chain and tensioner.

40. Verify that the crankshaft sprocket keyway is at the 9 o'clock position.

41. Align the camshaft timing marks so they are parallel to the cylinder head and aligned each other as shown.

42. If the timing chain guide was removed, install the timing chain guide and tighten the bolts to 105 inch lbs. (12 Nm).

43. Install the timing chain so plated links on chain align with timing marks on camshaft sprockets.

44. Align the timing mark on the crankshaft sprocket with the plated link on the timing chain. Position chain so slack will be on the tensioner side.

➡ **Keep the slack in the timing chain on the tensioner side.**

45. Install the moveable timing chain pivot guide, if removed, and tighten bolt to 105 inch lbs. (12 Nm).

46. Reset the timing chain tensioner by lifting up on the ratchet and pushing the plunger inward towards the tensioner body. Insert Special Tool 8514 Tensioner Pin into the slot to hold the tensioner plunger in the retracted position.

47. Install the timing chain tensioner and tighten bolts to 105 inch lbs. (12 Nm).

48. Remove the Tensioner Pin. Rotate the crankshaft CLOCKWISE two complete revolutions until the crankshaft is repositioned at the TDC position with the crankshaft keyway at the 9 o'clock position.

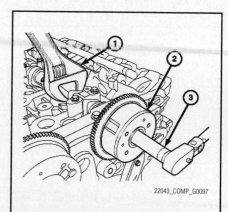

Fig. 103 Using a wrench (1) to hold the camshaft, remove the phaser assembly (2) using a suitable socket wrench (3)—2.0 & 2.4L Engines

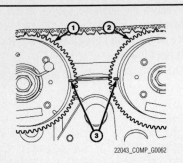

Fig. 104 Align the camshaft timing marks so they are parallel to the cylinder head and aligned each other as shown.

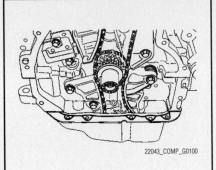

Fig. 107 Apply RTV to the oil pan as shown—Timing chain cover installation

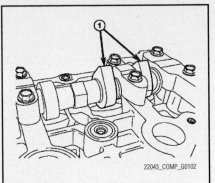

Fig. 109 To measure the valve lash, rotate camshaft so the lobes (1) are vertical.

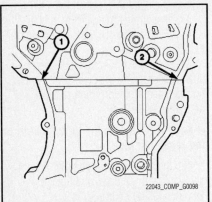

Fig. 105 Apply RTV to the cylinder head-to-engine block parting line (1,2) as shown—Timing chain cover installation

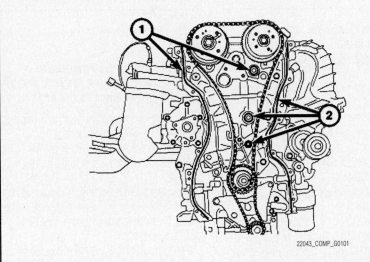

Fig. 108 Apply RTV to the engine block (1,2) as shown—Timing chain cover installation

49. Verify that the camshaft timing marks are in the proper position.

50. Clean all of the sealing surfaces of the timing chain cover.

51. Apply Mopar® engine sealant RTV or equivalent as shown at the cylinder head-to-block parting line.

52. Apply Mopar® engine sealant RTV or equivalent as shown at the ladder frame-to-block parting line.

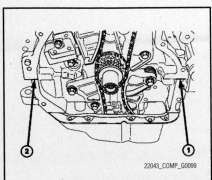

Fig. 106 Apply RTV to the ladder frame-to-engine block parting line (1,2) as shown—Timing chain cover installation

53. Apply Mopar® engine sealant RTV or equivalent in the corner of the oil pan and block.

54. Apply a 2 mm bead of Mopar® engine sealant RTV or equivalent to the oil pan as shown.

55. Apply a 2 mm bead of Mopar® engine sealant RTV or equivalent to the engine block as shown.

56. Install the timing chain cover upwards from under the vehicle. Tighten the M6 bolts to 105 inch lbs. (12 Nm) and tighten the M8 bolts to 17 ft. lbs. (23 Nm).

57. The remainder of the installation is the reverse order of removal procedure.

58. Refill the cooling system to the correct level.

59. Refill the engine with oil to the correct level.

60. Start the engine and check for leaks.

VALVE LASH

ADJUSTMENT

See Figure 109.

1. Remove the cylinder head cover.

2. Rotate the camshaft to the lobes are vertical.

3. Check the clearance using feeler gauges.

4. Repeat this procedure for all of the valve tappets and record the readings.

5. If the clearance was outside the required specification:

   a. Remove the camshaft. For additional information, refer to the following section, "Camshaft, Removal & Installation."

   b. Depending on if the clearance was too large or too small, increase or decrease the tappet thickness by the necessary amount.

   c. Install the camshafts and verify the valve lash is correct.

6. Install the cylinder head cover.

ACCELERATOR PEDAL POSITION (APP) SENSOR

LOCATION

See Figure 110.

Fig. 110 The APP sensor is an integral part of the pedal assembly.

OPERATION

The Accelerator Pedal Position (APP) Sensor is a variable resistor that provides the PCM with an input signal (voltage). The signal represents pedal angle position. As the position of the accelerator pedal changes, the resistance of the APP sensor changes.

REMOVAL & INSTALLATION

1. Disconnect the negative battery cable.
2. Disconnect the electrical connector form the pedal assembly.
3. Remove the mounting nuts.
4. Remove the pedal assembly from the mounting studs.
5. Installation is the reverse order of removal.

TESTING

1. Using a diagnostic scan tool, check for the presence of any Diagnostic Trouble Codes (DTCs). Record and address these codes as necessary.
2. If no codes are present, review the scan tool environmental data. If possible, try to duplicate the conditions under which the DTC set.

3. If applicable, actuate the component with the scan tool.
4. Monitor the scan tool data relative to this circuit and wiggle test the wiring and connectors.
5. Look for the data to change, the actuation to be interrupted, or for the DTC to reset during the wiggle test.
6. Refer to any Technical Service Bulletins (TSBs) that may apply.
7. Turn the ignition off.
8. Visually inspect the related wire harness. Disconnect all the related harness connectors. Look for any chafed, pierced, pinched, partially broken wires and broken, bent, pushed out, or corroded terminals.
9. Perform a voltage drop test on the related circuits between the suspected component and the Powertrain Control Module (PCM).
10. Inspect and clean all PCM, engine, and chassis grounds that are related to the most current DTC.
11. If numerous trouble codes were set, use a schematic and inspect any common ground or supply circuits.
12. For intermittent Misfire DTCs check for restrictions in the Intake and Exhaust system, proper installation of Sensors, vacuum leaks, and binding components that are run by the accessory drive belt.
13. Use the scan tool to perform a System Test if one applies to the component.

14. A co-pilot, data recorder, and/or lab scope should be used to help diagnose intermittent conditions.

CAMSHAFT POSITION (CMP) SENSOR

LOCATION

See Figure 111.

22043_COMP_G0104

Fig. 111 Location of the front camshaft position sensor—2.0L & 2.4L Engines

These engines utilize two camshaft position sensors mounted to the front and rear of the cylinder head.

OPERATION

The Powertrain Control Module (PCM) sends approximately 5 volts to the Hall-effect sensor. This voltage is required to operate the Hall-effect chip and the electronics inside the sensor. The input to the PCM occurs on a 5 volt output reference circuit. A ground for the sensor is provided through the sensor return circuit. The PCM identifies camshaft position by registering the change from 5 to 0 volts, as signaled from the camshaft position sensor.

The PCM determines fuel injection synchronization and cylinder identification from inputs provided by the camshaft position sensor and crankshaft position sensor. From the two inputs, the PCM determines crankshaft position.

REMOVAL & INSTALLATION

Front Sensor

1. Disconnect negative battery cable.
2. Remove the air cleaner hose to throttle body, disconnect the inlet air temperature sensor electrical connector.
3. Disconnect the electrical connector from the camshaft position sensor.

4. Remove the camshaft position (CMP) sensor mounting screws.

To install:

5. Lubricate the CMP sensor O-ring.
6. Install the CMP sensor using a twisting motion. Make sure the sensor is fully seated.

> ❈❈ **WARNING**
>
> **Do not drive the senior into the bore with the mounting screws.**

7. Carefully attach the electrical connector. Take care not to damage the sensor pins.
8. Install the air intake assembly.
9. Connect the negative battery cable.

Rear Sensor

See Figure 112.

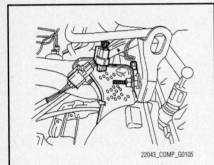

22043_COMP_G0105

Fig. 112 Disconnect the connector and remove the heat shield to access the rear CMP sensor.

1. Disconnect the negative battery cable.
2. Disconnect the sensor electrical connector.
3. Remove the heat shield retaining nut and remove the heat shield.
4. Remove the camshaft position (CMP) sensor mounting and remove the sensor.

To install:

5. Lubricate the CMP sensor O-ring.
6. Install the CMP sensor using a twisting motion. Make sure the sensor is fully seated.

> ❈❈ **WARNING**
>
> **Do not drive the senior into the bore with the mounting screws.**

7. Tighten the mounting bolt to 80 inch lbs. (9 Nm).
8. Carefully attach the electrical connector to the CMP sensor. Take care not to damage the sensor pins.

9. Install the heat shield onto the mounting stud and tighten the retaining nut.
10. Connect the electrical connector.
11. Connect the negative battery cable.

TESTING

1. Using the wiring diagram/schematic as a guide, inspect the wiring and connectors between the Camshaft 1/1 Position Sensor and the Powertrain Control Module (PCM).
2. Look for any chafed, pierced, pinched, or partially broken wires.
3. Look for broken, bent, pushed out or corroded terminals.
4. Inspect the Camshaft 1/1 Position Sensor for conditions such as loose mounting screws, damage, or cracks.
5. If no other problems are found, remove the Camshaft 1/1 Position Sensor.
6. Inspect the Camshaft 1/1 Position Sensor and mounting area for any condition that would result in an incorrect signal, such as damage, foreign material, or excessive movement.
7. Using a diagnostic scan tool, check for the presence of any Diagnostic Trouble Codes (DTCs). Record and address these codes as necessary.
8. If no codes are present, review the scan tool environmental data. If possible, try to duplicate the conditions under which the DTC set.
9. If applicable, actuate the component with the scan tool.
10. Monitor the scan tool data relative to this circuit and wiggle test the wiring and connectors.
11. Look for the data to change, the actuation to be interrupted, or for the DTC to reset during the wiggle test.
12. Refer to any Technical Service Bulletins (TSBs) that may apply.
13. Turn the ignition off.
14. Visually inspect the related wire harness. Disconnect all the related harness connectors. Look for any chafed, pierced, pinched, partially broken wires and broken, bent, pushed out, or corroded terminals.
15. Perform a voltage drop test on the related circuits between the suspected component and the Powertrain Control Module (PCM).
16. Inspect and clean all PCM, engine, and chassis grounds that are related to the most current DTC.
17. If numerous trouble codes were set, use a schematic and inspect any common ground or supply circuits.
18. For intermittent Misfire DTCs check for restrictions in the Intake and Exhaust

system, proper installation of Sensors, vacuum leaks, and binding components that are run by the accessory drive belt.
19. Use the scan tool to perform a System Test if one applies to the component.
20. A co-pilot, data recorder, and/or lab scope should be used to help diagnose intermittent conditions.

CRANKSHAFT POSITION (CKP) SENSOR

LOCATION

See Figure 113.

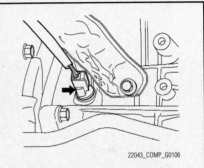

22043_COMP_G0106

Fig. 113 The crankshaft position sensor mounts to the rear of the engine block near the transmission.

OPERATION

The Powertrain Control Module (PCM) sends approximately 5 volts to the Hall-effect sensor. This voltage is required to operate the Hall-effect chip and the electronics inside the sensor. A ground for the sensor is provided through the sensor return circuit. The input to the PCM occurs on a 5 volt output reference circuit that operates as follows: The Hall-effect sensor contains a powerful magnet. As the magnetic field passes over the dense portion of the counterweight, the 5-volt signal is pulled to ground (0.3 volts) through a transistor in the sensor. When the magnetic field passes over the notches in the crankshaft counterweight, the magnetic field turns off the transistor in the sensor, causing the PCM to register the 5-volt signal. The PCM identifies crankshaft position by registering the change from 5 to 0 volts, as signaled from the Crankshaft Position sensor.

REMOVAL & INSTALLATION

1. Disconnect the negative battery cable.
2. Raise and safely support the vehicle.
3. If the vehicle is equipped with all wheel drive, the transfer case must be removed. For additional information, refer to Transfer Case, Removal & Installation.

4. Remove the heat shield retaining bolt and remove the heat shield.

5. Unlock and disconnect the crankshaft position (CKP) sensor electrical connector.

6. Remove the CKP sensor bolt and remove the sensor.

To install:

7. Lubricate the CKP sensor O-ring with clean engine oil.

8. Install the CKP sensor using a twisting motion. Make sure the sensor is fully seated.

✳✳ WARNING

Do not drive the senior into the bore with the mounting screws.

9. Tighten the mounting bolt to 80 inch lbs. (9 Nm).

10. Install the heat shield and tighten the retaining bolt.

11. If the vehicle is equipped with all wheel drive, install the transfer case.

12. Lower the vehicle.

13. Connect the negative battery cable.

TESTING

1. Using a diagnostic scan tool, check for the presence of any Diagnostic Trouble Codes (DTCs). Record and address these codes as necessary.

2. If no codes are present, review the scan tool environmental data. If possible, try to duplicate the conditions under which the DTC set.

3. If applicable, actuate the component with the scan tool.

4. Monitor the scan tool data relative to this circuit and wiggle test the wiring and connectors.

5. Look for the data to change, the actuation to be interrupted, or for the DTC to reset during the wiggle test.

6. Refer to any Technical Service Bulletins (TSBs) that may apply.

7. Turn the ignition off.

8. Visually inspect the related wire harness. Disconnect all the related harness connectors. Look for any chafed, pierced, pinched, partially broken wires and broken, bent, pushed out, or corroded terminals.

9. Perform a voltage drop test on the related circuits between the suspected component and the Powertrain Control Module (PCM).

10. Inspect and clean all PCM, engine, and chassis grounds that are related to the most current DTC.

11. If numerous trouble codes were set, use a schematic and inspect any common ground or supply circuits.

12. For intermittent Misfire DTCs check for restrictions in the Intake and Exhaust system, proper installation of Sensors, vacuum leaks, and binding components that are run by the accessory drive belt.

13. Use the scan tool to perform a System Test if one applies to the component.

14. A co-pilot, data recorder, and/or lab scope should be used to help diagnose intermittent conditions.

ENGINE COOLANT TEMPERATURE (ECT) SENSOR

LOCATION

See Figures 114 and 115.

There are two coolant temperature sensors. One is located in the coolant adapter and one is located in the cylinder head.

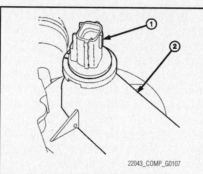

22043_COMP_G0107

Fig. 114 One the coolant temperature sensor (1) is located in the coolant adapter (2).

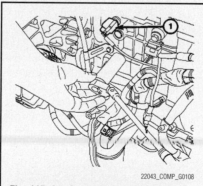

22043_COMP_G0108

Fig. 115 Another coolant temperature sensor (1) threads into the cylinder head.

OPERATION

The Engine Coolant Temperature (ECT) sensor provides an input to the Powertrain Control Module (PCM). As temperature increases, resistance of the sensor decreases. As coolant temperature varies, the ECT sensor resistance changes resulting in a different voltage value at the PCM ECT sensor signal circuit. The ECT sensor provides input for various PCM operations. The PCM uses the input to control air-fuel mixture, timing, and radiator fan on/off times.

REMOVAL & INSTALLATION

The following procedure can be used for removal and installation of either sensor.

1. Disconnect the negative battery cable.

2. Drain the cooling system.

3. Disconnect the Engine Coolant Temperature (ECT) sensor electrical connector.

4. Remove the ECT sensor.

To install:

5. Install the ECT sensor as follows:

  a. Coolant adapter mounted: Make sure the ECT sensor is locked in place.

  b. Cylinder head mounted: Tighten the sensor to 14 ft. lbs. (19 Nm).

6. Reconnect the ECT sensor electrical connector.

7. Refill the cooling system to the correct level.

8. Connect the negative battery cable.

TESTING

1. Using the wiring diagram/schematic as a guide, inspect the wiring and connectors between the Engine Coolant Temperature sensor(s) and the Powertrain Control Module (PCM).

2. Look for any chafed, pierced, pinched, or partially broken wires.

3. Look for broken, bent, pushed out or corroded terminals.

4. Turn the ignition on.

5. Monitor the scan tool data relative to the sensor(s) and wiggle test the wiring and connectors.

6. Look for the data to change or for a DTC to set during the wiggle test.

7. Check the engine coolant level and the condition of the engine coolant.

8. With the scan tool, read the Engine Coolant Temperature Sensor value for each sensor. If the engine was allowed to cool completely, the value should be approximately equal to the ambient temperature.

9. Monitor each sensor value on the scan tool and the actual coolant temperature with a thermometer.

10. Using a diagnostic scan tool, check for the presence of any Diagnostic Trouble Codes (DTCs). Record and address these codes as necessary.

11. If no codes are present, review the scan tool environmental data. If possible, try to duplicate the conditions under which the DTC set.

12. If applicable, actuate the component with the scan tool.

13. Monitor the scan tool data relative to

this circuit and wiggle test the wiring and connectors.

14. Look for the data to change, the actuation to be interrupted, or for the DTC to reset during the wiggle test.

15. Refer to any Technical Service Bulletins (TSBs) that may apply.

16. Turn the ignition off.

17. Visually inspect the related wire harness. Disconnect all the related harness connectors. Look for any chafed, pierced, pinched, partially broken wires and broken, bent, pushed out, or corroded terminals.

18. Perform a voltage drop test on the related circuits between the suspected component and the Powertrain Control Module (PCM).

19. Inspect and clean all PCM, engine, and chassis grounds that are related to the most current DTC.

20. If numerous trouble codes were set, use a schematic and inspect any common ground or supply circuits.

21. For intermittent Misfire DTCs check for restrictions in the Intake and Exhaust system, proper installation of Sensors, vacuum leaks, and binding components that are run by the accessory drive belt.

22. Use the scan tool to perform a System Test if one applies to the component.

23. A co-pilot, data recorder, and/or lab scope should be used to help diagnose intermittent conditions.

HEATED OXYGEN (HO2S) SENSOR

LOCATION

See Figures 116 and 117.

The upstream oxygen sensor threads into the outlet flange of the exhaust manifold. The downstream heated oxygen sensor threads into the system depending on emission package.

Fig. 116 The upstream sensor is located in the output flange of the exhaust manifold.

22043_COMP_G0110

Fig. 117 The downstream sensor is shown here threaded into the under floor catalytic converter.

OPERATION

As vehicles accumulate mileage, the catalytic converter deteriorates. The deterioration results in a less efficient catalyst. To monitor catalytic converter deterioration, the fuel injection system uses two heated oxygen sensors. One sensor is upstream of the catalytic converter, one is downstream of the converter. The Powertrain Control Module (PCM) compares the reading from the sensors to calculate the catalytic converter oxygen storage capacity and converter efficiency. Also, the PCM uses the upstream heated oxygen sensor input when adjusting injector pulse width.

When the catalytic converter efficiency drops below emission standards, the PCM stores a diagnostic trouble code and illuminates the malfunction indicator lamp (MIL).

The Heated Oxygen Sensors (HO2S) produce a constant 2.5 volts on NGC (4 cylinder) vehicles, depending upon the oxygen content of the exhaust gas. When a large amount of oxygen is present (caused by a lean air/fuel mixture, can be caused by misfire and exhaust leaks), the sensors produce a low voltage. When there is a lesser amount of oxygen present (caused by a rich air/fuel mixture, which can be caused by internal engine problems) it produces a higher voltage. By monitoring the oxygen content and converting it to electrical voltage, the sensors act as a rich-lean switch.

The oxygen sensors are equipped with a heating element that keeps the sensors at proper operating temperature during all operating modes. Maintaining correct sensor temperature at all times allows the system to enter into closed loop operation sooner. Also, it allows the system to remain in closed loop operation during periods of extended idle.

In Closed Loop operation the PCM monitors the HO2S input (along with other inputs) and adjusts the injector pulse width accordingly. During Open Loop operation the PCM ignores the HO2S input. The PCM adjusts injector pulse width based on preprogrammed (fixed) values and inputs from other sensors.

The NGC Controller has a common ground for the heater in the HO2S. 12 volts is supplied to the heater in the HO2S by the NGC controller. Both the upstream and downstream HO2S for NGC are pulse width modulation (PWM). NOTE: When replacing an HO2S, the PCM RAM memory must be cleared, either by disconnecting the PCM C-1 connector or momentarily disconnecting the Battery negative terminal. The NGC learns the characteristics of each HO2S heater element and these old values should be cleared when installing a new HO2S. You may experience driveability issues if this is not performed.

REMOVAL & INSTALLATION

Upstream Sensor

1. Remove the engine appearance cover.

2. Disconnect the negative battery cable.

3. Disconnect the Heated Oxygen Sensor (HO2S) electrical connector.

4. Remove the sensor using a Snap-On® tool YA8875 crow foot wrench or suitable oxygen sensor socket.

5. After removing the sensor, the exhaust manifold threads must be cleaned with an 18 mm x 1.5 + 6E tap.

To install:

6. If you are reusing the original sensor, coat the sensor threads with an anti-seize compound such as Loctite® 771-64 or equivalent. New sensors have the compound on the threads and not require an additional coating.

7. Install the sensor using a Snap-On® tool YA8875 crow foot wrench or suitable oxygen sensor socket. Tighten the sensor to 30 ft. lbs. (41 Nm).

8. Connect the HO2S electrical connector.

9. Connect the negative battery cable.

10. Install the engine appearance cover.

Downstream Sensor

1. Remove the negative battery cable.

2. Raise and safely support the vehicle.

3. Disconnect the Heated Oxygen Sensor (HO2S) electrical connector.

4. Disconnect the sensor electrical

wiring harness from the clips along the body.

5. Remove the sensor using a Snap-On® tool YA8875 crow foot wrench or suitable oxygen sensor socket.

6. After removing the sensor, the exhaust manifold threads must be cleaned with an 18 mm x 1.5 + 6E tap.

To install:

7. If you are reusing the original sensor, coat the sensor threads with an anti-seize compound such as Loctite® 771-64 or equivalent. New sensors have the compound on the threads and not require an additional coating.

8. Install the sensor using a Snap-On® tool YA8875 crow foot wrench or suitable oxygen sensor socket. Tighten the sensor to 30 ft. lbs. (41 Nm).

9. Connect the electrical wiring harness to the clips along the body.

10. Install the sensor using a Snap-On® tool YA8875 crow foot wrench or suitable oxygen sensor socket. Tighten the sensor to 30 ft. lbs. (41 Nm).

11. Connect the HO2S electrical connector.

12. Connect the negative battery cable.

13. Install the engine appearance cover.

TESTING

1. Using a diagnostic scan tool, check for the presence of any Diagnostic Trouble Codes (DTCs). Record and address these codes as necessary.

2. If no codes are present, review the scan tool environmental data. If possible, try to duplicate the conditions under which the DTC set.

3. If applicable, actuate the component with the scan tool.

4. Monitor the scan tool data relative to this circuit and wiggle test the wiring and connectors.

5. Look for the data to change, the actuation to be interrupted, or for the DTC to reset during the wiggle test.

6. Refer to any Technical Service Bulletins (TSBs) that may apply.

7. Turn the ignition off.

8. Visually inspect the related wire harness. Disconnect all the related harness connectors. Look for any chafed, pierced, pinched, partially broken wires and broken, bent, pushed out, or corroded terminals.

9. Perform a voltage drop test on the related circuits between the suspected component and the Powertrain Control Module (PCM).

10. Inspect and clean all PCM, engine, and chassis grounds that are related to the most current DTC.

11. If numerous trouble codes were set, use a schematic and inspect any common ground or supply circuits.

12. For intermittent Misfire DTCs check for restrictions in the Intake and Exhaust system, proper installation of Sensors, vacuum leaks, and binding components that are run by the accessory drive belt.

13. Use the scan tool to perform a System Test if one applies to the component.

14. A co-pilot, data recorder, and/or lab scope should be used to help diagnose intermittent conditions.

INTAKE AIR TEMPERATURE (IAT) SENSOR

LOCATION

See Figure 118.

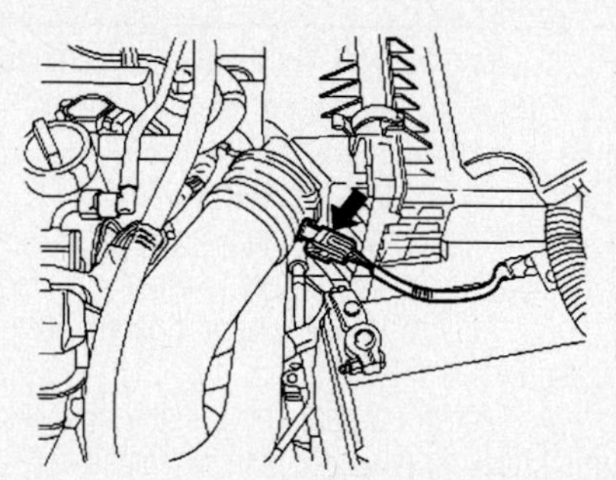

22043_COMP_G0111

Fig. 118 The Intake Air Temperature Sensor is located in the air intake tube of the air intake assembly.

OPERATION

The Intake Air Temperature (IAT) sensor is a negative coefficient sensor that provides information to the Powertrain Control Module regarding the temperature of the air entering the intake manifold.

REMOVAL & INSTALLATION

See Figure 119.

1. Disconnect the negative battery cable.

2. Disconnect the Intake Air Temperature (IAT) sensor electrical connector.

3. Remove the IAT sensor.

To install:

4. Install the IAT sensor and ensure the correct sensor orientation.

5. Attach the IAT sensor electrical connector.

6. Connect the negative battery cable.

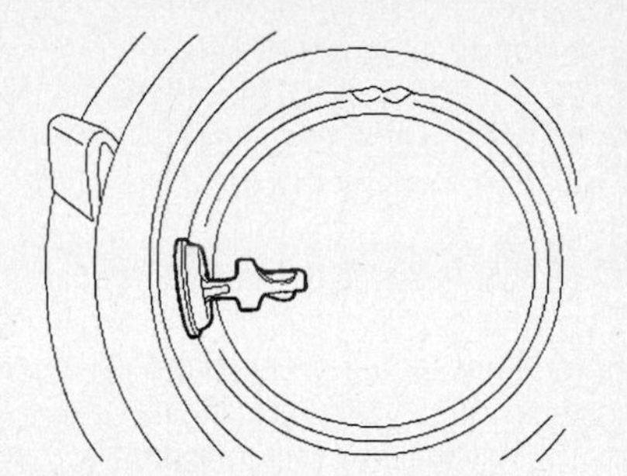

22043_COMP_G0112

Fig. 119 Showing the correct IAT sensor orientation—2.0L & 2.4L Engines

TESTING

1. Turn the ignition off. If possible, allow the vehicle to sit with the ignition off for more than 8 hours in an environment where the temperature is consistent and above 20°F (-7°C).

2. Test drive the vehicle. The vehicle must exceed 30 mph (48 km/h) during the test drive. Do not cycle the ignition off when the test drive is completed.

3. With a scan tool, select View DTCs.

4. If a DTC is not active, perform the following:

5. Refer to any Technical Service Bulletins (TSBs) that may apply.

6. Review the scan tool Freeze Frame information. If possible, try to duplicate the conditions under which the DTC set.

7. With the engine running at normal operating temperature, monitor the scan tool parameters related to the DTC while wiggling the wire harness. Look for parameter values to change and/or a DTC to set. Turn the ignition off.

8. Visually inspect the related wire harness. Disconnect all the related harness connectors. Look for any chafed, pierced, pinched, partially broken wires and broken, bent, pushed out, or corroded terminals. Perform a voltage drop test on the related circuits between the suspected inoperative component and the PCM.

CAUTION

Do not probe the PCM harness connectors. Probing the PCM harness connectors will damage the PCM terminals resulting in poor terminal to pin connection. Install Miller Special Tool #8815 to perform diagnosis.

9. Inspect and clean all PCM, engine, and chassis grounds that are related to the most current DTC.

10. If numerous trouble codes were set,

use a wire schematic and look for any common ground or supply circuits.

11. For any Relay DTCs, actuate the Relay with the scan tool and wiggle the related wire harness to try to interrupt the actuation.

12. For intermittent Evaporative Emission trouble codes perform a visual and physical inspection of the related parts including hoses and the Fuel Filler cap.

13. Use the scan tool to perform a System Test if one applies to failing component. A co-pilot, data recorder, and/or lab scope should be used to help diagnose intermittent conditions.

KNOCK SENSOR (KS)

LOCATION

See Figure 120.

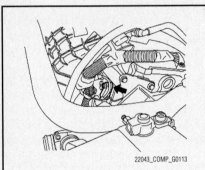

Fig. 120 The knock sensor is bolted to the engine block in front of the starter under the intake manifold.

OPERATION

When the Knock Sensor (KS) detects a knock in one of the cylinders, it sends an input signal to the Powertrain Control Module (PCM). In response, the PCM retards ignition timing for all cylinders by a scheduled amount.

Knock sensors contain a piezoelectric material which constantly vibrates and sends an input voltage (signal) to the PCM while the engine operates. As the intensity of the crystal's vibration increases, the knock sensor output voltage also increases.

The voltage signal produced by the knock sensor increases with the amplitude of vibration. The PCM receives as an input the knock sensor voltage signal. If the signal rises above a predetermined level, the PCM will store that value in memory and retard ignition timing to reduce engine knock. If the knock sensor voltage exceeds a preset value, the PCM retards ignition timing for all cylinders. It is not a selective cylinder retard.

The PCM ignores knock sensor input

during engine idle conditions. Once the engine speed exceeds a specified value, ignition timing retard is allowed.

REMOVAL & INSTALLATION

1. Disconnect the negative battery cable.
2. Remove the bolt holding the Knock Sensor (KS)
3. Remove the KS with the electrical connector attached.
4. Disconnect the electrical connector from the KS.

To install:
5. Attach the electrical connector to the KS.
6. Install the KS into the engine block. Tighten the bolt to 16 ft. lbs. (22 Nm).

❊❊ WARNING

Over or under-tightening affects the knock sensor performance.

7. Connect the negative battery cable.

TESTING

1. Using the wiring diagram/schematic as a guide, inspect the wiring and connectors between the Knock Sensor and the Powertrain Control Module (PCM).
2. Look for any chafed, pierced, pinched, or partially broken wires.
3. Look for broken, bent, pushed out or corroded terminals.
4. Monitor the scan tool data relative to this circuit and wiggle test the wiring and connectors.
5. Look for the data to change or for the DTC to reset during the wiggle test.
6. Refer to any Technical Service Bulletins that may apply.
7. Review the scan tool Freeze Frame information. If possible, try to duplicate the conditions under which the DTC set.
8. With the engine running at normal operating temperature, monitor the scan tool parameters related to the DTC while wiggling the wire harness. Look for parameter values to change and/or a DTC to set. Turn the ignition off.
9. Visually inspect the related wire harness. Disconnect all the related harness connectors. Look for any chafed, pierced, pinched, partially broken wires and broken, bent, pushed out, or corroded terminals. Perform a voltage drop test on the related circuits between the suspected inoperative component and the PCM.

❊❊ CAUTION

Do not probe the PCM harness connectors. Probing the PCM harness

connectors will damage the PCM terminals resulting in poor terminal to pin connection. Install Miller Special Tool #8815 to perform diagnosis.

10. Inspect and clean all PCM, engine, and chassis grounds that are related to the most current DTC.

11. If numerous trouble codes were set, use a wire schematic and look for any common ground or supply circuits.

12. For any Relay DTCs, actuate the Relay with the scan tool and wiggle the related wire harness to try to interrupt the actuation.

13. For intermittent Evaporative Emission trouble codes perform a visual and physical inspection of the related parts including hoses and the Fuel Filler cap.

14. Use the scan tool to perform a System Test if one applies to failing component. A co-pilot, data recorder, and/or lab scope should be used to help diagnose intermittent conditions.

MANIFOLD ABSOLUTE PRESSURE (MAP) SENSOR

LOCATION

See Figure 121.

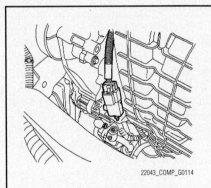

Fig. 121 The Manifold Absolute Pressure Sensor mounts to the intake manifold.

OPERATION

The Manifold Absolute Pressure (MAP) sensor serves as a Powertrain Control Module (PCM) input, using a silicon based sensing unit, to provide data on the manifold vacuum that draws the air/fuel mixture into the combustion chamber. The PCM requires this information to determine injector pulse width and spark advance. When MAP equals Barometric pressure, the pulse width will be at maximum.

Also like the cam and crank sensors, a 5 volt reference is supplied from the PCM and returns a voltage signal to the PCM that reflects manifold pressure. The zero pressure reading is 0.5 volt and full scale is 4.5 volt. For a pressure swing of 0 - 15 psi the voltage changes 4.0 volt. The sensor is supplied a regulated 4.8 to 5.1 volts to operate the sensor. Like the cam and crank sensors ground is provided through the sensor return circuit.

REMOVAL & INSTALLATION

1. Remove the air intake assembly.
2. Disconnect the negative battery cable.
3. Disconnect the electrical connector from the Manifold Absolute Pressure (MAP) sensor.
4. Remove the mounting screw from the MAP sensor and remove the sensor.

To install:

5. Install the MAP sensor to the intake manifold and tighten the screw.
6. Connect the electrical connector to the MAP sensor.
7. Connect the negative battery cable.
8. Install the air intake assembly.

TESTING

1. Turn the ignition off.
2. Using the wiring diagram/schematic as a guide, inspect the wiring and connectors between the MAP Sensor and the PCM.
3. Look for any chafed, pierced, pinched, or partially broken wires.
4. Look for broken, bent, pushed out or corroded terminals.
5. Turn the ignition on.
6. Monitor the scan tool data relative to the sensor and wiggle test the wiring and connectors.
7. Look for the data to change or for a DTC to set during the wiggle test. If necessary, check each sensor circuit for high resistance or a shorted condition.
8. With a scan tool, read the Barometric Pressure. The Barometric Pressure should be approximately equal to the actual barometric pressure. If necessary, compare the Barometric Pressure value of the tested vehicle to the value of a known good vehicle of a similar make and model.
9. Connect a vacuum gauge to a manifold vacuum source and start the engine.
10. With the scan tool, read the MAP Sensor vacuum. The scan tool reading for MAP vacuum should be within 1 inch of the vacuum gauge reading.
11. With the scan tool, monitor the MAP Sensor signal voltage. With the engine idling in neutral or park, snap the throttle. The MAP Sensor signal voltage should change from below 2.0 volts at idle to above 3.5 volts at wide open throttle.

POWERTRAIN CONTROL MODULE (PCM)

LOCATION

See Figure 122.

Fig. 122 The PCM is located in the engine compartment under the air cleaner housing.

OPERATION

The Powertrain Control Module (PCM) receives input signals from various switches and sensors that are referred to as PCM Inputs. Based on these inputs, the PCM adjusts various engine and vehicle operations through devices that are referred to as PCM Outputs .

Based on inputs it receives, the PCM adjusts fuel injector pulse width, idle speed, ignition spark advance, ignition coil dwell and EVAP canister purge operation. The PCM also determines the appropriate transmission shift schedule and shift points, depending on the present operating conditions and driver demand. The PCM regulates the cooling fan, air conditioning and speed control systems. The PCM changes generator charge rate by adjusting the generator field. The PCM also performs diagnostics.

The camshaft position sensor and crankshaft position sensor signals are sent to the PCM. If the PCM does not receive the signal within approximately 1 second of engine cranking, it deactivates the fuel pump. When these are deactivated, power is shut off to the fuel injectors, ignition coils, oxygen sensor heating elements and fuel pump.

The PCM contains a voltage converter that changes battery voltage to a regulated 5 volts direct current to power the camshaft position sensor, crankshaft position sensor, manifold absolute pressure sensor, throttle position sensor, A/C pressure switch, A/C pressure transducer, and vehicle speed sensor.

REMOVAL & INSTALLATION

1. Disconnect the negative battery cable.
2. Unlock and disconnect the electrical connectors from the Powertrain Control Module (PCM).
3. Remove the air intake assembly.
4. Remove the PCM mounting bolts.
5. Tip the module out and remove the PCM from the mounting bracket.

To install:

6. Tip the PCM module into the mounting bracket.
7. Install the mounting bolts and tighten to 80 inch lbs. (9 Nm).
8. Check the electrical connector pins for damage.
9. Connect the electrical connectors and lock them into place.
10. Install the air intake assembly.
11. Connect the negative battery cable.
12. Use a diagnostic scan tool to reprogram the PCM with the VIN and original mileage if PCM has been replaced.

TESTING

1. Turn the ignition on and with the scan tool, select ECU view.
2. A red X will be next to the module that is not communicating, indicating that the module is not active on the Bus network. A green check indicates that the module is active on the Bus network.
3. Visually inspect the related wire harness. Disconnect all the related harness connectors. Look for any chafed, pierced, pinched, partially broken wires and broken, bent, pushed out, or corroded terminals. Perform a voltage drop test on the related circuits between the suspected inoperative component and the PCM.

✳✳ CAUTION

Do not probe the PCM harness connectors. Probing the PCM harness connectors will damage the PCM terminals resulting in poor terminal to pin connection. Install Miller Special Tool #8815 to perform diagnosis.

4. Inspect and clean all PCM, engine, and chassis grounds that are related to the most current DTC.
5. If numerous trouble codes were set, use a wire schematic and look for any common ground or supply circuits.
6. For any Relay DTCs, actuate the Relay with the scan tool and wiggle the related wire harness to try to interrupt the actuation.
7. Use the scan tool to perform a System Test if one applies to failing component.

A co-pilot, data recorder, and/or lab scope should be used to help diagnose intermittent conditions.

THROTTLE POSITION SENSOR (TPS)

LOCATION

The Throttle Position Sensor is located on the throttle body assembly.

OPERATION

The Throttle Position Sensor (TPS) and throttle actuating DC motor are integral to the throttle body. The throttle body is a non serviceable item, replace the throttle body as an assembly.

The throttle blade will not close completely when engine is shut down. This engine off blade position is for start up. The electric throttle body will adjust the throttle blade for idle control as the idle air control valve adjusted idle speed previously on cable actuated throttle bodies. The electric throttle body will also adjust the throttle blade for normal driving operation. The throttle blade will move to the engine off blade position if throttle body codes are set to provide air for limp-in mode.

REMOVAL & INSTALLATION

The throttle position sensor and throttle actuating DC motor are integral to the throttle body. The throttle body is a non-serviceable item. The throttle body must be replaced as an assembly. For additional information, refer to the following section, "Throttle Body, Removal & Installation.

TESTING

1. Using the wiring diagram/schematic as a guide, inspect the wiring and connectors between the Throttle Body and the Powertrain Control Module (PCM).

2. Look for any chafed, pierced, pinched, or partially broken wires.

3. Look for broken, bent, pushed out or corroded terminals.

4. Inspect the Throttle Body for any condition that would result in an incorrect signal, such as damage or contamination.

5. Inspect and clean all PCM, engine, and chassis grounds that are related to the most current DTC.

6. If numerous trouble codes were set, use a wire schematic and look for any common ground or supply circuits.

7. For any Relay DTCs, actuate the Relay with the scan tool and wiggle the related wire harness to try to interrupt the actuation.

8. Use the scan tool to perform a System Test if one applies to failing component. A co-pilot, data recorder, and/or lab scope should be used to help diagnose intermittent conditions.

VEHICLE SPEED SENSOR (VSS)

LOCATION

The Vehicle Speed Sensor is mounted above the transaxle differential assembly.

OPERATION

The Vehicle Speed Sensor (VSS) is a Hall Effect sensor mounted above the transaxle differential. The sensor is triggered by the ring gear teeth passing below it. The VSS pulse signal to the speedometer/odometer is monitored by the PCM speed control circuitry to determine vehicle speed and to maintain speed control set speed.

REMOVAL & INSTALLATION

1. Disconnect the negative battery cable.
2. Remove the air intake assembly.
3. Disconnect the Vehicle Speed Sensor (VSS) electrical connector.

➡Clean the area around the VSS before removal to prevent dirt from the entering the transaxle.

4. Remove the VSS retaining bolt and remove the VSS.

To install:

5. Install the VSS using a new O-ring. Tighten the retaining bolt to 60 inch lbs. (7 Nm).

6. Connect the VSS electrical connector.
7. Install the air intake assembly.
8. Connect the negative battery cable.

TESTING

1. Using a diagnostic scan tool, check for the presence of any Diagnostic Trouble Codes (DTCs). Record and address these codes as necessary.

2. If no codes are present, review the scan tool environmental data. If possible, try to duplicate the conditions under which the DTC set.

3. If applicable, actuate the component with the scan tool.

4. Monitor the scan tool data relative to this circuit and wiggle test the wiring and connectors.

5. Look for the data to change, the actuation to be interrupted, or for the DTC to reset during the wiggle test.

6. Refer to any Technical Service Bulletins (TSBs) that may apply.

7. Turn the ignition off.

8. Visually inspect the related wire harness. Disconnect all the related harness connectors. Look for any chafed, pierced, pinched, partially broken wires and broken, bent, pushed out, or corroded terminals.

9. Perform a voltage drop test on the related circuits between the suspected component and the Powertrain Control Module (PCM).

10. Inspect and clean all PCM, engine, and chassis grounds that are related to the most current DTC.

11. If numerous trouble codes were set, use a schematic and inspect any common ground or supply circuits.

12. For intermittent Misfire DTCs check for restrictions in the Intake and Exhaust system, proper installation of Sensors, vacuum leaks, and binding components that are run by the accessory drive belt.

13. Use the scan tool to perform a System Test if one applies to the component.

14. A co-pilot, data recorder, and/or lab scope should be used to help diagnose intermittent conditions.

FUEL

GASOLINE FUEL INJECTION SYSTEM

FUEL SYSTEM SERVICE PRECAUTIONS

Safety is the most important factor when performing not only fuel system maintenance but any type of maintenance. Failure to conduct maintenance and repairs in a safe manner may result in serious personal injury or death. Maintenance and testing of the vehicle's fuel system components can be accomplished safely and effectively by adhering to the following rules and guidelines.

• To avoid the possibility of fire and personal injury, always disconnect the negative battery cable unless the repair or test procedure requires that battery voltage be applied.

• Always relieve the fuel system pressure prior to disconnecting any fuel system component (injector, fuel rail, pressure regulator, etc.), fitting or fuel line connection. Exercise extreme caution whenever relieving fuel system pressure to avoid exposing skin, face and eyes to fuel spray. Please be advised that fuel under pressure may penetrate the skin or any part of the body that it contacts.

• Always place a shop towel or cloth around the fitting or connection prior to loosening to absorb any excess fuel due to spillage. Ensure that all fuel spillage (should it occur) is quickly removed from engine surfaces. Ensure that all fuel soaked cloths or towels are deposited into a suitable waste container.

• Always keep a dry chemical (Class B) fire extinguisher near the work area.

• Do not allow fuel spray or fuel vapors to come into contact with a spark or open flame.

• Always use a back-up wrench when loosening and tightening fuel line connection fittings. This will prevent unnecessary stress and torsion to fuel line piping.

• Always replace worn fuel fitting O-rings with new Do not substitute fuel hose or equivalent where fuel pipe is installed.

Before servicing the vehicle, make sure to also refer to the precautions in the beginning of this section as well.

RELIEVING FUEL SYSTEM PRESSURE

1. Remove the lower rear seat cushion.
2. Remove the fuel pump module cover.
3. Disconnect the electrical connector for fuel pump module.

4. Start and run the engine until it stalls.
5. Attempt to restart the engine until it will no longer run.
6. Turn the ignition key to the **OFF** position.
7. Disconnect the negative battery cable.

➡**One or more Diagnostic Trouble Codes (DTCs) may have been stored in Powertrain Control Module (PCM) memory. The scan tool must be used to erase a DTC.**

FUEL FILTER

REMOVAL & INSTALLATION

The fuel filter is mounted inside the fuel pump module and is a non-serviceable part. For additional information, see Fuel Pump.

FUEL INJECTORS

REMOVAL & INSTALLATION

See Figures 123 through 125.

1. Properly relieve the fuel system pressure.
2. Disconnect the negative battery cable.
3. Disconnect the electrical connectors from the fuel injectors.
4. Disconnect the fuel line connection at the fuel rail.
5. Remove the hard fuel line from the fuel rail.
6. Remove the wiring harness clips from the fuel rail mounting studs.
7. Remove the two bolts holding the fuel rail at the lower manifold.
8. Remove the fuel rail.
9. Remove the clip holding the fuel injector to the fuel rail.
10. Remove the fuel injector, with the clip, from the fuel rail.

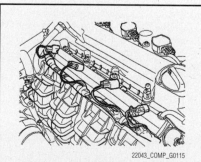

Fig. 123 Disconnect the electrical connectors from the fuel injectors—Fuel injector removal

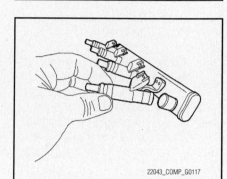

22043_COMP_G0116

Fig. 124 After removing the wiring harness and mounting bolts, remove the fuel rail—Fuel injector removal

22043_COMP_G0117

Fig. 125 Remove the fuel injector clip and fuel injector from the fuel rail—Fuel injector removal

To install:

11. Apply a light coating of clean engine oil to the upper O-ring of the fuel injector.
12. Install each injector in the cup on the fuel rail and then install the retaining clip.
13. Apply a light coating of clean engine oil to the O-ring on the nozzle each of each injector.
14. Install the fuel rail/injector assembly by inserting the fuel injector nozzles into the openings in the lower intake manifold.
15. Tighten the fuel rail mounting bolts to 20 ft. lbs. (27 Nm).
16. Install the wiring harness clips to the fuel rail mounting studs.
17. Attach the electrical connectors to the fuel injectors.
18. Install the fuel line to the fuel rail and connect the fuel supply tube.
19. Connect the negative battery cable.
20. Pressurize the fuel system with a diagnostic scan tool and check for leaks.

FUEL PUMP

REMOVAL & INSTALLATION

See Figures 126 through 128.

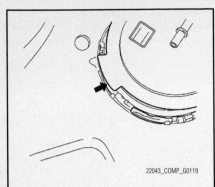

Fig. 126 Note the fuel pump location on the top of the fuel tank.

1. Properly relieve the fuel system pressure.

2. Remove the air cleaner housing lid and disconnect the Intake Air Temperature (IAT) sensor and make-up air hose.

3. Remove the rear seat cushion.

4. Remove the plastic access cover.

5. Disconnect the electrical connector.

6. Matchmark the orientation of the fuel pump module to the tank before removal.

7. Using Special Tool 9340 Spanner Wrench, remove the left side module lock ring.

8. Pull the fuel pump module up and out of the tank.

✳✳ WARNING

The fuel pump module will be filled fuel. Do not spill fuel inside the vehicle.

9. Tip the fuel pump module to the side and pour any fuel back into the tank.

10. Disconnect the internal line from the fuel pump module.

11. Tip the module on its side again to drain any remaining fuel from the reservoir into the tank.

12. Remove the fuel pump from the vehicle.

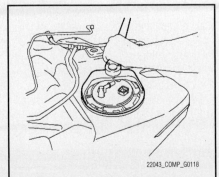

Fig. 127 Use a suitable spanner wrench to remove the lock ring of the fuel pump module.

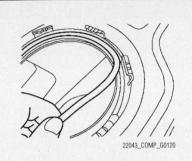

Fig. 128 Place a new seal between the tank threads and the pump module opening.

To install:

13. Remove the seal from the tank opening and discard.

14. Place a new seal between the tank threads and the pump module opening.

15. Connect the internal line to the fuel pump module

16. Install the module into the fuel tank.

17. Reposition the fuel pump module in the tank, aligning the matchmark made earlier.

18. While holding the fuel pump in position, install the lock ring using Special Tool 9340 Spanner Wrench.

19. Connect the electrical connector.

20. Install the plastic access cover.

21. Install the rear seat cushion.

22. Install the air cleaner housing lid and disconnect the Intake Air Temperature (IAT) sensor and make-up air hose.

23. Connect the negative battery cable.

24. Pressurize the fuel system with a diagnostic scan tool and check for leaks.

FUEL TANK

REMOVAL & INSTALLATION

1. Properly relieve the fuel system pressure.

2. Remove the air cleaner housing lid and disconnect the Intake Air Temperature (IAT) sensor and make-up air hose.

3. Remove the rear seat cushion.

4. Remove the plastic access cover.

5. Disconnect the electrical connector and fuel lines.

6. Drain the fuel from the fuel tank.

7. Raise and safely support the vehicle.

8. If equipped with All Wheel Drive, remove the driveshaft.

9. Remove the exhaust system.

10. Remove the rear suspension stay bars.

11. If equipped with All Wheel Drive, the rear differential module must be lowered as follows:

a. Tie the rear driveline module to the suspension crossmember.

b. Support rear differential module with a suitable jack.

c. Remove the three mounting bolts and lower rear differential module from the suspension crossmember

12. Remove all necessary splash shields.

13. Disconnect the vapor canister line.

14. Disconnect the filler tube recirculation vent and purge lines.

15. Disconnect the rubber fill hose from the fuel tank.

16. Remove the parking brake cable mounts from the fuel tank straps.

17. Support the fuel tank with a suitable jack and secure the fuel tank to the jack.

18. Remove the fuel tank strap mounting bolts.

19. Lower and remove the fuel tank from the vehicle.

To install:

20. Lift the fuel tank into position and install the fuel tank straps. Tighten the mounting bolts to 35 ft. lbs. (47 Nm).

➡ **Ensure the straps are not twisted or bent.**

21. Install the parking brake cable mounts.

22. Connect the filler tube recirculation vent and purge lines.

23. Connect the fill tube to the fuel tank inlet. Tighten the hose clamp to 38 inch lbs. (4 Nm).

24. Connect the vapor canister line.

25. Raise and install the rear differential module.

26. Install the rear suspension stay bars.

27. Install the splash shields.

28. Install the exhaust system.

29. Install the driveshaft.

30. Connect the electrical connectors and fuel lines to the fuel pump module.

31. Install the plastic access cover.

32. Install the rear seat cushion.

33. Install the air cleaner housing lid and disconnect the Intake Air Temperature (IAT) sensor and make-up air hose.

34. Connect the negative battery cable.

35. Pressurize the fuel system with a diagnostic scan tool and check for leaks.

IDLE SPEED

ADJUSTMENT

The idle speed is control by the Powertrain Control Module (PCM). No adjustment is necessary or possible.

THROTTLE BODY

REMOVAL & INSTALLATION

See Figure 129.

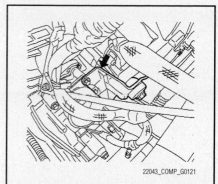

Fig. 129 Remove the throttle body support bracket.

1. Disconnect the negative battery cable.
2. Remove the engine appearance cover.
3. Remove the air intake assembly.
4. Disconnect the Intake Air Temperature (IAT) sensor and makeup air hose.
5. Disconnect the throttle body electrical connector.
6. Remove the throttle body support bracket.
7. Remove the throttle body mounting bolts.
8. Remove the throttle body assembly.

To install:

9. Ensure the throttle body O-ring is in place on the intake manifold.
10. Position the throttle body on the intake manifold alignment pins. Install, but do not tighten the mounting bolts.
11. Install the throttle body support bracket.
12. Tighten the throttle body mounting bolts in a criss-cross pattern to 80 inch lbs. (9 Nm).
13. Connect the throttle body electrical connector.
14. Install the air intake assembly.
15. Connect the IAT sensor and makeup air hose.
16. Connect the negative battery cable.
17. Install the engine appearance cover.

➡ **A Scan Tool may be used to learn electrical parameters. Go to the Miscellaneous Menu, and then select ETC Relearn. If the relearn is not performed, a Diagnostic Trouble Code (DTC) will be set. If necessary, use a scan tool to erase any Diagnostic Trouble Codes (DTCs) from the Powertrain Control Module (PCM).**

HEATING & AIR CONDITIONING SYSTEM

BLOWER MOTOR

REMOVAL & INSTALLATION

See Figure 130.

1. Disconnect the negative battery cable.
2. If equipped, remove the silencer from the below the passenger side of the instrument panel.
3. From underneath of the instrument panel, disengage the connector lock and disconnect the instrument panel wiring harness connector from the blower motor.
4. Remove the three screws that secure the blower motor and wire lead bracket.
5. Remove the blower motor.

To install:

6. Position the blower motor into the bottom of the HVAC housing.
7. Install the three mounting screws and tighten to 10 inch lbs. (1.2 Nm).
8. Connect the instrument panel wiring harness connector and engage the connector lock.
9. If equipped, install the silencer.
10. Connect the negative battery cable.

HEATER CORE

REMOVAL & INSTALLATION

See Figures 131 through 134.

1. Disconnect the negative battery cable.
2. Disable the air bag system.

3. Recover the refrigerant from the HVAC system.
4. Drain the cooling system.
5. Remove the heat shield located on the dash panel in the engine compartment.
6. Remove the bolt that secures the A/C liquid and suction line assembly to the A/C evaporator.
7. Disconnect the A/C liquid and suction line assembly from the A/C evaporator and remove and discard the dual-plane seals.
8. Cap the opened refrigerant line fittings and the evaporator ports.
9. Disconnect the heater hoses from the heater core tubes. Install plugs in, or tape over the opened heater core tubes to prevent coolant spillage during housing removal.
10. Remove the instrument panel as follows:

　a. Remove the left and right end caps using a trim stick to pry them off.
　b. Remove both left and right knee air bag covers, if equipped.
　c. Remove the two screws attaching the upper steering column shroud to the lower shroud. After removing the screws, unclip the shrouds from each other by applying hand pressure along the seams where the shrouds connect on the sides, then remove the upper shroud and lower steering column cover.
　d. Disconnect the steering column wiring harness.
　e. Remove the shift knob and remove the shifter bezel.

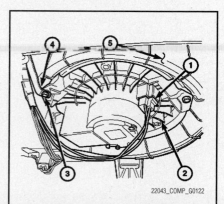

Fig. 130 Blower Motor (2) assembly— Wiring harness connector (1), Screws (3), Wire lead bracket (4), HVAC housing— Caliber

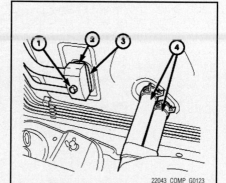

Fig. 131 Remove the bolt (1) that holds the A/C liquid and suction lines (2) to the evaporator (3). Disconnect the heater hoses and cap the open core tubes.

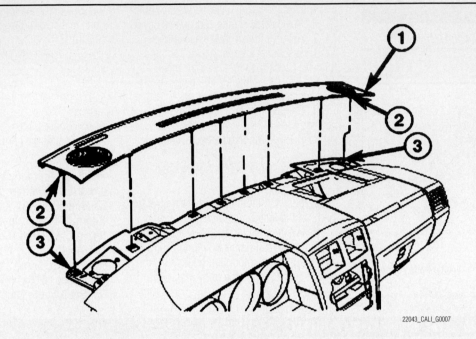

Fig. 132 Use a trim stick to disengage the panel clip (2) to remove the top cowl panel (1) from the instrument panel (3)—Instrument panel removal

f. Remove the center console shifter housing.

g. Remove the center bezel.

h. Remove the shifter assembly.

i. Remove the left and right A-pillar trim.

j. Remove the top cowl panel.

k. Remove the left cowl panel.

l. Disconnect the instrument panel wiring harness from the electrical connectors from behind the cowl panel.

m. Disconnect the wiring harness clipped along the A-pillar.

n. Remove the glove box.

o. Remove the right side cowl trim panel.

p. Disconnect the antenna wire from the radio harness.

q. Remove the mounting bolts and remove the front seats. Disconnect the electrical connectors before removal them from the vehicle.

r. Remove the center console.

s. Remove the left and right B-pillar trim panels.

t. Remove the left and right door sill scuff plate.

u. Pull back the carpet to gain access to the center console wiring harnesses.

v. Disconnect the instrument panel center console wiring harness.

w. Remove the left and right floor ducts.

x. Remove the four bolts behind the center bezel and one behind the glove box.

y. Remove the bolts holding the instrument panel to the cowl panel. Three bolts are located behind the left cap and one is at the bottom of the instrument panel.

z. Remove the condensation drain tube.

aa. Remove the fence line bolts from the upper cowl panel.

bb. Disconnect the HVAC wiring harness connectors.

cc. With the aid of an assistant, remove the instrument panel through the driver's side door.

11. Remove the nut that secures the passenger side of the HVAC housing to the dash panel.

12. Pull the HVAC housing rearward and remove the HVAC housing assembly from the passenger compartment.

13. Remove the foam seal from the flange located on the front of the HVAC housing.

14. Remove the screw that secures the

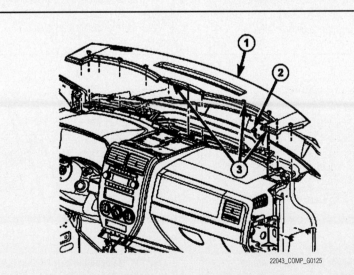

Fig. 133 Remove the fence line bolts (2) from the upper cowl panel (1)—Instrument panel removal

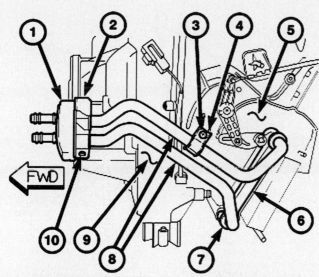

1. Foam seal
2. flange
3. screw
4. retaining bracket
5. air distribution housing
6. Heater core
8. heater core tubes
9. HVAC housing
10. screw

22043_COMP_G0128

Fig. 134 Heater core components—Foam seal (1), flange (2), screw (3), retaining bracket (4), air distribution housing (5), Heater core (6), heater core tubes (8), HVAC housing (9), screw (10)

flange to the front of the HVAC housing and remove the flange.

15. Remove the screw that secures the retaining bracket for the heater core tubes to the left side of the air distribution housing.

16. Carefully pull the heater core out of the driver's side of the air distribution housing.

To install:

17. Carefully install the heater core into the left side of the air distribution housing.

18. Install the retaining bracket that secures the heater core tubes. Tighten the screw to 10 inch lbs. (1.2 Nm).

19. Install the flange that secures the heater core tubes to the front of the HVAC housing.

20. Tighten the screw that secures the flange to the HVAC housing to 10 inch lbs. (1.2 Nm).

21. Install the foam seal onto the flange.

22. Installation is the reverse order of the removal process.

23. If the heater core was replaced, the cooling system must be flushed.

24. Charge the refrigerant system.

25. Refill the cooling system to the correct level.

26. Start the engine and check for leaks.

STEERING

POWER STEERING GEAR

REMOVAL & INSTALLATION

See Figures 135 through 139.

1. Siphon as much power steering fluid from the pump as possible.

2. Reposition the floor carpeting to access the intermediate shaft at the base of the column.

3. Position the front wheels in the straight-ahead position.

4. Turn the steering wheel to the right until the intermediate shaft coupling bolt at the base of the steering column can be accessed.

5. Remove the coupling bolt.

➡**Do not separate the intermediate shaft from the steering gear pinion shaft at this time.**

6. Return the front wheels to the straight-ahead position.

7. Use a steering wheel holder to lock the wheel into place.

8. Raise and safely support the vehicle.

9. Remove the front wheels.

10. On the side of the gear, remove the

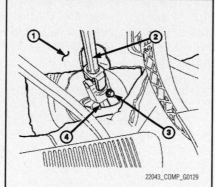

22043_COMP_G0129

Fig. 135 Under the carpet (1), remove the coupling bolt (3) that connects the intermediate shaft (2) to the steering gear pinion shaft (4).

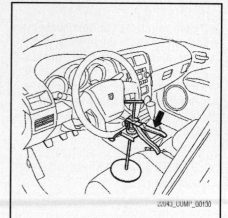

22043_COMP_G0130

Fig. 136 Use a steering wheel holder to lock the wheel into position.

nut from the outer tie rod end at the knuckle.

11. One the side of the gear, separate the tie rod end from the knuckle using Special Tool 9360 Remover or equivalent.

12. Remove the engine skid plate, if equipped.

13. Remove the rear engine mount.

14. Remove the front engine mount through-bolt.

15. Remove the three bolts securing the heat shield to the crossmember and remove the shield.

16. Disconnect the pressure and return hoses from the steering gear.

17. Remove the fasteners that secure the power steering hose routing clamps to the crossmember.

18. Remove the bolts securing the stabilizer bushing retainers to the

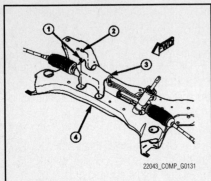

Fig. 137 Remove the bolts (1, 2) securing the heat shield (3) to the crossmember (4)

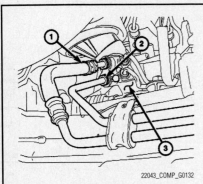

Fig. 138 Disconnect the pressure (2) and return (1) hoses from the steering gear

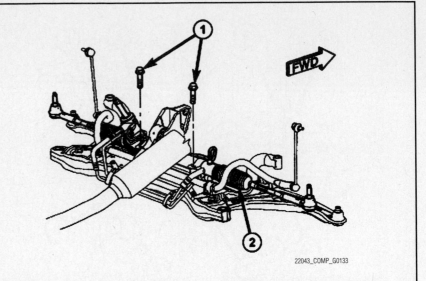

Fig. 139 Remove the mounting bolts (1) to remove the steering gear (2) from the front crossmember.

crossmember and remove the stabilizer bushing retainers.

➡Before removing the front suspension crossmember from the vehicle, the location of the crossmember must be marked on the body of the vehicle. If the front suspension crossmember is not reinstalled in exactly the same position, the preset wheel alignment settings will be lost.

19. Matchmark the location of the front crossmember on the body near each mounting bolt.
20. Support the front crossmember with a suitable jack.
21. Remove the mounting bolts securing the crossmember to the body.
22. Lower the crossmember enough to access the intermediate shaft coupling and slide it off the pinion shaft.
23. Remove the two bolts securing the steering gear to the crossmember.
24. Rotate the sway bar up in order to access the steering gear.
25. Remove the steering gear from the crossmember.

To install:
26. Rotate the sway bar up and install the steering gear on the crossmember.

Tighten the mounting bolts to 52 ft. lbs. (70 Nm).
27. Center the power steering gear rack in its travel as necessary.
28. Slowly raise the crossmember into its mounted position using a suitable jack matching the crossmember to the marked locations on the body made during removal.
29. Check the positioning of the seals at the dash panel and adjust as necessary.
30. Install the four mounting bolts (two each side) securing the front crossmember to the body and tighten the bolts to 140 ft. lbs. (190 Nm).
31. Install the retainers over the stabilizer bar cushions and tighten the bolts to 22 ft. lbs. (30 Nm).
32. Install the fasteners securing the power steering hose routing clamps to the crossmember. Use a new push clip on the left and tighten the screw on the right to 71 inch lbs. (8 Nm).
33. Install the pressure hose on the steering gear and tighten the tube nut to 24 ft. lbs. (32 Nm).
34. Install the return hose on the steering gear and tighten the tube nut to 15 ft. lbs. (20 Nm).
35. Position the heat shield on the crossmember. Tighten the two front mounting screws to 35 inch lbs. (4 Nm) and tighten the rear mounting screw to 13 ft. lbs. (17 Nm).
36. Install the front engine mount through-bolt.
37. Install the rear engine mount.
38. If equipped, install the engine skid plate.

➡Prior to attaching the outer tie rod end to the knuckle, inspect the tie rod seal boot. If the seal boot is damaged, replace the outer tie rod end.

39. On each side of the steering gear, install the outer tie rod end into the hole in the knuckle arm. Start a NEW tie rod mounting nut onto the stud. While holding the tie rod end stud with a wrench, tighten the nut with a wrench or crowfoot wrench to 97 ft. lbs. (132 Nm).
40. Install the front wheels.
41. Lower the vehicle.
42. Remove the steering wheel holder.
43. Verify the front wheels of vehicle are in the straight-ahead position.
44. Center the intermediate shaft over the steering gear pinion shaft, lining up the ends, then slide the intermediate shaft onto the steering gear pinion shaft.
45. From center, rotate the steering wheel to the right approximately 90° or until the intermediate shaft coupling bolt can be easily installed.
46. Install the intermediate shaft coupling bolt and tighten to 35 ft. lbs. (47 Nm).
47. Reposition the floor carpet in place.
48. Straighten the steering wheel to straight-ahead position.
49. Fill and bleed the power steering system.
50. Start the engine and check for leaks.
51. Check and adjust the alignment as necessary.

POWER STEERING PUMP

REMOVAL & INSTALLATION

See Figures 140 and 141.

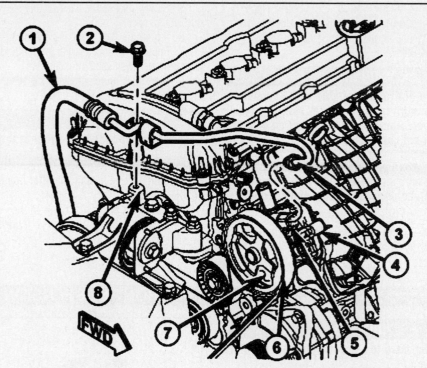

1. Supply hose
2. Routing bracket bolt
3. Pressure hose
4. Power steering pump
5. Pump pressure port
6. Accessory drive belt
7. Pump pulley
8. Upper mount

22043_COMP_G0135

Fig. 140 Power steering pump components—Supply hose (1), routing bracket bolt (2), pressure hose (3), power steering pump (4), pump pressure port (5), accessory drive belt (6), pump pulley (7), upper mount (8).

1. Siphon as much power steering fluid from the pump as possible.

2. Remove the engine appearance cover.

3. Remove the pressure hose routing bracket bolt from the upper mount.

4. Remove the pressure hose at the pump pressure port.

5. Remove the hose clamp securing the supply hose at the pump.

6. Remove the supply hose from the pump.

7. Remove the accessory drive belt. For additional information, refer to the following section, "Accessory drive belt, Removal & Installation."

8. Remove the three pump mounting bolts through the pulley openings.

9. Remove the power steering pump.

To install:

10. Using a lint free towel, wipe clean the open power steering pressure hose end and the power steering pump port. Replace any used O-rings with new. Lubricate the O-ring with clean power steering fluid.

11. Place the power steering pump into position and tighten the mounting bolts to 19 ft. lbs. (26 Nm).

12. Install the accessory drive belt.

13. Install the supply hose at the pump and secure the hose clamp.

14. Install the pressure hose at the pump pressure pump and tighten the tube nut to 24 ft. lbs. (32 Nm).

15. Install the pressure hose routing bracket bolt to the upper mount.

16. Fill and bleed and power steering system.

17. Start the engine and check for leaks.

18. Install the engine appearance cover.

BLEEDING

See Figure 142.

1. Check the fluid level. As measured on the side of the reservoir, the level should indicate between MAX and MIN when the fluid is at normal ambient temperature. Adjust the fluid level as necessary.

2. Tightly insert Special Tool 9688 Power Steering Cap Adapter into the mouth of the reservoir.

⁂ CAUTION

Failure to use a vacuum pump reservoir may allow power steering fluid to be sucked into the hand vacuum pump.

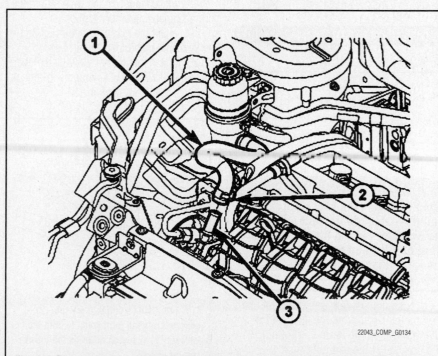

22043_COMP_G0134

Fig. 141 Remove the hose clamp (2) and supply hose (1) from the power steering pump (3).

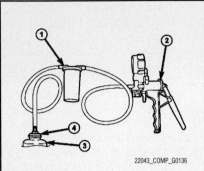

Fig. 142 Bleed the power steering system with a reservoir (1) Hand Vacuum Pump (2), Power Steering Cap Adapter (4) attached to the Power Steering Pump reservoir (3).

3. Attach Special Tool C-4207 Hand Vacuum Pump or equivalent, with reservoir attached, to the Power Steering Cap Adapter.

✳✳ WARNING

Do not run the engine while vacuum is applied to the power steering system. Damage to the power steering pump can occur.

➡ **When performing the following step make sure the vacuum level is maintained during the entire time period.**

4. Using a Hand Vacuum Pump, apply 68-85 kPa (20-25 in. Hg) of vacuum to the system for a minimum of three minutes.

5. Slowly release the vacuum and remove the special tools.

6. Adjust the fluid level as necessary.

7. Repeat the process until the fluid no longer drops when vacuum is applied.

8. Start the engine and cycle the steering wheel lock-to-lock three times.

✳✳ WARNING

Do not hold the steering wheel at the stops.

9. Stop the engine and check for leaks at all connections.

10. Check for any signs of air in the reservoir and check the fluid level. If air is present, repeat the procedure as necessary.

SUSPENSION

FRONT SUSPENSION

COIL SPRING

REMOVAL & INSTALLATION

The coil spring is part of the strut assembly. For additional information, See MacPherson Strut.

LOWER BALL JOINT

REMOVAL & INSTALLATION

The lower ball joint is an integral part of the lower control arm and is not serviceable. If the lower ball joint fails, the lower control arm must be replaced.

LOWER CONTROL ARM

REMOVAL & INSTALLATION

See Figures 143 and 144.

1. Raise and safely support the vehicle.

2. Remove the front wheel.

3. Remove the nut and pinch bolt that secures the ball joint stud to the knuckle.

✳ WARNING

Upon removing the knuckle from the ball joint stud, do not pull outward on the knuckle. Pulling the knuckle outward at this point can separate the inner CV-joint on the halfshaft, thus damaging it.

4. Using a suitable pry tool, separate the ball joint stud from the knuckle by prying down on the lower control arm and up against the ball joint on the knuckle.

✳✳ WARNING

Use care to not damage the ball joint seal.

5. Remove the front bolt attaching the lower control arm to the front suspension crossmember.

6. Remove the nut on the rear bolt attaching the lower control arm to the front suspension crossmember and remove the bolt.

7. Remove the lower control arm.

To install:

8. Place the lower control arm into the front suspension crossmember.

9. Insert the rear bolt up through the crossmember and lower control arm.

10. Install, but do not fully tighten, the nut on the rear bolt attaching the lower control arm to the crossmember.

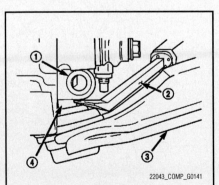

Fig. 143 Using a suitable pry tool (2), separate the ball joint stud (4) from the knuckle (1) by prying down on the lower control arm (3)

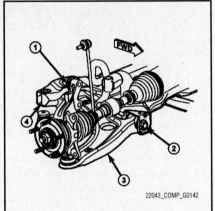

Fig. 144 Remove the front bolt (2) and nut (1) on the rear bolt that attaches the lower control arm (3) to the suspension crossmember (4) to remove the lower control arm.

11. Install, but do not fully tighten, the front bolt attaching the lower control arm to the crossmember.

12. With no weight on the lower control arm, tighten the lower control arm rear mounting bolt nut to 135 ft. lbs. (183 Nm) and the lower control arm front pivot bolt to 135 ft. lbs. (183 Nm).

13. Install the ball joint stud into the knuckle, aligning the bolt hole in the knuckle boss with the groove formed in the side of the ball joint stud. Install a new ball joint stud pinch bolt and nut and tighten the nut to 60 ft. lbs. (82 Nm).

14. Install the front wheel.

15. Lower the vehicle.

16. Check the alignment and adjust as necessary.

MACPHERSON STRUT

REMOVAL & INSTALLATION

See Figures 145 and 146.

1. Raise and safely support the vehicle.
2. Remove the front wheel.
3. Remove the bolt securing the brake hose routing bracket to the strut assembly.
4. While holding the stabilizer bar link stud stationary, remove the nut securing the link to the strut assembly.
5. While holding the bolt heads stationary, remove the nuts from the bolts that attach the strut to the knuckle.
6. Remove the two bolts attaching the strut assembly to the knuckle using a pin punch.

➡ **The bolts are serrated and cannot be turned.**

7. Remove the three nuts attaching the strut upper mount to the strut tower.
8. Remove the strut assembly from the vehicle.

To install:

9. Install the strut assembly into the strut tower. Tighten the three mounting nuts to 35 ft. lbs. (48 Nm).
10. Position the lower end of the strut assembly in line with the upper end of the knuckle. Align the holes and install the two

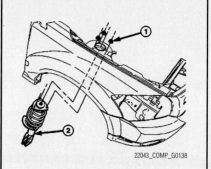

Fig. 146 Remove the three nuts (1) attaching the strut upper mount to the strut tower and remove the strut assembly (3).

attaching bolts. While holding the bolt heads stationary, tighten the nuts to 62 ft. lbs. (84 Nm).
11. Attach the stabilizer links to the strut and tighten the nuts to 43 ft. lbs. (58 Nm).
12. Secure the brake hose routing bracket to the strut and tighten the screws to 10 ft. lbs. (13 Nm).
13. Install the front wheels.
14. Lower the vehicle.
15. Check and adjust the alignment as necessary.

OVERHAUL

See Figures 147 and 148.

1. Position the strut assembly in the strut coil spring compressor following the manufacturer's instructions and set the lower and upper hooks of the compressor on the coil spring. Position the strut clevis bracket straight outward, away from the compressor.
2. Compress the coil spring until all coil spring tension is removed from the upper mount and bearing.
3. Once the spring is sufficiently compressed, install Strut Nut Wrench, Special Tool 9362, on the strut rod nut. Next, install Strut Shaft Socket, Special Tool 9894, on the end of the strut rod. While holding the strut rod from turning, remove the nut using the strut nut wrench.
4. Remove the clamp (if installed) from the bottom of the coil spring and remove the strut (damper) out through the bottom of the coil spring. The dust shield and jounce bumper will come out with the strut.
5. Remove the lower spring isolator from the strut seat.
6. Slide the dust shield and jounce bumper from the strut rod.
7. Remove the upper mount and bearing from the top of the upper spring seat and isolator.
8. Remove the upper spring seat and isolator from the top of the coil spring.
9. Release the tension from the coil spring by backing off the compressor drive completely. Push back the compressor hooks and remove the coil spring.

To assemble:

10. Place the coil spring in the spring compressor following the manufacturer's instructions. Before compressing the spring, rotate the spring so the end of the bottom coil is at approximately the 9 o'clock position as viewed from above (or to where the spring was when removed from the compressor). This action will allow the strut (damper) clevis bracket to be positioned outward, away from the compressor once installed.
11. Slowly compress the coil spring until enough room is available for strut assembly reassembly.
12. Install the upper spring seat and isolator on top of the coil spring.
13. Install the bearing and upper mount on top of the upper spring seat and isolator.
14. Install the lower spring isolator on the spring seat on the strut.
15. Slide the dust shield and jounce bumper onto the strut rod.
16. Install the strut up through the bottom of the coil spring and upper spring seat, mount, and bearing until the lower

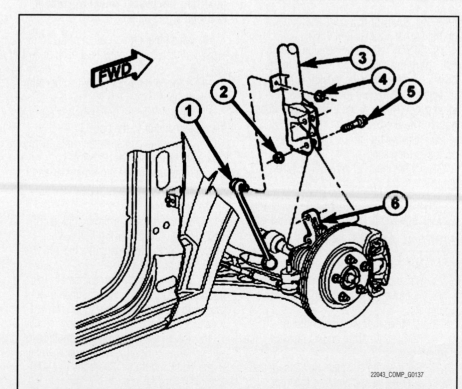

Fig. 145 Remove the nut (4) that secures the stabilizer link (1) to the strut (3). Hold the bolt heads (5) stationary while removing the nuts (2) that hold the strut (3) to the knuckle (6).

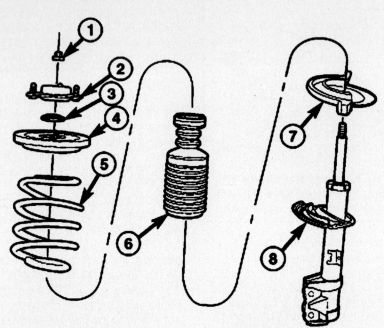

1. Upper mounting nut
2. Upper mount
3. Bearing
4. Isolator
5. Coil spring
6. Jounce bumper
7. Lower spring isolator
8. Strut

22043_COMP_G0139

Fig. 147 Strut assembly components—Upper mounting nut (1), Upper mount (2), Bearing (3), Isolator (4), Coil spring (5), Jounce bumper (6), Lower spring isolator (7), Strut (8).

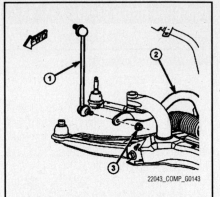

22043_COMP_G0143

Fig. 149 Hold the stabilizer bar link (1) lower stud stationary and remove the nut (3) that secures the link to the stabilizer bar (2).

spring seat contacts the lower end of the coil spring. Rotate the strut as necessary until the end of the bottom coil comes in contact with the stop built into the lower spring isolator.

17. While holding the strut in position, install the nut on the end of the strut rod.

18. Install Special Tool 9632 Strut Nut Wrench on the strut rod nut. Next, install Special Tool 9894 Strut Shaft Socket on the end of the strut rod. While holding the strut rod from turning, tighten the strut rod nut to 44 ft. lbs. (60 Nm) using a torque wrench on the end of Special Tool 9362.

19. Slowly release the tension from the coil spring by backing off the compressor drive completely. As the tension is relieved, make sure the upper mount and bearing align properly. Verify the upper mount does not bind when rotated.

20. Remove the strut assembly from the spring compressor.

21. Install the strut assembly on the vehicle

STABILIZER BAR

REMOVAL & INSTALLATION

See Figure 149.

1. Raise and safely support the vehicle.
2. Remove the engine skid plate, if equipped.
3. Remove the rear engine mount.
4. Remove the front engine mount through-bolt.
5. Remove the fasteners that secure the power steering hose clamps to the front suspension crossmember.
6. At each of the stabilizer bar, hold the stabilizer bar link lower stud stationary and remove the nut securing the link to the stabilizer bar.
7. Remove the bolts securing the stabilizer bar bushing retainers to the front suspension crossmember.
8. Remove the two stabilizer bushing retainers.

➡Before removing the front suspension crossmember from the vehicle, the location of the crossmember must be marked on the body of the vehicle. If the front suspension crossmember is not reinstalled in exactly the same position, the preset wheel alignment settings will be lost.

9. Matchmark the location of the front crossmember on the body near each mounting bolt.
10. Support the front crossmember with a suitable jack.
11. Remove the mounting bolts securing the crossmember to the body.
12. Lower the crossmember until there is clearance to remove the stabilizer bar between the rear of the crossmember and the body.

To install:

13. Install the stabilizer bar, link ends first, from the rear over top of the crossmember. Curve the ends of the bar over the steering gear.
14. Slowly raise the crossmember into its mounted position using a suitable jack matching the crossmember to the marked locations on the body made during removal.
15. Install the four mounting bolts (two each side) securing the front crossmember to the body and tighten the bolts to 140 ft. lbs. (190 Nm).
16. Install the retainers over the stabilizer bar cushions and tighten the bolts to 22 ft. lbs. (30 Nm).

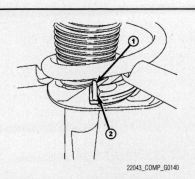

22043_COMP_G0140

Fig. 148 Rotate the strut until the end of the bottom coil (2) comes in contact with the stop (1).

17. Attach the stabilizer bar link at each end of the stabilizer bar. Tighten the nuts to 43 ft. lbs. (58 Nm).

18. Install the fasteners securing the power steering hose routing clamps to the crossmember. Use a new push clip on the left and tighten the screw on the right to 71 inch lbs. (8 Nm).

19. Install the rear engine mount.

20. Install the front engine mount through-bolt.

21. Install the engine skid plate, if equipped.

22. Lower the vehicle.

23. Check and adjust the alignment as necessary.

STEERING KNUCKLE

REMOVAL & INSTALLATION

1. Raise and safely support the vehicle.
2. Remove the front wheel.
3. Remove the cotter pin from the hub nut.
4. With an assistant applying the brakes to keep the hub from rotating, remove the hub nut and washer from the axle shaft.
5. Remove the brake rotor.
6. Remove the routing clip securing wheel speed sensor cable to the knuckle.
7. Remove the wheel speed sensor.
8. Remove the nut attaching the outer tie rod to the knuckle. To do this, hold the tie rod end stud with a wrench while loosening and removing the nut with a standard wrench or crowfoot wrench.
9. Release the outer tie rod end from the knuckle using Special Tool 9360 Ball Joint Remover.
10. Remove the outer tie rod from the knuckle.
11. Remove the nut and pinch bolt clamping the ball joint stud to the knuckle.

➡ The strut assembly-to-knuckle attaching bolts are serrated and must not be turned during removal.

12. While holding the bolt heads stationary, remove the two nuts from the bolts attaching the strut to the knuckle.
13. Remove the two bolts attaching the strut to the knuckle using a pin punch.

✳ WARNING
Use care when separating the ball joint stud from the knuckle, so the ball joint seal does not get cut.

14. Using a suitable pry tool, separate the ball joint stud from the knuckle by prying down on lower control arm and up against the ball joint boss on the knuckle.

✳ WARNING
Do not allow the half shaft to hang by the inner CV-joint. It must be supported to keep the joint from separating during this operation.

15. Pull the knuckle off the half shaft outer CV-joint splines and remove the knuckle from the vehicle.

To install:

16. Slide the hub of the knuckle onto the splines of the halfshaft outer CV-joint.
17. Install the knuckle onto the ball joint stud aligning the bolt hole in the knuckle boss with the groove formed into the side of the ball joint stud.
18. Install a new ball joint stud pinch bolt and nut. Tighten the nut to 60 ft. lbs. (82 Nm).
19. Position the lower end of the strut assembly in line with the upper end of the knuckle, aligning the mounting holes. Install the two mounting bolts. Install the nuts on the two bolts and tighten the nuts to 62 ft. lbs. (84 Nm).
20. Install the outer tie rod ball stud into the hole in the knuckle arm. Start the tie rod end-to-knuckle nut onto the stud. While holding the tie rod end stud with a wrench, tighten the nut with a wrench or crowfoot wrench to 97 ft. lbs. (132 Nm).
21. Install the wheel speed sensor.
22. Install the routing clip securing wheel speed sensor cable to the knuckle.
23. Install the brake rotor, disc brake caliper and adapter.
24. Clean all foreign matter from the threads of the halfshaft outer CV-joint.
25. Install the washer and hub nut on the end of the halfshaft and snug it.
26. Have an assistant apply the brakes to keep the hub from rotating and tighten the hub nut to 181 ft. lbs. (245 Nm).
27. Insert the cotter pin through the notches in the nut and the hole in halfshaft. If the notches in the nut do not line up with the hole in the halfshaft, continue to tighten the nut until they do. Do not loosen the nut.
28. Wrap the cotter pin ends tightly around the lock nut.
29. Install the front wheel.
30. Lower the vehicle.
31. Check the alignment and adjust as necessary.

WHEEL BEARINGS

REMOVAL & INSTALLATION
See Figures 150 through 154.

1. Raise and safely support the vehicle.
2. Remove the front wheel.
3. Remove the steering knuckle assembly from the vehicle.
4. Position the locator block for Special Tool 9712 Fixture, as follows:
   a. For left side knuckles, place the locator block to the left side on the Fixture. The side of the locator block with the angle cut goes downward, toward the Fixture. Install the mounting screws and tighten them to approximately 40 ft. lbs. (54 Nm).
   b. For right side knuckles, place the locator block to the right side on the Fixture. The side of the locator block with the angle cut goes downward, toward the Fixture. Install the mounting screws and tighten them to approximately 40 ft. lbs. (54 Nm).
5. Install the knuckle in the Fixture as shown, guiding the steering arm to rest on

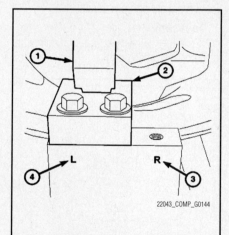

Fig. 150 Install the locator block (2) on Special Tool 9712 (1) for the left (4) or right (3) side knuckle as shown.

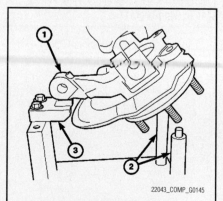

Fig. 151 Install the knuckle in the Fixture as shown, guiding the steering arm (1) to rest on the locator block (3) and the brake caliper mounting bosses on the two Fixture pins (2).

the locator block and the brake caliper mounting bosses on the two Fixture pins.

6. Place the Fixture with knuckle installed into an arbor press.

7. Position Special Tool 9712-2 Remover/Installer in the small end of the hub. Lower the arbor press ram and remove the hub from the wheel bearing and knuckle. The bearing race will normally come out of the wheel bearing with the hub as it is pressed out of the bearing.

8. Remove the knuckle from the Fixture and turn it over.

9. Remove the snap ring from the knuckle using an appropriate pair of snap ring pliers.

10. Place the knuckle back in the Fixture in the arbor press ram.

11. Place Special Tool MD-998334 Installer on the outer race of the wheel bearing. Lower the arbor press ram and remove the wheel bearing from the knuckle.

To install:

12. Wipe the bearing bore of the knuckle clean of any grease or dirt.

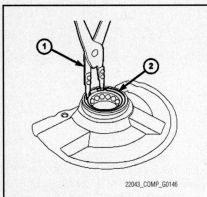

22043_COMP_G0146

Fig. 152 Remove the snap ring (2) from the knuckle using an appropriate pair of snap ring pliers (1).

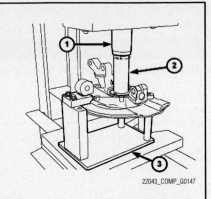

22043_COMP_G0147

Fig. 153 Put the knuckle assembly back into the fixture (3) and place Special Tool MD-998334 Installer (2) on the outer race of the wheel bearing. Lower the arbor press ram (1) and remove the wheel bearing from the knuckle.

13. Place the knuckle in an arbor press supporting the knuckle from underneath using Special Tool 6310-1 Cup.

14. Place the NEW wheel bearing magnetic encoder ring side down into the bore of the knuckle. Be sure the wheel bearing is placed squarely into the bore.

15. Place Special Tool 8498 Receiver, larger inside diameter end down, over the outer race of the wheel bearing.

16. Place Special Tool 6310-2 Disc, into the top of Receiver 8498. Lower the arbor press ram and press the wheel bearing into the knuckle until it is bottomed in the bore of the knuckle.

17. Remove the knuckle and tools from the arbor press.

18. Install a new snap ring in the knuckle using an appropriate pair of snap ring pliers.

19. Place the knuckle in an arbor press. Support the knuckle from underneath using Special Tool MB-990799 Remover/Installer,

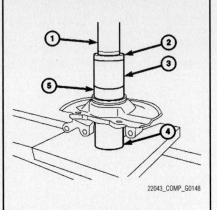

22043_COMP_G0148

Fig. 154 With knuckle installed on top of Special Tool 6310-1 (4), use a suitable shop press (1) and Special Tools 6310-2 (2) and 8498 (3) to press the new wheel bearing (5) into the knuckle.

with the smaller end up against the wheel bearing inner race.

20. Place the hub in the wheel bearing making sure it is square with the bearing inner race.

21. Position Special Tool 9712-2 Remover/Installer in the end of the hub. Lower the arbor press ram and press the hub into the wheel bearing until it bottoms out.

22. Remove the knuckle and tools from the press.

23. Verify the hub turns smoothly without rubbing or binding.

24. Install the knuckle on the vehicle

25. Check the alignment and adjust as necessary.

ADJUSTMENT

The wheel bearing is designed to last for the life of the vehicle and is unable to be adjusted. If the wheel bearing exhibits any roughness or resistance to rotation, the bearing must be replaced.

COIL SPRING

REMOVAL & INSTALLATION

The coil spring is part of the strut assembly.

CONTROL LINKS

REMOVAL & INSTALLATION

Trailing Arm

See Figures 155 through 157.

1. Raise and safely support the vehicle.
2. Remove the rear wheel.
3. Remove the screws that secures the brake hose to the trailing arm.
4. Remove the nut that secures the brake line routing bracket to the trailing arm. Remove the brake line from the routing bracket.
5. Remove the brake caliper and adapter as an assembly. Secure the caliper assembly out of the way.

✳ WARNING

Do not let the caliper assembly hang by the brake hose.

6. If equipped, remove the wheel speed sensor.
7. Remove the brake rotor.
8. Remove the hub and bearing assembly. For additional information, refer to the following section, "Wheel Bearings, Removal & Installation."
9. Remove the parking brake cable from the lever of the parking brake shoe.
10. Remove the hair pin securing the parking brake cable to the brake support plate.

11. Slide the brake support plate with parking brake shoes off the end of the parking brake cable and remove.
12. Pull the parking brake cable from the trailing arm.
13. Remove the bolt securing the lower control arm to the trailing arm.
14. Remove the bolt securing the upper control arm to the trailing arm.
15. Remove the bolts holding the leading end of the trailing arm to the body and remove the trailing arm.

To install:

16. Position the trailing arm and install the two bolts holding the leading end of trailing arm to the body. Tighten to 81 ft. lbs. (110 Nm).
17. Install the upper control arm to the trailing arm and tighten the bolt to 70 ft. lbs. (95 Nm).
18. Install the lower control arm to the

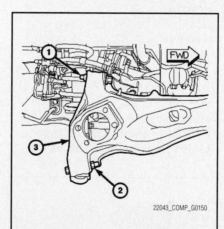

Fig. 156 Remove the nut (2) securing the lower control am and nut (1) securing the upper control arm to the trailing arm (3)— Trailing arm removal

trailing arm and tighten the bolt to 70 ft. lbs. (95 Nm).
19. Install the bolt securing the toe link to the trailing arm. It may be necessary to flex the trailing arm body mount bushing inward or outward using a suitable pry tool. Tighten the mounting bolts to 70 ft. lbs. (95 Nm).
20. Insert the parking brake cable through the trailing link from the inboard side.
21. Slide the parking brake cable into the brake support plate with parking brake shoes.
22. Install the hair pin securing the parking brake cable to the brake support plate.
23. Attach the parking brake cable onto the lever on the parking brake shoe.
24. Install the wheel speed sensor, if equipped.
25. Install the hub and bearing.
26. Install the brake rotor.
27. Install the caliper assembly and tighten the mounting bolts to 52 ft. lbs. (71 Nm).
28. Position the brake line on the trailing arm, inserting the routing clip and routing bracket over the welded stud. Tighten the nut on the welded stud to 11 ft. lbs. (15 Nm).
29. Position the brake hose on the trailing arm bracket and tighten the mounting bolts to 17 ft. lbs. (23 Nm).
30. Install the rear wheel.
31. Lower the vehicle.
32. Check and adjust the alignment as necessary.

Toe Link

See Figure 158.

1. Raise and safely support the vehicle.
2. Remove the bolt that secures the toe link to the trailing arm.
3. Matchmark the position of the cam bolt on the crossmember.
4. While holding the cam bolt head stationary, remove the toe link mounting cam bolt nut and washer. Remove the cam bolt.
5. Remove the toe link.

To install:

➡ **When installing the cam bolt (3) and washer make sure the cams stay inside the abutments built into the crossmember**

6. Install the toe link into position. Install the cam bolt from the front through crossmember and link. Match the cam to the marks made during the removal

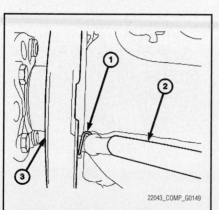

Fig. 155 Remove the hair pin (1) securing the parking brake cable (2) to the brake support plate (3)—Trailing Arm removal

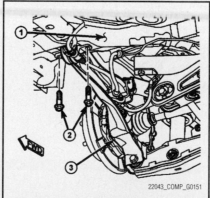

Fig. 157 Remove the two bolts (2) fastening the leading end of the trailing arm (3) to the body (1)—Trailing Arm removal

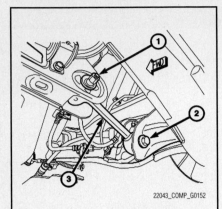

Fig. 158 Remove the bolt (2) that secures the toe link (3) to the trailing arm. Mark the position of the cam bolt (1) on the crossmember.

process. Only hand-tighten the nut at this time.

7. Install the bolt that secures the toe link to the trailing arm. It may be necessary to flex the trailing arm body mount bushing inward or outward using a suitable pry tool. Do not tighten the bolt at this time.

8. Lower the vehicle.

9. Tighten the toe link mounting bolt at the trailing arm to 70 ft. lbs. (95 Nm).

10. Check and adjust the alignment as necessary.

11. Once the rear toe is set, hold the cam bolt head stationary and tighten the toe link cam mounting bolt nut to 26 ft. lbs. (35 Nm).

LOWER CONTROL ARM

REMOVAL & INSTALLATION

See Figure 159.

1. Raise and safely support the vehicle.
2. Remove the rear wheel.
3. Hold the stabilizer bar link lower stud stationary and remove the nut securing the link to the lower control arm.
4. Remove the lower strut assembly nut and bolt.
5. Remove the stay brace.
6. Remove the bolt securing the lower control arm to the trailing arm.
7. Remove the bolt securing the lower control arm to the crossmember.
8. Remove the lower control arm.

To install:

9. Install the lower control arm to crossmember, install the nut and bolt but do not tighten.

10. Install the lower control arm to the trailing arm, install the nut and bolt but do not tighten.

11. Install the stay brace on the crossmember and tighten the mounting bolts to 18 ft. lbs. (25 Nm).

12. Install the mounting bolt holding the strut assembly to the lower control arm ,but do not tighten.

➡ **When attaching a stabilizer bar link to the lower control arm it is important that the lower mounting stud be posi-**

tioned properly. The lower mounting stud on the right side link needs to point toward the rear of the vehicle when inserted through the lower control arm mounting flange. The left side link lower stud needs to point toward the front of the vehicle.

13. Connect the stabilizer bar links to the lower control arm and tighten the nut to 43 ft. lbs. (58 Nm).

14. Install the rear wheel.

15. Lower the vehicle.

16. Tighten the lower control arm mounting bolt nut at the crossmember to 70 ft. lbs. (95 Nm).

17. Tighten the lower control arm mounting bolt nut at the trailing link to 70 ft. lbs. (95 Nm).

18. Tighten the strut assembly lower mounting bolt nut to 73 ft. lbs. (99 Nm).

19. Check and adjust the alignment as necessary.

STRUT & SPRING ASSEMBLY

REMOVAL & INSTALLATION

See Figures 160 and 161.

1. Remove the rear interior quarter panel trim as follows:

    a. Remove the rear quarter trim cargo loop retaining screw.

    b. Remove the subwoofer, if equipped.

    c. Remove the cargo floor.

    d. Remove the liftgate scuff plate.

    e. Remove the B-pillar lower trim.

    f. Remove the door sill scuff plate.

    g. Remove the upper C-pillar trim.

    h. Remove the rear quarter panel trim.

2. Remove the two nuts securing the strut assembly to the body bracket.

3. Raise and safely support the vehicle.

4. Remove the rear wheel.

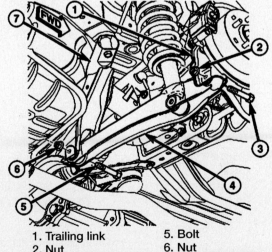

1. Trailing link
2. Nut
3. Bolt
4. Lower control arm
5. Bolt
6. Nut
7. Crossmember

Fig. 159 Remove the nut (2) and bolt (3) securing the lower control arm (4) to the trailing link (1) and remove the nut (6) and bolt (5) securing the lower control arm (4) to the cross-member (7).

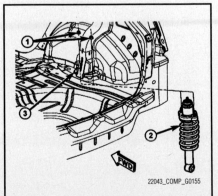

Fig. 160 Remove the two nuts (1) securing the shock assembly (2) to the body bracket (3)—Rear strut assembly

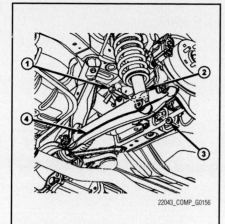

Fig. 161 Remove the strut assembly (2) lower mounting nut (3) and bolt (1) from the lower control arm (4)—Rear strut assembly

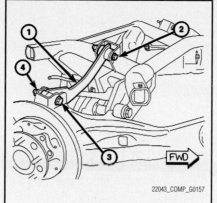

Fig. 162 Remove the nut (4) and bolt (3) securing the upper control arm (1) to the trailing arm and remove the bolt (2) securing the upper control arm (1) to the crossmember—Rear upper control arm

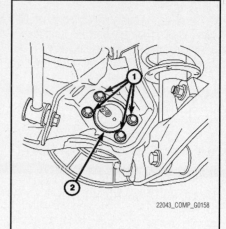

Fig. 163 Remove the four bolts (1) securing the hub and bearing (2) to the trailing arm—Rear wheel bearings

5. Remove the lower strut assembly mounting bolt.

6. Lower the strut assembly out of the body bracket and lift out over the rear suspension.

To install:

7. Insert the lower end of the strut assembly down through the lower control arm from above, just enough to clear the body, then lift it into position in the body bracket.

8. Install the mounting bolt at the lower control arm, but do not tighten.

9. Install the rear wheel.

10. Lower the vehicle.

11. Install the two upper mounting nuts to the strut assembly and tighten to 35 ft. lbs. (48 Nm).

12. Install the rear quarter panel trim.

13. Tighten the lower strut assembly mounting bolt to 73 ft. lbs. (99 Nm).

UPPER CONTROL ARM

REMOVAL & INSTALLATION

See Figure 162.

1. Raise and safely support the vehicle.

2. Remove the rear wheel.

3. Remove the bolt securing the upper control arm to the trailing arm.

4. Remove the bolt securing the upper control arm to the crossmember.

5. Remove the upper control arm.

To install:

6. Install the upper control arm and install the bolt securing the arm to the crossmember, but do not tighten.

7. Install bolt securing the upper control arm to the trailing arm, but do not tighten.

8. Install the rear wheel.

9. Lower the vehicle.

10. Tighten the upper control arm mounting bolt at the crossmember to 70 ft. lbs. (95 Nm).

11. Tighten the upper control arm mounting bolt at the trailing arm to 70 ft. lbs. (95 Nm).

12. Check and adjust the alignment as necessary.

WHEEL BEARINGS

REMOVAL & INSTALLATION

Front Wheel Drive

See Figure 163.

1. Raise and safely support the vehicle.

2. Remove the rear wheel.

3. Remove the brake caliper lower guide pin bolt.

4. Rotate the caliper upward, using the top guide bolt as a hinge. Hang the caliper assembly with mechanics wire or equivalent.

5. Remove any clips on the wheel mounting studs holding the rotor into place, and remove the rotor.

6. Remove the wheel speed sensor, if equipped.

7. Remove the bolts holding the hub and bearing assembly to the trailing arm.

8. Remove the hub and bearing assembly.

To install:

9. Install the hub and bearing assembly on the brake support plate and trailing arm. Tighten the bolts to 77 ft. lbs. (105 Nm).

10. Install the wheel speed sensor, if equipped.

11. Slide the brake rotor over the parking brake shoes and onto the wheel hub.

12. Rotate the caliper assembly downward over the rotor into the caliper adapter bracket.

13. Install the lower guide pin bolt and tighten to 32 ft. lbs. (43 Nm).

14. Install the rear wheel.

15. Lower the vehicle.

16. Pump the brake pedal several times to ensure the vehicle has a firm pedal.

All Wheel Drive

1. Raise and safely support the vehicle.

2. Remove the rear wheel.

3. Remove the cotter pin from the end of the hub nut.

4. With an assistant applying the brakes to keep the hub from rotating, remove the hub nut and washer from the end of the axle shaft.

5. Tap the end of the half shaft inward, loosening it from the hub and bearing assembly.

6. Remove the brake caliper lower guide pin bolt.

7. Rotate the caliper upward, using the top guide bolt as a hinge. Hang the caliper assembly with mechanics wire or equivalent.

8. Remove any clips on the wheel mounting studs holding the rotor into place, and remove the rotor.

9. Remove the wheel speed sensor, if equipped.

10. Remove the bolts holding the hub and bearing assembly to the trailing arm.

11. Remove the hub and bearing assembly.

To install:

12. Slide the hub and bearing assembly over the axle shaft and position it on the brake support plate and trailing arm. Tighten the bolts to 77 ft. lbs. (105 Nm).

13. Install the wheel speed sensor, if equipped.

14. Slide the brake rotor over the parking brake shoes and onto the wheel hub.

15. Rotate the caliper assembly downward over the rotor into the caliper adapter bracket.

16. Install the lower guide pin bolt and tighten to 32 ft. lbs. (43 Nm).

17. Install the washer and hub nut on the end of the halfshaft and hand tighten it.

18. With an assistant applying the brakes to keep the hub from rotating, tighten the hub nut to 181 ft. lbs. (245 Nm).

19. Install the cotter pin through the notches of the nut and the hole in the half shaft. If the notches do not line up with the hole in the axle shaft, continue tighten the nut until they do.

❊❊ WARNING

Do not loosen the nut to get the hole to line up.

20. Wrap the cotter pin tightly around the lock nut.

21. Install the rear wheel.

22. Lower the vehicle.

23. Pump the brake pedal several times to ensure the vehicle has a firm pedal.

ADJUSTMENT

The wheel bearing is designed to last for the life of the vehicle and is unable to be adjusted. If the wheel bearing exhibits any roughness or resistance to rotation, the bearing must be replaced.

CHRYSLER AND DODGE

Caravan • Town & Country

SPECIFICATIONS AND MAINTENANCE CHARTS

ENGINE AND VEHICLE IDENTIFICATION

Code	Liters (cc)	Cu. In.	Cyl.	Fuel Sys.	Engine Type	Eng. Mfg.
			Engine			
3	3.3 (3300)	201	6	FFV	OHV	Chrysler
B	2.4 (2429)	148	4	SMFI	DOHC	Chrysler
G	3.3 (3300)	201	6	FFV	OHV	Chrysler
L	3.8 (3785)	231	6	SMFI	OHV	Chrysler
R	3.3 (3300)	201	6	SMFI	OHV	Chrysler

Model Year	
Code ②	Year
5	2005
6	2006
7	2007

SMFI: Sequential Multi-port Fuel Injection

FFV: Flexible Fuel Vehicle

DOHC: Double Overhead Camshaft

OHV: Overhead Valve

22043_CARA_C0001

GENERAL ENGINE SPECIFICATIONS

Year	Model	Engine Displacement Liters	Net Horsepower (ft. lbs.)	Net Torque @ rpm (in.)	Bore x Stroke Ratio	Compression @ rpm	Oil Pressure @ rpm
2005	Caravan	2.4	150@5200	167@4000	3.44x3.98	9.5:1	25-80@3000
		3.3	180@5000	210@4000	3.66x3.19	9.3:1	30-80@3000
		3.8	215@5000	245@4000	3.78x3.43	9.6:1	30-80@3000
	Town & Country	3.3	180@5000	210@4000	3.66x3.19	9.3:1	30-80@3000
		3.8	207@5000	238@4000	3.78x3.43	9.6:1	30-80@3000
2006	Caravan	2.4	150@5200	167@4000	3.44x3.98	9.5:1	25-80@3000
		3.3	180@5000	210@4000	3.66x3.19	9.3:1	30-80@3000
		3.8	215@5000	245@4000	3.78x3.43	9.6:1	30-80@3000
	Town & Country	3.3	180@5000	210@4000	3.66x3.19	9.3:1	30-80@3000
		3.8	207@5000	238@4000	3.78x3.43	9.6:1	30-80@3000
2007	Caravan	2.4	150@5100	165@4000	3.44x3.98	9.5:1	25-80@3000
		3.3	180@5000	210@4000	3.66x3.19	9.3:1	30-80@3000
		3.8	200@5200	235@4000	3.78x3.43	9.6:1	30-80@3000
	Town & Country	3.3	170@5000	200@4000	3.66x3.19	9.3:1	30-80@3000
		3.8	200@5200	235@4000	3.78x3.43	9.6:1	30-80@3000

22043_CARA_C0002

ENGINE TUNE-UP SPECIFICATIONS

Year	Engine Displacement Liters	Spark Plug Gap (in.)	Ignition Timing (deg.)	Fuel Pump (psi)	Idle Speed (rpm)	Valve Clearance In.	Ex.
2005	2.4	0.048-0.053	①	49	②	HYD	HYD
	3.3	0.048-0.053	①	55	②	HYD	HYD
	3.8	0.048-0.053	①	49	②	HYD	HYD
2006	2.4	0.048-0.053	①	49	②	HYD	HYD
	3.3	0.048-0.053	①	55	②	HYD	HYD
	3.8	0.048-0.053	①	49	②	HYD	HYD
2007	2.4	0.048-0.053	①	49	②	HYD	HYD
	3.3	0.048-0.053	①	55	②	HYD	HYD
	3.8	0.048-0.053	①	49	②	HYD	HYD

NOTE: The Vehicle Emission Control Information label often reflects specification changes made during production.

The label figures must be used if they differ from those in this chart.

HYD: Hydraulic

① Ignition timing is regulated by the Powertrain Control Module (PCM), and cannot be adjusted.

② Idle speed is controled by the Powertrain Control Module (PCM), and cannot be adjusted.

22043_CARA_C0003

CAPACITIES

Year	Model	Engine Displacement Liters	Engine Oil with Filter (qts.)	Automatic Transaxle (qts.)	Transfer Case (qts.)	Rear Drive Axle (pts.)	Fuel Tank (gal.)	Cooling System (qts.)
2005	Caravan	2.4	4.5	8.5	—	—	20.0	9.5
		3.3	4.5	9.1	—	—	20.0	10.5
		3.8	4.5	9.1	1.22	4.0	20.0	10.5
	Town & Country	3.3	4.5	9.1	—	—	20.0	10.5
		3.8	4.5	9.1	1.22	4.0	20.0	10.5
2006	Caravan	2.4	4.5	8.5	—	—	20.0	9.5
		3.3	4.5	9.1	—	—	20.0	10.5
		3.8	4.5	9.1	1.22	4.0	20.0	10.5
	Town & Country	3.3	4.5	9.1	—	—	20.0	10.5
		3.8	4.5	9.1	1.22	4.0	20.0	10.5
2007	Caravan	2.4	4.5	8.5	—	—	20.0	9.5
		3.3	4.5	9.1	—	—	20.0	10.5
		3.8	4.5	9.1	1.22	4.0	20.0	10.5
	Town & Country	3.3	4.5	9.1	—	—	20.0	10.5
		3.8	4.5	9.1	1.22	4.0	20.0	10.5

NOTE: All capacities are approximate. Add fluid gradually and check to be sure a proper fluid level is obtained.

22043_CARA_C0004

FLUID SPECIFICATIONS

Year	Model	Engine Displacement Liters	Engine ID/VIN	Engine Oil	Auto. Trans.	Drive Axle	Power Steering Fluid	Brake Master Cylinder
2005	All	2.4	B	5W-30	Mopar ATF+4	NA	Mopar ATF+4	DOT-3
		3.3	①	5W-30	Mopar ATF+4	NA	Mopar ATF+4	DOT-3
		3.8	L	5W-30	Mopar ATF+4	②	Mopar ATF+4	DOT-3
2006	All	2.4	B	5W-30	Mopar ATF+4	NA	Mopar ATF+4	DOT-3
		3.3	①	5W-30	Mopar ATF+4	NA	Mopar ATF+4	DOT-3
		3.8	L	5W-30	Mopar ATF+4	②	Mopar ATF+4	DOT-3
2007	All	2.4	B	5W-30	Mopar ATF+4	NA	Mopar ATF+4	DOT-3
		3.3	①	5W-30	Mopar ATF+4	NA	Mopar ATF+4	DOT-3
		3.8	L	5W-30	Mopar ATF+4	②	Mopar ATF+4	DOT-3

DOT: Department Of Transpotation

NA: Not Applicable

① VIN 3, G and R

② Overunning clutch: Mopar ATF+4 Differential carrier: 80W-90 gear oil

22043_CARA_C0005

VALVE SPECIFICATIONS

Year	Engine Displacement Liters	Seat Angle (deg.)	Face Angle (deg.)	Spring Test Pressure (lbs. @ in.)	Spring Installed Height (in.)	Stem-to-Guide Clearance (in.)		Stem Diameter (in.)	
						Intake	Exhaust	Intake	Exhaust
2005	2.4	45	44.5-45.0	129-143@ 1.17	1.50	0.0018-0.0025	0.0029-0.0037	0.2340	0.2330
	3.3	45.0-45.5	①	207-229@ 1.169	1.62-1.68	0.0010-0.0030	0.0020-0.0060	0.3120-0.3130	0.3112-0.3119
	3.8	45.0-45.5	①	207-229@ 1.169	1.62-1.68	0.0010-0.0030	0.0020-0.0060	0.3120-0.3130	0.3112-0.3119
2006	2.4	45	44.5-45.0	129-143@ 1.17	1.50	0.0018-0.0025	0.0029-0.0037	0.2340	0.2330
	3.3	45.0-45.5	①	207-229@ 1.169	1.62-1.68	0.0010-0.0030	0.0020-0.0060	0.3120-0.3130	0.3112-0.3119
	3.8	45.0-45.5	①	207-229@ 1.169	1.62-1.68	0.0010-0.0030	0.0020-0.0060	0.3120-0.3130	0.3112-0.3119
2007	2.4	45	44.5-45.0	129-143@ 1.17	1.50	0.0018-0.0025	0.0029-0.0037	0.2340	0.2330
	3.3	45.0-45.5	①	207-229@ 1.169	1.62-1.68	0.0010-0.0030	0.0020-0.0060	0.3120-0.3130	0.3112-0.3119
	3.8	45.0-45.5	①	207-229@ 1.169	1.62-1.68	0.0010-0.0030	0.0020-0.0060	0.3120-0.3130	0.3112-0.3119

① Intake valve: 44.5 degrees

Exhaust valve: 45 degrees

22043_CARA_C0006

CAMSHAFT AND BEARING SPECIFICATIONS CHART

All measurements are given in inches.

Year	Engine Displ. Liters	Engine ID/VIN	Journal Dia.	Brg. Oil Clearance	Shaft End-play	Runout	Journal Bore	Lobe Height	
								Intake	Exhaust
2005	2.4	B	1.022-1.023	0.0009-0.0025	0.0019-0.0066	NA	1.024-1.025	0.324	0.259
	3.3	①	②	0.001-0.004	0.010-0.020	NA	NA	NA	NA
	3.8	L	②	0.001-0.004	0.010-0.020	NA	NA	NA	NA
2006	2.4	B	1.022-1.023	0.0009-0.0025	0.0019-0.0066	NA	1.024-1.025	0.324	0.259
	3.3	①	②	0.001-0.004	0.010-0.020	NA	NA	NA	NA
	3.8	L	②	0.001-0.004	0.010-0.020	NA	NA	NA	NA
2007	2.4	B	1.022-1.023	0.0009-0.0025	0.0019-0.0066	NA	1.024-1.025	0.324	0.259
	3.3	①	②	0.001-0.004	0.010-0.020	NA	NA	NA	NA
	3.8	L	②	0.001-0.004	0.010-0.020	NA	NA	NA	NA

NA: Not Available

① VIN 3, G and R

② Bore 1: 1.997-1.999

Bore 2: 1.9809-1.9829

Bore 3: 1.9659-1.9679

Bore 4: 1.9499-1.9520

22043_CARA_C0007

CRANKSHAFT AND CONNECTING ROD SPECIFICATIONS

All measurements are given in inches.

Year	Engine Displacement Liters	Crankshaft				Connecting Rod		
		Main Brg. Clearance	Main Brg. Oil End-play	Shaft on No.	Thrust Diameter	Journal Clearance	Oil Clearance	Side Clearance
2005	2.4	2.3610-2.3625	0.0007-0.0023	0.0035-0.0094	2	1.9670-1.9685	0.0009-0.0027	0.0051-0.0150
	3.3	2.5202-2.5195	0.0023-0.0043	0.0036-0.0095	2	2.1240-2.1250	0.0008-0.0026	0.0050-0.0150
	3.8	2.5202-2.5195	0.0023-0.0043	0.0036-0.0095	2	2.1240-2.1250	0.0008-0.0026	0.0050-0.0150
2006	2.4	2.3610-2.3625	0.0007-0.0023	0.0035-0.0094	2	1.9670-1.9685	0.0009-0.0027	0.0051-0.0150
	3.3	2.5202-2.5195	0.0023-0.0043	0.0036-0.0095	2	2.1240-2.1250	0.0008-0.0026	0.0050-0.0150
	3.8	2.5202-2.5195	0.0023-0.0043	0.0036-0.0095	2	2.1240-2.1250	0.0008-0.0026	0.0050-0.0150
2007	2.4	2.3610-2.3625	0.0007-0.0023	0.0035-0.0094	2	1.9670-1.9685	0.0009-0.0027	0.0051-0.0150
	3.3	2.5202-2.5195	0.0023-0.0043	0.0036-0.0095	2	2.1240-2.1250	0.0008-0.0026	0.0050-0.0150
	3.8	2.5202-2.5195	0.0023-0.0043	0.0036-0.0095	2	2.1240-2.1250	0.0008-0.0026	0.0050-0.0150

22043_CARA_C0008

PISTON AND RING SPECIFICATIONS

All measurements are given in inches.

Year	Engine Displacement Liters	Piston Clearance	Ring Gap			Ring Side Clearance		
			Top Compression	Bottom Compression	Oil Control	Top Compression	Bottom Compression	Oil Control
2005	2.4	0.0009-0.0022	0.0098-0.0200	0.0090-0.0180	0.0098-0.0250	0.0011-0.0031	0.0011-0.0031	0.0004-0.0070
	3.3	0.0010-0.0022	0.0118-0.0217	0.0118-0.0217	0.0098-0.0394	0.0012-0.0037	0.0012-0.0037	0.0005-0.0089
	3.8	0.0010-0.0022	0.0118-0.0217	0.0118-0.0217	0.0098-0.0394	0.0012-0.0037	0.0012-0.0037	0.0005-0.0089
2006	2.4	0.0009-0.0022	0.0098-0.0200	0.0090-0.0180	0.0098-0.0250	0.0011-0.0031	0.0011-0.0031	0.0004-0.0070
	3.3	0.0010-0.0022	0.0118-0.0217	0.0118-0.0217	0.0098-0.0394	0.0012-0.0037	0.0012-0.0037	0.0005-0.0089
	3.8	0.0010-0.0022	0.0118-0.0217	0.0118-0.0217	0.0098-0.0394	0.0012-0.0037	0.0012-0.0037	0.0005-0.0089
2007	2.4	0.0009-0.0022	0.0098-0.0200	0.0090-0.0180	0.0098-0.0250	0.0011-0.0031	0.0011-0.0031	0.0004-0.0070
	3.3	0.0010-0.0022	0.0118-0.0217	0.0118-0.0217	0.0098-0.0394	0.0012-0.0037	0.0012-0.0037	0.0005-0.0089
	3.8	0.0010-0.0022	0.0118-0.0217	0.0118-0.0217	0.0098-0.0394	0.0012-0.0037	0.0012-0.0037	0.0005-0.0089

22043_CARA_C0009

TORQUE SPECIFICATIONS
All readings in ft. lbs.

Year	Engine Displacement Liters	Cylinder Head Bolts	Main Bearing Bolts	Rod Bearing Bolts	Crankshaft Damper Bolts	Flywheel Bolts	Manifold Intake	Manifold Exhaust	Spark Plugs	Oil Pan Drain Plug
2005	2.4	①	②	③	100	70	④	15	20	20
	3.3	⑤	⑥	⑦	40	70	⑧	⑨	20	20
	3.8	⑤	⑥	⑦	40	70	⑧	⑨	20	20
2006	2.4	①	②	③	100	70	④	15	20	20
	3.3	⑤	⑥	⑦	40	70	⑧	⑨	20	20
	3.8	⑤	⑥	⑦	40	70	⑧	⑨	20	20
2007	2.4	①	②	③	100	70	④	15	20	20
	3.3	⑤	⑥	⑦	40	70	⑧	⑨	20	20
	3.8	⑤	⑥	⑦	40	70	⑧	⑨	20	20

① Step 1: 25 ft. lbs.
  Step 2: 50 ft. lbs.
  Step 3: 50 ft. lbs.
  Step 4: Plus 1/4 turn

② M8 bolts: 21 ft. lbs.
  M11 bolts: 30 ft. lbs. plus 90 degrees

③ Step 1: 20 ft. lbs.
  Step 2: Plus 90 degrees

④ 2.4L: Upper and lower 250 inch lbs

⑤ Step 1: 45 ft. lbs.
  Step 2: 65 ft. lbs.
  Step 3: 65 ft. lbs.
  Step 4: Plus 90 degrees

⑥ Step 1: 30 ft. lbs.
  Step 2: Plus 90 degrees

⑦ Step 1: 40 ft. lbs.
  Step 2: Plus 90 degrees

⑧ Step 1: 10 inch lbs.
  Step 2: 17 ft. lbs.
  Step 3: 17 ft. lbs.

⑨ Refer to procedure for torque sequence and specifications

22043_CARA_C0010

WHEEL ALIGNMENT

Year	Model			Caster Range (+/-Deg.)	Caster Preferred Setting (Deg.)	Camber Range (+/-Deg.)	Camber Preferred Setting (Deg.)	Toe-in (in.)
2005	All	①	F	1.00	+1.40	0.30	+0.05	0.10+/-0.20
			R	—	—	0.25	0	0+/-0.30
		②	F	1.00	+1.40	0.40	+0.15	0.10+/-0.20
			R	—	—	0.25	0	0+/-0.30
2006	All	①	F	1.00	+1.40	0.30	+0.05	0.10+/-0.20
			R	—	—	0.25	0	0+/-0.30
		②	F	1.00	+1.40	0.40	+0.15	0.10+/-0.20
			R	—	—	0.25	0	0+/-0.30
2007	All	①	F	1.00	+1.40	0.30	+0.05	0.10+/-0.20
			R	—	—	0.25	0	0+/-0.30
		②	F	1.00	+1.40	0.40	+0.15	0.10+/-0.20
			R	—	—	0.25	0	0+/-0.30

① P205/75R15, P215/65R16, P215/60R17

② All other tire sizes

22043_CARA_C0011

TIRE, WHEEL AND BALL JOINT SPECIFICATIONS

Year	Model	OEM Tires Standard	OEM Tires Optional	Tire Pressures (psi) Front	Tire Pressures (psi) Rear	Wheel Size	Ball Joint Inspection	Lug Nuts
2005	Town & Country base, LX	P215/70R15	None	①	①	6-J	0.030 in. ①	100
	Except Town & Country base, LX	P215/65R16	None	①	①	6.5-J	0.030 in. ①	100
	Caravan base	P215/65R16	None	①	①	6-J	0.030 in. ①	100
	Caravan SE	P215/70SR15	P215/65R16	①	①	6-J	0.030 in. ①	100
	Caravan SXT	P215/65R16	None	①	①	6-J	0.030 in. ①	100
2006	Town & Country base, LX	P215/70R15	None	①	①	6-J	0.030 in. ①	100
	Except Town & Country base, LX	P215/65R16	None	①	①	6.5-J	0.030 in. ①	100
	Caravan base	P215/65R16	None	①	①	6-J	0.030 in. ①	100
	Caravan SE	P215/70SR15	P215/65R16	①	①	6-J	0.030 in. ①	100
	Caravan SXT	P215/65R16	None	①	①	6-J	0.030 in. ①	100
2007	Town & Country base, LX	P215/70R15	None	①	①	6-J	0.030 in. ①	100
	Except Town & Country base, LX	P215/65R16	None	①	①	6.5-J	0.030 in. ①	100
	Caravan base	P215/65R16	None	①	①	6-J	0.030 in. ①	100
	Caravan SE	P215/70SR15	P215/65R16	①	①	6-J	0.030 in. ①	100
	Caravan SXT	P215/65R16	None	①	①	6-J	0.030 in. ①	100

OEM: Original Equipment Manufacturer

PSI: Pounds Per Square Inch

① Refer to label on drivers side door pillar

② Both upper and lower

22043_CARA_C0012

BRAKE SPECIFICATIONS

All measurements in inches unless noted

Year	Model		Brake Disc Original Thickness	Brake Disc Minimum Thickness	Brake Disc Maximum Run-out	Brake Drum Diameter Original Inside Diameter	Brake Drum Diameter Max. Wear Limit	Brake Drum Diameter Maximum Machine Diameter	Min. Lining Thickness	Caliper Guide Pin Bolts (ft. lbs.)
2005	Caravan	F	0.939-0.949	0.881	0.005	—	—	—	0.313	26
		R	0.482-0.502	0.443	0.005	9.84	9.93	9.90	①	26
	Town & Country	F	0.939-0.949	0.881	0.005	—	—	—	0.313	26
		R	0.482-0.502	0.443	0.005	9.84	9.93	9.90	①	26
2006	Caravan	F	0.939-0.949	0.881	0.005	—	—	—	0.313	26
		R	0.482-0.502	0.443	0.005	9.84	9.93	9.90	①	26
	Town & Country	F	0.939-0.949	0.881	0.005	—	—	—	0.313	26
		R	0.482-0.502	0.443	0.005	9.84	9.93	9.90	①	26
2007	Caravan	F	0.939-0.949	0.881	0.005	—	—	—	0.313	26
		R	0.482-0.502	0.443	0.005	9.84	9.93	9.90	①	26
	Town & Country	F	0.939-0.949	0.881	0.005	—	—	—	0.313	26
		R	0.482-0.502	0.443	0.005	9.84	9.93	9.90	①	26

F: Front

R: Rear

① Drum brakes: 0.031 in
  Disc brakes: 0.281 in.

22043_CARA_C0013

SCHEDULED MAINTENANCE INTERVALS
CHRYSLER—TOWN & COUNTRY, DODGE—CARAVAN

TO BE SERVICED	TYPE OF SERVICE	VEHICLE MILEAGE INTERVAL (x1000)												
		7.5	15	22.5	30	37.5	45	52.5	60	67.5	75	82.5	90	97.5
Engine oil & filter	R	✓	✓	✓	✓	✓	✓	✓	✓	✓	✓	✓	✓	✓
Driveshaft boots	S/I	✓	✓	✓	✓	✓	✓	✓	✓	✓	✓	✓	✓	✓
Exhaust system	S/I	✓	✓	✓	✓	✓	✓	✓	✓	✓	✓	✓	✓	✓
Engine coolant level, hoses & clamps	S/I	✓	✓	✓	✓	✓	✓	✓	✓	✓	✓	✓	✓	✓
Rotate tires	S/I	✓	✓	✓	✓	✓	✓	✓	✓	✓	✓	✓	✓	✓
Drive belts	S/I		✓		✓		✓		✓		✓		✓	
Brake hoses & linings	S/I			✓			✓			✓			✓	
Automatic transaxle fluid & filter	R				✓				✓				✓	
Air filter	R				✓				✓				✓	
Spark plugs ①	R				✓				✓				✓	
Serpentine belts	S/I								✓		✓		✓	
Lubricate tie rod ends	S/I			✓					✓				✓	
PCV valve	S/I			✓					✓				✓	
Engine coolant	R								✓			✓		

R: Replace   S/I: Service or Inspect

① Platinum tip spark plugs & ignition cables (3.3L & 3.8L): replace every 100,000 miles.

FREQUENT OPERATION MAINTENANCE (SEVERE SERVICE)

If a vehicle is operated under any of the following conditions it is considered severe service:

- Extremely dusty areas.

- 50% or more of the vehicle operation is in 32°C (90°F) or higher temperatures, or constant operation in temperatures below 0°C (32°F).

- Prolonged idling (vehicle operation in stop and go traffic.

- Frequent short running periods (engine does not warm to normal operating temperatures).

- Police, taxi, delivery usage or trailer towing usage.

Oil & oil filter change: change every 3000 miles.

Automatic transaxle fluid & filter: change every 15,000 miles.

Brake hoses & linings: check every 9000 miles.

CV-joints & front suspension ball joints: check every 3000 miles.

Tie rod ends & steering linkage: check every 15,000 miles.

Air filter: change every 15,000 miles.

22043_CARA_C0014

PRECAUTIONS

Before servicing any vehicle, please be sure to read all of the following precautions, which deal with personal safety, prevention of component damage, and important points to take into consideration when servicing a motor vehicle:

• Never open, service or drain the radiator or cooling system when the engine is hot; serious burns can occur from the steam and hot coolant.

• Observe all applicable safety precautions when working around fuel. Whenever servicing the fuel system, always work in a well–ventilated area. Do not allow fuel spray or vapors to come in contact with a spark, open flame, or excessive heat (a hot drop light, for example). Keep a dry chemical fire extinguisher near the work area. Always keep fuel in a container specifically designed for fuel storage; also, always properly seal fuel containers to avoid the possibility of fire or explosion. Refer to the additional fuel system precautions later in this section.

• Fuel injection systems often remain pressurized, even after the engine has been turned **OFF**. The fuel system pressure must be relieved before disconnecting any fuel lines. Failure to do so may result in fire and/or personal injury.

• Brake fluid often contains polyglycol ethers and polyglycols. Avoid contact with the eyes and wash your hands thoroughly after handling brake fluid. If you do get brake fluid in your eyes, flush your eyes with clean, running water for 15 minutes. If eye irritation persists, or if you have taken brake fluid internally, IMMEDIATELY seek medical assistance.

• The EPA warns that prolonged contact with used engine oil may cause a number of skin disorders, including cancer. You should make every effort to minimize your exposure to used engine oil. Protective gloves should be worn when changing oil. Wash your hands and any other exposed skin areas as soon as possible after exposure to used engine oil. Soap and water, or waterless hand cleaner should be used.

• All new vehicles are now equipped with an air bag system, often referred to as a Supplemental Restraint System (SRS) or Supplemental Inflatable Restraint (SIR) system. The system must be disabled before performing service on or around system components, steering column, instrument panel components, wiring and sensors. Failure to follow safety and disabling procedures could result in accidental air bag deployment, possible personal injury and unnecessary system repairs.

• Always wear safety goggles when working with, or around, the air bag system. When carrying a non–deployed air bag, be sure the bag and trim cover are pointed away from your body. When placing a non–deployed air bag on a work surface, always face the bag and trim cover upward, away from the surface. This will reduce the motion of the module if it is accidentally deployed. Refer to the additional air bag system precautions later in this section.

• Clean, high quality brake fluid from a sealed container is essential to the safe and proper operation of the brake system. You should always buy the correct type of brake fluid for your vehicle. If the brake fluid becomes contaminated, completely flush the system with new fluid. Never reuse any brake fluid. Any brake fluid that is removed from the system should be discarded. Also, do not allow any brake fluid to come in contact with a painted surface; it will damage the paint.

• Never operate the engine without the proper amount and type of engine oil; doing so WILL result in severe engine damage.

• Timing belt maintenance is extremely important. Many models utilize an interference–type, non–freewheeling engine. If the timing belt breaks, the valves in the cylinder head may strike the pistons, causing potentially serious (also time–consuming and expensive) engine damage. Refer to the maintenance interval charts for the recommended replacement interval for the timing belt, and to the timing belt section for belt replacement and inspection.

• Disconnecting the negative battery cable on some vehicles may interfere with the functions of the on–board computer system(s) and may require the computer to undergo a relearning process once the negative battery cable is reconnected.

• When servicing drum brakes, only disassemble and assemble one side at a time, leaving the remaining side intact for reference.

• Only an MVAC–trained, EPA–certified automotive technician should service the air conditioning system or its components.

BRAKES

GENERAL INFORMATION

PRECAUTIONS

• Certain components within the ABS system are not intended to be serviced or repaired individually.

• Do not use rubber hoses or other parts not specifically specified for and ABS system. When using repair kits, replace all parts included in the kit. Partial or incorrect repair may lead to functional problems and require the replacement of components.

• Lubricate rubber parts with clean, fresh brake fluid to ease assembly. Do not use shop air to clean parts; damage to rubber components may result.

• Use only DOT 3 brake fluid from an unopened container.

• If any hydraulic component or line is removed or replaced, it may be necessary to bleed the entire system.

- A clean repair area is essential. Always clean the reservoir and cap thoroughly before removing the cap. The slightest amount of dirt in the fluid may plug an orifice and impair the system function. Perform repairs after components have been thoroughly cleaned; use only denatured alcohol to clean components. Do not allow ABS components to come into contact with any substance containing mineral oil; this includes used shop rags.

• The Anti–Lock control unit is a microprocessor similar to other computer units in the vehicle. Ensure that the ignition switch is **OFF** before removing or installing controller harnesses. Avoid static electricity discharge at or near the controller.

• If any arc welding is to be done on the vehicle, the control unit should be unplugged before welding operations begin.

ANTI-LOCK BRAKE SYSTEM (ABS)

SPEED SENSORS

REMOVAL & INSTALLATION

Front

See Figure 1.

1. Before servicing the vehicle, refer to the Precautions Section.
2. Raise and safely support the vehicle.
3. Remove the tire and wheel assembly.
4. Remove the sensor cable routing clamp screws.

❈ CAUTION

When disconnecting the wheel speed sensor from vehicle wiring harness, be careful not to damage pins on connector

5. Remove the speed sensor cable grommets from the intermediate bracket on the strut.

6. Disconnect the speed sensor cable from the vehicle wiring harness behind the fender well shield.

7. Remove the wheel speed sensor head mounting bolt

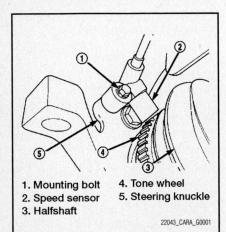

1. Mounting bolt   4. Tone wheel
2. Speed sensor   5. Steering knuckle
3. Halfshaft

22043_CARA_G0001

Fig. 1 Front wheel speed sensor mounting

8. Remove the sensor head from steering knuckle. If the sensor has seized due to corrosion, use a hammer and a punch to tap the edge of the sensor ear, rocking the sensor side–to–side until free.

9. Remove the front wheel speed sensor from vehicle.

10. Installation is the reverse of removal.

Rear
See Figure 2.

1. Before servicing the vehicle, refer to the Precautions Section.

2. Raise and safely support the vehicle.

3. Remove the grommet from the floor pan of the vehicle and unplug the speed sensor cable connector from the vehicle wiring harness.

❈ CAUTION

When removing the rear wheel speed sensor cable from the routing clips, be sure not to damage the routing clips. Routing clips that are molded onto the brake hose and will require replacement of the brake hose if damaged during removal or installation of the speed sensor cable.

4. Carefully remove the speed sensor cable from the press–in routing clips.

5. Remove the bolt securing the metal

routing clip to the rear of the axle and remove the sensor cable from the metal clip.

6. Remove the secondary (yellow) retaining clip at the rear of the wheel speed sensor head.

7. Push up on the metal retaining clip until it bottoms. This will release the wheel speed sensor head from the hub and bearing. While holding the metal clip up, pull back on the wheel speed sensor head, removing it from hub and bearing.

8. Installation is the reverse of removal. Lubricate the o–ring on the sensor with wheel bearing grease before installation.

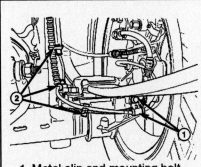

1. Metal clip and mounting bolt
2. Routing clips

22043_CARA_G0002

Fig. 2 Rear wheel speed sensor cable routing

BRAKES

BLEEDING PROCEDURE

BLEEDING PROCEDURE

See Figures 3 through 5.

When any part of the hydraulic system has been disconnected for repair or replacement, air may get into the lines and cause spongy pedal action (because air can be compressed and brake fluid cannot). To correct this condition, it is necessary to bleed the hydraulic system so to be sure all air is purged.

When bleeding the brake system, bleed one brake cylinder at a time, beginning with the left rear wheel cylinder first. ALWAYS Keep the master cylinder reservoir filled with brake fluid during the bleeding operation. Never use brake fluid that has been drained from the hydraulic system, no matter how clean it is.

The primary and secondary hydraulic brake systems are separate and are bled independently. During the bleeding operation, do not allow the reservoir to run dry. Keep the master cylinder reservoir filled with brake fluid.

BLEEDING THE BRAKE SYSTEM

1. Clean all dirt from around the master cylinder fill cap, remove the cap and fill the master cylinder with brake fluid until the level is within ¼ in. (6mm) of the top edge of the reservoir.

2. Clean the bleeder screws at all 4 wheels. The bleeder screws are located on the back of the brake backing plate (drum brakes) and on the top of the brake calipers (disc brakes).

3. Attach a length of rubber hose over the bleeder screw and place the other end of the hose in a glass jar, submerged in brake fluid.

4. Open the bleeder screw at least 1 full turn. Have an assistant slowly depress the brake pedal.

5. Close the bleeder screw and tell your assistant to allow the brake pedal to return slowly. Continue this process to purge all air from the system.

6. When bubbles cease to appear at the end of the bleeder hose, close the bleeder screw and remove the hose. Tighten the disc brake caliper bleeder screw to 11 ft. lbs. (15 Nm) and the drum brake wheel

cylinder bleeder screw to 80 inch lbs. (10 Nm).

7. The correct brake system bleeding sequence is:
- Left rear wheel
- Right front wheel
- Right rear wheel
- Left front wheel

91159P37

Fig. 3 With a clear plastic hose in a container of clean brake fluid, open the bleeder screw at least one full turn

Fig. 4 A vacuum bleeding kit can also be used to bleed the brakes

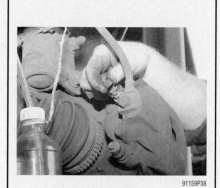

Fig. 5 Make sure to replace the bleeder screw caps after bleeding the brakes

8. Check the master cylinder fluid level and add fluid accordingly. Do this after bleeding each wheel.

9. Repeat the bleeding operation at the remaining 3 wheels, ending with the one closet to the master cylinder.

10. Fill the master cylinder reservoir to the proper level.

MASTER CYLINDER BLEEDING

See Figure 6.

⁂ CAUTION

When clamping the master cylinder in a vise, only clamp the master cylinder by its mounting flange. Do not clamp the master cylinder piston rod, reservoir, seal or body.

1. Clamp the master cylinder in a vise.

➡**Master cylinder outlet ports vary in size and type depending on whether master cylinder is for a vehicle equipped with ABS or not. ABS equipped master cylinders require the additional use of ISO style flare adapters supplied in Special Tool Package 8822 to be used in conjunction with the bleeder tubes in Special Tool Package 8358.**

2. Attach special tools for bleeding master cylinder in the following fashion:
    a. For non–ABS control equipped master cylinders, thread bleeder tube Special Tool 8358-1, into each outlet port. Tighten each tube to 145 inch lbs. (17 Nm).

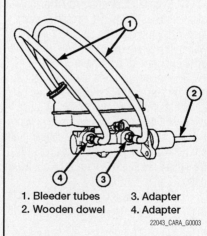

1. Bleeder tubes 3. Adapter
2. Wooden dowel 4. Adapter

22043_CARA_G0003

Fig. 6 Setup the master cylinder as shown to bleed it

Flex the bleeder tubes and place the open ends into the mouth of the fluid reservoir as far down as possible.
    b. For ABS equipped master cylinders, thread one adapter Special Tool 8822-2 in each outlet port. Tighten the adapters to 145 inch lbs. (17 Nm). Next, thread a bleeder tube Special Tool 8358-1 into each adapter. Flex the bleeder tubes and place the open ends into the mouth of the fluid reservoir as far down as possible .

➡**Make sure open ends of bleeder tubes stay below surface of brake fluid once reservoir is filled to proper level.**

3. Fill brake fluid reservoir with brake fluid meeting DOT 3 (DOT 4 and DOT 4+ are acceptable) specifications. Make sure fluid level is above tips of bleeder tubes in reservoir to ensure no air is ingested during bleeding.

4. Using a wooden dowel as a pushrod, slowly depress the master cylinder pistons, then release pressure, allowing the pistons to return to the released position.

5. Repeat several times until all air bubbles are expelled. Make sure the fluid level stays above the tips of the bleeder tubes in the reservoir while bleeding.

6. Remove the bleeder tubes from the master cylinder outlet ports, then plug the outlet ports and install the fill cap on the reservoir.

7. Install the master cylinder on vehicle then follow the brake bleeding procedure.

BLEEDING THE ABS SYSTEM

The bleeding procedure for the ABS System is the same as the Conventional Bleeding Procedure. Refer to the procedure located in this section.

❈❈ CAUTION

Dust and dirt accumulating on brake parts during normal use may contain asbestos fibers from production or aftermarket brake linings. Breathing excessive concentrations of asbestos fibers can cause serious bodily harm. Exercise care when servicing brake parts. Do not sand or grind brake lining unless equipment used is designed to contain the dust residue. Do not clean brake parts with compressed air or by dry brushing. Cleaning should be done by dampening the brake components with a fine mist of water, then wiping the brake components clean with a dampened cloth. Dispose of cloth and all residue containing asbestos fibers in an impermeable container with the appropriate label. Follow practices prescribed by the Occupational Safety and Health Administration (OSHA) and the Environmental Protection Agency (EPA) for the handling, processing, and disposing of dust or debris that may contain asbestos fibers.

BRAKE CALIPER

REMOVAL & INSTALLATION

See Figure 7.

1. Before servicing the vehicle, refer to the Precautions Section.

2. Raise and safely support the front of the vehicle. Remove the front wheels.

3. If the caliper is only being removed from the bracket (as for a brake pad change), move to Step 3. If the caliper is being removed from the vehicle (as for replacement or an overhaul and reseal), remove the brake hose attaching bolt from the caliper. Remove the hose from the caliper and discard the washers. New seal washers will be required at assembly. Plug the brake hose to prevent fluid leakage.

4. Remove the caliper guide pin bolts that secure the caliper to the steering knuckle.

5. Remove the caliper by slowly sliding it away from the steering knuckle. Slide the opposite end of the brake caliper out from under the machined abutment on the steering knuckle.

6. Using a strong piece of wire, support the brake caliper assembly off the strut unit. Do NOT allow the caliper to hang from the

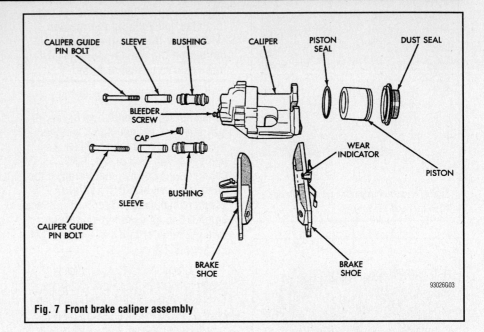

Fig. 7 Front brake caliper assembly

brake fluid flex hose or damage to the hose will result.

To install:

7. Clean both steering knuckle abutment surfaces of any dirt, grease or corrosion. Then lubricate the abutment surfaces with a liberal amount of MOPAR® Multipurpose Lubricant or equivalent.

8. Properly position the brake caliper over the brake pads and disc rotor. Be careful not to allow the caliper seals or guide pin bushings to get damaged by the steering knuckle bosses. Install the caliper guide pin bolts and torque to 26 ft. lbs. (35 Nm). Be careful not to cross thread the guide pin bolts.

9. If removed, attach the brake hose to the caliper using new washers. Tighten the banjo bolt to 35 ft. lbs. (47 Nm).

10. Bleed the brake system.

11. Install the front wheels and lug nuts. Torque the lug nuts, in a star pattern sequence, to ½ torque specifications. Then repeat the tightening sequence to the full torque specification of 100 ft. lbs. (135 Nm). Lower the vehicle.

12. Pump the brake pedal several times to insure that the brake pedal is firm. Road-test the vehicle

DISC BRAKE PADS

REMOVAL & INSTALLATION

1. Before servicing the vehicle, refer to the Precautions Section.

2. Remove brake fluid from the master cylinder brake fluid reservoir until the reservoir is approximately ½ full. Discard the removed fluid.

3. Raise and safely support the front of the vehicle. Remove the front wheels.

4. Remove or disconnect the following:

- Front brake caliper guide pin bolts
- Brake caliper by slowly sliding it up and off the adapter and brake rotor. Support the caliper out of the way with a strong piece of wire. Do not let the caliper hang by the brake hose or damage to the brake hose will result.

5. If necessary, compress the caliper piston into the bore using a C-clamp. Insert a suitable piece of wood between the C-clamp and caliper piston to protect the piston.

- Outboard disc brake pad from the caliper by prying the brake pad retaining clip over the raised area on the caliper. Slide the brake pad down and off the caliper.
- Inboard disc brake pad from the caliper by pulling the brake pad away from the caliper piston until the retaining clip on the pad is free from the caliper piston cavity

To install:

6. Be sure the caliper piston has been completely retracted into the piston bore of the caliper assembly. This is required when installing the brake caliper equipped with new brake pads.

7. If equipped, remove the protective paper from the noise suppression gaskets on the new disc brake pads.

8. Install or connect the following:
- New inboard disc brake pad into the caliper piston by pressing the pad firmly into the cavity of the caliper piston. Be sure the new

inboard brake pad is seated squarely against the face of the brake caliper piston.
- Outboard disc brake pad by sliding it onto the caliper assembly
- Brake caliper assembly over the brake rotor and onto the steering knuckle adapter

- Caliper guide pin bolts and torque to 26 ft. lbs. (35 Nm)
- Apply the brake pedal several times until a firm pedal is obtained.

9. Check the fluid level in the master cylinder and add fluid as necessary. Road–test the vehicle.

BRAKES

✳✳ CAUTION

Dust and dirt accumulating on brake parts during normal use may contain asbestos fibers from production or aftermarket brake linings. Breathing excessive concentrations of asbestos fibers can cause serious bodily harm. Exercise care when servicing brake parts. Do not sand or grind brake lining unless equipment used is designed to contain the dust residue. Do not clean brake parts with compressed air or by dry brushing. Cleaning should be done by dampening the brake components with a fine mist of water, then wiping the brake components clean with a dampened cloth. Dispose of cloth and all residue containing asbestos fibers in an impermeable container with the appropriate label. Follow practices prescribed by the Occupational Safety and Health Administration (OSHA) and the Environmental Protection Agency (EPA) for the handling, processing, and disposing of dust or debris that may contain asbestos fibers.

BRAKE CALIPER

REMOVAL & INSTALLATION
See Figure 8.

1. Before servicing the vehicle, refer to the Precautions Section.

2. Raise and safely support the rear of the vehicle. Remove the wheels.

3. If the caliper is only being removed from the bracket (as for a brake pad change), move to Step 3. If the caliper is being removed from the vehicle (as for replacement or an overhaul and reseal), remove the brake hose attaching bolt from the caliper. Remove the hose from the caliper and discard the washers. New seal washers will be required at assembly. Plug the brake hose to prevent fluid leakage.

4. Remove the caliper guide pin bolts that secure the caliper.

5. Remove the caliper by slowly sliding it away from the mount. Slide the opposite end of the brake caliper out from under the machined abutment.

6. Using a strong piece of wire, support the brake caliper assembly. Do NOT allow the caliper to hang from the brake fluid flex hose or damage to the hose will result.

To install:

7. Clean both abutment surfaces of any dirt, grease or corrosion. Then lubricate the abutment surfaces with a liberal amount of MOPAR® Multipurpose Lubricant or equivalent.

8. Properly position the brake caliper over the brake pads and disc rotor. Be careful not to allow the caliper seals or guide pin bushings to get damaged by the steering knuckle bosses. Install the caliper guide pin bolts and torque to 26 ft. lbs. (35 Nm). Be careful not to cross thread the guide pin bolts.

9. If removed, attach the brake hose to the caliper using new washers. Tighten the banjo bolt to 35 ft. lbs. (47 Nm).

10. Bleed the brake system.

REAR DISC BRAKES

11. Install the wheels and lug nuts. Torque the lug nuts, in a star pattern sequence, to ½ torque specifications. Then repeat the tightening sequence to the full torque specification of 100 ft. lbs. (135 Nm). Lower the vehicle.

12. Pump the brake pedal several times to insure that the brake pedal is firm. Road–test the vehicle

DISC BRAKE PADS

REMOVAL & INSTALLATION

1. Before servicing the vehicle, refer to the Precautions Section.

2. Remove brake fluid from the master cylinder brake fluid reservoir until the reservoir is approximately ½ full. Discard the removed fluid.

3. Raise and safely support the vehicle. Remove the wheels.

4. Remove or disconnect the following:
- Brake caliper guide pin bolts
- Brake caliper by slowly sliding it up and off the adapter and brake rotor.

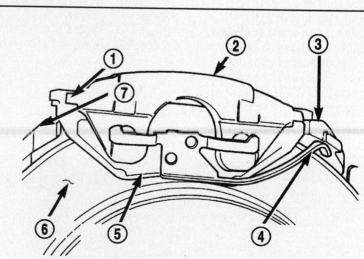

1. Lift this end of the caliper first
2. Caliper
3. Abutment
4. Outboard pad clip
5. Outboard pad
6. Rotor
7. Adapter

Fig. 8 Rear brake caliper removal

22043_CARA_G0004

Support the caliper out of the way with a strong piece of wire. Do not let the caliper hang by the brake hose or damage to the brake hose will result.

- Outboard disc brake pad from the caliper by prying the brake pad retaining clip over the raised area on the caliper. Slide the brake pad down and off the caliper.
- Inboard disc brake pad from the caliper by pulling the brake pad away from the caliper piston until the retaining clip on the pad is free from the caliper piston cavity

To install:

5. Be sure the caliper piston has been completely retracted into the piston bore of the caliper assembly. This is required when installing the brake caliper equipped with new brake pads.
6. If equipped, remove the protective paper from the noise suppression gaskets on the new disc brake pads.
7. Install or connect the following:
- New inboard disc brake pad into the caliper piston by pressing the pad firmly into the cavity of the caliper piston. Be sure the new inboard brake pad is seated

squarely against the face of the brake caliper piston.
- Outboard disc brake pad by sliding it onto the caliper assembly
- Brake caliper assembly over the brake rotor and onto the mount.
- Caliper guide pin bolts and torque to 26 ft. lbs. (35 Nm)
- Apply the brake pedal several times until a firm pedal is obtained.

8. Check the fluid level in the master cylinder and add fluid as necessary. Road–test the vehicle.

BRAKES

✳✳ CAUTION

Dust and dirt accumulating on brake parts during normal use may contain asbestos fibers from production or aftermarket brake linings. Breathing excessive concentrations of asbestos fibers can cause serious bodily harm. Exercise care when servicing brake parts. Do not sand or grind brake lining unless equipment used is designed to contain the dust residue. Do not clean brake parts with compressed air or by dry brushing. Cleaning should be done by dampening the brake components with a fine mist of water, then wiping the brake components clean with a dampened cloth. Dispose of cloth and all residue containing asbestos fibers in an impermeable container with the appropriate label. Follow practices prescribed by the Occupational Safety and Health Administration (OSHA) and the Environmental Protection Agency (EPA) for the handling, processing, and disposing of dust or debris that may contain asbestos fibers.

BRAKE DRUM

REMOVAL & INSTALLATION

1. Before servicing the vehicle, refer to the Precautions Section.
2. Raise and safely support the vehicle.
3. Remove or disconnect the following:
- Rear wheels
- Brake drum from the hub assembly by pulling the drum straight off the wheel studs

4. Inspect the brake drum for thickness and runout. Replace or machine as necessary.

To install:

5. Install the brake drum to the hub assembly.
6. Adjust the brake shoes.
7. Install the rear wheel.

BRAKE SHOES

REMOVAL & INSTALLATION

See Figure 9.

1. Before servicing the vehicle, refer to the Precautions Section.
2. Raise and safely support the vehicle.
3. Remove or disconnect the following:
- Rear wheels and the brake drums

4. Be sure the parking brake pedal is in the released position. Create slack in the rear parking brake cables by grasping an exposed section of the front parking brake cable, pulling it down and rearward. Maintain the slack in the brake cable by clamping a pair of locking pliers onto the parking brake cable just rearward of **the rear** body outrigger bracket.

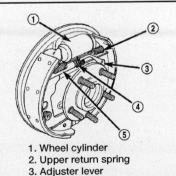

1. Wheel cylinder
2. Upper return spring
3. Adjuster lever
4. Tension clip
5. Adjuster

22043_CARA_G0005

Fig. 9 Drum brake components

REAR DRUM BRAKES

- Adjustment lever spring from the automatic adjustment lever and front brake shoe (leading brake shoe)
- Automatic adjustment lever from the front brake shoe (leading brake shoe)
- Brake shoe–to–brake shoe lower return spring
- Tension clip that secures the upper return spring to the automatic adjuster assembly
- Brake shoe–to–brake shoe upper return spring
- Rear brake shoe (trailing brake shoe) hold–down clip and pin
- Trailing brake shoe, parking brake actuating lever and parking brake actuator strut from the brake support plate
- Automatic adjuster assembly from the leading brake shoe
- Leading brake shoe hold–down clip and pin
- Leading brake shoe
- Parking brake actuator plate from the leading brake shoe and install onto the replacement brake shoe

To install:

5. Thoroughly clean and dry the backing plate. To prepare the backing plate, lubricate the 8 brake shoe contact areas and brake shoe anchor, using suitable grease.
6. Install or connect the following:
- Leading brake shoe into position on the brake shoe support plate. Secure the leading brake shoe by installing the brake shoe hold–down clip and pin.
- Parking brake actuating strut onto the leading brake shoe and then install the parking brake actuating lever onto the strut

7. Lubricate the shaft threads of the

automatic adjuster screw assembly with anti–seize lubricant.

- Automatic adjuster screw assembly onto the leading brake shoe
- Trailing brake shoe onto the parking brake actuating lever and parking brake actuating strut
- Trailing brake shoe into position on the brake support plate and install the brake shoe hold–down clip and pin
- Brake shoe–to–brake shoe upper return spring
- Tension clip that secures the upper return spring to the automatic adjuster assembly. Be sure the tension clip is positioned on the threaded area of the adjuster assembly or the function of the automatic adjuster will be affected.
- Brake shoe–to–brake shoe lower return spring
- Automatic adjustment lever onto the leading brake shoe

- Actuating spring onto the automatic adjustment lever and leading brake shoe. Make sure the automatic adjustment lever makes positive contact with the star wheel.

8. Once the brake shoes and all other brake system components are fully and correctly installed, remove the locking pliers from the front parking brake cable. This will remove the slack and correctly adjust the parking brake cables.

9. Make sure there is no grease on the brake shoe linings, then install the brake drums.

10. Adjust the rear brakes, then lower the vehicle and check the brakes for proper operation.

11. Install the wheels.

12. Road–test the vehicle. The automatic adjuster will continue to adjust the brake shoes during the road–test.

ADJUSTMENT

1. Raise the vehicle.

2. Remove rubber plug from rear brake adjusting hole in the rear brake support plate.

3. Insert a thin screwdriver through the adjusting hole in the support plate and against the star wheel of the adjusting screw. Move handle of the tool downward, rotating the star wheel until a slight drag is felt when tire and wheel assembly is rotated.

4. Insert a second thin screwdriver or piece of welding rod into brake adjusting hole and push the adjusting lever out of engagement with the star wheel. Care should be taken so as not to bend adjusting lever or distort lever spring.

5. While holding the adjusting lever out of engagement, back off the star wheel just enough to ensure a free wheel with no brake shoe drag.

6. Repeat the above adjustment at the other rear wheel.

7. Install the adjusting hole rubber plugs back in the rear brake support plates.

BRAKES
PARKING BRAKE

PARKING BRAKE CABLES

ADJUSTMENT

The park brake cables on this vehicle have an automatic self adjuster built into the park brake pedal mechanism. When the foot operated park brake pedal is in its released (upward most) position, a clock spring automatically adjusts the park brake cables. The park brake cables are adjusted (tensioned) just enough to remove all the slack from the cables. The automatic adjuster system will not over adjust the cables causing rear brake drag.

Due to the automatic adjust feature of the park brake pedal, adjustment of the parking brake cables on these vehicles relies on proper drum brake adjustment. Refer to the Brake Shoes adjustment procedure.

PARKING BRAKE SHOES

REMOVAL & INSTALLATION

See Figure 10.

1. Before servicing the vehicle, refer to the Precautions Section.

2. Raise and safely support the vehicle.

3. Remove the rotor from the hub/bearing.

4. Remove the park brake cable mounting bolt to adapter.

5. Remove the end of the park brake

cable from the actuator lever on the adapter.

6. Remove the end of the park brake cable from the adapter. Park brake cable is removed from adapter using a 1/2 wrench slipped over the park brake cable retainer.

7. Remove ABS wheel speed sensor head from hub/bearing.

8. Remove the hub/bearing.

✳✳ CAUTION

Corrosion may occur between the hub/bearing and the axle flange. If this occurs, the hub/bearing will be difficult to remove from the axle and disc brake caliper adapter. If the hub/bearing will not come out by pulling on it by hand, don't not pound on it with a hammer. Pounding on the hub/bearing will damage it. To remove a hub/bearing that is corroded in place, lightly tap the disc brake caliper adapter using a soft–face hammer. This will remove both the caliper adapter and hub/bearing together from the axle.

9. Remove the adapter from the rear axle.

10. Mount the adapter in a vise using the anchor boss for the park brake cable.

11. Remove the lower return spring from the leading and trailing park brake shoes.

12. Remove the hold down spring and pin from the leading park brake shoe.

13. Remove the adjuster from the leading and trailing park brake shoe.

14. Remove the leading park brake shoe from the adapter. Leading brake shoe is removed by rotating the bottom of the brake shoe inward until the top of the brake shoe can be removed from the brake shoe anchor. Then remove the upper return springs from the leading brake shoe.

15. Remove the upper return springs from the trailing park brake shoe.

16. Remove the hold down spring and pin from the trailing park brake shoe.

17. Remove the trailing park brake shoe from the adapter.

18. Remove the park brake shoe actuator from the adapter and inspect for signs of abnormal wear and binding at the pivot point.

19. Installation is the reverse of removal.

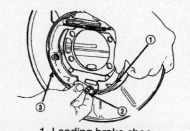

1. Leading brake shoe
2. Adjuster
3. Trailing brake shoe

22043_CARA_G0006

Fig. 10 Parking brake components

CHASSIS ELECTRICAL AIR BAG (SUPPLEMENTAL RESTRAINT SYSTEM)

GENERAL INFORMATION

❊❊ CAUTION

These vehicles are equipped with an air bag system. The system must be disarmed before performing service on, or around, system components, the steering column, instrument panel components, wiring and sensors. Failure to follow the safety precautions and the disarming procedure could result in accidental air bag deployment, possible injury and unnecessary system repairs.

SERVICE PRECAUTIONS

Disconnect and isolate the battery negative cable before beginning any airbag system component diagnosis, testing, removal, or installation procedures. Allow system capacitor to discharge for two minutes before beginning any component service. This will disable the airbag system. Failure to disable the airbag system may result in accidental airbag deployment, personal injury, or death.

Do not place an intact undeployed airbag face down on a solid surface. The airbag will propel into the air if accidentally deployed and may result in personal injury or death.

When carrying or handling an undeployed airbag, the trim side (face) of the airbag should be pointing towards the body to minimize possibility of injury if accidental deployment occurs. Failure to do this may result in personal injury or death.

Replace airbag system components with OEM replacement parts. Substitute parts may appear interchangeable, but internal differences may result in inferior occupant protection. Failure to do so may result in occupant personal injury or death.

Wear safety glasses, rubber gloves, and long sleeved clothing when cleaning powder residue from vehicle after an airbag deployment. Powder residue emitted from a deployed airbag can cause skin irritation. Flush affected area with cool water if irritation is experienced. If nasal or throat irritation is experienced, exit the vehicle for fresh air until the irritation ceases. If irritation continues, see a physician.

Do not use a replacement airbag that is not in the original packaging. This may result in improper deployment, personal injury, or death.

The factory installed fasteners, screws and bolts used to fasten airbag components have a special coating and are specifically designed for the airbag system. Do not use substitute fasteners. Use only original equipment fasteners listed in the parts catalog when fastener replacement is required.

During, and following, any child restraint anchor service, due to impact event or vehicle repair, carefully inspect all mounting hardware, tether straps, and anchors for proper installation, operation, or damage. If a child restraint anchor is found damaged in any way, the anchor must be replaced. Failure to do this may result in personal injury or death.

Deployed and non-deployed airbags may or may not have live pyrotechnic material within the airbag inflator.

Do not dispose of driver/passenger/curtain airbags or seat belt tensioners unless you are sure of complete deployment. Refer to the Hazardous Substance Control System for proper disposal.

Dispose of deployed airbags and tensioners consistent with state, provincial, local, and federal regulations.

After any airbag component testing or service, do not connect the battery negative cable. Personal injury or death may result if the system test is not performed first.

If the vehicle is equipped with the Occupant Classification System (OCS), do not connect the battery negative cable before performing the OCS Verification Test using the scan tool and the appropriate diagnostic information. Personal injury or death may result if the system test is not performed properly.

Never replace both the Occupant Restraint Controller (ORC) and the Occupant Classification Module (OCM) at the same time. If both require replacement, replace one, then perform the Airbag System test before replacing the other.

Both the ORC and the OCM store Occupant Classification System (OCS) calibration data, which they transfer to one another when one of them is replaced. If both are replaced at the same time, an irreversible fault will be set in both modules and the OCS may malfunction and cause personal injury or death.

If equipped with OCS, the Seat Weight Sensor is a sensitive, calibrated unit and must be handled carefully. Do not drop or handle roughly. If dropped or damaged, replace with another sensor. Failure to do so may result in occupant injury or death.

If equipped with OCS, the front passenger seat must be handled carefully as well. When removing the seat, be careful when setting on floor not to drop. If dropped, the sensor may be inoperative, could result in occupant injury, or possibly death.

If equipped with OCS, when the passenger front seat is on the floor, no one should sit in the front passenger seat. This uneven force may damage the sensing ability of the seat weight sensors. If sat on and damaged, the sensor may be inoperative, could result in occupant injury, or possibly death.

DISARMING THE SYSTEM

1. Disconnect and isolate the negative battery cable from the battery.
2. Allow the SIR system capacitor to discharge for at least two (2) minutes, before performing any repairs.
3. When repairs are completed, connect the negative battery cable.

ARMING THE SYSTEM

1. When repairs are completed, connect the negative battery cable.

CLOCKSPRING CENTERING

❊❊ CAUTION

If the rotating tape (wire coil) in the clockspring is not positioned properly with the steering wheel and the front wheels, the clockspring may fail. The following procedure MUST BE USED to center the clockspring if it is not known to be properly positioned, or if the front wheels were moved from the straight ahead position.

1. Position steering wheel and front wheels straight ahead.
2. Rotate the clockspring rotor clockwise until the rotor stops. Do not apply excessive force.
3. From the end of travel, rotate the rotor two turns counterclockwise until the wires end up at the top.
4. Install the clockspring.

DRIVETRAIN

AUTOMATIC TRANSAXLE ASSEMBLY

REMOVAL & INSTALLATION

41TE Transaxle

1. Before servicing the vehicle, refer to the Precautions Section.
2. Attach a support fixture to the engine lifting eyes.
3. Remove or disconnect the following:
   - Battery cables
   - Battery shield
   - Coolant recovery bottle
   - Dipstick tube and plug the opening
   - Torque converter clutch harness connector
   - Transaxle fluid cooler lines. Cut the lines flush with the fittings. A service kit will be used upon installation.
   - Input and output shaft sensor connectors
   - Transmission Range Sensor (TRS) connector
   - Solenoid/pressure switch connector
   - Shift cable
   - Crankshaft Position (CKP) sensor from the bell housing, if equipped
   - Position the leak detection pump harness and hoses aside
   - Rear mount bracket–to–case bolts
   - Upper transaxle bolts
   - Transaxle pan
   - Front wheels
   - Axle halfshafts
   - Power Transfer Unit (PTO), if equipped
   - Rear mount bracket–to–case lower bolt
   - Front mount/bracket assembly
   - Starter motor
   - Lateral bending brace
   - Inspection cover
   - Torque converter bolts
4. Support the engine with a screw jack and wood block.
   - Left wheel splash shield
   - Left upper mount through bolt
5. Lower the engine/transaxle assembly and attach a transmission jack to the transaxle.
   - Upper mount bracket from the transaxle
   - Remaining transaxle bolts
   - Transaxle

To install:
6. Install or connect the following:
   - Transaxle. Torque the flange bolts to 70 ft. lbs. (95 Nm).
   - Upper mount assembly and tighten the bolts to 40 ft. lbs. (54 Nm)
7. Raise the transaxle/engine assembly into position using a screw jack and a wood block.
   - Left upper mount through bolt and tighten to 55 ft. lbs. (75 Nm)
   - Left wheel splash shield
   - Torque converter bolts and tighten to 65 ft. lbs. (88 Nm)
   - Inspection cover
   - Lateral bending brace
   - Starter motor
   - Front mount/bracket assembly
   - Rear mount bracket–to–case lower bolt. Align the assembly, hand tighten the bolt first, then tighten to 75 ft. lbs. (102 Nm) on the assembly is aligned.
   - PTO, if equipped
   - Axle halfshafts
   - Front wheels
   - Transaxle pan
   - Rear mount bracket–to–case vertical bolts to 75 ft. lbs. (102 Nm)
   - Upper transaxle bolts to 70 ft. lbs. (95 Nm)
   - CKP sensor to the bell housing, if equipped
   - Shift cable
   - Attach the leak detection pump harness and hoses
   - Solenoid/pressure switch connector
   - TRS connector
   - Input and output shaft sensor connectors
   - Transaxle fluid cooler lines. Attach using the service kit supplied following the kit instructions.
   - Torque converter clutch harness connector
   - Dipstick tube
   - Coolant recovery bottle
   - Battery shield
   - Battery cables
8. Fill the transaxle with the correct type and amount of fluid
9. Start the engine and check for proper operation.

40TE Transaxle

1. Before servicing the vehicle, refer to the Precautions Section.
2. Attach a support fixture to the engine lifting eyes.
3. Remove or disconnect the following:
   - Battery cables
   - Battery shield
   - Coolant recovery bottle
   - Dipstick tube and plug the opening
   - Transaxle fluid cooler lines. Cut the lines flush with the fittings. A service kit will be used upon installation.
   - Input and output shaft sensor connectors
   - Transmission Range Sensor (TRS) connector
   - Solenoid/pressure switch connector
   - Shift cable
   - Crankshaft Position (CKP) sensor from the bell housing, if equipped
   - Position the leak detection pump harness and hoses aside
   - Rear mount bracket–to–case bolts
   - Upper transaxle bolts
   - Transaxle pan
   - Front wheels
   - Axle halfshafts
   - Power Transfer Unit (PTO), if equipped
   - Rear mount bracket–to–case lower bolt
   - Front mount/bracket assembly
   - Starter motor
   - Lateral bending brace
   - Inspection cover
   - Torque converter bolts
4. Support the engine with a screw jack and wood block.
   - Left wheel splash shield
   - Left upper mount through bolt
5. Lower the engine/transaxle assembly and attach a transmission jack to the transaxle.
   - Upper mount bracket from the transaxle
   - Remaining transaxle bolts
   - Transaxle

To install:
6. Install or connect the following:
   - Transaxle. Torque the flange bolts to 70 ft. lbs. (95 Nm).
   - Upper mount assembly and tighten the bolts to 40 ft. lbs. (54 Nm)
7. Raise the transaxle/engine assembly into position using a screw jack and a wood block.
   - Left upper mount through bolt and tighten to 55 ft. lbs. (75 Nm)
   - Left wheel splash shield
   - Torque converter bolts and tighten to 65 ft. lbs. (88 Nm)
   - Inspection cover
   - Lateral bending brace
   - Starter motor
   - Front mount/bracket assembly
   - Rear mount bracket–to–case lower

bolt. Align the assembly, hand tighten the bolt first, then tighten to 75 ft. lbs. (102 Nm) on the assembly is aligned.

- PTO, if equipped
- Axle halfshafts
- Front wheels
- Transaxle pan
- Rear mount bracket–to–case vertical bolts to 75 ft. lbs. (102 Nm)
- Upper transaxle bolts to 70 ft. lbs. (95 Nm)
- CKP sensor to the bell housing, if equipped
- Shift cable
- Attach the leak detection pump harness and hoses
- Solenoid/pressure switch connector
- TRS connector
- Input and output shaft sensor connectors
- Transaxle fluid cooler lines. Attach using the service kit supplied following the kit instructions.
- Dipstick tube
- Coolant recovery bottle
- Battery shield
- Battery cables

8. Fill the transaxle with the correct type and amount of fluid

9. Start the engine and check for proper operation.

MANUAL TRANSAXLE ASSEMBLY

REMOVAL & INSTALLATION

T850 Transaxle

1. Before servicing the vehicle, refer to the Precautions Section.

2. Raise hood.

3. Disconnect gearshift cables from shift levers/cover assembly.

4. Remove gearshift cable retaining clips from mounting bracket. Remove cables and secure out of way.

5. Remove three right engine mount bracket–to–transaxle bolts.

6. Raise vehicle on hoist.

7. Remove front wheel/tires and half-shafts.

8. Drain transaxle fluid into suitable container.

9. Remove front harness retainer and secure harness out of way.

10. Using Tool 6638A, disconnect clutch hydraulic circuit quick connect (located on slave cylinder tube). Remove clutch slave cylinder by depressing towards case and

rotating counter–clockwise, while lifting anti–rotation tab out of case slot with screwdriver.

11. Remove engine left mount bracket.

12. Remove starter motor.

13. Disconnect back–up lamp switch connector.

14. Remove structural collar.

15. Remove modular clutch assembly–to–drive plate bolts.

16. Position screw jack and wood block to engine oil pan.

17. Remove transmission upper mount through–bolt from left frame rail.

18. Lower engine/transaxle assembly on screw jack.

19. Remove four (4) upper mount–to–transaxle bolts and remove mount.

20. Secure transaxle to transmission jack and remove transaxle–to–engine bolts.

21. Remove transaxle from engine.

22. Inspect modular clutch assembly, clutch release components, and engine drive plate.

23. Installation is the reverse of removal. Tighten the engine to transaxle bolts to 70 ft. lbs. (95 Nm).

CLUTCH

REMOVAL & INSTALLATION

1. Before servicing the vehicle, refer to the Precautions Section.

2. Remove transaxle assembly.

3. Remove six (6) clutch pressure plate–to–flywheel bolts. Remove pressure plate and disc from flywheel.

4. Inspect flywheel. Resurface or replace as necessary.

5. Inspect clutch release bearing and lever. Replace as necessary.

To install:

6. Install clutch release bearing and lever (if removed).

7. Install clutch disc and pressure plate to flywheel. Install clutch alignment tool, and install and torque pressure plate–to–flywheel bolts to 250 inch lbs. (28 Nm.).

8. Install transaxle assembly.

TRANSFER CASE ASSEMBLY

REMOVAL & INSTALLATION

See Figure 11.

1. Before servicing the vehicle, refer to the Precautions Section.

2. Remove or disconnect the following:
- Right front wheel
- Right axle halfshaft
- Propeller shaft
- Cradle plate
- Power transfer unit brackets
- Power transfer unit

To install:

3. Install or connect the following:
- Power transfer unit and brackets. Tighten the bolts to 37 ft. lbs. (50 Nm).
- Rear driveshaft
- Cradle plate. Tighten the bolts to 123 ft. lbs. (166 Nm).
- Right axle halfshaft
- Right front wheel

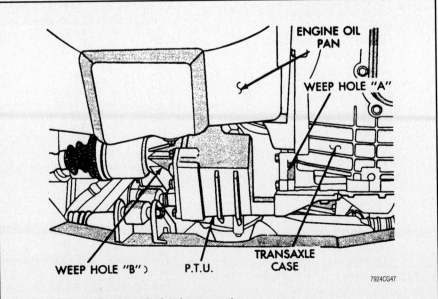

Fig. 11 Power transfer unit and related components

ENGINE OIL PAN

WEEP HOLE "A"

WEEP HOLE "B"   P.T.U.   TRANSAXLE CASE

7924CG47

FRONT HALFSHAFT

REMOVAL & INSTALLATION

1. Before servicing the vehicle, refer to the Precautions Section.
2. Remove or disconnect the following:
   - Front wheel
   - Split pin
   - Nut lock
   - Spring washer
   - Hub nut
   - Brake caliper and rotor
   - Outer tie rod end
   - Wheel speed sensor harness, if equipped
   - Lower ball joint
3. Separate the outer CV-joint stub shaft from the steering knuckle.
4. Pry the inner tri-pot joint out of the transaxle and remove the axle halfshaft.

To install:

5. Install the axle halfshaft so that the inner joint circlip seats in the transaxle side gear.
6. Guide the outer CV-joint stub shaft through the steering knuckle hub.
7. Install or connect the following:
   - Lower ball joint. Torque the nut to 65 ft. lbs. (88 Nm) plus a 90 degree turn.
   - Wheel speed sensor harness, if equipped
   - Outer tie rod end. Torque the nut to 55 ft. lbs. (75 Nm).
   - Brake caliper and rotor. Torque the caliper bolts to 35 ft. lbs. (47 Nm).
   - Hub nut. Torque the nut to 180 ft. lbs. (245 Nm).
   - Spring washer
   - Nut lock
   - Split pin
   - Front wheel
8. Check the wheel alignment and adjust as necessary.

CV-JOINTS OVERHAUL

Outer CV-Joint

The outer CV-joint and boot are serviced with the axle halfshaft as an assembly.

Inner Tri-pot Joint

1. Before servicing the vehicle, refer to the Precautions Section.
2. Remove or disconnect the following:
   - Negative battery cable
   - Axle halfshaft from the vehicle
   - Inner tri-pot joint boot clamps
   - Tri-pot joint housing
   - Snapring
   - Tri-pot joint

To install:

➡**Use new snaprings, clips, and boot clamps for assembly.**

3. Install or connect the following:
   - Tri-pot joint
   - Snapring
   - Tri-pot joint housing
4. Fill the tri-pot joint housing and boot with grease and tighten the boot clamps.
5. Install the axle halfshaft.
6. Connect the negative battery cable

REAR AXLE HOUSING

REMOVAL & INSTALLATION

1. Before servicing the vehicle, refer to the Precautions Section.
2. Raise vehicle on hoist.
3. Remove right and left inner half shaft joint mounting bolts
4. Support inner side of half shaft with mechanics wire or equivalent. Do not allow half shafts to hang freely.
5. Remove mounting bolts from the rear side of propeller shaft

❋❋ WARNING

CAUTION: Do not allow propeller shaft to hang freely

6. Support propeller shaft with mechanics wire and/or jack stand
7. Disconnect main vacuum line for rear drive line module assembly. Also disconnect electrical connections at the front of the module.
8. Support rear drive line module assembly with transmission jack or equivalent

❋❋ CAUTION

Be sure to chain rear drive line module assembly securely to the jack to prevent it from falling.

9. Remove rear drive line module assembly rear mounting bolts
10. Remove rear drive line module assembly front mounting bolts
11. Partially lower rear drive line module assembly and disconnect remote solenoid vent and remote carrier vent.
12. Remove the rear drive line module from the vehicle.

To install:

13. Position the drive line module in the vehicle. Install the front mounting bolts and tighten to 40 ft. lbs. (54 Nm).
14. Reconnect the vacuum line and electrical lead. Install the viscous coupling and nut. Tighten the nut to 120 ft. lbs. (162 Nm).

15. Connect the propeller shaft to the drive line module, tighten to 21 ft. lbs. (28 Nm).
16. Connect the rear halfshafts to the rear drive line module. Tighten the bolt to 45 ft. lbs. (61 Nm).
17. Lower the vehicle. Check the operation of the drive train.

REAR HALFSHAFT

REMOVAL & INSTALLATION

1. Before servicing the vehicle, refer to the Precautions Section.
2. Remove or disconnect the following:
   - Rear wheel
   - Cotter pin, nut lock and washer
   - Half shaft nut and washer
   - Rear halfshafts from the output flanges
   - Axle halfshaft

To install:

3. Guide the outer CV-joint stub shaft through the rear wheel hub.
4. Install or connect the following:
   - Inner joint to the differential. Torque the flange bolts to 45 ft. lbs. (61 Nm).
   - Half shaft nut and washer and tighten the nut to 180 ft. lbs. (244 Nm)
   - Waver washer, nut lock and new cotter pin
   - Rear wheel

CV-JOINT OVERHAUL

Outer CV-Joint

The outer CV-joint and boot are serviced with the axle halfshaft as an assembly.

Inner Tri-pot Joint

1. Before servicing the vehicle, refer to the Precautions Section.
2. Remove or disconnect the following:
   - Negative battery cable
   - Axle halfshaft from the vehicle
   - Inner tri-pot joint boot clamps
   - Tri-pot joint housing
   - Snapring
   - Tri-pot joint

To install:

➡**Use new snaprings, clips, and boot clamps for assembly.**

3. Install or connect the following:
   - Tri-pot joint
   - Snapring
   - Tri-pot joint housing
4. Fill the tri-pot joint housing and boot with grease and tighten the boot clamps.

5. Install the axle halfshaft.
6. Connect the negative battery cable

REAR PINION SEAL

REMOVAL & INSTALLATION

1. Before servicing the vehicle, refer to the Precautions Section.

ENGINE COOLING

ENGINE FAN

REMOVAL & INSTALLATION

See Figures 12 through 14.

➡The electric cooling fan assembly cannot be disassembled. If the fan is warped, cracked or otherwise damaged, it must be replaced as an assembly.

1. Before servicing the vehicle, refer to the Precautions Section.
2. Disconnect the negative battery cable.
3. Raise and safely support the vehicle.
4. Remove the radiator outlet hose from the radiator hose retaining clip and remove the retaining clip from the shroud.
5. If equipped, remove the lower auxiliary transaxle cooler lines from the retaining clips on the cooling fan module shroud.
6. Lower the vehicle.
7. Remove the entire air cleaner assembly and the air intake resonator.
8. Disconnect the fan motor electrical connector(s).
9. Remove the Coolant Recovery System (CRS) mounting screw from the upper radiator crossmember.
10. Disconnect the mounts to the upper radiator from the radiator crossmember.
11. Remove the upper radiator crossmember.

2. Raise vehicle on hoist.
3. Remove propeller shaft.
4. Using tool 6958, remove input flange nut and washer.
5. Remove inpuzt flange.
6. Using suitable screwdriver, remove input flange seal from overrunning clutch housing.

To install:

7. Using tool 8802, install input flange seal to overrunning clutch case.
8. Install input flange.
9. Install flange nut and washer. Using tool 6958, torque flange nut to 100 ft. lbs. (135 Nm).
10. Install propeller shaft.
11. Lower vehicle.

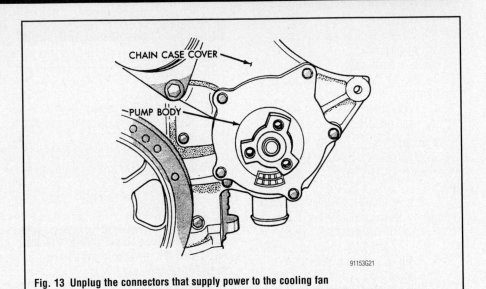

Fig. 13 Unplug the connectors that supply power to the cooling fan

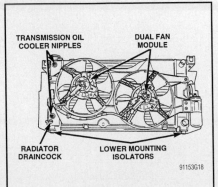

Fig. 12 Cooling fan assembly mounting points

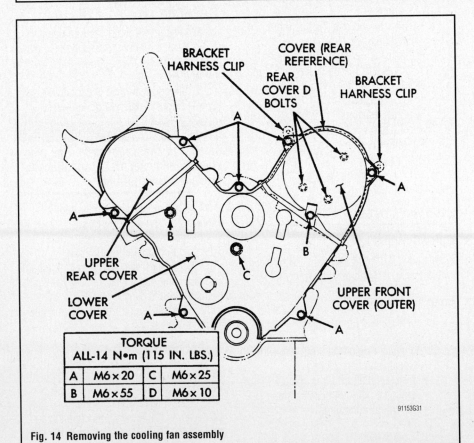

TORQUE ALL-14 N•m (115 IN. LBS.)			
A	M6 × 20	C	M6 × 25
B	M6 × 55	D	M6 × 10

Fig. 14 Removing the cooling fan assembly

12. Remove the cooling fan module mounting screws.

13. If equipped, remove the upper auxiliary transaxle cooler lines from the retaining clips on the cooling fan module shroud.

14. Disconnect and plug the transaxle oil cooler line from the radiator fitting on the lower left side.

15. Raise and safely support the vehicle.

16. Remove the filter/drier, cooling fan module and radiator mounting bolts located on the lower right of the cooling fan module.

17. Lower the vehicle. Remove the upper cooling fan module–to–radiator retaining clips.

18. Remove the cooling fan module from the vehicle.

To install:

19. Install the cooling fan module assembly into the retaining clips of the radiator.

20. Install the upper cooling fan module–to–radiator retaining clips.

21. Raise and safely support the vehicle.

22. Install the filter/drier, cooling fan module and radiator mounting bolts located on the lower right of the cooling fan module.

23. Lower the vehicle. Reconnect the transaxle cooler line to the radiator fitting on the lower left side.

24. If equipped, install the upper auxiliary transaxle cooler lines to the retaining clips on the cooling fan module shroud.

25. Install the cooling fan module retaining screws and torque to 105 inch lbs. (12 Nm).

26. Install the entire air cleaner assembly.

27. Install the upper radiator crossmember and connect the upper radiator mounts to the crossmember. Torque the mounting fasteners to 105 inch lbs. (12 Nm).

28. Install the Coolant Recovery System (CRS) mounting screw to the upper radiator crossmember. Torque the mounting screw to 18 inch lbs. (2 Nm).

29. Reconnect the fan motor electrical connector.

30. Install the air intake resonator to the air cleaner assembly.

31. Raise and safely support the vehicle.

32. If equipped, install the lower auxiliary transaxle cooler lines to the retaining clips on the cooling fan module shroud.

33. Install the radiator outlet hose retainer clip to the fan module shroud.

34. Install the radiator outlet hose to the retaining clip. Lower the vehicle.

35. Reconnect the negative battery cable. Run the engine and check for proper cooling fan operation when the engine reaches operating temperature.

RADIATOR

REMOVAL & INSTALLATION

See Figures 15 through 17.

1. Before servicing the vehicle, refer to the Precautions Section.

2. Disconnect the negative battery cable.

✳✳ CAUTION

Do not remove the radiator cap or drain with the cooling system hot and under pressure or serious personal injury can occur from hot pressurized coolant.

3. Place a drain pan under the radiator drain. Open the radiator drain plug and allow the coolant to drain.

4. Remove the air intake resonator from the air cleaner assembly.

5. Remove the Coolant Recovery System (CRS) overflow tank filler neck hose.

6. Disconnect the cooling fan electrical connector located on the left side of the cooling fan module.

7. Remove the CRS overflow tank mounting screw from the upper radiator crossmember.

8. Remove the upper radiator–to–crossmember mounting screws.

9. If equipped, disconnect the engine block heater wiring connector.

10. Remove the upper radiator crossmember.

11. Remove the entire air cleaner assembly.

12. Disconnect and plug the automatic transaxle oil cooler lines from the radiator.

13. Disconnect the upper and lower radiator hoses from the radiator. Remove the lower radiator hose clip from the cooling fan module.

14. Remove the A/C condenser mounting fasteners and separate the A/C condenser from the radiator. Be sure the condenser is supported in position.

15. Remove the A/C filter/drier mounting bracket, 2 mounting bolts to the cooling fan module and 2 mounting nuts to the filter/drier. Remove the mounting bracket.

16. Carefully lift the radiator out of the engine compartment. Be careful not to damage the radiator cooling fins or water tubes during removal.

To install:

17. Be sure the air seals are properly positioned before installation of the radiator. Lower the radiator into position and seat the radiator with the rubber isolators into the mounting holes provided.

18. Install the A/C filter/drier and mounting bracket onto the cooling fan module. Install the bracket mounting fasteners.

19. Install the A/C condenser to the radiator.

20. Unplug and connect the transaxle oil cooler lines to the radiator.

21. Connect the upper and lower radiator hoses to the radiator.

22. Connect the CRS overflow tank filler neck hose to the radiator.

23. Reconnect the cooling fan motor electrical connector.

24. Install the entire air cleaner assembly.

25. Install the upper radiator crossmember.

26. Install the upper radiator mounting screws and torque to 105 inch lbs. (12 Nm).

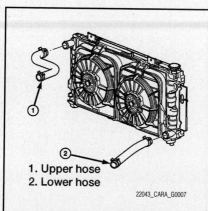

1. Upper hose
2. Lower hose

22043_CARA_G0007

Fig. 15 Radiator and cooling fan assemblies

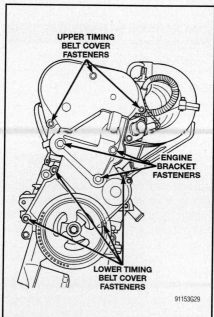

UPPER TIMING BELT COVER FASTENERS

ENGINE BRACKET FASTENERS

LOWER TIMING BELT COVER FASTENERS

91153G29

Fig. 16 Spring–type hose clamps can be removed with pliers

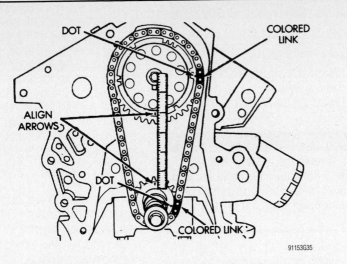

Fig. 17 Worm–type hose clamps can be removed with a screwdriver, or in some cases, a small socket

27. Reconnect the engine block heater electrical connector, if equipped.

28. Install the CRS overflow tank mounting screw to the upper radiator crossmember. Torque the screw to 18 inch lbs. (2 Nm).

29. Install the air intake resonator.

30. Refill the cooling system with a 50/50 mixture of clean, fresh ethylene glycol antifreeze and water to the proper level.

31. Reconnect the negative battery cable.

32. Start the engine and run until it reaches normal operating temperature, then check the coolant level and the automatic transmission fluid level. Add fluids, if necessary.

THERMOSTAT

REMOVAL & INSTALLATION

2.4L Engine

See Figure 18.

1. Before servicing the vehicle, refer to the Precautions Section.

2. Disconnect the negative battery cable.

3. Place a large drain pan under the radiator drain plug. Allow the cooling system to sufficiently cool down before opening the drain plug to avoid personal injury. Drain the coolant to below the thermostat level.

4. Disconnect the upper radiator hose at the thermostat housing.

5. Remove the thermostat housing bolts and coolant outlet connector of the thermostat housing.

6. Remove the thermostat assembly from the vehicle and discard. Discard the old thermostat gasket.

To install:

7. Clean all gasket mating surfaces.

8. Install the new thermostat in the correct position. If equipped, align the air bleed valve on top of thermostat to the vent recess in the water box (engine side) of the thermostat housing.

9. Dip the new gasket in clean water and install on the water box surface of the thermostat housing.

10. Install the thermostat housing over the gasket and thermostat, making sure the thermostat is in correct position.

11. Install the thermostat housing bolts and torque to 20 ft. lbs. (28 Nm).

12. Reconnect the radiator hose. Tighten the radiator hose clamp.

13. Connect the negative battery cable.

14. Fill and bleed the engine cooling system.

15. Pressure test for leaks.

3.3L and 3.8L Engines

See Figures 19 through 24.

1. Before servicing the vehicle, refer to the Precautions Section.

2. Disconnect the negative battery cable.

3. Place a drain pan under the radiator drain and drain the cooling system to just below the thermostat level. Close the drain.

4. Remove the upper radiator hose from the thermostat housing, then remove the housing.

5. Remove the thermostat and discard the gasket.

To install:

6. Clean the housing mating surfaces.

7. Dip the new gasket in clean water and place it on the water box surface.

8. Center the thermostat on the gasket, in the water box.

9. Make certain the bolt threads are clean. Threaded bolt holes exposed to coolant are subject to corrosion and should be cleaned with a small wire brush or correct size thread–cutting tap. Install the housing, making sure the thermostat is still in the recess, and tighten the retaining bolts to 21 ft. lbs. (28 Nm). Reconnect the upper radiator hose and tighten the hose clamp.

10. Connect the negative battery cable.

11. Fill and bleed the engine cooling system with a clean 50/50 mixture of ethylene glycol antifreeze and water.

12. Make sure the radiator is full and start the vehicle.

✳✳ CAUTION

Do not remove the radiator cap once the vehicle is warm. Coolant is under pressure and may cause scalding or personal injury.

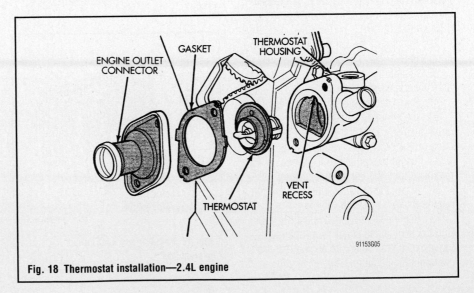

Fig. 18 Thermostat installation—2.4L engine

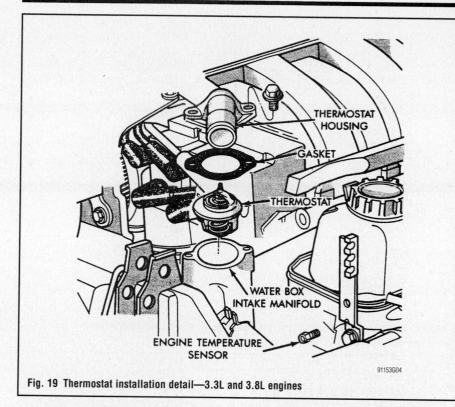

Fig. 19 Thermostat installation detail—3.3L and 3.8L engines

Fig. 20 Remove the radiator hose from the waterneck by loosening the hose clamp . . .

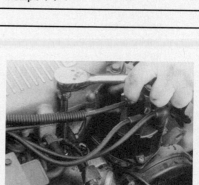

Fig. 21 . . . then loosen and remove the waterneck housing retaining bolts

Fig. 22 Lift the waterneck housing off of the lower intake manifold, then . . .

Fig. 23 . . . remove the thermostat out of its mounting flange

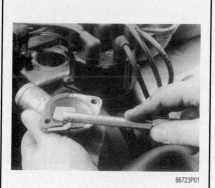

Fig. 24 Make sure to clean the waterneck before installation

13. Run the vehicle until the thermostat opens. Check the coolant level in the overflow tank and fill if necessary.
14. Pressure test for leaks.

WATER PUMP

REMOVAL & INSTALLATION

2.4L Engine

1. Before servicing the vehicle, refer to the Precautions Section.
2. Drain the cooling system.
3. Remove or disconnect the following:
   - Negative battery cable
   - Right inner splash shield
   - Accessory drive belts
   - Right motor mount and bracket, support the engine from below before removing the mount
   - Front cover
   - Timing belt.
   - Timing belt idler pulley
   - Camshaft sprockets
   - Timing belt rear cover
   - Alternator and bracket
   - Water pump

To install:

4. Install or connect the following:
   - Water pump with a new O–ring gasket. Tighten the bolts to 105 inch lbs. (12 Nm). Rotate the pump by hand to make sure it moves freely.
   - Timing belt rear cover
   - Camshaft sprockets. Tighten the bolts to 75 ft. lbs. (101 Nm).
   - Timing belt idler pulley. Tighten the bolt to 45 ft. lbs. (61 Nm).
   - Timing belt
   - Front cover
   - Alternator and bracket
   - Right motor mount
   - Accessory drive belts

- Right inner splash shield
- Negative battery cable
5. Fill the cooling system.
6. Start the engine and check for leaks.

3.3L and 3.8L Engines

See Figure 25.

1. Before servicing the vehicle, refer to the Precautions Section.
2. Drain the cooling system.
3. Remove or disconnect the following:

- Negative battery cable
- Right inner splash shield
- Accessory drive belt
- Water pump pulley bolts

➡**To remove the water pump it must be positioned between the pump housing and the drive hub. Refer to the accompanying illustration for further clarification.**

- Water pump with the pulley loosely positioned between the hub and pump body

To install:

4. Install or connect the following:
- New seal into the water pump housing groove

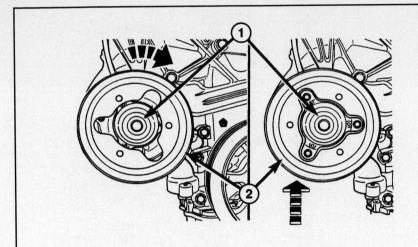

1 - HUB - WATER PUMP
2 - PULLEY - WATER PUMP

67189-MINV-G11

Fig. 25 The water pump must be positioned between the pump housing and the drive hub so it can be removed—3.3L and 3.8L engines

- Water pump with the pulley loosely positioned between the hub and pump body. Tighten the bolts to 105 inch lbs. (12 Nm).
- Water pump pulley and tighten the bolts to 250 inch lbs. (28 Nm).

Rotate the pump by hand to make sure it moves freely.
- Accessory drive belt
- Right inner splash shield
- Negative battery cable
5. Fill the cooling system.
6. Start the engine and check for leaks.

ENGINE ELECTRICAL

ALTERNATOR

REMOVAL & INSTALLATION

2.4L Engine

1. Before servicing the vehicle, refer to the Precautions Section.
2. Remove or disconnect the following:
- Negative battery cable
- Air inlet temperature sensor connector
- Air cleaner assembly
- Evaporative emissions (EVAP) purge solenoid from the bracket and position aside
- Alternator harness connections
- Accessory drive belt
- Alternator

To install:

3. Install or connect the following:
- Alternator

- Accessory drive belt. Tighten the alternator mounting fasteners to 20 ft. lbs. (28 Nm).
- Alternator harness connections
- EVAP purge solenoid
- Air cleaner assembly
- Air inlet temperature sensor connector
- Negative battery cable

3.3L and 3.8L Engines

1. Before servicing the vehicle, refer to the Precautions Section.
2. Remove or disconnect the following:

- Negative battery cable
- Alternator harness connectors
- Right front lower splash shield
- Accessory drive belt
- Lower oil dipstick tube bolt and the wiring harness from the tube

CHARGING SYSTEM

- 3 mounting bolts
- Dipstick tube
- Alternator

To install:

3. Install or connect the following:
- Alternator in position and the 3 mounting bolts. Tighten to 40 ft. lbs. (54 Nm).
- Dipstick tube, lubricate the O-ring with clean engine oil prior to installation, then tighten the upper dipstick tube bolt.
- Alternator harness connectors
- Lower oil dipstick tube bolt
- Accessory drive belt
- Right front lower splash shield
- Wiring harness to the dipstick tube
- Negative battery cable

ENGINE ELECTRICAL

IGNITION SYSTEM

FIRING ORDER

See Figures 26 and 27.

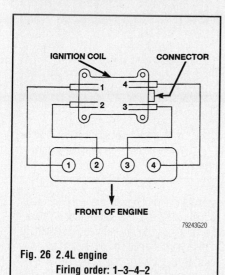

Fig. 26 2.4L engine
Firing order: 1–3–4–2
Distributorless ignition system

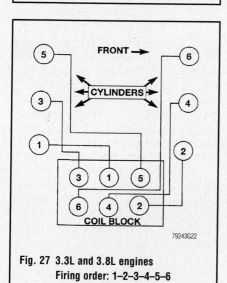

Fig. 27 3.3L and 3.8L engines
Firing order: 1–2–3–4–5–6
Distributorless ignition system

IGNITION COIL

REMOVAL & INSTALLATION

See Figures 28 and 29.

1. Disconnect the negative battery cable.

2. Label and disconnect the spark plug wires from each of the coil pack towers.

3. Disengage the electrical connector from the ignition coil pack.

4. Remove the coil pack mounting fasteners.

5. Remove the coil pack from the

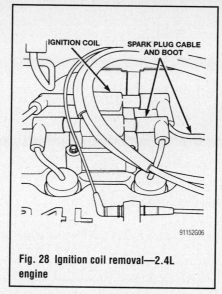

Fig. 28 Ignition coil removal—2.4L engine

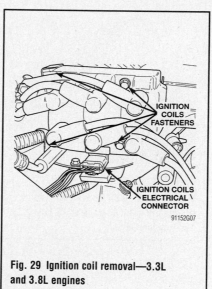

Fig. 29 Ignition coil removal—3.3L and 3.8L engines

vehicle. If equipped, remove the coil pack from the mounting bracket.

To install:

6. Place the coil pack into position on top of the engine valve cover, or mounting bracket, if equipped.

7. Install and tighten the coil pack mounting fasteners to 9 ft. lbs. (12 Nm).

8. Plug in the electrical connector to the ignition coil pack.

9. Connect each spark plug wire to each corresponding coil pack tower. The coil pack towers are numbered with the correct cylinder identification. Be sure that the spark plug wires snap firmly onto each coil tower.

10. Connect the negative battery cable.

IGNITION TIMING

ADJUSTMENT

The ignition timing is controlled by the Powertrain Control Module (PCM). No adjustment is necessary or possible.

SPARK PLUGS

REMOVAL & INSTALLATION

See Figures 30 through 32.

A set of spark plugs usually requires replacement after about 20,000–30,000 miles (32,000–48,000 km), depending on your style of driving. In normal operation plug gap increases about 0.001 in. (0.025mm) for every 2500 miles (4000 km). As the gap increases, the plug's voltage requirement also increases. It requires a greater voltage to jump the wider gap and about two to three times as much voltage to fire the plug at high speeds than at idle. The improved air/fuel ratio control of modern fuel injection combined with the higher voltage output of modern ignition systems will often allow an engine to run significantly longer on a set of standard spark plugs, but keep in mind that efficiency will drop as the gap widens (along with fuel economy and power).

When you're removing spark plugs, work on one at a time. Don't start by removing the plug wires all at once, because, unless you number them, they may become mixed up. Take a minute before you begin and number the wires with tape.

1. Disconnect the negative battery cable, and if the vehicle has been run recently, allow the engine to thoroughly cool.

➡**When removing the spark plugs on the V6 engine only on the firewall side, it may be necessary to remove the windshield wiper/motor module assembly from the vehicle. This will allow more room to work between the engine and the engine compartment firewall.**

2. On V6 models only, remove the windshield wiper/motor module assembly from the vehicle for access to the spark plugs on the firewall side.

3. Carefully twist the spark plug wire boot to loosen it, then pull upward and remove the boot from the plug. Be sure to pull on the boot and not on the wire, otherwise the connector located inside the boot may become separated.

Fig. 30 Hold the spark plug boot firmly, while giving it a slight ½ twist in each direction before pulling it off of the spark plug

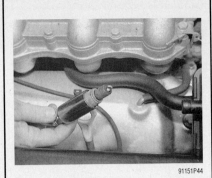

Fig. 32 Pull the used spark plug out of the cylinder head once it is completely loosened

4. Using compressed air, blow any water or debris from the spark plug well to assure that no harmful contaminants are allowed to enter the combustion chamber when the spark plug is removed. If compressed air is not available, use a rag or a brush to clean the area.

➡Remove the spark plugs when the engine is cold, if possible, to prevent damage to the threads. If removal of the plugs is difficult, apply a few drops of penetrating oil or silicone spray to the area around the base of the plug, and allow it a few minutes to work.

5. Using a spark plug socket that is equipped with a rubber insert to properly hold the plug, turn the spark plug counterclockwise to loosen and remove the spark plug from the bore.

✳✳ WARNING

Be sure not to use a flexible extension on the socket. Use of a flexible extension may allow a shear force to be applied to the plug. A shear force could break the plug off in the cylinder head, leading to costly and frustrating repairs.

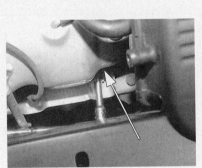

Fig. 31 Once all dirt is removed from around the spark plug, carefully loosen and remove the plug

To install:

6. Inspect the spark plug boot for tears or damage. If a damaged boot is found, the spark plug wire must be replaced.

7. Using a wire feeler gauge, check and adjust the spark plug gap. When using a gauge, the proper size should pass between the electrodes with a slight drag. The next larger size should not be able to pass while the next smaller size should pass freely.

8. Carefully thread the plug into the bore by hand. If resistance is felt before the plug is almost completely threaded, back the plug out and begin threading again. In small, hard to reach areas, an old spark plug wire and boot could be used as a threading tool. The boot will hold the plug while you twist the end of the wire and the wire is supple enough to twist before it would allow the plug to crossthread.

✳✳ WARNING

Do not use the spark plug socket to thread the plugs. Always carefully thread the plug by hand or using an old plug wire to prevent the possibility of crossthreading and damaging the cylinder head bore.

9. Carefully tighten the spark plug. If the plug you are installing is equipped with a crush washer, seat the plug, then tighten about ¼ turn to crush the washer. If you are installing a tapered seat plug, tighten the plug to specifications provided by the vehicle or plug manufacturer.

10. Apply a small amount of silicone dielectric compound to the end of the spark plug lead or inside the spark plug boot to prevent sticking, then install the boot to the spark plug and push until it clicks into place. The click may be felt or heard, then gently pull back on the boot to assure proper contact.

ENGINE ELECTRICAL

STARTER

REMOVAL & INSTALLATION

1. Before servicing the vehicle, refer to the Precautions Section.

2. Remove or disconnect the following:

- Negative battery cable
- Starter harness connectors
- Starter motor

To install:

3. Install or connect the following:

STARTING SYSTEM

- Starter motor. Torque the bolts to 35 ft. lbs. (47 Nm).
- Starter harness connectors. Torque the battery cable nut to 100 inch lbs. (11 Nm).
- Negative battery cable

ENGINE MECHANICAL

➡ Disconnecting the negative battery cable may interfere with the functions of the on board computer systems and may require the computer to undergo a relearning process, once the negative battery cable is reconnected.

ACCESSORY DRIVE BELTS

ACCESSORY BELT ROUTING

See Figures 33 and 34.

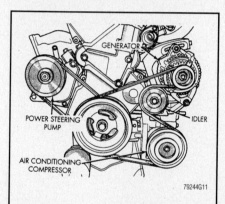

Fig. 33 Accessory V–belt routing—2.4L engine

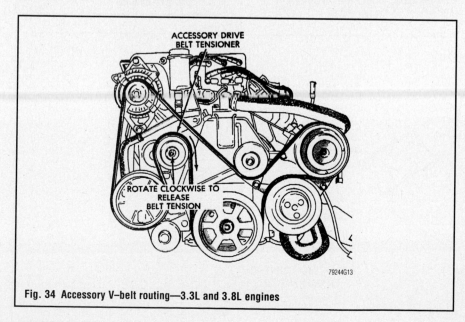

Fig. 34 Accessory V–belt routing—3.3L and 3.8L engines

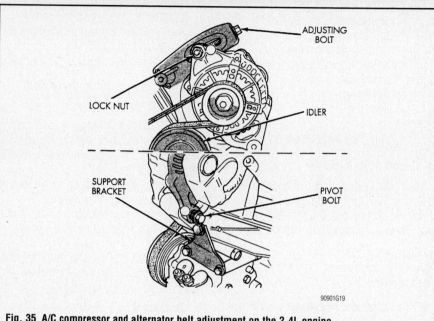

Fig. 35 A/C compressor and alternator belt adjustment on the 2.4L engine

INSPECTION

Inspect the drive belt for signs of glazing or cracking. A glazed belt will be perfectly smooth from slippage, while a good belt will have a slight texture of fabric visible. Cracks will usually start at the inner edge of the belt and run outward. All worn or damaged drive belts should be replaced immediately.

ADJUSTMENT

2.4L Engine

A/C Compressor and Alternator Drive Belt

See Figure 35.

1. Disconnect the negative battery cable.

2. Loosen the locknut at the top and pivot bolt at the bottom of the alternator.

3. Adjust the belt by rotating the adjusting bolt until the correct tension is reached. A new belt should be adjusted to 130–150 lbs. tension. A used belt should be adjusted to 80–90 lbs. tension.

4. After the belt is properly adjusted, tighten the pivot bolt and locknut to 40 ft. lbs. (54 Nm).

5. Connect the negative battery cable.

Power Steering Pump Drive Belt

1. Disconnect the negative battery cable.
2. From above the vehicle, loosen the locking nuts at the top of the power steering pump.
3. Raise and safely support the front of the vehicle securely on jackstands.
4. From underneath the vehicle, loosen the pivot bolt at the bottom of the power steering pump.
5. Rotate the adjusting bolt above the power steering pump to adjust the belt tension. A new belt should be adjusted to 130–150 lbs. tension. A used belt should be adjusted to 80–90 lbs. tension.
6. After the belt is adjusted properly, tighten the pivot bolt to 40 ft. lbs. (54 Nm).
7. Lower the vehicle.
8. Tighten the locking nuts to 40 ft. lbs. (54 Nm).
9. Connect the negative battery cable.

3.3L and 3.8L Engines

All of the belt driven accessories on the 3.3L and 3.8L engines are driven by a single serpentine belt. The belt tension is maintained by an automatic tensioner.

REMOVAL & INSTALLATION

2.4L Engine

A/C Compressor and Alternator Drive Belt

See Figure 36.

1. Disconnect the negative battery cable.
2. Loosen the locknut at the top and pivot bolt at the bottom of the alternator.
3. Rotate the adjuster screw, on top of the alternator, to decrease the belt tension.

4. Take note of the exact routing of the belt prior to removal. Lift the drive belt from the pulleys and remove it from the engine compartment.

To install:

5. Position the replacement belt around the pulleys, making sure the belt routing is correct.
6. Adjust the belt by rotating the adjusting bolt until the correct tension is reached. Refer to the procedure earlier in this section for belt adjustment.
7. After the belt is installed and/or properly adjusted, tighten the pivot bolt and locknut to 40 ft. lbs. (54 Nm).
8. Connect the negative battery cable.

Power Steering Pump Drive Belt

See Figure 36.

1. Disconnect the negative battery cable.
2. From above the vehicle, loosen the locking nuts at the top of the power steering pump.
3. Raise and safely support the front of the vehicle securely on jackstands.
4. From underneath the vehicle, loosen the pivot bolt at the bottom of the power steering pump.
5. Loosen the adjusting bolt above the power steering pump. With the tension released, remove the drive belt.

To install:

6. Install the drive belt around the crankshaft and power steering pump pulleys.
7. Rotate the adjusting bolt clockwise to adjust the belt tension. Refer to the procedure earlier in this section for belt adjustment.
8. After the belt is installed and/or adjusted properly, tighten the pivot bolt to 40 ft. lbs. (54 Nm).

9. Lower the vehicle.
10. Tighten the locking nuts to 40 ft. lbs. (54 Nm).
11. Connect the negative battery cable.

3.3L and 3.8L Engines

See Figure 38.

All of the belt driven accessories on the 3.3L and 3.8L engines are driven by a single serpentine belt. The belt tension is maintained by am automatic tensioner.

1. Disconnect the negative battery cable.
2. Raise the front of the vehicle and safely support it with jackstands.
3. Remove the right front splash shield.
4. Release tension by rotating the tensioner clockwise.
5. Remove the belt and install a replacement.
6. Proper belt tension is maintain by the dynamic tension.

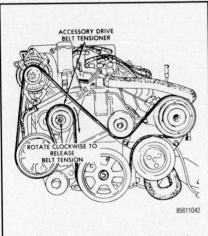

Fig. 38 Accessory drive belt adjustment— 3.3L and 3.8L engines

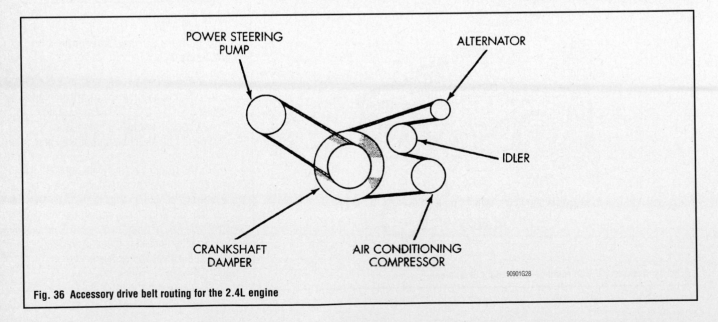

Fig. 36 Accessory drive belt routing for the 2.4L engine

7. Install the right front splash shield. Lower the front of the vehicle.

8. Connect the negative battery cable.

CAMSHAFT AND VALVE LIFTERS

INSPECTION

1. Inspect the camshaft bearing journals for wear or damage.

2. Inspect the cylinder head and check oil return holes.

3. Check the tooth surface of the distributor drive gear teeth of the right camshaft for wear or damage.

4. Check both camshaft surfaces for wear or damage.

5. Remove the distributor drive adapter seal.

6. Check camshaft lobe height and replace if out of limit. Standard value is 1.61 in. (41mm).

REMOVAL & INSTALLATION

2.4L Engine

See Figures 39 through 42.

1. Before servicing the vehicle, refer to the Precautions Section.

2. Remove or disconnect the following:

- Negative battery cable
- Valve cover
- Camshaft Position (CMP) sensor and camshaft target magnet
- Timing belt
- Camshaft sprockets
- Rear timing cover

➡ **The bearing caps are marked for location. Remove the outside caps**

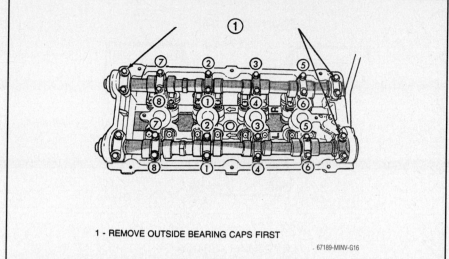

1 - REMOVE OUTSIDE BEARING CAPS FIRST

67189-MINV-G16

Fig. 40 Camshaft bearing caps removal sequence—2.4L engines

first. The caps are not interchangeable the intake cam # 6 thrust bearing face spacing is wider.

3. Make sure to identify the caps before removal, then loosen the caps in the sequence illustrated one at a time and remove the camshafts and cam followers. Always make sure to remove the outside bearing caps first.

To install:

➡ **Make sure none of the pistons are at Top Dead Center (TDC) when installing the camshafts.**

4. Install or connect the following:
- Lubricate then install the cam followers in their original positions
- Lubricate then install the camshafts

5. Install right and left camshaft bearing

caps 2–5 and right # 6. Tighten the M6 fasteners to 105 inch lbs. (12 Nm) in the sequence illustrated.

6. Apply a 0.060 (1–1.5mm) bead of gasket maker to the # 1 and # 6 bearing caps. Install the bearing caps in their original positions and tighten the M8 fasteners to 250 inch lbs. (28 Nm)

- Camshaft oil seals
- Camshaft target magnet and CMP sensor
- Valve cover
- Rear timing cover
- Timing belt idler pulley
- Camshaft sprockets. Tighten the bolts to 75 ft. lbs. (101 Nm).
- Timing belt
- Front cover
- Negative battery cable

7. Start the engine and check for proper operation.

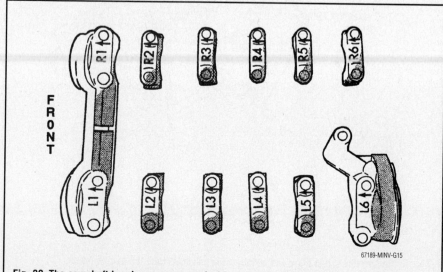

67189-MINV-G15

Fig. 39 The camshaft bearing caps are marked for location—2.4L engines

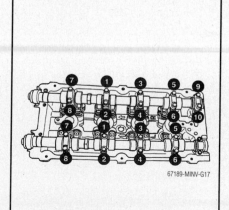

67189-MINV-G17

Fig. 41 Apply a 0.060 (1–1.5mm) bead of gasket maker to the # 1 and # 6 bearing caps—2.4L engines

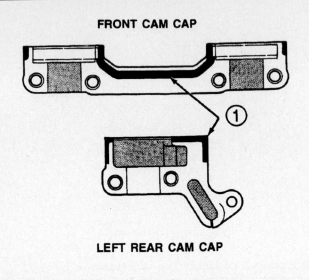

FRONT CAM CAP

LEFT REAR CAM CAP

1 - 1.5 mm (.060 in.) DIAMETER BEAD OF MOPAR GASKET MAKER

67189-MINV-G18

Fig. 42 Camshaft bearing caps tightening sequence—2.4L engines

3.3L and 3.8L Engines

See Figure 43.

➡**Keep all valvetrain components in order for assembly.**

1. Before servicing the vehicle, refer to the Precautions Section.

2. Remove the engine from the vehicle and mount it on a stand.

3. Remove or disconnect the following:

- Valve covers
- Rocker arm and shaft assemblies
- Pushrods
- Intake manifold
- Cylinder heads
- Yoke retainer
- Aligning yokes
- Hydraulic lifters
- Oil pan
- Oil pump pickup tube
- Crankshaft pulley
- Front cover
- Timing chain and sprockets
- Camshaft thrust plate
- Camshaft

To install:

4. Install or connect the following:

- Camshaft
- Camshaft thrust plate. Torque the bolts to 105 inch lbs. (12 Nm).
- Timing chain and sprockets. Torque the camshaft sprocket bolt to 40 ft. lbs. (54 Nm).
- Front cover. Torque the bolts to 20 ft. lbs. (27 Nm).

- Crankshaft pulley. Torque the bolt to 40 ft. lbs. (54 Nm).
- Oil pump pickup tube
- Oil pan
- Hydraulic lifters
- Aligning yokes
- Yoke retainer. Torque the bolts to 105 inch lbs. (12 Nm).
- Cylinder heads
- Intake manifold

- Pushrods
- Rocker arm and shaft assemblies
- Valve covers

5. Install the engine to the vehicle.

CRANKSHAFT FRONT SEAL

REMOVAL & INSTALLATION

2.4L Engine

The timing belt must be removed for this procedure. Use care that all timing marks are aligned after installation or the engine will become damaged.

1. Disconnect the negative battery cable.

2. Remove the accessory drive belts.

3. Raise and safely support the vehicle. Drain the engine oil.

4. Remove the crankshaft damper/pulley using a jaw puller tool.

5. Remove the timing belt cover and timing belt.

6. Remove the crankshaft timing belt sprocket using tool No. 6793 or equivalent.

❊❊ WARNING

WARNING! Do not nick the seal surface of the crankshaft or the seal bore.

7. Remove the front crankshaft seal using tool No. 6771 or equivalent seal puller. Be careful not to damage the seal contact area of the crankshaft.

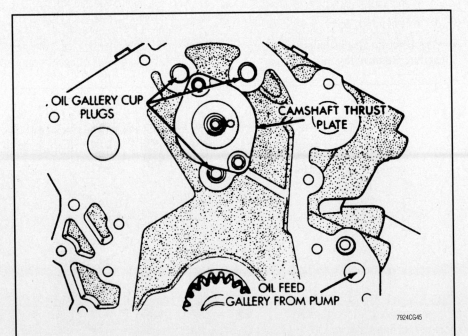

OIL GALLERY CUP PLUGS

CAMSHAFT THRUST PLATE

OIL FEED GALLERY FROM PUMP

7924CG45

Fig. 43 Remove the thrust plate and withdraw the camshaft from the engine—3.3L and 3.8L engines

To install:

8. Apply a light coating of clean engine oil to the lip of the new oil seal. Install the new front crankshaft oil seal using oil seal installer tool No. 6780–1 or equivalent. Install the new oil seal into the opening with the seal spring facing the inside of the engine. Be sure the oil seal is installed flush with the front cover.

9. Install the crankshaft timing belt sprocket using tool No. 6792.

Be sure the word "FRONT" on the timing belt sprocket is facing you.

10. Install the timing belt and timing belt cover.

11. Install the crankshaft damper/pulley onto the crankshaft. Use thrust bearing/washer and 12M–1.75 x 150mm bolt from special tool No. 6792. Install the crankshaft damper/pulley retaining bolt and torque to 105 ft. lbs. (142 Nm).

12. Lower the vehicle.

13. Install the accessory drive belts. Adjust the belts to the proper tension.

14. Refill the engine with the correct amount of clean engine oil.

15. Reconnect the negative battery cable. Start the engine and check for leaks.

3.3L and 3.8L Engines

1. Disconnect the negative battery cable.

2. Raise the vehicle and support safely.

3. Remove the right front wheel and the splash shield.

4. Remove the accessory drive belt.

5. Remove the crankshaft pulley bolt and remove the pulley using a suitable puller.

6. Remove the crankshaft oil seal from the cover using crankshaft seal removal tool C–4991 or equivalent. Be careful not to damage the crankshaft seal surface of the front timing chain cover.

To install:

7. Lubricate the lip of the new crankshaft oil seal with clean engine oil.

8. Use tool C–4992 or equivalent seal driver, to install the new crankshaft oil seal.

9. Install the crankshaft pulley using a bolt approximately 5.9 in. long and thrust bearing and washer plate. Make sure the pulley bottoms out on the crankshaft seal diameter. Install the bolt and torque to 40 ft. lbs. (54 Nm).

10. Install the accessory drive belt.

11. Install the inner splash shield and the wheel. Torque the wheel lug nuts, in a star pattern, to 95 ft. lbs. (129 Nm).

12. Lower the vehicle.

13. Reconnect the negative battery cable. Check the engine oil level; add oil as necessary.

14. Start the engine and check for leaks.

CYLINDER HEAD

REMOVAL & INSTALLATION

2.4L Engine

See Figures 44 through 47.

1. Before servicing the vehicle, refer to the Precautions Section.

2. Drain the cooling system.

3. Relieve the fuel system pressure.

4. Remove or disconnect the following:
- Negative battery cable
- Air cleaner and hoses
- Upper intake manifold
- Heater tube support bracket
- Upper radiator hose
- Heater hose
- Accessory drive belts
- Exhaust front pipe
- Power steering pump reservoir and line support bracket
- Ignition coil and spark plug wires
- Camshaft Position (CMP) sensor connector
- Fuel injector harness connectors
- Timing belt
- Camshaft sprockets
- Timing belt idler pulley
- Rear timing cover
- Valve cover

➡ **Keep all valvetrain components in order for assembly.**

- Camshafts and cam followers
- Cylinder head bolts in the reverse of the tightening sequence using several passes
- Cylinder head and gasket

To install:

5. Examine the cylinder head bolts and replace any that have stretched.

6. Install the cylinder head and tighten the bolts in sequence, as follows:

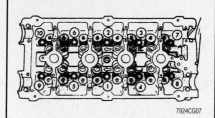

Fig. 45 Cylinder head torque sequence—2.4L engine

a. Step 1: 25 ft. lbs. (34 Nm).
b. Step 2: 50 ft. lbs. (68 Nm).
c. Step 3: 50 ft. lbs. (68 Nm).
d. Step 4: Plus 90 degrees.

7. Install or connect the following:
- Camshafts and cam followers

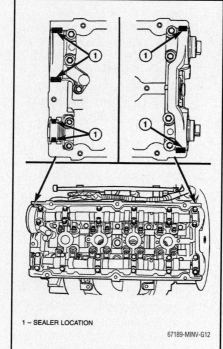

1 – SEALER LOCATION

67189-MINV-G12

Fig. 46 Apply sealant at these locations when installing the valve cover—2.4L engines

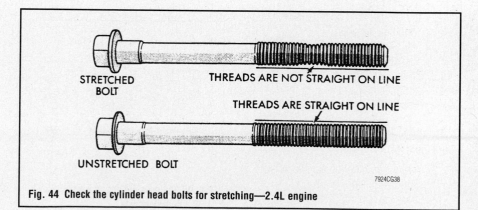

Fig. 44 Check the cylinder head bolts for stretching—2.4L engine

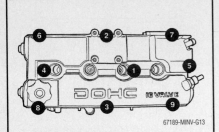

Fig. 47 Valve cover torque sequence. The stud should be located at the # 8 position—2.4L engines

67189-MINV-G13

8. Install the valve cover as follows:

  a. Install new head cover gaskets and spark plug well seals.

  b. Apply Mopar®RTV GEN II at the camshaft cap corners and the top edges of the ½ round seal.

  c. Valve cover and use new bolts making sure the single stud used to attach the upper intake manifold support bracket is located in the # 8 as shown in the illustration. Tighten the bolts in the sequence illustrated in 3 steps. First step to 40 inch lbs. (4.5 Nm). Second step to 80 inch lbs. (9 Nm) and the third step to 105 inch lbs. (12 Nm).

9. Install or connect the following:

  • Rear timing cover
  • Timing belt idler pulley. Tighten the bolt to 45 ft. lbs. (61 Nm).
  • Camshaft sprockets. Tighten the bolts to 75 ft. lbs. (101 Nm).
  • Timing belt
  • Front cover
  • CMP sensor connector
  • Fuel injector harness connectors
  • Ignition coil and spark plug wires
  • Power steering pump reservoir and line support bracket
  • Exhaust front pipe
  • Accessory drive belts
  • Upper radiator hose
  • Heater hose
  • Intake manifold and the EGR tube with new gaskets
  • Air cleaner and hoses
  • Negative battery cable

10. Fill the cooling system.

11. Start the engine, check for leaks and repair if necessary.

3.3L and 3.8L Engines

See Figure 48.

1. Before servicing the vehicle, refer to the Precautions Section.

2. Drain the cooling system.

3. Relieve the fuel system pressure.

4. Remove or disconnect the following:

  • Negative battery cable
  • Wiper module if removing the right cylinder head
  • Upper and lower intake manifolds

✳✳ CAUTION

The intake manifold gaskets are made of a very thin metal and can cause injury if not properly handled.

  • Valve covers.
  • Spark plugs
  • Dipstick tube
  • Exhaust manifolds

➡**Keep all valvetrain components in order for assembly**

  • Rocker arm and shaft assemblies
  • Cylinder head bolts, heads and gaskets

5. Clean all gasket mating surfaces.

To install:

6. Examine the cylinder head bolts and replace any that have stretched.

7. Install the cylinder head with a new gasket. The left bank gasket has an L on it and is located at the front of the engine. The right gasket has an R stamped on it and is located at the rear of the engine. Tighten the bolts in sequence, as follows:

  a. Step 1: Tighten bolts 1–8 to 45 ft. lbs. (61 Nm).
  b. Step 2: Tighten bolts 1–8 to 65 ft. lbs. (88 Nm).
  c. Step 3: Tighten bolts 1–8 to 65 ft. lbs. (88 Nm).
  d. Step 4: Bolts 1–8 plus 90 degrees.
  e. Step 5: Tighten bolt 9 to 25 ft. lbs. (33 Nm).

8. Check that the torque on bolts 1–8 has exceeded 90 ft. lbs. (122 Nm). If not, replace the bolt.

9. Install or connect the following:

  • Pushrods
  • Rocker arm and shaft assemblies
  • Valve covers

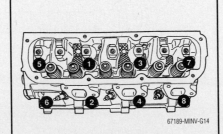

Fig. 48 Cylinder head torque sequence— 3.3L and 3.8L engines

67189-MINV-G14

  • Exhaust manifolds
  • Dipstick tube with a new O–ring
  • Spark plugs
  • Intake manifolds
  • Wiper module, if removed
  • Negative battery cable

10. Fill the cooling system.

11. Start the engine and check for leaks.

ENGINE ASSEMBLY

REMOVAL & INSTALLATION

2.4L Engine

See Figures 49 through 55.

1. Before servicing the vehicle, refer to the Precautions Section.

2. Drain the cooling system.

3. Drain the engine oil.

4. Relieve the fuel system pressure.

5. Recover the A/C refrigerant.

6. Remove or disconnect the following:

  • Negative battery cable
  • Air cleaner and hoses
  • Fuel line
  • Vacuum hoses
  • Radiator fans
  • Radiator hoses

➡**When the transaxle lines are removed from the fittings at the transaxle damage to the inner wall of the hose will occur. To prevent leakage, cut the cooler hoses off flush at the transaxle fitting and use a service cooler hose splice kit upon installation.**

  • Transaxle cooler lines, cut the lines flush at the transaxle fittings
  • Transaxle shift linkage
  • Throttle body linkage
  • Engine wiring harness
  • Heater hoses
  • Front wheels
  • Right inner splash shield
  • Drive belts
  • Axle halfshafts
  • Crossmember cradle plate
  • Exhaust front pipe
  • Front motor mount
  • Structural collar
  • Rear motor mount
  • Power steering pump. Pinch off the supply hose at the pump, disconnect the hose but leave the pressure line attached and then set the pump assembly aside.
  • A/C compressor lines
  • Body ground straps

7. Raise the vehicle enough to position dolly 6135, cradle tool 6710 with posts 6848 under vehicle.

8. Loosen the cradle posts to allow movement for proper positioning. Position the two rear posts (right side of engine) into the engine bedplate holes. Position the two front posts (left side of engine) on the oil pan rails. Lower the vehicle and position the cradle mounts until the engine is resting on the mounts and then tighten the mounts to the cradle frame to prevent mounts from moving when removing/installing the powertrain assembly.

9. Attach safety straps around the engine–to–cradle assembly. Lower the vehicle so the weight of the powertrain assembly, not the vehicle are on the cradle.

10. Remove the engine and transmission bolts.

11. Raise the vehicle away from the powertrain.

To install:

12. Lower the vehicle over the powertrain.

13. Align the engine and transmission mounts to their attaching points. Install and tighten the right mount–to–rail and engine and left mount–to–frame brackets as shown in the two accompanying illustrations.

14. Remove the safety straps and the dolly.

15. Install the rear mount bracket and through bolt.

16. Install or connect the following:
- Torque converter
- Axle halfshafts

17. Install the bending struts and structural collar, as follows:
   a. Step 1: Position the collar between the transaxle and oil pan and install bolts hand tight.
   b. Step 2: Position the collar to oil pan bolts and install bolts hand tight.

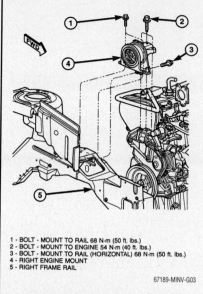

1 - BOLT - MOUNT TO RAIL 68 N·m (50 ft. lbs.)
2 - BOLT - MOUNT TO ENGINE 54 N·m (40 ft. lbs.)
3 - BOLT - MOUNT TO RAIL (HORIZONTAL) 68 N·m (50 ft. lbs.)
4 - RIGHT ENGINE MOUNT
5 - RIGHT FRAME RAIL

67189-MINV-G03

Fig. 50 Right mount–to–rail and engine installation—2.4L engine

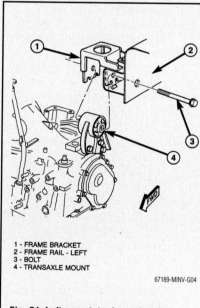

1 - FRAME BRACKET
2 - FRAME RAIL - LEFT
3 - BOLT
4 - TRANSAXLE MOUNT

67189-MINV-G04

Fig. 51 Left mount–to–frame bracket installation 2.4L engine

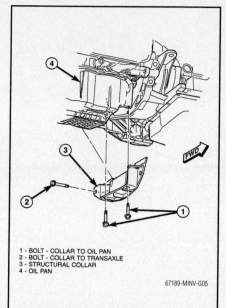

1 - BOLT - COLLAR TO OIL PAN
2 - BOLT - COLLAR TO TRANSAXLE
3 - STRUCTURAL COLLAR
4 - OIL PAN

67189-MINV-G05

Fig. 52 Structural collar and bending strut torque sequence—2.4L engine

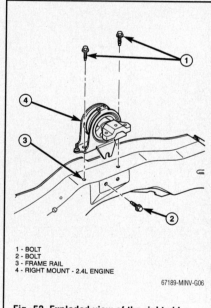

1 - BOLT
2 - BOLT
3 - FRAME RAIL
4 - RIGHT MOUNT - 2.4L ENGINE

67189-MINV-G06

Fig. 53 Exploded view of the right side engine hydro–type mount—2.4L engine

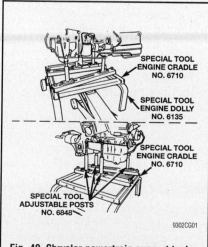

SPECIAL TOOL ENGINE CRADLE NO. 6710

SPECIAL TOOL ENGINE DOLLY NO. 6135

SPECIAL TOOL ENGINE CRADLE NO. 6710

SPECIAL TOOL ADJUSTABLE POSTS NO. 6848

9302CG01

Fig. 49 Chrysler powertrain support tools

   c. Step 3: Tighten collar to transaxle bolts to 75 ft. lbs. (101 Nm).
   d. Step 4: Tighten collar to oil pan bolts to 40 ft. lbs. (54 Nm).
   e. Step 5: Install the engine front mount assembly.

18. Install or connect the following:
- Exhaust front pipe
- Crossmember cradle plate
- Power steering pump and lines
- A/C compressor lines
- Drive belts
- Right inner splash shield
- Axle halfshafts

- Front wheels
- Transaxle cooler lines using a splice service kit
- Transaxle shift linkage
- Heater hoses
- Body ground straps
- Engine wiring harness
- Vacuum lines
- Throttle body linkage
- Engine cooling fans
- Fuel line
- Radiator hoses
- Air cleaner and hoses
- Negative battery cable

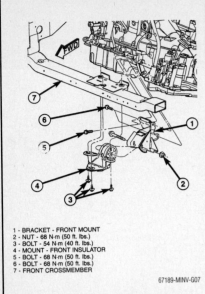

1 - BRACKET - FRONT MOUNT
2 - NUT - 68 N·m (50 ft. lbs.)
3 - BOLT - 54 N·m (40 ft. lbs.)
4 - MOUNT - FRONT INSULATOR
5 - BOLT - 68 N·m (50 ft. lbs.)
6 - BOLT - 68 N·m (50 ft. lbs.)
7 - FRONT CROSSMEMBER

67189-MINV-G07

Fig. 54 Exploded view of the front mount and bracket assembly—2.4L engine

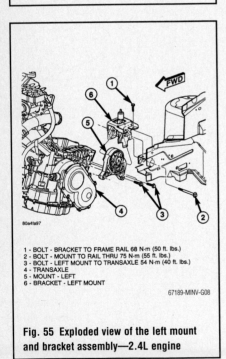

1 - BOLT - BRACKET TO FRAME RAIL 68 N·m (50 ft. lbs.)
2 - BOLT - MOUNT TO RAIL THRU 75 N·m (55 ft. lbs.)
3 - BOLT - LEFT MOUNT TO TRANSAXLE 54 N·m (40 ft. lbs.)
4 - TRANSAXLE
5 - MOUNT - LEFT
6 - BRACKET - LEFT MOUNT

80a4fa97

67189-MINV-G08

Fig. 55 Exploded view of the left mount and bracket assembly—2.4L engine

19. Fill the cooling system.
20. Fill the engine with clean oil.
21. Recharge the A/C system.
22. Start the engine and check for leaks.

3.3L and 3.8L Engines

See Figures 56 through 63.

1. Before servicing the vehicle, refer to the Precautions Section.
2. Drain the cooling system.
3. Drain the engine oil.
4. Relieve the fuel system pressure.
5. Recover the A/C refrigerant.

6. Remove or disconnect the following:
   - Battery and tray
   - Air cleaner and hoses
   - Fuel line from the rail
   - Wiper module

7. Block off the heater hoses to the rear system by using pinch off pliers, if equipped.
   - Heater hoses
   - Radiator upper support crossmember
   - Engine cooling fan
   - Throttle body linkage
   - Manifold Absolute Pressure (MAP) sensor connector
   - Idle Air Control (IAC) valve connector
   - Throttle Position (TPS) sensor connector
   - Exhaust Gas Recirculation (EGR) transducer connector
   - Vacuum lines from the throttle body, brake booster and speed control
   - Wiring harness clip from the right side mount
   - Power steering reservoir and set aside without disconnecting the lines
   - Ground strap from the rear of the cylinder head
   - Engine Coolant Temperature (ECT) sensor connector
   - Ignition coil connectors
   - Fuel injector connectors and clip from the bracket
   - Camshaft (CMP) and Crankshaft (CKP) position sensor connectors
   - A/C compressor electrical connectors and hoses. Cap the lines to avoid system contamination.
   - Radiator upper hose
   - Electrical connector at the transaxle dipstick tube
   - Transaxle dipstick tube and seal the opening to avoid system contamination

➡When the transaxle lines are removed from the fittings at the transaxle damage to the inner wall of the hose will occur. To prevent leakage, cut the cooler hoses off flush at the transaxle fitting and use a service cooler hose splice kit upon installation.

   - Transaxle cooler lines, cut the lines flush at the transaxle fittings
   - Transaxle shift linkage and electrical connectors
   - Axle halfshafts
   - Crossmember cradle plate
   - Power Transfer Unit (PTO), if equipped

   - Exhaust front pipe from the manifold
   - Front motor mount and bracket
   - Rear motor mount bracket
   - Engine–to–transaxle struts
   - Transaxle case cover
   - Torque converter
   - Power steering pressure hose clip bolt
   - Knock sensor connector, if equipped
   - Engine block heater connector, if equipped
   - Drive belt splash shield
   - Accessory drive belt
   - Lower radiator hose
   - A/C compressor
   - Alternator
   - Water pump pulley bolts and position the pulley between the pump and the housing
   - Oil pressure switch connector
   - Wiring harness clip from the dipstick tube

8. Install adapter tools on the right side of the engine block as illustrated
   - Power steering pump and set aside

9. Raise the vehicle enough to position dolly 6135, cradle tool 6710 with posts 6848 and adapter tool 6909 under vehicle.

10. Loosen the cradle posts to allow movement for proper positioning. Lower the vehicle and position the cradle/post mounts until the engine is resting on the posts and then tighten the mounts to the cradle frame to prevent mounts from moving when removing/installing the powertrain assembly.

11. Attach safety straps around the engine–to–cradle assembly. Lower the vehicle so the weight of the powertrain assembly, not the vehicle are on the cradle.

12. Remove or disconnect the following:
   - Engine right side mount–to–engine bolts
   - Left mount through bolt

13. Raise the vehicle away from the powertrain.

To install:

14. Lower the vehicle over the powertrain.

15. Align the engine and transmission mounts to their attaching points. Install and tighten the right mount and left transmission mounts as shown in the two accompanying illustrations.

16. Remove the safety straps and the dolly and adapters.

17. Install or connect the following:
   - Power steering pump and pressure line

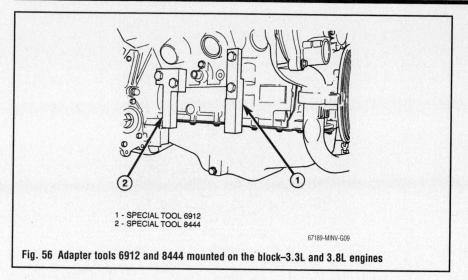

1 - SPECIAL TOOL 6912
2 - SPECIAL TOOL 8444

67189-MINV-G09

Fig. 56 Adapter tools 6912 and 8444 mounted on the block–3.3L and 3.8L engines

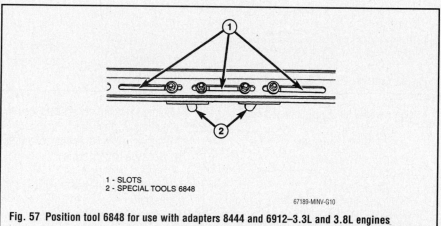

1 - SLOTS
2 - SPECIAL TOOLS 6848

67189-MINV-G10

Fig. 57 Position tool 6848 for use with adapters 8444 and 6912–3.3L and 3.8L engines

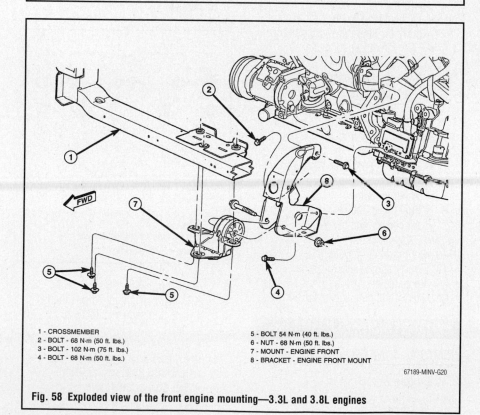

1 - CROSSMEMBER
2 - BOLT - 68 N·m (50 ft. lbs.)
3 - BOLT - 102 N·m (75 ft. lbs.)
4 - BOLT - 68 N·m (50 ft. lbs.)

5 - BOLT 54 N·m (40 ft. lbs.)
6 - NUT - 68 N·m (50 ft. lbs.)
7 - MOUNT - ENGINE FRONT
8 - BRACKET - ENGINE FRONT MOUNT

67189-MINV-G20

Fig. 58 Exploded view of the front engine mounting—3.3L and 3.8L engines

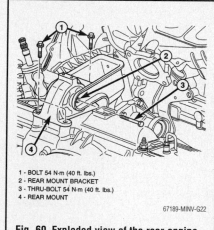

1 - BOLT
2 - BOLT
3 - FRAME RAIL
4 - RIGHT MOUNT - 3.3/3.8L ENGINE

67189-MINV-G21

Fig. 59 Exploded view of the right side hydro–type engine mounting—3.3L and 3.8L engines

1 - BOLT 54 N·m (40 ft. lbs.)
2 - REAR MOUNT BRACKET
3 - THRU-BOLT 54 N·m (40 ft. lbs.)
4 - REAR MOUNT

67189-MINV-G22

Fig. 60 Exploded view of the rear engine mounting—3.3L and 3.8L engines

- Alternator
- Wiring harness clip to the dipstick tube
- Oil pressure switch connector
- A/C compressor
- Water pump pulley
- Lower radiator hose
- Accessory drive belt
- Drive belt splash shield
- Engine block heater connector, if equipped
- Knock sensor connector, if equipped
- Power steering pressure hose clip bolt
- Torque converter
- Transaxle case cover
- Engine–to–transaxle struts
- Rear motor mount bracket

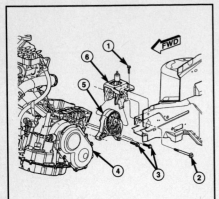

1 - BOLT - BRACKET TO FRAME RAIL 68 N·m (50 ft. lbs.)
2 - BOLT - MOUNT TO RAIL THRU 75 N·m (55 ft. lbs.)
3 - BOLT - LEFT MOUNT TO TRANSAXLE 54 N·m (40 ft. lbs.)
4 - TRANSAXLE
5 - MOUNT - LEFT
6 - BRACKET - LEFT MOUNT

67189-MINV-G23

Fig. 61 Exploded view of the left engine mounting—3.3L and 3.8L engines

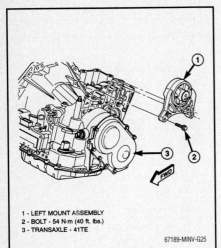

1 - LEFT MOUNT ASSEMBLY
2 - BOLT - 54 N·m (40 ft. lbs.)
3 - TRANSAXLE - 41TE

67189-MINV-G25

Fig. 62 Exploded view of the left engine mounting on models equipped with a 41TE transaxle—3.3L and 3.8L engines

- Front motor mount and bracket
- PTO, if equipped
- Axle halfshafts
- Exhaust front pipe to the manifold
- Crossmember cradle plate
- Transaxle shift linkage and electrical connectors
- Transaxle cooler lines using a splice kit
- Transaxle dipstick tube and
- Electrical connector at the transaxle dipstick tube
- A/C compressor electrical connectors and hoses
- CMP and CKP position sensor connectors

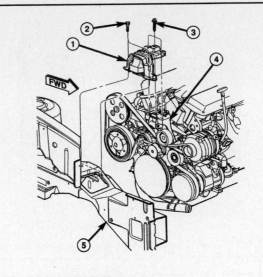

1 - RIGHT ENGINE MOUNT
2 - BOLT - MOUNT TO FRAME RAIL
3 - BOLT - MOUNT TO ENGINE
4 - ENGINE MOUNT BRACKET
5 - RIGHT FRAME RAIL

67189-MINV-G26

Fig. 63 Exploded view of the right engine mounting—3.3L and 3.8L engines

- Fuel injector connectors and clip to the bracket
- ECT sensor connector
- Ignition coil connectors
- Ground strap to the rear of the cylinder head
- Power steering reservoir
- Wiring harness clip to the right side mount
- Vacuum lines to the throttle body, brake booster and speed control
- EGR transducer connector
- TPS sensor connector
- IAC valve connector
- MAP sensor connector
- Throttle body linkage
- Engine cooling fan
- Radiator upper hose
- Heater hoses
- Radiator upper support crossmember
- Wiper module
- Fuel line to the rail
- Air cleaner and hoses
- Battery and tray
18. Fill the cooling system.
19. Fill the engine with clean oil.
20. Recharge the A/C system.
21. Start the engine and check for leaks.

EXHAUST MANIFOLD

REMOVAL & INSTALLATION

2.4L Engine

See Figure 64.

1. Before servicing the vehicle, refer to the Precautions Section.
2. Remove or disconnect the following:
- Negative battery cable
- Exhaust front pipe
- Heated Oxygen Sensor (HO2S) connector
- Exhaust manifold

To install:

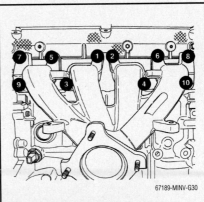

67189-MINV-G30

Fig. 64 Exhaust manifold torque sequence—2.4L engine

3. Install or connect the following:
- Exhaust manifold. Torque the fasteners in sequence to 15 ft. lbs. (20 Nm).
- HO2S connector
- Exhaust front pipe. Torque the fasteners to 27 ft. lbs. (37 Nm).
- Negative battery cable
4. Start the engine and check for leaks.

3.3L and 3.8L Engines

Right Side

1. Before servicing the vehicle, refer to the Precautions Section.
2. Remove or disconnect the following:
   - Negative battery cable
   - Wiper module
   - Spark plug wires
   - Crossover pipe
   - Upstream Oxygen Sensor (O_2S) connectors
   - Heat shield
   - Accessory drive belt
   - Power steering pump support strut lower bolt
   - Downstream O_2S connectors
   - Catalytic converter pipe from the manifold
   - Power steering support strut upper bolt and strut
   - Exhaust manifold bolt
   - Exhaust manifold and gasket

To install:

3. Position the exhaust manifold on the cylinder head and install the bolts to the center runner (cyl # 3), and temporarily tighten to 25 inch lbs. (2.8 Nm).

➡ **Examine the crossover pipe bolts for damage caused due to heat or corrosion and replace using new OEM bolts if found to be defective.**

4. Install a new gasket, attach the crossover pipe to the manifold and tighten the bolts to 30 ft. lbs. (41 Nm).
5. Install or connect the following:
   - Remaining manifold bolts. Torque the fasteners to 17 ft. lbs. (23 Nm).
   - Power steering support strut and upper bolt
   - Heat shield
   - Upstream O_2S connectors
   - Catalytic converter pipe to the manifold
   - Downstream O_2S connectors
   - Power steering pump support strut lower bolt
   - Accessory drive belt
   - Spark plug wires
   - Wiper module
   - Negative battery cable
6. Start the engine and check for leaks.

Left Side

1. Before servicing the vehicle, refer to the Precautions Section.
2. Remove or disconnect the following:
   - Negative battery cable
   - Crossover pipe
   - Spark plug wires
   - Heat shield
   - Exhaust manifold bolt
   - Exhaust manifold and gasket

To install:

3. Position the exhaust manifold on the cylinder head and install the bolts to the center runner (cyl # 4), and temporarily tighten to 25 inch lbs. (2.8 Nm).

➡ **Examine the crossover pipe bolts for damage caused due to heat or corrosion and replace using new OEM bolts if found to be defective.**

4. Install a new gasket, attach the crossover pipe to the manifold and tighten the bolts to 30 ft. lbs. (41 Nm).
5. Install or connect the following:
   - Remaining manifold bolts. Torque the fasteners to 17 ft. lbs. (23 Nm).
   - Heat shield
   - Negative battery cable
6. Start the engine and check for leaks.

INTAKE MANIFOLD

REMOVAL & INSTALLATION

See Figures 65 and 66.

1. Before servicing the vehicle, refer to the Precautions Section.
2. Drain the cooling system.
3. Relieve the fuel system pressure.
4. Remove or disconnect the following:
   - Negative battery cable
   - Air cleaner and tube
   - Throttle Position (TP) sensor connector
   - Idle Air Control (IAC) valve connector
   - Manifold Absolute Pressure (MAP) sensor connector
   - Evaporative Emissions (EVAP) canister purge solenoid vacuum line
   - Positive Crankcase Ventilation (PCV) valve and hose
   - Brake booster vacuum line
   - Cruise control vacuum reservoir line
   - Accelerator cable
   - Cruise control cable
   - Exhaust Gas Recirculation (EGR) tube
   - Front and rear intake manifold support brackets
   - Engine oil dipstick tube
   - Upper intake manifold
   - Fuel line
   - Upper radiator hose
   - Heater hose
   - Engine Coolant Temperature (ECT) sensor connector
   - Lower manifold support upper bolts and lower bolt

   - Fuel injector harness connectors
   - Power steering reservoir bolts and position aside without disconnecting the lines
   - Lower intake manifold bolts and the manifold

To install:

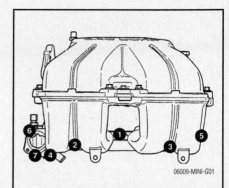

Fig. 65 Lower intake manifold torque sequence—2.4L engine

06009-MINI-G01

5. Install or connect the following:
   - Lower intake manifold using a new gasket. Tighten the bolts in several steps to 250 inch lbs. (28 Nm).
   - Fuel injector harness connectors
   - Intake manifold Y–bracket. Tighten the block bolts to 40 ft. lbs. (54 Nm) and the intake manifold bolts to 250 inch (28 Nm).
   - Power steering reservoir
   - Fuel line
   - ECT sensor connector
   - Heater hose
   - Upper radiator hose
6. Apply a 0.060 inch (1.5mm) bead of gasket maker to the perimeter of the lower intake manifold runner openings.
   - Upper intake manifold. Tighten the bolts in several passes to 250 inch lbs. (28 Nm)
   - Engine oil dipstick tube

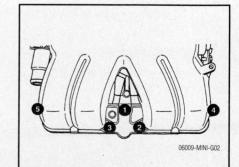

Fig. 66 Upper intake manifold torque sequence—2.4L engine

06009-MINI-G02

- Upper bolt on the manifold–to–front support bracket to 250 inch lbs. (28 Nm)
- EGR tube
- Cruise control cable
- Accelerator cable
- Cruise control vacuum reservoir line
- Brake booster vacuum line
- PCV valve and hose
- EVAP canister purge solenoid vacuum line
- MAP sensor connector
- IAC valve connector
- TP sensor connector
- Air cleaner and tube
- Negative battery cable

7. Fill the cooling system.

8. Start the engine, check for leaks and repair if necessary.

OIL PAN

REMOVAL & INSTALLATION

2.4L Engine

1. Before servicing the vehicle, refer to the Precautions Section.

2. Drain the engine oil.

3. Remove or disconnect the following:
- Negative battery cable
- Structural collar
- A/C compressor bracket to oil pan bolt
- Oil pan

4. Clean the oil pan and all gasket mating surfaces.

To install:

5. Install or connect the following:
- Oil pan gasket to the block after applying engine RTV at the oil pump parting line
- Oil pan. Torque the bolts to 105 inch lbs. (12 Nm).
- Structural collar
- Negative battery cable

6. Fill the crankcase to the correct level.

7. Start the engine, check for leaks and repair if necessary.

3.3L and 3.8L Engines

1. Before servicing the vehicle, refer to the Precautions Section.

2. Drain the engine oil.

3. Remove or disconnect the following:
- Negative battery cable
- Engine oil dipstick
- Drive belt splash shield
- Strut to transaxle attaching bolt and loosen the strut to engine attaching bolts

- Transaxle case cover
- Oil pan fasteners
- Oil pan and gasket

To install:

4. Clean the oil pan and all mating surfaces.

5. Apply a 1/8 inch bead of gasket material at the parting line of the chain case cover and the real seal retainer.

6. Install or connect the following:
- New gasket on the oil pan
- Oil pan. Torque the bolts to 105 inch lbs. (12 Nm).
- Transaxle case cover
- All bending brace bolts
- Drive belt splash shield
- Engine oil dipstick
- Negative battery cable

7. Fill the crankcase to the correct level.

8. Start the engine, check for leaks and repair if necessary.

OIL PUMP

REMOVAL & INSTALLATION

2.4L Engine

See Figures 67 through 70.

1. Before servicing the vehicle, refer to the Precautions Section.

2. Drain the engine oil.

3. Remove or disconnect the following:
- Negative battery cable
- Timing belt.
- Rear timing belt cover
- Oil pan
- Crankshaft sprocket using puller 6793 and insert C–4685–C2
- Crankshaft key
- Oil pump pickup tube
- Oil pump

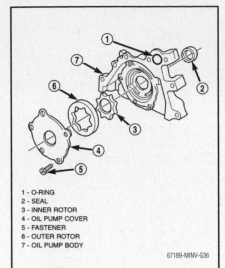

1 - O-RING
2 - SEAL
3 - INNER ROTOR
4 - OIL PUMP COVER
5 - FASTENER
6 - OUTER ROTOR
7 - OIL PUMP BODY

67189-MINV-G36

Fig. 68 Exploded view of the oil pump—2.4L engine

To install:

4. Clean all mating surfaces of any remaining gasket material.

5. Apply gasket maker material to the oil pump and replace the O–ring in the oil pump discharge passage.

6. Prime the pump with oil prior to installation.

7. Install or connect the following:
- Oil pump, align the flats on the rotor with the flats on the crankshaft. Torque the bolts to 21 ft. lbs. (28 Nm).

➡ **The front crankshaft seal must be out of the pump to align it or the pump may be damaged.**

- Front crankshaft seal using tool 6780
- Crankshaft key

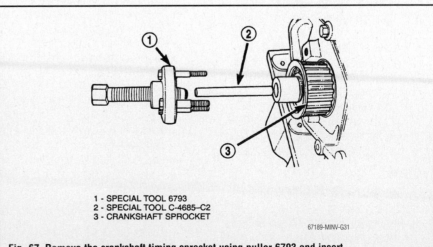

1 - SPECIAL TOOL 6793
2 - SPECIAL TOOL C-4685-C2
3 - CRANKSHAFT SPROCKET

67189-MINV-G31

Fig. 67 Remove the crankshaft timing sprocket using puller 6793 and insert C–4685–C2—2.4L engine

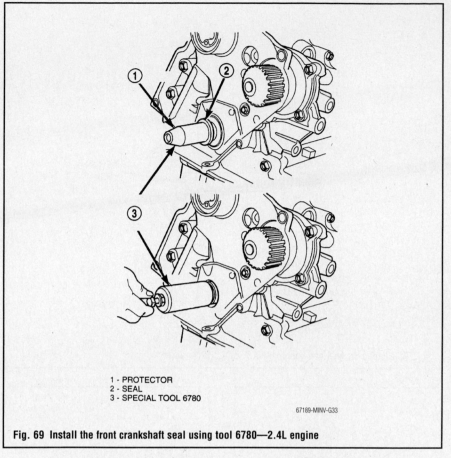

1 - PROTECTOR
2 - SEAL
3 - SPECIAL TOOL 6780

67189-MINV-G33

Fig. 69 Install the front crankshaft seal using tool 6780—2.4L engine

- Crankshaft sprocket using tool 6792
- Oil pump pickup tube. Torque the bolt to 21 ft. lbs. (28 Nm).
- Oil pan
- Rear timing belt cover
- Timing belt
- Negative battery cable
8. Fill the engine with clean oil.

9. Start the engine, check for leaks and repair if necessary.

3.3L and 3.8L Engines

See Figure 71.

1. Before servicing the vehicle, refer to the Precautions Section.

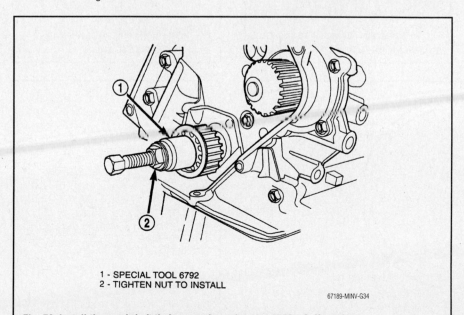

1 - SPECIAL TOOL 6792
2 - TIGHTEN NUT TO INSTALL

67189-MINV-G34

Fig. 70 Install the crankshaft timing sprocket using tool 6792—2.4L engine

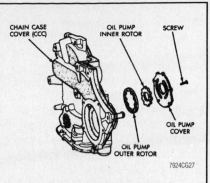

CHAIN CASE COVER (CCC)   OIL PUMP INNER ROTOR   SCREW

OIL PUMP OUTER ROTOR   OIL PUMP COVER

7924CG27

Fig. 71 Exploded view of the oil pump assembly—3.3L and 3.8L engines

2. Drain the cooling system.
3. Drain the engine oil.
4. Remove or disconnect the following:
   - Negative battery cable
   - Oil pan
   - Timing chain cover
   - Oil pump from the case cover

To install:

5. Install or connect the following:
   - Oil pump to the front cover. Torque the cover screws to 105 inch lbs. (12 Nm).
   - Front cover. Torque the bolts to 20 ft. lbs. (27 Nm).
   - Oil pan
   - Negative battery cable
6. Fill the engine with clean oil.
7. Fill the cooling system.
8. Start the engine, check for leaks and repair if necessary.

INSPECTION

1. Inspect mating surface of the chain case cover. Surface should be smooth. Replace cover if scratched or grooved.

2. Lay a straightedge across the pump cover surface. If a 0.025 mm (0.001 in.) feeler gauge can be inserted between cover and straight edge, cover should be replaced.

3. Measure thickness and diameter of outer rotor. If outer rotor thickness measures 7.64 mm (0.301 in.) or less, or if the diameter is 79.95 mm (3.148 in.) or less, replace outer rotor.

4. If inner rotor thickness measures 7.64 mm (0.301 in.) or less, replace inner rotor.

5. Install outer rotor into chain case cover. Press rotor to one side with fingers and measure clearance between rotor and chain case cover. If measurement is 0.39 mm (0.015 in.) or more, replace chain case cover, only if outer rotor is in specification.

6. Install inner rotor into chain case cover. If clearance between inner and outer rotors is 0.203 mm (0.008 in.) or more, replace both rotors.

7. Place a straightedge across the face of the chain case cover, between bolt holes. If a feeler gauge of 0.10 mm (0.004 in.) or more can be inserted between rotors and the straightedge, replace pump assembly.

8. Remove oil pressure relief valve.

9. Inspect oil pressure relief valve and bore. Inspect for scoring, pitting and free valve operation in bore. Small marks may be removed with 400–grit wet or dry sandpaper.

10. The relief valve spring has a free length of approximately 49.5 mm (1.95 inches) it should test between 19.5 and 20.5 pounds when compressed to 34 mm (1–11/32 inches). Replace spring that fails to meet specifications.

11. If oil pressure is low and pump is within specifications, inspect for worn engine bearings or other reasons for oil pressure loss.

PISTON AND RING

POSITIONING

See Figures 72 through 77.

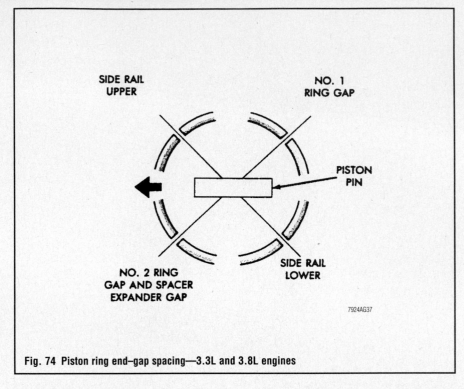

Fig. 74 Piston ring end–gap spacing—3.3L and 3.8L engines

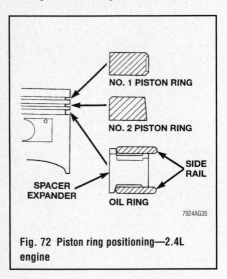

Fig. 72 Piston ring positioning—2.4L engine

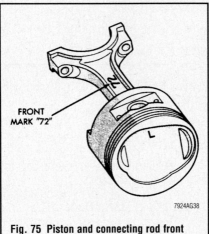

Fig. 75 Piston and connecting rod front mark locations—3.3L and 3.8L engines

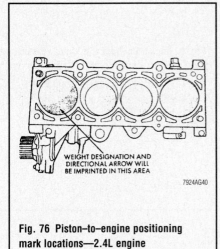

Fig. 76 Piston-to-engine positioning mark locations—2.4L engine

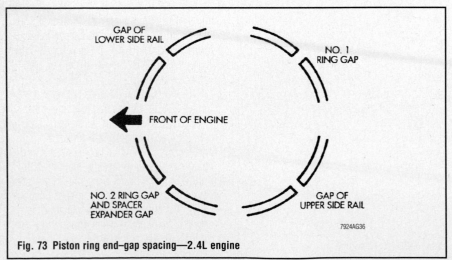

Fig. 73 Piston ring end–gap spacing—2.4L engine

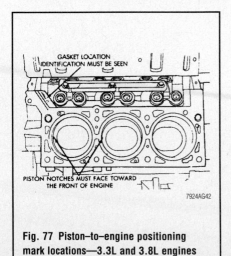

Fig. 77 Piston-to-engine positioning mark locations—3.3L and 3.8L engines

REAR MAIN SEAL

REMOVAL & INSTALLATION

See Figure 78.

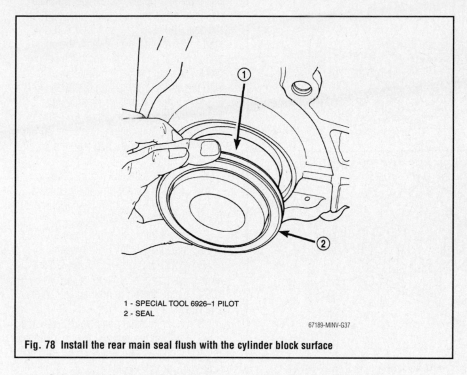

1 - SPECIAL TOOL 6926–1 PILOT
2 - SEAL

67189-MINV-G37

Fig. 78 Install the rear main seal flush with the cylinder block surface

1. Before servicing the vehicle, refer to the precautions at the beginning of this section.

2. Remove or disconnect the following:
   • Negative battery cable
   • Transaxle
   • Flexplate
   • Rear main seal

To install:

3. Place seal guide tool 6926–1 on the crankshaft and place the seal over the tool. Make sure the lip of the seal is facing towards the crankcase.

4. Install or connect the following:
   • Rear main seal flush with the cylinder block surface using the tools illustrated.
   • Flexplate
   • Transaxle
   • Negative battery cable

5. Run the engine and check for leaks.

TIMING BELT

REMOVAL & INSTALLATION

2.4L Engine

See Figures 79 through 82.

➡**You may need DRB scan tool to perform the crankshaft and camshaft relearn alignment procedure.**

1. Remove or disconnect the following:
   • Negative battery cable
   • Right front wheel and inner splash shield
   • Accessory drive belts
   • Crankshaft damper
   • A/C compressor/alternator tensioner and pulley assembly
   • Lower front timing cover
   • Upper front timing cover
   • Right engine mount
   • Engine mount bracket

➡**This is an interference engine. Do not rotate the crankshaft or the camshafts after the timing belt has been removed. Damage to the valve components may occur. Before removing the timing belt, always align the timing marks.**

2. Rotate the crankshaft until the Top Dead Center (TDC) mark on the oil pump housing aligns with the TDC mark on the camshaft sprocket (located on the trailing edge of the tooth).

3. Loosen the timing belt tensioner lock bolt.

4. Insert a 6mm Allen wrench into the hexagon opening located on the top plate of the belt tensioner pulley. Rotate the top plate clockwise until there is enough slack to remove the belt.

5. If necessary, remove the camshaft timing belt sprockets.

6. If necessary, remove the crankshaft

timing belt sprocket using removal tool No. 6793, or equivalent.

7. Place the tensioner into a soft–jawed vise to compress the tensioner.

8. After compressing the tensioner, insert a pin (a 5/64 in. Allen wrench will also work) into the plunger side hole to retain the plunger until installation.

To install:

9. If necessary, use tool No. 6792, or equivalent, to install the crankshaft timing belt sprocket onto the crankshaft.

10. If necessary, install the camshaft sprockets onto the camshafts. Install and tighten the camshaft sprocket bolts to 75 ft. lbs. (101 Nm).

11. Set the crankshaft sprocket to Top Dead Center (TDC) by aligning the notch on the sprocket with the arrow on the oil pump housing.

12. Set the camshafts timing marks so the exhaust camshaft is ½ notch below intake camshaft sprocket. Make sure the arrows on both camshaft sprockets are facing up

13. Install the timing belt starting at the crankshaft, then around the water pump sprocket, idler pulley, camshaft sprockets and around the tensioner pulley.

14. Move the exhaust camshaft sprocket counterclockwise to take up the belt slack.

15. Insert a 6mm Allen wrench into the hexagon opening located on the top plate of the belt tensioner pulley. Rotate the top plate counterclockwise until there is no slack on the belt. The tensioner setting notch will start to move clockwise. Watch the notch

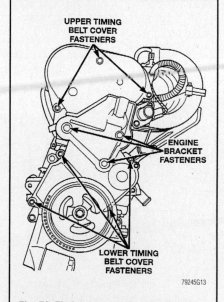

UPPER TIMING BELT COVER FASTENERS

ENGINE BRACKET FASTENERS

LOWER TIMING BELT COVER FASTENERS

79245G13

Fig. 79 Timing cover and engine mounting bracket bolt locations—2.4L engine

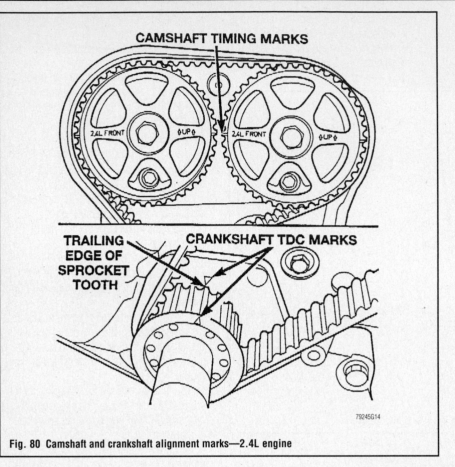

Fig. 80 Camshaft and crankshaft alignment marks—2.4L engine

17. Check the spring tang is within the tolerance window. If not within the window, reinsert the Allen wrench and into the hexagon opening located on the top plate of the belt tensioner pulley. Rotate the top plate counterclockwise until there is no slack on the belt. The tensioner setting notch will start to move clockwise. Watch the notch and continue rotating the top plate counterclockwise until the setting notch is aligned with the spring tang. Using the Allen wrench to prevent the top plate from moving, tighten the tensioner lock bolt to 220 inch lbs. (25 Nm). The setting notch and spring tang should remain aligned after the lock nut is tightened.

18. Install the engine mount bracket.

19. Install the front timing belt covers.

20. Install the A/C compressor/alternator tensioner and pulley assembly.

21. Install the right engine mount.

22. Install the crankshaft damper

23. Install the accessory drive belts and adjust to the proper tension.

24. Install the right inner splash shield and wheel.

25. Reconnect the negative battery cable.

26. Perform the crankshaft and camshaft relearn alignment procedure using the DRB scan tool, or equivalent.

and continue rotating the top plate counterclockwise until the setting notch is aligned with the spring tang. Using the Allen wrench to prevent the top plate from moving, tighten the tensioner lock bolt to 220 inch lbs. (25 Nm). The setting notch and spring tang should remain aligned after the lock nut is tightened.

16. Rotate the crankshaft 2 revolutions and recheck the timing marks.

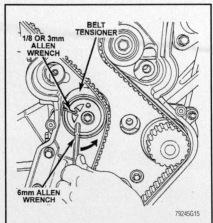

Fig. 81 To lock the timing belt tensioner, be sure to fully insert the smaller Allen wrench into the tensioner as shown—2.4L engine

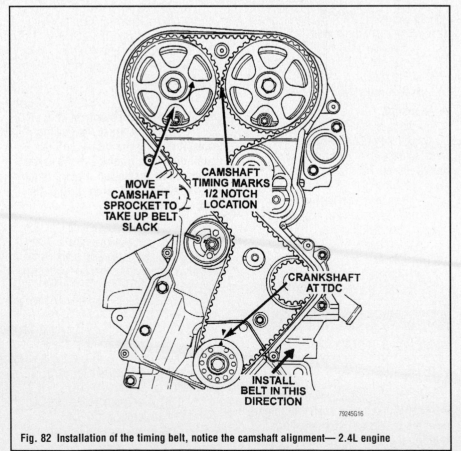

Fig. 82 Installation of the timing belt, notice the camshaft alignment— 2.4L engine

TIMING CHAIN, SPROCKETS, FRONT COVER AND SEAL

REMOVAL & INSTALLATION

3.3L and 3.8L Engines

See Figure 83.

1. Before servicing the vehicle, refer to the Precautions Section.
2. Drain the cooling system.
3. Drain the engine oil.
4. Remove the timing chain cover as follows:

- Negative battery cable
- Right wheel and splash shield
- Oil pan and pick up tube
- Drive belt
- A/C compressor and set aside with the lines still attached
- Crankshaft damper
- Lower radiator hose
- Camshaft Position (CMP), if necessary
- Heater hose from the timing cover or water pump inlet tub if equipped with an engine oil cooler
- Right side engine mount
- Idler pulley from the bracket
- Engine mount bracket
- Water pump
- Power steering support strut–to–cover bolt
- Timing chain cover bolts and the cover

5. Rotate the engine so that the timing marks are aligned.
6. Remove or disconnect the following:

- Camshaft sprocket attaching bolt
- Timing chain and camshaft sprocket
- Crankshaft sprocket with special tools 8539, 5048–6 and 5048–1

To install:

7. Rotate the engine so the timing arrow is at the 12 o'clock position.
8. Lubricate the chain and sprockets with clean oil.
9. Hold the camshaft sprocket and chain and place the chain around the sprocket aligning the plated link with the dot on the sprocket. Position the timing arrow at the 6 o'clock position.

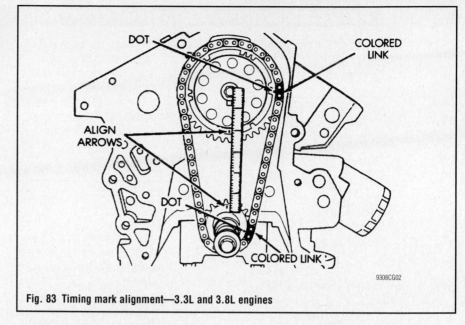

Fig. 83 Timing mark alignment—3.3L and 3.8L engines

10. Place the chain around the crankshaft sprocket with the plated link lined up with the dot on the sprocket and install the camshaft sprocket.
11. Use a straight edge to check the timing alignment marks.
12. Align the timing chain colored links with the dots on the timing sprockets.
13. Tighten the camshaft sprocket bolt to 40 ft. lbs. (54 Nm).
14. Rotate the crankshaft 2 revolutions and verify the proper timing chain alignment, if not remove the components and reinstall as described above.
15. Clean the timing cover mating surfaces.
16. Install or the front cover as follows:

- New gasket on the cover making sure the lower edge of the gasket is flush to 0.020 inch (0.5mm) past the lower edge of the cover. Rotate the crankshaft so the oil pump drive flats are in a vertical position.
- Position the oil pump inner rotor so the mating flats are in the same position as the crankshaft drive flats or damage may occur
- Timing chain cover and bolts. Tighten the M8 bolts to 20 ft. lbs. (27 Nm) and the M10 bolts to 40 ft. lbs. (54 Nm).
- Crankshaft front oil seal

- Water pump
- Power steering support strut–to–cover bolt
- Crankshaft damper
- Engine mount bracket. Tighten the M10 bolts to 40 ft. lbs. (54 Nm) and the M8 bolts to 21 ft. lbs. (28 Nm).
- Idler pulley on the bracket
- Right side engine mount
- CMP sensor, if removed
- Heater hose to the timing cover or water pump inlet tub if equipped with an engine oil cooler
- Lower radiator hose
- A/C compressor
- Drive belt
- Oil pick up tube and pan
- Right splash shield and wheel
- Negative battery cable

17. Fill the engine with clean oil.
18. Fill the cooling system.
19. Start the engine, check for leaks and repair if necessary.

VALVE LASH

ADJUSTMENT

All engines are equipped with hydraulic lash adjusters. No adjustment is necessary.

ENGINE PERFORMANCE & EMISSION CONTROL

COMPONENT LOCATIONS

See Figures 84 and 85.

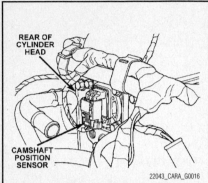

Fig. 84 Component locations—2.4L, 3.3L and 3.8L engines

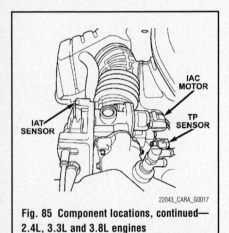

Fig. 85 Component locations, continued— 2.4L, 3.3L and 3.8L engines

CAMSHAFT POSITION (CMP) SENSOR

LOCATION

On the 2.4L engine, the Camshaft Position (CMP) sensor mounts to the rear of the cylinder head. The sensor also serves as a thrust plate to control endplay of the camshaft.

On 3.3L and 3.8L engines, the CMP mounts to the top of the timing case cover, in which the bottom of the sensor is positioned above the camshaft sprocket.

OPERATION

The Camshaft Position (CMP) sensor (along with the crankshaft position sensor) provides inputs to the PCM to determine fuel injection synchronization and cylinder identification. From these inputs, the PCM determines crankshaft position.

The CMP provides cylinder identification to the Powertrain Control Module (PCM).

The sensor generates pulses as groups of notches on the camshaft sprocket pass underneath it. The PCM keeps track of crankshaft rotation and identifies each cylinder by the pulses generated by the notches on the camshaft sprocket. Four crankshaft pulses follow each group of camshaft pulses.

REMOVAL & INSTALLATION

2.4L Engines

See Figure 86.

1. Unplug the electrical connector.
2. Remove the bolts securing the sensor.
3. Remove the sensor. If necessary, remove the magnet from the sensor.
4. Installation is the reverse of removal. Use a new o–ring; line up the dowels when installing the sensor.

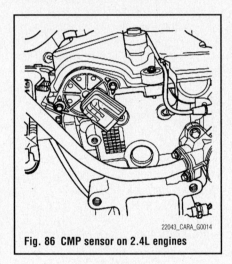

Fig. 86 CMP sensor on 2.4L engines

3.3L and 3.8L Engines

See Figure 87.

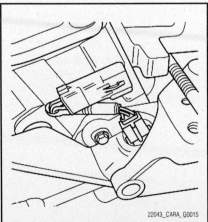

Fig. 87 CMP sensor location on 3.3L and 3.8L engines

1. Unplug the electrical connector.
2. Remove the bolt securing the sensor.
3. Remove the sensor; do not pull on the wire, only the sensor itself.
4. Installation is the reverse of removal. Use a new o–ring and be sure to use a new spacer on the face of the sensor.

TESTING

To test this sensor, you will need the use of an oscilloscope. Visually check the connector, making sure it is attached properly and that all of the terminals are straight, tight and free of corrosion. The output voltage of a properly operating camshaft position sensor switches from high (5.0 volts) to low (0.3 volts). By connecting an oscilloscope to the sensor output circuit, you can view the square wave pattern produced by the voltage swing.

CRANKSHAFT POSITION (CKP) SENSOR

LOCATION

On 4–cylinder engines, the Crankshaft Position (CKP) sensor is mounted to the engine block behind the alternator, just above the oil filter. On 6–cylinder engines, the crankshaft position sensor is mounted on the transaxle housing, above the vehicle speed sensor.

OPERATION

The PCM determines what cylinder to fire from the crankshaft position sensor input and the camshaft position sensor input. On 4–cylinder engines, the second crankshaft counterweight has two sets of four timing reference notches, including a 60 signature notch. From the crankshaft position sensor input, the PCM determines engine speed and crankshaft angle (position). On 6–cylinder engines, this sensor is a Hall effect device that detects notches in the flexplate.

The notches generate pulses from high to low in the crankshaft position sensor output voltage. When a metal portion of the notches line up with the crankshaft position sensor, the sensor output voltage goes low (less than 0.5 volts). When a notch aligns with the sensor, voltage goes high (5.0 volts). As a group of notches pass under the sensor, the output voltage switches from low (metal) to high (notch), then back to low.

REMOVAL & INSTALLATION

1. Unplug the electrical connector.
2. Remove the bolts securing the sensor.

3. Remove the sensor.

4. Installation is the reverse of removal.

TESTING

To test this sensor, you will need the use of an oscilloscope. Visually check the connector, making sure it is attached properly and that all of the terminals are straight, tight and free of corrosion. Also inspect the notches in the crankshaft (4–cylinder) or flywheel (6–cylinder) for damage, and replace if necessary. The output voltage of a properly operating crankshaft position sensor switches from high (5.0 volts) to low (0.3 volts). By connecting an oscilloscope to the sensor output circuit, you can view the square wave pattern produced by the voltage swing.

ELECTRONIC CONTROL MODULE (ECM)

LOCATION

The ECM is located in the left front corner of the engine compartment attached to the radiator support.

OPERATION

The Electronic Control Module (ECM) performs many functions on your vehicle. The module accepts information from various sensors and computes the required fuel flow rate necessary to maintain the correct amount of air/fuel ratio throughout the entire engine operational range and controls the shifting of the transmission.

Based on the information that is received and programmed into the ECM's memory, the ECM generates output signals to control relays, actuators and solenoids. The module automatically senses and compensates for any changes in altitude when driving your vehicle.

REMOVAL & INSTALLATION

1. Disconnect negative battery cable.

2. Remove left front headlamp module.

3. Remove ECM upper mounting bolts.

4. Lift ECM from radiator support.

5. Disconnect ECM electrical connectors.

6. Separate ECM from mounting bracket.

7. Installation is the reverse of removal.

TESTING

Service of the ECM should consist of either replacement of the ECM or programming of the Electrically Erasable Programmable Read Only Memory (EEPROM). If the diagnostic procedures call for the ECM to

be replaced, the replacement ECM should be checked to ensure that the correct part is being used. If the correct part is being used, remove the faulty ECM and install the new service ECM.

ENGINE COOLANT TEMPERATURE (ECT) SENSOR

LOCATION

The Engine Coolant Temperature (ECT) sensor is threaded into the cylinder head. Refer to the component location graphics.

OPERATION

1. The ECT sensor is a variable resistor with a range of –40°F–265°F (–5°C–129°C).

2. The engine coolant temperature sensor provides an input voltage to the PCM. As the coolant temperature varies, the sensor resistance changes resulting in a different input voltage to the PCM.

3. When the engine is cold, the PCM will demand slightly richer air/fuel mixtures and higher idle speeds until normal operating temperatures are reached.

4. The engine coolant temperature sensor is also utilized for control of the cooling fan.

REMOVAL & INSTALLATION

✳✳ CAUTION

Hot, pressurized coolant can cause injury by scalding. Cooling system must be partially drained before removing the coolant temperature sensor.

1. Drain the cooling system below thermostat level.

2. Unplug coolant temperature sensor electrical connector.

3. Remove coolant temperature sensor.

4. Installation is the reverse of removal. Tighten the sensor to 60 inch lbs. (7 Nm).

TESTING

1. Turn the ignition switch to the off position.

2. Disconnect the coolant temperature sensor electrical connector.

3. Using a DVOM set to the ohms scale, connect one lead to terminal A and the other lead to terminal B of the coolant temperature sensor connector.

4. With the engine at normal operating temperature, approximately 200°F (93°C), the ohmmeter should read approximately 700–1000 ohms.

5. With the engine at room temperature, approximately 70°F (21°C), the ohmmeter should read approximately 7000–13,000 ohms.

6. If not within specifications, replace the engine coolant temperature sensor.

NOTE: Test the resistance of the wiring harness between PCM terminal 26 and the sensor wiring harness connector. Also check for continuity between PCM connector terminal 43 and the sensor wiring harness connector. If the resistance measures greater than 1 ohm, repair the wiring harness as necessary.

HEATED OXYGEN (HO2S) SENSOR

LOCATION

Refer to the component locations. The Heated Oxygen Sensors (HO2S) are threaded into the exhaust pipes.

OPERATION

As a vehicle accrues mileage, the catalytic converter deteriorates. The deterioration results in a less effective catalyst. To monitor catalytic converter deterioration, the fuel injection system uses two heated oxygen sensors: one is upstream of the catalytic converter and one downstream of the converter.

The heated oxygen sensor, or HO2S sensor is usually located near the catalytic converter. It produces a voltage signal of 0.1–1.0 volts based on the amount of oxygen in the exhaust gas. When a low amount of oxygen is present (caused by a rich air/fuel mixture), the sensor produces a high voltage. When a high amount of oxygen is present (caused by a lean air/fuel mixture), the sensor produces a low voltage. Because an accurate voltage signal is only produced if the sensor temperature is above approximately 600F (315C), a fast–acting heating element is built into its body.

The PCM uses the HO2S sensor voltage signal to constantly adjust the amount of fuel injected that keeps the engine at its peak efficiency.

The PCM compares the reading from the sensors to calculate the catalytic converter oxygen storage capacity and storage efficiency. The PCM also uses the upstream heated oxygen sensor input when adjusting the injector pulse width. When the catalytic converter efficiency drops below preset emission criteria, the PCM stores a Diagnostic Trouble Code (DTC) and illuminates the Malfunction Indicator Lamp (MIL).

The automatic shutdown relay supplies battery voltage to both of the heated oxygen sensors. The sensors have heating elements that reduce the amount of time it takes for the sensors to reach operating temperature.

REMOVAL & INSTALLATION

✳✳ CAUTION

The exhaust manifold and catalytic converter may be extremely hot. Use care when servicing the oxygen sensor.

1. Disconnect the negative battery cable.
2. Raise and support the vehicle.
3. Disconnect the electrical connector.

✳✳ WARNING

Do NOT pull on the oxygen sensor wire when unplugging the electrical connector.

4. Use a special socket or crows foot wrench to remove the sensor.
5. When the sensor is removed, the exhaust manifold threads must be cleaned with an 18 mm X 1.5 + 6E tap.

➡ **If using the original sensor, coat the threads with Loctite 771–64 anti–seize compound or equivalent.**

To install:

➡ **Threads of new oxygen sensors are factory coated with anti–seize compound to aid in removal. DO NOT add any additional anti–seize compound to the threads of a new oxygen sensor.**

6. Install sensor and tighten to 20 ft. lbs. (27 Nm).
7. Connect the electrical connector.
8. Lower vehicle.
9. Install the negative battery cable.

TESTING

Heating Element

➡ **Before testing any electrical component, inspect the wiring and connectors for damage. Also wiggle the connectors to ensure a that they are firmly engaged.**

1. Disconnect the electrical harness from each of the sensors.
2. The white wires in the sensor connector are the power and ground circuits for the heater.
3. Connect the ohmmeter test leads to the terminals of the white wires in the heated oxygen sensor connector.
4. Check the resistance of the sensor, if it is not within 4–7 ohms, replace the sensor.

Sensor

See Figure 88.

1. Start the engine and bring it to normal operating temperature, then run the engine above 1200 RPM for two minutes.
2. Backprobe with a high impedance averaging voltmeter set to the DC voltage scale. Backprobe between the HO2S sensor signal wire (terminal 4) and battery ground.
3. Verify that the sensor voltage fluctuates rapidly between 0.40–0.60 volts.
4. If the sensor voltage is stabilized at the middle of the specified range (approximately 0.45–0.55 volts) or if the voltage fluctuates very slowly within the specified range (HO2S signal crosses 0.5 volts less than 5 times in ten seconds), the sensor may be faulty.
5. If the sensor voltage stabilizes at either end of the specified range, the PCM is probably not able to compensate for a mechanical problem such as a vacuum leak. These types of mechanical problems will cause the sensor to report a constant lean or constant rich mixture. The mechanical problem will first have to be repaired and then the HO2S sensor test repeated.
6. Pull a vacuum hose located after the throttle plate. Voltage should drop to approximately 0.12 volts (while still fluctuating rapidly). This tests the ability of the sensor to detect a lean mixture condition.
7. Reattach the vacuum hose.
8. Richen the mixture using a propane enrichment tool. Sensor voltage should rise to approximately 0.90 volts (while still fluctuating rapidly). This tests the ability of the sensor to detect a rich mixture condition.

If the sensor voltage is above or below the specified range, the sensor and/or the sensor wiring may be faulty. Check the wiring for any breaks, repair as necessary and repeat the test.

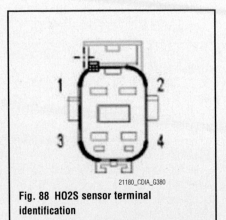

Fig. 88 HO2S sensor terminal identification

21180_CDIA_G380

➡**Further sensor operational testing requires the use of a special tester DRB scan tool or equivalent.**

INTAKE AIR TEMPERATURE (IAT) SENSOR

LOCATION

The Intake Air Temperature (IAT) sensor is located on the throttle body.

OPERATION

The IAT sensor threads into the intake manifold, where it measures the temperature of the intake air as it enters the engine. The sensor is a Negative Temperature Coefficient (NTC) thermistor–type sensor (resistance varies inversely with temperature). This means at high temperatures, resistance decreases and so the voltage will be low. At cold temperatures, the resistance is high and so the voltage will also be high. This allows the sensor to provide an analog voltage signal to the PCM. The PCM uses this signal to compensate for changes in air density due to temperature.

REMOVAL & INSTALLATION

See Figure 89.

1. Disconnect the electrical connector.
2. Remove the sensor from the throttle body.
3. Installation is the reverse of removal.

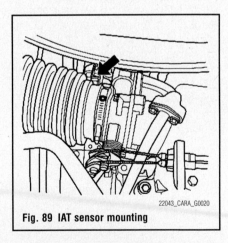

22043_CARA_G0020

Fig. 89 IAT sensor mounting

TESTING

1. Visually check the connector, making sure it is attached properly and all of the terminals are straight, tight and free of corrosion.
2. With the engine OFF, turn the ignition key to the ON position.
3. Do not allow more than 5 minutes delay between the next 2 steps.
4. Using a DRB, or equivalent scan

tool, read the information on the Intake Air Temperature (IAT) sensor and record the reading.

5. Turn the ignition switch OFF.

6. Remove the IAT sensor.

7. Using a temperature probe, quickly measure intake temperature inside the sensor opening.

8. Replace the IAT sensor if the scan tool reading is NOT within 10 of the probe reading.

9. Using a DRB, or equivalent scan tool, read the IAT sensor voltage.

10. If the voltage reading measures outside of the 0.5–4.5 volt range, disengage the IAT sensor connector.

11. Using the scan tool, read the IAT sensor voltage.

12. If the voltage reading measures greater than 4 volts, replace the IAT sensor.

13. Connect a jumper wire between the IAT signal and sensor ground circuits, then, along with the scan tool, read the sensor voltage.

14. If the voltage reading measures less than 1 volt, replace the IAT sensor.

KNOCK SENSOR (KS)

LOCATION

The knock sensor is threaded into the side of the cylinder block, in front of the starter.

OPERATION

When the knock sensor detects a knock in one of the cylinders, it sends an input signal to the PCM. In response, the PCM retards ignition timing for all cylinders by a specific amount. Knock sensors contain a piezoelectric material that sends an input signal (voltage) to the PCM. As the intensity of the engine knock vibration increases, the knock sensor output voltage also increases.

When the knock sensor detects a knock in one of the cylinders, it sends an input signal to the PCM. In response, the PCM retards ignition timing for all cylinders by a scheduled amount.

REMOVAL & INSTALLATION

See Figure 90.

1. Disconnect the negative battery cable.

2. Raise vehicle and support.

3. On All Wheel Drive vehicles remove the PTU (Power Transfer Unit).

4. Unplug the electrical connector from knock sensor.

5. Use a crow foot socket to remove the knock sensor.

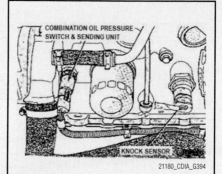
Fig. 90 Knock sensor used on 3.3L and 3.8L engines

6. Installation is the reverse of removal. Tighten the sensor to 7 ft. lbs. (10 Nm).

TESTING

1. Visually check the connector, making sure it is attached properly and that all of the terminals are straight, tight and free of corrosion.

2. A number of factors affect the engine knock sensor. A few of these are: ignition timing, cylinder pressure, fuel octane, etc. The knock sensor produces an AC voltage whose amplitude increases with the amount of engine knock. The knock sensor can be tested with a digital voltmeter.

3. The knock sensor output voltage should measure between 80mV and 4 volts with the engine running between 576 and 2208 rpm. If the output falls outside of this range, a Diagnostic Trouble Code (DTC) will set.

MANIFOLD ABSOLUTE PRESSURE (MAP) SENSOR

LOCATION

The MAP sensor is located on the intake manifold. Refer to the component location illustrations.

OPERATION

The PCM supplies 5 volts of direct current to the Manifold Absolute Pressure (MAP) sensor. The MAP sensor then converts the intake manifold pressure into voltage. The PCM monitors the MAP sensor output voltage. As vacuum increases, the MAP sensor voltage decreases proportionately. Also, as vacuum decreases, the MAP sensor voltage increases proportionally.

With the ignition key ON, before the engine is started, the PCM determines atmospheric air pressure from the MAP sensor voltage. While the engine operates,

the PCM figures out intake manifold pressure from the MAP sensor voltage. Based on the MAP sensor voltage and inputs from other sensors, the PCM adjusts spark advance and the air/fuel ratio. The MAP sensor is mounted to the intake manifold, near the throttle body inlet to the manifold. The sensor connects electrically to the PCM.

REMOVAL & INSTALLATION

1. Disconnect the electrical connector.

2. Remove the sensor from the intake manifold.

3. Installation is the reverse of removal.

TESTING

See Figure 91.

1. Visually check the connector, making sure it is attached properly and that all of the terminals are straight, tight and free of corrosion.

2. Test the MAP sensor output voltage at the sensor connector between terminals B and C.

3. With the ignition switch ON and the engine not running, the output voltage should be 4–5 volts. The voltage should fall to 1.5–2.1 volts with a hot, neutral idle speed condition. If OK, go to the next step. If not OK, go to Step 5.

4. Test the PCM terminal 36 for the same voltage described in the previous step to make sure the wire harness is OK. Repair as necessary.

5. Test the MAP sensor ground circuit at the sensor connector terminal A and PCM terminal 43. If OK, go to the next step. If not OK, repair as necessary.

6. Test the MAP sensor supply voltage between the sensor connector terminals A and B with the ignition key in the ON position. The voltage should be about 4.5–5.5 volts.

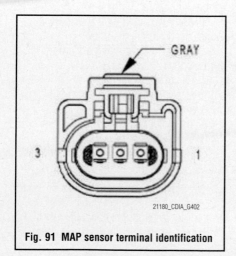
Fig. 91 MAP sensor terminal identification

7. There should also be 4.5–5.5 volts at terminal 61 of the PCM. If OK, replace the MAP sensor.

8. If not, repair or replace the wire harness as required.

THROTTLE POSITION SENSOR (TPS)

LOCATION

The Throttle Position Sensor (TPS) is mounted to the side of the throttle body

OPERATION

The TPS is a variable resistor that provides the PCM with an input signal (voltage). The signal represents throttle blade position. As the position of the throttle blade changes, the resistance of the TPS changes.

The PCM supplies about 5 volts of DC current to the TPS. The TPS output voltage (input signal to the PCM) represents throttle blade position. The TPS output voltage to the PCM varies from about 0.5 volt at idle to a maximum of 4.0 volts at wide open throttle. The PCM uses the TPS input, and other sensor input, to determine current engine operating conditions. The PCM also adjusts fuel injector pulse width and ignition timing based on these inputs.

REMOVAL & INSTALLATION

1. Disconnect the negative battery cable.

2. Remove the electrical connector from the IAT sensor.

3. Remove the air cleaner box lid. Remove hose from throttle body.

4. Disconnect the electrical connector at TPS.

5. Disconnect the electrical connector at Idle Air Control motor.

6. Remove the throttle and speed control cables from throttle body.

7. Remove 3 mounting bolts from throttle body.

8. Remove throttle body.

9. Disconnect the purge vacuum line from the throttle body.

10. Remove TPS from throttle body.

11. Installation is the reverse of removal.

TESTING

See Figure 92.

In order to perform a complete test of the TPS and related circuits, you must use a

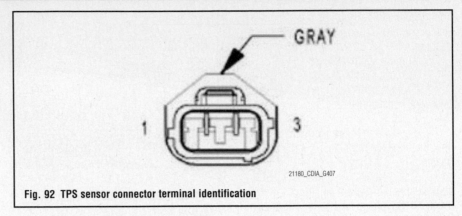

Fig. 92 TPS sensor connector terminal identification

DRB or equivalent scan tool, and follow the manufacturers directions. To check the Throttle Position Sensor (TPS) only, proceed with the following tests.

Visually check the connector, making sure it is attached properly and that all of the terminals are straight, tight and free of corrosion.

The TPS can be tested using a digital ohmmeter. The center terminal of the sensor supplies the output voltage. The outer terminal with the violet/white wire is the 5–volt supply terminal and the black/light blue wire is the sensor ground terminal.

1. Connect the DVOM between the center terminal and sensor ground.

2. With the ignition key to the **ON** position and the engine off, check the output voltage at the center terminal wire of the connector.

3. Check the output voltage at idle and at Wide Open Throttle (WOT):

4. The TPS output voltage should be about 0.38–1.20 volts. At WOT, the output voltage should be about 3.1–4.4 volts.

5. The output voltage should gradually increase as the throttle plate moves slowly from idle to WOT.

6. If voltage measures outside these values, replace the TPS.

7. Before replacing the TPS, check for spread terminals and also inspect the PCM connections.

VEHICLE SPEED SENSOR (VSS)

LOCATION

See Figures 93 and 94.

The PCM receives a signal from the VSS to indicate vehicle speed. On V6 manual transmission vehicles, the ABS speed sensors provides the signal to the PCM for vehicle speed. Refer to the illustrations for locations.

OPERATION

The VSS is a two–wire magnetic pickup device that generates an AC signal as rotation

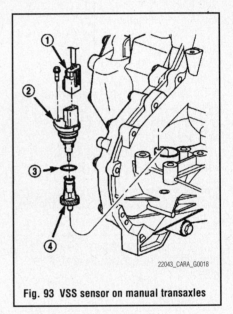

Fig. 93 VSS sensor on manual transaxles

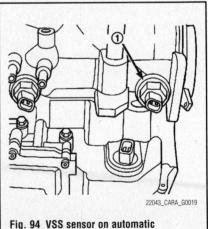

Fig. 94 VSS sensor on automatic transaxles

occurs. The PCM converts this signal into a pulse per mile signal and sends the vehicle speed message across the communication bus to the BCM. The BCM sends this signal to the instrument cluster to display vehicle speed to the driver. The vehicle speed signal pulse is roughly 8000 pulses per mile.

REMOVAL & INSTALLATION

1. Raise and safely support the vehicle.
2. Disconnect the electrical connector from the VSS.
3. On manual transaxles, remove the bolt securing the sensor, then remove the sensor from the transaxle.
4. On automatic transaxles, unscrew the sensor from the transaxle case.
5. Installation is the reverse of removal. Use a new o–ring when installing. On manual transaxles, tighten the mounting bolt until just snug. On automatics, tighten the sensor to 20 ft. lbs. (27 Nm).

FUEL — GASOLINE FUEL INJECTION SYSTEM

FUEL SYSTEM SERVICE PRECAUTIONS

Safety is the most important factor when performing not only fuel system maintenance but any type of maintenance. Failure to conduct maintenance and repairs in a safe manner may result in serious personal injury or death. Maintenance and testing of the vehicle's fuel system components can be accomplished safely and effectively by adhering to the following rules and guidelines.

• To avoid the possibility of fire and personal injury, always disconnect the negative battery cable unless the repair or test procedure requires that battery voltage be applied.

• Always relieve the fuel system pressure prior to disconnecting any fuel system component (injector, fuel rail, pressure regulator, etc.), fitting or fuel line connection. Exercise extreme caution whenever relieving fuel system pressure to avoid exposing skin, face and eyes to fuel spray. Please be advised that fuel under pressure may penetrate the skin or any part of the body that it contacts.

• Always place a shop towel or cloth around the fitting or connection prior to loosening to absorb any excess fuel due to spillage. Ensure that all fuel spillage (should it occur) is quickly removed from engine surfaces. Ensure that all fuel soaked cloths or towels are deposited into a suitable waste container.

• Always keep a dry chemical (Class B) fire extinguisher near the work area.

• Do not allow fuel spray or fuel vapors to come into contact with a spark or open flame.

• Always use a back–up wrench when loosening and tightening fuel line connection fittings. This will prevent unnecessary stress and torsion to fuel line piping.

• Always replace worn fuel fitting O–rings with new Do not substitute fuel hose or equivalent where fuel pipe is installed.

Before servicing the vehicle, make sure to also refer to the precautions in the beginning of this section as well.

RELIEVING FUEL SYSTEM PRESSURE

1. Before servicing the vehicle, refer to the Precautions Section.
2. Remove the fuel pump relay from the Power Distribution Center (PDC).
3. Start the vehicle until it stalls.
4. Try and start the vehicle several times to verify the system is fully relieved.
5. Reinstall the relay once all repair procedures have been completed.

FUEL FILTER

REMOVAL & INSTALLATION

➡ The fuel filter mounts to the top of the fuel tank.

1. Before servicing the vehicle, refer to the Precautions Section.
2. Relieve the fuel system pressure.
3. Remove or disconnect the following:
   • Negative battery cable
4. Raise the vehicle and support the fuel tank with a transmission jack.
   • Fuel line from the front of the tank
   • Ground strap
   • Inboard side of the fuel tank straps and front T strap fastener and lower the tank about 6 inches
   • Fuel lines from the fuel pump module
   • Fuel filter
5. Installation is the reverse of removal. Tighten the fuel filter bolts to 40 inch lbs. (4.5 Nm), the main tank straps to 40 ft. lbs. (54 Nm) and the T strap to 250 inch lbs. (28 Nm).
6. Start the engine and check for leaks.

FUEL INJECTORS

REMOVAL & INSTALLATION

2.4L Engine

1. Before servicing the vehicle, refer to the Precautions Section.
2. Relieve the fuel system pressure.
3. Remove or disconnect the following:
   • Negative battery cable
   • Wiring connectors for the injector harness
   • Wiring harness from the brackets
   • Fuel injector harness connectors
   • Harness from the vehicle
   • Quick connect fuel hose fittings from the chassis tube
   • Fuel rail bolts
   • Fuel rail with injectors attached
4. Rotate and pull the injectors to separate them from the fuel supply manifold.

To install:

5. Install or connect the following:
   • Injectors with new O–ring seals
   • Fuel rail with injectors attached. Tighten the bolts to 16 ft. lbs. (22 Nm).
   • Quick connect fuel hose fittings to the chassis tube
   • Harness from the vehicle
   • Fuel injector harness connectors
   • Wiring harness from the brackets
   • Wiring connectors to the injector harness
   • Negative battery cable
6. Start the engine, check for leaks and repair if necessary.

3.3L and 3.8L Engines

1. Before servicing the vehicle, refer to the Precautions Section.
2. Relieve the fuel system pressure.
3. Remove or disconnect the following:
   • Negative battery cable
   • Upper intake manifold
   • Quick connect fuel hose fittings from the chassis tube
   • Fuel rail bolts
   • Fuel rail with injectors attached
4. Rotate and pull the injectors to separate them from the fuel supply manifold.

To install:

5. Install or connect the following:
   • Injectors with new O–ring seals
   • Fuel rail with injectors attached. Tighten the bolts to 16 ft. lbs. (22 Nm).
   • Quick connect fuel hose fittings to the chassis tube
   • Upper intake manifold
   • Negative battery cable
6. Start the engine, check for leaks and repair if necessary.

FUEL PUMP

REMOVAL & INSTALLATION

1. Before servicing the vehicle, refer to the Precautions Section.
2. Relieve the fuel system pressure.
3. Drain the fuel tank.
4. Remove or disconnect the following:
   • Negative battery cable
   • Fuel tank straps. Support the fuel tank before loosening the strap bolts.
   • Fuel lines
   • Fuel pump module harness connector
5. Lower the tank for access and remove the fuel pump module locking ring and the fuel pump module.

To install:

6. Install or connect the following:
   • Fuel pump module. Tighten the locking ring to 40 ft. lbs. (54 Nm).
   • Fuel pump module harness connector
   • Fuel lines
   • Fuel tank straps. Tighten the main tank straps to 40 ft. lbs. (54 Nm) and the T strap to 250 inch lbs. (28 Nm).
   • Negative battery cable
7. Start the engine and check for leaks.

FUEL TANK

REMOVAL & INSTALLATION

1. Before servicing the vehicle, refer to the Precautions Section.
2. Remove the fuel filler cap and release the fuel system pressure.
3. Disconnect the negative cable from the battery.
4. Drain the fuel tank.
5. Raise and safely support the vehicle.
6. Use a transmission jack to support the fuel tank. Remove the bolts from the fuel tank straps.
7. Lower the tank slightly.
8. Disconnect the fuel filler vent tube. Squeeze the tabs and pull it apart.
9. Disconnect the fuel fill hose at the fuel tank filler metal tube; not at the fuel tank.
10. Disconnect the fuel line and vapor line at the front of the fuel tank.
11. Slide the fuel pump module electrical connector lock to the unlock position.
12. Push down on the connector retainer.
13. Lower the tank from the vehicle. Remove the fuel filler vent tube from the frame.

14. Installation is the reverse of removal. Tighten the strap bolts to 40 ft. lbs. (54 Nm) and the T strap bolt to 21 ft. lbs. (28 Nm).
15. Start the engine and check for leaks.

IDLE SPEED

ADJUSTMENT

Idle speed is maintained by the Powertrain Control Module (PCM). No adjustment is necessary or possible.

THROTTLE BODY

REMOVAL & INSTALLATION

See Figures 95 through 104.

1. Disconnect the negative battery cable.
2. Remove the air inlet–to–throttle body hose clamp.
3. Remove the 2 mounting screws and air inlet resonator.

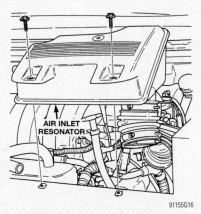

Fig. 95 Remove the air inlet resonator assembly

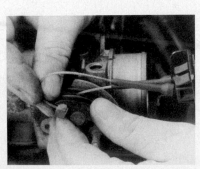

Fig. 96 Disconnect the throttle and speed control (if equipped) cables from the throttle lever

Fig. 97 Loosen the throttle cable bracket mounting nuts . . .

Fig. 98 . . . then remove the throttle cable bracket from the throttle body unit

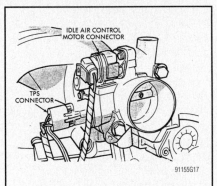

Fig. 99 Disengage the electrical connectors from the IAC motor and TPS—2.4L engine

4. Remove the throttle and speed control (if equipped) cables from the lever and bracket.
5. Disengage the electrical connectors from the Idle Air Control (IAC) motor and Throttle Position Sensor (TPS).
6. Disconnect the vacuum hoses from the throttle body.
7. Remove the throttle body mounting nuts.
8. Remove the throttle body assembly and mounting gasket.

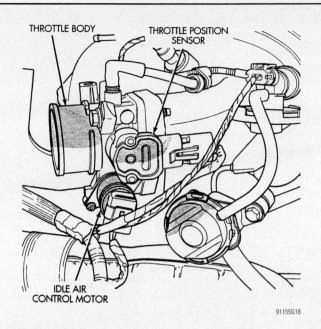

Fig. 100 Disengage the electrical connectors from the IAC motor and TPS—3.3L and 3.8L engines

Fig. 101 Disconnect the vacuum hoses from the throttle body

Fig. 103 . . . then remove the throttle body assembly

Fig. 102 Remove the throttle body mounting nuts . . .

Fig. 104 Be sure to replace the throttle body gasket

To install:

9. Position the throttle body, along with a new mounting gasket, onto the intake manifold.

10. Install the mounting nuts and tighten to 18 ft. lbs. (25 Nm).

11. Connect the vacuum hoses to the throttle body.

12. Attach the IAC motor and TPS electrical connections to the throttle body.

13. Connect the throttle and speed control (if equipped) cables.

14. Install the air cleaner/inlet resonator assembly.

15. Connect the negative battery cable.

HEATING & AIR CONDITIONING **SYSTEM**

BLOWER MOTOR

REMOVAL & INSTALLATION

See Figures 105 through 107.

✳✳ CAUTION

The Supplemental Inflatable Restraint (SIR) system must be disarmed before removing the blower motor assembly. Failure to do so may cause accidental deployment of the air bag, resulting in unnecessary SIR system repairs and/or personal injury.

1. Disconnect and isolate the negative battery cable, then wait 2 minutes before proceeding with the removal. This will effectively disable the air bag system preventing possible personal injury.
2. Remove the glove box from the instrument panel.
3. Remove the A/C–heater blower motor cover.
4. Disconnect the blower motor wiring connector.
5. Remove the blower motor wiring grommet and feed the wiring through the blower motor housing.
6. Remove the blower motor mounting screws.
7. Allow the blower motor assembly to drop downward to clear the instrument panel and remove from vehicle.

To install:
8. Place the blower motor assembly into position on the A/C heater unit and tighten the mounting screws.
9. Route the blower motor wiring through the blower motor housing and seat the wiring grommet in the hole of the blower motor housing.

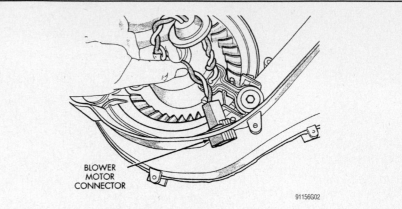

Fig. 106 Once the cover is removed, unplug the electrical connector and push it through the opening in the housing

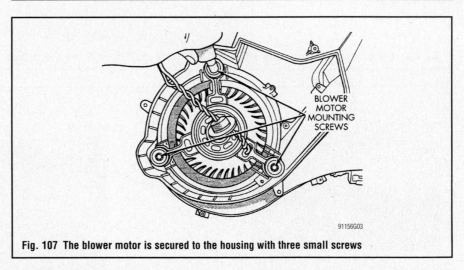

Fig. 107 The blower motor is secured to the housing with three small screws

10. Reconnect the blower motor electrical connector.
11. Install the A/C heater blower motor cover.
12. Install the glove box into the instrument panel.

13. Reconnect the negative battery cable. Check blower motor operation.

HEATER CORE

REMOVAL & INSTALLATION

See Figures 108 through 110.

1. Before servicing the vehicle, refer to the Precautions Section.
2. Align the wheels in the straight–ahead position.
3. Disconnect the negative battery cable.

✳✳ CAUTION

Before working around the steering wheel or the instrument panel all 2 minutes to pass to allow the air bag module to discharge.

4. Drain the cooling system into a clean container for reuse.
5. Remove the steering column, by removing or disconnect the following:

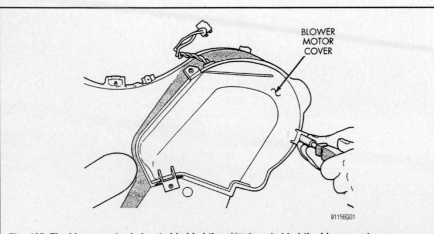

Fig. 105 The blower motor is located behind the glovebox, behind the blower motor cover

- Lower left side steering column cover
- Parking brake release cable from the parking brake lever
- 10 steering column cover liner–to–instrument panel bolts and the cover liner

6. Rotate the key to the LOCK position; then, rotate the steering wheel to the LOCKED position.

- Gear selector cable and its mounting bracket as an assembly from the upper steering column mounting bracket
- 2 instrument cluster trim bezel–to–instrument panel screws, retaining clips and bezel
- 2 steering column shroud–to–steering column screws and the shroud

- Steering column–to–intermediate steering shaft coupler

7. Loosen but do not remove the 2 lower steering column mounting bracket nuts/washers.

- 2 upper steering column mounting bracket nuts/washers
- Steering column assembly from the vehicle

8. Remove or disconnect the following:

- Instrument panel–to–chassis harness interconnect and bracket
- Lower silencer boot, at the base of the steering shaft

9. Working in the engine compartment, pinch off the heater hoses.

- Heater core cover. Position some towels under the heater core hoses.
- Heater core plate and the hoses

10. Depress the heater core retaining clips.

11. Lift the accelerator pedal and slide the heater core past it.

12. Depress the brake pedal and remove the heater core from the heater/air conditioning housing assembly.

To install:

13. Depress the brake pedal and install the heater core into the heater/air conditioning housing assembly.

14. Lift the accelerator pedal and slide the heater core past it.

15. Install or connect the following:

- Heater hoses (using new O–rings) and the heater core plate
- Heater core cover
- Heater hoses clamps, working in the engine compartment
- Lower silencer boot at the base of the steering shaft

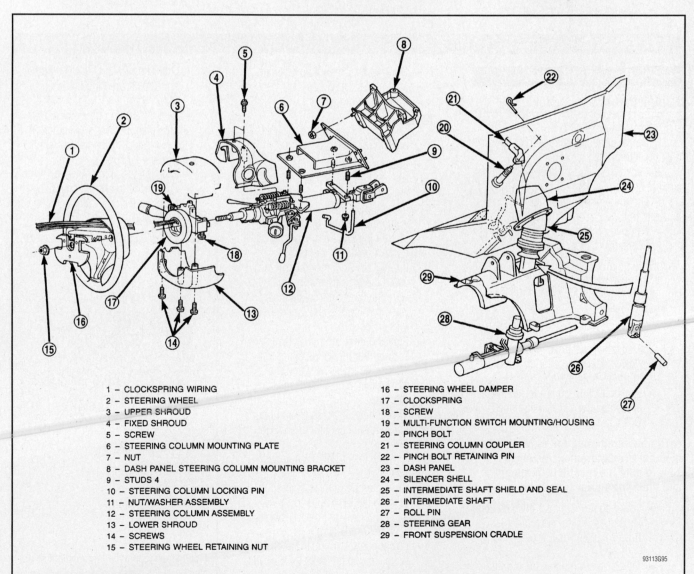

1 – CLOCKSPRING WIRING
2 – STEERING WHEEL
3 – UPPER SHROUD
4 – FIXED SHROUD
5 – SCREW
6 – STEERING COLUMN MOUNTING PLATE
7 – NUT
8 – DASH PANEL STEERING COLUMN MOUNTING BRACKET
9 – STUDS 4
10 – STEERING COLUMN LOCKING PIN
11 – NUT/WASHER ASSEMBLY
12 – STEERING COLUMN ASSEMBLY
13 – LOWER SHROUD
14 – SCREWS
15 – STEERING WHEEL RETAINING NUT
16 – STEERING WHEEL DAMPER
17 – CLOCKSPRING
18 – SCREW
19 – MULTI-FUNCTION SWITCH MOUNTING/HOUSING
20 – PINCH BOLT
21 – STEERING COLUMN COUPLER
22 – PINCH BOLT RETAINING PIN
23 – DASH PANEL
24 – SILENCER SHELL
25 – INTERMEDIATE SHAFT SHIELD AND SEAL
26 – INTERMEDIATE SHAFT
27 – ROLL PIN
28 – STEERING GEAR
29 – FRONT SUSPENSION CRADLE

93113G95

Fig. 108 View of the steering column assembly

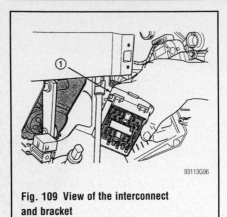

Fig. 109 View of the interconnect and bracket

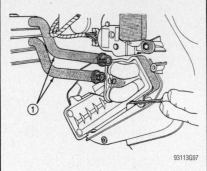

Fig. 110 View of the front heater core assembly

- Instrument panel–to–chassis harness interconnect and bracket
16. Install the steering column assembly by installing or connect the following:
- Steering column assembly, carefully into the vehicle.
- 2 upper and 2 lower steering

column mounting bracket nuts/washers. Torque the nuts to 105 inch lbs. (12 Nm).
- Steering column–to–intermediate steering shaft coupler and tighten the pinch bolt to 21 ft. lbs. (28 Nm)

- 2 steering column shroud and the shroud–to–steering column screws
- Bezel, the retaining clips and the 2 instrument cluster trim bezel–to–instrument panel screws
- Gear selector cable and its mounting bracket as an assembly to the upper steering column mounting bracket
- 10 steering column cover liner and the cover liner–to–instrument panel bolts
- Parking brake release cable to the parking brake lever
- Lower left side steering column cover.
- Lower left side steering column cover
17. Refill the cooling system.
18. Connect the negative battery cable.
19. Run the engine to normal operating temperatures; then, check the climate control operation and check for leaks.

STEERING

POWER STEERING GEAR

REMOVAL & INSTALLATION

See Figures 111 and 112.

1. Before servicing the vehicle, refer to the Precautions Section.
2. Lock the steering wheel to the straight ahead position.
3. Drain the power steering fluid from the reservoir.
4. Remove or disconnect the following:
- Negative battery cable
- Front wheels
- Steering column shaft coupler
- Front emissions vapor canister, if equipped
- Single hose at the power steering cooler and let the fluid drain into a suitable container
- Power steering cooler–to–cradle bolts, if equipped
- Leak detection pump–to–cradle crossmember bolts, if equipped
- Outer tie rod ends

➡The bolts retaining the cradle crossmember are different sizes, makes sure to note the locations of the bolts and their sizes prior to removal.

- Lower control arm rear bushing bolts
- Crossmember reinforcement
- Power transfer unit, if equipped with AWD
- Power steering pressure and return lines

- Steering gear mounting fasteners
- Intermediate shaft coupler
- Power steering gear

To install:
5. Install or connect the following:
- Power steering gear
- Intermediate shaft coupler. Start the roll pin into the coupler before installing the coupler, start the roll pin and then user a hammer to tap it into the coupler. Install the coupler on the shaft of the gear. Install removal/installer tool 6831A through the center of the roll pin, using the knurled nut to secure it. Hold the threaded rod stationary while turning the nut to pull the pin into the coupler.
- Steering gear mounting fasteners. Torque the 14mm fasteners to 135 ft. lbs. (183 Nm) and the 12mm fastener to 70 ft. lbs. (95 Nm).
- Power steering pressure and return lines. Torque the line to 25 ft. lbs. (31 Nm).
- Power transfer unit, if equipped with AWD
- Crossmember reinforcement. Tighten the M14 bolts to 113 ft. lbs. (153 Nm) and the M12 bolts to 78 ft. lbs. (106 Nm).
- Lower control arm rear bushing bolts. Torque the bolts to 45 ft. lbs. (61 Nm).

- Outer tie rod ends to the steering knuckle. Torque the nut to 55 ft. lbs. (75 Nm).
- Leak detection pump–to–cradle crossmember bolts, if equipped
- Power steering cooler–to–cradle bolts, if equipped
- Single hose at the power steering cooler and fasten the clamp
- Front emissions vapor canister, if equipped

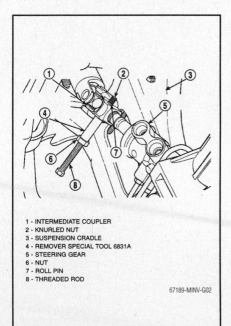

1 - INTERMEDIATE COUPLER
2 - KNURLED NUT
3 - SUSPENSION CRADLE
4 - REMOVER SPECIAL TOOL 6831A
5 - STEERING GEAR
6 - NUT
7 - ROLL PIN
8 - THREADED ROD

Fig. 111 Installing the intermediate shaft coupler to the gear

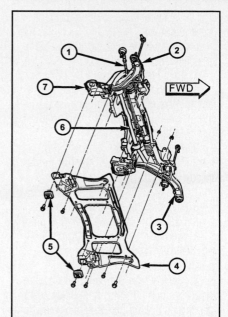

1 - STEERING GEAR
2 - RIGHT LOWER CONTROL ARM
3 - LEFT LOWER CONTROL ARM
4 - CRADLE CROSSMEMBER REINFORCEMENT
5 - REAR CRADLE CROSSMEMBER ISOLATOR BUSHING
6 - STABILIZER BAR
7 - CRADLE CROSSMEMBER

67189-MINV-G01

Fig. 112 Cradle crossmember reinforcement mounting

- Front wheels
- Steering column shaft coupler. Tighten the pinch bolt to 21 ft. lbs. (28 Nm).
- Negative battery cable

6. Fill and bleed the power steering reservoir

7. Inspect the power steering system for leaks and repair if necessary.

8. Check the wheel alignment and adjust as necessary.

POWER STEERING PUMP

REMOVAL & INSTALLATION

2.4L Engine

See Figures 113 through 119.

1. Disconnect and isolate the negative battery cable from the battery.

2. Remove the power steering drive belt. It is not necessary to remove the belt from the engine.

3. Loosen, but do not remove the nut securing the front bracket for the power steering pump to the aluminum mounting bracket.

4. Raise and safely support the vehicle.

5. Disconnect the wiring harness connector to the oxygen sensor which is accessible through the oxygen sensor wiring harness grommet in the vehicle floor pan.

6. Remove the catalytic converter from the exhaust manifold and remove all exhaust system hangers and isolators from the exhaust system brackets. Move the exhaust system out of the way as far rearward and to the left as possible to provide access to the power steering pump.

7. Place a drain pan under the power steering pump. Remove the power steering fluid return line hose on the front suspension cradle. Allow the fluid to drain from the pump and hose.

8. Remove the accessory drive belt splash shield.

9. Disconnect the power steering remote reservoir supply hose from the fitting on the power steering pump. Allow fluid to drain from the hose.

10. Remove power steering fluid pressure line from the power steering pump and drain any excess power steering fluid.

11. Remove the power steering fluid return hose from the power steering pump.

12. Remove the nut securing the rear of the power steering pump to the cast mounting bracket.

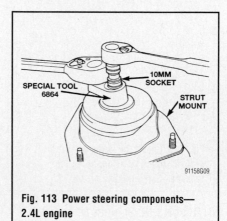

Fig. 113 Power steering components—2.4L engine

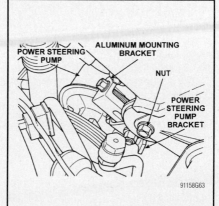

Fig. 114 After the belt is removed, loosen (but do not remove) the power steering pump-to-mounting bracket nut—2.4L engine

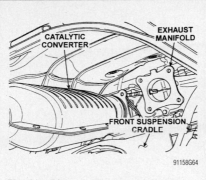

Fig. 115 Exhaust system positioned for pump removal—2.4L engine

13. Loosen the 3 bolts securing the power steering pump to the front mounting bracket and then remove the nut and bolt mounting the front of the power steering pump to the cast mounting bracket.

14. Remove the power steering pump and front bracket as an assembly from the cast bracket.

15. Remove the 3 mounting bolts securing the bracket to the power steering pump and separate the bracket from the power steering pump.

16. Remove the power steering pump from the vehicle. Transfer any parts from the power steering pump to the new replacement power steering pump.

To install:

17. Install the power steering pump into the vehicle and position the front of the pump onto the cast mounting bracket. Loosely install mounting nut to secure the pump in place.

18. Install the front mounting bracket on the power steering pump and loosely install the 3 mounting bolts, then install the nut and bolt securing the front bracket to the cast bracket.

19. Torque the 3 power steering pump mounting bracket bolts to 40 ft. lbs. (54 Nm).

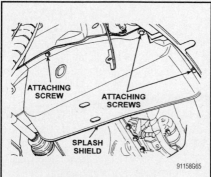

Fig. 116 Drive belt splash shield mounting detail—2.4L engine

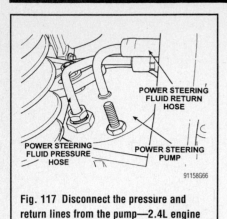

Fig. 117 Disconnect the pressure and return lines from the pump—2.4L engine

20. Install the high pressure fluid line to the pump output fitting. Torque the high pressure line–to–power steering pump fitting to 275 inch lbs. (31 Nm). Be sure to inspect the pressure line O–ring for any damage before connecting the pressure line to the steering pump.

21. Install the low pressure power steering fluid hose to the power steering pump low pressure fitting. Be sure the hose clamps are properly reinstalled and hoses are clear of the accessory drive belts.

22. Install the power steering fluid reservoir supply hose to the power steering pump fluid fitting. Be sure all hoses are clear of any accessory drive belts and hose clamps correctly installed.

23. Install the power steering drive belt.

24. Install the accessory drive belt splash shield.

25. Install the hose on the power steering fluid return line on the front suspension cradle. Be sure the hose clamps and heat shield tubes are correctly reinstalled.

26. Reconnect the exhaust pipe to the exhaust manifold. Install the hangers and isolators onto the exhaust system brackets. Torque the nuts and bolts to 250 inch lbs. (28 Nm).

27. Reconnect the wiring harness connectors to the oxygen sensor. Install the wiring harness grommet into the vehicle floor pan.

28. Remove the drain pan and lower the vehicle.

29. Torque the top mounting nut and bottom mounting bolt on the power steering pump front mounting bracket to 40 ft. lbs. (54 Nm).

30. Refill the power steering pump reservoir with the correct amount of clean power steering fluid.

31. Reconnect the negative battery cable. Bleed the power steering system.

32. Run the engine and check the system for leaks and proper steering operation.

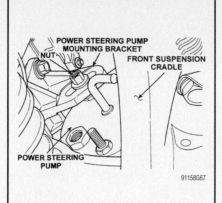

Fig. 118 After the pump and lines are disconnected and drained of excess fluid, remove the adjustment bracket nut—2.4L engine

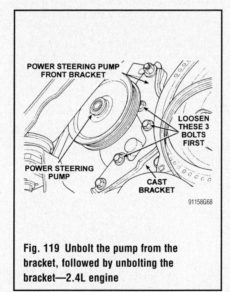

Fig. 119 Unbolt the pump from the bracket, followed by unbolting the bracket—2.4L engine

3.3L and 3.8L Engines

See Figures 120 and 121.

1. Remove and isolate the negative battery cable.

2. Raise and safely support the vehicle. Place a drain pan under the power steering pump.

3. Disconnect the wiring harness connector to the oxygen sensor which is accessible through the oxygen sensor wiring harness grommet in the vehicle floor pan.

4. Remove the catalytic converter from the exhaust manifold and remove all exhaust system hangers and isolators from the exhaust system brackets. Move exhaust system out of the way as far rearward and to the left as possible to provide access to the power steering pump.

5. Remove the power steering fluid return line hose on the front suspension

cradle. Allow the fluid to drain from the pump and hose.

6. Remove the accessory drive belt splash shield.

7. Remove accessory drive belt.

8. Disconnect the power steering remote reservoir supply hose from the fitting on the power steering pump. Allow fluid to drain from the hose.

9. Remove power steering fluid pressure line from the power steering pump and drain any excess power steering fluid.

10. Remove the power steering fluid return hose from the power steering pump.

11. Remove the rear support bracket mounted behind the power steering pump to the engine block.

12. Remove the 3 mounting bolts that secure the pump to the alternator/power steering pump and belt tensioner mounting bracket.

13. Remove the power steering pump and pulley assembly from the vehicle. Transfer all required parts from the pump to the new replacement pump before installation.

To install:

14. Position the front of the power steering pump up onto the mounting bracket.

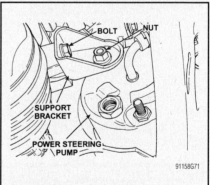

Fig. 120 Rear support bracket mounting detail—3.3L and 3.8L engines

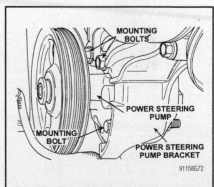

Fig. 121 Power steering pump mounting detail—3.3L and 3.8L engines

Torque the 3 power steering pump–to–mounting bracket bolts to 40 ft. lbs. (54 Nm).

15. Install the rear power steering pump–to–engine block support bracket. Torque the support bracket mounting bolts to 40 ft. lbs. (54 Nm). Install the nut to the mounting stud behind the pump and torque to 40 ft. lbs. (54 Nm).

16. Install the high pressure fluid line to the pump output fitting. Torque the high pressure line–to–power steering pump fitting to 275 inch lbs. (31 Nm). Be sure to inspect the pressure line O–ring for any damage before connecting the pressure line to the steering pump.

17. Install the low pressure power steering fluid hose to the power steering pump low pressure fitting. Be sure the hose clamps are properly reinstalled and hoses are clear of the accessory drive belts.

18. Install the accessory drive belt.

19. Install the hose on the power steering fluid return line on the front suspension cradle. Be sure the hose clamps and heat shield tubes are correctly reinstalled.

20. Reconnect the exhaust pipe to the exhaust manifold. Install the hangers and isolators onto the exhaust system brackets. Torque the nuts and bolts to 250 inch lbs. (28 Nm).

21. Reconnect the wiring harness con-nectors to the oxygen sensor. Install the wiring harness grommet into the vehicle floor pan.

22. Install the accessory drive belt splash shield.

23. Remove the drain pan and lower the vehicle.

24. Refill the power steering pump reservoir with the correct amount of clean power steering fluid.

25. Reconnect the negative battery cable. Bleed the power steering system.

26. Run the engine and check the system for leaks and proper steering operation.

BLEEDING

> ### ✳✳ CAUTION
>
> **The power steering fluid level should be checked with the engine OFF to prevent injury from moving components. Power steering oil, engine components and exhaust system may be extremely hot if the engine has been running. Do not start the engine with any loose or disconnected hoses or allow hoses to touch a hot exhaust manifold or catalyst.**

➡ **In all power steering pumps, use only MOPAR® Power Steering Fluid or** equivalent. **DO NOT use any type of automatic transmission fluid in the power steering system.**

Wipe the filler cap clean, then check the fluid level. The dipstick should indicate FULL COLD when the fluid is at normal room temperature of approximately 70–80°F.

1. Fill the power steering pump fluid reservoir to the proper level. Allow the fluid to settle for at least 2 minutes.

2. Start the engine and let run for a few seconds. Turn the engine OFF.

3. Add fluid if necessary. Repeat this procedure until the fluid level remains constant after running the engine.

4. Raise and safely support the vehicle so the front wheels of the vehicle are off the ground.

5. Start the engine. Slowly turn the steering wheel right and left, lightly contacting the wheel stops. Then turn the engine OFF.

6. Add power steering fluid if necessary.

7. Lower the vehicle and turn the steering wheel slowly from lock to lock.

8. Turn off the engine. Check the fluid level and refill as required.

9. If the fluid is extremely foamy, allow the vehicle to stand a few minutes and repeat the above procedure.

SUSPENSION

COIL SPRING

REMOVAL & INSTALLATION

See Figure 122.

1. Before servicing the vehicle, refer to the Precautions Section.

2. Remove the strut assembly from the vehicle.

3. Compress the coil spring and remove the piston rod nut.

4. Remove or disconnect the following:

- Upper strut mount
- Pivot bearing
- Spring upper seat
- Coil spring
- Jounce bumper and dust shield
- Lower spring isolator

To install:

5. Install or connect the following:

- Lower spring isolator
- Jounce bumper and dust shield
- Coil spring
- Spring upper seat
- Pivot bearing
- Upper strut mount. Torque the

piston rod nut to 75 ft. lbs. (100 Nm).

6. Remove the spring compressor and install the strut assembly to the vehicle.

FRONT SUSPENSION

LOWER BALL JOINT

REMOVAL & INSTALLATION

1. Before servicing the vehicle, refer to the Precautions Section.

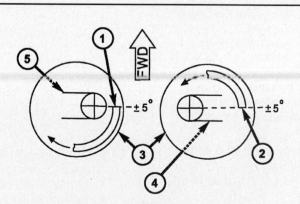

1 - END OF LEFT COIL SPRING AT STRUT LOWER SEAT
2 - END OF RIGHT COIL SPRING AT STRUT LOWER SEAT
3 - LOWER SEATS OF STRUTS
4 - RIGHT STRUT CLEVIS BRACKET
5 - LEFT STRUT CLEVIS BRACKET

06009-MINI-G03

Fig. 122 Position the coil spring as shown during assembly

2. Remove or disconnect the following:

- Front wheel
- Lower control arm
- Ball joint seal boot

3. Remove the ball joint from the control arm with a press.

To install:

4. Install the ball joint to the control arm with a press so that the ball joint flange contacts the control arm with no visible gaps.

5. Install or connect the following:

- Ball joint seal boot
- Lower control arm
- Front wheel

6. Check the wheel alignment and adjust as necessary.

LOWER CONTROL ARM

REMOVAL & INSTALLATION

1. Before servicing the vehicle, refer to the Precautions Section.

2. Remove or disconnect the following:

- Negative battery cable
- Front wheels
- Power steering cooler

➡**The bolts retaining the cradle cross-member are different sizes, makes sure to note the locations of the bolts and their sizes prior to removal.**

- Cradle plate
- Lower ball joints
- Rear control arm bushing retainers

3. Matchmark the suspension cradle and the frame rail.

4. Loosen the left suspension cradle bolts and lower the cradle to allow the pivot bolt to be removed.

5. Remove or disconnect the following:

- Front pivot bolts
- Lower control arms

To install:

➡**The suspension must be at curb height for final tightening of the control arm pivot bolts and the rear bushing retainer bolts.**

6. Install or connect the following:

- Lower control arms
- Front pivot bolts. Torque the M14 suspension cradle bolts to 113 ft. lbs. (153 Nm) and the M12 bolts to 78 ft. lbs. (106 Nm).
- Rear control arm bushing retainers. Torque the bolts to 45 ft. lbs. (61 Nm).
- Lower ball joints. Tighten the pinch bolts 105 ft. lbs. (145 Nm).

- Cradle plate. Tighten the bolts to 120 ft. lbs. (163 Nm).
- Power steering cooler and tighten the bolts to 100 inch lbs. (11 Nm)
- Front wheels
- Negative battery cable

7. Raise the suspension to curb height and tighten the pivot bolts to 135 ft. lbs. (183 Nm).

8. Check the wheel alignment and adjust as necessary.

CONTROL ARM BUSHING REPLACEMENT

1. Before servicing the vehicle, refer to the Precautions Section.

2. Remove the control arm from the vehicle.

3. Press the front bushing out of the control arm.

4. Cut the rear bushing lengthwise and remove it from the control arm.

To install:

5. Press the front bushing into the control arm until the bushing flange contacts the control arm.

6. Lubricate the rear bushing with silicone spray lubricant and push it onto the control arm.

7. Install the control arm to the vehicle.

MACPHERSON STRUT

REMOVAL & INSTALLATION

1. Before servicing the vehicle, refer to the Precautions Section.

2. Remove or disconnect the following:

- Front wheel
- Brake hose bracket
- Wheel speed sensor harness bracket, if equipped
- Stabilizer bar link
- Steering knuckle bracket bolts
- Upper strut mount nuts
- Strut assembly

To install:

3. Install or connect the following:

- Strut assembly. Torque the upper strut mount nuts to 21 ft. lbs. (28 Nm).
- Steering knuckle bracket bolts. Torque the bolts to 60 ft. lbs. (81 Nm) plus 90 degrees.
- Stabilizer bar link. Torque the nut to 65 ft. lbs. (88 Nm).
- Wheel speed sensor harness bracket, if equipped. Torque the bolt to 10 ft. lbs. (13 Nm).
- Brake hose bracket. Tighten the bolt to 10 ft. lbs. (13 Nm).
- Front wheel

4. Check the wheel alignment and adjust as necessary.

OVERHAUL

See Figures 123 through 126.

1. Before servicing the vehicle, refer to the Precautions Section.

➡**For the disassembly and assembly of the strut assembly, use of Strut Spring Compressor tool 223–7400, or the equivalent, is recommended to compress the coil spring. Follow the manufacturer's instructions closely.**

✳✳ CAUTION

Do not remove the strut shaft nut before the coil spring is compressed. The coil spring is held under pressure and must be compressed, removing spring tension from the upper mount and pivot bearing, before the shaft nut is removed.

2. Position the strut assembly in the strut coil spring compressor following the manufacturer's instructions. Position the lower hooks on the coil spring first. The strut clevis bracket should be positioned straight outward from the compressor.

3. Turn the upper mount of the strut assembly toward the inside of the compressor as shown to allow positioning of the compressor upper hooks. Position the upper hooks on top of the coil spring upper seat approximately 1 inch from outside diameter of seat. Do not allow hooks to be placed closer to edge. Place a clamp on the lower end of the coil spring, so the strut is held in place once the strut shaft nut is removed.

4. Compress the coil spring until all coil spring tension is removed from the upper mount.

5. Install Strut Nut Socket, Special Tool 6864, on the strut shaft retaining nut. Next, install a 10 mm socket on the hex on the end of the strut shaft. While holding the strut shaft from turning, remove the nut from the strut shaft.

6. Remove the upper mount from the strut shaft.

7. If the pivot bearing needs to be serviced, remove it from the top of the coil spring upper seat by pulling it straight up.

8. Remove the clamp from the bottom of the coil spring and remove the strut out through the bottom of the coil spring.

9. Release the tension from the coil spring by backing off the compressor drive fully. Push back the compressor upper hooks and remove the upper spring seat with upper spring isolator.

10. Remove the coil spring from the spring compressor.

11. Remove the dust shield and jounce bumper as an assembly from the strut shaft by pulling both straight up and off the strut shaft. The dust shield cannot be separated from the jounce bumper until after it is removed from strut shaft.

12. Remove the jounce bumper from the dust shield. The jounce bumper is removed from the dust shield by collapsing the dust shield until the jounce bumper can be pulled free from the dust boot.

13. Remove the spring isolator from the lower spring seat on the strut.

14. Inspect the strut assembly components for the following and replace as necessary:

   a. Inspect the strut for any condition of shaft binding over the full stroke of the shaft.

   b. Check the upper mount for cracks and distortion and its retaining studs for any sign of damage.

   c. Check the upper seat for stress cracks and wear.

   d. Check the upper spring isolator for severe deterioration.

   e. Check for binding of the strut assembly pivot bearing.

   f. Inspect the dust shield for rips and deterioration.

   g. Inspect the jounce bumper for cracks and signs of deterioration.

To assemble:

➡Coil springs on this vehicle are side–oriented. Left and right springs

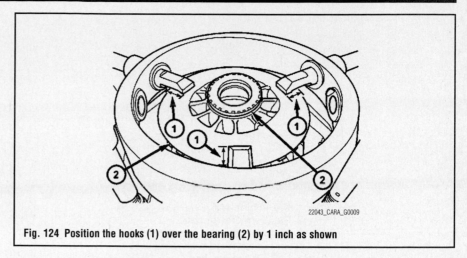

Fig. 124 Position the hooks (1) over the bearing (2) by 1 inch as shown

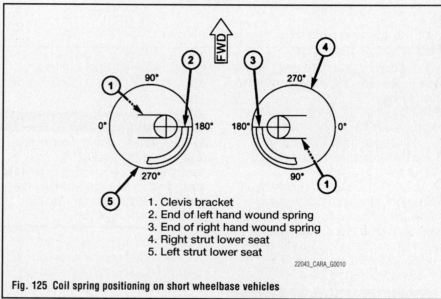

1. Clevis bracket
2. End of left hand wound spring
3. End of right hand wound spring
4. Right strut lower seat
5. Left strut lower seat

Fig. 125 Coil spring positioning on short wheelbase vehicles

must not be interchanged. On short wheel base vehicles the springs on the left side of the vehicle have a left–hand wind top–to–bottom while springs on the right side have a right–hand wind top–to–bottom. On long wheel base vehicles the springs on both the left side and right side of the vehicle have a left–hand wind top–to–bottom.

15. Place the coil spring in the compressor lower hooks following the manufacturer's instructions. Consider the following in terms of degrees when placing the coil spring in the compressor: From above, the compressor back is at the 180 degree position, and the operator, standing in the front of the compressor, is at the 0 degree position. On short–wheel–based vehicles, place the lower coil spring end at the 180 degree position for left springs and at the 180 degree position for right springs. On long–wheel–based vehicles, place the lower coil spring end at the 260 degree

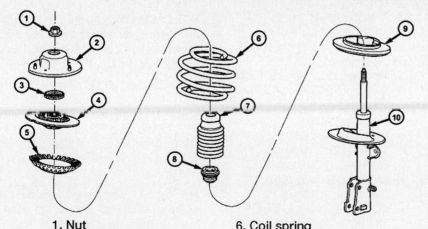

1. Nut
2. Upper mount
3. Pivot bearing
4. Upper spring seat
5. Upper spring isolator

6. Coil spring
7. Dust shield
8. Jounce bumper
9. Lower spring isolator
10. Strut

Fig. 123 Exploded view of the strut components

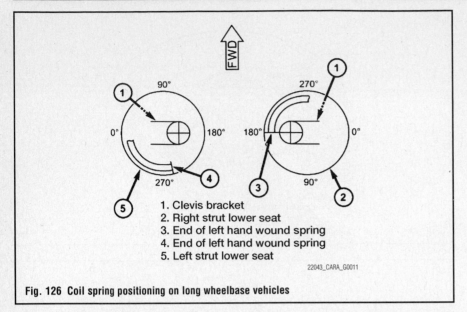

1. Clevis bracket
2. Right strut lower seat
3. End of left hand wound spring
4. End of left hand wound spring
5. Left strut lower seat

22043_CARA_G0011

Fig. 126 Coil spring positioning on long wheelbase vehicles

position (clockwise from 0 degrees) for left springs and at the 180 degree position for right springs.

16. Install the upper seat and upper isolator on top of the coil spring. Position the notch in the perimeter of the upper seat toward the front of the compressor (at 0 degree position).

17. Position the upper hooks on top of the coil spring upper seat so the upper hooks span approximately one inch past outside diameter of upper seat. This will allow proper clearance for upper mount installation without pinching the hooks in—between the two pieces.

✳✳ WARNING

Do not allow hooks to be placed closer to edge.

18. Compress the coil spring far enough to allow strut installation.

19. If the pivot bearing has been removed from the upper seat, install the pivot bearing on the top of the upper spring seat. The bearing must be installed on upper seat with the smaller diameter side of the pivot bearing toward the spring seat. Be sure the pivot bearing is sitting flat on the spring seat once mounted.

20. Install the spring isolator on the lower spring seat of the strut.

21. Install the jounce bumper on the strut shaft. The jounce bumper is to be installed with the small end pointing downward.

22. Install the dust shield on the strut. Collapse and stretch the dust shield down over the top of the jounce bumper until the dust shield snaps into the slot on the jounce bumper. The jounce bumper will

be at the top of the inner dust boot. Return the dust shield to its fully extended length.

✳✳ WARNING

In the following step it most important to properly position the coil spring on the lower spring seat of the strut. Failure to do so will alter the geometry of the vehicle possibly causing a pull condition.

23. Install the strut through the bottom of the coil spring until the lower spring seat contacts the lower end of the coil spring. If the coil spring is properly aligned, the clevis bracket on the strut should point straight outward away from the compressor (toward operator at 0 degree position). If necessary, reposition the strut or coil spring in the compressor so the strut clevis bracket lines up with the lower coil spring end as indicated in the following:

a Short wheel base vehicles: Position the end of the lower coil approximately 180 degrees from the center of the clevis bracket.

b Long wheel base vehicles: Position the end of the left side lower coil approximately 260 degrees clockwise from the center of the clevis bracket. Position the end of the right side lower coil approximately 180 degrees from the center of the clevis bracket.

24. Install the clamp to hold the strut and coil spring together.

25. Install the strut mount over the strut shaft and onto the top of the pivot bearing and upper seat. Loosely install the retaining nut on the strut shaft.

26. Install Strut Nut Socket (on the end of a torque wrench), Special Tool 6864, on the strut shaft retaining nut. Next, install a 10 mm socket on the hex on the end of the strut shaft. While holding the strut shaft from turning, tighten the strut shaft retaining nut to 75 ft. lbs. (100 Nm).

27. Before releasing the tension the compressor has on the spring, make sure the upper spring seat and strut clevis bracket are lined up properly (within 5 degrees of one another).

28. Slowly release the tension from the coil spring by backing off the compressor drive fully. As the tension is relieved, make sure the upper mount, pivot bearing and upper seat are align properly. Remove the clamp from the lower end of the coil spring and strut. Push back the spring compressor upper and lower hooks, then remove the strut assembly from the spring compressor.

29. Install the strut assembly on the vehicle.

STABILIZER BAR

REMOVAL & INSTALLATION

See Figure 127.

1. Before servicing the vehicle, refer to the Precautions Section.

2. Remove the bolts fastening the power steering cooler to the front suspension cradle crossmember reinforcement.

3. Remove the lower control arm rear bushing retainer bolts located on each side of each lower control arm rear bushing.

➡**The bolts fastening the cradle crossmember reinforcement are of two different thread sizes. Note the location of the various sizes.**

4. Remove the bolts attaching the cradle crossmember reinforcement to the front suspension cradle crossmember.

5. Remove the 2 bolts fastening the reinforcement and rear of cradle crossmember to the body of the vehicle. Remove the reinforcement.

➡**When removing the nut from the stud of the stabilizer bar link, do not allow the stud to rotate in it's socket. Hold the stud from rotating by placing an open—end wrench on the flat machined into the stud.**

6. Remove the stabilizer bar links from each end of the stabilizer bar. To do so, place an open—end wrench on the flat

machined into the link's mounting stud, then remove the nut while holding the wrench in place. Push each stud out of the hole in the stabilizer bar.

7. Remove the stabilizer bar bushing (cushion) retainers from the front suspension cradle crossmember.

8. Remove the stabilizer bar and bushings (cushions) as an assembly from the front suspension cradle crossmember.

9. Installation is the reverse of removal. Observe the following tightening specifications:

a. Link stud nuts: 65 ft. lbs. (88 Nm)
b. Stabilizer bar bushing retainer to cradle attaching bolts: 50 ft. lbs. (68 Nm)
c. Reinforcement on the front suspension cradle crossmember: M14 to 113 ft. lbs. (153 Nm), M12 78 ft. lbs. (16 Nm)
d. Lower control arm rear bushing retainer bolts: 45 ft. lbs. (61 Nm).
e. Cradle crossmember: 120 ft. lbs. (163 Nm)

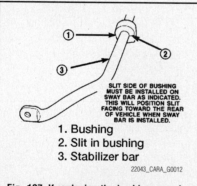

1. Bushing
2. Slit in bushing
3. Stabilizer bar

22043_CARA_G0012

Fig. 127 If replacing the bushings, position them as shown

STEERING KNUCKLE

REMOVAL & INSTALLATION

See Figure 128.

1. Before servicing the vehicle, refer to the Precautions Section.
2. Raise and support vehicle.
3. Remove the wheel and tire assembly from the vehicle.
4. Remove the cotter pin, nut lock and spring washer from the end of the stub axle and hub nut.
5. Have a helper apply the vehicle's

brakes to keep hub from turning, loosen and remove the hub nut.

6. Remove disc brake caliper and adapter as an assembly from knuckle.

7. Remove nut attaching outer tie rod end to steering knuckle by holding the tie rod end stud while loosening and removing nut with a wrench.

8. Remove tie rod end from steering knuckle.

9. If equipped with antilock brakes, remove the front wheel speed sensor from the steering knuckle.

10. Remove the two steering knuckle–to–strut clevis bracket attaching bolts.

11. Tip the knuckle outward and remove the driveshaft stub axle from the hub and bearing. Suspend driveshaft straight outward using a bungee cord or wire.

⁂ WARNING

Do not allow driveshaft to hang by inner joint.

12. Remove ball joint nut using a power impact wrench. Because the tapered stud is held sufficiently in the knuckle at this time, it is not necessary to hold the stud stationary to remove the nut.

13. Reinstall the ball joint nut until the top of the nut is even with the top of the ball joint stud. This will keep the stud from distorting while the stud is released from the knuckle in the following step.

⁂ WARNING

Do not remove ball joint stud from steering knuckle using a hammer. Damage to the aluminum knuckle, ball joint or control arm may result.

14. Release ball joint stud from steering knuckle.

➡ To ease remover installation and use, it may help to rotate the knuckle around so the inside of the knuckle faces outward.

15. Remove the steering knuckle from the vehicle.

16. If the hub and bearing needs to be transferred, remove the four bolts attaching the hub and bearing to the knuckle, then remove the hub and bearing.

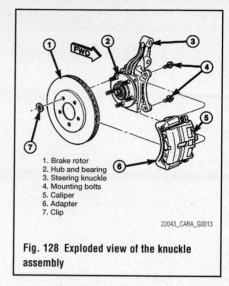

1. Brake rotor
2. Hub and bearing
3. Steering knuckle
4. Mounting bolts
5. Caliper
6. Adapter
7. Clip

22043_CARA_G0013

Fig. 128 Exploded view of the knuckle assembly

17. Installation is the reverse of removal.

WHEEL BEARINGS

REMOVAL & INSTALLATION

1. Before servicing the vehicle, refer to the Precautions Section.
2. Remove or disconnect the following:
   - Front wheel
   - Brake caliper and rotor
   - Hub retaining bolts
   - Hub and bearing assembly

To install:

3. Install or connect the following:
   - Hub and bearing assembly. Torque the bolts to 45 ft. lbs. (65 Nm).
   - Caliper and adapter to the brake rotor and align the assembly to the steering knuckle. Torque the mounting bolts to 125 ft. lbs. (169 Nm).
   - Hub retaining nut. Tighten the nut to 180 ft. lbs. (244 Nm).
   - Front wheel

4. Check and adjust the front end alignment, if necessary.

ADJUSTMENT

The front and rear wheel bearings are designed for the life of the vehicle and require no type of adjustment or periodic maintenance. The bearing is a sealed unit with the wheel hub and can only be removed and/or replaced as an assembly.

SUSPENSION

REAR SUSPENSION

LEAF SPRING

REMOVAL & INSTALLATION

1. Before servicing the vehicle, refer to the Precautions Section.
2. Remove the axle halfshaft, if equipped.
3. Support the vehicle at the frame rail with jackstands.
4. Support the axle with a floor jack.
5. Remove or disconnect the following:

  • Shock absorber
  • Axle plate from the axle and spring

6. Slowly lower the axle so that the leaf spring hangs free.
7. Remove or disconnect the following:

  • Front spring mount
  • Rear spring shackle plate
  • Leaf spring

To install:

8. Install or connect the following:

  • Leaf spring
  • Rear spring shackle plate. Torque the nuts to 45 ft. lbs. (61 Nm).
  • Axle plate. Torque the bolts to 75 ft. lbs. (101 Nm) on AWD models or 70 ft. lbs. (95 Nm) on FWD models.
  • Front spring mount. Torque the through bolt to 115 ft. lbs. (156 Nm) and the mount bolts to 45 ft. lbs. (61 Nm).
  • Shock absorber
  • Axle halfshaft, if equipped

SHOCK ABSORBER

REMOVAL & INSTALLATION

1. Before servicing the vehicle, refer to the Precautions Section.
2. Support the rear axle with a jackstand.
3. Remove the top and bottom shock absorber bolts.
4. Remove the shock absorber.

To install:

5. Install the shock absorber. Torque the mounting bolts to 65 ft. lbs. (88 Nm).
6. Remove the jackstand.

WHEEL BEARINGS

REMOVAL & INSTALLATION

Front Wheel Drive

1. Before servicing the vehicle, refer to the Precautions Section.
2. Remove or disconnect the following:

  • Rear wheel
  • Brake drum or caliper
  • Wheel speed sensor, if equipped
  • Hub and bearing assembly from the rear axle

To install:

3. Install or connect the following:

  • Hub and bearing assembly. Tighten the bolts to 95 ft. lbs. (129 Nm).
  • Wheel speed sensor, if equipped. Tighten the bolt to 105 inch lbs. (12 Nm).
  • Brake drum or caliper
  • Rear wheel

All Wheel Drive

1. Before servicing the vehicle, refer to the Precautions Section.
2. Set the parking brake.
3. Remove or disconnect the following:

  • Rear wheel
  • Brake caliper and rotor
  • Mounting bolts from the driveshaft inner joint to the output shaft
  • Wheel speed sensor and release the parking brake
  • Axle halfshaft
  • Hub and bearing assembly

To install:

4. Install or connect the following:

  • Hub and bearing assembly. Torque the bolts to 95 ft. lbs. (129 Nm).
  • Axle halfshaft
  • Wheel speed sensor and set the parking brake. Torque the fastener to 105 inch lbs. (12 Nm).
  • Driveshaft inner joint to output shaft mounting bolts. Torque the bolts to 45 ft. lbs. (61 Nm).
  • Torque the outer CV Joint hub nut to 180 ft. lbs. (244 Nm).
  • Brake caliper and rotor
  • Rear wheel

ADJUSTMENT

The front and rear wheel bearings are designed for the life of the vehicle and require no type of adjustment or periodic maintenance. The bearing is a sealed unit with the wheel hub and can only be removed and/or replaced as an assembly.

JEEP

Commander

5

SPECIFICATIONS AND MAINTENANCE CHARTS

ENGINE AND VEHICLE IDENTIFICATION

Code ①	Liters (cc)	Cu. In.	Cyl.	Fuel Sys.	Engine Type	Eng. Mfg.
K	3.7 (3701)	226	6	MFI	SOHC	Chrysler
N	4.7 (4701)	287	8	MFI	SOHC	Chrysler
P	4.7 (4701)	287	8	FF	SOHC	Chrysler
2	5.7 (5654)	345	8	MFI	OHV	Chrysler

Code ②	Year
6	2006
7	2007

MFI: Multi-port Fuel Injection
OHV: Over Head Valve
SOHC: Single Overhead Camshaft
FF: Flex Fuel

① 8th position of VIN
② 10th position of VIN

22043_COMM_C0001

GENERAL ENGINE SPECIFICATIONS

Year	Model	Engine Displ. Liters	Engine VIN	Net Horsepower @ rpm	Net Torque @ rpm (ft. lbs.)	Bore x Stroke (in.)	Comp. Ratio	Oil Pressure @ rpm
2006	Commander	3.7	K	211@5200	236@4000	3.66x3.40	9.6:1	25-110@3000
		4.7	N	235@4800	295@3200	3.66x3.40	9.0:1	35-105@3000
		5.7	2	330@5000	375@4000	3.91x3.58	9.6:1	25-110@3000
2007	Commander	3.7	K	211@5200	236@4000	3.66x3.40	9.6:1	25-110@3000
		4.7	N	235@4800	295@3200	3.66x3.40	9.0:1	35-105@3000
		4.7	P	235@4800	295@3200	3.66x3.40	9.0:1	35-105@3000
		5.7	2	330@5000	375@4000	3.91x3.58	9.6:1	25-110@3000

22043_COMM_C0002

GASOLINE ENGINE TUNE-UP SPECIFICATIONS

Year	Engine Displ. Liters	Engine VIN	Spark Plug Gap (in.)	Ignition Timing (deg.)	Fuel Pump (psi)	Idle Speed (rpm)	Valve Clearance Intake	Valve Clearance Exhaust
2006	3.7	K	0.042	①	56-60	①	HYD	HYD
	4.7	N	0.040	①	56-60	①	HYD	HYD
	5.7	2	0.045	①	56-60	①	HYD	HYD
2007	3.7	K	0.042	①	56-60	①	HYD	HYD
	4.7	N	0.040	①	56-60	①	HYD	HYD
	4.7	P	0.040	①	56-60	①	HYD	HYD
	5.7	2	0.045	①	56-60	①	HYD	HYD

Note: The information on the Vehicle Emission Control label must be used, if different from the figures in this chart.
HYD: Hydraulic

① Ignition timing and idle speed are controlled by the PCM. No adjustment is necessary.

22043_COMM_C0003

CAPACITIES

Year	Model	Engine Displ. Liters	Engine VIN	Engine Oil with Filter	Transmission (pts.) Man.	Transmission (pts.) Auto.**	Transfer Case (pts.)	Drive Axle Front (pts.)	Drive Axle Rear* (pts.)	Fuel Tank (gal.)	Cooling System (qts.)
2006	Commander	3.7	K	5.0	—	16.3	①	3.6	4.4	20.0	9.0
		4.7	N	6.0	—	28.0	3.8	3.6	4.4	20.0	14.5
		5.7	2	7.0	—	28.0	3.8	3.6	4.4	20.0	14.5
2007	Commander	3.7	K	5.0	—	16.3	①	3.6	4.4	20.0	9.0
		4.7	N	6.0	—	28.0	3.8	3.6	4.4	20.0	14.5
		4.7	P	6.0	—	28.0	3.8	3.6	4.4	20.0	14.5
		5.7	2	7.0	—	28.0	3.8	3.6	4.4	20.0	14.5

① NV140: 1.4 pts.
   NV245: 3.8 pts.

* When equipped with Trac Lok, add 4 oz. of limited slip additive
**Overhaul

22043_COMM_C0004

FLUID SPECIFICATIONS

Year	Model	Engine Displacement Liters	Engine ID/VIN	Engine Oil	Auto. Trans.	Front & Rear Axle	Power Steering Fluid	Brake Master Cylinder
2006	Commander	3.7	K	5W-30	Mopar® ATF +4	Mopar® Synthetic Gear Lube 75W-140	Mopar® Hydraulic System/Power Steering Fluid (MS-10838)	DOT 3
		4.7	N	5W-30	Mopar® ATF +4	Mopar® Synthetic Gear Lube 75W-140	Mopar® Hydraulic System/Power Steering Fluid (MS-10838)	DOT 3
		5.7	2	5W-20	Mopar® ATF +4	Mopar® Synthetic Gear Lube 75W-140	Mopar® Hydraulic System/Power Steering Fluid (MS-10838)	DOT 3
2007	Commander	3.7	K	5W-30	Mopar® ATF +4	Mopar® Synthetic Gear Lube 75W-140	Mopar® Hydraulic System/Power Steering Fluid (MS-10838)	DOT 3
		4.7	N	5W-30	Mopar® ATF +4	Mopar® Synthetic Gear Lube 75W-140	Mopar® Hydraulic System/Power Steering Fluid (MS-10838)	DOT 3
		4.7	P	5W-30	Mopar® ATF +4	Mopar® Synthetic Gear Lube 75W-140	Mopar® Hydraulic System/Power Steering Fluid (MS-10838)	DOT 3
		5.7	2	5W-20	Mopar® ATF +4	Mopar® Synthetic Gear Lube 75W-140	Mopar® Hydraulic System/Power Steering Fluid (MS-10838)	DOT 3

DOT: Department Of Transpotation

22043_COMM_C0005

VALVE SPECIFICATIONS

Year	Engine Displ. Liters	Engine VIN	Seat Angle (deg.)	Face Angle (deg.)	Spring Test Pressure (lbs. @ in.)	Spring Installed Height (in.)	Stem-to-Guide Clearance (in.)		Stem Diameter (in.)	
							Intake	Exhaust	Intake	Exhaust
2006	3.7	K	NA	45-45.5	213-234@ 1.107	1.579	0.0008-0.0028	0.0019-0.0039	0.2729-0.2739	0.2717-0.2728
	4.7	N	NA	45-45.5	174.5-195.6 @1.137	1.579	0.0008-0.0028	0.0019-0.0039	0.2729-0.2739	0.2717-0.2728
	5.7	2	NA	45-45.5	231-253@ 1.283	1.771	0.0008-0.0025	0.0009-0.0025	0.3120-0.3130	0.3120-0.3130
2007	3.7	K	NA	45-45.5	213-234@ 1.107	1.579	0.0008-0.0028	0.0019-0.0039	0.2729-0.2739	0.2717-0.2728
	4.7	N	NA	45-45.5	174.5-195.6 @1.137	1.579	0.0008-0.0028	0.0019-0.0039	0.2729-0.2739	0.2717-0.2728
	4.7	P	NA	45-45.5	174.5-195.6 @1.137	1.579	0.0008-0.0028	0.0019-0.0039	0.2729-0.2739	0.2717-0.2728
	5.7	2	NA	45-45.5	231-253@ 1.283	1.771	0.0008-0.0025	0.0009-0.0025	0.3120-0.3130	0.3120-0.3130

NA: Information not available

22043_COMM_C0006

CAMSHAFT AND BEARING SPECIFICATIONS CHART
All measurements are given in inches.

Year	Engine Displacement Liters	Engine VIN	Journal Diameter	Brg. Oil Clearance	Shaft End-play	Runout	Journal Bore	Lobe Lift	
								Intake	Exhaust
2006	3.7	K	1.0227-1.0235	0.0010-0.0026	0.0030-0.0079	NA	NA	NA	NA
	4.7	N	1.0227-1.0235	0.0010-0.0026	0.0030-0.0079	NA	NA	NA	NA
	5.7	2	①	②	0.0031-0.0114	NA	NA	0.2830	0.2830
2007	3.7	K	1.0227-1.0235	0.0010-0.0026	0.0030-0.0079	NA	NA	NA	NA
	4.7	N	1.0227-1.0235	0.0010-0.0026	0.0030-0.0079	NA	NA	NA	NA
	4.7	P	1.0227-1.0235	0.0010-0.0026	0.0039-0.0079	NA	NA	NA	NA
	5.7	2	①	②	0.0031-0.0114	NA	NA	0.2830	0.2830

NA: Not Available

① No. 1: 2.29 in.
   No. 2: 2.27 in.
   No. 3: 2.26 in.
   No. 4: 2.24 in.
   No. 5: 1.72 in.

② No. 1: 0.0015-0.0030 in.
   No. 2: 0.0019-0.0035 in.
   No. 3: 0.0015-0.0030 in.
   No. 4: 0.0019-0.0035 in.
   No. 5: 0.0015-0.0030 in.
   No. 5: 0.0031-0.0114 in.

22043_COMM_C0007

CRANKSHAFT AND CONNECTING ROD SPECIFICATIONS

All measurements are given in inches.

Year	Engine Displ. Liters	Engine VIN	Crankshaft				Connecting Rod		
			Main Brg. Journal Dia.	Main Brg. Oil Clearance	Shaft End-play	Thrust on No.	Journal Diameter	Oil Clearance	Side Clearance
2006	3.7	K	2.4996-2.5005	0.0001-0.0018	0.0021-0.0112	2	2.2792-2.2798	0.0002-0.0011	0.0040-0.0138
	4.7	N	2.4996-2.5005	0.0002-0.0013	0.0021-0.0112	2	2.0076-2.0082	0.0006-0.0022	0.0040-0.0138
	5.7	2	2.5585-2.5595	0.0009-0.0020	0.0020-0.0110	3	2.1250-2.1260	0.0007-0.0023	0.0030-0.0137
2007	3.7	K	2.4996-2.5005	0.0001-0.0018	0.0021-0.0112	2	2.2792-2.2798	0.0002-0.0011	0.0040-0.0138
	4.7	N	2.4996-2.5005	0.0002-0.0013	0.0021-0.0112	2	2.0076-2.0082	0.0006-0.0022	0.0040-0.0138
	4.7	P	2.4996-2.5005	0.0002-0.0013	0.0021-0.0112	2	2.0076-2.0082	0.0006-0.0022	0.0040-0.0138
	5.7	2	2.5585-2.5595	0.0009-0.0020	0.0020-0.0110	3	2.1250-2.1260	0.0007-0.0023	0.0030-0.0137

22043_COMM_C0008

PISTON AND RING SPECIFICATIONS

All measurements are given in inches.

Year	Engine Displ. Liters	Engine VIN	Piston Clearance	Ring Gap			Ring Side Clearance		
				Top Compression	Bottom Compression	Oil Control	Top Compression	Bottom Compression	Oil Control
2006	3.7	K	0.0002-0.0005	0.0079-0.0142	0.0146-0.0249	0.0099-0.0300	0.0020-0.0037	0.0016-0.0031	0.0007-0.0091
	4.7	N	0.0008-0.0020	0.0146-0.0249	0.0146-0.0249	0.0100-0.0500	0.0020-0.0041	0.0016-0.0032	0.0007-0.0091
	5.7	2	0.0008-0.0019	0.0090-0.0149	0.0137-0.0236	0.0059-0.0259	0.0007-0.0026	0.0007-0.0022	0.0007-0.0091
2007	3.7	K	0.0002-0.0005	0.0079-0.0142	0.0146-0.0249	0.0099-0.0300	0.0020-0.0037	0.0016-0.0031	0.0007-0.0091
	4.7	N	0.0008-0.0020	0.0146-0.0249	0.0146-0.0249	0.0100-0.0500	0.0020-0.0041	0.0016-0.0032	0.0007-0.0091
	4.7	P	0.0008-0.0020	0.0146-0.0249	0.0146-0.0249	0.0100-0.0500	0.0020-0.0041	0.0016-0.0032	0.0007-0.0091
	5.7	2	0.0008-0.0019	0.0090-0.0149	0.0137-0.0236	0.0059-0.0259	0.0007-0.0026	0.0007-0.0022	0.0007-0.0091

22043_COMM_C0009

TORQUE SPECIFICATIONS
All readings in ft. lbs.

Year	Engine Displ. Liters	Engine VIN	Cylinder Head Bolts	Main Bearing Bolts	Rod Bearing Bolts	Crankshaft Damper Bolts	Flywheel Bolts	Manifold		Spark Plugs	Oil Pan Drain Plug
								Intake	Exhaust		
2006	3.7	K	①	②	③	130	70	9	18	20	25
	4.7	N	④	⑤	③	130	45	9	18	20	25
	5.7	2	⑥	⑦	⑧	130	55	9	18	13	20
2007	3.7	K	①	②	③	130	70	9	18	20	25
	4.7	N	④	⑤	③	130	45	9	18	20	25
	4.7	P	④	⑤	③	130	45	9	18	20	25
	5.7	2	⑥	⑦	⑧	130	55	9	18	13	20

① Refer to procedure for illustration
  Step 1: Tighten bolts 1-8 to 20 ft. lbs. (27 Nm)
  Step 2: Verify bolts 1-8 at 20 ft. lbs. (27 Nm)
  Step 3: Tighten bolts 9-12 to 10 ft. lbs. (14 Nm)
  Step 4: Tighten bolts 1-8 an addt'l 90 degrees
  Step 5: Tighten bolts 1-8 another 90 degrees
  Step 6: Tighten bolts 9-12 to 19 ft. lbs. (26 Nm)

② Bed plate bolt sequence. Refer to illustration
  Step 1: Tighten bolts 1D,1G, 1F until bedplate contacts block
  Step 2: Tighten bolts 1A - 1J to 40 ft. lbs. (54 Nm)
  Step 3: Tighten bolts 1 - 8 to 5 ft. lbs. (7 Nm)
  Step 4: Turn bolts 1 - 8 an additional 90°.
  Step 5: Tighten bolts A - E to 20 ft. lbs. (27 Nm)

③ 20 ft. lbs. + 90 degrees

④ Refer to procedure for illustration
  Step 1: Tighten bolts 1-10 to 15 ft. lbs. (20 Nm)
  Step 2: Tighten bolts 1-10 at 35 ft. lbs. (47 Nm)
  Step 3: Tighten bolts 11-14 to 18 ft. lbs. (25 Nm)
  Step 4: Tighten bolts 1-10 an addt'l 90 degrees
  Step 5: Tighten bolts 11-14 to 22 ft. lbs. (30 Nm)

⑤ Bed plate bolt sequence. Refer to illustration
  Step 1: Tighten bolts A-L to 40 ft. lbs. (54 Nm)
  Step 2: Tighten bolts 1-10 to 25 inch lbs. (2.8 Nm)
  Step 3: Tighten bolts 1 - 10 an addt'l 90 degrees
  Step 4: Tighten bolts A1 - A6 to 20 ft. lbs. (27 Nm)

⑥ Refer to procedure for illustration
  Step 1: Tighten M12 bolts to 25 ft. lbs. (34 Nm)
  Step 2: Tighten M8 bolts 1-10 at 15 ft. lbs. (20 Nm)
  Step 3: Tighten M12 bolts to 40 ft. lbs. (54 Nm)
  Step 4: Tighten M8 bolts again to 15 ft. lbs. (20 Nm)
  Step 5: Tighten M12 bolts an addt'l 90 degrees
  Step 6: Tighten M8 bolts to 25 ft. lbs. (34 Nm)

⑦ Step 1: Tighten bolts to 20 ft. lbs. (27 Nm)
  Step 2: Tighten bolts an addt'l 90 degrees
  Step 3: Tighten crossbolts to 21 ft. lbs. (28 Nm)
  Step 4: Tighten crossbolts again to 21 ft. lbs. (28 Nm)

⑧ 15 ft. lbs., plus 90 degrees

WHEEL ALIGNMENT

Year	Model		Caster Range (+/-Deg.)	Caster Preferred Setting (Deg.)	Camber Range (+/-Deg.)	Camber Preferred Setting (Deg.)	Toe-in (deg.)
2006	Commander	F	0.45	+4.00	0.45	-0.25	0.25+/-0.25
		R	—	—	0.25	-0.25	0.25+/-0.25
2007	Commander	F	0.45	+4.00	0.45	-0.25	0.25+/-0.25
		R	—	—	0.25	-0.25	0.25+/-0.25

22043_COMM_C0011

TIRE, WHEEL AND BALL JOINT SPECIFICATIONS

Year	Model	OEM Tires Standard	OEM Tires Optional	Tire Pressures (psi) Front	Tire Pressures (psi) Rear	Wheel Size	Ball Joint Inspection	Lug Nut Torque (ft. lbs.)
2006	Commander	P245/65R17	-	①	①	①	②	85-115
2007	Commander	P245/65R17	-	①	①	①	②	85-115

OEM: Original Equipment Manufacturer

STD: Standard

OPT: Optional

① See placard on vehicle

② Replace if travel exceeds 0.020 in. (0.5 mm)

22043_COMM_C0012

BRAKE SPECIFICATIONS

All measurements in inches unless noted

Year	Model		Brake Disc Original Thickness	Brake Disc Minimum Thickness	Brake Disc Maximum Run-out	Minimum Lining Thickness Front	Minimum Lining Thickness Rear	Brake Caliper Bracket Bolts (ft. lbs.)	Brake Caliper Mounting Bolts (ft. lbs.)
2006	Commander	F	NA	1.122	0.0020	0.030	—	125	32
		R	NA	0.492	0.0001	—	0.030	—	18
2007	Commander	F	NA	1.122	0.0008	0.030	—	125	32
		R	NA	0.492	0.0008	—	0.030	—	18

F - Front

R - Rear

22043_COMM_C0013

SCHEDULED MAINTENANCE INTERVALS
2006-07 Commander

TO BE SERVICED	TYPE OF SERVICE	VEHICLE MILEAGE INTERVAL (x1000)												
		3	6	9	12	15	18	21	24	27	30	33	36	39
Engine oil & filter	R	✓	✓	✓	✓	✓	✓	✓	✓	✓	✓	✓	✓	✓
Tires	Rotate		✓		✓		✓		✓		✓		✓	
Brake hoses & linings	S/I				✓				✓				✓	
Lubricate steering and suspension ball joints	C/L		✓		✓		✓		✓		✓		✓	
Brake caliper pins	C/L				✓				✓				✓	
Air filter	I/R					✓					✓			
Spark plugs	R										✓			
Drive axle lubricant	R					✓			✓				✓	
Transfer case fluid	R	Every 60,000 miles												
PCV valve	I/R										✓			
Accessory drive belt	S/I	Every 60,000 miles												
Spark plug cables (5.7L)	I/R	Every 60,000 miles												
Automatic trans. fluid and filter (4.7L and 5.7L)	R	Every 60,000 miles												
Engine coolant	R	Every 60,000 miles												

R: Replace   S/I: Service or Inspect   C/L: Clean and lubricate   I/R: Inspect and rerplace if necessary

The above schedule is to be used if you drive under any of the following conditions:

Driving in temperatures under 32 degrees F
Stop and go traffic
Extensive engine idling
Driving in dusty conditions
Frequent trips under 10 miles
More than 50 % of your driving is in hot weather (90 deg. F) above 50 miles per hour
Trailer towing
Taxi, police or delivery service
Off-road driving
The vehicle is equipped for and operated with E85 (ethonol) fuel

If none of these conditions is met, double the maintenance intervals

22043_COMM_C0014

PRECAUTIONS

Before servicing any vehicle, please be sure to read all of the following precautions, which deal with personal safety, prevention of component damage, and important points to take into consideration when servicing a motor vehicle:

• Never open, service or drain the radiator or cooling system when the engine is hot; serious burns can occur from the steam and hot coolant.

• Observe all applicable safety precautions when working around fuel. Whenever servicing the fuel system, always work in a well-ventilated area. Do not allow fuel spray or vapors to come in contact with a spark, open flame, or excessive heat (a hot drop light, for example). Keep a dry chemical fire extinguisher near the work area. Always keep fuel in a container specifically designed for fuel storage; also, always properly seal fuel containers to avoid the possibility of fire or explosion. Refer to the additional fuel system precautions later in this section.

• Fuel injection systems often remain pressurized, even after the engine has been turned **OFF**. The fuel system pressure must be relieved before disconnecting any fuel lines. Failure to do so may result in fire and/or personal injury.

• Brake fluid often contains polyglycol ethers and polyglycols. Avoid contact with the eyes and wash your hands thoroughly after handling brake fluid. If you do get brake fluid in your eyes, flush your eyes with clean, running water for 15 minutes. If eye irritation persists, or if you have taken brake fluid internally, IMMEDIATELY seek medical assistance.

• The EPA warns that prolonged contact with used engine oil may cause a number of skin disorders, including cancer. You should make every effort to minimize your exposure to used engine oil. Protective gloves should be worn when changing oil. Wash your hands and any other exposed skin areas as soon as possible after exposure to used engine oil. Soap and water, or waterless hand cleaner should be used.

• All new vehicles are now equipped with an air bag system, often referred to as a Supplemental Restraint System (SRS) or Supplemental Inflatable Restraint (SIR) system. The system must be disabled before performing service on or around system components, steering column, instrument panel components, wiring and sensors. Failure to follow safety and disabling procedures could result in accidental air bag deployment, possible personal injury and unnecessary system repairs.

• Always wear safety goggles when working with, or around, the air bag system. When carrying a non-deployed air bag, be sure the bag and trim cover are pointed away from your body. When placing a non-deployed air bag on a work surface, always face the bag and trim cover upward, away from the surface. This will reduce the motion of the module if it is accidentally deployed. Refer to the additional air bag system precautions later in this section.

• Clean, high quality brake fluid from a sealed container is essential to the safe and proper operation of the brake system. You should always buy the correct type of brake fluid for your vehicle. If the brake fluid becomes contaminated, completely flush the system with new fluid. Never reuse any brake fluid. Any brake fluid that is removed from the system should be discarded. Also, do not allow any brake fluid to come in contact with a painted surface; it will damage the paint.

• Never operate the engine without the proper amount and type of engine oil; doing so WILL result in severe engine damage.

• Timing belt maintenance is extremely important. Many models utilize an interference-type, non-freewheeling engine. If the timing belt breaks, the valves in the cylinder head may strike the pistons, causing potentially serious (also time-consuming and expensive) engine damage. Refer to the maintenance interval charts for the recommended replacement interval for the timing belt, and to the timing belt section for belt replacement and inspection.

• Disconnecting the negative battery cable on some vehicles may interfere with the functions of the on-board computer system(s) and may require the computer to undergo a relearning process once the negative battery cable is reconnected.

• When servicing drum brakes, only disassemble and assemble one side at a time, leaving the remaining side intact for reference.

• Only an MVAC-trained, EPA-certified automotive technician should service the air conditioning system or its components.

BRAKES

GENERAL INFORMATION

PRECAUTIONS

• Certain components within the ABS system are not intended to be serviced or repaired individually.

• Do not use rubber hoses or other parts not specifically specified for and ABS system. When using repair kits, replace all parts included in the kit. Partial or incorrect repair may lead to functional problems and require the replacement of components.

• Lubricate rubber parts with clean, fresh brake fluid to ease assembly. Do not use shop air to clean parts; damage to rubber components may result.

• Use only DOT 3 brake fluid from an unopened container.

• If any hydraulic component or line is removed or replaced, it may be necessary to bleed the entire system.

• A clean repair area is essential. Always clean the reservoir and cap thoroughly before removing the cap. The slightest amount of dirt in the fluid may plug an orifice and impair the system function. Perform repairs after components have been thoroughly cleaned; use only denatured alcohol to clean components. Do not allow ABS components to come into contact with any substance containing mineral oil; this includes used shop rags.

• The Anti-Lock control unit is a microprocessor similar to other computer units in the vehicle. Ensure that the ignition switch is **OFF** before removing or

ANTI-LOCK BRAKE SYSTEM (ABS)

installing controller harnesses. Avoid static electricity discharge at or near the controller.

• If any arc welding is to be done on the vehicle, the control unit should be unplugged before welding operations begin.

SPEED SENSORS

REMOVAL & INSTALLATION

Front

See Figure 1.

1. Raise and safely support the vehicle.
2. Remove the front wheel.
3. Remove the brake caliper mounting bolts.

❋❋ WARNING

Support the brake caliper with mechanics wire. Do not let the caliper hang by the brake hose.

4. Remove the brake rotor.

5. Remove the front wheel speed sensor mounting nut and remove the speed sensor from the hub.

6. Disconnect the sensor wire routing clips.

7. Disconnect the speed sensor electrical connector.

To install:

8. Reconnect the speed sensor electrical connector.

9. Reconnect the speed sensor wire to the routing clips.

10. Install the speed sensor to the hub and tighten the mounting nut to 106–124 inch lbs. (12–14 Nm).

➡**Ensure the speed sensor wire is not kinked or twisted at any spot.**

11. Install the brake rotor.

12. Install the brake caliper and tighten the mounting bolts to 66–85 ft. lbs. (90–115 Nm).

13. Install the front wheel.

14. Lower the vehicle.

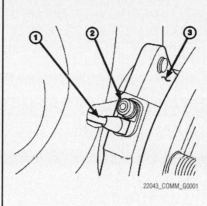

22043_COMM_G0001

Fig. 1 Remove the mounting nut (2) from to remove the speed sensor (1) from the hub (3)—Front wheels

Rear

See Figure 2.

1. Raise and safely support the vehicle.

2. Remove the rear wheel.

3. Remove the speed sensor mounting bolt from the rear support plate.

4. Pull out the speed sensor from the support plate and disconnect the electrical connector.

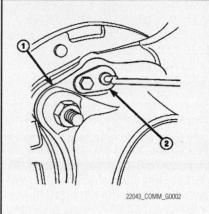

22043_COMM_G0002

Fig. 2 Remove the speed sensor mounting bolt (2) from the rear support plate (1)—Rear wheels

To install:

5. Install the speed sensor through the support plate and tighten the mounting bolt to 106–124 inch lbs. (12–14 Nm).

6. Reconnect the speed sensor electrical connector.

➡**Ensure the speed sensor wire is securely mounted in the routing clips and clear of any rotating components.**

7. Install the rear wheel.

8. Lower the vehicle.

BRAKES   **BLEEDING THE BRAKE SYSTEM**

BLEEDING PROCEDURE

BLEEDING PROCEDURE

Manual Bleeding

Use Mopar® brake fluid, or an equivalent quality fluid meeting SAE J1703-F and DOT 3 standards only. Use fresh, clean fluid from a sealed container at all times.

Do not pump the brake pedal at any time while bleeding. Air in the system will be compressed into small bubbles that are distributed throughout the hydraulic system. This will make additional bleeding operations necessary.

Do not allow the master cylinder to run out of fluid during bleed operations. An empty cylinder will allow additional air to be drawn into the system. Check the cylinder fluid level frequently and add fluid as needed.

Bleed only one brake component at a time in the following sequence:

1. Fill the master cylinder reservoir with brake fluid.

2. If calipers are overhauled, open all caliper bleed screws. Then close each bleed screw as fluid starts to drip from it. Top off master cylinder reservoir once more before proceeding.

3. Attach one end of bleed hose to bleed screw and insert opposite end in glass container partially filled with brake fluid. Be sure end of bleed hose is immersed in fluid.

4. Open up bleeder, then have a helper press down the brake pedal. Once the pedal is down, close the bleeder. Repeat bleeding until fluid stream is clear and free of bubbles. Then move to the next wheel.

Pressure Bleeding

Use Mopar® brake fluid, or an equivalent quality fluid meeting SAE J1703-F and DOT 3 standards only. Use fresh, clean fluid from a sealed container at all times.

➡**Do not pump the brake pedal at any time while bleeding.**

Air in the system will be compressed into small bubbles that are distributed throughout the hydraulic system. This will make additional bleeding operations necessary.

Do not allow the master cylinder to run out of fluid during bleed operations. An empty cylinder will allow additional air to be drawn into the system. Check the cylinder fluid level frequently and add fluid as needed.

Bleed only one brake component at a time in the following sequence: Follow the manufacturer's instructions carefully when using pressure equipment. Do not exceed the tank manufacturer's pressure recommendations. Generally, a tank pressure of 15-20 psi (51-67 kPa) is sufficient for bleeding.

1. Fill the bleeder tank with recommended fluid and purge air from the tank lines before bleeding.

2. Do not pressure bleed without a proper master cylinder adapter. The wrong adapter can lead to leakage, or drawing air back into the system. Use adapter provided with the equipment or Adapter 6921.

BLEEDING THE ABS SYSTEM

ABS system bleeding requires conventional bleeding methods plus use of the DRB scan tool. The procedure involves performing a base brake bleeding, followed by use of the scan tool to cycle and bleed the HCU pump and solenoids. A second base brake bleeding procedure is then required to remove any air remaining in the system.

1. Perform the manual or pressure brake bleeding procedure.
2. Connect a scan tool to the Data Link Connector (DLC).
3. Select ANTI-LOCK BRAKES, followed by MISCELLANEOUS, then ABS BRAKES. Follow the instructions that are displayed. When scan tool displays TEST COMPLETE, disconnect scan tool and proceed.
4. Perform the manual or pressure brake bleeding procedure a second time.
5. Top off master cylinder fluid level and verify proper brake operation before moving vehicle.

BRAKES

✳✳ CAUTION

Dust and dirt accumulating on brake parts during normal use may contain asbestos fibers from production or aftermarket brake linings. Breathing excessive concentrations of asbestos fibers can cause serious bodily harm. Exercise care when servicing brake parts. Do not sand or grind brake lining unless equipment used is designed to contain the dust residue. Do not clean brake parts with compressed air or by dry brushing. Cleaning should be done by dampening the brake components with a fine mist of water, then wiping the brake components clean with a dampened cloth. Dispose of cloth and all residue containing asbestos fibers in an impermeable container with the appropriate label. Follow practices prescribed by the Occupational Safety and Health Administration (OSHA) and the Environmental Protection Agency (EPA) for the handling, processing, and disposing of dust or debris that may contain asbestos fibers.

BRAKE CALIPER

REMOVAL & INSTALLATION

1. Raise and safely support the vehicle.
2. Remove the front wheel.
3. Siphon a small amount of brake fluid from the master cylinder reservoir.
4. Insert a small prybar through the caliper opening and pry the caliper cover (using the outboard brake pad) to bottom the piston in the caliper bore.
5. Remove the brake hose banjo bolt and gasket washers.

6. Remove the caliper slide bolts.
7. Remove the caliper assembly from the adapter.

To install:

8. Install the caliper assembly to the adapter.
9. Clean the slide bolts of any debris, lightly lubricate with silicon grease and tighten them to 32 ft. lbs. (44 Nm).

➡ **Verify the slide bolt boot is fully covering the bolt.**

✳✳ WARNING

Verify the brake hose is not twisted or kinked before fully tighten the banjo bolt.

10. Install the brake hose with new copper washers and tighten the banjo bolt to 23 ft. lbs. (31 Nm).
11. Fill and bleed the brake system.
12. Install the front wheel.
13. Lower the vehicle and recheck the brake fluid level.

DISC BRAKE PADS

REMOVAL & INSTALLATION

See Figure 3.

1. Raise and safely support the vehicle.
2. Remove the front wheel.
3. Siphon a small amount of brake fluid from the master cylinder reservoir.
4. Compress the brake caliper and remove it from the adapter.

✳✳ WARNING

Support the brake caliper with mechanics wire. Do not let the caliper hang by the brake hose.

FRONT DISC BRAKES

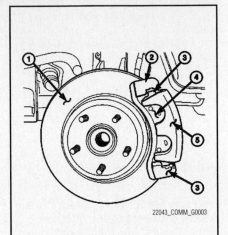

22043_COMM_G0003

Fig. 3 After removing the caliper (5), remove the pads (4) and anti-rattle clips (3) from the adapter (2)—Front brakes

5. Remove the brake pads from the caliper adapter.
6. Remove the anti-rattle clips from the caliper adapter.

To install:

7. Clean all of the anti-rattle clip mounting surfaces on the brake caliper adapter.
8. Install new anti-rattle clips into the caliper adapter.
9. Install the brake pads onto the caliper adapter.
10. Install the caliper on the caliper adapter and tighten the slide bolts to 32 ft. lbs. (44 Nm).
11. Install the front wheel.
12. Lower the vehicle.
13. Pump the brake pedal several times until a firm pedal is obtained in order to properly seat the pads.
14. Refill the brake fluid reservoir to the proper level.

BRAKES

✳ CAUTION

Dust and dirt accumulating on brake parts during normal use may contain asbestos fibers from production or aftermarket brake linings. Breathing excessive concentrations of asbestos fibers can cause serious bodily harm. Exercise care when servicing brake parts. Do not sand or grind brake lining unless equipment used is designed to contain the dust residue. Do not clean brake parts with compressed air or by dry brushing. Cleaning should be done by dampening the brake components with a fine mist of water, then wiping the brake components clean with a dampened cloth. Dispose of cloth and all residue containing asbestos fibers in an impermeable container with the appropriate label. Follow practices prescribed by the Occupational Safety and Health Administration (OSHA) and the Environmental Protection Agency (EPA) for the handling, processing, and disposing of dust or debris that may contain asbestos fibers.

BRAKE CALIPER

REMOVAL & INSTALLATION

1. Raise and safely support the vehicle.

2. Remove the rear wheel.
3. Siphon a small amount of brake fluid from the master cylinder reservoir.
4. Insert a small prybar through the caliper opening and pry the caliper cover (using the outboard brake pad) to bottom the piston in the caliper bore.
5. Remove the brake hose banjo bolt and discards the washers.
6. Remove the caliper slide pins.
7. Remove the rear caliper from the anchor.
8. Remove the brake pads from the caliper, if necessary.

To install:
9. Install the brake pads to the caliper, if removed.
10. Clean the slide pins of any debris and lightly lubricate them with silicon grease.
11. Install the caliper to the anchor and tighten the slide pin bolts to 18 ft. lbs. (25 Nm).

✳ WARNING

Verify the brake hose is not twisted or kinked before fully tighten the banjo bolt.

12. Install the brake hose with new gasket washers and tighten the banjo bolt to 23 ft. lbs. (31 Nm).
13. Fill and bleed the brake system.
14. Install the rear tire.
15. Lower the vehicle.

DISC BRAKE PADS

REMOVAL & INSTALLATION

1. Raise and safely support the vehicle.
2. Remove the rear wheel.
3. Siphon a small amount of brake fluid from the master cylinder reservoir.
4. Insert a small prybar through the caliper opening and pry the caliper cover (using the outboard brake pad) to bottom the piston in the caliper bore.
5. Remove the caliper slide bolts.
6. Remove the caliper from the anchor.

✳ WARNING

Support the brake caliper with mechanics wire. Do not let the caliper hang by the brake hose.

7. Remove the brake pads from the caliper.

To install:
8. Install the brake pads onto the caliper.
9. Lubricate the slide pin bolts with grease provided with the brake pads, or suitable silicon grease equivalent.
10. Install the caliper on the anchor and tighten the slide pin bolts to 18 ft. lbs. (25 Nm).
11. Install the rear wheel.
12. Pump the brake pedal several times until a firm pedal is obtained in order to properly seat the pads.
13. Refill the brake fluid reservoir to the proper level.

BRAKES

PARKING BRAKE CABLES

ADJUSTMENT

Parking brake cable adjustment is controlled by an automatic tensioner mechanism. The only adjustment possible is to the parking brake shoes using the star wheel adjuster. See Parking Brake Shoes.

PARKING BRAKE SHOES

REMOVAL & INSTALLATION

See Figures 4 and 5.

1. Remove and safely support the vehicle.
2. Remove the rear wheel.
3. Remove caliper mounting bolts to remove the caliper assembly.

✳ WARNING

Support the brake caliper with mechanics wire. Do not let the caliper hang by the brake hose.

4. Remove the rubber access plug from the back of the disc brake support plate.
5. If it is necessary to retract the parking brake shoes, use a suitable brake adjuster tool. Position the tool at the top of the star wheel and rotate the wheel.
6. Remove the rotor from the wheel hub.
7. Remove the axle shaft from the rear differential.
8. Remove the shoe to shoe return spring with needle nose pliers & then remove the adjuster.
9. Remove the shoe to shoe return spring with brake pliers.

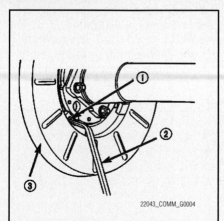

22043_COMM_G0004

Fig. 4 Remove the rubber access plug (1) from the support plate (3) and use a brake adjuster tool (2) to retract the parking brake shoes.

10. Remove the shoe hold-down clips and pins. The clips are held in place by a pin which fits in clip notch. Remove the clips as follows:

a. Push clip ends together and slide clip until head of pin clears narrow part of notch.

b. Remove the clip and pin.

11. Remove the shoes off the actuator lever for the park brake then remove the shoes.

To install:

12. Install the park brake shoes onto the actuator lever.

13. Install shoes on support plate with hold down clips and pins. Be sure shoes are properly engaged in the park brake actuator lever.

14. Install the return spring.

15. Lubricate and install adjuster screw assembly. Be sure notched ends of screw assembly are properly seated on shoes and that star wheel is aligned with access hole in the support plate.

16. Install shoe to shoe adjuster spring. Needle nose pliers can be used to connect spring to each shoe.

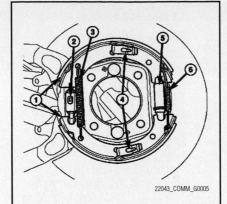

22043_COMM_G0005

Fig. 5 Remove the return springs (6,3), adjuster (5), hold-down clips (4) to remove the shoes (1) from the actuator lever (2).

17. install the rear axle shaft.

18. Install the brake rotor.

19. Install the brake caliper and tighten the mounting bolts to 32 ft. lbs. (44 Nm).

20. Install the rear wheel.

21. Adjust the parking brake shoes as follows:

a. Ensure parking brake lever is fully released.

b. Raise the vehicle so rear wheels can be rotated freely.

c. Remove the plug from each access hole in brake support plates.

d. Loosen parking brake cable adjustment nut until there is slack in front cable.

e. Insert adjusting tool through support plate access hole and engage tool in teeth of adjusting screw star wheel.

f. Rotate adjuster screw star wheel (move tool handle upward) until slight drag can be felt when wheel is rotated.

g. Push and hold adjuster lever away from star wheel with thin screwdriver.

h. Back off adjuster screw star wheel until brake drag is eliminated.

i. Repeat the adjustment at opposite wheel. Be sure adjustment is equal at both wheels.

j. Install support plate access hole plugs.

k. Lower the vehicle.

l. Depress park brake lever and make sure park brakes hold the vehicle stationary.

m. Release park brake lever.

CHASSIS ELECTRICAL

AIR BAG (SUPPLEMENTAL RESTRAINT SYSTEM)

GENERAL INFORMATION

※※ CAUTION

These vehicles are equipped with an air bag system. The system must be disarmed before performing service on, or around, system components, the steering column, instrument panel components, wiring and sensors. Failure to follow the safety precautions and the disarming procedure could result in accidental air bag deployment, possible injury and unnecessary system repairs.

SERVICE PRECAUTIONS

Disconnect and isolate the battery negative cable before beginning any airbag system component diagnosis, testing, removal, or installation procedures. Allow system capacitor to discharge for two minutes before beginning any component service. This will disable the airbag system. Failure to disable the airbag system may result in accidental airbag deployment, personal injury, or death.

Do not place an intact undeployed airbag face down on a solid surface. The airbag will propel into the air if accidentally deployed and may result in personal injury or death.

When carrying or handling an undeployed airbag, the trim side (face) of the airbag should be pointing towards the body to minimize possibility of injury if accidental deployment occurs. Failure to do this may result in personal injury or death.

Replace airbag system components with OEM replacement parts. Substitute parts may appear interchangeable, but internal differences may result in inferior occupant protection. Failure to do so may result in occupant personal injury or death.

Wear safety glasses, rubber gloves, and long sleeved clothing when cleaning powder residue from vehicle after an airbag deployment. Powder residue emitted from a deployed airbag can cause skin irritation. Flush affected area with cool water if irritation is experienced. If nasal or throat irritation is experienced, exit the vehicle for fresh air until the irritation ceases. If irritation continues, see a physician.

Do not use a replacement airbag that is not in the original packaging. This may result in improper deployment, personal injury, or death.

The factory installed fasteners, screws and bolts used to fasten airbag components have a special coating and are specifically designed for the airbag system. Do not use substitute fasteners. Use only original equipment fasteners listed in the parts catalog when fastener replacement is required.

During, and following, any child restraint anchor service, due to impact event or vehicle repair, carefully inspect all mounting hardware, tether straps, and anchors for proper installation, operation, or damage. If a child restraint anchor is found damaged in any way, the anchor must be replaced. Failure to do this may result in personal injury or death.

Deployed and non-deployed airbags may or may not have live pyrotechnic material within the airbag inflator.

Do not dispose of driver/passenger/curtain airbags or seat belt tensioners unless you are sure of complete deployment. Refer to the Hazardous Substance Control System for proper disposal.

Dispose of deployed airbags and tensioners consistent with state, provincial, local, and federal regulations.

After any airbag component testing or service, do not connect the battery negative cable. Personal injury or death may result if the system test is not performed first.

If the vehicle is equipped with the Occupant Classification System (OCS), do not connect the battery negative cable before performing the OCS Verification Test using the scan tool and the appropriate diagnostic information. Personal injury or death may result if the system test is not performed properly.

Never replace both the Occupant Restraint Controller (ORC) and the Occupant Classification Module (OCM) at the same time. If both require replacement, replace one, then perform the Airbag System test before replacing the other.

Both the ORC and the OCM store Occupant Classification System (OCS) calibration data, which they transfer to one another when one of them is replaced. If both are replaced at the same time, an irreversible fault will be set in both modules and the OCS may malfunction and cause personal injury or death.

If equipped with OCS, the Seat Weight Sensor is a sensitive, calibrated unit and must be handled carefully. Do not drop or handle roughly. If dropped or damaged, replace with another sensor. Failure to do so may result in occupant injury or death.

If equipped with OCS, the front passenger seat must be handled carefully as well. When removing the seat, be careful when setting on floor not to drop. If dropped, the sensor may be inoperative, could result in occupant injury, or possibly death.

If equipped with OCS, when the passenger front seat is on the floor, no one should sit in the front passenger seat. This uneven force may damage the sensing ability of the seat weight sensors. If sat on and damaged, the sensor may be inoperative, could result in occupant injury, or possibly death.

DISARMING THE SYSTEM

Disconnect and isolate the negative battery cable. Wait two minutes for the system capacitor to discharge before servicing the vehicle.

ARMING THE SYSTEM

Reconnect the negative battery cable.

CLOCKSPRING CENTERING

See Figure 6.

1. Place the front wheels in the straight-ahead position.
2. Remove the Steering Control Module (SCM) from the steering column.
3. Hold the SCM in one hand so that it is oriented as it would be when it is installed on the steering column.

4. Use your other hand to rotate the clockspring rotor counterclockwise to the end of its travel. Do not apply excessive torque.
5. From the end of the counterclockwise travel, rotate the rotor about three turns clockwise. Turn the rotor slightly clockwise or counterclockwise as necessary so that the clockspring airbag pigtail wires and connector receptacles are at the top and the holes for the clockspring locking pin are in alignment.
6. The clockspring is now centered. Secure the clockspring rotor to the SCM case to maintain clockspring centering until the SCM is reinstalled on the steering column.
7. The front wheels should still be in the straight-ahead position. Reinstall the SCM onto the steering column

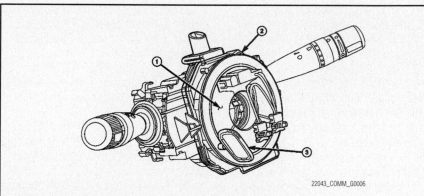

22043_COMM_G0006

Fig. 6 The steering control module (SCM) (2) must be removed to install the clockspring (1). Do not remove the locking pin (3) until the SCM is installed on the steering column.

DRIVETRAIN

AUTOMATIC TRANSMISSION ASSEMBLY

REMOVAL & INSTALLATION

NAG1 (3.7L Models)

See Figure 7.

1. Disconnect the negative battery cable.
2. Raise and safely support the vehicle.
3. Remove the front and rear drive-shafts.
4. Remove the starter.

➡**It is not necessary to disconnect the starter motor wires.**

5. Remove the structural cover by removing the mounting bolts.
6. Rotate the crankshaft in clockwise direction until the torque converter bolts are accessible. Then remove bolts one at a time. Rotate crankshaft with socket wrench on dampener bolt.

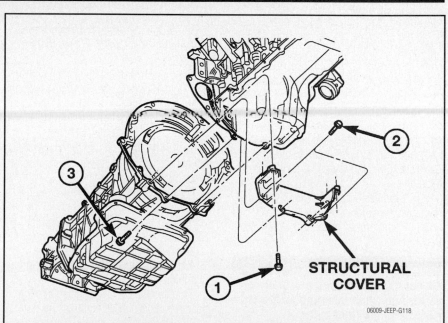

STRUCTURAL COVER

06009-JEEP-G118

Fig. 7 Structural cover and mounting bolts (1,2,3)—3.7L Commander w/NAG1

7. Disconnect the gearshift cable from the transmission manual valve lever.

8. Remove the shift cable from the gearshift cable bracket.

9. Disconnect the 13-pin plug connector. Turn bayonet lock of guide bushing counterclockwise.

10. Remove the 13-pin connector from the transmission.

11. Disconnect the transmission fluid cooler lines at the transmission.

12. Disconnect the transmission vent hose from the transmission.

13. Remove the bolts holding the transmission fill tube to the transmission.

14. Support rear of engine with safety stand or jack.

15. Raise transmission slightly with service jack to relieve load on crossmember and supports.

16. Remove bolts securing rear support and cushion to transmission crossmember.

17. Remove bolts attaching crossmember to frame and remove crossmember.

18. Remove all remaining bolts holding the engine to the transmission. Note the location of any wiring harness clips.

19. Carefully work transmission and torque converter assembly rearward off engine block dowels.

20. Hold torque converter in place during transmission removal.

21. Lower transmission and remove assembly from under the vehicle.

22. To remove torque converter, carefully slide torque converter out of the transmission.

To install:

23. Check torque converter hub and hub drive flats for sharp edges burrs, scratches, or nicks. Polish the hub and flats with 320/400 grit paper and crocus cloth if necessary. The hub must be smooth to avoid damaging pump seal at installation.

24. If a replacement transmission is being installed, transfer any components necessary, such as the manual shift lever and shift cable bracket, from the original transmission onto the replacement transmission.

25. Lubricate oil pump seal lip with transmission fluid.

26. Place torque converter in position on transmission.

❋❋ WARNING

Do not damage oil pump seal or converter hub while inserting torque converter into the front of the transmission.

27. Align torque converter to oil pump seal opening.

28. Insert torque converter hub into oil pump.

29. While pushing torque converter inward, rotate converter until converter is fully seated in the oil pump gears.

30. Check converter seating with a scale and straightedge. Surface of converter lugs should be at least 19mm (¾ in.) to rear of straightedge when converter is fully seated.

31. If necessary, temporarily secure converter with C-clamp attached to the converter housing.

32. Check condition of converter drive plate. Replace the plate if cracked, distorted or damaged. Also be sure transmission dowel pins are seated in engine block and protrude far enough to hold transmission in alignment.

33. Apply a light coating of Mopar® High Temp Grease to the torque converter hub pocket in the rear pocket of the engine's crankshaft.

34. Raise transmission and align the torque converter with the drive plate and the transmission converter housing with the engine block.

35. Move transmission forward. Then raise, lower, or tilt transmission to align the converter housing with the engine block dowels.

36. Carefully work transmission forward and over engine block dowels until converter hub is seated in crankshaft. Verify that no wires, or the transmission vent hose, have become trapped between the engine block and the transmission.

37. Install two bolts to attach the transmission to the engine.

38. Install remaining torque converter housing to engine bolts. Tighten to 29 ft. lbs. (36 Nm).

39. Install rear transmission crossmember. Tighten crossmember to frame bolts to 50 ft. lbs. (68 Nm).

40. Install rear support to transmission. Tighten bolts to 35 ft. lbs. (47 Nm).

41. Lower transmission onto crossmember and install bolts attaching transmission mount to crossmember. Tighten clevis bracket to crossmember bolts to 35 ft. lbs. (47 Nm). Tighten the clevis bracket to rear support bolt to 50 ft. lbs. (68 Nm).

42. Remove engine support fixture.

43. Install the engine to transmission structural cover.

44. Connect the gearshift cable to the gearshift cable bracket and transmission.

45. Check O-ring on plug connector, and replace if necessary.

46. Install the plug connector into the guide bushing. Turn bayonet lock of guide bushing clockwise to connect plug connector.

❋❋ WARNING

It is essential that correct length bolts be used to attach the converter to the drive plate. Bolts that are too long will damage the clutch surface inside the converter.

47. Install all torque converter-to-drive plate bolts by hand.

48. Verify the torque converter is pulled flush up to the drive plate. Tighten bolts to 30 ft. lbs. (42 Nm).

49. Install the starter motor.

50. Install the transmission fill tube.

51. Connect the cooler lines to transmission.

52. Align and connect drive shafts.

53. Adjust gearshift cable if necessary.

54. Lower the vehicle.

55. Connect negative battery cable.

56. Fill the transmission with the appropriate fluid to the correct level.

57. Start the engine, check for leaks and verify proper transmission operation.

545RFE (4.7L & 5.7L Models)

See Figures 8 through 11.

1. Disconnect the negative battery cable.

2. Raise and safely support the vehicle.

3. Remove the front and rear driveshafts.

4. Remove the engine to transmission structural cover.

5. Remove the exhaust support bracket from the rear of the transmission.

6. Disconnect and lower or remove any necessary exhaust components.

7. Rotate the crankshaft in clockwise direction until converter bolts are accessible. Then remove bolts one at a time. Rotate crankshaft with socket wrench on dampener bolt.

8. Disconnect wires from solenoid and pressure switch assembly, input and output speed sensors, and line pressure sensor.

9. Disconnect the gearshift cable from transmission manual valve lever.

10. Remove the clip securing the transfer case shift cable into the cable support bracket.

11. Remove the transfer case assembly from the transmission.

12. Remove the engine oil pan-to-transmission mounting bolts, 5.7L engine only.

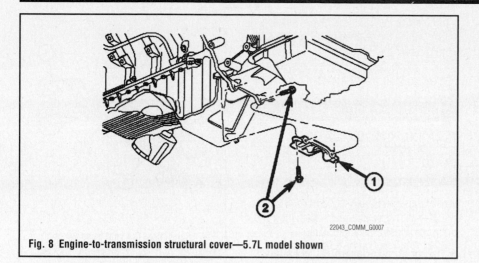

Fig. 8 Engine-to-transmission structural cover—5.7L model shown

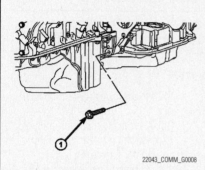

Fig. 9 Remove the engine oil pan-to-transmission mounting bolts—5.7L engine only.

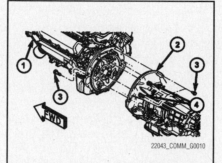

Fig. 11 Remove any remaining bolts (3,4) holding the transmission (2) to the engine (1).

13. Remove the bolt holding the transmission fill tube to the transmission and remove the fill tube and dipstick.

14. Disconnect the transmission fluid cooler lines at the transmission fittings and clips.

15. Disconnect the transmission vent hose from the transmission.

16. Support rear of engine with safety stand or jack.

17. Raise the transmission slightly with service jack to relieve load on crossmember and supports.

18. Remove bolts securing rear support and cushion to transmission and crossmember.

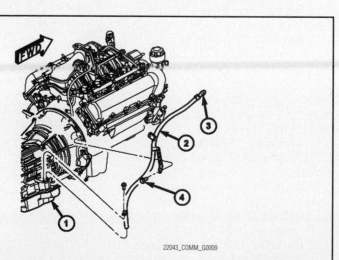

Fig. 10 Remove the bolt (4) holding the fill tube (2) to the transmission (1). Remove the fill tube and dipstick (3) assembly—545RFE transmission shown

19. Remove bolts attaching crossmember to frame and remove crossmember.

20. Remove all remaining transmission-to-engine bolts.

21. Carefully work transmission and torque converter assembly rearward off engine block dowels.

22. Hold torque converter in place during transmission removal.

23. Lower transmission and remove assembly from under the vehicle.

24. In order to remove torque converter, carefully slide the torque converter out of the transmission.

To install:

25. Check torque converter hub and hub drive flats for sharp edges burrs, scratches, or nicks. Polish the hub and flats with 320/400 grit paper and crocus cloth if necessary. Verify that the converter hub O-ring is properly installed and is free of any debris. The hub must be smooth to avoid damaging pump seal at installation.

26. If a replacement transmission is being installed, transfer any components necessary, such as the manual shift lever and shift cable bracket, from the original transmission onto the replacement transmission.

27. Lubricate oil pump seal lip with transmission fluid.

28. Align converter and oil pump.

29. Carefully insert converter in oil pump. Then rotate converter back and forth until fully seated in pump gears.

30. Check converter seating with steel scale and straightedge. Surface of converter lugs should be at least 13mm (½ in.) to rear of straightedge when converter is fully seated.

31. Temporarily secure converter with C-clamp.

32. Position transmission on jack and secure it with chains.

33. Check condition of converter drive plate. Replace the plate if cracked, distorted or damaged.

➡Be sure transmission dowel pins are seated in engine block and protrude far enough to hold transmission in alignment.

34. Apply a light coating of Mopar® High Temp Grease to the torque converter hub pocket in the rear pocket of the engine's crankshaft.

35. Raise transmission and align the torque converter with the drive plate and the transmission converter housing with the engine block.

36. Move transmission forward. Then raise, lower, or tilt transmission to align the converter housing with the engine block dowels.

37. Carefully work transmission forward and over engine block dowels until converter hub is seated in crankshaft. Verify that no wires, or the transmission vent hose, have become trapped between the engine block and the transmission.

38. Install two bolts to attach the transmission to the engine.

39. Install remaining torque converter housing to engine bolts. Tighten to 50 ft. lbs. (68 Nm).

40. Install the left and right side oil pan-to-transmission bolts and tighten to 40 ft. lbs. (54 Nm), 5.7L engines only.

41. Connect the cooler lines to transmission.

42. Install the transmission fill tube.

43. Install rear transmission crossmember. Tighten crossmember to frame bolts to 50 ft. lbs. (68 Nm).

44. Install rear support to transmission. Tighten bolts to 35 ft. lbs. (47 Nm).

45. Lower transmission onto crossmember and install bolts attaching transmission mount to crossmember.

46. Tighten clevis bracket to crossmember bolts to 35 ft. lbs. (47 Nm). Tighten the clevis bracket to rear support bolt to 50 ft. lbs. (68 Nm).

47. Remove engine support fixture.

48. Install new plastic retainer grommet on any shift cable that was disconnected. Grommets should not be reused. Use pry tool to remove rod from grommet and cut away old grommet. Use pliers to snap new grommet into cable and to snap grommet onto lever.

49. Connect the gearshift cable to transmission.

50. Connect wires to solenoid and pressure switch assembly connector, input and output speed sensors, and line pressure sensor. Be sure transmission harnesses are properly routed.

➡**It is essential that correct length bolts be used to attach the converter to the drive plate. Bolts that are too long will damage the clutch surface inside the converter.**

51. Verify the torque converter is pulled flush up to the drive plate. Tighten bolts to 270 inch lbs. (31 Nm).

52. Install the structural dust cover onto the transmission and the engine.

53. Install the transfer case.

54. Install the starter.

55. Install any exhaust components that were removed for access.

56. Install the front and rear driveshafts.

57. Adjust the gearshift cable if necessary.

58. Lower the vehicle.

59. Fill the transmission with the appropriate fluid to the correct level.

TRANSFER CASE ASSEMBLY

REMOVAL & INSTALLATION

NV140

See Figure 12.

1. Raise and safely support the vehicle.

2. Remove transfer case drain plug and drain the transfer case lubricant.

➡**Do not allow drive shafts to hang at attached end. Damage to joint can result.**

3. Remove the front and rear driveshafts.

4. Support the transmission with jack stand.

5. Remove rear crossmember and skid plate, if equipped.

6. Disconnect transfer case vent hose.

7. Support transfer case with transmission jack and secure with chains.

8. Remove the nuts attaching transfer case to transmission.

9. Pull transfer case and jack rearward to disengage transfer case.

10. Remove transfer case from under vehicle.

To install:

11. Mount transfer case on a transmission jack.

12. Secure transfer case to jack with chains.

13. Position transfer case under vehicle.

14. Align transfer case and transmission shafts and install transfer case onto the transmission.

15. Install and tighten transfer case attaching nuts to 26 ft. lbs .(35 Nm).

16. Connect front and rear drive shafts. Torque the front driveshaft-to-transfer case bolts to 24 ft. lbs. (32 Nm). Torque the rear driveshaft-to-transfer case bolts to 80 ft. lbs. (108 Nm).

17. Fill transfer case with correct fluid. Check transmission fluid level. Correct as necessary.

18. Install the transfer case fill plug. Tighten the plug to 15–25 ft. lbs. (20–34 Nm).

19. Install rear crossmember and skid plate, if equipped. Tighten crossmember bolts to 30 ft. lbs. (41 Nm).

20. Remove transmission jack and support stand.

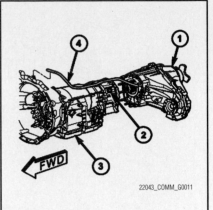

Fig. 12 Remove the vent hose (4) and mounting nuts (2) to remove the transfer case (1) from the transmission (3)— NV140 Transfer Case

22043_COMM_G0011

21. Lower vehicle and verify transfer case shift operation.

NV245

1. Shift the transfer case into NEUTRAL.

2. Raise and safely support the vehicle.

3. Remove the transfer case drain plug and drain transfer case lubricant.

4. Support the transmission with suitable jack stand.

5. Remove rear crossmember and skid plate, if equipped.

6. Disconnect front driveshaft from transfer case at companion flange. Remove rear driveshaft from vehicle.

➡**Do not allow driveshafts to hang at attached end. Damage to the joint can result.**

7. Disconnect the transfer case shift motor and mode sensor connector.

8. Disconnect the transfer case vent hose.

9. Support the transfer case with a suitable transmission jack.

10. Secure the transfer case to the jack with chains.

11. Remove the mounting nuts attaching transfer case to transmission.

12. Pull the transfer case and jack rearward to disengage transfer case.

13. Remove the transfer case from under the vehicle.

To install:

14. Mount the transfer case on a transmission jack.

15. Secure the transfer case to jack with chains.

16. Position the transfer case under vehicle.

17. Align the transfer case and transmission shafts and install transfer case onto transmission.

18. Install and tighten transfer case attaching nuts to 26 ft. lbs. (35 Nm).

19. Connect the transfer case vent hose to the transfer case.

20. Install the rear crossmember and skid plate, if equipped.

21. Remove the transmission jack and support stand.

22. Connect the front and rear driveshafts. Torque the front driveshaft-to-transfer case bolts to 24 ft. lbs. (32 Nm). Torque the rear driveshaft-to-transfer case bolts to 80 ft. lbs. (108 Nm).

23. Fill the transfer case with appropriate fluid to the correct level.

24. Install the transfer case fill plug and tighten to 15–25 ft. lbs. (20–34 Nm).

25. Connect the shift motor and mode sensor wiring connector.

26. Lower vehicle and verify transfer case shift operation.

FRONT AXLE TUBE BEARING

REMOVAL & INSTALLATION

See Figures 13 through 15.

1. Raise and safely support the vehicle.
2. Remove the front wheel.
3. Remove the axle shaft.
4. Remove the axle shaft tube seal with Seal Remover Tool 7794-A and a slide hammer.
5. Install axle bearing remover tool C-4660-A into the axle bearing in the axle tube and tighten the remover nut.
6. Install the Bearing Receiver C-4660-A washer and nut on the remover. Tighten the nut and draw the bearing into the receiver.

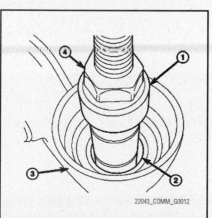

Fig. 13 Install the bearing remover tool (1) into the axle bearing (2) in the axle tube (3) and tighten the remover nut (4).

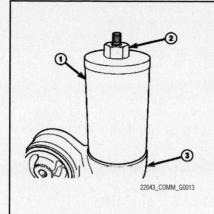

Fig. 14 Install the bearing receiver (1), washer and nut (2). Tighten the nut to draw the bearing from the axle tube (3).

To install:

7. Install the axle bearing with Special Tool 5063 and Handle C-4171 or suitable installer tool.
8. Install the axle shaft and seal.
9. Install the front wheel.
10. Lower the vehicle.

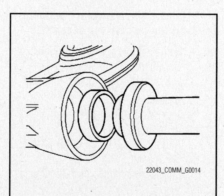

Fig. 15 Drive in the bearing with installer tool—Front Axle

FRONT AXLE SHAFT

REMOVAL & INSTALLATION

See Figure 16.

1. Remove the half shaft from the vehicle.
2. Clean axle seal area.
3. Remove snap ring and O-ring from the axle shaft.
4. Remove axle with Remover Tool 8420A and slide hammer.

To install:

5. Lubricate bearing bore and seal lip with gear lubricant.
6. Install axle shaft and engage shaft into side gear. Push firmly on axle shaft to engage snap ring.

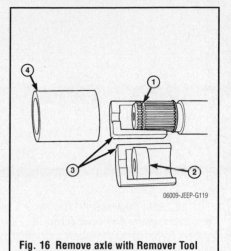

Fig. 16 Remove axle with Remover Tool 8420A and slide hammer

7. Check the differential fluid level and add fluid if necessary.
8. Install half shaft.
9. Install skid plate, if necessary.

FRONT DRIVESHAFT

REMOVAL & INSTALLATION

See Figures 17 through 19.

1. With the vehicle in neutral, raise and safely support the vehicle.
2. Mark a line across the axle pinion flange, driveshaft, flange yoke and transfer case for installation reference.
3. Support the transmission and the transmission crossmember with a suitable jack.
4. Remove the driveshaft from the transfer case flange.
5. Remove the driveshaft from axle pinion flange.

To install:

6. Install the driveshaft with reference marks aligned on companion flanges.

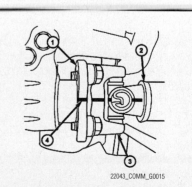

Fig. 17 Matchmark (4) the driveshaft (2) across the pinion flange (1), flange yoke (3) and transfer case.

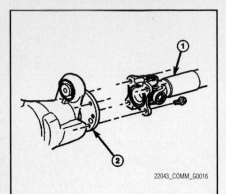

Fig. 18 Install the driveshaft (1) to the companion flange (2)—Front driveshaft

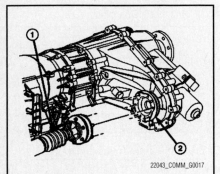

Fig. 19 Then install the driveshaft (1) to the transfer case flange (2)—Front driveshaft

7. Install the driveshaft flange bolts and tighten to 80 ft. lbs. (108 Nm).

8. Install the driveshaft on the transfer case flange.

9. Install the bolts to transfer case flange and tighten to 24 ft. lbs. (32 Nm).

10. Install the transmission crossmember.

FRONT HALFSHAFT

REMOVAL & INSTALLATION

1. Before servicing the vehicle, refer to the precautions section.

2. With vehicle in neutral, position vehicle on hoist.

3. Remove half shaft hub/bearing nut.

4. Remove wheel speed sensor from hub/bearing.

5. Remove brake calipers bolts and remove calipers from caliper adapters.

6. Remove lower stabilizer link bolt from control arm.

7. Remove outer tie rod end nuts and separate tie rods from knuckles with the proper tool.

8. Remove upper ball joint nuts and separate ball joints from knuckles with the proper tool.

9. Remove shock clevis bolt and nut from lower control arm

10. Lean the knuckle out and push half shaft out of the hub/bearing.

11. Pry half shafts from axle/axle tube with pry bar.

To install:

12. Install half shaft on the axle and through the hub/bearing. Verify halfshaft has engaged.

13. Install shock clevis on lower control arm and tighten nut to 60 ft. lbs. (81 Nm).

14. Install upper control arm on knuckle. Torque to 55 ft. lbs. (75 Nm).

15. Install tie rod end on knuckle. Torque to 70 ft. lbs. (95 Nm).

16. Install stabilizer link on lower control arm. Torque to 85 ft. lbs. (115 Nm).

17. Install caliper on caliper adapter.

18. Install wheel speed sensor on the hub/bearing.

19. Install half shaft hub/bearing nut and tighten to 100 ft. lbs. (135 Nm).

CV-JOINTS OVERHAUL

CV Boot, Outer

➡ **CV joint is serviced with the shaft, the boot can be serviced separately**

1. Remove inner CV boot and joint.

2. Cut outer CV boot clamps .

3. Cut boot off CV housing and shaft .

To install:

1. Clean the CV joint then apply new grease to the joint.

2. Slid the new boot on to the shaft and on the CV housing .

3. Install boot clamps in original locations.

4. Install inner CV joint and boot,

CV Joint/Boot, Inner

1. Clamp shaft in a vise (with soft jaws) and support C/V joint .

2. Remove clamps with a cut-off wheel or grinder.

3. Slide boot down the shaft.

4. Remove lubricant from housing to expose the C/V snap ring and remove snap ring.

5. Remove bearings from the cage.

6. Rotate cage 30° and slide cage off the inner race and down the shaft.

7. Remove spread inner race snap ring and remove race from the shaft.

8. Remove boot from the shaft and discard.

9. Clean and inspect housing, cage, bearings, housing snap-ring, inner race snap-ring and inner race for wear or damage.

To install:

1. Apply a coat of grease supplied with the joint/boot to the C/V joint components before assembling them.

2. Place new clamps on the new boot and slide boot down the shaft.

3. Slide cage onto the shaft with the small diameter end towards the boot.

4. Install the inner race onto the shaft . Pull on the race to verify snap ring has engaged.

5. Align cage with the inner race and slide over the race.

6. Turn the cage 30° to align the cage windows with the race .

7. Apply grease to the inner race and bearings and install the bearings.

8. Apply grease to the housing bore then install the bearing assembly into the housing .

9. Install the housing snap ring and verify it is seated in the groove.

10. Fill the housing and boot with the remaining grease.

11. Slide the boot onto the C/V housing into it's original position. Ensure boot is not twisted and remove any excess air.

12. Secure both boot clamps with Clamp Installer C-4975A. Place tool on clamp bridge and tighten tool until the jaws of the tool are closed.

FRONT PINION SEAL

REMOVAL & INSTALLATION

See Figures 20 and 21.

1. Remove the front wheels.

2. Push back the brake pads.

3. Remove the front driveshaft.

4. Rotate the pinion with an inch pound torque wrench. Record the torque required to rotate.

5. Mark the installation position of collared nut with respect to drive pinion.

6. Bend the pinion nut lock back with a punch and hammer.

7. Hold the pinion flange with Flange Wrench C-3281and remove the pinion nut.

8. Remove the pinion flange with Puller C-452.

9. Remove the pinion seal with a seal pick.

To install:

10. Install the pinion seal with seal Installer C-3972A and Handle C-4171.

11. Install the pinion flange on pinion with flange Installer 9616. Tap the flange on to the pinion, then thread the installer center bolt on pinion shaft and draw the flange onto the pinion.

12. Install the new pinion collared nut

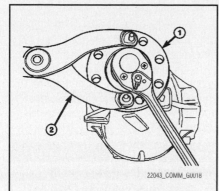

Fig. 20 Hold the flange (1) with Special Tool C-3281 (2) and remove the pinion nut.

and carefully tighten the nut in stages holding flange with flange Wrench C-3281. Check the torque required to rotate after each stage, until the value of torque to rotate recorded during the removal process is exceeded by 4.4 in. lbs. (0.5 Nm).

13. Cut the pinion nut collar.

14. Bend the nut collar so it touches the wall of the slot in the pinion shaft.

15. Connect the driveshaft to pinion flange.

16. Install the front wheels.

17. Operate brake pedal several times until brake pads contact brake discs (so brake pressure builds up).

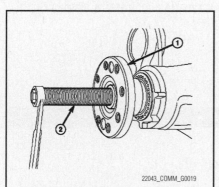

Fig. 21 Install the pinion flange (1) to the pinion using Special Tool 8616 (2)—Front pinion

REAR AXLE HOUSING

REMOVAL & INSTALLATION

1. With vehicle in neutral, raise and safely support the vehicle.

2. Remove the differential cover and drain the fluid.

3. Remove the calipers and rotors.

4. Remove the speed sensors from axle tube flange.

5. Remove the axle flange nuts from axle.

6. Pull the axle shaft and backing plate out of axle tube until axle bearing is exposed.

7. Remove the O-ring from the axle bearing.

8. Remove the axle shaft from axle tube and backing plate.

9. Remove the axle vent hose from axle vent and cover bracket.

10. Remove the propeller shaft.

11. Remove the stabilizer bar clamp from axle.

12. Support the axle with jack.

13. Remove the track bar from axle.

14. Remove the shock absorbers from axle brackets.

15. Remove the upper control arms from axle brackets.

16. Remove the lower control arms from axle brackets.

17. Lower the axle from vehicle and remove coil springs and insulators.

To install:

18. Install coil springs and insulators, then raise the axle into place.

19. Install the lower control arms to the axle brackets.

20. Install the upper control arms to the axle brackets.

21. Install the shock absorbers to the axle brackets.

22. Install the stabilizer bar and clamps to the axle.

23. Install the driveshaft.

24. Install the axle vent hose to the axle vent and cover bracket.

25. Install the axle shaft into the axle tube and backing plate with a new o-ring on the axle.

26. Slip the O-ring through the backing plate, then push the axle through the backing plate until the bearing is exposed.

27. Install the O-ring axle bearing.

28. Push the axle into axle tube.

29. Install the axle flange nuts and tighten to 88 ft. lbs. (119 Nm).

30. Install the speed sensors.

31. Install the calipers and rotors.

32. Install the differential cover, fill differential and install fill plug.

REAR AXLE SHAFT, BEARING & SEAL

REMOVAL & INSTALLATION

See Figure 22.

1. With the vehicle in neutral, raise and safely support the vehicle.

2. Remove the calipers and rotors.

3. Tap the axle end plug loose from the axle flange with a hammer and punch. Pull the plug out of axle flange.

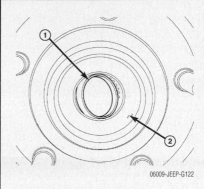

Fig. 22 Tap the axle end plug loose from the axle flange.

4. Remove the speed sensors from axle tube flange.

5. Remove the axle flange nuts from axle.

6. Pull the axle shaft and backing plate out of axle tube until axle bearing is exposed.

7. Remove O-ring from the axle bearing.

8. Slide axle shaft from axle tube and backing plate.

9. Tap the axle shaft out of the bearing and axle flange through the plug hole with a hammer and brass drift.

To install:

10. Tap the axle shaft into through axle bearing into the axle flange.

11. Install the axle shaft into axle tube and backing plate with new O-ring on axle.

12. Slip the O-ring through backing plate, then push the axle through backing plate until the bearing is exposed.

13. Install the O-ring axle bearing.

14. Push the axle into the axle tube.

15. Install the axle flange nuts and tighten to 88 ft. lbs. (119 Nm).

16. Install the speed sensors in the axle tube flange.

17. Coat the new axle flange plug with Mopar® Stud N' Bearing Mount Adhesive, or equivalent, and install the plug.

18. Install the calipers and rotors.

19. Lower the vehicle.

REAR DRIVESHAFT

REMOVAL & INSTALLATION

1. With the vehicle in neutral, raise and safely support the vehicle.

2. Matchmark the driveshaft in relation to the pinion flange and transmission/transfer case flanges for installation reference.

3. Remove the driveshaft from axle pinion flange.

4. Remove the driveshaft from vehicle transfer case flange or transmission flange.

5. Remove the driveshaft from vehicle.

To install:

6. Install the driveshaft on the transfer case or transmission with the reference marks aligned. Install the flange bolts and tighten to 80 ft. lbs. (108 Nm).

7. Install the driveshaft on the pinion flange with the reference marks aligned. Install the flange bolts and tighten to 80 ft. lbs. (108 Nm).

8. Lower the vehicle.

REAR PINION SEAL

REMOVAL & INSTALLATION

See Figure 23.

1. With the vehicle in neutral, raise and safely support the vehicle.

2. Mark a reference line across the axle flange and driveshaft flange.

3. Remove the driveshaft

4. Remove the brake calipers and rotors to prevent any drag.

5. Rotate the pinion flange three or four times and verify flange rotates smoothly.

6. Measure the torque needed to rotate the pinion flange with an inch pound torque wrench. Record the reading for installation reference.

7. Hold the pinion flange with Wrench C-3281 and remove pinion nut and washer.

8. Remove the flange with two jaw puller.

9. Remove the pinion seal with a seal pick or slide-hammer mounted screw.

To install:

10. Apply a light coating of gear lubricant on the lip of pinion seal.

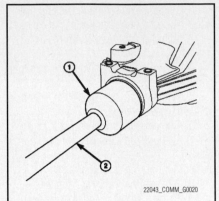

Fig. 23 Install a new pinion seal with Special Tool C-3972A (1) and Handle C-4171 (2)—Rear Pinion

22043_COMM_G0020

11. Install new pinion seal with Installer C-3972A and Handle C-4171.

12. Install flange on the end of the shaft with the reference marks aligned.

13. Install flange on pinion shaft with Installer C-3718 and Wrench C-3281.

14. Install pinion washer and a new pinion nut. The convex side of the washer must face outward.

✳✳ WARNING

Do not exceed the minimum tightening torque when installing the companion flange retaining nut at this point. Failure to follow these instructions can damage the collapsible spacer or bearings.

15. Hold flange with Wrench C-3281 and tighten pinion nut to 210 ft. lbs. (285 Nm). Rotate pinion several revolutions to ensure bearing rollers are seated.

16. Rotate the pinion flange with an inch pound torque wrench. Rotating torque should be equal to the reading recorded during removal plus an additional 5 inch lbs. (0.56 Nm).

✳✳ WARNING

Never loosen the pinion nut to decrease pinion bearing rotating torque and never exceed specified preload torque. If rotating torque is exceeded, a new collapsible spacer must be installed. Failure to follow these instructions can damage the collapsible spacer or bearings.

17. If the rotating torque is low use Wrench C-3281 to hold the flange and tighten the pinion nut in 60 inch lbs. (6.8 Nm) increments until the proper rotating torque is achieved.

➡ **The seal replacement is unacceptable if final pinion nut torque is less than 210 ft. lbs. (285 Nm).**

➡ **The bearing rotating torque should be constant during a complete revolution of the pinion. If the rotating torque varies, this indicates a binding condition.**

18. Install the driveshaft.
19. Install the rear brake components.
20. Lower the vehicle.

ENGINE COOLING

ENGINE FAN

REMOVAL & INSTALLATION

3.7L & 4.7L Engines

1. Disconnect the negative battery cable.

2. Disconnect the electric fan connector.

3. Remove the shroud mounting bolts.

4. Remove the fan shroud and fan assembly from vehicle.

5. Remove the fan assembly mounting bolts and remove the fan from the shroud.

To install:

6. Position the fan assembly on shroud.

7. Install the fan-to-fan shroud mounting nuts and tighten to 50 inch lbs. (6 Nm).

8. Position the fan and shroud assembly in vehicle.

9. Install the shroud mounting bolts and tighten to 50 inch lbs. (6 Nm).

10. Connect the electric fan electrical connector.

11. Connect the negative battery cable.

12. Start the engine and check fan operation.

5.7L Engine

1. Disconnect the negative battery cable.

2. Raise and safely support the vehicle.

3. Drain the cooling system.

4. Disconnect the two high pressure lines at hydraulic fan drive. Remove and discard the O-rings from line fittings.

5. Disconnect the low pressure return hose at hydraulic fan drive.

6. Remove the lower shroud mounting bolts.

7. Lower the vehicle.

8. Disconnect the fan control solenoid electrical connector.

9. Disconnect the upper radiator hose.

10. Disconnect the power steering gear output hose and return hose at the cooler.

11. Remove the upper mounting bolts from the shroud.

12. Remove the fan assembly from the vehicle.

To install:

13. Position the fan assembly in vehicle.

14. Install the fan shroud upper mounting bolts. Do not tighten at this time.

15. Install the radiator upper hose onto radiator.

16. Connect the power steering cooler hoses.

17. Raise and safely support the vehicle.

18. Install fan shroud lower mounting bolts and tighten to 50 inch lbs. (6 Nm).

➡When ever the high pressure line fittings are removed from the hydraulic fan drive, the O-rings located on the fittings must be replaced.

19. Lubricate the o-rings on the fittings with power steering fluid then connect the inlet and outlet high pressure lines to fan drive. Tighten the inlet line to 36 ft. lbs. (49 Nm) and tighten the outlet line to 21 ft. lbs. (29 Nm).

20. Connect the low pressure return hose to fan drive.

21. Lower the vehicle.

22. Install the radiator upper hose.

23. Connect the electrical connector for hydraulic fan control solenoid.

24. Tighten the fan shroud upper mounting bolts to 50 inch lbs. (6 Nm).

25. Refill the cooling system to the correct level.

✳✳ WARNING

Do not run the engine with power steering fluid below the full mark in the reservoir. Severe damage to the hydraulic cooling fan or the engine can occur.

26. Refill the power steering fluid reservoir and bleed air from steering system.

27. Start the engine and check for leaks

RADIATOR

REMOVAL & INSTALLATION

1. Disconnect the negative battery cable.

2. Drain the cooling system.

3. Remove the front grille as follows:

    a. Remove the six upper push pins.

    b. Tip the grill forward to remove.

4. Remove the two radiator mounting bolts.

5. Disconnect both transmission cooler lines from radiator.

6. Disconnect the electrical connector for the fan control solenoid.

7. Disconnect the power steering cooler line from the cooler and filter.

8. Disconnect the radiator upper and lower hoses.

9. Disconnect the overflow hose from radiator.

10. Remove the air inlet duct at the grille.

11. The lower part of radiator is equipped with two alignment dowel pins.

They are located on the bottom of radiator tank and fit into rubber grommets. These rubber grommets are pressed into the radiator lower crossmember.

✳✳ WARNING

The air conditioning system (if equipped) is under a constant pressure even with the engine off. Refer to refrigerant warnings in, heating and air conditioning before handling any air conditioning component.

➡The radiator and radiator cooling fan can be removed as an assembly. It is not necessary to remove the cooling fan before removing or installing the radiator.

12. Disconnect the two high pressure fluid lines at the hydraulic fan drive.

13. Disconnect the low pressure return hose at the hydraulic fan drive.

14. Gently lift up and remove radiator from vehicle. Be careful not to scrape the radiator fins against any other component. Also be careful not to disturb the air conditioning condenser (if equipped).

To install:

15. Gently lower the radiator and fan shroud into the vehicle. Guide the two radiator alignment dowels through the holes in the rubber air seals first and then through the A/C support brackets. Continue to guide the alignment dowels into the rubber grommets located in lower radiator crossmember. The holes in the L-shaped brackets (located on bottom of A/C condenser) must be positioned between bottom of rubber air seals and top of rubber grommets.

16. Connect the radiator hoses and hose clamps to the radiator.

➡The tangs on the hose clamps must be positioned straight down.

17. Install the coolant reserve/overflow tank hose at the radiator.

18. Connect both transmission cooler lines at the radiator.

19. Install both radiator mounting bolts.

20. Install the air inlet duct at grille.

21. Attach the electric connector for hydraulic fan control solenoid.

22. Install the grille

23. Connect the two high pressure lines to the hydraulic fan drive. Tighten ½ in. pressure line fitting to 36 ft. lbs. (49 Nm) and the ⅜ in. pressure line fitting to 21 ft. lbs. (29 Nm).

24. Connect the low pressure hose to the hydraulic fan drive. Position the spring clamp.

25. Connect the power steering filter hoses to the filter and install new hose clamps.

26. Rotate the fan blades (by hand) and check for any interference at the fan shroud.

27. Refill the cooling system to the correct level.

28. Refill the power steering reservoir and bleed air from system.

29. Connect the negative battery cable.

30. Start the engine and check for leaks.

THERMOSTAT

REMOVAL & INSTALLATION

3.7L & 4.7L Engines
See Figure 24.

✳✳ WARNING

Do not loosen radiator drain cock with system hot and pressurized. Serious burns from coolant can occur.

➡Do not waste reusable coolant. If the solution is clean, drain coolant into a clean container for reuse. If thermostat is being replaced, be sure that replacement is specified thermostat for vehicle model and engine type.

1. Disconnect the negative battery cable.

2. Drain the cooling system.

3. Raise and safely support the vehicle.

4. Remove the splash shield.

5. Remove the lower radiator hose clamp and lower radiator hose at thermostat housing.

6. Remove the thermostat housing mounting bolts, thermostat housing and thermostat.

To install:

7. Clean mating areas of timing chain cover and thermostat housing.

8. Install the thermostat (spring side down) into recessed machined groove on timing chain cover.

9. Position the thermostat housing on timing chain cover.

10. Install the two housing-to-timing chain cover bolts and tighten to 115 inch lbs. (13 Nm).

✳✳ CAUTION

Housing must be tightened evenly and thermostat must be centered into recessed groove in timing chain cover. If not, it may result in a cracked housing, damaged timing chain cover threads or coolant leaks.

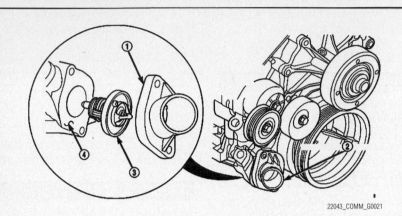

Fig. 24 Exploded view of the thermostat (3) showing the thermostat housing (1,2) location on the engine block (4)—3.7L & 4.7L engines

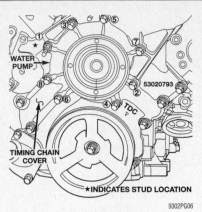

Fig. 26 Water pump tightening sequence—3.7L & 4.7L engines

11. Install the lower radiator hose on thermostat housing.

12. Install the splash shield.

13. Lower the vehicle.

14. Refill the cooling system to the correct level.

15. Connect the negative battery cable.

16. Start the engine and check for leaks.

5.7L Engine

See Figure 25.

> ✳✳ **WARNING**
>
> **Do not loosen radiator drain cock with system hot and pressurized. Serious burns from coolant can occur.**

➡**Do not waste reusable coolant . If solution is clean, drain coolant into a clean container for reuse. If thermostat is being replaced, be sure that replacement is specified thermostat for vehicle model and engine type.**

1. Disconnect the negative battery cable.

2. Drain the cooling system.

3. Remove the radiator hose clamp and radiator hose at the thermostat housing .

4. Remove the thermostat housing mounting bolts , thermostat housing and thermostat.

To install:

5. Position the thermostat and housing on the front cover.

6. Install the thermostat housing bolts and tighten the bolts to 112 inch lbs. (13 Nm).

7. Install the radiator hose onto the thermostat housing.

8. Refill the cooling system to the correct level.

9. Connect the negative battery cable.

10. Start the engine and check for leaks.

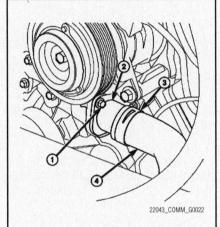

Fig. 25 Exploded view of the thermostat housing (2) and mounting bolts (1), lower radiator hose (4) and hose clamp (3)—5.7L engine

WATER PUMP

REMOVAL & INSTALLATION

3.7L Engine

See Figure 26.

1. Disconnect the negative battery cable.

2. Drain the cooling system.

3. Remove the two fan shroud-to-radiator screws.

4. Disconnect the coolant overflow hose.

5. Remove the accessory drive belt.

6. Remove the lower radiator hose from the water pump.

7. Remove the water pump mounting bolts.

8. Remove the water pump and gasket.

To install:

9. Clean all of the gasket mating surfaces.

10. Install the water pump, using a new gasket, and tighten the mounting bolts in sequence to 40 ft. lbs. (54 Nm).

11. Spin the water pump by hand to ensure the pump impeller does not rub against the timing chain cover.

12. Connect the lower radiator hose to the water pump.

13. Install the accessory drive belt.

14. Reposition the fan shroud and install the two fan shroud-to-radiator screws.

15. Refill the cooling system to the correct level.

16. Connect the negative battery cable.

17. Start the engine and check for leaks.

4.7L Engine

1. Disconnect the negative battery cable.

2. Drain the cooling system.

3. Remove the accessory drive belt.

4. Remove the lower radiator hose from the water pump.

5. Remove the water pump mounting bolts.

6. Remove the water pump and gasket.

To install:

7. Clean all of the gasket mating surfaces.

8. Install the water pump, using a new gasket, and tighten the mounting bolts in sequence to 43 ft. lbs. (58 Nm).

9. Spin the water pump by hand to ensure the pump impeller does not rub against the timing chain cover.

10. Connect the lower radiator hose to the water pump.

11. Install the accessory drive belt.

12. Refill the cooling system to the correct level.

13. Connect the negative battery cable.

14. Start the engine and check for leaks.

5.7L Engine

1. Disconnect the negative battery cable.
2. Drain the cooling system.
3. Remove the accessory drive belt.
4. Remove the fan clutch assembly.
5. Remove the coolant overflow bottle.
6. Disconnect the windshield washer bottle wiring and hose.
7. Remove the fan shroud assembly.
8. Remove the A/C compressor and alternator brace.
9. Remove the idler pulleys.
10. Remove the accessory drive belt tensioner.
11. Disconnect the upper and lower radiator hoses.
12. Disconnect the heater hoses.
13. Remove the water pump mounting bolts and remove the water pump.

To install:

14. Install the water pump and tighten the mounting bolts to 18 ft. lbs. (24 Nm).
15. Connect the heater hoses.
16. Connect the upper and lower radiator hoses.
17. Install the accessory drive belt tensioner.
18. Install the idler pulleys.
19. Install the A/C compress and alternator brace. Tighten the mounting bolts and nuts to 21 ft. lbs. (28 Nm).
20. Install the fan shroud assembly.
21. Connect the windshield washer bottle wiring and hose.
22. Install the coolant overflow bottle.
23. Install the fan clutch assembly.
24. Install the accessory drive belt.
25. Refill the cooling system to the correct level.
26. Connect the negative battery cable.
27. Start the engine and check for leaks.

ENGINE ELECTRICAL

ALTERNATOR

REMOVAL & INSTALLATION

3.7L & 4.7L Engines

See Figure 27.

1. Disconnect the negative battery cable.
2. Remove the accessory drive belt.
3. Unsnap the insulator cap from the B+ terminal and remove the mounting nut. Disconnect the B+ terminal from the alternator.
4. Disconnect the ground wire connector from the rear of the alternator by pushing on the connector tab.
5. Remove the rear vertical mounting bolt and front horizontal mounting bolts.
6. Remove the alternator.

To install:

7. Install the alternator and insert all of the mounting bolts. Tighten all three bolts to 40 ft. lbs. (55 Nm).
8. Snap the ground wire connector to the back of the alternator.
9. Install the B+ terminal eyelet to the output stud. Reinstall the mounting nut and tighten to 108 inch lbs. (12 Nm).
10. Snap the insulator for the B+ terminal back into place.
11. Install the accessory drive belt.
12. Connect the negative battery cable.

5.7L Engines

See Figure 28.

1. Disconnect the negative battery cable.
2. Remove the accessory drive belt.
3. Unsnap the insulator cap from the B+ terminal and remove the mounting nut. Disconnect the B+ terminal from the alternator.

CHARGING SYSTEM

4. Disconnect the ground wire connector from the rear of the alternator by pushing on the connector tab.
5. Remove the alternator mounting bolts.
6. Remove the alternator.

To install:

7. Install the alternator and tighten the mounting bolts to 30 ft. lbs. (41 Nm).
8. Snap the ground wire connector to the back of the alternator.
9. Install the B+ terminal eyelet to the output stud. Reinstall the mounting nut and tighten to 108 inch lbs. (12 Nm).
10. Snap the insulator for the B+ terminal back into place.
11. Install the accessory drive belt.
12. Connect the negative battery cable.

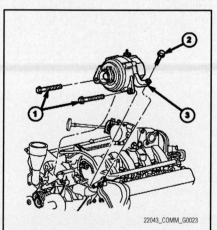

22043_COMM_G0023

Fig. 27 Remove the rear vertical mounting bolt (2) and front horizontal mounting bolts (1) to remove the alternator (3)—3.7L & 4.7L Engines

22043_COMM_G0024

Fig. 28 Disconnect the wiring harness (3) and remove the mounting bolts (1) to remove the alternator (2)—5.7L Engine

FIRING ORDER

See Figures 29 and 30.

IGNITION COIL

REMOVAL & INSTALLATION

See Figures 31 and 32.

An individual ignition coil is used for each spark plug. The coil fits into machined holes in the cylinder head. A mounting stud/nut secures each coil to the top of the intake manifold. The bottom of the coil is equipped with a rubber boot to seal the spark plug to the coil. Inside each rubber boot is a spring. The spring is used for a mechanical contact between the coil and the top of the spark plug. These rubber boots and springs are a permanent part of the coil and are not serviced separately. An O-ring is used to seal the coil at the opening into the cylinder head.

1. Depending on which coil is being removed, the throttle body air intake tube or intake box may need to be removed to gain access to coil.

2. Disconnect electrical connector from coil by pushing downward on release lock on top of connector and pull connector from coil.

3. Clean area at base of coil with compressed air before removal.

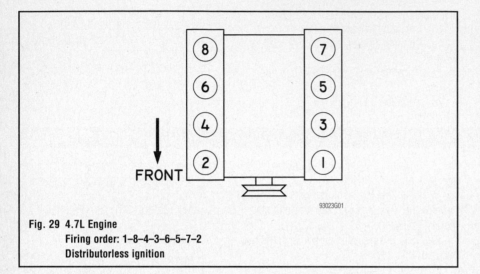

93023G01

Fig. 29 4.7L Engine
   Firing order: 1–8–4–3–6–5–7–2
   Distributorless ignition

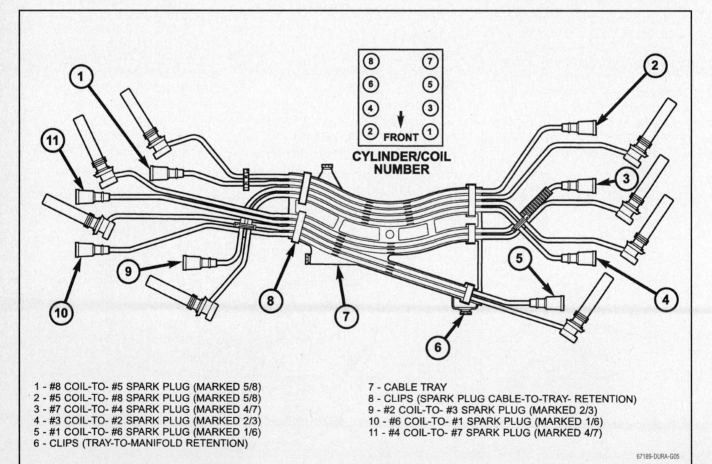

1 - #8 COIL-TO- #5 SPARK PLUG (MARKED 5/8)
2 - #5 COIL-TO- #8 SPARK PLUG (MARKED 5/8)
3 - #7 COIL-TO- #4 SPARK PLUG (MARKED 4/7)
4 - #3 COIL-TO- #2 SPARK PLUG (MARKED 2/3)
5 - #1 COIL-TO- #6 SPARK PLUG (MARKED 1/6)
6 - CLIPS (TRAY-TO-MANIFOLD RETENTION)

7 - CABLE TRAY
8 - CLIPS (SPARK PLUG CABLE-TO-TRAY- RETENTION)
9 - #2 COIL-TO- #3 SPARK PLUG (MARKED 2/3)
10 - #6 COIL-TO- #1 SPARK PLUG (MARKED 1/6)
11 - #4 COIL-TO- #7 SPARK PLUG (MARKED 4/7)

67189-DURA-G05

Fig. 30 5.7L Engine
   Firing order: 1–8–4–3–6–5–7–2
   Distributorless ignition

4. Remove coil mounting nut from mounting stud.

5. Carefully pull up coil from cylinder head opening with a slight twisting action.

6. Remove coil from vehicle

To install:

7. Using compressed air, blow out any dirt or contaminants from around top of spark plug.

8. Clean coil O-ring but do not apply any lubricant.

9. Position ignition coil into cylinder head opening and push onto spark plug. Do this while guiding coil base over mounting stud.

10. Install mounting stud nut and tighten as follows:

　　a. 3.7L & 4.7L Engines: 70 inch lbs. (8 Nm).

　　b. 5.7L Engines: 62 inch lbs. (7 Nm).

11. Connect electrical connector to coil by snapping into position.

12. If necessary, install throttle body air tube or box.

IGNITION TIMING

ADJUSTMENT

Ignition timing is controlled by the Powertrain Control Module (PCM). No adjustment is possible.

SPARK PLUGS

REMOVAL & INSTALLATION

Each individual spark plug is located under each ignition coil. The ignition coil must be removed in order to access the spark plug.

☆☆ WARNING

The 4.7L Engine is equipped with copper core ground electrode spark plugs. They must be replaced with the same type.

1. Remove the ignition coil.

2. Remove the spark plug from the cylinder using a spark plug socket with the appropriate rubber insert.

To install:

3. Start the spark plug by hand and then tighten as follows:

　　a. 3.7L & 4.7L Engines: 20 ft. lbs. (27 Nm)

　　b. 5.7L Engine: 13 ft. lbs. (18 Nm).

4. Install the ignition coil.

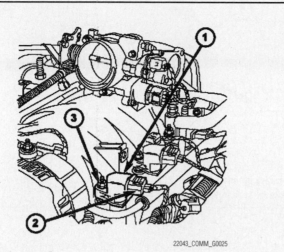

22043_COMM_G0025

Fig. 31 Install the mounting stud nut (3) and connect the electrical connector (2) when installing each ignition coil (1)—4.7L Engine shown

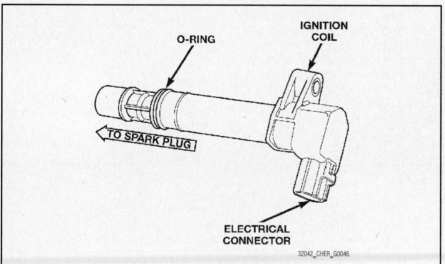

32042_CHER_G0046

Fig. 32 These engines use dedicated, and individually fired, coils for each spark plug. Each coil is mounted directly to the top of each spark plug.

STARTER

REMOVAL & INSTALLATION

3.7L & 4.7L Engines

See Figure 33.

1. Disconnect the negative battery cable.

2. Raise and safely support the vehicle.

3. If equipped with 4WD, remove the front driveshaft.

4. Note: If equipped with 4WD and certain transmissions, a support bracket is used between front axle and side of transmission. Remove 2 support bracket bolts at transmission. Pry support bracket slightly to gain access to lower starter mounting bolt.

5. Remove the two mounting bolts.

6. Move the starter towards front of vehicle far enough for nose of starter pinion housing to clear the housing. Always support the starter during this process, do not let it hang from the wiring harness.

7. Tilt the nose downwards and lower the starter far enough to access and remove the nut that secures the positive battery cable wiring harness connector eyelet to the solenoid battery terminal stud. Do not let starter hang from the wiring harness.

8. Remove the positive battery cable wire harness connector eyelet from the solenoid battery terminal stud.

9. Disconnect the positive battery cable wire harness connector from solenoid terminal connector receptacle.

10. Remove the starter.

To install:

11. Connect the solenoid wire to the starter(snaps on).

12. Position the battery cable to the solenoid stud. Install and tighten battery cable eyelet nut 19 ft. lbs. (25 Nm). Do not allow starter to hang from wire harness.

13. Position the starter to the transmission.

14. Slide the cooler tube bracket into position.

15. Install and tighten both bolts to 50 ft. lbs. (68 Nm).

16. If equipped with 4WD and certain transmissions, a support bracket is used between front axle and side of transmission. Install the two support bracket bolts at transmission.

17. If equipped with 4WD, install the front driveshaft.

18. Lower the vehicle.

19. Connect the negative battery cable.

5.7L Engines

See Figure 34.

1. Disconnect the negative battery cable.

2. Raise and safely support the vehicle.

3. If equipped with 4WD and certain transmissions, a support bracket is used between the front axle and side of the transmission. Remove the two support bracket bolts at transmission. Pry the support bracket slightly to gain access to the lower starter mounting bolt.

4. Remove the two mounting bolts.

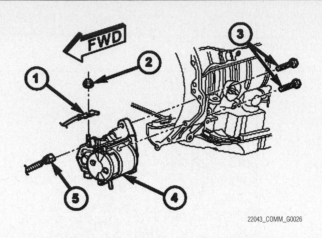

Fig. 33 Remove the mounting bolts (3), positive battery cable (1) and nut (2), and solenoid wire (5) in order to remove the starter (4)—3.7L & 4.7L Engines

5. Move the starter motor towards the front of vehicle far enough for the nose of starter pinion housing to clear the housing. Do not let starter motor hang from wire harness.

6. Tilt the nose downwards and lower starter motor far enough to access and remove nut that secures battery positive cable wire harness connector eyelet to solenoid battery terminal stud. Do not let starter motor hang from wire harness.

7. Remove the positive battery cable wire harness connector eyelet from solenoid battery terminal stud.

8. Disconnect the positive battery

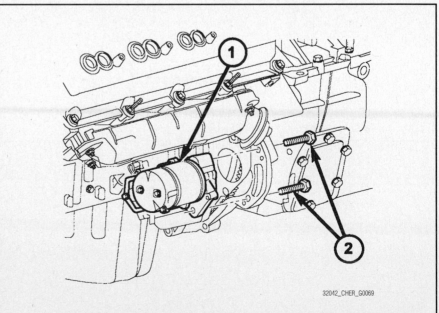

Fig. 34 Remove the starter mounting bolts (2) in order to remove the starter (1)—5.7L Engine

cable wire harness connector from the solenoid terminal connector receptacle.

9. Remove the starter.

To install:

10. Connect the solenoid wire to the starter (snaps on).

11. Position the battery cable to solenoid stud. Install and tighten the battery cable eyelet nut to 19 ft. lbs. (25 Nm). Do not allow the starter to hang from wire harness.

12. Position the starter to engine.

13. If equipped with automatic trans-

mission, slide cooler tube bracket into position.

14. Install and tighten both mounting bolts to 50 ft. lbs. (68 Nm).

15. Lower the vehicle.

16. Connect the negative battery cable.

ENGINE MECHANICAL

➡ **Disconnecting the negative battery cable may interfere with the functions of the on board computer systems and may require the computer to undergo a relearning process, once the negative battery cable is reconnected.**

ACCESSORY DRIVE BELTS

ACCESSORY BELT ROUTING

See Figures 35 and 36.

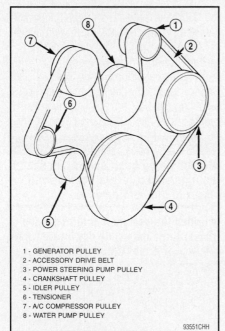

1 - GENERATOR PULLEY
2 - ACCESSORY DRIVE BELT
3 - POWER STEERING PUMP PULLEY
4 - CRANKSHAFT PULLEY
5 - IDLER PULLEY
6 - TENSIONER
7 - A/C COMPRESSOR PULLEY
8 - WATER PUMP PULLEY

93551CHH

Fig. 35 Accessory drive belt routing—Jeep 3.7L and 4.7L engines

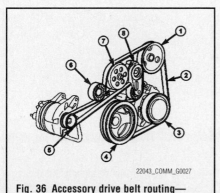

22043_COMM_G0027

Fig. 36 Accessory drive belt routing—5.7L Engines

INSPECTION

See Figure 37.

Although many manufacturers recommend that the drive belt(s) be inspected every 30,000 miles (48,000 km) or more, it is really a good idea to check them at least once a year, or at every major fluid change. Whichever interval you choose, the belts should be checked for wear or damage. Obviously, a damaged drive belt can cause problems should it give way while the vehicle is in operation. But, improper length belts (too short or long), as well as excessively worn belts, can also cause problems. Loose accessory drive belts can lead to poor engine cooling and diminished output from the alternator, air conditioning compressor or power steering pump. A belt that is too tight places a severe strain on the driven unit and can wear out bearings quickly.

Serpentine drive belts should be inspected for rib chunking (pieces of the ribs breaking off), severe glazing, frayed cords or other visible damage. Any belt which is missing sections of 2 or more adjacent ribs which are ½ in. (13mm) or longer must be replaced. You might want to note that serpentine belts do tend to form small cracks across the backing. If the only wear you find is in the form of one or more cracks are across the backing and NOT parallel to the ribs, the belt is still good and does not need to be replaced.

ADJUSTMENT

Periodic drive belt tensioning is not necessary, because an automatic spring-loaded

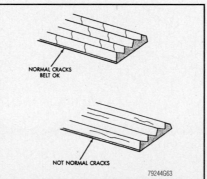

79244G63

Fig. 37 Typical wear patterns for a serpentine drive belt

tensioner is used with these belts to maintain proper adjustment at all times.

REMOVAL & INSTALLATION

3.7L & 4.7L Engines

1. Disconnect the negative battery cable.

2. Rotate the belt tensioner until it contacts the stop.

3. Remove the accessory drive belt, then slowly rotate the tensioner into the freearm position.

To install:

4. Check the condition of all the pulleys.

5. Install the accessory drive belt. Route the belt around all the pulleys except the idler pulley.

6. Rotate the tensioner arm until it contacts the stop position.

7. Route the belt around the idler and slowly let the tensioner rotate into the belt.

8. Ensure the belt is seated properly onto all of the pulleys.

5.7L Engine

1. Remove the air intake assembly.

2. Release the belt tension by rotating the tensioner counterclockwise with a 15mm wrench on the tensioner pulley bolt. Rotate the tensioner far enough until the belt can be removed.

3. Remove the belt and slowly release the tensioner.

To install:

4. Position the belt over all of the pulleys except for the water pump pulley.

5. Rotate the tensioner counterclockwise and install the belt over the water pump pulley.

6. Gently release the tensioner.

7. Install the air intake assembly.

8. Ensure the belt is seated properly on all of the pulleys.

CAMSHAFT AND VALVE LIFTERS

REMOVAL & INSTALLATION

3.7L Engine

See Figures 38 through 41.

Left Side

> **⁂ WARNING**
>
> When the timing chain is removed and the cylinder heads are still installed, DO NOT forcefully rotate the camshafts or crankshaft independently of each other. Severe valve and/or piston damage can occur.

> **⁂ WARNING**
>
> When removing the cam sprocket, timing chains or camshaft, Failure to use Special Tool 8379 will result in hydraulic tensioner ratchet over extension, requiring timing chain cover removal to reset the tensioner ratchet.

1. Remove the cylinder head cover.
2. Set engine to TDC cylinder No. 1, camshaft sprocket V6 marks at the 12 o'clock position.
3. Mark one link on the secondary timing chain on both sides of the V6 mark on the camshaft sprocket to aid in installation.

> **⁂ WARNING**
>
> Do not hold or pry on the camshaft target wheel (located on the right side camshaft sprocket) for any reason, severe damage will occur to the target wheel resulting in a vehicle no start condition.

4. Loosen but do not remove the camshaft sprocket retaining bolt. Leave the bolt snug against the sprocket.

> **⁂ WARNING**
>
> The timing chain tensioners must be secured prior to removing the

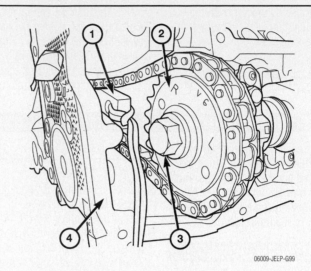

Fig. 39 Position Special Tool 8379 timing chain wedge between the timing chain strands—3.7L engine

camshaft sprockets. Failure to secure tensioners will allow the tensioners to extend, requiring timing chain cover removal in order to reset tensioners.

> **⁂ WARNING**
>
> Do not force wedge past the narrowest point between the chain strands. Damage to the tensioners may occur.

5. Position Special Tool 8379 timing chain wedge between the timing chain strands, tap the tool to securely wedge the timing chain against the tensioner arm and guide.
6. Hold the camshaft with Special Tool 8428 Camshaft Wrench, or equivalent, while removing the camshaft sprocket bolt and sprocket.

7. Using Special Tool 8428 Camshaft Wrench, gently allow the camshaft to rotate 5° clockwise until the camshaft is in the neutral position (no valve load).
8. Starting at the outside working inward, loosen the camshaft bearing cap retaining bolts ½ turn at a time. Repeat until all load is off the bearing caps.

> **⁂ WARNING**
>
> Do not stamp or strike the camshaft bearing caps. Severe damage will occur to the bearing caps.

➡ When the camshaft is removed the rocker arms may slide downward, mark the rocker arms before removing camshaft.

9. Remove the camshaft bearing caps and the camshaft.

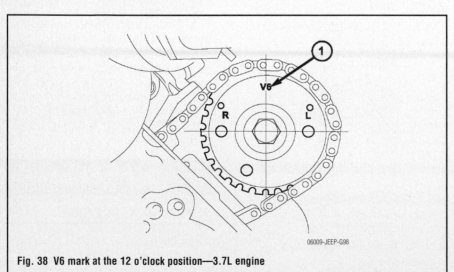

Fig. 38 V6 mark at the 12 o'clock position—3.7L engine

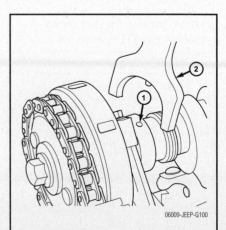

Fig. 40 Hold the camshaft with Special Tool 8428 Camshaft Wrench, or equivalent—3.7L engine

To install:

10. Lubricate the camshaft journals with clean engine oil.

➡**Position the left side camshaft so that the camshaft sprocket dowel is near the 1 o'clock position. This will place the camshaft at the neutral position easing the installation of the camshaft bearing caps.**

11. Position the camshaft into the cylinder head.

12. Install the camshaft bearing caps, hand tighten the retaining bolts.

➡**Caps should be installed so that the stamped numbers on the caps are in numerical order, (1 thru 4) from the front to the rear of the engine. All caps should be installed so that the stamped arrows on the caps point toward the front of the engine.**

13. Working in ½ turn increments, tighten the bearing cap retaining bolts starting with the middle cap working outward.

14. Torque the camshaft bearing cap retaining bolts to 100 inch lbs. (11 Nm).

15. Position the camshaft drive gear into the timing chain aligning the V6 mark between the two marked chain links (two links marked during removal).

16. Using Tool 8428 Camshaft Wrench, rotate the camshaft until the camshaft sprocket dowel is aligned with the slot in the camshaft sprocket. Install the sprocket onto the camshaft.

✳ WARNING

Remove excess oil from camshaft sprocket bolt. Failure to do so can cause bolt over-torque resulting in bolt failure.

17. Remove excess oil from bolt, then install the camshaft sprocket retaining bolt and hand tighten.

18. Remove Special Tool 8379 timing chain wedge.

19. Using Special Tool 6958 spanner wrench with adapter pins 8346, torque the camshaft sprocket retaining bolt to 90 ft. lbs. (122 Nm).

20. Install the cylinder head cover.

Right Side

✳ WARNING

When the timing chain is removed and the cylinder heads are still installed, do not forcefully rotate the camshafts or crankshaft independ-

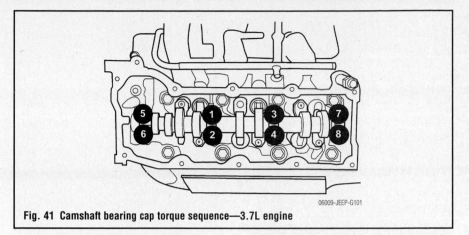

Fig. 41 Camshaft bearing cap torque sequence—3.7L engine

dently of each other. Severe valve and/or piston damage can occur.

✳ WARNING

When removing the cam sprocket, timing chains or camshaft, Failure to use special tool 8379 will result in hydraulic tensioner ratchet over extension, Requiring timing chain cover removal to re-set the tensioner ratchet.

1. Remove the cylinder head cover.
2. Set engine to TDC cylinder No. 1, camshaft sprocket V6 marks at the 12 o'clock position.
3. Mark one link on the secondary timing chain on both sides of the V6 mark on the camshaft sprocket to aid in installation.

✳ WARNING

Do not hold or pry on the camshaft target wheel for any reason, Severe damage will occur to the target wheel. A damaged target wheel could cause a vehicle no start condition.

4. Loosen but do not remove the camshaft sprocket retaining bolt. Leave bolt snug against sprocket.

➡**The timing chain tensioners must be secured prior to removing the camshaft sprockets. Failure to secure tensioners will allow the tensioners to extend, requiring timing chain cover removal in order to reset tensioners.**

✳ WARNING

Do not force wedge past the narrowest point between the chain strands. Damage to the tensioners may occur.

5. Position Special Tool 8379 timing

chain wedge between the timing chain strands. Tap the tool to securely wedge the timing chain against the tensioner arm and guide.

6. Remove the camshaft position sensor.
7. Hold the camshaft with Special Tool 8428 Camshaft Wrench, while removing the camshaft sprocket bolt and sprocket.
8. Starting at the outside working inward, loosen the camshaft bearing cap retaining bolts ½ turn at a time. Repeat until all load is off the bearing caps.

✳ WARNING

Do not stamp or strike the camshaft bearing caps. Severe damage will occur to the bearing caps.

➡**When the camshaft is removed the rocker arms may slide downward, mark the rocker arms before removing camshaft.**

9. Remove the camshaft bearing caps and the camshaft.

To install:

10. Lubricate camshaft journals with clean engine oil.

➡**Position the right side camshaft so that the camshaft sprocket dowel is near the 10 o'clock position. This will place the camshaft at the neutral position easing the installation of the camshaft bearing caps.**

11. Position the camshaft into the cylinder head.

12. Install the camshaft bearing caps, hand tighten the retaining bolts.

➡**Caps should be installed so that the stamped numbers on the caps are in numerical order, (1 thru 4) from the front to the rear of the engine. All caps should be installed so that the stamped arrows on the caps point toward the front of the engine.**

13. Working in ½ turn increments, tighten the bearing cap retaining bolts starting with the middle cap working outward.

14. Torque the camshaft bearing cap retaining bolts to 100 inch lbs. (11 Nm).

15. Position the camshaft drive gear into the timing chain aligning the V6 mark between the two marked chain links (two links marked during removal).

16. Using Special Tool 8428 Camshaft Wrench, rotate the camshaft until the camshaft sprocket dowel is aligned with the slot in the camshaft sprocket. Install the sprocket onto the camshaft.

✳✳ WARNING

Remove excess oil from camshaft sprocket bolt. Failure to do so can cause bolt over-torque resulting in bolt failure.

17. Remove excess oil from camshaft sprocket bolt, then install the camshaft sprocket retaining bolt and hand tighten.

18. Remove timing chain wedge special tool 8379.

19. Using Special Tool 6958 spanner wrench with adapter pins 8346, torque the camshaft sprocket retaining bolt to 90 ft. lbs. (122 Nm).

20. Install the camshaft position sensor.

21. Install the cylinder head cover.

4.7L Engine

See Figures 42 through 49.

Left Side

1. Remove the cylinder head cover.

✳✳ WARNING

When the timing chain is removed and the cylinder heads are still installed, DO NOT forcefully rotate the camshafts or crankshaft independently of each other. Severe valve and/or piston damage can occur.

✳✳ WARNING

When removing the cam sprocket, timing chains or camshaft, failure to use Special Tool 8350 will result in hydraulic tensioner ratchet over extension, requiring timing chain cover removal to reset the tensioner ratchet.

2. Set engine to TDC cylinder no.1, camshaft sprocket V8 marks at the 12 o'clock position.

3. Mark one link on the secondary timing

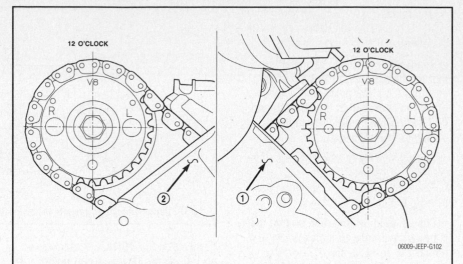

Fig. 42 Set engine to TDC cylinder no.1, camshaft sprocket V8 marks at the 12 o'clock position—4.7L engine

chain on both sides of the V8 mark on the camshaft sprocket to aid in installation.

✳✳ WARNING

Do not hold or pry on the camshaft target wheel (located on the right side camshaft sprocket) for any reason, severe damage will occur to the target wheel resulting in a vehicle no start condition.

4. Loosen but do not remove the camshaft sprocket retaining bolt. Leave the bolt snug against the sprocket.

➡The timing chain tensioners must be secured prior to removing the camshaft sprockets. Failure to secure tensioners will allow the tensioners to extend,

requiring timing chain cover removal in order to reset tensioners.

✳✳ WARNING

Do not force wedge past the narrowest point between the chain strands. Damage to the tensioners may occur.

5. Position Special Tool 8350 timing chain wedge between the timing chain strands, tap the tool to securely wedge the timing chain against the tensioner arm and guide.

➡When gripping the camshaft, place the pliers on the tube portion of the camshaft only. Do not grip the lobes or the sprocket areas.

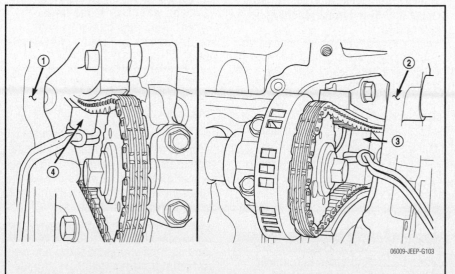

Fig. 43 The timing chain tensioners must be secured prior to removing the camshaft sprockets—4.7L engine

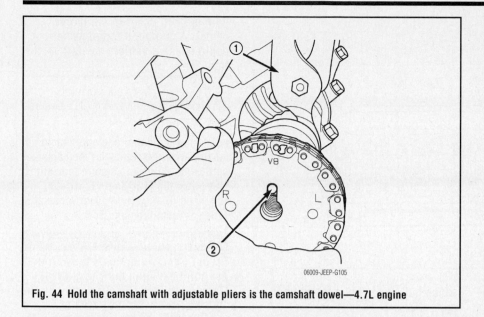

Fig. 44 Hold the camshaft with adjustable pliers is the camshaft dowel—4.7L engine

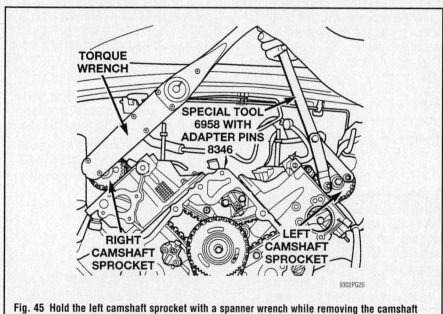

Fig. 45 Hold the left camshaft sprocket with a spanner wrench while removing the camshaft sprocket—4.7L engine

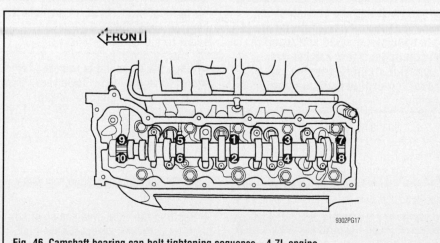

Fig. 46 Camshaft bearing cap bolt tightening sequence—4.7L engine

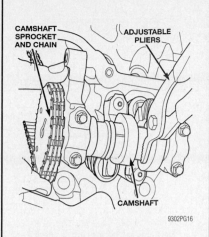

Fig. 47 Turn the camshaft with pliers, if needed, to align the dowel in the sprocket—4.7L engine

6. Hold the camshaft with adjustable pliers while removing the camshaft sprocket bolt and sprocket.

7. Using the pliers, gently allow the camshaft to rotate 15° clockwise until the camshaft is in the neutral position (no valve load).

8. Starting at the outside working inward, loosen the camshaft bearing cap retaining bolts ½ turn at a time. Repeat until all load is off the bearing caps.

✳✳ WARNING

Do not stamp or strike the camshaft bearing caps. Severe damage will occur to the bearing caps.

➡When the camshaft is removed the rocker arms may slide downward, mark the rocker arms before removing camshaft.

9. Remove the camshaft bearing caps and the camshaft.

To install:

10. Lubricate camshaft journals with clean engine oil.

➡Position the left side camshaft so that the camshaft sprocket dowel is near the 1 o'clock position. This will place the camshaft at the neutral position easing the installation of the camshaft bearing caps.

11. Position the camshaft into the cylinder head.

12. Install the camshaft bearing caps, hand tighten the retaining bolts.

13. Working in ½ turn increments, tighten the bearing cap retaining bolts starting with the middle cap working outward.

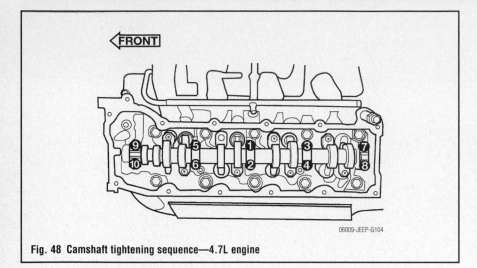

Fig. 48 Camshaft tightening sequence—4.7L engine

14. Torque the camshaft bearing cap retaining bolts to 100 inch lbs. (11 Nm).

15. Position the camshaft drive gear into the timing chain aligning the V8 mark between the two marked chain links (two links marked during removal).

➡When gripping the camshaft, place the pliers on the tube portion of the camshaft only. Do not grip the lobes or the sprocket areas.

16. Using the adjustable pliers, rotate the camshaft until the camshaft sprocket dowel is aligned with the slot in the camshaft sprocket. Install the sprocket onto the camshaft.

✳✳ WARNING

Remove excess oil from camshaft sprocket bolt. Failure to do so can

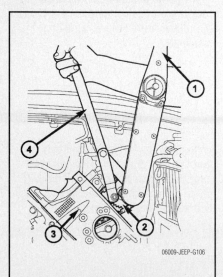

Fig. 49 Using Special Tool 6958 spanner wrench with adapter pins 8346, torque the camshaft sprocket retaining bolt is the torque wrench, is the head—4.7L engine

cause bolt over-torque resulting in bolt failure.

17. Remove excess oil from bolt, then install the camshaft sprocket retaining bolt and hand tighten.

18. Remove Special Tool 8350 timing chain wedge.

19. Using Special Tool 6958 spanner wrench with adapter pins 8346, torque the camshaft sprocket retaining bolt to 90 ft. lbs. (122 Nm).

20. Install the cylinder head cover.

Right Side

✳✳ WARNING

When the timing chain is removed and the cylinder heads are still installed, do not forcefully rotate the camshafts or crankshaft independently of each other. Severe valve and/or piston damage can occur.

✳✳ WARNING

When removing the cam sprocket, timing chains or camshaft, failure to use special tool 8350 will result in hydraulic tensioner ratchet over extension, requiring timing chain cover removal to reset the tensioner ratchet.

1. Set engine to TDC cylinder no.1, camshaft sprocket V8 marks at the 12 o'clock position.

2. Mark one link on the secondary timing chain on both sides of the V8 mark on the camshaft sprocket to aid in installation.

✳✳ WARNING

Do not hold or pry on the camshaft target wheel for any reason, severe

damage will occur to the target wheel. A damaged target wheel could cause a vehicle no start condition.

3. Loosen but do not remove the camshaft sprocket retaining bolt. Leave bolt snug against sprocket.

➡The timing chain tensioners must be secured prior to removing the camshaft sprockets. Failure to secure tensioners will allow the tensioners to extend, requiring timing chain cover removal in order to reset tensioners.

✳✳ WARNING

Do not force wedge past the narrowest point between the chain strands. Damage to the tensioners may occur.

4. Position Special Tool 8350 timing chain wedge between the timing chain strands. Tap the tool to securely wedge the timing chain against the tensioner arm and guide.

5. Remove the camshaft position sensor.

➡When gripping the camshaft, place the pliers on the tube portion of the camshaft only. Do not grip the lobes or the sprocket areas.

6. Hold the camshaft with adjustable pliers while removing the camshaft sprocket bolt and sprocket.

7. Using the pliers, gently allow the camshaft to rotate 45° counterclockwise until the camshaft is in the neutral position (no valve load).

8. Starting at the outside working inward, loosen the camshaft bearing cap retaining bolts ½ turn at a time. Repeat until all load is off the bearing caps.

✳✳ WARNING

Do not stamp or strike the camshaft bearing caps. Severe damage will occur to the bearing caps.

➡When the camshaft is removed the rocker arms may slide downward, mark the rocker arms before removing camshaft.

9. Remove the camshaft bearing caps and the camshaft.

To install:

10. Lubricate camshaft journals with clean engine oil.

➡Position the right side camshaft so that the camshaft sprocket dowel is near the 10 o'clock position. This will place the camshaft at the neutral position easing the installation of the camshaft bearing caps.

11. Position the camshaft into the cylinder head.

12. Install the camshaft bearing caps, hand tighten the retaining bolts.

13. Working in ½ turn increments, tighten the bearing cap retaining bolts starting with the middle cap working outward.

14. Torque the camshaft bearing cap retaining bolts to 100 inch lbs.(11 Nm).

15. Position the camshaft drive gear into the timing chain aligning the V8 mark between the two marked chain links (two links marked during removal).

➡When gripping the camshaft, place the pliers on the tube portion of the camshaft only. Do not grip the lobes or the sprocket areas.

16. Using the adjustable pliers, rotate the camshaft until the camshaft sprocket dowel is aligned with the slot in the camshaft sprocket. Install the sprocket onto the camshaft.

✳✳ WARNING

Remove the excess oil from camshaft sprocket bolt. Failure to do so can cause bolt over-torque resulting in bolt failure.

17. Remove excess oil from camshaft sprocket bolt, then install the camshaft sprocket retaining bolt and hand tighten.

18. Remove the timing chain wedge Special Tool 8350.

19. Using Special Tool 6958 spanner wrench with adapter pins 8346, torque the camshaft sprocket retaining bolt to 90 ft. lbs. (122 Nm).

20. Install the camshaft position sensor.
21. Install the cylinder head cover.

5.7L Engine

See Figure 51.

1. Remove the battery negative cable.
2. Remove the air cleaner assembly.
3. Drain the engine coolant.
4. Remove the accessory drive belt.
5. Remove the alternator.
6. Remove the A/C compressor, and set aside.
7. Remove the radiator.
8. Remove the intake manifold.
9. Remove the cylinder head covers.
10. Remove both left and right cylinder heads.
11. Remove the oil pan.
12. Remove the timing case cover.
13. Remove the oil pick up tube.
14. Remove the oil pump.
15. Remove the timing chain.
16. Remove the camshaft tensioner/thrust plate assembly.

➡Identify the lifters to ensure installation in original location.

17. Remove the tappets and retainer assembly.

18. Install a long bolt into front of camshaft to aid in removal of the camshaft. Remove camshaft, being careful not to damage cam bearings with the cam lobes.

To install:

➡The 5.7L LX engine uses a unique camshaft for use with the Multi Displacement System. When installing a new camshaft, the replacement

camshaft must be compatible with the Multi Displacement System.

19. Lubricate camshaft lobes and camshaft bearing journals and insert the camshaft.

20. Install the camshaft tensioner plate assembly. Tighten bolts to 250 inch lbs. (28 Nm).

21. Install the timing chain and sprockets.

22. Measure the camshaft end play. If not within limits install a new thrust plate.

23. Install the oil pump.

24. Install the oil pick-up tube.

25. Each tappet reused must be installed in the same position from which it was removed.

➡When camshaft is replaced, all of the tappets must be replaced.

✳✳ WARNING

The 5.7L engine uses both standard roller tappets and deactivating roller tappets, for use with the Multi Displacement System. The deactivating roller tappets must be used in cylinders 1, 4, 6, 7. The deactivating tappets can be identified by the two holes in the side of the tappet body, for the latching pins.

26. Install tappets and retaining yoke assembly.

27. Install both left and right cylinder heads.

28. Install the pushrods.
29. Install the rocker arms.
30. Install the timing case cover.
31. Install the oil pan.

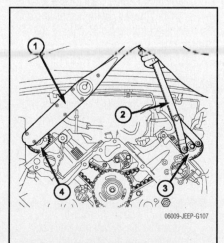

06009-JEEP-G107

Fig. 50 Tightening the right side camshaft sprocket retaining bolt—4.7L engine

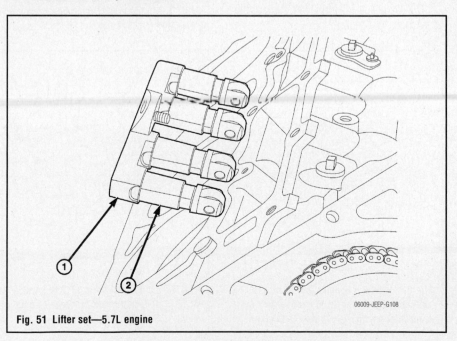

06009-JEEP-G108

Fig. 51 Lifter set—5.7L engine

32. Install the cylinder head covers.
33. Install the intake manifold.
34. Install the A/C compressor.
35. Install the alternator.
36. Install the accessory drive belt.
37. Install the radiator.
38. Install the air cleaner assembly.
39. Connect the negative battery cable.
40. Refill the cooling system to the correct level.
41. Refill the engine with oil to the correct level.
42. Start engine and check for leaks.

CRANKSHAFT FRONT SEAL

REMOVAL & INSTALLATION

3.7L & 4.7L Engines

See Figures 52 through 56.

1. Disconnect the negative battery cable.
2. Drain the cooling system.
3. Remove the accessory drive belt.
4. Remove the A/C compressor mounting bolts and set the compressor aside.

➡ **It is not necessary to disconnect the A/C lines from the compressor.**

5. Remove the upper radiator hose.
6. Disconnect the engine fan electrical connector, located inside the radiator shroud.
7. Remove the engine fan.
8. Remove the camshaft damper bolt.
9. Using Special Tool 8513 Insert and 1026 three-jaw puller, remove the crankshaft damper.
10. Using Special Tool 8511, remove the crankshaft front seal.

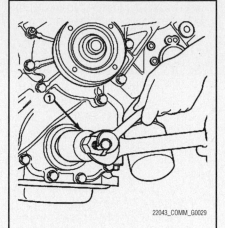

Fig. 53 Use Special Tool 8511 Seal Remover (1) to remove the crankshaft front seal—3.7L & 4.7L Engines

To install:

11. Using Special Tools 8348 and 8512, install the crankshaft front seal.
12. Install the crankshaft damper as follows:

a. Align the crankshaft damper slot with the key in the crankshaft. Slide the damper onto the crankshaft.

b. Assemble Special Tool 8512-A. The nut is threaded onto the threaded rod first. Then the roller bearing is placed onto the threaded rod (The hardened bearing surface of the bearing MUST face the nut). Then the hardened washer slides onto the threaded rod. Once assembled coat the threaded rod's threads with Mopar® Nickel Anti-Seize or equivalent.

c. Using Special Tool 8512-A, press the damper onto the crankshaft.

13. Install the crankshaft damper bolt and tighten to 130 ft. lbs. (175 Nm).

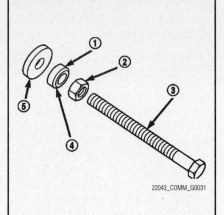

Fig. 55 Install the nut (2) to the threaded rod (3), then the roller bearing (1) with the hardened surface (4) facing the nut. Then install the washer (5).

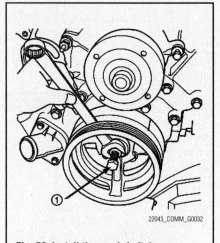

Fig. 56 Install the crankshaft damper using Special Tool 8512-A (1)—3.7L & 4.7L Engines

14. Install the engine fan.
15. Install the upper radiator hose.
16. Install the A/C compressor and tighten the mounting bolts to 40 ft. lbs. (54 Nm).
17. Install the accessory drive belt.
18. Refill the cooling system to the correct level.
19. Connect the negative battery cable.
20. Start the engine and check for leaks.

5.7L Engines

See Figures 57 and 58.

1. Disconnect the negative battery cable.
2. Drain the cooling system.
3. Remove the accessory drive belt.
4. Remove the upper radiator hose.
5. Remove the engine fan.
6. Remove the crankshaft damper bolt.

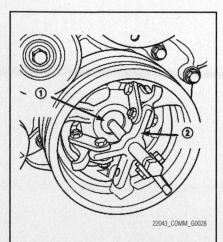

Fig. 52 Using the Special Tool Insert (1) and three-jaw puller (2) to remove the crankshaft damper—3.7L & 4.7L Engines

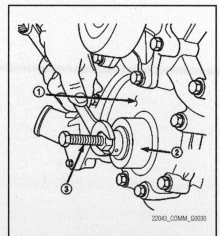

Fig. 54 Use Special Tools 8348 (2) and 8512 (3) to install a new crankshaft front seal—3.7L & 4.7L Engines

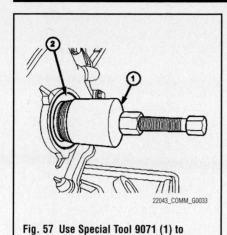

Fig. 57 Use Special Tool 9071 (1) to remove the crankshaft front seal (2)—5.7L Engine

7. Using Special Tool 8513 Insert and 1026 three-jaw puller, remove the crankshaft damper.

8. Using Special Tool 9071, remove the crankshaft front seal.

To install:

❈❈ WARNING

The front crankshaft seal must be installed dry, without any lubricant applied to the sealing lip or outer edge.

9. Using Special Tools 9072 and 8512-A, install the crankshaft front seal.

10. Install the crankshaft damper as follows:

   a. Align the crankshaft damper slot with the key in the crankshaft. Slide the damper onto the crankshaft.

   b. Assemble Special Tool 8512-A. The nut is threaded onto the threaded rod first. Then the roller bearing is placed onto the threaded rod (The hardened bearing surface of the bearing MUST face the nut). Then the hardened washer slides onto the threaded rod. Once assembled coat the threaded rod's threads with Mopar® Nickel Anti-Seize or equivalent.

   c. Using Special Tool 8512-A, press the damper onto the crankshaft.

11. Install the crankshaft damper bolt and tighten to 129 ft. lbs. (176 Nm).

12. Install the engine fan.

13. Install the upper radiator hose.

14. Install the accessory drive belt.

15. Refill the cooling system to the correct level.

16. Connect the negative battery cable.

17. Start the engine and check for leaks.

CYLINDER HEAD

REMOVAL & INSTALLATION

3.7L Engine

Left Side

1. Disconnect the negative battery cable.

2. Drain the cooling system.

3. Raise and safely support the vehicle.

4. Disconnect the exhaust pipe at the left side exhaust manifold.

5. Lower the vehicle.

6. Remove the intake manifold.

7. Siphon the master cylinder.

8. Remove the primary brake line at the master cylinder.

9. Remove the primary brake line from the HCU.

10. Remove the secondary brake line at the master cylinder.

11. Remove the secondary brake line at the HCU.

12. Remove the 4 chassis lines at the HCU.

13. Disconnect the HCU electrical connector.

14. Remove the 3 mounting nuts at the HCU bracket.

15. Remove the HCU with the bracket from the vehicle.

16. Disconnect the brake fluid level sensor electrical connector from the fluid reservoir.

17. Remove the 2 master cylinder mounting nuts.

18. Remove the master cylinder.

19. Disconnect vacuum hose at booster check valve.

20. Remove the hush panel.

21. Remove the steering column opening cover and hush panel.

22. Remove the retainer clip that holds booster push rod on pedal pin. Then slide push rod off pin.

23. Disconnect the brake lamp switch wire connector.

24. Remove the brake lamp switch.

25. Remove four nuts that attach booster to dash panel.

26. In the engine compartment, disconnect the wire harness routing clips and move the harness to the side and downward.

27. Remove the booster from the vehicle.

28. Remove the cylinder head cover

29. Remove the fan shroud and fan blade assembly

30. Remove the accessory drive belt.

31. Remove the power steering pump and set aside.

32. Rotate the crankshaft until the damper timing mark is aligned with TDC indicator mark.

33. Verify the V6 mark on the camshaft sprocket is at the 12 o'clock position, with the No. 1 cylinder at TDC on the exhaust stroke. Rotate the crankshaft one turn if necessary.

34. Remove the crankshaft damper.

35. Remove the timing chain cover.

36. Lock the secondary timing chains to the idler sprocket using Special Tool 8429 Timing Chain Holding Fixture.

➡**Mark the secondary timing chain prior to removal to aid in installation.**

37. Mark the secondary timing chain, one link on each side of the V6 mark on the camshaft drive gear.

38. Remove the left side secondary chain tensioner.

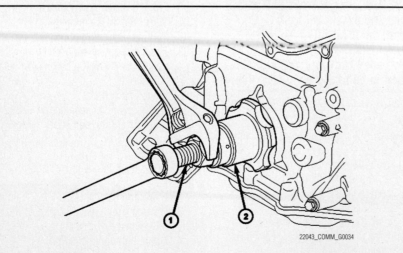

Fig. 58 Use Special Tools 8512-A (1) and 9072 (2) to install the front crankshaft seal—5.7L Engine

39. Remove the cylinder head access plug.

40. Remove the left side secondary chain guide.

41. Remove the retaining bolt and the camshaft drive gear.

⁕ WARNING

Do not allow the engine to rotate. Severe damage to the valve train can occur.

➡ **Do not overlook the four smaller bolts at the front of the cylinder head. Do not attempt to remove the cylinder head without removing these four bolts.**

➡ **The cylinder head is attached to the cylinder block with twelve bolts.**

42. Remove the cylinder head retaining bolts.

43. Remove the cylinder head and gasket. Discard the gasket.

⁕ WARNING

Do not lay the cylinder head on its gasket sealing surface, due to the design of the cylinder head gasket any distortion to the cylinder head sealing surface may prevent the gasket from properly sealing resulting in leaks.

To install:

➡ **The cylinder head bolts are tightened using a torque plus angle procedure. The bolts must be examined before reuse. If the threads are necked down the bolts should be replaced. Necking can be checked by holding a straight edge against the threads. If all the threads do not contact the scale, the bolt should be replaced.**

⁕⁕ WARNING

When cleaning cylinder head and cylinder block surfaces, DO NOT use a metal scraper because the surfaces could be cut or ground. Use only a wooden or plastic scraper.

44. Clean the cylinder head and cylinder block mating surfaces.

45. Position the new cylinder head gasket on the locating dowels.

⁕⁕ WARNING

When installing cylinder head, use care not damage the tensioner arm or the guide arm.

46. Position the cylinder head onto the cylinder block. Make sure the cylinder head seats fully over the locating dowels.

➡ **The four smaller cylinder head mounting bolts require sealant to be added to them before installing. Failure to do so may cause leaks.**

47. Lubricate the cylinder head bolt threads with clean engine oil and install the eight M11 bolts.

48. Coat the four M8 cylinder head bolts with Mopar® Lock and Seal Adhesive, or equivalent, then install the bolts.

➡ **The cylinder head bolts are tightened using an angle torque procedure, however, the bolts are not a torque-to-yield design.**

49. Tighten the bolts in sequence using the following steps and torque values:
- Step 1: Tighten bolts 1-8 to 20 ft. lbs. (27 Nm).
- Step 2: Verify that bolts 1-8, all reached 20 ft. lbs. (27 Nm), by repeating step 1 without loosening the bolts.
- Step 3: Tighten bolts 9-12 to 10 ft. lbs. (14 Nm).
- Step 4: Tighten bolts 1-8, 90 degrees.
- Step 5: Tighten bolts 1-8, 90 degrees, again.
- Step 6: Tighten bolts 9-12 to 19 ft. lbs. (26 Nm).

50. Position the secondary chain onto the camshaft drive gear, making sure one marked chain link is on either side of the V6 mark on the gear then using Special Tool 8428 Camshaft Wrench, position the gear onto the camshaft.

⁕⁕ WARNING

Remove any excess oil from camshaft sprocket retaining bolt before reinstalling bolt. Failure to do so may cause over-torquing of bolt resulting in bolt failure.

51. Install the camshaft drive gear retaining bolt.

52. Install the left side secondary chain guide.

53. Install the cylinder head access plug.

54. Re-set and install the left side secondary chain tensioner.

55. Install the timing chain cover.

56. Install the crankshaft damper. Tighten damper bolt 130 ft. lbs. (175 Nm).

57. Install the power steering pump.

58. Install the fan blade assembly and fan shroud.

59. Install the cylinder head cover.

60. Check condition of grommet that secures check valve in booster. Replace grommet if cut, torn, or loose.

61. Install a new booster dash seal.

62. Align and position the booster in the mounting holes of the dash panel.

63. Inside the vehicle, Lubricate pedal pin Mopar® multi-mileage grease.

64. Install the booster attaching nuts on studs. Tighten attaching nuts to 29 ft. lbs. (39Nm).

65. Slide booster push rod on pedal pin. Then secure rod to pin with retainer clip.

66. Install a new brake lamp switch and reconnect the electrical connector.

67. Install the steering column opening cover.

68. Install the hush panel.

69. In engine compartment, attach vacuum hose to booster check valve.

70. Install the master cylinder to the power brake booster with new gasket and nuts.

71. Reroute the wire harness back into position and install the routing clip.

72. Reconnect the brake fluid level electrical connector.

73. Install the HCU with bracket to the vehicle and tighten the 2 mounting nuts.

74. Reconnect the HCU electrical connector.

75. Install the 4 chassis lines at the HCU.

76. Install the secondary brake line at the HCU.

77. Install the secondary brake line at the master cylinder.

78. Install the primary brake line at the HCU.

79. Install the primary brake line at the master cylinder.

80. Fill and bleed brake system.

81. Install the intake manifold.

82. Refill the cooling system.

83. Raise and safely support the vehicle.

84. Install the exhaust pipe onto the left exhaust manifold.

85. Lower the vehicle.

86. Connect the negative battery cable.

87. Start the engine and check for leaks.

Right Side

1. Disconnect the negative battery cable.

2. Raise and safely support the vehicle.

3. Disconnect the exhaust pipe at the right side exhaust manifold.

4. Drain the engine coolant.

5. Lower the vehicle.

6. Remove the intake manifold.

7. Remove the cylinder head cover.

8. Remove the fan shroud.
9. Remove oil fill housing from cylinder head.
10. Remove the accessory drive belt.
11. Rotate the crankshaft until the damper timing mark is aligned with TDC indicator mark.
12. Verify the V6 mark on the camshaft sprocket is at the 12 o'clock position. Rotate the crankshaft one turn if necessary.
13. Remove the crankshaft damper.
14. Remove the timing chain cover.
15. Lock the secondary timing chains to the idler sprocket using Special Tool 8429 Timing Chain Holding Fixture.

➡Mark the secondary timing chain prior to removal to aid in installation.

16. Mark the secondary timing chain, one link on each side of the V6 mark on the camshaft drive gear.
17. Remove the right side secondary chain tensioner.
18. Remove the cylinder head access plug.
19. Remove the right side secondary chain guide.

✳✳ WARNING

The nut on the right side camshaft sprocket should not be removed for any reason, as the sprocket and camshaft sensor target wheel is serviced as an assembly. If the nut was removed, torque nut to 44 inch lbs. (5 Nm).

20. Remove the retaining bolt and the camshaft drive gear.

✳✳ WARNING

Do not allow the engine to rotate. Severe damage to the valve train can occur.

➡Do not overlook the four smaller bolts at the front of the cylinder head. Do not attempt to remove the cylinder head without removing these four bolts.

✳✳ WARNING

Do not hold or pry on the camshaft target wheel for any reason. A damaged target wheel can result in a vehicle no start condition.

➡The cylinder head is attached to the cylinder block with twelve bolts.

21. Remove the cylinder head retaining bolts.

22. Remove the cylinder head and gasket. Discard the gasket.

✳✳ WARNING

Do not lay the cylinder head on its gasket sealing surface, do to the design of the cylinder head gasket any distortion to the cylinder head sealing surface may prevent the gasket from properly sealing resulting in leaks.

To install:

➡The cylinder head bolts are tightened using a torque plus angle procedure. The bolts must be examined before reuse. If the threads are necked down the bolts should be replaced. Necking can be checked by holding a straight edge against the threads. If all the threads do not contact the scale, the bolt should be replaced.

✳✳ WARNING

When cleaning cylinder head and cylinder block surfaces, DO NOT use a metal scraper because the surfaces could be cut or ground. Use only a wooden or plastic scraper.

23. Clean the cylinder head and cylinder block mating surfaces.
24. Position the new cylinder head gasket on the locating dowels.

✳✳ WARNING

When installing cylinder head, use care not damage the tensioner arm or the guide arm.

25. Position the cylinder head onto the cylinder block. Make sure the cylinder head seats fully over the locating dowels.

➡The four M8 cylinder head mounting bolts require sealant to be added to them before installing. Failure to do so may cause leaks.

26. Lubricate the cylinder head bolt threads with clean engine oil and install the eight M10 bolts.
27. Coat the four M8 cylinder head bolts with Mopar® Lock and Seal Adhesive, or equivalent, then install the bolts.

➡The cylinder head bolts are tightened using an angle torque procedure, however, the bolts are not a torque-to-yield design.

28. Tighten the bolts in sequence using the following steps and torque values:

• Step 1: Tighten bolts 1-8, to 20 ft. lbs. (27 Nm).
• Step 2: Verify that bolts 1-8, all reached 20 ft. lbs. (27 Nm), by repeating step 1 without loosening the bolts.
• Step 3: Tighten bolts 9 through 12 to 10 ft. lbs. (14 Nm).
• Step 4: Tighten bolts 1-8, 90°.
• Step 5: Tighten bolts 1-8, 90°, again.
• Step 6: Tighten bolts 9-12, to 19 ft. lbs. (26 Nm)

✳✳ WARNING

The nut on the right side camshaft sprocket should not be removed for any reason, as the sprocket and camshaft sensor target wheel is serviced as an assembly. If the nut was removed, torque nut to 60 inch lbs. (5 Nm).

29. Position the secondary chain onto the camshaft drive gear, making sure one marked chain link is on either side of the V6 mark on the gear then using Special Tool 8428 Camshaft Wrench, position the gear onto the camshaft.

✳✳ WARNING

Remove any excess oil from camshaft sprocket retaining bolt before reinstalling bolt. Failure to do so may cause over-torquing of bolt resulting in bolt failure.

30. Install the camshaft drive gear retaining bolt.
31. Install the right side secondary chain guide.
32. Install the cylinder head access plug.
33. Re-set and install the right side secondary chain tensioner.
34. Remove Special Tool 8429.
35. Install the timing chain cover.
36. Install the crankshaft damper. Tighten damper bolt 130 ft. lbs. (175 Nm).
37. Install the accessory drive belt.
38. Install the fan shroud.
39. Install the cylinder head cover.
40. Install the intake manifold.
41. Install oil fill housing onto cylinder head.
42. Refill the cooling system to the correct level.
43. Raise and safely support the vehicle.
44. Install the exhaust pipe onto the right exhaust manifold.
45. Lower the vehicle.
46. Connect the negative battery cable.
47. Start the engine and check for leaks.

4.7L Engine

See Figures 59 through 64.

1. Drain the cooling system.
2. Properly relieve the fuel system pressure.
3. Remove or disconnect the following:
   - Negative battery cable
   - Exhaust Y-pipe
   - Intake manifold
   - Cylinder head covers
   - Engine cooling fan and shroud
   - Accessory drive belt
   - Oil fill housing from the cylinder head.
   - Power steering pump, left side only
   - Rocker arms
4. Rotate the crankshaft so that the crankshaft timing mark aligns with the Top Dead Center (TDC) mark on the front cover, and the **V8** marks on the camshaft sprockets are at 12 o'clock as shown.
5. Remove or disconnect the following:
   - Crankshaft damper
   - Front cover
6. Lock the secondary timing chains to the idler sprocket with Timing Chain Locking tool 8515.
7. Matchmark the secondary timing chains to the camshaft sprockets.
8. Remove or disconnect the following:
   - Secondary timing chain tensioners
   - Cylinder head access plugs
   - Secondary timing chain guides
   - Camshaft sprockets
   - Cylinder heads

➡**Each cylinder head is retained by ten 11mm bolts and four 8mm bolts.**

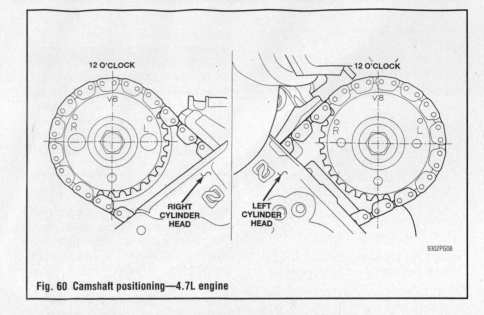

Fig. 60 Camshaft positioning—4.7L engine

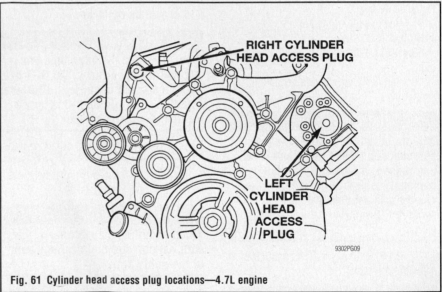

Fig. 61 Cylinder head access plug locations—4.7L engine

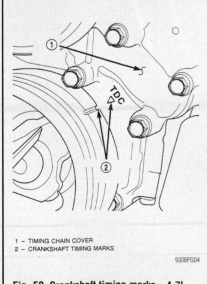

1 – TIMING CHAIN COVER
2 – CRANKSHAFT TIMING MARKS

Fig. 59 Crankshaft timing marks—4.7L engine

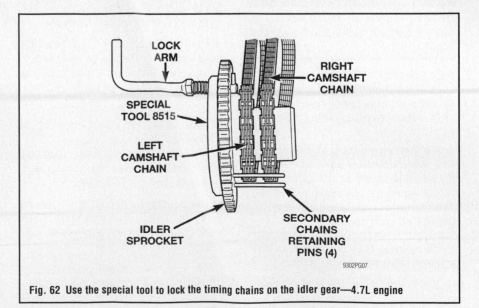

Fig. 62 Use the special tool to lock the timing chains on the idler gear—4.7L engine

To install:

9. Check the cylinder head bolts for signs of stretching and replace as necessary.

10. Lubricate the threads of the 11mm bolts with clean engine oil.

11. Coat the threads of the 8mm bolts with Mopar® Lock and Seal Adhesive.

12. Install the cylinder heads. Use new gaskets and tighten the bolts, in sequence, as follows:

   a. Step 1: Bolts 1–10 to 15 ft. lbs. (20 Nm)

   b. Step 2: Bolts 1–10 to 35 ft. lbs. (47 Nm)

   c. Step 3: Bolts 11–14 to 18 ft. lbs. (25 Nm)

   d. Step 4: Bolts 1–10 plus ¼ (90 degree) turn

   e. Step 5: Bolts 11–14 to 19 ft. lbs. (26 Nm)

13. Install or connect the following:
   • Camshaft sprockets. Align the secondary chain matchmarks and tighten the bolts to 90 ft. lbs. (122 Nm).
   • Secondary timing chain guides
   • Cylinder head access plugs
   • Secondary timing chain tensioners.

14. Remove the Timing Chain Locking tool 8515.

15. Install or connect the following:
   • Front cover
   • Crankshaft damper. Torque the bolt to 130 ft. lbs. (175 Nm).
   • Rocker arms
   • Power steering pump, if removed.
   • Oil fill housing
   • Accessory drive belt
   • Engine cooling fan and shroud
   • Valve covers
   • Intake manifold
   • Exhaust Y-pipe
   • Negative battery cable

16. Fill and bleed the cooling system.

17. Start the engine, check for leaks and repair if necessary.

5.7L Engine

See Figures 65 and 66.

1. Properly relieve the fuel system pressure. Disconnect the fuel supply line.

2. Disconnect the negative battery cable.

3. Drain the cooling system.

4. Remove the air cleaner resonator and duct work.

5. Remove closed crankcase ventilation system.

6. Disconnect the exhaust at the exhaust manifolds.

7. Disconnect the evaporation control system.

8. Disconnect the heater hoses.

9. Remove the power steering pump.

10. Remove the cylinder head covers, using the sequence provided, and gaskets.

11. Remove the intake manifold and throttle body as an assembly.

12. Remove the rocker arm assemblies and push rods. Identify to ensure installation in original locations.

13. Remove the head bolts from each cylinder head, using the sequence provided, and remove cylinder heads. Discard the cylinder head gasket.

To install:

14. Clean all surfaces of cylinder block and cylinder heads.

15. Clean cylinder block front and rear gasket surfaces using a suitable solvent.

➡The head gaskets are not interchangeable between left and right sides. They are marked "L" and "R" to indicate left and right sides. The head gaskets are also marked "TOP" to indicate which side goes up.

16. Position new cylinder head gaskets onto the cylinder block.

17. Position the cylinder heads onto head gaskets and cylinder block.

18. Tighten the cylinder head bolts in three steps using the sequence provided:
   • Step 1: Tighten M12 cylinder head bolts, in sequence, to 25 ft. lbs. (34 Nm) and M8 bolts to 20 Nm (15 ft. lbs.).
   • Step 2: Tighten M12 cylinder head bolts, in sequence, to 40 ft. lbs. (54 Nm) and verify M8 bolts to 15 ft. lbs. (20 Nm).
   • Step 3: Turn M12 cylinder head bolts, in sequence, 90 degrees and tighten M8 bolts to 25 ft. lbs. (34 Nm)

19. Install the pushrods and rocker arm assemblies in their original position.

20. Install the intake manifold and throttle body assembly.

21. If required, adjust spark plugs to specifications. Install the plugs.

22. Connect the heater hoses.

23. Install the fuel supply line.

24. Install the power steering pump.

25. Install the drive belt.

26. Install cylinder head covers.

27. Connect the evaporation control system.

28. Install the air cleaner.

29. Refill the cooling system to the correct level.

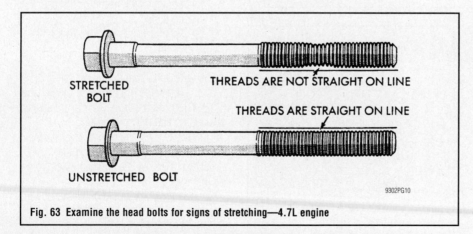

Fig. 63 Examine the head bolts for signs of stretching—4.7L engine

STRETCHED BOLT

THREADS ARE NOT STRAIGHT ON LINE

THREADS ARE STRAIGHT ON LINE

UNSTRETCHED BOLT

9302PG10

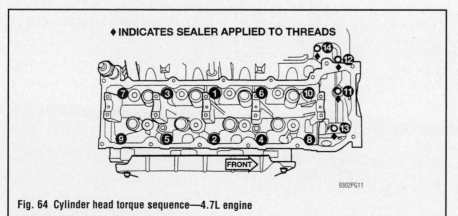

Fig. 64 Cylinder head torque sequence—4.7L engine

♦ INDICATES SEALER APPLIED TO THREADS

FRONT

9302PG11

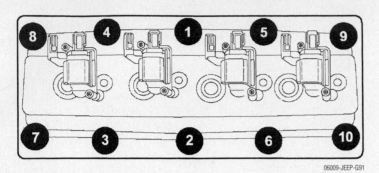

Fig. 65 Cylinder head cover bolt removal and tightening sequence—5.7L engine

06009-JEEP-G91

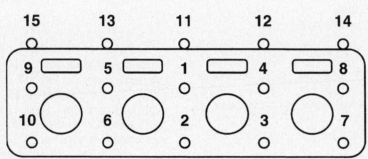

Fig. 66 Cylinder head bolt removal and tightening sequence—5.7L engine

06009-JEEP-G92

30. Connect the negative battery cable.
31. Start engine check for leaks.

ENGINE ASSEMBLY

REMOVAL & INSTALLATION

3.7L Engine

See Figure 67.

1. Properly relieve the fuel pressure and disconnect the fuel supply line at the fuel rail.
2. Disconnect the negative battery cable.
3. Drain the cooling system.
4. Remove the strut tower support.
5. Remove the air intake assembly.
6. Remove the engine fan.
7. Remove the accessory drive belt.
8. Remove the A/C compressor mounting bolts and secure away from the engine.

➡Leave A/C lines attached.

9. Remove the alternator and secure away from the engine.
10. Remove the power steering pump mounting bolts and secure away from the engine.

➡Leave power steering hoses attached.

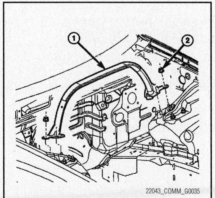

Fig. 67 Remove the mounting nuts (2) to remove the strut tower support (1)—3.7L Engine

22043_COMM_G0035

11. Disconnect the following:
   • Heater hoses from the engine
   • Heater hoses from the heater core
   • Throttle and speed control cables
12. Remove the upper and lower radiator hoses.
13. Remove the radiator assembly.
14. Disconnect the engine-to-body ground straps on the left side of the cowl.
15. Disconnect the engine wiring harness from the following components:

   • Intake air temperature (IAT) sensor
   • Fuel Injectors
   • Throttle Position (TPS) Switch
   • Idle Air Control (IAC) Motor
   • Engine Oil Pressure Switch
   • Engine Coolant Temperature (ECT) Sensor
   • Manifold Absolute Pressure MAP) Sensor
   • Camshaft Position (CMP) Sensor
   • Coil Over Plugs
   • Crankshaft Position Sensor
16. Remove the ignition coil packs.
17. Remove the fuel rail.
18. Remove or disconnect the following:
   • PCV hose
   • Breather hoses
   • Power brake booster vacuum hose
   • Knock sensors
   • Engine oil dipstick tube
   • Intake manifold
19. Install Special Tool 8427 Engine Lifting Fixture using the original mounting bolts from the intake manifold and fuel rail. Torque to the factory specifications for those components.
20. Remove or disconnect the following:
   • Oxygen sensor wiring
   • Crankshaft position sensor
   • Engine block heater power cable, if equipped
   • Front driveshaft at the front differential
   • Starter
   • Ground straps from the left and right side of the engine block
21. Remove the structural cover between the engine and transmission.
22. Disconnect the right and left exhaust pipes at the manifolds and from the crossover. Remove the exhaust pipes from the vehicle.
23. Remove the torque converter bolts, keeping them in order for reinstallation.
24. Remove the transmission bellhousing-to-engine bolts.
25. Remove the left and right engine mount through bolts.
26. Lower the vehicle.
27. Support the transmission with a suitable jack.
28. Connect a suitable engine host to the engine lift plate previously installed.
29. Carefully remove the engine from the vehicle.
30. Installation is the reverse order of removal.
31. Tighten the engine-to-transmission bellhousing bolts to 30 ft. lbs. (41 Nm).
32. Refill the cooling system to the correct level.

33. Refill the engine with oil to the correct level.

34. Start the engine and check for leaks.

4.7L Engine

See Figure 68.

1. Properly relieve the fuel pressure and disconnect the fuel supply line at the fuel rail.

2. Disconnect the battery cables.

3. Drain the cooling system.

4. Remove the strut tower support.

5. Disconnect the two ground straps from the lower left hand side and one ground strap form the lower right hand side of the engine.

6. Remove the through bolt from the left and right side engine mounts.

7. Disconnect the crankshaft position sensor.

8. Remove the exhaust crossover pipe from the exhaust manifolds.

9. Remove the structural cover between the engine and transmission.

10. Remove the starter.

11. Remove the torque converter bolts.

12. Remove the transmission-to-engine mounting bolts.

13. Disconnect the engine block heater power cable, if equipped.

14. Remove the throttle body resonator assembly and air intake hose.

15. Disconnect the throttle and speed control cables.

16. Disconnect the tube from the right and left side crankcase breathers and remove.

17. Properly discharge the A/C system.

18. Remove the A/C compressor.

19. Remove the engine fan.

20. Remove the accessory drive belt.

21. Disconnect the transmission oil cooler lines at the radiator

22. Disconnect the upper and lower radiator hoses.

23. Remove the radiator, A/C condenser, and transmission oil cooler.

24. Remove the alternator.

25. Disconnect the two heater hoses from the timing chain cover and heater core.

26. Unclip and remove the heater hoses from the intake manifold.

27. Disconnect the engine wiring harness from the following points:
- Intake air temperature (IAT) sensor
- Fuel Injectors
- Throttle Position (TPS) Switch
- Idle Air Control (IAC) Motor
- Engine Oil Pressure Switch
- Engine Coolant Temperature (ECT) Sensor

- Manifold absolute pressure (MAP) Sensor
- Camshaft Position (CMP) Sensor
- Coil Over Plugs

28. Disconnect the vacuum lines at the throttle body and intake manifold.

29. Remove the power steering pump and position out of the way.

➡Leave the power steering lines attached.

30. Install the Special Tool 8400 or equivalent Lifting Studs into the cylinder heads.

31. Install the Special Tool 8347 Engine Lifting Fixture as follows:

a. Holding the lifting fixture at a slight angle, slide the large bore in the front plate over the hex portion of the lifting stud.

b. Position the two remaining fixture arms onto the two Special Tools 8400 Lifting Studs, in the cylinder heads.

c. Pull forward and upward on the lifting fixture, so the lifting stud rests in the slotted area below the large bore.

d. Secure the lifting fixture to the three studs using three 7/16 – 14 N/C locknuts.

e. Make sure the lifting loop in the lifting fixture is in the last hole (closest to the throttle body) to minimize the angle of engine during removal.

32. Disconnect the body ground strap at the right and left side cowl.

Fig. 68 When using the engine lifting fixture (3), secure the three nuts (1, 4) on the studs and ensure the lifting loop (2) is in the last hole—4.7L Engine

33. Place a suitable jack under the transmission.

34. Connect an engine hoist to the engine lifting fixture and carefully remove the engine from the vehicle.

35. Installation is the reverse order of removal.

36. Tighten the engine mount through bolts to 70 ft. lbs. (95 Nm).

37. Tighten the transmission-to-engine mounting bolts to 30 ft. lbs. (41 Nm)>

38. Refill the cooling system to the correct level.

39. Start the engine and check for leaks.

5.7L Engine

See Figure 69.

1. Remove the strut tower support.

2. Remove the engine cover.

3. Properly relieve the fuel pressure and disconnect the fuel supply line at the fuel rail.

4. Disconnect the battery negative cable.

5. Remove the air cleaner resonator and duct work as an assembly.

6. Drain the cooling system.

7. Remove the accessory drive belt.

8. Remove the radiator fan shroud.

9. Remove the A/C compressor with the lines attached. Secure compressor out of the way.

10. Remove the alternator assembly.

11. Remove the intake manifold and IAFM as an assembly.

12. Remove the ground wires from the rear of each cylinder head.

13. Disconnect the heater hoses.

➡It is not necessary to disconnect P/S hoses from pump, for P/S pump removal.

14. Remove the power steering pump and set aside.

15. Disconnect the fuel supply line.

16. Raise and support the vehicle on a hoist and drain the engine oil.

17. Remove engine front mount to frame bolts and nuts.

18. Disconnect the transmission oil cooler lines from their retainers at the oil pan bolts.

19. Disconnect exhaust pipe at manifolds.

20. Disconnect the starter wires. Remove starter motor.

21. Remove the structural dust cover.

22. Remove drive plate to converter bolts.

23. Remove the oil pan to transmission bolts.

24. Remove transmission bell housing to engine block bolts.

25. Lower the vehicle.

26. Install Special Tools 8984 and 8984—UPD Engine Lifting Fixtures.

27. Separate engine from transmission, remove engine from vehicle, and install engine assembly on a repair stand.

To install:

28. Position the engine in the engine compartment.

29. Lower engine into compartment and align engine with transmission.

30. Mate engine and transmission and install two transmission-to-engine block mounting bolts finger tight.

31. Lower engine assembly until the engine mounts rests in frame perches.

32. Install remaining transmission to engine block mounting bolts and the oil pan to transmission bolts and tighten.

33. Install and tighten engine mount to frame bolts and nuts.

34. Install drive plate to torque converter bolts.

35. Install the structural dust cover.

36. Install the starter and connect the starter wires.

37. Install exhaust pipe to manifold.

38. Lower the vehicle.

39. Remove the engine lift fixture, special tool no. 8984 and 8984—UPD.

40. Connect the fuel supply line.

41. Reinstall the power steering pump.

42. Connect the heater hoses.

43. Reconnect the ground wires to the rear of each cylinder head.

44. Install the intake manifold.

45. Install the generator, and wire connections.

46. Install the A/C compressor.

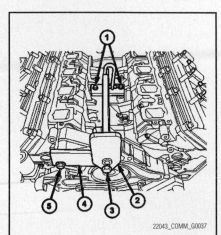

Fig. 69 Installation of the Special Tools 8984 (2) and 8984-UPD (4) and the bolt locations (1,3,5)—5.7L Engine

22043_COMM_G0037

47. Install the accessory drive belt.

48. Install the radiator fan shroud.

49. Connect the radiator lower hose.

50. Connect the transmission oil cooler lines to the radiator.

51. Connect the radiator upper hose.

52. Install the air cleaner resonator and duct work.

53. Add engine oil to crankcase.

54. Fill the cooling system to the correct level.

55. Install the engine cover.

56. Install the strut tower support.

57. Connect the negative battery cable.

58. Start engine and inspect for leaks.

EXHAUST MANIFOLD

REMOVAL & INSTALLATION

3.7L Engine

Right Side

1. Disconnect the negative battery cable.

2. Raise and safely support the vehicle.

3. Remove the bolts and nuts attaching the exhaust pipe to the engine exhaust manifold.

4. Lower the vehicle.

5. Remove the exhaust heat shield.

6. Remove bolts, nuts and washers attaching manifold to cylinder head.

7. Remove manifold and gasket from the cylinder head.

To install:

> ✳✳ **WARNING**
>
> **If the studs came out with the nuts when removing the engine exhaust manifold, install new studs. Apply sealer on the coarse thread ends. Water leaks may develop at the studs if this precaution is not taken.**

8. Position the engine exhaust manifold and gasket on the two studs located on the cylinder head. Install conical washers and nuts on these studs.

9. Install remaining conical washers. Starting at the center arm and working outward, tighten the bolts and nuts to 18 ft. lbs. (25 Nm).

10. Install the exhaust heat shields.

11. Raise and safely support the vehicle.

> ✳✳ **WARNING**
>
> **Over tightening heat shield fasteners, may cause shield to distort and/or crack.**

12. Assemble exhaust pipe to manifold and secure with bolts, nuts and retainers.

Tighten the bolts and nuts to 25 ft. lbs. (34 Nm).

13. Lower the vehicle.

14. Connect the negative battery cable.

Left Side

1. Disconnect the negative battery cable.

2. Raise and safely support the vehicle.

3. Remove the bolts and nuts attaching the exhaust pipe to the engine exhaust manifold.

4. Lower the vehicle.

5. Remove the exhaust heat shields.

6. Remove bolts, nuts and washers attaching manifold to cylinder head.

7. Remove manifold and gasket from the cylinder head.

To install:

> ✳✳ **WARNING**
>
> **If the studs came out with the nuts when removing the engine exhaust manifold, install new studs. Apply sealer on the coarse thread ends. Water leaks may develop at the studs if this precaution is not taken.**

8. Position the engine exhaust manifold and gasket on the two studs located on the cylinder head. Install conical washers and nuts on these studs.

9. Install remaining conical washers. Starting at the center arm and working outward, tighten the bolts and nuts to 18 ft. lbs. (25 Nm).

10. Install the exhaust heat shields.

11. Raise and safely support the vehicle.

> ✳✳ **WARNING**
>
> **Over tightening heat shield fasteners, may cause shield to distort and/or crack.**

12. Assemble exhaust pipe to manifold and secure with bolts, nuts and retainers. Tighten the bolts and nuts to 25 ft. lbs. (34 Nm).

13. Lower the vehicle.

14. Connect the negative battery cable.

4.7L Engine

Right Side

See Figure 70.

1. Disconnect the negative battery cable.

2. Remove the battery from the vehicle.

3. Remove the Power Distribution Center (PDC) fasteners.

4. Remove the battery tray.

5. Remove the washer bottle assembly.

6. Remove the accessory drive belt.

7. Remove the A/C compressor mounting bolts and set the compressor aside.

8. Remove the A/C accumulator support bracket mounting bolts.

9. Drain the cooling system.

10. Remove the heater hoses from the engine.

11. Remove the nuts holding the exhaust manifold heat shield.

12. Remove the heat shield.

13. Remove the upper exhaust manifold mounting bolts.

14. Using a suitable jack, raise the engine up enough to disconnect the exhaust pipe from the manifold.

15. Remove the starter mounting bolts and move the starter aside.

16. Remove the lower exhaust manifold mounting bolts.

17. Remove the exhaust manifold and gasket. Remove the manifold from below the engine compartment.

To install:

18. Install the exhaust manifold and gasket. Tighten the bolts from the center and working outward to 18 ft. lbs. (25 Nm).

✷✷ WARNING

Do not tighten the bolts until there are all in place.

19. Install the exhaust manifold heat shield and tighten the nuts to 72 inch lbs. (8 Nm) and the back off each nut 45°.

20. Install or connect the following:
- Starter
- Exhaust pipe to the exhaust manifold
- Heater hoses
- A/C compressor
- Accessory drive belt
- Washer bottle assembly
- PDC
- Battery tray
- Negative battery cable

21. Refill the cooling system to the correct level.

22. Start the engine and check for leaks.

Left Side

1. Disconnect the negative battery cable.

2. Raise and safely support the vehicle.

3. Disconnect the exhaust pipe from the manifold.

4. Lower the vehicle.

5. Remove the air intake assembly.

6. Remove the front two exhaust manifold heat shield mounting nuts. Raise and safely support the vehicle and remove the rear heat shield fasteners.

7. Remove the heat shield.

8. Lower the vehicle and remove the upper exhaust manifold bolts.

9. Raise and safely support the vehicle

and remove the lower exhaust manifold bolts.

10. Remove the exhaust manifold and gasket. Remove the manifold from below the engine compartment.

To install:

11. Install the exhaust manifold and gasket. Tighten the bolts from the center and working outward to 18 ft. lbs. (25 Nm).

✷✷ WARNING

Do not tighten the bolts until there are all in place.

12. Install the exhaust manifold heat shield and tighten the nuts to 72 inch lbs. (8 Nm) and the back off each nut 45°.

13. Install the air intake assembly.

14. Connect the exhaust pipe to the exhaust manifold.

15. Connect the negative battery cable.

16. Lower the vehicle.

5.7L Engine

See Figures 71 and 72.

1. Disconnect the negative battery cable.

2. Raise and safely support the vehicle.

3. Disconnect the exhaust pipe from the manifold.

4. Remove the engine mount to frame bolts.

5. Using a suitable jack, raise the engine enough to remove the manifolds.

6. Remove the engine mount.

7. Remove the heat shield.

8. Remove the manifold bolts using sequence provided.

9. Remove the manifold and gasket.

To install:

10. Inspect the manifold for cracks.

11. Inspect the mating surfaces of manifold for flatness with a straightedge. Gasket surfaces must be flat within 0.2mm per 300mm (0.008 inch per foot).

12. Install the manifold gasket and manifold and tighten the bolts in sequence to 25 ft. lbs. (34 Nm).

13. Install the heat shield and tighten nuts to 70 inch lbs (8 Nm).

14. Install the front engine mount. Torque to 70 ft. lbs. (95 Nm).

15. Lower the engine.

16. Install and tighten right and left side engine mount to frame fasteners. Torque to 70 ft. lbs. (95 Nm).

17. Install the exhaust flange to pipe bolts.

18. Lower the vehicle.

19. Connect negative battery cable.

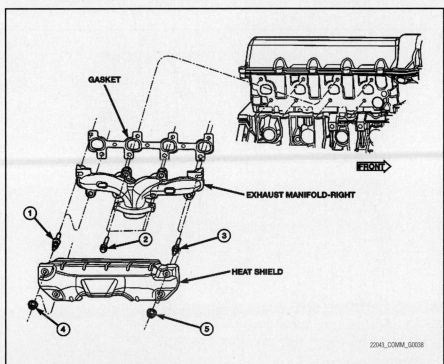

GASKET

FRONT

EXHAUST MANIFOLD-RIGHT

HEAT SHIELD

22043_COMM_G0038

Fig. 70 Exploded view of the heat shield mounting nuts (4,5) and exhaust manifold mounting studs (1,2,3)—4.7L Engine Right Side

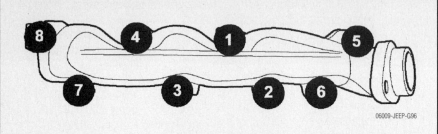

Fig. 71 Left side exhaust manifold bolt sequence—5.7L engine

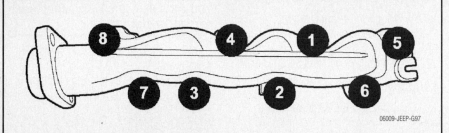

Fig. 72 Right side exhaust manifold bolt sequence—5.7L engine

INTAKE MANIFOLD

REMOVAL & INSTALLATION

3.7L & 4.7L Engines

See Figures 73 and 74.

1. Properly relieve the fuel system pressure.
2. Disconnect the negative battery cable.
3. Drain the cooling system.
4. Remove the air intake system.
5. Disconnect the throttle and speed control cables.
6. Disconnect the electrical connectors for the following components:
- Manifold Absolute Pressure (MAP) sensor connector
- Intake Air Temperature (IAT) sensor connector
- Throttle Position (TP) sensor connector
- Idle Air Control (IAC) valve connector
- Engine Coolant Temperature (ECT) sensor
7. Disconnect the following components:
- Positive Crankcase Ventilation (PCV) valve and hose
- Canister purge vacuum line
- Brake booster vacuum line
- Cruise control servo hose
8. Remove the alternator.
9. Remove the air conditioning compressor.
10. Disconnect the left and right radio suppressor straps.
11. Disconnect and remove the ignition coil packs.
12. Remove the top oil dipstick tube mounting bolt and ground strap.
13. Remove the fuel rail.
14. Remove the throttle body assembly and mounting bracket.
15. Remove the heater hoses from the engine front cover and heater core.
16. Unclip, then remove the hoses from the intake manifold.
17. Support the engine using Special Tool 8534 Engine Support Fixture.
18. Remove the right side engine mount-to-frame bolt.
19. With the bolt removed, carefully lower the engine until it resets in the frame mount.
20. Remove the intake manifold bolts in the reverse order of the tightening sequence.
21. Remove the intake manifold and gaskets.

To install:

22. Install the intake manifold gaskets.
23. Install the intake manifold and tighten the mounting bolts in the sequence shown to 105 inch lbs. (12 Nm).

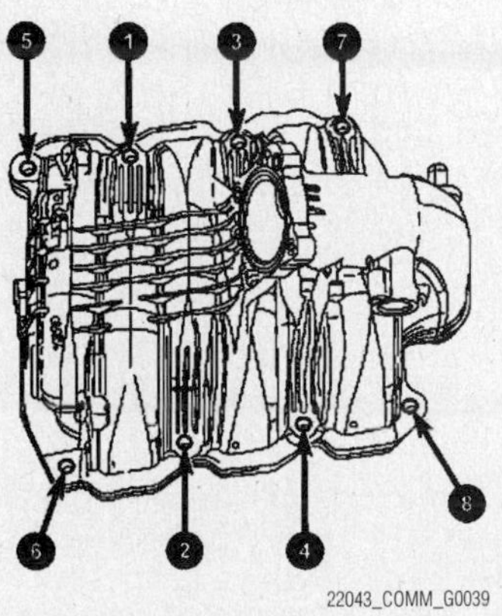

Fig. 73 Intake manifold bolt torque sequence—3.7L Engine

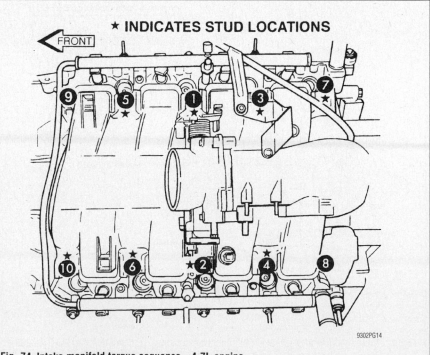

Fig. 74 Intake manifold torque sequence—4.7L engine

24. Install the left and right radio suppressor straps.

25. Install the throttle body assembly.

26. Connect the throttle and speed control cables to the throttle body.

27. Install the fuel rail.

28. Install and connect the ignition coil packs.

29. Position the heater hoses into the clips on the intake manifold, then connect the heater hoses to the heater core and front cover.

30. Connect the electrical connectors for the following components:
- MAP sensor
- IAT sensor
- TP sensor
- IAC valve
- ECT sensor

31. Install the top oil dipstick mounting bolt and ground strap.

32. Install the alternator.

33. Install the A/C compressor.

34. Connect the following components:
- Positive Crankcase Ventilation (PCV) valve and hose
- Canister purge vacuum line
- Brake booster vacuum line
- Cruise control servo hose

35. Raise the engine using the engine support fixture.

36. Install the right side engine mount through bolt and remove the engine support fixture.

37. Install the air intake assembly.

38. Refill the cooling system to the correct level.

39. Connect the negative battery cable.

39. Start the engine and check for leaks.

5.7L Engine

1. Properly relieve the fuel system pressure.

2. Disconnect the negative battery cable.

3. Remove the engine appearance cover.

4. Remove the air intake hose.

5. Remove the ignition wires from the top of the intake manifold.

6. Disconnect electrical connectors for the following components:
- Manifold Absolute Pressure (MAP) Sensor
- Fuel Injectors
- ETC (Electric Throttle Control)

7. Remove the wiring harness from the intake manifold.

8. Disconnect brake booster hose, purge hose, and the Make-Up Air (MUA) hose.

9. Remove the EGR tube from the intake manifold.

10. Remove the intake manifold retaining fasteners in a crisscross pattern starting from the outside bolts and ending at the middle bolts.

11. Remove the intake manifold as an assembly.

To install:

12. Position and install the intake manifold. Tighten the retaining bolts in sequence from the middle bolts towards the outside in a crisscross pattern to 105 inch lbs. (12 Nm).

13. Install the EGR rube.

14. Install the wiring harness to the intake manifold.

15. Connect the electrical connectors:
- MAP sensor
- Fuel Injectors
- ETC

16. Install the ignition wires.

17. Connect the brake booster hose, purge hose and MUA hose.

18. Install the air intake hose.

19. Install the engine appearance cover.

20. Connect the negative battery cable.

OIL PAN

REMOVAL & INSTALLATION

3.7L Engine

See Figures 75 and 76.

1. Disconnect the negative battery cable.

2. Drain the engine oil and remove the oil filter.

3. Remove the radiator fan.

4. Remove the intake manifold.

5. Install Special Tool 8534 Engine Lifting Fixture, or equivalent, to the engine.

➡**Do not raise engine at this time.**

6. Remove the structural cover using sequence shown.

7. Remove both left and right side engine mount through bolts.

8. Raise engine to provide enough clearance to remove the oil pan.

➡**Do not pry on oil pan or oil pan gasket. Gasket is mounted to engine and does not come out with oil pan.**

9. Remove the oil pan mounting bolts and oil pan.

10. Unbolt oil pump pickup tube and remove tube and oil pan gasket from engine.

To install:

11. Clean the oil pan gasket mating surface of the bedplate and oil pan.

12. Inspect integrated oil pan gasket, and replace as necessary.

13. Position the integrated oil pan gasket/windage tray assembly.

14. Install the oil pickup tube

15. If removed, install stud at position No. 9.

16. Install the mounting bolt and nuts. Tighten nuts to 20 ft. lbs. (28 Nm).

17. Position the oil pan and install the mounting bolts. Tighten the mounting bolts to 15 Nm (11 ft. lbs.) in the sequence shown.

18. Install structural dust cover

19. Lower the engine into mounts.

20. Remove the lifting tool.

21. Install both the left and right side engine mount through bolts. Tighten the nuts to 50 ft. lbs. (68 Nm).

22. Install the intake manifold.

23. Fill the engine oil to the correct level.

24. Reconnect the negative battery cable.

25. Start engine and check for leaks.

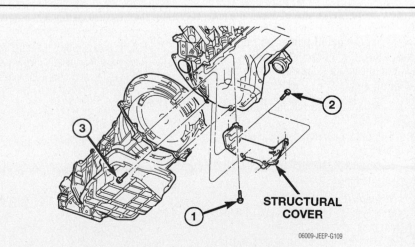

06009-JEEP-G109

Fig. 75 Structural cover removal and installation sequence—3.7L and 4.7L engines

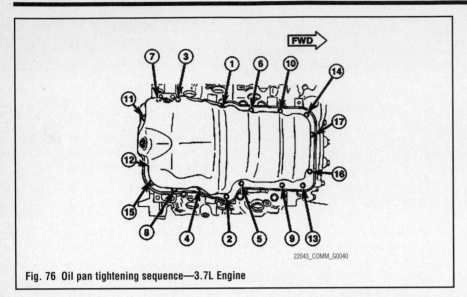

Fig. 76 Oil pan tightening sequence—3.7L Engine

4.7L Engine

See Figure 77.

1. Disconnect the negative battery cable.
2. Install engine support fixture special tool 8534, or equivalent.

➡**Do not raise engine at this time.**

3. Loosen both left and right side engine mount through bolts. Do not remove the bolts.
4. Remove the structural dust cover.
5. Drain engine oil.

⚹⚹ WARNING

Only raise the engine enough to provide clearance for oil pan removal. Check for proper clearance at fan shroud to fan and cowl to intake manifold.

6. Remove the engine mount through bolts and raise engine using special tool 8534 to provide clearance to remove oil pan.

➡**Do not pry on oil pan or oil pan gasket. Gasket is integral to engine windage tray and does not come out with oil pan.**

7. Remove the oil pan mounting bolts and oil pan.
8. Unbolt oil pump pickup tube and remove tube.
9. Inspect the integral windage tray and gasket and replace as needed.

To install:
10. Clean the oil pan gasket mating surface of the bedplate and oil pan.
11. Position the oil pan gasket and pickup tube with new O-ring. Install the

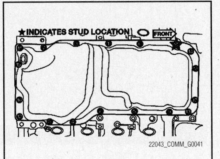

Fig. 77 Oil pan torque sequence—4.7L Engine

mounting bolt and nuts. Tighten bolt and nuts to 20 ft. lbs. (28 Nm).
12. Position the oil pan and install the mounting bolts. Tighten the mounting bolts to 15 Nm (11 ft. lbs.) in the sequence shown.
13. Lower the engine into mounts using special tool 8534.
14. Install both the left and right side engine mount through bolts. Tighten the nuts to 50 ft. lbs. (68 Nm).
15. Remove special tool 8534.
16. Install structural dust cover.
17. Fill the engine oil to the correct level.
18. Reconnect the negative battery cable.
19. Start engine and check for leaks.

5.7L Engine

See Figures 78 and 79.

1. Disconnect the negative battery cable.
2. Drain engine oil and remove the oil filter.
3. Remove the engine appearance cover.
4. Remove the intake manifold.
5. Raise and safely support the vehicle.

6. Remove both left and right side engine mount to frame bolts.
7. Remove the engine oil dipstick and tube from the oil pan.
8. Lower the vehicle.
9. Install engine support fixture special tool 8534, or equivalent.

➡**Do not use the third leg.**

10. Raise engine using special tool 8534 to provide clearance to remove oil pan.
11. Raise and safely support the vehicle.
12. Remove the front axle.
13. Remove the structural dust cover.

➡**Do not pry on oil pan or oil pan gasket. Gasket is integral to engine windage tray and does not come out with oil pan.**

➡**The horizontal M10 fasteners are 5mm longer in length, and must be reinstalled in original locations.**

14. Remove the M10 fasteners (vertical and horizontal) from the rear of the oil pan to the transmission and engine.
15. Remove the oil pan mounting bolts using the sequence provided, and oil pan.

➡**When the oil pan is removed, a new oil pan gasket/windage tray assembly must be installed. The old gasket cannot be reused.**

16. Discard the integral windage tray and gasket and replace.

To install:
17. Clean the oil pan gasket mating surface of the block and oil pan.

➡**Mopar® Engine RTV, or equivalent, must be applied to the 4 T-joints, (area where front cover, rear retainer, block, and oil pan gasket meet). The bead of RTV should cover the bottom of the gasket. This area is approximately 4.5mm x 25mm in each of the 4 T-joint locations.**

18. Apply Mopar® T Engine RTV at the 4 T-joints.

➡**When the oil pan is removed, a new oil pan gasket/windage tray assembly must be installed. The old gasket cannot be reused.**

19. Install a new oil pan gasket/windage tray assembly.
20. If removed, reinstall the oil pump pickup tube with new O-ring. Tighten tube to pump fasteners to 250 inch lbs. (28 Nm).

➡**The horizontal M10 fasteners are 5mm longer in length, and must be reinstalled in original locations.**

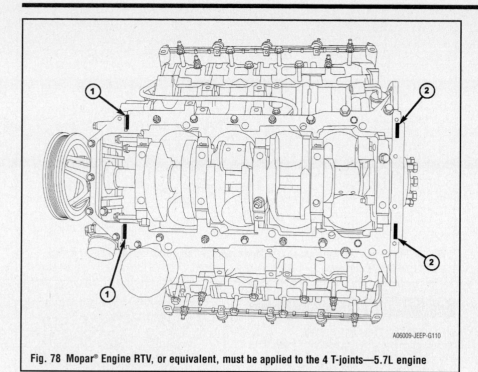

Fig. 78 Mopar® Engine RTV, or equivalent, must be applied to the 4 T-joints—5.7L engine

➡**The horizontal M10 fasteners are 5mm longer in length, and must be reinstalled in original locations.**

21. Align the rear of the oil pan with the rear face of the engine block, and install the M10 and M6 oil pan fasteners finger tight. Using the following torque sequence, torque the M6 mounting bolts to 44 inch lbs. (5 Nm).

22. Using the following torque sequence, torque the M10 oil pan fasteners to 39 ft. lbs. (54 Nm).

23. Using the following torque sequence, torque the M6 oil pan fasteners to 106 inch lbs. (12 Nm).

24. Install both the left and right side oil pan to transmission bolts. Torque the bolts to 39 ft. lbs. (54 Nm).

25. Lower the engine into mounts.

26. Install both the left and right side engine mount bolts and nuts. Torque the studs and nuts to 39 ft. lbs. (54 Nm).

27. Install the engine oil dipstick and tube.

28. Remove special tool 8534.

29. Install the intake manifold.

30. Install the front axle.

31. Install the engine appearance cover.

32. Install the oil filter.

33. Fill the engine with oil to the correct level.

34. Reconnect the negative battery cable.

35. Start engine and check for leaks.

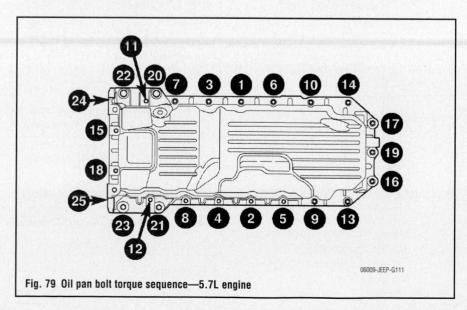

Fig. 79 Oil pan bolt torque sequence—5.7L engine

OIL PUMP

REMOVAL & INSTALLATION

3.7L & 4.7L Engines

See Figure 80.

1. Remove the oil pan.
2. Remove the timing chain cover.
3. Remove the timing chains and tensioners.
4. Remove the four bolts, primary chain tensioner and the oil pump.

To install:

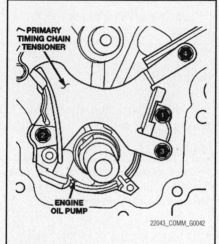

Fig. 80 Oil pump & primary chain tensioner bolt torque sequence—3.7L & 4.7L Engines

5. Position the oil pump onto the crankshaft and install one oil pump retaining bolts.

6. Position the primary timing chain tensioner and install three retaining bolts.

7. Tighten the oil pump and primary timing chain tensioner retaining bolts to 250 inch lbs. (28 Nm) in the sequence shown.

8. Install the secondary timing chain tensioners and timing chains.

9. Install the timing chain cover.

10. Install the oil pan.

11. Start the engine and check for leaks.

5.7L Engine

See Figure 81.

1. Remove the oil pan and pick-up tube.
2. Remove the timing chain cover.
3. Remove the four bolts, and the oil pump.

To install:

4. Position the oil pump onto the crankshaft and install the 4 oil pump retaining bolts.

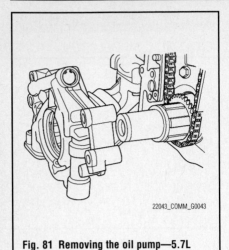

Fig. 81 Removing the oil pump—5.7L Engine

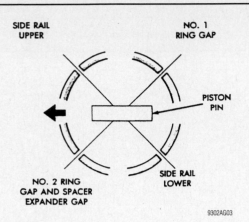

Fig. 82 Piston ring end-gap spacing. Position raised "F" on piston towards front of engine—3.7L, 4.7L & 5.7L engines

5. Tighten the oil pump retaining bolts to 250 inch lbs. (28 Nm).

6. Install the timing chain cover.

7. Install the pick-up tube and oil pan.

INSPECTION

➡In the event the oil pump is not functioning or out of specification it must be replaced as an assembly.

1. Remove the pump cover.

2. Clean all parts thoroughly. Mating surface of the oil pump housing should be smooth. If the pump cover is scratched or grooved the oil pump assembly should be replaced.

3. Slide the outer rotor into the body of the oil pump. Press the outer rotor to one side of the oil pump body and measure clearance between the outer rotor and the body. If the measurement is 0.235mm (0.009 in.) or more the oil pump assembly must be replaced.

4. Install the inner rotor in the into the oil pump body. Measure the clearance between the inner and outer rotors. If the clearance between the rotors is .150 mm (0.006 in.) or more the oil pump assembly must be replaced.

5. Place a straight edge across the body of the oil pump (between the bolt holes), if a feeler gauge of .095 mm (0.0038 in.) or greater can be inserted between the straight-edge and the rotors, the pump must be replaced.

6. Reinstall the pump cover. Torque the fasteners to 132 inch lbs. (15 Nm).

PISTON AND RING

POSITIONING

See Figure 82.

REAR MAIN SEAL

REMOVAL & INSTALLATION

See Figures 83 through 85.

1. Before servicing the vehicle, refer to the precautions section.

2. Remove or disconnect the following:
- Transmission
- Flexplate

3. Thread Oil Seal Remover 8506 into the rear main seal as far as possible and remove the rear main seal.

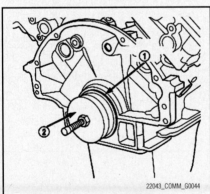

Fig. 83 Use Special Tool 8506 (2) to remove the rear main seal (1).

To install:

4. Install or connect the following:
- Seal Guide 8349-2 onto the crank-shaft
- Rear main seal on the seal guide
- Rear main seal, using the Crank-shaft Rear Oil Seal Installer 8349 and Driver Handle C-4171; tap it into place until the installer is flush with the cylinder block
- Flexplate. Torque the bolts to 45 ft. lbs. (60 Nm).
- Transmission

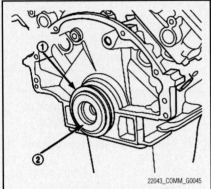

Fig. 84 Position the rear oil seal (1) onto the guide (2).

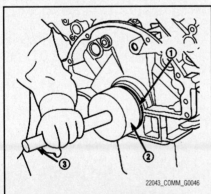

Fig. 85 Use Special Tools 8349 (2) and C-4171 (3) to drive the oil seal (1) into place.

5. Start the engine, check for leaks and repair if necessary.

TIMING CHAIN, SPROCKETS, FRONT COVER AND SEAL

REMOVAL & INSTALLATION

3.7L Engine

See Figure 86.

1. Before servicing the vehicle, refer to the precautions section.

2. Disconnect the battery negative cable.

3. Drain the cooling system.

4. Remove electric cooling fan and fan shroud assembly.

5. Remove the radiator fan.

6. Rotate engine until timing mark on crankshaft damper aligns with TDC mark on timing chain cover.

7. Make sure the camshaft sprocket "V6" marks are at the 12 o'clock position (No. 1 TDC exhaust stroke).

8. Remove power steering pump.

9. Remove access plugs from left and right cylinder heads for access to chain guide fasteners.

10. Remove the oil fill housing to gain access to the right side tensioner arm fastener.

11. Disconnect both heater hoses at timing cover.

12. Disconnect lower radiator hose at engine.

13. Remove the accessory drive belt tensioner assembly.

14. Remove the crankshaft damper.

15. Remove the generator.

16. Remove the A/C compressor.

✳✳ WARNING

The 3.7L engine uses an anaerobic sealer instead of a gasket to seal the front cover to the engine block, from the factory. For service, Mopar° Grey Engine RTV sealant must be substituted.

➡**It is not necessary to remove the water pump for timing cover removal.**

17. Remove the bolts holding the timing cover to engine block.

18. Remove the timing cover.

19. Collapse and pin primary chain tensioner.

✳✳ WARNING

Plate behind left secondary chain tensioner could fall into oil pan. Therefore, cover pan opening.

20. Remove the secondary chain tensioners.

21. Remove the camshaft position sensor.

✳✳ WARNING

Care should be taken not to damage camshaft target wheel. Do not hold target wheel while loosening or tightening camshaft sprocket. Do not

place the target wheel near a magnetic source of any kind. A damaged or magnetized target wheel could cause a vehicle no start condition.

✳✳ WARNING

Do not forcefully rotate the camshafts or crankshaft independently of each other. Damaging intake valve to piston contact will occur. Ensure negative battery cable is disconnected to guard against accidental starter engagement.

22. Remove left and right camshaft sprocket bolts.

23. While holding the left camshaft steel tube with Special Tool 8428 Camshaft Wrench, remove the left camshaft sprocket. Slowly rotate the camshaft approximately 5 degrees clockwise to a neutral position.

24. While holding the right camshaft steel tube with Special Tool 8428 Camshaft Wrench, remove the right camshaft sprocket.

25. Remove the idler sprocket assembly bolt.

26. Slide the idler sprocket assembly and crank sprocket forward simultaneously to remove the primary and secondary chains.

27. Remove both pivoting tensioner arms and chain guides.

28. Remove the primary chain tensioner.

To install:

29. Using a vise, lightly compress the secondary chain tensioner piston until the piston step is flush with the tensioner body. Using a pin or suitable tool, release ratchet pawl by pulling pawl back against spring force through access hole on side of tensioner. While continuing to hold pawl back, push ratchet device to approximately 2mm from the tensioner body. Install Special Tool 8514 lock pin into hole on front of tensioner. Slowly open vise to transfer piston spring force to lock pin.

30. Position primary chain tensioner over oil pump and insert bolts into lower two holes on tensioner bracket. Tighten bolts to 250 inch lbs. (28 Nm).

31. Install right side chain tensioner arm. Install Torx® bolt. Tighten bolt to 250 inch lbs. (28 Nm).

✳✳ WARNING

The silver bolts retain the guides to the cylinder heads and the black bolts retain the guides to the engine block.

32. Install the left side chain guide. Tighten the bolts to 250 inch lbs. (28 Nm).

33. Install left side chain tensioner arm, and Torx® bolt. Tighten bolt to 250 inch lbs. (28 Nm).

34. Install the right side chain guide. Tighten the bolts to 250 inch lbs. (28 Nm).

35. Install both secondary chains onto the idler sprocket. Align two plated links on the secondary chains to be visible through the two lower openings on the idler sprocket (4 o'clock and 8 o'clock). Once the secondary timing chains are installed, position special tool 8429 to hold chains in place for installation.

36. Align the primary chain double plated links with the timing mark at 12 o'clock on the idler sprocket. Align the primary chain single plated link with the timing mark at 6 o'clock on the crankshaft sprocket.

37. Lubricate the idler shaft and bushings with clean engine oil.

➡**The idler sprocket must be timed to the counterbalance shaft drive gear before the idler sprocket is fully seated.**

38. Install all chains, crankshaft sprocket, and idler sprocket as an assembly. After guiding both secondary chains through the block and cylinder head openings, affix chains with an elastic strap or equivalent. This will maintain tension on chains to aid in installation. Align the timing mark on the idler sprocket gear to the timing mark on the counterbalance shaft drive gear, then seat idler sprocket fully. Before installing idler sprocket bolt, lubricate washer with oil, and tighten idler sprocket assembly retaining bolt to 25 ft. lbs. (34 Nm).

➡**It will be necessary to slightly rotate camshafts for sprocket installation.**

39. Align left camshaft sprocket "L" dot to plated link on chain.

40. Align right camshaft sprocket "R" dot to plated link on chain.

✳✳ WARNING

Remove the excess oil from the camshaft sprocket bolt. Failure to do so can result in over torque of bolt resulting in bolt failure.

41. Remove Special Tool 8429, then attach both sprockets to camshafts. Remove excess oil from bolts, then install sprocket bolts, but do not tighten at this time.

42. Verify that all plated links are aligned with the marks on all sprockets and the

"V6" marks on camshaft sprockets are at the 12 o'clock position.

⁂ WARNING

Ensure the plate between the left secondary chain tensioner and block is correctly installed.

43. Install both secondary chain tensioners. Tighten bolts to 250 inch lbs. (28 Nm).

➡ **Left and right secondary chain tensioners are not common.**

44. Remove all locking pins from tensioners.

⁂ WARNING

After pulling locking pins out of each tensioner, do not manually extend the tensioner(s) ratchet. Doing so will over-tension the chains, resulting in noise and/or high timing chain loads.

45. Using Special Tool 6958, Spanner with Adapter Pins 8346, tighten left camshaft sprocket bolts to 90 ft. lbs. (122 Nm).

46. Using Special Tool 6958, Spanner with Adapter Pins 8346, tighten right camshaft sprocket bolts to 90 ft. lbs. (122 Nm).

47. Rotate engine two full revolutions. Verify timing marks are at the follow locations:

- Primary chain idler sprocket dot is at 12 o'clock
- Primary chain crankshaft sprocket dot is at 6 o'clock
- Secondary chain camshaft sprockets "V6" marks are at 12 o'clock
- Counterbalance shaft drive gear dot is aligned to the idler sprocket gear dot

48. Lubricate all three chains with engine oil.

49. After installing all chains, it is recommended that the idler gear end play be checked. The end play must be within 0.10–0.25mm (0.004–0.010 in.). If not within specification, the idler gear must be replaced.

⁂ WARNING

Do not use oil based liquids to clean timing cover or block surfaces. Use only rubbing alcohol, along with plastic or wooden scrapers. Use no wire brushes or abrasive wheels or metal scrapers, or damage to surfaces could result.

50. Clean the timing chain cover and block surface using rubbing alcohol.

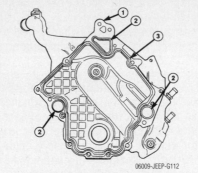

06009-JEEP-G112

Fig. 86 Front cover sealant application—3.7L engine

⁂ WARNING

The 3.7L uses a special anaerobic sealer instead of a gasket to seal the timing cover to the engine block, from the factory. For service repairs, Mopar® Engine RTV must be used as a substitute.

51. Inspect the water passage O-rings for any damage, and replace as necessary.

52. Apply Mopar® Engine RTV sealer to front cover as shown using a 3 to 4mm thick bead.

53. Install cover. Tighten fasteners in sequence as shown in to 43 ft. lbs. (58 Nm).

54. Install crankshaft damper.

55. Install the A/C compressor.

56. Install the generator.

57. Install accessory drive belt tensioner.

58. Install radiator upper and lower hoses.

59. Install both heater hoses.

60. Install radiator fan.

61. Install cylinder head covers.

➡ **Before installing threaded plug in right cylinder head, the plug must be coated with sealant to prevent leaks.**

62. Coat the large threaded access plug with Mopar® Thread Sealant with Teflon, then install into the right cylinder head and tighten to 60 ft. lbs. (81 Nm).

63. Install the oil fill housing.

64. Install access plug in left cylinder head.

65. Install power steering pump.

66. Refill the cooling system to the correct level.

67. Connect negative cable to battery.

4.7L Engine

See Figures 87 through 94.

1. Before servicing the vehicle, refer to the precautions section.

2. Disconnect the battery negative cable.

3. Drain the cooling system.

4. Disconnect both heater hoses at timing cover.

5. Disconnect lower radiator hose at engine.

6. Remove the crankshaft damper.

7. Remove the accessory drive belt tensioner assembly.

8. Rotate engine until timing mark on crankshaft damper aligns with TDC mark on timing chain cover cylinder exhaust stroke) and the camshaft sprocket "V8" marks are at the 12 o'clock position.

9. Remove power steering pump.

10. Remove access plugs from left and right cylinder heads for access to chain guide fasteners.

11. Remove the oil fill housing to gain access to the right side tensioner arm fastener.

12. Remove the generator and A/C compressor.

⁂ WARNING

The 4.7L engine uses an RTV sealer instead of a gasket to seal the front cover to the engine block, from the factory. For service, Mopar® Grey Engine RTV sealant must be substituted.

➡ **It is not necessary to remove the water pump for timing cover removal.**

13. Remove the bolts holding the timing cover to engine block.

14. Remove the cover.

15. Disconnect negative cable from battery.

16. Drain the cooling system.

17. Remove right and left cylinder head covers.

18. Remove the radiator fan.

19. Collapse and pin primary chain tensioner.

⁂ WARNING

Plate behind left secondary chain tensioner could fall into oil pan. Therefore, cover pan opening.

20. Remove the secondary chain tensioners.

21. Remove the camshaft position sensor from right cylinder head.

⁂ WARNING

Care should be taken not to damage camshaft target wheel. Do not hold target wheel while loosening or tight-

ening camshaft sprocket. Do not place the target wheel near a magnetic source of any kind. A damaged or magnetized target wheel could cause a vehicle no start condition.

✻✻ WARNING

Do not forcefully rotate the camshafts or crankshaft independently of each other. Damaging intake valve to piston contact will occur. Ensure negative battery cable is disconnected to guard against accidental starter engagement.

22. Remove left and right camshaft sprocket bolts.
23. While holding the left camshaft steel tube with adjustable pliers, remove the left camshaft sprocket. Slowly rotate the camshaft approximately 15 degrees clockwise to a neutral position.
24. While holding the right camshaft steel tube with adjustable pliers, remove the right camshaft sprocket. Slowly rotate the camshaft approximately 45 degrees counterclockwise to a neutral position.
25. Remove the idler sprocket assembly bolt.
26. Slide the idler sprocket assembly and crank sprocket forward simultaneously to remove the primary and secondary chains.
27. Remove both pivoting tensioner arms and chain guides.
28. Remove chain tensioner.

To install:

29. Using a vise, lightly compress the secondary chain tensioner piston until the piston step is flush with the tensioner body. Using a pin or suitable tool, release ratchet pawl by pulling pawl back against spring force through access hole on side of tensioner. While continuing to hold pawl back, push the ratchet device to approximately 2mm from the tensioner body. Install Special Tool 8514 lock pin into hole on front of the tensioner. Slowly open vise to transfer piston spring force to lock pin.
30. Position primary chain tensioner over oil pump and insert bolts into lower two holes on tensioner bracket. Tighten bolts to 250 inch lbs. (28 Nm).

✻✻ WARNING

Over-tightening the tensioner arm Torx® bolt can cause severe damage to the cylinder head. Tighten bolt to specified torque only.

31. Install right side chain tensioner arm. Apply Mopar® Lock N, Seal to Torx® bolt, tighten bolt to 150 inch lbs. (17 Nm).

➡The silver bolts retain the guides to the cylinder heads and the black bolts retain the guides to the engine block.

32. Install the left side chain guide. Tighten the bolts to 250 inch lbs. (28 Nm).

✻✻ WARNING

Over-tightening the tensioner arm can cause severe damage to the cylinder head. Tighten bolt to specified torque only.

33. Install left side chain tensioner arm. Apply Mopar® Lock N, Seal to bolt, tighten bolt to 150 inch lbs. (17 Nm).
34. Install the right side chain guide. Tighten the bolts to 250 inch lbs. (28 Nm).
35. Install both secondary chains onto the idler sprocket. Align two plated links on the secondary chains to be visible through the two lower openings on the idler sprocket (4 o'clock and 8 o'clock). Once the secondary timing chains are installed, position special tool 8515 to hold chains in place for installation.
36. Align the primary chain double plated links with the timing mark at 12 o'clock on the idler sprocket. Align the primary chain single plated link with the timing mark at 6 o'clock on the crankshaft sprocket.
37. Lubricate the idler shaft and bushings with clean engine oil.
38. Install all chains, crankshaft sprocket, and idler sprocket as an assembly. After guiding both secondary chains through the block and cylinder head openings, affix chains with an elastic strap or the equivalent, This will maintain tension on chains to aid in installation.

➡It will be necessary to slightly rotate camshafts for sprocket installation.

39. Align left camshaft sprocket "L" dot to plated link on chain.
40. Align right camshaft sprocket "R" dot to plated link on chain.

✻✻ WARNING

Remove the excess oil from the camshaft sprocket bolt. Failure to do so can result in over torque of bolt resulting in bolt failure.

41. Remove Special Tool 8515, then attach both sprockets to camshafts. Remove excess oil from bolts, then Install sprocket bolts, but do not tighten at this time.

42. Verify that all plated links are aligned with the marks on all sprockets and the "V8" marks on camshaft sprockets are at the 12 o'clock position.

✻✻ WARNING

Ensure the plate between the left secondary chain tensioner and block is correctly installed.

43. Install both secondary chain tensioners. Tighten bolts to 250 inch lbs. (28 Nm).

➡Left and right secondary chain tensioners are not common.

44. Before installing idler sprocket bolt, lubricate washer with oil, and tighten idler sprocket assembly retaining bolt to 25 ft. lbs. (34 Nm).
45. Remove all locking pins from tensioners.

✻✻ WARNING

After pulling locking pins out of each tensioner do not manually extend the tensioner(s) ratchet. Doing so will over-tension the chains, resulting in noise and/or high timing chain loads.

46. Using Special Tool 6958, Spanner with Adapter Pins 8346, tighten left and right. camshaft sprocket bolts to 90 ft. lbs. (122 Nm).
47. Rotate engine two full revolutions. Verify timing marks are at the following locations:
- primary chain idler sprocket dot is at 12 o'clock
- primary chain crankshaft sprocket dot is at 6 o'clock
- secondary chain camshaft sprockets "V8" marks are at 12 o'clock
48. Lubricate all three chains with engine oil.
49. After installing all chains, it is recommended that the idler gear end play be checked. The end play must be within 0.10–0.25mm (0.004–0.010 in.). If not within specification, the idler gear and idler shaft must be replaced.

✻✻ WARNING

Do not use oil based liquids to clean timing cover or block surfaces. Use only rubbing alcohol, along with plastic or wooden scrapers. Use no wire brushes or abrasive wheels or metal scrapers, or damage to surfaces could result.

50. Clean the timing chain cover and block surface using rubbing alcohol.

✳✳ WARNING

The 4.7L can use a special RTV sealer instead of a carrier gasket to seal the timing cover to the engine block, from the factory. For service repairs, Mopar® Grey Engine RTV must be used as a substitute, if RTV is present. If the front cover being used has no provisions for the water passage O-rings, then Mopar® Grey Engine RTV must be applied around the water passages.

51. Inspect the water passage O-rings, if equipped for any damage, and replace as necessary.

52. Apply Mopar® Grey Engine RTV sealer to the front cover following the path above, using a 3 to 4mm thick bead.

53. Install the cover. Tighten flange head fasteners in sequence as shown in to 43 ft. lbs. (58 Nm).

54. Install the A/C compressor and generator.

55. Install the crankshaft damper.

56. Install the accessory drive belt tensioner assembly. Tighten fastener to 40 ft. lbs. (54 Nm).

57. Install the lower radiator hose.

58. Install both heater hoses.

59. Install cylinder head covers.

➡Before installing threaded plug in right cylinder head, the plug must be coated with sealant to prevent leaks.

60. Coat the large threaded access plug with Mopar® Thread Sealant with Teflon, then install into the right cylinder head and tighten to 60 ft. lbs. (81 Nm).

61. Install the oil fill housing.

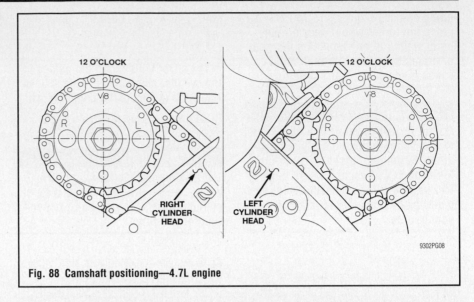

Fig. 88 Camshaft positioning—4.7L engine

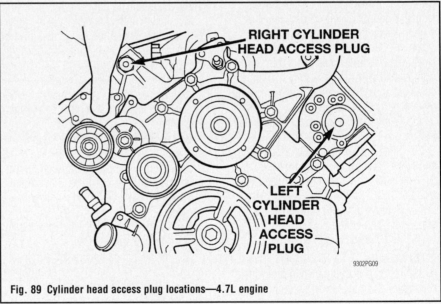

Fig. 89 Cylinder head access plug locations—4.7L engine

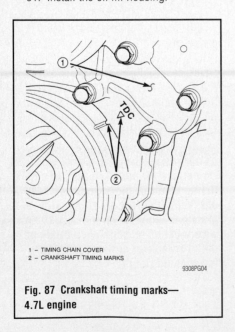

1 – TIMING CHAIN COVER
2 – CRANKSHAFT TIMING MARKS

9308PG04

Fig. 87 Crankshaft timing marks—
4.7L engine

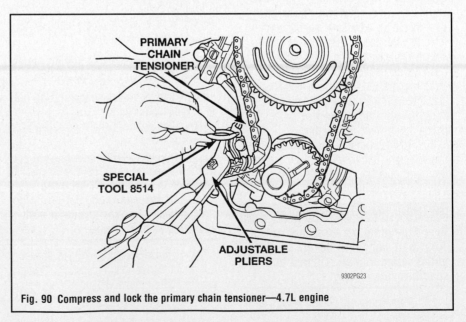

Fig. 90 Compress and lock the primary chain tensioner—4.7L engine

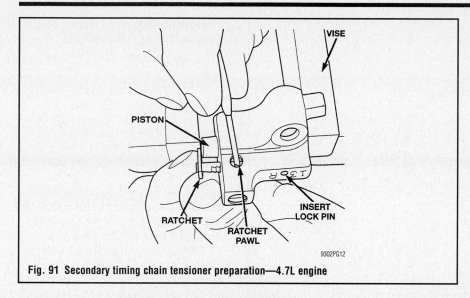

Fig. 91 Secondary timing chain tensioner preparation—4.7L engine

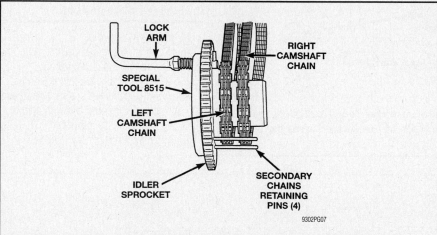

Fig. 92 Use the Timing Chain Locking tool to lock the timing chains on the idler gear—4.7L engine

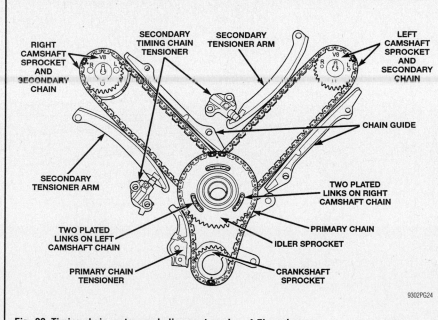

Fig. 93 Timing chain system and alignment marks—4.7L engine

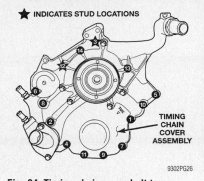

Fig. 94 Timing chain cover bolt torque sequence—4.7L engine

62. Install access plug in left cylinder head.

63. Install power steering pump.

64. Install the radiator fan.

65. Refill the cooling system to the correct level.

66. Connect negative cable to battery.

5.7L Engine

See Figures 95 and 96.

1. Before servicing the vehicle, refer to the precautions section.

2. Disconnect the battery negative cable.

3. Remove the engine cover.

4. Remove air cleaner assembly.

5. Drain the cooling system.

6. Remove the accessory drive belt.

7. Remove fan and fan drive assembly.

8. Remove the coolant bottle and washer bottle.

9. Remove fan shroud.

➡ **It is not necessary to disconnect A/C lines or discharge refrigerant.**

10. Remove A/C compressor and set aside.

11. Remove the generator.

12. Remove the upper radiator hose.

13. Disconnect both heater hoses at timing cover.

14. Disconnect lower radiator hose at engine.

15. Remove accessory drive belt tensioner and both idler pulleys.

16. Remove the crankshaft damper.

➡ **Do not remove the hoses from the power steering pump.**

17. Remove power steering pump and set aside.

18. Remove the dipstick support bolt.

19. Drain the engine oil.

20. Remove the oil pan and pick up tube.

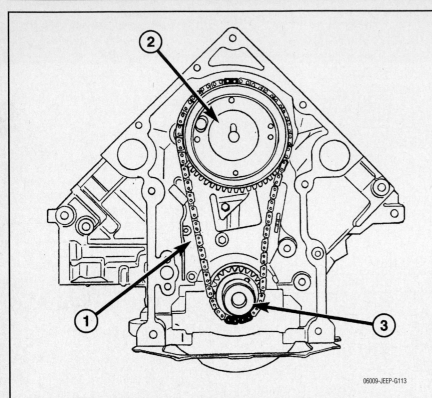

Fig. 95 The camshaft pin and the slot in the cam sprocket must be clocked at 12:00 (2). The crankshaft keyway must be clocked at 2:00 (3). The crankshaft sprocket must be installed so that the dots and or paint marking is at 6:00—5.7L Engine

➡It is not necessary to remove water pump for timing cover removal.

21. Remove the timing cover bolts and cover.

22. Verify that timing cover slide bushings are located in timing cover.

23. Reinstall the vibration damper bolt finger tight. Using a suitable socket and breaker bar, rotate the crankshaft to align timing chain sprockets and keyways as shown.

❈❈ WARNING

The camshaft pin and the slot in the cam sprocket must be clocked at 12:00 (2). The crankshaft keyway must be clocked at 2:00 (3). The crankshaft sprocket must be installed so that the dot and/or paint marking is at the 6 o'clock position.

24. Remove oil pump.

25. Retract tensioner shoe until hole in shoe lines up with hole in bracket.

26. Slide a suitable pin into the holes.

27. Remove camshaft sprocket attaching bolt and remove timing chain with crankshaft and camshaft sprockets.

28. If tensioner assembly is to be

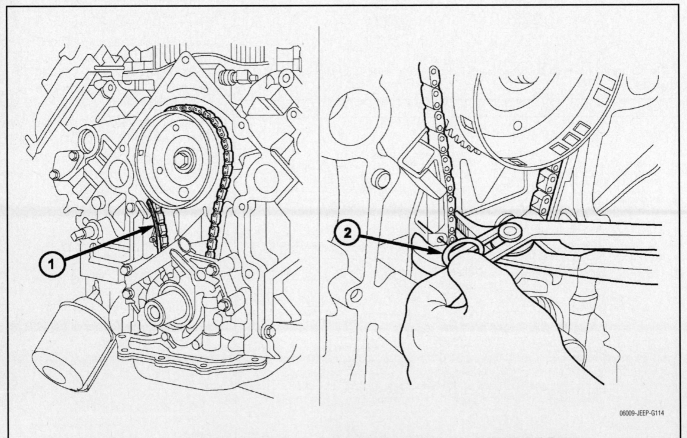

Fig. 96 Retract tensioner shoe until hole in shoe lines up with hole in bracket. Slide a suitable pin into the holes—5.7L Engine

replaced, remove the tensioner to block bolts and remove tensioner assembly.

To install:

29. If tensioner assembly is being replaced, install tensioner and mounting bolts. Torque bolts to 250 inch lbs. (28 Nm).

30. Retract the tensioner if necessary.

✳✳ WARNING

The timing chain must be installed with the single plated link aligned with the dot and or paint marking on the camshaft sprocket. The crankshaft sprocket is aligned with the dot and or paint marking on the sprocket between two plated timing chain links.

✳✳ WARNING

The camshaft pin and the slot in the cam sprocket must be clocked at 12:00. The crankshaft keyway must be clocked at 2:00. The crankshaft sprocket must be installed so that the dots and or paint marking is at 6:00.

31. Place both camshaft sprocket and crankshaft sprocket on the bench with tim-ing marks on exact imaginary center line through both camshaft and crankshaft bores.

32. Place the timing chain around both sprockets.

33. Lift the sprockets and chain (keep sprockets tight against the chain in position as shown).

34. Slide both sprockets evenly over their respective shafts and check alignment of timing marks.

35. Install the camshaft bolt. Tighten the bolt to 90 ft. lbs. (122 Nm).

36. Remove the tensioner pin. Again, verify alignment of timing marks.

37. Install the oil pump.

38. Install the oil pan and pick up.

39. Clean the timing chain cover and block surface.

➡**Always install a new gasket on tim-ing cover.**

40. Verify that the slide bushings are installed in the timing cover.

41. Install the cover and new gasket. Tighten fasteners to 250 inch lbs. (28 Nm).

➡**The large lifting stud is torqued to 40 ft. lbs. (55 Nm).**

42. Install the oil pan and pick up tube.

43. Install the A/C compressor.
44. Install the generator.
45. Install power steering pump.
46. Install the dipstick support bolt.
47. Install the thermostat housing.
48. Install the crankshaft damper.
49. Install the accessory drive belt ten-sioner assembly and both idler pulleys.
50. Install the radiator lower hose.
51. Install both heater hoses.
52. Install the radiator fan shroud.
53. Install the fan and fan drive assembly
54. Install the accessory drive belt.
55. Install the coolant bottle and washer bottle.
56. Install the upper radiator hose.
57. Install the air cleaner assembly.
58. Refill the cooling system to the cor-rect level.
59. Refill engine oil.
60. Connect the battery negative cable.
61. Install the engine cover.

VALVE LASH

ADJUSTMENT

These engines are equipped with hydraulic valve lifters. No valve clearance adjustments are necessary.

ENGINE PERFORMANCE & EMISSION CONTROL

CAMSHAFT POSITION (CMP) SENSOR

LOCATION

See Figures 97 and 98.

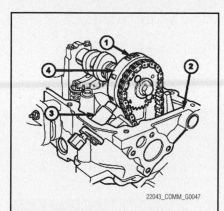

Fig. 97 The camshaft position sensor (3) bolts to the right-front side of the right cylinder (2)—3.7L & 4.7L Engines

OPERATION

The Camshaft Position Sensor (CMP) sensor contains a hall effect device referred

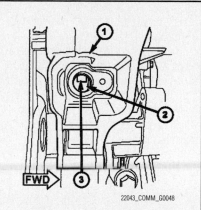

Fig. 98 The camshaft position sensor (2) is located below the alternator on the tim-ing chain cover (1) on the right-front side of the engine—5.7L Engine

to as a sync signal generator. A rotating tar-get wheel (tone wheel) for the CMP is located at the front of the camshaft for the right cylinder head. This sync signal gener-ator detects notches located on a tone wheel. As the tone wheel rotates, the notches pass through the sync signal gen-erator. The signal from the CMP sensor is

used in conjunction with the Crankshaft Position Sensor (CKP) to differentiate between fuel injection and spark events. It is also used to synchronize the fuel injectors with their respective cylinders.

When the leading edge of the target wheel notch enters the tip of the CMP, the interruption of magnetic field causes the voltage to switch high, resulting in a sync signal of approximately 5 volts. When the trailing edge of the target wheel notch leaves the tip of the CMP, the change of the magnetic field causes the sync signal volt-age to switch to 0 volts.

REMOVAL & INSTALLATION

1. Raise and safely support the vehicle.
2. Disconnect the Camshaft Position (CMP) sensor electrical connector.
3. Remove the CMP sensor mounting bolts.
4. Carefully twist the sensor from the cylinder.

To install:

5. Check the condition of the sensor O-ring.
6. Clean out the machined hole in the cylinder head.

7. Apply a small amount of clean engine oil to the sensor O-ring.

8. Install the CMP sensor into the cylinder head with a slight rocking and twisting action.

9. Install the mounting bolt and tighten to 106 inch lbs. (12 Nm).

10. Connect the electrical connector.

11. Lower the vehicle.

TESTING

1. Using a diagnostic scan tool, check for the presence of any Diagnostic Trouble Codes (DTCs). Record and address these codes as necessary.

2. Turn the ignition off and disconnect the Camshaft Position (CMP) Sensor harness connector.

➡️**If any of the test results fall outside of the specification, stop and repair the affected component.**

3. With the Ignition on, and engine not running, measure the voltage on the (F856) 5-volt Supply circuit in the CMP Sensor harness connector. Is the voltage between 4.5 and 5.2 volts?

4. If it is, measure the voltage on the (K44) CMP Signal circuit in the CMP Sensor harness connector. The voltage should be between 4.5 and 5.0 volts.

5. If it is, turn the ignition off and disconnect the C2 PCM harness connector.

❊❊ CAUTION

Do not probe the PCM harness connectors. Probing the PCM harness connectors will damage the PCM terminals resulting in poor terminal to pin connection. Install Miller Special Tool no. 8815 to perform diagnosis.

6. Measure the resistance of the (K900) Sensor ground circuit from the CMP Sensor harness connector to the appropriate terminal of special tool no. 8815. If the resistance is below 5.0 ohms, proceed to the next step, otherwise repair the open ground in the K900 sensor.

7. Measure the resistance between the (K44) CMP Signal circuit and the (F856) 5-volt Supply circuit in the CMP Sensor harness connector. If the resistance is below 5.0 ohms, repair the short between the (K44) CMP Signal circuit and the (F856) 5-volt Supply circuit.

➡️**Inspect the Camshaft sprocket for damage per the Service Information. If a problem is found repair as necessary.**

8. Replace the CMP sensor.

CRANKSHAFT POSITION (CKP) SENSOR

LOCATION

See Figure 99.

The Crankshaft Position (CKP) sensor is mounted into the right rear side of the cylinder block.

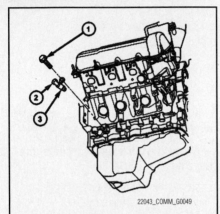

22043_COMM_G0049

Fig. 99 Location of the crankshaft position sensor (3), electrical connector (2) and mounting bolt (1)—3.7L engine shown, others similar

OPERATION

The sensor generates pulses that are the input sent to the Powertrain Control Module (PCM). The PCM interprets the sensor input to determine the crankshaft position and engine speed.

The sensor is a hall effect device combined with an internal magnet. It is also sensitive to steel within a certain distance from it. A tonewheel is bolted to the engine crankshaft. The tonewheel has notches which cause a pulse to be generated when they pass under the sensor.

REMOVAL & INSTALLATION

1. Raise and safely support the vehicle.

2. Disconnect the sensor electrical connector.

3. Remove the CKP sensor mounting bolt.

4. Carefully twist the CKP sensor from the cylinder block.

To install:

5. Check the condition of the O-ring.

6. Clean out the machined hole in the engine block.

7. Apply a small amount of clean engine oil to the sensor O-ring.

8. Install the CKP sensor into the engine block with a slight rocking and twisting action.

9. Install the mounting bolt and tighten to 21 ft. lbs. (28 Nm).

10. Connect the electrical connector.

11. Lower the vehicle.

TESTING

1. Using a diagnostic scan tool, check for the presence of any Diagnostic Trouble Codes (DTCs). Record and address these codes as necessary.

2. Turn the ignition off. Disconnect the Crankshaft Position (CKP) Sensor harness connector.

➡️**If the test results fall outside of the specification, stop and repair the affected component.**

3. With the Ignition on, and engine not running, measure the voltage on the (F855) 5-volt Supply circuit in the CKP Sensor harness connector. Voltage should be between 4.5 and 5.2 volts.

4. If it is, measure the voltage on the (K24) CKP Signal circuit in the CKP Sensor harness connector. The sensor voltage should be approximately 5.0 volts (plus or minus .1 volt) with the connector disconnected.

5. If it is, turn the ignition off and disconnect the C2 PCM harness connector.

❊❊ CAUTION

Do not probe the PCM harness connectors. Probing the PCM harness connectors will damage the PCM terminals resulting in poor terminal to pin connection. Install Miller Special Tool no. 8815 to perform diagnosis.

6. Measure the resistance of the (K900) Sensor ground circuit from the CKP Sensor harness connector to the appropriate terminal of special tool no. 8815. Resistance should be below 5.0 ohms.

7. If it is, measure the resistance between the (K24) CKP Signal circuit and the (F855) 5-volt Supply circuit in the CKP Sensor harness connector. If the resistance below 5.0 ohms, repair the short between the (K24) CKP Signal circuit and the (F855) 5-volt Supply circuit.

8. If not, replace the crankshaft position sensor.

ENGINE COOLANT TEMPERATURE (ECT) SENSOR

LOCATION

3.7 & 4.7L Engines

The Engine Coolant Temperature (ECT) sensor is installed into a water jacket at the front of the intake manifold.

5.7L Engine

The Engine Coolant Temperature (ECT) sensor is located under the air conditioning compressor. It is installed into a water jack at the front of the cylinder block.

OPERATION

The sensor provides an input to the Powertrain Control Module (PCM). As coolant temperature varies, the sensor resistance changes, resulting in a different input voltage to the PCM. When the engine is cold, the PCM will demand slightly richer air-fuel mixtures and higher idle speeds until normal operating temperatures are reached.

The engine coolant sensor input also determines operation of the low and high speed cooling fans.

REMOVAL & INSTALLATION

3.7 & 4.7L Engines

1. Drain the cooling system.
2. Disconnect the sensor electrical connector.
3. Remove the Engine Coolant Temperature (ECT) sensor.

To install:

4. Apply thread sealant to the sensor threads.
5. Install the ECT sensor into the engine block and tighten the mounting bolt to 8 ft. lbs. (11 Nm).
6. Connect the electrical connector.
7. Refill the cooling system to the correct level.

5.7L Engine

See Figure 100.

1. Drain the cooling system.
2. Remove the accessory drive belt.
3. Carefully unbolt the A/C compressor. Temporarily support the compressor to access the engine coolant temperature (ECT) sensor.

➡ **It is not necessary to disconnect the A/C lines from the compressor.**

4. Disconnect the sensor electrical connector.
5. Remove the ECT sensor from the engine block.

To install:

6. Apply thread sealant to the sensor threads.
7. Install the sensor into the engine block and tighten the mounting bolt to 8 ft. lbs. (11 Nm).
8. Connect the electrical connector.

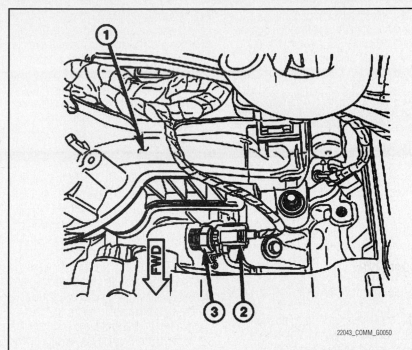

Fig. 100 Disconnect the electrical connector (2) and remove the ECT sensor (3) from the engine block (1)—5.7L Engine shown

9. Position the A/C compressor into place and tighten the mounting bolts.
10. Install the accessory drive belt.
11. Refill the cooling system to the correct level.

TESTING

1. Turn the ignition off. If possible, allow the vehicle to sit with the ignition off for more than 8 hours in an environment where the temperature is consistent and above 20°F (-7°C).
2. Test drive the vehicle. The vehicle must exceed 30 mph (48 km/h) during the test drive. Do not cycle the ignition off when the test drive is completed.
3. With a scan tool, select View DTCs.
4. Turn the ignition off. Allow the vehicle to sit with the ignition off in an environment where the temperature is consistent and above 20°F (-7°C) until the engine coolant temperature is equal to ambient temperature. Turn the ignition on. With a scan tool, compare the AAT, ECT, and IAT sensor values.
5. If the ECT sensor value is not within 18°F (10°C) of the other two sensor values, perform the following:
6. Refer to any Technical Service Bulletins (TSBs) that may apply.
7. Review the scan tool Freeze Frame information. If possible, try to duplicate the conditions under which the DTC set.
8. With the engine running at normal operating temperature, monitor the scan tool parameters related to the DTC while wiggling the wire harness. Look for parameter values to change and/or a DTC to set. Turn the ignition off.
9. Visually inspect the related wire harness. Disconnect all the related harness connectors. Look for any chafed, pierced, pinched, partially broken wires and broken, bent, pushed out, or corroded terminals.
10. Perform a voltage drop test on the related circuits between the suspected inoperative component and the PCM.

✳✳ CAUTION

Do not probe the PCM harness connectors. Probing the PCM harness connectors will damage the PCM terminals resulting in poor terminal to pin connection. Install Miller Special Tool no. 8815 to perform diagnosis.

11. Inspect and clean all PCM, engine, and chassis grounds that are related to the most current DTC.
12. If numerous trouble codes were set, use a wire schematic and look for any common ground or supply circuits.
13. For any Relay DTCs, actuate the Relay with the scan tool and wiggle the related wire harness to try to interrupt the actuation.
14. For intermittent Evaporative Emission trouble codes perform a visual and physical inspection of the related parts including hoses and the Fuel Filler cap.

15. Use the scan tool to perform a System Test if one applies to failing component. A co-pilot, data recorder, and/or lab scope should be used to help diagnose intermittent conditions.

HEATED OXYGEN (HO2S) SENSOR

LOCATION

See Figures 101 and 102.

If equipped with a Federal Emission Package, two sensors are used: upstream (referred to as 1/1) and downstream (referred to as 1/2). With this emission package, the upstream sensor (1/1) is located just before the main catalytic converter. The downstream sensor (1/2) is located just after the main catalytic converter.

If equipped with a California Emission Package, 4 sensors are used: 2 upstream (referred to as 1/1 and 2/1) and 2 downstream (referred to as 1/2 and 2/2). With this emission package, the right upstream sensor (2/1) is located in the right exhaust downpipe just before the mini-catalytic converter. The left upstream sensor (1/1) is located in the left exhaust downpipe just

before the mini-catalytic converter. The right downstream sensor (2/2) is located in the right exhaust downpipe just after the mini-catalytic converter, and before the main catalytic converter. The left downstream sensor (1/2) is located in the left exhaust downpipe just after the mini-catalytic converter, and before the main catalytic converter.

OPERATION

An O2 sensor is a galvanic battery that provides the PCM with a voltage signal (0-1 volt) inversely proportional to the amount of oxygen in the exhaust. In other words, if the oxygen content is low, the voltage output is high; if the oxygen content is high the output voltage is low. The PCM uses this information to adjust injector pulse-width to achieve the 14.7to1 air/fuel ratio necessary for proper engine operation and to control emissions.

The O2 sensor must have a source of oxygen from outside of the exhaust stream for comparison. Current O2 sensors receive their fresh oxygen (outside air) supply through the O2 sensor case housing.

Four wires (circuits) are used on each O2 sensor: a 12volt feed circuit for the sensor heating element; a ground circuit for the heater element; a low-noise sensor return circuit to the PCM, and an input circuit from the sensor back to the PCM to detect sensor operation.

REMOVAL & INSTALLATION

1. Raise and safely support the vehicle.
2. Disconnect the wire connector from oxygen sensor.

✳✳ WARNING

When disconnecting sensor electrical connector, do not pull directly on wire going into sensor.

3. Remove the sensor with an oxygen sensor removal and installation tool.
4. Clean threads in exhaust pipe using appropriate tap.

To install:

➡Threads of new oxygen sensors are factory coated with anti-seize compound.

✳✳ WARNING

Do not add any additional anti-seize compound to the threads of a new oxygen sensor.

5. Install the oxygen sensor and tighten to 22 ft. lbs. (30 Nm).
6. Connect the electrical connector.
7. Lower the vehicle.

TESTING

1. Start the engine and allow it to idle for at least 60 seconds. Using a diagnostic scan tool, check for the presence of any Diagnostic Trouble Codes (DTCs). Record and address these codes as necessary.
2. Turn the ignition off, allow the sensor to cool down to room temperature disconnect the oxygen sensor wiring harness. Measure the resistance across the sensor heater control terminal and ground terminal. If resistance is not between 2 and 30 ohms, replace the sensor.
3. Refer to any Technical Service Bulletins (TSBs) that may apply.
4. Review the scan tool Freeze Frame information. If possible, try to duplicate the conditions under which the DTC set.
5. With the engine running at normal operating temperature, monitor the scan tool parameters related to the DTC while wiggling the wire harness. Look for parameter values to change and/or a DTC to set. Turn the ignition off.
6. Visually inspect the related wire harness. Disconnect all the related harness connectors. Look for any chafed, pierced, pinched, partially broken wires and broken, bent, pushed out, or corroded terminals.
7. Perform a voltage drop test on the related circuits between the suspected inoperative component and the PCM.

✳✳ CAUTION

Do not probe the PCM harness connectors. Probing the PCM harness connectors will damage the PCM terminals resulting in poor terminal to pin connection. Install Miller Special Tool no. 8815 to perform diagnosis.

8. Inspect and clean all PCM, engine, and chassis grounds that are related to the most current DTC.
9. If numerous trouble codes were set, use a wire schematic and look for any common ground or supply circuits.
10. For any Relay DTCs, actuate the Relay with the scan tool and wiggle the related wire harness to try to interrupt the actuation.
11. For intermittent Evaporative Emission trouble codes perform a visual and physical inspection of the related parts including hoses and the Fuel Filler cap.
12. Use the scan tool to perform a System Test if one applies to failing component. A co-pilot, data recorder, and/or lab scope should be used to help diagnose intermittent conditions.

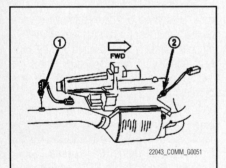

Fig. 101 Two oxygen sensors (1, 2) are used with a federal emissions equipped vehicle.

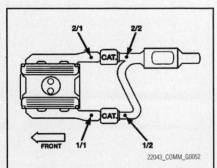

Fig. 102 Four oxygen sensors are used with a California emissions equipped vehicle.

INTAKE AIR TEMPERATURE (IAT) SENSOR

LOCATION

See Figure 103.

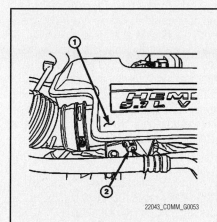

22043_COMM_G0053

Fig. 103 The 2-wire Intake Manifold Air Temperature (IAT) sensor (2) is installed in the air inlet tube (1)with the sensor element extending into the air stream—5.7L Engine shown

OPERATION

The IAT sensor is a two-wire Negative Thermal Coefficient (NTC) sensor. Meaning, as inlet air temperatures increase, resistance (voltage) in the sensor decreases. As temperature decreases, resistance (voltage) in the sensor increases.

The IAT sensor provides an input voltage to the Powertrain Control Module (PCM) indicating the density of the air entering the intake manifold based upon intake manifold temperature. At key-on, a 5volt power circuit is supplied to the sensor from the PCM. The sensor is grounded at the PCM through a low-noise, sensor-return circuit.

REMOVAL & INSTALLATION

1. Disconnect the electrical connector from the Intake Air Temperature (IAT) sensor.
2. Clean any dirt from the air inlet tube at the sensor base.
3. Gently lift the small plastic release tab and rotate the sensor about ¼ turn counter-clockwise to remove.

To install:

4. Check the condition of the sensor O-ring.
5. Clean the sensor mounting hole.
6. Position the sensor into the intake air tube and rotate clockwise until the release tab clicks into place.
7. Install the electrical connector.

TESTING

1. Turn the ignition off. If possible, allow the vehicle to sit with the ignition off for more than 8 hours in an environment where the temperature is consistent and above 20°F (-7°C).
2. Test drive the vehicle. The vehicle must exceed 30 mph (48 km/h) during the test drive. Do not cycle the ignition off when the test drive is completed.
3. With a scan tool, select View DTCs.
4. If a DTC is not active, perform the following:
5. Refer to any Technical Service Bulletins (TSBs) that may apply.
6. Review the scan tool Freeze Frame information. If possible, try to duplicate the conditions under which the DTC set.
7. With the engine running at normal operating temperature, monitor the scan tool parameters related to the DTC while wiggling the wire harness. Look for parameter values to change and/or a DTC to set. Turn the ignition off.
8. Visually inspect the related wire harness. Disconnect all the related harness connectors. Look for any chafed, pierced, pinched, partially broken wires and broken, bent, pushed out, or corroded terminals.
9. Perform a voltage drop test on the related circuits between the suspected inoperative component and the PCM.

✳✳ CAUTION

Do not probe the PCM harness connectors. Probing the PCM harness connectors will damage the PCM terminals resulting in poor terminal to pin connection. Install Miller Special Tool no. 8815 to perform diagnosis.

10. Inspect and clean all PCM, engine, and chassis grounds that are related to the most current DTC.
11. If numerous trouble codes were set, use a wire schematic and look for any common ground or supply circuits.
12. For any Relay DTCs, actuate the Relay with the scan tool and wiggle the related wire harness to try to interrupt the actuation.
13. For intermittent Evaporative Emission trouble codes perform a visual and physical inspection of the related parts including hoses and the Fuel Filler cap.
14. Use the scan tool to perform a System Test if one applies to failing component. A co-pilot, data recorder, and/or lab scope should be used to help diagnose intermittent conditions.

KNOCK SENSOR (KS)

LOCATION

3.7L & 4.7L Engines

Two knock sensors are bolted into the engine block under the intake manifold.

5.7L Engine

Two knock sensors are bolted into each side of the engine block under the exhaust manifolds.

OPERATION

Two knock sensors are used; one for each cylinder bank. When the knock sensor detects a knock in one of the cylinders on the corresponding bank, it sends an input signal to the Powertrain Control Module (PCM). In response, the PCM retards ignition timing for all cylinders by a scheduled amount.

Knock sensors contain a piezoelectric material which constantly vibrates and sends an input voltage (signal) to the PCM while the engine operates. As the intensity of the crystal's vibration increases, the knock sensor output voltage also increases

REMOVAL & INSTALLATION

3.7L & 4.7L Engines

See Figure 104.

1. Disconnect the knock sensor dual pigtail harness from engine wiring harness. This connection is made near rear of engine.
2. Remove the intake manifold
3. Remove the Knock Sensor (KS) mounting bolts.
4. Remove the sensors from engine.

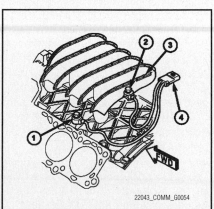

22043_COMM_G0054

Fig. 104 Disconnect the wiring harness (4) and remove the intake manifold (3) remove the knock sensors (1,2)—3.7L & 4.7L Engines

To install:

5. Thoroughly clean the KS mounting holes.

6. Install the sensors into the engine block. Tighten the mounting bolts to 15 ft. lbs. (20 Nm).

7. Install the intake manifold.

8. Connect the KS wiring harness to the engine wiring harness at the rear of the engine.

5.7L Engine

1. Raise and safely support the vehicle.

2. Disconnect the Knock Sensor (KS) electrical connector.

3. Remove the KS mounting bolt.

4. Remove the sensor from the engine.

To install:

5. Thoroughly clean the KS mounting holes.

6. Install the sensors into the engine block. Tighten the mounting bolts to 15 ft. lbs. (20 Nm).

7. Connect the KS electrical connectors.

8. Lower the vehicle.

TESTING

1. Start the engine and allow it to reach normal operating temperature. Using a diagnostic scan tool, check for the presence of any Diagnostic Trouble Codes (DTCs). Record and address these codes as necessary.

2. Refer to any Technical Service Bulletins (TSBs) that may apply.

3. Review the scan tool Freeze Frame information. If possible, try to duplicate the conditions under which the DTC set.

4. With the engine running at normal operating temperature, monitor the scan tool parameters related to the DTC while wiggling the wire harness. Look for parameter values to change and/or a DTC to set. Turn the ignition off.

5. Visually inspect the related wire harness. Disconnect all the related harness connectors. Look for any chafed, pierced, pinched, partially broken wires and broken, bent, pushed out, or corroded terminals.

6. Perform a voltage drop test on the related circuits between the suspected inoperative component and the PCM.

✳✳ CAUTION

Do not probe the PCM harness connectors. Probing the PCM harness connectors will damage the PCM terminals resulting in poor terminal to pin connection. Install Miller Special Tool no. 8815 to perform diagnosis.

7. Inspect and clean all PCM, engine, and chassis grounds that are related to the most current DTC.

8. If numerous trouble codes were set, use a wire schematic and look for any common ground or supply circuits.

9. For any Relay DTCs, actuate the Relay with the scan tool and wiggle the related wire harness to try to interrupt the actuation.

10. For intermittent Evaporative Emission trouble codes perform a visual and physical inspection of the related parts including hoses and the Fuel Filler cap.

11. Use the scan tool to perform a System Test if one applies to failing component. A co-pilot, data recorder, and/or lab scope should be used to help diagnose intermittent conditions.

MANIFOLD ABSOLUTE PRESSURE (MAP) SENSOR

LOCATION

3.7L & 4.7L Engines

The Manifold Absolute Pressure (MAP) sensor is mounted to the front of the intake manifold with two bolts.

5.7L Engine

The Manifold Absolute Pressure (MAP) sensor is mounted to the back of the intake manifold by a quarter turn fastener.

OPERATION

The MAP sensor is used as an input to the Powertrain Control Module (PCM). It contains a silicon based sensing unit to provide data on the manifold vacuum that draws the air/fuel mixture into the combustion chamber. The PCM requires this information to determine injector pulse width and spark advance. When manifold absolute pressure (MAP) equals Barometric pressure, the pulse width will be at maximum.

A 5-volt reference is supplied from the PCM and returns a voltage signal to the PCM that reflects manifold pressure. The zero pressure reading is 0.5V and full scale is 4.5V. For a pressure swing of 015 psi, the voltage changes 4.0V. To operate the sensor, it is supplied a regulated 4.8 to 5.1 volts. Ground is provided through the low-noise, sensor return circuit at the PCM.

The MAP sensor input is the number one contributor to fuel injector pulse width. The most important function of the MAP sensor is to determine barometric pressure. The PCM needs to know if the vehicle is at sea level or at a higher altitude, because the air density changes with altitude. It will also help to correct for varying barometric pressure. Barometric pressure and altitude have a direct inverse correlation; as altitude goes up, barometric goes down. At key-on, the PCM powers up and looks at MAP voltage, and based upon the voltage it sees, it knows the current barometric pressure (relative to altitude). Once the engine starts, the PCM looks at the voltage again, continuously every 12 milliseconds, and compares the current voltage to what it was at key-on. The difference between current voltage and what it was at Key On is the manifold vacuum.

During key-on (engine not running) the sensor reads (updates) barometric pressure. A normal range can be obtained by monitoring a known good sensor.

As the altitude increases, the air becomes thinner (less oxygen). If a vehicle is started and driven to a very different altitude than where it was at key-on, the barometric pressure needs to be updated. Any time the PCM sees Wide Open Throttle (WOT), based upon Throttle Position Sensor (TPS) angle and RPM, it will update barometric pressure in the MAP memory cell. With periodic updates, the PCM can make its calculations more effectively.

REMOVAL & INSTALLATION

3.7L & 4.7L Engines

1. Disconnect the sensor electrical connector.

2. Clean the area around the Manifold Absolute Pressure (MAP) sensor.

3. Remove the two mounting screws.

4. Remove the MAP sensor from the intake manifold.

To install:

5. Inspect the condition of the sensor O-ring and replace if necessary.

6. Position the MAP sensor into the manifold and install the two mounting screws.

7. Connect the electrical connector.

5.7L Engine

1. Disconnect the electrical connector at the Manifold Absolute Pressure (MAP) sensor by sliding the release lock out. Then press down on the lock tab.

2. Rotate the MAP sensor ¼ turn counter-clockwise to remove.

To install:

3. Inspect the condition of the sensor O-ring and replace if necessary.

4. Position the MAP sensor into the intake manifold and rotate ¼ turn clockwise.

5. Connect the electrical connector to the MAP sensor until it clicks into place.

TESTING

1. Start the engine and allow it to reach normal operating temperature. Using a diagnostic scan tool, check for the presence of any Diagnostic Trouble Codes (DTCs). Record and address these codes as necessary.

2. Refer to any Technical Service Bulletins (TSBs) that may apply.

3. Review the scan tool Freeze Frame information. If possible, try to duplicate the conditions under which the DTC set.

4. With the engine running at normal operating temperature, monitor the scan tool parameters related to the DTC while wiggling the wire harness. Look for parameter values to change and/or a DTC to set. Turn the ignition off.

5. Visually inspect the related wire harness. Disconnect all the related harness connectors. Look for any chafed, pierced, pinched, partially broken wires and broken, bent, pushed out, or corroded terminals.

6. Perform a voltage drop test on the related circuits between the suspected inoperative component and the PCM.

✳✳ CAUTION

Do not probe the PCM harness connectors. Probing the PCM harness connectors will damage the PCM terminals resulting in poor terminal to pin connection. Install Miller Special Tool no. 8815 to perform diagnosis.

7. Inspect and clean all PCM, engine, and chassis grounds that are related to the most current DTC.

8. If numerous trouble codes were set, use a wire schematic and look for any common ground or supply circuits.

9. For any Relay DTCs, actuate the Relay with the scan tool and wiggle the related wire harness to try to interrupt the actuation.

10. For intermittent Evaporative Emission trouble codes perform a visual and physical inspection of the related parts including hoses and the Fuel Filler cap.

11. Use the scan tool to perform a System Test if one applies to failing component. A co-pilot, data recorder, and/or lab scope should be used to help diagnose intermittent conditions.

POWERTRAIN CONTROL MODULE (PCM)

LOCATION
See Figure 105.

OPERATION

The Powertrain Control Module (PCM) receives input signals from various switches and sensors. Based on these inputs, the PCM regulates various engine and vehicle operations through different system components. These components are referred to as Powertrain Control Module (PCM) Outputs. The sensors and switches that provide inputs to the PCM are considered Powertrain Control Module (PCM) Inputs.

The PCM adjusts ignition timing based upon inputs it receives from sensors that react to: engine rpm, manifold absolute pressure, engine coolant temperature, throttle position, transmission gear selection (automatic transmission), vehicle speed and the brake switch.

The PCM adjusts idle speed based on inputs it receives from sensors that react to: throttle position, vehicle speed, transmission gear selection, engine coolant temperature and from inputs it receives from the air conditioning clutch switch and brake switch.

Based on inputs that it receives, the PCM adjusts ignition coil dwell. The PCM also adjusts the generator charge rate through control of the generator field and provides speed control operation.

REMOVAL & INSTALLATION
See Figure 106.

✳✳ WARNING

The use of a diagnostic scan tool is required the Powertrain Control Module (PCM) is being in order to reprogram the new PCM.

1. Disconnect the negative battery cable.

2. Unplug the 38-way connectors from the PCM.

➡**A locating pin is used in place of one of the mounting bolts.**

3. Pry the clip from the locating pin.

4. Remove the two remaining mounting bolts.

5. Remove the PCM from the vehicle.

To install:

6. Position the PCM to the body and install the two mounting bolts.

➡**Position the ground strap in place before tightening the mounting bolts.**

7. Install the clip to the locating pin.

8. Tighten the mounting bolts to 35 inch lbs. (4 Nm).

9. Carefully plug in the 38-way connectors to the PCM.

10. Connect the negative battery cable.

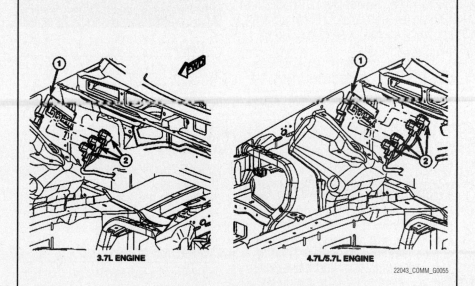

3.7L ENGINE   **4.7L/5.7L ENGINE**

22043_COMM_G0055

Fig. 105 The engine wiring harnesses (2) are plugged into the PCM (1), which is attached to the right-front inner fender located in the engine compartment—4.7L Engine shown

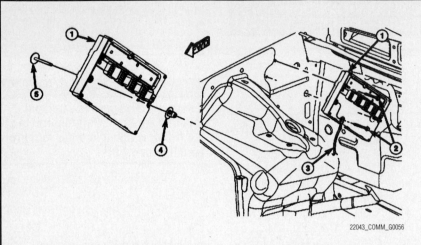

22043_COMM_G0056

Fig. 106 Pry the clip (4) from the pin (5), remove the mounting bolts (2) and place the ground strap (3) aside in order to remove the PCM (1).

11. Use a diagnostic scan tool to reprogram the PCM with the VIN and original mileage if PCM has been replaced.

TESTING

1. Start the engine and allow it to reach normal operating temperature. Using a diagnostic scan tool, check for the presence of any Diagnostic Trouble Codes (DTCs). Record and address these codes as necessary.

2. Refer to any Technical Service Bulletins (TSBs) that may apply.

3. Review the scan tool Freeze Frame information. If possible, try to duplicate the conditions under which the DTC set.

4. With the engine running at normal operating temperature, monitor the scan tool parameters related to the DTC while wiggling the wire harness. Look for parameter values to change and/or a DTC to set. Turn the ignition off.

5. Visually inspect the related wire harness. Disconnect all the related harness connectors. Look for any chafed, pierced, pinched, partially broken wires and broken, bent, pushed out, or corroded terminals.

6. Perform a voltage drop test on the related circuits between the suspected inoperative component and the PCM.

✳✳ CAUTION

Do not probe the PCM harness connectors. Probing the PCM harness connectors will damage the PCM terminals resulting in poor terminal to pin connection. Install Miller Special Tool no. 8815 to perform diagnosis.

7. Inspect and clean all PCM, engine, and chassis grounds that are related to the most current DTC.

8. If numerous trouble codes were set, use a wire schematic and look for any common ground or supply circuits.

9. For any Relay DTCs, actuate the Relay with the scan tool and wiggle the related wire harness to try to interrupt the actuation.

10. For intermittent Evaporative Emission trouble codes perform a visual and physical inspection of the related parts including hoses and the Fuel Filler cap.

11. Use the scan tool to perform a System Test if one applies to failing component. A co-pilot, data recorder, and/or lab scope should be used to help diagnose intermittent conditions.

THROTTLE POSITION SENSOR (TPS)

LOCATION

3.7L & 4.7L Engines

The Throttle Position Sensor (TPS) is mounted on the throttle body and connected to the throttle blade shaft.

5.7L Engine

The 5.7L engine does not use a separate Throttle Position Sensor (TPS) on the throttle body. If it is determined, that the TPS signal is bad, the throttle body assembly must be replaced.

OPERATION

The Throttle Position Sensor (TPS) is a 3-wire variable resistor that provides the Powertrain Control Module (PCM) with an input signal (voltage) that represents the throttle blade position of the throttle body. The sensor is connected to the throttle blade shaft. As the position of the throttle blade changes, the resistance (output voltage) of the TPS changes.

The PCM supplies approximately 5 volts to the TPS. The TPS output voltage (input signal to the PCM) represents the throttle blade position. The PCM receives an input signal voltage from the TPS. This will vary in an approximate range of from .26 volts at minimum throttle opening (idle), to 4.49 volts at wide-open throttle. Along with inputs from other sensors, the PCM uses the TPS input to determine current engine operating conditions. In response to engine operating conditions, the PCM will adjust fuel injector pulse width and ignition timing.

REMOVAL & INSTALLATION

See Figure 107.

1. Remove the air intake tube.
2. Disconnect the Throttle Position Sensor (TPS) electrical connector.
3. Remove the TPS mounting screws.
4. Remove the TPS.

To install:

➡**The throttle shaft end of throttle body slides into a socket in TPS. The TPS must be installed so that it can be rotated a few degrees. If sensor will not rotate, install the sensor with throttle shaft on other side of socket tangs. The TPS will be under slight tension when rotated.**

5. Install the TPS and tighten the mounting screws to 60 inch lbs. (7 Nm).
6. Connect the TPS electrical connector.
7. Manually operate the throttle by hand to check for any TPS binding before starting the engine.
8. Install the air intake tube.

22043_COMM_G0057

Fig. 107 The throttle shaft end (3) of the throttle body (1) slides into the socket (4) of the TPS (2)—3.7 & 4.7L Engines

TESTING

1. Start the engine and allow it to reach normal operating temperature. Using a diagnostic scan tool, check for the presence of any Diagnostic Trouble Codes (DTCs). Record and address these codes as necessary.

2. Refer to any Technical Service Bulletins (TSBs) that may apply.

3. Review the scan tool Freeze Frame information. If possible, try to duplicate the conditions under which the DTC set.

4. With the engine running at normal operating temperature, monitor the scan tool parameters related to the DTC while wiggling the wire harness. Look for parameter values to change and/or a DTC to set. Turn the ignition off.

5. Visually inspect the related wire harness. Disconnect all the related harness connectors. Look for any chafed, pierced, pinched, partially broken wires and broken, bent, pushed out, or corroded terminals.

6. Perform a voltage drop test on the related circuits between the suspected inoperative component and the PCM.

✳✳ CAUTION

Do not probe the PCM harness connectors. Probing the PCM harness connectors will damage the PCM terminals resulting in poor terminal to pin connection. Install Miller Special Tool no. 8815 to perform diagnosis.

7. Inspect and clean all PCM, engine, and chassis grounds that are related to the most current DTC.

8. If numerous trouble codes were set, use a wire schematic and look for any common ground or supply circuits.

9. For any Relay DTCs, actuate the Relay with the scan tool and wiggle the related wire harness to try to interrupt the actuation.

10. For intermittent Evaporative Emission trouble codes perform a visual and physical inspection of the related parts including hoses and the Fuel Filler cap.

11. Use the scan tool to perform a System Test if one applies to failing component. A co-pilot, data recorder, and/or lab scope should be used to help diagnose intermittent conditions.

VEHICLE SPEED SENSOR (VSS)

LOCATION

The Vehicle Speed Sensor (VSS) is located on the left side of the transmission case.

OPERATION

The VSS generates an AC signal as its coil is excited by rotation of the rear planetary carrier lugs. The Transmission Control Module (TCM) interprets this information as output shaft RPM.

REMOVAL & INSTALLATION

1. Raise and safely support the vehicle.

2. Place a suitable catch pan under the transmission for any fluid.

3. Remove the wiring connector from the output speed sensor.

4. Remove the mounting bolt and remove the speed sensor from the transmission case.

To install:

5. Install the speed sensor into the transmission case and tighten the bolt to 105 inch lbs. (12 Nm).

6. Install the wiring connector to the speed sensor.

7. Verify the proper transmission fluid level and refill as necessary.

8. Lower the vehicle.

TESTING

1. Start the engine and allow it to reach normal operating temperature. Using a diagnostic scan tool, check for the presence of any Diagnostic Trouble Codes (DTCs). Record and address these codes as necessary.

2. Refer to any Technical Service Bulletins (TSBs) that may apply.

3. Review the scan tool Freeze Frame information. If possible, try to duplicate the conditions under which the DTC set.

4. With the engine running at normal operating temperature, monitor the scan tool parameters related to the DTC while wiggling the wire harness. Look for parameter values to change and/or a DTC to set. Turn the ignition off.

5. Visually inspect the related wire harness. Disconnect all the related harness connectors. Look for any chafed, pierced, pinched, partially broken wires and broken, bent, pushed out, or corroded terminals.

6. Perform a voltage drop test on the related circuits between the suspected inoperative component and the PCM.

✳✳ CAUTION

Do not probe the PCM harness connectors. Probing the PCM harness connectors will damage the PCM terminals resulting in poor terminal to pin connection. Install Miller Special Tool no. 8815 to perform diagnosis.

7. Inspect and clean all PCM, engine, and chassis grounds that are related to the most current DTC.

8. If numerous trouble codes were set, use a wire schematic and look for any common ground or supply circuits.

9. For any Relay DTCs, actuate the Relay with the scan tool and wiggle the related wire harness to try to interrupt the actuation.

10. For intermittent Evaporative Emission trouble codes perform a visual and physical inspection of the related parts including hoses and the Fuel Filler cap.

11. Use the scan tool to perform a System Test if one applies to failing component. A co-pilot, data recorder, and/or lab scope should be used to help diagnose intermittent conditions.

FUEL SYSTEM SERVICE PRECAUTIONS

Safety is the most important factor when performing not only fuel system maintenance but any type of maintenance. Failure to conduct maintenance and repairs in a safe manner may result in serious personal injury or death. Maintenance and testing of the vehicle's fuel system components can be accomplished safely and effectively by adhering to the following rules and guidelines.

- To avoid the possibility of fire and personal injury, always disconnect the negative battery cable unless the repair or test procedure requires that battery voltage be applied.

- Always relieve the fuel system pressure prior to disconnecting any fuel system component (injector, fuel rail, pressure regulator, etc.), fitting or fuel line connection. Exercise extreme caution whenever relieving fuel system pressure to avoid exposing skin, face and eyes to fuel spray. Please be advised that fuel under pressure may penetrate the skin or any part of the body that it contacts.

- Always place a shop towel or cloth around the fitting or connection prior to loosening to absorb any excess fuel due to spillage. Ensure that all fuel spillage (should it occur) is quickly removed from engine surfaces. Ensure that all fuel soaked cloths or towels are deposited into a suitable waste container.

- Always keep a dry chemical (Class B) fire extinguisher near the work area.

- Do not allow fuel spray or fuel vapors to come into contact with a spark or open flame.

- Always use a back-up wrench when loosening and tightening fuel line connection fittings. This will prevent unnecessary stress and torsion to fuel line piping.

- Always replace worn fuel fitting O-rings with new Do not substitute fuel hose or equivalent where fuel pipe is installed.

Before servicing the vehicle, make sure to also refer to the precautions in the beginning of this section as well.

RELIEVING FUEL SYSTEM PRESSURE

1. Disconnect the negative battery cable.
2. Remove the fuel tank filler cap to release any fuel tank pressure.
3. Remove the fuel pump relay from the PDC.

4. Start and run the engine until it stops.
5. Unplug the connector from any injector and connect a jumper wire from either injector terminal to the positive battery terminal. Connect another jumper wire to the other terminal and momentarily touch the other end to the negative battery terminal.

⁂ WARNING

Just touch the jumper to the battery. Powering the injector for more than a few seconds will permanently damage it.

6. Place a rag below the quick-disconnect coupling at the fuel rail and disconnect it.
7. When service is complete, reinstall the fuel pump relay.

➡**A Diagnostic Trouble Code (DTC) may have been stored in the PCM due to the fuel pump relay removal. A diagnostic scan tool must be used to erase the DTC.**

FUEL FILTER

REMOVAL & INSTALLATION

Two fuel filters are used. One is located at the bottom of the fuel pump module. The other is located inside the module. A separate frame mounted fuel filter is not used with any engine.

Both filters are designed for extended service and do not require normally scheduled maintenance. They should only be replaced as part of a repair.

FUEL INJECTORS

REMOVAL & INSTALLATION
See Figures 108 through 110.

1. Before servicing the vehicle, refer to the precautions section.

⁂ CAUTION

the fuel system is under constant pressure even with engine off. Before servicing fuel rail, fuel system pressure must be released.

➡**The left and right fuel rails are replaced as an assembly. Do not attempt to separate rail halves at connector tube. Due to design of tube, it does not use any clamps. Never attempt to install a clamping device of any kind to tube. When removing fuel**

rail assembly for any reason, be careful not to bend or kink tube.

2. Remove fuel tank filler tube cap.
3. Properly relieve the fuel system pressure.
4. Disconnect the negative battery cable.
5. Remove the air duct at throttle body air box.
6. Remove the air box at throttle body.
7. Disconnect the fuel line latch clip and fuel line at fuel rail. A special tool will be necessary for fuel line disconnection.
8. Remove the necessary vacuum lines at throttle body.
9. Disconnect the electrical connectors at all of the fuel injectors. Push red colored slider away from injector. While pushing slider, depress tab and remove connector from injector. The factory fuel injection wiring harness is numerically tagged (INJ 1, INJ 2, etc.) for injector position identification. If the harness is not tagged, be sure to note the wiring location before removal.
10. Disconnect the electrical connectors at throttle body sensors.
11. Remove the ignition coils.
12. Remove the fuel rail mounting bolts.
13. Gently rock and pull left side of fuel rail until fuel injectors just start to clear machined holes in cylinder head. Gently rock and pull right side of rail until injectors just start to clear cylinder head holes.
14. Repeat this procedure (left/right) until all injectors have cleared cylinder head holes.
15. Remove fuel rail (with injectors attached) from engine.
16. Disconnect the clip that holds the fuel injector and remove the fuel injectors from the fuel rail.

To install:

➡**New O-rings should be used if the same injector is being reinstalled.**

17. Clean out fuel injector machined bores in intake manifold.
18. Apply a small amount of engine oil to each fuel injector O-ring. This will help in fuel rail installation.
19. Install the fuel injectors to the fuel rail.
20. Position the fuel rail/fuel injector assembly to machined injector openings in cylinder head.
21. Guide each injector into cylinder head. Be careful not to tear injector O-rings.
22. Push right side of fuel rail down until fuel injectors have bottomed on cylinder head shoulder. Push left fuel rail down until

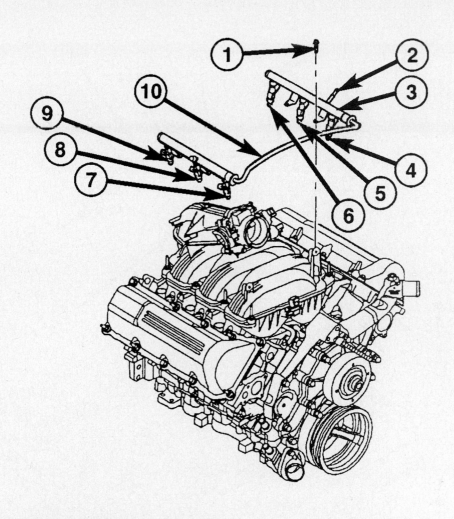

1 - MOUNTING BOLTS (4)
2 - QUICK-CONNECT FITTING
3 - FUEL RAIL
4 - INJ. #1
5 - INJ. #3
6 - INJ. #5
7 - INJ. #2
8 - INJ. #4
9 - INJ. #6
10 - CONNECTOR TUBE

67189-JEEP-G52

Fig. 108 Fuel rail assembly—3.7L engine

injectors have bottomed on cylinder head shoulder.

22. Install the fuel rail mounting bolts and tighten to 100 inch lbs. (11 Nm).

23. Install the ignition coils.

24. Connect the electrical connectors to throttle body.

25. Connect the electrical connectors at all fuel injectors. Push connector onto injector and then push and lock red colored slider. Verify connector is locked to injector by lightly tugging on connector.

26. Connect the necessary vacuum lines to throttle body.

27. Connect fuel line latch clip and fuel line to fuel rail.

28. Install air box to throttle body.

29. Install air duct to air box.

30. Connect the negative battery cable.

31. Start engine and check for leaks.

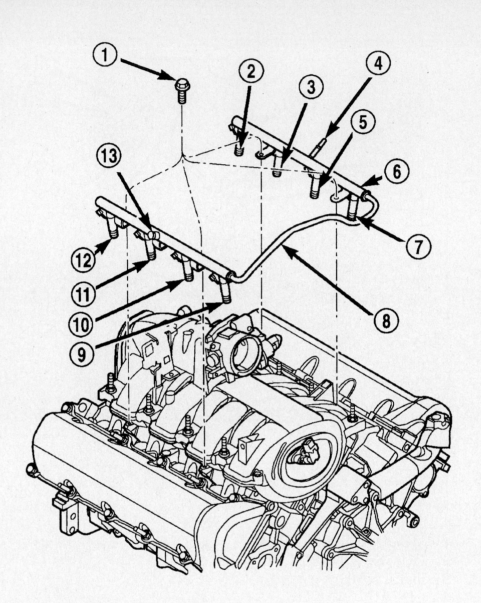

1 - MOUNTING BOLTS (4)
2 - INJ.#7
3 - INJ.#5
4 - QUICK-CONNECT FITTING
5 - INJ.#3
6 - FUEL INJECTOR RAIL
7 - INJ.#1
8 - CONNECTOR TUBE
9 - INJ.#2
10 - INJ.#4
11 - INJ.#6
12 - INJ.#8
13 - PRESSURE TEST PORT CAP

67189-JEEP-G56

Fig. 109 Fuel rail assembly—4.7L engine shown, 5.7L Engine similar

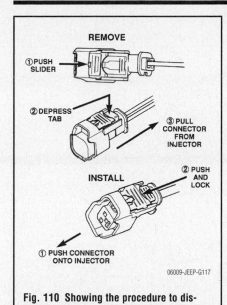

Fig. 110 Showing the procedure to disconnect the electrical connectors from the fuel injectors.

FUEL PUMP

REMOVAL & INSTALLATION

See Figure 111.

1. Drain and remove the fuel tank.
2. Note the rotational position of the fuel pump module before removing. Use the indexing arrow located on top of the module for reference.
3. Install Special Tool 9340 Locking Remover/Install into the notches on the outside edges of the lockring.
4. Install a ½ breaker bar to the lockring removal tool.
5. Rotate the breaker bar counter-clockwise to remove the lockring.
6. When the lockring is removed, the fuel pump module will spring up slightly from the tank.

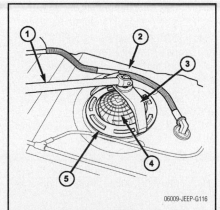

Fig. 111 Install Special Tool 9340 (3) and breaker bar (1) to the lockring (5) in order to remove the fuel pump (4).

7. Carefully remove the fuel pump assembly from the tank.

To install:

8. Install the fuel pump module into the fuel tank using a new gasket.
9. Position the lockring over the fuel pump module.
10. Rotate the fuel pump under the embossed alignment arrow points to the center of the alignment mark.
11. Install Special Tool 9340 and breaker bar over the lockring and turn clockwise until all seven notches have been engaged.
12. Install the fuel tank.
13. Start the engine and check for leaks.

FUEL TANK

REMOVAL & INSTALLATION

1. Properly relieve the fuel system pressure.
2. Raise and safely support the vehicle.
3. Thoroughly clean the area around fuel fill fitting and rubber fuel fill hose at rear of fuel tank.
4. Loosen the clamp at tank fitting and disconnect rubber fuel fill hose at fuel tank fitting. Using an approved gas holding tank, drain fuel tank through this fitting.
5. Loosen clamp and disconnect rubber fill hose at tank fitting.
6. At the rear of tank, disconnect fuel pump module electrical jumper connector from body connector.
7. At the rear of tank, disconnect the EVAP lines.
8. At the front of tank, disconnect the fuel and EVAP lines.
9. Support tank with a hydraulic jack.
10. Remove the mounting bolts and at right side of fuel tank.
11. Remove the mounting bolts at left side of fuel tank.
12. Carefully lower the tank to remove.

To install:

13. Position the fuel tank to the hydraulic jack.
14. Raise the tank until positioned to the body.
15. Install and tighten the mounting bolts to 50 ft. lbs. (68 Nm).
16. Remove the hydraulic jack.
17. Connect the EVAP, ORVR, fuel and NVLD lines at front and rear of tank.
18. Connect the fuel pump module electrical jumper connector to body connector.
19. Connect the rubber fill hose to tank fitting and tighten clamp.
20. Lower the vehicle.

21. Fill fuel tank with fuel.
22. Start engine and check for fuel leaks near top of module.

IDLE SPEED

ADJUSTMENT

The idle speed is control by the Powertrain Control Module (PCM). No adjustment is necessary or possible.

✳✳ WARNING

Never attempt to adjust the engine idle speed using the set screw on the throttle body. This screw is used to limit the position of the throttle body throttle plate and is set at the factory.

THROTTLE BODY

REMOVAL & INSTALLATION

3.7L Engine

2006 Models

See Figure 112.

1. Remove the air intake assembly from the throttle body.
2. Disconnect the throttle body electrical connectors at Idle Air Control (IAC) motor and Throttle Position Sensor (TPS).
3. Remove all control cables from throttle body (lever) arm.
4. Disconnect any necessary vacuum lines from the throttle body.
5. Remove the three throttle body mounting bolts.
6. Remove the throttle body from intake manifold.

To install:

7. Inspect the condition of the throttle body O-ring and replace if necessary.
8. Clean the mating surfaces of the throttle body and intake manifold.

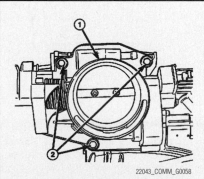

Fig. 112 Position of the three throttle body (1) mounting bolts (2)—2006 3.7L Engines

9. Install the throttle body to the intake manifold and tighten the mounting bolts to 105 inch lbs. (12 Nm).

10. Install the control cables.

11. Install the electrical connectors.

12. Install the necessary vacuum lines.

13. Install the air intake assembly.

2007 Models

See Figure 113.

1. Remove the air intake assembly from the throttle body.

2. Disconnect the throttle body electrical connector.

3. Disconnect any necessary vacuum lines from the throttle body.

4. Remove the four throttle body mounting bolts.

5. Remove the throttle body from the intake manifold.

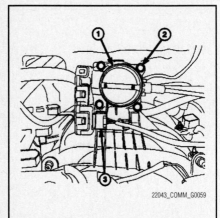

Fig. 113 Position of the four throttle body (1) mounting bolts (2) and electrical connector (3)—2007 3.7L Engine

22043_COMM_G0059

To install:

6. Inspect the condition of the throttle body O-ring and replace if necessary.

7. Clean the mating surfaces of the throttle body and intake manifold.

8. Install the throttle body to the intake manifold and tighten the mounting bolts to 60 inch lbs. (7 Nm).

9. Install the electrical connector.

10. Install the necessary vacuum lines.

11. Install the air intake assembly.

4.7L Engine

See Figure 114.

1. Remove the air duct and air resonator box at the throttle body.

2. Disconnect the throttle body electrical

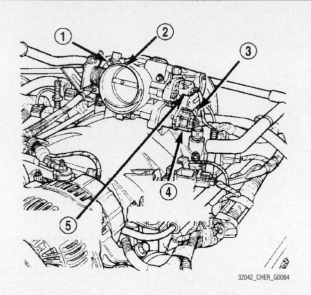

Fig. 114 Throttle body (2), mounting bolts (1) and sensor electrical connectors (3, 4, 5)—4.7L engine

32042_CHER_G0084

connectors at Idle Air Control (IAC) motor and Throttle Position Sensor (TPS).

3. Remove the vacuum line at throttle body.

4. Remove all control cables from throttle body (lever) arm.

5. Remove the three throttle body mounting bolts.

6. Remove throttle body from intake manifold.

To install:

7. Clean throttle body-to-intake manifold O-ring.

8. Clean mating surfaces of throttle body and intake manifold.

9. Install throttle body to intake manifold by positioning throttle body to manifold alignment pins.

10. Install three mounting bolts. Tighten bolts to 105 in. lbs. (12 Nm).

11. Install control cables.

12. Install vacuum line to throttle body.

13. Install the sensor electrical connectors.

14. Install air duct/air box at throttle body.

5.7L Engine

❋❋❋ CAUTION

Do not use spray (carburetor) cleaners on any part of the throttle body. Do not apply silicone lubricants to any part of the throttle body.

1. Remove the air duct and air resonator box at throttle body.

2. Disconnect the electrical connector at throttle body.

3. Remove the four throttle body mounting bolts.

4. Remove the throttle body from intake manifold.

To install:

❋❋❋ CAUTION

Do not use spray (carburetor) cleaners on any part of the throttle body. Do not apply silicone lubricants to any part of the throttle body.

5. Clean and check condition of throttle body-to-intake manifold O-ring.

6. Clean mating surfaces of throttle body and intake manifold.

7. Install the throttle body to intake manifold by positioning throttle body to manifold alignment pins.

8. Install the four mounting bolts.

9. Connect the electrical connector.

10. Install the air duct and box.

11. A Scan Tool may be used to learn electrical parameters.

12. If the previous step is not performed, a Diagnostic Trouble Code (DTC) will be set.

13. If necessary, use a scan tool to erase any Diagnostic Trouble Codes (DTCs) from PCM.

HEATING & AIR CONDITIONING SYSTEM

BLOWER MOTOR

REMOVAL & INSTALLATION

Front

See Figure 115.

1. Disconnect the negative battery cable.
2. Remove the instrument panel silencer from the passenger side of the instrument panel.
3. Remove the glove box from the instrument panel.
4. Disconnect the blower motor wire harness connector from the blower motor power module or resistor, depending on how equipped.
5. Remove the three screws that secure the blower motor to the HVAC housing.
6. Remove the blower motor from the HVAC housing.

To install:

7. Position the blower motor into the HVAC housing.
8. Install the three screws that secure the blower motor to the HVAC housing. Tighten the screws to 20 inch lbs. (2.2 Nm).
9. Connect the wire harness connector to the blower motor power module or resistor, depending on how equipped.
10. Install the glove box into the instrument panel.
11. Install the instrument panel silencer onto the passenger side of the instrument panel.
12. Reconnect the negative battery cable.

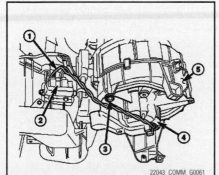

Fig. 115 Disconnect the wiring harness (1) form the motor power module (2) and remove the bolts (3) that secure the front blower motor (4) to the HVAC housing (5)—Front blower motor

Rear

1. Recover the refrigerant from the refrigerant system.
2. Drain the engine cooling system.
3. Disconnect the negative battery cable.
4. Raise and safely support the vehicle.
5. Remove the nut that secures the underbody refrigerant lines to the rear A/C expansion valve which extends through the rear floor panel behind the right rear wheel housing.
6. Disconnect the rear underbody refrigerant lines from the rear A/C expansion valve and remove and discard the O-ring seals.
7. Cap the opened underbody refrigerant line fittings and rear expansion valve ports.
8. Disconnect the rear heater hoses from the rear heater core tubes which extends through the rear floor panel.
9. Lower the vehicle.
10. Remove the right rear quarter panel trim.
11. Disengage the retainer that secures the distribution duct to the rear of the HVAC housing and remove the duct.
12. Disconnect the rear HVAC wire harness connector from the body wire harness connector.
13. Remove the nut and bolt that secure the rear HVAC housing to the rear interior quarter panel.
14. Remove the rear HVAC housing from the vehicle.
15. Disconnect the rear HVAC wiring harness connector from the rear blower motor.
16. Remove the bolts that secure the blower motor to the rear HVAC housing.

To install:

17. Position the blower motor into the rear HVAC housing and tighten the bolts to 17 inch lbs. (2 Nm).
18. Connect the wiring harness.
19. Position the rear HVAC housing into the vehicle and install the fasteners to 27 inch lbs. (3 Nm).
20. Connect the rear HVAC wire harness connector to the body wire harness connector.
21. Install the distribution duct onto the rear of the HVAC housing and engage the retainer to the housing.
22. Install the right rear quarter panel trim.
23. Raise and safely support the vehicle.
24. Connect the rear heater hoses to the rear heater core tubes which extend through the rear floor panel behind the right rear wheel housing and install the heater hose clamps securely.
25. Remove the caps from rear underbody refrigerant line fittings and rear expansion valve ports.
26. Lubricate new rubber O-ring seals with clean refrigerant oil and install them onto the rear underbody refrigerant line fittings.

✳✳ WARNING

Use only the specified O-rings as they are made of a special material for the R-134a refrigerant system.

✳✳ WARNING

Use only refrigerant oil of the type recommended for the A/C compressor in the vehicle.

27. Connect the underbody refrigerant lines to the rear A/C expansion valve.
28. Install the nut that secures the underbody refrigerant lines to the rear A/C expansion valve and tighten the nut to 17 ft. lbs. (23 Nm).
29. Lower the vehicle.
30. Connect the negative battery cable.
31. Refill the cooling system to the correct level.
32. Charge the refrigerant system.

HEATER CORE

REMOVAL & INSTALLATION

Front

See Figures 116 and 117.

1. Disconnect the negative battery cable.
2. Drain the engine cooling system.
3. Properly disable the airbag system.
4. If required, disconnect the heater hoses from the heater core tubes in the engine compartment.
5. Remove the instrument panel as follows:

   a. Remove the bolts and remove the driver's side hush panel.

   b. Using a trim stick C-4755 or equivalent, separate the upper clips and rotate the cover down and release the lower hinges at the bottom and remove the opening cover.

   c. Remove the three bolts in the lower shroud.

Use care not to break off the tangs on the shrouds.

d. Then unsnap the lower shroud from the upper shroud.

e. Disconnect the steering column electrical connectors.

Do not turn the steering wheel more than 90° or damage to the clock-spring may occur.

f. Position front wheels in the straight ahead position.

g. Remove the pinch bolt.

h. Remove the column support bolts.

i. Remove the column cross bolt and slide the column downward off the bracket and remove the steering column.

j. Remove the nuts attaching the instrument panel to the pedal support bracket.

k. Separate the door seal as necessary to access the side covers.

l. Using a trim stick C-4755 or equivalent, remove the left side cover.

m. Remove the left side door sill trim.

n. Remove the driver's side cowl trim panel.

o. Disconnect the electrical connectors.

p. Remove the bolts and disconnect the ground wires within the steering column opening to the left of the steering column.

q. Disconnect the white adjustable pedal electrical connector.

r. Disconnect the HVAC electrical connector.

s. Remove the bolts and remove the left a-pillar trim.

t. Remove the two left side bolts and one screw at the a-pillar support.

u. Using a trim stick C-4755 or equivalent, remove the shifter bezel ring.

v. Using a trim stick C-4755 or equivalent, remove the shifter bezel.

w. Remove the center console back cover and disconnect the electrical connector.

x. Remove the screws and remove the console.

y. Disconnect the electrical connectors under the console.

z. Separate the wire harness push pin hangers and remove the screw and disconnect the ground.

aa. Remove the shifter assembly.

bb. Remove the center HVAC duct.

cc. Separate the glove box damper

rod from the clove box by sliding the rod towards the rear of the vehicle to release it from the bin.

dd. Open the glove box and push the stop tabs down to drop the glove box out of the instrument panel.

ee. Rotate the box down and release the door hinges at the bottom and remove the glove box.

ff. Remove the passenger side hush panel.

gg. Remove the right side door sill trim.

hh. Remove the nut , separate the right cowl trim panel and remove.

ii. Separate the door seal as necessary to access the side covers.

jj. Remove the right side end cap.

kk. Disconnect the electrical connectors.

ll. Disconnect the antenna cable (1 and 2).

mm. Remove the bolts and remove the right a-pillar trim panel.

nn. Remove the two right side bolts and one screw at the a-pillar support.

oo. Using a trim stick C-4755 or equivalent, remove the defroster grill.

pp. Using a trim stick C-4755 or equivalent, remove the radio bezel.

qq. Remove the screw inside the lower storage bin, if equipped.

rr. Using a trim stick C-4755 or equivalent, remove the center bezel and disconnect the electrical connectors.

ss. Remove the nut from the HVAC support stud behind the center bezel.

tt. Remove the screw to the HVAC from under the glove box opening.

uu. Remove the HVAC bracket bolt from the glove box opening.

vv. Remove the left and right center support brackets. * Left side shown, right side similar.

ww. Remove the center floor duct.

xx. Remove the radio.

yy. Remove the two HVAC bolts from the radio opening.

zz. Remove the instrument panel assembly

6. Remove the five bolts that secure the heater core and tube cover to the HVAC housing.

7. Remove the heater core and tube cover from the HVAC housing.

8. If equipped with dual zone heating-A/C, remove the blend door actuator from the passenger side of the HVAC air distribution housing.

9. Remove the bolt that secure the heater core tubes and retaining bracket to the HVAC housing.

Protect the carpeting from engine coolant have absorbent towels readily available to clean up any spills.

10. Remove the bolt that secures the heater tubes to the heater core.

11. Disconnect the heater core tubes from the heater core and remove and discard the O-ring seals.

12. Cap the opened heater core ports.

13. Carefully pull the heater core out of the HVAC air distribution housing.

To install:

14. Carefully install the heater core into the passenger side of the HVAC air distribution housing.

15. Remove the caps from the heater core ports.

16. If removed, position the heater core tubes (4) into the vehicle.

17. Lubricate new rubber O-ring seals with clean engine coolant and install them onto the heater core tubes.

Use only the specified O-ring as they are made of a special material for the engine cooling system.

18. Connect the heater core tubes to the heater core.

19. Install the bolt that secures the heater core tubes to the heater core. Tighten the bolt securely.

20. Install the screw that secures the heater core tube retaining bracket to the HVAC housing and tighten to 20 inch lbs. (2.2 Nm).

21. If equipped with dual zone heating-A/C, install the blend door actuator onto the passenger side of the HVAC air distribution housing.

22. Install the heater core and tube cover onto the HVAC housing.

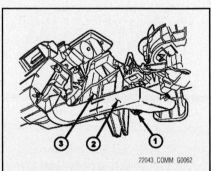

22043_COMM G0062

Fig. 116 Remove the bolts (1) that secure the heater core cover (2) to the HVAC housing (3)—Front heater core removal

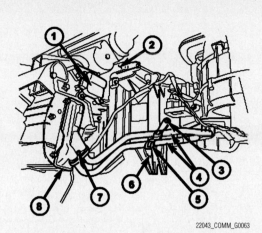

Fig. 117 Remove the blend door actuator (1) form the air distribution housing (2). Remove the screws (3) that hold the heater core tubes (4) and bracket (5) to the HVAC housing (6). Remove the bolt (7) that secures the tubes to heater core (8)—Front heater core removal

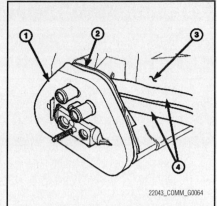

Fig. 118 Remove the foam seal (1) from the flange (2) on the rear HVAC housing (3). Remove the heater core tubes (4) from the flange—Rear heater core removal

23. Install the five screws that secure the heater core and tube cover to the HVAC housing and tighten to 20 inch lbs. (2.2 Nm).

24. The remainder of the installation is the reverse order of removal.

25. If the heater core is being replaced, flush the cooling system.

26. Refill the engine with coolant to the correct level.

Rear

See Figures 118 and 119.

1. Remove the rear HVAC housing.

2. Carefully remove the foam seal from the flange located at the bottom of the rear HVAC housing.

➡**If the seal is deformed or damaged, it must be replaced.**

3. Partially bend the inner half of the flange downward and remove the heater core tubes from the flange.

4. Release the two tabs that secure the rear heater core in the rear HVAC housing.

5. Carefully pull the rear heater core out of the end of the rear HVAC housing.

➡**If the foam seals on the heater core are deformed or damaged, they must be replaced.**

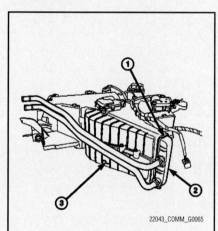

Fig. 119 Release the tubs (1) that secure the heater core (2) in the HVAC housing (3)—Rear heater core removal

To install:

6. Install the rear heater core into the end of the rear HVAC housing. Make sure that the foam seals are properly installed and that the two retaining tabs are fully engaged.

7. If the rear heater core tubes were removed from the heater core, lubricate new rubber O-ring seals with clean engine coolant and install them onto the heater core tubes. Connect the heater core tubes to the heater core and install two retaining clamps securely.

❈❈ WARNING

Use only the specified O-ring as they are made of a special material for the engine cooling system.

8. Partially bend the inner half of the flange located at the bottom of the rear HVAC housing downward and install the heater core tubes into the flange.

9. Install the foam seal onto the flange.

➡**If the seal is deformed or damaged, it must be replaced.**

10. Install the rear HVAC housing.

STEERING

POWER STEERING GEAR

REMOVAL & INSTALLATION

1. Place the front wheels in the straight ahead position with the steering wheel centered and locked with a steering wheel lock.
2. Drain or siphon the power steering system.
3. Remove the column coupler shaft bolt and remove the shaft from the gear.
4. Remove the oil drip tray.
5. Remove the pressure line at the gear.
6. Remove the return line at the gear.
7. Raise and safely support the vehicle.
8. Remove the front tires.
9. Loosen the tie rod end jam nuts.
10. Remove the outer tie rod end nut and separate the tie rod from the knuckle using Special Tool 8677.
11. Remove the front splash shield.
12. If equipped with 4WD, remove the front axle.
13. Remove the two steering gear mounting bolts.
14. Move the gear to the full right position to allow clearance over the control arm then lower the gear down, then turn the gear to the full left position then to allow clearance then remove from the vehicle.
15. Remove the outer tie rod ends from the steering gear (if needed).

To install:

16. Install the outer tie rod ends. (if removed).
17. Position the steering gear back into the vehicle the same way it was removed.
18. Install the steering gear mounting bolts and tighten to 180 ft. lbs. (244 Nm).
19. Install the front splash shield.
20. Install the outer tie rod ends jam nuts and only hand tighten at this time.
21. Install the outer tie rod ends to the knuckle and tighten the tie rod end nut to 70 ft. lbs. (95 Nm).
22. Install the pressure and return hoses to the steering gear and tighten to 21 ft. lbs. (28 Nm).
23. Install the oil filter drip tray.
24. Install the column coupler shaft into the lower coupling and install a new bolt Tighten to 36 ft. lbs. (49 Nm).
25. If equipped with 4WD, install the front axle.

26. Install the front tires.
27. Lower the vehicle.
28. Remove the steering wheel lock.
29. Fill the power steering pump.
30. Check and adjust the front wheel alignment as necessary.

POWER STEERING PUMP

REMOVAL & INSTALLATION

3.7L & 4.7L Engines

1. Siphon the fluid from the power steering reservoir.
2. Remove the cooler return hose at the reservoir.
3. Disconnect the pressure hose nut at the pump.
4. Remove the pressure hose at the pump.
5. Remove the accessory drive belt.
6. Remove the three power steering pump mounting bolts.

To install:

7. Install the power steering pump mounting bolts and tighten to 21 ft. lbs. (28 Nm).
8. Install the accessory drive belt.
9. Install the pressure hose on the pump and tighten the nut to 21 ft. lbs. (28 Nm).
10. Install the cooler return hose at the reservoir.
11. Add power steering fluid as necessary.
12. Bleed the power steering system.

5.7L Engine

1. Siphon the fluid from the power steering reservoir.
2. Remove the air intake assembly.
3. Remove the accessory drive belt.
4. Disconnect the power steering pump supply hose.
5. Disconnect the pressure line at the pump.
6. Remove the pump mounting bolts and remove the pump.

To install:

7. Position the pump to the engine and tighten the mounting bolts to 21 ft. lbs. (28 Nm).
8. Install the pressure hose on the pump and tighten the nut to 21 ft. lbs. 28 Nm).

9. Reconnect the supply hose.
10. Install the accessory drive belt.
11. Install the air intake assembly.
12. Fill the system with power steering fluid.
13. Bleed the power steering system.

BLEEDING

✳✳ WARNING

The fluid level should be checked with the engine off to prevent injury from any moving components.

✳✳ WARNING

Use Mopar® Power Steering Fluid or equivalent. Do not use automatic transmission fluid and do not overfill.

1. Wipe filler cap clean, then check the fluid level. The dipstick should indicate COLD when the fluid is at normal ambient temperature.
2. Fill the pump fluid reservoir to the proper level and let the fluid settle for at least two minutes.
3. Start the engine and let run for a few seconds then turn engine off.
4. Add fluid as necessary. Repeat the above procedure until the fluid level remains constant after running the engine.
5. Raise the front wheels off the ground.
6. Slowly turn the steering wheel right and left, lightly contacting the wheel stops at least 20 times.
7. Check the fluid level add if necessary.
8. Lower the vehicle, start the engine and turn the steering wheel slowly from lock to lock.
9. Stop the engine and check the fluid level and refill as required.

✳✳ CAUTION

Do not run a vehicle with foamy fluid for an extended period. This may cause pump damage.

10. If the fluid is extremely foamy or milky looking, allow the vehicle to stand a few minutes and repeat the procedure.

CLEVIS BRACKET

REMOVAL & INSTALLATION

See Figure 120.

1. Raise and safely support the vehicle.
2. Remove the front wheel.
3. Remove the brake caliper.

✳✳ WARNING

Support the caliper with mechanics wire or equivalent. Do not let the caliper hang by the brake hose.

4. Remove the brake rotor.
5. Remove the upper ball joint nut and separate the upper ball joint from the steering knuckle using Special Tool 8677.
6. Remove the clevis bolt from the bottom of the strut assembly.
7. Remove the lower clevis bolt and nut from the lower control arm.
8. Remove the lower stabilizer link bolt for access.
9. Remove the clevis bracket.

To install:

10. Install the clevis bracket to the strut assembly and tighten the bolt to 90 ft. lbs. (122 Nm).
11. Install the lower stabilizer link bolt and tighten to 85 ft. lbs. (115 Nm).
12. Install the lower clevis bolt/nut to the lower control arm and tighten to 125 ft. lbs. (169 Nm).
13. Install the upper ball joint into the knuckle and tighten to 70 ft. lbs. (95 Nm).
14. Install the brake rotor.
15. Install the brake caliper.
16. Install the front wheel.
17. Lower the vehicle.

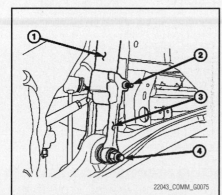

Fig. 120 Remove the upper bolt (2) from the strut assembly (1) and lower bolt (3) to remove the clevis bracket (3)—Clevis bracket removal.

COIL SPRING

REMOVAL & INSTALLATION

See Figures 121 and 122.

1. Remove the strut assembly from the vehicle.
2. Install the strut assembly in the Branick 7200® spring removal/installation tool or equivalent.
3. Compress the spring.
4. Remove the upper strut nut.

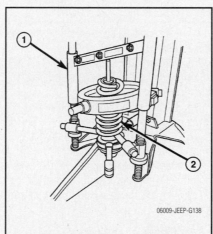

06009-JEEP-G138

Fig. 121 Strut installed in a spring compressor

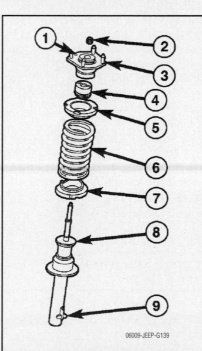

06009-JEEP-G139

Fig. 122 Strut components. (1) nub hole, (2) upper nut, (3) strut plate, (4) jounce bumper, (5) upper isolator, (6) spring, (7) lower isolator, (8) strut, (9) bracket

➡The nub in the upper strut mount must be 180° from the centerline of the lower bracket on the strut for proper installation.

5. Remove the strut.
6. Remove the strut upper mounting plate.
7. Remove and inspect the upper and lower spring isolators.

To install:

8. Compress the spring.
9. Install the lower isolator.
10. Position the strut into the coil spring. Make sure the jounce bumper is on the strut rod.
11. Install the upper isolator.

➡For proper orientation the nub hole in the upper strut plate must be 180° in a centerline from the bracket at the bottom of the strut.

12. Install the upper strut mounting plate.
13. Install the strut upper mounting nut. Tighten to 25 ft. lbs. (39 Nm).
14. Decompress the spring.
15. Remove the strut assembly from the spring compressor tool.
16. Install the strut assembly.

LOWER BALL JOINT

REMOVAL & INSTALLATION

See Figures 123 through 125.

1. Raise and safely support the vehicle.
2. Remove the front wheel.
3. Remove the brake caliper and rotor.
4. Disconnect the tie rod from the steering knuckle using Special Tool C-3894-A or equivalent.
5. Separate the lower ball joint from steering knuckle using Special Tool 8677.
6. Remove the steering knuckle.
7. If equipped with 4WD, remove the clevis bracket and move the halfshaft to the side and support it.
8. Press the lower ball joint from the lower control arm using Special Tools C-4212-F, C-4212-3 and 9654-3.

To install:

➡Extreme pressure lubrication must be used on the threaded portions of the tool. This will increase the longevity of the tool and insure proper operation during the removal and installation process.

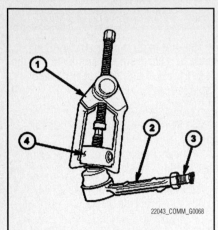

Fig. 123 Remove the tie rod (2) from the steering knuckle (4) using Special Tool C-3894-A (1)—Lower ball joint removal

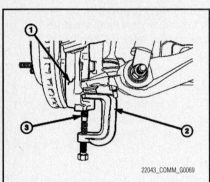

Fig. 124 Separate the lower ball joint (3) from steering knuckle (1) using Special Tool 8677 (2)—Lower ball joint removal

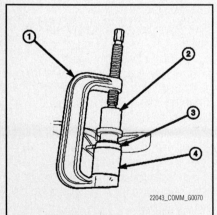

Fig. 125 Press the lower ball joint from the lower control arm (3)using Special Tools C-4212-F (1), C-4212-3 (2) and 9654-3 (4)—Lower ball joint removal

9. Install the ball joint into the control arm using Special Tools C-4212-F, 9654-1 and 9654-2.

10. Stake the ball joint flange in four evenly spaced places around the ball joint flange, using a chisel and hammer.

11. If equipped with 4WD, remove the support for the halfshaft and install into position.

12. Install the steering knuckle.

13. Install the tie rod end into the steering knuckle.

14. Install and tighten the halfshaft nut to 185 ft. lbs. (251 Nm) (if equipped).

15. Install the brake caliper and rotor.

16. Install the tire and wheel assembly.

17. Check the vehicle ride height

18. Perform a wheel alignment.

LOWER CONTROL ARM

REMOVAL & INSTALLATION

1. Raise and safely support the vehicle.

2. Remove the front wheel.

3. Remove the steering knuckle.

4. Remove the shock clevis bracket from the lower control arm.

5. Remove the stabilizer link at the lower control arm.

6. Remove the nut and bolt from the front of the lower control arm.

7. Remove the rear bolts and flag nuts from the lower control arm.

8. Remove the lower control arm from the vehicle.

To install:

9. Position the lower suspension arm into the frame rail bracket.

10. Install the rear bolts for the lower control arm to the frame and tighten to 65 ft. lbs. (88 Nm)..

11. Install the nut and bolt for the front of the lower control arm and tighten to 125 ft lbs (169 Nm).

12. Install the lower clevis bolt at the lower control arm and tighten to 125 ft. lbs. (169 Nm).

13. Install the stabilizer link at the lower control arm and tighten to 85 ft. lbs. (115 Nm).

14. Install the steering knuckle and tighten the nut to 70 ft. lbs. (95 Nm).

15. Install the front wheel.

16. Lower the vehicle.

17. Perform wheel alignment.

CONTROL ARM BUSHING REPLACEMENT

The lower control arm bushings are serviced with the control arms as complete assemblies.

STABILIZER BAR

REMOVAL & INSTALLATION

1. Raise and safely support the vehicle.

2. Remove the front splash shield.

3. Remove the stabilizer bar link upper nut and bolt.

4. Remove the two stabilizer bushing clamp bolts.

5. Remove the stabilizer bar.

To install:

6. Install the stabilizer bar into place under the vehicle.

7. Install the bushing clamps and tighten the bolts to 95 ft. lbs. (129 Nm).

8. Connect the upper stabilizer links to the stabilizer bar and tighten the nuts to 80 ft. lbs. (108 Nm).

9. Install the front splash shield.

10. Lower the vehicle.

STEERING KNUCKLE

REMOVAL & INSTALLATION

See Figure 126.

1. Raise and safely support the vehicle.

2. Remove the front wheel.

3. Remove the brake caliper.

4. Remove the caliper mounting adapter.

5. Remove the brake rotor.

6. Remove the wheel speed sensor.

7. If equipped with 4WD, remove the axleshaft nut.

8. Remove the wheel hub.

9. Remove the outer tie road retaining nut.

10. Separate the outer tie rod end from the steering knuckle using Special Tool 8677.

11. Remove the lower ball joint nut.

12. Separate the lower ball joint from the knuckle using Special Tool C-4150A.

13. Remove the upper ball joint nut.

14. Separate the upper ball joint from the knuckle using Special Tool 8677.

15. Remove the steering knuckle from the vehicle.

To install:

16. Position the steering knuckle into place on the vehicle.

17. Install the lower ball joint into the knuckle and tighten the nut to 70 ft. lbs. (95 Nm).

18. install the upper ball joint into the knuckle and tighten the nut to 70 ft. lbs. (95 Nm).

19. Install the outer tie rod end to the steering knuckle.

20. Install the wheel hub and tighten to 85 ft. lbs. (115 Nm).

21. If equipped with 4WD, install the axleshaft nut and tighten to 96 ft. lbs. (135 Nm).

22. Install the following front brake components:

- Wheel speed sensor
- Brake rotor

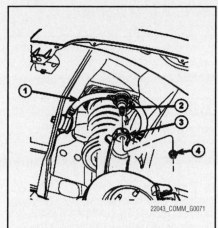

Fig. 126 Install the upper ball joint (2) into the knuckle (3) and tighten the upper ball joint nut (4)—Steering knuckle installation

- Caliper mounting adapter
- Caliper
23. Install the front wheel.
24. Lower the vehicle and perform a wheel alignment as necessary.

STRUT & SPRING ASSEMBLY

REMOVAL & INSTALLATION

See Figures 127 and 128.

1. Remove the air intake assembly.
2. If removing the right side strut assembly:
   a. Disconnect the cruise control servo electrical connector.
   b. Remove the coolant reservoir mounting bolt and move the coolant reservoir off to the side.
3. If removing the left side strut assembly.
   a. Remove the power distribution center (PDC) bracket nuts.
   b. Move the PDC over to the side in order to access the upper strut mounting nuts.
4. Remove the four upper strut mounting nuts.
5. Raise and support the vehicle.
6. Remove the front wheel.
7. Remove the two brake caliper adapter bolts.
8. Support the brake caliper adapter and caliper.

❊❊ WARNING

Do not allow the caliper to hang by the brake hose.

9. Remove the disc brake rotor.
10. Remove the upper ball joint nut.

11. Separate the upper ball joint from the knuckle using Special Tool 8677 or equivalent ball joint separator.
12. Remove the lower clevis bolt at the lower control arm.
13. Remove the lower stabilizer bolt at the lower control arm.
14. Remove the strut assembly from the vehicle.

To install:

15. Install the clevis bracket to the strut assembly and tighten to 90 ft. lbs. (122 Nm).
16. Install the strut assembly to the vehicle and tighten the upper mounting nuts to 70 ft. lbs. (95 Nm).
17. If installing the right side strut assembly:
   a. Install the coolant reservoir bolt.

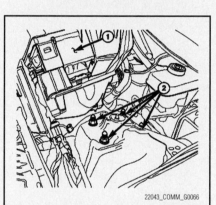

Fig. 127 Remove the upper strut mounting nuts (2) once the PDC (1) has been moved aside—Left side strut

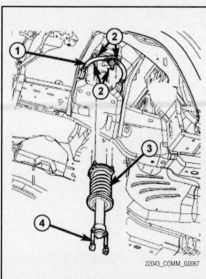

Fig. 128 Install the clevis bracket (1) to the strut assembly (3) and then tighten the upper mounting nuts (2)—Right strut shown, left side similar

   b. Reconnect the cruise control servo wiring connector.
18. If installing the left side strut assembly:
   a. Position the PDC into place and tighten the bracket nuts.
19. Install the air intake assembly.
20. Install the lower stabilizer bolt at the lower control arm and tighten to 85 ft. lbs. (115 Nm)..
21. Install the lower clevis bolt at the lower control arm and tighten to 125 ft. lbs. (169 Nm).
22. Install the upper ball joint into the knuckle and tighten the nut to 55 ft. lbs. (75 Nm).
23. Install the disc brake rotor.
24. Install the caliper adapter mounting bolts to 130 ft. lbs. (176 Nm).
25. Install the front wheel.
26. Lower the vehicle.

UPPER BALL JOINT

REMOVAL & INSTALLATION

See Figures 129 and 130.

1. Raise and safely support the vehicle.
2. Remove the front wheel.
3. Remove the upper ball joint retaining nut.
4. Separate the upper ball joint from the steering knuckle using Special Tool 8677.
5. Move the knuckle aside to allow access for the ball joint removal tool.

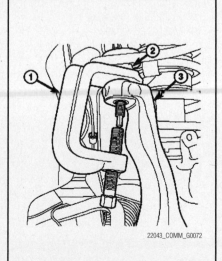

Fig. 129 Separate the upper ball joint (2) from the steering knuckle (3) using Special Tool 8677 (1)—Upper ball joint removal

➡Extreme pressure lubrication must be used on the threaded portions of the tool. This will increase the longevity of the tool and insure proper operation during the removal and installation process.

6. Press the ball joint from the upper control arm using Special Tools C-4212-F and 9652.

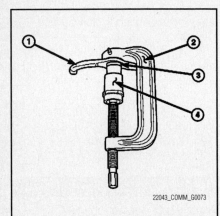

Fig. 130 Press the ball joint (3) from the upper control arm (1) using Special Tools C-4212-F (2) and 9652 (4)—Upper ball joint removal

To install:

7. Press the ball joint into the upper control arm using Special Tools C-4212-F Press, 9652 Driver, and 8975-2 Receiver.

8. Install the upper ball joint into the steering knuckle. Tighten the upper ball joint retaining nut to 70 ft. lbs. (95 Nm).

9. Install the front wheel.

10. Lower the vehicle.

11. Check and adjust the wheel alignment as necessary.

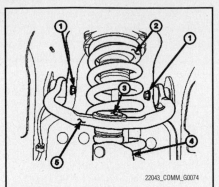

Fig. 131 Remove the nut and bolt (1) holding the upper control arm (5) to the body.

UPPER CONTROL ARM

REMOVAL & INSTALLATION

See Figure 131.

1. Raise and safely support the vehicle.

2. Remove the front wheel.

3. Remove the inner fender well splash shield.

4. Remove the upper ball joint nut.

5. Separate the upper ball joint from the steering knuckle using Special Tool 8677.

6. Remove the nut and bolt securing the upper control to the body.

7. Remove the upper control arm.

To install:

8. Position the upper control arm into place and tighten the bolt and nut to 80 ft. lbs. (108 Nm).

9. Install the upper ball joint into the steering knuckle and tighten the nut to 70 ft. lbs. (95 Nm).

10. Install the inner fender well.

11. Lower the vehicle.

12. Check and adjust the alignment as necessary.

CONTROL ARM BUSHING REPLACEMENT

The upper control arm bushings are serviced with the control arms as a complete assembly.

WHEEL BEARINGS

REMOVAL & INSTALLATION

1. Raise and safely support the vehicle.

2. Remove the front wheel.

3. Remove the disc brake caliper.

✳✳ WARNING

Support the caliper. Do not let the caliper hang by the hose.

4. Remove the brake caliper adapter

5. Remove the disc brake rotor.

6. Remove the wheel speed sensor nut.

7. Remove the wheel speed sensor.

8. Remove the 3 hub bearing mounting bolts from the back of the steering knuckle. Remove hub bearing from the steering knuckle.

To install:

9. Install the hub bearing to the knuckle.

10. Install the hub bearing to knuckle and the 3 bolts then tighten to 85 ft. lbs. (115 Nm).

11. Install the wheel speed sensor.

12. Install the wheel speed sensor nut.

13. Install the brake rotor.

14. Install the brake caliper adapter.

15. Install the caliper.

16. Install the front wheel.

17. Lower the vehicle.

18. Check and adjust the wheel alignment as necessary.

ADJUSTMENT

The wheel hub/bearing unit is not serviceable and must be replaced as an assembly.

COIL SPRING

REMOVAL & INSTALLATION

See Figures 132 and 133.

1. Raise and safely support the vehicle.
2. Position a suitable jack under the axle to support the axle.
3. Remove the wheel and tire assemblies.
4. Remove the lower shock bolt from the axle bracket.
5. Remove the stabilizer bar link from the body rail.
6. Lower the hydraulic jack and tilt the axle and remove the coil spring.
7. Remove and inspect the spring isolators.

To install:

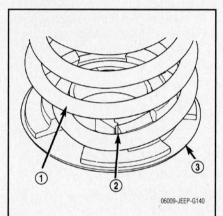

06009-JEEP-G140

Fig. 132 Position the coil spring (1) properly in the lower isolator (3)—Rear coil spring

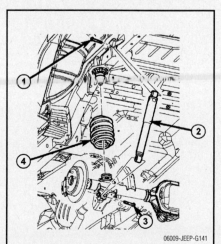

06009-JEEP-G141

Fig. 133 Rear spring and shock installation (1) upper shock bolt, (2) shock, (3) lower shock bolt, (4) spring—2006 Commander shown

8. Install the upper isolator.
9. Install the lower isolator.
10. Pull down on the axle and position the coil spring in the lower isolator.
11. Raise the axle with the hydraulic jack.
12. Install the shock absorber to the axle bracket and tighten to 85 ft. lbs. (115 Nm).
13. Install the stabilizer bar link to the body rail, tighten to 75 ft. lbs. (102 Nm).
14. Install the wheel and tire assemblies.
15. Lower the vehicle.

LOWER CONTROL ARM

REMOVAL & INSTALLATION

Left Side

1. Raise and safely support the vehicle.
2. Place a suitable jack under the axle to support it.
3. Remove the fuel tank.
4. Remove the lower suspension arm nut and bolt from the axle bracket.
5. Remove the nut and bolt from the frame rail and remove the lower suspension arm.

➡**All torques should be done with vehicle on the ground with full vehicle weight.**

To install:

6. Position the lower suspension arm in the frame rail.
7. Install the frame rail bracket bolt and nut. Tighten to130 ft. lbs. (176 Nm).
8. Position the lower suspension arm in the axle bracket.
9. Install the axle bracket bolt and nut. Tighten to 155 ft. lbs. (210 Nm).
10. Install the fuel tank.
11. Lower the vehicle.

Right Side

1. Raise and safely support the vehicle.
2. Place a suitable jack under the axle to support it.
3. Remove the lower suspension arm nut and bolt from the axle bracket.
4. Remove the nut and bolt from the frame rail and remove the lower suspension arm.

To install:

➡**All torques should be done with vehicle on the ground with full vehicle weight.**

5. Position the lower suspension arm in the frame rail.

6. Install the frame rail bracket bolt and nut tighten to to130 ft. lbs.(176 Nm).
7. Position the lower suspension arm in the axle bracket.
8. Install the axle bracket bolt and nut. Tighten to 155 ft. lbs. (210 Nm).
9. Lower the vehicle.

SHOCK ABSORBERS

REMOVAL & INSTALLATION

1. Raise and safely support the vehicle.
2. Place a suitable jack under the axle to support it.
3. Remove the shock bolt from the frame bracket.
4. Remove the lower bolt from the axle bracket and remove the shock absorber.

To install:

➡**Do not tighten the mounting bolts until both bolts are installed.**

5. Position the shock absorber to the vehicle and install the upper shock bolt.
6. Install the lower shock bolt.
7. Tighten the upper shock bolt to 70 ft. lbs. (95 Nm).
8. Tighten the lower shock bolt to 85 ft. lbs. (115 Nm).
9. Lower the vehicle.

STABILIZER BAR

REMOVAL & INSTALLATION

See Figure 134.

1. Raise and safely support the vehicle.
2. Remove both rear wheels.
3. Remove the stabilizer bar links from stabilizer bar.

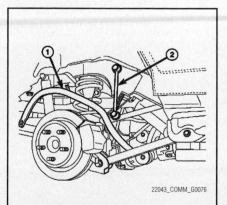

22043_COMM_G0076

Fig. 134 Remove the sway bar links (2) in order to remove the stabilizer bar (1)—Rear stabilizer bar removal

4. Remove the stabilizer bar retainer bolts from the retainer.

5. Remove the stabilizer bar by twisting it out and around the rotor and caliper from the right rear side of the vehicle.

To install:

6. Twist and rotate to position the stabilizer bar on the axle from the right rear side of the vehicle.

7. Install the retainers and bolts. Ensure the bar is centered with equal spacing on both sides. Tighten the bolts to 31 ft. lbs. (42 Nm).

8. Install the links to the stabilizer bar.

9. Tighten the nuts at the stabilizer bar to 90 ft. lbs. (122 Nm).

10. Install the tire and wheel assemblies.

11. Remove support and lower the vehicle.

UPPER CONTROL ARM

REMOVAL & INSTALLATION

Left Side

1. Raise and safely support the vehicle.

2. Place a suitable jack under the axle to support it.

3. Lower the fuel tank in order to gain access to the bolt.

4. Remove the upper suspension arm nut and bolt from the axle bracket.

5. Remove the nut and bolt from the frame rail and remove the upper suspension arm.

To install:

➡All torques should be done with vehicle on the ground with full vehicle weight.

6. Position the upper suspension arm in the frame rail bracket.

7. Install the mounting bolt and nut tighten to 95 ft. lbs. (129 Nm).

8. Position the upper suspension arm in the axle bracket.

9. Install the mounting bolt and nut tighten to 100 ft. lbs. (136 Nm).

10. Raise the fuel tank back into place and secure.

11. Remove the supports and lower the vehicle.

Right Side

1. Raise and safely support the vehicle.

2. Place a suitable jack under the axle to support it.

3. Remove the upper suspension arm nut and bolt from the axle bracket.

4. Remove the nut and bolt from the frame rail and remove the upper suspension arm.

To install:

➡All torques should be done with vehicle on the ground with full vehicle weight.

5. Position the upper suspension arm in the frame rail bracket.

6. Install the mounting bolt and nut tighten to 95 ft. lbs. (129 Nm).

7. Position the upper suspension arm in the axle bracket.

8. Install the mounting bolt and nut tighten to 100 ft. lbs. (136 Nm).

9. Remove the supports and lower the vehicle.

JEEP

Compass • Patriot

SPECIFICATIONS AND MAINTENANCE CHARTS

ENGINE AND VEHICLE IDENTIFICATION

Engine							Model Year	
Code ①	Liters (cc)	Cu. In.	Cyl.	Fuel Sys.	Engine Type	Eng. Mfg.	Code ②	Year
0	2.0 (1998)	122	4	MFI	DOHC	GEMA	7	2007
W	2.4 (2360)	146.5	4	MFI	DOHC	GEMA		

MFI: Multi-port Fuel Injection

DOHC: Dual Overhead Camshaft

① 8th position of VIN

② 10th position of VIN

22043_COMP_C0001

GENERAL ENGINE SPECIFICATIONS

Year	Model	Engine Displ. Liters	Engine VIN	Net Horsepower @ rpm	Net Torque @ rpm (ft. lbs.)	Bore x Stroke (in.)	Comp. Ratio	Oil Pressure @ rpm
2007	Compass	2.0	0	158@6400	141@5000	3.37x3.37	10.5:1	25-80@3000
		2.4	W	172@6000	165@4400	3.47x3.82	10.5:1	25-80@3000
	Patriot	2.0	0	158@6400	141@5000	3.37x3.37	10.5:1	25-80@3000
		2.4	W	172@6000	165@4400	3.47x3.82	10.5:1	25-80@3000

22043_COMP_C0002

GASOLINE ENGINE TUNE-UP SPECIFICATIONS

Year	Engine Displ. Liters	Engine VIN	Spark Plug Gap (in.)	Ignition Timing (deg.)	Fuel Pump (psi)	Idle Speed (rpm)	Valve Clearance	
							Intake	Exhaust
2007	2.0	0	0.038-0.043	①	NA	①	0.006-0.009	0.010-0.012
	2.4	W	0.038-0.043	①	NA	①	0.006-0.009	0.010-0.012

Note: The information on the Vehicle Emission Control label must be used, if different from the figures in this chart.

NA: Not Available

① Ignition timing and idle speed are controlled by the PCM. No adjustment is necessary.

22043_COMP_C0003

CAPACITIES

Year	Model	Engine Displ. Liters	Engine VIN	Engine Oil with Filter	Transmission (pts.) Man.	Transmission (pts.) Auto.**	Transfer Case (pts.)	Drive Axle Front (pts.)	Drive Axle Rear (pts.)	Fuel Tank (gal.)	Cooling System (qts.)
2007	Compass	2.0	0	4.5	4.2	15.4	2.2	-	2.0-2.2	13.5	7.2
		2.4	W	4.5	5.0-5.4	15.4	3.8	-	2.0-2.2	13.5	7.2
	Patriot	2.0	0	4.5	4.2	15.4	2.2	-	2.0-2.2	13.5	7.2
		2.4	W	4.5	5.0-5.4	15.4	3.8	-	2.0-2.2	13.5	7.2

22043_COMP_C0004

FLUID SPECIFICATIONS

Year	Model	Engine Displacement Liters	Engine ID/VIN	Engine Oil	Manual Trans.	Auto. Trans.	Front & Rear Axle	Power Steering Fluid	Brake Master Cylinder
2007	Compass	2.0	0	5W-20	Mopar® ATF +4	Mopar® CVT +4	Mopar® Gear & Axle Lube 80W-90 API GL 5	Mopar® Power Steering Fluid +4 or Mopar® ATF +4	DOT 3
		2.4	W	5W-20	Mopar® ATF +4	Mopar® ATF +4	Mopar® Gear & Axle Lube 80W-90 API GL 5	Mopar® Power Steering Fluid +4 or Mopar® ATF +4	DOT 3
	Patriot	2.0	0	5W-20	Mopar® ATF +4	Mopar® CVT +4	Mopar® Gear & Axle Lube 80W-90 API GL 5	Mopar® Power Steering Fluid +4 or Mopar® ATF +4	DOT 3
		2.4	W	5W-20	Mopar® ATF +4	Mopar® ATF +4	Mopar® Gear & Axle Lube 80W-90 API GL 5	Mopar® Power Steering Fluid +4 or Mopar® ATF +4	DOT 3

DOT: Department Of Transpotation

22043_COMP_C0005

VALVE SPECIFICATIONS

Year	Engine Displ. Liters	Engine VIN	Seat Angle (deg.)	Face Angle (deg.)	Spring Test Pressure (lbs. @ in.)	Spring Installed Height (in.)	Stem-to-Guide Clearance (in.) Intake	Stem-to-Guide Clearance (in.) Exhaust	Stem Diameter (in.) Intake	Stem Diameter (in.) Exhaust
2007	2.0	0	NA	45.25-45.75	78.2-85.8@ 1.152	1.378	0.0008-0.0021	0.0012-0.0024	0.2151-0.2157	0.2148-0.2153
	2.4	W	NA	45.25-45.75	78.2-85.8@ 1.152	1.378	0.0008-0.0021	0.0012-0.0024	0.2151-0.2157	0.2148-0.2153

NA: Information not available

22043_COMP_C0006

CAMSHAFT AND BEARING SPECIFICATIONS CHART
All measurements are given in inches.

Year	Engine Displacement Liters	Engine VIN	Journal Diameter	Brg. Oil Clearance	Shaft End-play	Runout	Journal Bore	Lobe Lift Intake	Lobe Lift Exhaust
2007	2.0	0	0.9430-0.9440	①	0.0040-0.0090	NA	NA	0.3620	0.3310
	2.4	W	0.9430-0.9440	①	0.0031-0.0114	NA	NA	0.2830	0.2830

NA: Not Available

① Front Intake Journal: 0.0008-0.0022 in.
Front Exhaust Journal: 0.0007-0.0020 in.
All Others: 0.0011-0.0026 in.

22043_COMP_C0007

CRANKSHAFT AND CONNECTING ROD SPECIFICATIONS
All measurements are given in inches.

Year	Engine Displ. Liters	Engine VIN	Crankshaft Main Brg. Journal Dia.	Main Brg. Oil Clearance	Shaft End-play	Thrust on No.	Connecting Rod Journal Diameter	Oil Clearance	Side Clearance
2007	2.0	0	①	0.0011-0.0018	0.0019-0.0098	3	2.0078-2.0084	0.0010-0.0020	0.0039-0.0098
	2.4	W	①	0.0011-0.0018	0.0019-0.0098	3	2.0078-2.0084	0.0012-0.0023	0.0039-0.0098

① 0: 2.0466-2.0467 in.
1: 2.0465-2.0466 in.
2: 2.0464-2.0465 in.
3: 2.0462-2.0464 in.
4: 2.0461-2.0462 in.

22043_COMP_C0008

PISTON AND RING SPECIFICATIONS
All measurements are given in inches.

Year	Engine Displ. Liters	Engine VIN	Piston Clearance	Ring Gap Top Compression	Ring Gap Bottom Compression	Ring Gap Oil Control	Ring Side Clearance Top Compression	Ring Side Clearance Bottom Compression	Ring Side Clearance Oil Control
2007	2.0	0	(-0.0006)-0.0006	0.0059-0.0118	0.0118-0.0177	0.0079-0.0276	0.0012-0.0028	0.0012-0.0028	0.0024-0.0059
	2.4	W	(-0.0006)-0.0006	0.0059-0.0118	0.0118-0.0177	0.0079-0.0276	0.0012-0.0028	0.0012-0.0028	0.0024-0.0059

22043_COMP_C0009

TORQUE SPECIFICATIONS
All readings in ft. lbs.

Year	Engine Displ. Liters	Engine VIN	Cylinder Head Bolts	Main Bearing Bolts	Rod Bearing Bolts	Crankshaft Damper Bolts	Flywheel Bolts	Manifold Intake	Manifold Exhaust	Spark Plugs	Oil Pan Drain Plug
2007	2.0	0	①	②	③	155	70	18	25	20	30
	2.4	W	①	②	③	155	70	18	25	20	30

① Refer to procedure for illustration
  Step 1: Tighten bolts to 25 ft. lbs. (30 Nm)
  Step 2:Tighten bolts to 45 ft. lbs. (61 Nm)
  Step 3: Verify all bolts at 45 ft. lbs. (60 Nm)
  Step 4: Tighten bolts an addt'l 90 degrees

② Refer to procedure for illustration
  Step 1: Tighten all bolts to 20 ft. lbs.
  Step 2: Tighten bolts an addt'l 45 degrees

③ Step 1: Tighten all bolts to 15 ft. lbs. (20 Nm)
  Step 2: Tighten bolts an addt'l 90 degrees

22043_COMP_C0010

WHEEL ALIGNMENT

Year	Model①		Caster Range (+/-Deg.)	Caster Preferred Setting (Deg.)	Camber Range (+/-Deg.)	Camber Preferred Setting (Deg.)	Toe-in (deg.)
2007	Compass/Patriot	F	1.00	②	0.40	-0.80	0.10+/-0.10
	16 inch wheels	R	—	—	0.40	-0.70	0.10+/-0.10
	Compass/Patriot	F	1.00	③	0.40	-0.70	0.10+/-0.10
	17 inch wheels	R	—	—	0.40	-0.60	0.10+/-0.10
	Compass/Patriot	F	1.00	②	0.40	-0.70	0.10+/-0.10
	18 inch wheels	R	—	—	0.40	-0.70	0.10+/-0.10

① Wheel size refers to OEM wheels only

② Left: +3.00
  Right: +2.70

③ Left: +2.90
  Right: +2.60

22043_COMP_C0011

TIRE, WHEEL AND BALL JOINT SPECIFICATIONS

Year	Model	OEM Tires Standard	OEM Tires Optional	Tire Pressures (psi) Front	Tire Pressures (psi) Rear	Wheel Size	Ball Joint Inspection	Lug Nut Torque (ft. lbs.)
2007	Compass	P215/60R17	P215/55R18	①	①	①	②	100
	Patriot	P205/70R16	P215/60R17	①	①	①	②	100

OEM: Original Equipment Manufacturer

STD: Standard

OPT: Optional

① See placard on vehicle

② The ball joint is not servicable. The entire lower control arm must be replaced.

22043_COMP_C0012

BRAKE SPECIFICATIONS
All measurements in inches unless noted

| Year | Model | | Brake Disc | | | Minimum Lining Thickness | | Brake Caliper | |
			Original Thickness	Minimum Thickness	Maximum Run-out	Front	Rear	Bracket Bolts (ft. lbs.)	Mounting Bolts (ft. lbs.)
2007	Compass	F	1.020	0.961	0.0020	NA	—	80	32
		R	0.386	0.331	0.0016	—	NA	52	32
	Patriot	F	NA	1.122	0.0008	NA	—	80	32
		R	NA	0.492	0.0008	—	NA	52	32

F - Front

R - Rear

NA - Not Available

22043_COMP_C0013

SCHEDULED MAINTENANCE INTERVALS
2007 Compass & Patriot

| TO BE SERVICED | TYPE OF SERVICE | VEHICLE MILEAGE INTERVAL (x1000) | | | | | | | | | | | | |
		3	6	9	12	15	18	21	24	27	30	33	36	39
Engine oil & filter	R	✓	✓	✓	✓	✓	✓	✓	✓	✓	✓	✓	✓	✓
Tires	Rotate		✓		✓		✓		✓		✓		✓	
Spare Tire - proper inflation	S/I		✓		✓		✓		✓		✓		✓	
Brake hoses & linings	S/I						✓						✓	
Lubricate steering and suspension ball joints	C/L		✓		✓		✓		✓		✓		✓	
Brake caliper pins	C/L				✓				✓				✓	
Air filter	R					✓					✓			
Cabin air filter	R				✓				✓				✓	
Spark plugs	R										✓			
Drive axle lubricant	R					✓			✓				✓	
Power Transfer Unit fluid	R	Every 60,000 miles												
PCV valve	I/R										✓			
Rear drive axle fluid	R	Every 60,000 miles												
Accessory drive belt	R	Every 120,000 miles												
Manual trans fluid	R	Every 48,000 miles												
Automatic trans. fluid and filter	R	Every 60,000 miles												
Engine coolant	R	Every 60,000 miles												

R: Replace   S/I: Service or Inspect   C/L: Clean and lubricate   I/R: Inspect and rerplace if necessary

The above schedule is to be used if you drive under any of the following conditions:

Driving in temperatures under 32 degrees F

Stop and go traffic

Extensive engine idling

Driving in dusty conditions

Frequent trips under 10 miles

More than 50 % of your driving is in hot weather (90 deg. F) above 50 miles per hour

Trailer towing

Taxi, police or delivery service

Off-road driving

The vehicle is equipped for and operated with E85 (ethonol) fuel

If none of these conditions is met, double the maintenance intervals

22043_COMP_C0014

PRECAUTIONS

Before servicing any vehicle, please be sure to read all of the following precautions, which deal with personal safety, prevention of component damage, and important points to take into consideration when servicing a motor vehicle:

• Never open, service or drain the radiator or cooling system when the engine is hot; serious burns can occur from the steam and hot coolant.

• Observe all applicable safety precautions when working around fuel. Whenever servicing the fuel system, always work in a well-ventilated area. Do not allow fuel spray or vapors to come in contact with a spark, open flame, or excessive heat (a hot drop light, for example). Keep a dry chemical fire extinguisher near the work area. Always keep fuel in a container specifically designed for fuel storage; also, always properly seal fuel containers to avoid the possibility of fire or explosion. Refer to the additional fuel system precautions later in this section.

• Fuel injection systems often remain pressurized, even after the engine has been turned **OFF**. The fuel system pressure must be relieved before disconnecting any fuel lines. Failure to do so may result in fire and/or personal injury.

• Brake fluid often contains polyglycol ethers and polyglycols. Avoid contact with the eyes and wash your hands thoroughly after handling brake fluid. If you do get brake fluid in your eyes, flush your eyes with clean, running water for 15 minutes. If eye irritation persists, or if you have taken brake fluid internally, IMMEDIATELY seek medical assistance.

• The EPA warns that prolonged contact with used engine oil may cause a number of skin disorders, including cancer. You should make every effort to minimize your exposure to used engine oil. Protective gloves should be worn when changing oil. Wash your hands and any other exposed skin areas as soon as possible after exposure to used engine oil. Soap and water, or waterless hand cleaner should be used.

• All new vehicles are now equipped with an air bag system, often referred to as a Supplemental Restraint System (SRS) or Supplemental Inflatable Restraint (SIR) system. The system must be disabled before performing service on or around system components, steering column, instrument panel components, wiring and sensors. Failure to follow safety and disabling procedures could result in accidental air bag deployment, possible personal injury and unnecessary system repairs.

• Always wear safety goggles when working with, or around, the air bag system. When carrying a non-deployed air bag, be sure the bag and trim cover are pointed away from your body. When placing a non-deployed air bag on a work surface, always face the bag and trim cover upward, away from the surface. This will reduce the motion of the module if it is accidentally deployed. Refer to the additional air bag system precautions later in this section.

• Clean, high quality brake fluid from a sealed container is essential to the safe and proper operation of the brake system. You should always buy the correct type of brake fluid for your vehicle. If the brake fluid becomes contaminated, completely flush the system with new fluid. Never reuse any brake fluid. Any brake fluid that is removed from the system should be discarded. Also, do not allow any brake fluid to come in contact with a painted surface; it will damage the paint.

• Never operate the engine without the proper amount and type of engine oil; doing so WILL result in severe engine damage.

• Timing belt maintenance is extremely important. Many models utilize an interference-type, non-freewheeling engine. If the timing belt breaks, the valves in the cylinder head may strike the pistons, causing potentially serious (also time-consuming and expensive) engine damage. Refer to the maintenance interval charts for the recommended replacement interval for the timing belt, and to the timing belt section for belt replacement and inspection.

• Disconnecting the negative battery cable on some vehicles may interfere with the functions of the on-board computer system(s) and may require the computer to undergo a relearning process once the negative battery cable is reconnected.

• When servicing drum brakes, only disassemble and assemble one side at a time, leaving the remaining side intact for reference.

• Only an MVAC-trained, EPA-certified automotive technician should service the air conditioning system or its components.

BRAKES

GENERAL INFORMATION

PRECAUTIONS

• Certain components within the ABS system are not intended to be serviced or repaired individually.

• Do not use rubber hoses or other parts not specifically specified for and ABS system. When using repair kits, replace all parts included in the kit. Partial or incorrect repair may lead to functional problems and require the replacement of components.

• Lubricate rubber parts with clean, fresh brake fluid to ease assembly. Do not use shop air to clean parts; damage to rubber components may result.

• Use only DOT 3 brake fluid from an unopened container.

• If any hydraulic component or line is removed or replaced, it may be necessary to bleed the entire system.

• A clean repair area is essential. Always clean the reservoir and cap thoroughly before removing the cap. The slightest amount of dirt in the fluid may plug an orifice and impair the system function. Perform repairs after components have been thoroughly cleaned; use only denatured alcohol to clean components. Do not allow ABS components to come into contact with any substance containing mineral oil; this includes used shop rags.

• The Anti-Lock control unit is a microprocessor similar to other computer units in the vehicle. Ensure that the ignition switch is **OFF** before removing or installing controller harnesses. Avoid static electricity discharge at or near the controller.

• If any arc welding is to be done on the vehicle, the control unit should be unplugged before welding operations begin.

ANTI-LOCK BRAKE SYSTEM (ABS)

SPEED SENSORS

REMOVAL & INSTALLATION

Front

See Figures 1 and 2.

1. Disconnect the wheel speed sensor cable connector from the wiring harness connector, located on top of the frame rail just inside the strut tower.

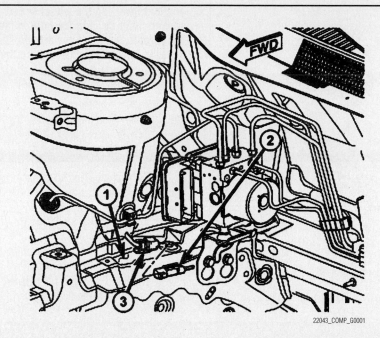

Fig. 1 Disconnect the speed sensor connector (2) from the wiring harness (3) on top of the frame rail (1)—Front speed sensor

2. Raise and safely support the vehicle.

3. Remove the grommet from the hole in the body and pull the wheel speed sensor cable out of the hole.

4. Remove the speed sensor cable routing clip from the outside frame rail.

5. Remove the screw fastening the cable routing clamp to the outside frame rail.

6. Remove the screw securing the wheel speed sensor routing bracket to the brake flex hose bracket.

7. Remove the mounting screws holding the speed sensor head to the steering knuckle.

8. Remove the routing clip and remove the speed sensor.

To install:

9. Install the wheel speed sensor head into the knuckle. Install the routing clip and

mounting screw and tighten it to 106 inch lbs. (12 Nm).

10. Position the wheel speed sensor routing bracket on the brake flex hose bracket and tighten the mounting screw to 13 ft. lbs. (18 Nm).

11. Position the wheel speed sensor cable routing clamp on the outside frame rail and tighten the mounting screw to 13 ft. lbs. (18 Nm).

12. Install the speed sensor cable routing clip on the outside frame rail.

13. Insert the wheel speed sensor cable through the hole in the body and install the grommet in the hole.

14. Lower the vehicle.

15. Connect the wheel speed sensor cable connector to the wiring harness connector on top of the frame rail.

16. Using a Diagnostic Scan Tool, clear any faults

Rear

All-Wheel Drive

See Figure 3.

1. Remove the cargo floor cover.

2. Remove the rear floor pan silencer.

3. If equipped, remove the nuts mounting the satellite receiver or amplifier to the rear floor pan. Move the component aside to allow access to the wheel speed sensor wiring connector through the opening in bottom of the quarter trim panel.

4. Through the opening in the bottom of the quarter trim panel, disconnect the wheel speed sensor cable connector at the body wiring harness connector.

5. Raise and safely support the vehicle.

6. Remove the rear wheel.

7. Remove the grommet from the hole in the body and pull the wheel speed sensor cable out through the hole.

8. Remove the speed sensor cable routing clip from the outside frame rail.

9. Remove the screw fastening the cable routing clamp to the rear suspension crossmember.

10. Remove the speed sensor cable routing clip from the trailing link.

11. Remove the screw fastening the cable routing clamp to the trailing link.

12. Unclip the wheel speed sensor head from the spring-loaded retainer on the rear of the hub and bearing. Remove the sensor from the vehicle.

To install:

❋❋ CAUTION

Be sure that cables are installed, routed, and clipped properly. Failure to install speed sensor cables properly may result in contact with moving parts or an over extension of cables causing an open circuit.

➡ When installing the sensor head to the spring-loaded retainer on the hub and bearing, make sure the head is held snug in the retainer. If there is any play, the clip is deformed and the hub and bearing must be replaced. The retainer is not serviced separately.

13. Clip the wheel speed sensor head (flat side to bearing rear face) into the spring-loaded retainer on the rear of the hub and bearing.

14. Position the wheel speed sensor on the trailing link and install the screw securing it in place. Tighten the mounting screw to 13 ft. lbs. (18 Nm).

15. Position the wheel speed sensor and install the routing clip fastening the sensor to the trailing link.

16. Position the wheel speed sensor cable routing clamp on the rear suspension crossmember and install the mounting screw. Tighten the mounting screw to 13 ft. lbs. (18 Nm).

17. Install the speed sensor cable routing clip on the outside frame rail.

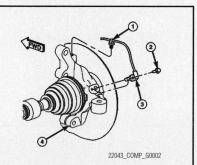

Fig. 2 Remove the screw (2) and routing clip (1) holding the speed sensor (3) to the steering knuckle (4)—Front speed sensor

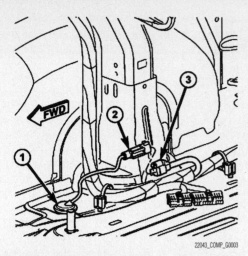

Fig. 3 Disconnect the speed sensor connector (2) from the body wiring harness (3)—Rear speed sensor

➡ **When inserting the wheel speed sensor cable through the hole in the body, route the cable toward the shock tower to make it easier to grasp the cable to connect it to the body wiring harness connector in a later step.**

18. Insert the wheel speed sensor cable through the hole in the body and install the grommet in the hole.

19. Install the rear wheel.

20. Lower the vehicle.

21. Through the opening in the bottom of the quarter trim panel, connect the wheel speed sensor cable connector to the body wiring harness connector.

22. If equipped, install the satellite receiver or amplifier to rear floor pan.

23. Install the rear floor pan silencer.

24. Install the cargo floor cover.

BRAKES   BLEEDING THE BRAKE SYSTEM

BLEEDING PROCEDURE

BLEEDING PROCEDURE

1. The following wheel sequence for bleeding the brake hydraulic system should be used to ensure adequate removal of all trapped air from the hydraulic system:
   • Left rear wheel
   • Right front wheel
   • Right rear wheel
   • Left front wheel

2. Attach a clear plastic hose (1) to the bleeder screw and feed the hose into a clear jar (2) containing enough fresh brake fluid to submerge the end of the hose.

3. Have a helper pump the brake pedal three or four times and hold it in the down position.

4. With the pedal in the down position, open the bleeder screw at least one full turn.

5. Once the brake pedal has dropped, close the bleeder screw. After the bleeder screw is closed, release the brake pedal.

6. Repeat the above steps until all trapped air is removed from that wheel circuit (usually four or five times).

7. Bleed the remaining wheel circuits in the same manner until all air is removed from the brake system. Monitor the fluid level in the master cylinder reservoir (2) to make sure it does not go dry.

8. Check and adjust brake fluid level to the FULL mark.

9. Check the brake pedal travel. If pedal travel is excessive or has not been improved, some air may still be trapped in the system. Re-bleed the brakes as necessary.

10. Test drive the vehicle to verify the brakes are operating properly and pedal feel is correct.

MASTER CYLINDER BLEEDING

See Figure 4.

1. Clamp the master cylinder in a vise with soft-jaw caps.

2. Attach the special tools for bleeding the master cylinder in the following fashion:

   a. Thread Special Tool 8822-2 Bleeder Tube Adapters into the primary and secondary outlet ports of the master cylinder. Tighten the Adapters to 150 inch lbs. (17 Nm).

   b. Thread Special Tool 8358-1 Bleeder Tube into each Adapter. Tighten tube nuts to 150 inch lbs. (17 Nm).

   c. Flex each Bleeder Tube and place the open ends into the neck of the master cylinder reservoir. Position the open ends of the tubes into the reservoir so their outlets are below the surface of the brake fluid in the reservoir when filled.

➡ **Make sure the ends of the Bleeder Tubes stay below the surface of the brake fluid in the reservoir at all times during the bleeding procedure.**

3. Fill the brake fluid reservoir with fresh Mopar® Brake Fluid DOT 3 Motor Vehicle, or equivalent.

4. Using an appropriately sized wooden dowel as a pushrod, slowly press the pistons inward discharging brake fluid through the Bleeder Tubes, then release the pressure, allowing the pistons to return to the released position. Repeat this several times

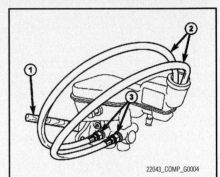

Fig. 4 The master cylinder shown with Bleeder Tube Adapters (3) and Bleeder Tubes (2) installed when bleeding the master cylinder.

until all air bubbles are expelled from the master cylinder bore and Bleeder Tubes.

5. Remove the Bleeder Tubes and Adapters from the master cylinder and plug the master cylinder outlet ports.

6. Install the fill cap on the reservoir.

7. Remove the master cylinder from the vise.

8. Install the master cylinder on the vehicle.

BLEEDING THE ABS SYSTEM

The ABS must always be bled anytime it is suspected that the Hydraulic Control Unit has ingested air.

1. Make sure all hydraulic fluid lines are installed and properly torqued.

2. Connect the scan tool to the diagnostics connector. The diagnostic connector is located under the lower steering column cover to the left of the steering column.

3. Using the scan tool, check to make sure the ABM does not have any fault codes stored. If it does, clear them.

2. Follow the standard brake bleeding procedure listed above.

3. Using the diagnostic scan tool, select ECU VIEW, followed by

ABS MISCELLANEOUS FUNCTIONS to access bleeding. Follow the instructions displayed. When finished, disconnect the scan tool and proceed.

4. Bleed the brake system a second time. Check brake fluid level in the reservoir periodically to prevent

emptying, causing air to enter the hydraulic system.

5. Fill the master cylinder fluid reservoir to the FULL level.

6. Test drive the vehicle to be sure the brakes are operating correctly and that the brake pedal does not feel spongy.

BRAKES

FRONT DISC BRAKES

✷ CAUTION

Dust and dirt accumulating on brake parts during normal use may contain asbestos fibers from production or aftermarket brake linings. Breathing excessive concentrations of asbestos fibers can cause serious bodily harm. Exercise care when servicing brake parts. Do not sand or grind brake lining unless equipment used is designed to contain the dust residue. Do not clean brake parts with compressed air or by dry brushing. Cleaning should be done by dampening the brake components with a fine mist of water, then wiping the brake components clean with a dampened cloth. Dispose of cloth and all residue containing asbestos fibers in an impermeable container with the appropriate label. Follow practices prescribed by the Occupational Safety and Health Administration (OSHA) and the Environmental Protection Agency (EPA) for the handling, processing, and disposing of dust or debris that may contain asbestos fibers.

BRAKE CALIPER

REMOVAL & INSTALLATION

See Figures 5 and 6.

1. Using a brake pedal holding tool as shown, depress the brake pedal past its first 1 inch (25 mm) of travel and hold it in this position. This will i solate the master cylinder from the brake hydraulic system and will not allow the brake fluid to drain out of the master cylinder reservoir when the lines are opened.

2. Raise and safely support the vehicle.

3. Remove the front wheel.

4. Remove the banjo bolt holding the brake hose to the brake caliper.

➡There are two washers that will come off with the banjo bolt. Discard the washers.

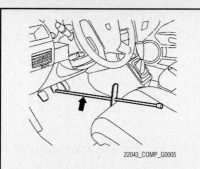

22043_COMP_G0005

Fig. 5 Use a brake pedal holding tool to depress the brake pedal when disconnecting brake hoses.

5. Remove the caliper guide pin bolts.

6. Slide the caliper assembly from the adapter bracket and brake pads to remove.

To install:

7. Using a C-clamp, completely retract the caliper piston back into the bore of the caliper.

✷ WARNING

Place a block of wood over the piston before using the C-clamp to prevent damage to the piston.

➡When installing the caliper guide pin bolts, ensure the one with the special sleeve on the end is installed in the upper mounting hole.

8. Install the caliper assembly over the brake pads on the caliper adapter bracket.

9. Align the guide pin bolt hose with the adapter bracket. Install the guide pin bolts and tighten to 32 ft. lbs. (43 Nm).

10. Reconnect the brake hose using the banjo bolt and two **new** washers. Tighten the banjo bolt to 18 ft. lbs. (24 Nm).

11. Install the front wheel.

12. Lower the vehicle.

13. Remove the brake pedal holding tool.

14. Bleed the brake system if necessary.

15. Test drive the vehicle to ensure proper brake operation.

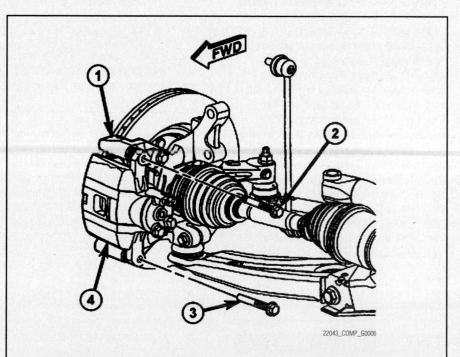

22043_COMP_G0006

Fig. 6 Remove the guide pins (2,3) to remove the caliper (4) from the adapter bracket (1)— Front caliper assembly

DISC BRAKE PADS

REMOVAL & INSTALLATION
See Figure 7.

1. Raise and safely support the vehicle.
2. Remove the front tire.
3. Remove the two brake caliper guide pin bolts.
4. Remove the brake caliper from the adapter brake and secure with mechanics wire or equivalent.

✳✳ WARNING

Do not let the caliper hang by the brake hose.

5. Remove the brake pads from the caliper bracket.

To install:

6. Install the brake pads in the brake shims clipped into the caliper adapter bracket. Place the pad with the wear indicator on the inboard side.

7. Using a C-clamp, completely retract the caliper piston back into the bore of the caliper.

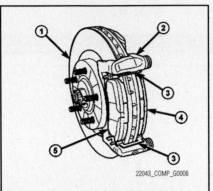

Fig. 7 Install the brake pads (4,5) into the brake shims (3) in the adapter bracket (2). Place the wear indicator (4) pad on the inboard side—Front brake assembly shown

✳✳ WARNING

Place a block of wood over the piston before using the C-clamp to prevent damage to the piston.

8. Install the caliper over the brake pads on the caliper adapter bracket.

➡ **When installing the caliper guide pin bolts, ensure the one with the special sleeve on the end is installed in the upper mounting hole.**

9. Align the guide pin bolt hose with the adapter bracket. Install the guide pin bolts and tighten to 32 ft. lbs. (43 Nm).
10. Install the front wheel.
11. Lower the vehicle.
12. Pump the pedal several times to set the pads to the brake rotor.
13. Test drive the vehicle to ensure proper brake operation.

BRAKES

✳✳ CAUTION

Dust and dirt accumulating on brake parts during normal use may contain asbestos fibers from production or aftermarket brake linings. Breathing excessive concentrations of asbestos fibers can cause serious bodily harm. Exercise care when servicing brake parts. Do not sand or grind brake lining unless equipment used is designed to contain the dust residue. Do not clean brake parts with compressed air or by dry brushing. Cleaning should be done by dampening the brake components with a fine mist of water, then wiping the brake components clean with a dampened cloth. Dispose of cloth and all residue containing asbestos fibers in an impermeable container with the appropriate label. Follow practices prescribed by the Occupational Safety and Health Administration (OSHA) and the Environmental Protection Agency (EPA) for the handling, processing, and disposing of dust or debris that may contain asbestos fibers.

BRAKE CALIPER

REMOVAL & INSTALLATION
See Figures 8 and 9.

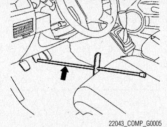

Fig. 8 Use a brake pedal holding tool to depress the brake pedal when disconnecting brake hoses.

1. Using a brake pedal holding tool as shown, depress the brake pedal past its first 1 inch (25 mm) of travel and hold it in this position. This will isolate the master cylinder from the brake hydraulic system and will not allow the brake fluid to drain out of the master cylinder reservoir when the lines are opened.
2. Raise and safely support the vehicle.
3. Remove the front wheel.
4. Loosen the brake tube nut at the rear brake hose.
5. Remove the clip holding the rear brake hose to the trailing link bracket, and remove the brake hose from the bracket.
6. Loosen and remove the brake hose from the brake caliper.

➡ **When removing the caliper guide pin bolts, note the location of the bolt with**

REAR DISC BRAKES

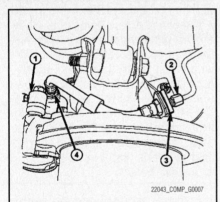

Fig. 9 Loosen the brake tube nut (2), remove the clip (3), and loosen the brake hose connection (4) to disconnect it from the caliper (1)—Rear brake caliper

the special sleeve on the tip. Depending on the build date, this special sleeve bolt can be located in either the top or bottom location. It must be reinstalled in its original position.

7. Remove the caliper guide pin bolts.
8. Slide and remove the caliper assembly with the outboard brake pad attached.
9. Remove the outboard brake pad from the caliper by prying the pad retaining clip over the raised area on the caliper.

To install:

10. Using a C-clamp, completely retract the caliper piston back into the bore of the caliper.

WARNING

Place a block of wood over the piston before using the C-clamp to prevent damage to the piston.

11. Slide the outboard brake pad onto the caliper. Be sure the retaining clip is squarely seated in the depressed areas on the caliper beyond the raised retaining bead.

12. Install the caliper with outboard brake pad attached over the inboard brake pad and rotor, onto the brake caliper adapter bracket.

➡**When installing the caliper guide pin bolts, make sure the bolts are put back in the same locations as when removed.**

13. Align the caliper guide pin bolt holes with the adapter bracket. Install the caliper guide pin bolts and tighten to 32 ft. lbs. (43 Nm).

14. Inspect the outboard brake pad to make sure it is correctly positioned. The retaining clip must be squarely seated in the depressed areas on the caliper fingers. Also, the nubs on the pad's steel backing plate must be fully seated in the depressions formed into the inside of the caliper fingers. There should be no gap between the pad backing plate and the caliper fingers.

15. Thread the brake hose connection into the brake caliper. Tighten the hose fitting at the caliper to 133 inch lbs. (15 Nm).

16. Route and install the brake hose into the trailing link mounted bracket and install the clip to secure it.

17. Thread the brake tube nut into brake hose and tighten to 150 inch lbs. (17 Nm).

18. Install the rear wheel.
19. Lower the vehicle.
20. Remove the brake pedal holding tool.
21. Bleed the brake system if necessary.
22. Test drive the vehicle to ensure proper brake operation.

DISC BRAKE PADS

REMOVAL & INSTALLATION

See Figure 10.

1. Raise and safely support the vehicle.
2. Remove the rear wheel.
3. Remove the brake caliper lower guide pin bolt.

4. Rotate the caliper upward, using the top guide bolt as a hinge. Hang the caliper assembly with mechanics wire or equivalent.

WARNING

Do not let the caliper hang by the brake hose.

5. Remove the inboard brake pad from the caliper adapter bracket.
6. Remove the outboard brake pad from the caliper by prying the retaining clip over the raised area on the caliper.

To install:

7. Using a C-clamp, completely retract

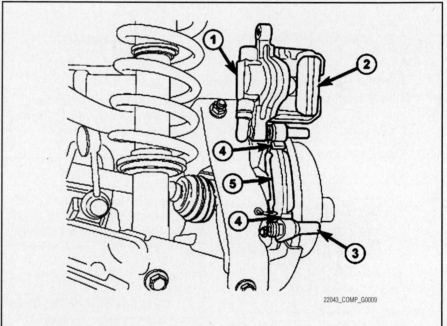

Fig. 10 Remove the inboard pad (5) from the adapter bracket (3) and remove the outboard pad (2) from the caliper (1)—Rear brake assembly

22043_COMP_G0009

the caliper piston back into the bore of the caliper.

WARNING

Place a block of wood over the piston before using the C-clamp to prevent damage to the piston.

➡**The brake pad with the wear indicator should be installed on the inboard side. The wear indicator should be positioned at the bottom when installed.**

8. Slide the outboard pad onto the caliper. Ensure the retaining clip is seated properly in the depressed areas of the caliper.
9. Place the inboard pad in the brake shims clipped into the caliper adapter bracket.
10. Rotate the caliper assembly downward over the rotor into the caliper adapter bracket.
11. Install the lower guide pin bolt and tighten to 32 ft. lbs. (43 Nm).
12. Inspect the outboard brake pad to make sure it is correctly positioned. The retaining clip must be squarely seated in the depressed areas on the caliper fingers.

Also, the nubs on the pad's steel backing plate must be fully seated in the depressions formed into the inside of the caliper fingers. There should be no gap between the pad backing plate and the caliper fingers.

13. Install the rear wheel.
14. Lower the vehicle.
15. Pump the pedal several times to set the pads to the brake rotor.
16. Test drive the vehicle to ensure proper brake operation.

PARKING BRAKE CABLES

ADJUSTMENT

Parking brake cable adjustment is controlled by an automatic tensioner mechanism. The only adjustment possible is to the parking brake shoes using the star wheel adjuster.

PARKING BRAKE SHOES

REMOVAL & INSTALLATION

See Figures 11 through 13.

1. Raise and safely support the vehicle.
2. Remove the rear wheel.
3. Remove the caliper assembly.
4. Remove any clips from the wheels studs and remove the brake rotor.
5. Turn the brake shoe adjuster wheel until the adjuster is at the shortest length.
6. Remove the upper return spring from the anchor pin and rear brake shoe.
7. Remove the second upper return

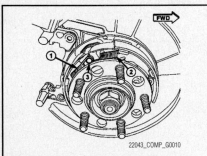

Fig. 11 Remove the upper return springs (1,2) from the anchor pin (3) and brake shoes—Parking brake assembly

spring from the anchor pin and front brake shoe.

8. Remove the brake shoe hold-down springs and pins. Rotate the pins 90° to disengage and remove.

9. Remove the parking brake cable from the lever on the rear parking brake shoe.
10. Remove the brake shoes, adjuster and lower return spring as an assembly from the support plate.
11. If necessary, remove the strut.
12. Remove the lower return spring and adjuster from the shoes.

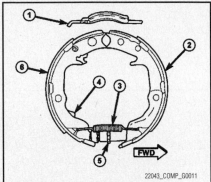

Fig. 12 Exploded view of the LEFT side parking brake assembly—Strut (1), Brake shoes (2,6), Lower return spring (3), Adjuster (5)

To install:

13. Install the lower return spring and adjuster between the parking brake shoes. The rear shoe will have the lever mounted on the inside. Make sure the threaded portion of the adjuster is mounted to the left on both right and left side parking brake assemblies.
14. If necessary, place the strut above the hub on the vehicle. The curved end of the strut is positioned to the rear.
15. Install the assembled brake shoes, adjuster and lower return spring over the hub and onto the support plate and anchor. Be sure to install the strut between the front shoe and the lever on the rear shoe.
16. Install the parking brake cable onto the lever on the parking brake shoe.
17. Install the brake hold-down springs and pins. Rotate the pins 90° to engage.

18. Install the front upper return spring hooking the front brake shoe and over the anchor pin.
19. Install the front upper return spring hooking the rear brake shoe and over the anchor pin.
20. Adjust the parking brake shows as follows:
    a. Using Special Tool C-3919 Brake Shoe Gauge or equivalent, measure the inside diameter of parking brake drum portion of rotor. Set the Gauge.
    b. Place the gauge over the parking brake shoes at their widest point.
    c. Using the adjuster wheel, adjust the parking brake shoes until the linings on both parking brake shoes just touch the jaws on the gauge.
21. Install the rotor.
22. Install the caliper assembly. Tighten the lower guide pin bolt to 32 ft. lbs. (43 Nm).
23. Install the rear wheel.
24. Lower the vehicle.
25. Verify proper operation of the parking brake.

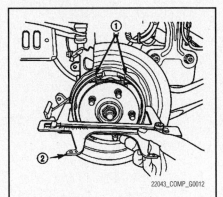

Fig. 13 Adjust the parking brake shoes (1) until linings touch the jaws of the gauge, set to the measurement (2) of the inside of the brake drum portion of the rotor—Parking brake adjustment

CHASSIS ELECTRICAL — AIR BAG (SUPPLEMENTAL RESTRAINT SYSTEM)

GENERAL INFORMATION

✳ CAUTION

These vehicles are equipped with an air bag system. The system must be disarmed before performing service on, or around, system components, the steering column, instrument panel components, wiring and sensors. Failure to follow the safety precautions and the disarming procedure could result in accidental air bag deployment, possible injury and unnecessary system repairs.

SERVICE PRECAUTIONS

Disconnect and isolate the battery negative cable before beginning any airbag system component diagnosis, testing, removal, or installation procedures. Allow system capacitor to discharge for two minutes before beginning any component service. This will disable the airbag system. Failure to disable the airbag system may result in accidental airbag deployment, personal injury, or death.

Do not place an intact undeployed airbag face down on a solid surface. The airbag will propel into the air if accidentally deployed and may result in personal injury or death.

When carrying or handling an undeployed airbag, the trim side (face) of the airbag should be pointing towards the body to minimize possibility of injury if accidental deployment occurs. Failure to do this may result in personal injury or death.

Replace airbag system components with OEM replacement parts. Substitute parts may appear interchangeable, but internal differences may result in inferior occupant protection. Failure to do so may result in occupant personal injury or death.

Wear safety glasses, rubber gloves, and long sleeved clothing when cleaning powder residue from vehicle after an airbag deployment. Powder residue emitted from a deployed airbag can cause skin irritation. Flush affected area with cool water if irritation is experienced. If nasal or throat irritation is experienced, exit the vehicle for fresh air until the irritation ceases. If irritation continues, see a physician.

Do not use a replacement airbag that is not in the original packaging. This may result in improper deployment, personal injury, or death.

The factory installed fasteners, screws and bolts used to fasten airbag components have a special coating and are specifically designed for the airbag system. Do not use substitute fasteners. Use only original equipment fasteners listed in the parts catalog when fastener replacement is required.

During, and following, any child restraint anchor service, due to impact event or vehicle repair, carefully inspect all mounting hardware, tether straps, and anchors for proper installation, operation, or damage. If a child restraint anchor is found damaged in any way, the anchor must be replaced. Failure to do this may result in personal injury or death.

Deployed and non-deployed airbags may or may not have live pyrotechnic material within the airbag inflator.

Do not dispose of driver/passenger/curtain airbags or seat belt tensioners unless you are sure of complete deployment. Refer to the Hazardous Substance Control System for proper disposal.

Dispose of deployed airbags and tensioners consistent with state, provincial, local, and federal regulations.

After any airbag component testing or service, do not connect the battery negative cable. Personal injury or death may result if the system test is not performed first.

If the vehicle is equipped with the Occupant Classification System (OCS), do not connect the battery negative cable before performing the OCS Verification Test using the scan tool and the appropriate diagnostic information. Personal injury or death may result if the system test is not performed properly.

Never replace both the Occupant Restraint Controller (ORC) and the Occupant Classification Module (OCM) at the same time. If both require replacement, replace one, then perform the Airbag System test before replacing the other.

Both the ORC and the OCM store Occupant Classification System (OCS) calibration data, which they transfer to one another when one of them is replaced. If both are replaced at the same time, an irreversible fault will be set in both modules and the OCS may malfunction and cause personal injury or death.

If equipped with OCS, the Seat Weight Sensor is a sensitive, calibrated unit and must be handled carefully. Do not drop or handle roughly. If dropped or damaged, replace with another sensor. Failure to do so may result in occupant injury or death.

If equipped with OCS, the front passenger seat must be handled carefully as well. When removing the seat, be careful when setting on floor not to drop. If dropped, the sensor may be inoperative, could result in occupant injury, or possibly death.

If equipped with OCS, when the passenger front seat is on the floor, no one should sit in the front passenger seat. This uneven force may damage the sensing ability of the seat weight sensors. If sat on and damaged, the sensor may be inoperative, could result in occupant injury, or possibly death.

DISARMING THE SYSTEM

Disconnect and isolate the negative battery cable. Wait two minutes to allow the system capacitor to discharge before servicing the vehicle.

ARMING THE SYSTEM

Reconnect the negative battery cable.

CLOCKSPRING CENTERING

See Figure 14.

1. Place the front wheels in the straight-ahead position and inhibit the steering column shaft from rotation.
2. Remove the steering wheel from the steering shaft.
3. Rotate the clockspring rotor clockwise to the end of its travel. Do not apply excessive torque.
4. From the end of the clockwise travel, rotate the rotor about two and one-half turns counterclockwise. Turn the rotor slightly clockwise or counterclockwise as necessary so that the clockspring airbag pigtail wires and connector receptacle are at the top and the dowel pin is at the bottom.
5. The clockspring is now centered. Secure the clockspring rotor to the clockspring case using a locking pin or some similar device to maintain clockspring centering until the steering wheel is reinstalled on the steering column.

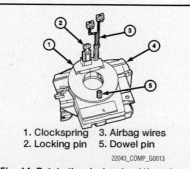

1. Clockspring   3. Airbag wires
2. Locking pin   5. Dowel pin

22043_COMP_G0013

Fig. 14 Rotate the clockspring (1) so the airbag wires (3) is at the top and dowel pin (5) is at the bottom. Secure the clockspring with a locking pin (2).

DRIVETRAIN

AUTOMATIC TRANSAXLE ASSEMBLY

REMOVAL & INSTALLATION

See Figures 15 through 18.

1. Disconnect the negative battery cable.
2. Drain the cooling system.
3. Drain the automatic transaxle.
4. Remove the air intake assembly.
5. Remove the battery.
6. Remove the battery tray.
7. Remove the air intake tube and vacuum supply lines.
8. Remove the shifter cable and mounting bracket.
9. Remove the coolant lines from the CVT fluid cooler.
10. Remove the heater hose from the CVT fluid cooler.
11. Remove the speed sensor connector.
12. Disconnect and remove the wiring harness from the top of the transaxle.
13. Remove the transmission vent tube.
14. Remove the throttle body support bracket.
15. Remove the upper bell housing bolts.
16. Remove the upper transmission mounting bolts, the upper transmission mount through-bolt and upper transmission bolt.
17. Raise and safely support the vehicle.
18. Remove the left and right front lower splash shield.
19. Remove the lower splash shield, if equipped.

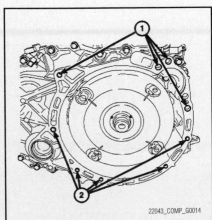

Fig. 15 View of the upper bell housing bolts (1) and lower bell housing bolts (2)—Automatic Transaxle

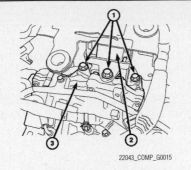

Fig. 16 View of the transaxle (3) upper mounting bolts (1) and upper mount (2)—Automatic Transaxle

20. Support the transaxle assembly with a suitable jack.
21. Remove the starter.
22. Remove the transaxle fill tube by removing the two mounting bolts.
23. Remove the both front wheels.
24. Remove the left and right halfshafts.
25. Remove the torque converter inspection cover.
26. Matchmark the torque converter to the flexplate for the correct alignment during installation.
27. Remove the torque converter bolts and discard the bolts.
28. Support the engine with a suitable jack.
29. Remove the front transaxle mount through-bolt.
30. Remove the transaxle crossmember mounting bolts and remove the crossmember.
31. Remove the transaxle rear mount through-bolt.
32. Remove the rear mount-to-transaxle bolts.
33. Remove the transfer case, if equipped.
34. Remove the lower transaxle bell housing bolts.
35. Carefully lower the transaxle assembly from the vehicle.

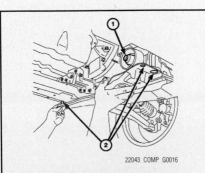

Fig. 17 Location of the front transaxle mount through-bolt and transaxle crossmember bolts—Automatic Transaxle

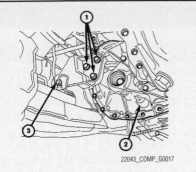

Fig. 18 Location of the rear mount through-bolt (3) and rear mount-to-transaxle bolts (1)—Automatic Transaxle

To install:

➡Ensure that both alignment pins are present into the engine before installing the transaxle.

36. Raise the transaxle assembly in the vehicle using a suitable jack.
37. Install the lower transaxle bell housing bolts and tighten to 35 ft. lbs. (48 Nm).
38. Connect the transaxle cooler lines.
39. Install the transaxle crossmember and tighten the mounting bolts to 55 ft. lbs. (75 Nm).
40. Install the through bolt at the front transaxle mount and tighten to 55 ft. lbs. (75 Nm).
41. Install the rear mount through-bolt and tighten to 55 ft. lbs. (75 Nm).
42. Install the rear mount-to-transaxle and tighten to 55 ft. lbs. (75 Nm).
43. Install new torque converter bolts and tighten to 35 ft. lbs. (48 Nm).
44. Install the torque converter inspection cover.
45. Install the transfer case, if equipped.
46. Install the splash shields.
47. Install the halfshafts.
48. Install the front wheels.
49. Lower the vehicle.
50. Install the upper bell housing bolts and tighten to 35 ft. lbs. (48 Nm).
51. Install the upper mount bolts and tighten to 55 ft. lbs. (75 Nm).
52. Install the upper mount through-bolt and tighten to 55 ft. lbs. (75 Nm).
53. Install the throttle body support bracket and tighten the bolts to 105 inch lbs. (11 Nm).
54. The remainder of the installation is the reverse order of removal.
55. Tighten the transaxle fill tube bolts to 79 inch lbs. (9 Nm).
56. Refill the transaxle with fluid to the correct level.

57. Refill the cooling system to the correct level.

58. Test drive the vehicle for proper operation and check for leaks.

MANUAL TRANSAXLE ASSEMBLY

REMOVAL & INSTALLATION

See Figures 19 through 22.

1. Remove the splash shields and drain the transaxle fluid.
2. Disconnect the negative battery cable.
3. Remove the engine appearance cover.
4. Remove the air intake assembly.
5. Unplug the speed sensor connector.
6. Disconnect the back-up lamp switch.
7. Remove the shift cables from the bracket clips.
8. Disconnect the shift selector and crossover cable from the levers. Remove the cables and secure them out of the way.
9. Remove the slave cylinder hose from the bracket.
10. Remove the air inlet tube from the throttle body.
11. Remove the throttle body support bracket.
12. Remove the upper bell housing bolts.
13. Remove the starter mounting bolts and secure the starter out of the way.
14. Support the transaxle with a suitable jack.
15. Loosen the left-upper transaxle mount through-bolt.
16. Remove the transaxle mount bolts.
17. Raise and safely support the vehicle.
18. Remove the halfshaft.

19. Remove the transfer case, if equipped.
20. Support the engine with a suitable jack.
21. Support the transaxle with a suitable transmission jack.
22. Remove the bell housing dust cover.
23. Remove four modular clutch-to-drive plate bolts. While removing bolts, one tight-tolerance (slotted) drive plate hole will be encountered. When this bolt is removed, mark drive plate and modular clutch assembly at this location, and be sure to align marks upon reassembly.
24. Remove the front transaxle mount through-bolt.

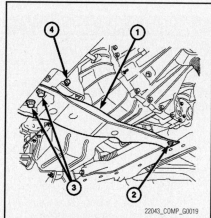

Fig. 20 Location of the front transaxle through-bolt (4) and transaxle crossmember mounting bolts (2,3) and crossmember (1)—Manual Transaxle

25. Remove the transaxle crossmember mounting bolts and remove the crossmember.
26. Remove the rear transaxle through-bolt.
27. Remove the rear transaxle mount bolts and mount from the frame.

28. Remove the rear transaxle mount bracket bolts and bracket from the transaxle.
29. Remove the remaining transaxle bell housing bolts.

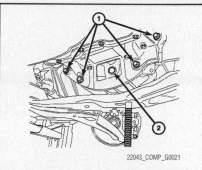

Fig. 22 Location of the lower transaxle bell housing bolts—Manual Transaxle

30. Carefully lower the engine/transaxle assembly on the two jacks until the enough clearance is obtained to remove the transaxle.
31. Obtain a helper to assist in holding transaxle assembly while removing transaxle-to-engine mounting bolts.
32. Remove the transaxle from the vehicle.

To install:

33. Using a suitable transmission jack, raise the transaxle assembly into position.
34. Install the transaxle bell housing bolts and tighten to 35 ft. lbs. (48 Nm).
35. Install the transfer case, if equipped.
36. Install the rear transaxle mount bracket and tighten the mounting bolts to 50 ft. lbs. (68 Nm).
37. Install the rear transaxle mount and tighten the bolts to 50 ft. lbs. (68 Nm).
38. Install the rear transaxle mount through-bolt and tighten to 50 ft. lbs. (68 Nm).
39. Install the front mount bracket to the transaxle and tighten the bolts to 50 ft. lbs. (68 Nm).
40. Install the transaxle crossmember and tighten the mounting bolts to 50 ft. lbs. (68 Nm).
41. Lower the vehicle slightly, and raise the engine/transaxle assembly until the upper mount bracket aligns with the upper mount. Tighten the upper mount bolts to 50 ft. lbs. (68 Nm).
42. Tighten the upper mount through-bolt to 50 ft. lbs. (68 Nm).
43. Remove the transaxle jack.
44. Raise and safely support the vehicle.
45. Install the four modular clutch-to-driveplate bolts. Align the driveplate and modular clutch alignment matchmarks made

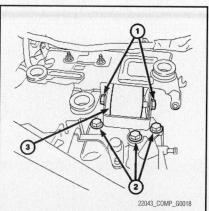

Fig. 19 Location of the left-upper transaxle mount through-bolt (1) and transaxle mount bolts (2)—Manual Transaxle

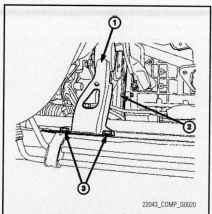

Fig. 21 Location of the rear transaxle mount (1), mount bracket (2), and transaxle mount bolts (3)—Manual Transaxle

during the removal process. Start with the tight-tolerance (slotted) hole and install the torque bolts to 65 ft. lbs. (88 Nm).

46. Install the starter.

47. Install the bell housing dust cover.

48. Install the axle shafts.

49. Fill the transaxle with fluid to the correct level.

50. Install the splash shields.

51. Lower the vehicle.

52. Install the top remaining bell housing bolts and tighten to 35 ft. lbs. (48 Nm).

53. Connect the hydraulic clutch slave cylinder.

54. Connect the shift and selector cables to shift lever. Install the cables to the bracket clips.

55. Connector the back-up lamp connector.

56. Connect the vehicle speed sensor.

57. Install the air intake tube and air intake assembly.

58. Connect the negative battery cable.

59. Test drive the vehicle for proper operation and check for leaks.

CLUTCH

REMOVAL & INSTALLATION

1. Remove the transaxle assembly from the vehicle.

2. Remove the clutch assembly from the transaxle input shaft.

To install:

3. Install the clutch assembly onto the input shaft of the transaxle.

4. Install the transaxle assembly.

BLEEDING

1. Verify the fluid level in the brake master cylinder. Top off with DOT 3 brake fluid as necessary. Leave cap off.

2. Raise and safely support the vehicle.

3. Remove the bleed port protective cap and install suitable size and length of clear hose to monitor and divert fluid into suitable container.

4. Open up the bleed circuit by turning the thumb screw counter clockwise this will start the air purge and fluid fill process.

5. Lower the vehicle, but only enough to gain access to and fill the brake master cylinder.

➡Do not allow the clutch master cylinder to run dry while fluid exits bleed port.

6. Top off the brake master cylinder fluid level while air is being purged and fluid drains from the bleed port. Continue

this until no air bubbles are seen and a solid column of fluid exists.

7. Close hydraulic bleed circuit, remove drain hose and replace dust cap on bleed port.

8. From driver's seat, actuate clutch pedal 60-100 times.

9. Apply the parking brake. Start engine and verify clutch operation and pedal feel. If pedal feels fine and clutch operates as designed, stop here. If pedal still feels spongy or clutch does not fully disengage, excessive air is still trapped within the system, most likely at the master cylinder.

10. Top off the brake master cylinder fluid level with DOT 3 brake fluid as necessary.

TRANSFER CASE ASSEMBLY

REMOVAL & INSTALLATION

See Figures 23 through 27.

➡Jeep refers to the transfer case as the Power Transfer Unit (PTU)

1. Disconnect the negative battery cable.

2. Remove the engine appearance cover.

3. Remove the air intake assembly.

4. Remove the Power Distribution Center (PDC) from the mounting bracket.

5. Raise and safely support the vehicle.

6. Remove the front halfshafts.

7. Drain the transfer case fluid and reinstall the drain plug.

8. Remove the driveshaft.

9. Remove the two exhaust flange mounting bolts and disconnect the downstream O_2 sensor to separate the exhaust system.

10. Lower the vehicle.

11. Unplug the upstream O_2 sensor connector.

12. Remove the upstream O_2 sensor from the exhaust manifold.

13. Remove the exhaust manifold top and side heat shields.

14. Remove the exhaust manifold retaining bolts. Slide the exhaust manifold up and to the right, and support the exhaust manifold with a bungee cord or equivalent.

15. Raise and safely support the vehicle.

16. Remove the engine-to-exhaust manifold bracket bolts.

17. Remove the rear engine mount through-bolt.

18. Remove the three front engine mount-to-frame bolts and mount through-bolt.

19. Remove the transfer case mounting bolts.

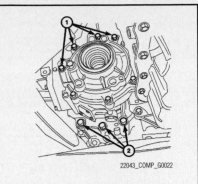

Fig. 23 Location of the upper (1) and lower (2) transfer case mounting bolts.

20. Using a suitable jack, support the engine on the front mount bracket.

21. Raise the front of the engine until the rear mount as dropped.

22. Separate the transfer case from the transaxle. Remove and discard the O-ring.

23. Roll the transfer case forward and down to remove.

To install:

24. Roll the transfer in, moving from front to back.

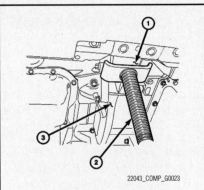

Fig. 24 Support the engine (3) using a suitable jack (2) by the front mount bracket (1)—Transfer case removal

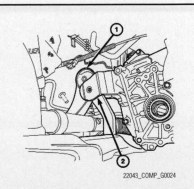

Fig. 25 Raise the front of the engine until the rear mount (1,2) has dropped—Transfer case removal

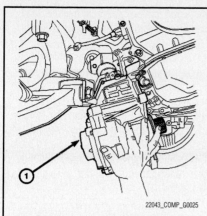

Fig. 26 Roll the transfer case (1) forward and down to remove—Transfer case removal

25. Rest the transfer case on the frame while the engine/transaxle assembly is raised into position.

26. Lower the jack on the front engine mount bracket until the rear mount through-bolt can be installed. Tighten the bolt to 55 ft. lbs. (75 Nm).

27. Install the transaxle crossmember and tighten the bolts to 55 ft. lbs. (75 Nm).

28. Install the front transaxle mount through-bolt and tighten to 55 ft. lbs. (75 Nm).

29. Install a new O-ring between the transfer case and transaxle.

➡ **Coat the O-ring in Vaseline or transaxle assembly grease.**

30. Slide the transfer completely into position. Tighten the mounting bolts to 43 ft. lbs. (58 Nm).

31. Lower the vehicle.

32. Install the exhaust manifold.
33. Install the air intake assembly.
34. Install the engine appearance cover.
35. Raise and safely support the vehicle.
36. Reconnect the exhaust system.
37. Install the rear driveshaft.
38. Install the axleshaft.
39. Refill the transfer case with fluid to the correct level.
40. Lower the vehicle.
41. Connect the negative battery cable.
42. Refill the transaxle with fluid to the correct level if necessary.
43. Test drive the vehicle to ensure proper operation and check for leaks.

FRONT HALFSHAFT

REMOVAL & INSTALLATION

See Figures 28 through 32.

1. Place the automatic transaxle, if equipped, in PARK.
2. Disconnect the negative battery cable.
3. Raise and safely support the vehicle.
4. Remove the front wheel.
5. Remove the cotter pin, nut lock, spring washer and hub nut from the outer axle.
6. If equipped with ABS, disconnect the front speed sensor.
7. Remove the ball joint retaining bolt and nut.
8. Carefully separate the ball joint stud from the steering knuckle by prying down on the lower control arm.
9. Remove the halfshaft from the steering knuckle by pulling outward on knuckle

while pressing in on halfshaft. Support the outer end of halfshaft assembly. If you have difficulty in separating halfshaft from hub is encountered, do not strike shaft with hammer, instead use Special Tool 1026 Puller to separate.

10. If equipped with 2WD:
   a. Remove the halfshaft bracket from the engine lower mounting bolt.
   b. Remove the halfshaft bracket from the upper engine mounting bolts.

11. Support the outer end of the halfshaft assembly.

➡**Removal of the inner tripod joints is made easier if you apply outward pressure on the joint as you strike the punch with a hammer. Do not pull on interconnecting shaft to remove, as the inner joint will become separated.**

12. Remove the inner tripod joints from the side gears of the transaxle using a punch to dislodge the inner tripod joint retaining ring from the transaxle side gear. If removing the right side inner tripod joint, position the punch to the inner tripod joint extraction groove, if equipped. Strike the punch sharply with a hammer to dislodge the right inner joint from the side gear. If removing the left side inner tripod joint, position the punch to the inner tripod joint extraction groove. Strike the punch sharply with a hammer to dislodge the left inner tripod joint from the side gear.

13. Hold the inner tripod joint and interconnecting shaft of halfshaft assembly. Remove inner tripod joint from transaxle by pulling it straight out of transaxle side gear and transaxle oil seal.

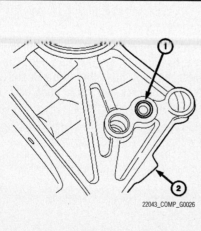

Fig. 27 Ensure the O-ring (1) between the transaxle and transfer case (2) is correct installed.

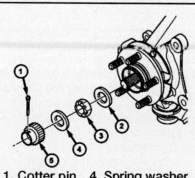

1. Cotter pin   4. Spring washer
2. Washer   5. Nut lock
3. Hub nut

Fig. 28 Exploded view of the halfshaft retaining hardware—Cotter pin (1), nut lock (5), spring washer (4) and hub nut (3) and washer (2)—Front halfshaft

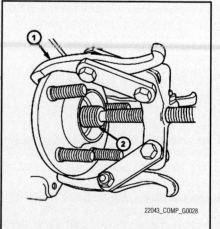

Fig. 29 If it is difficult to remove the halfshaft (2), use Special Tool 1026 (1) to pull the halfshaft out—Front halfshaft removal.

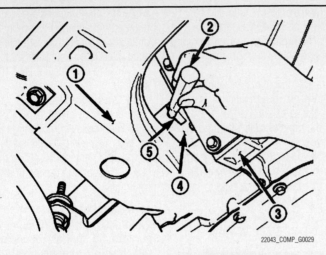

Fig. 30 Position a punch (2) to joint extraction groove (5) to remove the inner tripod joints (4) from the transaxle—Right side front halfshaft removal.

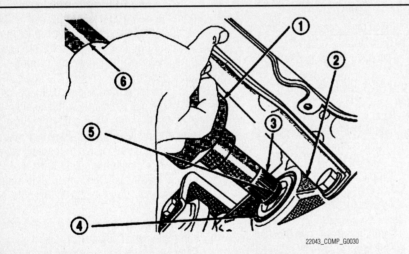

Fig. 31 Hold the inner tripod joint (1) and interconnecting shaft (6) and remove the joint by pulling it straight out of the transaxle oil seal (4)—Front halfshaft removal

⁂ **WARNING**

When removing the tripod joint, do not let spline or snap ring drag across sealing lip of the transaxle to tripod joint oil seal. When tripod joint is removed from transaxle, some fluid will leak out.

To install:

⁂ **WARNING**

The halfshaft, when installed, acts as a bolt and secures the front hub/bearing assembly. If vehicle is to be supported or moved on its wheels with a halfshaft removed, install a PROPER-SIZED BOLT AND NUT through front hub. Tighten the bolt and nut to 180 ft. lbs. (244 Nm). This will ensure that the hub bearing cannot loosen.

14. Clean all debris from the steering knuckle opening.

⁂ **WARNING**

Boot sealing is vital to retain special lubricants and to prevent foreign contaminants from entering the CV joint. Mishandling, such as allowing the assemblies to dangle unsupported, or pulling or pushing the ends can cut boots or damage CV joints. During removal and installation procedures, always support both ends of the halfshaft to prevent damage.

15. Thoroughly clean the spline and oil seal sealing surfaces on the tripod joint. Lightly lubricate the oil seal sealing surface on the tripod joint with clean transmission fluid.

16. Holding the halfshaft assembly by

the tripod joint and interconnecting shaft, install the tripod joint into transaxle side gear as far as possible by hand.

17. Carefully align the tripod joint with the transaxle side gears. Then grasp the halfshaft interconnecting shaft and push tripod joint into the transaxle side gear until fully seated. Test that the snap ring is fully engaged with the side gear by attempting to remove tripod joint from transaxle by hand. If the snap ring is fully engaged with side gear, the tripod joint will not be removable by hand.

18. If equipped with 2WD:
   a. Install the intermediate shaft bracket to the lower engine block and tighten to 55 ft. lbs. (75 Nm).
   b. Install the intermediate shaft bracket to the upper engine mounting bolts and tighten to 55 ft. lbs. (75 Nm).

19. Apply a light coating of Mopar® multipurpose wheel bearing grease on the facing flat surface of the outer CV-joint.

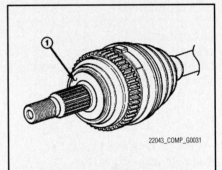

Fig. 32 Apply a light coating of Mopar® multipurpose wheel bearing grease on the facing flat surface (1) of the outer CV-joint—Front halfshaft installation

20. Install the steering knuckle onto the ball joint stud.

➡ At this point, the outer joint will not seat completely into the front hub. The outer joint will be pulled into hub and seated when the hub nut is installed and tightened.

21. Install a **NEW** ball joint bolt and nut and tighten to 70 ft. lbs. (95 Nm).

22. Install the washer and hub nut and tighten the hub nut to 180 ft. lbs. (244 Nm).

23. Install the spring washer, nut lock and cotter pin.

24. Install the front wheel.

25. Inspect the transaxle fluid level.

26. Lower the vehicle.

27. Connect the negative battery cable.

CV-JOINTS OVERHAUL

Inner Joint

See Figures 33 through 37.

1. Remove the halfshaft from the vehicle.

2. Remove large boot clamp that retains inner tripod joint sealing boot to tripod joint housing and discard. Then remove small clamp that retains inner tripod joint sealing boot to interconnecting shaft and discard. Remove the sealing boot from the tripod housing and slide it down the interconnecting shaft.

❋❋ WARNING

When removing the spider joint from the tripod joint housing, hold the rollers in place on the spider trunions to prevent the rollers and needle bearings from falling away.

3. Slide the interconnecting shaft and spider assembly out of the tripod joint housing.

4. Remove snap ring that retains spider assembly to interconnecting shaft.

5. Remove the spider assembly from interconnecting shaft. If spider assembly will not come off interconnecting shaft by hand, it can be removed by tapping spider assembly with a brass drift. Do not hit the outer tripod bearings in an attempt to remove spider assembly from interconnecting shaft.

6. Slide the sealing boot off the interconnecting shaft.

7. Thoroughly clean and inspect the spider assembly, tripod joint housing, and interconnecting shaft for any signs of excessive wear. If any parts show signs of excessive wear, the halfshaft assembly will require replacement.

➡ Component parts of these halfshaft assemblies are not serviceable.

To install:

➡ The inner tripod joint sealing boots are made from two different types of material. High-temperature applications (close to exhaust system) use silicone rubber whereas standard temperature applications use Hytrel plastic. The silicone sealing boots are soft and pliable. The Hytrel sealing boots are stiff and rigid. The replacement sealing boot MUST BE the same type of material as the sealing boot that was removed.

8. Slide the inner tripod joint seal boot retaining clamp onto the intercon-

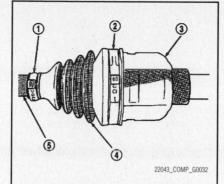

Fig. 33 Small clamp (1), Large boot clamp (2), tripod joint housing (3), sealing boot (4) and interconnecting shaft (5)—Front halfshaft inner joint

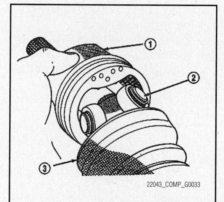

Fig. 34 Slide the interconnecting shaft and spider assembly (2) out of the tripod joint housing (1)—Front halfshaft inner joint

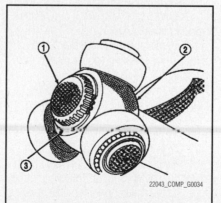

Fig. 35 Remove the snap ring (3) that holds the spider assembly (2) to the shaft (1)—Front halfshaft inner joint

necting shaft. Then slide the replacement inner tripod joint sealing boot onto interconnecting shaft. Inner tripod joint seal boot MUST be positioned on interconnecting shaft, so the raised bead on the inside of the seal boot is in groove on interconnecting shaft.

❋❋ WARNING

The rollers can fall off, use caution when installing the tripod

9. Install the spider assembly onto the interconnecting shaft with chamfer on the spider assembly toward the interconnecting shaft.

10. The spider assembly must be installed on the interconnecting shaft far enough to fully install spider retaining snap ring. If spider assembly will not fully install on interconnecting shaft by hand, it can be installed by tapping the spider body with a brass drift. Do not hit the outer tripod bearings in an attempt to install spider assembly on interconnecting shaft.

11. Install the spider assembly-to-interconnecting shaft retaining snap ring into the groove on end of the interconnecting shaft. Be sure the snap ring is fully seated into groove on interconnecting shaft.

12. Distribute ½ the amount of grease provided in the seal boot service package into tripod housing. Put the remaining amount into the sealing boot.

❋❋ WARNING

Use only the grease provided in the seal boot service package.

13. Align tripod housing with the spider assembly and then slide tripod housing over spider assembly and interconnecting shaft.

14. Install the inner tripod joint seal boot-to-interconnecting shaft clamp evenly on the sealing boot.

15. Clamp the sealing boot onto the interconnecting shaft using Special Tool C-4975-A Clamp and the following procedure. Place Clamp C-4975-A over bridge of clamp.

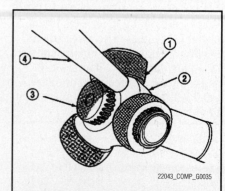

Fig. 36 If necessary, the spider assembly (2) can be installed on the shaft (3) using a brass drift (4)—Front halfshaft inner joint

16. Tighten the nut on Clamp C-4975-A until jaws on the tool are closed completely together, face to face.

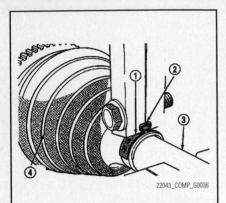

Fig. 37 Tighten the nut on Clamp C-4975-A (1) until completely closed to tighten the boot seal (2)—Front halfshaft inner joint

➡ Seal must not be dimpled, stretched, or out-of-shape in any way. If seal is NOT shaped correctly, equalize pressure in seal and shape it by hand.

17. Position the sealing boot into the tripod retaining groove. Install seal boot retaining clamp evenly on sealing boot.

✳✳ WARNING

The following positioning procedure determines the correct air pressure inside the inner tripod joint assembly prior to clamping the sealing boot to inner tripod joint housing. If this procedure is not done prior to clamping sealing boot to tripod joint housing, boot durability can be adversely affected.

✳✳ WARNING

When venting the inner tripod joint assembly, use care so inner tripod sealing boot does not get punctured or, in any other way, damaged. If sealing boot is punctured or damaged while being vented, the sealing boot can not be used.

18. Insert a trim stick between the tripod and the sealing boot to vent inner tripod joint assembly. When inserting trim stick between tripod housing and sealing boot, ensure trim stick is held flat and firmly against the tripod housing. If this is not done, damage to the sealing boot can occur. If inner tripod joint has a Hytrel (hard plastic) sealing boot, be sure the trim stick is inserted between soft rubber insert and tripod housing, and not the hard plastic sealing boot and soft rubber insert.

19. With the trim stick inserted between the sealing boot and tripod joint housing, position the inner tripod joint on halfshaft until correct sealing boot edge to edge length is obtained for type of sealing boot material being used. Then remove the trim stick.

20. Clamp the tripod joint sealing boot to tripod joint using required procedure for type of boot clamp application. If seal boot uses crimp type boot clamp, clamp sealing boot onto tripod housing using Special Tool C-4975-A Clamp. Place Clamp C-4975-A over bridge of clamp.

21. Tighten the nut on Clamp C-4975-A until jaws on tool are closed completely together, face-to-face.

22. If seal boot uses low profile latching type boot clamp, clamp sealing boot onto tripod housing using Clamping Tool, Snap-On® YA3050, or equivalent. Place the prongs of Clamp Locking Tool in the holes of the clamp.

23. Squeeze tool together until top band of clamp is latched behind the two tabs on lower band of clamp.

24. Install the halfshaft onto the vehicle.

Outer Joint

See Figures 38 through 41.

1. Remove the halfshaft from the vehicle.

2. Remove the large boot clamp retaining CV-joint sealing boot to CV-joint housing and discard.

3. Remove small clamp that retains outer CV-joint sealing boot to interconnecting shaft and discard.

4. Remove sealing boot from outer CV-joint housing and slide it down interconnecting shaft.

5. Wipe away the grease to expose outer CV-joint and interconnecting shaft.

6. Remove outer CV-joint from interconnecting shaft using the following procedure: Support interconnecting shaft in a vise equipped with protective caps on jaws of vise to prevent damage to interconnecting shaft. Then, using a soft-faced hammer, sharply hit the end of the CV-joint housing to dislodge housing from internal circlip on interconnecting shaft. Then slide outer CV-joint off end of interconnecting shaft, joint may have to be tapped off shaft using a soft-faced hammer.

7. Remove large circlip from the interconnecting shaft before attempting to remove outer CV-joint sealing boot.

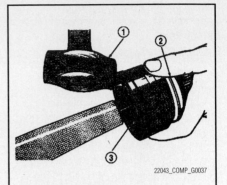

Fig. 38 Use a soft-faced hammer (1) to sharply hit the end of the CV-joint to dislodge the housing from the internal circlip (3)—Front halfshaft outer joint

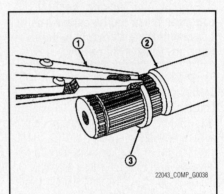

Fig. 39 Remove the large circlip (3) from the interconnecting shaft (2) using a suitable snapring pliers (1)—Front halfshaft outer joint

8. Slide the sealing boot off interconnecting shaft.

9. Thoroughly clean and inspect outer CV-joint assembly and interconnecting joint for any signs of excessive wear.

➡ If any parts show signs of excessive wear, the halfshaft assembly will require replacement. Component parts of these halfshaft assemblies are not serviceable.

To install:

10. Slide the new sealing boot clamp onto the interconnecting shaft. Slide the outer CV-joint assembly sealing boot onto the interconnecting shaft.

✳✳ WARNING

Seal boot MUST be positioned on the interconnecting shaft so the raised bead on the inside of the seal boot is in groove on the interconnecting shaft.

11. Align the splines on the interconnecting shaft with the splines on the cross

of the outer CV-joint assembly and start the outer CV-joint onto interconnecting shaft.

12. Install outer CV-joint assembly onto interconnecting shaft by using a soft-faced hammer and tapping end of stub axle (with hub nut installed) until outer CV-joint is fully seated on interconnecting shaft.

13. Outer CV-joint assembly must be installed on interconnecting shaft until cross of outer CV-joint assembly is seated against circlip on interconnecting shaft.

14. Distribute ½ the amount of grease provided in the seal boot service package into tripod housing. Put the remaining amount into the sealing boot.

15. Install the outer CV-joint sealing boot-to-interconnecting shaft clamp evenly on sealing boot.

16. Clamp the sealing boot onto the interconnecting shaft using crimper, Special Tool Clamp C-4975-A and the following procedure. Place Clamp C-4975-A over bridge of clamp.

17. Tighten nut on Clamp C-4975-A

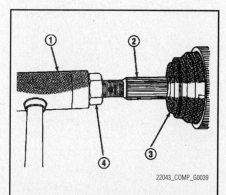

Fig. 40 Use a soft-face hammer (1) to tap the end of the stab axle (2) with the hub nut (4) installed until the CV-joint (3) is fully seated—Front halfshaft outer joint

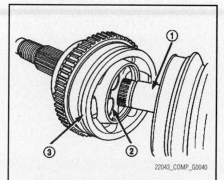

Fig. 41 Press the joint assembly (3) on the shaft until the cross (2) is seated against the circlip on the interconnecting shaft (1)—Front halfshaft outer joint

until jaws on tool are closed completely together, face to face.

❊❊ CAUTION

Seal must not be dimpled, stretched, or out-of-shape in any way. If seal is NOT shaped correctly, equalize pressure in seal and shape it by hand.

18. Position the outer CV-joint sealing boot into its retaining groove on outer CV joint housing. Install sealing boot-to-outer CV-joint retaining clamp evenly on sealing boot.

19. Clamp the sealing boot onto outer CV-joint housing using Clamp C-4975-A and the following procedure. Place Clamp C-4975-A over bridge of clamp.

20. Tighten nut on Clamp C-4975-A until jaws on tool are closed completely together, face to face.

21. Install the halfshaft onto the vehicle.

FRONT PINION SEAL

REMOVAL & INSTALLATION

➡Since no front differential is used, the equivalent of the front pinion seal is the output flange seal on the transfer case.

1. Remove the driveshaft. For additional information, refer to the following section, "Rear Driveshaft, Removal & Installation."

2. Using a suitable pry tool, remove the output seal.

To install:

3. Using Special Tool 9851 Installer and C-4171 Handle, drive the output shaft seal into the transfer case.

4. Install the driveshaft.

REAR DRIVESHAFT

REMOVAL & INSTALLATION

See Figures 42 and 43.

1. Raise and safely support the vehicle.

2. Matchmark the driveshaft and differential for alignment during reinstallation.

❊❊ CAUTION

Never allow driveshaft to hang while connected to transfer case, rear differential module flanges or center bearings. If propeller shaft section is hung unsupported, damage may occur to joint, boot and/or center bearing from over-angulation. This may result in vibration/balance issues.

3. Remove the rear driveshaft-to-rear axle retaining nuts.

4. Remove the three bolts from the center support heat shield.

5. Remove the heat shield.

6. Remove the two center support mounting bolts.

7. Remove the driveshaft.

To install:

8. Make sure transaxle is in Neutral (N) position.

9. Obtain a helper if needed and lift driveshaft assembly into position. Install driveshaft spline into transfer case.

10. Align marks on driveshaft with marks on rear axle flange. Slide driveshaft over studs on rear axle flange.

11. Install the four retaining nuts.

12. Raise the center support into position.

13. Install center support bolts and tighten to 30 ft. lbs. (41 Nm).

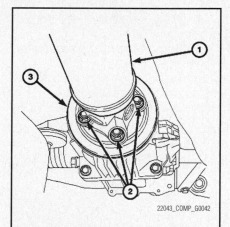

Fig. 42 Remove the driveshaft (1)-to-rear axle (3) retaining nuts (2)—Rear driveshaft

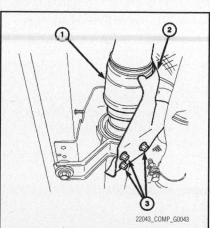

Fig. 43 Remove the mounting bolts (3) to remove the heat shield (2) from the driveshaft (1)—Rear driveshaft

14. Install driveshaft nuts and tighten to 43 ft. lbs. (58 Nm).

15. Install heat shield nuts and tighten to 15 ft. lbs. (21 Nm).

16. Check all fluid levels starting with transfer case.

REAR HALFSHAFT

REMOVAL & INSTALLATION

See Figure 44.

1. Raise and safely support the vehicle.
2. Remove the rear wheel.
3. Drain the fluid from the rear differential.
4. Remove the driveshaft.
5. Remove the sway bar connecting nuts and roll the sway bar down and out of the way, if equipped.
6. Remove the left and right rear halfshaft stay bracket bolts.
7. Remove the exhaust system up to the catalytic converter.
8. Support the rear differential module with a suitable jack.
9. Remove the rear bolt supporting the rear differential module.
10. Remove the two side bolts supporting the rear differential module.
11. Using the jack, lower the differential

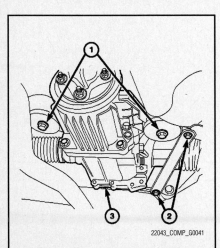

Fig. 44 Location of the two side bolts and left side stay bracket bolts (2) for the rear differential module (2)—Left side rear halfshaft removal

module enough to gain access to the electrical connector and bracket.

12. Remove the routing bracket bolt and unplug the electrical connector.
13. Lower the rear axle assembly.
14. Disengage the axle shaft.
15. Remove the nut and washer connecting the halfshaft to left rear hub.
16. Remove the halfshaft from the vehicle. If it's hard to remove, use a punch and hammer to tap it out.

To install:

17. Lift the rear axle assembly as the halfshaft is being installed.
18. Install the nut and washer connecting halfshaft to the left rear hub and tighten to 180 ft. lbs. (244 Nm).
19. Connect the electrical connector, route the wiring harness into the bracket. Tighten the bracket bolts to 89 inch lbs. (10 Nm).
20. Lift the rear axle assembly completely into place.
21. Install the two differential module side bolts and tighten to 75 ft. lbs. (102 Nm).
22. Install the rear differential module rear bolt and tighten to 75 ft. lbs. (102 Nm).
23. Install the halfshaft stay bracket and tighten the bolts to 45 ft. lbs. (61 Nm).
24. Install the driveshaft.
25. Refill the rear differential module to the correct level.
26. If equipped, roll the sway bar into place and tighten the nuts to 45 ft. lbs. (61 Nm).
27. Install any exhaust components removed.
28. Install the wheel.

REAR PINION SEAL

REMOVAL & INSTALLATION

See Figures 45 and 46.

1. Raise and safely support the vehicle.
2. Remove the driveshaft.
3. Disconnect the electrical connector from the rear differential module.
4. Disconnect the breather tube.
5. Remove the electronically control clutch (ECC)-to-rear differential module mounting bolts.

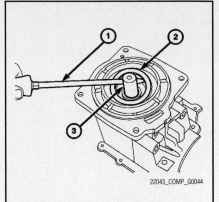

Fig. 45 Use a suitable pry tool (1) to remove the flange seal (2) from the input shaft (3).

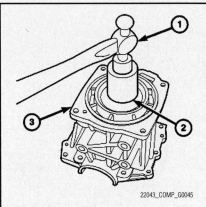

Fig. 46 Install the pinion seal using Special Tool 9931 (2) and hammer (1) to the ECC (3).

6. Separate and lower the ECC.
7. Remove all of the old gasket material on the mating surfaces of the ECC and rear differential mating surfaces.
8. Remove the wave washer.
9. Remove the flange seal.

To install:

10. Coat the edge face of the seal with liquid gasket and place over the input shaft.
11. Install the wave washer.
12. Install the pinion seal using Special Tool 9931 Installer tool.
13. The remainder of the installation is the reverse order of removal. Tighten the ECC-to-rear differential to 58 ft. lbs. (78 Nm).

ENGINE COOLING

ENGINE FAN

REMOVAL & INSTALLATION

✳✳ CAUTION

Do not open the radiator draincock with the system hot and under pressure because serious burns from coolant can occur.

1. Disconnect the negative battery cable.
2. Drain the cooling system.
3. Remove the radiator crossmember.
4. Disconnect the upper radiator hose from the radiator.
5. Remove the wiring harness bracket from the fan.
6. Disconnect the radiator fan electrical connector.
7. Detach the radiator fan assembly from the retaining clips.
8. Remove the radiator fan by lifting up and out of the engine compartment.

To install:

9. Install the radiator fan assembly into the J-clips.
10. Install the radiator fan fasteners. Tighten the screws to 55 inch lbs. (6 Nm).
11. Install the radiator crossmember.
12. Install the wiring harness bracket and connector the fan electrical connector.
13. Install the upper radiator hose.
14. Refill the cooling system to the correct level.
15. Connect the negative battery cable.

RADIATOR

REMOVAL & INSTALLATION

1. Drain the cooling system.
2. Remove the engine fan.
3. Disconnect the radiator hoses.
4. Remove the fasteners attaching the A/C condenser to the radiator. Reposition the A/C condenser out of the way.
5. Remove the radiator assembly by lifting it up and out of the engine compartment.
6. Installation is the reverse order of removal.
7. Refill the cooling system to the correct level.

THERMOSTAT

REMOVAL & INSTALLATION

These engines contain two thermostats. The primary thermostat is located on the front of the water plenum in the thermostat

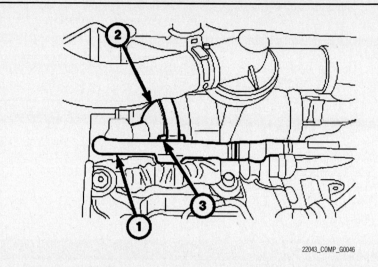

Fig. 47 Remove the coolant hose (1) and mounting bolts (3) from the thermostat housing (2)— Primary thermostat

housing. The secondary thermostat is located in the cylinder head under the water plenum.

Primary Thermostat

See Figure 47.

1. Drain the cooling system.
2. Remove the air intake assembly.
3. Disconnect the coolant hose from the thermostat housing.
4. Remove the housing mounting bolts.
5. Remove the thermostat assembly and clean the sealing surfaces.

To install:

6. Position the thermostat into the water plenum. Align the air bleed hole with the location notch on the thermostat housing.

7. Install the thermostat housing onto the coolant adapter and tighten the bolts to 79 inch lbs. (9 Nm).
8. Connect the coolant hose.
9. Install the air intake assembly.
10. Refill the cooling system to the correct level.

Secondary Thermostat

See Figure 48.

1. Drain the cooling system.
2. Remove the air intake assembly.
3. Disconnect the coolant hoses from the rear of the coolant adapter.
4. Remove the radiator hoses.
5. Remove the coolant adapter mounting bolts.

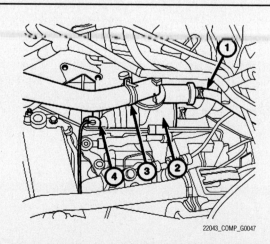

Fig. 48 Location of the coolant hose (1), radiator hoses (3,4) and coolant adapter (2)— Secondary thermostat

6. Carefully slide the coolant adapter off the water pump inlet tube to remove the coolant adapter and secondary thermostat.

To install:

7. Position the thermostat into the cylinder head.

8. Inspect the water pump inlet tube O-rings for damage before installing the tube in the coolant adapter. Replace O-ring as necessary.

9. Lubricate the O-rings with soapy water.

10. Position the coolant adapter on water pump inlet tube and cylinder head.

11. Install the coolant adapter mounting bolts and tighten to 159 inch lbs. (18 Nm).

12. Connect the front coolant hose.

13. Connect the two rear coolant hoses.

14. Connect the radiator hose.

15. Install the air intake assembly.

16. Refill the cooling system to the correct level.

WATER PUMP

REMOVAL & INSTALLATION

1. Disconnect the negative battery cable.

2. Drain the cooling system.

3. Remove the accessory drive belt.

4. Raise and safely support the vehicle.

5. Remove the accessory drive belt splash shield.

6. Remove the bolts securing the water pump pulley and remove the pulley.

7. Remove the water pump mounting bolts and remove the water pump.

To install:

8. Install the water pump and tighten the mounting bolts to 18 ft. lbs. (24 Nm).

9. Install the water pump pulley and tighten the pulley bolts to 79 inch lbs. (9 Nm).

10. Install the accessory drive belt splash shield.

11. Lower the vehicle.

12. Install the accessory drive belt.

13. Refill the cooling system to the correct level.

14. Connect the negative battery cable.

ENGINE ELECTRICAL

CHARGING SYSTEM

ALTERNATOR

REMOVAL & INSTALLATION

See Figure 49.

1. Disconnect the negative battery cable.

2. Raise and safely support the vehicle.

3. Remove the right front wheel.

4. Remove the engine splash shield.

5. Remove the accessory drive belt splash shield.

6. Remove the accessory drive belt.

7. Remove the idler pulley.

8. Loosen the alternator lower mounting bolt.

9. Remove the A/C compressor and secure out of the way.

➡**Do not disconnect the A/C lines.**

10. Unplug the ground wiring harness from the alternator.

11. Remove the battery positive terminal nut and wire.

12. Remove the upper and lower mounting bolts.

13. Move the A/C line to the other side of the battery terminal stud of the alternator.

14. Pull the alternator down and slide it out of the vehicle.

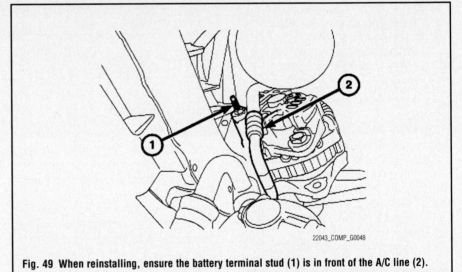

Fig. 49 When reinstalling, ensure the battery terminal stud (1) is in front of the A/C line (2).

22043_COMP_G0048

To install:

15. Slide the alternator up and rotate into place.

16. Move the A/C line back behind the battery terminal stud of the alternator.

17. Loosely install the lower mounting bolt.

18. Install the upper mounting bolt and tighten both mounting bolts to 40 ft. lbs. (54 Nm).

19. Install the battery positive cable and tighten the terminal nut to 89 inch lbs. (10 Nm).

20. Plug in the ground wiring harness.

21. Install the idler pulley.

22. Install the accessory drive belt.

23. Install the accessory drive belt splash shield.

24. Install the engine splash shield.

25. Install the right front wheel.

26. Lower the vehicle.

27. Connect the negative battery cable.

IGNITION COIL

REMOVAL & INSTALLATION
See Figures 50 and 51.

Fig. 50 There is an ignition coil mounted on the valve cover for each spark plug—All engines

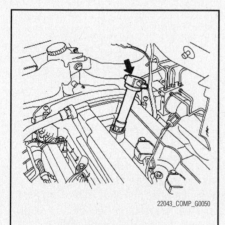

Fig. 51 Twist and pull straight up to remove the ignition coil.

1. Disconnect the negative battery cable.
2. Disconnect the electrical connector from the ignition coil.

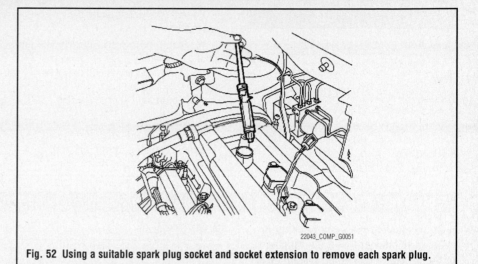

Fig. 52 Using a suitable spark plug socket and socket extension to remove each spark plug.

3. Remove the ignition coil mounting bolts.
4. Twist the ignition coil and then pull straight up.
5. Installation is the reverse order of removal. Tighten the mounting bolts to 80 inch lbs. (9 Nm).

IGNITION TIMING

ADJUSTMENT

Ignition timing is controlled by the Powertrain Control Module (PCM). No adjustment is possible.

SPARK PLUGS

REMOVAL & INSTALLATION
See Figure 52.

Each individual spark plug is located under each ignition coil. The ignition coil must be removed in order to access the spark plug.
1. Remove the ignition coil.
2. Remove the spark plug using a suitable spark plug socket with a rubber or foam insert.

To install:
3. Inspect the condition of the spark plug. Replace if necessary.

✳✳ WARNING
Special care should be used when installing spark plugs in the cylinder head spark plug wells. Be sure the plugs do not drop into the wells, damage to the electrodes can occur.

✳✳ WARNING
Always tighten spark plugs to the specified torque. Over tightening can cause distortion resulting in a change in the spark plug gap. Over tightening can also damage the cylinder head.

4. Install the spark plug and start threading it by hand. Tighten the spark plugs to 11–15 ft. lbs. (16–20 Nm).
5. Install the ignition coil to the spark plug. Tighten the mounting bolts to 80 inch lbs. (9 Nm).
6. Connect the negative battery cable.

ENGINE ELECTRICAL

STARTER

REMOVAL & INSTALLATION

1. Disconnect the negative battery cable.
2. Remove the air intake assembly.
3. Remove the starter mounting bolt.
4. Disconnect the throttle body electrical connector.
5. Remove the throttle body.

6. Push the starter under the intake manifold.
7. Tip the nose of the starter toward the cooling module.
8. Pull the starter up and out of the vehicle.
9. Disconnect the starter wiring.

To install:
10. Connect the starter wiring. Tighten the battery cable nut to 89 inch lbs. (10 Nm).

STARTING SYSTEM

11. Install the starter in the vehicle engine compartment and loosely place the starter into position.
12. Install the throttle body and throttle body bracket.
13. Install the starter mounting bolts and tighten to 40 ft. lbs. (54 Nm).
14. Connect the throttle body electrical connector.
15. Install the air intake assembly.
16. Connect the negative battery cable.

ENGINE MECHANICAL

➡Disconnecting the negative battery cable may interfere with the functions of the on board computer systems and may require the computer to undergo a relearning process, once the negative battery cable is reconnected.

ACCESSORY DRIVE BELTS

ACCESSORY BELT ROUTING
See Figure 53.

INSPECTION
See Figure 54.

Although many manufacturers recommend that the drive belt(s) be inspected every 30,000 miles (48,000 km) or more, it is really a good idea to check them at least once a year, or at every major fluid change. Whichever interval you choose, the belts should be checked for wear or damage. Obviously, a damaged drive belt

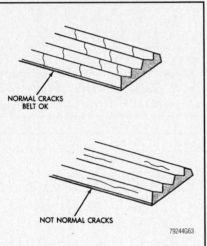

Fig. 54 Inspect the wear patterns for the serpentine drive belt.

can cause problems should it give way while the vehicle is in operation. But, improper length belts (too short or long), as well as excessively worn belts, can also cause problems. Loose accessory drive belts can lead to poor engine cooling and diminished output from the alternator, air conditioning compressor or power steering pump. A belt that is too tight places a severe strain on the driven unit and can wear out bearings quickly.

Serpentine drive belts should be inspected for rib chunking (pieces of the ribs breaking off), severe glazing, frayed cords or other visible damage. Any belt which is missing sections of 2 or more adjacent ribs which are ½ in. (13mm) or longer must be replaced. You might want to note that serpentine belts do tend to form small cracks across the backing. If the only wear you find is in the form of one or more cracks are across the backing and NOT parallel to the ribs, the belt is still good and does not need to be replaced.

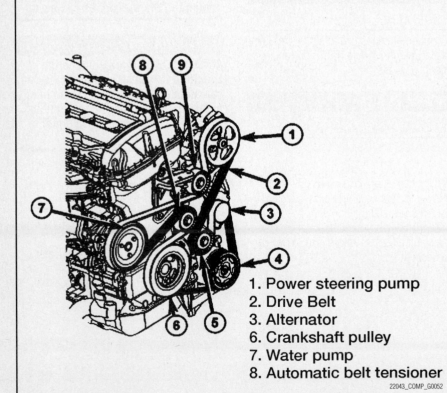

1. Power steering pump
2. Drive Belt
3. Alternator
6. Crankshaft pulley
7. Water pump
8. Automatic belt tensioner

Fig. 53 Drive belt (2) components: Power steering pump (1), Alternator (3), Crankshaft pulley (6), Water pump (7), Automatic belt tensioner (8)—2.0 & 2.4L Engines

ADJUSTMENT

Periodic drive belt tensioning is not necessary, because an automatic spring-loaded tensioner is used with these belts to maintain proper adjustment at all times.

REMOVAL & INSTALLATION

1. Using a wrench, rotate the accessory drive belt tensioner counterclockwise until the belt can be removed from the pulleys.
2. Remove the accessory drive belt.

To install:

3. Install the accessory drive belt around all of the pulleys except for the alternator.
4. Using a wrench, rotate the accessory drive belt tensioner counterclockwise until the belt can be installed over the alternator pulley.
5. Release the spring tensioner onto the accessory drive belt.

CAMSHAFT AND VALVE LIFTERS

INSPECTION

See Figure 55.

1. Inspect the camshaft bearing journals for damage. If journals are damaged, check the cylinder head for damage. Also check the cylinder head oil holes for clogging.
2. Check the cam lobe and bearing surfaces for abnormal wear and damage. Replace camshaft if defective.
3. Measure the camshaft end play as follows:

    a. Using a suitable tool, move camshaft as far rearward as it will go.

    b. Zero out the dial indicator.

    c. Move the camshaft as far forward as it will go.

    d. Record the reading on the dial indicator.

    e. If end play is exceeds the specification, check cylinder head and camshaft for wear; replace as necessary

REMOVAL & INSTALLATION

See Figures 56 through 69.

1. Remove the engine appearance cover.
2. Disconnect the negative battery cable.
3. Drain the cooling system.
4. Drain the engine oil.
5. Disconnect the ignition coil electrical connector.
6. Disconnect the Positive Crankcase Valve (PCV) and make-up air hoses from the cylinder head cover.
7. Remove the cylinder head cover bolts and cylinder head cover.
8. Remove the right side engine splash shield.
9. Rotate the engine to Top Dead Center (TDC).
10. Make sure camshaft timing marks are aligned.
11. Mark the chain link corresponding to timing marks with a paint marker.
12. Remove the timing tensioner plug from the front cover.
13. Insert a small Allen wrench through the timing tensioner plug hole and lift the ratchet upward to release the tensioner and push the Allen wrench inward. Leave the Allen wrench installed during the remainder of this procedure.
14. Insert Special Tool 9701 Locking Wedge between the camshaft phasers.
15. Lightly tap Special Tool 9701 into place with a suitable tool until it will no longer sink down.

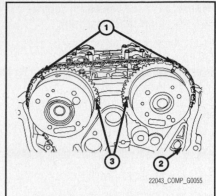

22043_COMP_G0055

Fig. 57 Make sure camshaft timing marks (3) are aligned and mark the chain link (1) corresponding to the timing marks with a paint marker.

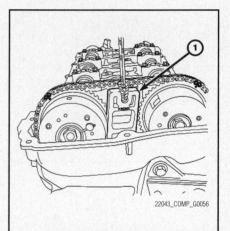

22043_COMP_G0056

Fig. 58 Insert Special Tool 9701 Locking Wedge (1) between the camshaft phasers

16. Remove the camshaft front bearing cap.
17. Slowly remove the remaining intake and exhaust camshafts cap bolts one turn at a time.

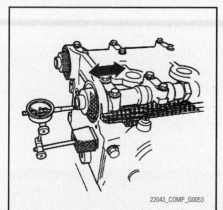

22043_COMP_G0053

Fig. 55 Measure the endplay of the camshaft with a dial indicator—2.0L & 2.4L Engines

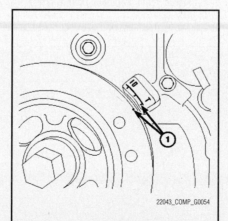

22043_COMP_G0054

Fig. 56 Align the timing mark (1) on the crankshaft with the reference line to ensure the engine is at TDC.

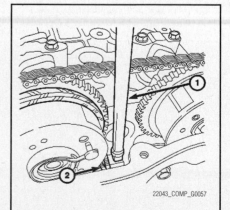

22043_COMP_G0057

Fig. 59 Lightly tap Special Tool 9701 (2) into place with a suitable tool (1) until it will no longer sink down.

➡Keep all of the valvetrain components in order for reassembly.

18. Remove the intake camshaft by lifting the rear of the camshaft upward.

19. Rotate the camshaft while lifting it out of the front bearing cradle.

20. Lift the timing chain off of the sprocket.

21. Remove the exhaust camshaft.

22. Secure the timing chain with wire so it does not fall into the timing chain cover.

23. Remove the valve lifters.

➡Keep all of the valvetrain components in order for reassembly.

To install:

24. Apply a light coat of clean engine oil to the valve lifters.

25. Install the lifters into their original positions in the cylinder head.

26. The camshaft cap is numbered 1, 2, or 3. This corresponds to the select fit bearing to use.

27. Install the corresponding select fit bearing.

28. Apply a light coat of clean engine oil to all of the camshaft journals.

Fig. 60 Remove the intake camshaft by lifting the rear of the camshaft upward.

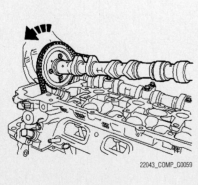

Fig. 61 Rotate the camshaft while lifting it out of the front bearing cradle.

29. Install the camshaft phasers on the camshafts, if removed.

  a. Install camshaft phaser making sure that the dowel is in the correct hole.

  b. Install camshaft phaser bolt and hand tighten.

30. Install the timing chain onto exhaust camshaft sprocket, making sure that the timing marks on the sprocket and the painted chain link are aligned.

31. Position the exhaust camshaft on the bearing journals in the cylinder head.

32. Align exhaust camshaft timing mark so it is parallel to the cylinder head as shown.

33. Install intake camshaft by raising the rear of the camshaft upward and roll the sprocket into the chain.

34. Align the timing marks on the intake cam sprocket with the painted chain link.

35. Position the intake camshaft into the bearing journals in the cylinder head.

36. Verify that the timing marks are aligned on both camshafts and that the timing marks are parallel with the cylinder head.

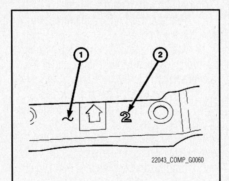

Fig. 62 The camshaft bearing cap (1) is numbered (2) to correspond to the select fit bearing.

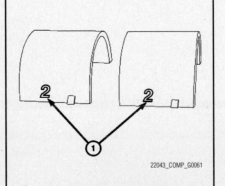

Fig. 63 Install the corresponding select fit bearing (1).

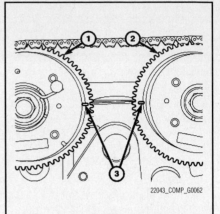

Fig. 64 When installing the exhaust (1) and intake (2) camshafts, make sure the timing marks (3) are aligned and parallel with the cylinder head.

✳✳ WARNING

Install the front intake and exhaust camshaft bearing cap last. Ensure that the dowels are seated and follow torque sequence or damage to engine could result.

➡If the front camshaft bearing cap is broken, the cylinder head MUST be replaced.

➡Verify that the exhaust bearing shells are correctly installed, and the dowels are seated in the head, prior to tightening bolts.

37. Install intake and exhaust camshaft bearing caps and slowly tighten bolts to 97 inch lbs. (11 Nm) in the sequence shown.

38. Install the front intake and exhaust bearing cap and tighten bolts to 18 ft. lbs. (25 Nm). in the sequence shown.

39. Verify that all of the timing marks are aligned.

40. Remove the Allen wrench from the timing chain tensioner.

41. Remove Special Tool 9701 Locking Wedge by pulling straight up on the pull rope.

42. Apply Mopar® thread sealant to the timing tensioner plug and install.

43. Install the right engine splash shield.

44. Clean any old RTV from the cylinder head cover gasket.

45. Inspect the cylinder head cover gaskets for damage. If they are not damaged, they may be reinstalled. Otherwise they must be replaced.

46. Install the studs in the cylinder head cover as shown.

47. Clean all RTV from the cylinder head.

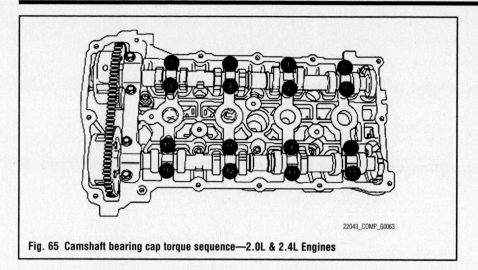

Fig. 65 Camshaft bearing cap torque sequence—2.0L & 2.4L Engines

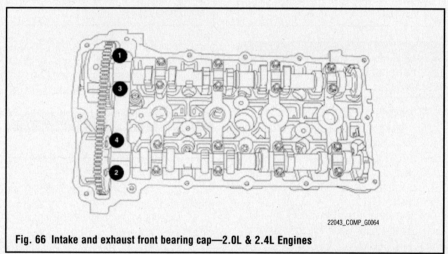

Fig. 66 Intake and exhaust front bearing cap—2.0L & 2.4L Engines

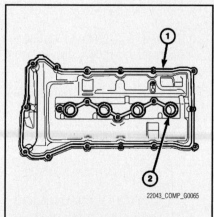

Fig. 67 Inspect the cylinder head covers for damage before installing.

48. Apply a dot of Mopar® engine sealant RTV or equivalent to the cylinder head front cover T-joint.

49. Install the cylinder head cover and tighten the bolts in sequence as follows:

a. Tighten all bolts in sequence to 44 inch lbs. (5 Nm).

50. Tighten all bolts in sequence to 90 inch lbs. (10 Nm).

51. Connect the ignition coil electrical connectors.

52. Connect the PCV and make-up air hoses

53. Refill the cooling system to the correct level.

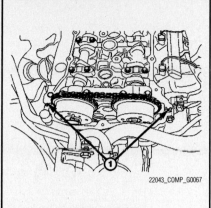

Fig. 69 Apply RTV to the cylinder head/front cover T-joints (1)

54. Refill the engine with oil to the correct level.

55. Install the engine appearance cover.

56. Connect the negative battery cable.

COMBINATION MANIFOLD

REMOVAL & INSTALLATION

All Wheel Drive
See Figure 70.

1. Remove the under floor catalytic converter as follows:

a. Raise and safely support the vehicle.

b. Remove the muffler assembly.

c. Disconnect the oxygen sensor electrical connectors.

d. Remove the flange bolts, springs and spherical gasket.

e. Remove the under floor catalytic converter.

2. Lower the vehicle.

3. Remove the secondary thermostat.

For additional information, refer to the fol-

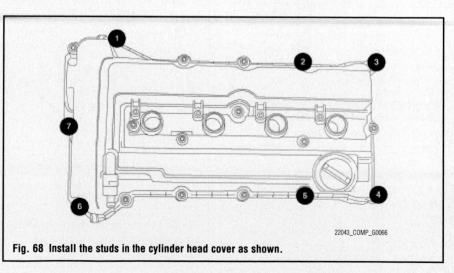

Fig. 68 Install the studs in the cylinder head cover as shown.

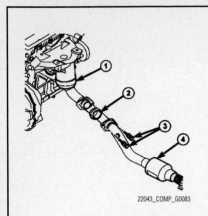

Fig. 70 Exploded view of the exhaust system—Maniverter (1), spherical gasket (2), flange bolts (3), under-floor catalytic converter (4)—AWD vehicles

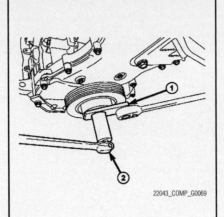

Fig. 71 Install Special Tool 9707 Damper Holder (1) to remove the crankshaft damper bolt.

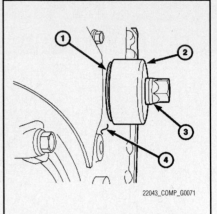

Fig. 73 Install the new seal (1) by tightening the crankshaft bolt (3) until the Seal Installer Tool (2) seats against the timing chain cover (4).

lowing section, "Thermostat, Removal & Installation."

4. Remove the maniverter mounting bolts.

5. Remove the maniverter and gasket.

To install:

6. Using a new flange gasket, install the maniverter to the engine. Tighten the mounting bolts to 21 ft. lbs. (28 Nm).

7. Install the secondary thermostat.

8. Install the under floor catalytic converter as follows:

   a. Install the under floor catalytic converter and the isolator supports to the underbody.

9. Position the spherical gasket with white side facing rear of vehicle, and install springs and tighten the bolts to 24 ft. lbs. (33 Nm).

10. Install the muffler assembly.

11. Working from the front of system; align each component to maintain position and proper clearance with underbody parts. Tighten all band clamps to 40 ft. lbs. (55 Nm).

12. Start the engine and check for exhaust leaks.

13. Check the exhaust system for contact with any of the body panels.

CRANKSHAFT FRONT SEAL

REMOVAL & INSTALLATION

See Figures 71 through 73.

1. Remove the accessory drive belt.

2. Install Special Tool 9707 Damper Holder to remove the crankshaft damper bolt.

3. Pull the damper off of the crankshaft.

4. Remove the crankshaft front seal by prying it out with a suitable pry tool.

✳✳ WARNING

Take care not to damage the cover seal surface.

To install:

5. Place the new seal onto Special Tool 9506 Seal Installer with the seal spring towards the inside of the engine.

6. Install the new crankshaft front seal using the Seal Installer tool and the crankshaft damper bolt.

7. Tighten the crankshaft bolt until the Seal Installer tool seats flush against the timing chain cover.

8. Remove the crankshaft bolt and Installer Tool.

9. Install the crankshaft damper. Oil the bolt threads between the bolt head and washer.

10. Using Special Tool 9707 Damper Holder told on the crankshaft damper

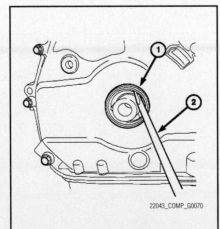

Fig. 72 Remove the crankshaft front seal (1) by prying it out with a suitable pry tool (2).

and tighten the bolt to 155 ft. lbs. (210 Nm).

11. Install the accessory drive belt.

12. Start the engine and check for leaks.

CYLINDER HEAD

REMOVAL & INSTALLATION

See Figures 74 through 77.

1. Properly relieve the fuel system pressure.

2. Disconnect the negative battery cable.

3. Drain the cooling system.

4. Remove the air intake assembly.

5. Remove the engine appearance cover.

6. Remove the coolant recovery bottle.

7. Disconnect the power steering pump and reposition out of the way.

➡ **Do not disconnect the power steering lines.**

8. Remove the windshield washer bottle.

9. Disconnect the following:

   • Breather hose
   • Positive Crankcase Valve (PCV) hose
   • Ignition coil electrical connectors

10. Remove the cylinder head cover.

11. Raise and safely support the vehicle.

12. Remove the right engine splash shield.

13. Rotate the engine to Top Dead Center (TDC).

14. Remove the accessory drive belt.

15. Remove the lower A/C compressor mounting bolts and lower mount.

16. Remove the lower idler pulley.

17. Remove the crankshaft damper.

18. Remove the water pump pulley.

19. Remove the right side engine mount bracket lower bolt.

20. Remove the timing chain cover lower bolts.

21. Disconnect the oxygen sensor electrical connector.

22. Remove exhaust pipe at manifold nuts and remove pipe.

23. Lower the vehicle.

24. Support the engine with suitable jack.

25. Remove right engine mount through bolt.

26. Remove right engine mount to mount bracket bolts.

27. Remove right engine mount adapter.

28. Remove accessory drive upper idler pulley.

29. Remove right upper engine mount bracket.

30. Remove the accessory drive belt tensioner.

31. Remove the upper timing chain cover retaining bolts.

32. Remove the timing chain cover.

➡**If the timing chain plated links can no longer be seen, the timing chain links corresponding to the timing marks must be marked prior to removal if the chain is to be reused.**

33. Mark chain link corresponding to camshaft timing mark.

34. Mark chain link corresponding to crankshaft timing mark.

35. Remove the timing chain tensioner.

36. Remove the timing chain.

37. Remove the timing chain guides.

38. Disconnect the fuel line at the fuel rail.

39. Disconnect the fuel injector electrical connectors.

40. Disconnect the top engine electrical connectors and reposition harness.

41. Remove the fuel rail.

42. Remove the throttle body support bracket retaining bolt.

43. Disconnect the electronic throttle control electrical connector.

44. Disconnect the MAP sensor electrical connector.

45. Disconnect the vacuum lines at intake.

46. Remove the intake manifold retaining bolts.

47. Remove the upper radiator hose retaining bolt.

48. Remove the intake manifold.

49. Remove the coolant outlet manifold and set aside.

50. Remove the ground strap at right rear of cylinder head.

51. Remove the exhaust manifold.

52. Remove the camshafts.

➡**All of the cylinder head bolts have captured washers EXCEPT the front two.**

53. Remove the cylinder head bolts.

54. Remove the cylinder head from engine block.

To install:

55. Replace the variable valve timing filter screen.

⁂ **WARNING**

Always replace the variable valve timing filter screen when servicing the head gasket or engine damage could result.

56. Place two pea size dots of Mopar® engine sealant RTV or equivalent (1) on cylinder block as shown.

57. Position the new cylinder head gasket on engine block with the part number

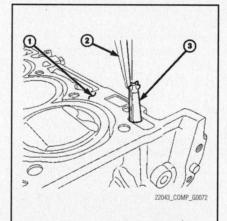

Fig. 74 Always replace the variable valve timing filter screen (3) in the cylinder head (1).

facing up. Ensure gasket is seated over the locating dowels in block.

58. Place two pea size dots of Mopar® engine sealant RTV or equivalent (1) on cylinder head gasket as shown.

59. Position the cylinder head onto the engine block.

60. Install washers for the front two cylinder head bolts.

61. Lightly coat the cylinder head bolts with clean engine oil.

62. Install the cylinder head bolts and tighten in sequence as follows:

   a. Tighten all bolts to 25 ft. lbs. (30 Nm).

   b. Tighten all bolts to 45 ft. lbs. (61 Nm).

   c. Tighten all bolts a second time to 45 ft. lbs. (61 Nm).

   d. Tighten all bolts an additional 90°

⁂ **WARNING**

Do not use a torque wrench for last torque step.

63. Install the exhaust manifold.

64. Install the ground strap at the right rear of the cylinder head.

65. Install the coolant adapter with new seals.

66. Connect the coolant hoses.

67. Connect the purge hose.

68. Install the intake manifold and tighten to 18 ft. lbs. (24 Nm).

69. Install the upper radiator hose retaining bracket bolt.

70. Install the timing chain.

71. Install the timing chain cover.

72. Remove the ignition coils from cylinder head cover.

73. Install the cylinder head cover.

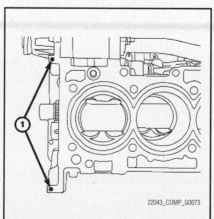

Fig. 75 Before installing the head gasket, place two dots of RTV (1) on the cylinder block as shown.

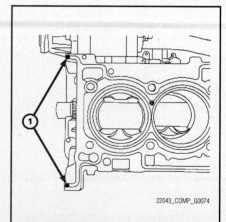

Fig. 76 After installing head gasket, place two more dots of RTV (1) on the cylinder block as shown.

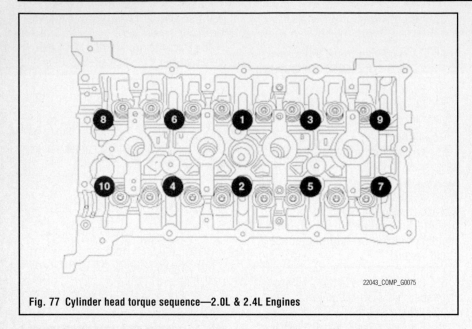

Fig. 77 Cylinder head torque sequence—2.0L & 2.4L Engines

22043_COMP_G0075

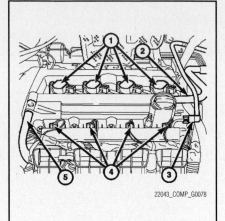

22043_COMP_G0078

Fig. 78 Location of the Ignition Coil electrical connectors (1), make-up air hose (2), fuel line (3), fuel injector electrical connectors (4), and PCV hose (5)—2.0L & 2.4L Engines

74. Connect the cam sensor wiring connector.

75. Install the spark plugs and tighten to 20 ft. lbs. (27 Nm).

76. Install ignition coils and tighten to 70 inch lbs. (8 Nm).

77. Install the power steering pump reservoir.

78. Install the windshield washer reservoir.

79. Install the coolant recovery reservoir

80. Install the accessory drive belt.

81. Connect the engine coolant temperature sensor connector.

82. Connect the coolant hoses to coolant adapter. Connect heater hoses to coolant adapter.

83. Connect the coolant temperature sensor and capacitor electrical connectors.

84. Install the heater tube support bracket to cylinder head.

85. Install the fastener attaching dipstick tube to lower intake manifold.

86. Connect the ignition coil and injector electrical connectors.

87. Install the fuel rail.

88. Connect fuel supply line quick-connect at the fuel rail assembly.

89. Install the air intake assembly.

90. Install the engine appearance cover.

91. Refill the cooling system to the correct level.

92. Refill the engine with oil to the correct level.

93. Connect the negative battery cable.

94. Start the engine and check for leaks.

ENGINE ASSEMBLY

REMOVAL & INSTALLATION

See Figures 78 through 81.

1. Drain the engine oil.

2. Drain the cooling system.

3. Properly relieve the fuel system pressure.

4. Remove the hood.

5. Remove the engine appearance cover.

6. Remove the air intake assembly.

7. Disconnect both cables from the battery.

8. Remove the battery and battery tray.

9. Remove the coolant reservoir.

10. Remove the power steering reservoir.

11. Remove the windshield washer reservoir.

12. Remove the coolant hoses from coolant adapter.

13. Remove the grill closure panel.

14. Remove the upper radiator hose support.

15. Disconnect the engine electrical connectors and reposition harness.

16. Remove the air intake tube from throttle body.

17. Disconnect the fuel line from fuel rail.

18. Remove the vacuum lines from throttle body and intake manifold.

19. Remove the wiring harness from the intake.

20. Remove the throttle body support bracket.

21. Disconnect the electronic throttle control and manifold flow control valve electrical connectors.

22. Remove the PCV hose, and make-up air hose from valve cover.

23. Remove the dipstick.

24. Remove the intake manifold mounting bolts and remove the intake manifold.

25. Disconnect electrical connectors and reposition harness.

26. Remove the accessory drive belt.

27. Remove the power steering line support at engine mount and exhaust manifold.

28. Remove the power steering pump and set aside.

29. Remove the upper idler pulley.

30. Remove the ground strap near right tower.

31. Raise and safely support the vehicle.

32. Remove the right front wheel.

33. Remove the engine splash shield.

34. Remove the torque converter inspection cover and matchmark the torque converter to the flywheel.

35. Remove the torque converter bolts.

36. Remove the lower bellhousing mounting bolts.

37. Remove the A/C compressor mounting bolts.

38. Remove the alternator and lower idler pulley.

39. Disconnect the crankshaft position (CKP) sensor electrical connector and remove the sensor.

40. Remove the exhaust variable valve timing solenoid.

41. Install an engine lift chain as shown to cylinder head.

42. Connect the chain to the rear engine lift hook.

43. Install engine lifting crane.

44. Remove the right engine mount through-bolt.

45. Remove the engine mount adapter retaining bolts and the mount adapter.

46. Carefully lift the engine from engine compartment.

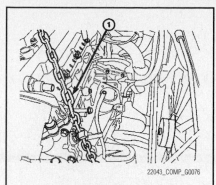

Fig. 79 Install an engine lift chain (1) to the cylinder head as shown.

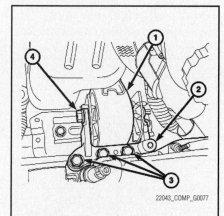

Fig. 80 Remove the right engine mount through-bolt (4), mount adapter retaining bolts (3) and mount adapter (2)—2.0L & 2.4L Engine removal

To install:

47. Position the engine assembly over the vehicle and slowly lower the engine into place.

48. Continue lowering engine until the engine/transaxle assembly are aligned to the mounting locations.

49. Install the engine mount adapter and tighten bolts. Install the mount through-bolt and tighten all bolts to 87 ft. lbs. (118 Nm).

50. Remove the engine lift chain.

51. Install the oil control valve.

52. Raise and safely support the vehicle.

53. Install the A/C compressor.

54. Install the exhaust manifold and heat shields.

55. Install the oxygen sensor and connect the electrical connector.

56. Install the crankshaft position sensor and connect connector.

57. Install the manifold to exhaust pipe bolts and tighten bolts.

58. Install the alternator.

59. Install lower bell housing bolts and tighten bolts.

60. Align the torque converter and flex plate matchmark. Install torque converter bolts and tighten.

61. Install the torque converter inspection cover.

62. Install the crankshaft damper, using Special Tool 9707 Damper holder. Apply clean engine oil to the crankshaft damper bolt threads and between bolt head and washer. Tighten bolt to 155 ft. (210 Nm).

63. Install the right engine splash shield.

64. Install the wheel.

65. Install the coolant hose to the oil cooler.

66. Install a new oil filter.

67. Lower the vehicle.

68. Install the upper idler pulley.

69. Install the coolant adapter assembly.

70. Install the ground strap near the right strut tower.

71. Install the power steering line support bracket and install the power steering pump.

72. Install the accessory drive belt.

73. Connect the electrical connectors at block ground, starter, A/C compressor, knock sensor, oil pressure sensor, generator, coolant temperature sensor at block, and block heater (if equipped).

74. Install the intake manifold

75. Install the throttle body support bracket and wiring harness retainer.

76. Install the dipstick.

77. Install the PCV hose to valve cover and make-up air hose.

78. Connect the manifold flow control valve and electronic throttle control electrical connectors.

79. Install the vacuum lines to the throttle body and intake manifold.

80. Install the intake air tube to the throttle body.

81. Connect the ignition coil electrical connectors.

82. Connect the injector electrical connectors.

83. Connect the fuel line to fuel rail.

84. Connect the intake and exhaust oil control valve electrical connectors.

85. Install the grill trim panel.

86. Install the upper radiator support bracket.

87. Connect the coolant temperature sensor.

88. Connect the capacitor electrical connector.

89. Install the coolant hoses at coolant adapter.

90. Install the coolant reservoir and connect hose.

91. Install the battery tray and battery.

92. Connect the battery cables.

Fig. 81 Location of the coolant temperature sensor (1), capacitor electrical connector (2) and coolant hoses connected to the coolant adapter (3)—2.0L & 2.4L Engines

93. Install the air intake assembly.

94. Refill the cooling system to the correct level.

95. Refill the engine with oil to the correct level.

96. Install the engine appearance cover.

97. Install the hood.

98. Start the engine and check for leaks.

EXHAUST MANIFOLD

REMOVAL & INSTALLATION

See Figures 82 through 84.

1. Disconnect the negative battery cable.
2. Remove the engine appearance cover.
3. Remove the upper heat shields mounting bolts.
4. Remove the upper heat shield.
5. Disconnect the exhaust pipe from the exhaust manifold.
6. Remove the exhaust manifold support bracket.

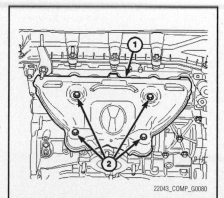

Fig. 82 Remove the upper heat shield mounting bolts (2) to remove the upper heat shield (1)

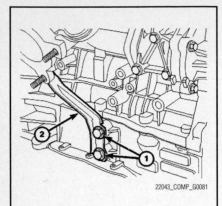

Fig. 83 Remove the bracket mounting bolts (1) and remove the exhaust manifold support bracket (2)

7. Disconnect the Oxygen sensor electrical connector.

8. Remove the exhaust manifold mounting bolts.

9. Remove the exhaust manifold and gasket.

To install:

10. Install the exhaust manifold with a new gasket. Tighten the bolts in sequence to 25 ft. lbs. (34 Nm).

11. Install the exhaust manifold heat shield. Tighten the bolts to 105 inch lbs. (12 Nm).

12. Install the exhaust manifold support bracket.

13. Install a new catalytic converter gasket and connect the exhaust pipe to the exhaust manifold. Tighten the flange bolts to 21 ft. lbs. (28 Nm).

14. Connect the oxygen sensor electrical connector.

15. Install the engine appearance cover.

16. Connect the negative battery cable.

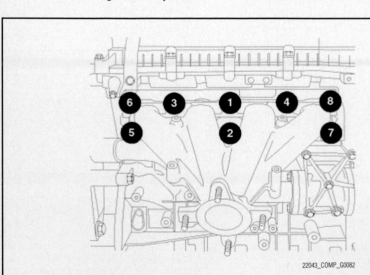

Fig. 84 Exhaust manifold torque sequence

INTAKE MANIFOLD

REMOVAL & INSTALLATION

See Figures 85 through 88.

1. Properly relieve the fuel system pressure.

2. Drain the cooling system.

3. Disconnect the negative battery cable.

4. Remove the engine appearance cover.

5. Remove the air intake assembly.

6. Disconnect the fuel line from the fuel rail.

7. Disconnect the fuel injector electrical connectors.

8. Remove the fuel rail. For additional information, refer to the following section, "Fuel Injectors, Removal & Installation."

9. Disconnect the electrical connectors for:

- Oil temperature sensor
- Variable valve timing solenoid
- Intake camshaft position sensor

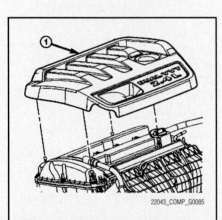

Fig. 85 Remove the engine appearance cover (1) by pulling upward—2.0L & 2.4L engines

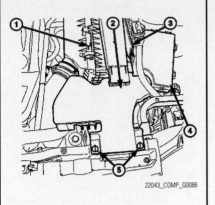

Fig. 86 Air intake components—Air cleaner housing (1), fresh air inlet (2), heat shield (3), retainers (5)—2.0L & 2.4L engines

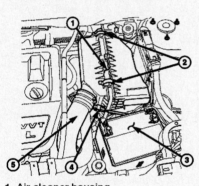

1. Air cleaner housing
2. Housing clasps
3. Battery
4. Intake Air Temperature (IAT) sensor electrical connector
5. Air inlet tube

Fig. 87 Air intake components—Air cleaner housing (1), housing clasps (2), battery (3), Intake Air Temperature (IAT) sensor electrical connector (4), Air inlet tube (5)—2.0L & 2.4L engines

10. Position the wiring harness out of the way.

11. Remove the throttle body support bracket.

12. Disconnect the electronic throttle control electrical connector.

13. Remove the wiring harness retainer from the intake manifold.

14. Disconnect the manifold absolute pressure (MAP) sensor electrical connector.

15. Disconnect the vacuum lines from the intake manifold.

16. Remove the upper radiator hose retaining bracket.

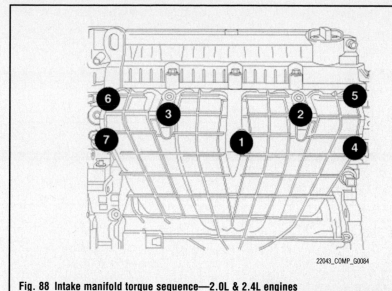

Fig. 88 Intake manifold torque sequence—2.0L & 2.4L engines

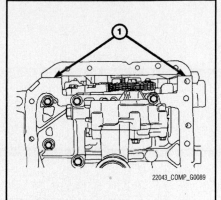

Fig. 90 Apply Mopar® Engine RTV GEN II to the front cover-to-engine block parting lines(1) as shown

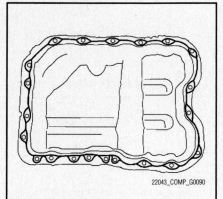

Fig. 91 Apply a 2 mm bead of Mopar® Engine RTV GEN II on the oil pan mating surface as shown

17. Remove the intake manifold retaining bolts.

18. Remove the intake manifold and gasket.

To install:

19. Clean all of the gasket surfaces.

20. Using a new gasket, install the intake manifold bolts in sequence to 18 ft. lbs. (25 Nm).

21. Install the upper radiator hose support bracket.

22. Connect the vacuum lines to the intake manifold.

23. Install the fuel rail assembly and tighten the mounting bolts to 17 ft. lbs. (23 Nm).

24. Connect the fuel injector electrical connectors.

25. Connect the fuel supply hose.

26. Reconnect the electrical connectors previously removed.

27. Install the air intake assembly.

28. Refill the cooling system to the correct level.

29. Install the engine appearance cover.

OIL PAN

REMOVAL & INSTALLATION

See Figures 89 through 91.

1. Raise and safely support the vehicle.
2. Drain the engine oil.
3. Remove the accessory drive belt splash shield.
4. Remove the lower A/C compressor mounting bolt and remove the A/C mounting bracket.
5. Remove the oil pan mounting bolts.
6. Using a putty knife, loosen the seal around the oil pan.

✳ WARNING

Do not use the pry points in the engine block to remove the oil pan.

7. Remove the oil pan.

To install:

8. Clean any old gasket material from the mating surfaces.

9. Apply Mopar® Engine RTV GEN II at the front cover-to-engine block parting lines.

10. Apply a 2 mm bead of Mopar® Engine RTV GEN II around the oil pan mating surface as shown in the illustration.

11. Install the oil pan into position and tighten the bolts as follows:

- The two long bolts to 16 ft. lbs. (22 Nm).
- All other bolts to 105 ft. lbs. (12 Nm).

12. Install the oil drain plug.
13. Install the A/C compressor mounting

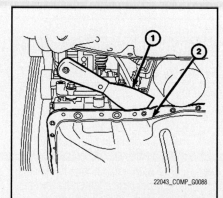

Fig. 89 Use a putty knife (1) to the loose the seal around the oil pan (2)—2.0L & 2.4L Engine

bracket and A/C compressor lower mounting bolt.

14. Lower the vehicle.

15. Refill the engine with oil to the correct level.

16. Start the engine and check for leaks.

OIL PUMP

REMOVAL & INSTALLATION

See Figure 92.

1. Rotate the engine to put cylinder no. 1 at Top Dead Center (TDC).

2. Remove the oil pan.

3. Matchmark the position of the timing chain to the crankshaft sprocket and the timing chain on the oil pump sprocket.

4. Push the tensioner piston back into the tensioner body.

5. With the piston held back, insert Special Tool 9703 Tensioner Pin into the tensioner body to hold the piston in the retracted position.

6. Remove the balance shaft module (BSM) mounting bolts and discard the bolts.

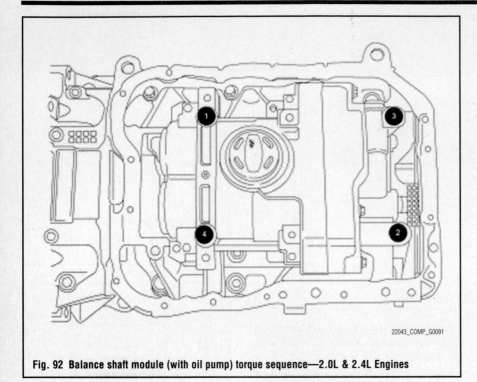

Fig. 92 Balance shaft module (with oil pump) torque sequence—2.0L & 2.4L Engines

7. Lower the back of the BSM and remove the timing chain from the oil pump sprocket.

8. Remove the BSM from the engine.

To install:

9. Clean the BSM mounting holes with brake cleaner.

10. If removed, position the timing chain over the sprocket, aligning the matchmarks.

11. Align the matchmarks and install the chain over the oil pump sprocket.

12. Pivot the BSM assembly upwards and position on the ladder frame.

13. Using new bolts, install them first only finger tight. Then tighten as follows:

   a. Tighten the bolts in the sequence shown to 11 ft. lbs. (15 Nm).

   b. Then tighten them to 22 ft. lbs. (29 Nm) in sequence.

   c. Rotate each bolt an additional 90° in the sequence shown

14. Remove the tensioner pin.

15. Install the oil pan.

16. Refill the engine with oil to the correct level.

17. Start the engine and check for leaks.

INSPECTION

The oil pump is integral to the balance shaft module. The oil pump cannot be disassembled for inspection

PISTON AND RING

POSITIONING

See Figure 93.

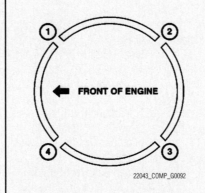

Fig. 93 Position the piston ring end gaps as shown—Top compression ring gap (1), Upper oil ring side rail gap (2), Second compression ring gap (3), Lower oil ring side rail gap (4)—2.0L & 2.4L Engines

REAR MAIN SEAL

REMOVAL & INSTALLATION

See Figure 94.

1. Remove the transaxle assembly.
2. Remove the flexplate.
3. Insert a suitable pry tool between the dust lip and metal case of the crankshaft seal. Angle the pry tool through the dust lip against the metal case and pry out the seal.

To install:

4. Lightly coat Special Tool 9509 Seal Guide with clean engine oil. Place the seal guide on the crankshaft.

5. Position a new rear seal over the seal guide. Ensure the lip of the seal is facing towards the crankcase during installation.

6. Drive the seal into the block using Special Tool 9706 Seal Driver and Handle C-4171. When the seal driver bottoms out against the block, the seal is installed.

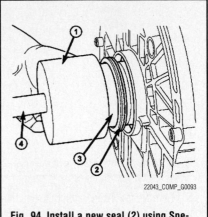

Fig. 94 Install a new seal (2) using Special Tools 9509 (3), 9706 (1) and C-4171 (4)—2.0L & 2.4L Engines

7. Install the flexplate. Tighten the new bolts to 70 ft. lbs. (95 Nm).

8. Install the transaxle assembly.

TIMING CHAIN, SPROCKETS, FRONT COVER AND SEAL

REMOVAL & INSTALLATION

See Figures 95 through 103.

1. Disconnect the negative battery cable.

2. Turn the crankshaft until cylinder no. 1 is at Top Dead Center (TDC).

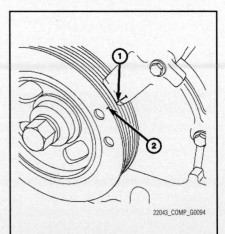

Fig. 95 The timing mark on the crankshaft (2) should align with the reference mark (1) to indicate that cylinder no. 1 is at TDC—2.0L & 2.4L Engines

3. Remove the engine appearance cover.
4. Properly relieve the fuel system pressure.
5. Drain the cooling system.
6. Drain the engine oil.
7. Remove the coolant recovery bottle.
8. Remove the power steering reservoir mounting bolts and secure it aside.

➡**Do not disconnect the power steering lines.**

9. Disconnect the fuel, make-up air hose, PCV hose and ignition coil electrical connectors.
10. Remove the cylinder head cover.
11. Raise and safely support the vehicle.
12. Remove the lower right engine splash shield.
13. Remove the accessory drive belt.
14. Remove the lower A/C compressor mounting bolt and remove the A/C compressor lower bracket.
15. Remove the lower idler pulley and crankshaft pulley.
16. Remove the front crankshaft oil seal by prying it out with a suitable pry tool.
17. Remove the water pump pulley.
18. Remove the engine mount bracket lower mounting bolt.
19. Remove the timing chain cover lower mounting bolts.
20. Lower the vehicle.
21. Remove the power steering line support, then remove the power steering pump mounting bolts and secure it out of the way.

➡**Do not disconnect the power steering lines.**

22. Support the engine with a suitable jack.

➡**When support the engine, use a block a wood between the jack and oil pan to avoid damage to the engine.**

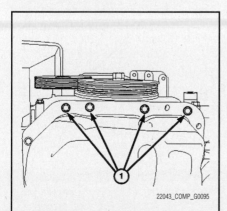

Fig. 96 Lower timing chain cover mounting bolts (1) (looking from the bottom up)—2.0L & 2.4L Engines

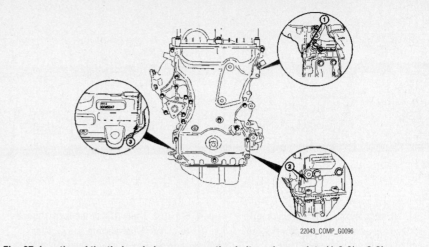

Fig. 97 Location of the timing chain cover mounting bolts and pry points (1,2,3)—2.0L & 2.4L Engines

23. Remove the remaining right engine mount-to-mount bracket bolts.
24. Remove the upper idler pulley.
25. Remove the right engine mount bracket.
26. Remove the accessory drive belt tensioner.
27. Remove the timing chain cover mounting bolts.
28. Using the pry points indicated, remove the timing chain cover out through the bottom of the vehicle.
29. Matchmark the chain links corresponding to the camshaft timing marks.
30. Match mark the chain link corresponding to the crankshaft timing mark.
31. Remove the timing chain tensioner.
32. Remove the timing chain.
33. Remove the oil pump drive chain tensioner and oil pump drive chain.
34. Remove the crankshaft sprocket.
35. Hold the camshaft in place on the camshaft flats using a wrench.
36. Remove the camshaft phaser assembly from the camshaft.

❊❊ WARNING

The camshaft phasers and camshaft sprockets are supplied as an assembly and should not be disassembled.

To install:
37. Using a wrench to hold the camshaft in place, install the phaser assembly to the camshaft.

➡**Ensure the dowel is seated in the dowel hose and not in an oil feed hole. The dowel hole is larger than the four oil feed holes.**

38. Install the crankshaft sprocket onto the crankshaft.

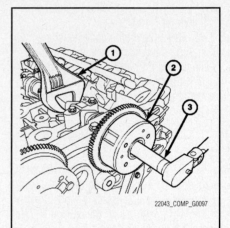

Fig. 98 Using a wrench (1) to hold the camshaft, remove the phaser assembly (2) using a suitable socket wrench (3)—2.0 & 2.4L Engines

39. Install the oil pump drive chain and tensioner.
40. Verify that the crankshaft sprocket keyway is at the 9 o'clock position.
41. Align the camshaft timing marks so they are parallel to the cylinder head and aligned each other as shown.
42. If the timing chain guide was removed, install the timing chain guide and tighten the bolts to 105 inch lbs. (12 Nm).
43. Install the timing chain so plated links on chain align with timing marks on camshaft sprockets.
44. Align the timing mark on the crankshaft sprocket with the plated link on the timing chain. Position chain so slack will be on the tensioner side.

➡**Keep the slack in the timing chain on the tensioner side.**

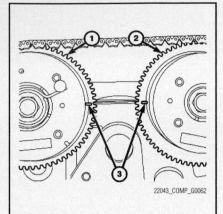

Fig. 99 Align the camshaft timing marks so they are parallel to the cylinder head and aligned each other as shown.

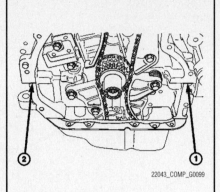

Fig. 101 Apply RTV to the ladder frame-to-engine block parting line (1,2) as shown—Timing chain cover installation

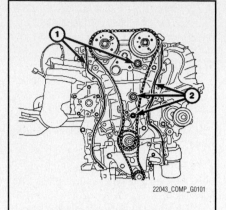

Fig. 103 Apply RTV to the engine block (1,2) as shown—Timing chain cover installation

45. Install the moveable timing chain pivot guide, if removed, and tighten bolt to 105 inch lbs. (12 Nm).

46. Reset the timing chain tensioner by lifting up on the ratchet and pushing the plunger inward towards the tensioner body. Insert Special Tool 8514 Tensioner Pin into the slot to hold the tensioner plunger in the retracted position.

47. Install the timing chain tensioner and tighten bolts to 105 inch lbs. (12 Nm).

48. Remove the Tensioner Pin. Rotate the crankshaft CLOCKWISE two complete revolutions until the crankshaft is repositioned at the TDC position with the crankshaft keyway at the 9 o'clock position.

49. Verify that the camshaft timing marks are in the proper position.

50. Clean all of the sealing surfaces of the timing chain cover.

51. Apply Mopar® engine sealant RTV or equivalent as shown at the cylinder head-to-block parting line.

52. Apply Mopar® engine sealant RTV or equivalent as shown at the ladder frame-to-block parting line.

53. Apply Mopar® engine sealant RTV or equivalent in the corner of the oil pan and block.

54. Apply a 2 mm bead of Mopar® engine sealant RTV or equivalent to the oil pan as shown.

55. Apply a 2 mm bead of Mopar® engine sealant RTV or equivalent to the engine block as shown.

56. Install the timing chain cover upwards from under the vehicle. Tighten the M6 bolts to 105 inch lbs. (12 Nm) and tighten the M8 bolts to 17 ft. lbs. (23 Nm).

57. The remainder of the installation is the reverse order of removal procedure.

58. Refill the cooling system to the correct level.

59. Refill the engine with oil to the correct level.

60. Start the engine and check for leaks.

VALVE LASH

ADJUSTMENT

See Figure 104.

1. Remove the cylinder head cover.

2. Rotate the camshaft to the lobes are vertical.

3. Check the clearance using feeler gauges.

4. Repeat this procedure for all of the valve tappets and record the readings.

5. If the clearance was outside the required specification:

   a. Remove the camshaft. For additional information, refer to the following section, "Camshaft, Removal & Installation."

   b. Depending on if the clearance was too large or too small, increase or decrease the tappet thickness by the necessary amount.

   c. Install the camshafts and verify the valve lash is correct.

6. Install the cylinder head cover.

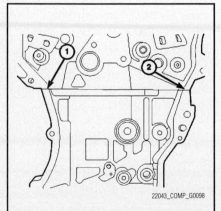

Fig. 100 Apply RTV to the cylinder head-to-engine block parting line (1,2) as shown—Timing chain cover installation

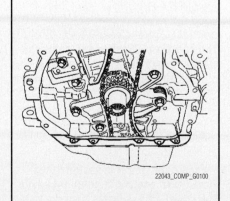

Fig. 102 Apply RTV to the oil pan as shown—Timing chain cover installation

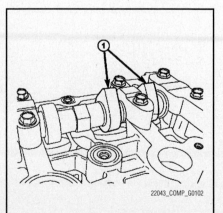

Fig. 104 To measure the valve lash, rotate camshaft so the lobes (1) are vertical.

ENGINE PERFORMANCE & EMISSION CONTROL

CAMSHAFT POSITION (CMP) SENSOR

LOCATION

See Figure 105.

These engines utilize two Camshaft Position (CMP) sensors mounted to the front and rear of the cylinder head.

Fig. 105 Location of the front camshaft position sensor—2.0L & 2.4L Engines

OPERATION

The Powertrain Control Module (PCM) sends approximately 5 volts to the Hall-effect sensor. This voltage is required to operate the Hall-effect chip and the electronics inside the sensor. The input to the PCM occurs on a 5 volt output reference circuit. A ground for the sensor is provided through the sensor return circuit. The PCM identifies camshaft position by registering the change from 5 to 0 volts, as signaled from the camshaft position sensor.

The PCM determines fuel injection synchronization and cylinder identification from inputs provided by the camshaft position sensor and crankshaft position sensor. From the two inputs, the PCM determines crankshaft position.

REMOVAL & INSTALLATION

Front Sensor

1. Disconnect negative battery cable.
2. Remove the air cleaner hose to throttle body, disconnect the inlet air temperature sensor electrical connector.
3. Disconnect the electrical connector from the camshaft position sensor.
4. Remove the CMP sensor mounting screws.

To install:
5. Lubricate the CMP sensor O-ring.
6. Install the CMP sensor using a twisting motion. Make sure the sensor is fully seated.

> **✷✷ WARNING**
>
> **Do not drive the sensor into the bore with the mounting screws.**

7. Carefully attach the electrical connector. Take care not to damage the sensor pins.
8. Install the air intake assembly.
9. Connect the negative battery cable.

Rear Sensor

See Figure 106.

1. Disconnect the negative battery cable.
2. Disconnect the sensor electrical connector.
3. Remove the heat shield retaining nut and remove the heat shield.
4. Remove the CMP sensor mounting and remove the sensor.

To install:
5. Lubricate the CMP sensor O-ring.
6. Install the CMP sensor using a twisting motion. Make sure the sensor is fully seated.

> **✷✷ WARNING**
>
> **Do not drive the sensor into the bore with the mounting screws.**

7. Tighten the mounting bolt to 80 inch lbs. (9 Nm).
8. Carefully attach the electrical connector to the CMP sensor. Take care not to damage the sensor pins.

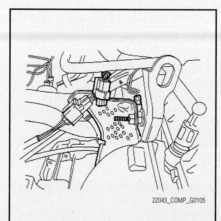

Fig. 106 Disconnect the connector and remove the heat shield to access the rear CMP sensor.

9. Install the heat shield onto the mounting stud and tighten the retaining nut.
10. Connect the electrical connector.
11. Connect the negative battery cable.

TESTING

1. Using the wiring diagram/schematic as a guide, inspect the wiring and connectors between the Camshaft 1/1 Position Sensor and the Powertrain Control Module (PCM).
2. Look for any chafed, pierced, pinched, or partially broken wires.
3. Look for broken, bent, pushed out or corroded terminals.
4. Inspect the Camshaft 1/1 Position Sensor for conditions such as loose mounting screws, damage, or cracks.
5. If no other problems are found, remove the Camshaft 1/1 Position Sensor.
6. Inspect the Camshaft 1/1 Position Sensor and mounting area for any condition that would result in an incorrect signal, such as damage, foreign material, or excessive movement.
7. Using a diagnostic scan tool, check for the presence of any Diagnostic Trouble Codes (DTCs). Record and address these codes as necessary.
8. If no codes are present, review the scan tool environmental data. If possible, try to duplicate the conditions under which the DTC set.
9. If applicable, actuate the component with the scan tool.
10. Monitor the scan tool data relative to this circuit and wiggle test the wiring and connectors.
11. Look for the data to change, the actuation to be interrupted, or for the DTC to reset during the wiggle test.
12. Refer to any Technical Service Bulletins (TSBs) that may apply.
13. Turn the ignition off.
14. Visually inspect the related wire harness. Disconnect all the related harness connectors. Look for any chafed, pierced, pinched, partially broken wires and broken, bent, pushed out, or corroded terminals.
15. Perform a voltage drop test on the related circuits between the suspected component and the Powertrain Control Module (PCM).
16. Inspect and clean all PCM, engine, and chassis grounds that are related to the most current DTC.
17. If numerous trouble codes were set, use a schematic and inspect any common ground or supply circuits.

18. For intermittent Misfire DTCs check for restrictions in the Intake and Exhaust system, proper installation of Sensors, vacuum leaks, and binding components that are run by the accessory drive belt.

19. Use the scan tool to perform a System Test if one applies to the component.

20. A co-pilot, data recorder, and/or lab scope should be used to help diagnose intermittent conditions.

CRANKSHAFT POSITION (CKP) SENSOR

LOCATION

See Figure 107.

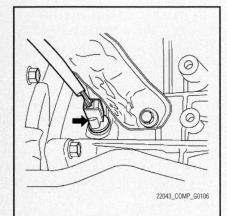

Fig. 107 The Crankshaft Position (CKP) sensor mounts to the rear of the engine block near the transmission.

OPERATION

The Powertrain Control Module (PCM) sends approximately 5 volts to the Hall-effect sensor. This voltage is required to operate the Hall-effect chip and the electronics inside the sensor. A ground for the sensor is provided through the sensor return circuit. The input to the PCM occurs on a 5 volt output reference circuit that operates as follows: The Hall-effect sensor contains a powerful magnet. As the magnetic field passes over the dense portion of the counterweight, the 5-volt signal is pulled to ground (0.3 volts) through a transistor in the sensor. When the magnetic field passes over the notches in the crankshaft counterweight, the magnetic field turns off the transistor in the sensor, causing the PCM to register the 5-volt signal. The PCM identifies crankshaft position by registering the change from 5 to 0 volts, as signaled from the Crankshaft Position sensor.

REMOVAL & INSTALLATION

1. Disconnect the negative battery cable.

2. Raise and safely support the vehicle.

3. If the vehicle is equipped with all wheel drive, the transfer case must be removed.

4. Remove the heat shield retaining bolt and remove the heat shield.

5. Unlock and disconnect the CKP sensor electrical connector.

6. Remove the CKP sensor bolt and remove the sensor.

To install:

7. Lubricate the CKP sensor O-ring with clean engine oil.

8. Install the CKP sensor using a twisting motion. Make sure the sensor is fully seated.

✳✳ WARNING

Do not drive the sensor into the bore with the mounting screws.

9. Tighten the mounting bolt to 80 inch lbs. (9 Nm).

10. Install the heat shield and tighten the retaining bolt.

11. If the vehicle is equipped with all wheel drive, install the transfer case.

12. Lower the vehicle.

13. Connect the negative battery cable.

TESTING

1. Using a diagnostic scan tool, check for the presence of any Diagnostic Trouble Codes (DTCs). Record and address these codes as necessary.

2. If no codes are present, review the scan tool environmental data. If possible, try to duplicate the conditions under which the DTC set.

3. If applicable, actuate the component with the scan tool.

4. Monitor the scan tool data relative to this circuit and wiggle test the wiring and connectors.

5. Look for the data to change, the actuation to be interrupted, or for the DTC to reset during the wiggle test.

6. Refer to any Technical Service Bulletins (TSBs) that may apply.

7. Turn the ignition off.

8. Visually inspect the related wire harness. Disconnect all the related harness connectors. Look for any chafed, pierced, pinched, partially broken wires and broken, bent, pushed out, or corroded terminals.

9. Perform a voltage drop test on the related circuits between the suspected component and the Powertrain Control Module (PCM).

10. Inspect and clean all PCM, engine, and chassis grounds that are related to the most current DTC.

11. If numerous trouble codes were set, use a schematic and inspect any common ground or supply circuits.

12. For intermittent Misfire DTCs check for restrictions in the Intake and Exhaust system, proper installation of Sensors, vacuum leaks, and binding components that are run by the accessory drive belt.

13. Use the scan tool to perform a System Test if one applies to the component.

14. A co-pilot, data recorder, and/or lab scope should be used to help diagnose intermittent conditions.

ENGINE COOLANT TEMPERATURE (ECT) SENSOR

LOCATION

See Figures 108 and 109.

There are two Engine Coolant Temperature (ECT) sensors. One is located in the coolant adapter and one is located in the cylinder head.

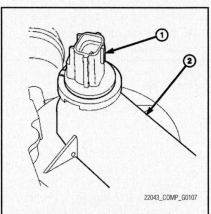

Fig. 108 One of the coolant temperature sensor (1) is located in the coolant adapter (2).

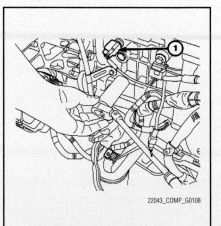

Fig. 109 Another coolant temperature sensor (1) threads into the cylinder head.

OPERATION

The Engine Coolant Temperature (ECT) sensor provides an input to the Powertrain Control Module (PCM). As temperature increases, resistance of the sensor decreases. As coolant temperature varies, the ECT sensor resistance changes resulting in a different voltage value at the PCM ECT sensor signal circuit. The ECT sensor provides input for various PCM operations. The PCM uses the input to control air-fuel mixture, timing, and radiator fan on/off times.

REMOVAL & INSTALLATION

The following procedure can be used for removal and installation of either sensor.

1. Disconnect the negative battery cable.
2. Drain the cooling system.
3. Disconnect the ECT sensor electrical connector.
4. Remove the ECT sensor.

To install:

5. Install the ECT sensor as follows:
   a. Coolant adapter mounted: Make sure the ECT sensor is locked in place.
   b. Cylinder head mounted: Tighten the sensor to 14 ft. lbs. (19 Nm).
6. Reconnect the ECT sensor electrical connector.
7. Refill the cooling system to the correct level.
8. Connect the negative battery cable.

TESTING

1. Using the wiring diagram/schematic as a guide, inspect the wiring and connectors between the Engine Coolant Temperature sensor(s) and the Powertrain Control Module (PCM).
2. Look for any chafed, pierced, pinched, or partially broken wires.
3. Look for broken, bent, pushed out or corroded terminals.
4. Turn the ignition on.
5. Monitor the scan tool data relative to the sensor(s) and wiggle test the wiring and connectors.
6. Look for the data to change or for a DTC to set during the wiggle test.
7. Check the engine coolant level and the condition of the engine coolant.
8. With the scan tool, read the Engine Coolant Temperature Sensor value for each sensor. If the engine was allowed to cool completely, the value should be approximately equal to the ambient temperature.

9. Monitor each sensor value on the scan tool and the actual coolant temperature with a thermometer.
10. Using a diagnostic scan tool, check for the presence of any Diagnostic Trouble Codes (DTCs). Record and address these codes as necessary.
11. If no codes are present, review the scan tool environmental data. If possible, try to duplicate the conditions under which the DTC set.
12. If applicable, actuate the component with the scan tool.
13. Monitor the scan tool data relative to this circuit and wiggle test the wiring and connectors.
14. Look for the data to change, the actuation to be interrupted, or for the DTC to reset during the wiggle test.
15. Refer to any Technical Service Bulletins (TSBs) that may apply.
16. Turn the ignition off.
17. Visually inspect the related wire harness. Disconnect all the related harness connectors. Look for any chafed, pierced, pinched, partially broken wires and broken, bent, pushed out, or corroded terminals.
18. Perform a voltage drop test on the related circuits between the suspected component and the Powertrain Control Module (PCM).
19. Inspect and clean all PCM, engine, and chassis grounds that are related to the most current DTC.
20. If numerous trouble codes were set, use a schematic and inspect any common ground or supply circuits.
21. For intermittent Misfire DTCs check for restrictions in the Intake and Exhaust system, proper installation of Sensors, vacuum leaks, and binding components that are run by the accessory drive belt.
22. Use the scan tool to perform a System Test if one applies to the component.
23. A co-pilot, data recorder, and/or lab scope should be used to help diagnose intermittent conditions.

HEATED OXYGEN (HO2S) SENSOR

LOCATION

See Figures 110 and 111.

The upstream oxygen sensor threads into the outlet flange of the exhaust manifold. The downstream heated oxygen sensor threads into the system depending on emission package.

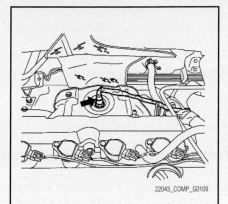

22043_COMP_G0109

Fig. 110 The upstream sensor is located in the output flange of the exhaust manifold.

22043_COMP_G0110

Fig. 111 The downstream sensor is shown here threaded into the under floor catalytic converter.

OPERATION

As vehicles accumulate mileage, the catalytic converter deteriorates. The deterioration results in a less efficient catalyst. To monitor catalytic converter deterioration, the fuel injection system uses two heated oxygen sensors. One sensor is upstream of the catalytic converter, one is downstream of the converter. The Powertrain Control Module (PCM) compares the reading from the sensors to calculate the catalytic converter oxygen storage capacity and converter efficiency. Also, the PCM uses the upstream heated oxygen sensor input when adjusting injector pulse width.

When the catalytic converter efficiency drops below emission standards, the PCM stores a diagnostic trouble code and illuminates the malfunction indicator lamp (MIL).

The Heated Oxygen Sensors (HO2S) produce a constant 2.5 volts on NGC (4 cylinder) vehicles, depending upon the oxygen content of the exhaust gas. When a large amount of oxygen is present (caused by a lean air/fuel mixture, can be caused by misfire and exhaust leaks), the sensors produce a low voltage. When there is a lesser amount of oxygen present (caused by a rich air/fuel mixture, which can be caused by internal engine problems) it produces a higher voltage. By monitoring the oxygen content and converting it to electrical voltage, the sensors act as a rich-lean switch.

The oxygen sensors are equipped with a heating element that keeps the sensors at proper operating temperature during all operating modes. Maintaining correct sensor temperature at all times allows the system to enter into closed loop operation sooner. Also, it allows the system to remain in closed loop operation during periods of extended idle.

In Closed Loop operation the PCM monitors the HO2S input (along with other inputs) and adjusts the injector pulse width accordingly. During Open Loop operation the PCM ignores the HO2S input. The PCM adjusts injector pulse width based on pre-programmed (fixed) values and inputs from other sensors.

The NGC Controller has a common ground for the heater in the HO2S. 12 volts is supplied to the heater in the HO2S by the NGC controller. Both the upstream and downstream HO2S for NGC are pulse width modulation (PWM). NOTE: When replacing an HO2S, the PCM RAM memory must be cleared, either by disconnecting the PCM C-1 connector or momentarily disconnecting the Battery negative terminal. The NGC learns the characteristics of each HO2S heater element and these old values should be cleared when installing a new HO2S. You may experience driveability issues if this is not performed.

REMOVAL & INSTALLATION

Upstream Sensor

1. Remove the engine appearance cover.
2. Disconnect the negative battery cable.
3. Disconnect the Heated Oxygen Sensor (HO2S) electrical connector.
4. Remove the sensor using a Snap-On® tool YA8875 crow foot wrench or suitable oxygen sensor socket.
5. After removing the sensor, the exhaust manifold threads must be cleaned with an 18 mm x 1.5 + 6E tap.

To install:

6. If you are reusing the original sensor, coat the sensor threads with an anti-seize compound such as Loctite® 771-64 or equivalent. New sensors have the compound on the threads and not require an additional coating.

7. Install the sensor using a Snap-On® tool YA8875 crow foot wrench or suitable oxygen sensor socket. Tighten the sensor to 30 ft. lbs. (41 Nm).
8. Connect the HO2S electrical connector.
9. Connect the negative battery cable.
10. Install the engine appearance cover.

Downstream Sensor

1. Remove the negative battery cable.
2. Raise and safely support the vehicle.
3. Disconnect the Heated Oxygen Sensor (HO2S) electrical connector.
4. Disconnect the sensor electrical wiring harness from the clips along the body.
5. Remove the sensor using a Snap-On® tool YA8875 crow foot wrench or suitable oxygen sensor socket.
6. After removing the sensor, the exhaust manifold threads must be cleaned with an 18 mm x 1.5 + 6E tap.

To install:

7. If you are reusing the original sensor, coat the sensor threads with an anti-seize compound such as Loctite® 771-64 or equivalent. New sensors have the compound on the threads and not require an additional coating.
8. Install the sensor using a Snap-On® tool YA8875 crow foot wrench or suitable oxygen sensor socket. Tighten the sensor to 30 ft. lbs. (41 Nm).
9. Connect the electrical wiring harness to the clips along the body.
10. Install the sensor using a Snap-On® tool YA8875 crow foot wrench or suitable oxygen sensor socket. Tighten the sensor to 30 ft. lbs. (41 Nm).
11. Connect the HO2S electrical connector.
12. Connect the negative battery cable.
13. Install the engine appearance cover.

TESTING

1. With the scan tool, read the Engine Coolant Temperature Sensor value for each sensor. If the engine was allowed to cool completely, the value should be approximately equal to the ambient temperature.
2. Monitor each sensor value on the scan tool and the actual coolant temperature with a thermometer.
3. Using a diagnostic scan tool, check for the presence of any Diagnostic Trouble Codes (DTCs). Record and address these codes as necessary.
4. If no codes are present, review the scan tool environmental data. If possible, try to duplicate the conditions under which the DTC set.

5. If applicable, actuate the component with the scan tool.
6. Monitor the scan tool data relative to this circuit and wiggle test the wiring and connectors.
7. Look for the data to change, the actuation to be interrupted, or for the DTC to reset during the wiggle test.
8. Refer to any Technical Service Bulletins (TSBs) that may apply.
9. Turn the ignition off.
10. Visually inspect the related wire harness. Disconnect all the related harness connectors. Look for any chafed, pierced, pinched, partially broken wires and broken, bent, pushed out, or corroded terminals.
11. Perform a voltage drop test on the related circuits between the suspected component and the Powertrain Control Module (PCM).
12. Inspect and clean all PCM, engine, and chassis grounds that are related to the most current DTC.
13. If numerous trouble codes were set, use a schematic and inspect any common ground or supply circuits.
14. For intermittent Misfire DTCs check for restrictions in the Intake and Exhaust system, proper installation of Sensors, vacuum leaks, and binding components that are run by the accessory drive belt.
15. Use the scan tool to perform a System Test if one applies to the component.
16. A co-pilot, data recorder, and/or lab scope should be used to help diagnose intermittent conditions.

INTAKE AIR TEMPERATURE (IAT) SENSOR

LOCATION
See Figure 112.

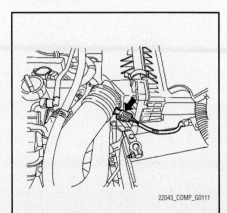

22043_COMP_G0111

Fig. 112 The Intake Air Temperature (IAT) Sensor is located in the air intake tube of the air intake assembly.

OPERATION

The IAT sensor is a negative coefficient sensor that provides information to the Powertrain Control Module regarding the temperature of the air entering the intake manifold.

REMOVAL & INSTALLATION

See Figure 113.

1. Disconnect the negative battery cable.
2. Disconnect the IAT sensor electrical connector.
3. Remove the IAT sensor.

To install:

4. Install the IAT sensor and ensure the correct sensor orientation.

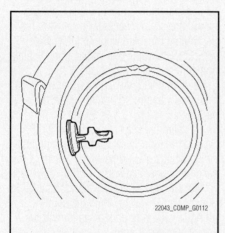

Fig. 113 Showing the correct IAT sensor orientation—2.0L & 2.4L Engines

5. Attach the IAT sensor electrical connector.
6. Connect the negative battery cable.

TESTING

1. Turn the ignition off. If possible, allow the vehicle to sit with the ignition off for more than 8 hours in an environment where the temperature is consistent and above 20°F (-7°C).
2. Test drive the vehicle. The vehicle must exceed 30 mph (48 km/h) during the test drive. Do not cycle the ignition off when the test drive is completed.
3. With a scan tool, select View DTCs.
4. If a DTC is not active, perform the following:
5. Refer to any Technical Service Bulletins (TSBs) that may apply.
6. Review the scan tool Freeze Frame information. If possible, try to duplicate the conditions under which the DTC set.
7. With the engine running at normal operating temperature, monitor the scan tool parameters related to the DTC while

wiggling the wire harness. Look for parameter values to change and/or a DTC to set. Turn the ignition off.

8. Visually inspect the related wire harness. Disconnect all the related harness connectors. Look for any chafed, pierced, pinched, partially broken wires and broken, bent, pushed out, or corroded terminals. Perform a voltage drop test on the related circuits between the suspected inoperative component and the PCM.

✳✳ CAUTION

Do not probe the PCM harness connectors. Probing the PCM harness connectors will damage the PCM terminals resulting in poor terminal to pin connection. Install Miller Special Tool no. 8815 to perform diagnosis.

9. Inspect and clean all PCM, engine, and chassis grounds that are related to the most current DTC.
10. If numerous trouble codes were set, use a wire schematic and look for any common ground or supply circuits.
11. For any Relay DTCs, actuate the Relay with the scan tool and wiggle the related wire harness to try to interrupt the actuation.
12. For intermittent Evaporative Emission trouble codes perform a visual and physical inspection of the related parts including hoses and the Fuel Filler cap.
13. Use the scan tool to perform a System Test if one applies to failing component. A co-pilot, data recorder, and/or lab scope should be used to help diagnose intermittent conditions.

KNOCK SENSOR (KS)

LOCATION

See Figure 114.

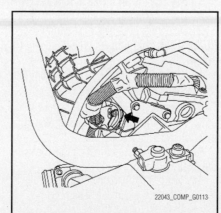

Fig. 114 The Knock Sensor (KS) is bolted to the engine block in front of the starter under the intake manifold.

OPERATION

When the Knock Sensor (KS) detects a knock in one of the cylinders, it sends an input signal to the Powertrain Control Module (PCM). In response, the PCM retards ignition timing for all cylinders by a scheduled amount.

Knock sensors contain a piezoelectric material which constantly vibrates and sends an input voltage (signal) to the PCM while the engine operates. As the intensity of the crystal's vibration increases, the knock sensor output voltage also increases.

The voltage signal produced by the knock sensor increases with the amplitude of vibration. The PCM receives as an input the knock sensor voltage signal. If the signal rises above a predetermined level, the PCM will store that value in memory and retard ignition timing to reduce engine knock. If the knock sensor voltage exceeds a preset value, the PCM retards ignition timing for all cylinders. It is not a selective cylinder retard.

The PCM ignores knock sensor input during engine idle conditions. Once the engine speed exceeds a specified value, ignition timing retard is allowed.

REMOVAL & INSTALLATION

1. Disconnect the negative battery cable.
2. Remove the bolt holding the KS.
3. Remove the KS with the electrical connector attached.
4. Disconnect the electrical connector from the KS.

To install:

5. Attach the electrical connector to the KS.
6. Install the KS into the engine block. Tighten the bolt to 16 ft. lbs. (22 Nm).

✳✳ WARNING

Over or under-tightening affects the knock sensor performance.

7. Connect the negative battery cable.

TESTING

1. Using the wiring diagram/schematic as a guide, inspect the wiring and connectors between the Knock Sensor and the Powertrain Control Module (PCM).
2. Look for any chafed, pierced, pinched, or partially broken wires.
3. Look for broken, bent, pushed out or corroded terminals.

4. Monitor the scan tool data relative to this circuit and wiggle test the wiring and connectors.

5. Look for the data to change or for the DTC to reset during the wiggle test.

6. Refer to any Technical Service Bulletins that may apply.

7. Review the scan tool Freeze Frame information. If possible, try to duplicate the conditions under which the DTC set.

8. With the engine running at normal operating temperature, monitor the scan tool parameters related to the DTC while wiggling the wire harness. Look for parameter values to change and/or a DTC to set. Turn the ignition off.

9. Visually inspect the related wire harness. Disconnect all the related harness connectors. Look for any chafed, pierced, pinched, partially broken wires and broken, bent, pushed out, or corroded terminals. Perform a voltage drop test on the related circuits between the suspected inoperative component and the PCM.

✳✳ CAUTION

Do not probe the PCM harness connectors. Probing the PCM harness connectors will damage the PCM terminals resulting in poor terminal to pin connection. Install Miller Special Tool no. 8815 to perform diagnosis.

10. Inspect and clean all PCM, engine, and chassis grounds that are related to the most current DTC.

11. If numerous trouble codes were set, use a wire schematic and look for any common ground or supply circuits.

12. For any Relay DTCs, actuate the Relay with the scan tool and wiggle the related wire harness to try to interrupt the actuation.

13. For intermittent Evaporative Emission trouble codes perform a visual and physical inspection of the related parts including hoses and the Fuel Filler cap.

14. Use the scan tool to perform a System Test if one applies to failing component. A co-pilot, data recorder, and/or lab scope should be used to help diagnose intermittent conditions.

MANIFOLD ABSOLUTE PRESSURE (MAP) SENSOR

LOCATION

See Figure 115.

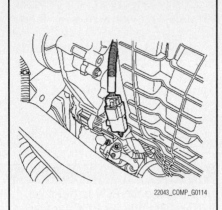

Fig. 115 The Manifold Absolute Pressure Sensor mounts to the intake manifold.

22043_COMP_G0114

OPERATION

The Manifold Absolute Pressure (MAP) sensor serves as a Powertrain Control Module (PCM) input, using a silicon based sensing unit, to provide data on the manifold vacuum that draws the air/fuel mixture into the combustion chamber. The PCM requires this information to determine injector pulse width and spark advance. When MAP equals Barometric pressure, the pulse width will be at maximum.

Also like the cam and crank sensors, a 5 volt reference is supplied from the PCM and returns a voltage signal to the PCM that reflects manifold pressure. The zero pressure reading is 0.5 volt and full scale is 4.5 volt. For a pressure swing of 0 - 15 psi the voltage changes 4.0 volt. The sensor is supplied a regulated 4.8 to 5.1 volts to operate the sensor. Like the cam and crank sensors ground is provided through the sensor return circuit.

REMOVAL & INSTALLATION

1. Remove the air intake assembly.
2. Disconnect the negative battery cable.
3. Disconnect the electrical connector from the Manifold Absolute Pressure (MAP) sensor.
4. Remove the mounting screw from the MAP sensor and remove the sensor.

To install:

5. Install the MAP sensor to the intake manifold and tighten the screw.
6. Connect the electrical connector to the MAP sensor.
7. Connect the negative battery cable.
8. Install the air intake assembly.

TESTING

1. Turn the ignition off.
2. Using the wiring diagram/schematic as a guide, inspect the wiring and connectors between the MAP Sensor and the PCM.

3. Look for any chafed, pierced, pinched, or partially broken wires.

4. Look for broken, bent, pushed out or corroded terminals.

5. Turn the ignition on.

6. Monitor the scan tool data relative to the sensor and wiggle test the wiring and connectors.

7. Look for the data to change or for a DTC to set during the wiggle test. If necessary, check each sensor circuit for high resistance or a shorted condition.

8. With a scan tool, read the Barometric Pressure. The Barometric Pressure should be approximately equal to the actual barometric pressure. If necessary, compare the Barometric Pressure value of the tested vehicle to the value of a known good vehicle of a similar make and model.

9. Connect a vacuum gauge to a manifold vacuum source and start the engine.

10. With the scan tool, read the MAP Sensor vacuum. The scan tool reading for MAP vacuum should be within 1 inch of the vacuum gauge reading.

11. With the scan tool, monitor the MAP Sensor signal voltage. With the engine idling in neutral or park, snap the throttle. The MAP Sensor signal voltage should change from below 2.0 volts at idle to above 3.5 volts at wide open throttle.

THROTTLE POSITION SENSOR (TPS)

LOCATION

The Throttle Position Sensor (TPS) is located on the throttle body assembly.

OPERATION

The Throttle Position Sensor (TPS) and throttle actuating DC motor are integral to the throttle body. The throttle body is a non serviceable item, replace the throttle body as an assembly.

The throttle blade will not close completely when engine is shut down. This engine off blade position is for start up. The electric throttle body will adjust the throttle blade for idle control as the idle air control valve adjusted idle speed previously on cable actuated throttle bodies. The electric throttle body will also adjust the throttle blade for normal driving operation. The throttle blade will move to the engine off blade position if throttle body codes are set to provide air for limp-in mode.

REMOVAL & INSTALLATION

The TPS and throttle actuating DC motor are integral to the throttle body. The throttle body is a non-serviceable item. The throttle body must be replaced as an assembly.

TESTING

1. Using the wiring diagram/schematic as a guide, inspect the wiring and connectors between the Throttle Body and the Powertrain Control Module (PCM).

2. Look for any chafed, pierced, pinched, or partially broken wires.

3. Look for broken, bent, pushed out or corroded terminals.

4. Inspect the Throttle Body for any condition that would result in an incorrect signal, such as damage or contamination.

5. Inspect and clean all PCM, engine, and chassis grounds that are related to the most current DTC.

6. If numerous trouble codes were set, use a wire schematic and look for any common ground or supply circuits.

7. For any Relay DTCs, actuate the Relay with the scan tool and wiggle the related wire harness to try to interrupt the actuation.

8. Use the scan tool to perform a System Test if one applies to failing component. A co-pilot, data recorder, and/or lab scope should be used to help diagnose intermittent conditions.

VEHICLE SPEED SENSOR (VSS)

LOCATION

The Vehicle Speed Sensor (VSS) is mounted above the transaxle differential assembly.

OPERATION

The Vehicle Speed Sensor (VSS) is a Hall Effect sensor mounted above the transaxle differential. The sensor is triggered by the ring gear teeth passing below it. The VSS pulse signal to the speedometer/odometer is monitored by the PCM speed control circuitry to determine vehicle speed and to maintain speed control set speed.

REMOVAL & INSTALLATION

1. Disconnect the negative battery cable.
2. Remove the air intake assembly.
3. Disconnect the Vehicle Speed Sensor (VSS) electrical connector.

➡**Clean the area around the VSS before removal to prevent dirt from the entering the transaxle.**

4. Remove the VSS retaining bolt and remove the VSS.

To install:

5. Install the VSS using a new O-ring. Tighten the retaining bolt to 60 inch lbs. (7 Nm).
6. Connect the VSS electrical connector.
7. Install the air intake assembly.
8. Connect the negative battery cable.

FUEL   GASOLINE FUEL INJECTION SYSTEM

FUEL SYSTEM SERVICE PRECAUTIONS

Safety is the most important factor when performing not only fuel system maintenance but any type of maintenance. Failure to conduct maintenance and repairs in a safe manner may result in serious personal injury or death. Maintenance and testing of the vehicle's fuel system components can be accomplished safely and effectively by adhering to the following rules and guidelines.

• To avoid the possibility of fire and personal injury, always disconnect the negative battery cable unless the repair or test procedure requires that battery voltage be applied.

• Always relieve the fuel system pressure prior to disconnecting any fuel system component (injector, fuel rail, pressure regulator, etc.), fitting or fuel line connection. Exercise extreme caution whenever relieving fuel system pressure to avoid exposing skin, face and eyes to fuel spray. Please be advised that fuel under pressure may penetrate the skin or any part of the body that it contacts.

• Always place a shop towel or cloth around the fitting or connection prior to loosening to absorb any excess fuel due to spillage. Ensure that all fuel spillage (should it occur) is quickly removed from engine surfaces. Ensure that all fuel soaked cloths or towels are deposited into a suitable waste container.

• Always keep a dry chemical (Class B) fire extinguisher near the work area.

• Do not allow fuel spray or fuel vapors to come into contact with a spark or open flame.

• Always use a back-up wrench when loosening and tightening fuel line connection fittings. This will prevent unnecessary stress and torsion to fuel line piping.

• Always replace worn fuel fitting O-rings with new Do not substitute fuel hose or equivalent where fuel pipe is installed.

Before servicing the vehicle, make sure to also refer to the precautions in the beginning of this section as well.

RELIEVING FUEL SYSTEM PRESSURE

1. Remove the lower rear seat cushion.
2. Remove the fuel pump module cover.
3. Disconnect the electrical connector for fuel pump module.
4. Start and run the engine until it stalls.
5. Attempt to restart the engine until it will no longer run.
6. Turn the ignition key to the **OFF** position.
7. Disconnect the negative battery cable.

➡**One or more Diagnostic Trouble Codes (DTCs) may have been stored in Powertrain Control Module (PCM) memory. The scan tool must be used to erase a DTC.**

FUEL FILTER

REMOVAL & INSTALLATION

The fuel filter is mounted inside the fuel pump module and is a non-serviceable part.

FUEL INJECTORS

REMOVAL & INSTALLATION

See Figures 116 through 118.

1. Properly relieve the fuel system pressure.
2. Disconnect the negative battery cable.
3. Disconnect the electrical connectors from the fuel injectors.

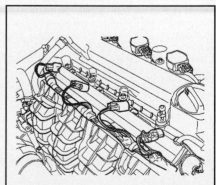

22043_COMP_G0115

Fig. 116 Disconnect the electrical connectors from the fuel injectors—Fuel injector removal

4. Disconnect the fuel line connection at the fuel rail.

5. Remove the hard fuel line from the fuel rail.

6. Remove the wiring harness clips from the fuel rail mounting studs.

7. Remove the two bolts holding the fuel rail at the lower manifold.

8. Remove the fuel rail.

9. Remove the clip holding the fuel injector to the fuel rail.

10. Remove the fuel injector, with the clip, from the fuel rail.

To install:

11. Apply a light coating of clean engine oil to the upper O-ring of the fuel injector.

12. Install each injector in the cup on the fuel rail and then install the retaining clip.

13. Apply a light coating of clean engine oil to the O-ring on the nozzle each of each injector.

Fig. 117 After removing the wiring harness and mounting bolts, remove the fuel rail—Fuel injector removal

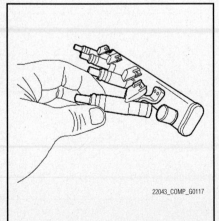

Fig. 118 Remove the fuel injector clip and fuel injector from the fuel rail—Fuel injector removal

14. Install the fuel rail/injector assembly by inserting the fuel injector nozzles into the openings in the lower intake manifold.

15. Tighten the fuel rail mounting bolts to 20 ft. lbs. (27 Nm).

16. Install the wiring harness clips to the fuel rail mounting studs.

17. Attach the electrical connectors to the fuel injectors.

18. Install the fuel line to the fuel rail and connect the fuel supply tube.

19. Connect the negative battery cable.

20. Pressurize the fuel system with a diagnostic scan tool and check for leaks.

FUEL PUMP

REMOVAL & INSTALLATION

See Figures 119 through 121.

1. Properly relieve the fuel system pressure.

2. Remove the air cleaner housing lid and disconnect the Intake Air Temperature (IAT) sensor and make-up air hose.

3. Remove the rear seat cushion.

4. Remove the plastic access cover.

5. Disconnect the electrical connector.

6. Matchmark the orientation of the fuel pump module to the tank before removal.

7. Using Special Tool 9340 Spanner Wrench, remove the left side module lock ring.

8. Pull the fuel pump module up and out of the tank.

✳✳ WARNING

The fuel pump module will be filled fuel. Do not spill fuel inside the vehicle.

9. Tip the fuel pump module to the side and pour any fuel back into the tank.

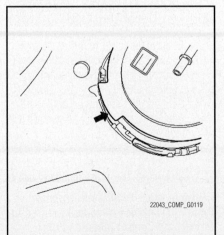

Fig. 119 Not the fuel pump location on the top of the fuel tank.

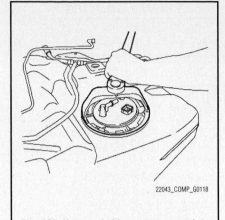

Fig. 120 Use a suitable spanner wrench to remove the lock ring of the fuel pump module.

10. Disconnect the internal line from the fuel pump module.

11. Tip the module on its side again to drain any remaining fuel from the reservoir into the tank.

12. Remove the fuel pump from the vehicle.

To install:

13. Remove the seal from the tank opening and discard.

14. Place a new seal between the tank threads and the pump module opening.

15. Connect the internal line to the fuel pump module

16. Install the module into the fuel tank.

17. Reposition the fuel pump module in the tank, aligning the matchmark made earlier.

18. While holding the fuel pump in position, install the lock ring using Special Tool 9340 Spanner Wrench.

19. Connect the electrical connector.

20. Install the plastic access cover.

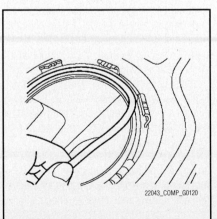

Fig. 121 Place a new seal between the tank threads and the pump module opening.

21. Install the rear seat cushion.

22. Install the air cleaner housing lid and disconnect the Intake Air Temperature (IAT) sensor and make-up air hose.

23. Connect the negative battery cable.

24. Pressurize the fuel system with a diagnostic scan tool and check for leaks.

FUEL TANK

REMOVAL & INSTALLATION

1. Properly relieve the fuel system pressure.

2. Remove the air cleaner housing lid and disconnect the Intake Air Temperature (IAT) sensor and make-up air hose.

3. Remove the rear seat cushion.

4. Remove the plastic access cover.

5. Disconnect the electrical connector and fuel lines.

6. Drain the fuel from the fuel tank.

7. Raise and safely support the vehicle.

8. If equipped with All Wheel Drive, remove the driveshaft.

9. Remove the exhaust system.

10. Remove the rear suspension stay bars.

11. If equipped with All Wheel Drive, the rear differential module must be lowered as follows:

    a. Tie the rear driveline module to the suspension crossmember.

    b. Support rear differential module with a suitable jack.

    c. Remove the three mounting bolts and lower rear differential module from the suspension crossmember

12. Remove all necessary splash shields.

13. Disconnect the vapor canister line.

14. Disconnect the filler tube recirculation vent and purge lines.

15. Disconnect the rubber fill hose from the fuel tank.

16. Remove the parking brake cable mounts from the fuel tank straps.

17. Support the fuel tank with a suitable jack and secure the fuel tank to the jack.

18. Remove the fuel tank strap mounting bolts.

19. Lower and remove the fuel tank from the vehicle.

To install:

20. Lift the fuel tank into position and install the fuel tank straps. Tighten the mounting bolts to 35 ft. lbs. (47 Nm).

➡Ensure the straps are not twisted or bent.

21. Install the parking brake cable mounts.

22. Connect the filler tube recirculation vent and purge lines.

23. Connect the fill tube to the fuel tank inlet. Tighten the hose clamp to 38 inch lbs. (4 Nm).

24. Connect the vapor canister line.

25. Raise and install the rear differential module.

26. Install the rear suspension stay bars.

27. Install the splash shields.

28. Install the exhaust system.

29. Install the driveshaft.

30. Connect the electrical connectors and fuel lines to the fuel pump module.

31. Install the plastic access cover.

32. Install the rear seat cushion.

33. Install the air cleaner housing lid and disconnect the Intake Air Temperature (IAT) sensor and make-up air hose.

34. Connect the negative battery cable.

35. Pressurize the fuel system with a diagnostic scan tool and check for leaks.

IDLE SPEED

ADJUSTMENT

The idle speed is control by the Powertrain Control Module (PCM). No adjustment is necessary or possible.

THROTTLE BODY

REMOVAL & INSTALLATION

See Figure 122.

1. Disconnect the negative battery cable.

2. Remove the engine appearance cover.

3. Remove the air intake assembly.

4. Disconnect the Intake Air Temperature (IAT) sensor and makeup air hose.

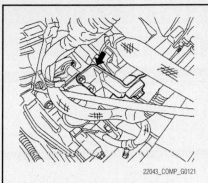

22043_COMP_G0121

Fig. 122 Remove the throttle body support bracket.

5. Disconnect the throttle body electrical connector.

6. Remove the throttle body support bracket.

7. Remove the throttle body mounting bolts.

8. Remove the throttle body assembly.

To install:

9. Ensure the throttle body O-ring is in place on the intake manifold.

10. Position the throttle body on the intake manifold alignment pins. Install, but do not tighten the mounting bolts.

11. Install the throttle body support bracket.

12. Tighten the throttle body mounting bolts in a criss-cross pattern to 80 inch lbs. (9 Nm).

13. Connect the throttle body electrical connector.

14. Install the air intake assembly.

15. Connect the IAT sensor and makeup air hose.

16. Connect the negative battery cable.

17. Install the engine appearance cover.

➡**A Scan Tool may be used to learn electrical parameters. Go to the Miscellaneous Menu, and then select ETC Relearn. If the relearn is not performed, a Diagnostic Trouble Code (DTC) will be set. If necessary, use a scan tool to erase any Diagnostic Trouble Codes (DTCs) from the Powertrain Control Module (PCM).**

HEATING & AIR CONDITIONING SYSTEM

BLOWER MOTOR

REMOVAL & INSTALLATION

See Figure 123.

1. Disconnect the negative battery cable.

2. If equipped, remove the silencer from the below the passenger side of the instrument panel.

3. From underneath of the instrument panel, disengage the connector lock and disconnect the instrument panel wiring harness connector from the blower motor.

4. Remove the three screws that secure the blower motor and wire lead bracket.

5. Remove the blower motor.

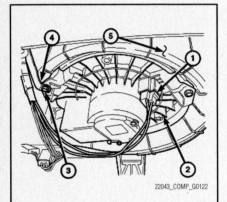

Fig. 123 Blower Motor (2) assembly—Wiring harness connector (1), Screws (3), Wire lead bracket (4), HVAC housing

To install:

6. Position the blower motor into the bottom of the HVAC housing.

7. Install the three mounting screws and tighten to 10 inch lbs. (1.2 Nm).

8. Connect the instrument panel wiring harness connector and engage the connector lock.

9. If equipped, install the silencer.

10. Connect the negative battery cable.

HEATER CORE

REMOVAL & INSTALLATION

See Figures 124 through 129.

1. Disconnect the negative battery cable.

2. Disable the air bag system.

3. Recover the refrigerant from the HVAC system.

4. Drain the cooling system.

5. Remove the heat shield located on the dash panel in the engine compartment.

6. Remove the bolt that secures the A/C liquid and suction line assembly to the A/C evaporator.

7. Disconnect the A/C liquid and suction line assembly from the A/C evaporator and remove and discard the dual-plane seals.

8. Cap the opened refrigerant line fittings and the evaporator ports.

9. Disconnect the heater hoses from the heater core tubes. Install plugs in, or tape over the opened heater core tubes to prevent coolant spillage during housing removal.

10. Remove the instrument panel as follows:

   a. Remove the floor console.

   b. Remove the shift mechanism.

   c. Remove the side cowl panels.

   d. Remove the passenger side air bag.

   e. Using a trim stick, separate the snap clips and remove the steering column opening cover.

   f. Remove the screws and remove the steering column reinforcement.

   g. Using a trim stick, remove the upper trim cover over the center bezel and radio.

   h. Remove the compass module from under the upper cover.

   i. Remove the HVAC housing-to-instrument panel screws.

   j. Disconnect the electrical connectors from the A-pillar.

   k. Remove the passenger side end cap and remove the support bolts.

   l. Remove the passenger side silencer pad.

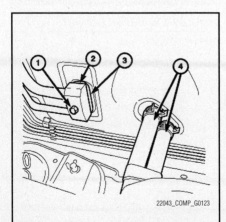

Fig. 124 Remove the bolt (1) that holds the A/C liquid and suction lines (2) to the evaporator (3). Disconnect the heater hoses and cap the open core tubes.

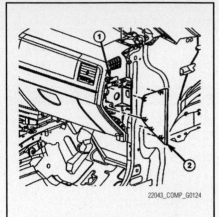

Fig. 125 Remove the passenger side end cap (2) and remove the support bolts (1)

   m. Disconnect the radio antenna.

   n. Disconnect the HVAC wiring harness connectors.

   o. Remove the fence line bolts from the upper cowl panel.

   p. Separate the center wiring harness.

   q. Disconnect the main wiring harness connectors at the driver's side cowl.

   r. Disconnect the wiring harness connectors at the driver's side A-pillar.

   s. Remove the center support bolts.

   t. Remove the end cap and remove the driver's side support bolts.

   u. Remove the instrument panel from the vehicle.

11. Remove the rear floor ducts.

12. Remove the condensation drain tube.

13. Remove the nut that secures the passenger side of the HVAC housing to the dash panel.

14. Pull the HVAC housing rearward and remove the HVAC housing assembly from the passenger compartment.

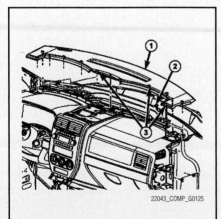

Fig. 126 Remove the fence line bolts (2) from the upper cowl panel (1)

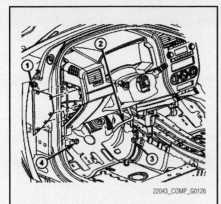

Fig. 127 Remove the center support bolts (3), end cap (1) and driver's side support bolts (4)

15. Remove the left side front floor duct.

16. Remove the foam seal from the flange located on the front of the HVAC housing.

17. Remove the screw that secures the flange to the front of the HVAC housing and remove the flange.

18. Remove the screw that secures the retaining bracket for the heater core tubes to the left side of the air distribution housing.

19. Carefully pull the heater core out of the driver's side of the air distribution housing.

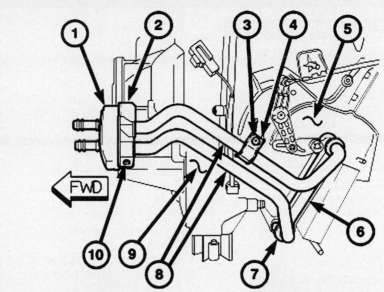

1. Foam seal
2. flange
3. screw
4. retaining bracket
5. air distribution housing
6. Heater core
8. heater core tubes
9. HVAC housing
10. screw

Fig. 129 Heater core components—Foam seal (1), flange (2), screw (3), retaining bracket (4), air distribution housing (5), Heater core (6), heater core tubes (8), HVAC housing (9), screw (10)

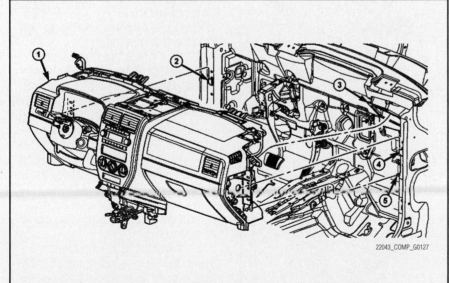

Fig. 128 Lift the instrument panel (1) off the support clips (2,4) and pins (5) to remove.

To install:

20. Carefully install the heater core into the left side of the air distribution housing.

21. Install the retaining bracket that secures the heater core tubes. Tighten the screw to 10 inch lbs. (1.2 Nm).

22. Install the flange that secures the heater core tubes to the front of the HVAC housing.

23. Tighten the screw that secures the flange to the HVAC housing to 10 inch lbs. (1.2 Nm).

24. Install the foam seal onto the flange.

25. Installation is the reverse order of the removal process.

26. If the heater core was replaced, the cooling system must be flushed.

27. Charge the refrigerant system.

28. Refill the cooling system to the correct level.

29. Start the engine and check for leaks.

STEERING

POWER STEERING GEAR

REMOVAL & INSTALLATION

See Figures 130 through 134.

1. Siphon as much power steering fluid from the pump as possible.

2. Reposition the floor carpeting to access the intermediate shaft at the base of the column.

3. Position the front wheels in the straight-ahead position.

4. Turn the steering wheel to the right until the intermediate shaft coupling bolt at the base of the steering column can be accessed.

5. Remove the coupling bolt.

➡**Do not separate the intermediate shaft from the steering gear pinion shaft at this time.**

6. Return the front wheels to the straight-ahead position.

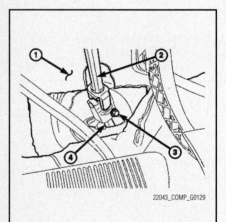

Fig. 130 Under the carpet (1), remove the coupling bolt (3) that connects the intermediate shaft (2) to the steering gear pinion shaft (4).

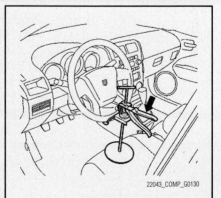

Fig. 131 Use a steering wheel holder to lock the wheel into position.

7. Use a steering wheel holder to lock the wheel into place.

8. Raise and safely support the vehicle.

9. Remove the front wheels.

10. On the side of the gear, remove the nut from the outer tie rod end at the knuckle.

11. One the side of the gear, separate the tie rod end from the knuckle using Special Tool 9360 Remover or equivalent.

12. Remove the engine skid plate, if equipped.

13. Remove the rear engine mount.

14. Remove the front engine mount through-bolt.

15. Remove the three bolts securing the heat shield to the crossmember and remove the shield.

16. Disconnect the pressure and return hoses from the steering gear.

17. Remove the fasteners that secure the power steering hose routing clamps to the crossmember.

18. Remove the bolts securing the stabilizer bushing retainers to the crossmem-

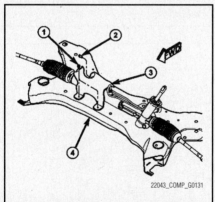

Fig. 132 Remove the bolts (1, 2) securing the heat shield (3) to the crossmember (4)

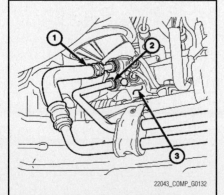

Fig. 133 Disconnect the pressure (2) and return (1) hoses from the steering gear (3)

ber and remove the stabilizer bushing retainers.

➡**Before removing the front suspension crossmember from the vehicle, the location of the crossmember must be marked on the body of the vehicle. If the front suspension crossmember is not reinstalled in exactly the same position, the preset wheel alignment settings will be lost.**

19. Matchmark the location of the front crossmember on the body near each mounting bolt.

20. Support the front crossmember with a suitable jack.

21. Remove the mounting bolts securing the crossmember to the body.

22. Lower the crossmember enough to access the intermediate shaft coupling and slide it off the pinion shaft.

23. Remove the two bolts securing the steering gear to the crossmember.

24. Rotate the sway bar up in order to access the steering gear.

25. Remove the steering gear from the crossmember.

To install:

26. Rotate the sway bar up and install the steering gear on the crossmember. Tighten the mounting bolts to 52 ft. lbs. (70 Nm).

27. Center the power steering gear rack in its travel as necessary.

28. Slowly raise the crossmember into its mounted position using a suitable jack matching the crossmember to the marked locations on the body made during removal.

29. Check the positioning of the seals at the dash panel and adjust as necessary.

30. Install the four mounting bolts (two each side) securing the front crossmember to the body and tighten the bolts to 140 ft. lbs. (190 Nm).

31. Install the retainers over the stabilizer bar cushions and tighten the bolts to 22 ft. lbs. (30 Nm).

32. Install the fasteners securing the power steering hose routing clamps to the crossmember. Use a new push clip on the left and tighten the screw on the right to 71 inch lbs. (8 Nm).

33. Install the pressure hose on the steering gear and tighten the tube nut to 24 ft. lbs. (32 Nm).

34. Install the return hose on the steering gear and tighten the tube nut to 15 ft. lbs. (20 Nm).

35. Position the heat shield on the crossmember. Tighten the two front

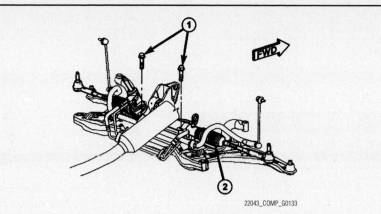

Fig. 134 Remove the mounting bolts (1) to remove the steering gear (2) from the front crossmember.

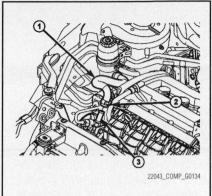

Fig. 136 Remove the hose clamp (2) and supply hose (1) from the power steering pump (3).

mounting screws to 35 inch lbs. (4 Nm) and tighten the rear mounting screw to 13 ft. lbs. (17 Nm).

36. Install the front engine mount through-bolt.

37. Install the rear engine mount.

38. If equipped, install the engine skid plate.

➡**Prior to attaching the outer tie rod end to the knuckle, inspect the tie rod seal boot. If the seal boot is damaged, replace the outer tie rod end.**

39. On each side of the steering gear, install the outer tie rod end into the hole in the knuckle arm. Start a NEW tie rod mounting nut onto the stud. While holding the tie rod end stud with a wrench, tighten the nut with a wrench or crowfoot wrench to 97 ft. lbs. (132 Nm).

40. Install the front wheels.

41. Lower the vehicle.

42. Remove the steering wheel holder.

43. Verify the front wheels of vehicle are in the straight-ahead position.

44. Center the intermediate shaft over the steering gear pinion shaft, lining up the ends, then slide the intermediate shaft onto the steering gear pinion shaft.

45. From center, rotate the steering wheel to the right approximately 90° or until the intermediate shaft coupling bolt can be easily installed.

46. Install the intermediate shaft coupling bolt and tighten to 35 ft. lbs. (47 Nm).

47. Reposition the floor carpet in place.

48. Straighten the steering wheel to straight-ahead position.

49. Fill and bleed the power steering system.

50. Start the engine and check for leaks.

51. Check and adjust the alignment as necessary.

POWER STEERING PUMP

REMOVAL & INSTALLATION

See Figures 135 and 136.

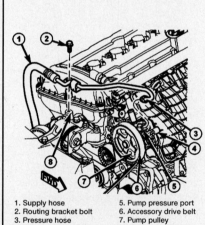

1. Supply hose
2. Routing bracket bolt
3. Pressure hose
4. Power steering pump
5. Pump pressure port
6. Accessory drive belt
7. Pump pulley
8. Upper mount

Fig. 135 Power steering pump components—Supply hose (1), routing bracket bolt (2), pressure hose (3), power steering pump (4), pump pressure port (5), accessory drive belt (6), pump pulley (7), upper mount (8).

1. Siphon as much power steering fluid from the pump as possible.

2. Remove the engine appearance cover.

3. Remove the pressure hose routing bracket bolt from the upper mount.

4. Remove the pressure hose at the pump pressure port.

5. Remove the hose clamp securing the supply hose at the pump.

6. Remove the supply hose from the pump.

7. Remove the accessory drive belt. For additional information, refer to the following

section, "Accessory drive belt, Removal & Installation."

8. Remove the three pump mounting bolts through the pulley openings.

9. Remove the power steering pump.

To install:

10. Using a lint free towel, wipe clean the open power steering pressure hose end and the power steering pump port. Replace any used O-rings with new. Lubricate the O-ring with clean power steering fluid.

11. Place the power steering pump into position and tighten the mounting bolts to 19 ft. lbs. (26 Nm).

12. Install the accessory drive belt.

13. Install the supply hose at the pump and secure the hose clamp.

14. Install the pressure hose at the pump pressure pump and tighten the tube nut to 24 ft. lbs. (32 Nm).

15. Install the pressure hose routing bracket bolt to the upper mount.

16. Fill and bleed and power steering system.

17. Start the engine and check for leaks.

18. Install the engine appearance cover.

BLEEDING

See Figure 137.

1. Check the fluid level. As measured on the side of the reservoir, the level should indicate between MAX and MIN when the fluid is at normal ambient temperature. Adjust the fluid level as necessary.

2. Tightly insert Special Tool 9688 Power Steering Cap Adapter into the mouth of the reservoir.

✳✳ CAUTION

Failure to use a vacuum pump reservoir may allow power steering fluid to be sucked into the hand vacuum pump.

3. Attach Special Tool C-4207 Hand Vacuum Pump or equivalent, with reservoir attached, to the Power Steering Cap Adapter.

> ### ⁕ WARNING
> **Do not run the engine while vacuum is applied to the power steering system. Damage to the power steering pump can occur.**

➡ **When performing the following step make sure the vacuum level is maintained during the entire time period.**

4. Using a Hand Vacuum Pump, apply 68-85 kPa (20-25 in. Hg) of vacuum to the system for a minimum of three minutes.

5. Slowly release the vacuum and remove the special tools.

6. Adjust the fluid level as necessary.

7. Repeat the process until the fluid no longer drops when vacuum is applied.

8. Start the engine and cycle the steering wheel lock-to-lock three times.

> ### ⁕⁕ WARNING
> **Do not hold the steering wheel at the stops.**

9. Stop the engine and check for leaks at all connections.

10. Check for any signs of air in the reservoir and check the fluid level. If air is present, repeat the procedure as necessary.

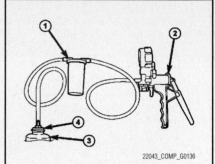

Fig. 137 Bleed the power steering system with a reservoir (1) Hand Vacuum Pump (2), Power Steering Cap Adapter (4) attached to the Power Steering Pump reservoir (3).

SUSPENSION

FRONT SUSPENSION

COIL SPRING

REMOVAL & INSTALLATION

The coil spring is part of the strut assembly.

LOWER BALL JOINT

REMOVAL & INSTALLATION

The lower ball joint is an integral part of the lower control arm and is not serviceable. If the lower ball joint fails, the lower control arm must be replaced.

LOWER CONTROL ARM

REMOVAL & INSTALLATION

See Figures 138 and 139.

1. Raise and safely support the vehicle.
2. Remove the front wheel.
3. Remove the nut and pinch bolt that secures the ball joint stud to the knuckle.

> ### ⁕ WARNING
> **Upon removing the knuckle from the ball joint stud, do not pull outward on the knuckle. Pulling the knuckle outward at this point can separate the inner CV-joint on the halfshaft, thus damaging it.**

4. Using a suitable pry tool, separate the ball joint stud from the knuckle by prying down on the lower control arm and up against the ball joint on the knuckle.

> ### ⁕ WARNING
> **Use care to not damage the ball joint seal.**

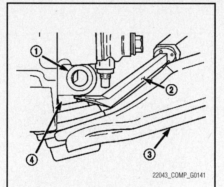

Fig. 138 Using a suitable pry tool (2), separate the ball joint stud (4) from the knuckle (1) by prying down on the lower control arm (3)

5. Remove the front bolt attaching the lower control arm to the front suspension crossmember.

6. Remove the nut on the rear bolt attaching the lower control arm to the front suspension crossmember and remove the bolt.

7. Remove the lower control arm.

To install:

8. Place the lower control arm into the front suspension crossmember.

9. Insert the rear bolt up through the crossmember and lower control arm.

10. Install, but do not fully tighten, the nut on the rear bolt attaching the lower control arm to the crossmember.

11. Install, but do not fully tighten, the front bolt attaching the lower control arm to the crossmember.

12. With no weight on the lower control arm, tighten the lower control arm rear mounting bolt nut to 135 ft. lbs. (183 Nm)

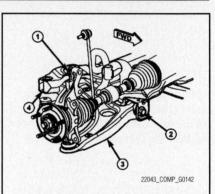

Fig. 139 Remove the front bolt (2) and nut (1) on the rear bolt that attaches the lower control arm (3) to the suspension crossmember (4) to remove the lower control arm.

and the lower control arm front pivot bolt to 135 ft. lbs. (183 Nm).

13. Install the ball joint stud into the knuckle, aligning the bolt hole in the knuckle boss with the groove formed in the side of the ball joint stud. Install a new ball joint stud pinch bolt and nut and tighten the nut to 60 ft. lbs. (82 Nm).

14. Install the front wheel.

15. Lower the vehicle.

16. Check the alignment and adjust as necessary.

MACPHERSON STRUT

REMOVAL & INSTALLATION

See Figures 140 and 141.

1. Raise and safely support the vehicle.
2. Remove the front wheel.
3. Remove the bolt securing the brake hose routing bracket to the strut assembly.

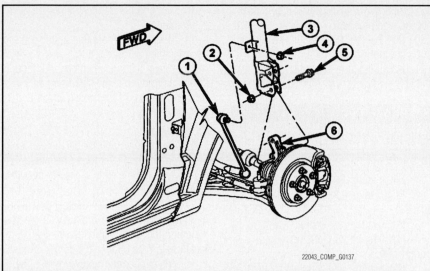

Fig. 140 Remove the nut (4) that secures the stabilizer link (1) to the strut (3). Hold the bolt heads (5) stationary while removing the nuts (2) that hold the strut (3) to the knuckle (6).

4. While holding the stabilizer bar link stud stationary, remove the nut securing the link to the strut assembly.

5. While holding the bolt heads stationary, remove the nuts from the bolts that attach the strut to the knuckle.

6. Remove the two bolts attaching the strut assembly to the knuckle using a pin punch.

➡**The bolts are serrated and cannot be turned.**

7. Remove the three nuts attaching the strut upper mount to the strut tower.

8. Remove the strut assembly from the vehicle.

To install:

9. Install the strut assembly into the strut tower. Tighten the three mounting nuts to 35 ft. lbs. (48 Nm).

10. Position the lower end of the strut assembly in line with the upper end of the knuckle. Align the holes and install the two attaching bolts. While holding the bolt heads stationary, tighten the nuts to 62 ft. lbs. (84 Nm).

11. Attach the stabilizer links to the strut and tighten the nuts to 43 ft. lbs. (58 Nm).

12. Secure the brake hose routing bracket to the strut and tighten the screws to 10 ft. lbs. (13 Nm).

13. Install the front wheels.

14. Lower the vehicle.

15. Check and adjust the alignment as necessary.

OVERHAUL

See Figures 142 and 143.

1. Position the strut assembly in the strut coil spring compressor following the manufacturer's instructions and set the lower and upper hooks of the compressor on the coil spring. Position the strut clevis bracket straight outward, away from the compressor.

2. Compress the coil spring until all coil spring tension is removed from the upper mount and bearing.

3. Once the spring is sufficiently compressed, install Strut Nut Wrench, Special Tool 9362, on the strut rod nut. Next, install Strut Shaft Socket, Special Tool 9894, on the end of the strut rod. While holding the strut rod from turning, remove the nut using the strut nut wrench.

4. Remove the clamp (if installed) from the bottom of the coil spring and remove the strut (damper) out through the bottom of the coil spring. The dust shield and jounce bumper will come out with the strut.

5. Remove the lower spring isolator from the strut seat.

6. Slide the dust shield and jounce bumper from the strut rod.

7. Remove the upper mount and bearing from the top of the upper spring seat and isolator.

8. Remove the upper spring seat and isolator from the top of the coil spring.

9. Release the tension from the coil spring by backing off the compressor drive completely. Push back the compressor hooks and remove the coil spring.

To assemble:

10. Place the coil spring in the spring compressor following the manufacturer's

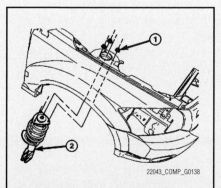

Fig. 141 Remove the three nuts (1) attaching the strut upper mount to the strut tower and remove the strut assembly (3).

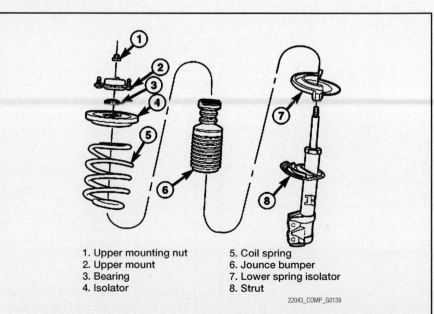

1. Upper mounting nut
2. Upper mount
3. Bearing
4. Isolator
5. Coil spring
6. Jounce bumper
7. Lower spring isolator
8. Strut

Fig. 142 Strut assembly components—Upper mounting nut (1), Upper mount (2), Bearing (3), Isolator (4), Coil spring (5), Jounce bumper (6), Lower spring isolator (7), Strut (8).

instructions. Before compressing the spring, rotate the spring so the end of the bottom coil is at approximately the 9 o'clock position as viewed from above (or to where the spring was when removed from the compressor). This action will allow the strut (damper) clevis bracket to be positioned outward, away from the compressor once installed.

11. Slowly compress the coil spring until enough room is available for strut assembly reassembly.

12. Install the upper spring seat and isolator on top of the coil spring.

13. Install the bearing and upper mount on top of the upper spring seat and isolator.

14. Install the lower spring isolator on the spring seat on the strut.

15. Slide the dust shield and jounce bumper onto the strut rod.

16. Install the strut up through the bottom of the coil spring and upper spring seat, mount, and bearing until the lower spring seat contacts the lower end of the coil spring. Rotate the strut as necessary until the end of the bottom coil comes in contact with the stop built into the lower spring isolator.

17. While holding the strut in position, install the nut on the end of the strut rod.

18. Install Special Tool 9632 Strut Nut Wrench on the strut rod nut. Next, install Special Tool 9894 Strut Shaft Socket on the end of the strut rod. While holding the strut rod from turning, tighten the strut rod nut to 44 ft. lbs. (60 Nm) using a torque wrench on the end of Special Tool 9362.

19. Slowly release the tension from the coil spring by backing off the compressor drive completely. As the tension is relieved, make sure the upper mount and bearing

align properly. Verify the upper mount does not bind when rotated.

20. Remove the strut assembly from the spring compressor.

21. Install the strut assembly on the vehicle

STABILIZER BAR

REMOVAL & INSTALLATION

See Figure 144.

1. Raise and safely support the vehicle.
2. Remove the engine skid plate, if equipped.
3. Remove the rear engine mount.
4. Remove the front engine mount through-bolt.
5. Remove the fasteners that secure the power steering hose clamps to the front suspension crossmember.
6. At each of the stabilizer bar, hold the stabilizer bar link lower stud stationary and remove the nut securing the link to the stabilizer bar.
7. Remove the bolts securing the stabilizer bar bushing retainers to the front suspension crossmember.
8. Remove the two stabilizer bushing retainers.

➡**Before removing the front suspension crossmember from the vehicle, the location of the crossmember must be marked on the body of the vehicle. If the front suspension crossmember is not reinstalled in exactly the same position, the preset wheel alignment settings will be lost.**

9. Matchmark the location of the front crossmember on the body near each mounting bolt.

10. Support the front crossmember with a suitable jack.

11. Remove the mounting bolts securing the crossmember to the body.

12. Lower the crossmember until there is clearance to remove the stabilizer bar between the rear of the crossmember and the body.

To install:

13. Install the stabilizer bar, link ends first, from the rear over top of the crossmember. Curve the ends of the bar over the steering gear.

14. Slowly raise the crossmember into its mounted position using a suitable jack matching the crossmember to the marked locations on the body made during removal.

15. Install the four mounting bolts (two each side) securing the front crossmember to the body and tighten the bolts to 140 ft. lbs. (190 Nm).

16. Install the retainers over the stabilizer bar cushions and tighten the bolts to 22 ft. lbs. (30 Nm).

17. Attach the stabilizer bar link at each end of the stabilizer bar. Tighten the nuts to 43 ft. lbs. (58 Nm).

18. Install the fasteners securing the power steering hose routing clamps to the crossmember. Use a new push clip on the left and tighten the screw on the right to 71 inch lbs. (8 Nm).

19. Install the rear engine mount.

20. Install the front engine mount through-bolt.

21. Install the engine skid plate, if equipped.

22. Lower the vehicle.

23. Check and adjust the alignment as necessary.

STEERING KNUCKLE

REMOVAL & INSTALLATION

1. Raise and safely support the vehicle.
2. Remove the front wheel.
3. Remove the cotter pin from the hub nut.
4. With an assistant applying the brakes to keep the hub from rotating, remove the hub nut and washer from the axle shaft.
5. Remove the brake rotor.
6. Remove the routing clip (1) securing wheel speed sensor cable to the knuckle (4).
7. Remove the wheel speed sensor.
8. Remove the nut attaching the outer tie rod to the knuckle. To do this, hold the tie rod end stud with a wrench while loosening and removing the nut with a standard wrench or crowfoot wrench.

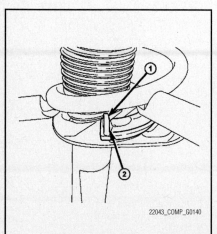

22043_COMP_G0140

Fig. 143 Rotate the strut until the end of the bottom coil (2) comes in contact with the stop (1).

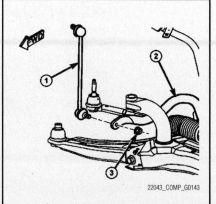

22043_COMP_G0143

Fig. 144 Hold the stabilizer bar link (1) lower stud stationary and remove the nut (3) that secures the link to the stabilizer bar (2).

9. Release the outer tie rod end from the knuckle using Special Tool 9360 Ball Joint Remover.

10. Remove the outer tie rod from the knuckle.

11. Remove the nut and pinch bolt clamping the ball joint stud to the knuckle.

➡**The strut assembly-to-knuckle attaching bolts are serrated and must not be turned during removal.**

12. While holding the bolt heads stationary, remove the two nuts from the bolts attaching the strut to the knuckle.

13. Remove the two bolts attaching the strut to the knuckle using a pin punch.

❊❊ WARNING

Use care when separating the ball joint stud from the knuckle, so the ball joint seal does not get cut.

14. Using a suitable pry tool, separate the ball joint stud from the knuckle by prying down on lower control arm and up against the ball joint boss on the knuckle.

❊❊ WARNING

Do not allow the half shaft to hang by the inner CV-joint. It must be supported to keep the joint from separating during this operation.

15. Pull the knuckle off the half shaft outer CV-joint splines and remove the knuckle from the vehicle.

To install:

16. Slide the hub of the knuckle onto the splines of the halfshaft outer CV-joint.

17. Install the knuckle onto the ball joint stud aligning the bolt hole in the knuckle boss with the groove formed into the side of the ball joint stud.

18. Install a new ball joint stud pinch bolt and nut. Tighten the nut to 60 ft. lbs. (82 Nm).

19. Position the lower end of the strut assembly in line with the upper end of the knuckle, aligning the mounting holes. Install the two mounting bolts. Install the nuts on the two bolts and tighten the nuts to 62 ft. lbs. (84 Nm).

20. Install the outer tie rod ball stud into the hole in the knuckle arm. Start the tie rod end-to-knuckle nut onto the stud. While holding the tie rod end stud with a wrench, tighten the nut with a wrench or crowfoot wrench to 97 ft. lbs. (132 Nm).

21. Install the wheel speed sensor.

22. Install the routing clip securing the wheel speed sensor cable to the knuckle.

23. Install the brake rotor, disc brake caliper and adapter.

24. Clean all foreign matter from the threads of the halfshaft outer CV-joint.

25. Install the washer and hub nut on the end of the halfshaft and snug it.

26. Have an assistant apply the brakes to keep the hub from rotating and tighten the hub nut to 181 ft. lbs. (245 Nm.

27. Insert the cotter pin through the notches in the nut and the hole in halfshaft. If the notches in the nut do not line up with the hole in the halfshaft, continue to tighten the nut until they do. Do not loosen the nut.

28. Wrap the cotter pin ends tightly around the lock nut.

29. Install the front wheel.

30. Lower the vehicle.

31. Check the alignment and adjust as necessary.

WHEEL BEARINGS

REMOVAL & INSTALLATION
See Figures 145 through 149.

1. Raise and safely support the vehicle.
2. Remove the front wheel.
3. Remove the steering knuckle assembly from the vehicle.
4. Position the locator block for Special Tool 9712 Fixture, as follows:

a. For left side knuckles, place the locator block to the left side on the Fixture. The side of the locator block with the angle cut goes downward, toward the Fixture. Install the mounting screws and tighten them to approximately 40 ft. lbs. (54 Nm).

b. For right side knuckles, place the locator block to the right side on the Fixture. The side of the locator block with the angle cut goes downward, toward the Fixture. Install the mounting screws and tighten them to approximately 40 ft. lbs. (54 Nm).

5. Install the knuckle in the Fixture as shown, guiding the steering arm to rest on the locator block and the brake caliper mounting bosses on the two Fixture pins.

6. Place the Fixture with knuckle installed into an arbor press.

7. Position Special Tool 9712-2 Remover/Installer in the small end of the hub. Lower the arbor press ram and remove the hub from the wheel bearing and knuckle. The bearing race will normally come out of the wheel bearing with the hub as it is pressed out of the bearing.

8. Remove the knuckle from the Fixture and turn it over.

9. Remove the snap ring from the knuckle using an appropriate pair of snap ring pliers.

10. Place the knuckle back in the Fixture in the arbor press ram.

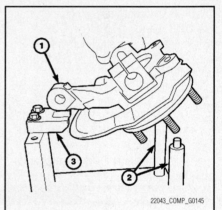
22043_COMP_G0145

Fig. 146 Install the knuckle in the Fixture as shown, guiding the steering arm (1) to rest on the locator block (3) and the brake caliper mounting bosses on the two Fixture pins (2).

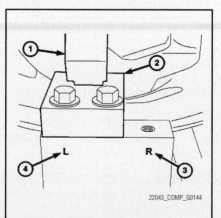
22043_COMP_G0144

Fig. 145 Install the locator block (2) on Special Tool 9712 (1) for the left (4) or right (3) side knuckle as shown.

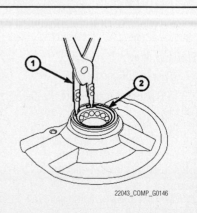
22043_COMP_G0146

Fig. 147 Remove the snap ring (2) from the knuckle using an appropriate pair of snap ring pliers (1).

11. Place Special Tool MD-998334 Installer on the outer race of the wheel bearing. Lower the arbor press ram and remove the wheel bearing from the knuckle.

To install:

12. Wipe the bearing bore of the knuckle clean of any grease or dirt.

13. Place the knuckle in an arbor press supporting the knuckle from underneath using Special Tool 6310-1 Cup.

14. Place the NEW wheel bearing magnetic encoder ring side down into the bore of the knuckle. Be sure the wheel bearing is placed squarely into the bore.

15. Place Special Tool 8498 Receiver, larger inside diameter end down, over the outer race of the wheel bearing.

16. Place Special Tool 6310-2 Disc, into the top of Receiver 8498. Lower the arbor press ram and press the wheel bearing into the knuckle until it is bottomed in the bore of the knuckle.

17. Remove the knuckle and tools from the arbor press.

18. Install a new snap ring in the knuckle using an appropriate pair of snap ring pliers.

19. Place the knuckle in an arbor press. Support the knuckle from underneath using Special Tool MB-990799 Remover/Installer, with the smaller end up against the wheel bearing inner race.

20. Place the hub in the wheel bearing

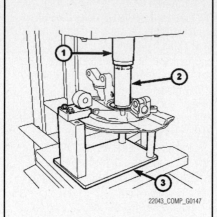

Fig. 148 Put the knuckle assembly back into the fixture (3) and place Special Tool MD-998334 Installer (2) on the outer race of the wheel bearing. Lower the arbor press ram (1) and remove the wheel bearing from the knuckle.

making sure it is square with the bearing inner race.

21. Position Special Tool 9712-2 Remover/Installer in the end of the hub. Lower the arbor press ram and press the hub into the wheel bearing until it bottoms out.

22. Remove the knuckle and tools from the press.

23. Verify the hub turns smoothly without rubbing or binding.

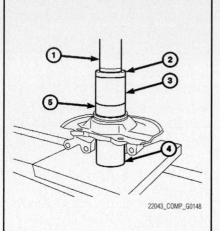

Fig. 149 With knuckle installed on top of Special Tool 6310-1 (4), use a suitable shop press (1) and Special Tools 6310-2 (2) and 8498 (3) to press the new wheel bearing (5) into the knuckle.

24. Install the knuckle on the vehicle

25. Check the alignment and adjust as necessary.

ADJUSTMENT

The wheel bearing is designed to last for the life of the vehicle and is unable to be adjusted. If the wheel bearing exhibits any roughness or resistance to rotation, the bearing must be replaced.

SUSPENSION

COIL SPRING

REMOVAL & INSTALLATION

The coil spring is part of the strut assembly.

CONTROL LINKS

REMOVAL & INSTALLATION

Trailing Arm

See Figures 150 through 152.

1. Raise and safely support the vehicle.

2. Remove the rear wheel.

3. Remove the screws that secures the brake hose to the trailing arm.

4. Remove the nut that secures the brake line routing bracket to the trailing arm. Remove the brake line from the routing bracket.

5. Remove the brake caliper and adapter as an assembly. Secure the caliper assembly out of the way.

✳ WARNING

Do not let the caliper assembly hang by the brake hose.

6. If equipped, remove the wheel speed sensor.

7. Remove the brake rotor.

8. Remove the hub and bearing assembly.

9. Remove the parking brake cable from the lever of the parking brake shoe.

10. Remove the hair pin securing the parking brake cable to the brake support plate.

11. Slide the brake support plate with parking brake shoes off the end of the parking brake cable and remove.

12. Pull the parking brake cable from the trailing arm.

13. Remove the bolt securing the lower control arm to the trailing arm.

14. Remove the bolt securing the upper control arm to the trailing arm.

15. Remove the bolts holding the

REAR SUSPENSION

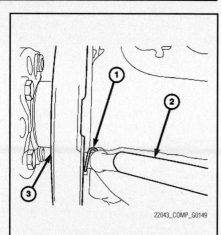

Fig. 150 Remove the hair pin (1) securing the parking brake cable (2) to the brake support plate (3)—Trailing Arm removal

leading end of the trailing arm to the body and remove the trailing arm.

To install:

16. Position the trailing arm and install the two bolts holding the leading end of the

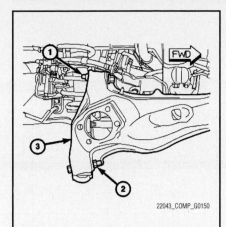

Fig. 151 Remove the nut (2) securing the lower control arm and nut (1) securing the upper control arm to the trailing arm (3)

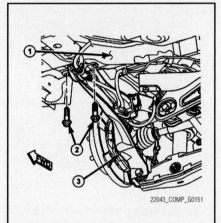

Fig. 152 Remove the two bolts (2) fastening the leading end of the trailing arm (3) to the body (1)

trailing arm to the body. Tighten to 81 ft. lbs. (110 Nm).

17. Install the upper control arm to the trailing arm and tighten the bolt to 70 ft. lbs. (95 Nm).

18. Install the lower control arm to the trailing arm and tighten the bolt to 70 ft. lbs. (95 Nm).

19. Install the bolt securing the toe link to the trailing arm. It may be necessary to flex the trailing arm body mount bushing inward or outward using a suitable pry tool. Tighten the mounting bolts to 70 ft. lbs. (95 Nm).

20. Insert the parking brake cable through the trailing link from the inboard side.

21. Slide the parking brake cable into the brake support plate with parking brake shoes.

22. Install the hair pin securing the parking brake cable to the brake support plate.

23. Attach the parking brake cable onto the lever on the parking brake shoe.

24. Install the wheel speed sensor, if equipped.

25. Install the hub and bearing.

26. Install the brake rotor.

27. Install the caliper assembly and tighten the mounting bolts to 52 ft. lbs. (71 Nm).

28. Position the brake line on the trailing arm, inserting the routing clip and routing bracket over the welded stud. Tighten the nut on the welded stud to 11 ft. lbs. (15 Nm).

29. Position the brake hose on the trailing arm bracket and tighten the mounting bolts to 17 ft. lbs. (23 Nm).

30. Install the rear wheel.

31. Lower the vehicle.

32. Check and adjust the alignment as necessary.

Toe Link

See Figure 153.

1. Raise and safely support the vehicle.

2. Remove the bolt that secures the toe link to the trailing arm.

3. Matchmark the position of the cam bolt on the crossmember.

4. While holding the cam bolt head stationary, remove the toe link mounting cam bolt nut and washer. Remove the cam bolt.

5. Remove the toe link.

To install:

➡**When installing the cam bolt (3) and washer make sure the cams stay inside the abutments built into the crossmember**

6. Install the toe link into position. Install the cam bolt from the front through crossmember and link. Match the cam to

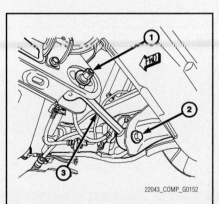

Fig. 153 Remove the bolt (2) that secures the toe link (3) to the trailing arm. Mark the position of the cam bolt (1) on the crossmember.

the marks made during the removal process. Only hand-tighten the nut at this time.

7. Install the bolt that secures the toe link to the trailing arm. It may be necessary to flex the trailing arm body mount bushing inward or outward using a suitable pry tool. Do not tighten the bolt at this time.

8. Lower the vehicle.

9. Tighten the toe link mounting bolt at the trailing arm to 70 ft. lbs. (95 Nm).

10. Check and adjust the alignment as necessary.

11. Once the rear toe is set, hold the cam bolt head stationary and tighten the toe link cam mounting bolt nut to 26 ft. lbs. (35 Nm).

LOWER CONTROL ARM

REMOVAL & INSTALLATION

See Figure 154.

1. Raise and safely support the vehicle.

2. Remove the rear wheel.

3. Hold the stabilizer bar link lower stud stationary and remove the nut securing the link to the lower control arm.

4. Remove the lower strut assembly nut and bolt.

5. Remove the stay brace.

6. Remove the bolt securing the lower control arm to the trailing arm.

7. Remove the bolt securing the lower control arm to the crossmember.

8. Remove the lower control arm.

To install:

9. Install the lower control arm to crossmember, install the nut and bolt but do not tighten.

10. Install the lower control arm to the trailing arm, install the nut and bolt but do not tighten.

11. Install the stay brace on the crossmember and tighten the mounting bolts to 18 ft. lbs. (25 Nm).

12. Install the mounting bolt holding the strut assembly to the lower control arm ,but do not tighten.

➡**When attaching a stabilizer bar link to the lower control arm it is important that the lower mounting stud be positioned properly. The lower mounting stud on the right side link needs to point toward the rear of the vehicle when inserted through the lower control arm mounting flange. The left side link lower stud needs to point toward the front of the vehicle.**

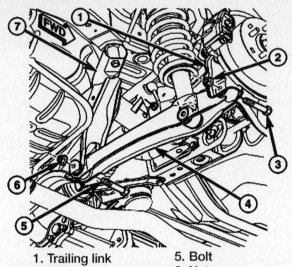

1. Trailing link
2. Nut
3. Bolt
4. Lower control arm
5. Bolt
6. Nut
7. Crossmember

22043_COMP_G0153

Fig. 154 Remove the nut (2) and bolt (3) securing the lower control arm (4) to the trailing link (1) and remove the nut (6) and bolt (5) securing the lower control arm (4) to the crossmember (7).

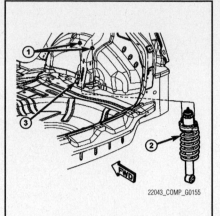

22043_COMP_G0155

Fig. 156 Remove the two nuts (1) securing the shock assembly (2) to the body bracket (3)—Rear strut assembly

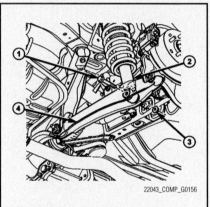

22043_COMP_G0156

Fig. 157 Remove the strut assembly (2) lower mounting nut (3) and bolt (1) from the lower control arm (4)—Rear strut assembly

13. Connect the stabilizer bar links to the lower control arm and tighten the nut to 43 ft. lbs. (58 Nm).

14. Install the rear wheel.

15. Lower the vehicle.

16. Tighten the lower control arm mounting bolt nut at the crossmember to 70 ft. lbs. (95 Nm).

17. Tighten the lower control arm mounting bolt nut at the trailing link to 70 ft. lbs. (95 Nm).

18. Tighten the strut assembly lower mounting bolt nut to 73 ft. lbs. (99 Nm).

19. Check and adjust the alignment as necessary.

STRUT & SPRING ASSEMBLY

REMOVAL & INSTALLATION

See Figures 155 through 157.

1. Remove the cargo floor cover.

2. Remove the rear floor pan silencer.

3. If equipped, remove the nuts mounting the satellite receiver or amplifier to the rear floor pan. Move the component aside to allow access to the wheel speed sensor wiring connector through the opening in bottom of the quarter trim panel.

4. Remove the spare tire.

5. Fold the strut assembly upper mounting nut access door upward. Use this opening and the one created when the rear floor pan silencer was removed to access the upper mounting nuts.

6. Remove the two nuts securing the strut assembly to the body bracket.

7. Raise and safely support the vehicle.

8. Remove the rear wheel.

9. Remove the lower strut assembly mounting bolt.

10. Lower the strut assembly out of the body bracket and lift out over the rear suspension.

To install:

11. Insert the lower end of the strut assembly down through the lower control arm from above, just enough to clear the body, then lift it into position in the body bracket.

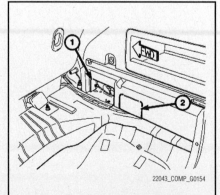

22043_COMP_G0154

Fig. 155 Use the upper mounting nut access door (2) and opening from the floor pan silencer (1) to access the strut upper mounting nuts—Rear strut assembly

12. Install the mounting bolt at the lower control arm, but do not tighten.

13. Install the rear wheel.

14. Lower the vehicle.

15. Install the two upper mounting nuts to the strut assembly and tighten to 35 ft. lbs. (48 Nm).

16. Close the upper mounting nut access door.

17. If equipped, install the satellite receiver or amplifier to the rear floor pan.

18. Install the rear floor pan silencer.

19. Install the cargo floor cover.

20. Tighten the lower strut assembly mounting bolt to 73 ft. lbs. (99 Nm).

UPPER CONTROL ARM

REMOVAL & INSTALLATION

See Figure 158.

1. Raise and safely support the vehicle.

2. Remove the rear wheel.

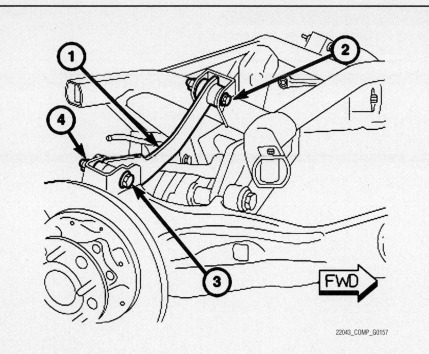

Fig. 158 Remove the nut (4) and bolt (3) securing the upper control arm (1) to the trailing arm and remove the bolt (2) securing the upper control arm (1) to the crossmember—Rear upper control arm

3. Remove the bolt securing the upper control arm to the trailing arm.
4. Remove the bolt securing the upper control arm to the crossmember.
5. Remove the upper control arm.

To install:

6. Install the upper control arm and install the bolt securing the arm to the crossmember, but do not tighten.
7. Install bolt securing the upper control arm to the trailing arm, but do not tighten.
8. Install the rear wheel.
9. Lower the vehicle.
10. Tighten the upper control arm mounting bolt at the crossmember to 70 ft. lbs. (95 Nm).
11. Tighten the upper control arm mounting bolt at the trailing arm to 70 ft. lbs. (95 Nm).
12. Check and adjust the alignment as necessary.

WHEEL BEARINGS

REMOVAL & INSTALLATION

Front Wheel Drive

See Figure 159.

1. Raise and safely support the vehicle.
2. Remove the rear wheel.
3. Remove the brake caliper lower guide pin bolt.

4. Rotate the caliper upward, using the top guide bolt as a hinge. Hang the caliper assembly with mechanics wire or equivalent.
5. Remove any clips on the wheel mounting studs holding the rotor into place, and remove the rotor.
6. Remove the wheel speed sensor, if equipped.
7. Remove the bolts holding the hub and bearing assembly to the trailing arm.
8. Remove the hub and bearing assembly.

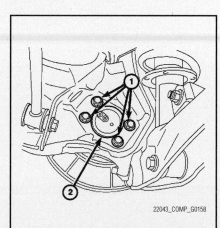

Fig. 159 Remove the four bolts (1) securing the hub and bearing (2) to the trailing arm—Rear wheel bearings

To install:

9. Install the hub and bearing assembly on the brake support plate and trailing arm. Tighten the bolts to 77 ft. lbs. (105 Nm).
10. Install the wheel speed sensor, if equipped.
11. Slide the brake rotor over the parking brake shoes and onto the wheel hub.
12. Rotate the caliper assembly downward over the rotor into the caliper adapter bracket.
13. Install the lower guide pin bolt and tighten to 32 ft. lbs. (43 Nm).
14. Install the rear wheel.
15. Lower the vehicle.
16. Pump the brake pedal several times to ensure the vehicle has a firm pedal.

All Wheel Drive

1. Raise and safely support the vehicle.
2. Remove the rear wheel.
3. Remove the cotter pin from the end of the hub nut.
4. With an assistant applying the brakes to keep the hub from rotating, remove the hub nut and washer from the end of the axle shaft.
5. Tap the end of the half shaft inward, loosening it from the hub and bearing assembly.
6. Remove the brake caliper lower guide pin bolt.
7. Rotate the caliper upward, using the top guide bolt as a hinge. Hang the caliper assembly with mechanics wire or equivalent.
8. Remove any clips on the wheel mounting studs holding the rotor into place, and remove the rotor.
9. Remove the wheel speed sensor, if equipped.
10. Remove the bolts holding the hub and bearing assembly to the trailing arm.
11. Remove the hub and bearing assembly.

To install:

12. Slide the hub and bearing assembly over the axle shaft and position it on the brake support plate and trailing arm. Tighten the bolts to 77 ft. lbs. (105 Nm).
13. Install the wheel speed sensor, if equipped.
14. Slide the brake rotor over the parking brake shoes and onto the wheel hub.
15. Rotate the caliper assembly downward over the rotor into the caliper adapter bracket.
16. Install the lower guide pin bolt and tighten to 32 ft. lbs. (43 Nm).
17. Install the washer and hub nut on the end of the halfshaft and hand tighten it.

18. With an assistant applying the brakes to keep the hub from rotating, tighten the hub nut to 181 ft. lbs. (245 Nm).

19. Install the cotter pin through the notches of the nut and the hole in the half shaft. If the notches do not line up with the hole in the axle shaft, continue tighten the nut until they do.

❊❊ WARNING

Do not loosen the nut to get the hole to line up.

20. Wrap the cotter pin tightly around the lock nut.
21. Install the rear wheel.
22. Lower the vehicle.

23. Pump the brake pedal several times to ensure the vehicle has a firm pedal.

ADJUSTMENT

The wheel bearing is designed to last for the life of the vehicle and is unable to be adjusted. If the wheel bearing exhibits any roughness or resistance to rotation, the bearing must be replaced.

SPECIFICATIONS AND MAINTENANCE CHARTS

ENGINE AND VEHICLE IDENTIFICATION

		Engine							Model Year	
Code	Liters (cc)	Cu. In.	Cyl.	Fuel Sys.	Engine Type	Eng. Mfg.			Code ①	Year
L	3.2 (3199)	195	6	MFI	SOHC	Chrysler			5	2005
N ②	3.2 (3199)	195	6	MFI	SOHC	Chrysler			6	2006
									7	2007
									8	2008

MFI: Multi-point Fuel Injection

SOHC: Single Overhead Camshaft

① 10th digit of the Vehicle Identification Number (VIN)

② Supercharged

22043_CSFR_C0001

GENERAL ENGINE SPECIFICATIONS

Year	Model	Engine Displacement Liters (VIN)	Net Horsepower @ rpm	Net Torque @ rpm (ft. lbs.)	Bore x Stroke (in.)	Compression Ratio	Oil Pressure @ rpm
2005	Crossfire	3.2 (L)	215@5700	230@3000	3.54x3.31	10.0:1	45-105@3000
		3.2 (N)	330@6100	310@3500	3.54x3.31	9.0:1	45-105@3000
2006	Crossfire	3.2 (L)	215@5700	230@3000	3.54x3.31	10.0:1	45-105@3000
		3.2 (N)	330@6100	310@3500	3.54x3.31	9.0:1	45-105@3000
2007	Crossfire	3.2 (L)	215@5700	230@3000	3.54x3.31	10.0:1	45-105@3000
2008	Crossfire	3.2 (L)	215@5700	230@3000	3.54x3.31	10.0:1	45-105@3000

22043_CSFR_C0002

ENGINE TUNE-UP SPECIFICATIONS

Year	Engine Displacement Liters (VIN)	Spark Plug Gap (in.)	Ignition Timing (deg.) MT	AT	Fuel Pump (psi)	Idle Speed (rpm) MT	AT	Valve Clearance In.	Ex.
2005	3.2 (L)	0.040	①	①	54-60	①	①	HYD	HYD
	3.2 (N)	0.040	①	①	54-60	①	①	HYD	HYD
2006	3.2 (L)	0.040	①	①	54-60	①	①	HYD	HYD
	3.2 (N)	0.040	①	①	54-60	①	①	HYD	HYD
2007	3.2 (L)	0.040	①	①	54-60	①	①	HYD	HYD
2008	3.2 (L)	0.040	①	①	54-60	①	①	HYD	HYD

NOTE: The Vehicle Emission Control Information label reflects specification changes made during production and must be used if differnent from this chart.

HYD: Hydraulic

① The basic setting is controlled by the PCM and is not adjustable

22043_CSFR_C0003

CAPACITIES

Year	Model	Engine Displacement Liters (VIN)	Engine Oil with Filter	Transmission (pts.) 6-Spd	Transmission (pts.) Auto	Drive Axle Front (pts.)	Drive Axle Rear (pts.)	Fuel Tank (gal.)	Cooling System (qts.)
2005	Crossfire	3.2 (L)	8.5	3.8	17.0	—	2.8	15.8	11.8
		3.2 (N)	8.5	3.8	17.0	—	2.8	15.8	15.3
2006	Crossfire	3.2 (L)	8.5	3.8	17.0	—	2.8	15.8	11.8
		3.2 (N)	8.5	3.8	17.0	—	2.8	15.8	15.3
2007	Crossfire	3.2 (L)	8.5	3.8	17.0	—	2.8	15.8	11.8
2008	Crossfire	3.2 (L)	8.5	3.8	17.0	—	2.8	15.8	11.8

22043_CSFR_C0004

FLUID SPECIFICATIONS

Year	Model	Engine Displacement Liters (cc)	Engine ID/VIN	Engine Oil	Auto. Trans.	Drive Axle	Power Steering Fluid	Brake Master Cylinder
2005	Crossfire	3.2 (3231)	L	①	②	80W-90	③	DOT 4
		3.2 (3231)	N	①	②	80W-90	③	DOT 4
2006	Crossfire	3.2 (3231)	L	①	②	80W-90	③	DOT 4
		3.2 (3231)	N	①	②	80W-90	③	DOT 4
2007	Crossfire	3.2 (3231)	L	①	②	80W-90	③	DOT 4
2008	Crossfire	3.2 (3231)	L	①	②	80W-90	③	DOT 4

DOT: Department Of Transpotation

① See owners manual. Synthetic SAE 0W-40 or SAE 5W-40 may be used.

② Mopar part number 05127382AA. Synthetic Dexron III may be substituted.

③ Mopar part number 05127381AA. System filled at factory with Pentosin CHF 11S.

22043_CSFR_C0016

VALVE SPECIFICATIONS

Year	Engine Displacement Liters (VIN)	Seat Angle (deg.)	Face Angle (deg.)	Spring Test Pressure (lbs. @ in.)	Spring Installed Height (in.)	Stem-to-Guide Clearance (in.) Intake	Stem-to-Guide Clearance (in.) Exhaust	Stem Diameter (in.) Intake	Stem Diameter (in.) Exhaust
2005	3.2 (L)	45	45+/-1.5	NA	NA	NA	NA	0.2740	0.2740
	3.2 (N)	45	45+/-1.5	NA	NA	NA	NA	0.2740	0.2740
2006	3.2 (L)	45	45+/-1.5	NA	NA	NA	NA	0.2740	0.2740
	3.2 (N)	45	45+/-1.5	NA	NA	NA	NA	0.2740	0.2740
2007	3.2 (L)	45	45+/-1.5	NA	NA	NA	NA	0.2740	0.2740
2008	3.2 (L)	45	45+/-1.5	NA	NA	NA	NA	0.2740	0.2740

NA: Information not available

22043_CSFR_C0006

CAMSHAFT SPECIFICATIONS
All measurements are given in inches.

Year	Engine Displ. Liters	Engine VIN	Journal Dia.	Brg. Oil Clearance	Shaft End-play	Runout	Lobe Height Intake	Exhaust
2005	3.2	L	NA	NA	NA	NA	①	①
	3.2	N	NA	NA	NA	NA	①	①
2006	3.2	L	NA	NA	NA	NA	①	①
	3.2	N	NA	NA	NA	NA	①	①
2007	3.2	L	NA	NA	NA	NA	①	①
2008	3.2	L	NA	NA	NA	NA	①	①

NA: Information not available

① Standard value is 0.001, wear limit is 0.010 inch

22043_CSFR_C0015

CRANKSHAFT AND CONNECTING ROD SPECIFICATIONS
All measurements are given in inches.

Year	Engine Displacement Liters (VIN)	Main Brg. Journal Dia.	Main Brg. Oil Clearance	Shaft End-play	Thrust on No.	Journal Diameter	Oil Clearance	Side Clearance
2005	3.2 (L)	NA	①	NA	3	NA	0.0010-0.0020	NA
	3.2 (N)	NA	①	NA	3	NA	0.0010-0.0020	NA
2006	3.2 (L)	NA	①	NA	3	NA	0.0010-0.0020	NA
	3.2 (N)	NA	①	NA	3	NA	0.0010-0.0020	NA
2007	3.2 (L)	NA	①	NA	3	NA	0.0010-0.0020	NA
2008	3.2 (L)	NA	①	NA	3	NA	0.0010-0.0020	NA

NA: Information not available

① Radial: 0.0010-0.0020 Axial: 0.0030-0.0100

22043_CSFR_C0005

PISTON AND RING SPECIFICATIONS
All measurements are given in inches

Year	Engine Displacement Liters (VIN)	Piston Clearance	Ring Gap Top Compression	Bottom Compression	Oil Control	Ring Side Clearance Top Compression	Bottom Compression	Oil Control
2005	3.2 (L)	NA	0.0070-0.0130	0.0070-0.0150	NA	NA	NA	NA
	3.2 (N)	NA	0.0070-0.0130	0.0070-0.0150	NA	NA	NA	NA
2006	3.2 (L)	NA	0.0070-0.0130	0.0070-0.0150	NA	NA	NA	NA
	3.2 (N)	NA	0.0070-0.0130	0.0070-0.0150	NA	NA	NA	NA
2007	3.2 (L)	NA	0.0070-0.0130	0.0070-0.0150	NA	NA	NA	NA
2008	3.2 (L)	NA	0.0070-0.0130	0.0070-0.0150	NA	NA	NA	NA

NA: Information not available

22043_CSFR_C0007

TORQUE SPECIFICATIONS
All readings in ft. lbs.

Year	Engine Displacement Liters (VIN)	Cylinder Head Bolts	Main Bearing Bolts	Rod Bearing Bolts	Crankshaft Damper Bolts	Flywheel Bolts	Manifold		Spark Plugs	Oil Pan Drain Plug
							Intake	Exhaust		
2005	3.2 (L)	①	②	③	④	⑤	15	26	21	22
	3.2 (N)	①	②	③	④	⑤	15	26	21	22
2006	3.2 (L)	①	②	③	④	⑤	15	26	21	22
	3.2 (N)	①	②	③	④	⑤	15	26	21	22
2007	3.2 (L)	①	②	③	④	⑤	15	26	21	22
2008	3.2 (L)	①	②	③	④	⑤	15	26	21	22

① Step 1: 7 ft. lbs.
Step 2: 22 ft. lbs.
Step 3: 90 degrees
Step 4: 90 degrees

② M8 Bolt
Step 1: 15 ft. lbs.
Step 2: plus 90 degres
M10 bolt
Step 1: 22 ft. lbs.
Step 2: plus 90 degres

③ Step 1: 44 inch lbs.
Step 2: 18 ft. lbs.
Step 3: 90 degrees
④ Step 1: 148 ft. lbs.
Step 2: 90 degrees

⑤ Step 1: 33 ft. lbs.
Step 2: 90 degrees

22043_CSFR_C0008

WHEEL ALIGNMENT

Year	Model		Caster Range (+/-Deg.)	Caster Preferred Setting (Deg.)	Camber Range (+/-Deg.)	Camber Preferred Setting (Deg.)	Toe-in (in.)
2005	Crossfire	F	—	5.20	0.33	-1.22	0.16 +/- 0.12
		R	—	—	—	-1.13	—
2006	Crossfire	F	—	5.20	0.33	-1.22	0.16 +/- 0.12
		R	—	—	—	-1.13	—
2007	Crossfire	F	—	5.20	0.33	-1.22	0.16 +/- 0.12
		R	—	—	—	-1.13	—
2008	Crossfire	F	—	5.20	0.33	-1.22	0.16 +/- 0.12
		R	—	—	—	-1.13	—

22043_CSFR_C0009

TIRE, WHEEL AND BALL JOINT SPECIFICATIONS

Year	Model	OEM Tires Standard	OEM Tires Optional	Tire Pressures (psi) Front	Tire Pressures (psi) Rear	Wheel Size (in.)	Lug Nut Torque (ft. lbs.)
2005	Crossfire	Front-225/40ZR18	—	32	—	18	81
		Rear-255/35ZR19	—	—	33	19	81
2006	Crossfire	Front-225/40ZR18	—	32	—	18	81
		Rear-255/35ZR19	—	—	33	19	81
2007	Crossfire	Front-225/40ZR18	—	26	—	18	81
		Rear-255/35ZR19	—	—	26	19	81
2008	Crossfire	Front-225/40ZR18	—	26	—	18	81
		Rear-255/35ZR19	—	—	26	19	81

OEM: Original Equipment Manufacturer

PSI: Pounds Per Square Inch

NOTE: If specification on door differs from this chart, use specification on door.

22043_CSFR_C0010

BRAKE SPECIFICATIONS
All measurements in inches unless noted

| Year | Model | | Brake Disc | | | Minimum Lining Thickness | Brake Caliper | |
			Original Thickness	Minimum Thickness	Maximum Runout		Bracket Bolts (ft. lbs.)	Mounting Bolts (ft. lbs.)
2005	Crossfire	F	1.100	0.990	0.001	0.080	85	18
		R	0.350	0.290	0.001	0.080	—	41
	Crossfire SRT	F	1.250	1.160	0.001	0.080	85	18
		R	0.870	0.790	0.001	0.080	—	41
2006	Crossfire	F	1.100	0.990	0.001	0.080	85	18
		R	0.350	0.290	0.001	0.080	—	41
	Crossfire SRT	F	1.250	1.160	0.001	0.080	85	18
		R	0.870	0.790	0.001	0.080	—	41
2007	Crossfire	F	1.100	0.990	0.001	0.080	85	18
		R	0.350	0.290	0.001	0.080	—	41
2008	Crossfire	F	1.100	0.990	0.001	0.080	85	18
		R	0.350	0.290	0.001	0.080	—	41

22043_CSFR_C0011

7-8   **CHRYSLER**
CROSSFIRE

SCHEDULED MAINTENANCE INTERVALS
Chrysler—Crossfire

TO BE SERVICED	TYPE OF SERVICE	VEHICLE MILEAGE INTERVAL (x1000)										
		5	10	20	30	40	50	60	70	80	90	100
Engine oil & filter ①	R	✔	✔	✔	✔	✔	✔	✔	✔	✔	✔	✔
Automatic shiftlock operation	S/I		✔	✔	✔	✔	✔	✔	✔	✔	✔	✔
Cooling system	S/I			✔		✔		✔		✔		✔
Passenger compartment air filter	R			✔		✔		✔		✔		✔
Automatic transmission fluid, filter & final drive	S/I			✔		✔		✔		✔		✔
Battery electrolyte level	S/I			✔		✔		✔		✔		✔
Brake system (brake pads & fluid level)	S/I		✔	✔	✔	✔	✔	✔	✔	✔	✔	✔
Drive axle shaft boots	S/I			✔		✔		✔		✔		✔
Engine (check for leaks)	S/I			✔		✔		✔		✔		✔
Exhaust system	S/I			✔		✔		✔		✔		✔
Idle speed	S/I											
Manual transmission fluid	S/I											
OBD System check for codes	S/I			✔		✔		✔		✔		✔
V-belts	S/I		✔			✔				✔		✔
Air cleaner element	R					✔				✔		
Spark plugs	R					✔				✔		
Power steering fluid level	S/I					✔				✔		
Automatic transmission fluid	R					✔				✔		
Timing belt	R											
Brake Fluid ②	R					✔				✔		
Front axle dust seals on ball joints & tie rod ends	S/I					✔				✔		✔
Poly-ribbed belt	S/I					✔				✔		
Rotate tires	S/I		✔	✔	✔	✔	✔	✔	✔	✔	✔	✔

R: Replace   S/I: Service or Inspect

① Reset service interval display, if equipped.

② Replace every 2 years regardless of mileage.

FREQUENT OPERATION MAINTENANCE (SEVERE SERVICE)

If a vehicle is operated under any of the following conditions it is considered severe service:

- Extremely dusty areas.
- 50% or more of the vehicle operation is in 32°C (90°F) or higher temperatures, or constant operation in temperatures below 0°C (32°F).
- Prolonged idling (vehicle operation in stop and go traffic).
- Frequent short running periods (engine does not warm to normal operating temperatures).
- Police, taxi, delivery usage or trailer towing usage.

Oil & oil filter: change every 5000 miles.

22043_CSFR_C0012

PRECAUTIONS

Before servicing any vehicle, please be sure to read all of the following precautions, which deal with personal safety, prevention of component damage, and important points to take into consideration when servicing a motor vehicle:

• Never open, service or drain the radiator or cooling system when the engine is hot; serious burns can occur from the steam and hot coolant.

• Observe all applicable safety precautions when working around fuel. Whenever servicing the fuel system, always work in a well-ventilated area. Do not allow fuel spray or vapors to come in contact with a spark, open flame, or excessive heat (a hot drop light, for example). Keep a dry chemical fire extinguisher near the work area. Always keep fuel in a container specifically designed for fuel storage; also, always properly seal fuel containers to avoid the possibility of fire or explosion. Refer to the additional fuel system precautions later in this section.

• Fuel injection systems often remain pressurized, even after the engine has been turned OFF. The fuel system pressure must be relieved before disconnecting any fuel lines. Failure to do so may result in fire and/or personal injury.

• Brake fluid often contains polyglycol ethers and polyglycols. Avoid contact with the eyes and wash your hands thoroughly after handling brake fluid. If you do get brake fluid in your eyes, flush your eyes with clean, running water for 15 minutes. If eye irritation persists, or if you have taken

brake fluid internally, IMMEDIATELY seek medical assistance.

• The EPA warns that prolonged contact with used engine oil may cause a number of skin disorders, including cancer. You should make every effort to minimize your exposure to used engine oil. Protective gloves should be worn when changing oil. Wash your hands and any other exposed skin areas as soon as possible after exposure to used engine oil. Soap and water, or waterless hand cleaner should be used.

• All new vehicles are now equipped with an air bag system, often referred to as a Supplemental Restraint System (SRS) or Supplemental Inflatable Restraint (SIR) system. The system must be disabled before performing service on or around system components, steering column, instrument panel components, wiring and sensors. Failure to follow safety and disabling procedures could result in accidental air bag deployment, possible personal injury and unnecessary system repairs.

• Always wear safety goggles when working with, or around, the air bag system. When carrying a non-deployed air bag, be sure the bag and trim cover are pointed away from your body. When placing a non-deployed air bag on a work surface, always face the bag and trim cover upward, away from the surface. This will reduce the motion of the module if it is accidentally deployed. Refer to the additional air bag system precautions later in this section.

• Clean, high quality brake fluid from a sealed container is essential to the safe and

proper operation of the brake system. You should always buy the correct type of brake fluid for your vehicle. If the brake fluid becomes contaminated, completely flush the system with new fluid. Never reuse any brake fluid. Any brake fluid that is removed from the system should be discarded. Also, do not allow any brake fluid to come in contact with a painted surface; it will damage the paint.

• Never operate the engine without the proper amount and type of engine oil; doing so WILL result in severe engine damage.

• Timing belt maintenance is extremely important. Many models utilize an interference-type, non-freewheeling engine. If the timing belt breaks, the valves in the cylinder head may strike the pistons, causing potentially serious (also time-consuming and expensive) engine damage. Refer to the maintenance interval charts for the recommended replacement interval for the timing belt, and to the timing belt section for belt replacement and inspection.

• Disconnecting the negative battery cable on some vehicles may interfere with the functions of the on-board computer system(s) and may require the computer to undergo a relearning process once the negative battery cable is reconnected.

• When servicing drum brakes, only disassemble and assemble one side at a time, leaving the remaining side intact for reference.

• Only an MVAC-trained, EPA-certified automotive technician should service the air conditioning system or its components.

BRAKES

GENERAL INFORMATION

PRECAUTIONS

• Certain components within the ABS system are not intended to be serviced or repaired individually.

• Do not use rubber hoses or other parts not specifically specified for and ABS system. When using repair kits, replace all parts included in the kit. Partial or incorrect repair may lead to functional problems and require the replacement of components.

• Lubricate rubber parts with clean, fresh brake fluid to ease assembly. Do not use shop air to clean parts; damage to rubber components may result.

• Use only DOT 3 brake fluid from an unopened container.

• If any hydraulic component or line is removed or replaced, it may be necessary to bleed the entire system.

• A clean repair area is essential. Always clean the reservoir and cap thoroughly before removing the cap. The slightest amount of dirt in the fluid may plug an orifice and impair the system function. Perform repairs after components have been thoroughly cleaned; use only denatured alcohol to clean components. Do not allow ABS components to come into contact with any substance containing mineral oil; this includes used shop rags.

• The Anti-Lock control unit is a microprocessor similar to other computer units in

ANTI-LOCK BRAKE SYSTEM (ABS)

the vehicle. Ensure that the ignition switch is OFF before removing or installing controller harnesses. Avoid static electricity discharge at or near the controller.

• If any arc welding is to be done on the vehicle, the control unit should be unplugged before welding operations begin.

SPEED SENSORS

REMOVAL & INSTALLATION

Front

See Figure 1.

1. Before servicing the vehicle, refer to the Precautions Section.

2. Raise and support the vehicle safely.

3. Remove or disconnect the following:
- Bolts attaching the flange to the steering knuckle
- Wheel speed sensor from the steering knuckle
- Wheel speed/brake wear indicator wire harness connector from the body mount connector

To install:

4. Install or connect the following:
- Wheel speed sensor/brake wear indicator wire harness connector to the body mount connector
- Wheel speed sensor to the steering knuckle
- Bolts attaching the flange to the steering knuckle and tighten to 106 inch lbs. (12 Nm)

Rear

See Figure 1.

1. Before servicing the vehicle, refer to the Precautions Section.
2. Raise and support the vehicle safely.
3. Remove or disconnect the following:
- Bolt attaching the wheel speed sensor to the rear knuckle
- Rear wheel speed sensor from the knuckle
- Rubber grommet

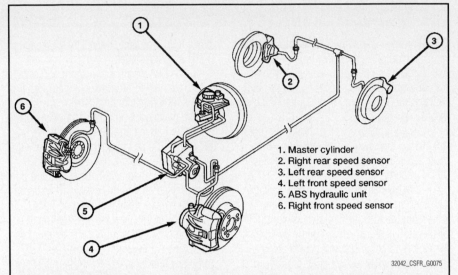

Fig. 1 Wheel speed sensors are located in each wheel knuckle—master cylinder (1), right rear speed sensor (2), left rear speed sensor (3), left front speed sensor (4), ABS hydraulic unit (5) and right front speed sensor (6)

1. Master cylinder
2. Right rear speed sensor
3. Left rear speed sensor
4. Left front speed sensor
5. ABS hydraulic unit
6. Right front speed sensor

32042_CSFR_G0075

- Wheel speed sensor wire harness from the mount
- Wheel speed sensor harness connector

To install:

4. Install or connect the following:
- Wheel speed sensor wire harness connector

- Rubber grommet
- Wheel speed sensor wire harness to the mount
- Wheel speed sensor to the knuckle and tighten the bolt to 106 inch lbs. (12 Nm)

BRAKES

BLEEDING THE BRAKE SYSTEM

BLEEDING PROCEDURE

BLEEDING PROCEDURE

See Figure 2.

Manual Bleeding

1. Before servicing the vehicle, refer to the Precautions Section.
2. Bleed only one brake component at a time in the following sequence:
- Fill the master cylinder reservoir with brake fluid
- Open the caliper bleed screws and allow the brakes to gravity bleed
- Close each bleed screw as fluid starts to drip from it
- Top off master cylinder reservoir once more before proceeding
- Attach one end of the bleed hose to the bleed screw and insert the opposite end in a glass container partially filled with brake fluid
- Be sure the end of the bleed hose is immersed in the brake fluid
- Open up the bleeder screw, then have a helper press down on the brake pedal

- Once the pedal is down, close the bleeder screw
- Repeat bleeding until fluid stream is clear and free of bubbles, then move to the next wheel.

Pressure Bleeding

1. Before servicing the vehicle, refer to the Precautions Section.

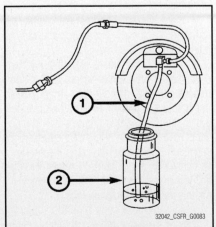

Fig. 2 Submerse the brake bleeding hose (1) into a jar of clean brake fluid (2)

32042_CSFR_G0083

2. Follow the manufactures instructions carefully when using pressure equipment. DO NOT exceed the tank manufacturer's pressure recommendations. Generally, a tank pressure of 15–20 psig (51-67 kPa) is sufficient for bleeding.

3. Fill the bleeder tank with recommended brake fluid and purge air from the tank lines before bleeding.

4. Do not pressure bleed without a proper master cylinder adapter. The wrong adapter can lead to leakage, or drawing air back into the system. Use an adapter provided with the equipment.

BLEEDING THE ABS SYSTEM

✳✳ WARNING

Do not spill brake fluid on any painted surface. Brake fluid can damage paint.

Use brake fluid approved to MB 331.0, such as Mopar part number 0454925AC, or a DOT 4 brake fluid with minimum dry boiling point of 500°F and minimum wet boiling point of 356°F.

Do not pump brake pedal at any time while bleeding. Air in the system will be compressed into small bubbles that are distributed throughout the hydraulic system.

This will make additional bleeding operations necessary.

Do not allow the master cylinder to run out of fluid during bleeding operations. An

empty cylinder will allow additional air to be drawn into the system. Check the cylinder fluid level frequently and add fluid as needed.

BRAKES   FRONT DISC BRAKES

✳✳ CAUTION

Dust and dirt accumulating on brake parts during normal use may contain asbestos fibers from production or aftermarket brake linings. Breathing excessive concentrations of asbestos fibers can cause serious bodily harm. Exercise care when servicing brake parts. Do not sand or grind brake lining unless equipment used is designed to contain the dust residue. Do not clean brake parts with compressed air or by dry brushing. Cleaning should be done by dampening the brake components with a fine mist of water, then wiping the brake components clean with a dampened cloth. Dispose of cloth and all residue containing asbestos fibers in an impermeable container with the appropriate label. Follow practices prescribed by the Occupational Safety and Health Administration (OSHA) and the Environmental Protection Agency (EPA) for the handling, processing, and disposing of dust or debris that may contain asbestos fibers.

BRAKE CALIPER

REMOVAL & INSTALLATION

See Figures 3 and 4.

1. Raise and support the vehicle safely.
2. Drain a small amount of fluid from the master cylinder reservoir.
3. Remove the wheels.
4. Remove the brake pad wear indicator.
5. Press the caliper piston back into the bore with a suitable prytool. Use a large C-clamp to drive the piston into the bore of additional force is required.
6. Remove the caliper support spring.
7. Remove the caliper mounting pins.
8. Loosen the bolt that secures the front brake hose fitting bolt in the caliper.
9. Slide the caliper off the rotor and out from its mount.
10. Remove the front brake hose fitting bolt completely, then remove the caliper with the pads installed as an assembly. Take care not to drip fluid onto the pad surfaces.

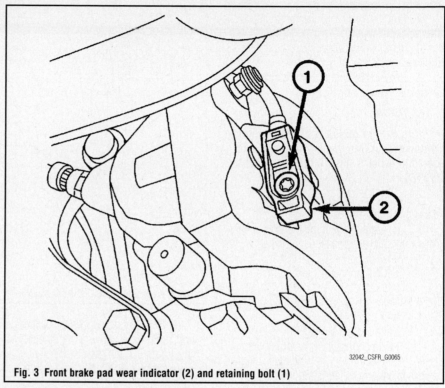

32042_CSFR_G0065

Fig. 3 Front brake pad wear indicator (2) and retaining bolt (1)

11. Cover the open end of the front brake hose fitting to prevent dirt entry.

To install:

12. Lubricate the caliper slide pins and bushings with silicone grease.
13. Install the caliper over the rotor and seat it in its original position until flush.
14. Install the slide pins by hand, and then tighten them to 18 ft. lbs. (25 Nm).
15. Connect the brake hose.

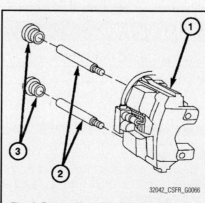

32042_CSFR_G0066

Fig. 4 Front caliper (1) slide pins (2) and slide pin caps (3)

16. Install the brake pad wear indicator. Tighten the bolt to 6 ft. lbs. (8 Nm).
17. Install the caliper support spring.
18. Install the wheels.
19. Lower the vehicle.
20. Pump the brakes several times to seat the pads.

DISC BRAKE PADS

REMOVAL & INSTALLATION

See Figure 5.

1. Before servicing the vehicle, refer to the Precautions Section.
2. Raise and support the vehicle safely.
3. Remove the wheel and tire assembly.
4. Drain a small amount of fluid from master cylinder brake reservoir with a clean suction gun.
5. Bottom the caliper pistons into the caliper by prying the caliper over.
6. Remove the caliper support spring by prying the spring out of the holes in the caliper.
7. Disconnect the brake pad wear indicator harness connector.

8. Remove the caliper slide pin caps and then remove the caliper slide pins from the caliper.

Never allow the disc brake caliper to hang from the brake hose. Damage to the brake hose will result.

9. Provide a suitable support to hang the caliper securely.

10. Remove the caliper from the mounting bracket.

11. Remove the inboard and outboard brake pads from the caliper.

To install:

➡**If the caliper piston is not completely bottomed out into the caliper, you must do so in order to install the caliper onto the rotor.**

12. Install the inboard and outboard brake pads onto the caliper.

13. Lubricate the slide pins and slide pin caps with silicone grease.

14. Install or connect the following:
   • Caliper on the caliper mounting bracket
   • Caliper slide pins and tighten to 18 ft. lbs. (25 Nm)
   • Caliper slide pin caps
   • Brake pad wear indicator harness connector

15. Install the caliper support spring in the top end of the caliper under the caliper mounting bracket, then install the other end into the lower caliper hole.

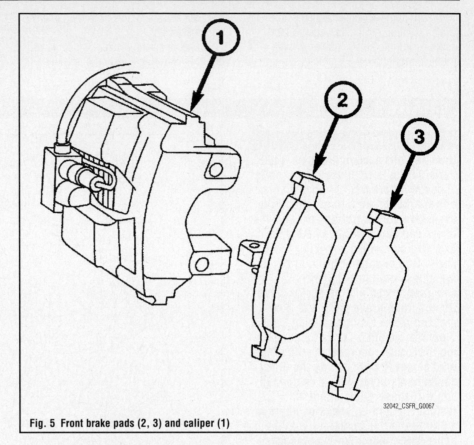

Fig. 5 Front brake pads (2, 3) and caliper (1)

32042_CSFR_G0067

a. Hold the spring into the caliper with your thumb while prying the end of the spring out and down under the caliper mounting bracket with a screwdriver.

16. Install wheel and tire assembly.

17. Lower the vehicle.

18. Pump the brake pedal until the caliper pistons and the brake pads are seated and a firm brake pedal is achieved.

19. Top off the brake fluid reservoir with new fluid if necessary and check for leaks.

BRAKES

Dust and dirt accumulating on brake parts during normal use may contain asbestos fibers from production or aftermarket brake linings. Breathing excessive concentrations of asbestos fibers can cause serious bodily harm. Exercise care when servicing brake parts. Do not sand or grind brake lining unless equipment used is designed to contain the dust residue. Do not clean brake parts with compressed air or by dry brushing. Cleaning should be done by dampening the brake components with a fine mist of water, then wiping the brake components clean with a dampened cloth. Dispose of cloth and all residue containing asbestos fibers in an impermeable container with the appropriate label. Follow practices prescribed by the Occupational Safety and Health Administration (OSHA) and the Environmental Protection Agency (EPA) for the handling, processing, and disposing of dust or debris that may contain asbestos fibers.

BRAKE CALIPER

REMOVAL & INSTALLATION

See Figure 6.

1. Before servicing the vehicle, refer to the Precautions Section.

2. Raise and support the vehicle.

3. Remove the rear tire and wheel assembly.

4. Drain a small amount of fluid from the master cylinder brake reservoir with a clean suction gun.

5. Remove or disconnect the following:
   • Caliper mounting bolts

REAR DISC BRAKES

   • Caliper from the knuckle

DO NOT spill the brake fluid on any painted surfaces. Brake fluid can damage paint.

   • Brake hose by rotating the caliper while holding the brake hose with a wrench
   • Brake pads retaining pin by knocking out with a punch
   • Anti-rattle clip and remove the brake pads from the caliper

To install:

6. Install or connect the following:
   • Rear brake pads
   • Brake hose to caliper by holding the brake hose with a wrench and rotating caliper until snug and fully tighten the brake hose

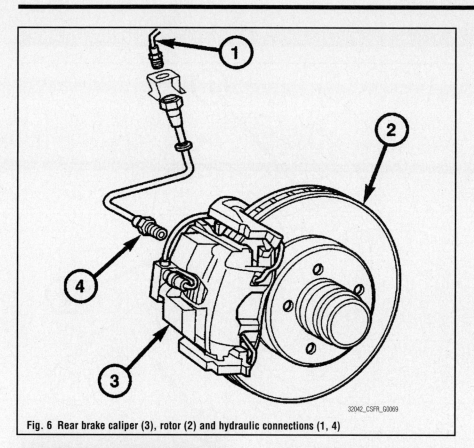

Fig. 6 Rear brake caliper (3), rotor (2) and hydraulic connections (1, 4)

✳✳ WARNING

Verify the brake hose is not twisted or kinked before installing the caliper to the knuckle.

- Caliper to the knuckle and tighten the bolts to 41 ft. lbs. (55 Nm)
7. Fill and bleed the brake system.
8. Install the wheel and tire assembly.

✳✳ CAUTION

Do not move the vehicle until a firm brake pedal is obtained.

9. Lower the vehicle.
10. Pump the brake pedal until the caliper pistons and the brake pads are seated and a firm brake pedal is achieved.
11. Top off the brake fluid reservoir with new fluid if necessary, and check for leaks.

DISC BRAKE PADS

REMOVAL & INSTALLATION

See Figure 7.

1. Before servicing the vehicle, refer to the Precautions Section.
2. Disconnect battery negative cable from battery and properly isolate to prevent accidental reconnection.

3. Raise and support the vehicle.
4. Remove the wheel and tire assembly.
5. Drain a small amount of fluid from the master cylinder brake reservoir with a clean suction gun.
6. Remove or disconnect the following:
   - Caliper mounting bolts and remove the caliper from the knuckle

- Brake hose from the caliper by rotating the caliper while holding the brake hose with a line wrench.
- Pad retaining pin by knocking out with a punch
- Anti-rattle clip

To install:

➡ **If the caliper piston is not completely bottomed out into the caliper, you must do so in order to install the caliper onto the rotor.**

7. Use a C-clamp to bottom out caliper piston.
8. Install or connect the following:
   - Brake pads into the caliper by sliding them through the hole in the top of the caliper
   - Anti-rattle clip

➡**Hold the anti-rattle clip down with your thumb while tapping the retaining clip into position.**

- Retaining pin through the hole in the side of the caliper and tap the pin into the caliper until it is threaded through both brake pads and over the anti-rattle clip
- Wheel and tire assembly
9. Lower the vehicle.
10. Pump the brake pedal until the caliper pistons and the brake pads are seated and a firm brake pedal is achieved.
11. Top off the brake fluid reservoir with new fluid if necessary, and check for leaks.

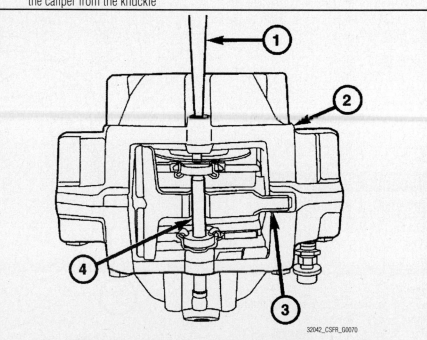

Fig. 7 Using a suitable punch (1) knock out the retaining pin (4) that holds the pads in place. Remove the anti-rattle clip (3) and remove the rear brake pads from the rear caliper (2).

PARKING BRAKE CABLES

ADJUSTMENT

See Figure 8.

Adjust the parking brake only if the hand brake lever can be pulled up more than 3 notches without having an adequate solid braking effect.

1. Before servicing the vehicle, refer to the Precautions Section.

2. Raise and support the vehicle safely.

3. Loosen the parking brake cable tensioning bolt.

4. Remove one wheel bolt on each rear wheel.

5. Rotate the rear wheel until the parking brake adjuster wheel can be seen through the removed rear wheel bolt.

6. Use a suitable tool to turn the adjusting wheel until the parking brake shoes are applied and the rear wheel no longer turns freely.

- Right side: Turn the adjusting wheel from the bottom to top.
- Left side: Turn the adjusting wheel from the top to bottom.

➡ **When slackening the adjusting wheels ensure that both sides are turned back by the same number of teeth.**

7. Turn the adjusting wheel back until the rear wheel turns freely.

8. Tighten the parking brake cable tensioning bolt until the parking brake cables no longer sag.

9. Firmly apply the parking brake several times.

10. To fine adjust the parking brake, tighten the parking brake tensioning bolt until the parking brake lever can be moved one tooth with moderate effort.

11. Install the wheel bolt and tighten to 81 ft. lbs. (110 Nm).

PARKING BRAKE SHOES

REMOVAL & INSTALLATION

See Figures 9 and 10.

1. Before servicing the vehicle, refer to the Precautions Section.

2. Raise and support the vehicle safely.

3. Remove or disconnect the following:

- Wheel and tire assembly
- Caliper assembly bolts
- Disc brake rotor

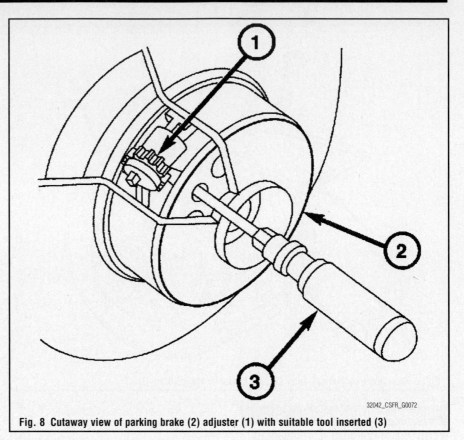

Fig. 8 Cutaway view of parking brake (2) adjuster (1) with suitable tool inserted (3)

32042_CSFR_G0072

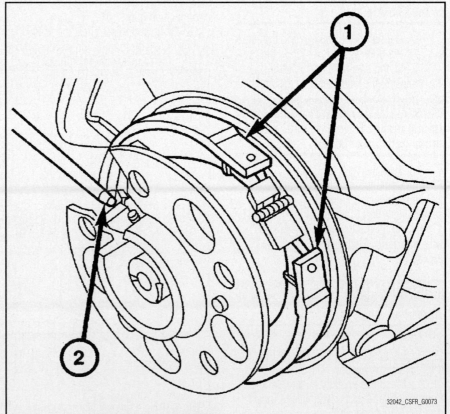

Fig. 9 Parking brake shoes (1) and springs (2)

32042_CSFR_G0073

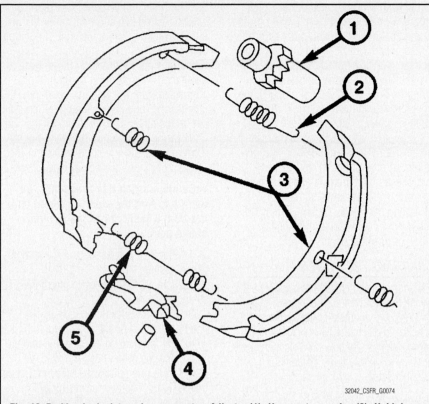

Fig. 10 Parking brake internal components—Adjuster (1), Upper return spring (2), Hold-down spring (3), Expanding lock (4) and Lower return spring (5)

them over rear axle shaft flange
- Upper parking brake shoe return spring
- Expanding lock

5. The parking brake shoe assembly consists of the following components:
- Adjuster
- Upper return spring
- Hold down spring
- Expanding lock
- Lower return spring

To install:

➡ **Coat all bearing and sliding surfaces on the expanding lock with anti-seize compound.**

6. Install or connect the following:
- Parking brake adjuster
- Upper return spring
- Parking brake shoes by placing the assembly over rear axle shaft flange
- Hold down spring by using a pair of needle-nose pliers
- Return spring by using a hooked tool or needle-nose pliers

7. Securely tighten the bolt on the parking brake cable equalizer.

8. Continue installing:
- Disc brake rotors
- Caliper bolts
- Wheel and tire assembly

4. Release the parking brake equalizer tensioning bolt.
- Parking brake shoe return spring using a hooked pick
- Parking brake shoe hold down spring using a pair of needle-nose pliers
- Parking brake shoes by lifting

CHASSIS ELECTRICAL

AIR BAG (SUPPLEMENTAL RESTRAINT SYSTEM)

GENERAL INFORMATION

❋❋ CAUTION

These vehicles are equipped with an air bag system. The system must be disarmed before performing service on, or around, system components, the steering column, instrument panel components, wiring and sensors. Failure to follow the safety precautions and the disarming procedure could result in accidental air bag deployment, possible injury and unnecessary system repairs.

SERVICE PRECAUTIONS

Disconnect and isolate the battery negative cable before beginning any airbag system component diagnosis, testing, removal, or installation procedures. Allow system capacitor to discharge for two minutes before beginning any component service.

This will disable the airbag system. Failure to disable the airbag system may result in accidental airbag deployment, personal injury, or death.

Do not place an intact undeployed airbag face down on a solid surface. The airbag will propel into the air if accidentally deployed and may result in personal injury or death.

When carrying or handling an undeployed airbag, the trim side (face) of the airbag should be pointing towards the body to minimize possibility of injury if accidental deployment occurs. Failure to do this may result in personal injury or death.

Replace airbag system components with OEM replacement parts. Substitute parts may appear interchangeable, but internal differences may result in inferior occupant protection. Failure to do so may result in occupant personal injury or death.

Wear safety glasses, rubber gloves, and long sleeved clothing when cleaning powder residue from vehicle after an airbag

deployment. Powder residue emitted from a deployed airbag can cause skin irritation. Flush affected area with cool water if irritation is experienced. If nasal or throat irritation is experienced, exit the vehicle for fresh air until the irritation ceases. If irritation continues, see a physician.

Do not use a replacement airbag that is not in the original packaging. This may result in improper deployment, personal injury, or death.

The factory installed fasteners, screws and bolts used to fasten airbag components have a special coating and are specifically designed for the airbag system. Do not use substitute fasteners. Use only original equipment fasteners listed in the parts catalog when fastener replacement is required.

During, and following, any child restraint anchor service, due to impact event or vehicle repair, carefully inspect all mounting hardware, tether straps, and anchors for proper installation, operation, or damage. If a child restraint anchor is found damaged in any way, the anchor must be replaced. Failure to do this may result in personal injury or death.

Deployed and non-deployed airbags may or may not have live pyrotechnic material within the airbag inflator.

Do not dispose of driver/passenger/curtain airbags or seat belt tensioners unless you are sure of complete deployment. Refer to the Hazardous Substance Control System for proper disposal.

Dispose of deployed airbags and tensioners consistent with state, provincial, local, and federal regulations.

After any airbag component testing or service, do not connect the battery negative cable. Personal injury or death may result if the system test is not performed first.

If the vehicle is equipped with the Occupant Classification System (OCS), do not connect the battery negative cable before performing the OCS Verification Test using the scan tool and the appropriate diagnostic information. Personal injury or death may result if the system test is not performed properly.

Never replace both the Occupant Restraint Controller (ORC) and the Occupant Classification Module (OCM) at the same time. If both require replacement, replace one, then perform the Airbag System test before replacing the other.

Both the ORC and the OCM store Occupant Classification System (OCS) calibration data, which they transfer to one another when one of them is replaced. If both are replaced at the same time, an irreversible fault will be set in both modules and the OCS may malfunction and cause personal injury or death.

If equipped with OCS, the Seat Weight Sensor is a sensitive, calibrated unit and must be handled carefully. Do not drop or handle roughly. If dropped or damaged, replace with another sensor. Failure to do so may result in occupant injury or death.

If equipped with OCS, the front passenger seat must be handled carefully as well. When removing the seat, be careful when setting on floor not to drop. If dropped, the sensor may be inoperative, could result in occupant injury, or possibly death.

If equipped with OCS, when the passenger front seat is on the floor, no one should sit in the front passenger seat. This uneven force may damage the sensing ability of the seat weight sensors. If sat on and damaged, the sensor may be inoperative, could result in occupant injury, or possibly death.

DISARMING THE SYSTEM

Disconnect and isolate the negative battery cable to prevent accidental reconnection. Wait two minutes for the system capacitor to discharge before performing further diagnosis or service. This is the only sure way to disable the supplemental restraint system.

ARMING THE SYSTEM

Perform Supplemental Restraint System (SRS) verification test. Reconnect the battery. The supplemental restraint system will self-initialize.

CLOCKSPRING CENTERING

The clockspring is designed to wind and unwind when the steering wheel is rotated, but is only designed to rotate the same number of turns (about five complete rotations) as the steering wheel can be turned from stop to stop. Centering the clockspring indexes the clockspring tape to other steering components so that it can operate within its designed travel limits. The rotor of a centered clockspring can be rotated two and one-half turns in either direction from the centered position, without damaging the clockspring tape. However, if the clockspring is removed for service or if the steering column is disconnected from the steering gear, the clockspring tape can change position relative to the other steering components. The clockspring must then be re-centered following completion of such service or the clockspring tape may be damaged.

➡**Before starting this procedure, be certain to turn the steering wheel until the front wheels are in the straight-ahead position.**

1. Place the front wheels in the straight-ahead position.
2. Remove the clockspring from the steering column.
3. Hold the clockspring case in one hand so that it is oriented as it would be when it is installed on the steering column.
4. Use your other hand to rotate the clockspring rotor clockwise to the end of its travel. Do not apply excessive torque.
5. From the end of the clockwise travel, rotate the rotor about two and one-half turns counterclockwise, until the arrows on the clockspring rotor label and the clockspring case are aligned. The uppermost pin on the lower surface of the clockspring rotor should now be aligned with the oblong pin.
6. The clockspring is now centered. Secure the clockspring rotor to the clockspring case to maintain clockspring centering until it is reinstalled on the steering column.
   a. The front wheels should still be in the straight-ahead position.
7. Reinstall the clockspring onto the steering column.

DRIVETRAIN

AUTOMATIC TRANSMISSION ASSEMBLY

REMOVAL & INSTALLATION

1. Before servicing the vehicle, refer to the Precautions Section.
2. Drain the transmission fluid.
3. Remove or disconnect the following:
   - Negative battery cable
   - Exhaust system
   - Center exhaust heat shield
   - Transmission support bracket
   - Transmission mount and cross-member. Support the transmission with a jack.
   - Driveshaft
   - Front engine undercover
   - Transmission ground bolt
   - Shift rod
   - Transmission oil cooler fittings
   - Torque converter access cover
   - Torque converter bolts
   - Oxygen sensor connectors
   - Heat shield
   - Controller harness connector
4. Support the transmission with a jack under the transmission oil pan rail.
5. Remove or disconnect:
   - Starter
   - Engine to transmission retaining bolts
   - Transmission

To install:
6. Ensure the torque converter is fully seated in the transmission.
7. Install or connect the following:
   - Transmission. Torque the mounting bolts to 28 ft. lbs. (38 Nm).
   - Torque converter. Torque the mounting bolts to 37 ft. lbs. (50 Nm).
   - Torque converter access cover
   - Starter. Torque the mounting bolts to 31 ft. lbs. (42 Nm).
   - Controller harness connector
   - Heat shield. Torque the mounting bolts to 15 ft. lbs. (20 Nm).
   - Oxygen sensor connector
   - Transmission cooler fittings. Torque the mounting bolts to 25 ft. lbs. (34 Nm).
   - Shift rod
   - Driveshaft. Torque the mounting bolts to 44 ft. lbs. (60 Nm).
   - Transmission support bracket. Torque the mounting bolts to 15 ft. lbs. (20 Nm).
   - Transmission mount and cross-

member. Torque the mounting bolts to 33 ft. lbs. (45 Nm).
   - Center heat shield
   - Exhaust system
   - Engine undercover
   - Negative battery cable
8. Fill the transmission to the correct level.
9. Start engine and check for proper transmission operation.

MANUAL TRANSMISSION ASSEMBLY

REMOVAL & INSTALLATION

See Figures 11 through 13.

1. Before servicing the vehicle, refer to the Precautions Section.
2. Remove or disconnect the following:
   - Negative battery cable
   - Exhaust system
   - Center exhaust heat shield
   - Driveshaft
   - Transmission support bracket
   - Transmission mount and cross-member. Support the transmission with a jack stand.
   - Reverse light switch connector
   - Clutch slave cylinder pressure line
   - Reverse lockout cable
   - Shift rod
   - Ground cable
   - Transmission

To install:
3. Raise the transmission into place.
4. Install or connect the following:
   - Ground cable. Tighten the bolt to 30 ft. lbs. (40 Nm).
   - Transmission to engine block retaining bolts. Tighten the bolts to 30 ft. lbs. (40 Nm).
   - Transmission mount bolts to the transmission. Tighten to 22 ft. lbs. (30 Nm).
   - Rear crossmember retaining bolts. Tighten to 30 ft. lbs. (40 Nm).
   - Shift rod
   - Reverse lockout cable
   - Reverse light connector
   - Clutch slave cylinder pressure line
   - Driveshaft. Torque the mounting bolts to 44 ft. lbs. (60 Nm).
   - Center exhaust heat shield
   - Exhaust system
   - Negative battery cable
5. Fill transmission to the correct level.
6. Check for proper clutch operation.

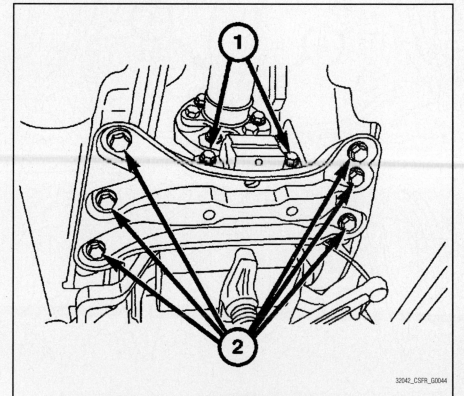

Fig. 11 Rear transmission mount (1) and crossmember (2) bolts

32042_CSFR_G0044

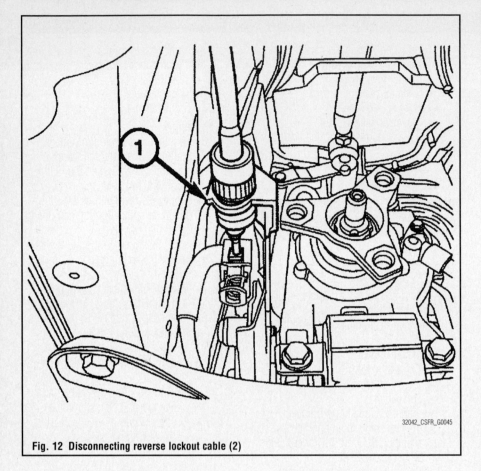

Fig. 12 Disconnecting reverse lockout cable (2)

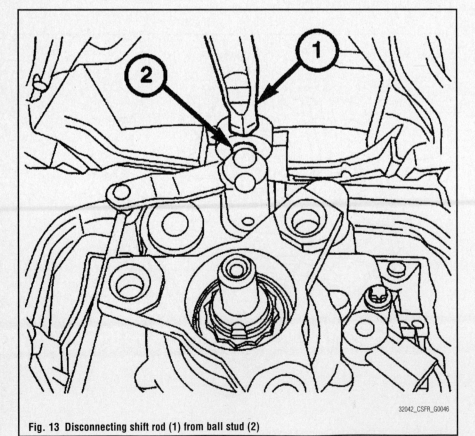

Fig. 13 Disconnecting shift rod (1) from ball stud (2)

CLUTCH

REMOVAL & INSTALLATION

See Figure 14.

1. Before servicing the vehicle, refer to the Precautions Section.
2. Disconnect battery negative cable from battery and properly isolate to prevent accidental reconnection.
3. Remove the transmission.
4. Gradually remove the clutch cover bolts 1 to 1 ½ turns at a time.
5. Loosen the bolts on the clutch cover.
6. Mark the relation of the clutch cover to the flywheel.
7. Remove the bolts on the clutch cover.

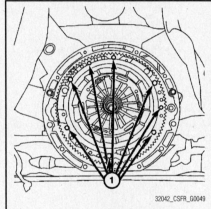

Fig. 14 Location of pressure plate bolts (1)

8. Remove the clutch cover and the clutch disc.

To install:

9. If the clutch cover is to be reused, adjustment is required on the clutch disc. See adjustment.
10. Position the clutch disc and clutch cover on the flywheel.
11. Loosely install the clutch cover bolts.
12. Install a universal clutch alignment tool.
13. Align the clutch disc to the flywheel.
14. Gradually tighten the clutch cover bolts 1 to 1 ½ turns at a time.
15. Tighten the clutch cover bolts until all bolts are fully seated.
   a. Tighten the bolts to 18 ft. lbs. (25 Nm)
16. Remove the clutch alignment tool.
17. Install the transmission.

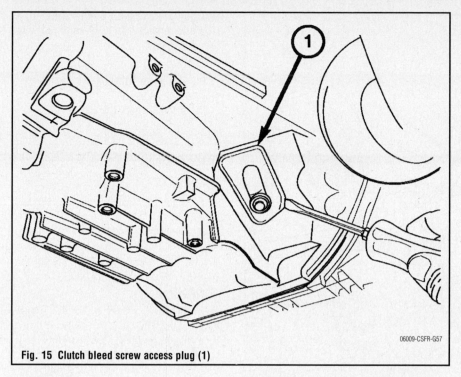

Fig. 15 Clutch bleed screw access plug (1)

06009-CSFR-G57

BLEEDING

See Figure 15.

1. Before servicing the vehicle, refer to the Precautions Section.
2. Connect a pressure bleeder to the brake master cylinder.
3. Open the bleed screw on the clutch slave cylinder.
4. Allow the fluid to flow until there are no bubbles and the fluid is clear.
5. Close the bleed screw and disconnect the pressure bleeder.
6. Check the clutch for proper operation.

REAR AXLE HOUSING

REMOVAL & INSTALLATION

1. Before servicing the vehicle, refer to the Precautions Section.
2. Raise and support the vehicle safely.
3. Remove the driveshaft.
4. Drain the rear differential housing.
5. Support the differential housing, using a suitable jack.
6. Remove the housing front mounting bolt.
7. Remove the two rear housing mounting bolts.
8. Carefully remove the differential housing from the vehicle.

To install:

9. Installation is the reverse of the removal procedure.

➡**Always replace the self locking bolts and shims. Lightly oil the bolt at the thread and bolt head contact surfaces.**

10. Tighten the housing rear mounting bolts to 82 ft. lbs. Tighten the front housing mounting bolt to 33 ft. lbs.

11. Be sure to fill the assembly with the proper grade and type fluid.
12. Check for leaks, correct as required.

REAR AXLE SHAFT, BEARING & SEAL

REMOVAL & INSTALLATION

1. Before servicing the vehicle, refer to the Precautions Section.
2. Remove the halfshaft.

➡**Do not scrape or damage the surface of the seal bore.**

3. Using the proper removal tool, remove the axle shaft seal.

To install:

4. Lubricate the new seal with hypoid gear oil.
5. Using tool 9223 (drift) drive the seal into the differential housing.
6. Install the halfshaft.

REAR HALFSHAFT

REMOVAL & INSTALLATION

See Figures 16 and 17.

1. Before servicing the vehicle, refer to the Precautions Section.

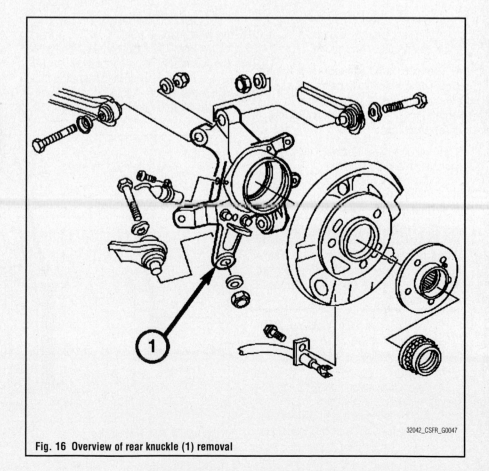

Fig. 16 Overview of rear knuckle (1) removal

32042_CSFR_G0047

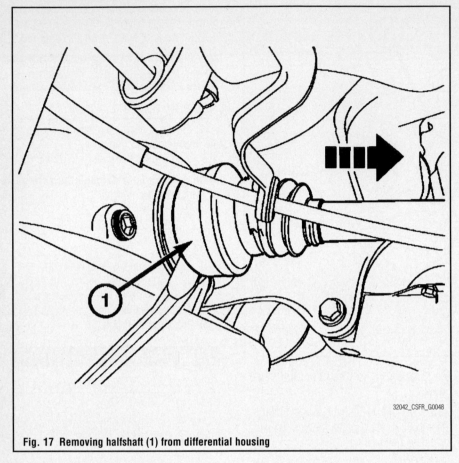

Fig. 17 Removing halfshaft (1) from differential housing

2. Raise and support the vehicle.
3. Remove the rear wheels.
4. Remove the rear knuckle.

➡ **The axle halfshafts are seated in the differential side gears using expandable snap rings. It is necessary to forcefully pry the halfshaft out of the differential.**

5. Insert a pry bar between the differential housing and the halfshaft.
6. Pry against differential housing until the halfshaft retaining snap ring is disengaged from the differential side gear.

✷✷ WARNING

When removing the halfshaft assembly do not allow the snap ring to drag across the sealing lip of the differential oil seal.

7. Carefully pull the halfshaft out of the differential housing and remove the halfshaft from the vehicle.

To install:

8. Thoroughly clean the spline and oil sealing surface of the halfshaft.
9. Lightly lubricate the oil seal sealing surface of the halfshaft with clean lubricant.

10. Insert the halfshaft outer end through the wheel hub.
11. Install the halfshaft into the differential side gear as far as possible by hand.
12. Forcefully push the halfshaft into the differential side gear until the snap ring is engaged with the differential side gear.

➡ **Grasp the halfshaft and test the snap ring and ensure it is fully engaged with the side gear.**

13. Install the rear knuckle.
14. Use a new halfshaft outer retaining nut and tighten to 164 ft. lbs. (220 Nm).
15. Install the rear wheels.

CV-JOINT OVERHAUL

Outer CV-Joint

See Figure 18.

1. Before servicing the vehicle, refer to the Precautions Section.
2. Remove or disconnect the following:
   • Axle halfshaft from the vehicle
   • Inner CV-joint boot and clamps
   • Outer CV-joint and boot

To install:

3. Pack the outer CV-joint with grease supplied in repair kit.
4. Install or connect the following:
   • CV-joint into inner seal
5. Crimp the retaining boot clamps.
6. Install the axle halfshaft.

Inner CV-Joint

See Figure 19.

1. Before servicing the vehicle, refer to the Precautions Section.
2. Remove or disconnect the following:
   • Axle halfshaft from the vehicle
   • CV joint boot clamps
3. Clamp the halfshaft in a vise.
4. Pry the joint cover from the bearing retainer.
5. Remove the boot from the inner seal.

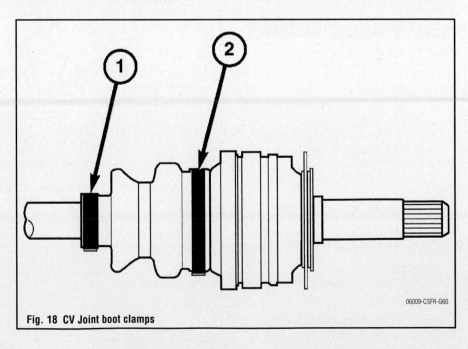

Fig. 18 CV Joint boot clamps

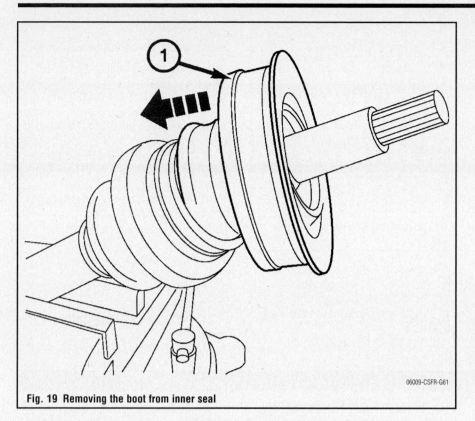

Fig. 19 Removing the boot from inner seal

06009-CSFR-G61

6. Pry the inner seal from the bearing retainer.

7. Slide the boot, inner seal and bearing retainer off the halfshaft.

8. Remove the circlip from the axle shaft.

9. Using a press, remove the inner joint bearing from the halfshaft.

To install:

➡**Use new circlips and boot clamps for assembly.**

10. Install or connect the following:
   • Inner boot
   • Inner joint bearing
   • Inner seal
   • Circlip
11. Fill the bearing housing with grease.
12. Apply a bead of sealant to the outer sealing surface of the joint ring.
13. Using a mallet, tap on a NEW joint cover.
14. Install the boot into the sealing groove of the inner seal.
15. Install the retaining clamps and crimp in place.
16. Install the axle halfshaft.

REAR PINION SEAL

REMOVAL & INSTALLATION
See Figures 20 through 22.

1. Before servicing the vehicle, refer to the Precautions Section.
2. Drain the differential of fluid.
3. Remove or disconnect the following:

   • Wheels

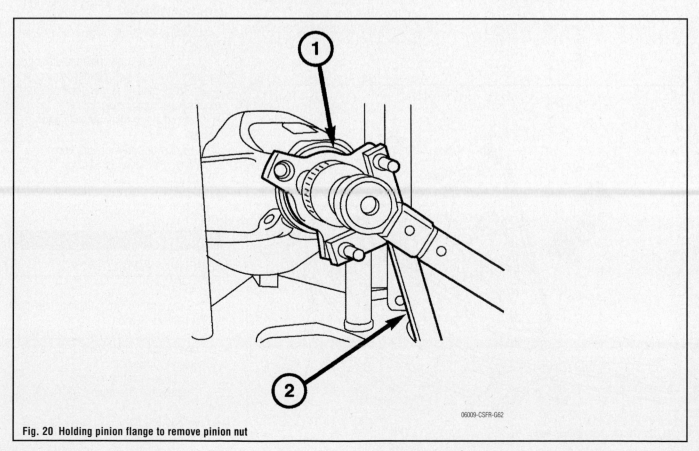

06009-CSFR-G62

Fig. 20 Holding pinion flange to remove pinion nut

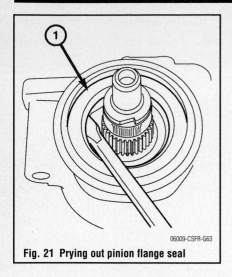

Fig. 21 Prying out pinion flange seal

06009-CSFR-G63

- Muffler
- Driveshaft from the rear differential
- Halfshafts at differential

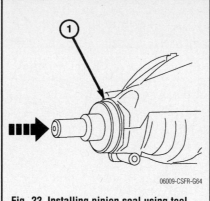

06009-CSFR-G64

Fig. 22 Installing pinion seal using tool 9321

4. Check and record the bearing preload with an inch lb. torque wrench.

5. Hold the pinion flange using special tool C-3281 or equivalent and remove the collared nut.

6. Pry out the pinion flange seal.

To install:

➡ Use a new pinion nut for assembly.

7. Install the new pinion seal using special tool 9321 drift and a mallet. Tighten the pinion nut to 133 ft. lbs. (180 Nm).

8. Check the bearing preload. The bearing preload should be equal to the reading taken earlier.

9. If the preload torque is low, tighten the pinion nut in 44 inch lb. (5 Nm) increments until the torque value is reached.

10. If the pinion bearing preload torque cannot be attained at maximum pinion nut torque, replace the collapsible spacer.

11. Install or connect the following:
- Halfshafts
- Driveshaft
- Muffler
- Wheels

12. Fill the axle assembly to correct level.

ENGINE COOLING

ENGINE FAN

REMOVAL & INSTALLATION

See Figure 23.

1. Before servicing the vehicle, refer to the Precautions Section.

2. Disconnect battery negative cable from battery and properly isolate to prevent accidental reconnection.

3. Remove or disconnect the following:
- Radiator fan harness connector
- Coolant return hose from the mounting bracket
- Radiator fan hold down clamps with suitable tool

4. Carefully pry the upper radiator hose and return hoses away from the cooling fan.

5. Gently lift the radiator fan up and out of the vehicle.

To install:

➡ Lightly lubricate the two locating studs on the bottom of the radiator fan prior to installation.

6. Gently lower the radiator fan into the vehicle.

7. Carefully pry the upper radiator hose and return hoses away from the cooling fan.

8. Install the radiator fan locating studs into the lower rubber mounts.

9. Install the radiator fan hold down clamps.

10. Route the coolant return hose through the bracket on the radiator fan.

11. Connect the radiator fan harness connector.

12. Connect the negative battery cable.

RADIATOR

REMOVAL & INSTALLATION

See Figure 24.

1. Before servicing the vehicle, refer to the Precautions Section.

2. Disconnect battery negative cable from battery and properly isolate to prevent accidental reconnection.

3. Drain the cooling system.

4. Remove or disconnect the following:
- Radiator fan
- Air cleaner inlet tubes

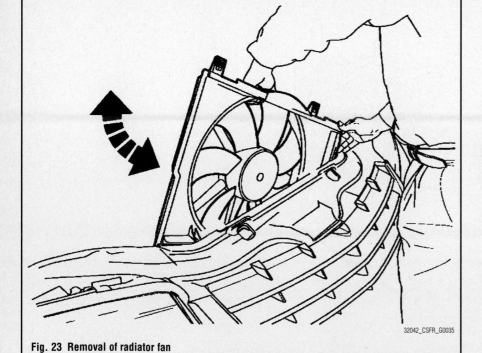

Fig. 23 Removal of radiator fan

32042_CSFR_G0035

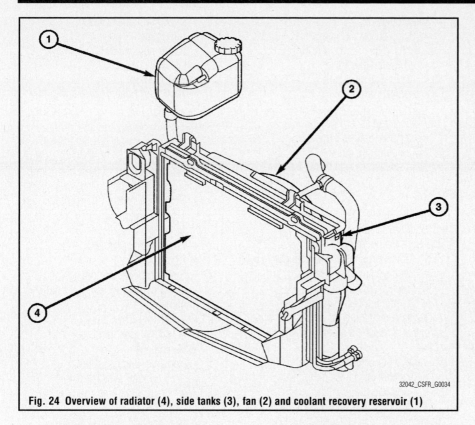

Fig. 24 Overview of radiator (4), side tanks (3), fan (2) and coolant recovery reservoir (1)

- Upper and lower radiator hoses
- Coolant recovery reservoir hose
- Transmission cooler line located on the right side of the radiator (automatic transmissiononly)
- Transmission cooler line located in the middle front of the vehicle (automatic transmission only)

5. Using a suitable tool, grasp the radiator hold down clamps and pull up to remove the clamps from the mounting holes.

6. Remove the condenser retaining bolts from the radiator support.

7. Carefully lean the radiator back toward the engine.

8. Gently lift and remove the radiator from the vehicle.

To install:

9. Carefully lower the radiator into the vehicle.

10. Install or connect the following:
- Coolant recovery reservoir hose
- Transmission cooler line (automatic transmission only) and tighten the line to 89 inch lbs. (10 Nm)
- Upper radiator hose
- Transmission cooler line located in the middle front of the vehicle (automatic transmission only)
- Radiator retaining clamps, using a suitable tool

- Condenser retainer bolts into the radiator support and tighten to 89 inch lbs. (10 Nm)
- Radiator fan
- Air inlet tubes

11. Refill the cooling system.

12. Connect the negative battery cable.

13. Start the engine and check for coolant leaks.

14. Recheck the coolant level.

THERMOSTAT

REMOVAL & INSTALLATION

See Figure 25.

1. Before servicing the vehicle, refer to the Precautions Section.

2. Disconnect battery negative cable from battery and properly isolate to prevent accidental reconnection.

3. Remove the air cleaner housing.

4. Partially drain the cooling system.

5. Disconnect the upper radiator hose.

➡**The thermostat housing and the thermostat are serviced as an assembly. The thermostat cannot beserviced separately.**

6. Remove the thermostat housing retaining bolts and remove the thermostat and housing from the engine.

To install:

7. Install the thermostat housing with a new O-ring and tighten the bolts to 89 inch lbs. (10 Nm)

8. Connect the upper radiator hose.

9. Fill the cooling system.

10. Start the engine and check for coolant leaks.

11. Recheck the coolant level and adjust as necessary.

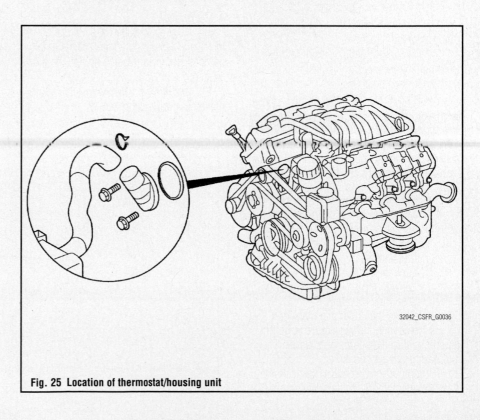

Fig. 25 Location of thermostat/housing unit

WATER PUMP

REMOVAL & INSTALLATION

Except SRT

1. Before servicing the vehicle, refer to the Precautions Section.
2. Drain the cooling system.
3. Disconnect the negative battery cable.
4. Remove the engine cover, as required.
5. Remove or disconnect the following:
   - Air intake assembly
   - Radiator fan
   - Accessory drive belt
   - Belt tensioner
   - Lower radiator hoses
   - Coolant by-pass hose
   - Alternator
   - Pump pulley and idler pulley
   - Water pump (16 bolts)
6. Installation is the reverse of removal. Tighten the bolts to 28 ft. lbs. (35 Nm).

To install:

7. Install or connect the following:
   - Water pump with a new gasket. Tighten bolts to 26 ft. lbs. (35 Nm).
   - Alternator

- Belt tensioner
- Pump pulley and idler pulley. Tighten bolts to 89 inch lbs. (10 Nm).
- Lower radiator hoses
- Accessory drive belt
- Radiator fan
- Engine cover, as required
- Air intake assembly
- Negative battery cable.
8. Fill cooling system.
9. Start the engine and check for leaks.

SRT

1. Before servicing the vehicle, refer to the Precautions Section.
2. Drain the cooling system.
3. Remove or disconnect the following:
   - Negative battery cable
   - Radiator fan
   - Air pump tube assembly
4. Release the tension on the accessory drive belt and remove the belt from the pulleys.
5. Remove or disconnect the following:
   - Supercharger idler pulley
   - Accessory drive belt
   - Belt tensioner pulley and belt tensioner

- Lower radiator hoses
- Alternator
- Pump pulley and idler pulley
- Oil cooler hose clamp
- Water pump
- Oil cooler hose from water pump

To install:

6. Install or connect the following:
   - Water pump with a new gasket. Tighten bolts to 26 ft. lbs. (35 Nm).
   - Oil cooler hose to the water pump and hose clamp
   - Pump pulley and idler pulley. Tighten bolts to 89 inch lbs. (10 Nm).
   - Lower radiator hoses
   - Alternator
   - Supercharger idler pulley
   - Belt tensioner pulley and belt tensioner
   - Accessory drive belt
   - Air pump tube assembly
   - Radiator fan
   - Negative battery cable
7. Fill the cooling system.
8. Start the engine and check for leaks.

ENGINE ELECTRICAL

ALTERNATOR

REMOVAL & INSTALLATION

See Figure 26.

1. Before servicing the vehicle, refer to the Precautions Section.
2. Disconnect battery negative cable from battery and properly isolate to prevent accidental reconnection.
3. Remove the right side air inlet tube.

✳✳ CAUTION

The accessory drive belt tensioner pulley is spring loaded and can injure hands and fingers if allowed to spring back.

4. Remove the accessory drive belt from the alternator pulley.
   a. Pull the tensioning pulley in a counter clockwise direction.
   b. Lock the tensioning pulley with a pin or slowly release the pulley after the belt is free from the area.
5. Remove the upper alternator bolt (2).
6. Remove the lower alternator bolt (3) and reposition the alternator to access the alternator harness connectors.
7. Remove the protective plastic cap from the alternator B+ cable retaining nut (5).

8. Disconnect the alternator B+ cable and the alternator harness connectors (4) from the rear of the alternator.
9. Remove the alternator (1).

To install:

10. Connect the alternator B+ cable with the retaining nut and connect the alternator harness connector (4) and tighten the nut to 11 ft. lbs. (15 Nm).
11. Install the protective plastic cap on the alternator B+ cable nut (5).

CHARGING SYSTEM

12. Continue installing:
   - Upper and lower alternator mounting bolts and torque to 31 ft. lbs. (42 Nm).

✳✳ WARNING

Be sure to check proper installation on all pulleys.

- Accessory drive belt
- Right side air inlet tube
- Negative battery cable

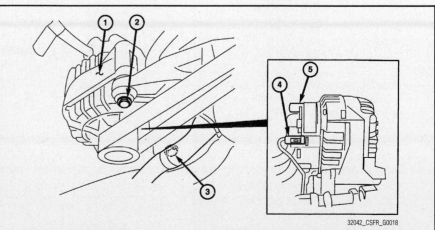

Fig. 26 Detailed view of alternator (1), upper mounting bolt (2), lower mounting bolt (3) and electrical connectors (4, 5)

32042_CSFR_G0018

ENGINE ELECTRICAL

IGNITION SYSTEM

FIRING ORDER

See Figure 27.

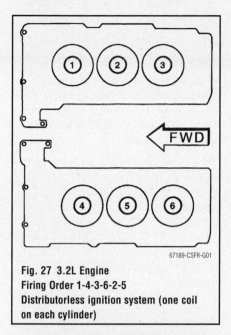

67189-CSFR-G01

**Fig. 27 3.2L Engine
Firing Order 1-4-3-6-2-5
Distributorless ignition system (one coil
on each cylinder)**

IGNITION COIL

REMOVAL & INSTALLATION

The ignition coils are mounted on the cylinder head covers. They are connected to the spark plugs via short spark plug cables. The coils are a dual coil type construction utilizing two separate coils in one coil pack.

Except SRT

See Figure 28.

1. Before servicing the vehicle, refer to the Precautions Section.
2. Disconnect battery negative cable from battery and properly isolate to prevent accidental reconnection.
3. Remove the air cleaner inlet tubes.
4. Remove the engine cover. Grasp both corners of the engine cover and pull up firmly.
5. Disconnect the ignition coil wire harness connector (1).
6. Disconnect the spark plug cables (4) from the spark plugs.
7. Remove the ignition coil retaining bolt (2).
8. Remove the ignition coil (3) from the cylinder head cover.

To install:

9. Position the ignition coil (3) on the cylinder head cover.

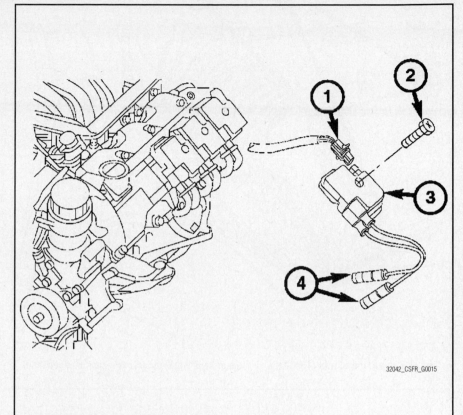

32042_CSFR_G0015

Fig. 28 Ignition coil (3), mounting bolts (2), electrical connector (1) and spark plug cables (4)—non-supercharged models

10. Install the ignition coil retaining bolt (2) and tighten to 71 inch lbs. (8 Nm).
11. Connect the ignition coil wire harness connector (1) to the coil pack.

➡**When installing the spark plug cables, route the cables correctly. Failure to route the cables properly can cause improper phase shift in the dual spark plug system.**

12. Install the spark plug cables to the appropriate coil tower (A & B) (coil side).
13. Install the spark plug cables to the appropriate spark plug location (G & K) (plug side).
    a. Refer to the reference pad cast into the cylinder head cover to identify proper spark plug/spark plug cable orientation.
    b. When installing spark plug cables, insure a positive connection is made. A snap should be felt when a good connection is made between the spark plug cable and the spark plug.
14. Install the engine cover. Align the engine cover retaining clips to the rubber mounts and push down firmly to connect engine cover to rubber mounts.

    c. To ease the installation of the engine cover, apply a small amount of lubricant to the engine cover rubber mounts.
15. Connect the negative battery cable.

SRT

See Figures 29 and 30.

1. Before servicing the vehicle, refer to the Precautions Section.
2. Disconnect battery negative cable from battery and properly isolate to prevent accidental reconnection.
3. Disconnect the negative battery cable.
4. Remove the engine cover. Grasp both corners of the engine cover and pull up firmly.
5. Remove the upper air cleaner housing by removing the inlet tube and the retaining screws.
6. Disconnect the ignition coil harness connector.
7. Disconnect both the spark plug cables from the spark plugs.
8. Remove the ignition coil mounting bolt.

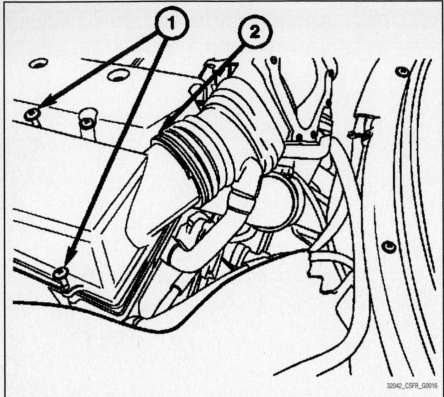

Fig. 29 Remove the screws (1) and the air cleaner housing (2) for access—supercharged models

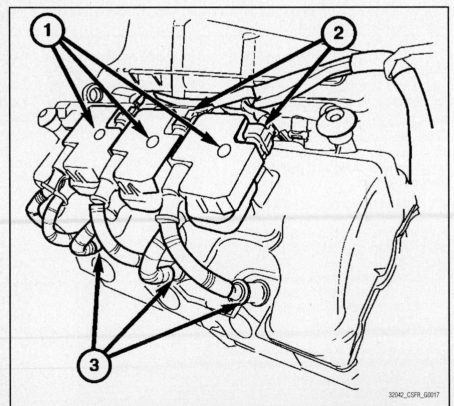

Fig. 30 Ignition coil (3), retaining bolts (2) and connectors (1)—supercharged models

9. Remove the ignition coil from the engine.

To install:

10. Position the ignition coil (3) on the cylinder head cover.

11. Install the ignition coil retaining bolt (2) and tighten to 71 inch lbs. (8 Nm).

12. Connect the ignition coil wire harness connector (1) to the coil pack.

➡ **When installing the spark plug cables, route the cables correctly. Failure to route the cables properly can cause improper phase shift in the dual spark plug system.**

13. Install the spark plug cables to the appropriate coil tower (A & B) (coil side).

14. Install the spark plug cables to the appropriate spark plug location (G & K) (plug side).

   a. Refer to the reference pad cast into the cylinder head cover to identify proper spark plug/spark plug cable orientation.

   b. When installing spark plug cables, insure a positive connection is made. A snap should be felt when a good connection is made between the spark plug cable and the spark plug.

15. Insure a firm connection is made from the spark plug cables to the spark plugs.

16. Install the upper air cleaner housing.

17. Install the engine cover. Align the engine cover retaining clips to the rubber mounts and push down firmly to connect engine cover to rubber mounts.

   c. To ease the installation of the engine cover, apply a small amount of lubricant to the engine cover rubber mounts.

18. Connect the negative battery cable.

IGNITION TIMING

ADJUSTMENT

The ignition system for the 3.2L and the 3.2L SRT-6 engines utilize a Distributorless Ignition System design. The ignition system uses a separate ignition coil pack for each cylinder. The one piece coil pack bolts directly to the cylinder head cover. The coil packs are designed with two secondary towers for each spark plug wire. Rubber boots seal the secondary terminal ends of the spark plug wires. A separate electrical connector is used for each coil pack. The camshaft position sensor is a hall effect device, and the crankshaft position sensor is an inductive device. The camshaft position sensor and crankshaft position sensor generate pulses that are inputs to the PCM. The PCM determines engine position from these sensors. The PCM calculates injector sequence and ignition timing based on crankshaft & camshaft position. The two spark plugs per cylinder are fired slightly out of phase to prevent the cylinder pressures from rising too quickly, which could cause knocking. To prevent one spark plug from eroding more quickly than the other, they alternately lead each other. Under normal conditions, the timing is the same for all cylinders, but the timing can be delayed in individual cylinders if knocking is present in one or more. Two knock sensors are used to control spark knock. Highly sensitive knock sensors can distinguish knocking conditions in individual cylinders and retard the ignition timing as needed on the cylinders that are knocking.

➡All engines use a fixed ignition timing system. Basic ignition timing is not adjustable. All spark advance is determined by the Powertrain Control Module (PCM).

SPARK PLUGS

REMOVAL & INSTALLATION

See Figure 31.

✳✳ WARNING

When disconnecting a high tension cable from a spark plug or from the ignition coil, twist the rubber boot slightly (1/2 turn) to break it loose. Grasp the boot (not the cable) and pull it off with a steady, even force.

1. Before servicing the vehicle, refer to the Precautions Section.
2. Disconnect battery negative cable

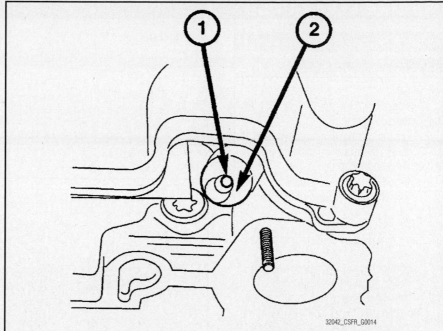

Fig. 31 Keep debris out of the spark plug (1) well (2)—any dirt here will go straight into the engine.

from battery and properly isolate to prevent accidental reconnection.

3. Twist and pull the metal clad spark plug cable boots to remove them from the spark plugs.

➡Avoid allowing debris to fall into the spark plug holes during replacement.

4. Clean the cylinder head spark plug recesses using low-pressure compressed air.

✳✳ WARNING

Do not use power tools to replace spark plugs. Damage to the cylinder head can result.

5. Use a rubber insulated spark plug socket and a hand ratchet to remove the spark plugs.
6. Remove the spark plugs from the engine.

To install:

7. Gap the spark plugs with a spark plug gap gauge to 0.040-inch (1.02 mm) before installation.
8. Start the spark plugs into the cylinder head by hand to avoid cross threading and tighten to 21 ft. lbs. (28 Nm)

➡When installing the spark plug cables, route the cables correctly. Failure to route the cables properly can cause improper spark plug phase shift (inductive cross fire).

9. Install the spark plug cables to the appropriate spark plug location.
   a. Refer to the reference pad cast into the cylinder head cover to identify proper spark plug/spark plug cable orientation.
   b. Insure a positive connection is made. A snap should be felt when a good connection is made between the spark plug cable and the spark plug.

ENGINE ELECTRICAL
STARTING SYSTEM

STARTER

REMOVAL & INSTALLATION

See Figure 32.

1. Before servicing the vehicle, refer to the Precautions Section.

2. Disconnect battery negative cable from battery and properly isolate to prevent accidental reconnection.

3. Raise and support the vehicle.

4. Remove or disconnect the following:

- Lower engine panel
- Right O2 sensor electrical connector
- Right side exhaust pipe from the exhaust manifold to the rear exhaust system
- Starter bolts (1) and reposition the starter to access the starter electrical cables
- Starter positive cable protective plastic cap (3)
- Starter cables by removing the ground cable nut (2) and the positive cable nut
- Starter (4) from the vehicle

To install:

5. Install or connect the following:

- Starter (4)
- Starter cable and torque the nut to 10 ft. lbs. (14 Nm)
- Ground cable and torque the nut to 52 inch lbs. (6 Nm)
- Starter positive cable protective plastic cap (3)
- Starter bolts and torque to 31 ft. lbs. (42 Nm)
- Right side exhaust pipe
- Right side O2 sensor
- Lower engine panel

6. Lower the vehicle and connect the negative battery cable.

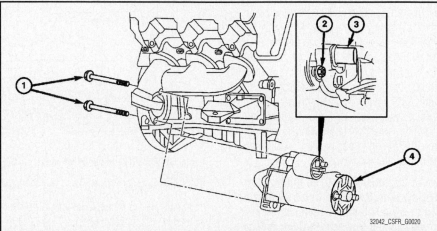

Fig. 32 Exploded view of starter mounting bolts (1), starter (4), cable cap (3) and ground cable nut (2)

ENGINE MECHANICAL

→Disconnecting the negative battery cable may interfere with the functions of the on board computer systems and may require the computer to undergo a relearning process, once the negative battery cable is reconnected.

ACCESSORY DRIVE BELTS

ACCESSORY BELT ROUTING

See Figures 33 and 34.

INSPECTION

See Figure 35.

Belt replacement is necessary for any or all of the following conditions:
- Excessive wear
- Frayed cords
- Severe glazing

The accessory drive belt may develop minor cracks across the ribbed side (1) due to reverse bending. These minor cracks are considered normal and acceptable. Parallel cracks (2) are not considered normal and should be cause for belt replacement.

→Do not use any type of belt dressing or restorer on the accessory drive belt.

ADJUSTMENT

The accessory drive belt is automatically adjusted by the non-adjustable tensioner.

REMOVAL & INSTALLATION

See Figure 36.

Except SRT

1. Before servicing the vehicle, refer to the Precautions Section.

2. Remove the engine cover. Grasp both corners of the engine cover and pull up firmly.

✳✳ CAUTION

The accessory drive belt tensioner pulley is spring loaded and can injure hands and fingers if allowed to spring back.

3. Rotate the belt tensioner counterclockwise and release the tension on the drive belt.

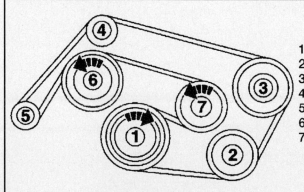

1. Crankshaft
2. A/C compressor
3. Power steering pump
4. Idler Pulley
5. Alternator
6. Water pump
7. Tensioner (7)

Fig. 33 Accessory drive belt routing—except SRT

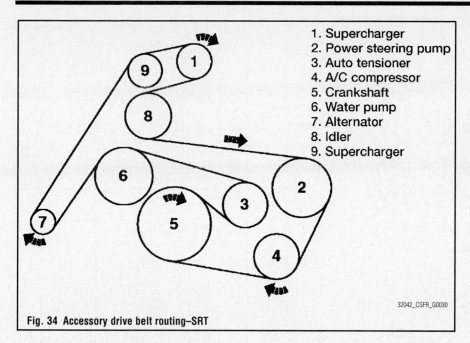

1. Supercharger
2. Power steering pump
3. Auto tensioner
4. A/C compressor
5. Crankshaft
6. Water pump
7. Alternator
8. Idler
9. Supercharger

32042_CSFR_G0030

Fig. 34 Accessory drive belt routing–SRT

4. Remove the drive belt from the pulleys.

5. Carefully release the wrench tension on the belt tensioner.

To install:

6. Route the accessory drive belt onto the engine pulleys.

7. Rotate the belt tensioner counterclockwise and install the accessory drive belt over the tensioner pulley.

8. Release the belt tensioner and remove the wrench.

9. Install the engine cover. Align the engine cover retaining clips to the rubber mounts, and push down firmly to connect engine cover to rubber mounts.

➡**To ease the installation of the engine cover, apply a small amount of lubricant to the engine cover rubber mounts.**

10. Start the engine and verify the accessory drive belt is properly routed and seated.

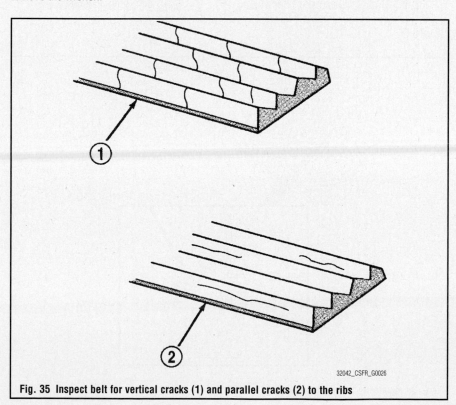

32042_CSFR_G0026

Fig. 35 Inspect belt for vertical cracks (1) and parallel cracks (2) to the ribs

SRT

1. Before servicing the vehicle, refer to the Precautions Section.

2. Remove the engine cover. Grasp both corners of the engine cover and pull up firmly.

❊❊ CAUTION

The accessory drive belt tensioner pulley is spring loaded and can injure hands and fingers if allowed to spring back.

3. Pull the tensioning pulley in a counter clockwise direction.

4. Lock the tensioning pulley with a pin or slowly release the pulley after the belt is free from the area.

5. Remove the belt.

To install:

6. Route the accessory drive belt onto the engine pulleys.

7. Install the supercharger idler pulley upper and lower mounting bolts and torque to 15 ft. lbs. (20 Nm).

8. Rotate the belt tensioner counterclockwise and install the accessory drive belt over the tensioner pulley.

9. Release the belt tensioner and remove the wrench.

10. Install the air pump tube assembly to the engine.

11. Install the engine cover. Align engine cover retaining clips to the rubber mounts, and push down firmly to connect engine cover to rubber mounts.

➡ **To ease the installation of the engine cover, apply a small amount of lubricant to the engine cover rubber mounts.**

12. Start the engine and verify the accessory drive belt is properly routed and seated.

CAMSHAFT AND VALVE LIFTERS

INSPECTION

1. Before servicing the vehicle, refer to the Precautions Section.

2. Remove the camshaft from the engine.

3. Inspect the camshaft bearing journals for damage or binding.

➡**If the journals are binding, check the cylinder head for damage. Also check the cylinder head oil holes for clogging.**

4. Check the camshaft lobe and bearing surfaces for wear and damage. Replace as required.

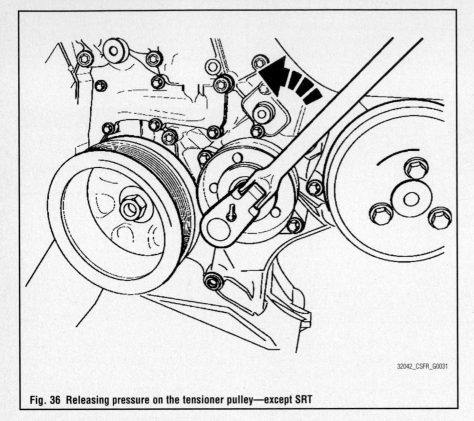

Fig. 36 Releasing pressure on the tensioner pulley—except SRT

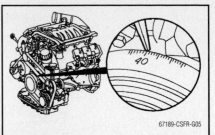

Fig. 37 Crankshaft timing mark set to 40 degrees ATDC

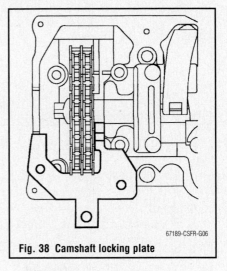

Fig. 38 Camshaft locking plate

5. Measure the lobe actual wear and replace the camshaft if it is out of limit. The standard value is 0.001 inch. The wear limit is 0.010 inch.

REMOVAL & INSTALLATION

See Figures 37 through 42.

1. Before servicing the vehicle, refer to the Precautions Section.
2. Drain the cooling system.
3. Drain the engine oil
4. Properly relieve the fuel system pressure.
5. Remove or disconnect the following:
- Negative battery cable
- Air intake assembly
- Mass Air Flow (MAF) sensor
- Radiator and radiator fan
- Camshaft position sensor
- Intake manifold
- Cylinder head cover
- Exhaust pipes from exhaust manifold

6. Rotate the crankshaft so that the crankshaft timing mark aligns with the 40 degree After Top Dead Center (ATDC) mark on the front cover as shown. Grooves in the camshafts must be toward the inside of the wedge.
7. Lock the camshafts in place with Camshaft Locking Plates 9104 and 9105.
8. Remove the timing chain tensioner as shown.

9. Use a cable tie and secure the timing chain the camshaft sprocket.
10. Remove the camshaft sprockets.
11. Remove the camshaft locking plate tools.
12. Loosen and remove the camshaft bearing cap bolts in the sequence shown.
13. Remove the rocker arms and the camshafts.

To install:

14. Install the rocker arms and the camshafts.
15. Install the camshaft bearing cap bolts in the sequence shown. Tighten the

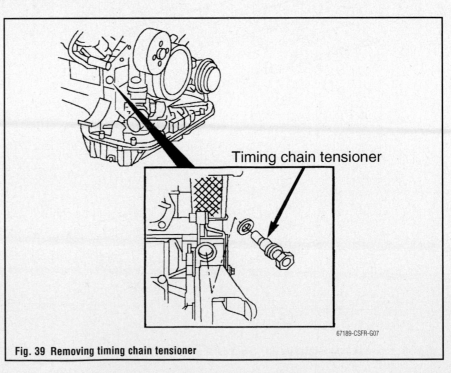

Timing chain tensioner

Fig. 39 Removing timing chain tensioner

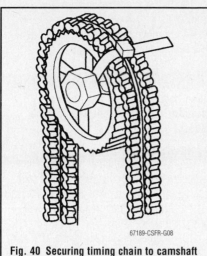

Fig. 40 Securing timing chain to camshaft sprocket

bolts to 11 ft. lbs. (15 Nm), plus an additional 90 degrees.

16. Lock the camshafts in place with Camshaft Locking Plates 9104 and 9105.

17. Install the camshaft sprockets. Tighten the bolts to 37 ft. lbs. (50 Nm), plus an additional 90 degrees.

18. Remove cable tie from timing chain.

19. Install the timing chain tensioner. Tighten the bolt to 59 ft. lbs. (80 Nm).

20. Remove camshaft locking plates

21. Ensure crankshaft is set to 40 degrees ATDC

22. Install or connect the following:
  • Exhaust pipes to manifold. Tighten the bolts to 15 ft. lbs. (20 Nm).
  • Cylinder head covers. Tighten the bolts to 89 inch lbs. (10 Nm).
  • Intakc manifold.
  • Ignition coils
  • Accessory drive belt
  • Camshaft position sensor
  • Radiator and radiator fan
  • Mass Air Flow (MAF) sensor
  • Air intake assembly
  • Negative battery cable

23. Fill and bleed the cooling system.

24. Fill the engine with oil.

25. Start the engine and check for leaks.

CRANKSHAFT FRONT SEAL

REMOVAL & INSTALLATION

See Figure 43.

1. Before servicing the vehicle, refer to the Precautions Section.

2. Disconnect battery negative cable from battery and properly isolate to prevent accidental reconnection.

3. Remove or disconnect the following:
  • Engine cooling fan and shroud
  • Accessory drive belt
  • Vibration damper

4. Protect the crankshaft with a rag and pry out the front crankshaft oil seal with a suitable tool.

To install:

5. Remove any burrs from the seal's mounting surface.
  a. The circumference and the sealing lip of the front crankshaft oil seal and its mating surface MUST be free of oil and grease.

6. Fit the front crankshaft oil seal onto the Special Tool 9103 or a suitable crankshaft seal driver.
  a. If using Special Tool 9103, align the slot in the tool with the crankshaft key and install the vibration damper bolt to press in the new seal until it bottoms.
  b. Remove the seal driver and damper bolt.

7. Install the vibration damper.

8. Install or connect the following:

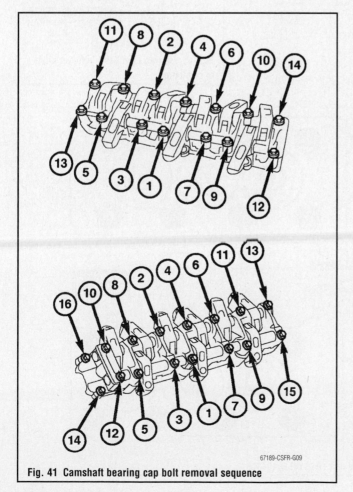

Fig. 41 Camshaft bearing cap bolt removal sequence

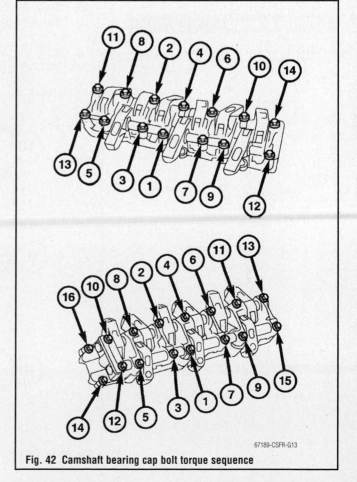

Fig. 42 Camshaft bearing cap bolt torque sequence

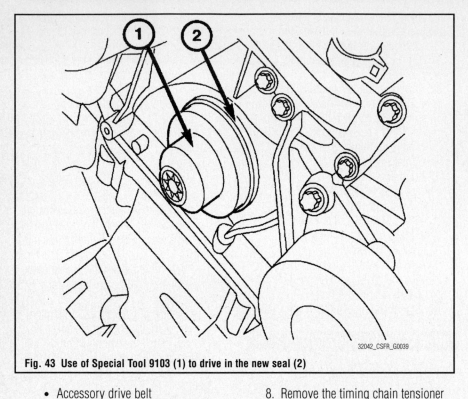

Fig. 43 Use of Special Tool 9103 (1) to drive in the new seal (2)

- Accessory drive belt
- Engine cooling fan and shroud
- Negative battery cable
9. Start the engine and check for leaks.

CYLINDER HEAD

REMOVAL & INSTALLATION

See Figures 37 through 41 and 44 through 46.

1. Before servicing the vehicle, refer to the Precautions Section.
2. Drain the cooling system.
3. Drain the engine oil
4. Properly relieve the fuel system pressure.
5. Remove or disconnect the following:
- Negative battery cable
- Air intake assembly
- Mass Air Flow (MAF) sensor
- Radiator and radiator fan
- Camshaft position sensor
- Intake manifold
- Cylinder head cover
- Exhaust pipes from exhaust manifold
6. Rotate the crankshaft so that the crankshaft timing mark aligns with the 40 degree After Top Dead Center (ATDC) mark on the front cover as shown. Grooves in the camshafts must be toward the inside of the wedge.
7. Lock the camshafts in place with Camshaft Locking Plates 9104 and 9105.

8. Remove the timing chain tensioner as shown.
9. Use a cable tie and secure the timing chain the camshaft sprocket.
10. Remove the camshaft sprockets.
11. Remove the camshaft locking plate tools.
12. Loosen and remove the camshaft bearing cap bolts in the sequence shown.

13. Remove the rocker arms and the camshafts.
14. Remove the cylinder head bolts in the sequence shown.
15. Remove the cylinder head.

➡**The cylinder head is retained by sixteen bolts. Eight of the bolts are smaller and are at the front of the head.**

To install:

16. Check the cylinder head bolts for signs of stretching. If length exceeds 5.67 inches (144 mm), replace bolts as necessary.
17. Lubricate the threads of the bolts with clean engine oil.
18. Install the cylinder heads. Use new gaskets and tighten the bolts, in sequence, as follows:
   a. Step 1: 7 ft. lbs. (10 Nm)
   b. Step 2: 22 ft. lbs. (30 Nm)
   c. Step 3: rotate bolts 90 degrees clockwise
   d. Step 4: rotate bolts 90 degrees clockwise

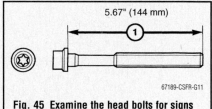

Fig. 45 Examine the head bolts for signs of stretching

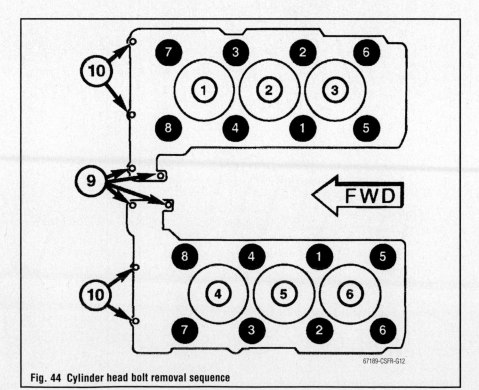

Fig. 44 Cylinder head bolt removal sequence

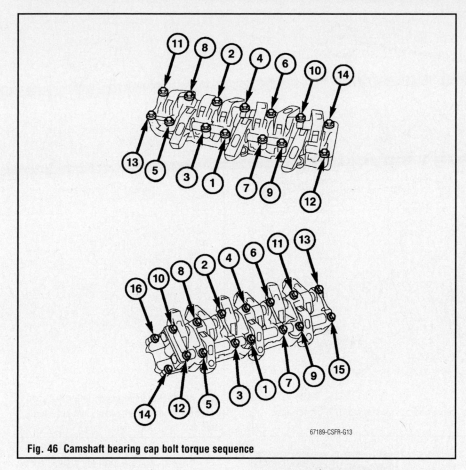

Fig. 46 Camshaft bearing cap bolt torque sequence

67189-CSFR-G13

e. Step 5: Bolts 9 and 10 to 7–15 ft. lbs. (10–20 Nm)

19. Install the rocker arms and the camshafts.

20. Install the camshaft bearing cap bolts in the sequence shown. Tighten the bolts to 11 ft. lbs. (15 Nm), plus an additional 90 degrees.

21. Lock the camshafts in place with Camshaft Locking Plates 9104 and 9105.

22. Install the camshaft sprockets. Tighten the bolts to 37 ft. lbs. (50 Nm), plus an additional 90 degrees.

23. Remove cable tie from timing chain.

24. Install the timing chain tensioner. Tighten the bolt to 59 ft. lbs. (80 Nm).

25. Remove camshaft locking plates

26. Ensure crankshaft is set to 40 degrees ATDC

27. Install or connect the following:
- Exhaust pipes to manifold. Tighten the bolts to 15 ft. lbs. (20 Nm).
- Cylinder head covers. Tighten the bolts to 89 inch lbs. (10 Nm).
- Intake manifold.
- Ignition coils
- Accessory drive belt
- Camshaft position sensor
- Radiator and radiator fan
- Mass Air Flow (MAF) sensor

- Air intake assembly
- Negative battery cable

28. Fill and bleed the cooling system.
29. Fill the engine with oil.
30. Start the engine and check for leaks.

ENGINE ASSEMBLY

REMOVAL & INSTALLATION

See Figures 47 and 48.

1. Before servicing the vehicle, refer to the Precautions Section.
2. Drain the cooling system.
3. Recover the A/C refrigerant, if equipped.
4. Drain the engine oil.
5. Relieve the fuel system pressure.
6. Remove or disconnect the following:
- Negative battery cable
- Air cleaner housing assembly
- Radiator hoses
- Radiator and fan shroud
- Accessory drive belt
- Vacuum hoses from brake booster, intake manifold and purge valve
- Power steering fluid from pump
- Ground lead at power steering pump
- Power steering pressure and return lines at pump

- Oxygen (O$_2$) sensors
- Mass Air Flow (MAF) sensor
- Heater hose
- Fuel supply line
- Engine wiring harness and all electrical connectors
- Lower radiator hose and coolant bypass hose from water pump
- Upper radiator hose from thermostat housing

7. Raise and support vehicle on jack stands.

8. Remove or disconnect the following:
- Engine undercover
- Front exhaust pipes
- Ground cable at transmission
- Driveshaft
- Starter

9. Place a transmission jack under the transmission.

10. Remove or disconnect the following:
- Transmission assembly
- A/C compressor and place aside with lines attached
- Front engine mount bolts

11. Lower the vehicle.

12. Attach a suitable engine lifting device to the engine lifting eyes.

13. Remove engine assembly from the vehicle.

To install:

14. Lower the engine into the vehicle.

15. Install or connect the following:
- Front engine mount. Tighten the bolt to 41 ft. lbs. (55 Nm).
- Transmission
- A/C compressor. Tighten the bolts to 17 ft. lbs. (23 Nm).

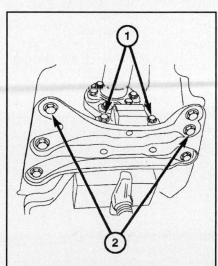

1. Transmission mount bolts
2. Crossmember bolts

67189-CSFR-G03

Fig. 47 Rear crossmember/transmission mount

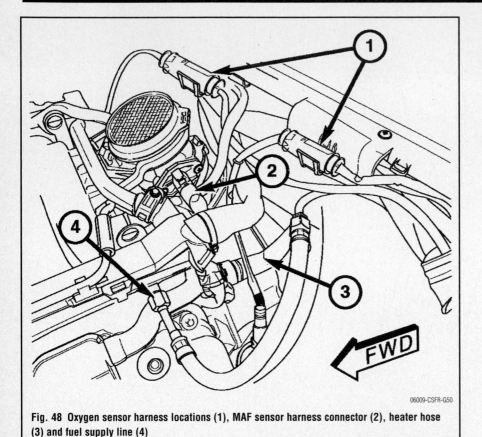

Fig. 48 Oxygen sensor harness locations (1), MAF sensor harness connector (2), heater hose (3) and fuel supply line (4)

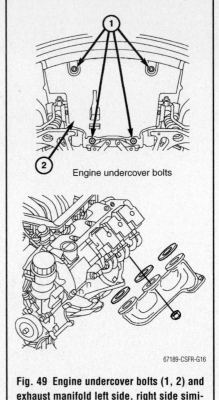

Fig. 49 Engine undercover bolts (1, 2) and exhaust manifold left side, right side similar

- Transmission ground cable. Tighten to 30 ft. lbs. (40 Nm).
- Starter
- Driveshaft
- Front exhaust pipes
- Engine undercover
- Lower radiator hose and coolant bypass hose
- Heater hoses to the rear of the intake manifold
- Upper radiator hose
- Engine wiring harness
- Fuel supply line. Tighten fitting to 28 ft. lbs. (38 Nm).
- O_2 sensors, MAF sensor and heater hose
- Power steering lines. Tighten fittings to 33 ft. lbs. (45 Nm).
- Power steering pump ground. Tighten bolt to 18 ft. lbs. (25 Nm).
- Vacuum hoses
- Accessory drive belt
- Radiator and fan
- Air cleaner housing
- Negative battery cable

16. Fill the power steering pump to the correct level.
17. Fill the crankcase to the correct level.
18. Fill the cooling system.
19. Start the engine and check for leaks.

EXHAUST MANIFOLD

REMOVAL & INSTALLATION

See Figure 49.

1. Before servicing the vehicle, refer to the Precautions Section.
2. Remove or disconnect the following:
   - Negative battery cable
   - Air intake assembly
   - Engine undercover
   - Catalytic converters
   - Exhaust manifolds

To install:
3. Install or connect the following:
   - Exhaust manifolds, using new gaskets. Tighten the bolts to 26 ft. lbs. (35 Nm).
   - Catalytic converters
   - Engine undercover
   - Air intake assembly
4. Start the engine and check for leaks.

INTAKE MANIFOLD

REMOVAL & INSTALLATION

See Figure 50.

1. Before servicing the vehicle, refer to the Precautions Section.
2. Drain the cooling system.

3. Properly relieve the fuel system pressure.
4. Remove or disconnect the following:
   - Negative battery cable
   - Air intake assembly
   - Mass Air Flow (MAF) sensor
   - Fuel rail and injectors
   - Vacuum lines
   - Engine wiring connectors
   - EGR pipe at EGR valve
   - Air pump switchover valves
   - Intake manifold

To install:
5. Install or connect the following:
   - Intake manifold using new gaskets. Torque the bolts to 15 ft. lbs. (20 Nm).
   - Air pump switchover valves
   - EGR pipe at EGR valve and tighten to 30 ft. lbs. (40 Nm)
   - MAF sensor
   - Engine wiring connectors
   - Vacuum lines
   - Fuel rail and injectors
   - Air intake assembly
   - Negative battery cable
6. Fill and bleed the cooling system.
7. Start the engine and check for leaks.

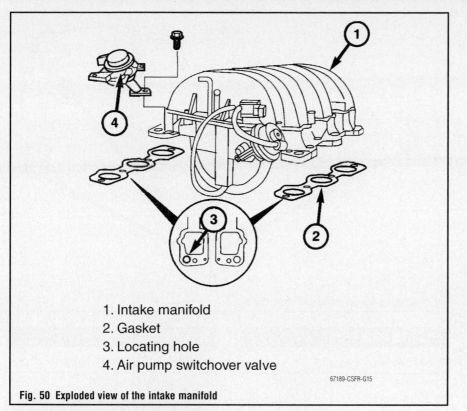

1. Intake manifold
2. Gasket
3. Locating hole
4. Air pump switchover valve

67189-CSFR-G15

Fig. 50 Exploded view of the intake manifold

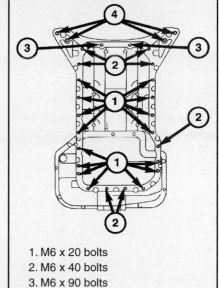

1. M6 x 20 bolts
2. M6 x 40 bolts
3. M6 x 90 bolts
4. M6 x 30 bolts

67189-CSFR-G17

Fig. 52 Upper oil pan mounting bolt locations

OIL PAN

REMOVAL & INSTALLATION

Lower Oil Pan

See Figure 51.

1. Before servicing the vehicle, refer to the Precautions Section.
2. Drain the engine oil.
3. Remove or disconnect the following:

• Negative battery cable
• Engine undercover
• Transmission oil cooler line retainer bolts and place line aside
• Oil pan
• Oil pan gasket

To install:

4. Install a bead of sealant around oil pan perimeter.
5. Install or connect the following:
• Oil pan. Tighten the bolts to 10 ft. lbs. (14 Nm).
• Transmission oil cooler lines
• Oil drain plug. Tighten to 22 ft. lbs. (30 Nm).
• Engine undercover
• Negative battery cable
6. Fill the engine with oil.
7. Start the engine and check for leaks.

Upper Oil Pan

See Figure 52.

1. Before servicing the vehicle, refer to the Precautions Section.

2. Drain the engine oil.
3. Remove or disconnect the following:
• Negative battery cable
• Engine undercover
• Lower oil pan
• Front exhaust pipes

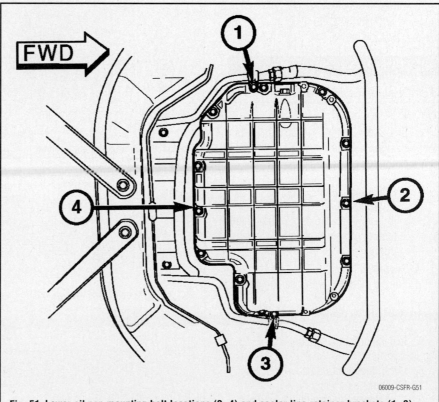

06009-CSFR-G51

Fig. 51 Lower oil pan mounting bolt locations (2, 4) and cooler line retainer brackets (1, 3)

- Oil level/temperature sensor harness connector
- Front engine mount bolts
- Oil dipstick tube assembly

4. Install an engine support bracket and attach a suitable lifting device.

5. Raise the engine slightly to provide clearance to upper oil pan bolts.

➡**Take care not to damage coolant, power steering and A/C lines when lifting the raising the engine.**

6. Remove the upper oil pan bolts.

7. Separate the oil pan from the engine block.

To install:

8. Install a bead of sealant around oil pan perimeter.

9. Install the correct bolts in the proper locations as shown. Torque the M6 bolts to 89 inch lbs. (10 Nm), and M8 bolts to 15 ft. lbs. (20 Nm).

10. Install the lower oil pan.

11. Lower the engine back into position.

12. Remove the engine support bracket.

13. Install or connect the following:
- Dipstick tube assembly
- Front engine mount bolts. Tighten to 26 ft. lbs. (35 Nm).
- Oil level/temperature sensor harness connector
- Front exhaust pipes
- Engine undercover
- Negative battery cable

14. Fill the engine with oil.

15. Start the engine and check for leaks.

OIL PUMP

REMOVAL & INSTALLATION

See Figure 53.

1. Before servicing the vehicle, refer to the Precautions Section.

2. Remove or disconnect the following:
- Lower oil pan
- Oil pump bolts
- Release the oil pump timing chain tensioner and remove the oil pump

To install:

3. Fill the oil pump with clean engine oil.

4. Position the pump driven sprocket into the drive chain.

5. Install and torque the bolts to 15 ft. lbs. (20 Nm).

6. Install the lower oil pan.

7. Fill the engine with oil.

8. Start the engine and check for leaks.

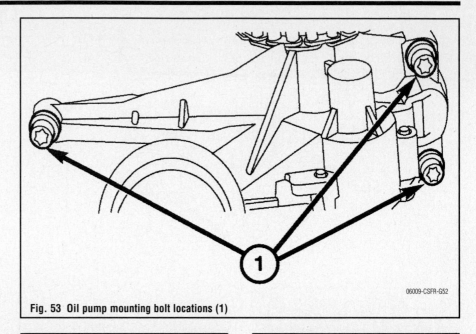

Fig. 53 Oil pump mounting bolt locations (1)

06009-CSFR-G52

PISTON AND RING

POSITIONING

See Figures 54 and 55.

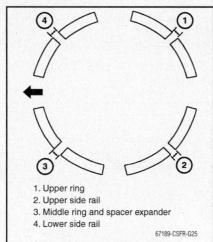

1. Upper ring
2. Upper side rail
3. Middle ring and spacer expander
4. Lower side rail

67189-CSFR-G25

Fig. 54 Piston ring end-gap spacing

REAR MAIN SEAL

REMOVAL & INSTALLATION

See Figures 56 through 58.

1. Before servicing the vehicle, refer to the Precautions Section.

➡**The rear main seal cannot be replaced separately. The crankshaft end cover and oil seal are replaced as a set.**

2. Remove or disconnect the following:
- Transmission
- Flywheel
- Crankshaft end cover

3. Clean the engine block and oil pan sealing surfaces.

To install:

4. Install a bead of sealant as shown on the NEW end cover.

5. Install the end cover. Torque the bolts to 89 inch lbs. (10 Nm).

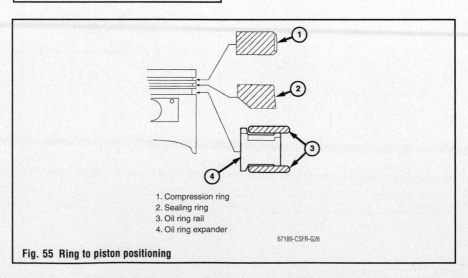

1. Compression ring
2. Sealing ring
3. Oil ring rail
4. Oil ring expander

67189-CSFR-G26

Fig. 55 Ring to piston positioning

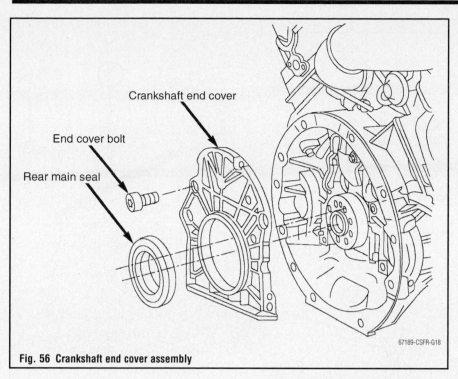

Crankshaft end cover

End cover bolt

Rear main seal

67189-CSFR-G18

Fig. 56 Crankshaft end cover assembly

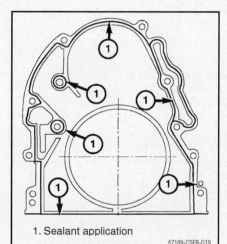

1. Sealant application

67189-CSFR-G19

Fig. 57 Crankshaft end cover sealant application

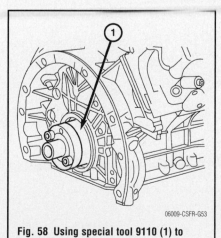

06009-CSFR-G53

Fig. 58 Using special tool 9110 (1) to install the seal

6. Use Special Tool 9100 and install the real seal into the end cover.

7. Remove the seal installer.

8. Install the following:
- Flywheel
- Transmission

TIMING CHAIN, SPROCKETS, FRONT COVER AND SEAL

REMOVAL & INSTALLATION

See Figures 59 through 66.

1. Before servicing the vehicle, refer to the Precautions Section.
2. Drain the cooling system.
3. Drain the power steering pump fluid.
4. Remove or disconnect the following:
- Negative battery cable
- Radiator fan
- Accessory drive belt
- Idler pulley
- Accessory drive belt tensioner

- Vibration damper
- Coolant and heater hoses from water pump
- Power steering pump
- AIR pump
- Cylinder head covers
- Front cylinder head to timing chain cover retaining bolts
- Alternator
- Lower oil pan
- Upper oil pan
- Starter

5. Rotate crankshaft to 40 degrees After Top Dead Center (ATDC).

6. Lock the flywheel in place using Special Tool 9102 by inserting the tool into the starter opening.

7. Remove or disconnect the following:
- Timing chain tensioner
- Timing chain cover
- Oil pump drive chain and tensioner
- Left and right camshaft sprocket bolts
- Timing chain and camshaft sprockets
- Timing chain camshaft sprocket
- Rear main seal

8. Hold the balance shaft rear counter weight using a drift, and remove the rear retaining bolt.

9. Remove the balance shaft counterweight.

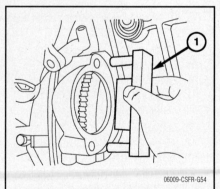

06009-CSFR-G54

Fig. 60 Locking the flywheel in place with tool 9102

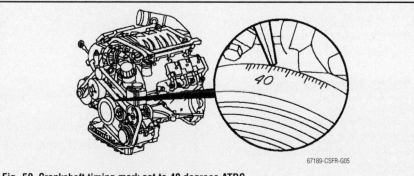

67189-CSFR-G05

Fig. 59 Crankshaft timing mark set to 40 degrees ATDC

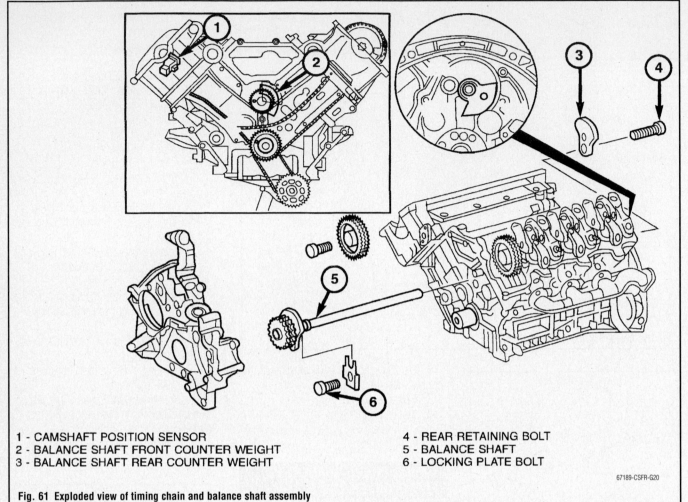

1 - CAMSHAFT POSITION SENSOR
2 - BALANCE SHAFT FRONT COUNTER WEIGHT
3 - BALANCE SHAFT REAR COUNTER WEIGHT

4 - REAR RETAINING BOLT
5 - BALANCE SHAFT
6 - LOCKING PLATE BOLT

67189-CSFR-G20

Fig. 61 Exploded view of timing chain and balance shaft assembly

10. Remove the balance shaft locking plate at the front of the engine block.

11. Remove the balance shaft.

12. Pry out the front crankshaft seal using a suitable pry tool.

To install:

13. Position the front crankshaft seal into Special Tool 9103 as shown.

14. Align the slot of the installation tool into the crankshaft keyway.

15. Tap the tool in until the crankshaft damper bolt can be inserted.

16. Tighten the damper bolt until the seal is installed.

17. Remove the installer tool.

18. Place the balance shaft into the bore in the block from the front of the engine.

19. Install the rear counter weight onto the shaft and torque the retaining bolt to 15 ft. lbs. (20 Nm), plus an additional 90 degrees.

20. Install the balance shaft locking plate and bolt and torque to 15 ft. lbs. (20 Nm).

21. Install the rear crankshaft seal/end cover assembly.

22. Install the crankshaft sprocket.

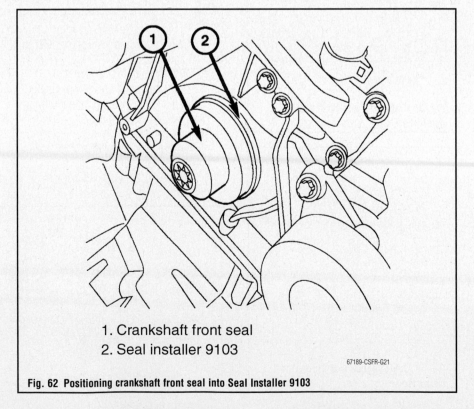

1. Crankshaft front seal
2. Seal installer 9103

67189-CSFR-G21

Fig. 62 Positioning crankshaft front seal into Seal Installer 9103

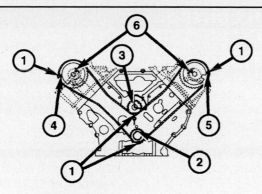

1. Copper teeth
2. Crankshaft sprocket
3. Balance shaft timing mark
4. Camshaft sprocket timing mark
5. Camshaft sprocket timing mark
6. Camshaft sprockets

67189-CSFR-G22

Fig. 63 Positioning timing chain on camshaft sprockets

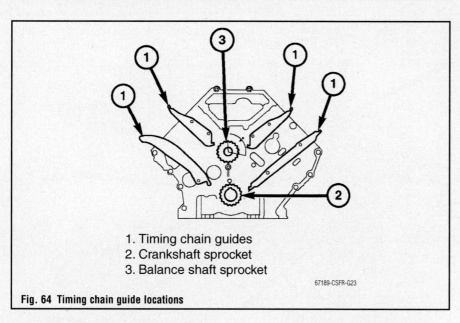

1. Timing chain guides
2. Crankshaft sprocket
3. Balance shaft sprocket

67189-CSFR-G23

Fig. 64 Timing chain guide locations

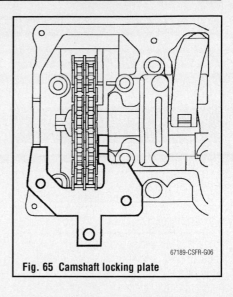

67189-CSFR-G06

Fig. 65 Camshaft locking plate

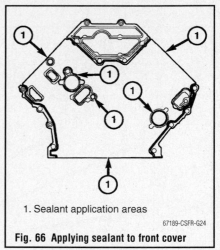

1. Sealant application areas

67189-CSFR-G24

Fig. 66 Applying sealant to front cover

23. Ensure that the crankshaft is still positioned at 40 degrees ATDC.

24. Align the balance shaft sprocket with the timing chain (3) and check that the copper teeth (1) of the timing chain are aligned on the camshaft sprockets (6).

25. Route the timing chain within the timing chain guides as shown.

26. Lock the camshafts in place with Camshaft Locking Plates 9104 and 9105.

27. Install the oil pump drive chain and tensioner.

28. Apply sealant to timing chain cover as shown.

29. Install or connect the following:
- Timing chain cover. Torque the bolts to 15 ft. lbs. (20 Nm).
- Timing chain tensioner. Torque the bolt to 59 ft. lbs. (80 Nm).

30. Remove Special Tool 9102 to unlock the flywheel.

31. Install or connect the following:
- Starter
- Upper and lower oil pans
- Alternator
- Front cylinder head to timing chain cover bolts. Tighten to 15 ft. lbs. (20 Nm).
- Cylinder head covers
- AIR pump
- Power steering pump
- Coolant and heater hoses to water pump
- Vibration damper. Tighten to 148 ft. lbs. (200 Nm) plus 90 degrees clockwise.
- Idler pulley
- Accessory belt tensioner
- Accessory drive belt
- Radiator fan
- Negative battery cable

32. Fill the power steering pump with fluid.

33. Fill and bleed the cooling system.

VALVE LASH

ADJUSTMENT

All engines use hydraulic valve lash adjusters; no adjustment is possible or required.

ENGINE PERFORMANCE & EMISSION CONTROL

COMPONENT LOCATIONS

See Figure 67.

CAMSHAFT POSITION (CMP) SENSOR

LOCATION

The Camshaft Position (CMP) sensor is located on the right front cylinder head

OPERATION

The CMP sensor is a hall effect type sensor and is used to determine when number one cylinder is on the compression stroke.

REMOVAL & INSTALLATION

1. Before servicing the vehicle, refer to the Precautions Section.
2. Disconnect the negative battery cable.
3. Remove the air cleaner housing.
4. Disconnect the sensor electrical connector.
5. Remove the sensor retaining bolt.
6. Remove the sensor from its mounting.

To install:

7. Installation is the reverse of the removal procedure.
8. Inspect the sensor O-ring for damage, replace as required.
9. Lubricate the O-ring with clean engine oil prior to installation.

10. Tighten the retaining bolt to 71 inch lbs.

CRANKSHAFT POSITION (CKP) SENSOR

LOCATION

The Crankshaft Position (CKP) sensor is located on the left side of the engine just forward of the transmission housing. The bottom of the sensor is positioned above the flywheel.

OPERATION

The CKP sensor generates pulses that are signals sent to the PCM. The PCM interprets these signals to determine the

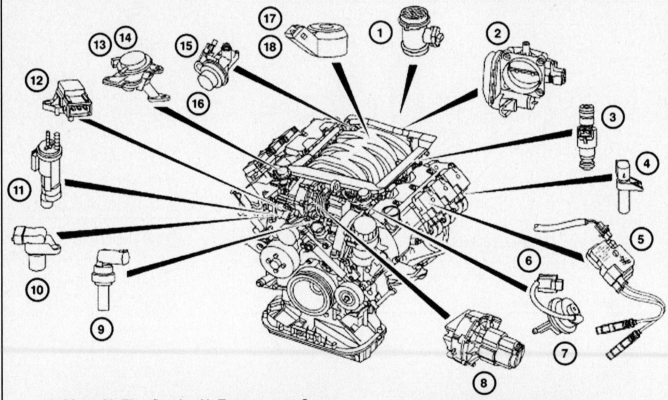

1. Mass Air Flow/Intake Air Temperature Sensor
2. Throttle Body (Includes Electronic Throttle Control and Throttle Position Sensor)
3. Fuel Injector
4. Crankshaft Position Sensor
5. Ignition Coil
6. Short Runner Valve Solenoid
7. Short Runner Valve
8. Air Pump
9. Coolant Temperature Sensor
10. Camshaft Position Sensor
11. Air Pump Switchover Solenoid
12. Manifold Absolute Pressure Sensor
13. Right Air Pump Switchover Valve
14. Left Air Pump Switchover Valve
15. Exhaust Gas Recirculation Solenoid
16. Exhaust Gas Recirculation Valve
17. Right Knock Sensor
18. Left Knock Sensor

Fig. 67 Component Locations

22043_CSFR_G0003

crankshaft position. The PCM uses this data along with other inputs to determine injector sequence and ignition timing.

REMOVAL & INSTALLATION

1. Before servicing the vehicle, refer to the Precautions Section.
2. Disconnect the negative battery cable.
3. Remove the air cleaner housing.
4. Disconnect the sensor electrical connector.
5. Remove the sensor retaining bolt.
6. Remove the sensor from its mounting.

To install:

7. Installation is the reverse of the removal procedure.
8. Tighten the retaining bolt to 71 inch lbs.

ELECTRONIC CONTROL MODULE (ECM)

LOCATION

The Electronic Control Module (ECM) is located in the engine compartment inside the control module box, located next to the battery.

OPERATION

The ECM controls the vehicle engine operating system.

REMOVAL & INSTALLATION

1. Before servicing the vehicle, refer to the Precautions Section.
2. Disconnect the negative battery cable.
3. Slide the clips forward to remove the plastic control module box cover.
4. Holding the retaining clip back, pull the PCM module up and out of the control module box.
5. Disconnect the electrical connectors.
6. Remove the PCM from the vehicle.

To install:

7. Installation is the reverse of the removal procedure.

ENGINE COOLANT TEMPERATURE (ECT) SENSOR

LOCATION

The Engine Coolant Temperature (ECT) sensor is located on top of the engine, near the upper radiator hose.

OPERATION

The ECT sensor provides coolant temperature data the PCM. When the engine is cold the PCM will demand slightly richer air/fuel mixtures and higher idle speeds until normal operating temperature is reached. This sensor also determines the operation of the radiator fan.

REMOVAL & INSTALLATION

Except SRT

1. Before servicing the vehicle, refer to the Precautions Section.
2. Disconnect the negative battery cable.
3. Partially drain the cooling system. Be sure to collect and dispose of used coolant, as required.
4. Remove the engine cover.
5. Disconnect the sensor electrical connector.
6. Pull up on the sensor retaining clip. Slide the sensor out of the housing.
7. Remove the sensor from its mounting.

To install:

8. Installation is the reverse of the removal procedure.
9. Use a small amount of petroleum jelly to lubricate the sensor seal.
10. Be sure to fill the engine with the proper grade and type coolant.
11. Start the engine and check for leaks.

SRT

1. Before servicing the vehicle, refer to the Precautions Section.
2. Disconnect the negative battery cable.
3. Partially drain the cooling system. Be sure to collect and dispose of used coolant, as required.
4. Remove the engine cover.
5. Remove the air pump tube retaining bolts. Remove the air pump from the engine.
6. Remove the tension on the accessory drive belt. Remove the drive belt.
7. Remove the supercharger idler pulley upper retaining bolt and lower retaining bolt. Remove the idler pulley.
8. Remove the accessory drive belt idler pulley.
9. Disconnect the sensor electrical connector.
10. Pull up on the sensor retaining clip. Slide the sensor out of the housing.
11. Remove the sensor from its mounting.

To install:

12. Installation is the reverse of the removal procedure.
13. Use a small amount of petroleum jelly to lubricate the sensor seal.
14. Tighten the accessory drive belt idler pulley bolt to 15 ft. lbs.
15. Tighten the supercharger idler pulley bolts to 15 ft. lbs.
16. Be sure to fill the engine with the proper grade and type coolant.
17. Start the engine and check for leaks.

HEATED OXYGEN (HO2S) SENSOR

LOCATION

The Heated Oxygen (HO2S) sensors are attached to and protrude into the exhaust system. This vehicle uses four sensors.

OPERATION

The oxygen sensor senses the oxygen concentration in the exhaust gas then converts it into a voltage and sends it on to the PCM. The PCM controls fuel injection based on the signal so that the air fuel ratio is maintained at the theoretical ration.

REMOVAL & INSTALLATION

Upstream Sensor

1. Before servicing the vehicle, refer to the Precautions Section.
2. Disconnect the negative battery cable.
3. Remove the engine cover.
4. Disconnect the sensor electrical connector.
5. Remove the sensor retaining bolt.
6. Remove the sensor from its mounting.

To install:

7. Installation is the reverse of the removal procedure.
8. Apply anti-seize compound to the threaded portion of the sensor.
9. Tighten the retaining bolt to 37 ft. lbs.

Downstream Sensor

1. Before servicing the vehicle, refer to the Precautions Section.
2. Disconnect the negative battery cable.
3. Raise and support the vehicle safely.
4. Disconnect the sensor electrical connector.
5. Remove the sensor retaining bolt.
6. Remove the sensor from its mounting.

To install:

7. Installation is the reverse of the removal procedure.
8. Apply anti-seize compound to the threaded portion of the sensor.
9. Tighten the retaining bolt to 37 ft. lbs.

INTAKE AIR TEMPERATURE (IAT) SENSOR

LOCATION

The Intake Air Temperature (IAT) sensor is located on the rear of the engine and attached to the throttle body, under the air cleaner housing. This sensor also houses the MAF sensor.

OPERATION

The IAT sensor detects the intake air temperature. According to the intake air temperature reading the PCM will control the necessary amount of fuel injection.

REMOVAL & INSTALLATION

1. Before servicing the vehicle, refer to the Precautions Section.
2. Disconnect the negative battery cable.
3. Remove the engine cover.
4. Disconnect the sensor electrical connector.
5. Remove the vent hose.
6. Disengage the lock ring that attaches the sensor to the intake by inserting a suitable tool into the locking ring and moving the tabs on the intake away from their locked position.
7. Press the locking tab on the bottom right of the sensor down, using a suitable tool thereby unlocking it from the intake.
8. Press the locking tab on the upper left of the sensor upward with a suitable tool, unlocking it from the intake manifold.
9. Remove the sensor from the intake manifold.

To install:
10. Installation is the reverse of the removal procedure.
11. Inspect the sealing ring, replace if necessary.
12. Inspect the sealing ring between the air inlet and the sensor, replace if necessary.
13. Inspect the locking tabs, replace if necessary.

KNOCK SENSOR (KS)

LOCATION

This engine is equipped with two Knock Sensors (KS). They are located below the intake manifold in the engine valley.

OPERATION

The KS is used to detect engine vibrations caused by preignition or detonation and provides information to the PCM, which then retards the timing to eliminate detonation.

REMOVAL & INSTALLATION

1. Before servicing the vehicle, refer to the Precautions Section.
2. Disconnect the negative battery cable.
3. Remove the intake manifold.
4. Disconnect the sensor electrical connector.
5. Remove the sensor retaining bolt.
6. Remove the sensor from its mounting.

To install:

➡ **The knock sensor bolt torque is higher than the other sensors. If the proper torque is not applied driveability can be affected.**

7. Installation is the reverse of the removal procedure.
8. Tighten the retaining bolt to 15 ft. lbs.

MANIFOLD ABSOLUTE PRESSURE (MAP) SENSOR

LOCATION

Except SRT

The Manifold Absolute Pressure (MAP) sensor is mounted to the front of the engine on the right side, next to the air pump.

SRT

The MAP sensor is mounted in the charge air cooler below the throttle body.

OPERATION

Except SRT

The MAP sensor monitors the pressure in the intake manifold. The pressure in the manifold moves a diaphragm which is connected to piezo resistors which alter their resistance values. The output voltage of the resistors provides information to the PCM about the pressure in the intake manifold.

SRT

On the supercharged engine, the MAP sensor serves as a PCM input, using a silicon based sensing unit to provide data on the manifold vacuum pressure that draws/pushes the air/fuel mixture into the combustion chambers. The PCM uses this data combined the intake air temperature to determine the volume of air entering the engine.

REMOVAL & INSTALLATION

Except SRT

1. Before servicing the vehicle, refer to the Precautions Section.
2. Disconnect the negative battery cable.
3. Remove the engine cover.
4. Disconnect the sensor electrical connector.
5. Remove the sensor retaining bolt.
6. Remove the sensor from its mounting.

To install:
7. Installation is the reverse of the removal procedure.

SRT

1. Before servicing the vehicle, refer to the Precautions Section.
2. Disconnect the negative battery cable.
3. Remove the engine cover.
4. Remove the upper air cleaner housing. Remove the lower air cleaner housing.
5. Remove the right and left intake plenums.
6. Remove the throttle body.
7. Remove the supercharger outlet housing hose clamps. Remove the outlet housing.
8. Disconnect the sensor electrical connector.
9. Remove the sensor retaining bolt.
10. Remove the sensor from its mounting.

To install:
11. Installation is the reverse of the removal procedure.
12. Tighten the retaining bolt to 40 inch lbs.

MASS AIR FLOW (MAF) SENSOR

LOCATION

The Mass Air Flow (MAF) sensor is located on the rear of the engine and attached to the throttle body, under the air cleaner housing. This sensor also houses the IAT sensor.

OPERATION

The MAF sensor controls the temperature of the heating resistor by means of a variable voltage so its temperature is 160 degrees centigrade above the intake air temperature which is detected by the temperature resistor. The temperature of the heating resistor is detected by the sensor resistor. If a temperature change occurs as a result of an increased or decreased air flow, the PCM adapts the voltage at the heating resistor until the temperature difference is again achieved. This control voltage is used by the PCM as a measure for the metered mass. The intake air temperature is detected by an additional Negative Temperature Coefficient (NTC) resistor.

REMOVAL & INSTALLATION

1. Before servicing the vehicle, refer to the Precautions Section.
2. Disconnect the negative battery cable.
3. Remove the engine cover.
4. Disconnect the sensor electrical connector.
5. Remove the vent hose.
6. Disengage the lock ring that attaches the sensor to the intake by inserting a suitable tool into the locking ring and moving the tabs on the intake away from their locked position.
7. Press the locking tab on the bottom right of the sensor down, using a suitable tool thereby unlocking it from the intake.
8. Press the locking tab on the upper left of the sensor upward with a suitable tool, unlocking it from the intake manifold.
9. Remove the sensor from the intake manifold.

To install:
10. Installation is the reverse of the removal procedure.
11. Inspect the sealing ring, replace if necessary.
12. Inspect the sealing ring between the air inlet and the sensor, replace if necessary.
13. Inspect the locking tabs, replace if necessary.

THROTTLE POSITION SENSOR (TPS)

LOCATION

The Throttle Position Sensor (TPS) is part of the throttle body.

OPERATION

The TPS contains two actual potentiometers for detecting the position of the throttle valve. The system will switch to the second potentiometer if the first one fails. This sensor cannot be serviced separately. If the TPS fails, the throttle body must be replaced.

REMOVAL & INSTALLATION

Except SRT

1. Before servicing the vehicle, refer to the Precautions Section.
2. Remove or disconnect the following:
   - Negative battery cable
   - Throttle body intake tube
   - Electrical connector
   - PCV hose from the throttle body
   - Throttle body retaining bolts and PCV hose bracket
   - Throttle body with gasket

To install:
3. Install or connect the following:
   - PCV hose to the throttle body
   - Throttle body with new gasket. Tighten bolts to 15 ft. lbs. (20 Nm).

- Electrical connector
- Throttle body intake tube
- Negative battery cable

SRT

1. Before servicing the vehicle, refer to the Precautions Section.
2. Remove or disconnect the following:
   - Negative battery cable
   - Upper air intake assembly
   - Throttle body intake tube by lifting up on the inlet tube lever
   - Electrical connector
   - PCV hose from throttle body
   - Throttle body retaining bolts and PCV hose bracket
   - Throttle body and gasket

To install:
3. Install or connect the following:
   - PCV hose to the throttle body
   - Throttle body and gasket. Tighten to 15 ft. lbs. (20 Nm).
   - Electrical connector
   - Throttle body intake tube as follows:
   f. Install the upper air intake assembly.
   g. Install the throttle body intake tube by firmly inserting tube into the throttle body.
   h. Ensure the intake tube lever is attached.
   - Negative battery cable

FUEL   GASOLINE FUEL INJECTION SYSTEM

FUEL SYSTEM SERVICE PRECAUTIONS

Safety is the most important factor when performing not only fuel system maintenance but any type of maintenance. Failure to conduct maintenance and repairs in a safe manner may result in serious personal injury or death. Maintenance and testing of the vehicle's fuel system components can be accomplished safely and effectively by adhering to the following rules and guidelines.

- To avoid the possibility of fire and personal injury, always disconnect the negative battery cable unless the repair or test procedure requires that battery voltage be applied.
- Always relieve the fuel system pressure prior to disconnecting any fuel system component (injector, fuel rail, pressure regulator, etc.), fitting or fuel line connection. Exercise extreme caution whenever relieving

fuel system pressure to avoid exposing skin, face and eyes to fuel spray. Please be advised that fuel under pressure may penetrate the skin or any part of the body that it contacts.

- Always place a shop towel or cloth around the fitting or connection prior to loosening to absorb any excess fuel due to spillage. Ensure that all fuel spillage (should it occur) is quickly removed from engine surfaces. Ensure that all fuel soaked cloths or towels are deposited into a suitable waste container.
- Always keep a dry chemical (Class B) fire extinguisher near the work area.
- Do not allow fuel spray or fuel vapors to come into contact with a spark or open flame.
- Always use a back-up wrench when loosening and tightening fuel line connection fittings. This will prevent unnecessary stress and torsion to fuel line piping.
- Always replace worn fuel fitting O-rings with new Do not substitute fuel hose

or equivalent where fuel pipe is installed.
Before servicing the vehicle, make sure to also refer to the precautions in the beginning of this section as well.

RELIEVING FUEL SYSTEM PRESSURE

See Figure 68.

Relieve residual high pressure in the fuel system when performing any type of service that will expose you to liquid fuel.
1. Remove the fuel filler cap from the fuel filler neck.
2. Remove the fuel pump fuse from the relay control module located next to the PCM.
3. Start and run engine until it stalls.
4. Attempt restarting engine until it will no longer run.
5. Turn ignition key to OFF position.
6. Return the fuel pump fuse to the relay control module.

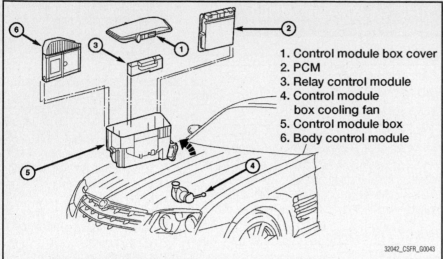

Fig. 68 Parts access to relieve fuel pressure—Control module box cover (1), PCM (2), Relay control module (3), Control module box cooling fan (4), Control module box (5), Body control module (6)

1. Control module box cover
2. PCM
3. Relay control module
4. Control module box cooling fan
5. Control module box
6. Body control module

32042_CSFR_G0043

7. One or more Diagnostic Trouble Codes may have been stored in PCM memory due to fuel pump fuse removal.

   a. The DRB IIIT scan tool must be used to erase any DTCs.

FUEL FILTER

REMOVAL & INSTALLATION

See Figure 69.

1. Before servicing the vehicle, refer to the Precautions Section.

➡**The fuel filter is integral with the fuel pressure regulator. Both must be replaced as an assembly.**

2. Relieve the fuel system pressure.
3. Raise and support the vehicle safely.

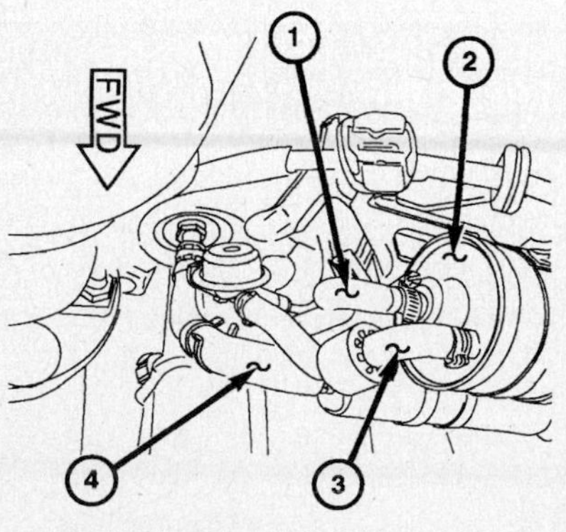

4. Remove or disconnect the following:

- Fuel pump splash shield
- Degassing line
- Fuel supply line
- Fuel delivery line
- Fuel return line

5. Pull the filter/regulator out of the mounting clamp.

To install:

6. Install the filter/regulator into the mounting clamp.

7. Install or connect the following in order:

- Fuel return line
- Fuel delivery line
- Fuel supply line
- Degassing line
- Splash shield

8. Start the engine and check for leaks.

FUEL INJECTORS

REMOVAL & INSTALLATION

See Figure 70.

1. Before servicing the vehicle, refer to the Precautions Section.
2. Relieve the fuel system pressure.
3. Remove or disconnect the following:

- Negative battery cable
- Wiring harness cover

4. Open fuel rail service valve.
5. Remove or disconnect:

- Fuel feed line
- Fuel injector retaining clamps
- Fuel supply manifold with injectors attached
- Fuel injectors

To install:

6. Install or connect the following:

- Fuel injectors, using new O-rings
- Fuel supply manifold with injectors attached. Tighten the bolts to 80 inch lbs. (9 Nm).
- Injector retaining clamps

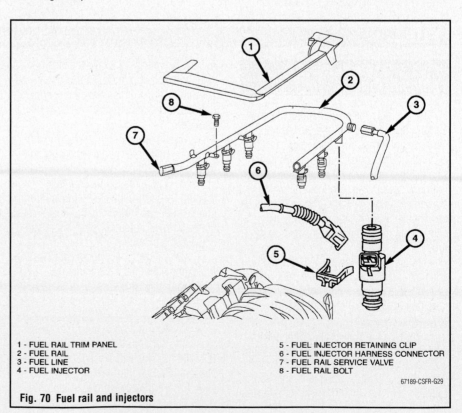

1. Degaussing line
2. Fuel filter/pressure regulator
3. Fuel supply line
4. Fuel return line

67189-CSFR-G27

Fig. 69 Fuel filter/pressure regulator assembly

1 - FUEL RAIL TRIM PANEL
2 - FUEL RAIL
3 - FUEL LINE
4 - FUEL INJECTOR
5 - FUEL INJECTOR RETAINING CLIP
6 - FUEL INJECTOR HARNESS CONNECTOR
7 - FUEL RAIL SERVICE VALVE
8 - FUEL RAIL BOLT

67189-CSFR-G29

Fig. 70 Fuel rail and injectors

- Fuel feed line. Tighten the fuel line to 28 ft. lbs. (38 Nm).
7. Close fuel rail service valve
8. Install or connect:
    - Fuel rail trim cover
    - Air cleaner housing
    - Negative battery cable
9. Start the engine and check for leaks.

FUEL PUMP

REMOVAL & INSTALLATION

See Figure 71.

1. Before servicing the vehicle, refer to the Precautions Section.
2. Relieve the fuel system pressure.
3. Raise and support the vehicle safely.
4. Remove or disconnect the following:
    - Negative battery cable
    - Splash shield
    - Fuel suction hose
    - Fuel delivery hose
    - Fuel pump electrical connectors
    - Fuel pump retaining clamp
    - Fuel pump

To install:
5. Install or connect the following:
    - Fuel pump
    - Fuel pump retaining clamp
    - Electrical connectors
    - Fuel delivery hose
    - Fuel suction hose
    - Splash shield
    - Negative battery cable
6. Start the engine and check for leaks.

FUEL TANK

REMOVAL & INSTALLATION

See Figure 72.

1. Before servicing the vehicle, refer to the Precautions Section.
2. Relieve the fuel system pressure.
3. Disconnect the negative battery cable.
4. Raise and support the vehicle safely.
5. Remove the fuel pump splash shield.
6. Properly drain the fuel from the tank in an approved fuel container.
7. Disconnect the fuel feed hose from the bottom of the fuel tank.
8. Disconnect the fuel return hose from the bottom of the fuel tank.
9. Remove the cargo trim panels.
10. Remove the fuel tank partition retaining bolts. Remove the partition.
11. Disconnect the fuel tank level and pressure sensor connectors from the sending unit.

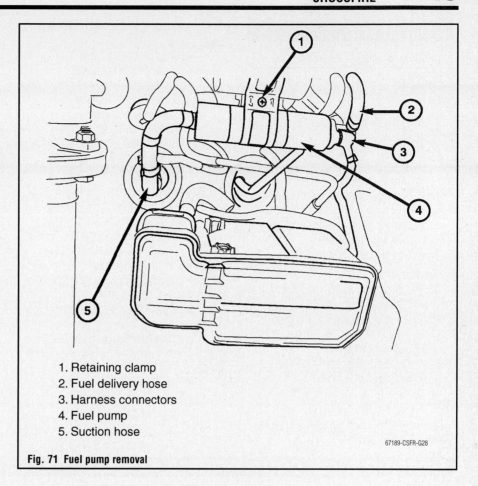

1. Retaining clamp
2. Fuel delivery hose
3. Harness connectors
4. Fuel pump
5. Suction hose

67189-CSFR-G28

Fig. 71 Fuel pump removal

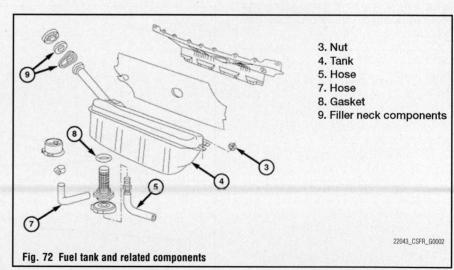

3. Nut
4. Tank
5. Hose
7. Hose
8. Gasket
9. Filler neck components

22043_CSFR_G0002

Fig. 72 Fuel tank and related components

12. Disconnect the fuel tank filler neck cup seals from the body.
13. Carefully remove the fuel tank from its mounting.
14. As required, remove the fuel strainer.

To install:
15. Be sure to inspect the strainer and O-ring for damage. Replace defective components as necessary.
16. Installation is the reverse of the removal procedure.

17. Be sure to use new gaskets and fuel line hose, as required.
18. Start the engine and check for leaks. Correct as required.

IDLE SPEED

ADJUSTMENT

Idle speed is maintained by the Powertrain Control Module (PCM). No adjustment is necessary or possible.

THROTTLE BODY

REMOVAL & INSTALLATION

Except SRT

See Figure 73.

1. Before servicing the vehicle, refer to the Precautions Section.
2. Remove or disconnect the following:
   - Negative battery cable
   - Throttle body intake tube
   - Electrical connector
   - PCV hose from the throttle body
   - Throttle body retaining bolts and PCV hose bracket
   - Throttle body with gasket

To install:

3. Install or connect the following:
   - PCV hose to the throttle body
   - Throttle body with new gasket. Tighten bolts to 15 ft. lbs. (20 Nm).
   - Electrical connector
   - Throttle body intake tube
   - Negative battery cable

SRT

1. Before servicing the vehicle, refer to the Precautions Section.

2. Remove or disconnect the following:
   - Negative battery cable
   - Upper air intake assembly
   - Throttle body intake tube by lifting up on the inlet tube lever
   - Electrical connector
   - PCV hose from throttle body
   - Throttle body retaining bolts and PCV hose bracket
   - Throttle body and gasket

To install:

3. Install or connect the following:
   - PCV hose to the throttle body
   - Throttle body and gasket. Tighten to 15 ft. lbs. (20 Nm).
   - Electrical connector
   - Throttle body intake tube as follows:

   b. Install the upper air intake assembly.

   c. Install the throttle body intake tube by firmly inserting tube into the throttle body.

   d. Ensure the intake tube lever is attached.
   - Negative battery cable

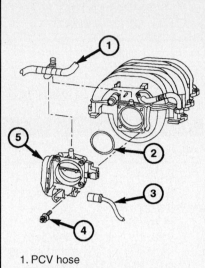

1. PCV hose
2. O ring
3. Harness connector
4. Bolts (4)
5. Throttle body

67189-CSFR-G30

Fig. 73 Throttle body

HEATING & AIR CONDITIONING SYSTEM

BLOWER MOTOR

REMOVAL & INSTALLATION

See Figures 74 and 75.

1. Before servicing the vehicle, refer to the Precautions Section.

2. Disconnect battery negative cable from battery and properly isolate to prevent accidental reconnection.

3. Remove or disconnect the following:
   - Lower instrument panel cover from the instrument panel
   - Blower motor electrical connector from the relief in the blower motor door
   - Blower motor door catch mounts
4. Swing the blower motor door down.
   - Screws attaching the blower motor to the heater housing
   - Blower motor and squirrel cage as an assembly

To install:

5. Install or connect the following:
   - Blower motor and squirrel cage as an assembly
   - Screws attaching the blower motor to the heater housing
6. Swing the blower motor door up.

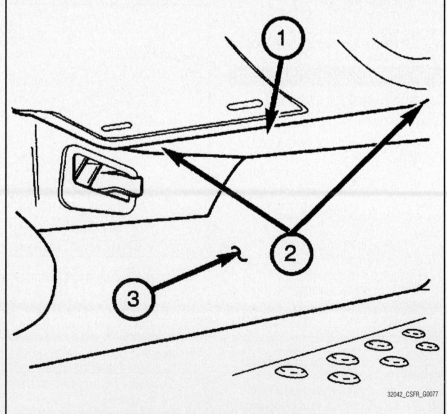

Fig. 74 Lower instrument panel cover (2) instrument panel (1, 3)

32042_CSFR_G0077

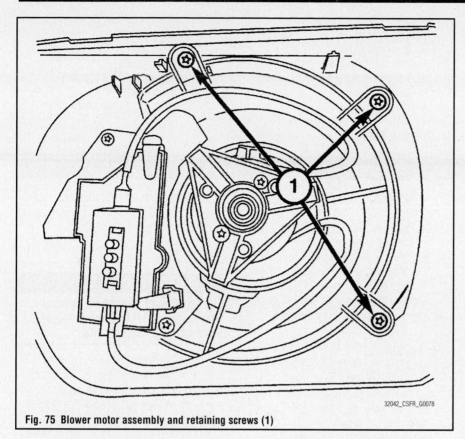

Fig. 75 Blower motor assembly and retaining screws (1)

32042_CSFR_G0078

- Blower motor door catch mounts by sliding them over to the detents
- Blower motor electrical connector
- Lower instrument panel cover

HEATER CORE

REMOVAL & INSTALLATION

See Figure 76.

1. Disconnect the negative battery cable.

✳✳ CAUTION

After disconnecting the negative battery cable, wait 2 minutes for the driver's/passenger's air bag system capacitor to discharge before attempting to do any work around the steering column or instrument panel.

2. Drain the cooling system.
3. Recover the A/C refrigerant, if equipped.
4. Remove or disconnect the following:
   - Heater hoses
   - A pillar trim
   - Fuse block covers
   - Left and right air vents
   - Center console-to-instrument top panel screws
   - Glove box
   - Defroster vents
   - A pillar sheet metal clips

- Instrument panel top section
- Steering column cover
- Lower instrument panel
- Instrument cluster cover
- Instrument cluster
- Steering wheel
- Sentry Key Remote Entry Module (SKREEM)
- Wiring connectors at transmission tunnel

- Steering column bolts-to-instrument panel support
- Position steering column aside
- Electrical harness connector on passenger airbag module
- Left and right heater ducts
- Heater core attaching nuts
- Instrument panel support bolts
- Vacuum reservoir lines
- Instrument panel support
- HVAC housing electrical connectors
- HVAC housing

5. Separate heater core from HVAC housing

To install:

6. Install or connect the following:
   - Heater core to HVAC housing
   - HVAC housing
   - HVAC housing electrical connectors
   - Instrument panel support
   - Instrument panel support bolts
   - Steering column bolts-to-instrument panel support
   - Wiring connectors at transmission tunnel
   - Sentry Key Remote Entry Module (SKREM)
   - Instrument cluster
   - Instrument cluster cover
   - Steering wheel
   - Left and right heater ducts
   - Vacuum reservoir lines
   - Instrument panel support bolts
   - HVAC housing attaching nuts
   - Position steering column into place
   - Steering column bolts-to-instrument panel support

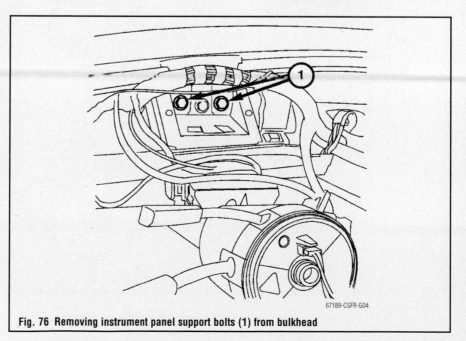

67189-CSFR-G04

Fig. 76 Removing instrument panel support bolts (1) from bulkhead

- Wiring connectors at transmission tunnel
- Sentry Key Remote Entry Module (SKREM)
- Steering wheel
- Instrument cluster
- Instrument cluster cover
- Left and right heater ducts
- Lower instrument panel cover

- Lower instrument panel screws
- Steering column cover
- Instrument panel top section
- A pillar sheet metal clips
- Defroster vents
- Glove box
- Center console-to-instrument top panel screws

- Left and right air vents
- Fuse block covers
- A pillar trim
- Heater hoses
7. Recharge the A/C refrigerant.
8. Fill the cooling system.
9. Start the engine and check for leaks.

STEERING

POWER STEERING GEAR

REMOVAL & INSTALLATION

POWER STEERING PUMP

REMOVAL & INSTALLATION
See Figure 77.

1. Before servicing the vehicle, refer to the Precautions Section.
2. Disconnect battery negative cable from battery and properly isolate to prevent accidental reconnection.
3. Remove or disconnect the following:

- Accessory drive belt
- Oil in the power steering reservoir
- Power steering supply line from the reservoir

- Return hose from the power steering pump
- High-pressure hose from the power steering pump
- Power steering pump by removing the two bolts attaching it to the engine block

4. Remove the reservoir if necessary by pressing out the C-clip using a suitable tool.

To install:
5. Install or connect the following:

- Reservoir, if removed
- Power steering pump and bolts to the engine block and tighten to 15 ft. lbs. (20 Nm)
- High-pressure hose on the pump
- Return hose on the pump
- Power steering supply line to the reservoir
- Accessory drive belt

6. Fill the power steering pump reservoir and bleed the system by performing the initial operation.

BLEEDING

✳✳ CAUTION

The fluid level should be checked with engine OFF to prevent injury from moving components.

Use MOPAR power steering fluid or equivalent. Do not use automatic transmission fluid and do not overfill.

1. Wipe filler cap clean and check the fluid level. The dipstick should indicate COLD when the fluid is at normal ambient temperature.
2. Fill the pump fluid reservoir to the proper level and let the fluid settle for at least two minutes.

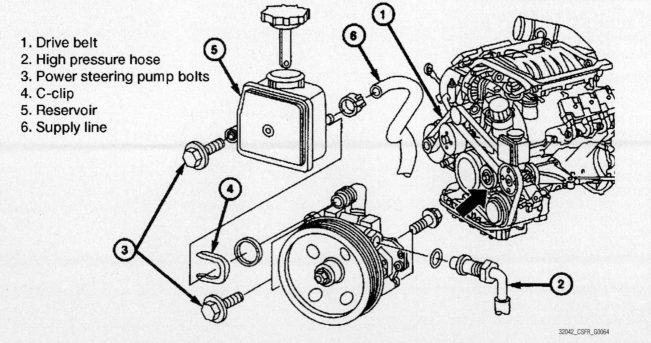

1. Drive belt
2. High pressure hose
3. Power steering pump bolts
4. C-clip
5. Reservoir
6. Supply line

32042_CSFR_G0064

Fig. 77 Power steering pump location and overview—Drive belt (1), high pressure hose (2), power steering pump bolts (3), c-clip (4), reservoir (5) and supply line (6)

3. Start the engine and let run for a few seconds then turn engine off.

4. Add fluid if necessary.

5. Repeat the above procedure until the fluid level remains constant after running the engine.

6. Raise the front wheels off the ground.

7. Slowly turn the steering wheel right and left, lightly contacting the wheel stops at least 20 times.

8. Check the fluid level and add if necessary.

9. Lower the vehicle, start the engine and turn the steering wheel slowly from lock to lock.

10. Stop the engine and check the fluid level and refill as required.

✳✳ WARNING

DO NOT run a vehicle with foamy fluid for an extended period. This may cause pump damage.

11. If the fluid is extremely foamy or milky looking, allow the vehicle to stand a few minutes and repeat the procedure.

SUSPENSION

COIL SPRING

REMOVAL & INSTALLATION

1. Before servicing the vehicle, refer to the Precautions Section.

➡ **The vehicle must be sitting on its wheels when removing the upper shock mount nut.**

2. Remove or disconnect the following:
- Front wheel
- Shock absorber

3. Support the lower control arm on a floor jack.

4. Compress the spring using special tools 9151 and 9152 or equivalent.

5. Remove the lower control arm mounting nuts and bolts.

6. Lower the jack while holding the spring. When enough clearance is obtained, remove the spring.

To install:

7. Install the coil spring and raise the control arm into position.

8. Install or connect the following:
- Lower control arm bolts and nuts
- Shock absorber
- Tighten lower control arm nuts to 88 ft. lbs. (120 Nm)

LOWER BALL JOINT

REMOVAL & INSTALLATION

See Figure 78.

1. Before servicing the vehicle, refer to the Precautions Section.

2. Raise and support the vehicle.

3. Remove or disconnect the following:
- Front wheels
- Brake caliper
- Brake rotor
- Dust shield
- Lower shock mount bolt
- Coil spring
- Ball joint nuts

- Outer ball joint stud from steering knuckle using special tool 9168 or equivalent puller
- Upper ball joint stud from lower control arm using special tool 9168 or equivalent puller

To install:

4. Install or connect the following:
- Ball joint. Tighten ball joint nuts to 77 ft. lbs. (105 Nm).
- Coil spring
- Lower shock bolt
- Dust shield
- Brake rotor and caliper
- Front wheel

LOWER CONTROL ARM

REMOVAL & INSTALLATION

1. Before servicing the vehicle, refer to the Precautions Section.

2. Remove or disconnect the following:

FRONT SUSPENSION

- Front wheel
- Coil spring
- Lower shock bolt
- Stabilizer bar clamp
- Lower ball joint nuts
- Press ball joint out of steering knuckle using special tool 9168 or equivalent puller
- Lower control arm bolts
- Lower control arm

To install:

3. Install or connect the following:
- Lower control arm. Tighten the bolts to the frame to 88 ft. lbs. (120 Nm).
- Lower control arm to steering knuckle lower ball joint. Tighten the nut to 33 ft. lbs. (45 Nm).
- Stabilizer bar clamp. Tighten the nuts to 15 ft. lbs. (20 Nm).
- Lower shock bolt. Tighten the nut to 41 ft. lbs. (55 Nm).

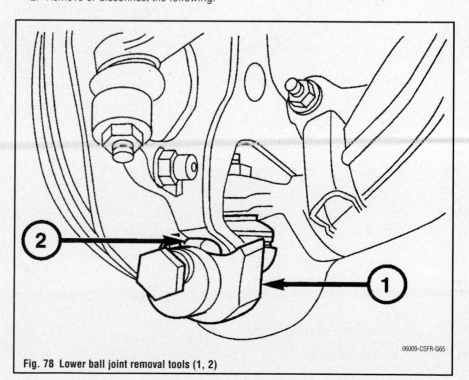

06009-CSFR-G65

Fig. 78 Lower ball joint removal tools (1, 2)

- Coil spring
- Front wheel

STABILIZER BAR

REMOVAL & INSTALLATION

See Figure 79.

1. Before servicing the vehicle, refer to the Precautions Section.
2. Raise and support the vehicle safely.
3. Remove or disconnect the following:
   - Stabilizer bar brackets on both sides
   - Retainer bracket and mounting plate
   - Stabilizer bar
   - Stabilizer bar bushings

To install:

4. Assemble the stabilizer bushings onto the bar.

➡ **The lower control arms may have to be raised to allow the stabilizer bar bushings to be inserted into their mating surfaces.**

5. Install the stabilizer bar by loosely installing the bolts and nuts to all 4 brackets.

6. Align the stabilizer bar so it is centered in the vehicle.
7. Due to the preload of the bracket, install the hexagon bolt first.
8. Tighten both stabilizer bolts to the frame.
9. Tighten the hexagon socket bolts to the retainer.
10. Tighten both bar bracket nuts to the lower control arm. Torque the bolts to 15 ft. lbs. (20 Nm).
11. Install the bar retainer and mounting plate.
12. Tighten the retainer bolts to 44 ft. lbs. 60 Nm).
13. Tighten the lower retainer bracket nut to 15 ft. lbs. (20 Nm).
14. Tighten the upper retainer nuts to 29 ft. lbs. (40 Nm).

STEERING KNUCKLE

REMOVAL & INSTALLATION

See Figure 80.

1. Before servicing the vehicle, refer to the Precautions Section.
2. Raise and support the vehicle safely.
3. Remove or disconnect the following:

- Front wheel
- Brake caliper
- Brake rotor
- Wheel hub
- Dust shield
- Wheel speed sensor
- Tie rod end
- Upper and lower ball joints from knuckle
- Steering knuckle

To install:

4. Install or connect the following:
   - Steering knuckle to upper ball joint stud. Tighten the nut to 33 ft. lbs. (45 Nm).
   - Steering knuckle to lower ball joint stud. Tighten the nut to 77 ft. lbs. (105 Nm).
   - Tie rod end. Tighten the nut to 37 ft. lbs. (50 Nm).
   - Wheel speed sensor. Tighten bolt to 16 ft. lbs. (22 Nm).
   - Dust shield. Tighten bolts to 16 ft. lbs. (22 Nm).
   - Wheel hub
   - Brake rotor
   - Brake caliper
   - Wheel

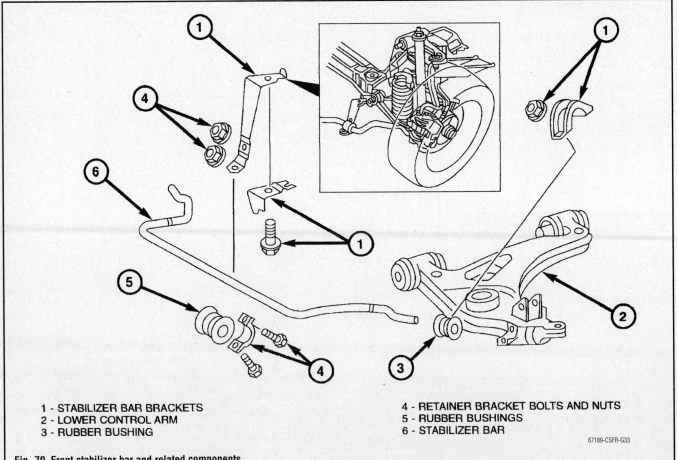

1 - STABILIZER BAR BRACKETS
2 - LOWER CONTROL ARM
3 - RUBBER BUSHING
4 - RETAINER BRACKET BOLTS AND NUTS
5 - RUBBER BUSHINGS
6 - STABILIZER BAR

67189-CSFR-G33

Fig. 79 Front stabilizer bar and related components

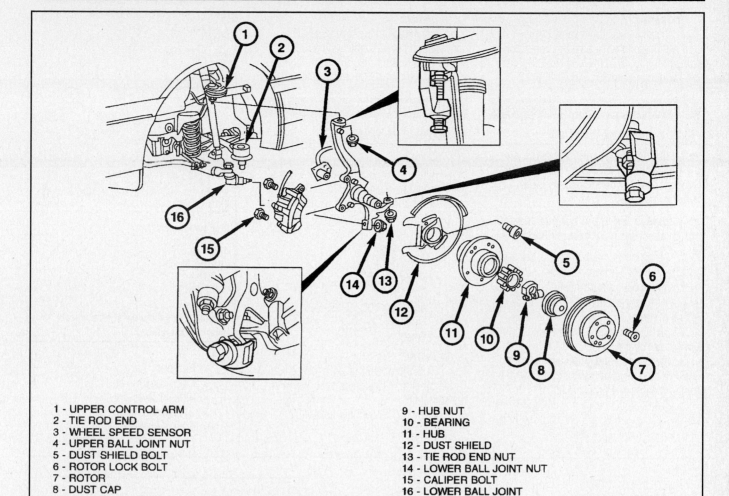

1 - UPPER CONTROL ARM
2 - TIE ROD END
3 - WHEEL SPEED SENSOR
4 - UPPER BALL JOINT NUT
5 - DUST SHIELD BOLT
6 - ROTOR LOCK BOLT
7 - ROTOR
8 - DUST CAP

9 - HUB NUT
10 - BEARING
11 - HUB
12 - DUST SHIELD
13 - TIE ROD END NUT
14 - LOWER BALL JOINT NUT
15 - CALIPER BOLT
16 - LOWER BALL JOINT

67189-CSFR-G39

Fig. 80 Exploded view of front steering knuckle assembly

UPPER BALL JOINT

REMOVAL & INSTALLATION

See Figure 81.

➡️ **If replacing the ball joint on the right side, the air cleaner housing must be removed for access. The shock absorbers must remain installed.**

➡️ **To remove the upper control arm the shock absorber must remain installed.**

1. Before servicing the vehicle, refer to the Precautions Section.
2. Remove the front wheel.
3. Wire tie the steering knuckle to the shock absorber.
4. Remove the ball joint nut from the upper control arm.
5. Using special tool 9168 or an equivalent puller, press the ball joint out of the steering knuckle.
6. If removing the upper control arm, from inside the engine compartment, remove the upper control arm nut and bolt, and remove the control arm.

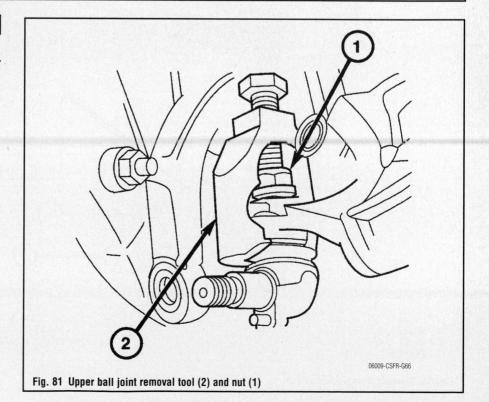

06009-CSFR-G66

Fig. 81 Upper ball joint removal tool (2) and nut (1)

To install:

7. Installation is the reverse of the removal procedure. Tighten the upper control arm nut to 48 ft. lbs. (65 Nm). Tighten the ball joint nut to 33 ft. lbs. (45 Nm).

UPPER CONTROL ARM

REMOVAL & INSTALLATION

➡ If working on the right side, the air cleaner housing must be removed for access. The shock absorbers must remain installed.

➡ To remove the upper control arm the shock absorber must remain installed.

1. Before servicing the vehicle, refer to the Precautions Section.
2. Remove the front wheel.
3. Wire tie the steering knuckle to the shock absorber.
4. Remove the ball joint nut from the upper control arm.
5. As required and using special tool 9168 or an equivalent puller, press the ball joint out of the steering knuckle.
6. From inside the engine compartment, remove the upper control arm nut and bolt, and remove the control arm.

To install:

7. Installation is the reverse of the removal procedure. Tighten the upper control arm nut to 48 ft. lbs. (65 Nm). Tighten the ball joint nut to 33 ft. lbs. (45 Nm).

WHEEL BEARINGS

REMOVAL & INSTALLATION

See Figure 82.

1. Before servicing the vehicle, refer to the Precautions Section.
2. Raise and support the vehicle safely.
3. Remove or disconnect the following:

- Front wheel
- Brake caliper
- Brake rotor
- Grease cap
- Adjusting nut
- Bearing
- Wheel hub

To install:

4. Pack the wheel hub with grease and install the hub, bearing and seal ring onto the spindle.
5. Install or connect the following:

- Brake rotor

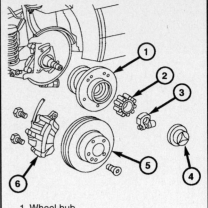

1. Wheel hub
2. Bearing
3. Hub nut
4. Grease cap
5. Rotor
6. Caliper

67189-CSFR-G38

Fig. 82 Exploded view of front wheel bearing assembly

- Hub nut
- Adjust bearing end play
- Brake caliper
- Grease cap
- Front wheel

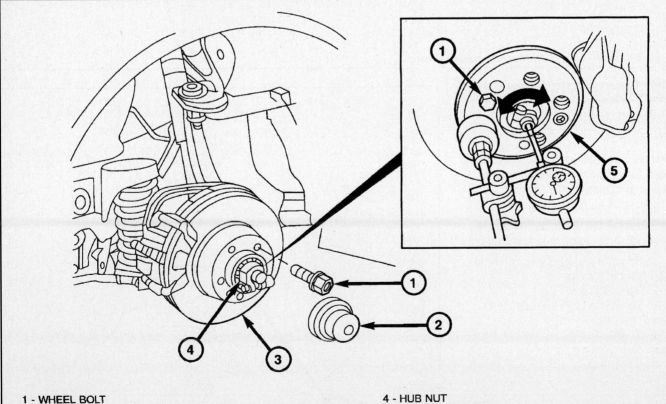

1 - WHEEL BOLT
2 - DUST CAP
3 - ROTOR

4 - HUB NUT
5 - ROTOR LOCK BOLT

67189-CSFR-G37

Fig. 83 Adjusting front wheel bearing

ADJUSTMENT

See Figure 83.

1. Before servicing the vehicle, refer to the Precautions Section.

2. With the wheel removed, install a wheel bolt on the opposite side from the brake rotor retaining bolt

3. Press the brake pads back into the caliper so the rotor turns free.

4. Remove the bearing grease cap.

5. Loosen the wheel bearing adjusting nut until some end play is present.

6. Attach a dial indicator to the hub.

7. Turn the hub nut in stages while pushing and pulling the rotor firmly back and forth. Adjust the end play to 0.0004–0.0008 inches (0.01–0.02mm).

8. Tighten the hub nut to 97 inch lbs. (11 Nm).

9. Remove dial indicator and install grease cap.

10. Remove the wheel bolt from rotor and install the wheel.

SUSPENSION

COIL SPRING

REMOVAL & INSTALLATION

See Figure 84.

1. Before servicing the vehicle, refer to the Precautions Section.

2. Raise and support the vehicle safely.

3. Remove or disconnect the following:
   • Rear wheel
   • Lower control arm cover
   • Lower shock absorber bolts

4. Raise the lower control arm with a jack until the halfshaft is horizontal.

5. Using a spring compressor, compress the rear spring.

6. Remove the rear lower control arm attaching bolts, and then lower the jack allowing the control arm to swing away from the mounting tabs.

7. Remove the rear spring.

To install:

8. Install the coil spring and raise the control arm into position.

9. Install or connect the following:
   • Lower control arm bolts and nuts.
   • Lower shock absorber bolt. Torque the bolt to 41 ft. lbs. (55 Nm).
   • Control arm cover
   • Rear wheel

LOWER CONTROL ARM

REMOVAL & INSTALLATION

See Figure 85.

1. Before servicing the vehicle, refer to the Precautions Section.

2. Raise and support the vehicle safely.

3. Remove or disconnect the following:
   • Rear wheel
   • Lower control arm cover
   • Coil spring
   • Shock absorber
   • Stabilizer bar link
   • Lower control arm

To install:

4. Install or connect the following:
   • Lower control arm to wheel carrier bolt. Tighten to 52 ft. lbs. (70 Nm).

• Shock absorber
• Coil spring
• Lower control arm to frame bolt. Tighten to 52 ft. lbs. (70 Nm).
• Stabilizer bar link. Tighten the nut to 15 ft. lbs. (20 Nm).

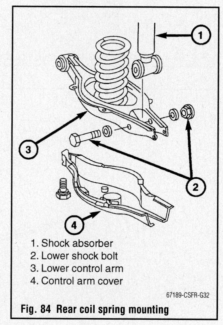

1. Shock absorber
2. Lower shock bolt
3. Lower control arm
4. Control arm cover

67189-CSFR-G32

Fig. 84 Rear coil spring mounting

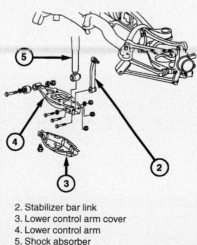

2. Stabilizer bar link
3. Lower control arm cover
4. Lower control arm
5. Shock absorber

67189-CSFR-G36

Fig. 85 Exploded view of rear lower control arm

REAR SUSPENSION

• Lower control arm cover
• Rear wheel

SHOCK ABSORBER

REMOVAL & INSTALLATION

➡**The vehicle must be resting on its wheels, before removing the top shock absorber mounting hardware.**

1. Before servicing the vehicle, refer to the Precautions Section.

2. Raise and support the vehicle safely.

3. Remove or disconnect the following:

   • Rear wheel
   • Upper mounting bolt
   • Lower control arm cover
   • Lower mounting bolts
   • Shock absorber

To install:

4. Install or connect the following:
   • Shock absorber. Tighten the upper bolt nut to 13 ft. lbs. (18 Nm) and the lower bolt to 41 ft. lbs. (55 Nm).
   • Lower control arm cover
   • Rear wheel

WHEEL BEARINGS

REMOVAL & INSTALLATION

1. Before servicing the vehicle, refer to the Precautions Section.

2. Disconnect battery negative cable from battery and properly isolate to prevent accidental reconnection.

3. Raise and support the vehicle safely.

4. Remove or disconnect the following:

   • Disc brake calipers and bolts
   • Rear disc brake rotor
   • Parking brake shoes
   • Rear axle halfshaft nut
   • Rear axle halfshaft
   • Snap ring from the rear hub assembly housing

5. Use Special Tool 9181 or a suitable bearing tool to remove the bearing on the hub.

⁂ WARNING

Be sure not to mar or damage the rear axle halfshaft flange while in vise.

6. Remove the inner bearing race from the rear axle halfshaft flange by screwing the clamping pliers onto the puller then tighten.

7. Clamp the rear axle halfshaft flange in vise.

   a. Fit the thrust piece with the large diameter on the rear axle halfshaft flange.

   b. Place the complete puller over the inner bearing race.

   c. Clamp it firmly at the upper grooves of the clamping pliers over the tapered sleeve of the puller.

   d. Pull the inner bearing race off the rear axle halfshaft flange using the puller.

8. Check the lateral and radial runout of the rear axle halfshaft flange. Replace rear axle halfshaft flange if test values are exceeded.

   a. Permissible lateral runout: 0.0011 in. (0.03mm).

   b. Permissible radial runout: 0.0011 in. (0.03mm).

To install:

9. Use Special Tool 9199 or a suitable bearing tool to install the bearing by pulling it into the wheel carrier until it touches the shoulder of the wheel carrier.

➡**Insure that the snap ring is correctly fitted in the rear wheel carrier.**

10. Install the snap ring into the rear wheel carrier.

   a. Verify the pressure plate lies flush against the bearings inner race during insertion.

11. Install or connect the following:
- Rear axle halfshaft flange
- Parking brake shoes
- Disc brake rotor
- Rear disc brake caliper bolts
- Rear halfshaft
- Wheel and tire assembly

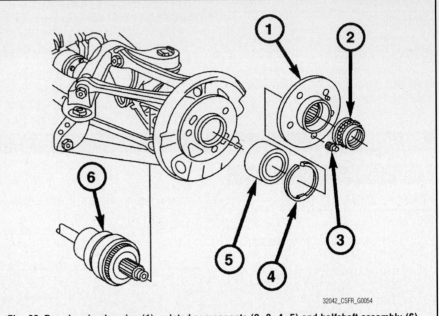

Fig. 86 Rear bearing housing (1), related components (2, 3, 4, 5) and halfshaft assembly (6)

32042_CSFR_G0054

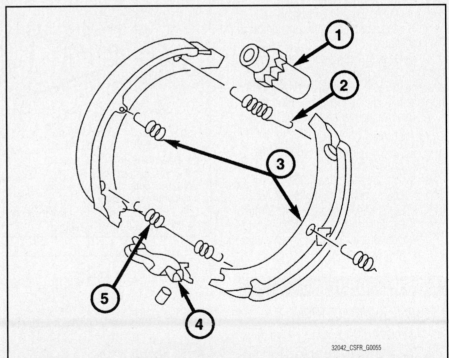

Fig. 87 Rear parking brake shoes—Adjuster (1), Upper return spring (2), Hold-down spring (3), Expanding lock (4) and Lower return spring (5)

32042_CSFR_G0055

DODGE

Dakota

8

SPECIFICATIONS AND MAINTENANCE CHARTS

ENGINE AND VEHICLE IDENTIFICATION

	Engine							Model Year	
Code	Liters (cc)	Cu. In.	Cyl.	Fuel Sys.	Engine Type	Eng. Mfg.		Code	Year
K	3.7 (3701)	226	6	MFI	SOHC	Chrysler		5	2005
J	4.7 (4701)	287	8	MFI	SOHC	Chrysler		6	2006
N	4.7 (4701)	287	8	MFI	SOHC	Chrysler		7	2007
P	4.7 (4701)	287	8	FFV	SOHC	Chrysler			

OHV: Overhead Valve

MFI: Multi-port Fuel Injection

FFV: Flexible Fuel Vehicle

22043_DAKO_C0001

GENERAL ENGINE SPECIFICATIONS

Year	Engine Displacement Liters	Engine VIN	Net Horsepower @ rpm	Net Torque @ rpm (ft. lbs.)	Bore x Stroke (in.)	Com- pression Ratio	Oil Pressure @ rpm
2005	3.7	K	210@5200	235@4000	3.66x3.40	9.2:1	25-110@3000
	4.7	J	250@5200	300@3500	3.66x3.40	9.7:1	35-105@3000
	4.7	N	230@4600	295@4000	3.66x3.40	9.0:1	25-110@3000
2006	3.7	K	210@5200	235@4000	3.66x3.40	9.2:1	25-110@3000
	4.7	J	260@5200	310@3600	3.66x3.40	9.7:1	35-105@3000
	4.7	N	230@4600	290@3600	3.66x3.40	9.0:1	25-110@3000
2007	3.7	K	210@5200	235@4000	3.66x3.40	9.2:1	25-110@3000
	4.7	J	260@5200	310@3600	3.66x3.40	9.7:1	35-105@3000
	4.7	N	230@4600	290@3600	3.66x3.40	9.0:1	25-110@3000
	4.7	P	235@4800	300@3200	3.66x3.40	9.0:1	35-105@3000

22043_DAKO_C0002

GASOLINE ENGINE TUNE-UP SPECIFICATIONS

Year	Engine Displacement Liters	Engine VIN	Spark Plug Gap (in.)	Ignition Timing (deg.)	Fuel Pump (psi)	Idle Speed (rpm)	Valve Clearance Intake	Valve Clearance Exhaust
2005	3.7	K	0.042	①	56-60	②	HYD	HYD
	4.7	J	0.040	①	56-60	②	HYD	HYD
	4.7	N	0.040	①	56-60	②	HYD	HYD
2006	3.7	K	0.042	①	56-60	②	HYD	HYD
	4.7	J	0.040	①	56-60	②	HYD	HYD
	4.7	N	0.040	①	56-60	②	HYD	HYD
2007	3.7	K	0.042	①	56-60	②	HYD	HYD
	4.7	J	0.040	①	56-60	②	HYD	HYD
	4.7	N	0.040	①	56-60	②	HYD	HYD
	4.7	P	0.040	①	56-60	②	HYD	HYD

NOTE: The Vehicle Emission Control Information (VECI) label often reflects specification changes made during production.

The label figures must be used if they differ from those in this chart.

HYD: Hydraulic

① Ignition timing is controlled by the PCM and is not adjustable.

② Idle speed is controlled by the PCM and is not adjustable

22043_DAKO_C0003

CAPACITIES

Year	Engine Displ. Liters	Engine VIN	Oil with Filter (qts.)	Transmission (pts.) Manual	Transmission (pts.) Auto.	Transfer Case (pts.)	Drive Axle Front (pts.)	Drive Axle Rear (pts.)	Fuel Tank (gal.)	Cooling System (qts.)
2005	3.7	K	5.0	4.65	①	②	3.5	③	25.0	16.2
	4.7	J	6.0	—	①	②	3.5	③	25.0	16.2
	4.7	N	6.0	—	①	②	3.5	③	25.0	16.2
2006	3.7	K	5.0	4.65	①	②	3.5	③	25.0	16.2
	4.7	J	6.0	—	①	②	3.5	③	25.0	16.2
	4.7	N	6.0	—	①	②	3.5	③	25.0	16.2
2007	3.7	K	5.0	4.65	①	②	3.5	③	25.0	16.2
	4.7	J	6.0	—	①	②	3.5	③	25.0	16.2
	4.7	N	6.0	—	①	②	3.5	③	25.0	16.2
	4.7	P	6.0	—	①	②	3.5	③	25.0	16.2

NOTE: All capacities are approximate. Add fluid gradually and check to be sure a proper fluid level is obtained.

① 42RLE: 8.0 pts.
545RFE 2wd: 11.0
545RFE 4wd: 13 pts.

② NV233: 2.5 pts.
NV244: 2.85 pts.

③ The following values include 0.25 pt. of friction modifier for LSD axles.
8.25 in. axle: 4.4 pts.
9.25 in. axle: 4.9 pts.

22043_DAKO_C0004

FLUID SPECIFICATIONS

Year	Model	Engine Displacement Liters	Engine ID/VIN	Engine Oil	Auto. Trans.	Drive Axle	Power Steering Fluid	Brake Master Cylinder
2005	Dakota	3.7	K	5W-30	Mopar ATF+4	①	Mopar ATF+4	DOT-3
		4.7	J	5W-30	Mopar ATF+4	①	Mopar ATF+4	DOT-3
		4.7	N	5W-30	Mopar ATF+4	①	Mopar ATF+4	DOT-3
2006	Dakota	3.7	K	5W-30	Mopar ATF+4	①	Mopar ATF+4	DOT-3
		4.7	J	5W-30	Mopar ATF+4	①	Mopar ATF+4	DOT-3
		4.7	N	5W-30	Mopar ATF+4	①	Mopar ATF+4	DOT-3
2007	Dakota	3.7	K	5W-20	Mopar ATF+4	①	Mopar ATF+4	DOT-3
		4.7	J	5W-20	Mopar ATF+4	①	Mopar ATF+4	DOT-3
		4.7	N	5W-20	Mopar ATF+4	①	Mopar ATF+4	DOT-3
		4.7	P	5W-20	Mopar ATF+4	①	Mopar ATF+4	DOT-3

DOT: Department Of Transpotation

NA: Not Applicable

① Front: Mopar Gear Lube 75W-90
Rear: Mopar Synthetic Gear Lube 75W-140

22043_DAKO_C0005

VALVE SPECIFICATIONS

Year	Engine Displ. Liters	Engine VIN	Seat Angle (deg.)	Face Angle (deg.)	Spring Test Pressure (lbs. @ in.)	Spring Installed Height (in.)	Stem-to-Guide Clearance (in.)		Stem Diameter (in.)	
							Intake	Exhaust	Intake	Exhaust
2005	3.7	K	44.5-45	45-45.5	①	1.579	0.0008-0.0028	0.0019-0.0039	0.2729-0.2739	0.2717-0.2728
	4.7	J	44.5-45	45-45.5	②	1.579	0.0008-0.0028	0.0019-0.0039	0.2729-0.2739	0.2717-0.2728
	4.7	N	44.5-45	45-45.5	174.4-195.5 @1.1370	1.579	0.0008-0.0028	0.0019-0.0039	0.2729-0.2739	0.2717-0.2728
2006	3.7	K	44.5-45	45-45.5	①	1.579	0.0008-0.0028	0.0019-0.0039	0.2729-0.2739	0.2717-0.2728
	4.7	J	44.5-45	45-45.5	②	1.579	0.0008-0.0028	0.0019-0.0039	0.2729-0.2739	0.2717-0.2728
	4.7	N	44.5-45	45-45.5	174.4-195.5 @1.1370	1.579	0.0008-0.0028	0.0019-0.0039	0.2729-0.2739	0.2717-0.2728
2007	3.7	K	44.5-45	45-45.5	①	1.579	0.0008-0.0028	0.0019-0.0039	0.2729-0.2739	0.2717-0.2728
	4.7	J	44.5-45	45-45.5	②	1.579	0.0008-0.0028	0.0019-0.0039	0.2729-0.2739	0.2717-0.2728
	4.7	N	44.5-45	45-45.5	174.4-195.5 @1.1370	1.579	0.0008-0.0028	0.0019-0.0039	0.2729-0.2739	0.2717-0.2728
	4.7	P	44.5-45	45-45.5	174.4-195.5 @1.1370	1.579	0.0008-0.0028	0.0019-0.0039	0.2729-0.2739	0.2717-0.2728

① Intake: 213-234@1.107
Exhaust: 215-219@1.067
② Intake: 221.2-233.8@1.107
Exhaust: 216.9-237.1@1.146

22043_DAKO_C0006

CAMSHAFT AND BEARING SPECIFICATIONS CHART

All measurements are given in inches.

Year	Engine Displacement Liters	Engine VIN	Journal Diameter	Brg. Oil Clearance	Shaft End-play	Runout	Journal Bore	Lobe Lift Intake	Lobe Lift Exhaust
2005	3.7	K	1.0227-1.0235	0.0010-0.0026	0.0030-0.0079	NA	NA	NA	NA
	4.7	J	1.0227-1.0235	0.0010-0.0026	0.0030-0.0079	NA	NA	NA	NA
	4.7	N	1.0227-1.0235	0.0010-0.0026	0.0030-0.0079	NA	NA	NA	NA
2006	3.7	K	1.0227-1.0235	0.0010-0.0026	0.0030-0.0079	NA	NA	NA	NA
	4.7	J	1.0227-1.0235	0.0010-0.0026	0.0030-0.0079	NA	NA	NA	NA
	4.7	N	1.0227-1.0235	0.0010-0.0026	0.0030-0.0079	NA	NA	NA	NA
2007	3.7	K	1.0227-1.0235	0.0010-0.0026	0.0030-0.0079	NA	NA	NA	NA
	4.7	J	1.0227-1.0235	0.0010-0.0026	0.0030-0.0079	NA	NA	NA	NA
	4.7	N	1.0227-1.0235	0.0010-0.0026	0.0030-0.0079	NA	NA	NA	NA
	4.7	P	1.0227-1.0235	0.0010-0.0026	0.0030-0.0079	NA	NA	NA	NA

NA: Not Available

22043_DAKO_C0007

CRANKSHAFT AND CONNECTING ROD SPECIFICATIONS

All measurements are given in inches.

Year	Engine Displ. Liters	Engine VIN	Crankshaft Main Brg. Journal Dia.	Crankshaft Main Brg. Oil Clearance	Crankshaft Shaft End-play	Crankshaft Thrust on No.	Connecting Rod Journal Diameter	Connecting Rod Oil Clearance	Connecting Rod Side Clearance
2005	3.7	K	2.4996-2.5005	0.0008-0.0018	0.0021-0.0112	2	2.2792-2.2798	0.0002-0.0011	0.0040-0.0138
	4.7	J	2.4996-2.5005	0.0008-0.0021	0.0021-0.0112	2	2.0076-2.0082	0.0006-0.0022	0.0040-0.0138
	4.7	N	2.4996-2.5005	0.0008-0.0021	0.0021-0.0112	2	2.0076-2.0082	0.0006-0.0022	0.0040-0.0138
2006	3.7	K	2.4996-2.5005	0.0008-0.0018	0.0021-0.0112	2	2.2792-2.2798	0.0002-0.0011	0.0040-0.0138
	4.7	J	2.4996-2.5005	0.0008-0.0021	0.0021-0.0112	2	2.0076-2.0082	0.0006-0.0022	0.0040-0.0138
	4.7	N	2.4996-2.5005	0.0008-0.0021	0.0021-0.0112	2	2.0076-2.0082	0.0006-0.0022	0.0040-0.0138
2007	3.7	K	2.4996-2.5005	0.0008-0.0018	0.0021-0.0112	2	2.2792-2.2798	0.0002-0.0011	0.0040-0.0138
	4.7	J	2.4996-2.5005	0.0008-0.0021	0.0021-0.0112	2	2.0076-2.0082	0.0006-0.0022	0.0040-0.0138
	4.7	N	2.4996-2.5005	0.0008-0.0021	0.0021-0.0112	2	2.0076-2.0082	0.0006-0.0022	0.0040-0.0138
	4.7	P	2.4996-2.5005	0.0008-0.0021	0.0021-0.0112	2	2.0076-2.0082	0.0006-0.0022	0.0040-0.0138

22043_DAKO_C0008

PISTON AND RING SPECIFICATIONS
All measurements are given in inches.

Year	Engine Displ. Liters	Engine VIN	Piston Clearance	Ring Gap			Ring Side Clearance		
				Top Comp.	Bottom Comp.	Oil Control	Top Comp.	Bottom Comp.	Oil Control
2005	3.7	K	0.0014	0.0079-0.0142	0.0146-0.0249	0.0100-0.0300	0.0020-0.0037	0.0016-0.0031	0.0007-0.0091
	4.7	J	0.0014	0.0146-0.0249	0.0146-0.0249	0.0099-0.0300	0.0020-0.0037	0.0016-0.0031	0.0175-0.0185
	4.7	N	0.0014	0.0146-0.0249	0.0146-0.0249	0.0099-0.0300	0.0020-0.0037	0.0016-0.0031	0.0175-0.0185
2006	3.7	K	0.0014	0.0079-0.0142	0.0146-0.0249	0.0100-0.0300	0.0020-0.0037	0.0016-0.0031	0.0007-0.0091
	4.7	J	0.0014	0.0146-0.0249	0.0146-0.0249	0.0099-0.0300	0.0020-0.0037	0.0016-0.0031	0.0175-0.0185
	4.7	N	0.0014	0.0146-0.0249	0.0146-0.0249	0.0099-0.0300	0.0020-0.0037	0.0016-0.0031	0.0175-0.0185
2007	3.7	K	0.0014	0.0079-0.0142	0.0146-0.0249	0.0100-0.0300	0.0020-0.0037	0.0016-0.0031	0.0007-0.0091
	4.7	J	0.0014	0.0146-0.0249	0.0146-0.0249	0.0099-0.0300	0.0020-0.0037	0.0016-0.0031	0.0175-0.0185
	4.7	N	0.0014	0.0146-0.0249	0.0146-0.0249	0.0099-0.0300	0.0020-0.0037	0.0016-0.0031	0.0175-0.0185
	4.7	P	0.0014	0.0146-0.0249	0.0146-0.0249	0.0099-0.0300	0.0020-0.0037	0.0016-0.0031	0.0175-0.0185

22043_DAKO_C0009

TORQUE SPECIFICATIONS

All readings in ft. lbs.

Year	Engine Displ. Liters	Engine VIN	Cylinder Head Bolts	Main Bearing Bolts	Rod Bearing Bolts	Crankshaft Damper Bolts	Flywheel Bolts	Manifold Intake	Manifold Exhaust	Spark Plugs	Oil Pan Drain Plug
2005	3.7	K	①	②	③	130	70	④	18	20	25
	4.7	J	⑤	⑥	③	130	45	④	18	20	25
	4.7	N	⑤	⑥	③	130	45	④	18	20	25
2005	3.7	K	①	②	③	130	70	④	18	20	25
	4.7	J	⑤	⑥	③	130	45	④	18	20	25
	4.7	N	⑤	⑥	③	130	45	④	18	20	25
2005	3.7	K	①	②	③	130	70	④	18	20	25
	4.7	J	⑤	⑥	③	130	45	④	18	20	25
	4.7	N	⑤	⑥	③	130	45	④	18	20	25
	4.7	P	⑤	⑥	③	130	45	④	18	20	25

① See illustration in text section
- Step 1: bolts 1-8 to 20 ft. lbs.
- Step 2: bolts 1-8: verify torque without loosening
- Step 3: bolts 9-12 to 10 ft. lbs.
- Step 4: bolts 1-8 90 degree turn
- Step 5: bolts 9-12 to 19 ft. lbs.

② See the illustration
- Step 1: Hand tighten bolts 1D, 1G and 1F until bedplate contacts the block
- Step 2: tighten bolts 1A-1J to 40 ft. lbs.
- Step 3: Tighten bolts 1-8 to 60 inch lbs.
- Step 4: Tighten bolts 1-8 an additional 90 degrees
- Step 5: Tighten bolts A-E to 20 ft. lbs.

③ 20 ft. lbs. plus 90 degrees

④ 105 inch lbs.

⑤ See illustration in text section
- Step 1: bolts 1-10 to 15 ft. lbs.
- Step 2: bolts 1-10 35 ft. lbs.
- Step 3: bolts 11-14 to 18 ft. lbs.
- Step 4: bolts 1-10 90 degree turn
- Step 5: bolts 11-14 to 22 ft. lbs.

⑥ Bed plate bolt sequence. Refer to illustration
- Step 1: Bolts A-L to 40 ft. lbs.
- Step 2: Bolts 1-10 25 inch lbs.
- Step 3: Bolts 1-10 plus 90 degrees
- Step 4: Bolts A1-A6 20 ft. lbs.

22043_DAKO_C0010

WHEEL ALIGNMENT SPECIFICATIONS

Year	Model	Wheel Base (in.)	Caster Range (+/-Deg.)	Caster Preferred Setting (Deg.)	Camber Range (+/-Deg.)	Camber Preferred Setting (Deg.)	Toe-in (in.)
2005	Dakota	131	0.50	+3.50	0.50	+0.25	0.20+/-0.50
2006	Dakota	131	0.50	+3.50	0.50	+0.25	0.20+/-0.50
2007	Dakota	131	0.50	+3.50	0.50	+0.25	0.20+/-0.50

22043_DAKO_C0011

TIRE, WHEEL AND BALL JOINT SPECIFICATIONS

Year	Model	OEM Tires Standard	OEM Tires Optional	Tire Pressures (psi) Front	Tire Pressures (psi) Rear	Wheel Size	Ball Joint Inspection	Lug Nut Torque (ft. lbs.)
2005	2WD/4WD ST Club Cab	P245/70R16	none	①	①	NA	0.020 in.	135
	2WD/4WD SLT Club Cab	P245/70R16	P255/65R16	①	①	NA		
	Laramie 2WD Club Cab	P255/65R17	P265/65R17	①	①	NA		
	Laramie 4WD Club Cab	P265/70R16	P265/65R17	①	①	NA		
	2WD/4WD ST Quad Cab	P245/70R16	none	①	①	NA		
	2WD SLT Quad Cab	P245/70R16	P255/65R16	①	①	NA		
	Laramie 2WD Quad Cab	P255/65R16	P265/65R17	①	①	NA		
	Laramie 4WD Quad Cab	P245/70R16	P265/70R16	①	①	NA		
			P255/65R16	①	①	NA		
			P265/75R17	①	①	NA		
2006	2WD/4WD ST Club Cab	P245/70R16	none	①	①	NA	0.020 in.	135
	2WD/4WD SLT Club Cab	P245/70R16	P255/65R16	①	①	NA		
	Laramie 2WD Club Cab	P255/65R17	P265/65R17	①	①	NA		
	Laramie 4WD Club Cab	P265/70R16	P265/65R17	①	①	NA		
	2WD/4WD ST Quad Cab	P245/70R16	none	①	①	NA		
	2WD SLT Quad Cab	P245/70R16	P255/65R16	①	①	NA		
	Laramie 2WD Quad Cab	P255/65R16	P265/65R17	①	①	NA		
	Laramie 4WD Quad Cab	P245/70R16	P265/70R16	①	①	NA		
			P255/65R16	①	①	NA		
			P265/75R17	①	①	NA		
2007	2WD/4WD ST Club Cab	P245/70R16	none	①	①	NA	0.020 in.	135
	2WD/4WD SLT Club Cab	P245/70R16	P255/65R16	①	①	NA		
	Laramie 2WD Club Cab	P255/65R17	P265/65R17	①	①	NA		
	Laramie 4WD Club Cab	P265/70R16	P265/65R17	①	①	NA		
	2WD/4WD ST Quad Cab	P245/70R16	none	①	①	NA		
	2WD SLT Quad Cab	P245/70R16	P255/65R16	①	①	NA		
	Laramie 2WD Quad Cab	P255/65R16	P265/65R17	①	①	NA		
	Laramie 4WD Quad Cab	P245/70R16	P265/70R16	①	①	NA		
			P255/65R16	①	①	NA		
			P265/75R17	①	①	NA		

OEM: Original Equipment Manufacturer

PSI: Pounds Per Square Inch

① See the tire placard on the vehicle

22043_DAKO_C0012

BRAKE SPECIFICATIONS
All measurements in inches unless noted

| Year | | Brake Disc | | | Brake Drum | | | Minimum Lining Thickness | | Brake Caliper | |
		Original Thickness	Minimum Thickness	Maximum Run-out	Original Inside Diameter	Max. Wear Limit	Maximum Machine Diameter	Front	Rear	Bracket Bolts (ft. lbs.)	Mounting Bolts (ft. lbs.)
2005	F	1.102	1.039	0.0010	—	—	—	①	—	130	26
	R	1.102	1.039	0.0010	11.50	②	②	①	③	130	26
2006	F	1.102	1.039	0.0010	—	—	—	①	—	130	26
	R	1.102	1.039	0.0010	11.50	②	②	①	③	130	26
2007	F	1.102	1.039	0.0010	—	—	—	①	—	130	26
	R	1.102	1.039	0.0010	11.50	②	②	①	③	130	26

F: Front

R: Rear

① Riveted brake pads: 0.0625 in.
Bonded brake pads: 0.1875 in.

② Maximum allowable drum diameter, either from wear or machining, is stamped on the drum.

③ Riveted brake shoes: 0.031 in.
Bonded brake shoes: 0.0625 in.

22043_DAKO_C0013

SCHEDULED MAINTENANCE INTERVALS
DODGE DAKOTA

TO BE SERVICED	TYPE OF SERVICE	VEHICLE MILEAGE INTERVAL (x1000)													
		6	12	18	24	30	36	42	48	54	60	66	72	78	84
Engine coolant	R	Replace every 60 months, regardless of milage													
Accessory drive belt ①	S/I										✓				
Engine oil & filter	R	✓	✓	✓	✓	✓	✓	✓	✓	✓	✓	✓	✓	✓	✓
Tires	Rotate	✓	✓	✓	✓	✓	✓	✓	✓	✓	✓	✓	✓	✓	✓
PCV valve ①	S/I										✓				
Brake linings	S/I			✓			✓			✓			✓		
Air cleaner element	S/I					✓					✓				
Air cleaner element	R										✓				
Spark plugs	R					✓					✓				
Transfer case fluid level ②	I					✓					✓				

R: Replace   S/I: Service or Inspect   L: Lubricate   Adj: Adjust

① Replace if necessary.

② Replace every 120,000 miles

FREQUENT OPERATION MAINTENANCE (SEVERE SERVICE)

If a vehicle is operated under any of the following conditions it is considered severe service:

- Extremely dusty areas.
- 50% or more of the vehicle operation is in 32°C (90°F) or higher temperatures, or constant operation in temperatures below 0°C (32°F).
- Prolonged idling (vehicle operation in stop and go traffic.
- Frequent short running periods (engine does not warm to normal operating temperatures).
- Police, taxi, delivery usage or trailer towing usage.

Oil & oil filter change: change every 3000 miles.

Air filter/air pump air filter: change every 24,000 miles.

Engine coolant level, hoses & clamps: check every 6,000 miles.

Exhaust system: check every 6000 miles.

Drive belts: check every 18,000 miles; replace every 24,000 miles.

Crankcase inlet air filter (6 & 8 cyl.): clean every 24,000 miles.

Oxygen sensor: replace every 82,500 miles.

Automatic transmission fluid, filter & bands: change & adjust every 12,000 miles.

Steering linkage: lubricate every 6000 miles.

Rear axle fluid: change every 12,000 miles.

22043_DAKO_C0014

PRECAUTIONS

Before servicing any vehicle, please be sure to read all of the following precautions, which deal with personal safety, prevention of component damage, and important points to take into consideration when servicing a motor vehicle:

• Never open, service or drain the radiator or cooling system when the engine is hot; serious burns can occur from the steam and hot coolant.

• Observe all applicable safety precautions when working around fuel. Whenever servicing the fuel system, always work in a well-ventilated area. Do not allow fuel spray or vapors to come in contact with a spark, open flame, or excessive heat (a hot drop light, for example). Keep a dry chemical fire extinguisher near the work area. Always keep fuel in a container specifically designed for fuel storage; also, always properly seal fuel containers to avoid the possibility of fire or explosion. Refer to the additional fuel system precautions later in this section.

• Fuel injection systems often remain pressurized, even after the engine has been turned **OFF**. The fuel system pressure must be relieved before disconnecting any fuel lines. Failure to do so may result in fire and/or personal injury.

• Brake fluid often contains polyglycol ethers and polyglycols. Avoid contact with the eyes and wash your hands thoroughly after handling brake fluid. If you do get brake fluid in your eyes, flush your eyes with clean, running water for 15 minutes. If eye irritation persists, or if you have taken

brake fluid internally, IMMEDIATELY seek medical assistance.

• The EPA warns that prolonged contact with used engine oil may cause a number of skin disorders, including cancer. You should make every effort to minimize your exposure to used engine oil. Protective gloves should be worn when changing oil. Wash your hands and any other exposed skin areas as soon as possible after exposure to used engine oil. Soap and water, or waterless hand cleaner should be used.

• All new vehicles are now equipped with an air bag system, often referred to as a Supplemental Restraint System (SRS) or Supplemental Inflatable Restraint (SIR) system. The system must be disabled before performing service on or around system components, steering column, instrument panel components, wiring and sensors. Failure to follow safety and disabling procedures could result in accidental air bag deployment, possible personal injury and unnecessary system repairs.

• Always wear safety goggles when working with, or around, the air bag system. When carrying a non-deployed air bag, be sure the bag and trim cover are pointed away from your body. When placing a non-deployed air bag on a work surface, always face the bag and trim cover upward, away from the surface. This will reduce the motion of the module if it is accidentally deployed. Refer to the additional air bag system precautions later in this section.

• Clean, high quality brake fluid from a sealed container is essential to the safe and

proper operation of the brake system. You should always buy the correct type of brake fluid for your vehicle. If the brake fluid becomes contaminated, completely flush the system with new fluid. Never reuse any brake fluid. Any brake fluid that is removed from the system should be discarded. Also, do not allow any brake fluid to come in contact with a painted surface; it will damage the paint.

• Never operate the engine without the proper amount and type of engine oil; doing so WILL result in severe engine damage.

• Timing belt maintenance is extremely important. Many models utilize an interference-type, non-freewheeling engine. If the timing belt breaks, the valves in the cylinder head may strike the pistons, causing potentially serious (also time-consuming and expensive) engine damage. Refer to the maintenance interval charts for the recommended replacement interval for the timing belt, and to the timing belt section for belt replacement and inspection.

• Disconnecting the negative battery cable on some vehicles may interfere with the functions of the on-board computer system(s) and may require the computer to undergo a relearning process once the negative battery cable is reconnected.

• When servicing drum brakes, only disassemble and assemble one side at a time, leaving the remaining side intact for reference.

• Only an MVAC-trained, EPA-certified automotive technician should service the air conditioning system or its components.

BRAKES

GENERAL INFORMATION

PRECAUTIONS

• Certain components within the ABS system are not intended to be serviced or repaired individually.

• Do not use rubber hoses or other parts not specifically specified for and ABS system. When using repair kits, replace all parts included in the kit. Partial or incorrect repair may lead to functional problems and require the replacement of components.

• Lubricate rubber parts with clean, fresh brake fluid to ease assembly. Do not use shop air to clean parts; damage to rubber components may result.

• Use only DOT 3 brake fluid from an unopened container.

• If any hydraulic component or line is removed or replaced, it may be necessary to bleed the entire system.

• A clean repair area is essential. Always clean the reservoir and cap thoroughly before removing the cap. The slightest amount of dirt in the fluid may plug an orifice and impair the system function. Perform repairs after components have been thoroughly cleaned; use only denatured alcohol to clean components. Do not allow ABS components to come into contact with any substance containing mineral oil; this includes used shop rags.

• The Anti-Lock control unit is a microprocessor similar to other computer units in the vehicle. Ensure that the ignition switch is **OFF** before removing or

ANTI-LOCK BRAKE SYSTEM (ABS)

installing controller harnesses. Avoid static electricity discharge at or near the controller.

• If any arc welding is to be done on the vehicle, the control unit should be unplugged before welding operations begin.

SPEED SENSORS

REMOVAL & INSTALLATION

Front Wheel Speed Sensor

See Figure 1.

1. Raise and support the vehicle.
2. Remove the wheel.
3. Remove the brake caliper.
4. Remove the rotor.

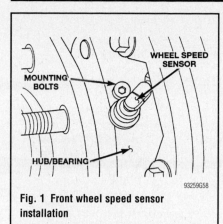

Fig. 1 Front wheel speed sensor installation

5. Remove the sensor attaching bolts.
6. Disconnect the wire and remove the sensor from the vehicle.

To install:
7. Tighten the bolts to 13 ft. lbs. (18 Nm).

➡**Use the original or replacement sensor bolts only. The bolts are special and must not be substituted under any circumstances.**

8. The remainder of the procedure is the reverse of removal.

Rear Wheel Speed Sensor

1. Raise the vehicle.
2. Remove the brake line mounting nut, if fitted, and remove the brake line from the sensor stud.
3. Remove the mounting stud from the sensor and shield.
4. Remove the sensor and shield from the differential housing.

5. Disconnect the wire and remove the sensor.

To install:
6. Connect harness to sensor. Be sure the seal is securely in place between the sensor and wiring connector.
7. Install O—ring on sensor if removed.
8. Install sensor on differential; housing, sensor shield, mounting stud. Tighten to 18 ft. lbs. (24 Nm).
9. Install the brake line on the sensor stud and install the nut.

➡**Use the original or replacement sensor bolt only. The bolt is special and must not be substituted.**

10. Lower the vehicle.

BRAKES

BLEEDING THE BRAKE SYSTEM

BLEEDING PROCEDURE

BLEEDING PROCEDURE

➡**Add only fresh, clean brake fluid from a sealed container when bleeding the brakes. If pressure bleeding equipment is used, the front brake metering valve will have to be held open to bleed the front brakes. The valve stem is located in the forward end or top of the combination valve. The stem must either be pressed inward or held outward slightly. Follow equipment manufacturer's instructions carefully when using pressure equipment. Do not exceed the maker's pressure recommendations. Generally, a tank pressure of 15—20 psi is sufficient. Do not pressure bleed without the proper master cylinder adapter.**

When any part of the hydraulic system has been disconnected for repair or replacement, air may get into the lines and cause spongy pedal action (because air can be compressed and brake fluid cannot). To correct this condition, it is necessary to bleed the hydraulic system so to be sure all air is purged.

Bleeding must start where the lines were disconnected. If lines were disconnected at the master cylinder, for example, bleeding must be done at that point before proceeding downstream.

When bleeding the brake system, bleed one brake bleeder point at a time. Failure to do so may result in more air being drawn into the lines.

If the existing system fluid seems dirty or

if the vehicle has covered considerable mileage, it is recommended that the system be completely purged and refilled with fresh, clean fluid. The best way to start is to siphon the old fluid out of the master cylinder reservoir and fill it completely with fresh fluid.

Brake fluid tends to darken over time. This does not necessarily indicate contamination. Examine fluid closely for foreign matter.

The primary and secondary hydraulic brake systems are separate and are bled independently. During the bleeding operation, do not allow the reservoir to run dry. Keep the master cylinder reservoir filled with brake fluid. Never use brake fluid that has been drained from the hydraulic system, no matter how clean it seems.

1. Clean all dirt from around the master cylinder fill cap, remove the cap and fill the master cylinder with brake fluid until the level is within ¼ in. (6mm) of the top edge of the reservoir.
2. Clean the bleeder screws at all 4 wheels. The bleeder screws are located on the back of the brake calipers.
3. Bleeder screws should be protected with rubber caps. If they are missing, the orifice may easily become clogged with road dirt. If the screw refuses to bleed when loosened, remove it and blow clear. Aftermarket caps are readily available.

Manual Bleeding

See Figures 2 through 4.

Manual bleeding requires two people and a degree of patience and cooperation. Bleeding should be performed in this order:

(1) Right rear, (2) Left rear, (3) Right front, (4) Left front.

1. Follow the preparatory steps, above.
2. Attach a length of rubber hose over the bleeder screw and place the other end of the hose in a glass jar, submerged in brake fluid.
3. Have your assistant press down on the brake pedal, then open the bleeder screw ½–¾ turn.
4. The brake pedal will go to the floor.
5. Close the bleeder screw—preferably before the pedal reaches the floor. Tell your assistant to allow the brake pedal to return slowly.
6. Repeat these steps to purge all air from the system.
7. When bubbles cease to appear at the end of the bleeder hose, close the bleeder screw and remove the hose. Check that the pedal is firm or at least more firm than it was when you started. If not, continue the procedure.
8. Check the master cylinder fluid level and add fluid accordingly. Do this after bleeding each wheel.
9. Repeat the bleeding operation at the remaining three wheels, ending with the one closet to the master cylinder.
10. Fill the master cylinder reservoir to the proper level.

➡**If there is excessive air in the system, it is possible that the stroke of the brake pedal will be insufficient to purge the lines. In this case a pressure bleeder or vacuum bleeder is the easiest solution.**

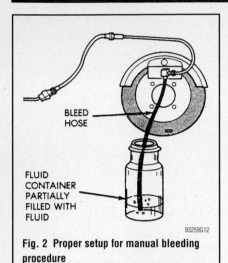

Fig. 2 Proper setup for manual bleeding procedure

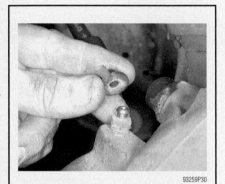

Fig. 3 Bleed screw caps are a must to keep the bleed screw passages clear

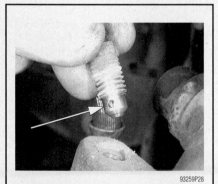

Fig. 4 Lack of cap may cause bleeder screw passages to become clogged

Vacuum Bleeding

See Figure 5.

Vacuum bleeding can be carried out by one person. Since a good vacuum bleeder will normally move more fluid than a brake pedal stroke, this procedure is preferred. These tools are inexpensive and readily available at auto parts outlets. Bleeding should be performed in this order: (1) Right rear, (2) Left rear, (3) Right front, (4) Left front.

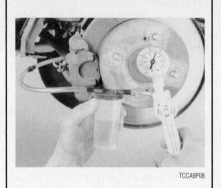

Fig. 5 There are tools, such as this Mighty-Vac, available to assist in vacuum bleeding of the brake system

1. Follow the preparatory steps, above.

2. Attach the vacuum bleeder according to the manufacturer's recommendations.

3. Pump up the unit until maximum vacuum is reached. Loosen the bleeder screw slightly until bubbles and fluid issue forth. Close the screw before the vacuum is equalized.

4. Repeat the procedure until fluid without bubbles issues from the bleeder screw.

5. Keep a close check on master cylinder fluid level during this procedure as vacuum bleeders move considerable amounts of fluid.

MASTER CYLINDER BLEEDING

See Figure 6.

✳✳ CAUTION

When clamping the master cylinder in a vise, only clamp the master cylinder by its mounting flange. Do not clamp the master cylinder piston rod, reservoir, seal or body.

1. Clamp the master cylinder in a vise.

➡**Master cylinder outlet ports vary in size and type depending on whether master cylinder is for a vehicle equipped with ABS or not. ABS equipped master cylinders require the additional use of ISO style flare adapters supplied in Special Tool Package 8822 to be used in conjunction with the bleeder tubes in Special Tool Package 8358.**

2. Attach special tools for bleeding master cylinder in the following fashion:

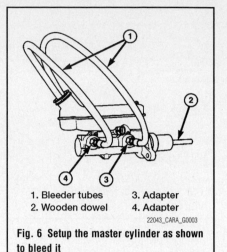

1. Bleeder tubes   3. Adapter
2. Wooden dowel   4. Adapter

Fig. 6 Setup the master cylinder as shown to bleed it

a. For non–ABS control equipped master cylinders, thread bleeder tube Special Tool 8358-1, into each outlet port. Tighten each tube to 145 inch lbs. (17 Nm). Flex the bleeder tubes and place the open ends into the mouth of the fluid reservoir as far down as possible.

b. For ABS equipped master cylinders, thread one adapter Special Tool 8822-2 in each outlet port. Tighten the adapters to 145 inch lbs. (17 Nm). Next, thread a bleeder tube Special Tool 8358-1 into each adapter. Flex the bleeder tubes and place the open ends into the mouth of the fluid reservoir as far down as possible .

➡**Make sure open ends of bleeder tubes stay below surface of brake fluid once reservoir is filled to proper level.**

3. Fill brake fluid reservoir with brake fluid meeting DOT 3 (DOT 4 and DOT 4+ are acceptable) specifications. Make sure fluid level is above tips of bleeder tubes in reservoir to ensure no air is ingested during bleeding.

4. Using a wooden dowel as a pushrod, slowly depress the master cylinder pistons, then release pressure, allowing the pistons to return to the released position.

5. Repeat several times until all air bubbles are expelled. Make sure the fluid level stays above the tips of the bleeder tubes in the reservoir while bleeding.

6. Remove the bleeder tubes from the master cylinder outlet ports, then plug the outlet ports and install the fill cap on the reservoir.

7. Install the master cylinder on vehicle then follow the brake bleeding procedure.

BLEEDING THE ABS SYSTEM

ABS system bleeding requires conventional bleeding methods plus use of the DRB scan tool. The procedure involves performing a base brake bleeding, followed by use of the scan tool to cycle and bleed the HCU pump and solenoids. A second base brake bleeding procedure is then required to remove any air remaining in the system.

1. Perform base brake bleeding. Refer to the appropriate section.
2. Connect the scan tool to the data link connector beneath the dashboard.
3. Select "Anti-lock Brakes" followed by "Miscellaneous", then "Bleed Brakes". Follow the instructions displayed until the unit displays "Test Complete", then disconnect the scan tool and proceed.
4. Perform a base brake bleeding a second time.
5. Top up the master cylinder.

✳✳ CAUTION

Dust and dirt accumulating on brake parts during normal use may contain asbestos fibers from production or aftermarket brake linings. Breathing excessive concentrations of asbestos fibers can cause serious bodily harm. Exercise care when servicing brake parts. Do not sand or grind brake lining unless equipment used is designed to contain the dust residue. Do not clean brake parts with compressed air or by dry brushing. Cleaning should be done by dampening the brake components with a fine mist of water, then wiping the brake components clean with a dampened cloth. Dispose of cloth and all residue containing asbestos fibers in an impermeable container with the appropriate label. Follow practices prescribed by the Occupational Safety and Health Administration (OSHA) and the Environmental Protection Agency (EPA) for the handling, processing, and disposing of dust or debris that may contain asbestos fibers.

BRAKE CALIPER

REMOVAL & INSTALLATION

See Figure 7.

1. Before servicing the vehicle, refer to the precautions in the beginning of this manual.

✳✳ CAUTION

Never allow the disc brake caliper to hang from the brake hose. Damage to the brake hose with result. Provide a suitable support to hang the caliper securely.

2. Raise and support the vehicle.
3. Remove the tire and wheel assembly.
4. Compress the disc brake caliper.
5. Remove the banjo bolt and discard the copper washers.

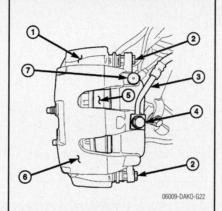

06009-DAKO-G22

Fig. 7 Brake caliper: (1) caliper mounting adapter, (2) caliper mounting bolts, (3) brake line, (4) banjo bolt, (5) pad, (6) caliper

6. Remove the caliper slide pin bolts.
7. Remove the disc brake caliper from the caliper adapter.
8. Remove the caliper slide pins from the adapter.

To install:

✳✳ WARNING

Petroleum based grease should not be used on any of the rubber components of the caliper, Use only Non-Petroleum based grease.

➡**Clean slide pin bores thoroughly to remove any old grease.**

➡**Use grease packets included with kit or Dow Corning-807T grease.**

9. Thoroughly coat the new slide pins on all working surfaces.
10. Install the boot onto the slide pin and then insert into the adapter.
11. Push the pin all the way into the adapter and carefully expel the trapped air by gently pushing on the boot near the slide pin head.

➡**Install a new copper washers on the banjo bolt when installing**

12. Install the disc brake caliper to the brake caliper adapter.
13. Install the banjo bolt with new copper washers to the caliper. Tighten to 28 Nm (250 inch lbs.)
14. Install the caliper slide pin bolts. Tighten to 32 Nm (24 ft. lbs.).
15. Bleed the base brake system.
16. Install the tire and wheel assembly.
17. Lower the vehicle.

DISC BRAKE PADS

REMOVAL & INSTALLATION

See Figures 8 and 9.

1. Before servicing the vehicle, refer to the precautions in the beginning of this manual.
2. Raise and support vehicle.
3. Remove the wheel and tire assemblies.
4. Compress the caliper.
5. Remove the caliper slide pin bolts.
6. Remove the caliper from the caliper adapter.

➡**Do not allow brake hose to support caliper assembly.**

7. Support and hang the caliper.
8. Remove the inboard brake pad from the caliper adapter.
9. Remove the outboard brake pad from the caliper adapter.
10. Remove the anti-rattle clips from the pad.

To install:
11. Bottom pistons in caliper bore with C-clamp. Place an old brake shoe between a C-clamp and caliper piston.
12. Clean caliper mounting adapter.
13. Install new anti-rattle clips to the brake pads.
14. Install inboard brake pad in adapter.
15. Install outboard brake pad in adapter.
16. Install the caliper over rotor. Then, push the caliper onto the adapter.
17. Install caliper slide pin bolts.

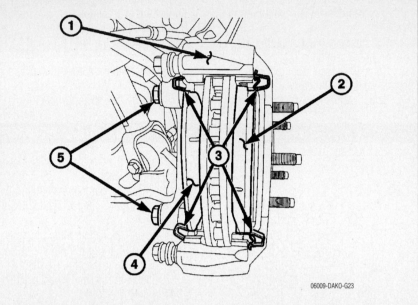

Fig. 8 Brake pad: (1) caliper adapter, (2) outboard pad, (3) anti-rattle clips, (4) inboard pad, (5) caliper mounting bolts

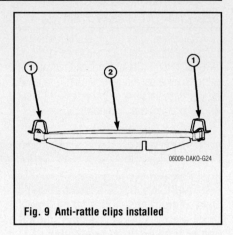

Fig. 9 Anti-rattle clips installed

18. Install wheel and tire assemblies and lower vehicle.

19. Apply brakes several times to seat caliper pistons and brake shoes and obtain firm pedal.

20. Top off master cylinder fluid level.

BRAKES

✳✳ CAUTION

Dust and dirt accumulating on brake parts during normal use may contain asbestos fibers from production or aftermarket brake linings. Breathing excessive concentrations of asbestos fibers can cause serious bodily harm. Exercise care when servicing brake parts. Do not sand or grind brake lining unless equipment used is designed to contain the dust residue. Do not clean brake parts with compressed air or by dry brushing. Cleaning should be done by dampening the brake components with a fine mist of water, then wiping the brake components clean with a dampened cloth. Dispose of cloth and all residue containing asbestos fibers in an impermeable container with the appropriate label. Follow practices prescribed by the Occupational Safety and Health Administration (OSHA) and the Environmental Protection Agency (EPA) for the handling, processing, and disposing of dust or debris that may contain asbestos fibers.

BRAKE CALIPER

REMOVAL & INSTALLATION

See Figure 10.

1. Before servicing the vehicle, refer to the precautions in the beginning of this manual.

2. Install prop rod on the brake pedal to keep pressure on the brake system.

3. Raise and support vehicle.

4. Remove the wheel and tire assembly.

5. Drain small amount of fluid from master cylinder brake reservoir with suction gun.

6. Remove the brake hose banjo bolt if replacing caliper.

7. Remove the caliper mounting slide pin bolts.

8. Remove the caliper from vehicle.

To install:

9. Install the brake pads if removed.

10. Lubricate anti-rattle clips for the disc brake pads.

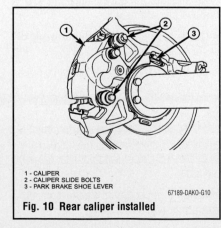

1 - CALIPER
2 - CALIPER SLIDE BOLTS
3 - PARK BRAKE SHOE LEVER

Fig. 10 Rear caliper installed

REAR DISC BRAKES

11. Install the caliper to the brake caliper adapter.

12. Coat the caliper mounting slide pin bolts with silicone grease. Then install and tighten the bolts to 25 Nm (18 ft. lbs.).

13. Install the brake hose banjo bolt if removed.

14. Install the brake hose to the caliper with new seal washers and tighten fitting bolt to 31 Nm (23 ft. lbs.).

➡**Verify brake hose is not twisted or kinked before tightening fitting bolt.**

15. Remove the prop rod from the vehicle.

16. Bleed the base brake system.

17. Install the wheel and tire assemblies.

DISC BRAKE PADS

REMOVAL & INSTALLATION

1. Raise and support vehicle.

2. Remove the wheel.

3. Drain small amount of fluid from master cylinder brake reservoir with suction gun.

4. Pry the piston side pad away from the rotor with a tool that won't scratch the rotor surface.

5. Remove the caliper mounting slide pin bolts.

6. Remove the caliper by tilting the top up and off the caliper adapter.

Do not allow brake hose to support caliper assembly.

7. Support and hang the caliper with a piece of wire or twine.

8. Remove the outboard brake pad from the caliper.

9. Remove the inboard brake pad from the caliper.

To install:

10. Install new anti—rattle clips.

➡When servicing the rear brake pads, replace the anti-rattle clips on the brake adapter. Anti-rattle clips are provided with the shoe & lining kit.

11. Install inboard brake pad in caliper.

12. Install outboard brake pad in caliper.

13. Lubricate rail clips for the disc brake pads.

14. Tilt the top of the caliper over rotor and secure to the mounting holes on the brake caliper adapter.

15. Install the caliper to the brake caliper adapter.

16. Coat the caliper mounting slide pin bolts with silicone grease. Then install and tighten the bolts to 25 Nm (19 ft. lbs.).

Verify brake hose is not twisted or kinked before tightening fitting bolt.

17. Install the wheel.

18. Remove the supports and lower the vehicle.

19. Apply brakes several times to seat caliper pistons and brake shoes and obtain firm pedal.

20. Top off master cylinder fluid level.

BRAKES

REAR DRUM BRAKES

Dust and dirt accumulating on brake parts during normal use may contain asbestos fibers from production or aftermarket brake linings. Breathing excessive concentrations of asbestos fibers can cause serious bodily harm. Exercise care when servicing brake parts. Do not sand or grind brake lining unless equipment used is designed to contain the dust residue. Do not clean brake parts with compressed air or by dry brushing. Cleaning should be done by dampening the brake components with a fine mist of water, then wiping the brake components clean with a dampened cloth. Dispose of cloth and all residue containing asbestos fibers in an impermeable container with the appropriate label. Follow practices prescribed by the Occupational Safety and Health Administration (OSHA) and the Environmental Protection Agency (EPA) for the handling, processing, and disposing of dust or debris that may contain asbestos fibers.

BRAKE DRUM

REMOVAL & INSTALLATION

1. Before servicing the vehicle, refer to the precautions in the beginning of this manual.

2. Remove the axle shaft nuts, washers and cones. If the cones do not readily release, rap the axle shaft sharply in the center.

3. Remove the axle shaft.

4. Remove the outer hub nut.

5. Straighten the lockwasher tab and remove it along with the inner nut and bearing.

6. Carefully remove the drum.

To install:

7. Position the drum on the axle housing.

8. Install the bearing and inner nut. While rotating the wheel and tire, tighten the adjusting nut until a slight drag is felt.

9. Back off the adjusting nut ⅛ turn so that the wheel rotates freely without excessive end-play.

10. Install the lockrings and nut. Place a new gasket on the hub and install the axle shaft, cones, lockwashers and nuts.

11. Install the wheel and tire.

12. Road-test the vehicle.

BRAKE SHOES

REMOVAL & INSTALLATION

See Figures 11 and 12.

1. Before servicing the vehicle, refer to the precautions in the beginning of this manual.

2. Raise and support vehicle.

3. Remove wheel and tire assembly.

4. Remove clip nuts securing brake drum to wheel studs.

5. Remove drum. If drum is difficult to remove, remove rear plug from access hole in support plate. Back-off self adjusting by inserting a thin screwdriver into access hole and push lever away from adjuster star wheel. Then insert an adjuster tool into brake adjusting hole rotate adjuster star wheel to retract brake shoes.

6. Vacuum brake components to remove brake lining dust.

7. Remove shoe return spring with brake spring pliers tool.

8. Remove adjuster spring and lever. Disengage lever from spring by sliding lever forward to clear pivot and work lever out from under spring.

9. Disengage and remove shoe return spring from brake shoes.

10. Remove brake shoe hold down clips.

11. Remove rear brake shoe from support plate.

12. Remove front brake shoe from support plate.

13. Remove park brake lever from the brake shoe.

To install:

14. Clean and inspect individual brake components.

15. Lubricate where the brake shoe contacts the support plate with high temperature grease or Lubriplate®.

16. Lubricate adjuster screw socket, nut, button and screw thread surfaces with grease or Lubriplate®.

17. Install parking brake lever to the rear shoe and install the hold down clip.

18. Install the adjuster strut onto the shoes and park brake lever.

19. Install the front shoe on support plate, and install the hold down clip.

20. Install the adjuster spring and lever in the slot in the adjuster strut.

21. Install the lower return spring to the shoes.

22. Verify adjuster operation. Pull both shoes outward to move the adjuster lever to rotate the star wheel. Be sure adjuster lever properly engages star wheel teeth.

23. Adjust brake shoes to drum with brake gauge.

24. Install wheel and tire assembly.

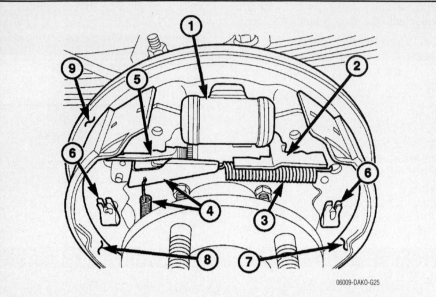

Fig. 11 Rear brake parts. (1) wheel cylinder, (2) parking brake lever, (3) return spring, (4 & 5) adjuster spring and lever, (6) hold-down clips, (7 & 8) brake shoes, (9) backing plate

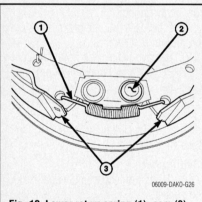

06009-DAKO-G26

Fig. 12 Lower return spring (1), cam (2) and brake shoes (3)

ADJUSTMENT

The rear drum brakes are equipped with a self-adjusting mechanism. Under normal circumstances, the only time adjustment is required is when the shoes are replaced, removed for access to other parts, or when one or both drums are replaced. Adjustment can be made with a standard brake gauge or with adjusting tool. Adjustment is performed with the complete brake assembly installed on the backing plate.

Adjustment with a Brake Gauge

See Figures 13 and 14.

1. Before servicing the vehicle, refer to the precautions in the beginning of this manual.

2. Be sure parking brakes are fully released.

3. Raise rear of vehicle and remove wheels and brake drums.

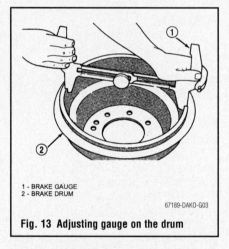

1 - BRAKE GAUGE
2 - BRAKE DRUM

67189-DAKO-G03

Fig. 13 Adjusting gauge on the drum

4. Verify that left and right automatic adjuster levers and cables are properly connected.

5. Insert brake gauge in drum. Expand gauge until gauge inner legs contact drum braking surface. Then lock gauge in position.

6. Reverse gauge and install it on brake shoes. Position gauge legs at shoe centers as shown. If gauge does not fit (too loose/too tight), adjust shoes.

7. Pull shoe adjuster lever away from adjuster screw star wheel.

8. Turn adjuster screw star wheel (by hand) to expand or retract brake shoes. Continue adjustment until gauge outside legs are light drag-fit on shoes.

9. Install brake drums and wheels and lower vehicle.

10. Drive vehicle and make one forward stop followed by one reverse stop. Repeat procedure 8-10 times to operate automatic adjusters and equalize adjustment.

➡ **Bring vehicle to complete standstill at each stop. Incomplete, rolling stops will not activate automatic adjusters.**

Adjustment with an Adjusting Tool

See Figure 15.

1. Before servicing the vehicle, refer to the precautions in the beginning of this manual.

2. Be sure parking brake lever is fully released.

3. Raise vehicle so rear wheels can be rotated freely.

4. Remove plug from each access hole in brake support plates.

5. Loosen parking brake cable adjustment nut until there is slack in front cable.

6. Insert adjusting tool through support plate access hole and engage tool in teeth of adjusting screw star wheel.

7. Rotate adjuster screw star wheel (move tool handle upward) until slight drag can be felt when wheel is rotated.

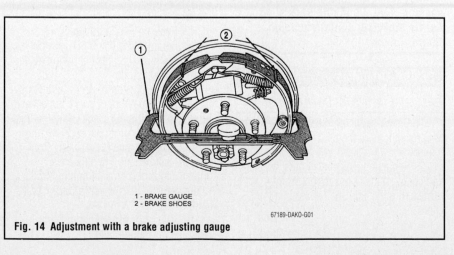

1 - BRAKE GAUGE
2 - BRAKE SHOES

67189-DAKO-G01

Fig. 14 Adjustment with a brake adjusting gauge

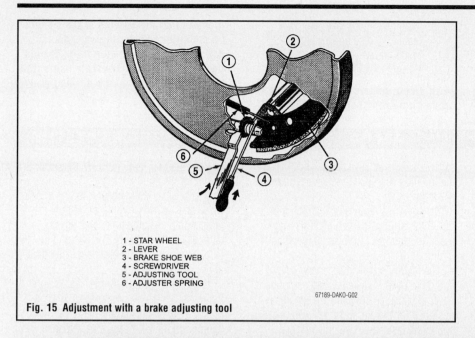

1 - STAR WHEEL
2 - LEVER
3 - BRAKE SHOE WEB
4 - SCREWDRIVER
5 - ADJUSTING TOOL
6 - ADJUSTER SPRING

67189-DAKO-G02

Fig. 15 Adjustment with a brake adjusting tool

8. Push and hold adjuster lever away from star wheel with thin screwdriver.

9. Back off adjuster screw star wheel until brake drag is eliminated.

10. Repeat adjustment at opposite wheel. Be sure adjustment is equal at both wheels.

11. Install support plate access hole plugs.

12. Adjust parking brake cable and lower vehicle.

13. Drive vehicle and make one forward stop followed by one reverse stop. Repeat procedure 8-10 times to operate automatic adjusters and equalize adjustment.

➡**Bring vehicle to complete standstill at each stop. Incomplete, rolling stops will not activate automatic adjusters.**

BRAKES

PARKING BRAKE CABLES

ADJUSTMENT
See Figure 16.

➡**Adjustment is only needed when the tensioner or a cable has been replaced or disconnected for service. To avoid faulty operation, only the procedure below should be carried out.**

1. Brakes must be operating correctly and properly adjusted.
2. Check that the parking brake cables operate freely.
3. Raise the vehicle and check that the wheels turn without drag with the parking brake released.
4. Apply the parking brake fully.
5. Mark the tensioner rod ¼in. (6.35mm) from the edge of the tensioner. There may be a factory mark already here.

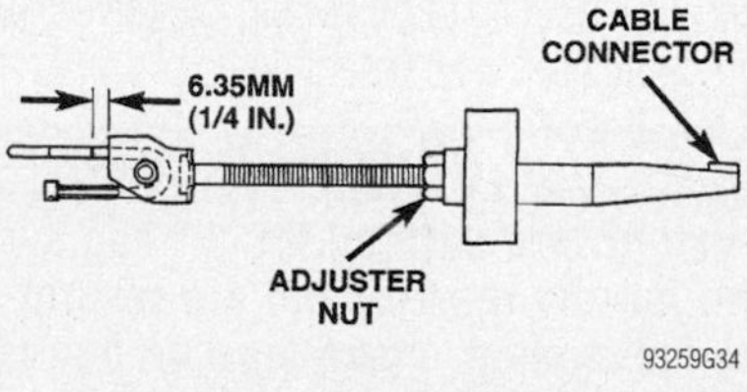

6. Tighten the adjusting nut on the tensioner until the mark is no longer visible.

7. Release the parking brake and ensure that the wheels turn without drag.

PARKING BRAKE SHOES

REMOVAL & INSTALLATION

With Rear Drum Brakes

The rear drum brake shoes serve as the parking brakes. Refer to the procedures under Rear Drum Brakes for service.

With Rear Disc Brakes
See Figure 17.

Rear disc parking brakes ("drum in hat") are dual shoe, internal expanding units with an automatic self adjusting mechanism. When the parking brake pedal is depressed the brake cable pulls the brake shoes outward against the brake drum. When the brake pedal is released the return springs attached to the brake shoes pull the shoes back to their original position.

1. Raise and support the vehicle.
2. Remove the tire and wheel assembly.
3. Remove the disc brake caliper.
4. Remove the disc brake rotor.
5. Disengage the park brake cable from behind the rotor assembly to allow easier disassembly of the park brake shoes.
6. Disassemble the rear park brake shoes.

PARKING BRAKE

To install:

7. Reassemble the rear park brake shoes.
8. Install park brake cable to the lever behind support plate.
9. Adjust the rear brake shoes:
   a. Measure the drum diameter with the gauge and lock it into position.
   b. Turn the gauge around and check the shoe diameter diagonally across at the top of one shoe and bottom of the opposite shoe (widest point). The gauge

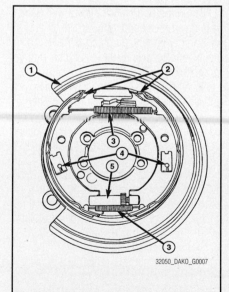

32050_DAKO_G0007

Fig. 17 Rear disc brake parking brake assembly. (1) Support plate, (2) Brake shoes, (3) Return springs, (4) Holddown clips, (5) Adjuster

CABLE
CONNECTOR

6.35MM
(1/4 IN.)

ADJUSTER
NUT

93259G34

Fig. 16 Parking brake adjustment mark

should be a light drag fit over the shoes.

c. If the gauge is not a light drag fit over the shoes, turn the star wheel by hand to move the shoes in or out so that the correct clearance can be achieved.

10. Install the disc brake rotor.
11. Install the disc brake caliper.
12. Install the wheel.
13. Lower the vehicle.

→On a new vehicle or after parking brake lining replacement, it is recom-

mended that the parking brake system be conditioned prior to use. This is done by making one stop from 25 mph on dry pavement or concrete using light to moderate force on the parking brake foot pedal.

CHASSIS ELECTRICAL

GENERAL INFORMATION

✳✳ CAUTION

These vehicles are equipped with an air bag system. The system must be disarmed before performing service on, or around, system components, the steering column, instrument panel components, wiring and sensors. Failure to follow the safety precautions and the disarming procedure could result in accidental air bag deployment, possible injury and unnecessary system repairs.

SERVICE PRECAUTIONS

Disconnect and isolate the battery negative cable before beginning any airbag system component diagnosis, testing, removal, or installation procedures. Allow system capacitor to discharge for two minutes before beginning any component service. This will disable the airbag system. Failure to disable the airbag system may result in accidental airbag deployment, personal injury, or death.

Do not place an intact undeployed airbag face down on a solid surface. The airbag will propel into the air if accidentally deployed and may result in personal injury or death.

When carrying or handling an undeployed airbag, the trim side (face) of the airbag should be pointing towards the body to minimize possibility of injury if accidental deployment occurs. Failure to do this may result in personal injury or death.

Replace airbag system components with OEM replacement parts. Substitute parts may appear interchangeable, but internal differences may result in inferior occupant protection. Failure to do so may result in occupant personal injury or death.

Wear safety glasses, rubber gloves, and long sleeved clothing when cleaning powder residue from vehicle after an airbag deployment. Powder residue emitted from a deployed airbag can cause skin irritation. Flush affected area with cool water if irritation is experienced. If nasal or throat irritation is

AIR BAG (SUPPLEMENTAL RESTRAINT SYSTEM)

experienced, exit the vehicle for fresh air until the irritation ceases. If irritation continues, see a physician.

Do not use a replacement airbag that is not in the original packaging. This may result in improper deployment, personal injury, or death.

The factory installed fasteners, screws and bolts used to fasten airbag components have a special coating and are specifically designed for the airbag system. Do not use substitute fasteners. Use only original equipment fasteners listed in the parts catalog when fastener replacement is required.

During, and following, any child restraint anchor service, due to impact event or vehicle repair, carefully inspect all mounting hardware, tether straps, and anchors for proper installation, operation, or damage. If a child restraint anchor is found damaged in any way, the anchor must be replaced. Failure to do this may result in personal injury or death.

Deployed and non-deployed airbags may or may not have live pyrotechnic material within the airbag inflator.

Do not dispose of driver/passenger/curtain airbags or seat belt tensioners unless you are sure of complete deployment. Refer to the Hazardous Substance Control System for proper disposal.

Dispose of deployed airbags and tensioners consistent with state, provincial, local, and federal regulations.

After any airbag component testing or service, do not connect the battery negative cable. Personal injury or death may result if the system test is not performed first.

If the vehicle is equipped with the Occupant Classification System (OCS), do not connect the battery negative cable before performing the OCS Verification Test using the scan tool and the appropriate diagnostic information. Personal injury or death may result if the system test is not performed properly.

Never replace both the Occupant Restraint Controller (ORC) and the Occupant Classification Module (OCM) at the same time. If both require replacement, replace one, then perform the Airbag System test before replacing the other.

Both the ORC and the OCM store Occupant Classification System (OCS) calibration data, which they transfer to one another when one of them is replaced. If both are replaced at the same time, an irreversible fault will be set in both modules and the OCS may malfunction and cause personal injury or death.

If equipped with OCS, the Seat Weight Sensor is a sensitive, calibrated unit and must be handled carefully. Do not drop or handle roughly. If dropped or damaged, replace with another sensor. Failure to do so may result in occupant injury or death.

If equipped with OCS, the front passenger seat must be handled carefully as well. When removing the seat, be careful when setting on floor not to drop. If dropped, the sensor may be inoperative, could result in occupant injury, or possibly death.

If equipped with OCS, when the passenger front seat is on the floor, no one should sit in the front passenger seat. This uneven force may damage the sensing ability of the seat weight sensors. If sat on and damaged, the sensor may be inoperative, could result in occupant injury, or possibly death.

DISARMING THE SYSTEM

1. Disconnect and isolate the negative battery cable. Wait 2 minutes for the system capacitor to discharge before performing any service.

2. When repairs are completed, connect the negative battery cable.

ARMING THE SYSTEM

Assuming that the system components (air bag control module, sensors, air bag, etc.) are installed correctly and are in good working order, the system is armed whenever the battery's positive and negative battery cables are connected.

✳✳ WARNING

If you have disarmed the air bag system for any reason, and are re-arming the system, make sure no one is in the vehicle (as an added safety measure), then connect the negative battery cable.

CLOCKSPRING CENTERING

See Figure 18.

Disconnect and isolate the battery negative cable before beginning any airbag system component diagnosis, testing, removal, or installation procedures. Allow system capacitor to discharge for two minutes before beginning any component service. This will disable the airbag system. Failure to disable the airbag system may result in accidental airbag deployment, personal injury, or death.

The clockspring is mounted on the steering column behind the steering wheel. Its purpose is to maintain a continuous electrical circuit between the wiring harness and the driver's side air bag module. This assembly consists of a flat, ribbon-like electrically conductive tape that winds and unwinds with the steering wheel rotation.

Service replacement clocksprings are shipped pre-centered and with a molded plastic locking pin that snaps into a receptacle on the rotor and is engaged between two tabs on the upper surface of the rotor case. The locking pin secures the centered clockspring rotor to the clockspring case during shipment, but the locking pin must be removed from the clockspring after it is installed on the steering column. This locking pin should not be removed until the clockspring has been installed on the steering column. If the locking pin is removed before the clockspring is installed on a steering column, the clockspring centering procedure must be performed.

➡**The clockspring cannot be repaired. If the clockspring is faulty, damaged, or if the driver airbag has been deployed, the clockspring must be replaced.**

Before starting this procedure, be certain to turn the steering wheel until the front wheels are in the straight-ahead position.

1. Place the front wheels in the straight-ahead position.
2. Remove the clockspring from the steering column.
3. Rotate the clockspring rotor clockwise to the end of its travel. Do not apply excessive torque.
4. From the end of the clockwise travel, rotate the rotor about two and one-half turns counterclockwise.
5. The engagement dowel and yellow rubber boot should end up at the bottom, and the arrows on the clockspring rotor and case should be in alignment. The clockspring is now centered.
6. The front wheels should still be in the straight-ahead position. Reinstall the clockspring onto the steering column.

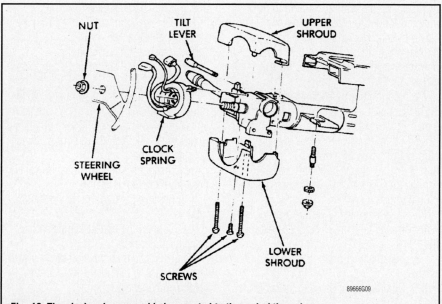

Fig. 18 The clockspring assembly is mounted to the end of the column, behind the steering wheel

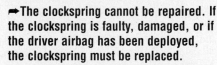

DRIVETRAIN

AUTOMATIC TRANSMISSION ASSEMBLY

REMOVAL & INSTALLATION

545RFE Transmission

1. Before servicing the vehicle, refer to the precautions in the beginning of this manual.
2. Disconnect the negative battery cable.
3. Raise and support the vehicle.
4. Remove any necessary skid plates.
5. Mark propeller shaft and axle companion flanges for assembly alignment.
6. Remove the rear propeller shaft.
7. Remove the front propeller shaft, if necessary.
8. Remove the engine to transmission collar.
9. Remove the exhaust support bracket from the rear of the transmission.
10. Disconnect and lower or remove any necessary exhaust components.
11. Remove the starter motor.
12. Rotate crankshaft in clockwise direction until converter bolts are accessible. Then remove bolts one at a time. Rotate crankshaft with socket wrench on dampener bolt.
13. Disengage the output speed sensor connector from the output speed sensor.
14. Disengage the input speed sensor connector from the input speed sensor.
15. Disengage the transmission solenoid/TRS assembly connector from the transmission solenoid/TRS assembly.
16. Disengage the line pressure sensor connector from the line pressure sensor.
17. Disconnect gearshift cable from transmission manual valve lever.
18. Disconnect transmission fluid cooler lines at transmission fittings and clips.
19. Disconnect the transmission vent hose from the transmission.
20. Support rear of engine with safety stand or jack.
21. Raise transmission slightly with service jack to relieve load on crossmember and supports.
22. Remove bolts securing rear support and cushion to transmission and crossmember.
23. Remove bolts attaching crossmember to frame and remove crossmember.
24. Remove transfer case on 4WD models.
25. Remove all remaining converter housing bolts.
26. Carefully work transmission and torque converter assembly rearward off engine block dowels.

27. Hold torque converter in place during transmission removal.

28. Lower transmission and remove assembly from under the vehicle.

29. To remove torque converter, carefully slide torque converter out of the transmission.

To install:

30. Check torque converter hub and hub drive flats for sharp edges burrs, scratches, or nicks. Polish the hub and flats with 320/400 grit paper and crocus cloth if necessary. Verify that the converter hub O-ring is properly installed and is free of any debris. The hub must be smooth to avoid damaging pump seal at installation.

31. If a replacement transmission is being installed, transfer any components necessary, such as the manual shift lever and shift cable bracket, from the original transmission onto the replacement transmission.

32. Lubricate oil pump seal lip with transmission fluid.

33. Align converter and oil pump.

34. Carefully insert converter in oil pump. Then rotate converter back and forth until fully seated in pump gears.

35. Check converter seating with steel scale and straightedge. Surface of converter lugs should be at least 13mm (½ in.) to rear of straightedge when converter is fully seated.

36. Temporarily secure converter with C-clamp.

37. Position transmission on jack and secure it with chains.

38. Check condition of converter driveplate. Replace the plate if cracked, distorted or damaged. Also be sure transmission dowel pins are seated in engine block and protrude far enough to hold transmission in alignment.

39. Apply a light coating of high temperature grease to the torque converter hub pocket in the rear pocket of the engine's crankshaft.

40. Raise transmission and align the torque converter with the drive plate and transmission converter housing with the engine block.

41. Move transmission forward. Then raise, lower or tilt transmission to align the converter housing with engine block dowels.

42. Carefully work transmission forward and over engine block dowels until converter hub is seated in crankshaft. Verify that no wires, or the transmission vent hose, have become trapped between the engine block and the transmission.

43. Install two bolts to attach the transmission to the engine.

44. Install remaining torque converter housing to engine bolts. Tighten to 68 Nm (50 ft. lbs.).

45. Install transfer case, if equipped. Tighten transfer case nuts to 35 Nm (26 ft. lbs.).

46. Install rear transmission crossmember. Tighten crossmember to frame bolts to 68 Nm (50 ft. lbs.).

47. Install rear support to transmission. Tighten bolts to 47 Nm (35 ft. lbs.).

48. Lower transmission onto crossmember and install bolts attaching transmission mount to crossmember. Tighten clevis bracket to crossmember bolts to 47 Nm (35 ft. lbs.). Tighten the clevis bracket to rear support bolt to 68 Nm (50 ft. lbs.).

49. Remove engine support fixture.

50. Connect gearshift cable to transmission.

51. Connect wires to solenoid and pressure switch assembly connector, input and output speed sensors, and line pressure sensor. Be sure transmission harnesses are properly routed.

52. Install torque converter-to-driveplate bolts. Tighten bolts to 31 Nm (270 inch lbs.).

53. Install starter motor and cooler line bracket.

54. Connect cooler lines to transmission.

55. Install transmission fill tube.

56. Install exhaust components.

57. Install the engine collar onto the transmission and the engine. Tighten the bolts to 54 Nm (40 ft. lbs.).

58. Align and connect propeller shaft(s).

59. Adjust gearshift cable if necessary.

60. Install any skid plates removed previously.

61. Lower vehicle.

62. Fill transmission with Mopar® ATF +4, Automatic Transmission Fluid.

42RLE Transmission

1. Before servicing the vehicle, refer to the precautions in the beginning of this manual.

2. Disconnect the negative battery cable.

3. Raise and support the vehicle.

4. Remove any necessary skid plates.

5. Mark the propeller shaft and axle companion flanges for assembly alignment.

6. Remove the rear propeller shaft.

7. Remove the front propeller shaft, if necessary.

8. Disconnect the wires from the input and output speed sensors.

9. Disconnect the wires from the transmission range sensor and the solenoid/pressure switch assembly.

10. Remove the bolts holding the exhaust crossover pipe to the pre-catalytic converter pipe flanges.

11. Remove the bolts holding the exhaust crossover pipe to the catalytic converter flange.

12. Disconnect gearshift cable from transmission manual valve lever.

13. Disengage the shift cable from the cable support bracket.

14. Remove the starter motor.

15. Remove the engine to transmission collar.

16. Rotate the crankshaft in clockwise direction until the converter bolts are accessible. Then remove the bolts one at a time. Rotate the crankshaft with a socket wrench on dampener bolt.

17. Disconnect the transmission vent hose from the transmission.

18. Remove the transfer case on 4WD models.

19. Support the rear of engine with a safety stand or jack.

20. Raise the transmission slightly with a service jack to relieve the load on the crossmember and supports.

21. Remove the bolts securing the rear support and cushion to the transmission and crossmember.

22. Remove the bolts attaching the crossmember to frame and remove crossmember.

23. Disconnect the transmission fluid cooler lines at the transmission fittings and clips.

24. Remove all remaining converter housing bolts.

25. Carefully work the transmission and torque converter assembly rearward off the engine block dowels.

26. Hold the torque converter in place during transmission removal.

27. Lower the transmission and remove the assembly from under the vehicle.

28. To remove the torque converter, carefully slide the torque converter out of the transmission.

To install:

29. Check the torque converter hub and hub drive flats for sharp edges burrs, scratches, or nicks. Polish the hub and flats with 320/400 grit paper and crocus

cloth if necessary. Verify that the converter hub O-ring is properly installed and is free of any debris. The hub must be smooth to avoid damaging pump seal at installation.

30. If a replacement transmission is being installed, transfer any components necessary, such as the manual shift lever and shift cable bracket, from the original transmission onto the replacement transmission.

31. Lubricate the oil pump seal lip with transmission fluid.

32. Align the converter and oil pump.

33. Carefully insert the converter in the oil pump. Then rotate the converter back and forth until fully seated in the pump gears.

34. Check the converter seating with a steel scale and straightedge. The surface of the converter lugs should be at least 13mm (½ in.) to the rear of straightedge when the converter is fully seated.

35. Temporarily secure the converter with a C-clamp.

36. Position the transmission on the jack and secure it with chains.

37. Check the condition of the converter driveplate. Replace the plate if cracked, distorted or damaged. Also, be sure the transmission dowel pins are seated in the engine block and protrude far enough to hold the transmission in alignment.

38. Apply a light coating of high temperature grease to the torque converter hub pocket in the rear pocket of the engine's crankshaft.

39. Raise the transmission and align the torque converter with the drive plate and transmission converter housing with the engine block.

40. Move the transmission forward. Then raise, lower or tilt transmission to align the converter housing with engine block dowels.

41. Carefully work the transmission forward and over the engine block dowels until the converter hub is seated in the crankshaft. Verify that no wires, or the transmission vent hose, have become trapped between the engine block and the transmission.

42. Install the two bolts to attach the transmission to the engine.

43. Install the remaining torque converter housing to engine bolts. Tighten to 68 Nm (50 ft. lbs.).

44. Install the transfer case, if equipped. Tighten the transfer case nuts to 35 Nm (26 ft. lbs.).

45. Install the rear transmission crossmember. Tighten the crossmember to frame bolts to 68 Nm (50 ft. lbs.).

46. Install the rear support to the transmission. Tighten the bolts to 47 Nm (35 ft. lbs.).

47. Lower the transmission onto the crossmember and install the bolts attaching the transmission mount to the crossmember. Tighten clevis bracket to crossmember bolts to 47 Nm (35 ft. lbs.). Tighten the clevis bracket to rear support bolt to 68 Nm (50 ft. lbs.).

48. Remove the engine support fixture.

49. Connect the gearshift cable to the support bracket and transmission manual lever.

50. Connect the input and output speed sensor wires.

51. Connect the wires to the transmission range sensor and the solenoid/pressure switch assembly.

52. Install the torque converter-to-driveplate bolts. Tighten the bolts to 88 Nm (65 inch lbs.).

53. Install the starter motor and cooler line bracket.

54. Connect the cooler lines to transmission.

55. Install the transmission fill tube.

56. Install the exhaust components.

57. Align and connect the propeller shaft(s).

58. Adjust the gearshift cable if necessary.

59. Install any skid plates removed previously.

60. Lower the vehicle.

61. Fill the transmission with the required amount of Mopar® ATF +4, Automatic Transmission Fluid.

MANUAL TRANSMISSION ASSEMBLY

REMOVAL & INSTALLATION

2WD Models

1. Before servicing the vehicle, refer to the precautions in the beginning of this manual.

2. Disconnect battery negative cable.

3. Shift transmission into Neutral.

4. Remove floor console.

5. Remove shift lever boot.

6. Remove the shift lever extension from the shift tower and lever assembly.

7. Raise vehicle.

8. Remove skid plate, if equipped.

9. If transmission will be disassembled for repair, remove drain plug and drain lubricant from transmission.

10. Mark propeller shafts and companion flange for assembly reference.

11. Disconnect and remove propeller shafts.

12. Disconnect and remove exhaust system Y-pipe. Then disconnect and lower

remaining exhaust pipes for clearance as necessary.

13. Disconnect backup light switch wires.

14. Remove bolts/nuts attaching transmission to rear mount.

15. Support transmission with a transmission jack. Secure transmission to jack with safety chains.

16. Remove rear crossmember.

17. Remove bolts attaching clutch slave cylinder to clutch housing. Then move cylinder aside for working clearance.

18. Remove starter.

19. Remove transmission dust shield.

20. Remove transmission harness wires from clips on transmission shift cover.

21. Lower transmission slightly.

22. Remove the bolts attaching the shift tower and lever assembly to the transmission housing. Then remove the shift tower and lever assembly.

23. Remove bolts attaching transmission to engine.

24. Slide transmission and jack rearward until input shaft clears clutch disc.

25. Lower transmission jack and remove transmission from under vehicle.

To install:

➡ **If a new transmission is being installed, be sure to use all components supplied with the new transmission. For example, if a new shift tower is supplied with the new transmission, do not re-use the original shift tower.**

26. Apply light coat of Mopar® high temperature bearing grease to contact surfaces of following components:
- Input shaft splines
- Release bearing slide surface of front retainer
- Release bearing bore
- Release fork
- Release fork ball stud
- Propeller shaft slip yoke

27. Apply sealer to threads of drain plug, then install plug in case.

28. Mount transmission on jack and position transmission under vehicle. Secure transmission to jack with safety chains.

29. Raise transmission until input shaft is centered in clutch disc hub.

30. Move transmission forward and start input shaft in clutch disc.

31. Work transmission forward until seated against engine. Do not allow transmission to remain unsupported after input shaft has entered clutch disc.

32. Install and tighten transmission to engine bolts to 108 Nm (80 ft. lbs.).

33. Position transmission harness wires in clips on shift cover.

34. Install slave cylinder and shield, if equipped.

35. Install transmission mount on transmission or rear crossmember.

4WD Models

1. Before servicing the vehicle, refer to the precautions in the beginning of this manual.

2. Disconnect battery negative cable.

3. Shift transmission into Neutral.

4. Remove floor console.

5. Remove shift lever boot.

6. Remove the shift lever extension from the shift tower and lever assembly.

7. Raise vehicle.

8. Remove skid plate, if equipped.

9. If transmission will be disassembled for repair, remove drain plug and drain lubricant from transmission.

10. Mark propeller shafts and companion flange for assembly reference.

11. Disconnect and remove propeller shafts.

12. Disconnect and remove exhaust system Y-pipe. Then disconnect and lower remaining exhaust pipes for clearance as necessary.

13. Disconnect backup light switch wires.

14. Support engine with adjustable safety stand.

15. Disconnect transfer case shift linkage at transfer case range lever.

16. Remove transfer case shift lever from transmission.

17. Remove bolts/nuts attaching transmission to rear support.

18. Remove crossmember bolts/nuts and remove crossmember.

19. Support transfer case with transmission jack. Secure transfer case to jack with safety chains.

20. Remove transfer case attaching nuts.

21. Move transfer case rearward until input gear clears transmission output shaft.

22. Lower transfer case assembly and move it from under vehicle.

23. Support transmission with transmission jack. Secure transmission to jack with safety chains.

24. Remove transmission harness from retaining clips on transmission shift cover.

25. Remove clutch slave cylinder splash shield, if equipped.

26. Remove clutch slave cylinder attaching nuts. Move cylinder aside for working clearance.

27. Remove starter.

28. Remove transmission splash shield.

29. Lower transmission slightly.

30. Remove bolts attaching shift tower and lever assembly to rear case. Then remove shift tower and lever as an assembly.

31. Remove bolts attaching transmission to engine.

32. Move transmission rearward until the input shaft clears the clutch disc.

33. Lower transmission and remove it from under vehicle.

To install:

➡ **If a new transmission is being installed, be sure to use all components supplied with the new transmission. For example, if a new shift tower is supplied with the new transmission, do not re-use the original shift tower.**

34. Apply light coat of Mopar® high temperature bearing grease to contact surfaces of following components:
- Input shaft splines
- Release bearing slide surface of front retainer
- Release bearing bore
- Release fork
- Release fork ball stud
- Propeller shaft slip yoke

35. Apply sealer to threads of drain plug, then install plug in case.

36. Mount transmission on jack and position transmission under vehicle. Secure transmission to jack with safety chains.

37. Raise transmission until input shaft is centered in clutch disc hub.

38. Move transmission forward and start input shaft in clutch disc.

39. Work transmission forward until seated against engine. Do not allow transmission to remain unsupported after input shaft has entered clutch disc.

40. Install and tighten transmission to engine bolts to 108 Nm (80 ft. lbs.).

41. Position transmission harness wires in clips on shift cover.

42. Install slave cylinder and shield, if equipped.

43. Install transmission mount on transmission or rear crossmember.

44. Install transfer case shift lever on transmission.

45. Install rear crossmember.

➡ **Ensure wiring harness is clear before installing crossmember.**

46. Remove transmission jack and engine support fixture.

47. Install transfer case on transmission jack. Secure transfer case to jack with safety chains.

48. Raise jack and align transfer case input gear with transmission output shaft.

49. Move transfer case forward and seat it on transmission.

50. Install and tighten transfer case attaching nuts. Tighten nuts to 41–47 Nm (30–35 ft. lbs.) if case has ⅜ studs, or 30–41 Nm (22–30 ft. lbs.) if case has 5⁄16 studs.

51. Connect backup light switch wires.

52. Install transmission dust cover.

53. Install starter.

54. Install transfer case shift lever to side of transfer case.

55. Connect transfer case shift lever to range lever on transfer case.

56. Align and connect propeller shafts.

57. Fill transmission with required lubricant. Check lubricant level in transfer case and add lubricant if necessary.

58. Install transfer case skid plate, if equipped, and crossmember. Tighten attaching bolts/nuts to 41 Nm (30 ft. lbs.).

59. Install exhaust system components.

60. Lower vehicle.

61. Install shift tower and lever assembly. Tighten shift tower bolts to 7–10 Nm (5–7 ft. lbs.).

62. Install shift lever boot.

63. Install floor console.

64. Connect battery negative cable.

CLUTCH

REMOVAL & INSTALLATION

See Figure 19.

1. Before servicing the vehicle, refer to the precautions in the beginning of this manual.

2. Raise vehicle.

3. Remove transmission and clutch housing as assembly.

4. If pressure plate is being removed for access to another component, mark position of pressure plate cover on flywheel with small punch marks.

5. Loosen pressure plate cover bolts evenly and in rotation to relieve spring tension. Loosen bolts a few threads at a time to avoid warping cover.

6. Remove cover bolts, pressure plate and clutch disc.

To install:

➡ **Clean flywheel surface with solvent. Scuff sand surface with 120/180 grit emery cloth to remove minor scratches and glazing.**

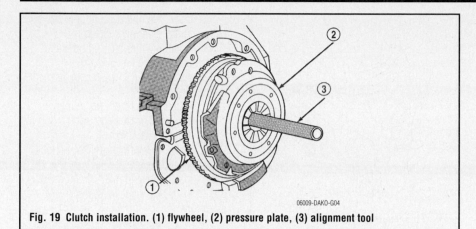

Fig. 19 Clutch installation. (1) flywheel, (2) pressure plate, (3) alignment tool

7. Check new clutch disc for runout and free operation on input shaft splines.

8. Lubricate crankshaft pilot bearing with a NLGI - 2 rated grease.

9. Position clutch disc on the flywheel.

10. Insert alignment tool or spare input shaft through clutch disc and into pilot bearing.

11. Verify that disc hub is positioned correctly. The raised portion of the hub faces away from the flywheel.

12. Position pressure plate cover over disc and on flywheel.

13. Install cover bolts finger tight.

14. Tighten cover bolts evenly (and in rotation) a few threads at a time. Cover bolts must be tightened evenly and to specified torque to avoid distorting cover.

15. Tighten cover bolts to:
- 5/16 in. bolts to 23 Nm (17 ft. lbs.).
- 3/8 in. bolts to 41 Nm (30 ft. lbs.).

16. Apply light coat of high temperature bearing grease to splines of transmission input shaft and to release bearing slide surface of front bearing retainer.

➡**Do not over-lubricate shaft splines. This could result in grease contamination of disc.**

17. Install transmission as assembly.

BLEEDING

The system is self-bleeding. Press the clutch pedal repeatedly to release air from the fluid. The air will be vented from the reservoir.

TRANSFER CASE ASSEMBLY

REMOVAL & INSTALLATION

NV233

See Figure 20.

1. Before servicing the vehicle, refer to the precautions in the beginning of this manual.

2. Shift the transfer case into 2WD.
3. Raise the vehicle.
4. Drain the transfer case lubricant.
5. Mark the front and rear propeller shafts for alignment reference.
6. Support the transmission with jack stand.
7. Remove the rear crossmember and skid plate, if equipped.
8. Disconnect the front and rear propeller shafts at transfer case.
9. Disconnect the transfer case shift motor and mode sensor wire connectors.
10. Disconnect the transfer case vent hose.
11. Support the transfer case with a transmission jack.
12. Secure the transfer case to the jack with chains.
13. Remove the nuts attaching transfer case to the transmission.
14. Pull the transfer case and jack rearward to disengage the transfer case.

15. Remove the transfer case from under the vehicle.

To install:

16. Mount the transfer case on a transmission jack.
17. Secure the transfer case to the jack with chains.
18. Position transfer case under vehicle.
19. Align the transfer case and transmission shafts and install the transfer case onto the transmission.
20. Install and tighten the transfer case attaching nuts to 27–34 Nm (20–25 ft. lbs.).
21. Connect the vent hose.
22. Connect the shift motor and mode sensor wiring connectors. Secure the wire harness to clips on the transfer case.
23. Align and connect the propeller shafts.
24. Fill the transfer case with the correct fluid.
25. Install the rear crossmember and skid plate, if equipped. Tighten the crossmember bolts to 41 Nm (30 ft. lbs.).
26. Remove the transmission jack and support stand.
27. Lower the vehicle and verify transfer case shift operation.

NV244

1. Before servicing the vehicle, refer to the precautions in the beginning of this manual.
2. Shift transfer case into AWD.
3. Raise vehicle.
4. Drain transfer case lubricant.

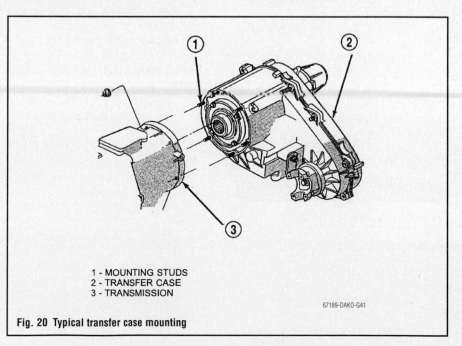

1 - MOUNTING STUDS
2 - TRANSFER CASE
3 - TRANSMISSION

Fig. 20 Typical transfer case mounting

5. Mark front and rear propeller shafts for alignment reference.

6. Disconnect front and rear propeller shafts at transfer case.

7. Support transmission with jack stand.

8. Remove rear crossmember and skid plate, if equipped.

9. Disconnect transfer case shift motor and mode sensor wire connectors.

10. Disconnect transfer case vent hose.

11. Support transfer case with transmission jack.

12. Secure transfer case to jack with chains.

13. Remove nuts attaching transfer case to transmission.

14. Pull transfer case and jack rearward to disengage transfer case from the transmission adapter housing and output shaft.

15. Remove transfer case from under vehicle.

To install:

16. Mount transfer case on a transmission jack.

17. Secure transfer case to jack with chains.

18. Position transfer case under vehicle.

19. Align transfer case and transmission shafts and install transfer case onto the transmission.

20. Install and tighten transfer case attaching nuts to 27–34 Nm (20–25 ft. lbs.). Connect the vent hose.

21. Connect the shift motor and mode sensor wiring connectors. Secure wire harness to clips on transfer case.

22. Align and connect the propeller shafts.

23. Fill transfer case with correct fluid.

24. Install rear crossmember and skid plate, if equipped. Tighten crossmember bolts to 41 Nm (30 ft. lbs.).

25. Remove transmission jack and support stand.

26. Lower vehicle and verify transfer case shift operation.

FRONT DRIVESHAFT

REMOVAL & INSTALLATION

See Figure 21.

1. Before servicing the vehicle, refer to the precautions in the beginning of this manual.

2. Mark propeller shaft and pinion flange for installation reference.

3. Remove front propeller shaft.

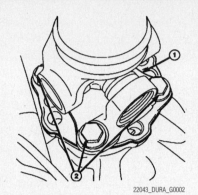

Fig. 21 Shaft flange (1) and mounting bolts (2)

To install:

4. Install propeller shaft with reference marks aligned.

5. Using new bolts, tighten them to 85 ft. lbs. (115 Nm).

FRONT HALFSHAFT

REMOVAL & INSTALLATION

1. Before servicing the vehicle, refer to the precautions in the beginning of this manual.

2. Raise the vehicle.

3. Remove the wheel and tire assembly.

4. Remove the skid plate, if equipped.

5. Remove the cotter pin, nut lock, and spring washer from the stub shaft.

6. Remove the hub nut and washer from the stub shaft.

7. Remove the brake caliper and rotor.

8. Remove the ABS wheel speed sensor if equipped.

9. Remove the hub bearing bolts and hub bearing from the knuckle.

10. Support the half shaft at the CV joint housings.

11. Position two pry bars behind the inner CV housing and disengage the CV joint from the axle.

12. Remove the half shaft from the vehicle.

To install:

13. Apply a light coating of wheel bearing grease on the axle splines.

14. Insert the half shaft stub through the steering knuckle and onto the axle. Verify the shaft snapring engages with the groove on the inside of the joint housing.

15. Clean the hub bearing bore and hub bearing mating surface of all foreign materials. Apply a light coating of grease to all mating surfaces.

16. Install the hub bearing onto the axle half shaft and steering knuckle.

17. Install the hub bearing bolts and tighten to 120 ft. lbs. (163 Nm).

18. Install the ABS wheel speed sensor, if equipped.

19. Install brake rotor and caliper.

20. Apply the brakes and tighten hub nut to 185 ft. lbs. (251 Nm).

21. Install the spring washer, nut lock and cotter pin.

22. Install the skid plate, if equipped.

23. Install the wheel and tire assembly.

CV-JOINTS OVERHAUL

Outer Joint

See Figures 22 through 27.

1. Before servicing the vehicle, refer to the precautions in the beginning of this manual.

2. Place shaft in vise with soft jaws and support CV-joint.

✳✳ CAUTION

Do not damage CV-joint housing or halfshaft.

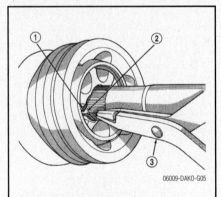

Fig. 22 Removing the snapring (1) from the shaft (2) with snapring pliers (3)

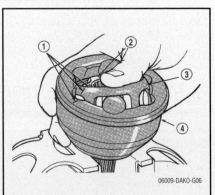

Fig. 23 Make alignment marks (1) on the inner race/hub (2) and cage (3)

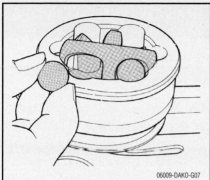

Fig. 24 Removing the balls from the bearing cage

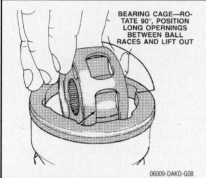

Fig. 25 Removing the cage and inner race from the housing

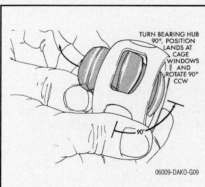

Fig. 26 Removing the inner race/hub from the cage

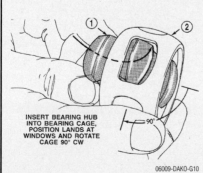

Fig. 27 Assembling the inner race cage and housing

3. Remove clamps with a cut-off wheel or grinder.

4. Slide the boot down the shaft.

5. Remove lubricant to expose the CV-joint snapring.

6. Spread snapring and slide the joint off the shaft.

7. Slide boot off the shaft and discard old boot.

8. Mark alignment marks on the inner race/hub, bearing cage and housing with dabs of paint.

9. Clamp CV-joint in a vertical position in a soft jawed vise.

10. Press down one side of the bearing cage to gain access to the ball at the opposite side.

➡If joint is tight, use a hammer and brass drift to loosen the bearing hub. Do not contact the bearing cage with the drift.

11. Remove ball from the bearing cage.

12. Repeat step above until all six balls are removed from the bearing cage.

13. Lift cage and inner race upward and out from the housing.

14. Turn inner race 90° in the cage and rotate the inner race/hub out of the cage.

To install:

15. Apply a light coat of grease to the CV-joint components before assembling them.

16. Align inner race, cage and housing according to the alignment reference marks.

17. Insert inner race into the cage and rotate race into the cage.

18. Rotate inner race/hub in the cage.

19. Insert cage into the housing.

20. Rotate cage 90° into the housing.

21. Apply lubricant included with replacement boot/joint to the ball races. Spread lubricant equally among all the races.

22. Tilt inner race/hub and cage and install the balls.

23. Place new clamps onto new boot and slide boot onto the shaft to its original position.

24. Apply the rest of lubricant to the CV-joint and boot.

25. Push the joint onto the shaft until the snapring seats in the groove. Pull on the joint to verify the span ring has engaged.

26. Position boot on the joint in its original position. Ensure boot is not twisted and remove any excess air.

27. Secure both boot clamps with Clamp

Installer C-4975A, or equivalent. Place tool on clamp bridge and tighten tool until the jaws of the tool are closed.

Inner Joint

1. Before servicing the vehicle, refer to the precautions in the beginning of this manual.

2. Clamp the shaft in a vise with soft jaws and support the CV joint.

3. Remove the clamps with a cut-off wheel or grinder.

❋❋ WARNING

Do not damage the CV housing or half shaft with the cut-off wheel or grinder.

4. Remove the housing from the half shaft and slide the boot down shaft.

5. Remove the housing bushing from the housing.

6. Remove the tripod snapring.

7. Remove the tripod and boot from the halfshaft.

8. Clean and inspect the CV components for excessive wear and damage. Replace the tripod as a unit only if necessary.

To install:

9. Slide a new boot down the halfshaft.

10. Install the tripod and tripod snapring on the halfshaft.

11. Pack the grease supplied with the joint/boot into the housing and boot.

12. Coat the tripod with the supplied grease.

13. Install new bushing onto the housing.

14. Insert the tripod and shaft in the housing.

15. Position the boot on the joint in its original position.

➡Verify the boot is not twisted and remove any excess air.

16. Secure both boot clamps with Clamp Installer C-4975A, or equivalent. Place the tool on the clamp bridge and tighten the tool until the jaws of the tool are closed.

FRONT PINION SEAL

REMOVAL & INSTALLATION

1. Before servicing the vehicle, refer to the precautions in the beginning of this manual.

2. Raise and support the vehicle.

3. Remove skid plate, if equipped.

4. Remove both half shafts.

5. Mark the propeller shaft and pinion companion flange for installation reference.

6. Remove the front propeller shaft.

7. Rotate the pinion gear three or four times and verify pinion rotates smoothly.

8. Record pinion rotating torque with an inch pound torque wrench, for installation reference.

9. Position Holder 6719, or equivalent, against the companion flange and install a four bolts and washers into the threaded holes and tighten the bolts.

10. Remove the pinion nut.

11. Remove the companion flange with Remover C-452, or equivalent.

12. Remove pinion seal with a pry tool or a slide hammer mounted screw.

To install:

13. Apply a light coating of gear lubricant on the lip of pinion seal.

14. Install seal with Installer C-3972-A and Handle C-4171, or equivalent,

15. Install the companion flange onto the pinion with Installer C-3718 and Holder 6719A, or equivalent.

16. Position holder against the companion flange and install four bolts and washers into the threaded holes. Tighten the bolt and washer so that the holder is held to the flange.

17. Install a new pinion nut onto the pinion shaft and tighten the pinion nut until there is zero bearing end-play.

➡**Do not exceed the minimum tightening torque when installing the companion flange at this point. Damage to the collapsible spacer or bearings may result.**

18. Tighten the nut to 200 ft. lbs. (271 Nm).

➡**Never loosen pinion nut to decrease pinion bearing rotating torque and never exceed specified preload torque. If preload torque or rotating torque is exceeded a new collapsible spacer must be installed.**

19. Record the pinion rotating torque using a torque wrench. The rotating torque should be equal to the reading recorded during removal plus an additional 0.56 Nm (5 inch lbs.).

20. If the rotating torque is low, tighten the pinion nut in 6.8 Nm (5 ft. lbs.) increments until the proper rotating torque is achieved.

➡**If the maximum tightening torque is reached prior to reaching the required**

rotating torque, the collapsible spacer may have been damaged. Replace the collapsible spacer.

21. Install propeller shaft with reference marks aligned.

22. Add gear lubricant to differential housing if necessary.

23. Install half shafts.

REAR AXLE HOUSING

REMOVAL & INSTALLATION

1. Before servicing the vehicle, refer to the precautions in the beginning of this manual.

2. Raise and support the vehicle.

3. Position a lift under axle and secure axle to lift.

4. Remove the wheels and rear brake components.

5. Remove ABS sensor from the differential housing.

6. Disconnect the brake hose at the axle junction block.

7. Disconnect the vent hose from the axle shaft tube.

8. Mark the propeller shaft and companion flange for installation alignment reference.

9. Remove propeller shaft.

10. Remove shock absorbers axle mounting bolts.

11. Remove stabilizer bar retainer clamp bolts and retainer clamps from the axle.

12. Remove spring clamps nuts and spring plates.

13. Remove the axle from the vehicle

To install:

14. Raise axle with lifting device and align to the leaf spring centering bolts.

15. Install spring clamps and spring plates. Tighten the U-bolt nuts to 149 Nm (110 ft. lbs.).

16. Install shock absorbers and tighten nuts to 102 Nm (75 ft. lbs.).

17. Install ABS sensor into the differential housing.

18. Install rear brake and park brake components.

19. Connect brake hose to axle junction block.

20. Install stabilizer bar and center it with equal spacing on both sides. Tighten retainer clamp bolts to 61 Nm (45 ft. lbs.).

21. Install axle vent hose.

22. Install propeller shaft with reference marks aligned. Tighten bolts to 108 Nm (80 ft. lbs.).

23. Add gear lubricant, if necessary.

REAR AXLE SHAFT, BEARING & SEAL

REMOVAL & INSTALLATION

8¼ Inch Axle

Axle Shafts

See Figures 28 and 29.

1. Before servicing the vehicle, refer to the precautions in the beginning of this manual.

2. Place the transmission in neutral and raise and support the vehicle.

3. Remove the brake drum/caliper and rotor.

4. Remove the differential cover and drain the lubricant.

5. Rotate the differential case to access the pinion shaft lock screw. Remove the lock screw and pinion shaft from the differential case.

6. Push the axle shaft inward then remove axle shaft C-lock.

7. Remove the axle shaft being careful not to damage the shaft bearing and seal.

8. Inspect the axle shaft seal for leakage or damage.

9. Inspect the axle shaft bearing contact surface for signs of brinelling, galling and pitting.

To install:

10. Lubricate the bearing bore and seal lip with gear lubricant. Insert the axle shaft through the seal, bearing and engage it into side gear splines.

➡**Use care to prevent shaft splines from damaging axle shaft seal lip.**

11. Insert the C-lock in end of axle shaft. Push the axle shaft outward to seat the C-lock in side gear.

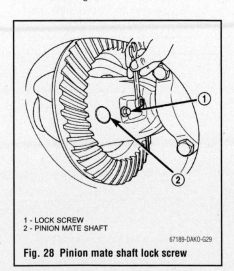

1 - LOCK SCREW
2 - PINION MATE SHAFT

67189-DAK0-G29

Fig. 28 Pinion mate shaft lock screw

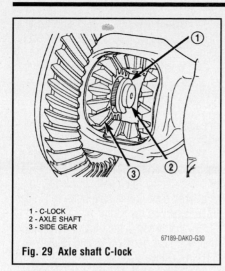

1 - C-LOCK
2 - AXLE SHAFT
3 - SIDE GEAR

67189-DAKO-G30

Fig. 29 Axle shaft C-lock

12. Insert the pinion shaft into differential case and through thrust washers and differential pinions.

13. Align hole in shaft with the hole in the differential case and install the lock screw with Loctite® on the threads. Tighten the lock screw to 11 Nm (8 ft. lbs.).

14. Apply a bead of Mopar red silicone rubber sealant or equivalent to the housing cover.

➡**If the cover is not installed within 3 to 5 minutes, the cover must be cleaned and new RTV applied or adhesion quality will be compromised.**

15. Install the cover and tighten the bolts in a criss-cross pattern to 41 Nm (30 ft. lbs.).

16. Fill the differential with gear lubricant to the bottom of the fill plug hole.

17. Install the fill hole plug.

18. Install the brake drum/rotor and caliper.

Axle Shaft Seals

1. Before servicing the vehicle, refer to the precautions in the beginning of this manual.

2. Remove the axle shaft.

3. Remove the axle shaft seal from the end of the axle tube with a small pry bar.

To install:

4. Wipe the axle tube bore clean. Remove any old sealer or burrs from the tube.

5. Install a new axle seal with Installer C-4076-B and Handle C-4735-1, or equivalent. When the tool contacts the axle tube, the seal is installed to the correct depth.

6. Coat the lip of the seal with axle lubricant for protection prior to installing the axle shaft.

7. Install the axle shaft.

8. Apply a bead of Mopar red Silicone

Rubber Sealant or equivalent to the housing cover.

➡**If the cover is not installed within 3 to 5 minutes, the cover must be cleaned and new RTV applied or adhesion quality will be compromised.**

9. Install the cover and tighten the bolts in a criss-cross pattern to 41 Nm (30 ft. lbs.).

10. Fill the differential with gear lubricant to the bottom of the fill plug hole and install the fill plug.

Axle Bearings

See Figures 30 and 31.

1. Before servicing the vehicle, refer to the precautions in the beginning of this manual.

2. Remove the axle shaft.

3. Remove the axle shaft seal from the axle tube with a small pry bar.

➡**The seal and bearing can be removed at the same time with the bearing removal tool.**

4. Remove the axle shaft bearing with Bearing Removal Tool Set 6310 and Adapter Foot 6310-9, or equivalent.

To install:

5. Wipe the axle tube bore clean. Remove any old sealer or burrs from the tube.

6. Install the axle shaft bearing with Installer C-4198 and Handle C-4171, or equivalent.

➡**Install the bearing with part number against the installer.**

7. Install a new axle seal with Installer C-4076-B and Handle C-4735-1, or equivalent. When the tool contacts the axle tube, the seal is installed to the correct depth.

8. Coat the lip of the seal with axle lubricant and install the axle shaft.

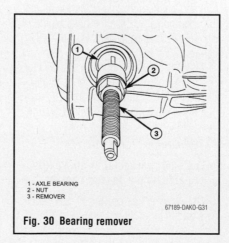

1 - AXLE BEARING
2 - NUT
3 - REMOVER

67189-DAKO-G31

Fig. 30 Bearing remover

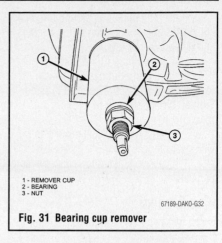

1 - REMOVER CUP
2 - BEARING
3 - NUT

67189-DAKO-G32

Fig. 31 Bearing cup remover

9. Apply a bead of Mopar red Silicone Rubber Sealant or equivalent to the housing cover.

➡**If the cover is not installed within 3 to 5 minutes, the cover must be cleaned and new RTV applied or adhesion quality will be compromised.**

10. Install the cover and tighten the bolts in a criss-cross pattern to 41 Nm (30 ft. lbs.).

11. Fill the differential with gear lubricant to bottom of the fill plug hole and install fill plug.

9¼ Inch Axle

Axle Shafts

1. Before servicing the vehicle, refer to the precautions in the beginning of this manual.

2. Place the transmission in neutral.

3. Remove the brake caliper, adapter and rotor.

4. Remove the differential housing cover and drain lubricant.

5. Rotate the differential case so the pinion mate shaft lock screw is accessible. Remove the lock screw and pinion mate shaft from the differential case.

6. Push the axle shaft inward and remove the axle shaft C-lock from the axle shaft.

7. Remove the axle shaft. Use care to prevent damage to the axle shaft bearing and seal in the axle tube.

To install:

8. Lubricate the bearing bore and seal lip with gear lubricant. Insert the axle shaft through seal, bearing, and engage it into the side gear splines.

➡**Use care to prevent the shaft splines from damaging the axle shaft seal.**

9. Insert the C-lock in end of the axle shaft then push the axle shaft outward to seat the C-lock in the side gear.

10. Insert the pinion shaft into the differential case and through the thrust washers and differential pinions.

11. Align the hole in shaft with the hole in the differential case and install the lock screw with Loctite® on the threads. Tighten the lock screw to 11 Nm (8 ft. lbs.).

12. Install the differential cover and fill with gear lubricant.

13. Install the brake rotor, caliper adapter and caliper.

Axle Bearings

1. Before servicing the vehicle, refer to the precautions in the beginning of this manual.

2. Remove the axle shaft.

3. Remove the axle shaft seal from the end of the axle tube with a small pry bar.

➡ **The seal and bearing can be removed at the same time with the bearing removal tool.**

4. Remove the axle shaft bearing with Bearing Remover 6310 and Foot 6310-9, or equivalent.

To install:

5. Wipe the axle tube bore clean. Remove any old sealer or burrs from the tube.

6. Install the axle shaft bearing with Installer C-4198 and Handle C-4171, or equivalent. Drive the bearing in until tool contacts the axle tube.

➡ **Bearing is installed with the bearing part number against the installer.**

7. Coat the lip of the new axle seal with axle lubricant and install with Installer C-4076-B and Handle C-4735-1, or equivalent.

8. Install the axle shaft.

Axle Shaft Seals

1. Before servicing the vehicle, refer to the precautions in the beginning of this manual.

2. Remove the axle shaft.

3. Remove the axle shaft seal from the end of the axle tube with a small pry bar.

To install:

4. Wipe the axle tube bore clean. Remove any old sealer or burrs from the tube.

5. Coat the lip of the new seal with axle lubricant and install a seal with Installer C-4076-B and Handle C-4735-1, or equivalent. When the tool contacts the axle tube, the seal is installed to the correct depth.

6. Install the axle shaft.

REAR DRIVESHAFT

REMOVAL & INSTALLATION

1. Before servicing the vehicle, refer to the precautions in the beginning of this manual.

2. Mark propeller shaft and pinion flange for installation reference.

3. Remove the front propeller shaft.

To install:

4. Install the propeller shaft with reference marks aligned.

5. Using new bolts, tighten them to 80 ft. lbs. (108 Nm).

REAR PINION SEAL

REMOVAL & INSTALLATION

8¼ Inch Axle

1. Before servicing the vehicle, refer to the precautions in the beginning of this manual.

2. Raise and support the vehicle.

3. Mark the universal joint, companion flange and pinion shaft for installation reference.

4. Remove companion flange bolts and secure the shaft in an upright position to prevent damage to the rear universal joint.

5. Remove the wheel and tire assemblies.

6. Remove brake drums to prevent any drag.

7. Rotate companion flange three or four times and verify flange rotates smoothly.

8. Measure rotating torque of the pinion with an inch pound torque wrench and record the reading for installation reference.

9. Install bolts into two of the threaded holes in the companion flange 180° apart.

10. Position Holder 6719, or equivalent, against the companion flange and install a bolt and washer into one of the remaining threaded holes. Tighten the bolts so the Holder 6719, or equivalent, is held to the flange.

11. Remove the pinion nut and washer.

12. Remove companion flange with Remover C-452, or equivalent.

13. Remove pinion seal with a pry tool or slide hammer mounted screw.

To install:

➡ **The outer perimeter of the seal is pre-coated with a special sealant.**

14. Apply a light coating of gear lubricant on the lip of pinion seal.

15. Install new pinion seal with Installer C-4076-B and Handle C-4735-1, or equivalent.

16. Install companion flange on the end of the shaft with the reference marks aligned.

17. Install bolts into two of the threaded holes in the companion flange 180° apart.

18. Position Holder 6719, or equivalent, against the companion flange and install a bolt and washer into one of the remaining threaded holes. Tighten the bolts so Holder 6719 is held to the flange.

19. Install companion flange on pinion shaft with Installer C-3718 and Holder 6719, or equivalent.

20. Install the pinion washer and a new pinion nut. The convex side of the washer must face outward.

➡ **Do not exceed the minimum tightening torque when installing the companion flange retaining nut at this point. Damage to collapsible spacer or bearings may result.**

21. Hold companion flange with Holder 6719 and tighten the pinion nut to 285 Nm (210 ft. lbs.). Rotate pinion several revolutions to ensure the bearing rollers are seated.

22. Rotate pinion with an inch pound torque wrench. Rotating torque should be equal to the reading recorded during removal plus an additional 0.56 Nm (5 inch lbs.).

➡ **Never loosen pinion nut to decrease pinion bearing rotating torque and never exceed specified preload torque. If rotating torque is exceeded, a new collapsible spacer must be installed.**

23. If rotating torque is low use Holder 6719 to hold the companion flange and tighten pinion nut in 6.8 Nm (5 ft. lbs.) increments until proper rotating torque is achieved.

➡ **The seal replacement is unacceptable if final pinion nut torque is less than 285 Nm (210 ft. lbs.).**

➡ **The bearing rotating torque should be constant during a complete revolution of the pinion. If the rotating torque varies, this indicates a binding condition.**

24. Install propeller shaft with the installation reference marks aligned.

25. Tighten companion flange bolts to 108 Nm (80 ft. lbs.).

26. Install the brake drums.

27. Check the differential housing lubricant level.

28. Install wheel and tire assemblies and lower the vehicle.

9¼ Inch Axle

1. Before servicing the vehicle, refer to the precautions in the beginning of this manual.

2. Raise and support the vehicle.

3. Remove the wheel and tire assemblies.

4. Mark the universal joint, companion flange and pinion shaft for installation reference.

5. Remove the propeller shaft from the companion flange.

6. Remove the brake drums to prevent any drag.

7. Rotate the companion flange three or four times and record the pinion rotating torque with an inch pound torque wrench.

8. Install two bolts into the companion flange threaded holes, 180° apart. Position Holder 6719A, or equivalent, against the companion flange and install and tighten two bolts and washers into the remaining holes.

9. Hold the companion flange with Holder 6719A, or equivalent, and remove pinion nut and washer.

10. Remove the companion flange with Remover C-452, or equivalent.

11. Remove the pinion seal with pry tool or slide hammer mounted screw.

To install:

12. Apply a light coating of gear lubricant on the lip of pinion seal.

13. Install a new pinion seal with Installer C-3860-A and Handle C-4171, or equivalent.

14. Install the companion flange on the end of the shaft with the reference marks aligned.

15. Install two bolts into the threaded holes in the companion flange, 180° apart.

16. Position Holder 6719, or equivalent, against the companion flange and install a bolt and washer into one of the remaining threaded holes. Tighten the bolts so holder is held to the flange.

17. Install the companion flange on the pinion shaft with Installer C-3718 and Holder 6719, or equivalent.

18. Install the pinion washer and a new pinion nut. The convex side of the washer must face outward.

➡**Never exceed the minimum tightening torque 285 Nm (210 ft. lbs.) when installing the companion flange retaining nut at this point. Damage to the collapsible spacer or bearings may result.**

19. Hold the companion flange with Holder 6719 and tighten the pinion nut with a torque set to 285 Nm (210 ft. lbs.). Rotate the pinion several revolutions to ensure the bearing rollers are seated.

20. Rotate the pinion with an inch pound torque wrench. Rotating torque should be equal to the reading recorded during removal plus an additional 0.56 Nm (5 inch lbs.).

➡**Never loosen the pinion nut to decrease pinion bearing rotating torque and never exceed the specified preload torque. If the rotating torque is exceeded, a new collapsible spacer must be installed.**

21. If the rotating torque is low, use Holder 6719 to hold the companion flange and tighten the pinion nut in 6.8 Nm (5 ft. lbs.) increments until the proper rotating torque is achieved.

➡**The bearing rotating torque should be constant during a complete revolution of the pinion. If the rotating torque varies, this indicates a binding condition.**

➡**The seal replacement is unacceptable if the final pinion nut torque is less than 285 Nm (210 ft. lbs.).**

22. Install the propeller shaft with the installation reference marks aligned.

23. Tighten the companion flange bolts to 108 Nm (80 ft. lbs.).

24. Install the brake drums, wheel and tire assemblies and lower the vehicle.

25. Check the differential lubricant level.

ENGINE COOLING

ENGINE FAN

REMOVAL & INSTALLATION

See Figures 32 through 36.

1. Before servicing the vehicle, refer to the precautions in the beginning of this manual.

2. Partially drain the cooling system.

3. Remove the upper radiator hose.

4. Remove the air filter housing assembly.

5. Stop the water pump from turning with a special tool or prybar on the nuts. Loosen the fan nut (36mm). Turn CCW to loosen.

6. Position the fan/fan drive assembly in the radiator shroud.

7. Remove the two shroud mounting screws.

8. Remove the radiator shroud and fan drive assembly.

➡**After removing fan blade/viscous fan drive assembly, do not place viscous fan drive in horizontal position. If stored horizontally, silicone fluid in the viscous fan drive could drain into its bearing assembly and contaminate lubricant.**

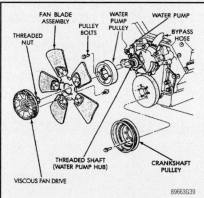

Fig. 32 Typical engine fan assembly

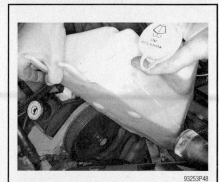

Fig. 33 Remove the windshield washer bottle from the fan shroud

9. Remove four bolts securing fan blade assembly to viscous fan drive .

To install:

10. If drive and fan were separated, tighten the bolts to 17 ft. lbs. (23 Nm).

11. The remainder of the installation procedure is the reverse of removal.

Fig. 34 Loosening the fan nut

Fig. 35 To loosen the fan nut, stop the pump shaft from turning. This tool will do it; you could also use a prybar. In this photo, the fan has been removed for clarity

Fig. 36 Removing fan and shroud together

12. If a new viscous drive has been fitted, start and run the engine at 2,000 rpm for about 2 minutes to distribute fluid within the drive.

RADIATOR

REMOVAL & INSTALLATION
See Figure 37.

✻✻ CAUTION

Never open, service or drain the radiator or cooling system when hot;

serious burns can occur from the steam and hot coolant. Avoid physical contact with the coolant. Wear protective clothing and eye protection. Always drain coolant into a sealable container. Clean up spills as soon as possible. Coolant should be reused unless it is contaminated or is several years old.

1. Before servicing the vehicle, refer to the precautions in the beginning of this manual.
2. Disconnect the battery negative cable(s).
3. Drain the radiator.
4. Remove any cables or lines clipped to the radiator or shrouds.
5. Remove the upper and lower heater hoses.

✻✻ WARNING

Most cooling system hoses use "constant tension" hose clamps. When removing or installing, use a tool designed for servicing this type of clamp. The clamps are stamped with a letter or number on the tongue. If replacement is necessary, use only an OEM clamp with a matching ID.

✻✻ CAUTION

Always wear safety glasses when servicing constant tension clamps.

6. If coolant overflow and windshield washer fluid bottles are fitted to the fan shroud, disconnect the lines and remove them. Pull straight up to remove the bottles from shroud.
7. Remove the upper fan shroud. Disconnect the electric fan wiring.
8. Label, then disconnect the automatic transmission lines if the fluid cooler is incorporated into the radiator. Plug the lines to prevent spillage. Be sure to note which line goes to which fitting.
9. Check for rubber shields on the sides of the radiator. Remove them if fitted. These are normally secured with non-reusable plastic pins.
10. Remove the radiator bolts (usually two at the top). Lift the radiator up and out of the vehicle, being careful that the cooling fins do not bang against anything. They are easily damaged.
11. Some vehicles may have an auxiliary automatic transmission fluid cooler which will come away with the radiator.

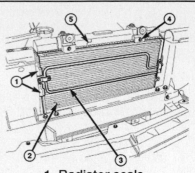

1. Radiator seals
2. Radiator
3. Condenser tube
4. Mounting bolt
5. Radiator tank

Fig. 37 Radiator mounting

To install:
12. Lower the radiator into place. There are two alignment pins at the bottom which fit into holes in the lower support.
13. Tighten radiator mounting bolts to 17 ft. lbs. (23 Nm).
14. The remainder of the procedure is the reverse of removal. Double-check the connection of all hoses and lines before adding fluids or operating the vehicle.

THERMOSTAT

REMOVAL & INSTALLATION
See Figures 38 and 39.

✻✻ WARNING

Most cooling system hoses use "constant tension" hose clamps. When removing or installing, use a tool designed for servicing this type of clamp. The clamps are stamped with a letter or number on the tongue. If replacement is necessary, use only an OEM clamp with a matching ID.

✻✻ CAUTION

Always wear safety glasses when servicing contact tension clamps.

1. Locate the thermostat. On the 3.7L and 4.7L engines, the thermostat is located on the engine side of the **lower** radiator hose.
2. Disconnect the negative battery cable.
3. Drain the engine coolant from the block until the level is below the thermostat.
4. On most models the alternator must be removed or repositioned for access to the thermostat housing.

5. Remove the radiator hose from the thermostat housing.

6. Disconnect any sensors fitted to the thermostat housing.

7. Remove the retaining bolts from the thermostat housing. Note lengths of each for ease of installation.

8. Remove the thermostat housing, thermostat, and gasket, if fitted.

9. Note the relative positions of all components, especially gaskets and seals. Note the orientation of the thermostat in the housing.

To install:

10. Be sure the new thermostat is the correct one for your engine.

11. Clean the gasket or seal mating surfaces.

12. Paper gaskets must be replaced.

13. Install the thermostat, gasket or seals.

14. Install the thermostat housing on the engine.

15. Be sure all components are properly seated before tightening.

16. Tighten the housing bolts to 18 ft. lbs. (24 Nm). Fasteners should be tightened evenly to avoid leaks or damage.

17. Reinstall the radiator hose onto the housing.

Fig. 38 Safe removal of constant tension clamps requires the proper tool

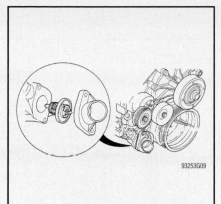

Fig. 39 On the 3.7L and 4.7L engine, the thermostat is at the bottom of the engine

➡**Ensure that you have secured the system drain plug(s) before refilling with coolant.**

18. Refill the radiator with a proper coolant mixture.

19. Connect the negative battery cable(s).

20. Start the engine and bleed the cooling system.

21. Ensure that the thermostat is operational (by checking the upper radiator hose for warmth), and that there are no leaks.

WATER PUMP

REMOVAL & INSTALLATION

3.7L Engine

See Figure 40.

1. Before servicing the vehicle, refer to the precautions in the beginning of this manual.

2. Drain the cooling system.

3. Remove or disconnect the following:
   - Negative battery cable
   - Fan and clutch assembly from the pump
   - Fan shroud and fan assembly. If you're reusing the fan clutch, keep it upright to avoid silicone fluid loss!
   - Lower hose
   - Water pump (8 bolts)

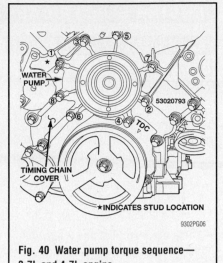

Fig. 40 Water pump torque sequence— 3.7L and 4.7L engine

4. Installation is the reverse of removal. Tighten the bolts, in sequence, to 40 ft. lbs. (54 Nm).

4.7L Engine

1. Before servicing the vehicle, refer to the precautions in the beginning of this manual.

2. Drain the cooling system.

3. Remove or disconnect the following:
   - Negative battery cable
   - Fan and fan drive assembly from the pump. Don't attempt to remove it from the vehicle, yet.

➡**If a new pump is being installed; don't separate the fan from the drive.**

   - Shroud and fan

❋ WARNING

Keep the fan upright to avoid fluid loss from the drive.

   - Accessory drive belt
   - Lower radiator hose
   - Water pump

4. Installation is the reverse of removal. Tighten the bolts in sequence to 40 ft. lbs. (54 Nm).

ALTERNATOR

REMOVAL & INSTALLATION

See Figure 41.

1. Before servicing the vehicle, refer to the precautions in the beginning of this manual.

2. Remove or disconnect the following:
   - Negative battery cable
   - Accessory drive belt
   - Alternator harness connectors
   - Mounting bolts and alternator

➡ **There are 1 vertical and 2 horizontal bolts.**

To install:

3. Before servicing the vehicle, refer to the precautions in the beginning of this manual.

4. Install the alternator and tighten the bolts to the following specifications:
   - Short horizontal bolt to 55 ft. lbs. (74 Nm)
   - Vertical bolt and long horizontal bolt to 40 ft. lbs. (55 Nm)

5. Install or connect the following:
   - Alternator harness connectors
   - Accessory drive belt
   - Negative battery cable

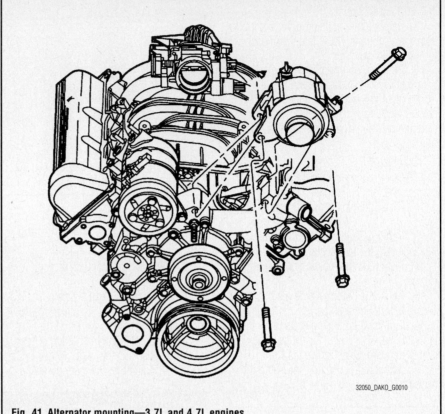

32050_DAKO_G0010

Fig. 41 Alternator mounting—3.7L and 4.7L engines

FIRING ORDER

See Figures 42 and 43.

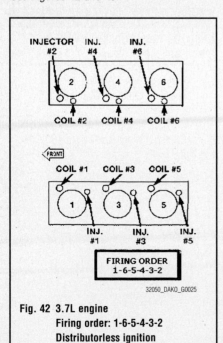

32050_DAKO_G0025

Fig. 42 3.7L engine
Firing order: 1-6-5-4-3-2
Distributorless ignition

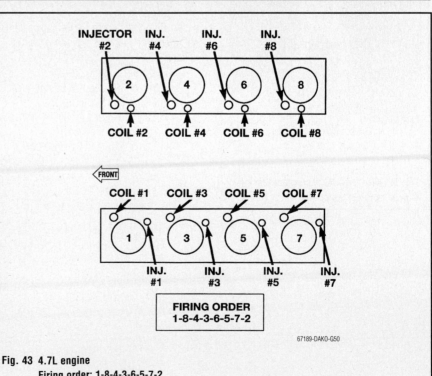

67189-DAKO-G50

Fig. 43 4.7L engine
Firing order: 1-8-4-3-6-5-7-2
Distributorless ignition

IGNITION COIL

REMOVAL & INSTALLATION

See Figures 44 and 45.

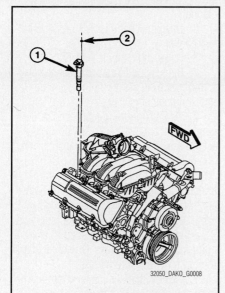

Fig. 44 3.7L V-6 Coil Location: (1) Ignition Coil (2) Coil Mounting Nut

1. Certain coils may require removal of the throttle body air intake tube or intake box for access.

2. Disconnect the negative battery cable.

3. Detach the electrical connector from the coil by pushing downward on the release lock on top of the connector and pulling the connector from the coil.

4. Clean the area at the base of each coil with compressed air.

5. Remove the coil mounting nut. Pull the coil up with a slight twisting action and remove it from the vehicle.

6. Installation is the reverse of removal. Smear the coil O–ring with silicone grease. Tighten the mounting nut to 70 inch lbs. (8 Nm). Connect the wiring.

IGNITION TIMING

ADJUSTMENT

The ignition timing is controlled by the Powertrain Control Module (PCM). No adjustment is necessary or possible.

SPARK PLUGS

REMOVAL & INSTALLATION

Each individual spark plug is located under each ignition coil. Each individual ignition coil must be removed to gain access to each spark plug. Refer to Ignition Coil Removal/Installation. Prior to removing a spark plug, spray compressed air around base of the ignition coil at cylinder head. This will help prevent foreign material from entering combustion chamber.

1. Remove spark plug from cylinder head using a quality socket with a rubber or foam insert.

2. Inspect spark plug condition.

To install:

3. Start the spark plug into the cylinder head by hand to avoid cross threading.

4. Before installing coil(s), check condition of coil O–ring and replace as necessary. To aid in coil installation, apply silicone to coil O–ring.

5. Tighten spark plugs to 20 ft. lbs. (27 Nm).

6. Install ignition coil(s). Refer to Ignition Coil Removal/Installation.

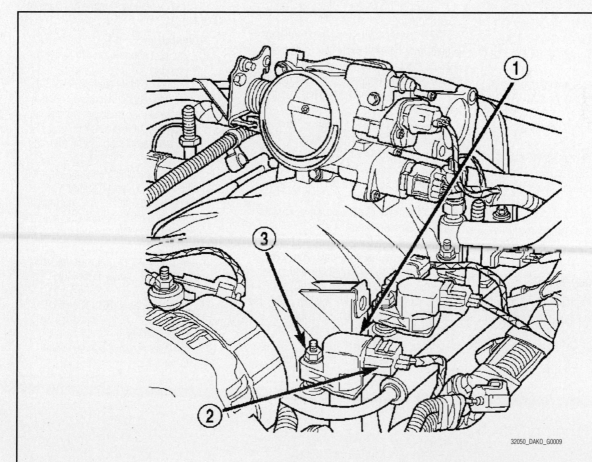

Fig. 45 4.7L V-8 Coil Location: (1) Ignition Coil (2) Coil Electrical Connector (3) Coil Mounting Stud/Nut

STARTER

REMOVAL & INSTALLATION

3.7L Engine

1. Before servicing the vehicle, refer to the precautions in the beginning of this manual.

2. Disconnect and isolate negative battery cable.

3. Raise and support vehicle.

4. Remove 2 starter heat shield bolts at side of starter.

5. Remove starter heat shield nut at front of starter.

6. Remove starter heat shield.

7. Remove solenoid wire from solenoid terminal.

8. Remove battery cable from stud on starter solenoid.

9. Remove 2 starter mounting bolts.

10. Position front of starter to face rear of vehicle. Rotate starter until solenoid position is located below starter.

11. Remove starter from vehicle by passing it between exhaust pipe and transmission bellhousing.

To install:

12. Position starter into bellhousing and install 2 bolts. Torque to 68 Nm (50 ft. lbs.).

13. Install battery cable and nut to stud on starter solenoid. Tighten nut to 13.6 Nm (120 inch lbs.).

14. Install solenoid wire connector to solenoid terminal.

15. Position starter heat shield and install nut at front of starter.

16. Install 2 starter heat shield bolts at side of starter.

17. Lower vehicle.

18. Connect negative battery cable.

4.7L Engine

With Manual Transmission

1. Before servicing the vehicle, refer to the precautions in the beginning of this manual.

2. Disconnect and isolate negative battery cable.

3. Raise and support vehicle.

4. Remove nut securing starter motor to stud on transmission housing.

5. While supporting starter motor, remove bolt securing starter motor to transmission housing.

6. If equipped with automatic transmission, slide transmission cooler tube bracket forward on tubes far enough for starter motor to be removed from lower mounting stud.

7. Lower starter motor from front transmission housing far enough to access and remove nut securing battery cable eyelet to starter solenoid stud. Always support starter motor during this process. Do not let starter motor hang from wire harness.

8. Remove solenoid wire solenoid terminal stud.

9. Disconnect battery cable solenoid wire from receptacle on starter solenoid.

10. Remove starter motor from transmission housing.

To install:

11. Position starter motor to transmission housing.

12. Connect battery cable solenoid terminal wire harness connector to connector receptacle on starter solenoid. Always support the starter motor during this process. Do not let the starter motor hang from the wire harness.

13. Install battery cable eyelet terminal onto solenoid B(+) terminal stud.

14. Install and tighten nut securing battery cable eyelet terminal to starter solenoid B (+) terminal stud. Tighten nut to 13.6 Nm (120 inch lbs.).

15. Position starter motor over stud on transmission housing.

16. If equipped with automatic transmission, slide automatic transmission cooler tube bracket rearward on tubes and into position over starter motor flange.

17. Loosely install the washers, bolt, and nut to starter. Tighten bolt and nut to 67.8 Nm (50 ft. lbs.).

18. Lower vehicle.

19. Connect negative battery cable.

With Automatic Transmission

1. Before servicing the vehicle, refer to the precautions in the beginning of this manual.

2. Disconnect and isolate negative battery cable.

3. Raise and support vehicle.

4. Remove bolt and washer (rearward facing) securing starter motor to the transmission housing.

5. While supporting starter motor, remove bolt and washer (rearward facing) securing starter motor to the transmission housing.

6. Lower starter motor from front of transmission housing far enough to access and remove nut securing battery positive cable eyelet terminal to the starter solenoid B (+) terminal stud. Always support starter motor during this process. Do not let starter motor hang from wire harness.

7. Remove battery cable eyelet terminal from solenoid B (+) terminal stud.

8. Disconnect battery cable solenoid terminal wire harness connector from receptacle on starter solenoid.

9. Remove starter motor from transmission housing.

To install:

10. Position starter motor to transmission housing.

11. Connect battery cable solenoid terminal wire harness connector to connector receptacle on starter solenoid. Always support the starter motor during this process. Do not let the starter motor hang from the wire harness.

12. Install battery cable eyelet terminal onto solenoid B (+) terminal stud.

13. Install and tighten nut securing battery cable eyelet terminal to starter solenoid B (+) terminal stud. Tighten nut to 13.6 Nm (120 inch lbs.).

14. Position starter motor to transmission housing and loosely install two bolts/washers.

15. Tighten bolts to 67.8 Nm (50 ft. lbs.).

16. Lower vehicle.

17. Connect negative battery cable.

ENGINE MECHANICAL

➡Disconnecting the negative battery cable may interfere with the functions of the on board computer systems and may require the computer to undergo a relearning process, once the negative battery cable is reconnected.

ACCESSORY DRIVE BELTS

ACCESSORY BELT ROUTING

See Figure 46.

➡The belt routing schematics are published from the latest information available at the time of publication. If anything differs between these schematics and the Belt Routing Label, use the schematics on Belt Routing Label. This label is located in the engine compartment, usually on the fan shroud.

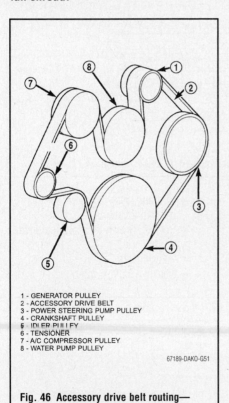

1 - GENERATOR PULLEY
2 - ACCESSORY DRIVE BELT
3 - POWER STEERING PUMP PULLEY
4 - CRANKSHAFT PULLEY
5 - IDLER PULLEY
6 - TENSIONER
7 - A/C COMPRESSOR PULLEY
8 - WATER PUMP PULLEY

67189-DAKO-G51

Fig. 46 Accessory drive belt routing—3.7L and 4.7L engines

INSPECTION

Inspect the drive belt for signs of glazing or cracking. A glazed belt will be perfectly smooth from slippage, while a good belt will have a slight texture of fabric visible. Cracks will usually start at the inner edge of the belt and run outward. All worn or damaged drive belts should be replaced immediately.

ADJUSTMENT

It is not necessary to adjust belt tension on the 3.7L or 4.7L engines. These engines are equipped with an automatic belt tensioner. The tensioner maintains correct belt tension at all times; consequently, do not attempt to use a belt tension gauge on these engines.

REMOVAL & INSTALLATION

See Figures 47 and 48.

1. Attach a socket/wrench to pulley mounting bolt of automatic tensioner.
2. Rotate tensioner assembly clockwise (as viewed from front) until tension has been relieved from belt.
3. Remove belt from idler pulley first.
4. Remove belt from vehicle.

To install:

✱✱ WARNING

When installing the serpentine accessory drive belt, the belt MUST be routed correctly. If not, the engine may overheat due to the water pump rotating in the wrong direction.

5. Install new belt. Route the belt around all pulleys except the idler pulley. Rotate the tensioner arm until it contacts its stop position. Route the belt around the idler and slowly let the tensioner rotate into the belt. Make sure the belt is seated onto all pulleys.

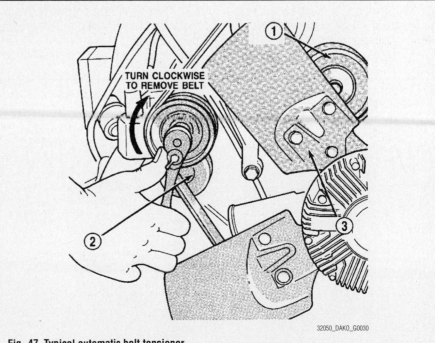

TURN CLOCKWISE TO REMOVE BELT

32050_DAKO_G0030

Fig. 47 Typical automatic belt tensioner

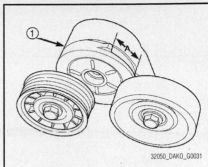

32050_DAKO_G0031

Fig. 48 Measurement (A) point on 4.7L engines

6. With the drive belt installed, inspect the belt wear indicator.
7. On 4.7L engines only, the gap between the tang and the housing stop (measurement A) must not exceed 0.94 inches (24 mm). If the measurement exceeds this specification replace the serpentine accessory drive belt.

CAMSHAFT AND VALVE LIFTERS

INSPECTION

1. Inspect the camshaft bearing journals for wear or damage.
2. Inspect the cylinder head and check oil return holes.
3. Check the tooth surface of any drive gear teeth for wear or damage.

4. Check both camshaft surfaces for wear or damage.

5. Check camshaft lobe height and replace if out of limit.

REMOVAL & INSTALLATION

See Figures 49 through 52.

1. Before servicing the vehicle, refer to the precautions in the beginning of this manual.

2. Remove or disconnect the following:
- Negative battery cable
- Valve covers
- Rocker arms
- Hydraulic lash adjusters

➡**Keep all valvetrain components in order for assembly.**

3. Set the engine at Top Dead Center (TDC) of the compression stroke for the No. 1 cylinder.

4. Install Timing Chain Wedge 8350 to retain the chain tensioners.

5. Matchmark the timing chains to the camshaft sprockets.

6. Install Camshaft Holding Tool 6958 and Adapter Pins 8346 to the left camshaft sprocket.

7. Remove or disconnect the following:
- Right camshaft timing sprocket and target wheel
- Left camshaft sprocket
- Camshaft bearing caps, by reversing the tightening sequence
- Camshafts

To install:

8. Install or connect the following:
- Camshafts. Tighten the bearing cap bolts in ½ turn increments, in sequence, to 100 inch lbs. (11 Nm).
- Target wheel to the right camshaft

- Camshaft timing sprockets and chains, by aligning the matchmarks

9. Remove the tensioner wedges and tighten the camshaft sprocket bolts to 90 ft. lbs. (122 Nm).

10. Install or connect the following:

- Hydraulic lash adjusters in their original locations
- Rocker arms in their original locations
- Valve covers
- Negative battery cable

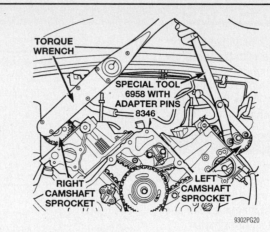

Fig. 50 Hold the left camshaft sprocket with a spanner wrench while removing or installing the camshaft sprocket bolts—3.7L and 4.7L engine

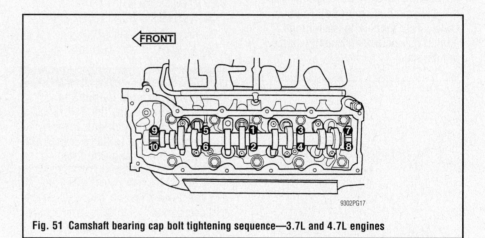

Fig. 51 Camshaft bearing cap bolt tightening sequence—3.7L and 4.7L engines

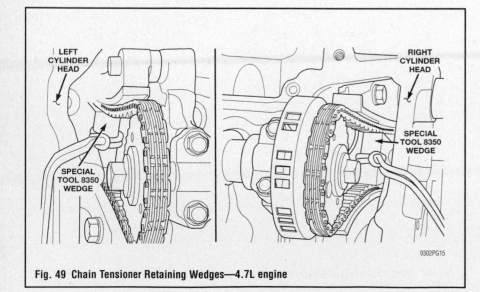

Fig. 49 Chain Tensioner Retaining Wedges—4.7L engine

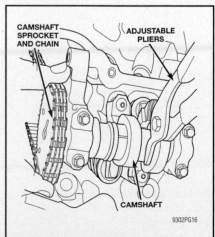

Fig. 52 Turn the camshaft with pliers, if needed, to align the dowel in the sprocket—4.7L engine

CRANKSHAFT FRONT SEAL

REMOVAL & INSTALLATION

See Figure 53.

1. Disconnect the negative battery cable.
2. Drain the cooling system.
3. Remove the accessory drive belt.
4. Remove the A/C compressor mounting bolts and set the compressor aside.

➡ **It is not necessary to disconnect the A/C lines from the compressor.**

5. Remove the upper radiator hose.
6. Disconnect the engine fan electrical connector, located inside the radiator shroud.
7. Remove the engine fan.
8. Remove the camshaft damper bolt.
9. Using Special Tool 8513 Insert and 1026 three-jaw puller, remove the crankshaft damper.
10. Remove the seal using Special Tool 8511.

To install:

11. Using Special Tools 8348 and 8512, install the crankshaft front seal.
12. Install the crankshaft damper as follows:

a. Align the crankshaft damper slot with the key in the crankshaft. Slide the damper onto the crankshaft.

b. Assemble Special Tool 8512-A. The nut is threaded onto the threaded rod first. Then the roller bearing is placed onto the threaded rod (The hardened bearing surface of the bearing MUST face the nut). Then the hardened washer slides onto the threaded rod. Once assembled coat the threaded rod's

threads with Mopar® Nickel Anti-Seize or equivalent.

c. Using Special Tool 8512-A, press the damper onto the crankshaft.

13. Install the crankshaft damper bolt and tighten to 130 ft. lbs. (175 Nm).
14. Install the engine fan.
15. Install the upper radiator hose.
16. Install the A/C compressor and tighten the mounting bolts to 40 ft. lbs. (54 Nm).
17. Install the accessory drive belt.
18. Refill the cooling system to the correct level.
19. Connect the negative battery cable.
20. Start the engine and check for leaks.

CYLINDER HEAD

REMOVAL & INSTALLATION

3.7L Engine

See Figures 54 through 58.

Left Side

1. Before servicing the vehicle, refer to the precautions in the beginning of this manual.
2. Drain the cooling system.
3. Properly relieve the fuel system pressure.
4. Remove or disconnect the following:
- Negative battery cable
- Exhaust Y-pipe
- Intake manifold
- Cylinder head cover
- Engine cooling fan and shroud
- Accessory drive belt
- Power steering pump
5. Rotate the crankshaft so that the crankshaft timing mark aligns with the Top Dead Center (TDC) mark on the front cover,

and the **V6** marks on the camshaft sprockets are at 12 o'clock as shown.
- Crankshaft damper
- Front cover

6. Lock the secondary timing chain to the idler sprocket with Timing Chain Locking tool 8429.

7. Matchmark the secondary timing chain one link on each side of the V6 mark to the camshaft sprocket.
- Left secondary timing chain tensioner
- Cylinder head access plug
- Secondary timing chain guide
- Camshaft sprocket
- Cylinder head

➡ **The cylinder head is retained by twelve bolts. Four of the bolts are smaller and are at the front of the head.**

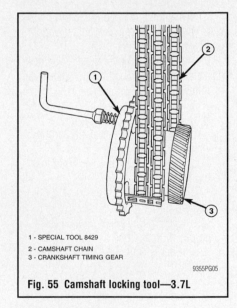

1 - SPECIAL TOOL 8429
2 - CAMSHAFT CHAIN
3 - CRANKSHAFT TIMING GEAR

9355PG05

Fig. 55 Camshaft locking tool—3.7L

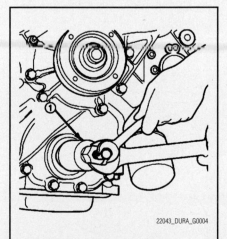

22043_DURA_G0004

Fig. 53 A special tool is required to remove and install the seal without removing the front timing cover

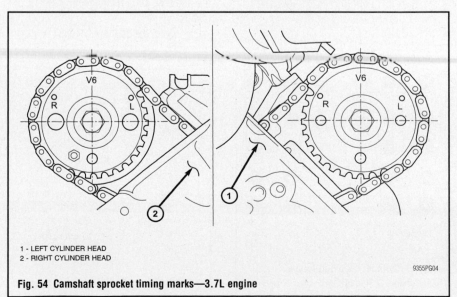

1 - LEFT CYLINDER HEAD
2 - RIGHT CYLINDER HEAD

9355PG04

Fig. 54 Camshaft sprocket timing marks—3.7L engine

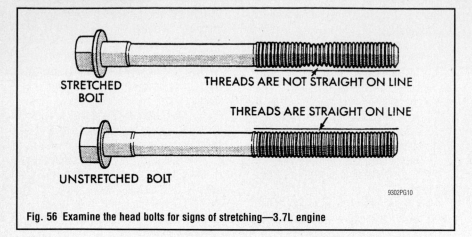

Fig. 56 Examine the head bolts for signs of stretching—3.7L engine

To install:

8. Check the cylinder head bolts for signs of stretching and replace as necessary.

9. Lubricate the threads of the 11mm bolts with clean engine oil.

10. Coat the threads of the 8mm bolts with Mopar® Lock and Seal Adhesive, or equivalent.

11. Install the cylinder heads. Use new gaskets and tighten the bolts, in sequence, as follows:

   a. Step 1: Bolts 1–8 to 20 ft. lbs. (27 Nm)

   b. Step 2: Bolts 1–8 verify torque without loosening

   c. Step 3: Bolts 9–12 to 10 ft. lbs. (14 Nm)

   d. Step 4: Bolts 1–8 plus ¼ (90 degree) turn

   e. Step 5: Bolts 1–8 plus ¼ (90 degree) turn again

   f. Step 6: Bolts 9–12 to 19 ft. lbs. (26 Nm)

12. Install or connect the following:
   • Camshaft sprocket. Align the secondary chain matchmarks and tighten the bolt to 90 ft. lbs. (122 Nm).

• Secondary timing chain guide
• Cylinder head access plug
• Secondary timing chain tensioner. Refer to the timing chain procedure in this section.

13. Remove the Timing Chain Locking tool.

14. Install or connect the following:
   • Front cover
   • Crankshaft damper. Torque the bolt to 130 ft. lbs. (175 Nm).
   • Power steering pump
   • Accessory drive belt
   • Engine cooling fan and shroud
   • Cover
   • Intake manifold
   • Exhaust Y-pipe
   • Negative battery cable

15. Fill and bleed the cooling system.

16. Start the engine, check for leaks and repair if necessary.

Right Side

1. Before servicing the vehicle, refer to the precautions in the beginning of this manual.

2. Drain the cooling system.

3. Properly relieve the fuel system pressure.

4. Remove or disconnect the following:
   • Negative battery cable
   • Exhaust Y-pipe
   • Intake manifold
   • Valve cover
   • Engine cooling fan and shroud
   • Accessory drive belt
   • Oil fill housing
   • Power steering pump

5. Rotate the crankshaft so that the crankshaft timing mark aligns with the Top Dead Center (TDC) mark on the front cover, and the **V6** marks on the camshaft sprockets are at 12 o'clock as shown.

6. Remove or disconnect the following:
   • Crankshaft damper
   • Front cover

7. Lock the secondary timing chains to the idler sprocket with Timing Chain Locking tool 8429.

8. Matchmark the secondary timing chains to the camshaft sprockets.

9. Remove or disconnect the following:
   • Secondary timing chain tensioners
   • Cylinder head access plugs
   • Secondary timing chain guides
   • Camshaft sprockets
   • Cylinder heads

➡ **Each cylinder head is retained by eight 11mm bolts and four 8mm bolts.**

To install:

10. Check the cylinder head bolts for signs of stretching and replace as necessary.

11. Lubricate the threads of the 11mm bolts with clean engine oil.

12. Coat the threads of the 8mm bolts with Mopar® Lock and Seal Adhesive, or equivalent.

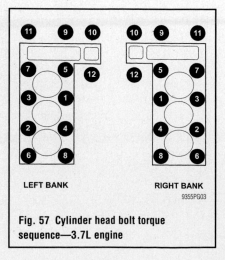

Fig. 57 Cylinder head bolt torque sequence—3.7L engine

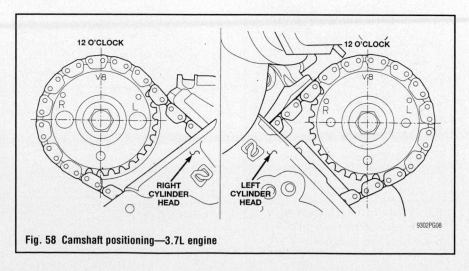

Fig. 58 Camshaft positioning—3.7L engine

13. Install the cylinder heads. Use new gaskets and tighten the bolts, in sequence, as follows:

  a. Step 1: Bolts 1–8 to 20 ft. lbs. (27 Nm)

  b. Step 2: Bolts 1–8 verify torque without loosening

  c. Step 3: Bolts 9–12 to 10 ft. lbs. (14 Nm)

  d. Step 4: Bolts 1–8 plus ¼ (90 degree) turn

  e. Step 5: Bolts 9–12 to 19 ft. lbs. (26 Nm)

14. Install or connect the following:

- Camshaft sprockets. Align the secondary chain matchmarks and tighten the bolts to 90 ft. lbs. (122 Nm).
- Secondary timing chain guides
- Cylinder head access plugs
- Secondary timing chain tensioners. Refer to the timing chain procedure in this section.

15. Remove the Timing Chain Locking tool.

16. Install or connect the following:

- Front cover
- Crankshaft damper. Torque the bolt to 130 ft. lbs. (175 Nm).
- Rocker arms
- Power steering pump
- Oil fill housing
- Accessory drive belt
- Engine cooling fan and shroud
- Valve covers
- Intake manifold
- Exhaust Y-pipe
- Negative battery cable

17. Fill and bleed the cooling system.

18. Start the engine, check for leaks and repair if necessary.

4.7L Engine

Left Side

See Figure 59.

1. Before servicing the vehicle, refer to the precautions in the beginning of this manual.

2. Drain the cooling system.

3. Remove or disconnect the following:

- Negative battery cable
- Exhaust pipe
- Intake manifold
- Cylinder head cover
- Fan shroud and fan
- Accessory drive belt
- Power steering pump

4. Rotate the crankshaft until the damper mark is aligned with the TDC mark. Verify that the V8 mark on the camshaft sprocket is at the 12 o'clock position.

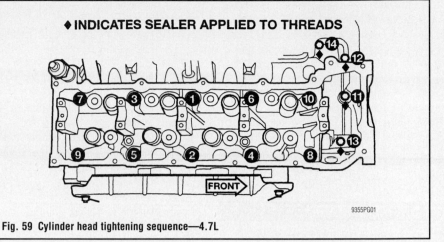

◆ **INDICATES SEALER APPLIED TO THREADS**

Fig. 59 Cylinder head tightening sequence—4.7L

5. Remove or disconnect the following:

- Vibration damper
- Timing chain cover

6. Lock the secondary timing chains to the idler sprocket with tool 8515, or equivalent.

7. Mark the secondary timing chain, on link on either side of the V8 mark on the cam sprocket.

8. Remove the left side secondary chain tensioner.

9. Remove the cylinder head access plug.

10. Remove the chain guide.

11. Remove the camshaft sprocket.

➡**There are 4 smaller bolts at the front of the head. Don't overlook these.**

12. Remove the head bolts and head.

> ✳✳ **WARNING**
>
> **Don't lay the head on its sealing surface. Due to the design of the head gasket, any distortion to the head sealing surface will result in leaks.**

13. Installation is the reverse of removal. Observe the following:

- Check the head bolts. If any necking is observed, replace the bolt.
- The 4 small bolts must be coated with sealer.
- The head bolts are tightened in the following sequence:

Step 1: Bolts 1-10 to 15 ft. lbs. (20 Nm)
Step 2: Bolts 1-10 to 35 ft. lbs. (47 Nm)
Step 3: Bolts 11-14 to 18 ft. lbs. (25 Nm)
Step 4: Bolts 1-10 90 degrees
Step 5: Bolts 11-14 to 22 ft. lbs.

Right Side

1. Before servicing the vehicle, refer to the precautions in the beginning of this manual.

2. Drain the cooling system.

3. Remove or disconnect the following:

- Negative battery cable
- Exhaust pipe
- Intake manifold
- Cylinder head cover
- Fan shroud and fan
- Oil filler housing
- Accessory drive belt

4. Rotate the crankshaft until the damper mark is aligned with the TDC mark. Verify that the V8 mark on the camshaft sprocket is at the 12 o'clock position.

5. Remove or disconnect the following:

- Vibration damper
- Timing chain cover

6. Lock the secondary timing chains to the idler sprocket with tool 8515, or equivalent.

7. Mark the secondary timing chain, on link on either side of the V8 mark on the cam sprocket.

8. Remove the left side secondary chain tensioner.

9. Remove the cylinder head access plug.

10. Remove the chain guide.

11. Remove the camshaft sprocket.

> ✳✳ **WARNING**
>
> **Do not pry on the target wheel for any reason!**

➡**There are 4 smaller bolts at the front of the head. Don't overlook these.**

12. Remove the head bolts and head.

> ✳✳ **WARNING**
>
> **Do not lay the head on its sealing surface. Due to the design of the head gasket, any distortion to the head sealing surface will result in leaks.**

13. Installation is the reverse of removal. Observe the following:

- Check the head bolts. If any necking is observed, replace the bolt.
- The 4 small bolts must be coated with sealer.
- The head bolts are tightened in the following sequence:

Step 1: Bolts 1-10 to 15 ft. lbs. (20 Nm)
Step 2: Bolts 1-10 to 35 ft. lbs. (47 Nm)
Step 3: Bolts 11-14 to 18 ft. lbs. (25 Nm)
Step 4: Bolts 1-10 90 degrees
Step 5: Bolts 11-14 to 22 ft. lbs.

ENGINE ASSEMBLY

REMOVAL & INSTALLATION

3.7L Engine

See Figures 60 through 63.

1. Before servicing the vehicle, refer to the precautions in the beginning of this manual.
2. Discharge the A/C system.
3. Drain the cooling system.
4. Release the fuel rail pressure.
5. Remove the air cleaner assembly.
6. Disconnect the battery.
7. Remove the upper fan shroud.
8. Remove the accessory drive belt.
9. Remove the viscous fan.
10. Remove the A/C compressor and position out of the way.
11. Remove the generator and secure away from engine.

➡**Do not remove the phenolic pulley from the P/S pump. It is not required for P/S pump removal.**

12. Remove the power steering pump with lines attached and secure away from engine.
13. Disconnect the heater hoses from the engine.
14. Disconnect the heater hoses from heater core and remove the hose assembly.
15. Remove the upper radiator hose from engine.
16. Remove the lower radiator hose from engine.
17. Disconnect the transmission oil cooler lines at the radiator.
18. Remove the radiator core support bracket.
19. Remove the radiator assembly, A/C Condenser and transmission oil cooler.
20. Disconnect throttle and speed control cables.
21. Disconnect the engine to body ground straps at the left side of cowl.

22. Disconnect the engine wiring harness at the following points:

- Intake air temperature (IAT) sensor
- Fuel Injectors
- Throttle Position (TPS) Switch
- Idle Air Control (IAC) Motor
- Engine Oil Pressure Switch
- Engine Coolant Temperature (ECT) Sensor
- Manifold Absolute Pressure MAP) Sensor
- Camshaft Position (CMP) Sensor
- Coil Over Plugs
- Crankshaft Position Sensor

23. Remove the coil over plugs.
24. Remove fuel rail and secure away from engine.

➡**It is not necessary to release the quick connect fitting from the fuel supply line for engine removal.**

25. Remove the PCV hose.
26. Remove the breather hoses.
27. Remove the vacuum hose for the power brake booster.
28. Disconnect the knock sensors.
29. Remove the engine oil dipstick tube.
30. Remove the intake manifold.
31. Install the engine lifting fixture, special tool 8247, using original fasteners from the removed intake manifold, and fuel rail.
32. Raise the vehicle on hoist.
33. Remove the exhaust crossover pipe from exhaust manifolds.
34. On 4WD vehicles, disconnect the axle vent tube from the left side engine mount.
35. Remove the through bolt retaining nut and bolt from both the left and right side engine mounts.
36. On 4WD vehicles, remove the locknut from the left and right side engine mount brackets.
37. Disconnect two ground straps from the lower left hand side and one ground strap from the lower right hand side of the engine.
38. Disconnect the crankshaft position sensor.

➡**The following step applies to 4WD vehicles equipped with automatic transmission only.**

39. On 4WD vehicles, remove the axle isolator bracket from the engine, transmission and the axle.
40. Remove the structural cover.
41. Remove the starter.
42. Remove the torque converter bolts (automatic transmission only).
43. Remove transmission to engine mounting bolts.

44. Disconnect the engine block heater power cable from the block heater, if equipped.
45. Lower the vehicle.
46. Remove throttle body resonator assembly and air inlet hose.
47. Disconnect the throttle and speed control cables.
48. Disconnect the tube from both the left and right side crankcase breathers. Remove the breathers.
49. Remove the generator.
50. Disconnect the two heater hoses from the timing chain cover and heater core.
51. Unclip and remove the heater hoses and tubes from the intake manifold.
52. Disconnect the engine harness at the following points:

- Intake air temperature (IAT) sensor
- Fuel Injectors
- Throttle Position (TPS) Switch
- Idle Air Control (IAC) Motor
- Engine Oil Pressure Switch
- Engine Coolant Temperature (ECT) Sensor
- Manifold absolute pressure (MAP) Sensor
- Camshaft Position (CMP) Sensor
- Coil Over Plugs

53. Disconnect the vacuum lines at the throttle body and intake manifold.
54. Remove the power steering pump and position out of the way.
55. Disconnect the body ground strap at the right side cowl.
56. Disconnect the body ground strap at the left side cowl.

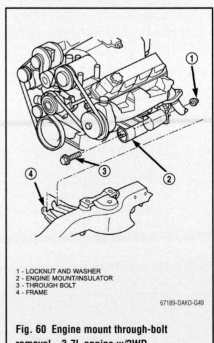

1 - LOCKNUT AND WASHER
2 - ENGINE MOUNT/INSULATOR
3 - THROUGH BOLT
4 - FRAME

67189-DAKO-G49

Fig. 60 Engine mount through-bolt removal—3.7L engine w/2WD

→It will be necessary to support the transmission in order to remove the engine.

57. Position a suitable jack under the transmission.

58. Remove the engine from the vehicle.

To install:

59. Position the engine in the vehicle. Position both the left and right side engine mount brackets and install the through bolts and nuts. On 2WD vehicles, tighten nuts to 95 Nm (70 ft. lbs.); on 4WD vehicles, to 102 Nm (75 ft. lbs.).

60. On 4WD vehicles, install the locknuts onto the engine mount brackets. Tighten the locknuts to 41 Nm (30 ft. lbs.).

61. Remove the jack from under the transmission.

62. Remove Engine Lifting Fixture Tool 8347.

63. Remove Special Tools 8400 Lifting Studs.

64. Position the generator wiring behind the oil dipstick tube, then install the oil dipstick tube upper mounting bolt.

65. Connect both left and right side body ground straps.

66. Install the power steering pump.

67. Connect the fuel supply line quick connect fitting.

68. Connect the vacuum lines at the throttle body and intake manifold.

69. Connect the engine harness at the following points:

- Intake Air Temperature (IAT) Sensor

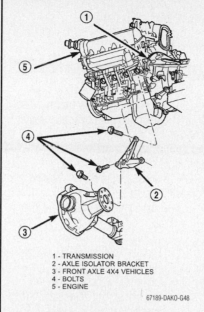

Fig. 62 Axle isolator bracket removal—3.7L engine w/4WD

1 - TRANSMISSION
2 - AXLE ISOLATOR BRACKET
3 - FRONT AXLE 4X4 VEHICLES
4 - BOLTS
5 - ENGINE

67189-DAKO-G48

- Idle Air Control (IAC) Motor
- Fuel Injectors
- Throttle Position (TPS) Switch
- Engine Oil Pressure Switch
- Engine Coolant Temperature (ECT) Sensor
- Manifold Absolute Pressure (MAP) Sensor
- Camshaft Position (CMP) Sensor
- Coil Over Plugs

70. Position and install the heater hoses and tubes onto intake manifold.

71. Install the heater hoses onto the heater core and the engine front cover.

72. Install the generator.

73. Install the A/C condenser, radiator and transmission oil cooler.

74. Connect the radiator upper and lower hoses.

75. Connect the transmission oil cooler lines to the radiator.

76. Install the accessory drive belt, fan assembly and shroud.

77. Install A/C compressor.

78. Install both breathers. Connect the tube to both crankcase breathers.

79. Connect the throttle and speed control cables.

80. Install the throttle body resonator assembly and air inlet hose. Tighten the clamps to 4 Nm (35 inch lbs.).

81. Raise the vehicle.

82. Install the transmission to engine mounting bolts. Tighten the bolts to 41 Nm (30 ft. lbs.).

83. Install the torque converter bolts (automatic transmission only).

84. Connect the crankshaft position sensor.

85. On 4WD vehicles, position and install the axle isolator bracket onto the axle, transmission and engine block.

86. Install the starter.

✳✳ WARNING

The structural cover requires a specific torque sequence. Failure to follow this sequence may cause severe damage to the cover.

87. Install the structural cover.

88. Install the exhaust crossover pipe.

89. Install the engine block heater power cable, if equipped.

90. On 4WD vehicles, connect the axle vent tube to the left side engine mount.

91. Lower the vehicle.

92. Check and fill engine oil.

93. Recharge the A/C system.

94. Refill the engine cooling system.

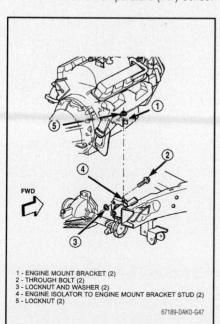

1 - ENGINE MOUNT BRACKET (2)
2 - THROUGH BOLT (2)
3 - LOCKNUT AND WASHER (2)
4 - ENGINE ISOLATOR TO ENGINE MOUNT BRACKET STUD (2)
5 - LOCKNUT (2)

67189-DAKO-G47

Fig. 61 Engine mount through-bolt removal—3.7L engine w/4WD

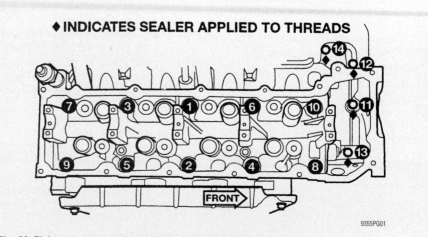

◆ INDICATES SEALER APPLIED TO THREADS

FRONT

9355PG01

Fig. 63 Tighten the structural cover bolts in this order—3.7L Engine

95. Install the battery tray and battery.

96. Connect the battery positive and negative cables.

97. Start the engine and check for leaks.

4.7L Engine

See Figure 64.

1. Before servicing the vehicle, refer to the precautions in the beginning of this manual.

2. Disconnect the battery negative and positive cables.

3. Remove the battery and the battery tray.

4. Raise the vehicle on hoist.

5. Remove exhaust crossover pipe from the exhaust manifolds.

6. On 4WD vehicles, disconnect the axle vent tube from left side engine mount.

7. Remove the through bolt retaining nut and bolt from both the left and right side engine mounts.

8. On 4WD vehicles, remove the locknut from left and right side engine mount brackets.

9. Disconnect two ground straps from the lower left hand side and one ground strap from the lower right hand side of the engine.

10. Disconnect the crankshaft position sensor.

➡**The following step applies to 4WD vehicles equipped with automatic transmission only.**

11. On 4WD vehicles, remove the axle isolator bracket from the engine, transmission and the axle.

12. Remove the structural cover.

13. Remove the starter.

14. Drain the cooling system.

15. Remove the torque converter bolts (automatic transmission only).

16. Remove the transmission to engine mounting bolts.

17. Disconnect the engine block heater power cable from the block heater, if equipped.

18. Lower the vehicle.

19. Remove the throttle body resonator assembly and air inlet hose.

20. Disconnect the throttle and speed control cables.

21. Disconnect the tube from both the left and right side crankcase breathers. Remove breathers.

22. Discharge the A/C system.

23. Remove the A/C compressor.

24. Remove the shroud, fan assembly and accessory drive belt.

25. Disconnect the transmission oil cooler lines at the radiator.

26. Disconnect the radiator upper and lower hoses.

27. Remove the radiator, A/C condenser and transmission oil cooler.

28. Remove the generator.

29. Disconnect the two heater hoses from the timing chain cover and heater core.

30. Unclip and remove the heater hoses and tubes from the intake manifold.

31. Disconnect the engine harness at the following points :
- Intake air temperature (IAT) sensor
- Fuel Injectors
- Throttle Position (TPS) Switch
- Idle Air Control (IAC) Motor
- Engine Oil Pressure Switch
- Engine Coolant Temperature (ECT) Sensor
- Manifold Absolute Pressure (MAP) Sensor
- Camshaft Position (CMP) Sensor
- Coil Over Plugs

32. Disconnect the vacuum lines at the throttle body and intake manifold.

33. Release the fuel rail pressure then disconnect the fuel supply quick connect fitting at the fuel rail.

34. Remove the power steering pump and position out of the way.

35. Install Special Tools 8400 Lifting Studs, into the cylinder heads.

36. Install Engine Lifting Fixture Special Tool 8347 following these steps:
- Holding the lifting fixture at a slight angle, slide the large bore in the front plate over the hex portion of the lifting stud.
- Position the two remaining fixture arms onto the two Special Tools 8400 Lifting Studs, in the cylinder heads.
- Pull forward and upward on the lifting fixture so that the lifting stud rest in the slotted area below the large bore.
- Secure the lifting fixture to the three studs using three 7/16 - 14 N/C locknuts.
- Make sure the lifting loop in the lifting fixture is in the last hole (closest to the throttle body) to minimize the angle of engine during removal.

37. Disconnect the body ground strap at the right side cowl.

38. Disconnect the body ground strap at the left side cowl.

➡**It will be necessary to support the transmission in order to remove the engine.**

39. Position a suitable jack under the transmission.

40. Remove the engine from the vehicle.

To install:

41. Position the engine in the vehicle. Position both the left and right side engine mount brackets and install the through bolts and nuts. On 2WD vehicles, tighten nuts to 95 Nm (70 ft. lbs.); On 4WD vehicles, tighten to 102 Nm (75 ft. lbs.).

42. On 4WD vehicles, install locknuts onto the engine mount brackets. Tighten the locknuts to 41 Nm (30 ft. lbs.).

43. Remove the jack from under the transmission.

44. Remove Engine Lifting Fixture Special Tool 8347.

45. Remove Special Tools 8400 Lifting Studs.

46. Position the generator wiring behind the oil dipstick tube, then install the oil dipstick tube upper mounting bolt.

47. Connect both left and right side body ground straps.

48. Install the power steering pump.

49. Connect the fuel supply line quick connect fitting.

50. Connect the vacuum lines at the throttle body and intake manifold.

51. Connect the engine harness at the following points:
- Intake Air Temperature (IAT) Sensor
- Idle Air Control (IAC) Motor
- Fuel Injectors
- Throttle Position (TPS) Switch
- Engine Oil Pressure Switch
- Engine Coolant Temperature (ECT) Sensor
- Manifold Absolute Pressure (MAP) Sensor
- Camshaft Position (CMP) Sensor
- Coil Over Plugs

52. Position and install the heater hoses and tubes onto intake manifold.

53. Install the heater hoses onto the heater core and the engine front cover.

54. Install the generator.

55. Install the A/C condenser, radiator and transmission oil cooler.

56. Connect the radiator upper and lower hoses.

57. Connect the transmission oil cooler lines to the radiator.

58. Install the accessory drive belt, fan assembly and shroud.

59. Install the A/C compressor.

60. Install both breathers. Connect the tube to both crankcase breathers.

61. Connect the throttle and speed control cables.

62. Install the throttle body resonator assembly and air inlet hose. Tighten clamps 4 Nm (35 inch lbs.).

63. Raise the vehicle.

64. Install transmission to engine mounting bolts. Tighten the bolts to 41 Nm (30 ft. lbs.).

65. Install the torque converter bolts (automatic transmission only).

66. Connect crankshaft position sensor.

67. On 4WD vehicles, position and install the axle isolator bracket onto the axle, transmission and engine block. Tighten the bolts to specification.

68. Install the starter.

✳ WARNING

The structural cover requires a specific torque sequence. Failure to follow this sequence may cause severe damage to the cover.

69. Install the structural cover.

70. Install the exhaust crossover pipe.

71. Install the engine block heater power cable, if equipped.

72. On 4WD vehicles, connect the axle vent tube to left side engine mount.

73. Lower the vehicle.

74. Check and fill the engine oil.

75. Recharge the A/C system.

76. Refill the engine cooling system.

77. Install the battery tray and battery.

78. Connect the battery positive and negative cables.

79. Start the engine and check for leaks.

EXHAUST MANIFOLD

REMOVAL & INSTALLATION

3.7L Engine
See Figure 65.

1. Before servicing the vehicle, refer to the precautions in the beginning of this manual.

2. Remove or disconnect the following:
   • Negative battery cable
   • Exhaust manifold heat shields
   • Exhaust Gas Recirculation (EGR) tube
   • Exhaust Y-pipe
   • Exhaust manifolds

To install:

➡**If the exhaust manifold studs came out with the nuts when removing the**

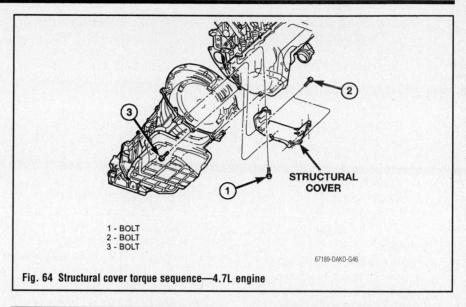

Fig. 64 Structural cover torque sequence—4.7L engine

1 - BOLT
2 - BOLT
3 - BOLT

67189-DAKO-G46

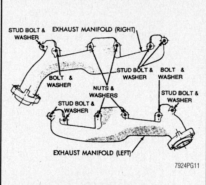

Fig. 65 Exhaust manifold fastener locations—3.7L engines

7924PG11

exhaust manifolds, replace them with new studs.

3. Install or connect the following:
   • Exhaust manifolds. Torque the fasteners to 20 ft. lbs. (27 Nm), starting with the center nuts and work out to the ends.
   • Exhaust Y-pipe
   • EGR tube
   • Exhaust manifold heat shields
   • Negative battery cable

4. Start the engine, check for leaks and repair if necessary.

4.7L Engine
See Figure 66.

1. Before servicing the vehicle, refer to the precautions in the beginning of this manual.

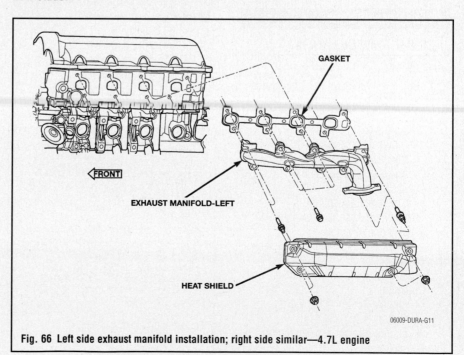

Fig. 66 Left side exhaust manifold installation; right side similar—4.7L engine

06009-DURA-G11

2. Drain the cooling system.
3. Remove or disconnect the following:
   - Battery
   - Power distribution center
   - Battery tray
   - Windshield washer fluid bottle
   - Air cleaner assembly
   - Accessory drive belt
   - A/C compressor
   - A/C accumulator bracket
   - Heater hoses
   - Exhaust manifold heat shields
   - Exhaust Y-pipe
   - Starter motor
   - Exhaust manifolds

To install:

4. Install or connect the following:
   - Exhaust manifolds, using new gaskets. Tighten the bolts to 18 ft. lbs. (25 Nm), starting with the inner bolts and work out to the ends.
   - Starter motor
   - Exhaust Y-pipe
   - Exhaust manifold heat shields
   - Heater hoses
   - A/C accumulator bracket
   - A/C compressor
   - Accessory drive belt
   - Air cleaner assembly
   - Windshield washer fluid bottle
   - Battery tray
   - Power distribution center
   - Battery
5. Fill the cooling system.
6. Start the engine and check for leaks.

INTAKE MANIFOLD

REMOVAL & INSTALLATION

See Figure 67.

1. Before servicing the vehicle, refer to the precautions in the beginning of this manual.
2. Drain the cooling system.
3. Remove or disconnect the following:
   - Negative battery cable
   - Air cleaner assembly
   - Accelerator cable
   - Cruise control cable
   - Manifold Absolute Pressure (MAP) sensor connector
   - Intake Air Temperature (IAT) sensor connector
   - Throttle Position (TP) sensor connector
   - Idle Air Control (IAC) valve connector
   - Engine Coolant Temperature (ECT) sensor

- Positive Crankcase Ventilation (PCV) valve and hose
- Canister purge vacuum line
- Brake booster vacuum line
- Cruise control servo hose
- Accessory drive belt
- Alternator
- A/C compressor
- Engine ground straps
- Ignition coil towers
- Oil dipstick tube
- Fuel line
- Fuel supply manifold
- Throttle body and mounting bracket
- Cowl seal
- Right engine lifting stud
- Intake manifold. Remove the fasteners in reverse of the tightening sequence.

To install:

4. Install or connect the following:
   - Intake manifold using new gaskets. Tighten the bolts, in sequence, to 105 inch lbs. (12 Nm).
   - Right engine lifting stud
   - Cowl seal
   - Throttle body and mounting bracket
   - Fuel supply manifold
   - Fuel line
   - Oil dipstick tube
   - Ignition coil towers
   - Engine ground straps
   - A/C compressor
   - Alternator
   - Accessory drive belt
   - Cruise control servo hose
   - Brake booster vacuum line
   - Canister purge vacuum line
   - PCV valve and hose
   - ECT sensor
   - IAC valve connector
   - TP sensor connector
   - IAT sensor connector
   - MAP sensor connector
   - Cruise control cable

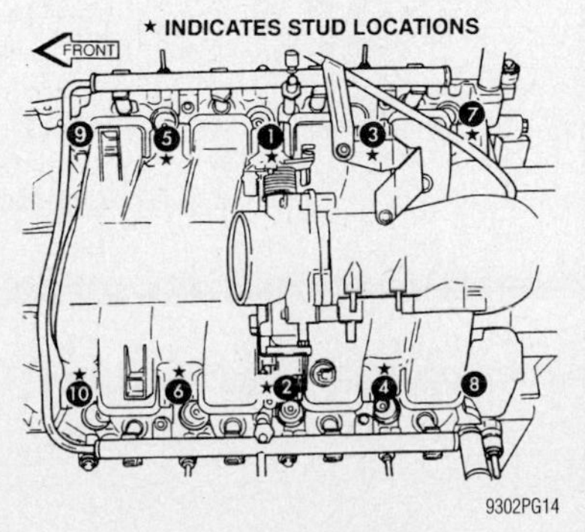

Fig. 67 Intake manifold torque sequence—3.7L and 4.7L engine

- Accelerator cable
- Air cleaner assembly
- Negative battery cable
5. Fill the cooling system.
6. Start the engine and check for leaks.

OIL PAN

REMOVAL & INSTALLATION

3.7L Engine

See Figures 68 and 69.

1. Before servicing the vehicle, refer to the precautions in the beginning of this manual.
2. Disconnect the negative battery cable.
3. Install an engine support fixture. Do not raise engine at this time.
4. Loosen both left and right side engine mount through bolts. Do not remove bolts.
5. Remove the structural dust cover, if equipped.
6. Drain engine oil.
7. Remove the front crossmember.

➡ **Raise the engine just enough to provide clearance for oil pan removal. Check for proper clearance at fan shroud to fan and cowl to intake manifold.**

8. Raise engine to provide clearance to remove oil pan.

➡ **Do not pry on oil pan or oil pan gasket. Gasket is integral to engine windage tray and does not come out with oil pan.**

9. Remove the oil pan mounting bolts and oil pan.
10. Unbolt oil pump pickup tube and remove tube.
11. Inspect the integral windage tray and gasket and replace as needed.

To install:

12. Clean the oil pan gasket mating surface of the bedplate and oil pan.
13. Inspect integrated oil pan gasket, and replace as necessary.
14. Position the integrated oil pan gasket/windage tray assembly.
15. Install the oil pickup tube.
16. If removed, install stud at position No. 9.
17. Install the mounting bolt and nuts. Tighten nuts to 28 Nm (20 ft. lbs.).
18. Position the oil pan and install the mounting bolts. Tighten the mounting bolts to 15 Nm (11 ft. lbs.) in the sequence shown.

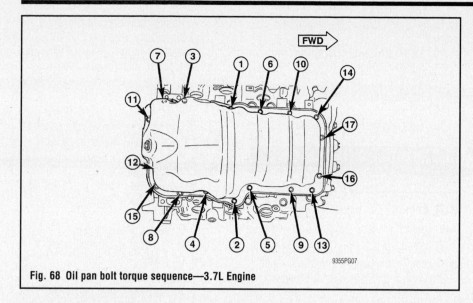

Fig. 68 Oil pan bolt torque sequence—3.7L Engine

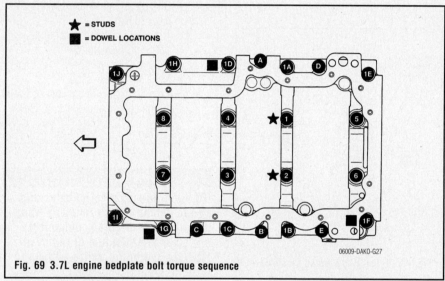

★ = STUDS
■ = DOWEL LOCATIONS

Fig. 69 3.7L engine bedplate bolt torque sequence

19. Lower the engine into mounts.
20. Install both the left and right side engine mount through bolts. Tighten the nuts to 68 Nm (50 ft. lbs.).
21. Remove the lifting device.
22. Install structural dust cover, If equipped.
23. Install the front crossmember.
24. Fill engine oil.
25. Reconnect the negative battery cable.
26. Start engine and check for leaks.

4.7L Engine

2WD

See Figure 70.

1. Before servicing the vehicle, refer to the precautions in the beginning of this manual.
2. Drain the cooling system.
3. Remove the upper fan shroud.

4. Remove the throttle body resonator and air inlet hose.
5. Remove the intake manifold.
6. Raise vehicle on hoist.
7. Disconnect exhaust pipe at exhaust manifolds.
8. Remove the structural dust cover using sequence shown.
9. Drain engine oil and remove oil filter.
10. Position suitable jack under engine.
11. Remove both left and right side engine mount through bolts.
12. Raise engine to provide clearance to remove oil pan.
13. Place blocks of wood between engine brackets and lower mounts to provide stability to engine.

➡ Do not pry on oil pan or oil pan gasket. Gasket is mounted to engine and does not come out with oil pan.

14. Remove the oil pan mounting bolts and oil pan.
15. Unbolt oil pump pickup tube and remove tube and oil pan gasket from engine.

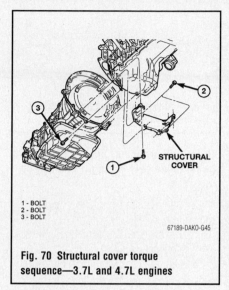

1 - BOLT
2 - BOLT
3 - BOLT

Fig. 70 Structural cover torque sequence—3.7L and 4.7L engines

To install:

16. Clean the oil pan gasket mating surface of the bedplate and oil pan.
17. Position the oil pan gasket and pickup tube with new o-ring. Install the mounting bolt and nuts. Tighten bolt and nuts to 28 Nm (20 ft. lbs.).
18. Position the oil pan and install the mounting bolts. Tighten the mounting bolts to 15 Nm (11 ft. lbs.) in the sequence shown.
19. Raise the engine and remove the blocks of wood.
20. Lower engine and install both the left and right side engine mount through bolts. Tighten the nuts to 68 Nm (50 ft. lbs.).
21. Remove jack and install oil filter.
22. Install structural dust cover.
23. Install exhaust pipe onto exhaust manifolds.
24. Lower vehicle.
25. Install intake manifold.
26. Install throttle body resonator and air inlet hose.
27. Install upper fan shroud.
28. Fill cooling system.
29. Fill engine oil.
30. Start engine and check for leaks.

4WD

See Figures 71 and 72.

1. Before servicing the vehicle, refer to the precautions in the beginning of this manual.

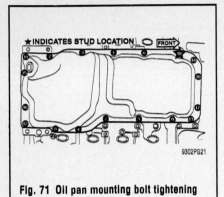

Fig. 71 Oil pan mounting bolt tightening sequence—4.7L engine

➡ **On 4WD vehicles, the front axle must be removed before the oil pan can be removed.**

2. Remove the front axle from vehicle.

3. Remove the structural dust cover using sequence shown.

4. Drain the engine oil and remove oil filter.

5. Remove the oil pan mounting bolts and oil pan.

6. Unbolt oil pump pickup tube and remove tube and oil pan gasket from engine.

To install:

7. Clean the oil pan gasket mating surface of the bedplate and oil pan.

8. Position the oil pan gasket and pickup tube with new o–ring. Install the mounting bolt and nuts. Tighten bolt and nuts to 28 Nm (20 ft. lbs.).

9. Position the oil pan and install the mounting bolts. Tighten the mounting bolts

to 15 Nm (11 ft. lbs.) in the sequence shown.

10. Install structural dust cover.
11. Install oil filter.
12. Install front axle.
13. Lower vehicle.
14. Fill engine oil.
15. Start engine check for leaks.

OIL PUMP

REMOVAL & INSTALLATION

3.7L Engine

See Figure 73.

1. Before servicing the vehicle, refer to the precautions in the beginning of this manual.

2. Remove or disconnect the following:
- Oil Pan
- Timing chain cover

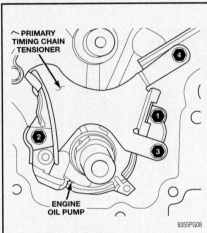

Fig. 73 Oil pump bolt torque sequence—3.7L

- Timing chains and tensioners
- Oil pump

3. Installation is the reverse of removal. Torque the pump bolts, in sequence, to 21 ft. lbs. (28 Nm),

4.7L Engine

1. Before servicing the vehicle, refer to the precautions in the beginning of this manual.

2. Drain the engine oil.

3. Remove or disconnect the following:
- Negative battery cable
- Oil pan
- Oil pump pick-up tube
- Timing chains and tensioners
- Oil pump

To install:

4. Install or connect the following:
- Oil pump. Tighten the bolts to 21 ft. lbs. (28 Nm).
- Timing chains and tensioners
- Oil pump pick-up tube
- Oil pan
- Negative battery cable

5. Fill the crankcase to the correct level.

6. Start the engine and check for leaks.

INSPECTION

See Figures 74 through 79.

✳✳ WARNING

Oil pump pressure relief valve and spring should not be removed from the oil pump. If these components are disassembled and or removed from the pump the entire oil pump assembly must be replaced.

1. Clean all parts thoroughly. Mating surface of the oil pump housing should be smooth. If the pump cover is scratched or grooved the oil pump assembly should be replaced.

2. Lay a straight edge across the pump cover surface. If a 0.025 mm (0.001 in.) feeler gauge can be inserted between the cover and the straight edge the oil pump assembly should be replaced.

3. Measure the thickness of the outer rotor. If the outer rotor thickness measures at 12.005 mm (0.472 in.) or less the oil pump assembly must be replaced.

4. Measure the diameter of the outer rotor. If the outer rotor diameter measures at 85.925 mm (3.382 in.) or less the oil pump assembly must be replaced.

5. Measure the thickness of the inner rotor. If the inner rotor thickness measures at 12.005 mm (0.472 in.) or less then the oil pump assembly must be replaced.

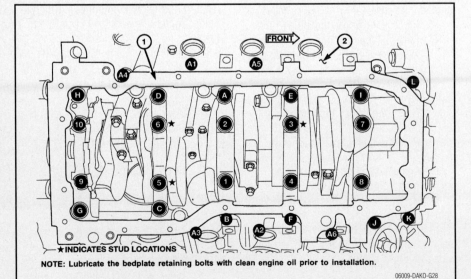

★INDICATES STUD LOCATIONS

NOTE: Lubricate the bedplate retaining bolts with clean engine oil prior to installation.

Fig. 72 4.7L engine bedplate bolt torque sequence

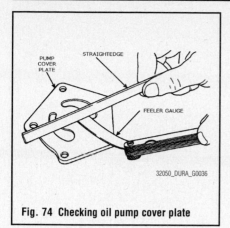

Fig. 74 Checking oil pump cover plate

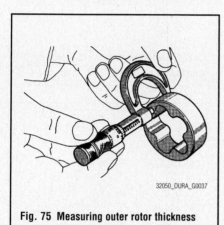

Fig. 75 Measuring outer rotor thickness

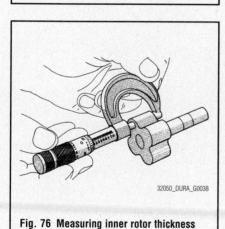

Fig. 76 Measuring inner rotor thickness

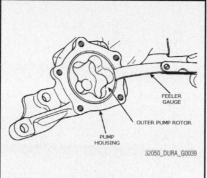

Fig. 77 Measuring clearance between pump housing and outer rotor

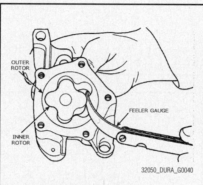

Fig. 78 Measuring clearance between inner and outer rotor

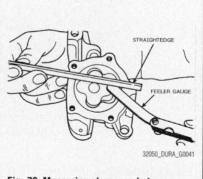

Fig. 79 Measuring clearance between rotors and pump body cover

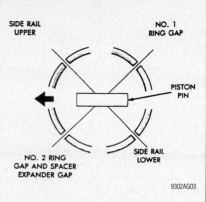

Fig. 80 Piston ring end-gap spacing. Position raised "F" on piston toward front of engine—3.7L and 4.7L engine

6. Slide outer rotor into the body of the oil pump. Press the outer rotor to one side of the oil pump body and measure clearance between the outer rotor and the body. If the measurement is 0.235mm (0.009 in.) or more the oil pump assembly must be replaced.

7. Install the inner rotor in the into the oil pump body. Measure the clearance between the inner and outer rotors. If the clearance between the rotors is .150 mm (0.006 in.) or more the oil pump assembly must be replaced.

8. Place a straight edge across the body of the oil pump (between the bolt holes); if a feeler gauge of .095 mm (0.0038 in.) or

greater can be inserted between the straight-edge and the rotors, the pump must be replaced.

➡ The 3.7L/4.7L oil pump is released as an assembly; there are no sub-assembly components. In the event the oil pump is not functioning or out of specification it must be replaced as an assembly.

PISTON AND RING

POSITIONING

See Figure 80.

REAR MAIN SEAL

REMOVAL & INSTALLATION

1. Before servicing the vehicle, refer to the precautions in the beginning of this manual.
2. Remove or disconnect the following:
    *   Transmission
    *   Flexplate
3. Thread Oil Seal Remover 8506 into the rear main seal as far as possible and remove the rear main seal.

To install:

4. Install or connect the following:
    *   Seal Guide 8349-2 onto the crankshaft
    *   Rear main seal on the seal guide
    *   Rear main seal, using the Crankshaft Rear Oil Seal Installer 8349 and Driver Handle C-4171; tap it into place until the installer is flush with the cylinder block
    *   Flexplate. Tighten the bolts to 45 ft. lbs. (60 Nm) for 4.7L; 70 ft. lbs. (95 Nm) for the 3.7L engine.
    *   Transmission
5. Start the engine and check for leaks.

TIMING CHAIN, SPROCKETS, FRONT COVER AND SEAL

REMOVAL & INSTALLATION

3.7L Engines

See Figures 81 through 91.

1. Before servicing the vehicle, refer to the precautions in the beginning of this manual.
2. Drain the cooling system.
3. Remove or disconnect the following:
    *   Negative battery cable
    *   Valve covers
    *   Radiator fan

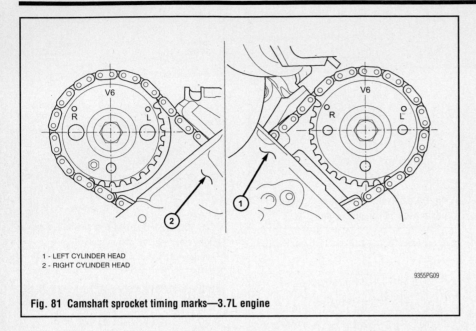

1 - LEFT CYLINDER HEAD
2 - RIGHT CYLINDER HEAD

9355PG09

Fig. 81 Camshaft sprocket timing marks—3.7L engine

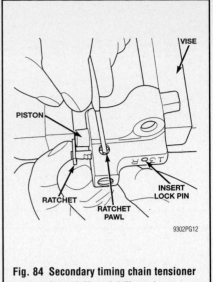

9302PG12

Fig. 84 Secondary timing chain tensioner preparation—3.7L and 4.7L engines

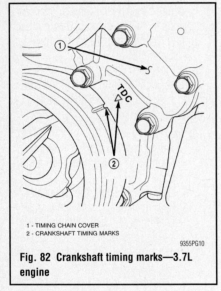

1 - TIMING CHAIN COVER
2 - CRANKSHAFT TIMING MARKS

9355PG10

Fig. 82 Crankshaft timing marks—3.7L engine

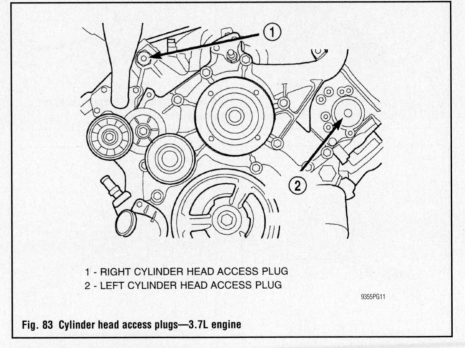

1 - RIGHT CYLINDER HEAD ACCESS PLUG
2 - LEFT CYLINDER HEAD ACCESS PLUG

9355PG11

Fig. 83 Cylinder head access plugs—3.7L engine

4. Rotate the crankshaft so that the crankshaft timing mark aligns with the Top Dead Center (TDC) mark on the front cover, and the**V6** marks on the camshaft sprockets are at 12 o'clock.
- Power steering pump
- Access plugs from the cylinder heads
- Oil fill housing
- Crankshaft damper

5. Compress the primary timing chain tensioner and install a lockpin.

6. Remove the secondary timing chain tensioners.

7. Hold the left camshaft with adjustable pliers and remove the sprocket and chain. Rotate the **left** camshaft 15 degrees **clockwise** to the neutral position.

8. Hold the right camshaft with adjustable pliers and remove the camshaft

sprocket. Rotate the **right** camshaft 45 degrees **counterclockwise** to the neutral position.

9. Remove the primary timing chain and sprockets.

To install:

10. Use a small prytool to hold the ratchet pawl and compress the secondary timing chain tensioners in a vise and install locking pins.

➡**The black bolts fasten the guide to the engine block and the silver bolts fasten the guide to the cylinder head.**

11. Install or connect the following:

- Secondary timing chain guides. Tighten the bolts to 21 ft. lbs. (28 Nm).
- Secondary timing chains to the idler sprocket so that the double plated links on each chain are visible through the slots in the primary idler sprocket

12. Lock the secondary timing chains to the idler sprocket with Timing Chain Locking tool as shown.

13. Align the primary chain double plated links with the idler sprocket timing mark and the single plated link with the crankshaft sprocket timing mark.

14. Install the primary chain and sprock-

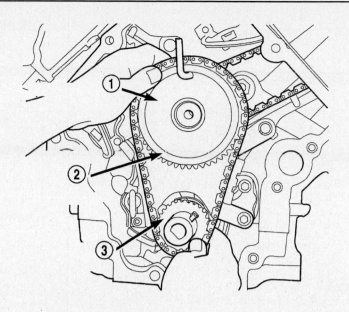

1 - SPECIAL TOOL 8429
2 - PRIMARY CHAIN IDLER SPROCKET
3 - CRANKSHAFT SPROCKET

9355PG12

Fig. 85 Installing the idler gear and timing chain—3.7L engine

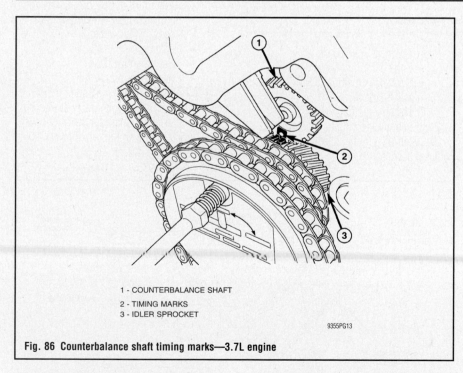

1 - COUNTERBALANCE SHAFT
2 - TIMING MARKS
3 - IDLER SPROCKET

9355PG13

Fig. 86 Counterbalance shaft timing marks—3.7L engine

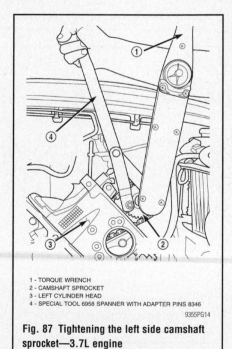

1 - TORQUE WRENCH
2 - CAMSHAFT SPROCKET
3 - LEFT CYLINDER HEAD
4 - SPECIAL TOOL 6958 SPANNER WITH ADAPTER PINS 8346

9355PG14

Fig. 87 Tightening the left side camshaft sprocket—3.7L engine

ets. Tighten the idler sprocket bolt to 25 ft. lbs. (34 Nm).

15. Align the secondary chain single plated links with the timing marks on the secondary sprockets. Align the dot at the **L** mark on the left sprocket with the plated link on the left chain and the dot at the **R** mark on the right sprocket with the plated link on the right chain.

16. Rotate the camshafts back from the neutral position and install the camshaft sprockets.

17. Remove the secondary chain locking tool.

18. Remove the primary and secondary timing chain tensioner locking pins.

19. Hold the camshaft sprockets with a

spanner wrench and tighten the retaining bolts to 90 ft. lbs. (122 Nm).

20. Install or connect the following:
   • Front cover. Tighten the bolts, in sequence, to 40 ft. lbs. (54 Nm).
   • Front crankshaft seal
   • Cylinder head access plugs
   • A/C compressor

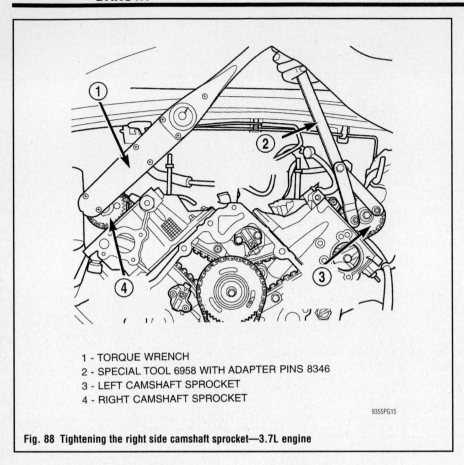

1 - TORQUE WRENCH
2 - SPECIAL TOOL 6958 WITH ADAPTER PINS 8346
3 - LEFT CAMSHAFT SPROCKET
4 - RIGHT CAMSHAFT SPROCKET

9355PG15

Fig. 88 Tightening the right side camshaft sprocket—3.7L engine

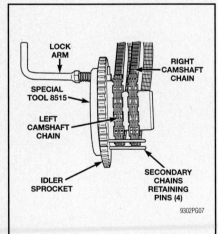

9302PG07

Fig. 89 Use the Timing Chain Locking tool to lock the timing chains on the idler gear—3.7L and 4.7L engines

- Alternator
- Accessory drive belt tensioner. Tighten the bolt to 40 ft. lbs. (54 Nm).
- Oil fill housing
- Crankshaft damper. Tighten the bolt to 130 ft. lbs. (175 Nm).
- Power steering pump
- Lower radiator hose
- Heater hoses

- Accessory drive belt
- Engine cooling fan and shroud
- Camshaft Position (CMP) sensor
- Valve covers
- Negative battery cable
21. Fill and bleed the cooling system.
22. Start the engine, check for leaks and repair if necessary.

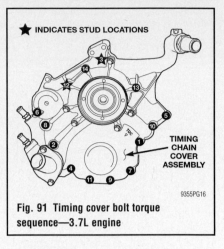

★ INDICATES STUD LOCATIONS

9355PG16

Fig. 91 Timing cover bolt torque sequence—3.7L engine

4.7L Engine

See Figures 92 through 95, 85, 89 and 90.

1. Before servicing the vehicle, refer to the precautions in the beginning of this manual.
2. Drain the cooling system.
3. Remove or disconnect the following:
- Negative battery cable
- Valve covers
- Camshaft Position (CMP) sensor
- Engine cooling fan and shroud
- Accessory drive belt
- Heater hoses
- Lower radiator hose
- Power steering pump
4. Rotate the crankshaft so that the crankshaft timing mark aligns with the Top Dead Center (TDC) mark on the front cover, and the **V8** marks on the camshaft sprockets are at 12 o'clock.

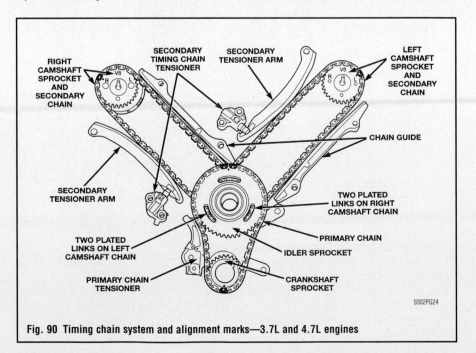

9302PG24

Fig. 90 Timing chain system and alignment marks—3.7L and 4.7L engines

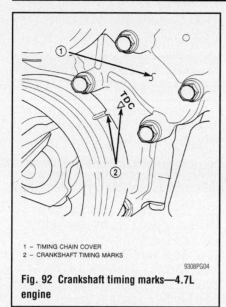

1 – TIMING CHAIN COVER
2 – CRANKSHAFT TIMING MARKS

Fig. 92 Crankshaft timing marks—4.7L engine

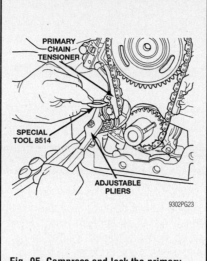

Fig. 95 Compress and lock the primary chain tensioner—4.7L engine

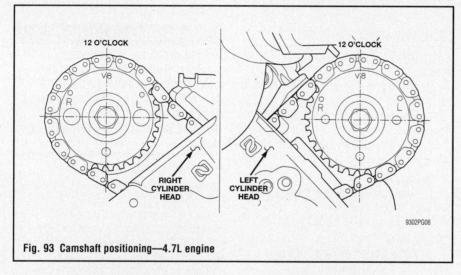

Fig. 93 Camshaft positioning—4.7L engine

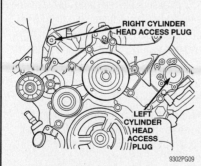

Fig. 94 Cylinder head access plug locations—4.7L engine

5. Remove or disconnect the following:
   • Crankshaft damper
   • Oil fill housing
   • Accessory drive belt tensioner
   • Alternator
   • A/C compressor
   • Front cover

   • Front crankshaft seal
   • Cylinder head access plugs
   • Secondary timing chain guides
6. Compress the primary timing chain tensioner and install a lockpin.
7. Remove the secondary timing chain tensioners.
8. Hold the left camshaft with adjustable pliers and remove the sprocket and chain. Rotate the **left** camshaft 15 degrees **clockwise** to the neutral position.
9. Hold the right camshaft with adjustable pliers and remove the camshaft sprocket. Rotate the **right** camshaft 45 degrees **counterclockwise** to the neutral position.
10. Remove the primary timing chain and sprockets.

To install:

11. Use a small prytool to hold the ratchet pawl and compress the secondary timing chain tensioners in a vise and install locking pins.

➡The black bolts fasten the guide to the engine block and the silver bolts fasten the guide to the cylinder head.

12. Install or connect the following:
    • Secondary timing chain guides. Tighten the bolts to 21 ft. lbs. (28 Nm).
    • Secondary timing chains to the idler sprocket so that the double plated links on each chain are visible through the slots in the primary idler sprocket
13. Lock the secondary timing chains to the idler sprocket with Timing Chain Locking tool 8515 as shown.
14. Align the primary chain double plated links with the idler sprocket timing mark and the single plated link with the crankshaft sprocket timing mark.
15. Install the primary chain and sprockets. Tighten the idler sprocket bolt to 25 ft. lbs. (34 Nm).
16. Align the secondary chain single plated links with the timing marks on the secondary sprockets. Align the dot at the **L** mark on the left sprocket with the plated link on the left chain and the dot at the **R** mark on the right sprocket with the plated link on the right chain.
17. Rotate the camshafts back from the neutral position and install the camshaft sprockets.
18. Remove the secondary chain locking tool.
19. Remove the primary and secondary timing chain tensioner locking pins.
20. Hold the camshaft sprockets with a spanner wrench and tighten the retaining bolts to 90 ft. lbs. (122 Nm).
21. Install or connect the following:
    • Front cover. Tighten the bolts, in sequence, to 40 ft. lbs. (54 Nm).

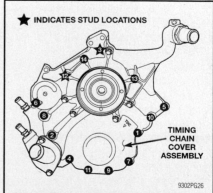

★ INDICATES STUD LOCATIONS

TIMING CHAIN COVER ASSEMBLY

Fig. 96 Timing chain cover bolt torque sequence—4.7L engine

- Front crankshaft seal
- Cylinder head access plugs
- A/C compressor
- Alternator
- Accessory drive belt tensioner. Tighten the bolt to 40 ft. lbs. (54 Nm).
- Oil fill housing
- Crankshaft damper. Tighten the bolt to 130 ft. lbs. (175 Nm).

- Power steering pump
- Lower radiator hose
- Heater hoses
- Accessory drive belt
- Engine cooling fan and shroud
- Camshaft Position (CMP) sensor
- Valve covers
- Negative battery cable

22. Fill the cooling system.

23. Start the engine and check for leaks.

ENGINE PERFORMANCE & EMISSION CONTROL

CAMSHAFT POSITION (CMP) SENSOR

LOCATION

See Figure 97.

The Camshaft Position (CMP) sensor is bolted to the right-front side of the right cylinder head on 3.7L and 4.7L engines.

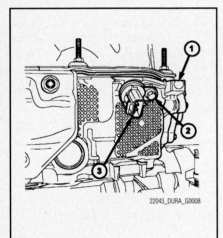

22043_DURA_G0008

Fig. 97 CMP sensor mounting on 3.7L and 4.7L engines

OPERATION

The Camshaft Position Sensor (CMP) sensor contains a hall effect device referred to as a sync signal generator. A rotating target wheel (tone wheel) for the CMP is located at the front of the camshaft for the right cylinder head. This sync signal generator detects notches located on a tone wheel. As the tone wheel rotates, the notches pass through the sync signal generator. The signal from the CMP sensor is used in conjunction with the Crankshaft Position Sensor (CKP) to differentiate between fuel injection and spark events. It is also used to synchronize the fuel injectors with their respective cylinders.

When the leading edge of the target wheel notch enters the tip of the CMP, the interruption of magnetic field causes the voltage to switch high, resulting in a sync signal of approximately 5 volts. When the trailing edge of the target wheel notch leaves the tip of the CMP, the change of the magnetic field causes the sync signal voltage to switch to 0 volts.

REMOVAL & INSTALLATION

1. Raise and safely support the vehicle.
2. Disconnect the camshaft position sensor (CMP) electrical connector.
3. Remove the CMP sensor mounting bolts.
4. Carefully twist the sensor from the cylinder.

To install:

5. Check the condition of the sensor O–ring.
6. Clean out the machined hole in the cylinder head.
7. Apply a small amount of clean engine oil to the sensor O–ring.
8. Install the CMP sensor into the cylinder head with a slight rocking and twisting action.
9. Install the mounting bolt and tighten to 106 inch lbs. (12 Nm).
10. Connect the electrical connector.
11. Lower the vehicle.

TESTING

1. Using a diagnostic scan tool, check for the presence of any Diagnostic Trouble Codes (DTCs). Record and address these codes as necessary.
2. Turn the ignition **OFF** and disconnect the Camshaft Position (CMP) Sensor harness connector.

➡**If any of the test results fall outside of the specification, stop and repair the affected component.**

3. With the Ignition on, and engine not running, measure the voltage on the (F856)

5-volt Supply circuit in the CMP Sensor harness connector. Is the voltage between 4.5 and 5.2 volts?

4. If it is, measure the voltage on the (K44) CMP Signal circuit in the CMP Sensor harness connector. The voltage should be between 4.5 and 5.0 volts.

5. If it is, turn the ignition off and disconnect the C2 ECM harness connector.

✳✳ CAUTION

Do not probe the ECM harness connectors. Probing the ECM harness connectors will damage the ECM terminals resulting in poor terminal to pin connection. Install Miller Special Tool #8815 to perform diagnosis.

6. Measure the resistance of the (K900) Sensor ground circuit from the CMP Sensor harness connector to the appropriate terminal of special tool #8815. If the resistance is below 5.0 ohms, proceed to the next step, otherwise repair the open ground in the K900 sensor.

7. Measure the resistance between the (K44) CMP Signal circuit and the (F856) 5-volt Supply circuit in the CMP Sensor harness connector. If the resistance is below 5.0 ohms, repair the short between the (K44) CMP Signal circuit and the (F856) 5-volt Supply circuit.

➡**Inspect the Camshaft sprocket for damage per the Service Information. If a problem is found repair as necessary.**

CRANKSHAFT POSITION (CKP) SENSOR

LOCATION

See Figure 98.

The Crankshaft Position (CKP) sensor is mounted into the right rear side of the cylinder block.

VALVE LASH

ADJUSTMENT

These engines use hydraulic lifters. No maintenance or periodic adjustment is required.

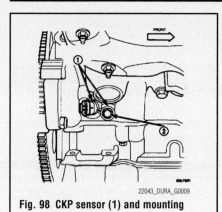

Fig. 98 CKP sensor (1) and mounting bolt (2)

OPERATION

The CKP sensor generates pulses that are the input sent to the Electronic Control Module (ECM). The ECM interprets the sensor input to determine the crankshaft position and engine speed.

The sensor is a hall effect device combined with an internal magnet. It is also sensitive to steel within a certain distance from it. A tonewheel is bolted to the engine crankshaft. The tonewheel has notches that cause a pulse to be generated when they pass under the sensor.

REMOVAL & INSTALLATION

1. Raise and safely support the vehicle.
2. Disconnect the sensor electrical connector.
3. Remove the Crankshaft Position (CKP) sensor mounting bolt.
4. Carefully twist the CKP sensor from the cylinder block.

To install:

5. Check the condition of the O-ring.
6. Clean out the machined hole in the engine block.
7. Apply a small amount of clean engine oil to the sensor O-ring.
8. Install the CKP sensor into the engine block with a slight rocking and twisting action.
9. Install the mounting bolt and tighten to 21 ft. lbs. (28 Nm).
10. Connect the electrical connector.
11. Lower the vehicle.

TESTING

1. Using a diagnostic scan tool, check for the presence of any Diagnostic Trouble Codes (DTCs). Record and address these codes as necessary.
2. Turn the ignition off. Disconnect the Crankshaft Position (CKP) Sensor harness connector.

➡ **If the test results fall outside of the specification, stop and repair the affected component.**

3. With the Ignition on, and engine not running, measure the voltage on the (F855) 5-volt Supply circuit in the CKP Sensor harness connector. Voltage should be between 4.5 and 5.2 volts.
4. If it is, measure the voltage on the (K24) CKP Signal circuit in the CKP Sensor harness connector. The sensor voltage should be approximately 5.0 volts (plus or minus .1 volt) with the connector disconnected.
5. If it is, turn the ignition off and disconnect the C2 ECM harness connector.

✳✳ CAUTION

Do not probe the ECM harness connectors. Probing the ECM harness connectors will damage the ECM terminals resulting in poor terminal to pin connection. Install Miller Special Tool #8815 to perform diagnosis.

6. Measure the resistance of the (K900) Sensor ground circuit from the CKP Sensor harness connector to the appropriate terminal of special tool #8815. Resistance should be below 5.0 ohms.
7. If it is, measure the resistance between the (K24) CKP Signal circuit and the (F855) 5-volt Supply circuit in the CKP Sensor harness connector. If the resistance below 5.0 ohms, repair the short between the (K24) CKP Signal circuit and the (F855) 5-volt Supply circuit.
8. If not, replace the crankshaft position sensor.

ELECTRONIC CONTROL MODULE (ECM)

LOCATION

The Electronic Control Module (ECM) is attached to the inner fender located in the engine compartment

OPERATION

The Electronic Control Module (ECM) receives input signals from various switches and sensors. Based on these inputs, the ECM regulates various engine and vehicle operations through different system components. These components are referred to as Electronic Control Module (ECM) Outputs. The sensors and switches that provide inputs to the ECM are considered Electronic Control Module (ECM) Inputs.

The ECM adjusts ignition timing based upon inputs it receives from sensors that react to: engine rpm, manifold absolute pressure, engine coolant temperature, throttle position, transmission gear selection (automatic transmission), vehicle speed and the brake switch.

The ECM adjusts idle speed based on inputs it receives from sensors that react to: throttle position, vehicle speed, transmission gear selection, engine coolant temperature and from inputs it receives from the air conditioning clutch switch and brake switch.

Based on inputs that it receives, the ECM adjusts ignition coil dwell. The ECM also adjusts the generator charge rate through control of the generator field and provides speed control operation.

REMOVAL & INSTALLATION

✳✳ WARNING

The use of a diagnostic scan tool is required the Electronic Control Module (ECM) is being in order to reprogram the new ECM.

1. Disconnect the negative battery cable.
2. Unplug the 38-way connectors from the ECM.

➡ **A locating pin is used in place of one of the mounting bolts.**

3. Pry the clip from the locating pin.
4. Remove the two remaining mounting bolts.
5. Remove the ECM from the vehicle.

To install:

6. Position the ECM to the body and install the two mounting bolts.

➡ **Position the ground strap in place before tightening the mounting bolts.**

7. Install the clip to the locating pin.
8. Tighten the mounting bolts to 35 inch lbs. (4 Nm).
9. Carefully plug in the 38-way connectors to the ECM.
10. Connect the negative battery cable.
11. Use a diagnostic scan tool to reprogram the ECM with the VIN and original mileage if ECM has been replaced.

TESTING

1. Start the engine and allow it to reach normal operating temperature. Using a diagnostic scan tool, check for the presence of any Diagnostic Trouble Codes (DTCs). Record and address these codes as necessary.
2. Refer to any Technical Service Bulletins (TSBs) that may apply.

3. Review the scan tool Freeze Frame information. If possible, try to duplicate the conditions under which the DTC set.

4. With the engine running at normal operating temperature, monitor the scan tool parameters related to the DTC while wiggling the wire harness. Look for parameter values to change and/or a DTC to set. Turn the ignition off.

5. Visually inspect the related wire harness. Disconnect all the related harness connectors. Look for any chafed, pierced, pinched, partially broken wires and broken, bent, pushed out, or corroded terminals. Perform a voltage drop test on the related circuits between the suspected inoperative component and the ECM.

✳✳ CAUTION

Do not probe the ECM harness connectors. Probing the ECM harness connectors will damage the ECM terminals resulting in poor terminal to pin connection. Install Miller Special Tool #8815 to perform diagnosis.

6. Inspect and clean all ECM, engine, and chassis grounds that are related to the most current DTC.

7. If numerous trouble codes were set, use a wire schematic and look for any common ground or supply circuits.

8. For any Relay DTCs, actuate the Relay with the scan tool and wiggle the related wire harness to try to interrupt the actuation.

9. For intermittent Evaporative Emission trouble codes perform a visual and physical inspection of the related parts including hoses and the Fuel Filler cap.

10. Use the scan tool to perform a System Test if one applies to failing component. A co-pilot, data recorder, and/or lab scope should be used to help diagnose intermittent conditions.

ENGINE COOLANT TEMPERATURE (ECT) SENSOR

LOCATION

The Engine Coolant Temperature (ECT) sensor is installed into a water jacket at the front of the intake manifold.

OPERATION

The ECT sensor provides an input to the Electronic Control Module (ECM). As coolant temperature varies, the sensor resistance changes, resulting in a different input voltage to the ECM. When the engine is cold, the ECM will demand slightly richer air-fuel mixtures and higher idle speeds until normal operating temperatures are reached.

The engine coolant sensor input also determines operation of the low and high speed cooling fans.

REMOVAL & INSTALLATION

1. Drain the cooling system.
2. Disconnect the sensor electrical connector.
3. Remove the Engine Coolant Temperature (ECT) sensor.

To install:

4. Apply thread sealant to the sensor threads.
5. Install the ECT sensor into the engine block and tighten the mounting bolt to 8 ft. lbs. (11 Nm).
6. Connect the electrical connector.
7. Refill the cooling system to the correct level.

TESTING

1. Turn the ignition **OFF**. If possible, allow the vehicle to sit with the ignition off for more than 8 hours in an environment where the temperature is consistent and above 20°F (-7°C).

2. Test drive the vehicle. The vehicle must exceed 30 mph (48 km/h) during the test drive. Do not cycle the ignition off when the test drive is completed.

3. With a scan tool, select View DTCs.

4. Turn the ignition off. Allow the vehicle to sit with the ignition off in an environment where the temperature is consistent and above 20°F (-7°C) until the engine coolant temperature is equal to ambient temperature. Turn the ignition on. With a scan tool, compare the AAT, ECT, and IAT sensor values.

5. If the ECT sensor value is not within 18°F (10°C) of the other two sensor values, perform the following:

6. Refer to any Technical Service Bulletins (TSBs) that may apply.

7. Review the scan tool Freeze Frame information. If possible, try to duplicate the conditions under which the DTC set.

8. With the engine running at normal operating temperature, monitor the scan tool parameters related to the DTC while wiggling the wire harness. Look for parameter values to change and/or a DTC to set. Turn the ignition off.

9. Visually inspect the related wire harness. Disconnect all the related harness connectors. Look for any chafed, pierced, pinched, partially broken wires and broken, bent, pushed out, or corroded terminals.

Perform a voltage drop test on the related circuits between the suspected inoperative component and the ECM.

✳✳ CAUTION

Do not probe the ECM harness connectors. Probing the ECM harness connectors will damage the ECM terminals resulting in poor terminal to pin connection. Install Miller Special Tool #8815 to perform diagnosis.

10. Inspect and clean all ECM, engine, and chassis grounds that are related to the most current DTC.

11. If numerous trouble codes were set, use a wire schematic and look for any common ground or supply circuits.

12. For any Relay DTCs, actuate the Relay with the scan tool and wiggle the related wire harness to try to interrupt the actuation.

13. For intermittent Evaporative Emission trouble codes perform a visual and physical inspection of the related parts including hoses and the Fuel Filler cap.

14. Use the scan tool to perform a System Test if one applies to failing component. A co-pilot, data recorder, and/or lab scope should be used to help diagnose intermittent conditions.

HEATED OXYGEN (HO2S) SENSOR

LOCATION

See Figure 99.

If equipped with a Federal Emission Package, two sensors are used: upstream (referred to as 1/1) and downstream (referred to as 1/2). With this emission package, the upstream sensor (1/1) is located just before the main catalytic converter. The downstream sensor (1/2) is located just after the main catalytic converter.

If equipped with a California Emission Package, 4 sensors are used: 2 upstream (referred to as 1/1 and 2/1) and 2 downstream (referred to as 1/2 and 2/2). With this emission package, the right upstream sensor (2/1) is located in the right exhaust downpipe just before the mini-catalytic converter. The left upstream sensor (1/1) is located in the left exhaust downpipe just before the mini-catalytic converter. The right downstream sensor (2/2) is located in the right exhaust downpipe just after the mini-catalytic converter, and before the main catalytic converter. The left downstream sensor (1/2) is located in the left exhaust downpipe just

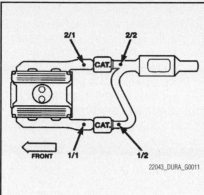

Fig. 99 Oxygen sensor mounting points

after the mini-catalytic converter, and before the main catalytic converter.

OPERATION

An O2 sensor is a galvanic battery that provides the ECM with a voltage signal (0-1 volt) inversely proportional to the amount of oxygen in the exhaust. In other words, if the oxygen content is low, the voltage output is high; if the oxygen content is high the output voltage is low. The ECM uses this information to adjust injector pulse-width to achieve the 14.7 to1 air/fuel ratio necessary for proper engine operation and to control emissions.

The O2 sensor must have a source of oxygen from outside of the exhaust stream for comparison. Current O2 sensors receive their fresh oxygen (outside air) supply through the O2 sensor case housing.

Four wires (circuits) are used on each O2 sensor: a 12volt feed circuit for the sensor heating element; a ground circuit for the heater element; a low-noise sensor return circuit to the ECM, and an input circuit from the sensor back to the ECM to detect sensor operation.

REMOVAL & INSTALLATION

1. Raise and safely support the vehicle.
2. Disconnect the wire connector from oxygen sensor.

❋❋ WARNING

When disconnecting sensor electrical connector, do not pull directly on wire going into sensor.

3. Remove the sensor with an oxygen sensor removal and installation tool.
4. Clean threads in exhaust pipe using appropriate tap.

To install:

➡**Threads of new oxygen sensors are factory coated with anti-seize compound.**

❋❋ WARNING

Do not add any additional anti-seize compound to the threads of a new oxygen sensor.

5. Install the oxygen sensor and tighten to 22 ft. lbs. (30 Nm).
6. Connect the electrical connector.
7. Lower the vehicle.

TESTING

1. Start the engine and allow it to idle for at least 60 seconds. Using a diagnostic scan tool, check for the presence of any Diagnostic Trouble Codes (DTCs). Record and address these codes as necessary.
2. Turn the ignition off, allow the sensor to cool down to room temperature disconnect the oxygen sensor wiring harness. Measure the resistance across the sensor heater control terminal and ground terminal. If resistance is not between 2 and 30 ohms, replace the sensor.
3. Refer to any Technical Service Bulletins (TSBs) that may apply.
4. Review the scan tool Freeze Frame information. If possible, try to duplicate the conditions under which the DTC set.
5. With the engine running at normal operating temperature, monitor the scan tool parameters related to the DTC while wiggling the wire harness. Look for parameter values to change and/or a DTC to set. Turn the ignition off.
6. Visually inspect the related wire harness. Disconnect all the related harness connectors. Look for any chafed, pierced, pinched, partially broken wires and broken, bent, pushed out, or corroded terminals. Perform a voltage drop test on the related circuits between the suspected inoperative component and the PCM.

❋❋ CAUTION

Do not probe the PCM harness connectors. Probing the PCM harness connectors will damage the PCM terminals resulting in poor terminal to pin connection. Install Miller Special Tool #8815 to perform diagnosis.

7. Inspect and clean all PCM, engine, and chassis grounds that are related to the most current DTC.
8. If numerous trouble codes were set, use a wire schematic and look for any common ground or supply circuits.
9. For any Relay DTCs, actuate the Relay with the scan tool and wiggle the related wire harness to try to interrupt the actuation.

10. For intermittent Evaporative Emission trouble codes perform a visual and physical inspection of the related parts including hoses and the Fuel Filler cap.
11. Use the scan tool to perform a System Test if one applies to failing component. A co-pilot, data recorder, and/or lab scope should be used to help diagnose intermittent conditions.

INTAKE AIR TEMPERATURE (IAT) SENSOR

LOCATION

The Intake Air Temperature (IAT) sensor is installed in the air inlet tube.

OPERATION

The IAT sensor is a two-wire Negative Thermal Coefficient (NTC) sensor. Meaning, as inlet air temperatures increase, resistance (voltage) in the sensor decreases. As temperature decreases, resistance (voltage) in the sensor increases.

The IAT sensor provides an input voltage to the Electronic Control Module (ECM) indicating the density of the air entering the intake manifold based upon intake manifold temperature. At key-on, a 5volt power circuit is supplied to the sensor from the ECM. The sensor is grounded at the ECM through a low-noise, sensor-return circuit.

REMOVAL & INSTALLATION

See Figure 100.

1. Disconnect the electrical connector form the Intake Air Temperature (IAT) sensor.
2. Clean any dirt from the air inlet tube at the sensor base.
3. Gently lift the small plastic release tab and rotate the sensor about ¼ turn counterclockwise to remove.

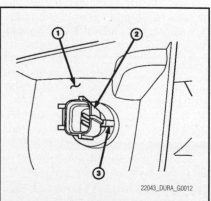

Fig. 100 The IAT sensor (2) is located in the air inlet (1). Lift the tab (3) to remove it

To install:

4. Check the condition of the sensor O–ring.
5. Clean the sensor mounting hole.
6. Position the sensor into the intake air tube and rotate clockwise until the release tab clicks into place.
7. Install the electrical connector.

TESTING

1. Turn the ignition off. If possible, allow the vehicle to sit with the ignition off for more than 8 hours in an environment where the temperature is consistent and above 20°F (-7°C).
2. Test drive the vehicle. The vehicle must exceed 30 mph (48 km/h) during the test drive. Do not cycle the ignition off when the test drive is completed.
3. With a scan tool, select View DTCs.
4. If a DTC is not active, perform the following:
5. Refer to any Technical Service Bulletins (TSBs) that may apply.
6. Review the scan tool Freeze Frame information. If possible, try to duplicate the conditions under which the DTC set.
7. With the engine running at normal operating temperature, monitor the scan tool parameters related to the DTC while wiggling the wire harness. Look for parameter values to change and/or a DTC to set. Turn the ignition off.
8. Visually inspect the related wire harness. Disconnect all the related harness connectors. Look for any chafed, pierced, pinched, partially broken wires and broken, bent, pushed out, or corroded terminals. Perform a voltage drop test on the related circuits between the suspected inoperative component and the ECM.

⁂ CAUTION

Do not probe the ECM harness connectors. Probing the ECM harness connectors will damage the ECM terminals resulting in poor terminal to pin connection. Install Miller Special Tool #8815 to perform diagnosis.

9. Inspect and clean all ECM, engine, and chassis grounds that are related to the most current DTC.
10. If numerous trouble codes were set, use a wire schematic and look for any common ground or supply circuits.
11. For any Relay DTCs, actuate the Relay with the scan tool and wiggle the related wire harness to try to interrupt the actuation.
12. For intermittent Evaporative Emission trouble codes perform a visual and physical inspection of the related parts including hoses and the Fuel Filler cap.
13. Use the scan tool to perform a System Test if one applies to failing component. A co-pilot, data recorder, and/or lab scope should be used to help diagnose intermittent conditions.

KNOCK SENSOR (KS)

LOCATION

Two knock sensors are bolted into the engine block under the intake manifold.

OPERATION

Two knock sensors are used; one for each cylinder bank. When the knock sensor detects a knock in one of the cylinders on the corresponding bank, it sends an input signal to the Electronic Control Module (ECM). In response, the ECM retards ignition timing for all cylinders by a scheduled amount.

Knock sensors contain a piezoelectric material which constantly vibrates and sends an input voltage (signal) to the ECM while the engine operates. As the intensity of the crystal's vibration increases, the knock sensor output voltage also increases.

REMOVAL & INSTALLATION

1. Disconnect the knock sensor dual pigtail harness from engine wiring harness. This connection is made near rear of engine.
2. Remove the intake manifold
3. Remove the Knock Sensor (KS) mounting bolts.
4. Remove the sensors from engine.

To install:

5. Thoroughly clean the KS mounting holes.
6. Install the sensors into the engine block. Tighten the mounting bolts to 15 ft. lbs. (20 Nm).
7. Install the intake manifold.
8. Connect the KS wiring harness to the engine wiring harness at the rear of the engine.

TESTING

1. Start the engine and allow it to reach normal operating temperature. Using a diagnostic scan tool, check for the presence of any Diagnostic Trouble Codes (DTCs). Record and address these codes as necessary.
2. Refer to any Technical Service Bulletins (TSBs) that may apply.
3. Review the scan tool Freeze Frame information. If possible, try to duplicate the conditions under which the DTC set.
4. With the engine running at normal operating temperature, monitor the scan tool parameters related to the DTC while wiggling the wire harness. Look for parameter values to change and/or a DTC to set. Turn the ignition off.
5. Visually inspect the related wire harness. Disconnect all the related harness connectors. Look for any chafed, pierced, pinched, partially broken wires and broken, bent, pushed out, or corroded terminals. Perform a voltage drop test on the related circuits between the suspected inoperative component and the ECM.

⁂ CAUTION

Do not probe the ECM harness connectors. Probing the ECM harness connectors will damage the ECM terminals resulting in poor terminal to pin connection. Install Miller Special Tool #8815 to perform diagnosis.

6. Inspect and clean all ECM, engine, and chassis grounds that are related to the most current DTC.
7. If numerous trouble codes were set, use a wire schematic and look for any common ground or supply circuits.
8. For any Relay DTCs, actuate the Relay with the scan tool and wiggle the related wire harness to try to interrupt the actuation.
9. For intermittent Evaporative Emission trouble codes perform a visual and physical inspection of the related parts including hoses and the Fuel Filler cap.
10. Use the scan tool to perform a System Test if one applies to failing component. A co-pilot, data recorder, and/or lab scope should be used to help diagnose intermittent conditions.

MANIFOLD ABSOLUTE PRESSURE (MAP) SENSOR

LOCATION

The Manifold Absolute Pressure (MAP) sensor is mounted to the front of the intake manifold with two bolts.

OPERATION

The MAP sensor is used as an input to the Electronic Control Module (ECM). It contains a silicon based sensing unit to provide data on the manifold vacuum that draws the air/fuel mixture into the combustion chamber. The ECM requires this information to determine injector pulse width and spark advance. When manifold absolute pressure (MAP) equals Barometric pressure, the pulse width will be at maximum.

A 5-volt reference is supplied from the ECM and returns a voltage signal to the ECM that reflects manifold pressure. The zero pressure reading is 0.5V and full scale is 4.5V. For a pressure swing of 015 psi, the voltage changes 4.0V. To operate the sensor, it is supplied a regulated 4.8 to 5.1 volts. Ground is provided through the low-noise, sensor return circuit at the ECM.

The MAP sensor input is the number one contributor to fuel injector pulse width. The most important function of the MAP sensor is to determine barometric pressure. The ECM needs to know if the vehicle is at sea level or at a higher altitude, because the air density changes with altitude. It will also help to correct for varying barometric pressure. Barometric pressure and altitude have a direct inverse correlation; as altitude goes up, barometric goes down. At key-on, the ECM powers up and looks at MAP voltage, and based upon the voltage it sees, it knows the current barometric pressure (relative to altitude). Once the engine starts, the ECM looks at the voltage again, continuously every 12 milliseconds, and compares the current voltage to what it was at key-on. The difference between current voltage and what it was at Key On is the manifold vacuum.

During key-on (engine not running) the sensor reads (updates) barometric pressure. A normal range can be obtained by monitoring a known good sensor.

As the altitude increases, the air becomes thinner (less oxygen). If a vehicle is started and driven to a very different altitude than where it was at key-on, the barometric pressure needs to be updated. Any time the ECM sees Wide Open Throttle (WOT), based upon Throttle Position Sensor (TPS) angle and RPM, it will update barometric pressure in the MAP memory cell. With periodic updates, the ECM can make its calculations more effectively.

REMOVAL & INSTALLATION

See Figure 101.

1. Disconnect the sensor electrical connector.
2. Clean the area around the Manifold Absolute Pressure (MAP) sensor.
3. Remove the two mounting screws.
4. Remove the MAP sensor from the intake manifold.

To install:

5. Inspect the condition of the sensor O–ring and replace if necessary.
6. Position the MAP sensor into the manifold and install the two mounting screws.
7. Connect the electrical connector.

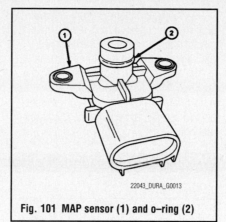

Fig. 101 MAP sensor (1) and o–ring (2)

TESTING

1. Start the engine and allow it to reach normal operating temperature. Using a diagnostic scan tool, check for the presence of any Diagnostic Trouble Codes (DTCs). Record and address these codes as necessary.
2. Refer to any Technical Service Bulletins (TSBs) that may apply.
3. Review the scan tool Freeze Frame information. If possible, try to duplicate the conditions under which the DTC set.
4. With the engine running at normal operating temperature, monitor the scan tool parameters related to the DTC while wiggling the wire harness. Look for parameter values to change and/or a DTC to set. Turn the ignition off.
5. Visually inspect the related wire harness. Disconnect all the related harness connectors. Look for any chafed, pierced, pinched, partially broken wires and broken, bent, pushed out, or corroded terminals. Perform a voltage drop test on the related circuits between the suspected inoperative component and the ECM.

✳✳ CAUTION

Do not probe the ECM harness connectors. Probing the ECM harness connectors will damage the ECM terminals resulting in poor terminal to pin connection. Install Miller Special Tool #8815 to perform diagnosis.

6. Inspect and clean all ECM, engine, and chassis grounds that are related to the most current DTC.
7. If numerous trouble codes were set, use a wire schematic and look for any common ground or supply circuits.
8. For any Relay DTCs, actuate the Relay with the scan tool and wiggle the related wire harness to try to interrupt the actuation.
9. For intermittent Evaporative Emission trouble codes perform a visual and physical inspection of the related parts including hoses and the Fuel Filler cap.
10. Use the scan tool to perform a System Test if one applies to failing component. A co-pilot, data recorder, and/or lab scope should be used to help diagnose intermittent conditions.

THROTTLE POSITION SENSOR (TPS)

LOCATION

The Throttle Position Sensor (TPS) is mounted on the throttle body and connected to the throttle blade shaft.

OPERATION

The Throttle Position Sensor (TPS) is a 3-wire variable resistor that provides the Electronic Control Module (ECM) with an input signal (voltage) that represents the throttle blade position of the throttle body. The sensor is connected to the throttle blade shaft. As the position of the throttle blade changes, the resistance (output voltage) of the TPS changes.

The ECM supplies approximately 5 volts to the TPS. The TPS output voltage (input signal to the ECM) represents the throttle blade position. The ECM receives an input signal voltage from the TPS. This will vary in an approximate range of from .26 volts at minimum throttle opening (idle), to 4.49 volts at wide-open throttle. Along with inputs from other sensors, the ECM uses the TPS input to determine current engine operating conditions. In response to engine operating conditions, the ECM will adjust fuel injector pulse width and ignition timing.

REMOVAL & INSTALLATION

1. Remove the air intake tube.
2. Disconnect the Throttle Position Sensor (TPS) electrical connector.
3. Remove the TPS mounting screws.
4. Remove the TPS.

To install:

➡**The throttle shaft end of throttle body slides into a socket in TPS. The TPS must be installed so that it can be rotated a few degrees. If sensor will not rotate, install the sensor with throttle shaft on other side of socket tangs. The TPS will be under slight tension when rotated.**

5. Install the TPS and tighten the mounting screws to 60 inch lbs. (7 Nm).
6. Connect the TPS electrical connector.

7. Manually operate the throttle by hand to check for any TPS binding before starting the engine.

8. Install the air intake tube.

TESTING

1. Start the engine and allow it to reach normal operating temperature. Using a diagnostic scan tool, check for the presence of any Diagnostic Trouble Codes (DTCs). Record and address these codes as necessary.

2. Refer to any Technical Service Bulletins (TSBs) that may apply.

3. Review the scan tool Freeze Frame information. If possible, try to duplicate the conditions under which the DTC set.

4. With the engine running at normal operating temperature, monitor the scan tool parameters related to the DTC while wiggling the wire harness. Look for parameter values to change and/or a DTC to set. Turn the ignition off.

5. Visually inspect the related wire harness. Disconnect all the related harness connectors. Look for any chafed, pierced, pinched, partially broken wires and broken, bent, pushed out, or corroded terminals. Perform a voltage drop test on the related circuits between the suspected inoperative component and the ECM.

❋❋ CAUTION

Do not probe the ECM harness connectors. Probing the ECM harness connectors will damage the ECM terminals resulting in poor terminal to pin connection. Install Miller Special Tool #8815 to perform diagnosis.

6. Inspect and clean all ECM, engine, and chassis grounds that are related to the most current DTC.

7. If numerous trouble codes were set, use a wire schematic and look for any common ground or supply circuits.

8. For any Relay DTCs, actuate the Relay with the scan tool and wiggle the related wire harness to try to interrupt the actuation.

9. For intermittent Evaporative Emission trouble codes perform a visual and physical inspection of the related parts including hoses and the Fuel Filler cap.

10. Use the scan tool to perform a System Test if one applies to failing component. A co-pilot, data recorder, and/or lab scope should be used to help diagnose intermittent conditions.

VEHICLE SPEED SENSOR (VSS)

LOCATION

The Vehicle Speed Sensor (VSS) is located on the left side of the transmission case. The VSS may also be referred to as an output shaft speed sensor.

OPERATION

The VSS generates an AC signal as its coil is excited by rotation of the rear planetary carrier lugs. The Transmission Control Module (TCM) interprets this information as output shaft RPM.

REMOVAL & INSTALLATION

1. Raise and safely support the vehicle.

2. Place a suitable catch pan under the transmission for any fluid.

3. Remove the wiring connector from the output speed sensor.

4. Remove the mounting bolt and remove the speed sensor from the transmission case.

To install:

5. Install the speed sensor into the transmission case and tighten the bolt to 105 inch lbs. (12 Nm).

6. Install the wiring connector to the speed sensor.

7. Verify the proper transmission fluid level and refill as necessary.

8. Lower the vehicle.

TESTING

1. Start the engine and allow it to reach normal operating temperature. Using a diagnostic scan tool, check for the presence of any Diagnostic Trouble Codes

(DTCs). Record and address these codes as necessary.

2. Refer to any Technical Service Bulletins (TSBs) that may apply.

3. Review the scan tool Freeze Frame information. If possible, try to duplicate the conditions under which the DTC set.

4. With the engine running at normal operating temperature, monitor the scan tool parameters related to the DTC while wiggling the wire harness. Look for parameter values to change and/or a DTC to set. Turn the ignition off.

5. Visually inspect the related wire harness. Disconnect all the related harness connectors. Look for any chafed, pierced, pinched, partially broken wires and broken, bent, pushed out, or corroded terminals. Perform a voltage drop test on the related circuits between the suspected inoperative component and the ECM.

❋❋ CAUTION

Do not probe the ECM harness connectors. Probing the PCM harness connectors will damage the PCM terminals resulting in poor terminal to pin connection. Install Miller Special Tool #8815 to perform diagnosis.

6. Inspect and clean all ECM, engine, and chassis grounds that are related to the most current DTC.

7. If numerous trouble codes were set, use a wire schematic and look for any common ground or supply circuits.

8. For any Relay DTCs, actuate the Relay with the scan tool and wiggle the related wire harness to try to interrupt the actuation.

9. For intermittent Evaporative Emission trouble codes perform a visual and physical inspection of the related parts including hoses and the Fuel Filler cap.

10. Use the scan tool to perform a System Test if one applies to failing component. A co-pilot, data recorder, and/or lab scope should be used to help diagnose intermittent conditions.

FUEL SYSTEM SERVICE PRECAUTIONS

Safety is the most important factor when performing not only fuel system maintenance but any type of maintenance. Failure to conduct maintenance and repairs in a safe manner may result in serious personal injury or death. Maintenance and testing of the vehicle's fuel system components can be accomplished safely and effectively by adhering to the following rules and guidelines.

• To avoid the possibility of fire and personal injury, always disconnect the negative battery cable unless the repair or test procedure requires that battery voltage be applied.

• Always relieve the fuel system pressure prior to disconnecting any fuel system component (injector, fuel rail, pressure regulator, etc.), fitting or fuel line connection. Exercise extreme caution whenever relieving fuel system pressure to avoid exposing skin, face and eyes to fuel spray. Please be advised that fuel under pressure may penetrate the skin or any part of the body that it contacts.

• Always place a shop towel or cloth around the fitting or connection prior to loosening to absorb any excess fuel due to spillage. Ensure that all fuel spillage (should it occur) is quickly removed from engine surfaces. Ensure that all fuel soaked cloths or towels are deposited into a suitable waste container.

• Always keep a dry chemical (Class B) fire extinguisher near the work area.

• Do not allow fuel spray or fuel vapors to come into contact with a spark or open flame.

• Always use a back-up wrench when loosening and tightening fuel line connection fittings. This will prevent unnecessary stress and torsion to fuel line piping.

• Always replace worn fuel fitting O–rings with new Do not substitute fuel hose or equivalent where fuel pipe is installed.

Before servicing the vehicle, make sure to also refer to the precautions in the beginning of this section as well.

RELIEVING FUEL SYSTEM PRESSURE

1. Before servicing the vehicle, refer to the precautions in the beginning of this manual.

2. Remove the fuel tank filler cap to release any fuel tank pressure.

3. Remove the fuel pump relay from the Power Distribution Center (PDC).

4. Start and run the engine until it stops.

5. Continue to restart the engine until it will not run.

6. Turn the key to **OFF**.

7. Unplug the connector from any injector and connect a jumper wire from either injector terminal to the positive battery terminal. Connect another jumper wire to the other terminal and momentarily touch the other end to the negative battery terminal.

✳✳ WARNING

Just touch the jumper to the battery. Powering the injector for more than a few seconds will permanently damage it.

8. Place a rag below the quick-disconnect coupling at the fuel rail and disconnect it.

FUEL FILTER

REMOVAL & INSTALLATION
See Figure 102.

These vehicles incorporate the use of a fuel pump module which comprises:
• An internal fuel filter
• A separate fuel pick-up, or inlet filter
• A fuel pressure regulator
• An electric fuel pump

• A fuel gauge sending unit (fuel level sensor)

If the filter(s), regulator, pump or sending unit requires service, the fuel pump module must be replaced.

FUEL INJECTORS

REMOVAL & INSTALLATION

3.7L Engine
See Figures 103 and 104.

✳✳ CAUTION

The fuel system is under constant pressure even with engine off. Before servicing fuel rail, fuel system pressure must be released.

✳✳ CAUTION

The left and right fuel rails are replaced as an assembly. Do not attempt to separate rail halves at connector tube. Due to design of tube, it does not use any clamps. Never attempt to install a clamping device of any kind to tube. When removing fuel rail assembly for any reason, be careful not to bend or kink tube.

1. Before servicing the vehicle, refer to the precautions in the beginning of this manual.

2. Remove fuel tank filler tube cap.

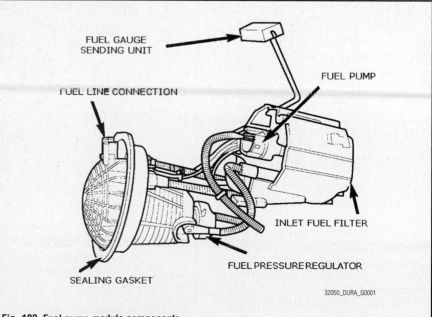

Fig. 102 Fuel pump module components

FUEL GAUGE SENDING UNIT

FUEL PUMP

FUEL LINE CONNECTION

INLET FUEL FILTER

FUEL PRESSURE REGULATOR

SEALING GASKET

32050_DURA_G0001

3. Perform Fuel System Pressure Release Procedure.

4. Remove negative battery cable at battery.

5. Remove air duct at throttle body air box.

6. Remove air box at throttle body.

7. Disconnect fuel line latch clip and fuel line at fuel rail. A special tool will be necessary for fuel line disconnection.

8. Remove necessary vacuum lines at throttle body.

9. Disconnect electrical connectors at all 6 fuel injectors. To remove connector, push red colored slider away from injector. While pushing slider, depress tab and remove connector from injector. The factory fuel injection wiring harness is numerically tagged (INJ 1, INJ 2, etc.) for injector position identification. If harness is not tagged, note wiring location before removal.

10. Disconnect electrical connectors at throttle body sensors.

11. Remove 6 ignition coils.

12. Remove 4 fuel rail mounting bolts.

13. Gently rock and pull left side of fuel rail until fuel injectors just start to clear machined holes in cylinder head. Gently rock and pull right side of rail until injectors just start to clear cylinder head holes. Repeat this procedure (left/right) until all injectors have cleared cylinder head holes.

14. Remove fuel rail (with injectors attached) from engine.

15. Disconnect clip(s) that retain fuel injector(s) to fuel rail.

To install:

16. Apply a small amount of clean engine oil to each fuel injector o–ring. This will help in fuel rail installation.

17. Install injector(s) and injector clip(s) to fuel rail.

18. Apply a small amount of engine oil to each fuel injector o–ring. This will help in fuel rail installation.

19. Position fuel rail/fuel injector assembly to machined injector openings in cylinder head.

20. Guide each injector into cylinder head. Be careful not to tear injector o–rings.

21. Push right side of fuel rail down until fuel injectors have bottomed on cylinder head shoulder. Push left fuel rail down until injectors have bottomed on cylinder head shoulder.

22. Install 4 fuel rail mounting bolts and tighten to 27 Nm (20 ft. lbs.).

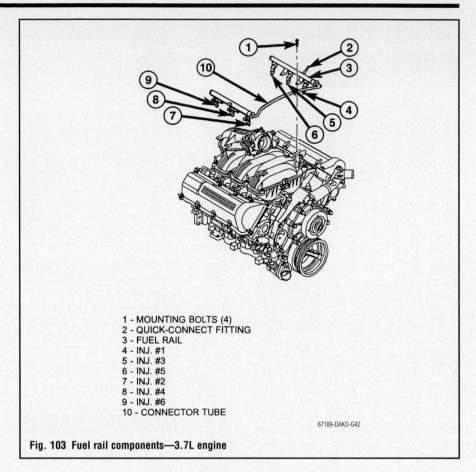

1 - MOUNTING BOLTS (4)
2 - QUICK-CONNECT FITTING
3 - FUEL RAIL
4 - INJ. #1
5 - INJ. #3
6 - INJ. #5
7 - INJ. #2
8 - INJ. #4
9 - INJ. #6
10 - CONNECTOR TUBE

67189-DAKO-G42

Fig. 103 Fuel rail components—3.7L engine

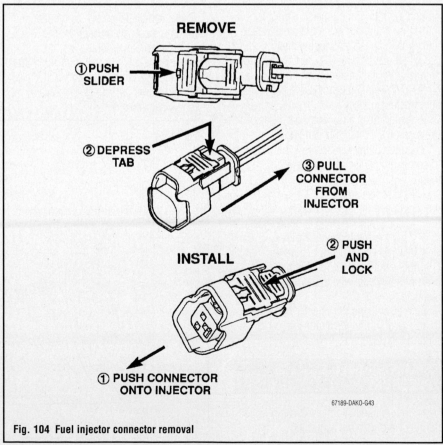

REMOVE

① PUSH SLIDER

② DEPRESS TAB

③ PULL CONNECTOR FROM INJECTOR

INSTALL

② PUSH AND LOCK

① PUSH CONNECTOR ONTO INJECTOR

67189-DAKO-G43

Fig. 104 Fuel injector connector removal

23. Install ignition coils.
24. Connect electrical connectors to throttle body.
25. Connect electrical connectors to MAP and IAT sensors.
26. Connect electrical connectors at all fuel injectors. To install connector, push connector onto injector and then push and lock red colored slider. Verify connector is locked to injector by lightly tugging on connector.
27. Connect vacuum lines to throttle body.
28. Connect fuel line latch clip and fuel line to fuel rail.
29. Connect wiring to rear of generator.
30. Install air box to throttle body.
31. Install air duct to air box.
32. Connect battery cable to battery.
33. Start engine and check for leaks.

4.7L Engine

See Figure 105.

> ✳✳ **CAUTION**
>
> **The fuel system is under constant pressure even with engine off. Before servicing fuel rail, fuel system pressure must be released.**

> ✳✳ **WARNING**
>
> **The left and right fuel rails are replaced as an assembly. Do not attempt to separate rail halves at connector tube. Due to design of tube, it does not use any clamps. Never attempt to install a clamping device of any kind to tube. When removing fuel rail assembly for any reason, be careful not to bend or kink tube.**

1. Before servicing the vehicle, refer to the precautions in the beginning of this manual.
2. Remove fuel tank filler tube cap.
3. Perform Fuel System Pressure Release Procedure.
4. Remove negative battery cable at battery.
5. Remove air duct at throttle body air box.
6. Remove air box at throttle body.
7. Remove wiring at rear of generator.
8. Disconnect fuel line latch clip and fuel line at fuel rail. A special tool will be necessary for fuel line disconnection.
9. Remove vacuum lines at throttle body.
10. Disconnect electrical connectors at all 8 fuel injectors. To remove, push red colored slider away from injector. While pushing slider, depress tab and remove

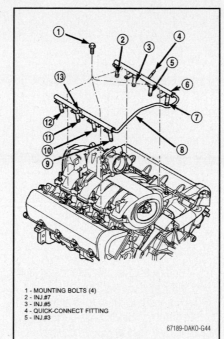

1 - MOUNTING BOLTS (4)
2 - INJ.#7
3 - INJ.#5
4 - QUICK-CONNECT FITTING
5 - INJ.#3

67189-DAKO-G44

Fig. 105 Fuel rail components—4.7L engine

connector from injector. The factory fuel injection wiring harness is numerically tagged (INJ 1, INJ 2, etc.) for injector position identification. If harness is not tagged, note wiring location before removal.
11. Disconnect electrical connectors at throttle body.
12. Disconnect electrical connectors at MAP and IAT sensors.
13. Remove first three ignition coils on each bank (cylinders #1, 3, 5, 2, 4 and 6).
14. Remove 4 fuel rail mounting bolts.
15. Gently rock and pull left side of fuel rail until fuel injectors just start to clear machined holes in cylinder head. Gently rock and pull right side of rail until injectors just start to clear cylinder head holes. Repeat this procedure (left/right) until all injectors have cleared cylinder head holes.
16. Remove fuel rail (with injectors attached) from engine.
17. Disconnect clip(s) that retain fuel injector(s) to fuel rail.

To install:

18. Apply a small amount of clean engine oil to each fuel injector O—ring. This will help in fuel rail installation.
19. Install injector(s) and injector clip(s) to fuel rail.
20. Apply a small amount of engine oil to each fuel injector o—ring. This will help in fuel rail installation.

21. Position fuel rail/fuel injector assembly to machined injector openings in cylinder head.
22. Guide each injector into cylinder head. Be careful not to tear injector o—rings.
23. Push right side of fuel rail down until fuel injectors have bottomed on cylinder head shoulder. Push left fuel rail down until injectors have bottomed on cylinder head shoulder.
24. Install 4 fuel rail mounting bolts and tighten to 27 Nm (20 ft. lbs.).
25. Install ignition coils.
26. Connect electrical connectors to throttle body.
27. Connect electrical connectors to MAP and IAT sensors.
28. Connect electrical connectors at all fuel injectors. To install connector, push connector onto injector and then push and lock red colored slider. Verify connector is locked to injector by lightly tugging on connector.
29. Connect vacuum lines to throttle body.
30. Connect fuel line latch clip and fuel line to fuel rail.
31. Connect wiring to rear of generator.
32. Install air box to throttle body.
33. Install air duct to air box.
34. Connect battery cable to battery.
35. Start engine and check for leaks.

FUEL PUMP

REMOVAL & INSTALLATION

See Figure 106.

1. Before servicing the vehicle, refer to the precautions in the beginning of this manual.
2. Release fuel system pressure.
3. Raise vehicle.
4. Remove left rear tire/wheel
5. Remove plastic fender liner in front of left-rear tire/wheel.
6. Thoroughly clean area around fuel fill fitting and rubber fuel fill hose at fuel tank.
7. Loosen clamp and disconnect rubber fuel fill hose at fuel tank fitting. Using an approved gas holding tank, drain fuel tank through this fitting.
8. Disconnect vent line from tank.
9. If equipped, remove fuel tank skid plate.
10. Disconnect NVLD, ORVR and EVAP lines at front of tank.
11. Disconnect electrical connector at NVLD pump.

12. Support tank with a hydraulic jack.

13. Remove two fuel tank strap nuts and remove both tank support straps.

14. Carefully lower tank a few inches and disconnect fuel pump module electrical connector at top of tank. To disconnect electrical connector: Push upward on red colored tab to unlock. Push on black colored tab while removing connector.

15. Disconnect fuel line at fuel pump module fitting by pressing on tabs at side of quick-connect fitting.

16. Continue to lower tank for removal.

17. Note rotational position of module before attempting removal. An indexing arrow is located on top of module for this purpose.

18. Position Special Tool 9340 into notches on outside edge of lockring.

19. Install ½ inch drive breaker bar to tool 9340.

20. Rotate breaker bar counter-clockwise to remove lockring.

21. Remove lockring. The module will spring up slightly when lockring is removed.

22. Remove module from fuel tank. Be careful not to bend float arm while removing.

To install:

23. Using a new seal (gasket), position fuel pump module into opening in fuel tank.

24. Position lockring over top of fuel pump module.

25. Rotate module until embossed alignment arrow points to center alignment mark. This step must be performed to prevent float from contacting side of fuel tank. Also be sure fuel fitting on top of pump module is pointed to driver's side of vehicle.

26. Install Special Tool 9340 to lockring.

27. Install breaker into Special Tool 9340.

28. Tighten lockring (clockwise) until all seven notches have engaged.

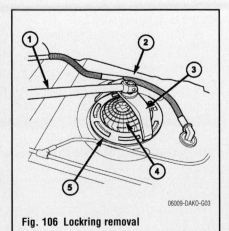

Fig. 106 Lockring removal

06009-DAKO-G03

29. Install fuel tank.

30. Position fuel tank to hydraulic jack.

31. Raise tank until positioned near body.

32. Connect fuel pump module electrical connector at top of tank.

33. Connect NVLD pump electrical connector to NVLD pump.

34. Connect fuel line quick-connect fitting to pump module.

35. Continue raising tank until positioned snug to body.

36. Install and position both tank support straps. Install two fuel tank strap nuts and tighten to 30 ft. lbs. (41 Nm).

37. Connect EVAP, ORVR and NVLD lines at front of tank.

38. Connect vent line.

39. Connect rubber fill hose to fuel tank fitting and tighten hose clamps.

40. The vapor/vacuum lines and hoses must be firmly connected. Also check the vapor/vacuum lines at the NVLD pump, NVLD filter and EVAP canister purge solenoid for damage or leaks. If a leak is present, a Diagnostic Trouble Code (DTC) may be set.

41. If equipped, install fuel tank skid plate.

42. Install plastic liner in front of left-rear tire/wheel.

43. Install left rear tire/wheel.

44. Lower vehicle.

45. Fill fuel tank with fuel.

46. Start engine and check for fuel leaks near top of module.

FUEL TANK

REMOVAL & INSTALLATION

See Figure 107.

1. Before servicing the vehicle, refer to the precautions in the beginning of this manual.

2. Release the fuel system pressure.

3. Raise and safely support the vehicle.

4. Drain the fuel tank. This is done by removing the clamp and hose from the fuel tank fill fitting at the rear of the tank. Position a draining hose from an approved gasoline draining station into the open fuel tank fill fitting.

5. Unplug the electrical connector from the ESIM switch.

6. Disconnect the quick connect fittings at front of fuel tank.

7. Disconnect the quick connect fitting at the rear of the fuel tank.

8. Support the tank with a hydraulic jack.

9. Remove the two fuel tank strap bolts and remove both tank support straps.

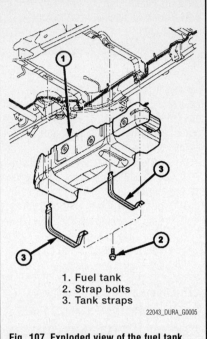

1. Fuel tank
2. Strap bolts
3. Tank straps

22043_DURA_G0005

Fig. 107 Exploded view of the fuel tank mounting

10. Carefully lower the tank a few inches and disconnect the fuel pump module electrical connector at the top of the tank. To disconnect the electrical connector, push upward on the red colored tab to unlock. Push on the black colored tab while removing the connector.

11. Disconnect the fuel line at the fuel pump module fitting by pressing on the tabs at the side of the quick connect fitting.

12. Disconnect the remaining lines from the tank.

13. Continue to lower the tank for removal.

14. Installation is the reverse of removal. Tighten the strap bolts to 30 ft. lbs. (41 Nm).

IDLE SPEED

ADJUSTMENT

Idle speed is maintained by the Powertrain Control Module (PCM). No adjustment is necessary or possible.

THROTTLE BODY

REMOVAL & INSTALLATION

See Figures 108 and 109.

1. Remove the air cleaner assembly.

2. Perform the fuel system depressurization procedure.

3. Disconnect the battery negative cable.

4. Disconnect all vacuum lines and electrical connectors from the throttle

body. Tag for location, if necessary. Electrical connectors include TPS, MAP and IAC motor.

5. Disconnect cables: throttle, cruise control and others fitted.

6. Remove the throttle body bolts.

7. Lift the throttle body from the intake manifold.

8. Put a clean rag into the intake manifold to prevent the entry of foreign matter.

To install:

9. Always use a new gasket. Inspect the O–ring between the throttle body and intake manifold.

10. Reverse the removal procedure.

11. Tighten the throttle body bolts to 9 ft. lbs. (12 Nm).

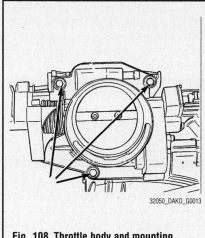

Fig. 108 Throttle body and mounting bolts—3.7L and 4.7L engines

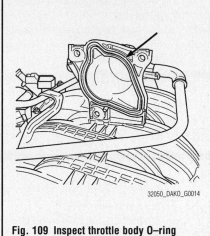

Fig. 109 Inspect throttle body O–ring and replace if necessary

HEATING & AIR CONDITIONING SYSTEM

BLOWER MOTOR

REMOVAL & INSTALLATION

➡**Removal of the blower motor on these models requires that the A/C lines be disconnected. According to law, refrigerant must be captured and reused which requires the use of special equipment and training. This procedure must be performed by a certified MVAC technician.**

1. Disconnect the battery negative cable.

2. Remove the instrument panel.

3. Recover the refrigerant.

4. Disconnect the liquid line refrigerant line fitting from the evaporator inlet tube.

5. Disconnect the accumulator inlet tube.

6. Drain the cooling system.

7. Disconnect the heater hoses from the heater core tubes.

8. Remove the four nuts from the heater–A/C mounting studs on the engine compartment side of the dash panel.

9. Remove the nut that secures the heater–A/C housing mounting brace to the stud on the passenger compartment side of the dash board.

10. Pull the housing rearward far enough for the mounting studs and evaporator condensate drain tube to clear the dash panel holes.

11. Remove the housing from the vehicle.

12. Remove the three screws that secure the motor to the housing.

13. Remove the wheel, if desired, by removing the clip from the motor shaft.

14. Installation is the reverse of removal. Note the following points:

a. When installing the wheel onto the shaft, be sure to line up the flats.

b. The ears of the retaining clip must be on the shaft flat.

c. Be sure the blower motor seal is in place.

HEATER CORE

REMOVAL & INSTALLATION

See Figure 110.

1. Before servicing the vehicle, refer to the precautions in the beginning of this manual.

2. Drain the engine cooling system.

3. Raise and support the vehicle.

4. Remove the right front wheelhouse splash shield.

5. Remove the heater hoses from the heater core tubes in the engine compartment.

6. Lower the vehicle.

☀ WARNING

To avoid personal injury or death, on vehicles equipped with airbags, disable the Supplemental Restraint System (SRS) before attempting any steering wheel, steering column, airbag, occupant classification system, seat belt tensioner, impact sensor, or Instrument panel component diagnosis or service. Disconnect and isolate the battery negative (ground) cable, then wait two minutes for the system capacitor to discharge before performing further diagnosis or service. This is the only sure way to disable the Supplemental Restraint System (SRS). Failure to take the proper precautions could result in accidental airbag deployment.

7. Before proceeding with the following repair procedure, review all warnings and cautions at the beginning of this chapter.

8. Disconnect and isolate battery negative cable.

9. Using a trim stick C-4755 or equivalent, remove the left door sill trim cover.

10. Remove the screw and remove the left cowl trim cover.

11. Remove the left instrument panel end cap.

12. Remove the two screws and remove the steering column opening cover.

13. Remove the screws and position aside the hood release handle.

14. Remove the four screws and remove the steering column opening reinforcement.

15. Remove the steering column tilt lever.

16. Remove the upper and lower column shrouds.

17. Disconnect the wiring harness connectors to the column.

18. Remove the shift cable from the column shift lever actuator.

19. Release the shift cable from the column bracket and remove it from the bracket.

20. Remove the SKIM module in order to disconnect the electrical connector.

21. Remove the upper steering shaft coupler bolt and slide the shaft down.

22. Remove the brake light switch and discard.

23. Remove the four steering column mounting nuts.

24. Lower the column from the mounting studs.

25. Remove the steering column assembly from the vehicle.

26. Remove the pedal support bracket bolts.

27. Disengage the release rod from the arm on the pedal assembly.

28. Disconnect the electrical connectors from the fuse block.

29. Remove the bolt and remove the ground wire.

30. Open the trim covers in the drivers side a-pillar grab handle and remove the bolts.

31. Remove the a-pillar trim panel.

32. Remove the floor console.

33. Disconnect the two body wire harness connectors from the Occupant Restraint Controller (ORC) connector receptacles located on the forward facing side of the module. To disconnect the wire harness connectors from the ORC, depress the release tab and lift the lever arm on each connector.

34. Position the carpet aside and remove the center harness screws. Pull instrument panel wiring harness from under the carpet.

35. Remove the center support bolts.

36. Remove the driver's seat.

37. Remove the drivers side floor duct.

38. Remove the drivers side support bolts.

39. Remove the right instrument panel end cap.

40. Remove the passenger side support bolts.

41. Using a trim stick C-4755 or equivalent, remove the right door sill trim cover.

42. Remove the screw and remove the right cowl trim cover.

43. Remove the bolts and remove the amplifier.

44. Disconnect the amplifier and antenna electrical connectors.

45. Remove the harness bolt and the ground wire bolt.

46. Remove the passenger side rear floor duct.

47. Open the trim covers in the passenger side a-pillar grab handle and remove the bolts.

48. Remove the a-pillar trim panel.

49. Using a trim stick C-4755 or equivalent, remove the instrument panel defroster grille.

50. Disconnect the sensor electrical connector.

51. Remove the four fenceline bolts.

52. Lift the instrument panel assembly off the side support pins and remove assembly through the driver's door.

53. Remove the bolt that secures the HVAC housing bracket to the dash panel.

54. Remove the two screws that secure the HVAC housing bracket to the top of the HVAC housing.

55. Remove the HVAC housing bracket from the vehicle.

56. Remove the screw that secures the heater core tube retaining bracket to the top of the HVAC housing.

57. Remove the heater core tube retaining bracket from the HVAC housing.

58. Remove the screw that secures the heater core tubes to the heater core.

59. Remove the heater core tubes from the heater core and the dash panel. Remove the O–ring seals from the heater core tube fittings and discard.

60. Remove the two screws that secure the heater core retaining bracket to the top of the HVAC housing.

61. Remove the heater core retaining bracket from the top of the HVAC housing.

62. Carefully lift the heater core out of the HVAC housing.

To install:

63. Carefully install the heater core and the heater core retaining bracket to the top of the HVAC housing. Make sure that the heater core insulator is properly positioned.

64. Install the two screws that secure the heater core and retaining bracket to the HVAC housing. Tighten the screws to 20 inch lbs. (2.2 Nm).

65. Lubricate new rubber O–ring seals with clean engine coolant and install them onto the heater core tube fittings. Use only the specified O–ring as it is made of a special material for the engine cooling system.

66. Install the heater core tubes through the dash panel and to the heater core.

67. Install the screw that secures heater core tubes to the heater core. Tighten the screw securely.

68. Install the heater core tube retaining bracket to the top of the HVAC housing.

69. Install the screw that secures the heater core tube retaining bracket to the HVAC housing. Tighten the screw to 20 inch lbs. (2.2 Nm).

70. Install the HVAC housing bracket to the top of HVAC housing and to the dash panel.

71. Install the two screws that secure the HVAC housing bracket to the HVAC housing. Tighten the screws to 20 inch lbs. (2.2 Nm).

72. Install the bolt that secures the HVAC housing bracket to the dash panel. Tighten the bolt to 26 inch lbs. (3 Nm).

73. Position the instrument panel assembly into the vehicle through the driver's side door and install onto the side support pins.

74. Install the four fenceline bolts and tighten to 70 inch lbs. (8 Nm).

75. Connect the sensor electrical connector.

76. Install the instrument panel defroster grille and seat fully.

77. Position the passenger side a-pillar trim panel into place and seat fully.

78. Install the bolts and tighten to 55 inch lbs. (6 Nm).

79. Install the passenger side rear floor duct.

80. Install the screws for the ground wire and passenger side wire harness.

81. Tighten the ground wire and harness bolts to 10 ft. lbs. (14 Nm).

82. Connect the amplifier and antenna electrical connectors.

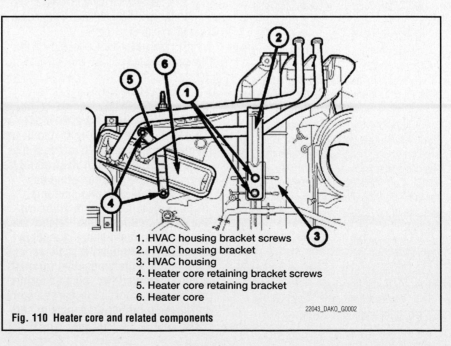

1. HVAC housing bracket screws
2. HVAC housing bracket
3. HVAC housing
4. Heater core retaining bracket screws
5. Heater core retaining bracket
6. Heater core

22043_DAKO_G0002

Fig. 110 Heater core and related components

83. Install the amplifier and install the bolts.

84. Tighten the bolts to 50 inch lbs. (6 Nm).

85. Install the right cowl trim cover and install the screw.

86. Install the right door sill trim cover.

87. Install the passenger side support bolts and tighten to 20 ft. lbs. (27 Nm).

88. Install the right instrument panel end cap.

89. Install the drivers side support bolts and tighten to 20 ft. lbs. (27 Nm).

90. Install the drivers side floor duct.

91. Install the driver's seat.

92. Install the center support bolts and tighten to 95 inch lbs. (11 Nm).

93. Position the center instrument panel wiring harness under the carpet and install the bolts.

⁂ CAUTION

The lever arms of the wire harness connectors for the ORC MUST be in the unlatched position before they are inserted into their connector receptacles on the ORC or they may become damaged.

94. Reconnect the two body wire harness connectors to the ORC connector receptacles located on the forward facing side of the module. Be certain that the latches on both connectors are each fully engaged.

95. Install the floor console.

96. Position the driver's side a-pillar trim into place and seat the retaining clips fully.

97. Install the bolts and tighten to 55 inch lbs. (6 Nm).

98. Install the ground wire and install the bolt.

99. Tighten the ground wire bolts to 10 ft. lbs. (14 Nm).

100. Connect the electrical connectors at the fuse block.

101. Connect the brake release rod to the arm on the pedal assembly.

102. Install the pedal support bolts and tighten to 10 ft. lbs. (14 Nm).

⁂ CAUTION

All fasteners must be torqued to specification to ensure proper operation of the steering column.

103. Position the steering column on the dash panel support and loosely install the mounting nuts.

104. Firmly slide the steering column upward against the studs in dash panel and hand tighten the nuts.

105. Install the steering shaft coupler on the steering shaft and loosely install a new bolt.

106. Center steering column in dash opening and tighten mounting nuts to 21 ft. lbs. (28 Nm).

➡**Torque the upper left nut first then the lower right nut. Then torque the lower left nut then the upper right nut.**

➡**A new bolt must be used for reinstallation.**

107. Tighten the coupler bolt to 28 ft. lbs. (38 Nm).

108. Install a new brake light switch.

109. Install the shifter cable.

110. Connect the wiring harness to the column.

111. Install the SKIM module.

112. Install the upper and lower column shrouds and install the screws.

113. Install the column tilt lever.

114. Install the steering column opening reinforcement and install the four screws.

115. Install the hood release handle and install the screws.

116. Install the steering column opening cover and install the two screws.

117. Install the left instrument panel end cap.

118. Install the left cowl trim cover and install the screw.

119. Install the left door sill trim cover and seat fully.

120. Do not reconnect the battery negative cable at this time. The supplemental restraint system verification test procedure should be performed following service of any supplemental restraint system component.

121. Raise the vehicle and install the heater hoses to the heater core tubes in the engine compartment.

122. Install the right front wheelhouse splash shield.

123. Lower the vehicle.

124. Refill the engine cooling system.

STEERING

POWER STEERING GEAR

REMOVAL & INSTALLATION

1. Before servicing the vehicle, refer to the precautions in the beginning of this manual.

2. Siphon out as much power steering fluid as possible from the pump.

3. Lock the steering wheel.

4. Raise and support the vehicle.

5. Remove the front tires.

6. Remove the nuts from the tie rod ends.

7. Separate tie rod ends from the knuckles.

8. Remove the steering gear pinch bolt.

9. Remove the lower steering coupling from the steering gear.

10. Turn the steering gear to the full right position.

➡**Protect the end of hoses to prevent contamination to the system and damage to the O-rings.**

11. Remove the power steering lines from the gear.

12. Remove the steering gear mounting bolts and nuts.

13. Tip the gear forward to allow clearance and move to the right then tip the gear downward on the left side to remove from the vehicle.

To install:

➡**Before installing gear inspect bushings and replace if worn or damaged.**

14. Install gear to the vehicle and tighten mounting nuts and bolts to 190 ft. lbs. (258 Nm).

15. Install power steering lines to steering gear and tighten the pressure

hose to 23 ft. lbs. (31 Nm) and tighten the return hose to 27 ft. lbs. (37 Nm).

16. Slide the shaft coupler onto gear. Install new bolt and tighten to 36 ft. lbs. (49 Nm).

17. Clean tie rod end studs and knuckle tapers.

18. Install tie rod ends into the steering knuckles and tighten the nuts to 55 ft. lbs. (75 Nm).

19. Install the front tires.

20. Remove the support and lower the vehicle.

21. Unlock the steering wheel.

22. Fill system with fluid.

23. Adjust the toe position.

POWER STEERING PUMP

REMOVAL & INSTALLATION

See Figure 111.

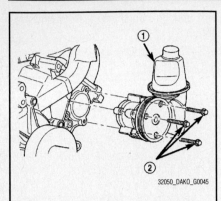

Fig. 111 Pump assembly (1) and mounting bolts (2), which are accessible through holes in the pump pulley

1. Drain and siphon the power steering fluid from the pump.
2. Remove the serpentine drive belt.
3. Remove the reservoir return hose at the reservoir.
4. Remove the pressure hose from the pump.
5. Remove the three pump mounting bolts through pulley access holes.
6. Remove the pump from the engine.

To install:

7. Align the pump with the mounting holes on the engine.

8. Install the three pump mounting bolts through the pulley access holes. Tighten the bolts to 28 Nm (21 ft. lbs.).
9. Install the pressure hose to the pump. Tighten the tube nut to 23 ft. lbs. (31 Nm).
10. Install reservoir return hose to the reservoir.
11. Install the serpentine drive belt.
12. Fill the power steering pump.

BLEEDING

✳✳ CAUTION

The fluid level should be checked with engine OFF to prevent injury from moving components.

✳✳ WARNING

MOPAR® ATF+4 is to be used in the power steering system. No other power steering or automatic transmission fluid is to be used in the system. Damage may result to the power steering pump and system if any other fluid is used. Do not overfill.

1. Wipe filler cap clean, then check the fluid level. The dipstick should indicate COLD when the fluid is at normal temperature (before engine has been operated).
2. Turn steering wheel all the way to the left
3. Fill the pump fluid reservoir to the proper level and let the fluid settle for at least two (2) minutes.
4. Raise the front wheels off the ground.
5. Slowly turn the steering wheel lock-to-lock 20 times with the engine **OFF** while checking the fluid level.

➡**Vehicles with long return lines or oil coolers turn wheel 40 times.**

6. Start the engine. With the engine idling maintain the fluid level.
7. Lower the front wheels and let the engine idle for two minutes.
8. Turn the steering wheel in both direction and verify power assist and quiet operation of the pump.
9. If the fluid is extremely foamy or milky looking, allow the vehicle to stand a few minutes and repeat the procedure.

✳✳ WARNING

Do not run a vehicle with foamy fluid for an extended period. This may cause pump damage.

SUSPENSION   FRONT SUSPENSION

COIL SPRING

REMOVAL & INSTALLATION

See Figures 112 and 113.

The front suspension utilizes coil over shock design; the shock absorber and coil spring are removed as a unit. A Branick 7200® or equivalent spring removal/installation tool will be required to service the spring.

1. Before servicing the vehicle, refer to the precautions in the beginning of this manual.
2. Remove the shock.
3. Install the shock assembly in the Branick 7200T spring removal/installation tool or equivalent.
4. Compress the spring.
5. Position Wrench, Special Tool 9362, or equivalent, on shock shaft retaining nut. Next, insert 8 mm socket though Wrench onto hex located on end of shock shaft. While holding shock shaft from turning, remove nut from shock shaft using Wrench.
6. Remove the upper shock nut.
7. Remove the shock.

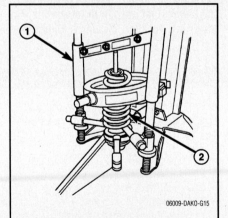

Fig. 112 Spring/shock assembly (2) mounted in the tool (1)

8. Remove the shock upper mounting plate.
9. Remove and inspect the upper and lower spring isolators.

To install:

10. Install the lower isolator.
11. Install the upper isolator.
12. Position the shock into the coil spring.

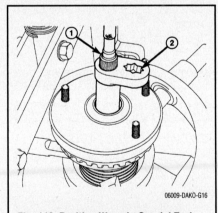

Fig. 113 Position Wrench, Special Tool 9362 (2), or equivalent, on shock shaft retaining nut (1)

13. Install the upper shock mounting plate.
14. Install Wrench (on end of a torque wrench), Special Tool 9362, on shock shaft retaining nut. Next, insert 8 mm socket though Wrench onto hex located on end of shock shaft. While holding shock shaft from turning, tighten nut using Wrench to 90 Nm (66 ft. lbs.) torque.

15. Install the shock upper mounting nut.

16. Decompress the spring.

17. Remove the shock assembly from the spring compressor tool.

18. Install the shock assembly.

LOWER BALL JOINT

REMOVAL & INSTALLATION

See Figures 114 and 115.

1. Before servicing the vehicle, refer to the precautions in the beginning of this manual.

2. Remove the tire and wheel assembly.

3. Remove the brake caliper and rotor.

4. Remove the outer tie rod retaining nut from the knuckle.

5. Separate the tie rod from the steering knuckle using special tool C-3894-A.

6. Remove the upper ball joint nut, then separate the upper ball joint from the knuckle using special tool 8677, or equivalent.

7. Remove the lower ball joint nut, then separate the lower ball joint from the steering knuckle using special tool 8677.

8. Remove the steering knuckle.

9. Move the halfshaft to the side and support the halfshaft out of the way on 4WD models.

10. Remove the snapring from the ball joint flange.

➡Extreme pressure lubrication must be used on the threaded portions of the tool. This will increase the longevity of the tool and insure proper operation during the removal and installation process.

11. Press the ball joint from the lower control arm using special tools C-4212-F (Press), 8445-3 (Driver) and 9604 (Receiver).

To install:

12. Install the ball joint into the control arm and press in using special tools C-4212-F (press), 8441-4 (Receiver) and 9654-1 (Driver).

13. Install the snapring around the ball joint flange.

14. Remove the support for the halfshaft and install into position on 4WD models.

15. Install the steering knuckle.

16. Install the tie rod end into the steering knuckle, then install the retaining nut and tighten to 55 ft. lbs. (75 Nm).

17. Install and tighten the halfshaft nut (if equipped) to 185 ft. lbs. (251 Nm).

18. Install the brake caliper and rotor.

19. Install the tire and wheel assembly.

20. Check the vehicle ride height.

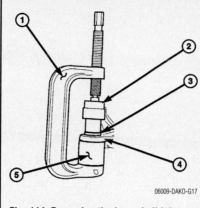

Fig. 114 Removing the lower ball joint from the control arm

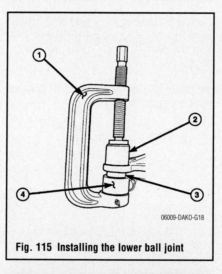

Fig. 115 Installing the lower ball joint

LOWER CONTROL ARM

REMOVAL & INSTALLATION

See Figure 116.

1. Before servicing the vehicle, refer to the precautions in the beginning of this manual.

2. Raise and support the vehicle.

3. Remove the wheel and tire assembly.

4. Remove the disc brake caliper assembly.

5. Remove the disc brake rotor.

6. Disconnect the wheel speed sensor at the wheel well.

7. Remove tie rod end jam nut.

8. Disconnect the tie rod from the knuckle using special tool C-3894-A, or equivalent.

9. Remove the front halfshaft nut (4WD models).

10. Remove the upper ball joint nut. Separate the upper ball joint from the steering knuckle with a remover.

11. Remove the lower ball joint nut. Separate the lower ball joint from the steering knuckle with a remover.

12. Remove the steering knuckle.

13. Remove the stabilizer bar link

14. Remove the shock absorber lower bolt and nut.

15. Remove the lower control arm bolts, nuts and washers.

16. Remove the lower control arm from the vehicle.

To install:

➡All suspension components should be tightened with the weight of the vehicle on them (curb height).

17. Position the lower control arm at the frame rail brackets. Install the pivot bolts washers and nuts. Tighten the nuts finger-tight.

✳✳ WARNING

The ball joint stud taper must be CLEAN and DRY before installing the knuckle. Clean the stud taper with mineral spirits to remove dirt and grease.

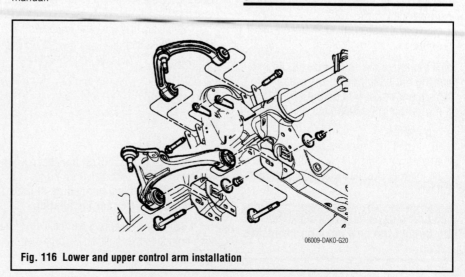

Fig. 116 Lower and upper control arm installation

18. Install the steering knuckle.
19. Insert the lower ball joint into the steering knuckle. Install and tighten the retaining nut to 60 ft. lbs. (81 Nm).
20. Install shock absorber lower bolt and nut. Tighten to 60 ft. lbs. (81 Nm).
21. Install the front halfshaft nut (4WD models).
22. Insert the upper ball joint into the steering knuckle. Install and tighten the retaining nut to 55 ft. lbs. (75 Nm).
23. Install the stabilizer bar link and tighten to 169 Nm (125 ft. lbs.).
24. Tighten the lower control arm pivot nut and bolts to 244 Nm (180 ft. lbs.).
25. Insert the outer tie rod end into the steering knuckle. Install and tighten the retaining nut to 55 ft. lbs. (75 Nm).
26. Install the disc brake rotor.
27. Install the disc brake caliper and adapter assembly and tighten to 135 Nm (100 ft. lbs.).
28. Install the wheel and tire assembly.
29. Remove the support and lower the vehicle.
30. Perform a wheel alignment.

CONTROL ARM BUSHING REPLACEMENT

The control arm bushings are serviced with the control arm as an assembly.

STABILIZER BAR

REMOVAL & INSTALLATION

2WD Models

Bar

1. Raise and support the vehicle.
2. Remove the upper link nut, retainer and grommet from each link.
3. Remove the stabilizer bar retainer bolts and remove the retainers and stabilizer bar from the vehicle.
4. Remove the bushings from the stabilizer bar.

➡If bushings are to be reused, do not cut the old bushings off the stabilizer bar; use a mixture of soapy water to aid in sliding the bushings off the bar.

To install:
5. Install the bushings on the stabilizer bar using a mixture of soapy water or equivalent in order to slide the bushing over the bar with ease.

⁂ WARNING

Do not cut the new bushing for installation.

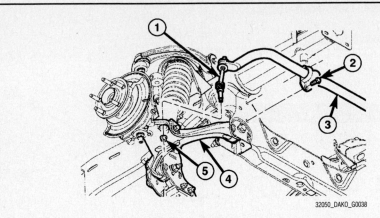

Fig. 117 2WD stabilizer components: link (1), retainer (2), stabilizer bar (3), lower control arm (4), and lower nut (5)

6. Install the stabilizer bar on the frame and install the retainers and the bolts.
7. Tighten the bolts to 45 ft. lbs. (60 Nm).

➡Ensure the bar is centered with equal spacing on both sides.

8. Install the upper link grommet, retainer and nut and tighten to 27 ft. lbs. (37 Nm).
9. Remove support and lower vehicle.

Links

See Figure 117.

1. Raise and support the vehicle.
2. Remove the lower nut.
3. Remove the upper nut, retainers and grommets from the stabilizer bar.
4. Remove the stabilizer link from the vehicle.

To install:
5. Install the stabilizer link to the vehicle.
6. Install the retainers, grommets and upper nut to the stabilizer bar and tighten to 23 Nm (17 ft. lbs.).
7. Install the lower nut and tighten to 102 Nm (75 ft. lbs.).
8. Remove the support and lower the vehicle.

4WD Models

Bar

See Figure 118.

➡To service the stabilizer bar the vehicle must be on a drive on hoist. The vehicle suspension must be at curb height for stabilizer bar installation.

1. Remove the stabilizer bar retainer bolts from the lower suspension arms and remove the retainers.

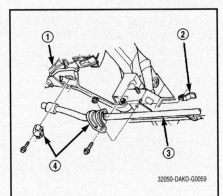

Fig. 118 4WD stabilizer components: lower control arm (1), nut (2), stabilizer bar (3) and retainers (4)

2. Remove the stabilizer bar retainer nuts, bolts and retainers from the frame crossmember and remove the bar.
3. If necessary, remove the bushings from the stabilizer bar.

➡If bushings are to be reused, do not cut the old bushings off the stabilizer bar; use a mixture of soapy water to aid in sliding the bushings off the bar.

To install:

➡To service the stabilizer bar the vehicle must be on a drive on hoist. The vehicle suspension must be at curb height for stabilizer bar installation.

4. If removed, install the bushings on the stabilizer bar using a mixture of soapy water or equivalent in order to slide the bushing over the bar with ease.

⁂ WARNING

Do not cut the new bushing for installation.

5. Position the stabilizer bar on the frame crossmember brackets and install the retainers and nuts and bolts finger-tight.

➡ **Ensure the bar is centered with equal spacing on both sides.**

6. Install the stabilizer bar to the lower suspension arm.

7. Install the retainers and bolts to the lower suspension arm and tighten to 34 Nm (25 ft. lbs.).

8. Tighten the frame retainer nuts to 190 Nm (140 ft. lbs.).

9. Tighten the frame retainer bolts to 108 Nm (80 ft. lbs.).

Links

Control links are not utilized on 4WD models; the stabilizer end is mounted directly to the lower control arm.

STEERING KNUCKLE

REMOVAL & INSTALLATION

1. Raise and support the vehicle.
2. Remove the wheel and tire assembly.
3. Remove the brake caliper, rotor, shield and ABS wheel speed sensor if equipped.
4. Remove the front halfshaft nut on 4WD models.
5. Remove the tie rod end nut.
6. Separate the tie rod from the knuckle with puller C-3894-A or equivalent.

❊❊ WARNING

Be careful not to damage the ball joint seal.

7. Remove the upper ball joint nut.
8. Separate the ball joint from the knuckle with puller 8677 or equivalent.
9. Install a hydraulic jack to support the lower control arm.
10. Remove the lower ball joint nut.
11. Separate the ball joint from the knuckle with puller 8677 or equivalent and remove the knuckle.
12. Remove the hub/bearing bolts from the knuckle.
13. Remove the hub/bearing from the steering knuckle.
14. Remove the steering knuckle.

To install:

❊❊ CAUTION

The ball joint stud tapers must be CLEAN and DRY before installing the knuckle. Clean the stud tapers with mineral spirits to remove dirt and grease.

15. Install the hub/bearing to the steering knuckle and tighten the bolts to 163 Nm (120 ft. lbs.).
16. Install the knuckle onto the upper and lower ball joints.
17. Install the upper ball joint nut . Tighten the nut to 95 Nm (70 ft. lbs.).
18. Install the lower ball joint nut. Tighten the nut to 129 Nm (95 ft. lbs.).
19. Remove the hydraulic jack from the lower control arm.
20. Install the tie rod end and tighten the nut to 75 Nm (55 ft. lbs.).
21. Install the front halfshaft into the hub/bearing on 4WD models.
22. Install the ABS wheel speed sensor if equipped, brake shield, rotor and caliper.
23. Install the wheel and tire assembly.
24. Remove the support and lower the vehicle.
25. Perform a wheel alignment.

UPPER BALL JOINT

REMOVAL & INSTALLATION

These models utilize an upper control arm with an integral ball joint. If the ball joint is damaged or worn, the upper control arm must be replaced.

UPPER CONTROL ARM

REMOVAL & INSTALLATION
See Figure 119.

1. Before servicing the vehicle, refer to the precautions in the beginning of this manual.
2. Raise and support vehicle.
3. Remove wheel and tire assembly.
4. Remove the nut from upper ball joint.
5. Separate upper ball joint from the steering knuckle with a ball joint tool.

❊❊ WARNING

When installing the tool to separate the ball joint, be careful not to damage the ball joint seal.

6. Remove the wheel speed sensor wire from the retaining brackets to the upper control arm.
7. Remove the control arm pivot bolts and nuts and remove control arm.

To install:

➡ **All suspension components should be tightened with the weight of the vehicle on them (curb height).**

8. Position the control arm into the frame brackets. Install bolts and nuts. Tighten to 102 Nm (75 ft. lbs.).
9. Reposition the wheel speed wire into the retaining brackets.
10. Insert ball joint in steering knuckle and tighten ball joint nut to 55 ft. lbs. (75 Nm).
11. Install the wheel and tire assembly.

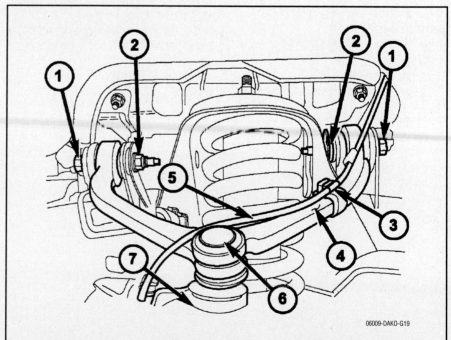

06009-DAKO-G19

Fig. 119 Upper control arm mounting: (1) bolts, (2) nuts, (3) brackets, (4) control arm, (5) ABS wheel speed wire, (6) ball joint, (7) knuckle

12. Remove the support and lower vehicle.

13. Perform a wheel alignment.

CONTROL ARM BUSHING REPLACEMENT

The control arm bushings are serviced with the control arm as an assembly.

WHEEL BEARINGS

REMOVAL & INSTALLATION

See Figure 120.

1. Before servicing the vehicle, refer to the precautions in the beginning of this manual.

2. Raise and support the vehicle.

3. Remove the wheel and tire assembly.

4. Remove the brake caliper and rotor.

5. Remove the ABS wheel speed sensor if equipped.

6. Remove the halfshaft nut on 4WD models.

➡**Do not strike the knuckle with a hammer to remove the tie rod end or the ball joint. Damage to the steering knuckle will occur.**

7. Pull down on the steering knuckle to separate the halfshaft from the hub/bearing on 4WD models.

8. Remove the three hub/bearing mounting bolts from the steering knuckle.

9. Slide the hub/bearing out of the steering knuckle.

10. Remove the brake dust shield.

To install:

11. Install the brake dust shield.

12. Install the hub/bearing into the steer-

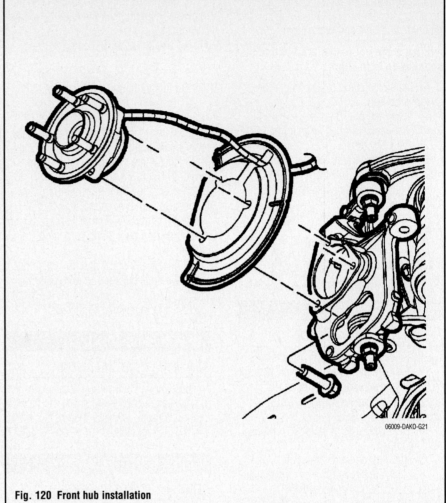

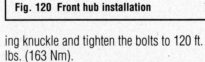

06009-DAKO-G21

Fig. 120 Front hub installation

ing knuckle and tighten the bolts to 120 ft. lbs. (163 Nm).

13. Install the brake rotor and caliper.

14. Install the ABS wheel speed sensor if equipped.

15. Install the halfshaft on 4WD models.

16. Install the wheel and tire assembly.

17. Remove the support and lower vehicle.

ADJUSTMENT

These models utilize a sealed hub/bearing assembly which is not adjustable.

LEAF SPRING

REMOVAL & INSTALLATION

1. Before servicing the vehicle, refer to the precautions in the beginning of this manual.

✳✳ CAUTION

The rear of the vehicle must be lifted only with a jack or hoist. The lift must be placed under the frame rail crossmember located aft of the rear axle. Use care to avoid bending the side rail flange.

2. Raise the vehicle at the frame.
3. Use a hydraulic jack to relieve the axle weight.
4. Remove the wheel and tire assemblies.
5. Remove the nuts, the U-bolts and spring plate from the axle.
6. Loosen and remove the bolt and then remove the flag nut through the access hole in the bracket from the spring front eye.
7. Remove the nut and bolt that attaches the spring shackle to the rear frame bracket.
8. Remove the spring from the vehicle.
9. Remove the shackle from the spring.

To install:

10. Install the spring shackle on the spring finger tight.
11. Position the spring on the rear axle pad. Make sure the spring center bolt is inserted in the pad locating hole.
12. Align front spring eye with the bolt hole in the front frame bracket. Install the spring eye bolt and flag nut through the access hole in the frame and tighten the bolt finger-tight.
13. Align spring shackle eye with the bolt hole in the rear frame bracket. Install the bolt and nut and tighten the spring shackle eye nut finger-tight.
14. Install the U-bolts, spring plate and nuts.
15. Tighten the U-bolt nuts to 149 Nm (110 ft. lbs.).
16. Install the wheel and tire assemblies.
17. Remove the support stands from under the frame rails. Lower the vehicle until the springs are supporting the weight of the vehicle.
18. Tighten the spring eye pivot bolt and flag nut to 163 Nm (120 ft. lbs.).
19. Tighten the upper shackle bolt and

nut and the lower shackle bolt and nut to 163 Nm (120 ft. lbs.).

SHOCK ABSORBER

REMOVAL & INSTALLATION

1. Before servicing the vehicle, refer to the precautions in the beginning of this manual.
2. Raise the vehicle and support rear axle.
3. Remove the shock absorber lower nut and bolt from the axle bracket.
4. Remove the shock absorber upper nut and bolt from the frame bracket and remove the shock absorber.

To install:

5. Install the shock absorber and upper mounting bolt and nut. Tighten the nut to 102 Nm (75 ft. lbs.).
6. Install the shock absorber into the axle bracket. Install the bolt and nut and tighten the nut to 102 Nm (75 ft. lbs.).
7. Remove the axle support and lower the vehicle.

STABILIZER BAR

REMOVAL & INSTALLATION

Bar

See Figure 121.

1. Raise and support vehicle.
2. Remove nuts and bolts from the links at the stabilizer bar.
3. Remove stabilizer bar retainer bolts and retainers.
4. Remove stabilizer bar and replace worn, cracked or distorted bushings.
5. Remove links upper mounting nuts and bolts and remove links.

To install:

6. Install the stabilizer bar and center it with equal spacing on both sides. Install stabilizer bar retainers and tighten bolts to 54 Nm (40 ft. lbs.).
7. Install link into frame brackets and the stabilizer bar. Install mounting nuts and bolts.
8. Remove support and lower vehicle.
9. Tighten stabilizer link nuts to 54 Nm (40 ft. lbs.).
10. Remove supports and lower vehicle.

Links

1. Raise and support the vehicle.
2. Remove the rear tire.
3. Support the rear axle with a jack.
4. Remove the lower link nut at the stabilizer bar.
5. Remove the upper link nut and bolt at the frame. On the left side stabilizer

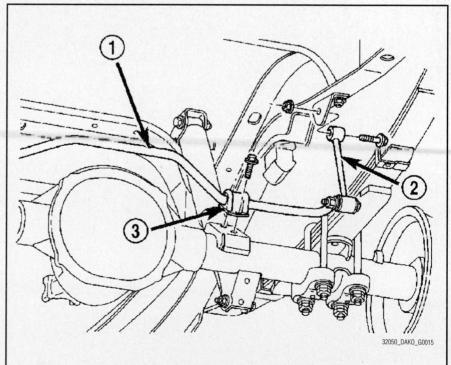

32050_DAKO_G0015

Fig. 121 Rear stabilizer and links: stabilizer bar (1), link (2), retainer (3)

link upper bolt, pull the bolt back after the nut is removed and then pull the link downward with the bolt still in the link to allow clearance from the fuel tank.

6. Remove stabilizer link.

To install:

7. Install the upper bolt into the stabilizer link then raise the link into position with the frame and install the nut for the stabilizer link to the frame and tighten to 54 Nm (40 ft. lbs.).

8. Install the stabilizer link to the stabilizer bar.

9. Install the nut and tighten to 54 Nm (40 ft. lbs.).

10. Remove supports and lower the vehicle.

CHRYSLER, DODGE AND JEEP

Diagnostic Trouble Codes

DIAGNOSTIC TROUBLE CODES

OBD II VEHICLE APPLICATIONS

CHRYSLER CORP.

300
2005–2007
- 2.7L ....VIN R
- 2.7L ....VIN 6
- 3.5L ....VIN G
- 3.5L ....VIN V
- 5.7L ....VIN H
- 5.7L ....VIN 2

300C
2005–2007
- 2.7L ....VIN R
- 2.7L ....VIN 6
- 3.5L ....VIN G
- 3.5L ....VIN V
- 5.7L ....VIN H
- 5.7L ....VIN 2

Aspen
2007
- 4.7L ....VIN N
- 4.7L ....VIN P
- 5.7L ....VIN 2

Caliber
2007
- 1.8L ....VIN C
- 2.0L ....VIN B
- 2.4L ....VIN K

Caravan
2005–2007
- 2.4L ....VIN B
- 3.3L ....VIN 3
- 3.3L ....VIN G
- 3.3L ....VIN R
- 3.8L ....VIN L

Charger
2005–2007
- 2.7L ....VIN R

- 2.7L ....VIN 6
- 3.5L ....VIN G
- 3.5L ....VIN V
- 5.7L ....VIN H
- 5.7L ....VIN 2

Commander
2006–2007
- 3.7L ....VIN K
- 4.7L ....VIN N
- 4.7L ....VIN P
- 5.7L ....VIN 2

Compass
2007
- 2.0L ....VIN 0
- 2.4L ....VIN W

Crossfire
2005–2007
- 3.2L ....VIN L
- 3.2L ....VIN N

Dakota
2005–2007
- 3.7L ....VIN K
- 4.7L ....VIN J
- 4.7L ....VIN N
- 4.7L ....VIN P

Durango
2005–2007
- 3.7L ....VIN K
- 4.7L ....VIN N
- 4.7L ....VIN P
- 5.7L ....VIN D
- 5.7L ....VIN 2

Magnum
2005–2007
- 2.7L ....VIN R
- 2.7L ....VIN 6
- 3.5L ....VIN G
- 3.5L ....VIN V
- 5.7L ....VIN H
- 5.7L ....VIN 2

Town & Country
2005–2007
- 2.4L ....VIN B
- 3.3L ....VIN 3
- 3.3L ....VIN G
- 3.3L ....VIN R
- 3.8L ....VIN L

REFERENCE INFORMATION

OBD II TROUBLE CODE LIST

To use this information, first read and record All codes in memory along with Freeze Frame data. *If a PCM Reset function is done prior to recording this data,* All *codes and freeze frame data are lost!*

Look up the appropriate trouble code in the list on the following pages. The left hand column includes the code number, the number of trips to set the code (e.g., **1T or 2T**), the year, model description and type of OBD II Monitor that failed (e.g., **CCM or O2S**). This data can be used to determine how to drive a vehicle after a repair in order to validate the repair has been completed.

The **(N/MIL)** designator in the left hand column indicates the trouble code does not turn on the Malfunction Indicator Lamp or MIL. The **(STS Lamp)** indicator in the left column indicates a code that turns on the Service Transmission Soon lamp. This code may or may not turn "on" the MIL.

OBD II Trouble Code List (P0XXX Codes)

DTC	Trouble Code Title, Conditions & Possible Causes
DTC: P0016 **1T CCM** **Years:** 2005, 2006, 2007 **Models:** 300, 300C, Aspen, Caliber, Caravan, Charger, Commander, Compass, Crossfire, Dakota, Durango, Magnum, Town & Country **Engines:** All **Transmissions:** All	**Crankshaft/Camshaft Timing Misalignment** Engine cranking or running; and the PCM detected the camshaft was out of phase with the crankshaft during the CCM test period. **Possible Causes:** • Base engine problem (i.e., the camshaft timing is not correct) • Intermittent condition • CKP or CMP Sensor signal is erratic (check with lab scope) • Tone wheel or pulse wheel is damaged or contains debris • CKP or CMP Sensor, harness or connector has failed • PCM has failed
DTC: P0030 **1T CCM** **Years:** 2000-03 **Models:** 300, 300C, Charger, Magnum **Engines:** All **Transmissions:** All	**O2 (B1 S1) Heater Circuit Fault** Engine started; system voltage over 10.6v, and the PCM detected a fault in the O2 heater element feedback sense circuit. **Possible Causes:** • O2 assembly is damaged or it has failed • O2 heater control circuit is open, shorted to ground or B+ • O2 heater ground circuit is open • O2 heater element is damaged or has failed • PCM has failed
DTC: P0031 **1T CCM** **Years:** 2005, 2006, 2007 **Models:** 300, 300C, 300M, Aspen, Caravan, Charger, Commander, Compass, Crossfire, Dakota, Durango, Magnum, Town & Country **Engines:** All **Transmissions:** All	**O2 (B1 S1) Heater Circuit Low** Key on; system voltage over 10.6v; ASD relay on; O2 heater "on". The PCM detected the O2 Heater circuit is out of acceptable range low. **Possible Causes:** • O2 assembly is damaged or it has failed • O2 heater element is damaged or has failed • O2 heater control circuit is shorted to ground • PCM has failed
DTC: P0032 **1T CCM** **Years:** 2005, 2006, 2007 **Models:** 300, 300C, 300M, Aspen, Caravan, Charger, Commander, Compass, Crossfire, Dakota, Durango, Magnum, Town & Country **Engines:** All **Transmissions:** All	**O2 (B1 S1) Heater Circuit High** Key on; system voltage over 10.6v; ASD relay on; O2 heater "off". The PCM detected the O2 Heater circuit is out of range high. **Possible Causes:** • O2 heater element is damaged or the heater has failed • O2 heater control circuit is open or it is shorted to power • O2 heater ground circuit is open • PCM has failed
DTC: P0037 **1T CCM** **Years:** 2005, 2006, 2007 **Models:** 300, 300C, 300M, Aspen, Caravan, Charger, Commander, Compass, Crossfire, Dakota, Durango, Magnum, Town & Country **Engines:** All **Transmissions:** All	**O2 (B1 S2) Heater Circuit Low** Key on; system voltage over 10.6v; ASD relay on; O2 heater "on". The PCM detected the O2 Heater circuit is out of acceptable range (i.e., below 0.0926v). **Possible Causes:** • O2 assembly is damaged or it has failed • O2 heater element is damaged or has failed • O2 heater control circuit is shorted to ground • PCM has failed
DTC: P0038 **1T CCM** **Years:** 2005, 2006, 2007 **Models:** 300, 300C, 300M, Aspen, Caravan, Charger, Commander, Compass, Crossfire, Dakota, Durango, Magnum, Town & Country **Engines:** All **Transmissions:** All	**O2 (B1 S2) Heater Circuit High** Key on; system voltage over 10.6v; ASD relay on; O2 heater "off". The PCM detected the O2 heater voltage is out of range high. **Possible Causes:** • O2 Sensor failed or improper operation • O2 heater element is damaged or failed • O2 heater control circuit is open or it is shorted to power • O2 heater ground circuit is open • PCM has failed

DTC	Trouble Code Title, Conditions & Possible Causes
DTC: P0051 **1T CCM** **Years:** 2005, 2006, 2007 **Models:** 300, 300C, 300M, Aspen, Caravan, Charger, Commander, Compass, Crossfire, Dakota, Durango, Magnum, Town & Country **Engines:** All **Transmissions:** All	**O2 (B2 S1) Heater Relay Circuit Low** Key on, system voltage over 10.6v, ASD relay on, O2 heater "on", and the PCM detected the Heater Relay circuit Actual state did not match the Desired state (low circuit). 3 good trips are required to turn off the MIL. **Possible Causes:** • O2 assembly is damaged or it has failed • O2 heater element is damaged or has failed • O2 heater control circuit is shorted to ground • PCM has failed
DTC: P0051 **1T CCM** **Years:** 2005, 2006, 2007 **Models:** Aspen, Dakota, Durango **Engines:** All **Transmissions:** All	**O2 (B2 S1) Heater Circuit Low** Key on; system voltage over 10.6v; ASD relay on; O2 heater "on". The PCM detected the O2 Heater circuit is below acceptable range. **Possible Causes:** • O2 assembly is damaged or it has failed • O2 heater control circuit is shorted to ground • PCM has failed
DTC: P0052 **1T CCM** **Years:** 2005, 2006, 2007 **Models:** 300, 300C, 300M, Aspen, Caravan, Charger, Commander, Compass, Crossfire, Dakota, Durango, Magnum, Town & Country **Engines:** All **Transmissions:** All	**O2 (B2 S1) Heater Relay Circuit High** Key on, system voltage over 10.6v, ASD relay on, O2 heater "off", and the PCM detected the Heater Relay circuit Actual state did not match the Desired state (high circuit). **Possible Causes:** • O2 heater element is damaged or the heater has failed • O2 heater control circuit is open or it is shorted to power • O2 heater ground circuit is open • PCM has failed
DTC: P0052 **1T CCM** **Years:** 2005, 2006, 2007 **Models:** Aspen, Dakota, Durango **Engines:** All **Transmissions:** All	**O2 (B2 S1) Heater Circuit High** Key on; system voltage over 10.6v; ASD relay on; O2 heater "off". The PCM detected the O2 Heater circuit is above acceptable range. **Possible Causes:** • O2 heater control circuit is open or is shorted to battery voltage • O2 heater ground circuit is open • O2 Sensor has failed • PCM has failed
DTC: P0057 **1T CCM** **Years:** 2005, 2006, 2007 **Models:** 300, 300C, 300M, Aspen, Caravan, Charger, Commander, Compass, Crossfire, Dakota, Durango, Magnum, Town & Country **Engines:** All **Transmissions:** All	**O2 (B2 S2) Heater Relay Circuit Low** Key on, system voltage over 10.6v, ECT input under test condition value, and the PCM detected the Heater Relay signal was too low. **Possible Causes:** • O2 assembly is damaged or it has failed • O2 heater element is damaged or has failed • O2 heater control circuit is shorted to ground • PCM has failed
DTC: P0057 **1T CCM** **Years:** 2005, 2006, 2007 **Models:** Aspen, Dakota, Durango **Engines:** All **Transmissions:** All	**O2 (B2 S2) Heater Circuit Low** Key on; system voltage over 10.6v; ASD relay on; O2 heater "on". The PCM detected the O2 Heater circuit is below acceptable range. **Possible Causes:** • O2 assembly is damaged or it has failed • O2 heater control circuit is shorted to ground • PCM has failed
DTC: P0058 **1T CCM** **Years:** 2005, 2006, 2007 **Models:** 300, 300C, 300M, Aspen, Caravan, Charger, Commander, Compass, Crossfire, Dakota, Durango, Magnum, Town & Country **Engines:** All **Transmissions:** All	**O2 (B2 S2) Heater Relay Circuit High** Key on, system voltage over 10.6v, ASD powered up, and O2 heater is off. ECT input under test condition value and the PCM detected the Heater Relay signal was too high. **Possible Causes:** • O2 heater element is damaged or the heater has failed • O2 heater control circuit is open or it is shorted to power • O2 heater ground circuit is open • PCM has failed

DTC	Trouble Code Title, Conditions & Possible Causes
DTC: P0058 **1T CCM** **Years:** 2005, 2006, 2007 **Models:** Aspen, Dakota, Durango **Engines:** All **Transmissions:** All	**O2 (B2 S2) Heater Circuit High** Key on; system voltage over 10.6v; ASD relay on; O2 heater "off". The PCM detected the O2 Heater circuit is above acceptable range. **Possible Causes:** • O2 heater control circuit is open or is shorted to battery voltage • O2 heater ground circuit is open • O2 Sensor has failed • PCM has failed
DTC: P0068 **1T CCM** **Years:** 2005, 2006, 2007 **Models:** 300, 300C, Aspen, Caliber, Charger, Dakota, Durango, Magnum **Engines:** All **Transmissions:** All	**MAP Sensor/TP Sensor Correction – High Flow/Vacuum Leak** Engine started; engine speed over 2000 RPM, and the PCM detected the Manifold Air Pressure (MAP) value dropped to less than 1.5" Hg with the throttle closed during the test. **Possible Causes:** • An engine vacuum leak present • High resistance in the MAP ground circuit, MAP Sensor signal or VREF (5v) circuit • High resistance in the TP ground, TP circuit or the TP Sensor VREF (5v) circuit • MAP Sensor is damaged or it has failed • TP Sensor is damaged or it has failed • PCM has failed
DTC: P0068 **2T CCM** **Years:** 2005, 2006, 2007 **Models:** Caravan, Town & Country **Engines:** All **Transmissions:** A/T	**MAP Sensor/TP Sensor Correlation** Engine started; no MAP Sensor or TP Sensor DTCs are present. The PCM determines a valid range in which the TP Sensor should be, at a given RPM/engine load. The actual TP Sensor voltage is then compared to this value. If the TP Sensor voltage does not fall within the expected range within a predetermined time, an error is detected. The DTC will set after 2 trips. **Possible Causes:** • An engine vacuum leak present • High resistance in the MAP ground circuit, MAP Sensor signal or VREF (5v) circuit • High resistance in the TP ground, TP circuit or the TP Sensor VREF (5v) circuit • MAP Sensor is damaged or it has failed • TP Sensor is damaged or it has failed • PCM has failed
DTC: P0068 **1T CCM** **Years:** 2005, 2006, 2007 **Models:** Aspen, Dakota, Durango **Engines:** All **Transmissions:** All	**MAP Sensor/TP Sensor Correlation** Condition is monitored during all drive modes. This DTC will set when an unexpectedly high intake manifold airflow condition exists that can lead to increased engine speed and which then puts the Next Generation Controller into a High Airflow Protection Limiting Mode. This feature includes RPM limits whenever a TP and/or MAP Sensor limp-in fault is present. If vacuum drops below 1.5 in. Hg, with engine speed greater than 2000 RPM and closed throttle, this DTC will set. **Possible Causes:** • An engine vacuum leak present • High resistance in the 5v supply circuit • 5v supply circuit is shorted to ground • High resistance in the MAP signal circuit or the TP signal circuit • TP signal circuit is shorted to ground • High resistance in the Sensor ground circuit • MAP Sensor is damaged or it has failed • TP Sensor is damaged or it has failed • PCM has failed
DTC: P0071 **2T CCM** **Years:** 2005, 2006, 2007 **Models:** 300, 300C, 300M, Aspen, Caliber, Caravan, Charger, Dakota, Durango, Magnum, Town & Country **Engines:** All **Transmissions:** A/T	**Ambient Temperature Sensor Performance** Engine "off" time over 8 hours; DTC P0072 and P0073 not set; ambient temperature more than 38°F (4C). The PCM determined the Ambient Air Temperature (AAT) Sensor was not within calibrated temperature of the ECT and IAT Sensor signals after a cool down period. **Possible Causes:** • AAT Sensor circuit open, shorted to ground or VREF • AAT Sensor voltage below 1.0v • AAT signal circuit is open or is shorted to ground, to battery voltage or to Sensor ground • AAT Sensor ground circuit is open • AAT Sensor is damaged or it has failed • PCM High or Low circuit is damaged or it has failed

DTC	Trouble Code Title, Conditions & Possible Causes
DTC: P0072 **1T CCM** **Years:** 2005, 2006, 2007 **Models:** 300, 300C, 300M, Aspen, Caliber, Caravan, Charger, Dakota, Durango, Magnum, Town & Country **Engines:** All **Transmissions:** All	**Ambient Temperature Sensor Circuit Low Input** Related DTCs not set, key on or engine running; system voltage over 10.5v, at least 5 warm-up cycles completed, odometer mileage change at least 196.6 miles, and the PCM detected the AAT Sensor signal was less than 0.3v at PCM. 3 good trips required to turn off MIL. **Possible Causes:** • AAT Sensor internal failure • AAT signal circuit shorted to ground • AAT signal circuit shorted to Sensor ground • PCM has failed
DTC: P0072 **1T CCM** **Years:** 2005, 2006, 2007 **Models:** Aspen, Dakota, Durango **Engines:** All **Transmissions:** All	**Ambient Temperature Sensor Circuit Low Input** Ignition is on. When the Ambient Temperature Sensor is less than 0.078v at the PCM for 2.8 seconds this DTC with set. 3 good trips required to turn off MIL. **Possible Causes:** • AAT Sensor internal failure • AAT signal circuit shorted to ground • AAT signal circuit shorted to Sensor ground • Front Control Module has failed
DTC: P0073 **1T CCM** **Years:** 2005, 2006, 2007 **Models:** 300, 300C, 300M, Aspen, Caliber, Caravan, Charger, Dakota, Durango, Magnum, Town & Country **Engines:** All **Transmissions:** All	**Ambient Temperature Sensor Circuit High Input** Key on or engine running; system voltage over 10.0v and the PCM detected the Ambient Air Temperature (AAT) Sensor signal was more than 4.9v for more than 2.8 seconds. Note that this code can be set due to an intermittent failure. 3 good trips are required to turn off the MIL. **Possible Causes:** • AAT Sensor signal shorted to VREF (5v) or battery voltage • AAT Sensor signal circuit or Sensor ground circuit is open • AAT Sensor is damaged (it may be open) • PCM has failed
DTC: P0107 **1T CCM** **Years:** 2005, 2006, 2007 **Models:** 300, 300C, 300M, Aspen, Caliber, Caravan, Charger, Dakota, Durango, Magnum, Town & Country **Engines:** All **Transmissions:** All	**MAP Sensor Circuit Low Input** Ignition on or engine from 600-3500 RPM, TP Sensor input less than 1.2v . Battery voltage greater than 10v. MAP Sensor signal voltage was less than 0.782v for 1.7 seconds (exc. Aspen, Dakota, Durango,) or less than 0.08v for 3 seconds (Aspen, Dakota, Durango). If equipped, ETC light will flash. **Possible Causes:** • 5-volt supply circuit is open or shorted to ground • MAP Sensor signal circuit is shorted to ground or shorted to Sensor ground circuit • MAP Sensor has failed • PCM 5-volt supply circuit has failed
DTC: P0108 **1T CCM** **Years:** 2005, 2006, 2007 **Models:** 300, 300C, 300M, Aspen, Caliber, Caravan, Charger, Dakota, Durango, Magnum, Town & Country **Engines:** All **Transmissions:** All	**MAP Sensor Circuit High Input** Ignition on or engine speed from 600-3500 RPM; TP Sensor input more than 1.2v, for more than 1.7 seconds; battery voltage over 10.0v. The PCM detected the MAP Sensor signal voltage (input) was over 4.92v . **Possible Causes:** • MAP Sensor signal circuit is open • MAP Sensor ground circuit is open • MAP Sensor signal circuit shorted to 5-volt supply circuit or to battery voltage • MAP Sensor has failed or it has failed (possible open circuit) • MAP Sensor has failed • PCM has failed
DTC: P0111 **1T CCM** **Years:** 2005, 2006, 2007 **Models:** 300, 300C, 300M, Aspen, Caliber, Caravan, Charger, Dakota, Durango, Magnum, Town & Country **Engines:** All **Transmissions:** All	**IAT Sensor Performance** DTC P0112 and P0113 not set, key on, ECT Sensor input more than 160°F at startup, at least 5 warm-up cycles have occurred with vehicle mileage change of more than 196.6 miles, and the PCM detected the IAT input changed less than 5.4°F during this period. **Possible Causes:** • IAT Sensor signal circuit is open, shorted to ground or VREF • IAT Sensor ground circuit is open • IAT Sensor is damaged or it has failed • PCM High or Low circuit is damaged or it has failed

DTC	Trouble Code Title, Conditions & Possible Causes
DTC: P0111 **2T CCM** **Years:** 2005, 2006, 2007 **Models:** 300, 300C, 300M, Aspen, Caliber, Caravan, Charger, Dakota, Durango, Magnum, Town & Country **Engines:** All **Transmissions:** All	**IAT Sensor Performance** Engine off. After calibrated amount of cool down (over 8 hours). PCM detects IAT Sensor is not within calibrated temperature amount of ECT Sensor and AAT Sensor. Engine time off when monitored is more than 8 hours and ambient temperature is more than 38F (4C). 3 good trips are required to turn off the MIL. **Possible Causes:** • IAT Sensor signal circuit is open, shorted to ground, to Sensor ground, or to battery voltage • IAT Sensor voltage is below 1.0v • IAT Sensor ground circuit is open • IAT Sensor is damaged or has failed • PCM High or Low circuit is damaged or has failed
DTC: P0112 **1T CCM** **Years:** 2005, 2006, 2007 **Models:** 300, 300C, 300M, Aspen, Caliber, Caravan, Charger, Dakota, Durango, Magnum, Town & Country **Engines:** All **Transmissions:** A/T	**IAT Sensor Circuit Low Input** Ignition on or engine started; battery voltage greater than 10v. If the PCM detected an IAT Sensor input of less than 0.157v (Caravan/Town & Country) or less than 0.078v (Aspen, Dakota, Durango) for 3 seconds, this DTC will set. **Possible Causes:** • IAT Sensor signal circuit is shorted to chassis ground • IAT Sensor signal circuit is shorted to Sensor ground • IAT Sensor is damaged or it has failed (an internal short circuit) • PCM has failed
DTC: P0113 **1T CCM** **Years:** 2005, 2006, 2007 **Models:** 300, 300C, 300M, Aspen, Caliber, Caravan, Charger, Dakota, Durango, Magnum, Town & Country **Engines:** All **Transmissions:** All	**IAT Sensor Circuit High Input** Check with ignition on or engine running; battery voltage more than 10v; The PCM detected the IAT Sensor input was over 4.90v (exc. Aspen, Dakota, Durango) or 4.98v (Aspen, Dakota, Durango) for 3 seconds. **Possible Causes:** • IAT Sensor signal circuit shorted to VREF (5v) • IAT Sensor signal circuit is open, or the ground circuit is open • IAT Sensor is damaged or it has failed (an internal open circuit) • PCM has failed
DTC: P0116 **2T CCM** **Years:** 2005, 2006, 2007 **Models:** 300, 300C, 300M, Aspen, Caliber, Caravan, Charger, Dakota, Durango, Magnum, Town & Country **Engines:** All **Transmissions:** All	**ECT Sensor Circuit Performance** Engine off time is more than 8 hours; ambient temperature is more than 38F (4C); and after a calibrated amount of cool-down time, the PCM compares the ECT Sensor, IAT Sensor and AAT Sensor values; if ECT Sensor is not within a calibrated temperature amount of the other 2 Sensors, an error is detected. 3 good trips are required to turn off the MIL. If equipped, the ECT light will also illuminate when the MIL illuminates. **Possible Causes:** • ECT Sensor signal circuit is open or it is shorted battery voltage or to ground • ECT Sensor signal circuit is shorted to Sensor ground • ECT Sensor ground circuit is open • ECT Sensor is damaged or it has failed • PCM High or Low circuit is damaged or it has failed
DTC: P0117 **1T CCM** **Years:** 2005, 2006, 2007 **Models:** 300, 300C, 300M, Aspen, Caliber, Caravan, Charger, Dakota, Durango, Magnum, Town & Country **Engines:** All **Transmissions:** All	**ECT Sensor Circuit Low Input** Ignition on or engine started. The PCM detected the ECT Sensor input voltage was below 0.51v for 3 seconds. **Possible Causes:** • ECT Sensor signal circuit is shorted to chassis ground • ECT Sensor signal circuit is shorted to Sensor ground • ECT Sensor is damaged or it has failed (it may be shorted) • PCM has failed
DTC: P0118 **1T CCM** **Years:** 2005, 2006, 2007 **Models:** 300, 300C, 300M, Aspen, Caliber, Caravan, Charger, Dakota, Durango, Magnum, Town & Country **Engines:** All **Transmissions:** All	**ECT Sensor Circuit High Input** Ignition on or engine started and the PCM detected the ECT Sensor input was over 4.9v for 3 seconds. If equipped, the ETC lamp will illuminate with the MIL. 3 good trips are required to turn off the MIL. **Possible Causes:** • ECT Sensor signal circuit is shorted to VREF (5v) • ECT Sensor signal circuit is open • ECT Sensor ground circuit is open • ECT Sensor is damaged or it has failed (possible open circuit) • PCM has failed

DTC	Trouble Code Title, Conditions & Possible Causes
DTC: P0121 **1T CCM** **Years:** 2005, 2006, 2007 **Models:** 300, 300C, 300M, Aspen, Charger, Dakota, Durango, Magnum **Engines:** All **Transmissions:** All	**TP Sensor No. 1 Does Not Agree With MAP** Ignition is on and no MAP Sensor DTCs are set. The PCM determines the TP Sensor signals do not correlate with the MAP Sensor signal. The ECT light will illuminate. DTC P2135 should also set with this DTC. **Possible Causes:** • TP Sensor No. 1 signal circuit shorted to battery voltage • Resistance in either TP Sensor No. 1 or 2 signal circuit, 5v supply circuit or TP Sensor return circuit • TP Sensor No. 1 signal circuit shorted to group or to TP Sensor No. 2 signal circuit • 5v supply circuit shorted to ground • TP Sensor or throttle body damaged or failed • PCM has failed
DTC: P0122 **1T CCM** **Years:** 2005, 2006, 2007 **Models:** 300, 300C, 300M, Aspen, Caliber, Caravan, Charger, Dakota, Durango, Magnum, Town & Country **Engines:** All **Transmissions:** All	**TP Sensor No. 1 Circuit Low Input** Key on; system voltage over 10v; and the PCM detected the TP Sensor indicated less than 0.16v for 0.7 second . 3 good trips are required to turn off the MIL. If equipped, the ETC light will illuminate. **Possible Causes:** • TP Sensor sweep • Intermittent condition • 5v supply circuit open or shorted to ground • TP Sensor No. 1 signal circuit shorted to ground or to Sensor return circuit • TP Sensor or throttle body damaged or has failed • PCM has failed
DTC: P0122 **1T CCM** **Years:** 2005, 2006, 2007 **Models:** Aspen, Dakota, Durango **Engines:** All **Transmissions:** All	**TP Sensor No. 1 Circuit Low Input** Key on; system voltage over 10.4v. The PCM detected the TP Sensor voltage is less than 0.0978v for 1.3 seconds (3.7L, 4.7L), or less than 0.16v for 0.7 second (5.7L). 3 good trips are required to turn off the MIL. If equipped, the ETC light will illuminate. **Possible Causes:** • 5v supply circuit open or shorted to ground • TP Sensor No. 1 signal circuit shorted to ground or to Sensor ground circuit • TP Sensor has failed • Throttle body is damaged • PCM has failed
DTC: P0123 **1T CCM** **Years:** 2005, 2006, 2007 **Models:** 300, 300C, 300M, Aspen, Caliber, Caravan, Charger, Dakota, Durango, Magnum, Town & Country **Engines:** All **Transmissions:** All	**TP Sensor/APPS Circuit High Input** Key on or engine running; system voltage over 10v. The PCM detected the TP Sensor indicated more than 4.494v for 0.48 second. If equipped, ETC light will illuminate. **Possible Causes:** • Related TP Sensor engine DTCs present • Intermittent wiring or connector problem • TP signal circuit is open or is shorted to battery voltage or to 5v supply circuit • TP sensor has failed • TP sensor ground circuit is open • PCM has failed
DTC: P0124 **1T CCM** **Years:** 2005, 2006, 2007 **Models:** Caravan, Town & Country **Engines:** All **Transmissions:** All	**TP Sensor/APPS Circuit Intermittent** Key on or engine running; system voltage over 10.5v. This DTC will set if the monitored TP Sensor angle between 6-120 and the degree change is greater than 5 within a period of less than 7.0ms. **Possible Causes:** • Related TP Sensor engine DTCs present • TP Sensor has failed • Intermittent wiring or connector problem • PCM has failed
DTC: P0125 **2T CCM** **Years:** 2005, 2006, 2007 **Models:** 300, 300C, 300M, Aspen, Caliber, Caravan, Charger, Dakota, Durango, Magnum, Town & Country **Engines:** All **Transmissions:** All	**Closed Loop Temperature Not Reached** Engine running; battery over 10v. Engine temperature does not enable closed loop. Failure time depends on start-up coolant temperature and ambient temperature (i.e., 2 minutes for a start temperature of 50°F (10C), or up to 10 minutes for a vehicle with start-up temperature of −18F (−28C). **Possible Causes:** • Low coolant level • Improper thermostat operation or thermostat failure • ECT has failed

DTC	Trouble Code Title, Conditions & Possible Causes
DTC: P0128 **2T CCM** **Years:** 2005, 2006, 2007 **Models:** 300, 300C, 300M, Aspen, Caliber, Caravan, Charger, Dakota, Durango, Magnum, Town & Country **Engines:** All **Transmissions:** All	**Thermostat Rationality Test** With engine running after cold start. PCM predicts a coolant temperature value that it will compare to the actual coolant temperature. If the 2 coolant temperature values are not within 50°F (10°C) of each other, an error is detected. **Possible Causes:** • Low coolant level • Thermostat has failed • Signal circuit shorted to battery voltage • ECT Sensor has failed or voltage is below 1.0v • Signal circuit is open, shorted to ground or shorted to Sensor ground • ECT Sensor ground circuit or signal circuit is open • PCM has failed
DTC: P0129 **1T CCM** **Years:** 2005, 2006, 2007 **Models:** 300, 300C, 300M, Aspen, Caravan, Charger, Dakota, Durango, Magnum, Town & Country **Engines:** All **Transmissions:** All	**Barometric Pressure Out-Of-Range** Engine cranking at less than 250 RPM; no CKP or CMP Sensor signals within 75ms. The PCM detected the MAP/BARO Sensor signal range was 0.04-2.2v for 300ms during testing. If equipped, the ETC lamp will be illuminated. 3 good trips are required to turn off the MIL. **Possible Causes:** • IAC motor control low or control high circuit has failed • MAP Sensor VREF (5v) circuit is open or shorted to ground • MAP Sensor signal circuit is open or shorted to ground • MAP Sensor is damaged or it has failed • May be an intermittent condition • PCM has failed
DTC: P0131 **2T CCM** **Years:** 2005, 2006, 2007 **Models:** 300, 300C, 300M, Aspen, Caravan, Charger, Dakota, Durango, Magnum, Town & Country **Engines:** All **Transmissions:** All	**O2 (B1 S1) Circuit Short to Ground** Engine running; cold start. O2 Sensor signal voltage is below 2.402v for 9 seconds (exc. Aspen, Dakota, Durango), or below 2.52v for 6 seconds (Aspen, Dakota, Durango). **Possible Causes:** • O2 signal circuit is shorted to chassis or Sensor ground • O2 return circuit is shorted to ground or to signal circuit • O2 signal circuit is shorted to O2 return upstream circuit • O2 may be contaminated or it has failed • PCM has failed
DTC: P0132 **1T CCM** **Years:** 2005, 2006, 2007 **Models:** 300, 300C, 300M, Charger, Magnum **Engines:** All **Transmissions:** All	**O2 Sensor (B1 S1) Voltage High** Engine started; battery voltage above 10.4v; O2 Sensor heater temperature is more than 925F (496C). O2 Sensor is more than 3.7v for 40 seconds. 3 good trips are required to turn the MIL off. **Possible Causes:** • O2 Sensor signal circuit and/or return circuit shorted to voltage • O2 Sensor has failed • O2 Sensor signal or return circuit open • PCM has failed
DTC: P0133 **2T O2** **Years:** 2005, 2006, 2007 **Models:** 300, 300C, 300M, Aspen, Caravan, Charger, Dakota, Durango, Magnum, Town & Country **Engines:** All **Transmissions:** All	**O2 (B1 S1) Slow Response** Vehicle driven at speeds between 20-55 mph, with throttle open for minimum of 120 seconds; coolant temperature is greater than 158F (70C); catalytic converter temperature is greater than 1112F (600C). PCM compared differences (state of change) between front and rear O2 Sensors indicate difference is greater than calibrated amount. **Possible Causes:** • Exhaust leak present in the exhaust manifold or exhaust pipes • O2 signal circuit or return circuit has failed • O2 element has failed
DTC: P0133 **2T O2** **Years:** 2005, 2006, 2007 **Models:** Aspen, Dakota, Durango **Engines:** All **Transmissions:** All	**O2 (B1 S1) Slow Response** Vehicle driven at speeds between 20-55 mph, with throttle open for minimum of 120 seconds; coolant temperature is greater than 158F (70C); catalytic converter temperature is greater than 1112F (600C); EVAP purge is active. The PCM detects the O2 Sensor signal voltage switches less than 16 times from lean to rich with 20 seconds during monitoring. 3 good trips are required to turn off MIL. **Possible Causes:** • Exhaust leak present in the exhaust manifold or exhaust pipes • O2 signal circuit or upstream circuit has failed • O2 element has failed

DTC	Trouble Code Title, Conditions & Possible Causes
DTC: P0135 **2T CCM** **Years:** 2005, 2006, 2007 **Models:** 300, 300C, 300M, Aspen, Caravan, Charger, Dakota, Durango, Magnum, Town & Country **Engines:** All **Transmissions:** All	**O2 (B1 S1) Heater Circuit** Engine running and O2 heater duty cycle is greater than 0%. O2 heater temperature does not reach 959F (575C), during monitoring conditions. No Sensor output is received when the PCM powers up the Sensor heater. 3 good trips are required to turn off the MIL. **Possible Causes:** • O2 heater ground circuit open or O2 signal circuit is open • O2 heater element has failed • PCM has failed
DTC: P0135 **2T CCM** **Years:** 2005, 2006, 2007 **Models:** Aspen, Dakota, Durango **Engines:** All **Transmissions:** All	**O2 (B1 S1) Heater Circuit** Engine running and O2 heater duty cycle is greater than 0%; battery voltage is more than 11v. No O2 sensor output signal is received when the PCM powers up the sensor heater. 3 good trips are required to turn off the MIL. **Possible Causes:** • O2 heater ground circuit open or heater control circuit is open • O2 heater element has failed • PCM has failed
DTC: P0137 **1T CCM** **Years:** 2005, 2006, 2007 **Models:** 300, 300C, 300M, Aspen, Caliber, Caravan, Charger, Dakota, Durango, Magnum, Town & Country **Engines:** All **Transmissions:** All	**O2 (B1 S2) Sensor Circuit Low** Engine running; battery voltage over 10.9v; O2 heater temperature below 484°F (251C) or ECT above 170F from previous key off. The PCM detected the O2 Sensor signal voltage was less than 1.5v for 3 seconds 300, 300C, Charger, less than 2.402v for 9 seconds (Caravan, Town & Country), or 2.5194v for 3 seconds (Aspen, Dakota, Durango). **Possible Causes:** • O2 return circuit is shorted to ground • O2 signal circuit is shorted to ground, or to O2 return circuit, or O2 heater ground circuit • O2 Sensor has failed • PCM has failed
DTC: P0138 **2T CCM** **Years:** 2005, 2006, 2007 **Models:** 300, 300C, Aspen, Caliber, Caravan, Charger, Commander, Compass, Crossfire, Dakota, Durango, Magnum, Town & Country **Engines:** All **Transmissions:** All	**O2 (B1 S2) Sensor Voltage High Condition:** Engine runtime for 119 seconds; O2 Sensor heater temperature is more than 662°F (350°C); Battery voltage more than 10.99v. O2 Sensor voltage is above 3.7v for 60 seconds (300, 300C, 300M, Charger. Magnum), above 3.9902v for 30 seconds (Aspen, Caravan, Dakota, Durango, Town & Country). **Possible Causes:** • O2 Sensor signal circuit or return circuit shorted to voltage • O2 Sensor has failed • O2 Sensor signal circuit or return circuit open • PCM has failed
DTC: P0139 **2T O2** **Years:** 2005, 2006, 2007 **Models:** 300, 300C, Aspen, Caliber, Caravan, Charger, Commander, Compass, Crossfire, Dakota, Durango, Magnum, Town & Country **Engines:** All **Transmissions:** All	**O2 (B1 S2) Slow Response** Engine started; vehicle driven at 20-55 mph with the throttle open for 2 minutes; ECT at more than 158°F (70C); catalytic converter temperature is more than 1112F (600C); and EVAP purge is active. O2 Sensor signal voltage switches less than 16 times from lean to rich within 20 seconds during monitoring, or will compare the state of change between the front and rear O2 Sensors and if the differences are greater than a calibrated amount, the DTC will set. 3 good trips are required to turn off the MIL. **Possible Causes:** • Exhaust leak • O2 element is contaminated, deteriorated or it has failed • O2 signal circuit or return circuit has failed
DTC: P0141 **2T CCM** **Years:** 2005, 2006, 2007 **Models:** 300, 300C, Aspen, Caliber, Caravan, Charger, Commander, Compass, Crossfire, Dakota, Durango, Magnum, Town & Country **Engines:** All **Transmissions:** All	**O2 (B1 S2) Heater Circuit** Engine running and O2 heater duty cycle is greater than 0%. O2 heater temperature does not reach 959F (575C), exc. 300, 300C, 300M, Charger, Magnum, or 662F (350C), all other models, within 90 seconds (45 seconds for Sebring, Stratus), or no O2 Sensor output is received when the PCM attempts to power up the Sensor heater. 3 good trips are required to turn off the MIL. **Possible Causes:** • O2 heater ground circuit open or O2 signal circuit is open • O2 heater element has failed • O2 heater ground circuit or control circuit is open • PCM has failed

DTC	Trouble Code Title, Conditions & Possible Causes
DTC: P0151 **1T CCM** **Years:** 2005, 2006, 2007 **Models:** 300, 300C, Aspen, Caliber, Caravan, Charger, Commander, Compass, Crossfire, Dakota, Durango, Magnum, Town & Country **Engines:** All **Transmissions: All**	**O2 (B2 S1) Circuit Short to Ground** Engine runtime under 30 seconds, system voltage over 10.99v, O2 heater temperature below 484°F. The PCM detected the O2 signal was below 1.5v (300, 300C, 300M, Charger, Magnum) or below 2.5196v (Aspen, Dakota, Durango) for 3 seconds after engine start. **Possible Causes:** • O2 upstream circuit is shorted to ground • O2 signal circuit is shorted to ground or to O2 upstream return circuit • O2 signal circuit is shorted to the heater ground circuit • O2 may be contaminated or it has failed • PCM has failed
DTC: P0152 **1T CCM** **Years:** 2005, 2006, 2007 **Models:** 300, 300C, Aspen, Caliber, Caravan, Charger, Commander, Compass, Crossfire, Dakota, Durango, Magnum, Town & Country **Engines:** All **Transmissions: All**	**O2 (B2 S1) Circuit High** O2 Sensor heater temperature is more than 925F (496C) on 300, 300C, 300M, Charger, Magnum; battery voltage is more than 10.99v. O2 Sensor voltage is more than 3.7v for 30 seconds (300, 300C, 300M, Charger, Magnum), more than 3.99v for 30 seconds (Aspen, Dakota, Durango). 3 good trips are required to turn off the MIL. **Possible Causes:** • O2 signal circuit is open or is shorted to battery voltage. • O2 upstream return circuit is open or is shorted to battery voltage • O2 Sensor is damaged or has failed • PCM has failed
DTC: P0153 **2T CCM** **Years:** 2005, 2006, 2007 **Models:** 300, 300C, Aspen, Caliber, Caravan, Charger, Commander, Compass, Crossfire, Dakota, Durango, Magnum, Town & Country **Engines:** All **Transmissions: All**	**O2 (B2 S1) Slow Response** Engine started; vehicle driven at a steady speed of 20-55 mph with the throttle open for at least 2 minutes, ECT Sensor more than 158°F (70C), Catalytic Converter temperature more than 1112°F (600C), EVAP purge is active, and the PCM detected the O2 signal switched from lean to rich less than 16 times (3.5L, 3.7L, 4.7L, 5.7L) or 11 times (2.7L) within a 20 second period during monitoring. 3 good trips are required to turn off MIL. **Possible Causes:** • Exhaust leak • O2 signal circuit has an open or grounded condition • O2 upstream return circuit has an open or grounded condition • O2 element is deteriorated or it has failed
DTC: P0155 **2T CCM** **Years:** 2005, 2006, 2007 **Models:** 300, 300C, Aspen, Caliber, Caravan, Charger, Commander, Compass, Crossfire, Dakota, Durango, Magnum, Town & Country **Engines:** All **Transmissions: All**	**O2 (B2 S1) Heater Circuit** Engine running and heater duty cycle is greater than 0%; battery voltage is more than 11v. O2 heater temperature does not reach 959F (575C) within 90 seconds, or no Sensor output is received when the PCM powers up the Sensor heater. 3 good trips required to turn off MIL. **Possible Causes:** • O2 heater control circuit is open • O2 heater ground circuit is open • O2 heater element is damaged or has failed • PCM has failed
DTC: P0157 **1T CCM** **Years:** 2005, 2006, 2007 **Models:** 300, 300C, Aspen, Caliber, Caravan, Charger, Commander, Compass, Crossfire, Dakota, Durango, Magnum, Town & Country **Engines:** **Transmissions:**	**O2 (B2 S2) Circuit Low** Engine runtime under 30 seconds; system voltage over 10.99v; O2 heater temperature below 484°F (251°C); O2 Sensor signal was less than 1.5v (300, 300C, 300M, Charger, Magnum) or less than 2.5196v (Aspen, Dakota, Durango) for 3 seconds after engine start. 3 good trips are required to turn off the MIL. **Possible Causes:** • O2 signal circuit is shorted to chassis or Sensor ground • O2 is damaged or it has failed • PCM has failed
DTC: P0158 **1T CCM** **Years:** 2005, 2006, 2007 **Models:** 300, 300C, Aspen, Caliber, Caravan, Charger, Commander, Compass, Crossfire, Dakota, Durango, Magnum, Town & Country **Engines:** All **Transmissions: All**	**O2 (B2 S2) Circuit High** Engine is running; system voltage over 10.99v; O2 heater temperature more than 925°F (496°C). The PCM detected the O2 signal was more than 3.70v for 30 seconds (300, 300C, 300M, Charger, Magnum), more than 3.99v for 30 seconds (Aspen, Dakota, Durango). 3 good trips required to turn off MIL. **Possible Causes:** • O2 signal circuit is open or is shorted to battery • O2 downstream return circuit is open or is shorted to battery • O2 is damaged or it has failed • PCM has failed

DTC	Trouble Code Title, Conditions & Possible Causes
DTC: P0159 2T O2 **Years:** 2005, 2006, 2007 **Models:** 300, 300C, Aspen, Caliber, Caravan, Charger, Commander, Compass, Crossfire, Dakota, Durango, Magnum, Town & Country **Engines:** All **Transmissions:** All	**O2 (B2 S2) Slow Response** Engine is driven at 20-55 mph with throttle open for 2 minutes; ECT Sensor over 158°F (70C); catalytic converter temperature over 1112°F (600C); EVAP purge is active. The O2 Sensor signal voltage switches less than 16 times or 11 times from lean to rich with 20 seconds during monitoring. 3 good trips required to turn off MIL. **Possible Causes:** • Exhaust leak • O2 signal circuit is open or shorted • O2 downstream return circuit is open or shorted • O2 Sensor is damaged or has failed
DTC: P0171 2T Fuel **Years:** 2005, 2006, 2007 **Models:** 300, 300C, Aspen, Caliber, Caravan, Charger, Commander, Compass, Crossfire, Dakota, Durango, Magnum, Town & Country **Engines:** All **Transmissions:** All	**Fuel System Lean (B1 S1)** Engine running in closed loop. AAT Sensor signal over 20°F (−7C). Altitude less than 8,500 feet. Fuel level greater than 15%. If PCM multiplies short-term compensation by long-term adaptive and a certain percentage is exceeded for 2 trips, a freeze frame is stored, the MIL illuminates, and a DTC is stored. **Possible Causes:** • Restricted fuel supply line • Fuel pump inlet strainer plugged or fuel pump has failed • O2 Sensor has failed • O2 signal circuit or return circuit has failed • O2 Sensor heater operation is faulty • TP Sensor sweep has failed • MAP Sensor operation has failed • ECT Sensor operation has failed • Engine mechanical problem is present • Fuel is contaminated • Exhaust leak exists
DTC: P0172 2T Fuel **Years:** 2005, 2006, 2007 **Models:** 300, 300C, Aspen, Caliber, Caravan, Charger, Commander, Compass, Crossfire, Dakota, Durango, Magnum, Town & Country **Engines:** All **Transmissions:** All	**Fuel System (S1 B1) Rich** Engine running in closed loop. IAT Sensor signal over 20°F (−7C). Altitude less than 8,500 feet. PCM multiplies short-term compensation by long-term adaptive, as well as a purge fuel multiplier, and the result is below a certain value for 30 seconds over 2 trips, a freeze frame is stored. MIL illuminates and DTC is stored. **Possible Causes:** • O2 Sensor heater or O2 Sensor has failed • EVAP purge solenoid failed or improper operation • O2 signal circuit or return circuit has failed • MAP Sensor has failed or circuit malfunction • ECT Sensor has failed or circuit malfunction • Engine mechanical problem • Fuel filter/pressure regulator has failed or needs repair • PCM has failed
DTC: P0174 2T Fuel **Years:** 2005, 2006, 2007 **Models:** 300, 300C, Aspen, Caliber, Caravan, Charger, Commander, Compass, Crossfire, Dakota, Durango, Magnum, Town & Country **Engines:** All **Transmissions:** All	**Fuel System (S2 B1) Lean** Engine running in closed loop. IAT Sensor signal over 20°F (−7C). Altitude less than 8,500 feet. PCM multiplies short-term compensation by long-term adaptive, and a certain percentage is exceeded in 2 trips, a freeze frame is stored. MIL illuminates and DTC is stored. 3 good trips required to turn off MIL. **Possible Causes:** • Restricted fuel supply line • Fuel pump inlet strainer plugged • Fuel pump is damaged or has failed • O2 signal circuit or return circuit has failed • MAP Sensor has failed or circuit malfunction • ECT Sensor has failed or circuit malfunction • Engine mechanical problem • Fuel filter/pressure regulator has failed or needs repair • O2 Sensor has failed • PCM has failed

DTC	Trouble Code Title, Conditions & Possible Causes
DTC: P0175 **2T Fuel** **Years:** 2005, 2006, 2007 **Models:** 300, 300C, Aspen, Caliber, Caravan, Charger, Commander, Compass, Crossfire, Dakota, Durango, Magnum, Town & Country **Engines:** All **Transmissions:** All	**Fuel System (S2 B1) Rich** Engine running in closed loop. IAT Sensor signal over 20°F (−7C). Altitude less than 8,500 feet. If the PCM multiplies short-term compensation by long-term adaptive, and a purge fuel multiplier, and the result is below a certain value for 30 seconds in 2 trips, a freeze frame is stored. MIL illuminates and DTC is stored. 3 good trips required to turn off MIL. **Possible Causes:** • Restricted fuel supply line • Fuel pump inlet strainer plugged • Fuel pump is damaged or has failed • O2 signal circuit or return circuit has failed • MAP Sensor has failed or circuit malfunction • ECT Sensor has failed or circuit malfunction • Engine mechanical problem • Fuel filter/pressure regulator has failed or needs repair • O2 Sensor has failed • PCM has failed
DTC: P0196 **1T CCM** **Years:** 2005, 2006, 2007 **Models:** 300, 300C, Aspen, Caliber, Caravan, Charger, Commander, Compass, Crossfire, Dakota, Durango, Magnum, Town & Country **Engines:** All **Transmissions:** All	**Engine Oil Temperature Sensor Circuit Performance** Engine off time is more than 8 hours; ambient temperature is more than 38F (4C). If the PCM detects the engine oil temperature value is incorrect, by comparing it with other engine inputs, then the DTC will set. 3 good trips required to turn off MIL. **Possible Causes:** • Engine oil temp signal circuit is open or is shorted to ground or to battery voltage • Engine oil temp Sensor ground circuit is open • Engine oil temp signal circuit is shorted to Sensor ground • Engine oil temp Sensor has failed • PCM has failed
DTC: P0197 **1T CCM** **Years:** 2005, 2006, 2007 **Models:** 300, 300C, Aspen, Caliber, Caravan, Charger, Commander, Compass, Crossfire, Dakota, Durango, Magnum, Town & Country **Engines:** All **Transmissions:** All	**Engine Oil Temperature Sensor Circuit Low** Ignition is on; battery voltage is more than 10.4v. The engine oil temperature Sensor circuit voltage at the PCM is less than the calibrated amount. 3 good trips required to turn off MIL. **Possible Causes:** • Engine oil temp signal circuit is shorted to ground • Engine oil temp signal circuit is shorted to Sensor ground • Engine oil temp Sensor has failed • PCM has failed
DTC: P0198 **1T CCM** **Years:** 2005, 2006, 2007 **Models:** 300, 300C, Aspen, Caliber, Caravan, Charger, Commander, Compass, Crossfire, Dakota, Durango, Magnum, Town & Country **Engines:** All **Transmissions:** All	**Engine Oil Temperature Sensor Circuit High** Ignition is on; battery voltage is more than 10.4v. The engine oil temperature Sensor circuit voltage at the PCM is higher than the calibrated amount. 3 good trips required to turn off MIL. **Possible Causes:** • Engine oil temp signal circuit is open or is shorted to battery voltage • Engine oil temp Sensor ground circuit is open • Engine oil temp Sensor has failed • PCM has failed
DTC: P0201-DTC: P0206 **1T CCM** **Years:** 2005, 2006, 2007 **Models:** 300, 300C, Aspen, Caliber, Caravan, Charger, Commander, Compass, Crossfire, Dakota, Durango, Magnum, Town & Country **Engines:** All **Transmissions:** All	**Injector 1, 2, 3, 4, 5, or 6 Control** ASD relay "on"; engine speed under 3000 RPM; battery voltage greater than 10v. No inductive spike is detected after injector turns off. **Possible Causes:** • ASD relay output circuit failure • Fuel injector has malfunctioned or failed • Fuel injector control circuit is open or shorted to ground • PCM has failed

DTC	Trouble Code Title, Conditions & Possible Causes
DTC: P0201-DTC: P0208 **1T CCM** **Years:** 2005, 2006, 2007 **Models:** 300, 300C, Aspen, Caliber, Caravan, Charger, Commander, Compass, Crossfire, Dakota, Durango, Magnum, Town & Country **Engines:** All **Transmissions:** All	**Injector 1, 2, 3, 4, 5, 6, 7 or 8 Control** ASD relay "on", engine speed under 3000 RPM, battery voltage greater than 10v. No inductive spike is detected after injector turn off. **Possible Causes:** • ASD relay output circuit failure • Fuel injector has malfunctioned or failed • Fuel injector control circuit is open or shorted to ground • PCM has failed
DTC: P0218 **1T CCM** **Years:** 2005, 2006, 2007 **Models:** 300, 300C, Aspen, Caliber, Caravan, Charger, Commander, Compass, Crossfire, Dakota, Durango, Magnum, Town & Country **Engines:** All **Transmissions:** All	**A/T High Temperature Operation Activated** Engine started; vehicle driven in gear, and the TCM indicated the Overheat shift schedule was activated (i.e., the TCM had detected a transmission oil temperature of more than 240°F). **Note: This is an informational DTC, designed to aid the technician in diagnosing shift quality complaints.** **Possible Causes:** • Engine cooling system malfunction present • High temperature operations activated • Transmission oil pump flow is too low or it is restricted
DTC: P0221 **1T CCM** **Years:** 2005, 2006, 2007 **Models:** 300, 300C, Aspen, Caliber, Caravan, Charger, Commander, Compass, Crossfire, Dakota, Durango, Magnum, Town & Country **Engines:** All **Transmissions:** All	**Throttle Position Sensor No. 2 Performance** Ignition on; No MAP Sensor DTCs are set. TP Sensor signals Do NOT correlate to the MAP Sensor signal. If equipped, ETC light will illuminate. P2135 should also set. **Possible Causes:** • TP Sensor No. 1 or 2 signal circuit is shorted to battery voltage or to ground • TP Sensor No. 1 or 2 signal circuit has high resistance • 5v supply circuit is shorted to ground • TP Sensor return circuit has high resistance • TP Sensor No. 1 signal circuit shorted to TP Sensor No. 2 signal circuit • TP Sensor or throttle body damaged or has failed • PCM has failed
DTC: P0223 **1T CCM** **Years:** 2005, 2006, 2007 **Models:** 300, 300C, Aspen, Caliber, Caravan, Charger, Commander, Compass, Crossfire, Dakota, Durango, Magnum, Town & Country **Engines:** All **Transmissions:** All	**Throttle Position Sensor No. 2 Circuit High** Ignition on; battery voltage is more than 10v. TP Sensor voltage at the PCM is more than 4.9v for 25ms. If equipped, ETC light will illuminate. **Possible Cause:** • TP Sensor No. 2 signal circuit shorted to battery voltage or to 5v supply circuit • TP Sensor return circuit is open • TP Sensor or throttle body is damaged or has failed • PCM has failed
DTC: P0300 **2T CCM** **Years:** 2005, 2006, 2007 **Models:** 300, 300C, Aspen, Caliber, Caravan, Charger, Commander, Compass, Crossfire, Dakota, Durango, Magnum, Town & Country **Engines:** All **Transmissions:** All	**Multiple Cylinder Misfire** Any time engine is running and Adaptive Numerator (Target Learning Coefficient) has been successfully updated. If more than 1.5% (300, 300C, 300M, Charger, Magnum) or 1.8% (Caravan, Town & Country), 2% (Aspen, Dakota, Durango), misfire rate is measured during 2 trips. 3 good trips required to turn off MIL. **Possible Causes:** • ASD relay output circuit fault • Injector control circuit fault • Coil control circuit fault • Ignition wiring, coil control circuit or coil fault • Fuel pump inlet strainer plugged • Restricted fuel supply line • Fuel pump module is damaged • Fuel pressure leakdown fault • Fuel injector damaged or has failed • Engine mechanical problems exist • PCM has failed

DTC	Trouble Code Title, Conditions & Possible Causes
DTC: P0301-P0306 **2T Catalyst** **2T CCM** **Years:** 2005, 2006, 2007 **Models:** 300, 300C, Aspen, Caliber, Caravan, Charger, Commander, Compass, Crossfire, Dakota, Durango, Magnum, Town & Country **Engines:** All **Transmissions:** All	**Cylinder 1-6 Misfire Detected** Any time engine is running and Target Learning Coefficient (TLC) has been successfully updated, if more than 1.8% (Caravan, Town & Country), 2% (Aspen, Dakota, Durango), 2.5% (Durango LEV), misfire rate is measured during 2 trips or with 10-30% misfire rate during one trip. **Possible Causes:** • Intermittent misfire • Base engine mechanical fault that affects only 1 cylinder • Ignition wiring, coil control circuit or coil fault • ASD relay output circuit (coil or injector) problem • Spark plug malfunction or failure on 1 cylinder • CMP Sensor, Sensor wiring harness or tone wheel is damaged • Fuel delivery component fault that affects only 1 cylinder (e.g., a dirty fuel injector) • Injector or control circuit failure • PCM has failed
DTC: P0301- P0308 **2TCatalyst** **Years:** 2005, 2006, 2007 **Models:** 300, 300C, Aspen, Caliber, Caravan, Charger, Commander, Compass, Crossfire, Dakota, Durango, Magnum, Town & Country **Engines:** All **Transmissions:** All	**Cylinder 1-8 Misfire Detected** Any time engine is running and the adaptive numerator has been successfully updated. When more than 1.5% (300, 300C, 300M, Charger, Magnum), 2% (Aspen, Dakota, Durango), 2.5% (Durango LEV), misfire rate is measured during 2 trips, or with 10-30% misfire during 1 trip. 3 good trips required to turn off MIL. **Possible Causes:** • ASD relay output 2 circuit fault • Injector control 1 circuit fault • Coil control 1 circuit fault • Ignition wiring, spark plug, or ignition coil fault • Fuel pump inlet strainer plugged • Restricted fuel supply line • Fuel pump module fault • Fuel pressure leakdown fault • Fuel injector is damaged or has failed • Engine mechanical problems exist • PCM has failed
DTC: P0315 **1T CCM** **Years:** 2005, 2006, 2007 **Models:** 300, 300C, Aspen, Caliber, Caravan, Charger, Commander, Compass, Crossfire, Dakota, Durango, Magnum, Town & Country **Engines:** All **Transmissions:** All	**No Crankshaft Position Sensor Learned** Engine started; engine runtime more than 50 seconds under closed throttle conditions; A/C off; ECT Sensor more than 167°F (75C). The PCM detected that one of the CKP Sensor windows had too much variance (e.g., over 2.86%) from its calibrated reference point. **Possible Causes:** • Crankshaft tone wheel flex plate is damaged • Tone wheel/pulse ring may be damaged • Erratic CKP Sensor signals (wiring/connector problem) • CKP Sensor has failed • PCM has failed
DTC: P0325 **1T CCM** **Years:** 2005, 2006, 2007 **Models:** 300, 300C, Aspen, Caliber, Caravan, Charger, Commander, Compass, Crossfire, Dakota, Durango, Magnum, Town & Country **Engines:** All **Transmissions:** All	**Knock Sensor No. 1 Circuit** Engine running at idle or in deceleration mode, and the PCM detected the Knock Sensor signal was below a minimum value (value depends on engine speed), or if Sensor voltage was about 5.0v with engine within idle range. **Possible Causes:** • Knock Sensor connector is damaged or shorted • Knock Sensor signal circuit open or grounded • Knock Sensor signal circuit shorted to return circuit • Knock Sensor return circuit is open • Knock Sensor not tightened properly • Knock Sensor damaged or has failed (it may be open internally) • PCM has failed
DTC: P0330 **1T CCM** **Years:** 2005, 2006, 2007 **Models:** 300, 300C, Aspen, Caliber, Caravan, Charger, Commander, Compass, Crossfire, Dakota, Durango, Magnum, Town & Country **Engines:** **Transmissions:**	**Knock Sensor No. 2 Circuit** Engine running. The Knock Sensor circuit voltage falls below a minimum value at idle or deceleration. The minimum value is from a lookup table internal to the PCM and is based on engine RPM. This DTC will also set if the Sensor voltage goes above 5v. 3 good trips required to turn off MIL. **Possible Causes:** • Knock Sensor No. 2 signal circuit shorted to battery voltage or to KS 2 return circuit • Knock Sensor No. 2 signal circuit or return circuit is open • Knock Sensor No. 2 signal circuit is shorted to KS 2 return circuit or to ground • Knock Sensor damaged or has failed • PCM has failed

DTC	Trouble Code Title, Conditions & Possible Causes
DTC: P0335 **1T CCM** **Years:** 2005, 2006, 2007 **Models:** 300, 300C, Aspen, Caliber, Caravan, Charger, Commander, Compass, Crossfire, Dakota, Durango, Magnum, Town & Country **Engines:** All **Transmissions:** All	**Crankshaft Position Sensor Circuit** Engine cranking with at least 8 CMP Sensor signals detected. The PCM did not detect any CKP Sensor signals for 2 seconds. **Possible Causes:** • Intermittent CKP signal • CKP Sensor signal circuit is open or it is shorted to ground or voltage • CKP Sensor 5v supply circuit is open or shorted to ground or voltage • CKP Sensor ground circuit is open • CKP Sensor or CMP Sensor is damaged or has failed • PCM has failed
DTC: P0339 **1T CCM** **Years:** 2005, 2006, 2007 **Models:** 300, 300C, Aspen, Caliber, Caravan, Charger, Commander, Compass, Crossfire, Dakota, Durango, Magnum, Town & Country **Engines:** **Transmissions:**	**Crankshaft Position Sensor Circuit Intermittent** Engine cranking or running; CMP Sensor signals detected. The PCM detected an intermittent loss of the CKP Sensor signal. The Failure counter must reach 20 before this code will set. **Possible Causes:** • Check the tone wheel/pulse ring for damage or debris collection • CKP Sensor signal circuit is open or shorted to ground • CKP Sensor 5v supply circuit is open or shorted to ground • CKP Sensor is damaged or it has failed • PCM has failed
DTC: P0340 **1T CCM** **Years:** 2005, 2006, 2007 **Models:** 300, 300C, Aspen, Caliber, Caravan, Charger, Commander, Compass, Crossfire, Dakota, Durango, Magnum, Town & Country **Engines:** All **Transmissions:** All	**No Camshaft Position Sensor Circuit Failure** Engine cranking or running, system voltage over 10v. The PCM detected CKP pulses without detecting any CMP Sensor pulses for 5 seconds or 2.5 engine revolutions. **Possible Causes:** • CMP Sensor connector is damaged, open or it is shorted • CMP Sensor signal circuit is open or shorted to ground or to battery voltage or 5v supply circuit • CMP Sensor 5v supply circuit is open or shorted to ground or to battery voltage • CMP Sensor ground circuit is open • CMP Sensor is damaged or has failed • CKP Sensor is damaged or has failed • PCM has failed
DTC: P0344 **1T CCM** **Years:** 2005, 2006, 2007 **Models:** 300, 300C, Aspen, Caliber, Caravan, Charger, Commander, Compass, Crossfire, Dakota, Durango, Magnum, Town & Country **Engines:** All **Transmissions:** All	**Camshaft Position Sensor Circuit Intermittent** Engine cranking or running; system voltage over 10.5v. The PCM detected an intermittent loss of the CMP Sensor signal during the period of 2.5 complete engine revolutions. The failure counter must reach 20 before this code matures and a code is set. **Possible Causes:** • Wiring harness fault • 5v supply circuit open or shorted to ground • Tone wheel/pulse ring is damaged or corroded • CMP Sensor has failed • CMP Sensor signal circuit is open, shorted to ground or battery voltage or 5v supply • CMP Sensor ground circuit is open • PCM has failed
DTC: P0401 **2T EGR** **Years:** 2005, 2006, 2007 **Models:** 300, 300C, Aspen, Caliber, Caravan, Charger, Commander, Compass, Crossfire, Dakota, Durango, Magnum, Town & Country **Engines:** All **Transmissions:** All	**EGR System Fault** Engine running for more than 2 minutes with ECT more than 158°F (70C). EGR is active. Vehicle is at less than 8500 feet altitude. Ambient temperature more than 20F (−6C). PCM closes EGR valve while monitoring O2 Sensor signal. Once a closed EGR fueling sample has been established, PCM then ramps in EGR and additional fueling, while monitoring the O2 Sensor signal in the open state. A fueling sample is again established. The PCM then compares the 2 different O2 Sensor signal readings (fueling samples). If a larger than expected variation is detected, a soft failure is recorded. Three soft failures set a one-trip (1T) failure. After 2 failed trips (2T), a DTC is set and the MIL illuminated. **Possible Causes:** • EGR valve is open at idle • EGR solenoid ground circuit is open • EGR solenoid control circuit is open, shorted to ground or to voltage • ASD relay power circuit open to the EGR solenoid • EGR valve or solenoid is damaged or has failed • PCM has failed (EGR open or EGR closed)

DTC	Trouble Code Title, Conditions & Possible Causes
DTC: P0403 **1T CCM** **Years:** 2005, 2006, 2007 **Models:** 300, 300C, Aspen, Caliber, Caravan, Charger, Commander, Compass, Crossfire, Dakota, Durango, Magnum, Town & Country **Engines:** All **Transmissions:** All	**EGR Solenoid Circuit** Engine started; system voltage over 10.5v. The EGR solenoid control circuit was not in its expected state when requested to operate by the PCM. **Possible Causes:** • EGR solenoid ground circuit is open • EGR solenoid control circuit is open or shorted to ground or to voltage • EGR solenoid power circuit is open • EGR solenoid is damaged or has failed • PCM has failed
DTC: P0404 **1T CCM** **Years:** 2005, 2006, 2007 **Models:** 300, 300C, Aspen, Caliber, Caravan, Charger, Commander, Compass, Crossfire, Dakota, Durango, Magnum, Town & Country **Engines:** All **Transmissions:** All	**EGR Position Sensor Signal Performance** Engine started; system voltage over 10.5v and the PCM detected that the EGR flow (or valve movement) was not what was expected during the test period. **Possible Causes:** • EGR Sensor signal circuit is open or shorted to ground • EGR Sensor 5v supply circuit is open or has high resistance • EGR Sensor ground circuit is open • EGR solenoid control circuit has a problem • EGR valve actuator loose, sticking, blocked or improperly grounded • EGR Sensor is damaged or has failed • Intermittent condition • PCM has failed
DTC: P0405 **1T CCM** **Years:** 2005, 2006, 2007 **Models:** 300, 300C, Aspen, Caliber, Caravan, Charger, Commander, Compass, Crossfire, Dakota, Durango, Magnum, Town & Country **Engines:** All **Transmissions:** All	**EGR Position Sensor Circuit Low Input** Key on or engine running; system voltage over 10v. The PCM detected that the EGR Sensor signal indicated less than 0.1v. **Possible Causes:** • EGR Sensor signal circuit is shorted to ground or open • EGR Sensor VREF (5v) circuit is open or shorted to ground • EGR Sensor is damaged (shorted internally) or it has failed • EGR position internal failure • PCM has failed
DTC: P0406 **1T CCM** **Years:** 2005, 2006, 2007 **Models:** 300, 300C, Aspen, Caliber, Caravan, Charger, Commander, Compass, Crossfire, Dakota, Durango, Magnum, Town & Country **Engines:** All **Transmissions:** All	**EGR Position Sensor Circuit High Input** Key on or engine running; system voltage over 10.5v. The PCM detected the EGR Sensor indicated more than 4.89v for 6 seconds. **Possible Causes:** • Intermittent condition • EGR Sensor signal is shorted to VREF (5v) supply circuit or to battery voltage • EGR Sensor ground circuit is open • EGR Sensor signal circuit is open • EGR Sensor is damaged (it may have an internal open circuit) • EGR solenoid failure • PCM has failed
DTC: P0420 **2T Catalyst** **Years:** 2005, 2006, 2007 **Models:** 300, 300C, Aspen, Caliber, Caravan, Charger, Commander, Compass, Crossfire, Dakota, Durango, Magnum, Town & Country **Engines:** All **Transmissions:** All	**Catalyst Efficiency Below Normal (Bank 1)** Engine speed at 1200-1700 RPM in closed loop with the throttle open for over 2 minutes, ECT Sensor more than 147°F, MAP Sensor signal from 15.0-21.0 in. Hg, and the PCM detected the switch rate of the rear O2 reached 70% of the switch rate of the front O2. **Possible Causes:** • Air leaks in at the exhaust manifold or exhaust pipes • Base engine problems (high coolant or engine oil consumption) • Catalytic converter damaged or has failed • Front O2 older (aged) than the rear O2 (O2 is lazy)

DTC	Trouble Code Title, Conditions & Possible Causes
DTC: P0420 **1T Catalyst** **Years:** 2005, 2006, 2007 **Models:** Aspen, Caravan, Dakota, Durango, Town & Country **Engines:** All **Transmissions:** All	**Catalyst Efficiency Below Normal (Bank 1)** Engine is running for more than 90 seconds; engine coolant is more than 158F (70C); vehicle speed is 20-55 mph; engine speed is 1200-1900 RPM; MAP vacuum at 15-20 in. Hg. As catalyst efficiency deteriorates, the switch rate of the downstream O2 Sensor approaches that of the upstream O2 Sensor. If at any point during the test, the switch ratio reaches a predetermined value, a counter is incremented by one. **Possible Causes:** • Catalytic converter damaged or has failed • Air leaks in at the exhaust manifold or exhaust pipes • Base engine problems (high coolant or engine oil consumption) • Front O2 older (aged) than the rear O2 (O2 is lazy)
DTC: P0430 **1T Catalyst** **Years:** 2005, 2006, 2007 **Models:** 300, 300C, Aspen, Caliber, Caravan, Charger, Commander, Compass, Crossfire, Dakota, Durango, Magnum, Town & Country **Engines:** All **Transmissions:** All	**Catalyst (2/1) Efficiency Below Normal** After engine warm-up, ECT Sensor more than 170°F for 180 seconds of open throttle operation and over 20 mph (engine between 1200-1700 RPM and MAP vacuum between 15-20 in. Hg). As catalyst efficiency deteriorates, the switch rate of the downstream O2 Sensor approaches that of the upstream O2 Sensor. If, at any point during the test, the switch ratio reaches a predetermined value, a counter is incremented by one. 3 good trips required to turn off MIL. **Possible Causes:** • Exhaust leaks • Base engine problems • Catalytic converter damaged or has failed • Front O2 older (aged) than the rear O2 (O2 is lazy)
DTC: P0432 **2T Catalyst** **Years:** 2005, 2006, 2007 **Models:** 300, 300C, Aspen, Caliber, Caravan, Charger, Commander, Compass, Crossfire, Dakota, Durango, Magnum, Town & Country **Engines:** All **Transmissions:** All	**Catalyst Efficiency Below Normal (Bank 2)** Engine speed at 1200-1700 RPM in closed loop with the throttle open for over 2 minutes, ECT Sensor more than 147°F, MAP Sensor signal from 15.0-21.0" Hg, and the PCM detected the switch rate of the rear O2 reached 70% of the switch rate of the front O2. **Possible Causes:** • Air leaks in at the exhaust manifold or exhaust pipes • Base engine problems (high coolant or engine oil consumption) • Catalytic converter damaged or has failed • Front O2 older (aged) than the rear O2 (O2 is lazy)
DTC: P0440 **2T EVAP** **Years:** 2005, 2006, 2007 **Models:** 300, 300C, Aspen, Caliber, Caravan, Charger, Commander, Compass, Crossfire, Dakota, Durango, Magnum, Town & Country **Engines:** All **Transmissions:** All	**EVAP Purge System Fault** Ambient Air Temperature from 39-89°F (4-32C); engine running; Fuel level over 12%. The PCM detected that the NVLD switch did not close during medium/large leak test. Once this event occurs, the PCM will increase the amount of vacuum in the system that flows past the purge valve. If the NVLD switch does not close under these conditions, the PCM will set this code. **Possible Causes:** • EVAP purge valve vacuum supply is leaking or clogged • EVAP purge valve is stuck closed • EVAP purge solenoid has failed • NVLD assembly (leak detection) is damaged or has failed • NVLD switch circuit is open or the NVLD switch has failed • Ground circuit is open • PCM has failed
DTC: P0441 **2T EVAP** **Years:** 2005, 2006, 2007 **Models:** 300, 300C, Aspen, Caliber, Caravan, Charger, Commander, Compass, Crossfire, Dakota, Durango, Magnum, Town & Country **Engines:** All **Transmissions:** All	**EVAP Purge Flow Monitor Fault** Engine at idle speed in closed loop for 200 seconds, BARO Sensor signal less than 8,000 feet, ECT Sensor more than 160°F, no Low Fuel, MAP Sensor signal less than 23.7" Hg, and the PCM did not detect any purge flow through the EVAP system during this test. **Possible Causes:** • EVAP purge solenoid vacuum line loose, leaking or restricted • EVAP purge solenoid stuck leaking, stuck open or stuck closed • EVAP purge vacuum line to canister leaking or disconnected • EVAP canister leaking, damaged or has failed

DTC	Trouble Code Title, Conditions & Possible Causes
DTC: P0441 **2T EVAP** **Years:** 2005, 2006, 2007 **Models:** 300, 300C, Aspen, Caliber, Caravan, Charger, Commander, Compass, Crossfire, Dakota, Durango, Magnum, Town & Country **Engines:** All **Transmissions:** All	**EVAP Purge System Performance** Check with cold start test. Engine running. Small leak test passed. The PCM activates the EVAP purge solenoid and it gradually increases to maximum flow. During flow, the PCM looks for the NVLD switch to close. If the PCM does not see the NVLD switch close at maximum flow, an error is detected. **Possible Causes:** • Intermittent condition • EVAP purge solenoid functioning improperly • EVAP purge solenoid vacuum supply leaking or clogged
DTC: P0442 **2T EVAP** **Years:** 2005, 2006, 2007 **Models:** 300, 300C, Aspen, Caliber, Caravan, Charger, Commander, Compass, Crossfire, Dakota, Durango, Magnum, Town & Country **Engines:** All **Transmissions:** All	**EVAP System Medium Leak Detected** Monitor with engine running. Cold start test. Fuel level more than 12%. Ambient temperature between 39-89F (4-32C). Closed loop fuel system. Test runs when small leak test is maturing. The PCM activates EVAP purge solenoid to pull EVAP system into a vacuum to close the NVLD switch. Once this switch is closed, the PCM turns the EVAP purge solenoid off to seal the EVAP system. If the NVLD switch re-opens before the calibrated amount of time for a Medium leak, an error is detected. **Possible Causes:** • Intermittent condition • Vacuum hoses, connections or switches have come loose or malfunctioned • EVAP emission system has a leak • EVAP purge solenoid operation has malfunctioned • NVLD switch operation has malfunctioned
DTC: P0443 **1T CCM** **Years:** 2005, 2006, 2007 **Models:** 300, 300C, Aspen, Caliber, Caravan, Charger, Commander, Compass, Crossfire, Dakota, Durango, Magnum, Town & Country **Engines:** All **Transmissions:** All	**EVAP Purge Solenoid Circuit Fault** Ignition on or engine running. Battery voltage more than 10v. The PCM will set a trouble code if the actual state of the solenoid does not match the intended state. **Possible Causes:** • EVAP purge solenoid control circuit open or shorted to ground • EVAP purge solenoid return circuit open or shorted to ground • EVAP purge solenoid is damaged or it has failed • PCM has failed
DTC: P0452 **1T CCM** **Years:** 2005, 2006, 2007 **Models:** 300, 300C, Aspen, Caliber, Caravan, Charger, Commander, Compass, Crossfire, Dakota, Durango, Magnum, Town & Country **Engines:** All **Transmissions:** All	**NVLD Pressure Switch Sense Circuit Low Input** Engine started; and immediately after the engine is running. The PCM activates the NVLD solenoid to test the NVLD switch circuit. If the switch is not open, the PCM sets this code. **Possible Causes:** • EVAP purge solenoid control circuit is shorted to ground • EVAP purge solenoid is leaking or it is stuck in open position • NVLD assembly or NVLD switch is damaged or it has failed • NVLD switch signal circuit is shorted to ground • PCM has failed
DTC: P0453 **1T CCM** **Years:** 2005, 2006, 2007 **Models:** 300, 300C, Aspen, Caliber, Caravan, Charger, Commander, Compass, Crossfire, Dakota, Durango, Magnum, Town & Country **Engines:** All **Transmissions:** All	**NVLD Pressure Switch Sense Circuit High Input** Engine started; and immediately after the engine is running, the PCM activates the NVLD solenoid to test the NVLD switch circuit. If the switch does not close under these conditions, this code is set. **Possible Causes:** • NVLD assembly ground circuit is open • NVLD switch signal circuit is open or shorted to power (B+) or to NVLD solenoid control circuit • NVLD assembly or switch is damaged or it has failed • PCM has failed
DTC: P0455 **2T EVAP** **Years:** 2005, 2006, 2007 **Models:** 300, 300C, Aspen, Caliber, Caravan, Charger, Commander, Compass, Crossfire, Dakota, Durango, Magnum, Town & Country **Engines:** All **Transmissions:** All	**EVAP Large Leak Detected** Ambient Air Temperature from 39-89°F at engine startup, engine running under closed loop conditions, Fuel Level over 12%, then with the EVAP purge solenoid enabled (to pull vacuum into the system to close the NVLD switch) and the EVAP "small leak" test maturing, the PCM turns "off" the EVAP purge solenoid once the NVLD switch closes. If the NVLD switch reopens before a calibrated amount of time expires, a "large" leak in the system is detected (larger than 0.080 in.). **Possible Causes:** • EVAP purge solenoid is damaged or it has failed • Fuel tank cap is damaged, missing or the wrong part number • NVLD switch is damaged or it has failed

DTC	Trouble Code Title, Conditions & Possible Causes
DTC: P0456 **2T EVAP** **Years:** 2005, 2006, 2007 **Models:** 300, 300C, Aspen, Caliber, Caravan, Charger, Commander, Compass, Crossfire, Dakota, Durango, Magnum, Town & Country **Engines:** All **Transmissions:** All	**EVAP System Small Leak Detected** Ambient Air Temperature from 39-109°F at engine startup, engine running under closed loop conditions, Fuel Level below 88%, then with the EVAP system sealed, the PCM monitors the NVLD switch. If the NVLD switch does not close within a calibrated amount of time expires, a "small" leak in the EVAP system was detected. **Possible Causes:** • Fuel tank cap is damaged, loose or the wrong part number • Small leak present somewhere in the EVAP system
DTC: P0457 **2T EVAP** **Years:** 2005, 2006, 2007 **Models:** 300, 300C, Aspen, Caliber, Caravan, Charger, Commander, Compass, Crossfire, Dakota, Durango, Magnum, Town & Country **Engines:** All **Transmissions:** All	**Loose Fuel Cap Condition:** Monitor with ignition on. Ambient temperature should be between 39-109F (4-43C). Vehicle should be in closed loop fuel system. The PCM has detected an EVAP system leak after a fuel level increase. If the NVLD switch reopens before the calibrated amount of time after a fuel tank fill, an error is detected. MIL will illuminate. Condition requires 3 good trips to turn off MIL. **Possible Causes:** • Loose or missing fuel fill cap • Intermittent condition • NVLD system or switch malfunction • EVAP system leaking • EVAP purge solenoid malfunction
DTC: P0461 **2T CCM** **Years:** 2005, 2006, 2007 **Models:** 300, 300C, Aspen, Caliber, Caravan, Charger, Commander, Compass, Crossfire, Dakota, Durango, Magnum, Town & Country **Engines:** All **Transmissions:** All	**Fuel Level Sensor No. 1 Malfunction** Test No. 1: With ignition on, fuel level is compared to the previous key-down after a 20-second delay. If the PCM does not see a difference in the fuel level of more than 0.1v, the test will fail. Test No. 2: The PCM monitors the fuel level with ignition on. If the PCM does not see a change in the fuel level of 0.1765 in. over a set amount of miles, the test will fail. **Possible Causes:** • Fuel tank or internal siphon hose damage • Fuel level signal circuit open or shorted to ground • Ground circuit is open • Fuel level Sensor malfunction
DTC: P0462 **1T CCM** **Years:** 2005, 2006, 2007 **Models:** 300, 300C, Aspen, Caliber, Caravan, Charger, Commander, Compass, Crossfire, Dakota, Durango, Magnum, Town & Country **Engines:** All **Transmissions:** All	**Fuel Level Sensor No. 1 Low Input** Key on. Battery voltage over 10.4v. Fuel level Sensor signal goes below 0.1961v (exc. Aspen, Dakota, Durango) for more than 5 seconds, or below 0.4v for more than 90 seconds (Aspen, Dakota, Durango). DTC is recorded. **Possible Causes:** • Intermittent condition • Fuel level sending unit signal circuit shorted to Sensor or chassis ground • Fuel level sensing unit is damaged or the fuel tank is damaged • Instrument cluster problem
DTC: P0463 **1T CCM** **Years:** 2005, 2006, 2007 **Models:** 300, 300C, Aspen, Caliber, Caravan, Charger, Commander, Compass, Crossfire, Dakota, Durango, Magnum, Town & Country **Engines:** All **Transmissions:** All	**Fuel Level Sensor No. 1 High Input** Key on. Battery voltage over 10.4v. If Fuel Level Sensor signal goes above 4.7v for more than 5 seconds (exc. Aspen, Dakota, Durango), above 4.9v for more than 90 seconds (Aspen, Dakota, Durango), this DTC is recorded. **Possible Causes:** • Fuel level sending unit signal circuit is open or is shorted to battery voltage • Fuel level Sensor ground circuit is open • Fuel level Sensor is damaged or the fuel tank is damaged • Instrument cluster is faulty • BCM or PCM has failed
DTC: P0480 **1T CCM** **Years:** 2005, 2006, 2007 **Models:** 300, 300C, Aspen, Caliber, Caravan, Charger, Commander, Compass, Crossfire, Dakota, Durango, Magnum, Town & Country **Engines:** All **Transmissions:** All	**Low Speed (No.1) Fan Control Relay Circuit** Key on. Battery voltage over 10v. An open or shorted circuit is detected in the Low Speed Fan Relay control circuit system. **Possible Causes:** • Fan relay intermittent condition • Ground circuit is open • Fused B+ output circuit malfunction • Fan relay control circuit is open or shorted to battery voltage or ground • Fan relay is damaged or has failed • PCM has failed

DTC	Trouble Code Title, Conditions & Possible Causes
DTC: P0481 **1T CCM** **Years:** 2005, 2006, 2007 **Models:** 300, 300C, Aspen, Caliber, Caravan, Charger, Commander, Compass, Crossfire, Dakota, Durango, Magnum, Town & Country **Engines:** All **Transmissions:** All	**High Speed (No. 2) Fan Relay Control Circuit** Key on or engine running; and the PCM detected an unexpected low or high voltage condition (open or shorted condition) on the High Speed Fan Relay circuit. **Possible Causes:** • HFAN relay power circuit is open from the relay to fused power • HFAN relay control circuit is open or shorted to chassis ground • Fan relay(s) failed • PCM has failed.
DTC: P0498 **1T CCM** **Years:** 2005, 2006, 2007 **Models:** 300, 300C, Aspen, Caliber, Caravan, Charger, Commander, Compass, Crossfire, Dakota, Durango, Magnum, Town & Country **Engines:** All **Transmissions:** All	**NVLD Canister Vent Solenoid Circuit Low** Key on or engine running; and the PCM detected an unexpected low voltage condition on the Natural Vacuum Leak Detection (NVLD) control circuit during the CCM test period. **Possible Causes:** • NVLD canister vent solenoid control circuit is shorted to ground • NVLD canister vent solenoid is damaged or it has failed • PCM has failed
DTC: P0499 **1T CCM** **Years:** 2005, 2006, 2007 **Models:** 300, 300C, Aspen, Caliber, Caravan, Charger, Commander, Compass, Crossfire, Dakota, Durango, Magnum, Town & Country **Engines:** All **Transmissions:** All	**NVLD Canister Vent Solenoid Circuit High** Key on or engine running. The PCM detected an open or unexpected high voltage condition on the Natural Vacuum Leak Detection (NVLD) circuit. **Possible Causes:** • NVLD canister vent solenoid control circuit is open or is shorted to power • NVLD canister vent solenoid ground circuit is open • NVLD canister vent solenoid is damaged or it has failed • PCM has failed
DTC: P0501 **2T CCM** **Years:** 2005, 2006, 2007 **Models:** 300, 300C, Aspen, Caliber, Caravan, Charger, Commander, Compass, Crossfire, Dakota, Durango, Magnum, Town & Country **Engines:** All **Transmissions:** All	**Vehicle Speed Sensor Performance** Engine started; vehicle driven at over 1500 RPM for 10 seconds, gear selector not in Park or Neutral (or clutch is not depressed on M/T); brakes not applied. The PCM did not receive any VSS signals from the TCM for 11 seconds for 2 consecutive trips. 3 good trips required to turn off MIL. **Possible Causes:** • Check for any ABS/RWAL or TCM codes related to the VSS • VSS connector is damaged, open or it is shorted • VSS signal is open, shorted to ground or shorted to power • Incorrect tire circumference • ABS/RWAL controller, BCM, ECM, TCM or PCM has failed
DTC: P0503 **1T or 2T CCM** **Years:** 2005, 2006, 2007 **Models:** 300, 300C, Aspen, Caliber, Caravan, Charger, Commander, Compass, Crossfire, Dakota, Durango, Magnum, Town & Country **Engines:** All **Transmissions:** All	**Vehicle Speed Sensor No. 1 Erratic Performance** Ignition is on; battery voltage over 10v; transmission in Drive or Reverse; brakes not applied. Vehicle speed signal is erratic during road load conditions. One-trip fault for ETC vehicles; Two-trip fault for ETC vehicles. 3 good trips required to turn off MIL. **Possible Causes:** • Check for active Bus or Communication DTCs • Incorrect Tire Circumference • PCM has failed
DTC: P0505 **Years:** 2005, 2006, 2007 **Models:** 300, 300C, Aspen, Caliber, Caravan, Charger, Commander, Compass, Crossfire, Dakota, Durango, Magnum, Town & Country **Engines:** All **Transmissions:** All	**Idle Air Control Motor Circuit** Engine started; system voltage over 11.5v and the PCM detected an unexpected voltage condition on one or more of the IAC motor circuits for 2.75 seconds with the IAC motor active. **Possible Causes:** • Stepper motor Coil No. 1, 2, 3 or 4 circuit open or shorted to ground • Stepper motor coil circuit(s) shorted to system power (B+) • Stepper motor is damaged or has failed • PCM has failed

DTC	Trouble Code Title, Conditions & Possible Causes
DTC: P0506 **2T CCM** **Years:** 2005, 2006, 2007 **Models:** 300, 300C, Aspen, Caliber, Caravan, Charger, Commander, Compass, Crossfire, Dakota, Durango, Magnum, Town & Country **Engines:** All **Transmissions:** All	**Idle Speed Low Performance** Engine running at idle speed in closed loop. If engine RPM does not come within a calibratable low limit of the target idle speed, a failure timer will increment. When the appropriate failure timer reaches its maximum threshold without sign of RPM trending toward control, a soft-fail is generated. When a calibratable number of the soft-fails is reached, a 1-trip fault is set. When two 1-trip faults occur in a row, the DTC is set and the MIL illuminates. **Possible Causes:** • PCV system malfunction • Air induction system restrictions (clogged air filter, etc.) • Idle air control passage is clogged or dirty (clean and retest) • Air induction system malfunction • Throttle body or linkage is binding, damaged or sticking
DTC: P0506 **1T CCM** **Years:** 2005, 2006, 2007 **Models:** Aspen, Dakota, Durango **Engines:** All **Transmissions:** All	**Idle Speed Low Performance** Engine running at idle speed; MAF is less than 250 mg/tdc; air temperature is greater than 0F (−18C) and less than 19F (−7C) enable after coolant temperature is greater than 158F (70C) or air temperature is greater than 19F (−7C); coolant temperature is between 19 to 266F (−7 to 130C); canister purge is less than 100% duty cycle; no DTCs are present for VSS, MAF/MAP, ECT, TPS, ECT and CKP Sensors; also no fuel system or injector related DTCs are present. If the DTC detects that engine speed is 100 RPM or more below the normal idle speed for 7 seconds, this DTC will set. **Possible Causes:** • Air induction system restrictions • Throttle body or linkage is binding, damaged or sticking • Intermittent condition • PCM has failed
DTC: P0507 **2T CCM** **Years:** 2005, 2006, 2007 **Models:** 300, 300C, Aspen, Caliber, Caravan, Charger, Commander, Compass, Crossfire, Dakota, Durango, Magnum, Town & Country **Engines:** All **Transmissions:** All	**Idle Speed High Performance** Engine running at idle speed in closed loop. If engine RPM does not come within a calibratable high limit of the target idle speed, a failure timer will increment. When the appropriate failure timer reaches its maximum threshold without sign of RPM trending toward control, a soft-fail is generated. When a calibratable number of the soft-fails is reached, a 1-trip fault is set. When two 1-trip faults occur in a row, the DTC is set and the MIL illuminates. **Possible Causes:** • PCV system malfunction • Air induction system restrictions (clogged air filter, etc.) • Idle air control passage is clogged or dirty (clean and retest) • Air induction system malfunction • Throttle body or linkage is binding, damaged or sticking
DTC: P0507 **1T CCM** **Years:** 2005, 2006, 2007 **Models:** Aspen, Dakota, Durango **Engines:** All **Transmissions:** All	**Idle Speed High Performance Higher Than Expected** Engine running at idle speed; MAF is less than 250 mg/tdc; air temperature is greater than 0F (−18C) and less than 19F (−7C) enable after coolant temperature is greater than 158F (70C) or air temperature is greater than 19F (−7C); coolant temperature is between 19 to 266F (−7 to 130C); canister purge is less than 100% duty cycle; no DTCs are present for VSS, MAF/MAP, ECT, TPS, ECT and CKP Sensors; also no fuel system or injector related DTCs are present. If the DTC detects that engine speed is 200 RPM or more above the normal idle speed for 7 seconds, this DTC will set. **Possible Causes:** • Air induction system restrictions (clogged air filter, etc.) • Vacuum leaks • Intermittent condition • Throttle body or linkage is binding, damaged or sticking • PCM has failed
DTC: P0508 **2T CCM** **Years:** 2005, 2006, 2007 **Models:** 300, 300C, Aspen, Caliber, Caravan, Charger, Commander, Compass, Crossfire, Dakota, Durango, Magnum, Town & Country **Engines:** All **Transmissions:** All	**Idle Air Control Motor Sense Circuit Low Input** Engine started; system voltage over 10.5v; IAC motor operating. The PCM detected the IAC Motor Sense circuit current was less than 175mA during the CCM test period. **Possible Causes:** • IAC motor driver circuit is open or shorted to ground • IAC motor sense circuit is open or shorted to ground • IAC motor is damaged or it has failed • PCM has failed

DTC	Trouble Code Title, Conditions & Possible Causes
DTC: P0508 **1 CCM** **Years:** 2005, 2006, 2007 **Models:** Aspen, Dakota, Durango **Engines:** All **Transmissions:** All	**Idle Air Control Motor Sense Circuit Low Input** Engine running; system voltage over 10v; IAC motor operating. The PCM senses an open or short to ground on any of the Linear Idle Air Control (LIAC) control circuits for 2.75 seconds while the IAC motor is active. 3 good trips are required to turn off the MIL. **Possible Causes:** • IAC motor control circuit is open or shorted to ground • IAC motor signal circuit is open or shorted to ground • IAC motor is damaged or it has failed • PCM has failed
DTC: P0509 **2T CCM** **Years:** 2005, 2006, 2007 **Models:** 300, 300C, Aspen, Caliber, Caravan, Charger, Commander, Compass, Crossfire, Dakota, Durango, Magnum, Town & Country **Engines:** All **Transmissions:** All	**Idle Air Control Motor Circuit High** Engine started; system voltage over 10.5v, IAC motor activated, and the PCM detected a high voltage on one or more of the IAC motor circuits (over 980mA) during the CCM test period. **Possible Causes:** • IAC motor driver circuit is shorted to power • IAC motor sense circuit is shorted to power • IAC motor is damaged or it has failed • PCM has failed
DTC: P0509 **1 CCM** **Years:** 2005, 2006, 2007 **Models:** Aspen, Dakota, Durango **Engines:** All **Transmissions:** All	**Idle Air Control Motor Sense Circuit High** Engine running; system voltage over 10v; IAC motor operating. The PCM senses a short-to-power on any of the Linear Idle Air Control (LIAC) control circuits for 2.75 seconds while the IAC motor is active. 3 good trips are required to turn off the MIL. **Possible Causes:** • IAC motor control circuit is shorted to battery power • IAC motor signal circuit is open or shorted to battery power • IAC control circuit is shorted to IAC return circuit • IAC motor is damaged or it has failed • PCM has failed
DTC: P0513 **1T PCM** **Years:** 2005, 2006, 2007 **Models:** 300, 300C, Aspen, Caliber, Caravan, Charger, Commander, Compass, Crossfire, Dakota, Durango, Magnum, Town & Country **Engines:** All **Transmissions:** All	**Invalid SKIM Key Detected** Key on, and the PCM detected an invalid Sentry Key Immobilizer key had been inserted into the ignition key assembly. **Possible Causes:** • Incorrect VIN in the PCM • No communication between the PCM and the SKIM • SKIM trouble codes present (check for any SKIM codes) • Valid SKIM key not present • VIN not programmed into the PCM • PCM has failed
DTC: P0516 **1T CCM** **Years:** 2005, 2006, 2007 **Models:** 300, 300C, Aspen, Caliber, Caravan, Charger, Commander, Compass, Crossfire, Dakota, Durango, Magnum, Town & Country **Engines:** All **Transmissions:** All	**Battery Temperature Sensor Circuit Low Input** Key on or engine running; and the PCM detected a Battery Temperature Sensor signal that indicated less than 0.10v. 3 good trips required to turn off MIL. **Possible Causes:** • BTS signal circuit is shorted to Sensor or chassis ground • BTS assembly is damaged or it has failed • PCM has failed
DTC: P0517 **1T CCM** **Years:** 2005, 2006, 2007 **Models:** 300, 300C, Aspen, Caliber, Caravan, Charger, Commander, Compass, Crossfire, Dakota, Durango, Magnum, Town & Country **Engines:** All **Transmissions:** All	**Battery Temperature Sensor Circuit High Input** Key on or engine running; and the PCM detected a Battery Temperature Sensor signal that indicated more than 4.8v. **Possible Causes:** • BTS signal circuit is shorted to VREF (5v) • BTS signal circuit is open or the BTS ground circuit is open • BTS assembly is damaged or it has failed • PCM has failed

DTC	Trouble Code Title, Conditions & Possible Causes
DTC: P0520 **1T CCM** **Years:** 2005, 2006, 2007 **Models:** 300, 300C, Aspen, Caliber, Caravan, Charger, Commander, Compass, Crossfire, Dakota, Durango, Magnum, Town & Country **Engines:** All **Transmissions:** All	**Engine Oil Pressure Sensor Out of Range** Key on (engine not started). The PCM detected an engine oil pressure reading out of the calibrated range. **Possible Causes:** • Oil pressure Sensor signal circuit is open or shorted to ground • Oil pressure Sensor signal circuit has high resistance • 5v supply circuit has high resistance • 5v supply circuit is shorted to ground • Oil pressure Sensor ground circuit has high resistance • Oil pressure Sensor is damaged or has failed • PCM has failed
DTC: P0521 **1T CCM** **Years:** 2005, 2006, 2007 **Models:** 300, 300C, Aspen, Caliber, Caravan, Charger, Commander, Compass, Crossfire, Dakota, Durango, Magnum, Town & Country **Engines:** All **Transmissions:** All	**Engine Oil Pressure Sensor Does Not Reach Range** Engine running. The PCM detected an engine oil pressure reading never reaches the calibrated specification when engine is at 1250 RPM. **Possible Causes:** • Engine oil or engine mechanical fault • Oil pressure Sensor signal circuit is shorted to battery • Oil pressure Sensor signal circuit has high resistance • 5v supply circuit has high resistance • 5v supply circuit is shorted to ground • Oil pressure Sensor return circuit has high resistance • Oil pressure Sensor is damaged or has failed • PCM has failed
DTC: P0522 **1T CCM** **Years:** 2005, 2006, 2007 **Models:** 300, 300C, Aspen, Caliber, Caravan, Charger, Commander, Compass, Crossfire, Dakota, Durango, Magnum, Town & Country **Engines:** All **Transmissions:** All	**Engine Oil Pressure Sensor Rationality** Engine running; battery voltage over 10.4v. If the PCM detected an engine oil pressure voltage reading of less than 0.1v for 0.5 second. **Possible Causes:** • 5v supply circuit is open or is shorted to ground • Oil pressure Sensor signal circuit is shorted to ground or to sensor ground • Oil pressure Sensor is damaged or has failed • PCM has failed
DTC: P0523 **1T CCM** **Years:** 2005, 2006, 2007 **Models:** 300, 300C, Aspen, Caliber, Caravan, Charger, Commander, Compass, Crossfire, Dakota, Durango, Magnum, Town & Country **Engines:** All **Transmissions:** All	**Engine Oil Pressure Sensor Circuit High** Key on (engine not started). The PCM detected an engine oil pressure reading greater than the calibrated amount. **Possible Causes:** • Oil pressure Sensor signal circuit is open or shorted to battery voltage or to 5v supply circuit • Oil pressure Sensor ground circuit is open • Oil pressure Sensor is damaged or has failed • PCM has failed
DTC: P0524 **1T CCM** **Years:** 2005, 2006, 2007 **Models:** 300, 300C, Aspen, Caliber, Caravan, Charger, Commander, Compass, Crossfire, Dakota, Durango, Magnum, Town & Country **Engines:** All **Transmissions:** All	**Engine Oil Pressure Low** Engine running. The PCM detected that the engine oil pressure never reaches the calibrated specification to allow the MDS activation. **Possible Causes:** • Engine oil system or engine mechanical faults • Oil pressure Sensor signal circuit is shorted to battery voltage or to ground • Oil pressure Sensor signal circuit has high resistance • 5v supply circuit has high resistance • 5v supply circuit is shorted to ground • Oil pressure Sensor return circuit has high resistance • Oil pressure Sensor is damaged or has failed • PCM has failed

DTC	Trouble Code Title, Conditions & Possible Causes
DTC: P0532 **1T CCM** **Years:** 2005, 2006, 2007 **Models:** 300, 300C, Aspen, Caliber, Caravan, Charger, Commander, Compass, Crossfire, Dakota, Durango, Magnum, Town & Country **Engines:** All **Transmissions:** All	**Air Conditioning Pressure Sensor Circuit Low Input** Engine running with the A/C relay energized. The PCM detected the signal from the A/C Pressure Sensor indicated less than 0.58v for over 2.6 seconds during the CCM test period. **Possible Causes:** • A/C pressure Sensor 5v power supply (VREF) circuit is open or is shorted to ground • A/C pressure Sensor signal circuit is shorted to ground or to Sensor ground circuit • A/C pressure Sensor is damaged or it has failed • Front A/C control module damaged or has failed • PCM has failed
DTC: P0533 **1T CCM** **Years:** 2005, 2006, 2007 **Models:** 300, 300C, Aspen, Caliber, Caravan, Charger, Commander, Compass, Crossfire, Dakota, Durango, Magnum, Town & Country **Engines:** All **Transmissions:** All	**Air Conditioning Pressure Sensor Circuit High Input** Engine running with the A/C relay energized, and the PCM detected the signal from the A/C Pressure Sensor indicated less than 4.92v for over 2.6 seconds during the CCM test period. **Possible Causes:** • A/C pressure Sensor signal circuit is shorted to 5v VREF power • A/C pressure Sensor signal circuit or ground circuit is open • A/C pressure Sensor is damaged or it has failed • Front A/C control module is damaged or has failed • PCM has failed
DTC: P0551 **1T CCM** **Years:** 2005, 2006, 2007 **Models:** 300, 300C, Aspen, Caliber, Caravan, Charger, Commander, Compass, Crossfire, Dakota, Durango, Magnum, Town & Country **Engines:** All **Transmissions:** All	**Power Steering Pressure Switch Circuit Failure** Engine running and vehicle driven at more than 40 mph for 30 seconds. If the PCM detected the PSPS signal remains open for 2 consecutive trips, this DTC will set. 3 good trips required to turn off MIL. **Possible Causes:** • PSPS sense circuit is open between the switch and the PCM • PSPS ground circuit is open between the switch and ground • PSPS is damaged or it has failed • PCM has failed
DTC: P0562 **1T CCM** **Years:** 2005, 2006, 2007 **Models:** 300, 300C, Aspen, Caliber, Caravan, Charger, Commander, Compass, Crossfire, Dakota, Durango, Magnum, Town & Country **Engines:** All **Transmissions:** All	**Battery Voltage Low Input** Engine running at a speed over 1000 RPM. If battery voltage is 1v less than desired voltage for a set period of time, this DTC will set. The ETC light is flashing. **Possible Causes:** • Resistance in battery positive circuit • Resistance in the generator case ground • Generator field ground circuit is open or shorted to ground • Generator is damaged or it has failed • Ground circuit is open • PCM has failed
DTC: P0562 **1T CCM** **Years:** 2005, 2006, 2007 **Models:** Caravan, Town & Country **Engines:** All **Transmissions:** All	**Charging System Voltage Low** PCM: Engine is running for over 30 sec. If the PCM detects battery voltage is under 11.5v for more than 5 sec., this DTC will set. Other charging system DTCs may be present. TCM w/NGC: Engine is running and PCM has closed the Transmission Control Relay. If battery voltage of the TC Relay output sense circuit is less than 10v for 15 seconds, this DTC will set. **Note: P0562 usually indicates failing battery voltage or resistive connection to the PCM. This DTC also sets if battery voltage sensed at PCM is less than 6.5v for 200ms or when the TC Relay output circuit is less than 7.2v for 200ms.** **Possible Causes:** • Resistance is high in battery positive circuit or in generator case ground • Ground circuit is open or has high resistance • Fused B+ circuit to TC relay or to PCM has high resistance • Intermittent wiring or connector condition • TC relay output to TCM is open or has high resistance • TC relay has failed • Generator field driver circuit is open • ASD relay output circuit is open • Generator has failed • PCM has failed

DTC	Trouble Code Title, Conditions & Possible Causes
DTC: P0563 **1T CCM** **Years:** 2005, 2006, 2007 **Models:** 300, 300C, Aspen, Caliber, Caravan, Charger, Commander, Compass, Crossfire, Dakota, Durango, Magnum, Town & Country **Engines:** All **Transmissions:** All	**Battery Sense Circuit High Input** Engine running at a speed over 380 RPM, and the PCM detected the Battery Sense circuit voltage indicated 1v higher than the Charging system "goal" during the CCM test. **Possible Causes:** • Generator field control circuit is shorted to system power (B+) • Generator is damaged or it has failed • PCM has failed
DTC: P0563 **1T CCM** **Years:** 2005, 2006, 2007 **Models:** 300, 300C, Aspen, Charger, Dakota, Durango, Magnum **Engines:** **Transmissions:**	**Battery (Charging System) Voltage High Input** Engine running at a speed over 1000 RPM. No other charging system codes are set. If battery voltage is 1v more than desired voltage for a set period of time, this DTC will set. 3 good trips required to turn off MIL. **Possible Causes:** • Intermittent condition • Generator field ground circuit is shorted to battery voltage • Generator is damaged or it has failed • PCM has failed
DTC: P0571 **1T CCM** **Years:** 2005, 2006, 2007 **Models:** 300, 300C, Aspen, Charger, Dakota, Durango, Magnum **Engines:** All **Transmissions:** All	**Brake Switch No. 1 No Output Signal** Ignition is on. If output of BS 1 to PCM looks like brake is not applied, while BS 2 circuit is applied, the fault will mature in 60ms. **Possible Causes:** • BS 1 signal open or shorted to ground • BS 2 signal open or shorted to ground • Ground circuit is open • Fused ignition switch output is open • Stop lamp switch is damaged or has failed • PCM has failed
DTC: P0572 **1T CCM** **Years:** 2005, 2006, 2007 **Models:** 300, 300C, Aspen, Caliber, Caravan, Charger, Commander, Compass, Crossfire, Dakota, Durango, Magnum, Town & Country **Engines:** All **Transmissions:** All	**Brake Switch Signal No. 1 Circuit Low** Ignition is on. When PCM recognizes that brake switch is mechanically stuck in the low/on position, a DTC will set. Three global good trips are necessary to turn off MIL. **Possible Causes:** • Brake switch signal circuit is shorted to ground • BS No. 2 signal open (5.7L) • Brake switch is damaged or has failed • PCM has failed
DTC: P0573 **1T CCM** **Years:** 2005, 2006, 2007 **Models:** 300, 300C, Aspen, Caliber, Caravan, Charger, Commander, Compass, Crossfire, Dakota, Durango, Magnum, Town & Country **Engines:** All **Transmissions:** All	**Brake Switch No. 1 Stuck High/Off** Ignition is on. If PCM recognizes BS No. 11 is mechanically stuck in the high/off position, this DTC will set. **Possible Causes:** • BS No. 2 signal open or shorted to ground • BS No. 1 signal shorted to ground or to voltage • Ground circuit is open • Fused ignition switch output is open • Stop lamp switch is damaged or has failed • PCM has failed
DTC: P0580 **1T CCM** **Years:** 2005, 2006, 2007 **Models:** 300, 300C, Aspen, Caliber, Caravan, Charger, Commander, Compass, Crossfire, Dakota, Durango, Magnum, Town & Country **Engines:** All **Transmissions:** All	**Speed Control Switch No. 1 Circuit Low Input** Key on or engine started; system voltage over 10.0v and the PCM detected the Speed Control Switch No. 1 signal indicated less than 0.43v for 2 minutes. 3 good trips required to turn off MIL. **Possible Causes:** • Intermittent condition • S/C switch signal circuit is shorted to chassis or Sensor ground • S/C On/Off switch is damaged or it has failed • S/C Resume/Accel switch is damaged or it has failed • PCM has failed.

DTC	Trouble Code Title, Conditions & Possible Causes
DTC: P0580 **1T CCM** **Years:** 2005, 2006, 2007 **Models:** Aspen, Dakota, Durango **Engines:** All **Transmissions:** All	**Speed Control Switch No. 1 Circuit Low Input** Key on. The PCM detected the Speed Control Switch No. 1 signal is below the minimum acceptable voltage. **Possible Causes:** • S/C switch No. 1 signal circuit is shorted to S/C switch return circuit • S/C switch No. 1 signal circuit is shorted to ground • Clockspring is damaged or it has failed • Speed control switch No. 1 has failed • PCM has failed
DTC: P0581 **1T CCM** **Years:** 2005, 2006, 2007 **Models:** 300, 300C, Aspen, Caliber, Caravan, Charger, Commander, Compass, Crossfire, Dakota, Durango, Magnum, Town & Country **Engines:** All **Transmissions:** All	**Speed Control Switch No. 1 Circuit High Input** Engine started; system voltage over 10v and the PCM detected an open or shorted condition, or above maximum acceptable S/C switch voltage, in the Speed Control Switch signal circuit. **Possible Causes:** • S/C switch No.1 signal circuit is shorted to system power (B+) • S/C switch ground circuit is open • S/C switch signal circuit is open between PCM and clockspring • S/C Sensor ground circuit is open between PCM and clockspring or clockspring and S/C switch • Clockspring has failed • S/C switch (one or more) is damaged or has failed • PCM has failed
DTC: P0582 **1T CCM** **Years:** 2005, 2006, 2007 **Models:** 300, 300C, Aspen, Caliber, Caravan, Charger, Commander, Compass, Crossfire, Dakota, Durango, Magnum, Town & Country **Engines:** All **Transmissions:** All	**Speed Control Vacuum Solenoid Circuit Malfunction** Ignition on or engine started; Speed Control (S/C) system activated, and the PCM detected an open or short to voltage condition on the S/C Vacuum solenoid circuit during the CCM test period. **Possible Causes:** • S/C supply circuit is open or is short to ground or to battery voltage • S/C vacuum solenoid control circuit is open • S/C vacuum solenoid control circuit is shorted to ground • S/C vacuum solenoid is damaged or has failed • PCM has failed
DTC: P0585 **1T CCM** **Years:** 2005, 2006, 2007 **Models:** Aspen, Dakota, Durango **Engines:** All **Transmissions:** All	**Speed Control Vacuum Solenoid Circuit Malfunction** Ignition on; Speed Control (S/C) system activated. The PCM detected the C/S switch inputs are not coherent with each other; for example, the PCM is reading C/S switch No. 1 as Accel and switch No. 2 as Coast at the same time. **Possible Causes:** • S/C signal circuits shorted to battery voltage • High resistance in the S/C switch signal or return circuits • S/C switch No. 1 signal circuit is shorted to switch No. 2 signal circuit • S/C signal circuits shorted to ground • Clockspring is damaged or has failed • S/C switch(es) has failed • PCM has failed
DTC: P0586 **1T CCM** **Years:** 2005, 2006, 2007 **Models:** 300, 300C, Aspen, Caliber, Caravan, Charger, Commander, Compass, Crossfire, Dakota, Durango, Magnum, Town & Country **Engines:** All **Transmissions:** All	**Speed Control Vent Solenoid Circuit Malfunction** Engine started; battery voltage over 10v; Speed Control (S/C) system activated. The PCM detected an unexpected voltage condition on the S/C Vent solenoid circuit during the CCM test period. **Possible Causes:** • S/C supply circuit is open or is short to ground • S/C vent solenoid control circuit is open • S/C vent solenoid control circuit is shorted to ground • S/C vent solenoid is damaged or has failed • PCM has failed
DTC: P0591 **1T CCM** **Years:** 2005, 2006, 2007 **Models:** Aspen, Dakota, Durango **Engines:** All **Transmissions:** All	**Speed Control Switch No. 2 Malfunction** Ignition on; Speed Control (S/C) system activated. The PCM detected S/C switch No. 2 output voltage is not out of range, but it does not equal any of the values for any of the button positions. **Possible Causes:** • S/C switch No. 2 signal circuit is open or is shorted to ground or to battery voltage • S/C return circuit is open • S/C switch No. 2 signal circuit is shorted to switch return circuit • S/C switch No. 2 has failed • Clockspring has failed • PCM has failed

DTC	Trouble Code Title, Conditions & Possible Causes
DTC: P0592 **1T CCM** **Years:** 2005, 2006, 2007 **Models:** Aspen, Dakota, Durango **Engines:** All **Transmissions:** All	**Speed Control Switch No. 2 Circuit Low** Ignition on; Speed Control (S/C) system activated. The PCM detected S/C switch No. 2 input voltage is below minimum acceptable voltage at the PCM. **Possible Causes:** • S/C switch No. 2 signal circuit is shorted to ground or to switch return circuit • S/C switch No. 2 has failed • Clockspring has failed • PCM has failed
DTC: P0593 **1T CCM** **Years:** 2005, 2006, 2007 **Models:** Aspen, Dakota, Durango **Engines:** All **Transmissions:** All	**Speed Control Switch No. 2 Circuit High** Ignition on; Speed Control (S/C) system activated. The PCM detected S/C switch No. 2 input voltage is above maximum acceptable voltage at the PCM. **Possible Causes:** • S/C switch No. 2 signal circuit shorted to voltage or open between PCM and clockspring • S/C switch No. 2 signal circuit is open between the clockspring and S/C switch • S/C switch return circuit is open between PCM and clockspring or S/C switch • S/C switch No. 2 or clockspring has failed • PCM has failed
DTC: P0594 **1T CCM** **Years:** 2005, 2006, 2007 **Models:** 300, 300C, Aspen, Caliber, Caravan, Charger, Commander, Compass, Crossfire, Dakota, Durango, Magnum, Town & Country **Engines:** All **Transmissions:** All	**Speed Control Servo Power Circuit Malfunction** Engine started; Speed Control (S/C) system activated. The PCM detected an unexpected voltage condition on the S/C Vent solenoid circuit during the CCM test period. **Possible Causes:** • S/C solenoid or vent solenoid has failed • Brake switch is damaged or it has failed • S/C brake switch circuit is open or it is shorted to ground • S/C power circuit is open or it is shorted to ground • PCM has failed
DTC: P0600 **1T PCM** **Years:** 2005, 2006, 2007 **Models:** 300, 300C, Aspen, Caliber, Caravan, Charger, Commander, Compass, Crossfire, Dakota, Durango, Magnum, Town & Country **Engines:** All **Transmissions:** All	**Serial Communication Link Malfunction** Ignition on. Internal Bus communication failure is recognized between engine and transmission processors. **Possible Causes:** • PCM or SPI failure
DTC: P0601 **1T PCM** **Years:** 2005, 2006, 2007 **Models:** 300, 300C, Aspen, Caliber, Caravan, Charger, Commander, Compass, Crossfire, Dakota, Durango, Magnum, Town & Country **Engines:** All **Transmissions:** All	**PCM Internal Controller Failure** Ignition on. Internal CHECKSUM (or Bus communication) for software has failed; no communication between processors; cannot match calculated value. **Possible Causes:** • PCM or SPI failure
DTC: P0606 **1T PCM** **Years:** 2005, 2006, 2007 **Models:** 300, 300C, Aspen, Charger, Dakota, Durango, Magnum **Engines:** All **Transmissions:** All	**Engine Control Module Processor Malfunction** Engine running. When the PCM detected an internal failure to communicate with the ECM, or the CMP and CKP Sensor count periods are too short, the DTC will set. The ETC light will be flashing. **Possible Causes:** • PCM has failed

DTC	Trouble Code Title, Conditions & Possible Causes
DTC: P060B **1T PCM** **Years:** 2005, 2006, 2007 **Models:** 300, 300C, Aspen, Charger, Dakota, Durango, Magnum **Engines:** **Transmissions:**	**Engine Temperature Control A-D Ground Malfunction** When throttle motor is powered, if A to D reading does not return to ground within a set period of time from the test activation, this DTC will set. The test typically runs a couple of times per second, and is the reason why the APP2 signal spikes to ground a couple of times per second in normal running. Reprogramming the module may not always fix this fault. The ETC lamp will flash. **Possible Causes:** • PCM need to be reprogrammed • PCM has failed
DTC: P060D **1T PCM** **Years:** 2005, 2006, 2007 **Models:** Aspen, Dakota, Durango **Engines:** All **Transmissions:** All	**Engine Temperature Control Level 2 Performance** When throttle motor is powered and no matured faults related to APP Sensors are present. When secondary software determines that APPS 1 and APPS 2 signals do not match for a period of time, this DTC will set. The ETC lamp will flash. **Possible Causes:** • PCM need to be reprogrammed • PCM has failed
DTC: P060E **1T PCM** **Years:** 2005, 2006, 2007 **Models:** Aspen, Dakota, Durango **Engines:** All **Transmissions:** All	**Engine Temperature Control Level 2 TPS Performance** When throttle motor is powered and no matured faults related to TP Sensors are present. When secondary software determines that TP Sensor No. 1 and TP Sensor No. 2 signals do not match for a period of time, this DTC will set. The ETC lamp will flash. **Possible Causes:** • PCM need to be reprogrammed • PCM has failed
DTC: P060F **1T PCM** **Years:** 2005, 2006, 2007 **Models:** Aspen, Dakota, Durango **Engines:** All **Transmissions:** All	**Engine Temperature Control Level 2 ETC Performance** When throttle motor is powered and no matured faults related to ETC Sensor is present. When secondary software determines that - ETC Sensor signal is implausible for a period of time, this DTC will set. The ETC lamp will flash. **Possible Causes:** • PCM need to be reprogrammed • PCM has failed
DTC: P061C **1T PCM** **Years:** 2005, 2006, 2007 **Models:** 300, 300C, Aspen, Charger, Dakota, Durango, Magnum **Engines:** All **Transmissions:** All	**Engine Temperature Control Level 2 RPM Performance** When throttle motor is powered, and no CMP or CKP electrical signal related DTCs are set, if the secondary software determines that the engine speed is implausible for a period of time, this DTC will set. The ETC lamp will flash. **Possible Causes:** • PCM need to be reprogrammed • PCM has failed
DTC: P0622 **1T CCM** **Years:** 2005, 2006, 2007 **Models:** 300, 300C, Aspen, Caliber, Caravan, Charger, Commander, Compass, Crossfire, Dakota, Durango, Magnum, Town & Country **Engines:** All **Transmissions:** All	**Generator Field Control Circuit Malfunction** Engine running. The PCM detected the Generator Field control circuit had malfunctioned (PCM tries to regulate the generator field with no result). **Possible Causes:** • Generator field control circuit is open or is shorted to ground • Generator field control circuit is shorted to system power (B+) • Generator field ground circuit is open • Generator is damaged or PCM has failed • PCM has failed
DTC: P0627 **1T CCM** **Years:** 2005, 2006, 2007 **Models:** 300, 300C, Aspen, Caliber, Caravan, Charger, Commander, Compass, Crossfire, Dakota, Durango, Magnum, Town & Country **Engines:** All **Transmissions:** All	**Fuel Pump Relay Control Circuit Malfunction** Engine started; system voltage over 10.5v. The PCM detected an unexpected voltage condition (open or short) on the Fuel Pump relay control circuit during the CCM test period. **Possible Causes:** • Fuel pump relay control circuit is open or is shorted to ground • Fuel pump relay control circuit is shorted to system power (B+) • Fuel pump relay power circuit (fused ignition) circuit is open • Fuel pump relay is damaged or it has failed • PCM has failed

DTC	Trouble Code Title, Conditions & Possible Causes
DTC: P062C **1T PCM** **Years:** 2005, 2006, 2007 **Models:** 300, 300C, Aspen, Charger, Dakota, Durango, Magnum **Engines:** All **Transmissions:** All	**Engine Temperature Control Level 2 MPH Performance** When throttle motor is powered, and no vehicle speed related DTCs are set, if the secondary software determines that the vehicle speed is implausible for a period of time, this DTC will set. The ETC lamp will flash. **Possible Causes:** • PCM need to be reprogrammed • PCM has failed
DTC: P0630 **1T CCM** **Years:** 2005, 2006, 2007 **Models:** 300, 300C, Aspen, Caliber, Caravan, Charger, Commander, Compass, Crossfire, Dakota, Durango, Magnum, Town & Country **Engines:** All **Transmissions:** All	**VIN Not Programmed Into The PCM** Key on, and the PCM determined that the Vehicle Identification Number (VIN) had not been programmed into its memory. **Possible Causes:** • Reprogram the correct VIN into the PCM • PCM has failed
DTC: P0632 **1T CCM** **Years:** 2005, 2006, 2007 **Models:** 300, 300C, Aspen, Caliber, Caravan, Charger, Commander, Compass, Crossfire, Dakota, Durango, Magnum, Town & Country **Engines:** All **Transmissions:** All	**Odometer Not Programmed Into The PCM** Key on, and the PCM detected the vehicle mileage had not been programmed into memory. **Possible Causes:** • Reprogram the correct mileage into the PCM • PCM has failed
DTC: P0633 **1T CCM** **Years:** 2005, 2006, 2007 **Models:** 300, 300C, Aspen, Caliber, Caravan, Charger, Commander, Compass, Crossfire, Dakota, Durango, Magnum, Town & Country **Engines:** All **Transmissions:** All	**SKIM Key Not Programmed Into The PCM** Key on, and the PCM determined that the Security Key Immobilizer (SKIM) information had not been programmed into its memory. **Possible Causes:** • Reprogram the SKIM key into the PCM • PCM has failed
DTC: P0642 **1T CCM** **Years:** 2005, 2006, 2007 **Models:** 300, 300C, Aspen, Charger, Dakota, Durango, Magnum **Engines:** All **Transmissions:** All	**Sensor Reference Voltage 1 Circuit Low** Ignition is on. When the PCM recognizes the primary 5v supply circuit voltage is too low, this DTC will set. The ETC light is flashing. **Possible Causes:** • Primary 5v supply shorted to ground • Sensor is shorted to ground • 5v Sensor has failed • PCM has failed
DTC: P0643 **1T CCM** **Years:** 2005, 2006, 2007 **Models:** 300, 300C, Aspen, Charger, Dakota, Durango, Magnum **Engines:** All **Transmissions:** All	**Sensor Reference Voltage 1 Circuit High** Ignition is on. When the PCM recognizes the primary 5v supply circuit voltage is too high, this DTC will set. The ETC light is flashing. **Possible Causes:** • Primary 5v supply shorted to battery voltage • PCM has failed

DTC	Trouble Code Title, Conditions & Possible Causes
DTC: P0645 **1T CCM** **Years:** 2005, 2006, 2007 **Models:** 300, 300C, Aspen, Caliber, Caravan, Charger, Commander, Compass, Crossfire, Dakota, Durango, Magnum, Town & Country **Engines:** All **Transmissions:** All	**A/C Clutch Relay Circuit Malfunction** Engine started; system voltage over 10.0v, A/C switch "on". The PCM detected an unexpected voltage condition (open or shorted condition) on the A/C Clutch relay control circuit during the CCM test. **Possible Causes:** • Internally fused ignition switch output circuit is faulty • A/C relay clutch control circuit is open or it is shorted to ground • A/C relay clutch power supply (fused ignition) circuit is open • A/C relay is damaged or it has failed • PCM has failed
DTC: P0652 **1T CCM** **Years:** 2005, 2006, 2007 **Models:** 300, 300C, Aspen, Charger, Dakota, Durango, Magnum **Engines:** **Transmissions:**	**Sensor Reference Voltage 2 Circuit Low** Ignition is on. When the PCM recognizes the auxiliary 5v supply circuit voltage is too low, this DTC will set. The ETC light is flashing. **Possible Causes:** • Auxiliary 5v supply shorted to ground • Sensor is shorted to ground • CMP Sensor has failed • PCM has failed
DTC: P0653 **1T CCM** **Years:** 2005, 2006, 2007 **Models:** 300, 300C, 300M, Aspen, Charger, Dakota, Durango, Magnum **Engines:** All **Transmissions:** All	**Sensor Reference Voltage 2 Circuit High** Ignition is on. When the PCM recognizes the auxiliary 5v supply circuit voltage is too high, this DTC will set. The ETC light is flashing. **Possible Causes:** • Auxiliary 5v supply shorted to battery voltage • PCM has failed
DTC: P0660 **1T CCM** **Years:** 2005, 2006, 2007 **Models:** 300, 300C, 300M, Aspen, Caliber, Caravan, Charger, Commander, Compass, Crossfire, Dakota, Durango, Magnum, Patriot, Town & Country **Engines:** All **Transmissions:** All	**Manifold Tune Valve Solenoid Circuit Malfunction** Engine started; ASD relay "on", system voltage over 10.0v, and the PCM detected an unexpected voltage condition on the Manifold Tune Valve (MTV) solenoid control circuit. **Possible Causes:** • Fused B+ circuit has failed • MTV solenoid/relay circuit is open or it is shorted to ground • MTV solenoid/relay circuit is shorted to power • MTV solenoid/relay ground circuit is open • MTV solenoid/relay is damaged or it has failed • PCM has failed
DTC: P0660 **1T CCM** **Years:** 2005, 2006, 2007 **Models:** 300, 300C, 300M, Charger, Magnum **Engines:** All **Transmissions:** All	**Manifold Tune Valve Solenoid Circuit Malfunction** Ignition on; ASD relay energized; battery voltage more than 10v. If the PCM senses the MTV is not at the desired state, this DTC will set. **Possible Causes:** • MTV ground circuit is open • MTV control circuit is open or is shorted to ground or to battery voltage • MTV solenoid has failed • PCM has failed
DTC: P0685 **1T CCM** **Years:** 2005, 2006, 2007 **Models:** 300, 300C, 300M, Aspen, Caliber, Caravan, Charger, Commander, Compass, Crossfire, Dakota, Durango, Magnum, Patriot, Town & Country **Engines:** All **Transmissions:** All	**ASD Relay Control Circuit Malfunction** Key on; system voltage over 10.0v. The PCM detected an unexpected voltage condition (open or short) on the Automatic Shutdown (ASD) relay control circuit during the CCM test period (ASD actual state is not equal to the desired state). 3 good trips are required to turn off MIL. P0688 may also set. **Possible Causes:** • Fused B+ circuit faults • ASD relay connector is damaged, loose or shorted • ASD relay control circuit is open or it is shorted to ground • ASD power supply (fused B+) circuit is open • ASD relay is damaged, has high resistance, or it has failed • PCM has failed

DTC	Trouble Code Title, Conditions & Possible Causes
DTC: P0688 **1T CCM** **Years:** 2005, 2006, 2007 **Models:** 300, 300C, 300M, Aspen, Caliber, Caravan, Charger, Commander, Compass, Crossfire, Dakota, Durango, Magnum, Patriot, Town & Country **Engines:** All **Transmissions:** All	**ASD Relay Sense Circuit Low** Key on, ASD relay energized, system voltage over 10.0v, and the PCM did not detect any voltage on the Automatic Shutdown (ASD) Sense circuit during the CCM test period. **Possible Causes:** • ASD relay output circuit is open • ASD power supply (fused B+) circuit is open • ASD relay is damaged or it has failed • Problem in fuse/relay center • PCM no start condition • PCM has failed
DTC: P0689 **1T CCM** **Years:** 2005, 2006, 2007 **Models:** Aspen, Dakota, Durango **Engines:** All **Transmissions:** All	**ASD Relay Sense Circuit Low** Key on; ASD relay energized; system voltage 9-16v. The ASD output circuit voltage drops below an acceptable value at the Front Control Module (FCM). This circuit is continuously monitored. **Possible Causes:** • ASD power supply (fused B+) problem • ASD relay output circuit is open or is shorted to ground • ASD relay has failed • PCM has failed
DTC: P0690 **1T CCM** **Years:** 2005, 2006, 2007 **Models:** Aspen, Dakota, Durango **Engines:** All **Transmissions:** All	**ASD Relay Sense Circuit High** Key on, ASD relay energized, system voltage over 10.0v, and the PCM (PT Cruiser) or FCM (Durango) detects high voltage on the Automatic Shutdown (ASD) Sense circuit during the CCM test period. **Possible Causes:** • Intermittent condition • ASD relay output circuit is shorted to voltage • ASD relay is damaged or it has failed • PCM internal short to voltage • PCM has failed
DTC: P0691 **1T CCM** **Years:** 2005, 2006, 2007 **Models:** Aspen, Dakota, Durango **Engines:** All **Transmissions:** All	**Low Speed Fan (Fan No. 1) Relay Control Circuit Low** Key on; No. 1 cooling fan relay is actuated. If the PCM (PT Cruiser) or FCM (Durango) detects no voltage (open or shorted to ground) on the Radiator Fan Relay control circuit for more than 3 seconds, this DTC will set. **Possible Causes:** • Intermittent condition • Fused ignition switch output circuit problems • Radiator fan relay has failed • Radiator fan control circuit is open or is shorted to ground • PCM has failed
DTC: P0692 **1T CCM** **Years:** 2005, 2006, 2007 **Models:** Aspen, Dakota, Durango **Engines:** All **Transmissions:** All	**Low Speed Fan (Fan No. 1) Relay Control Circuit High** Key on; radiator fan commanded ON. If the PCM (PT Cruiser) or FCM (Durango) detects an open or high voltage on the Radiator Fan Relay circuit for more than 3 seconds, this DTC will set. **Possible Causes:** • Intermittent condition • Radiator fan relay has failed • Radiator fan control circuit is shorted to battery voltage • PCM has failed
DTC: P0693 **1T CCM** **Years:** 2005, 2006, 2007 **Models:** Aspen, Dakota, Durango **Engines:** All **Transmissions:** All	**High Speed Fan (Fan No. 2) Relay Control Circuit Low** Key on; fan relay is powered on. If the PCM (PT Cruiser) or FCM (Durango) detects no voltage (open or shorted) on the Radiator Fan Relay control circuit for more than 3 seconds, this DTC will set. Circuit is continuously monitored. **Possible Causes:** • Intermittent condition • Fused ignition switch output circuit problems • Radiator fan relay has failed • Radiator fan control circuit is open or is shorted to ground • PCM has failed

DTC	Trouble Code Title, Conditions & Possible Causes
DTC: P0694 **1T CCM** **Years:** 2005, 2006, 2007 **Models:** Aspen, Dakota, Durango **Engines:** All **Transmissions:** All	**High Speed Fan (Fan No. 2) Relay Control Circuit High** Key on; radiator fan commanded ON. If the PCM (PT Cruiser) or FCM (Durango) detects an open, short or high voltage on the Radiator Fan Relay circuit for more than 3 seconds, this DTC will set. This circuit is continuously monitored. **Possible Causes:** • Intermittent condition • Radiator fan relay has failed • Radiator fan control circuit is open or shorted to battery voltage • PCM has failed
DTC: P0700 **2T TCM** **Years:** 2005, 2006, 2007 **Models:** 300, 300C, 300M, Aspen, Caliber, Caravan, Charger, Commander, Compass, Crossfire, Dakota, Durango, Magnum, Patriot, Town & Country **Engines:** All **Transmissions:** All	**Automatic Transmission Control System Malfunction** Ignition on or engine started. The PCM received a message over the CCD Bus from the Transmission Control Module (TCM) that it had detected a problem and set a trouble code in memory. **Possible Causes:** • The presence of this code means the TCM detected a problem • TCM related Sensor has solenoid is damaged or has failed • This code is for information only - check for other TCM codes • TCM or PCM has failed
DTC: P0703 **1T CCM** **Years:** 2005, 2006, 2007 **Models:** 300, 300C, 300M, Aspen, Charger, Dakota, Durango, Magnum **Engines:** All **Transmissions:** All	**A/T Brake Switch No. 2 Performance Malfunction** Ignition is on. When the PCM recognizes brake switch No.2 voltage is not equal to applied value at the PCM when brake switch No. 1 is applied, this DTC will set. **Note: This could be a normal condition; however, if this condition is seen repeatedly by the PCM, the DTC will be set. Cruise control will not work for the rest of the key cycle.** **Possible Causes:** • Fused B+ circuit malfunction • Brake switch output circuit is open or is shorted to battery voltage or to ground • Brake switch 1 signal circuit is open • Brake switch has failed • PCM has failed
DTC: P0706 **1T CCM** **Years:** 2005, 2006, 2007 **Models:** 300, 300C, 300M, Aspen, Caliber, Caravan, Charger, Commander, Compass, Crossfire, Dakota, Durango, Magnum, Patriot, Town & Country **Engines:** All **Transmissions:** All	**A/T Check Shifter Signal Circuit Malfunction** Key on. After 3 occurrences in one ignition cycle of an invalid PRNDL DDTC which last for more than 0.1 second. **Note: All indicator lights on the instrument cluster will illuminate boxed when the vehicle engine is not running, ignition on, or engine running in Park or Neutral if a problem exists.** **Possible Causes:** • Shifter out of adjustment • TRS T1, T3, T41 or T42 sense circuit is open, shorted to ground or to voltage • TRS Sensor has failed • Intermittent wiring or connector problems • PCM has failed
DTC: P0711 **1T CCM** **Years:** 2005, 2006, 2007 **Models:** 300, 300C, 300M, Aspen, Caliber, Caravan, Charger, Commander, Compass, Crossfire, Dakota, Durango, Magnum, Patriot, Town & Country **Engines:** All **Transmissions:** All	**A/T Transmission Fluid Temperature Sensor Signal - No Rise After Startup** Engine started. This DTC will set when the desired transmission temperature does not reach a normal operation temperature within a given time frame. Time is variable due to ambient temperature at cold engine start: from 35 minutes at 40F (−40C) to 10 minutes at 60F (15C). **Possible Causes:** • Related DTCs will be present • Transmission temperature Sensor has failed • Intermittent wiring or connector problems • PCM has failed
DTC: P0712 **1T CCM** **Years:** 2005, 2006, 2007 **Models:** 300, 300C, 300M, Aspen, Caliber, Caravan, Charger, Commander, Compass, Crossfire, Dakota, Durango, Magnum, Patriot, Town & Country **Engines:** All **Transmissions:** All	**A/T Transmission Fluid Temperature Sensor Low Input** Engine started and the PCM detected the TFT Sensor signal was under 0.078v for 0.45 second. **Possible Causes:** • Related DTCs are present • TFT Sensor signal circuit is shorted to ground • TFT Sensor is damaged or has failed (it may be shorted) • Intermittent wiring or connector problems • PCM has failed

DTC	Trouble Code Title, Conditions & Possible Causes
DTC: P0713 **1T CCM** **Years:** 2005, 2006, 2007 **Models:** 300, 300C, 300M, Aspen, Caliber, Caravan, Charger, Commander, Compass, Crossfire, Dakota, Durango, Magnum, Patriot, Town & Country **Engines:** All **Transmissions:** All	**A/T Transmission Fluid Temperature Sensor High Input** Engine started and the PCM detected the TFT Sensor signal was over 4.94v for 0.45 second. **Possible Causes:** • Related DTCs are present • TFT Sensor signal circuit is open or is shorted to voltage • TFT Sensor is damaged or has failed (it may be shorted) • Intermittent wiring or connector problems • PCM has failed
DTC: P0714 **1T CCM** **Years:** 2005, 2006, 2007 **Models:** 300, 300C, 300M, Aspen, Caliber, Caravan, Charger, Commander, Compass, Crossfire, Dakota, Durango, Magnum, Patriot, Town & Country **Engines:** All **Transmissions:** All	**A/T Transmission Fluid Temperature Sensor Intermittent** Engine started and the PCM detected the TFT Sensor signal was fluctuating or changes abruptly within a predetermined period of time. **Possible Causes:** • Related DTCs are present • TFT Sensor is damaged or has failed (it may be shorted) • Intermittent wiring or connector problems • PCM has failed
DTC: P0715 **1T CCM** **Years:** 2005, 2006, 2007 **Models:** 300, 300C, 300M, Aspen, Caliber, Caravan, Charger, Commander, Compass, Crossfire, Dakota, Durango, Magnum, Patriot, Town & Country **Engines:** All **Transmissions:** All	**TCM Input Speed Sensor Circuit Malfunction** Engine started; the transmission gear ratio is monitored continuously while the transmission is in gear. This DTC will set if there is an excessive change in the Input RPM in any gear. **Possible Causes:** • ISS ground circuit is open or is shorted to voltage • ISS signal circuit is open, shorted to ground or to power • ISS Sensor is damaged or it has failed • Intermittent wiring or connector problems • PCM has failed
DTC: P0720 **1T CCM** **Years:** 2005, 2006, 2007 **Models:** 300, 300C, 300M, Aspen, Caliber, Caravan, Charger, Commander, Compass, Crossfire, Dakota, Durango, Magnum, Patriot, Town & Country **Engines:** All **Transmissions:** All	**TCM Output Speed Sensor Circuit Malfunction** Engine started; the transmission gear ratio is monitored continuously while the transmission is in gear. This DTC will set if there is an excessive change in the Output RPM in any gear. On some models, this DTC can take up to 5 minutes of problem identification before lighting the MIL. **Possible Causes:** • OSS ground circuit is open or is shorted to voltage or to ground • Speed Sensor ground circuit is open, shorted to ground or to voltage • OSS Sensor is damaged or it has failed • Intermittent wiring or connector problems • PCM or TCM has failed
DTC: P0725 **1T CCM** **Years:** 2005, 2006, 2007 **Models:** 300, 300C, 300M, Aspen, Caliber, Caravan, Charger, Commander, Compass, Crossfire, Dakota, Durango, Magnum, Patriot, Town & Country **Engines:** All **Transmissions:** All	**A/T Engine Speed Sensor Circuit Malfunction** Engine running; and the PCM detected an Engine Speed Sensor reading of less than 390 RPM or more than 8000 RPM occurred for 2 seconds during the CCM test. **Possible Causes:** • Check for trouble codes related to the CKP Sensor • CKP Sensor signal circuit open, shorted to ground or to power • CKP Sensor is damaged or has failed (open or shorted) • Intermittent wiring or connector problems • PCM has failed
DTC: P0731 **1T CCM** **Years:** 2005, 2006, 2007 **Models:** 300, 300C, 300M, Aspen, Caliber, Caravan, Charger, Commander, Compass, Crossfire, Dakota, Durango, Magnum, Patriot, Town & Country **Engines:** All **Transmissions:** All	**A/T Additional Gear Ratio Error In First Gear** The transmission gear ratio is monitored continuously while the transmission is in gear. If the ratio of the Input RPM to the Output RPM does not match the current gear ratio, this DTC will set. **Possible Causes:** • Related DTCs will be present • Internal transmission mechanical problems may exist • Intermittent gear ratio errors are present

DTC	Trouble Code Title, Conditions & Possible Causes
DTC: P0732 **1T CCM** **Years:** 2005, 2006, 2007 **Models:** 300, 300C, 300M, Aspen, Caliber, Caravan, Charger, Commander, Compass, Crossfire, Dakota, Durango, Magnum, Patriot, Town & Country **Engines:** All **Transmissions:** All	**A/T Additional Gear Ratio Error In Second Gear** The transmission gear ratio is monitored continuously while the transmission is in gear. If the ratio of the Input RPM to the Output RPM does not match the current gear ratio, this DTC will set. **Possible Causes:** • Related DTCs will be present • Transmission solenoid/pressure switch assembly has malfunctioned or failed • Internal transmission mechanical problems may exist • Intermittent gear ratio errors are present
DTC: P0733 **1T CCM** **Years:** 2005, 2006, 2007 **Models:** 300, 300C, 300M, Aspen, Caliber, Caravan, Charger, Commander, Compass, Crossfire, Dakota, Durango, Magnum, Patriot, Town & Country **Engines:** All **Transmissions:** All	**A/T Additional Gear Ratio Error In Third Gear** The transmission gear ratio is monitored continuously while the transmission is in gear. If the ratio of the Input RPM to the Output RPM does not match the current gear ratio, this DTC will set. **Possible Causes:** • Related DTCs will be present • Transmission solenoid/pressure switch assembly has malfunctioned or failed • Internal transmission mechanical problems may exist • Intermittent gear ratio errors are present
DTC: P0734 **1T CCM** **Years:** 2005, 2006, 2007 **Models:** 300, 300C, 300M, Aspen, Caliber, Caravan, Charger, Commander, Compass, Crossfire, Dakota, Durango, Magnum, Patriot, Town & Country **Engines:** All **Transmissions:** All	**A/T Additional Gear Ratio Error In Fourth Gear** The transmission gear ratio is monitored continuously while the transmission is in gear. If the ratio of the Input RPM to the Output RPM does not match the current gear ratio, this DTC will set. **Possible Causes:** • Related DTCs will be present • Transmission solenoid/pressure switch assembly has malfunctioned or failed • Internal transmission mechanical problems may exist • Intermittent gear ratio errors are present
DTC: P0735 **1T CCM** **Years:** 2005, 2006, 2007 **Models:** 300, 300C, 300M, Aspen, Caliber, Caravan, Charger, Commander, Compass, Crossfire, Dakota, Durango, Magnum, Patriot, Town & Country **Engines:** All **Transmissions:** All	**A/T Gear Ratio Error Fourth Prime** Vehicle driven any forward Gear, and the TCM detected the ratio of the Input speed to the Output Speed did not match the current Gear Ratio (this test can take up to 5 minutes). **Possible Causes:** • Related Gear Ratio trouble codes may be stored (note that some of these Gear Ratio trouble codes may be intermittent) • Transmission has internal problems or damage present
DTC: P0736 **1T CCM** **Years:** 2005, 2006, 2007 **Models:** 300, 300C, 300M, Aspen, Caliber, Caravan, Charger, Commander, Compass, Crossfire, Dakota, Durango, Magnum, Patriot, Town & Country **Engines:** All **Transmissions:** All	**A/T Additional Gear Ratio Error In Reverse Gear** The transmission gear ratio is monitored continuously while the transmission is in gear. If the ratio of the Input RPM to the Output RPM does not match the current gear ratio, this DTC will set. **Possible Causes:** • Related DTCs will be present • Internal transmission mechanical problems may exist • Intermittent gear ratio errors are present
DTC: P0740 **1T CCM** **Years:** 2005, 2006, 2007 **Models:** 300, 300C, 300M, Aspen, Caliber, Caravan, Charger, Commander, Compass, Crossfire, Dakota, Durango, Magnum, Patriot, Town & Country **Engines:** All **Transmissions:** All	**A/T Torque Converter Clutch System Out of Range** The TCC is in FEMCC or PEMCC, transmission temperature is hot, engine temperature is more than 100F (38C), transmission input speed is more than 1750 RPM, with TPS less than 30. The TCC is modulated by controlling the duty cycle of the L/R solenoid, until the difference between the engine and transmission input speed RPM or duty cycle is within desired range. The DTC is set after the period of 10 seconds and 3 occurrences of either: FEMCC with slip greater than 100 RPM or PEMCC duty cycle is more than 85%. **Possible Causes:** • Related DTCs will be present • Internal transmission mechanical problems may exist • Intermittent gear ratio errors are present

DTC	Trouble Code Title, Conditions & Possible Causes
DTC: P0750 **1T CCM** **Years:** 2005, 2006, 2007 **Models:** 300, 300C, 300M, Aspen, Caliber, Caravan, Charger, Commander, Compass, Crossfire, Dakota, Durango, Magnum, Patriot, Town & Country **Engines:** All **Transmissions:** All	**A/T Low/Reverse Solenoid Circuit Failure** Solenoids are tested initially at power-up, then every 10 seconds thereafter, the solenoids will also be tested immediately after a gear ratio or pressure switch error is detected. 3 consecutive solenoid continuity test failures, or one failure if test is run in response to a gear ratio or pressure switch error. **Possible Causes:** • Related relay DTCs present • Transmission control relay output circuit open • L/R solenoid control circuit open or shorted to ground or to voltage • L/R solenoid/pressure switch assembly has malfunctioned or failed • Intermittent wiring and connectors • PCM has failed
DTC: P0755 **1T CCM** **Years:** 2005, 2006, 2007 **Models:** 300, 300C, 300M, Aspen, Caliber, Caravan, Charger, Commander, Compass, Crossfire, Dakota, Durango, Magnum, Patriot, Town & Country **Engines:** All **Transmissions:** All	**A/T 2/4 Solenoid Circuit Failure** 2/4 solenoid in monitored initially at power-up, then every 10 seconds thereafter. Also, immediately after a gear ratio or pressure switch error is detected. 3 consecutive solenoid continuity test failures, or one failure if test is run in response to a gear ratio or pressure switch error. **Possible Causes:** • Related DTCs present • Transmission control relay output circuit open • 2/4 Solenoid control circuit is open or shorted to ground • 2/4 Solenoid control circuit is shorted to system power • 2/4 Solenoid is damaged or has failed • Intermittent wiring or connector problems • PCM has failed
DTC: P0760 **1T CCM** **Years:** 2005, 2006, 2007 **Models:** 300, 300C, 300M, Aspen, Caliber, Caravan, Charger, Commander, Compass, Crossfire, Dakota, Durango, Magnum, Patriot, Town & Country **Engines:** All **Transmissions:** All	**A/T Overdrive Solenoid Circuit Failure** O/D solenoid in monitored initially at power-up, then every 10 seconds thereafter. Also, immediately after a gear ratio or pressure switch error is detected. 3 consecutive solenoid continuity test failures, or one failure if test is run in response to a gear ratio or pressure switch error. **Possible Causes:** • Related DTCs present • Transmission control relay output circuit open • O/D Solenoid control circuit is open or shorted to ground • O/D Solenoid control circuit is shorted to system power • O/D Solenoid is damaged or has failed • PCM has failed
DTC: P0765 **1T CCM** **Years:** 2005, 2006, 2007 **Models:** 300, 300C, 300M, Aspen, Caliber, Caravan, Charger, Commander, Compass, Crossfire, Dakota, Durango, Magnum, Patriot, Town & Country **Engines:** All **Transmissions:** All	**A/T Underdrive Solenoid Circuit Failure** U/D solenoid in monitored initially at power-up, then every 10 seconds thereafter. Also, immediately after a gear ratio or pressure switch error is detected. 3 consecutive solenoid continuity test failures, or one failure if test is run in response to a gear ratio or pressure switch error. **Possible Causes:** • Related DTCs present • Transmission control relay output circuit open • U/D Solenoid control circuit is open or shorted to ground • U/D Solenoid control circuit is shorted to system power • U/D Solenoid is damaged or has failed • Intermittent wiring or connector problems • PCM has failed
DTC: P0841 **1T CCM** **Years:** 2005, 2006, 2007 **Models:** 300, 300C, 300M, Aspen, Caliber, Caravan, Charger, Commander, Compass, Crossfire, Dakota, Durango, Magnum, Patriot, Town & Country **Engines:** All **Transmissions:** All	**Low/Reverse Pressure Switch Sense Circuit Malfunction** Switches are monitored whenever engine is running. This DTC will set if one of the pressure switches in open or closed at the wrong time in a given gear. **Possible Causes:** • Related DTCs present • Loss of Prime P0944 DTC present • Transmission control relay output circuit open • L/R switch sense circuit is open or is shorted to ground or to voltage • L/R pressure switch is damaged or has failed • Intermittent wiring or connector problems • PCM has failed

DTC	Trouble Code Title, Conditions & Possible Causes
DTC: P0845 **1T CCM** **Years:** 2005, 2006, 2007 **Models:** 300, 300C, 300M, Aspen, Caliber, Caravan, Charger, Commander, Compass, Crossfire, Dakota, Durango, Magnum, Patriot, Town & Country **Engines:** All **Transmissions:** All	**A/T 2/4 Hydraulic Pressure Test Malfunction** Engine speed over 1000 RPM, then immediately after a shift event, the PCM detected a failure in one or more of the Pressure Switch circuits (i.e., it tests switches that are not operating). **Possible Causes:** • 2/4 pressure is incorrect, or internal transmission faults exist • 2/4 pressure switch circuit is open, shorted to ground or power • 2/4 pressure switch is damaged or it has failed • Transmission solenoids/TRS assembly is damaged or have failed • TCM relay power circuit to 2/4 switch is open (loss of B+) • Intermittent wiring or connector problems exist • PCM or TCM has failed
DTC: P0846 **1T CCM** **Years:** 2005, 2006, 2007 **Models:** 300, 300C, 300M, Aspen, Caliber, Caravan, Charger, Commander, Compass, Crossfire, Dakota, Durango, Magnum, Patriot, Town & Country **Engines:** All **Transmissions:** All	**A/T 2/4 Pressure Switch Circuit Malfunction** Engine started; vehicle driven in a forward gear, and the PCM detected that the 2/4 Pressure Switch circuit indicated open or closed at the wrong time. Related relay DTCs may be present. **Possible Causes:** • 2/4 pressure is incorrect, or internal transmission faults exist • 2/4 pressure switch circuit is open, shorted to ground or power • 2/4 pressure switch is damaged or it has failed • TCM relay power circuit to L/R switch is open (loss of B+) • PCM/TCM has failed
DTC: P0850 **2T CCM** **Years:** 2005, 2006, 2007 **Models:** 300, 300C, 300M, Aspen, Caliber, Caravan, Charger, Commander, Compass, Crossfire, Dakota, Durango, Magnum, Patriot, Town & Country **Engines:** All **Transmissions:** All	**A/T Park/Neutral Switch Performance** Engine running; gearshift selector in Park, Neutral or Drive position (not Limp-In mode). The PCM detected an invalid Park/Neutral switch state during vehicle operation. **Possible Causes:** • Check for any TCM related codes stored in the TCM controller • PCM has failed
DTC: P0870 **1T CCM** **Years:** 2005, 2006, 2007 **Models:** 300, 300C, 300M, Aspen, Caliber, Caravan, Charger, Commander, Compass, Crossfire, Dakota, Durango, Magnum, Patriot, Town & Country **Engines:** All **Transmissions:** All	**A/T Hydraulic Pressure Line Malfunction** Engine started; vehicle driven at over 1000 RPM, then immediately after a shift, the PCM detected a malfunction in one or more of the Pressure Switch circuits (it detected the switch did not close twice). DTC P0944 may be present. **Possible Causes:** • Check for related line pressure trouble codes • Check for related speed ratio and pressure switch codes • 5v supply circuit is open or is shorted to ground • Transmission Control Relay output circuit is open • OD Pressure Switch sense circuit is shorted to ground or to voltage • Excessive debris in the oil pan • Line pressure Sensor connector is loose or damaged • Oil pressure switch is damaged or has failed • Intermittent wiring or connector problems exist • PCM or TCM has failed
DTC: P0871 **1T CCM** **Years:** 2005, 2006, 2007 **Models:** 300, 300C, 300M, Aspen, Caliber, Caravan, Charger, Commander, Compass, Crossfire, Dakota, Durango, Magnum, Patriot, Town & Country **Engines:** All **Transmissions:** All	**A/T O/D Pressure Switch Circuit Malfunction** Engine started; vehicle driven in a forward gear, and the PCM detected that the O/D Pressure Switch circuit indicated open or closed at the wrong time. **Possible Causes:** • Related DTCs may be present • O/D pressure is incorrect, or internal transmission faults exist • O/D pressure switch circuit is open, shorted to ground or power • O/D pressure switch is damaged or it has failed • TCM relay power circuit to O/D switch is open (loss of B+) • Intermittent wiring or connector problems exist • PCM or TCM has failed

DTC	Trouble Code Title, Conditions & Possible Causes
DTC: P0884 **1T CCM** **Years:** 2005, 2006, 2007 **Models:** 300, 300C, 300M, Aspen, Caliber, Caravan, Charger, Commander, Compass, Crossfire, Dakota, Durango, Magnum, Patriot, Town & Country **Engines:** All **Transmissions:** All	**Power-Up Automatic Transmission Speed Malfunction** Engine started, TCM relay enabled; and the TCM detected a valid forward gear PNDRL signal with the Output Speed more than 800 RPM indicating a vehicle speed of over 20 mph. **Note: The TCM has separate powers and grounds specifically to its portion of the PCM.** **Possible Causes:** • TCM power supply circuit to direct battery is open • TCM power supply circuit to the ignition switch is open • TCM power ground circuit is open or the connector is loose • TCM has failed
DTC: P0888 **1T CCM** **Years:** 2005, 2006, 2007 **Models:** 300, 300C, 300M, Aspen, Caliber, Caravan, Charger, Commander, Compass, Crossfire, Dakota, Durango, Magnum, Patriot, Town & Country **Engines:** All **Transmissions:** All	**A/T Relay Output Malfunction** Engine started, TCM relay enabled and monitored continuously. This DTC sets when less than 3v are present at the relay output circuits at the TCM when the TCM is energizing the relay. **Note: Due to the integration of the PCM and TCM, the transmission part of the PCM has its own specific power and ground circuits.** **Possible Causes:** • Fused B+ circuit is open • TC relay output circuit is open or is shorted to ground • TC relay control circuit is open or is shorted to ground • TC relay ground circuit is open • TC relay has failed • Intermittent wiring or connector problems exist • Transmission solenoid/pressure switch assembly has malfunctioned or failed • PCM/TCM has failed
DTC: P0890 **1T CCM** **Years:** 2005, 2006, 2007 **Models:** 300, 300C, 300M, Aspen, Caliber, Caravan, Charger, Commander, Compass, Crossfire, Dakota, Durango, Magnum, Patriot, Town & Country **Engines:** All **Transmissions:** All	**A/T TCM Switched Battery Circuit Malfunction** Ignition switch position is changed from one position to another. TCM relay "not" energized, and the TCM detected voltage present at any of the Pressure Switch input circuits. **Note: Due to the integration of the PCM and TCM, the transmission part of the PCM has its own specific power and ground circuits.** **Possible Causes:** • 2/4 switch circuit is shorted to system power (B+) • L/R switch circuit is shorted to system power (B+) • O/D switch circuit is shorted to system power (B+) • TCM switched battery circuit is damaged • Intermittent wiring or connector problems exist • PCM/TCM has failed
DTC: P0891 **1T CCM** **Years:** 2005, 2006, 2007 **Models:** 300, 300C, 300M, Aspen, Caliber, Caravan, Charger, Commander, Compass, Crossfire, Dakota, Durango, Magnum, Patriot, Town & Country **Engines:** All **Transmissions:** All	**A/T TCM Relay Always On** Key on or engine cranking; TCM relay "not" energized, and the TCM detected voltage present at the TCM output circuit during the test. **Note: Due to the integration of the PCM and TCM, the transmission part of the PCM has its own specific power and ground circuits.** **Possible Causes:** • TCM relay output circuit is shorted to system power (B+) • TCM relay control circuit is shorted to system power (B+) • TCM relay is damaged or it has failed (it may be stuck closed) • Intermittent wiring or connector problems exist • PCM/TCM has failed
DTC: P0897 **1T CCM** **Years:** 2005, 2006, 2007 **Models:** 300, 300C, 300M, Aspen, Caliber, Caravan, Charger, Commander, Compass, Crossfire, Dakota, Durango, Magnum, Patriot, Town & Country **Engines:** All **Transmissions:** All	**A/T Transmission Fluid Burnt Or Worn Out** Engine started; vehicle driven, and immediately after a transition from full TCC lockup to partial TCC engagement (for A/C bump prevention), the TCM detected vehicle shutter during engagement. **Possible Causes:** • Automatic transmission fluid is burnt or contaminated • Automatic transmission fluid is worn out

DTC	Trouble Code Title, Conditions & Possible Causes
DTC: P0944 **1T CCM** **Years:** 2005, 2006, 2007 **Models:** 300, 300C, 300M, Aspen, Caliber, Caravan, Charger, Commander, Compass, Crossfire, Dakota, Durango, Magnum, Patriot, Town & Country **Engines:** All **Transmissions:** All	**A/T Loss Of Prime Pressure** Engine started; vehicle driven, and immediately after a slipping condition is detected with the pressure switches "not" indicating pressure, the PCM detected a loss of prime pressure. In effect, the TCM turns "on" available elements to detect if prime pressure exists. The DTC sets if no pressure switches respond. **Possible Causes:** • A/T pressure switch connector is damaged, loose or shorted • Invalid PRNDL code (shift lever position error) • Automatic transmission fluid level is too low • Transmission oil filter is clogged or severely restricted • Transmission oil pump is damaged or weak • Intermittent wiring or connector problems exist
DTC: P0952 **1T CCM** **Years:** 2005, 2006, 2007 **Models:** 300, 300C, 300M, Aspen, Caliber, Caravan, Charger, Commander, Compass, Crossfire, Dakota, Durango, Magnum, Patriot, Town & Country **Engines:** All **Transmissions:** All	**A/T AutoStick Sensor Circuit Malfunction** Engine started; vehicle driven, transmission not in AutoStick position, and the TCM that either the Upshift or Downshift switch was closed (below 0.3v), or if both the Upshift and Downshift switches are closed at the same time. **Possible Causes:** • AutoStick assembly is damaged or has failed • Intermittent wiring or connector problems exist • Downshift sense or Upshift sense circuit is shorted to ground • PCM/TCM has failed
DTC: P0953 **1T CCM** **Years:** 2005, 2006, 2007 **Models:** 300, 300C, 300M, Aspen, Caliber, Caravan, Charger, Commander, Compass, Crossfire, Dakota, Durango, Magnum, Patriot, Town & Country **Engines:** All **Transmissions:** All	**A/T AutoStick Sensor Circuit High** The AutoStick circuit is checked every .007 second, with the ignition on and in both AutoStick and non-AutoStick modes. If the TCM detects circuit voltage rises above 4.8v, this DTC will set. **Possible Causes:** • AutoStick assembly is damaged or has failed • Intermittent wiring or connector problems exist • Downshift sense or Upshift sense circuit is shorted to ground • PCM/TCM has failed
DTC: P0992 **1T CCM** **Years:** 2005, 2006, 2007 **Models:** 300, 300C, 300M, Aspen, Caliber, Caravan, Charger, Commander, Compass, Crossfire, Dakota, Durango, Magnum, Patriot, Town & Country **Engines:** All **Transmissions:** All	**A/T 2/4 & O/D Hydraulic Pressure Test Malfunction** Engine started; vehicle driven at over 1000 RPM, then immediately after a shift, the PCM detected a malfunction in one or more of the Pressure Switch circuits (it tests the switches that are not operating). If the pressure switch does not close 2 times, the DTC will set. **Possible Causes:** • 2/4 pressure switch circuit is open, shorted to ground or power • 2/4 pressure switch is damaged or it has failed • O/D pressure switch circuit is open, shorted to ground or power • O/D pressure switch is damaged or it has failed • Internal transmission faults exist • TCM relay power circuit to 2/4 or O/D switch open (loss of B+) • PCM/TCM has failed

OBD II Trouble Code List (P1XXX Codes)

DTC	Trouble Code Title, Conditions & Possible Causes
DTC: P1115 **1T CCM** **Years:** 2005, 2006, 2007 **Models:** 300, 300C, 300M, Aspen, Caliber, Caravan, Charger, Commander, Compass, Crossfire, Dakota, Durango, Magnum, Patriot, Town & Country **Engines:** All **Transmissions:** All	**General Temperature Sensor Performance** Engine "off" more than 8 hours, then engine started, ambient temperature above −10°F; and after a calibrated amount of cool-down time, the PCM compares the values from the Ambient Air Temperature (AAT), Engine Coolant Temperature (ECT) and Intake Air Temperature (IAT) Sensors. If the PCM detects that the value of any combination of these Sensors (AAT-IAT, AAT-ECT or ECT-IAT) is less than a calibrated value, it will set this trouble code. **Possible Causes:** • Sensor signal circuit is open or shorted to ground • Sensor ground circuit is open or shorted to VREF (5v) • One or more of the identified Sensors is out-of-calibration • Ambient air temperature Sensor is damaged or it has failed • PCM High or Low circuit is damaged or it has failed

DTC	Trouble Code Title, Conditions & Possible Causes
DTC: P1196 **1T CCM** **Years:** 2005, 2006, 2007 **Models:** 300, 300C, 300M, Aspen, Caliber, Caravan, Charger, Commander, Compass, Crossfire, Dakota, Durango, Magnum, Patriot, Town & Country **Engines:** All **Transmissions:** All	**O2 (B2 S1) Circuit Insufficient Activity** Engine started, vehicle driven with the throttle open at a speed over 18-55 mph at light engine load for over 5 minutes, ECT Sensor more than 170°F, and the PCM detected the O2 signal switched from 0.39v to 0.60v too few times in the Oxygen Sensor Monitor test. **Possible Causes:** • Base engine mechanical fault affecting more than one cylinder • Exhaust leak present in exhaust manifold or exhaust pipes • O2 element fuel contamination or has deteriorated • O2 signal circuit or ground circuit has high resistance
DTC: P1281 **2T ECT** **Years:** 2005, 2006, 2007 **Models:** 300, 300C, 300M, Aspen, Caliber, Caravan, Charger, Commander, Compass, Crossfire, Dakota, Durango, Magnum, Patriot, Town & Country **Engines:** All **Transmissions:** All	**Engine Is Cold Too Long** Engine started, engine runtime more than 20 minutes, and the PCM detected the engine temperature did not exceed 176°F in the period. **Possible Causes:** • Check the operation of the thermostat (it may be stuck open) • ECT Sensor signal circuit has high resistance • ECT Sensor is damaged or it has failed • Inspect for low coolant level or an incorrect coolant mixture
DTC: P1282 **1T CCM** **Years:** 2005, 2006, 2007 **Models:** 300, 300C, 300M, Aspen, Caliber, Caravan, Charger, Commander, Compass, Crossfire, Dakota, Durango, Magnum, Patriot, Town & Country **Engines:** All **Transmissions:** All	**Fuel Pump Relay Control Circuit Malfunction** Key on or engine started, system voltage over 10.5v, and the PCM detected an unexpected voltage condition on the Fuel Pump Relay control circuit during the CCM test period. **Possible Causes:** • Fuel pump relay control circuit is open or shorted to ground • Fuel pump relay power circuit is open (test power from Ignition) • Fuel pump relay is damaged or has failed • PCM has failed
DTC: P1294 **1T CCM** **Years:** 2005, 2006, 2007 **Models:** 300, 300C, 300M, Aspen, Caliber, Caravan, Charger, Commander, Compass, Crossfire, Dakota, Durango, Magnum, Patriot, Town & Country **Engines:** All **Transmissions:** All	**Target Idle Speed Not Reached** DTC P0106, P0107, P0108, P0121, P0122 and P0123 not set, engine started, running at idle in Drive or Neutral, and the PCM detected the Actual idle speed was more than 200 RPM over or more than 100 RPM less than the Target speed for over 14 seconds. **Possible Causes:** • Engine vacuum leak in a hose, brake booster or in the engine • IAC motor control circuits open or grounded in the wire harness • Throttle body dirty or restricted (trying cleaning it and retesting) • Throttle linkage or throttle plate not in the correct position • PCM has failed
DTC: P1296 **1T CCM** **Years:** 2005, 2006, 2007 **Models:** 300, 300C, 300M, Aspen, Caliber, Caravan, Charger, Commander, Compass, Crossfire, Dakota, Durango, Magnum, Patriot, Town & Country **Engines:** All **Transmissions:** All	**5-Volt VREF Supply Not Present** Key on, altitude indicating zero feet above seal level, then the PCM detected the MAP Sensor was near 101 kPa; or with altitude at 1200 feet above sea level, the MAP Sensor was near 88 kPa. **Possible Causes:** • MAP Sensor VREF circuit open between the Sensor and PCM • MAP Sensor ground circuit open between the Sensor and PCM • MAP Sensor is damaged or has failed • PCM has failed
DTC: P1297 **1T CCM** **Years:** 2005, 2006, 2007 **Models:** 300, 300C, 300M, Aspen, Caliber, Caravan, Charger, Commander, Compass, Crossfire, Dakota, Durango, Magnum, Patriot, Town & Country **Engines:** All **Transmissions:** All	**No Change In MAP Signal From Start To Run Transition** Engine started, and with the engine speed within 64 RPM of the Target idle speed, the PCM detected too small a difference between the BARO and MAP Sensor signals for 8.80 seconds. **Possible Causes:** • Engine vacuum port to MAP Sensor clogged, dirty or restricted • MAP Sensor signal is skewed or the Sensor is out-of-calibration • MAP Sensor VREF circuit open or grounded (intermittent fault) • PCM has failed

DTC	Trouble Code Title, Conditions & Possible Causes
DTC: P1388 **1T CCM** **Years:** 2005, 2006, 2007 **Models:** 300, 300C, 300M, Aspen, Caliber, Caravan, Charger, Commander, Compass, Crossfire, Dakota, Durango, Magnum, Patriot, Town & Country **Engines:** All **Transmissions:** All	**Auto Shutdown Relay Control Circuit Malfunction** Key on or engine cranking; and the PCM detected an unexpected voltage condition on the ASD Relay Control circuit. The ASD Relay coil resistance is 95-105ohms at 68°F. **Possible Causes:** • ASD relay control circuit is open between the relay and PCM • ASD relay control circuit is shorted to ground • ASD relay power circuit is open (test power from Fused B+) • ASD relay is damaged or has failed • PCM has failed
DTC: P1389 **1T CCM** **Years:** 2005, 2006, 2007 **Models:** 300, 300C, 300M, Aspen, Caliber, Caravan, Charger, Commander, Compass, Crossfire, Dakota, Durango, Magnum, Patriot, Town & Country **Engines:** All **Transmissions:** All	**No Auto Shutdown Relay Output Voltage To PCM** Engine cranking; and the PCM did not detect any voltage on the ASD Relay Output circuit to the PCM during the CCM test. **Possible Causes:** • ASD relay connector is damaged, loose or shorted • ASD relay output circuit is open between the relay and PCM • ASD relay power circuit is open (test power from Fused B+) • ASD relay is damaged or has failed • PCM has failed
DTC: P1391 **1T CCM** **Years:** 2005, 2006, 2007 **Models:** 300, 300C, 300M, Aspen, Caliber, Caravan, Charger, Commander, Compass, Crossfire, Dakota, Durango, Magnum, Patriot, Town & Country **Engines:** All **Transmissions:** All	**CKP Or CMP Sensor Signal Intermittent** Engine started, engine running, and after every 69-degree CKP Sensor leading edge and trailing signal edge is determined, the PCM updates this data and compares it to the true CMP Sensor port level. If the PCM detects a disagreement between these two values 20 times in succession, this trouble code is set. **Possible Causes:** • Camshaft Sensor is not installed properly • Engine valve timing is not within specifications • Perform a CKP and CMP Sensor relearn with the scan tool • Tone wheel or pulse ring is damaged
DTC: P1398 **1T CCM** **Years:** 2005, 2006, 2007 **Models:** 300, 300C, 300M, Aspen, Caliber, Caravan, Charger, Commander, Compass, Crossfire, Dakota, Durango, Magnum, Patriot, Town & Country **Engines:** All **Transmissions:** All	**Misfire Adaptive Numerator At Limit** Engine started; ECT Sensor under 75°F; engine runtime over 50 sec.; A/C "OFF"; vehicle speed over 36 mph in 1st gear, or over 65 mph in high gear, followed by a closed throttle decel period. This code sets if the PCM detects one of the CKP Sensor target windows varies more than 2.86% from the reference window. • Background - PCM needs to learn any variation in engine machining to detect when a misfire is present. CKP Sensor has 2 40 windows that are 180 apart. The window for Cylinders 1 and 4 is the reference window. It is checked against the window for Cylinders 2 and 3. The PCM checks for any variation to make engine speed adjustments. **Possible Causes:** • Base engine problem (i.e., low cylinder compression) • CKP Sensor crankshaft target variation too large • CKP Sensor improperly installed or the CKP Sensor has failed • CKP Sensor signal circuit open or shorted (intermittent fault) • Tone wheel or pulse ring is damaged
DTC: P1411 **1T CCM** **Years:** 2005, 2006, 2007 **Models:** 300, 300C, 300M, Charger, Magnum **Engines:** All **Transmissions:** All	**Cylinder No. 1 Reactivation Control Performance Malfunction** This condition is monitored when transitioning from 8 cylinder to 4-cylinder mode. If the MDS solenoid fails to activate for cylinder No. 1. By actuating the solenoid, oil pressure is raised to the pair of lifters that coincide with each particular solenoid. The oil pressure pushes in the locking pins that allow the lifter to collapse, decoupling the valves and camshaft. If this does not occur, the DTC will set. **Possible Causes:** • MDS solenoid No. 1 control is open or is shorted to ground • MDS solenoid ground circuit is open • Insufficient oil pressure acting on the lifter locking pins • Oil passages restricted • Lifter is damaged or has failed • MDS solenoid No. 1 has failed • PCM has failed

DTC	Trouble Code Title, Conditions & Possible Causes
DTC: P1414 **1T CCM** **Years:** 2005, 2006, 2007 **Models:** 300, 300C, 300M, Charger, Magnum **Engines:** All **Transmissions:** All	**Cylinder No. 4 Reactivation Control Performance Malfunction** This condition is monitored when transitioning from 8-cylinder to 4-cylinder mode. If the MDS solenoid fails to activate for cylinder No. 4. By actuating the solenoid, oil pressure is raised to the pair of lifters that coincide with each particular solenoid. The oil pressure pushes in the locking pins that allow the lifter to collapse, decoupling the valves and camshaft. If this does not occur, the DTC will set. **Possible Causes:** • MDS solenoid No. 4 control is open or is shorted to ground • MDS solenoid ground circuit is open • Insufficient oil pressure acting on the lifter locking pins • Oil passages restricted • Lifter is damaged or has failed • MDS solenoid No. 4 has failed • PCM has failed
DTC: P1416 **1T CCM** **Years:** 2005, 2006, 2007 **Models:** 300, 300C, 300M, Charger, Magnum **Engines:** All **Transmissions:** All	**Cylinder No. 6 Reactivation Control Performance Malfunction** This condition is monitored when transitioning from 8-cylinder to 4-cylinder mode. If the MDS solenoid fails to activate for cylinder No. 6. By actuating the solenoid, oil pressure is raised to the pair of lifters that coincide with each particular solenoid. The oil pressure pushes in the locking pins that allow the lifter to collapse, decoupling the valves and camshaft. If this does not occur, the DTC will set. **Possible Causes:** • MDS solenoid No. 6 control is open or is shorted to ground • MDS solenoid ground circuit is open • Insufficient oil pressure acting on the lifter locking pins • Oil passages restricted • Lifter is damaged or has failed • MDS solenoid No. 6 has failed • PCM has failed
DTC: P1417 **1T CCM** **Years:** 2005, 2006, 2007 **Models:** 300, 300C, 300M, Charger, Magnum **Engines:** All **Transmissions:** All	**Cylinder No. 7 Reactivation Control Performance Malfunction** This condition is monitored when transitioning from 8-cylinder to 4-cylinder mode. If the MDS solenoid fails to activate for cylinder No. 7. By actuating the solenoid, oil pressure is raised to the pair of lifters that coincide with each particular solenoid. The oil pressure pushes in the locking pins that allow the lifter to collapse, decoupling the valves and camshaft. If this does not occur, the DTC will set. **Possible Causes:** • MDS solenoid No. 7 control is open or is shorted to ground • MDS solenoid ground circuit is open • Insufficient oil pressure acting on the lifter locking pins • Oil passages restricted • Lifter is damaged or has failed • MDS solenoid No. 7 has failed • PCM has failed
DTC: P1486 2T EVAP **Years:** 2005, 2006, 2007 **Models:** 300, 300C, 300M, Aspen, Caliber, Caravan, Charger, Commander, Compass, Crossfire, Dakota, Durango, Magnum, Patriot, Town & Country **Engines:** All **Transmissions:** All	**EVAP Leak Detection Monitor Pinched Hose Detected** BTS from 40-96°F and ECT Sensor within 20°F of the BTS signal at startup (cold engine), engine started, and after the EVAP Leak Detection test was enabled, the PCM detected the LDP switch did not reach 3 closures (i.e., a "no flow" condition was present). **Possible Causes:** • EVAP vapor hose blocked between the fuel tank and the LDP (i.e., in the OLFV, rollover or vapor hose) • EVAP canister is clogged or full of dirt or moisture • EVAP ventilation solenoid is damaged or has failed • Purge line is loose, damaged or incorrectly routed • PCM has failed
DTC: P1492 **1T CCM** **Years:** 2005, 2006, 2007 **Models:** 300, 300C, 300M, Aspen, Caliber, Caravan, Charger, Commander, Compass, Crossfire, Dakota, Durango, Magnum, Patriot, Town & Country **Engines:** All **Transmissions:** All	**Battery Temperature Sensor Circuit High Input** Key on or engine running; and the PCM detected the BTS signal indicated more than 4.90v for 3 seconds during the CCM test. **Possible Causes:** • BTS signal circuit is open between the Sensor and the PCM • BTS ground circuit is open between the Sensor and the PCM • BTS (Sensor) is damaged or the PCM has failed

DTC	Trouble Code Title, Conditions & Possible Causes
DTC: P1493 **1T CCM** **Years:** 2005, 2006, 2007 **Models:** 300, 300C, 300M, Aspen, Caliber, Caravan, Charger, Commander, Compass, Crossfire, Dakota, Durango, Magnum, Patriot, Town & Country **Engines:** All **Transmissions:** All	**Battery Temperature Sensor Circuit Low Input** Key on or engine running; and the PCM detected the BTS signal indicated less than 0.30v for 3 seconds during the CCM test. **Possible Causes:** • BTS circuit is shorted to ground between Sensor and the PCM • BTS (Sensor) is damaged or has failed • PCM has failed
DTC: P1494 **1T CCM** **Years:** 2005, 2006, 2007 **Models:** 300, 300C, 300M, Aspen, Caliber, Caravan, Charger, Commander, Compass, Crossfire, Dakota, Durango, Magnum, Patriot, Town & Country **Engines:** All **Transmissions:** All	**EVAP Leak Detection Pump Switch Or Mechanical Fault** BTS from 40-96°F and ECT Sensor within 10°F of the BTS signal at startup (cold engine), engine started, and the PCM detected the LDP switch was not in its expected state at key "on" or engine running. **Possible Causes:** • LDP switch signal circuit is open or shorted to ground • LDP switch power circuit is open (test power to Fused Ignition) • LDP vacuum hose is clogged, loose or restricted • LDP assembly is damaged or has failed (the switch has failed)
DTC: P1495 **1T CCM** **Years:** 2005, 2006, 2007 **Models:** 300, 300C, 300M, Aspen, Caliber, Caravan, Charger, Commander, Compass, Crossfire, Dakota, Durango, Magnum, Patriot, Town & Country **Engines:** All **Transmissions:** All	**Leak Detection Pump Solenoid Circuit Malfunction** Engine started, ECT Sensor from 40-90°F and within 10°F of the Battery Temperature Sensor signal, engine running, and the PCM detected the Actual state of the Leak Detection Pump solenoid did not match the Intended state of the solenoid during the test period. **Possible Causes:** • LDP power supply circuit from the ignition switch is open • LDP solenoid control circuit is open or shorted to ground • LDP assembly is damaged or it has failed • PCM has failed
DTC: P1501 **1T CCM** **Years:** 2005, 2006, 2007 **Models:** 300, 300C, 300M, Aspen, Dakota, Durango, Magnum **Engines:** All **Transmissions:** All	**Vehicle Speed Sensor No. 1/2 Drive Wheel Correlation** Engine is running and vehicle is moving. Speed control is learned and the speed control is trying to be activated. If the PCM recognizes the rear wheel speed is greater than the front wheel speed, this DTC will set. **Possible Causes:** • Other active Bus or Communication DTCs • Incorrect tire circumference • PCM has failed
DTC: P1502 **1T CCM** **Years:** 2005, 2006, 2007 **Models:** 300, 300C, 300M, Aspen, Dakota, Durango, Magnum **Engines:** **Transmissions:**	**Vehicle Speed Sensor No. 1/2 Non-Drive Wheel Correlation** Engine is running and vehicle is moving; brake pedal must not be applied. If the PCM recognizes the rear wheel speed is greater than the front wheel speed, this DTC will set. **Possible Causes:** • Other active Bus or Communication DTCs • Incorrect tire circumference • PCM has failed
DTC: P1521 **1T CCM** **Years:** 2005, 2006, 2007 **Models:** 300, 300C, 300M, Charger, Magnum **Engines:** All **Transmissions:** All	**Incorrect Engine Oil Type** Engine is running. The PCM will use oil pressure, oil temperature and other vital engine inputs to determine the engine oil viscosity. Incorrect viscosity will affect the operation of the MDS by delaying cylinder activation. **Possible Causes:** • Incorrect engine oil type • Engine oil contamination • Engine oil has aged and is breaking down
DTC: P1572 **1T CCM** **Years:** 2005, 2006, 2007 **Models:** 300, 300C, 300M, Charger, Dakota, Durango, Magnum **Engines:** All **Transmissions:** All	**Brake Switch Stuck ON** Ignition is on. The PCM recognizes that brake switch 1 is mechanically stuck in the Low/On position. **Possible Causes:** • Brake switch 1 signal is shorted to ground • Brake switch 2 signal is open • Stop lamp switch has failed • PCM has failed

DTC	Trouble Code Title, Conditions & Possible Causes
DTC: P1573 **1T CCM** **Years:** 2005, 2006, 2007 **Models:** 300, 300C, 300M, Aspen, Dakota, Durango, Magnum **Engines:** All **Transmissions:** All	**Brake Switch Stuck ON** Ignition is on. The PCM recognizes that brake switch 1 is mechanically stuck in the High/Off position. **Possible Causes:** • Brake switch 1 signal is shorted to ground or to voltage • Brake switch 2 signal is open or is shorted to ground • Ground circuit is open • Fused ignition switch output is open • Stop lamp switch has failed • PCM has failed
DTC: P1593 **1T CCM** **Years:** 2005, 2006, 2007 **Models:** 300, 300C, 300M, Aspen, Caliber, Caravan, Charger, Commander, Compass, Crossfire, Dakota, Durango, Magnum, Patriot, Town & Country **Engines:** All **Transmissions:** All	**Speed Control Switch Stuck Operation** Ignition on. Either S/C switch is mechanically stuck in On/Off, Resume/Accel or Set position for too long. **Possible Causes:** • Intermittent speed control switch 1/2 stuck DTC • S/C switches or Steering Column Control Module malfunctioning • S/C signal circuit open or shorted ground or to battery voltage • S/C switch signal circuit shorted to switch return circuit • S/C Sensor ground open • PCM has failed
DTC: P1598 **1T CCM** **Years:** 2005, 2006, 2007 **Models:** 300, 300C, 300M, Aspen, Caliber, Caravan, Charger, Commander, Compass, Crossfire, Dakota, Durango, Magnum, Patriot, Town & Country **Engines:** All **Transmissions:** All	**A/C Pressure Sensor Circuit High Input** Engine started, engine running, A/C Relay is "on", and the PCM detected the A/C Pressure Sensor indicated more than 4.90v. **Possible Causes:** • A/C pressure Sensor circuit is open or shorted to VREF (5v) • A/C pressure Sensor ground circuit is open • A/C pressure Sensor is damaged or has failed • PCM has failed
DTC: P1599 **1T CCM** **Years:** 2005, 2006, 2007 **Models:** 300, 300C, 300M, Aspen, Caliber, Caravan, Charger, Commander, Compass, Crossfire, Dakota, Durango, Magnum, Patriot, Town & Country **Engines:** All **Transmissions:** All	**A/C Pressure Sensor Circuit Low Input** Engine started, engine running, A/C Relay is "on", and the PCM detected the A/C Pressure Sensor indicated less than 0.70v. **Possible Causes:** • A/C pressure Sensor circuit is shorted to ground • A/C pressure Sensor power circuit is open • A/C pressure Sensor is damaged or has failed • PCM has failed
DTC: P1602 **1T PCM** **Years:** 2005, 2006, 2007 **Models:** 300, 300C, 300M, Aspen, Caliber, Caravan, Charger, Commander, Compass, Crossfire, Dakota, Durango, Magnum, Patriot, Town & Country **Engines:** All **Transmissions:** All	**PCM Not Programmed** Key on. The PCM detected that it had not been programmed. **Possible Causes:** • Program the PCM and then retest for this same trouble code • PCM has failed
DTC: P1603 **1T PCM** **Years:** 2005, 2006, 2007 **Models:** 300, 300C, 300M, Aspen, Caliber, Caravan, Charger, Commander, Compass, Crossfire, Dakota, Durango, Magnum, Patriot, Town & Country **Engines:** All **Transmissions:** All	**Powertrain Control Module Internal Dual-Port Ram Communication** Key on; and the PCM detected an error message that indicated that it had not been programmed or that it was programmed properly. **Possible Causes:** • Fused ignition switch output is missing (off-start-run circuit) • PCM is damaged or it has an internal failure

DTC	Trouble Code Title, Conditions & Possible Causes
DTC: P1604 **1T PCM** **Years:** 2005, 2006, 2007 **Models:** 300, 300C, 300M, Aspen, Caliber, Caravan, Charger, Commander, Compass, Crossfire, Dakota, Durango, Magnum, Patriot, Town & Country **Engines:** All **Transmissions:** All	**PCM Internal Dual-Port Ram Read/Write Integrity Failure** Key on; and the PCM detected an error message that indicated it had not been programmed, or it was not programmed properly. **Possible Causes:** • Fused ignition switch output is missing (off-start-run circuit) • PCM is damaged or it has an internal failure
DTC: P1607 **1T PCM** **Years:** 2005, 2006, 2007 **Models:** 300, 300C, 300M, Aspen, Caliber, Caravan, Charger, Commander, Compass, Crossfire, Dakota, Durango, Magnum, Patriot, Town & Country **Engines:** All **Transmissions:** All	**Powertrain Control Module Internal Shutdown Timer Rationality** Cold engine startup, and after the PCM compared the coolant temperature to the shutdown time, it detected a rationality fault. **Possible Causes:** • Fused ignition switch output is missing (off-start-run circuit) • PCM is damaged or it has an internal failure
DTC: P1618 **1T PCM** **Years:** 2005, 2006, 2007 **Models:** 300, 300C, 300M, Aspen, Dakota, Durango, Magnum **Engines:** All **Transmissions:** All	**Primary 5v Sensor Reference Voltage Malfunction** Key on. The PCM recognizes the primary 5v supply circuit voltage is varying too much too quickly. ETC light is flashing. **Possible Causes:** • Primary 5v supply circuit open or shorted to ground or to battery voltage • 5v Sensor has failed • PCM has failed
DTC: P1628 **1T PCM** **Years:** 2005, 2006, 2007 **Models:** 300, 300C, 300M, Aspen, Dakota, Durango, Magnum **Engines:** All **Transmissions:** All	**Auxiliary 5v Sensor Reference Voltage Malfunction** Key on. The PCM recognizes the auxiliary 5v supply circuit voltage is varying too much too quickly. ETC light is flashing. **Possible Causes:** • Auxiliary 5v supply circuit open or shorted to ground or to battery voltage • 5v Sensor has failed • PCM has failed
DTC: P1652 **1T CCM** **Years:** 2005, 2006, 2007 **Models:** 300, 300C, 300M, Aspen, Caliber, Caravan, Charger, Commander, Compass, Crossfire, Dakota, Durango, Magnum, Patriot, Town & Country **Engines:** All **Transmissions:** All	**Serial Communication Link Malfunction** Engine started; and after the TCM did not detect any signals on the Serial Communication Line for more than 20 seconds. **Note: Due to the integration of the PCM and TCM, Bus communication between the modules is internal.** **Possible Causes:** • TCM cannot communicate with the Instrument Cluster (MIC) • TCM cannot communicate with the Powertrain Control Module • PCM/TCM is damaged or it has an internal failure
DTC: P1682 **1T CCM** **Years:** 2005, 2006, 2007 **Models:** 300, 300C, 300M, Aspen, Caliber, Caravan, Charger, Commander, Compass, Crossfire, Dakota, Durango, Magnum, Patriot, Town & Country **Engines:** All **Transmissions:** All	**Charging System Voltage Too Low** Engine started; engine speed over 1152 RPM, and the PCM detected the Battery Sense circuit was 1.0v less than the Charging System circuit for 25 seconds during the CCM test (Generator Lamp is "on"). **Possible Causes:** • Battery positive or Fused Ignition circuit has high resistance • Generator drive belt out-of-adjustment or worn out • Generator field circuit has a high resistance condition • PCM has failed

DTC	Trouble Code Title, Conditions & Possible Causes
DTC: P1684 **1T PCM** **Years:** 2005, 2006, 2007 **Models:** 300, 300C, 300M, Aspen, Caliber, Caravan, Charger, Commander, Compass, Crossfire, Dakota, Durango, Magnum, Patriot, Town & Country **Engines:** All **Transmissions:** All	**Battery Has Been Disconnected** Key on, and the TCM detected that it had been disconnected from the Battery Direct (B+) circuit or its Power Ground circuit. This DTC will also set during the scan tool Quick Battery Disconnect procedure. **Note: Due to the integration of the PCM and TCM, the transmission part of the PCM has its own specific power and ground circuits.** **Possible Causes:** • Quick Learn procedure was performed with scan tool • TCM battery direct (B+) circuit is open or disconnected • TCM power ground circuit is open • PCM/TCM was disconnected or it has been replaced
DTC: P1687 **1T PCM** **Years:** 2005, 2006, 2007 **Models:** 300, 300C, 300M, Aspen, Caliber, Caravan, Charger, Commander, Compass, Crossfire, Dakota, Durango, Magnum, Patriot, Town & Country **Engines:** All **Transmissions:** All	**No Cluster Bus Messages** Key on or engine running; and the PCM determined that it did not receive any Security Key Bus Messages over the Data Bus line for 20 seconds. This malfunction may be an intermittent problem. **Possible Causes:** • Data Bus circuit from SKIM to PCM is damaged or it is open • PCM unable to communicate with the Body Control Module • PCM has failed, or the SKIM is damaged or has failed
DTC: P1687 **1T PCM** **Years:** 2005, 2006, 2007 **Models:** 300, 300C, 300M, Aspen, Caliber, Caravan, Charger, Commander, Compass, Crossfire, Dakota, Durango, Magnum, Patriot, Town & Country **Engines:** All **Transmissions:** All	**No Communication with MIC** Communications are monitored continuously with engine running. The DTC sets in about 25 seconds if no Bus messages are received from the MIC. **Possible Causes:** • Other Bus problems exist • Intermittent wiring or connector problems exist • PCM has failed
DTC: P1694 2005, 2006, 2007 **Models:** 300, 300C, 300M, Aspen, Caliber, Caravan, Charger, Commander, Compass, Crossfire, Dakota, Durango, Magnum, Patriot, Town & Country **Engines:** All **Transmissions:** All	**No PCM Bus Messages** Ignition on or engine started; system voltage over 10.5v and the PCM determined that it did not receive any Bus messages for 10 seconds. **Note: Due to the integration of the PCM and TCM, Bus communication between the modules is internal.** **Possible Causes:** • Data Bus circuit connector is damaged, open or it is shorted • Data Bus circuit to the PCM is damaged or it is open • PCM unable to communicate with the body control module • Intermittent wiring or connector problems exist • PCM has failed
DTC: P1695 **1T PCM** **Years:** 2005, 2006, 2007 **Models:** 300, 300C, 300M, Aspen, Caliber, Caravan, Charger, Commander, Compass, Crossfire, Dakota, Durango, Magnum, Patriot, Town & Country **Engines:** All **Transmissions:** All	**No BCM Bus Messages** Engine started; system voltage over 10.5v and the TCM determined that it did not receive any BCM messages for 20 seconds. **Possible Causes:** • Data Bus circuit from BCM to the PCM is damaged or it is open • BCM is damaged or has failed • TCM unable to communicate with the TCM • TCM has failed
DTC: P1696 **1T PCM** **Years:** 2005, 2006, 2007 **Models:** 300, 300C, 300M, Aspen, Caliber, Caravan, Charger, Commander, Compass, Crossfire, Dakota, Durango, Magnum, Patriot, Town & Country **Engines:** All **Transmissions:** All	**PCM EEPROM Write Operation Denied/Invalid** Engine started or ignition on continuously. PCM detected an unsuccessful attempt to program/write to the internal EEPROM. Occurred at initialization or shutdown. **Possible Causes:** • DRB or scan tool displays a "write" failure occurred • DRB or scan tool displays "write" refused a second time • DRB or scan tool displays SRI mileage invalid (compare the SRI mileage reading to the reading on the odometer) • PCM has failed

DTC	Trouble Code Title, Conditions & Possible Causes
DTC: P1697 **1T PCM** **Years:** 2005, 2006, 2007 **Models:** 300, 300C, 300M, Aspen, Caliber, Caravan, Charger, Commander, Compass, Crossfire, Dakota, Durango, Magnum, Patriot, Town & Country **Engines:** All **Transmissions:** All	**PCM Failure (EMR/SRI Mileage Not Stored)** Key on, and the PCM detected an unsuccessful attempt to "write" the Service Reminder Indicator (SRI) or Emission Mileage Request (EMR) mileage to an EEPROM located occurred during initialization. **Possible Causes:** • Clear the trouble codes and retest for the same trouble code. If DTC P1697 resets, replace the PCM and then reprogram it.
DTC: P1775 **1T CCM** **Years:** 2005, 2006, 2007 **Models:** 300, 300C, 300M, Aspen, Caliber, Caravan, Charger, Commander, Compass, Crossfire, Dakota, Durango, Magnum, Patriot, Town & Country **Engines:** All **Transmissions:** All	**A/T Solenoid Switch Latched In TCC Position** Engine started; vehicle driven to over 15 mph and the TCM detected the Transmission did not shift into 1st Gear (test must fail 3 times). **Possible Causes:** • Related DTC P0841 may be present. • Intermittent wiring or connector problems • Extremely low battery (system) voltage • L/R Solenoid pressure switch circuit is open or switch has failed • Transmission solenoid pack is damaged or has failed • Transmission control relay circuit is shorted to L/R solenoid • Valve body engine idle too high • Valve body solenoid switch stuck in "lockup" position • PCM has failed
DTC: P1776 **2T CCM** **Years:** 2005, 2006, 2007 **Models:** 300, 300C, 300M, Aspen, Caliber, Caravan, Charger, Commander, Compass, Crossfire, Dakota, Durango, Magnum, Patriot, Town & Country **Engines:** All **Transmissions:** All	**A/T Solenoid Switch Latched In Low/Reverse Position** Engine started; vehicle driven to over 30 mph and the TCM detected the L/R switch was closed while performing partial or full PEMCC or FEMCC. **Possible Causes:** • Related DTC P0841 may be present. • Intermittent wiring or connector problems • L/R pressure switch sense circuit is open, shorted to ground or to voltage • Extremely low battery (system) voltage • Transmission pan has debris caused by valve body damage • Transmission internal problems, SSV sticking, or valve body damage • PCM has failed
DTC: P1790 **1T CCM** **Years:** 2005, 2006, 2007 **Models:** 300, 300C, 300M, Aspen, Caliber, Caravan, Charger, Commander, Compass, Crossfire, Dakota, Durango, Magnum, Patriot, Town & Country **Engines:** All **Transmissions:** All	**A/T Malfunction Immediately After Shift Event** Engine started; vehicle driven to a speed over 10 mph in Drive, and the TCM detected a Speed Ratio error within 1.3 seconds of a shift. **Possible Causes:** • Transmission internal mechanical problem
DTC: P1793 **1T CCM** **Years:** 2005, 2006, 2007 **Models:** 300, 300C, 300M, Aspen, Caliber, Caravan, Charger, Commander, Compass, Crossfire, Dakota, Durango, Magnum, Patriot, Town & Country **Engines:** All **Transmissions:** All	**TCM TRD Link Communication Error** The TCM pulses the 12v TRD signal from the PCM to ground, during torque managed shifts, with the throttle angle above 54 degrees. The TRD system is also tested whenever the vehicle is stopped and the engine is at idle. This DTC is set when the TCM sends 2 subsequent torque reduction messages to the PCM and the TCM does not receive a confirmation from the PCM. **Note: Due to the integrations of the PCM and TCM, Bus communication between the modules is internal. Related DTCs are present.** **Possible Causes:** • Torque Management Request (TMR) sense circuit is open or is shorted to ground or to voltage • PCM or TCM has failed • Intermittent wiring and connector problems

DTC	Trouble Code Title, Conditions & Possible Causes
DTC: P1794 **1T CCM** **Years:** 2005, 2006, 2007 **Models:** 300, 300C, 300M, Aspen, Caliber, Caravan, Charger, Commander, Compass, Crossfire, Dakota, Durango, Magnum, Patriot, Town & Country **Engines:** All **Transmissions:** All	**A/T Speed Sensor Ground Circuit Malfunction** Engine started; gear selector position indicating Neutral, and the PCM an error in the Output Speed Sensor signal during the test. **Possible Causes:** • Extremely low battery (system) voltage • TCM "reset" function has just been performed
DTC: P1797 **1T CCM** **Years:** 2005, 2006, 2007 **Models:** 300, 300C, 300M, Aspen, Caliber, Caravan, Charger, Commander, Compass, Crossfire, Dakota, Durango, Magnum, Patriot, Town & Country **Engines:** All **Transmissions:** All	**A/T Manual Shift Overheat Malfunction** Whenever the engine is running and the transmission is in the AutoStick mode, if the engine temperature exceeds 275F (135C), this DTC will set. **Note: Aggressive driving or driving in Low for extended periods in AutoStick mode will set this DTC.** **Possible Causes:** • ATF fluid level too high (transmission may be overfilled) • Engine Cooling System or engine cooling fan malfunction • Excessive drive time in low gear, or aggressive drive patterns • Transmission oil cooler is clogged or restricted
DTC: P1797 **1T CCM** **Years:** 2005, 2006, 2007 **Models:** Caravan, Town & Country **Engines:** All **Transmissions:** All	**Manual Shift Overheat** Engine running; transmission in AutoStick mode. If the ECT Sensor exceeds 255F (123C), or the transmission temperature exceeds 275F (135C) while in AutoStick mode, this DTC will set. **Note: Aggressive driving or driving in Low for extended periods of time in AutoStick will set this DTC.** **Possible Causes:** • Aggressive driving/shift patterns • Driving in Low for extended periods

OBD II Trouble Code List (P2XXX Codes)

DTC	Trouble Code Title, Conditions & Possible Causes
DTC: P2008 **1T CCM** **Years:** 2005, 2006, 2007 **Models:** 300, 300C, 300M, Charger, Magnum **Engines:** All **Transmissions:** All	**Short Runner Solenoid Circuit Malfunction** Engine started. ASD relay energized. PCM detected the Short Runner solenoid circuit was not in its expected voltage state. **Possible Causes:** • S/R solenoid control circuit is open • S/R solenoid control circuit is shorted to ground or power (B+) • S/R solenoid power supply circuit is open to the ASD relay • Short runner solenoid is damaged or it has failed • PCM has failed
DTC: P2066 **2T CCM** **Years:** 2005, 2006, 2007 **Models:** 300, 300C, 300M, Charger, Magnum **Engines:** All **Transmissions:** All	**Fuel Level Sensor No. 2 Malfunction** Test No. 1: With ignition on, fuel level is compared to the previous key-down after a 20-second delay. If the PCM does not see a difference in the fuel level of more than 0.1v, the test will fail. Test No. 2: The PCM monitors the fuel level with ignition on. If the PCM does not see a change in the fuel level of 0.1765 in. over a set amount of miles, the test will fail. **Possible Causes:** • Fuel tank or internal siphon hose damage • Fuel level signal circuit open or shorted to ground • Ground circuit is open • Fuel level Sensor malfunction
DTC: P2067 **1T CCM** **Years:** 2005, 2006, 2007 **Models:** 300, 300C, 300M, Charger, Magnum **Engines:** All **Transmissions:** All	**Fuel Level Sensor No. 2 Low Input** Key on. Battery voltage over 10.4v. Fuel level Sensor signal goes below 0.4v for more than 90 seconds (300M, Magnum), or below 0.1961v for more than 5 seconds (Pacifica). DTC is recorded. **Possible Causes:** • Intermittent condition • Fuel level sending unit signal circuit shorted to Sensor or chassis ground • Fuel level sensing unit is damaged or the fuel tank is damaged • BCM or PCM has failed

DTC	Trouble Code Title, Conditions & Possible Causes
DTC: P2068 **1T CCM** **Years:** 2005, 2006, 2007 **Models:** 300, 300C, 300M, Charger, Magnum **Engines:** All **Transmissions:** All	**Fuel Level Sensor No. 2 High Input** Key on. Battery voltage over 10.4v. Fuel level Sensor signal goes above 4.9v for more than 90 seconds (300M, Magnum) or above 4.7v for more than 5 seconds (Pacifica). DTC is recorded. **Possible Causes:** • Fuel level sending unit signal circuit shorted to Sensor or chassis ground • Fuel level sensing unit is damaged or the fuel tank is damaged • Instrument cluster module faulty • BCM or PCM has failed
DTC: P2072 **1T CCM** **Years:** 2005, 2006, 2007 **Models:** 300, 300C, 300M, Aspen, Dakota, Durango, Magnum **Engines:** All **Transmissions:** All	**Electronic Throttle Control System Malfunction** Key on. The PCM recognizes the throttle plate is stuck during extremely cold ambient temperature conditions. The throttle plate goes through a de-icing procedure, but if the throttle plate still does not move, this DTC will set. The MIL will not illuminate. The vehicle will be in the Limp Home mode, limiting RPM and vehicle speed. **Possible Causes:** • Throttle plate frozen
DTC: P2074 **1T CCM** **Years:** 2005, 2006, 2007 **Models:** 300, 300C, 300M, Aspen, Caliber, Caravan, Charger, Commander, Compass, Crossfire, Dakota, Durango, Magnum, Patriot, Town & Country **Engines:** All **Transmissions:** All	**Manifold Pressure/Throttle Position Correlation; High Flow/Vacuum Leak** Engine running in all drive modes. The relationship between the MAP Sensor and TP Sensor exceeds a predetermined value for a given engine speed. If vacuum drops below 1.5 in. Hg with engine RPM at more than 2000 RPM at closed throttle, or if an unexpectedly high intake manifold airflow exists that can lead to increased engine speed and puts the NGC (Ram) into a High Airflow Protection Limiting mode; in this case, RPM limits for when a TP Sensor and/or MAP Sensor limp-in fault is present. **Possible Causes:** • Vacuum leak in hoses or component connections • High resistance or resistance to ground in MAP 5v supply or signal circuit • MAP Sensor has failed • High resistance in MAP ground circuit • TP Sensor has failed or is improperly adjusted • High resistance or resistance to ground in TP Sensor 5v supply or signal circuit • High resistance in TP Sensor ground circuit • PCM has failed
DTC: P2096 **2T CCM** **Years:** 2005, 2006, 2007 **Models:** 300, 300C, 300M, Aspen, Caliber, Caravan, Charger, Commander, Compass, Crossfire, Dakota, Durango, Magnum, Patriot, Town & Country **Engines:** All **Transmissions:** All	**Downstream Fuel System 1/2 Lean** Engine running in closed loop mode. Ambient/battery temperature above 20F (−7C). Altitude below 8500 feet. Fuel level is more than 15%. If the PCM adds downstream short-term compensation to long-term adaptive, and a certain percentage is exceeded for 2 trips, a freeze frame is stored, the MIL illuminates and a DTC is set. **Possible Causes:** • Exhaust leak • Engine mechanical problem • O2 Sensor has failed • O2 Sensor signal circuit or return circuit problem • Fuel contamination
DTC: P2097 **2T CCM** **Years:** 2005, 2006, 2007 **Models:** 300, 300C, 300M, Aspen, Caravan, Charger, Dakota, Durango, Magnum, Town & Country **Engines:** All **Transmissions:** All	**Downstream Fuel System 1/2 Rich** Engine running in closed loop mode. Ambient/battery temperature above 20F (−7C). Altitude below 8500 feet. Fuel level is more than 15%. If the PCM adds downstream short-term compensation to long-term adaptive, and a certain percentage is exceeded for 2 trips, a freeze frame is stored, the MIL illuminates and a DTC is set. **Possible Causes:** • Exhaust leak • Engine mechanical problem • O2 Sensor No. 1/2 has failed • O2 Sensor No. 1/2 signal circuit or return circuit problem • Fuel contamination
DTC: P2098 **2T CCM** **Years:** 2005, 2006, 2007 **Models:** 300, 300C, 300M, Aspen, Caliber, Caravan, Charger, Commander, Compass, Crossfire, Dakota, Durango, Magnum, Patriot, Town & Country **Engines:** All **Transmissions:** All	**Downstream Fuel System 2/2 Lean** Engine running in closed loop mode. Ambient/battery temperature above 20F (−7C). Altitude below 8500 feet. Fuel level is more than 15%. If the PCM adds downstream short-term compensation to long-term adaptive, and a certain percentage is exceeded for 2 trips, a freeze frame is stored, the MIL illuminates and a DTC is set. **Possible Causes:** • Exhaust leak • Engine mechanical problem • O2 Sensor No. 2/2 has failed • O2 Sensor No. 2/2 signal circuit or return circuit problem • Fuel contamination

DTC	Trouble Code Title, Conditions & Possible Causes
DTC: P2099 **2T CCM** **Years:** 2005, 2006, 2007 **Models:** 300, 300C, 300M, Aspen, Caliber, Caravan, Charger, Commander, Compass, Crossfire, Dakota, Durango, Magnum, Patriot, Town & Country **Engines:** All **Transmissions:** All	**Downstream Fuel System 2/2 Rich** Engine running in closed loop mode. Ambient/battery temperature above 20F (−7C). Altitude below 8500 feet. Fuel level is more than 15%. If the PCM adds downstream short-term compensation to long-term adaptive, and a certain percentage is exceeded for 2 trips, a freeze frame is stored, the MIL illuminates and a DTC is set. **Possible Causes:** • Exhaust leak • Engine mechanical problem • O2 Sensor No. 2/2 has failed • O2 Sensor No. 2/2 signal circuit or return circuit problem • Fuel contamination
DTC: P2100 **1T CCM** **Years:** 2005, 2006, 2007 **Models:** 300, 300C, 300M, Aspen, Charger, Dakota, Durango, Magnum **Engines:** All **Transmissions:** All	**Electronic Throttle Control Motor Circuit Malfunction** Ignition on and the ETC motor is not is Limp Home mode. When the PCM detects an internal error or a short between the ETC Motor and the ETC Motor positive circuit in the ETC Motor Driver, this DTC will set. The ETC light will be flashing. **Possible Causes:** • Intermittent condition • Throttle plate or bore may have foreign object blockage • ETC positive circuit is open or is shorted to battery voltage, to ground, or to ETC negative circuit • ETC negative circuit is open or is shorted to battery voltage or to ground • Low battery voltage • ETC Motor or Throttle Body has failed • PCM has failed
DTC: P2101 **1T CCM** **Years:** 2005, 2006, 2007 **Models:** 300, 300C, 300M, Aspen, Dakota, Durango, Magnum **Engines:** All **Transmissions:** All	**Electronic Throttle Control Motor Malfunction** With vehicle running and ETC motor is not is Limp Home mode, and the TPS adaptation is complete. The PCM recognizes too large of an error between the actual position of the throttle plate and the set point position. This DTC will set within 5 seconds. 3 good trips required to turn off MIL. The ETC light will be flashing. **Possible Causes:** • Throttle body assembly may have failed • Low battery voltage • PCM has failed
DTC: P2107 **1T CCM** **Years:** 2005, 2006, 2007 **Models:** 300, 300C, 300M, Aspen, Charger, Dakota, Durango, Magnum **Engines:** All **Transmissions:** All	**Electronic Throttle Control Module Processor Malfunction** Ignition is on. This condition is caused by an internal PCM failure. The module will attempt to reset, so you will be able to hear the throttle relearning. If the condition is continuous, the vehicle may not be drivable. The ETC light will be flashing. **Possible Causes:** • PCM requires reprogramming
DTC: P2108 **1T CCM** **Years:** 2005, 2006, 2007 **Models:** 300, 300C, 300M, Aspen, Dakota, Durango, Magnum **Engines:** All **Transmissions:** All	**Electronic Throttle Control Module Processor Malfunction** Ignition is on. This condition is caused by an internal PCM failure. Customer may experience an extended cranking condition, with limited driving and a rough idle. This code will set within 5 seconds. The ETC light will be flashing. **Possible Causes:** • PCM requires reprogramming
DTC: P2110 **1T CCM** **Years:** 2005, 2006, 2007 **Models:** 300, 300C, 300M, Aspen, Dakota, Durango, Magnum **Engines:** All **Transmissions:** All	**Electronic Throttle Control Forced Limited RPM** Ignition is on and ETC motor is working. When the PCM requests to limit engine speed, if the PWM is too high for 20.5 seconds and before P2118 sets. This one-trip fault will set within 5 seconds. The ETC light will be illuminated. **Possible Causes:** • Throttle plate stuck • ETC positive circuit is open or is shorted to ground • ETC negative circuit is open or is shorted to ground • ETC motor has failed • PCM has failed

DTC	Trouble Code Title, Conditions & Possible Causes
DTC: P2111 **1T CCM** **Years:** 2005, 2006, 2007 **Models:** 300, 300C, 300M, Aspen, Dakota, Durango, Magnum **Engines:** All **Transmissions:** All	**Electronic Throttle Control Forced Limited RPM** Ignition is on and battery voltage is more than 10v. If the TP Sensor does not return to Limp Home position at the end of this test, the DTC will set. This one-trip fault will set within 5 seconds. The ETC light will be flashing. **Possible Causes:** • Throttle plate stuck above Limp Home position • TP Sensors 1 & 2 both read 2.5v • ETC positive circuit is open or is shorted to ground or to battery voltage • ETC negative circuit is open or is shorted to ground • PCM has failed
DTC: P2112 **1T CCM** **Years:** 2005, 2006, 2007 **Models:** 300, 300C, 300M, Aspen, Dakota, Durango, Magnum **Engines:** All **Transmissions:** All	**Electronic Throttle Control Unable To Open** Ignition is on and battery voltage is more than 10v. Just after the ignition is turned on, the throttle is opened and closed to test the system. If the TP Sensor does not return to Limp Home position at the end of this test, the DTC will set. This one-trip fault will set within 5 seconds. The ETC light will be flashing. **Possible Causes:** • Throttle plate stuck at or below Limp Home position • ETC positive circuit is open or is shorted to ground • ETC negative circuit is open or is shorted to ground or to battery voltage • PCM has failed
DTC: P2115 **1T CCM** **Years:** 2005, 2006, 2007 **Models:** 300, 300C, 300M, Aspen, Dakota, Durango, Magnum **Engines:** All **Transmissions:** All	**Accelerator Pedal Position Sensor No. 1 Minimum Stop Performance** Ignition is on. During in-plant mode the APP Sensors need to be checked to make sure that idle and full pedal travel can be reached on both Sensors. The test for this DTC is enabled once the test for DTC P2166 has passed. This DTC will set if the APP Sensor No. 1 has failed to achieve the required minimum value during in-plant testing. This one-trip fault will set within 5 seconds. The engine will only idle. **Possible Causes:** • APP Sensors must be reprogrammed to relearn
DTC: P2116 **1T CCM** **Years:** 2005, 2006, 2007 **Models:** 300, 300C, 300M, Aspen, Dakota, Durango, Magnum **Engines:** All **Transmissions:** All	**Accelerator Pedal Position Sensor No. 2 Minimum Stop Performance** Ignition is on. During in-plant mode the APP Sensors need to be checked to make sure that idle and full pedal travel can be reached on both Sensors. The test for this DTC is enabled once the test for DTC P2167 has passed. This DTC will set if the APP Sensor No. 2 has failed to achieve the required minimum value during in-plant testing. This one-trip fault will set within 5 seconds. The engine will only idle. **Possible Causes:** • APP Sensors must be reprogrammed to relearn
DTC: P2118 **1T CCM** **Years:** 2005, 2006, 2007 **Models:** 300, 300C, 300M, Aspen, Dakota, Durango, Magnum **Engines:** All **Transmissions:** All	**Electronic Throttle Control Motor Circuit Malfunction** Ignition is on and ETC motor is not in limp-home mode. When the PCM detects an internal error or short between the ETC motor and ETC motor positive circuits in the ETC motor driver. The ETC light will be flashing. **Possible Causes:** • Throttle plate or bore malfunctions • ETC positive circuit is open or is shorted to ground, battery voltage or ETC negative circuit • ETC negative circuit is open or is shorted to ground or to battery voltage • ETC motor has malfunctioned • PCM has failed
DTC: P2122 **1T CCM** **Years:** 2005, 2006, 2007 **Models:** 300, 300C, 300M, Aspen, Dakota, Durango, Magnum **Engines:** All **Transmissions:** All	**Accelerator Pedal Position Sensor No. 1 Circuit Low** Ignition is on and no other APP Sensor No. 1 DTCs are present. When APP Sensor No. 1 voltage is too low, the engine will additionally idle, if the brake pedal is pressed or has failed. Acceleration rate and engine output are limited. This one-trip fault will set within 5 seconds. The ETC light will be flashing. **Possible Causes:** • 5v supply circuit is open or shorted to ground • APP Sensor No. 1 signal circuit is open, shorted to ground or to Sensor return circuit • APP Sensor No. 1 has failed • PCM has failed
DTC: P2123 **1T CCM** **Years:** 2005, 2006, 2007 **Models:** 300, 300C, 300M, Aspen, Dakota, Durango, Magnum **Engines:** All **Transmissions:** All	**Accelerator Pedal Position Sensor No. 1 Circuit High** Ignition is on and no other APP Sensor No. 1 DTCs are present. When APP Sensor No. 1 voltage is too high, the engine will additionally idle, if the brake pedal is pressed or has failed. Acceleration rate and engine output are limited. This one-trip fault will set within 5 seconds. The ETC light will be flashing. **Possible Causes:** • APP Sensor No. 1 return circuit is open • APP Sensor No. 1 signal circuit is shorted to either 5v supply circuit • APP Sensor No. 1 has failed • PCM has failed

DTC	Trouble Code Title, Conditions & Possible Causes
DTC: P2127 **1T CCM** **Years:** 2005, 2006, 2007 **Models:** 300, 300C, 300M, Aspen, Dakota, Durango, Magnum **Engines:** All **Transmissions:** All	**Accelerator Pedal Position Sensor No. 2 Circuit Low** Ignition is on and no other APP Sensor No. 2 DTCs are present. When APP Sensor No. 2 voltage is too high, the engine will additionally idle, if the brake pedal is pressed or has failed. Acceleration rate and engine output are limited. This one-trip fault will set within 5 seconds. The ETC light will be flashing. **Possible Causes:** • 5v supply circuit is open or shorted to ground • APP Sensor No. 2 signal circuit is open, shorted to ground or to Sensor return circuit • APP Sensor No. 2 has failed • PCM has failed
DTC: P2128 **1T CCM** **Years:** 2005, 2006, 2007 **Models:** 300, 300C, 300M, Aspen, Dakota, Durango, Magnum **Engines:** All **Transmissions:** All	**Accelerator Pedal Position Sensor No. 2 Circuit High** Ignition is on and no other APP Sensor No. 2 DTCs are present. When APP Sensor No. 2 voltage is too high, the engine will additionally idle, if the brake pedal is pressed or has failed. Acceleration rate and engine output are limited. This one-trip fault will set within 5 seconds. The ETC light will be flashing. **Possible Causes:** • APP Sensor No. 2 return circuit is open • APP Sensor No. 2 signal circuit is shorted to either 5v supply circuit • APP Sensor No. 2 has failed • PCM has failed
DTC: P2135 **1T CCM** **Years:** 2005, 2006, 2007 **Models:** 300, 300C, 300M, Aspen, Dakota, Durango, Magnum **Engines:** All **Transmissions:** All	**Throttle Position Sensors 1 & 2 Correlation** Ignition is on and no other TP Sensor DTCs are present. The PCM recognizes that TP Sensors 1 and 2 are not coherent, this one-trip fault will set within 5 seconds. The ETC light will be illuminated. **Possible Causes:** • TP Sensor No. 1 or 2 signal circuit is shorted to ground or to battery voltage • TP Sensor No. 1 or 2 signal circuit has high resistance • 5v supply circuit has high resistance • 5v supply circuit shorted to ground • TP Sensor ground circuit has high resistance • TP Sensor No. 1 signal circuit is shorted to Sensor No. 2 signal circuit • TP Sensor has failed • PCM has failed
DTC: P2138 **1T CCM** **Years:** 2005, 2006, 2007 **Models:** 300, 300C, 300M, Aspen, Dakota, Durango, Magnum **Engines:** All **Transmissions:** All	**Accelerator Pedal Position Sensors 1 & 2 Correlation** Ignition is on and no other APP Sensor DTCs are present. The PCM recognizes that APP Sensors 1 and 2 are not coherent. Acceleration rate and engine output are limited. This one-trip fault will set within 5 seconds. The ETC light will be flashing. **Possible Causes:** • APP Sensor No. 1 or 2 signal circuit has high resistance • APP Sensor No. 1 or 2 return circuit has high resistance • 5v supply circuit has high resistance • APP Sensor has failed • PCM has failed
DTC: P2161 **1T CCM** **Years:** 2005, 2006, 2007 **Models:** 300, 300C, 300M, Aspen, Dakota, Durango, Magnum **Engines:** All **Transmissions:** All	**Vehicle Speed Sensor No. 2 Erratic** Ignition is on and battery voltage is greater than 10v. Transmission is in Drive or Reverse. The PCM recognizes the VSS 2 speed signal is erratic or high. No MIL and no ETC light. The cruise control is disabled. **Possible Causes:** • Active Bus or Communications DTCs • Incorrect tire circumference • PCM has failed
DTC: P2166 **1T CCM** **Years:** 2005, 2006, 2007 **Models:** 300, 300C, 300M, Aspen, Dakota, Durango, Magnum **Engines:** All **Transmissions:** All	**Accelerator Pedal Position Sensor No. 1 Maximum Stop Performance** Ignition is on. During in-plant mode the APP Sensors need to be checked to make sure that idle and full pedal travel can be reached on both Sensors. This DTC will set if the APP Sensor No. 1 has failed to achieve the required maximum value during in-plant testing. This one-trip fault will set within 5 seconds. The engine will only idle. **Possible Causes:** • In-Plant test failure • APP Sensors must be reprogrammed to relearn
DTC: P2167 **1T CCM** **Years:** 2005, 2006, 2007 **Models:** 300, 300C, 300M, Aspen, Dakota, Durango, Magnum **Engines:** All **Transmissions:** All	**Accelerator Pedal Position Sensor No. 2 Maximum Stop Performance** Ignition is on. During in-plant mode the APP Sensors need to be checked to make sure that idle and full pedal travel can be reached on both Sensors. This DTC will set if the APP Sensor No. 2 has failed to achieve the required maximum value during in-plant testing. This one-trip fault will set within 5 seconds. The engine will only idle. **Possible Causes:** • In-Plant test failure • APP Sensors must be reprogrammed to relearn

DTC	Trouble Code Title, Conditions & Possible Causes
DTC: P2172 **1T CCM** **Years:** 2005, 2006, 2007 **Models:** 300, 300C, 300M, Aspen, Dakota, Durango, Magnum **Engines:** All **Transmissions:** All	**High Airflow/Vacuum Leak Detected (Instantaneous Accumulation)** Ignition is on and engine running with no MAP Sensor DTCs present. A large vacuum leak has been detected or both of the TP Sensors have failed, based on their position being 2.5v and the calculated MAP value is less than the actual MAP, minus an Offset value. This one-trip fault will set within 5 seconds. The ETC light will flash. **Possible Causes:** • Vacuum leak • 5v supply circuit has high resistance or is shorted to ground • MAP signal circuit has high resistance or is shorted to ground • TP Sensor ground circuit has high resistance • TP Sensor signal circuit is shorted to ground • TP Sensor return circuit has high resistance • MAP Sensor has failed • TP Sensor has failed • PCM has failed
DTC: P2173 **1T CCM** **Years:** 2005, 2006, 2007 **Models:** 300, 300C, 300M, Aspen, Dakota, Durango, Magnum **Engines:** All **Transmissions:** All	**High Airflow/Vacuum Leak Detected (Slow Accumulation)** Ignition is on and engine running with no MAP Sensor DTCs present. A large vacuum leak has been detected or both of the TP Sensors have failed, based on their position being 2.5v and the calculated MAP value is less than the Gas Flow Adaptation value. This one-trip fault will set within 5 seconds. The ETC light will flash. **Possible Causes:** • Vacuum leak • 5v supply circuit has high resistance or is shorted to ground • MAP signal circuit has high resistance or is shorted to ground • TP Sensor ground circuit has high resistance • TP Sensor signal circuit is shorted to ground • TP Sensor return circuit has high resistance • MAP Sensor has failed • TP Sensor has failed • PCM has failed
DTC: P2174 **1T CCM** **Years:** 2005, 2006, 2007 **Models:** 300, 300C, 300M, Aspen, Dakota, Durango, Magnum **Engines:** All **Transmissions:** All	**Low Airflow/Vacuum Leak Detected (Instantaneous Accumulation)** Ignition is on and engine running with no MAP Sensor DTCs present. The PCM calculated the MAP value is greater than actual MAP value, plus an Offset value. 3 good trips required to turn off MIL. The ETC light will flash. **Possible Causes:** • Restricted air inlet system • 5v supply circuit has high resistance or is shorted to ground • MAP signal circuit has high resistance or is shorted to ground • TP Sensor ground circuit has high resistance • TP Sensor signal circuit is shorted to ground • TP Sensor return circuit has high resistance • MAP Sensor has failed • TP Sensor has failed • PCM has failed
DTC: P2175 **1T CCM** **Years:** 2005, 2006, 2007 **Models:** 300, 300C, 300M, Aspen, Dakota, Durango, Magnum **Engines:** All **Transmissions:** All	**Low Airflow/Vacuum Leak Detected (Slow Accumulation)** Ignition is on and engine running with no MAP Sensor DTCs present. The PCM calculated the MAP value is greater than actual MAP value, plus an Offset value. This DTC will set in 5 seconds after occurrence. 3 good trips required to turn off MIL. The ETC light will flash. **Possible Causes:** • Restricted air inlet system • 5v supply circuit has high resistance or is shorted to ground • MAP signal circuit has high resistance or is shorted to ground • TP Sensor ground circuit has high resistance • TP Sensor signal circuit is shorted to ground • TP Sensor return circuit has high resistance • MAP Sensor has failed • TP Sensor has failed • PCM has failed

DTC	Trouble Code Title, Conditions & Possible Causes
DTC: P2181 **2T CCM** **Years:** 2005, 2006, 2007 **Models:** 300, 300C, 300M, Aspen, Dakota, Durango, Magnum **Engines:** All **Transmissions:** All	**Cooling System Performance** Ignition is on and engine running with no ECT Sensor DTCs present. The PCM recognizes that the ECT has failed its self-coherence test. The coolant temperature should only change at a certain rate. If this rate is too slow or too fast, this DTC will set. 3 good trips required to turn off MIL. The ETC light will illuminate on first trip failure. **Possible Causes:** • Low coolant level • ECT signal circuit is open or shorted to ground, Sensor ground, or battery voltage • ECT Sensor ground circuit is open • Thermostat has failed • ECT Sensor has failed • PCM has failed
DTC: P2299 **1T CCM** **Years:** 2005, 2006, 2007 **Models:** 300, 300C, 300M, Aspen, Dakota, Durango, Magnum **Engines:** All **Transmissions:** All	**Brake Pedal Position/Accelerator Pedal Position Incompatible** Ignition is on and no Brake or APPS DTCs present. The PCM recognizes that a brake application following the APPS showing a fixed pedal opening. Temporary or permanent in nature. Internally, the PCM will reduce throttle opening below driver demand. This one-trip fault code will set in 5 seconds. The ETC light will illuminate and will only stay on while the DTC is active. **Possible Causes:** • Customer pressing accelerator pedal, then pressing brake pedal and holds both down at the same time • Stop lamp switch has failed • APP Sensor has failed
DTC: P2302 **1T CCM** **Years:** 2005, 2006, 2007 **Models:** 300, 300C, 300M, Aspen, Caliber, Caravan, Charger, Commander, Compass, Crossfire, Dakota, Durango, Magnum, Patriot, Town & Country **Engines:** All **Transmissions:** All	**Ignition Coil No. 1 Secondary Circuit Insufficient Ionization** Engine started; and the PCM detected the Ignition Coil No. 1 secondary "burn time" was insufficient, or it was missing. **Possible Causes:** • Intermittent condition • Cylinder No. 1 spark plug or wire is damaged or it has failed • Ignition Coil No. 1 is damaged or it has failed • Ignition coil control circuit is open or shorted to ground • ASD relay output circuit problems • PCM has failed
DTC: P2305 **1T CCM** **Years:** 2005, 2006, 2007 **Models:** 300, 300C, 300M, Aspen, Caliber, Caravan, Charger, Commander, Compass, Crossfire, Dakota, Durango, Magnum, Patriot, Town & Country **Engines:** All **Transmissions:** All	**Ignition Coil No. 2 Secondary Circuit Insufficient Ionization** Engine started; and the PCM detected the Ignition Coil No. 2 secondary "burn time" was insufficient, or it was missing. **Possible Causes:** • Intermittent condition • Cylinder No. 2 spark plug or wire is damaged or it has failed • Ignition Coil No. 2 is damaged or it has failed • Ignition coil control circuit is open or shorted to ground • ASD relay output circuit problems • PCM has failed
DTC: P2308 **1T CCM** **Years:** 2005, 2006, 2007 **Models:** 300, 300C, 300M, Aspen, Caliber, Caravan, Charger, Commander, Compass, Crossfire, Dakota, Durango, Magnum, Patriot, Town & Country **Engines:** All **Transmissions:** All	**Ignition Coil No. 3 Secondary Circuit Insufficient Ionization** Engine started; and the PCM detected the Ignition Coil No. 3 secondary "burn time" was insufficient, or it was missing. **Possible Causes:** • Intermittent condition • Cylinder No. 3 spark plug or wire is damaged or it has failed • Ignition Coil No. 3 is damaged or it has failed • Ignition coil control circuit is open or shorted to ground • ASD relay output circuit problems • PCM has failed
DTC: P2311 **1T CCM** **Years:** 2005, 2006, 2007 **Models:** 300, 300C, 300M, Aspen, Caliber, Caravan, Charger, Commander, Compass, Crossfire, Dakota, Durango, Magnum, Patriot, Town & Country **Engines:** All **Transmissions:** All	**Ignition Coil No. 4 Secondary Circuit Insufficient Ionization** Engine started; and the PCM detected the Ignition Coil No. 4 secondary "burn time" was insufficient, or it was missing. **Possible Causes:** • Intermittent condition • Cylinder No. 4 spark plug or wire is damaged or it has failed • Ignition Coil No. 4 is damaged or it has failed • Ignition coil control circuit is open or shorted to ground • ASD relay output circuit problems • PCM has failed

DTC	Trouble Code Title, Conditions & Possible Causes
DTC: P2314 **1T CCM** **Years:** 2005, 2006, 2007 **Models:** 300, 300C, 300M, Aspen, Caliber, Caravan, Charger, Commander, Compass, Crossfire, Dakota, Durango, Magnum, Patriot, Town & Country **Engines:** All **Transmissions:** All	**Ignition Coil No. 5 Secondary Circuit Insufficient Ionization** Engine started; and the PCM detected the Ignition Coil No. 5 secondary "burn time" was insufficient, or it was missing. **Possible Causes:** • Intermittent condition • Cylinder No. 5 spark plug or wire is damaged or it has failed • Ignition Coil No. 5 is damaged or it has failed • Ignition coil control circuit is open or shorted to ground • ASD relay output circuit problems • PCM has failed
DTC: P2317 **1T CCM** **Years:** 2005, 2006, 2007 **Models:** 300, 300C, 300M, Aspen, Caliber, Caravan, Charger, Commander, Compass, Crossfire, Dakota, Durango, Magnum, Patriot, Town & Country **Engines:** All **Transmissions:** All	**Ignition Coil No. 6 Secondary Circuit Insufficient Ionization** Engine started; and the PCM detected the Ignition Coil No. 6 secondary "burn time" was insufficient, or it was missing. **Possible Causes:** • Intermittent condition • Cylinder No. 6 spark plug or wire is damaged or it has failed • Ignition Coil No. 6 is damaged or it has failed • Ignition coil control circuit is open or shorted to ground • ASD relay output circuit problems • PCM has failed
DTC: P2320 **1T CCM** **Years:** 2005, 2006, 2007 **Models:** 300, 300C, 300M, Aspen, Caliber, Caravan, Charger, Commander, Compass, Crossfire, Dakota, Durango, Magnum, Patriot, Town & Country **Engines:** All **Transmissions:** All	**Ignition Coil No. 7 Secondary Circuit Insufficient Ionization** Engine started; and the PCM detected the Ignition Coil No. 7 secondary "burn time" was insufficient, or it was missing. **Possible Causes:** • Cylinder No. 7 spark plug or wire is damaged or it has failed • Ignition Coil No. 7 is damaged or it has failed • Ignition coil control circuit is open or shorted to ground • PCM has failed
DTC: P2323 **1T CCM** **Years:** 2005, 2006, 2007 **Models:** 300, 300C, 300M, Aspen, Caliber, Caravan, Charger, Commander, Compass, Crossfire, Dakota, Durango, Magnum, Patriot, Town & Country **Engines:** All **Transmissions:** All	**Ignition Coil No. 8 Secondary Circuit Insufficient Ionization** Engine started; and the PCM detected the Ignition Coil No. 8 secondary "burn time" was insufficient, or it was missing. **Possible Causes:** • Cylinder No. 8 spark plug or wire is damaged or it has failed • Ignition Coil No. 8 is damaged or it has failed • Ignition coil control circuit is open or shorted to ground • PCM has failed
DTC: P2503 **1T CCM** **Years:** 2005, 2006, 2007 **Models:** 300, 300C, 300M, Aspen, Caliber, Caravan, Charger, Commander, Compass, Crossfire, Dakota, Durango, Magnum, Patriot, Town & Country **Engines:** All **Transmissions:** All	**Charging System Voltage Low** Engine started; engine speed over 1157 RPM; PCM detected the Battery Sense voltage was 1v less than the Charging system voltage "goal" for 13.47 seconds during the CCM test. The PCM senses the battery voltage turns off the field driver and then senses the battery voltage again. If the voltages are the same, the DTC is set. **Possible Causes:** • Battery sense circuit has a high resistance condition • Generator ground circuit has a high resistance condition • Generator field ground circuit is open • Generator field control circuit is open or shorted to ground • Generator is damaged or it has failed
DTC: P2700 **1T CCM** **Years:** 2005, 2006, 2007 **Models:** Aspen, Dakota, Durango, **Engines:** 3.7L **Transmissions:** All	**A/T L/R Inadequate Element Volume Detected** Engine started; transmission fluid temperature more than 110°F, vehicle driven, and the PCM updated the L/R volume (during a 3-1 or 2-1 Manual downshift) with the throttle angle less than 5 degrees, and it detected that the L/R volume fell below 16 during the test. **Possible Causes:** • L/R volume clutch index is too low • TCM L/R volume clutch circuit is damaged or has failed

DTC	Trouble Code Title, Conditions & Possible Causes
DTC: P2701 **1T CCM** **Years:** 2005, 2006, 2007 **Models:** Aspen, Dakota, Durango, **Engines:** 3.7L **Transmissions:** All	**A/T 2C Inadequate Element Volume Detected** Engine started; transmission fluid temperature more than 110°F, vehicle driven, then after the PCM updated the 2C volume (during a 3-2 kickdown event) with the throttle angle from 10-54 degrees, the PCM detected that the 2C volume fell below 5 during the CCM test. **Possible Causes:** • 2C volume clutch index is too low • TCM 2C volume clutch circuit is damaged or has failed
DTC: P2702 **1T CCM** **Years:** 2005, 2006, 2007 **Models:** Aspen, Dakota, Durango, **Engines:** 3.7L **Transmissions:**	**A/T O/D Inadequate Element Volume Detected** Engine started; transmission fluid temperature more than 110°F, vehicle driven, then after he PCM updated the O/D volume (during a 2-3 Upshift event) with the throttle angle from 10-54 degrees, the PCM detected that the O/D volume fell below 5 during the CCM test. **Possible Causes:** • O/D volume clutch index is too low • TCM O/D volume clutch circuit is damaged or has failed
DTC: P2703 **1T CCM** **Years:** 2005, 2006, 2007 **Models:** Aspen, Dakota, Durango, **Engines:** 3.7L **Transmissions:**	**A/T U/D Inadequate Element Volume Detected** Engine started; transmission fluid temperature more than 110°F, vehicle driven, and the TCM updated the U/D volume (during a 4-3 kickdown) with the throttle angle from 10-54 degrees, and it detected that the U/D volume fell below 11 during the test. **Possible Causes:** • U/D volume clutch index is too low • TCM U/D volume clutch circuit is damaged or has failed
DTC: P2704 **1T CCM** **Years:** 2005, 2006, 2007 **Models:** Aspen, Dakota, Durango, **Engines:** 3.7L **Transmissions:**	**A/T 4C Inadequate Element Volume Detected** Engine started; transmission fluid temperature more than 110°F, vehicle driven, then after the TCM updated the 4C volume (during a 3-4 Upshift event) with the throttle angle from 10-54 degrees, the PCM detected that the 4C volume fell below 5 during the CCM test. **Possible Causes:** • 4C volume clutch index is too low • TCM 4C volume clutch circuit is damaged or has failed
DTC: P2706 **1T CCM** **Years:** 2005, 2006, 2007 **Models:** Aspen, Dakota, Durango, **Engines:** 3.7L **Transmissions:**	**A/T MS Solenoid Circuit Malfunction** Engine started; vehicle driven in a forward gear, and immediately after a gear ratio or pressure switch change, the TCM detected a detected a MS solenoid error. The PCM sets this code when it detects three consecutive solenoid continuity test faults; or 1 failure if the test is run in response to a gear ratio of pressure switch fault. **Possible Causes:** • Check for a loose connector to the MS solenoid (intermittent) • MS solenoid control circuit is open or shorted to ground • MS solenoid control circuit is shorted to system power (B+) • MS solenoid is damaged or it has failed • Transmission control relay output supply circuit is open • TCM MS solenoid circuit is damaged or it has failed

OBD II Trouble Code List (P3XXX Codes)

DTC	Trouble Code Title, Conditions & Possible Causes
DTC: P3400 **1T CCM** **Years:** 2005, 2006, 2007 **Models:** 300, 300C, 300M, Charger, Magnum **Engines:** All **Transmissions:** All	**MDS Rationality Bank 1** Engine running and is in transition from 8 to 4-cylinder operation. The O2 Sensor readings on Bank 1 side indicate a lean condition while in the 4-cylinder mode. **Possible Causes:** • Insufficient oil pressure acting on the lifter locking pins • Oil passages restricted • Lifter has failed • MDS solenoid has failed

DTC	Trouble Code Title, Conditions & Possible Causes
DTC: P3401 **1T CCM** **Years:** 2005, 2006, 2007 **Models:** 300, 300C, 300M, Charger, Magnum **Engines:** All **Transmissions:** All	**MDS Solenoid 1 Circuit Malfunction** Engine running and is in transition from 8 to 4-cylinder operation. The PCM recognizes a problem with the solenoid control circuit. **Possible Causes:** • MDS solenoid 1 control circuit is open, or is shorted to ground or to battery voltage • Ground circuit is open • MDS solenoid 1 has failed • PCM has failed
DTC: P3402 **1T CCM** **Years:** 2005, 2006, 2007 **Models:** 300, 300C, 300M, Charger, Magnum **Engines:** All **Transmissions:** All	**Cylinder 1 Deactivation Control Performance** Engine running and is in transition from 8 to 4-cylinder operation. The MDS fails to disengage for cylinder 1. **Possible Causes:** • MDS solenoid 1 control circuit is shorted to voltage • Oil passages restricted • Lifter has failed • MDS solenoid 1 has failed • PCM has failed
DTC: P3425 **1T CCM** **Years:** 2005, 2006, 2007 **Models:** 300, 300C, 300M, Charger, Magnum **Engines:** All **Transmissions:** All	**MDS Solenoid 4 Circuit Malfunction** Engine running and is in transition from 8 to 4-cylinder operation. The PCM recognizes a problem with the solenoid control circuit. **Possible Causes:** • MDS solenoid 4 control circuit is open, or is shorted to ground or to battery voltage • Ground circuit is open • MDS solenoid 4 has failed • PCM has failed
DTC: P3426 **1T CCM** **Years:** 2005, 2006, 2007 **Models:** 300, 300C, 300M, Charger, Magnum **Engines:** All **Transmissions:** All	**Cylinder 4 Deactivation Control Performance** Engine running and is in transition from 8 to 4-cylinder operation. The MDS fails to disengage for cylinder 4. **Possible Causes:** • MDS solenoid 4 control circuit is shorted to voltage • Oil passages restricted • Lifter has failed • MDS solenoid 4 has failed • PCM has failed
DTC: P3441 **1T CCM** **Years:** 2005, 2006, 2007 **Models:** 300, 300C, 300M, Charger, Magnum **Engines:** All **Transmissions:** All	**MDS Solenoid 6 Circuit Malfunction** Engine running and is in transition from 8 to 4-cylinder operation. The PCM recognizes a problem with the solenoid control circuit. **Possible Causes:** • MDS solenoid 6 control circuit is open, or is shorted to ground or to battery voltage • Ground circuit is open • MDS solenoid 6 has failed • PCM has failed
DTC: P3442 **1T CCM** **Years:** 2005, 2006, 2007 **Models:** 300, 300C, 300M, Charger, Magnum **Engines:** All **Transmissions:** All	**Cylinder 6 Deactivation Control Performance** Engine running and is in transition from 8 to 4-cylinder operation. The MDS fails to disengage for cylinder 6. **Possible Causes:** • MDS solenoid 6 control circuit is shorted to voltage • Oil passages restricted • Lifter has failed • MDS solenoid 6 has failed • PCM has failed

DTC	Trouble Code Title, Conditions & Possible Causes
DTC: P3449 **1T CCM** **Years:** 2005, 2006, 2007 **Models:** 300, 300C, 300M, Charger, Magnum **Engines:** All **Transmissions:** All	**MDS Solenoid 7 Circuit Malfunction** Engine running and is in transition from 8 to 4-cylinder operation. The PCM recognizes a problem with the solenoid control circuit. **Possible Causes:** • MDS solenoid 7 control circuit is open, or is shorted to ground or to battery voltage • Ground circuit is open • MDS solenoid 7 has failed • PCM has failed
DTC: P3450 **1T CCM** **Years:** 2005, 2006, 2007 **Models:** 300, 300C, 300M, Charger, Magnum **Engines:** All **Transmissions:** All	**Cylinder 7 Deactivation Control Performance** Engine running and is in transition from 8 to 4-cylinder operation. The MDS fails to disengage for cylinder 7. **Possible Causes:** • MDS solenoid 7 control circuit is shorted to voltage • Oil passages restricted • Lifter has failed • MDS solenoid 7 has failed • PCM has failed
DTC: P3497 **1T CCM** **Years:** 2005, 2006, 2007 **Models:** 300, 300C, 300M, Charger, Magnum **Engines:** All **Transmissions:** All	**MDS Rationality Bank 2** Engine running and is in transition from 8 to 4-cylinder operation. The O2 Sensor readings on Bank 2 side indicate a lean condition while in the 4-cylinder mode. **Possible Causes:** • Insufficient oil pressure acting on the lifter locking pins • Oil passages restricted • Lifter has failed • MDS solenoid has failed

OBD II Trouble Code List (UXXXX Codes)

DTC	Trouble Code Title, Conditions & Possible Causes
DTC: U0001 **1T TCM** **Years:** 2005, 2006, 2007 **Models:** 300, 300C, 300M, Charger, Magnum **Engines:** All **Transmissions:** All	**CAN C Bus Circuit Malfunction** Ignition is on and battery voltage is 9-16v. Engine is running for more than 3 seconds. The PCM loses communication over the CAN C Bus circuit. The circuit is continuously monitored. **Possible Causes:** • CAN C Bus failure open or shorted • PCM has failed
DTC: U0101 **1T TCM** **Years:** 2005, 2006, 2007 **Models:** 300, 300C, 300M, Aspen, Caliber, Caravan, Charger, Commander, Compass, Crossfire, Dakota, Durango, Magnum, Patriot, Town & Country **Engines:** All **Transmissions:** All	**No TCM Bus Message** Engine running. Battery voltage more than 10v. No Bus messages are received from the TCM for 20 seconds. 2 trips required. **Possible Causes:** • PCI Bus unable to communicate with (DRBIII) scan tool • Fused ignition switch output incorrect (off-run-start) • Intermittent condition • PCM has failed

DTC	Trouble Code Title, Conditions & Possible Causes
DTC: U0101 **1T TCM** **Years:** 2005, 2006, 2007 **Models:** 300, 300C, 300M, Aspen, Dakota, Durango, Magnum **Engines:** All **Transmissions:** All	**No TCM Bus Message** Ignition is on and battery voltage is 9-16v. Engine is running for more than 3 seconds. The PCM does not receive a Bus message from the TCM for 7 consecutive seconds. The circuit is continuously monitored. **Possible Causes:** • CAN C Bus failure open or shorted • PCM has failed
DTC: U0103 **1T TCM** **Years:** 2005, 2006, 2007 **Models:** 300, 300C, 300M, Charger, Magnum **Engines:** All **Transmissions:** All	**Lost Communication With Electric Gear Shift Module** Ignition is on and battery voltage is 9-16v. Engine is running for more than 3 seconds. The PCM does not receive an Electric Gear Shift Module message over the CAN C circuit. The circuit is continuously monitored. **Possible Causes:** • CAN C Bus failure open or shorted • Electric gear shift module has failed • PCM has failed
DTC: U0121 **1T TCM** **Years:** 2005, 2006, 2007 **Models:** 300, 300C, 300M, Charger, Magnum **Engines:** All **Transmissions:** All	**Lost Communication With ABS Module** Ignition is on and battery voltage is 9-16v. Engine is running for more than 3 seconds. The PCM does not receive an ABS message over the CAN C circuit for 7 consecutive seconds. The circuit is continuously monitored. **Possible Causes:** • CAN C Bus failure open or shorted • ABS module has failed • PCM has failed
DTC: U0140 1T BCM 2005, 2006, 2007 **Models:** Caravan, Town & Country **Engines:** All **Transmissions:** All	**No Body Bus Message** Engine running. Battery voltage more than 10v. No Bus messages are received from the BCM for 20 seconds. **Possible Causes:** • Communication link with BCM has failed • PCI Bus circuit open • PCM has failed
DTC: U0141 **1T TCM** **Years:** 2005, 2006, 2007 **Models:** 300, 300C, 300M, Charger, Magnum **Engines:** All **Transmissions:** All	**Lost Communication With Front Control Module** Ignition is on and battery voltage is 9-16v. Engine is running for more than 3 seconds. The PCM does not receive an FCM message over the CAN C circuit for 7 consecutive seconds. The circuit is continuously monitored. **Possible Causes:** • CAN C Bus failure open or shorted • Front control module has failed • PCM has failed
DTC: U0155 **1T MIC** 2005, 2006, 2007 **Models:** 300, 300C, 300M, Aspen, Caliber, Caravan, Charger, Commander, Compass, Crossfire, Dakota, Durango, Magnum, Patriot, Town & Country **Engines:** All **Transmissions:** All	**No Cluster Bus Message** Engine running. Battery voltage more than 10v. No Bus messages are received from the MIC (instrument cluster) for 20 seconds. **Possible Causes:** • Communication link with instrument cluster has failed • Instrument cluster operation improper or has failed • PCM has failed

DTC	Trouble Code Title, Conditions & Possible Causes
DTC: U0155 **1T TCM** **Years:** 2005, 2006, 2007 **Models:** 300, 300C, 300M, Charger, Magnum **Engines:** All **Transmissions:** All	**Lost Communication With Instrument Cluster/CCN** Ignition is on and battery voltage is 9-16v. Engine is running for more than 3 seconds. The PCM does not receive a Cluster message over the CAN C circuit. The circuit is continuously monitored. **Possible Causes:** • CAN C Bus failure open or shorted • Front control module has failed • PCM has failed
DTC: U0168 **1T MIC** 2005, 2006, 2007 **Models:** 300, 300C, 300M, Aspen, Caliber, Caravan, Charger, Commander, Compass, Crossfire, Dakota, Durango, Magnum, Patriot, Town & Country **Engines:** All **Transmissions:** All	**No SKIM Bus Message** Engine running or ignition on. Battery voltage more than 10v. No Bus or J1850 messages are received from the SKIM for 20 seconds. **Possible Causes:** • Intermittent operation • PCI Bus circuit open or shorted from PCM to SKIM • Loss of communication between PCM and SKIM • SKIM or PCM has failed
DTC: U0168 **1T TCM** **Years:** 2005, 2006, 2007 **Models:** 300, 300C, 300M, Charger, Magnum **Engines:** All **Transmissions:** All	**Lost Communication With Vehicle Security Control Module (SKREEM/WCM)** Ignition is on and battery voltage is 9-16v. Engine is running for more than 3 seconds. Bus message not received from the SKREEM/WCM from about 2-5 seconds. **Possible Causes:** • CAN C Bus failure open or shorted • SKREEM/WCM module has failed • PCM has failed
DTC: U110A **1T TCM** **Years:** 2005, 2006, 2007 **Models:** 300, 300C, 300M, Charger, Magnum **Engines:** All **Transmissions:** All	**Lost Communication With Steering Control Module (SCCM)** Ignition is on and battery voltage is 9-16v. Engine is running for more than 3 seconds. Bus message not received from the SCCM from about 2-5 seconds. **Possible Causes:** • CAN C Bus failure open or shorted • SCCM module has failed • PCM has failed
DTC: U110C 1T MIC 2005, 2006, 2007 **Models:** Caravan, Town & Country **Engines:** All **Transmissions:** All	**No Fuel Level Bus Message** Ignition on. Battery voltage more than 10v. No fuel level Bus messages are received from the PCM for 20 seconds. **Possible Causes:** • PCI Bus circuit open between PCM and BCM • Fuel level Bus message circuit failure • BCM has failed
DTC: U110C **1T TCM** **Years:** 2005, 2006, 2007 **Models:** 300, 300C, 300M, Charger, Magnum **Engines:** All **Transmissions:** All	**No Fuel Level Bus Message** Ignition is on. PCM does not receive a fuel level signal from the FCM over the CAN C circuit. The circuit is constantly monitored. **Possible Causes:** • CAN C Bus failure open or shorted • Front Control Module (FCM) has failed • PCM has failed
DTC: U110E **1T TCM** **Years:** 2005, 2006, 2007 **Models:** 300, 300C, 300M, Charger, Magnum **Engines:** All **Transmissions:** All	**No Ambient Temperature Message** Ignition is on. PCM does not receive an ambient temperature signal over the CAN C circuit from the FCM. The circuit is constantly monitored. **Possible Causes:** • CAN C Bus failure open or shorted • Front Control Module (FCM) has failed • PCM has failed

DTC	Trouble Code Title, Conditions & Possible Causes
DTC: U110F **1T TCM** **Years:** 2005, 2006, 2007 **Models:** 300, 300C, 300M, Charger, Magnum **Engines:** All **Transmissions:** All	**No Fuel Volume Message** Ignition is on. PCM does not receive a fuel volume signal over the CAN C circuit from the FCM. The circuit is constantly monitored. **Possible Causes:** • CAN C Bus failure open or shorted • Front Control Module (FCM) has failed • PCM has failed
DTC: U1110 **1T TCM** **Years:** 2005, 2006, 2007 **Models:** 300, 300C, 300M, Charger, Magnum **Engines:** All **Transmissions:** All	**No Vehicle Speed Message** Ignition is on. PCM does not receive a vehicle speed signal from the ABS module or FCM (non-ABS) over the CAN C circuit. **Possible Causes:** • CAN C Bus failure open or shorted • Front Control Module (FCM) has failed • ABS Module has failed • PCM has failed
DTC: U1120 **1T TCM** **Years:** 2005, 2006, 2007 **Models:** 300, 300C, 300M, Charger, Magnum **Engines:** All **Transmissions:** All	**No Wheel Distance Message** Ignition is on. PCM does not receive a wheel distance signal from the ABS module or FCM (non-ABS) over the CAN C circuit. **Possible Causes:** • CAN C Bus failure open or shorted • Front Control Module (FCM) has failed • ABS Module has failed • PCM has failed
DTC: U1403 **1T TCM** **Years:** 2005, 2006, 2007 **Models:** 300, 300C, 300M, Charger, Magnum **Engines:** All **Transmissions:** All	**Implausible Fuel Level Signal** Ignition is on. The fuel level message that the PCM is receiving is implausible. The circuit is continuously monitored. **Possible Causes:** • CAN B Bus failure open or shorted • Instrument Cluster Module has failed • Front Control Module has failed • PCM has failed
DTC: U1411 **1T TCM** **Years:** 2005, 2006, 2007 **Models:** 300, 300C, 300M, Charger, Magnum **Engines:** All **Transmissions:** All	**Implausible Fuel Volume Signal** Ignition is on. The fuel volume message that the PCM is receiving is implausible. The circuit is continuously monitored. **Possible Causes:** • CAN B Bus failure open or shorted • Instrument Cluster Module has failed • Front Control Module has failed • PCM has failed
DTC: U1412 **1T TCM** **Years:** 2005, 2006, 2007 **Models:** 300, 300C, 300M, Charger, Magnum **Engines:** All **Transmissions:** All	**Implausible Vehicle Speed Signal** Ignition is on. The vehicle speed message that the PCM is receiving over the CAN C circuit from the ABS module or FCM (non-ABS) is implausible. The circuit is continuously monitored. **Possible Causes:** • CAN C Bus failure open or shorted • ABS Module has failed • Front Control Module has failed • PCM has failed
DTC: U1417 **1T TCM** **Years:** 2005, 2006, 2007 **Models:** 300, 300C, 300M, Charger, Magnum **Engines:** All **Transmissions:** All	**Implausible Left Wheel Distance Signal** Ignition is on. The left wheel distance message that the PCM is receiving over the CAN C circuit from the ABS module or FCM (non-ABS) is implausible. The circuit is continuously monitored. **Possible Causes:** • Vehicle speed Sensor fault active in ABS module • CAN C Bus failure open or shorted • ABS Module has failed • Front Control Module has failed • PCM has failed

DTC	Trouble Code Title, Conditions & Possible Causes
DTC: U1418 **1T TCM** **Years:** 2005, 2006, 2007 **Models:** 300, 300C, 300M, Charger, Magnum **Engines:** All **Transmissions:** All	**Implausible Right Wheel Distance Signal** Ignition is on. The left wheel distance message that the PCM is receiving over the CAN C circuit from the ABS module or FCM (non-ABS) is implausible. The circuit is continuously monitored. **Possible Causes:** • Vehicle speed Sensor fault active in ABS module • CAN C Bus failure open or shorted • ABS Module has failed • Front Control Module has failed • PCM has failed

GLOSSARY

ABS: Anti-lock braking system. An electro-mechanical braking system which is designed to minimize or prevent wheel lock-up during braking.

ABSOLUTE PRESSURE: Atmospheric (barometric) pressure plus the pressure gauge reading.

ACCELERATOR PUMP: A small pump located in the carburetor that feeds fuel into the air/fuel mixture during acceleration.

ACCUMULATOR: A device that controls shift quality by cushioning the shock of hydraulic oil pressure being applied to a clutch or band.

ACTUATING MECHANISM: The mechanical output devices of a hydraulic system, for example, clutch pistons and band servos.

ACTUATOR: The output component of a hydraulic or electronic system.

ADVANCE: Setting the ignition timing so that spark occurs earlier before the piston reaches top dead center (TDC).

ADAPTIVE MEMORY (ADAPTIVE STRATEGY): The learning ability of the TCM or PCM to redefine its decision-making process to provide optimum shift quality.

AFTER TOP DEAD CENTER (ATDC): The point after the piston reaches the top of its travel on the compression stroke.

AIR BAG: Device on the inside of the car designed to inflate on impact of crash, protecting the occupants of the car.

AIR CHARGE TEMPERATURE (ACT) SENSOR: The temperature of the airflow into the engine is measured by an ACT sensor, usually located in the lower intake manifold or air cleaner.

AIR CLEANER: An assembly consisting of a housing, filter and any connecting ductwork. The filter element is made up of a porous paper, sometimes with a wire mesh screening, and is designed to prevent airborne particles from entering the engine through the carburetor or throttle body.

AIR INJECTION: One method of reducing harmful exhaust emissions by injecting air into each of the exhaust ports of an engine. The fresh air entering the hot exhaust manifold causes any remaining fuel to be burned before it can exit the tailpipe.

AIR PUMP: An emission control device that supplies fresh air to the exhaust manifold to aid in more completely burning exhaust gases.

AIR/FUEL RATIO: The ratio of air-to-gasoline by weight in the fuel mixture drawn into the engine.

ALDL (assembly line diagnostic link): Electrical connector for scanning ECM/PCM/TCM input and output devices.

ALIGNMENT RACK: A special drive-on vehicle lift apparatus/measuring device used to adjust a vehicle's toe, caster and camber angles.

ALL WHEEL DRIVE: Term used to describe a full time four wheel drive system or any other vehicle drive system that continuously delivers power to all four wheels. This system is found primarily on station wagon vehicles and SUVs not utilized for significant off road use.

ALTERNATING CURRENT (AC): Electric current that flows first in one direction, then in the opposite direction, continually reversing flow.

ALTERNATOR: A device which produces AC (alternating current) which is converted to DC (direct current) to charge the car battery.

AMMETER: An instrument, calibrated in amperes, used to measure the flow of an electrical current in a circuit. Ammeters are always connected in series with the circuit being tested.

AMPERAGE: The total amount of current (amperes) flowing in a circuit.

AMPLIFIER: A device used in an electrical circuit to increase the voltage of an output signal.

AMP/HR. RATING (BATTERY): Measurement of the ability of a battery to deliver a stated amount of current for a stated period of time. The higher the amp/hr. rating, the better the battery.

AMPERE: The rate of flow of electrical current present when one volt of electrical pressure is applied against one ohm of electrical resistance.

ANALOG COMPUTER: Any microprocessor that uses similar (analogous) electrical signals to make its calculations.

ANODIZED: A special coating applied to the surface of aluminum valves for extended service life.

ANTIFREEZE: A substance (ethylene or propylene glycol) added to the coolant to prevent freezing in cold weather.

ANTI-FOAM AGENTS: Minimize fluid foaming from the whipping action encountered in the converter and planetary action.

ANTI-WEAR AGENTS: Zinc agents that control wear on the gears, bushings, and thrust washers.

ANTI-LOCK BRAKING SYSTEM: A supplementary system to the base hydraulic system that prevents sustained lock-up of the wheels during braking as well as automatically controlling wheel slip.

ANTI-ROLL BAR: See stabilizer bar.

ARC: A flow of electricity through the air between two electrodes or contact points that produces a spark.

ARMATURE: A laminated, soft iron core wrapped by a wire that converts electrical energy to mechanical energy as in a motor or relay. When rotated in a magnetic field, it changes mechanical energy into electrical energy as in a generator.

ATDC: After Top Dead Center.

ATF: Automatic transmission fluid.

ATMOSPHERIC PRESSURE: The pressure on the Earth's surface caused by the weight of the air in the atmosphere. At sea level, this pressure is 14.7 psi at 32°F (101 kPa at 0°C).

ATOMIZATION: The breaking down of a liquid into a fine mist that can be suspended in air.

AUXILIARY ADD-ON COOLER: A supplemental transmission fluid cooling device that is installed in series with the heat exchanger (cooler), located inside the radiator, to provide additional support to cool the hot fluid leaving the torque converter.

AUXILIARY PRESSURE: An added fluid pressure that is introduced into a regulator or balanced valve system to control valve movement. The auxiliary pressure itself can be either a fixed or a variable value. (See balanced valve; regulator valve.)

AWD: All wheel drive.

AXIAL FORCE: A side or end thrust force acting in or along the same plane as the power flow.

AXIAL PLAY: Movement parallel to a shaft or bearing bore.

AXLE CAPACITY: The maximum load-carrying capacity of the axle itself, as specified by the manufacturer. This is usually a higher number than the GAWR.

AXLE RATIO: This is a number (3.07:1, 4.56:1, for example) expressing the ratio between driveshaft revolutions and wheel revolutions. A low numerical ratio allows the engine to work easier because it doesn't have to turn as fast. A high numerical ratio means that the engine has to turn more rpm's to move the wheels through the same number of turns.

BACKFIRE: The sudden combustion of gases in the intake or exhaust system that results in a loud explosion.

BACKLASH: The clearance or play between two parts, such as meshed gears.

BACKPRESSURE: Restrictions in the exhaust system that slow the exit of exhaust gases from the combustion chamber.

BAKELITE®: A heat resistant, plastic insulator material commonly used in printed circuit boards and transistorized components.

BALANCED VALVE: A valve that is positioned by opposing auxiliary hydraulic pressures and/or spring force. Examples include mainline regulator, throttle, and governor valves. (See regulator valve.)

BAND: A flexible ring of steel with an inner lining of friction material. When tightened around the outside of a drum, a planetary member is held stationary to the transmission/transaxle case.

BALL BEARING: A bearing made up of hardened inner and outer races between which hardened steel balls roll.

BALL JOINT: A ball and matching socket connecting suspension components (steering knuckle to lower control arms). It permits rotating movement in any direction between the components that are joined.

BARO (BAROMETRIC PRESSURE SENSOR): Measures the change in the intake manifold pressure caused by changes in altitude.

BAROMETRIC MANIFOLD ABSOLUTE PRESSURE (BMAP) SENSOR: Operates similarly to a conventional MAP sensor; reads intake manifold pressure and is also responsible for determining altitude and barometric pressure prior to engine operation.

BAROMETRIC PRESSURE: (See atmospheric pressure.)

BALLAST RESISTOR: A resistor in the primary ignition circuit that lowers voltage after the engine is started to reduce wear on ignition components.

BATTERY: A direct current electrical storage unit, consisting of the basic active materials of lead and sulfuric acid, which converts chemical energy into electrical energy. Used to provide current for the operation of the starter as well as other equipment, such as the radio, lighting, etc.

BEAD: The portion of a tire that holds it on the rim.

BEARING: A friction reducing, supportive device usually located between a stationary part and a moving part.

BEFORE TOP DEAD CENTER (BTDC): The point just before the piston reaches the top of its travel on the compression stroke.

BELTED TIRE: Tire construction similar to bias-ply tires, but using two or more layers of reinforced belts between body plies and the tread.

BEZEL: Piece of metal surrounding radio, headlights, gauges or similar components; sometimes used to hold the glass face of a gauge in the dash.

BIAS-PLY TIRE: Tire construction, using body ply reinforcing cords which run at alternating angles to the center line of the tread.

BI-METAL TEMPERATURE SENSOR: Any sensor or switch made of two dissimilar types of metal that bend when heated or cooled due to the different expansion rates of the alloys. These types of sensors usually function as an on/off switch.

BLOCK: See Engine Block.

BLOW-BY: Combustion gases, composed of water vapor and unburned fuel, that leak past the piston rings into the crankcase during normal engine operation. These gases are removed by the PCV system to prevent the buildup of harmful acids in the crankcase.

BOOK TIME: See Labor Time.

BOOK VALUE: The average value of a car, widely used to determine trade-in and resale value.

BOOST VALVE: Used at the base of the regulator valve to increase mainline pressure.

BORE: Diameter of a cylinder.

BRAKE CALIPER: The housing that fits over the brake disc. The caliper holds the brake pads, which are pressed against the discs by the caliper pistons when the brake pedal is depressed.

BRAKE HORSEPOWER (BHP): The actual horsepower available at the engine flywheel as measured by a dynamometer.

BRAKE FADE: Loss of braking power, usually caused by excessive heat after repeated brake applications.

BRAKE HORSEPOWER: Usable horsepower of an engine measured at the crankshaft.

BRAKE PAD: A brake shoe and lining assembly used with disc brakes.

BRAKE PROPORTIONING VALVE: A valve on the master cylinder which restricts hydraulic brake pressure to the wheels to a specified amount, preventing wheel lock-up.

BREAKAWAY: Often used by Chrysler to identify first-gear operation in D and 2 ranges. In these ranges, first-gear operation depends on a one-way roller clutch that holds on acceleration and releases (breaks away) on deceleration, resulting in a freewheeling coast-down condition.

BRAKE SHOE: The backing for the brake lining. The term is, however, usually applied to the assembly of the brake backing and lining.

BREAKER POINTS: A set of points inside the distributor, operated by a cam, which make and break the ignition circuit.

BRINNELLING: A wear pattern identified by a series of indentations at regular intervals. This condition is caused by a lack of lube, overload situations, and/or vibrations.

BTDC: Before Top Dead Center.

BUMP: Sudden and forceful apply of a clutch or band.

BUSHING: A liner, usually removable, for a bearing; an anti-friction liner used in place of a bearing.

CALIFORNIA ENGINE: An engine certified by the EPA for use in California only; conforms to more stringent emission regulations than Federal engine.

CALIPER: A hydraulically activated device in a disc brake system, which is mounted straddling the brake rotor (disc). The caliper contains at least one piston and two brake pads. Hydraulic pressure on the piston(s) forces the pads against the rotor.

CAPACITY: The quantity of electricity that can be delivered from a unit, as from a battery in ampere-hours, or output, as from a generator.

CAMBER: One of the factors of wheel alignment. Viewed from the front of the car, it is the inward or outward tilt of the wheel. The top of the tire will lean outward (positive camber) or inward (negative camber).

CAMSHAFT: A shaft in the engine on which are the lobes (cams) which operate the valves. The camshaft is driven by the crankshaft, via a belt, chain or gears, at one half the crankshaft speed.

CAPACITOR: A device which stores an electrical charge.

CARBON MONOXIDE (CO): A colorless, odorless gas given off as a normal byproduct of combustion. It is poisonous and extremely dangerous in confined areas, building up slowly to toxic levels without warning if adequate ventilation is not available.

CARBURETOR: A device, usually mounted on the intake manifold of an engine, which mixes the air and fuel in the proper proportion to allow even combustion.

CASTER: The forward or rearward tilt of an imaginary line drawn through the upper ball joint and the center of the wheel. Viewed from the sides, positive caster (forward tilt) lends directional stability, while negative caster (rearward tilt) produces instability.

CATALYTIC CONVERTER: A device installed in the exhaust system, like a muffler, that converts harmful byproducts of combustion into carbon dioxide and water vapor by means of a heat-producing chemical reaction.

CENTRIFUGAL ADVANCE: A mechanical method of advancing the spark timing by using flyweights in the distributor that react to centrifugal force generated by the distributor shaft rotation.

CENTRIFUGAL FORCE: The outward pull of a revolving object, away from the center of revolution. Centrifugal force increases with the speed of rotation.

CETANE RATING: A measure of the ignition value of diesel fuel. The higher the cetane rating, the better the fuel. Diesel fuel cetane rating is roughly comparable to gasoline octane rating.

CHECK VALVE: Any one-way valve installed to permit the flow of air, fuel or vacuum in one direction only.

CHOKE: The valve/plate that restricts the amount of air entering an engine on the induction stroke, thereby enriching the air/fuel ratio.

CHUGGLE: Bucking or jerking condition that may be engine related and may be most noticeable when converter clutch is engaged; similar to the feel of towing a trailer.

CIRCLIP: A split steel snapring that fits into a groove to hold various parts in place.

CIRCUIT BREAKER: A switch which protects an electrical circuit from overload by opening the circuit when the current flow exceeds a pre-determined level. Some circuit breakers must be reset manually, while most reset automatically.

CIRCUIT: Any unbroken path through which an electrical current can flow. Also used to describe fuel flow in some instances.

CIRCUIT, BYPASS: Another circuit in parallel with the major circuit through which power is diverted.

CIRCUIT, CLOSED: An electrical circuit in which there is no interruption of current flow.

CIRCUIT, GROUND: The non-insulated portion of a complete circuit used as a common potential point. In automotive circuits, the ground is composed of metal parts, such as the engine, body sheet metal, and frame and is usually a negative potential.

CIRCUIT, HOT: That portion of a circuit not at ground potential. The hot circuit is usually insulated and is connected to the positive side of the battery.

CIRCUIT, OPEN: A break or lack of contact in an electrical circuit, either intentional (switch) or unintentional (bad connection or broken wire).

CIRCUIT, PARALLEL: A circuit having two or more paths for current flow with common positive and negative tie points. The same voltage is applied to each load device or parallel branch.

CIRCUIT, SERIES: An electrical system in which separate parts are connected end to end, using one wire, to form a single path for current to flow.

CIRCUIT, SHORT: A circuit that is accidentally completed in an electrical path for which it was not intended.

CLAMPING (ISOLATION) DIODES: Diodes positioned in a circuit to prevent self-induction from damaging electronic components.

CLEARCOAT: A transparent layer which, when sprayed over a vehicle's paint job, adds gloss and depth as well as an additional protective coating to the finish.

CLUTCH: Part of the power train used to connect/disconnect power to the rear wheels.

CLUTCH, FLUID: The same as a fluid coupling. A fluid clutch or coupling performs the same function as a friction clutch by utilizing fluid friction and inertia as opposed to solid friction used by a friction clutch. (See fluid coupling.)

CLUTCH, FRICTION: A coupling device that provides a means of smooth and positive engagement and disengagement of engine torque to the vehicle powertrain. Transmission of power through the clutch is accomplished by bringing one or more rotating drive members into contact with complementing driven members.

COAST: Vehicle deceleration caused by engine braking conditions.

COEFFICIENT OF FRICTION: The amount of surface tension between two contacting surfaces; identified by a scientifically calculated number.

COIL: Part of the ignition system that boosts the relatively low voltage supplied by the car's electrical system to the high voltage required to fire the spark plugs.

COMBINATION MANIFOLD: An assembly which includes both the intake and exhaust manifolds in one casting.

COMBINATION VALVE: A device used in some fuel systems that routes fuel vapors to a charcoal storage canister instead of venting them into the atmosphere. The valve relieves fuel tank pressure and allows fresh air into the tank as the fuel level drops to prevent a vapor lock situation.

COMBUSTION CHAMBER: The part of the engine in the cylinder head where combustion takes place.

COMPOUND GEAR: A gear consisting of two or more simple gears with a common shaft.

COMPOUND PLANETARY: A gearset that has more than the three elements found in a simple gearset and is constructed by combining members of two planetary gearsets to create additional gear ratio possibilities.

COMPRESSION CHECK: A test involving removing each spark plug and inserting a gauge. When the engine is cranked, the gauge will record a pressure reading in the individual cylinder. General operating condition can be determined from a compression check.

COMPRESSION RATIO: The ratio of the volume between the piston and cylinder head when the piston is at the bottom of its stroke (bottom dead center) and when the piston is at the top of its stroke (top dead center).

COMPUTER: An electronic control module that correlates input data according to prearranged engineered instructions; used for the management of an actuator system or systems.

CONDENSER: An electrical device which acts to store an electrical charge, preventing voltage surges.
2. A radiator-like device in the air conditioning system in which refrigerant gas condenses into a liquid, giving off heat.

CONDUCTOR: Any material through which an electrical current can be transmitted easily.

CONNECTING ROD: The connecting link between the crankshaft and piston.

CONSTANT VELOCITY JOINT: Type of universal joint in a halfshaft assembly in which the output shaft turns at a constant angular velocity without variation, provided that the speed of the input shaft is constant.

CONTINUITY: Continuous or complete circuit. Can be checked with an ohmmeter.

CONTROL ARM: The upper or lower suspension components which are mounted on the frame and support the ball joints and steering knuckles.

CONVENTIONAL IGNITION: Ignition system which uses breaker points.

CONVERTER: (See torque converter.)

CONVERTER LOCKUP: The switching from hydrodynamic to direct mechanical drive, usually through the application of a friction element called the converter clutch.

COOLANT: Mixture of water and anti-freeze circulated through the engine to carry off heat produced by the engine.

CORROSION INHIBITOR: An inhibitor in ATF that prevents corrosion of bushings, thrust washers, and oil cooler brazed joints.

COUNTERSHAFT: An intermediate shaft which is rotated by a mainshaft and transmits, in turn, that rotation to a working part.

COUPLING PHASE: Occurs when the torque converter is operating at its greatest hydraulic efficiency. The speed differential between the impeller and the turbine is at its minimum. At this point, the stator freewheels, and there is no torque multiplication.

CRANKCASE: The lower part of an engine in which the crankshaft and related parts operate.

CRANKSHAFT: Engine component (connected to pistons by connecting rods) which converts the reciprocating (up and down) motion of pistons to rotary motion used to turn the driveshaft.

CURB WEIGHT: The weight of a vehicle without passengers or payload, but including all fluids (oil, gas, coolant, etc.) and other equipment specified as standard.

CURRENT: The flow (or rate) of electrons moving through a circuit. Current is measured in amperes (amp).

CURRENT FLOW CONVENTIONAL: Current flows through a circuit from the positive terminal of the source to the negative terminal (plus to minus).

CURRENT FLOW, ELECTRON: Current or electrons flow from the negative terminal of the source, through the circuit, to the positive terminal (minus to plus).

CV-JOINT: Constant velocity joint.

CYCLIC VIBRATIONS: The off-center movement of a rotating object that is affected by its initial balance, speed of rotation, and working angles.

CYLINDER BLOCK: See engine block.

CYLINDER HEAD: The detachable portion of the engine, usually fastened to the top of the cylinder block and containing all or most of the combustion chambers. On overhead valve engines, it contains the valves and their operating parts. On overhead cam engines, it contains the camshaft as well.

CYLINDER: In an engine, the round hole in the engine block in which the piston(s) ride.

DATA LINK CONNECTOR (DLC): Current acronym/term applied to the federally mandated, diagnostic junction connector that is used to monitor ECM/PC/TCM inputs, processing strategies, and outputs including diagnostic trouble codes (DTCs).

DEAD CENTER: The extreme top or bottom of the piston stroke.

DECELERATION BUMP: When referring to a torque converter clutch in the applied position, a sudden release of the accelerator pedal causes a forceful reversal of power through the drivetrain (engine braking), just prior to the apply plate actually being released.

DELAYED (LATE OR EXTENDED): Condition where shift is expected but does not occur for a period of time, for example, where clutch or band engagement does not occur as quickly as expected during part throttle or wide open throttle apply of accelerator or when manually downshifting to a lower range.

DETENT: A spring-loaded plunger, pin, ball, or pawl used as a holding device on a ratchet wheel or shaft. In automatic transmissions, a detent mechanism is used for locking the manual valve in place.

DETENT DOWNSHIFT: (See kickdown.)

DETERGENT: An additive in engine oil to improve its operating characteristics.

DETONATION: An unwanted explosion of the air/fuel mixture in the combustion chamber caused by excess heat and compression, advanced timing, or an overly lean mixture. Also referred to as "ping".

DEXRON®: A brand of automatic transmission fluid.

DIAGNOSTIC TROUBLE CODES (DTCs): A digital display from the control module memory that identifies the input, processor, or output device circuit that is related to the powertrain emission/driveability malfunction detected. Diagnostic trouble codes can be read by the MIL to flash any codes or by using a handheld scanner.

DIAPHRAGM: A thin, flexible wall separating two cavities, such as in a vacuum advance unit.

DIESELING: The engine continues to run after the car is shut off; caused by fuel continuing to be burned in the combustion chamber.

DIFFERENTIAL: A geared assembly which allows the transmission of motion between drive axles, giving one axle the ability to rotate faster than the other, as in cornering.

DIFFERENTIAL AREAS: When opposing faces of a spool valve are acted upon by the same pressure but their areas differ in size, the face with the larger area produces the differential force and valve movement. (See spool valve.)

DIFFERENTIAL FORCE: (See differential areas)

DIGITAL READOUT: A display of numbers or a combination of numbers and letters.

DIGITAL VOLT OHMMETER: An electronic diagnostic tool used to measure voltage, ohms and amps as well as several other functions, with the readings displayed on a digital screen in tenths, hundredths and thousandths.

DIODE: An electrical device that will allow current to flow in one direction only.

DIRECT CURRENT (DC): Electrical current that flows in one direction only.

DIRECT DRIVE: The gear ratio is 1:1, with no change occurring in the torque and speed input/output relationship.

DISC BRAKE: A hydraulic braking assembly consisting of a brake disc, or rotor, mounted on an axle shaft, and a caliper assembly containing, usually two brake pads which are activated by hydraulic pressure. The pads are forced against the sides of the disc, creating friction which slows the vehicle.

DISPERSANTS: Suspend dirt and prevent sludge buildup in a liquid, such as engine oil.

DOUBLE BUMP (DOUBLE FEEL): Two sudden and forceful applies of a clutch or band.

DISPLACEMENT: The total volume of air that is displaced by all pistons as the engine turns through one complete revolution.

DISTRIBUTOR: A mechanically driven device on an engine which is responsible for electrically firing the spark plug at a pre-determined point of the piston stroke.

DOHC: Double overhead camshaft.

DOUBLE OVERHEAD CAMSHAFT: The engine utilizes two camshafts mounted in one cylinder head. One camshaft operates the exhaust valves, while the other operates the intake valves.

DOWEL PIN: A pin, inserted in mating holes in two different parts allowing those parts to maintain a fixed relationship.

DRIVELINE: The drive connection between the transmission and the drive wheels.

DRIVE TRAIN: The components that transmit the flow of power from the engine to the wheels. The components include the clutch, transmission, driveshafts (or axle shafts in front wheel drive), U-joints and differential.

DRUM BRAKE: A braking system which consists of two brake shoes and one or two wheel cylinders, mounted on a fixed backing plate, and a brake drum, mounted on an axle, which revolves around the assembly.

DRY CHARGED BATTERY: Battery to which electrolyte is added when the battery is placed in service.

DVOM: Digital volt ohmmeter

DWELL: The rate, measured in degrees of shaft rotation, at which an electrical circuit cycles on and off.

DYNAMIC: An application in which there is rotating or reciprocating motion between the parts.

EARLY: Condition where shift occurs before vehicle has reached proper speed, which tends to labor engine after upshift.

EBCM: See Electronic Control Unit (ECU).

ECM: See Electronic Control Unit (ECU).

ECU: Electronic control unit.

ELECTRODE: Conductor (positive or negative) of electric current.

ELECTROLYSIS: A surface etching or bonding of current conducting transmission/transaxle components that may occur when grounding straps are missing or in poor condition.

ELECTROLYTE: A solution of water and sulfuric acid used to activate the battery. Electrolyte is extremely corrosive.

ELECTROMAGNET: A coil that produces a magnetic field when current flows through its windings.

ELECTROMAGNETIC INDUCTION: A method to create (generate) current flow through the use of magnetism.

ELECTROMAGNETISM: The effects surrounding the relationship between electricity and magnetism.

ELECTROMOTIVE FORCE (EMF): The force or pressure (voltage) that causes current movement in an electrical circuit.

ELECTRONIC CONTROL UNIT: A digital computer that controls engine (and sometimes transmission, brake or other vehicle system) functions based on data received from various sensors. Examples used by some manufacturers include Electronic Brake Control Module (EBCM), Engine Control Module (ECM), Powertrain Control Module (PCM) or Vehicle Control Module (VCM).

ELECTRONIC IGNITION: A system in which the timing and firing of the spark plugs is controlled by an electronic control unit, usually called a module. These systems have no points or condenser.

ELECTRONIC PRESSURE CONTROL (EPC) SOLENOID: A specially designed solenoid containing a spool valve and spring assembly to control fluid mainline pressure. A variable current flow, controlled by the ECM/PCM, varies the internal force of the solenoid on the spool valve and resulting mainline pressure. (See variable force solenoid.)

ELECTRONICS: Miniaturized electrical circuits utilizing semiconductors, solid-state devices, and printed circuits. Electronic circuits utilize small amounts of power.

ELECTRONIFICATION: The application of electronic circuitry to a mechanical device. Regarding automatic transmissions, electrification is incorporated into converter clutch lockup, shift scheduling, and line pressure control systems.

ELECTROSTATIC DISCHARGE (ESD): An unwanted, high-voltage electrical current released by an individual who has taken on a static charge of electricity. Electronic components can be easily damaged by ESD.

ELEMENT: A device within a hydrodynamic drive unit designed with a set of blades to direct fluid flow.

ENAMEL: Type of paint that dries to a smooth, glossy finish.

END BUMP (END FEEL OR SLIP BUMP): Firmer feel at end of shift when compared with feel at start of shift.

END-PLAY: The clearance/gap between two components that allows for expansion of the parts as they warm up, to prevent binding and to allow space for lubrication.

ENERGY: The ability or capacity to do work.

ENGINE: The primary motor or power apparatus of a vehicle, which converts liquid or gas fuel into mechanical energy.

ENGINE BLOCK: The basic engine casting containing the cylinders, the crankshaft main bearings, as well as machined surfaces for the mounting of other components such as the cylinder head, oil pan, transmission, etc.

ENGINE BRAKING: Use of engine to slow vehicle by manually downshifting during zero-throttle coast down.

ENGINE CONTROL MODULE (ECM): Manages the engine and incorporates output control over the torque converter clutch solenoid. (Note: Current designation for the ECM in late model vehicles is PCM.)

ENGINE COOLANT TEMPERATURE (ECT) SENSOR: Prevents converter clutch engagement with a cold engine; also used for shift timing and shift quality.

EP LUBRICANT: EP (extreme pressure) lubricants are specially formulated for use with gears involving heavy loads (transmissions, differentials, etc.).

ETHYL: A substance added to gasoline to improve its resistance to knock, by slowing down the rate of combustion.

ETHYLENE GLYCOL: The base substance of antifreeze.

EXHAUST MANIFOLD: A set of cast passages or pipes which conduct exhaust gases from the engine.

FAIL-SAFE (BACKUP) CONTROL: A substitute value used by the PCM/TCM to replace a faulty signal from an input sensor. The temporary value allows the vehicle to continue to be operated.

FAST IDLE: The speed of the engine when the choke is on. Fast idle speeds engine warm-up.

FEDERAL ENGINE: An engine certified by the EPA for use in any of the 49 states (except California).

FEEDBACK: A circuit malfunction whereby current can find another path to feed load devices.

FEELER GAUGE: A blade, usually metal, of precisely predetermined thickness, used to measure the clearance between two parts.

FILAMENT: The part of a bulb that glows; the filament creates high resistance to current flow and actually glows from the resulting heat.

FINAL DRIVE: An essential part of the axle drive assembly where final gear reduction takes place in the powertrain. In RWD applications and north-south FWD applications, it must also change the power flow direction to the axle shaft by ninety degrees. (Also see axle ratio).

FIRING ORDER: The order in which combustion occurs in the cylinders of an engine. Also the order in which spark is distributed to the plugs by the distributor.

FIRM: A noticeable quick apply of a clutch or band that is considered normal with medium to heavy throttle shift; should not be confused with harsh or rough.

FLAME FRONT: The term used to describe certain aspects of the fuel explosion in the cylinders. The flame front should move in a controlled pattern across the cylinder, rather than simply exploding immediately.

FLARE (SLIPPING): A quick increase in engine rpm accompanied by momentary loss of torque; generally occurs during shift.

FLAT ENGINE: Engine design in which the pistons are horizontally opposed. Porsche, Subaru and some old VW are common examples of flat engines.

FLAT RATE: A dealership term referring to the amount of money paid to a technician for a repair or diagnostic service based on that particular service versus dealership's labor time (NOT based on the actual time the technician spent on the job).

FLAT SPOT: A point during acceleration when the engine seems to lose power for an instant.

FLOODING: The presence of too much fuel in the intake manifold and combustion chamber which prevents the air/fuel mixture from firing, thereby causing a no-start situation.

FLUID: A fluid can be either liquid or gas. In hydraulics, a liquid is used for transmitting force or motion.

FLUID COUPLING: The simplest form of hydrodynamic drive, the fluid coupling consists of two look-alike members with straight radial varies referred to as the impeller (pump) and the turbine. Input torque is always equal to the output torque.

FLUID DRIVE: Either a fluid coupling or a fluid torque converter. (See hydrodynamic drive units.)

FLUID TORQUE CONVERTER: A hydrodynamic drive that has the ability to act both as a torque multiplier and fluid coupling. (See hydrodynamic drive units; torque convertor.)

FLUID VISCOSITY: The resistance of a liquid to flow. A cold fluid (oil) has greater viscosity and flows more slowly than a hot fluid (oil).

FLYWHEEL: A heavy disc of metal attached to the rear of the crankshaft. It smoothes the firing impulses of the engine and keeps the crankshaft turning during periods when no firing takes place. The starter also engages the flywheel to start the engine.

FOOT POUND (ft. lbs., lbs. ft. or sometimes, ft. lb.): The amount of energy or work needed to raise an item weighing one pound, a distance of one foot.

FREEZE PLUG: A plug in the engine block which will be pushed out if the coolant freezes. Sometimes called expansion plugs, they protect the block from cracking should the coolant freeze.

FRICTION: The resistance that occurs between contacting surfaces. This relationship is expressed by a ratio called the coefficient of friction (CL).

FRICTION, COEFFICIENT OF: The amount of surface tension between two contacting surfaces; expressed by a scientifically calculated number.

FRONT END ALIGNMENT: A service to set caster, camber and toe-in to the correct specifications. This will ensure that the car steers and handles properly and that the tires wear properly.

FRICTION MODIFIER: Changes the coefficient of friction of the fluid between the mating steel and composition clutch/band surfaces during the engagement process and allows for a certain amount of intentional slipping for a good "shift-feel".

FRONTAL AREA: The total frontal area of a vehicle exposed to air flow.

FUEL FILTER: A component of the fuel system containing a porous paper element used to prevent any impurities from entering the engine through the fuel system. It usually takes the form of a canister-like housing, mounted in-line with the fuel hose, located anywhere on a vehicle between the fuel tank and engine.

FUEL INJECTION: A system replacing the carburetor that sprays fuel into the cylinder through nozzles. The amount of fuel can be more precisely controlled with fuel injection.

FULL FLOATING AXLE: An axle in which the axle housing extends through the wheel giving bearing support on the outside of the housing. The front axle of a four-wheel drive vehicle is usually a full floating axle, as are the rear axles of many larger (1 ton and over) pick-ups and vans.

FULL-TIME FOUR-WHEEL DRIVE: A four-wheel drive system that continuously delivers power to all four wheels. A differential between the front and rear driveshafts permits variations in axle speeds to control gear wind-up without damage.

FULL THROTTLE DETENT DOWNSHIFT: A quick apply of accelerator pedal to its full travel, forcing a downshift.

FUSE: A protective device in a circuit which prevents circuit overload by breaking the circuit when a specific amperage is present. The device is constructed around a strip or wire of a lower amperage rating than the circuit it is designed to protect. When an amperage higher than that stamped on the fuse is present in the circuit, the strip or wire melts, opening the circuit.

FUSIBLE LINK: A piece of wire in a wiring harness that performs the same job as a fuse. If overloaded, the fusible link will melt and interrupt the circuit.

FWD: Front wheel drive.

GAWR: (Gross axle weight rating) the total maximum weight an axle is designed to carry.

GCW: (Gross combined weight) total combined weight of a tow vehicle and trailer.

GARAGE SHIFT: initial engagement feel of transmission, neutral to reverse or neutral to a forward drive.

GARAGE SHIFT FEEL: A quick check of the engagement quality and responsiveness of reverse and forward gears. This test is done with the vehicle stationary.

GEAR: A toothed mechanical device that acts as a rotating lever to transmit power or turning effort from one shaft to another. (See gear ratio.)

GEAR RATIO: A ratio expressing the number of turns a smaller gear will make to turn a larger gear through one revolution. The ratio is found by dividing the number of teeth on the smaller gear into the number of teeth on the larger gear.

GEARBOX: Transmission

GEAR REDUCTION: Torque is multiplied and speed decreased by the factor of the gear ratio. For example, a 3:1 gear ratio changes an input torque of 180 ft. lbs. and an input speed of 2700 rpm to 540 Ft. lbs. and 900 rpm, respectively. (No account is taken of frictional losses, which are always present.)

GEARTRAIN: A succession of intermeshing gears that form an assembly and provide for one or more torque changes as the power input is transmitted to the power output.

GEL COAT: A thin coat of plastic resin covering fiberglass body panels.

GENERATOR: A device which produces direct current (DC) necessary to charge the battery.

GOVERNOR: A device that senses vehicle speed and generates a hydraulic oil pressure. As vehicle speed increases, governor oil pressure rises.

GROUND CIRCUIT: (See circuit, ground.)

GROUND SIDE SWITCHING: The electrical/electronic circuit control switch is located after the circuit load.

GVWR: (Gross vehicle weight rating) total maximum weight a vehicle is designed to carry including the weight of the vehicle, passengers, equipment, gas, oil, etc.

HALOGEN: A special type of lamp known for its quality of brilliant white light. Originally used for fog lights and driving lights.

HARD CODES: DTCs that are present at the time of testing; also called continuous or current codes.

HARSH(ROUGH): An apply of a clutch or band that is more noticeable than a firm one; considered undesirable at any throttle position.

HEADER TANK: An expansion tank for the radiator coolant. It can be located remotely or built into the radiator.

HEAT RANGE: A term used to describe the ability of a spark plug to carry away heat. Plugs with longer nosed insulators take longer to carry heat off effectively.

HEAT RISER: A flapper in the exhaust manifold that is closed when the engine is cold, causing hot exhaust gases to heat the intake manifold providing better cold engine operation. A thermostatic spring opens the flapper when the engine warms up.

HEAVY THROTTLE: Approximately three-fourths of accelerator pedal travel.

HEMI: A name given an engine using hemispherical combustion chambers.

HERTZ (HZ): The international unit of frequency equal to one cycle per second (10,000 Hertz equals 10,000 cycles per second).

HIGH-IMPEDANCE DVOM (DIGITAL VOLT-OHMMETER): This styled device provides a built-in resistance value and is capable of limiting circuit current flow to safe milliamp levels.

HIGH RESISTANCE: Often refers to a circuit where there is an excessive amount of opposition to normal current flow.

HORSEPOWER: A measurement of the amount of work; one horsepower is the amount of work necessary to lift 33,000 lbs. one foot in one minute. Brake horsepower (bhp) is the horsepower delivered by an engine on a dynamometer. Net horsepower is the power remaining (measured at the flywheel of the engine) that can be used to turn the wheels after power is consumed through friction and running the engine accessories (water pump, alternator, air pump, fan etc.)

HOT CIRCUIT: (See circuit, hot; hot lead.)

HOT LEAD: A wire or conductor in the power side of the circuit. (See circuit, hot.)

HOT SIDE SWITCHING: The electrical/electronic circuit control switch is located before the circuit load.

HUB: The center part of a wheel or gear.

HUNTING (BUSYNESS): Repeating quick series of up-shifts and downshifts that causes noticeable change in engine rpm, for example, as in a 4-3-4 shift pattern.

HYDRAULICS: The use of liquid under pressure to transfer force of motion.

HYDROCARBON (HC): Any chemical compound made up of hydrogen and carbon. A major pollutant formed by the engine as a by-product of combustion.

HYDRODYNAMIC DRIVE UNITS: Devices that transmit power solely by the action of a kinetic fluid flow in a closed recirculating path. An impeller energizes the fluid and discharges the high-speed jet stream into the turbine for power output.

HYDROMETER: An instrument used to measure the specific gravity of a solution.

HYDROPLANING: A phenomenon of driving when water builds up under the tire tread, causing it to lose contact with the road. Slowing down will usually restore normal tire contact with the road.

HYPOID GEARSET: The drive pinion gear may be placed below or above the centerline of the driven gear; often used as a final drive gearset.

IDLE MIXTURE: The mixture of air and fuel (usually about 14:1) being fed to the cylinders. The idle mixture screw(s) are sometimes adjusted as part of a tune-up.

IDLER ARM: Component of the steering linkage which is a geometric duplicate of the steering gear arm. It supports the right side of the center steering link.

IMPELLER: Often called a pump, the impeller is the power input (drive) member of a hydrodynamic drive. As part of the torque converter cover, it acts as a centrifugal pump and puts the fluid in motion.

INCH POUND (inch lbs.; sometimes in. lb. or in. lbs.): One twelfth of a foot pound.

INDUCTANCE: The force that produces voltage when a conductor is passed through a magnetic field.

INDUCTION: A means of transferring electrical energy in the form of a magnetic field. Principle used in the ignition coil to increase voltage.

INITIAL FEEL: A distinct firmer feel at start of shift when compared with feel at finish of shift.

INJECTOR: A device which receives metered fuel under relatively low pressure and is activated to inject the fuel into the engine under relatively high pressure at a predetermined time.

INPUT: In an automatic transmission, the source of power from the engine is absorbed by the torque converter, which provides the power input into the transmission. The turbine drives the input(turbine)shaft.

INPUT SHAFT: The shaft to which torque is applied, usually carrying the driving gear or gears.

INTAKE MANIFOLD: A casting of passages or pipes used to conduct air or a fuel/air mixture to the cylinders.

INTERNAL GEAR: The ring-like outer gear of a planetary gearset with the gear teeth cut on the inside of the ring to provide a mesh with the planet pinions.

ISOLATION (CLAMPING) DIODES: Diodes positioned in a circuit to prevent self-induction from damaging electronic components.

IX ROTARY GEAR PUMP: Contains two rotating members, one shaped with internal gear teeth and the other with external gear teeth. As the gears separate, the fluid fills the gaps between gear teeth, is pulled across a crescent-shaped divider, and then is forced to flow through the outlet as the gears mesh.

IX ROTARY LOBE PUMP: Sometimes referred to as a gerotor type pump. Two rotating members, one shaped with internal lobes and the other with external lobes, separate and then mesh to cause fluid to flow.

JOURNAL: The bearing surface within which a shaft operates.

JUMPER CABLES: Two heavy duty wires with large alligator clips used to provide power from a charged battery to a discharged battery mounted in a vehicle.

JUMPSTART: Utilizing the sufficiently charged battery of one vehicle to start the engine of another vehicle with a discharged battery by the use of jumper cables.

KEY: A small block usually fitted in a notch between a shaft and a hub to prevent slippage of the two parts.

KICKDOWN: Detent downshift system; either linkage, cable, or electrically controlled.

KILO: A prefix used in the metric system to indicate one thousand.

KNOCK: Noise which results from the spontaneous ignition of a portion of the air-fuel mixture in the engine cylinder caused by overly advanced ignition timing or use of incorrectly low octane fuel for that engine.

KNOCK SENSOR: An input device that responds to spark knock, caused by over advanced ignition timing.

LABOR TIME: A specific amount of time required to perform a certain repair or diagnostic service as defined by a vehicle or after-market manufacturer.

LACQUER: A quick-drying automotive paint.

LATE: Shift that occurs when engine is at higher than normal rpm for given amount of throttle.

LIGHT-EMITTING DIODE (LED): A semiconductor diode that emits light as electrical current flows through it; used in some electronic display devices to emit a red or other color light.

LIGHT THROTTLE: Approximately one-fourth of accelerator pedal travel.

LIMITED SLIP: A type of differential which transfers driving force to the wheel with the best traction.

LIMP-IN MODE: Electrical shutdown of the transmission/ transaxle output solenoids, allowing only forward and reverse gears that are hydraulically energized by the manual valve. This permits the vehicle to be driven to a service facility for repair.

LIP SEAL: Molded synthetic rubber seal designed with an outer sealing edge (lip) that points into the fluid containing area to be sealed. This type of seal is used where rotational and axial forces are present.

LITHIUM-BASE GREASE: Chassis and wheel bearing grease using lithium as a base. Not compatible with sodium-base grease.

LOAD DEVICE: A circuit's resistance that converts the electrical energy into light, sound, heat, or mechanical movement.

LOAD RANGE: Indicates the number of plies at which a tire is rated. Load range B equals four-ply rating; C equals six-ply rating; and, D equals an eight-ply rating.

LOAD TORQUE: The amount of output torque needed from the transmission/transaxle to overcome the vehicle load.

LOCKING HUBS: Accessories used on part-time four-wheel drive systems that allow the front wheels to be disengaged from the drive train when four-wheel drive is not being used. When four-wheel drive is desired, the hubs are engaged, locking the wheels to the drive train.

LOCKUP CONVERTER: A torque converter that operates hydraulically and mechanically. When an internal apply plate (lockup plate) clamps to the torque converter cover, hydraulic slippage is eliminated.

LOCK RING: See Circlip or Snapring

MAGNET: Any body with the property of attracting iron or steel.

MAGNETIC FIELD: The area surrounding the poles of a magnet that is affected by its attraction or repulsion forces.

MAIN LINE PRESSURE: Often called control pressure or line pressure, it refers to the pressure of the oil leaving the pump and is controlled by the pressure regulator valve.

MALFUNCTION INDICATOR LAMP (MIL): Previously known as a check engine light, the dash-mounted MIL illuminates and signals the driver that an emission or driveability problem with the powertrain has been detected by the ECM/PCM. When this occurs, at least one diagnostic trouble code (DTC) has been stored into the control module memory.

MANIFOLD ABSOLUTE PRESSURE (MAP) SENSOR: Reads the amount of air pressure (vacuum) in the engine's intake manifold system; its signal is used to analyze engine load conditions.

MANIFOLD VACUUM: Low pressure in an engine intake manifold formed just below the throttle plates. Manifold vacuum is highest at idle and drops under acceleration.

MANIFOLD: A casting of passages or set of pipes which connect the cylinders to an inlet or outlet source.

MANUAL LEVER POSITION SWITCH (MLPS): A mechanical switching unit that is typically mounted externally to the transmission/transaxle to inform the PCM/ECM which gear range the driver has selected.

MANUAL VALVE: Located inside the transmission/transaxle, it is directly connected to the driver's shift lever. The position of the manual valve determines which hydraulic circuits will be charged with oil pressure and the operating mode of the transmission.

MANUAL VALVE LEVER POSITION SENSOR (MVLPS): The input from this device tells the TCM what gear range was selected.

MASS AIR FLOW (MAF) SENSOR: Measures the airflow into the engine.

MASTER CYLINDER: The primary fluid pressurizing device in a hydraulic system. In automotive use, it is found in brake and hydraulic clutch systems and is pedal activated, either directly or, in a power brake system, through the power booster.

MacPherson STRUT: A suspension component combining a shock absorber and spring in one unit.

MEDIUM THROTTLE: Approximately one-half of accelerator pedal travel.

MEGA: A metric prefix indicating one million.

MEMBER: An independent component of a hydrodynamic unit such as an impeller, a stator, or a turbine. It may have one or more elements.

MERCON: A fluid developed by Ford Motor Company in 1988. It contains a friction modifier and closely resembles operating characteristics of Dexron.

METAL SEALING RINGS: Made from cast iron or aluminum, their primary application is with dynamic components involving pressure sealing circuits of rotating members. These rings are designed with either butt or hook lock end joints.

METER (ANALOG): A linear-style meter representing data as lengths; a needle-style instrument interfacing with logical numerical increments. This style of electrical meter uses relatively low impedance internal resistance and cannot be used for testing electronic circuitry.

METER (DIGITAL): Uses numbers as a direct readout to show values. Most meters of this style use high impedance internal resistance and must be used for testing low current electronic circuitry.

MICRO: A metric prefix indicating one-millionth (0.000001).

MILLI: A metric prefix indicating one-thousandth (0.001).

MINIMUM THROTTLE: The least amount of throttle opening required for upshift; normally close to zero throttle.

MISFIRE: Condition occurring when the fuel mixture in a cylinder fails to ignite, causing the engine to run roughly.

MODULE: Electronic control unit, amplifier or igniter of solid state or integrated design which controls the current flow in the ignition primary circuit based on input from the pick-up coil. When the module opens the primary circuit, high secondary voltage is induced in the coil.

MODULATED: In an electronic-hydraulic converter clutch system (or shift valve system), the term modulated refers to the pulsing of a solenoid, at a variable rate. This action controls the buildup of oil pressure in the hydraulic circuit to allow a controlled amount of clutch slippage.

MODULATED CONVERTER CLUTCH CONTROL (MCCC): A pulse width duty cycle valve that controls the converter lockup apply pressure and maximizes smoother transitions between lock and unlock conditions.

MODULATOR PRESSURE (THROTTLE PRESSURE): A hydraulic signal oil pressure relating to the amount of engine load, based on either the amount of throttle plate opening or engine vacuum.

MODULATOR VALVE: A regulator valve that is controlled by engine vacuum, providing a hydraulic pressure that varies in relation to engine torque. The hydraulic torque signal functions to delay the shift pattern and provide a line pressure boost. (See throttle valve.)

MOTOR: An electromagnetic device used to convert electrical energy into mechanical energy.

MULTIPLE-DISC CLUTCH: A grouping of steel and friction lined plates that, when compressed together by hydraulic pressure acting upon a piston, lock or unlock a planetary member.

MULTI-WEIGHT: Type of oil that provides adequate lubrication at both high and low temperatures.

needed to move one amp through a resistance of one ohm.

MUSHY: Same as soft; slow and drawn out clutch apply with very little shift feel.

MUTUAL INDUCTION: The generation of current from one wire circuit to another by movement of the magnetic field surrounding a current-carrying circuit as its ampere flow increases or decreases.

NEEDLE BEARING: A bearing which consists of a number (usually a large number) of long, thin rollers.

NITROGEN OXIDE (NOx): One of the three basic pollutants found in the exhaust emission of an internal combustion engine. The amount of NOx usually varies in an inverse proportion to the amount of HC and CO.

NONPOSITIVE SEALING: A sealing method that allows some minor leakage, which normally assists in lubrication.

O2 SENSOR: Located in the engine's exhaust system, it is an input device to the ECM/PCM for managing the fuel delivery and ignition system. A scanner can be used to observe the fluctuating voltage readings produced by an O2 sensor as the oxygen content of the exhaust is analyzed.

O-RING SEAL: Molded synthetic rubber seal designed with a circular cross-section. This type of seal is used primarily in static applications.

OBD II (ON-BOARD DIAGNOSTICS, SECOND GENERATION): Refers to the federal law mandating tighter control of 1996 and newer vehicle emissions, active monitoring of related devices, and standardization of terminology, data link connectors, and other technician concerns.

OCTANE RATING: A number, indicating the quality of gasoline based on its ability to resist knock. The higher the number, the better the quality. Higher compression engines require higher octane gas.

OEM: Original Equipment Manufactured. OEM equipment is that furnished standard by the manufacturer.

OFFSET: The distance between the vertical center of the wheel and the mounting surface at the lugs. Offset is positive if the center is outside the lug circle; negative offset puts the center line inside the lug circle.

OHM'S LAW: A law of electricity that states the relationship between voltage, current, and resistance. Volts = amperes x ohms

OHM: The unit used to measure the resistance of conductor-to-electrical flow. One ohm is the amount of resistance that limits current flow to one ampere in a circuit with one volt of pressure.

OHMMETER: An instrument used for measuring the resistance, in ohms, in an electrical circuit.

ONE-WAY CLUTCH: A mechanical clutch of roller or sprag design that resists torque or transmits power in one direction only. It is used to either hold or drive a planetary member.

ONE-WAY ROLLER CLUTCH: A mechanical device that transmits or holds torque in one direction only.

OPEN CIRCUIT: A break or lack of contact in an electrical circuit, either intentional (switch) or unintentional (bad connection or broken wire).

ORIFICE: Located in hydraulic oil circuits, it acts as a restriction. It slows down fluid flow to either create back pressure or delay pressure buildup downstream.

OSCILLOSCOPE: A piece of test equipment that shows electric impulses as a pattern on a screen. Engine performance can be analyzed by interpreting these patterns.

OUTPUT SHAFT: The shaft which transmits torque from a device, such as a transmission.

OUTPUT SPEED SENSOR (OSS): Identifies transmission/transaxle output shaft speed for shift timing and may be used to calculate TCC slip; often functions as the VSS (vehicle speed sensor).

OVERDRIVE: (1.) A device attached to or incorporated in a transmission/transaxle that allows the engine to turn less than one full revolution for every complete revolution of the wheels. The net effect is to reduce engine rpm, thereby using less fuel. A typical overdrive gear ratio would be .87:1, instead of the normal 1:1 in high gear. (2.) A gear assembly which produces more shaft revolutions than that transmitted to it.

OVERDRIVE PLANETARY GEARSET: A single planetary gearset designed to provide a direct drive and overdrive ratio. When coupled to a three-speed transmission/transaxle configuration, a four-speed/overdrive unit is present.

OVERHEAD CAMSHAFT (OHC): An engine configuration in which the camshaft is mounted on top of the cylinder head and operates the valve either directly or by means of rocker arms.

OVERHEAD VALVE (OHV): An engine configuration in which all of the valves are located in the cylinder head and the camshaft is located in the cylinder block. The camshaft operates the valves via lifters and pushrods.

OVERRUNCLUTCH: Another name for a one-way mechanical clutch. Applies to both roller and sprag designs.

OVERSTEER: The tendency of some vehicles, when steering into a turn, to over-respond or steer more than required, which could result in excessive slip of the rear wheels. Opposite of under-steer.

OXIDATION STABILIZERS: Absorb and dissipate heat. Automatic transmission fluid has high resistance to varnish and sludge buildup that occurs from excessive heat that is generated primarily in the torque converter. Local temperatures as high as 6000F (3150C) can occur at the clutch plates during engagement, and this heat must be absorbed and dissipated. If the fluid cannot withstand the heat, it burns or oxidizes, resulting in an almost immediate destruction of friction materials, clogged filter screen and hydraulic passages, and sticky valves.

OXIDES OF NITROGEN: See nitrogen oxide (NOx).

OXYGEN SENSOR: Used with a feedback system to sense the presence of oxygen in the exhaust gas and signal the computer which can use the voltage signal to determine engine operating efficiency and adjust the air/fuel ratio.

PARALLEL CIRCUIT: (See circuit, parallel.)

PARTS WASHER: A basin or tub, usually with a built-in pump mechanism and hose used for circulating chemical solvent for the purpose of cleaning greasy, oily and dirty components.

PART-TIME FOUR WHEEL DRIVE: A system that is normally in the two wheel drive mode and only runs in four-wheel drive when the system is manually engaged because more traction is desired. Two or four wheel drive is normally selected by a lever to engage the front axle, but if locking hubs are used, these must also be manually engaged in the Lock position. Otherwise, the front axle will not drive the front wheels.

PASSIVE RESTRAINT: Safety systems such as air bags or automatic seat belts which operate with no action required on the part of the driver or passenger. Mandated by Federal regulations on all vehicles sold in the U.S. after 1990.

PAYLOAD: The weight the vehicle is capable of carrying in addition to its own weight. Payload includes weight of the driver, passengers and cargo, but not coolant, fuel, lubricant, spare tire, etc.

PCM: Powertrain control module.

PCV VALVE: A valve usually located in the rocker cover that vents crankcase vapors back into the engine to be reburned.

PERCOLATION: A condition in which the fuel actually "boils," due to excessive heat. Percolation prevents proper atomization of the fuel causing rough running.

PICK-UP COIL: The coil in which voltage is induced in an electronic ignition.

PING: A metallic rattling sound produced by the engine during acceleration. It is usually due to incorrect ignition timing or a poor grade of gasoline.

PINION: The smaller of two gears. The rear axle pinion drives the ring gear which transmits motion to the axle shafts.

PINION GEAR: The smallest gear in a drive gear assembly.

PISTON: A disc or cup that fits in a cylinder bore and is free to move. In hydraulics, it provides the means of converting hydraulic pressure into a usable force. Examples of piston applications are found in servo, clutch, and accumulator units.

PISTON RING: An open-ended ring which fits into a groove on the outer diameter of the piston. Its chief function is to form a seal between the piston and cylinder wall. Most automotive pistons have three rings: two for compression sealing; one for oil sealing.

PITMAN ARM: A lever which transmits steering force from the steering gear to the steering linkage.

PLANET CARRIER: A basic member of a planetary gear assembly that carries the pinion gears.

PLANET PINIONS: Gears housed in a planet carrier that are in constant mesh with the sun gear and internal gear. Because they have their own independent rotating centers, the pinions are capable of rotating around the sun gear or the inside of the internal gear.

PLANETARY GEAR RATIO: The reduction or overdrive ratio developed by a planetary gearset.

PLANETARY GEARSET: In its simplest form, it is made up of a basic assembly group containing a sun gear, internal gear, and planet carrier. The gears are always in constant mesh and offer a wide range of gear ratio possibilities.

PLANETARY GEARSET (COMPOUND): Two planetary gearsets combined together.

PLANETARY GEARSET (SIMPLE): An assembly of gears in constant mesh consisting of a sun gear, several pinion gears mounted in a carrier, and a ring gear. It provides gear ratio and direction changes, in addition to a direct drive and a neutral.

PLY RATING: A. rating given a tire which indicates strength (but not necessarily actual plies). A two-ply/four-ply rating has only two plies, but the strength of a four-ply tire.

POLARITY: Indication (positive or negative) of the two poles of a battery.

PORT: An opening for fluid intake or exhaust.

POSITIVE SEALING: A sealing method that completely prevents leakage.

POTENTIAL: Electrical force measured in volts; sometimes used interchangeably with voltage.

POWER: The ability to do work per unit of time, as expressed in horsepower; one horsepower equals 33,000 ft. lbs. of work per minute, or 550 ft. lbs. of work per second.

POWER FLOW: The systematic flow or transmission of power through the gears, from the input shaft to the output shaft.

POWER-TO-WEIGHT RATIO: Ratio of horsepower to weight of car.

POWERTRAIN: See Drivetrain.

POWERTRAIN CONTROL MODULE (PCM): Current designation for the engine control module (ECM). In many cases, late model vehicle control units manage the engine as well as the transmission. In other settings, the PCM controls the engine and is interfaced with a TCM to control transmission functions.

Ppm: Parts per million; unit used to measure exhaust emissions.

PREIGNITION: Early ignition of fuel in the cylinder, sometimes due to glowing carbon deposits in the combustion chamber. Preignition can be damaging since combustion takes place prematurely.

PRELOAD: A predetermined load placed on a bearing during assembly or by adjustment.

PRESS FIT: The mating of two parts under pressure, due to the inner diameter of one being smaller than the outer diameter of the other, or vice versa; an interference fit.

PRESSURE: The amount of force exerted upon a surface area.

PRESSURE CONTROL SOLENOID (PCS): An output device that provides a boost oil pressure to the mainline regulator valve to control line pressure. Its operation is determined by the amount of current sent from the PCM.

PRESSURE GAUGE: An instrument used for measuring the fluid pressure in a hydraulic circuit.

PRESSURE REGULATOR VALVE: In automatic transmissions, its purpose is to regulate the pressure of the pump output and supply the basic fluid pressure necessary to operate the transmission. The regulated fluid pressure may be referred to as mainline pressure, line pressure, or control pressure.

PRESSURE SWITCH ASSEMBLY (PSA): Mounted inside the transmission, it is a grouping of oil pressure switches that inputs to the PCM when certain hydraulic passages are charged with oil pressure.

PRESSURE PLATE: A spring-loaded plate (part of the clutch) that transmits power to the driven (friction) plate when the clutch is engaged.

PRIMARY CIRCUIT: The low voltage side of the ignition system which consists of the ignition switch, ballast resistor or resistance wire, bypass, coil, electronic control unit and pick-up coil as well as the connecting wires and harnesses.

PROFILE: Term used for tire measurement (tire series), which is the ratio of tire height to tread width.

PROM (PROGRAMMABLE READ-ONLY MEMORY): The heart of the computer that compares input data and makes the engineered program or strategy decisions about when to trigger the appropriate output based on stored computer instructions.

PULSE GENERATOR: A two-wire pickup sensor used to produce a fluctuating electrical signal. This changing signal is read by the controller to determine the speed of the object and can be used to measure transmission/transaxle input speed, output speed, and vehicle speed.

PSI: Pounds per square inch; a measurement of pressure.

PULSE WIDTH DUTY CYCLE SOLENOID (PULSE WIDTH MODULATED SOLENOID): A computer-controlled solenoid that turns on and off at a variable rate producing a modulated oil pressure; often referred to as a pulse width modulated (PWM) solenoid. Employed in many electronic automatic transmissions and transaxles, these solenoids are used to manage shift control and converter clutch hydraulic circuits.

PUSHROD: A steel rod between the hydraulic valve lifter and the valve rocker arm in overhead valve (OHV) engines.

PUMP: A mechanical device designed to create fluid flow and pressure buildup in a hydraulic system.

QUARTER PANEL: General term used to refer to a rear fender. Quarter panel is the area from the rear door opening to the tail light area and from rear wheel well to the base of the trunk and roof-line.

RACE: The surface on the inner or outer ring of a bearing on which the balls, needles or rollers move.

RACK AND PINION: A type of automotive steering system using a pinion gear attached to the end of the steering shaft. The pinion meshes with a long rack attached to the steering linkage.

RADIAL TIRE: Tire design which uses body cords running at right angles to the center line of the tire. Two or more belts are used to give tread strength. Radials can be identified by their characteristic sidewall bulge.

RADIATOR: Part of the cooling system for a water-cooled engine, mounted in the front of the vehicle and connected to the engine with rubber hoses. Through the radiator, excess combustion heat is dissipated into the atmosphere through forced convection using a water and glycol based mixture that circulates through, and cools, the engine.

RANGE REFERENCE AND CLUTCH/BAND APPLY CHART: A guide that shows the application of clutches and bands for each gear, within the selector range positions. These charts are extremely useful for understanding how the unit operates and for diagnosing malfunctions.

RAVIGNEAUX GEARSET: A compound planetary gearset that features matched dual planetary pinions (sets of two) mounted in a single planet carrier. Two sun gears and one ring mesh with the carrier pinions.

REACTION MEMBER: The stationary planetary member, in a planetary gearset, that is grounded to the transmission/transaxle case through the use of friction and wedging devices known as bands, disc clutches, and one-way clutches.

REACTION PRESSURE: The fluid pressure that moves a spool valve against an opposing force or forces; the area on which the opposing force acts. The opposing force can be a spring or a combination of spring force and auxiliary hydraulic force.

REACTOR, TORQUE CONVERTER: The reaction member of a fluid torque converter, more commonly called a stator. (See stator.)

REAR MAIN OIL SEAL: A synthetic or rope-type seal that prevents oil from leaking out of the engine past the rear main crankshaft bearing.

RECIRCULATING BALL: Type of steering system in which recirculating steel balls occupy the area between the nut and worm wheel, causing a reduction in friction.

RECTIFIER: A device (used primarily in alternators) that permits electrical current to flow in one direction only.

REDUCTION: (See gear reduction.)

REGULATOR VALVE: A valve that changes the pressure of the oil in a hydraulic circuit as the oil passes through the valve by bleeding off (or exhausting) some of the volume of oil supplied to the valve.

REFRIGERANT 12 (R-12) or 134 (R-134): The generic name of the refrigerant used in automotive air conditioning systems.

REGULATOR: A device which maintains the amperage and/or voltage levels of a circuit at predetermined values.

RELAY: A switch which automatically opens and/or closes a circuit.

RELAY VALVE: A valve that directs flow and pressure. Relay valves simply connect or disconnect interrelated passages without restricting the fluid flow or changing the pressure.

RELIEF VALVE: A spring-loaded, pressure-operated valve that limits oil pressure buildup in a hydraulic circuit to a predetermined maximum value.

RELUCTOR: A wheel that rotates inside the distributor and triggers the release of voltage in an electronic ignition.

RESERVOIR: The storage area for fluid in a hydraulic system; often called a sump.

RESIN: A liquid plastic used in body work.

RESIDUAL MAGNETISM: The magnetic strength stored in a material after a magnetizing field has been removed.

RESISTANCE: The opposition to the flow of current through a circuit or electrical device, and is measured in ohms. Resistance is equal to the voltage divided by the amperage.

RESISTOR SPARK PLUG: A spark plug using a resistor to shorten the spark duration. This suppresses radio interference and lengthens plug life.

RESISTOR: A device, usually made of wire, which offers a preset amount of resistance in an electrical circuit.

RESULTANT FORCE: The single effective directional thrust of the fluid force on the turbine produced by the vortex and rotary forces acting in different planes.

RETARD: Set the ignition timing so that spark occurs later (fewer degrees before TDC).

RHEOSTAT: A device for regulating a current by means of a variable resistance.

RING GEAR: The name given to a ring-shaped gear attached to a differential case, or affixed to a flywheel or as part of a planetary gear set.

ROADLOAD: grade.

ROCKER ARM: A lever which rotates around a shaft pushing down (opening) the valve with an end when the other end is pushed up by the pushrod. Spring pressure will later close the valve.

ROCKER PANEL: The body panel below the doors between the wheel opening.

ROLLER BEARING: A bearing made up of hardened inner and outer races between which hardened steel rollers move.

ROLLER CLUTCH: A type of one-way clutch design using rollers and springs mounted within an inner and outer cam race assembly.

ROTARY FLOW: The path of the fluid trapped between the blades of the members as they revolve with the rotation of the torque converter cover (rotational inertia).

ROTOR: (1.) The disc-shaped part of a disc brake assembly, upon which the brake pads bear; also called, brake disc. (2.) The device mounted atop the distributor shaft, which passes current to the distributor cap tower contacts.

ROTARY ENGINE: See Wankel engine.

RPM: Revolutions per minute (usually indicates engine speed).

RTV: A gasket making compound that cures as it is exposed to the atmosphere. It is used between surfaces that are not perfectly machined to one another, leaving a slight gap that the RTV fills and in which it hardens. The letters RTV represent room temperature vulcanizing.

RUN-ON: Condition when the engine continues to run, even when the key is turned off. See dieseling.

SEALED BEAM: A automotive headlight. The lens, reflector and filament from a single unit.

SEATBELT INTERLOCK: A system whereby the car cannot be started unless the seatbelt is buckled.

SECONDARY CIRCUIT: The high voltage side of the ignition system, usually above 20,000 volts. The secondary includes the ignition coil, coil wire, distributor cap and rotor, spark plug wires and spark plugs.

SELF-INDUCTION: The generation of voltage in a current-carrying wire by changing the amount of current flowing within that wire.

SEMI-CONDUCTOR: A material (silicon or germanium) that is neither a good conductor nor an insulator; used in diodes and transistors.

SEMI-FLOATING AXLE: In this design, a wheel is attached to the axle shaft, which takes both drive and cornering loads. Almost all solid axle passenger cars and light trucks use this design.

SENDING UNIT: A mechanical, electrical, hydraulic or electromagnetic device which transmits information to a gauge.

SENSOR: Any device designed to measure engine operating conditions or ambient pressures and temperatures. Usually electronic in nature and designed to send a voltage signal to an on-board computer, some sensors may operate as a simple on/off switch or they may provide a variable voltage signal (like a potentiometer) as conditions or measured parameters change.

SERIES CIRCUIT: (See circuit, series.)

SERPENTINE BELT: An accessory drive belt, with small multiple v-ribs, routed around most or all of the engine-powered accessories such as the alternator and power steering pump. Usually both the front and the back side of the belt comes into contact with various pulleys.

SERVO: In an automatic transmission, it is a piston in a cylinder assembly that converts hydraulic pressure into mechanical force and movement; used for the application of the bands and clutches.

SHIFT BUSYNESS: When referring to a torque converter clutch, it is the frequent apply and release of the clutch plate due to uncommon driving conditions.

SHIFT VALVE: Classified as a relay valve, it triggers the automatic shift in response to a governor and a throttle signal by directing fluid to the appropriate band and clutch apply combination to cause the shift to occur.

SHIM: Spacers of precise, predetermined thickness used between parts to establish a proper working relationship.

SHIMMY: Vibration (sometimes violent) in the front end caused by misaligned front end, out of balance tires or worn suspension components.

SHORT CIRCUIT: An electrical malfunction where current takes the path of least resistance to ground (usually through damaged insulation). Current flow is excessive from low resistance resulting in a blown fuse.

SHUDDER: Repeated jerking or stick-slip sensation, similar to chuggle but more severe and rapid in nature, that may be most noticeable during certain ranges of vehicle speed; also used to define condition after converter clutch engagement.

SIMPSON GEARSET: A compound planetary gear train that integrates two simple planetary gearsets referred to as the front planetary and the rear planetary.

SINGLE OVERHEAD CAMSHAFT: See overhead camshaft.

SKIDPLATE: A metal plate attached to the underside of the body to protect the fuel tank, transfer case or other vulnerable parts from damage.

SLAVE CYLINDER: In automotive use, a device in the hydraulic clutch system which is activated by hydraulic force, disengaging the clutch.

SLIPPING: Noticeable increase in engine rpm without vehicle speed increase; usually occurs during or after initial clutch or band engagement.

SLUDGE: Thick, black deposits in engine formed from dirt, oil, water, etc. It is usually formed in engines when oil changes are neglected.

SNAP RING: A circular retaining clip used inside or outside a shaft or part to secure a shaft, such as a floating wrist pin.

SOFT: Slow, almost unnoticeable clutch apply with very little shift feel.

SOFTCODES: DTCs that have been set into the PCM memory but are not present at the time of testing; often referred to as history or intermittent codes.

SOHC: Single overhead camshaft.

SOLENOID: An electrically operated, magnetic switching device.

SPALLING: A wear pattern identified by metal chips flaking off the hardened surface. This condition is caused by foreign particles, overloading situations, and/or normal wear.

SPARK PLUG: A device screwed into the combustion chamber of a spark ignition engine. The basic construction is a conductive core inside of a ceramic insulator, mounted in an outer conductive base. An electrical charge from the spark plug wire travels along the conductive core and jumps a preset air gap to a grounding point or points at the end of the conductive base. The resultant spark ignites the fuel/air mixture in the combustion chamber.

SPECIFIC GRAVITY (BATTERY): The relative weight of liquid (battery electrolyte) as compared to the weight of an equal volume of water.

SPLINES: Ridges machined or cast onto the outer diameter of a shaft or inner diameter of a bore to enable parts to mate without rotation.

SPLIT TORQUE DRIVE: In a torque converter, it refers to parallel paths of torque transmission, one of which is mechanical and the other hydraulic.

SPONGY PEDAL: A soft or spongy feeling when the brake pedal is depressed. It is usually due to air in the brake lines.

SPOOLVALVE: A precision-machined, cylindrically shaped valve made up of lands and grooves. Depending on its position in the valve bore, various interconnecting hydraulic circuit passages are either opened or closed.

SPRAG CLUTCH: A type of one-way clutch design using cams or contoured-shaped sprags between inner and outer races. (See one-way clutch.)

SPRUNG WEIGHT: The weight of a car supported by the springs.

SQUARE-CUT SEAL: Molded synthetic rubber seal designed with a square- or rectangular-shaped cross-section. This type of seal is used for both dynamic and static applications.

SRS: Supplemental restraint system

STABILIZER (SWAY) BAR: A bar linking both sides of the suspension. It resists sway on turns by taking some of added load from one wheel and putting it on the other.

STAGE: The number of turbine sets separated by a stator. A turbine set may be made up of one or more turbine members. A three-element converter is classified as a single stage.

STALL: In fluid drive transmission/transaxle applications, stall refers to engine rpm with the transmission/transaxle engaged and the vehicle stationary; throttle valve can be in any position between closed and wide open.

STALL SPEED: In fluid drive transmission/transaxle applications, stall speed refers to the maximum engine rpm with the transmission/transaxle engaged and vehicle stationary, when the throttle valve is wide open. (See stall; stall test.)

STALL TEST: A procedure recommended by many manufacturers to help determine the integrity of an engine, the torque converter stator, and certain clutch and band combinations. With the shift lever in each of the forward and reverse positions and with the brakes firmly applied, the accelerator pedal is momentarily pressed to the wide open throttle (WOT) position. The engine rpm reading at full throttle can provide clues for diagnosing the condition of the items listed above.

STALL TORQUE: The maximum design or engineered torque ratio of a fluid torque converter, produced under stall speed conditions. (See stall speed.)

STARTER: A high-torque electric motor used for the purpose of starting the engine, typically through a high ratio geared drive connected to the flywheel ring gear.

STATIC: A sealing application in which the parts being sealed do not move in relation to each other.

STATOR (REACTOR): The reaction member of a fluid torque converter that changes the direction of the fluid as it leaves the turbine to enter the impeller vanes. During the torque multiplication phase, this action assists the impeller's rotary force and results in an increase in torque.

STEERING GEOMETRY: Combination of various angles of suspension components (caster, camber, toe-in); roughly equivalent to front end alignment.

STRAIGHT WEIGHT: Term designating motor oil as suitable for use within a narrow range of temperatures. Outside the narrow temperature range its flow characteristics will not adequately lubricate.

STROKE: The distance the piston travels from bottom dead center to top dead center.

SUBSTITUTION: Replacing one part suspected of a defect with a like part of known quality.

SUMP: The storage vessel or reservoir that provides a ready source of fluid to the pump. In an automatic transmission, the sump is the oil pan. All fluid eventually returns to the sump for recycling into the hydraulic system.

SUN GEAR: In a planetary gearset, it is the center gear that meshes with a cluster of planet pinions.

SUPERCHARGER: An air pump driven mechanically by the engine through belts, chains, shafts or gears from the crankshaft. Two general types of supercharger are the positive displacement and centrifugal type, which pump air in direct relationship to the speed of the engine.

SUPPLEMENTAL RESTRAINT SYSTEM: See air bag.

SURGE: Repeating engine-related feeling of acceleration and deceleration that is less intense than chuggle.

SWITCH: A device used to open, close, or redirect the current in an electrical circuit.

SYNCHROMESH: A manual transmission/transaxle that is equipped with devices (synchronizers) that match the gear speeds so that the transmission/transaxle can be downshifted without clashing gears.

SYNTHETIC OIL: Non-petroleum based oil.

TACHOMETER: A device used to measure the rotary speed of an engine, shaft, gear, etc., usually in rotations per minute.

TDC: Top dead center. The exact top of the piston's stroke.

TEFLON SEALING RINGS: Teflon is a soft, durable, plastic-like material that is resistant to heat and provides excellent sealing. These rings are designed with either scarf-cut joints or as one-piece rings. Teflon sealing rings have replaced many metal ring applications.

TERMINAL: A device attached to the end of a wire or cable to make an electrical connection.

TEST LIGHT, CIRCUIT-POWERED: Uses available circuit voltage to test circuit continuity.

TEST LIGHT, SELF-POWERED: Uses its own battery source to test circuit continuity.

THERMISTOR: A special resistor used to measure fluid temperature; it decreases its resistance with increases in temperature.

THERMOSTAT: A valve, located in the cooling system of an engine, which is closed when cold and opens gradually in response to engine heating, controlling the temperature of the coolant and rate of coolant flow.

THERMOSTATIC ELEMENT: A heat-sensitive, spring-type device that controls a drain port from the upper sump area to the lower sump. When the transaxle fluid reaches operating temperature, the port is closed and the upper sump fills, thus reducing the fluid level in the lower sump.

THROTTLE POSITION (TP) SENSOR: Reads the degree of throttle opening; its signal is used to analyze engine load conditions. The ECM/PCM decides to apply the TCC, or to disengage it for coast or load conditions that need a converter torque boost.

THROTTLE PRESSURE/MODULATOR PRESSURE: A hydraulic signal oil pressure relating to the amount of engine load, based on either the amount of throttle plate opening or engine vacuum.

THROTTLE VALVE: A regulating or balanced valve that is controlled mechanically by throttle linkage or engine vacuum. It sends a hydraulic signal to the shift valve body to control shift timing and shift quality. (See balanced valve; modulator valve.)

THROW-OUT BEARING: As the clutch pedal is depressed, the throwout bearing moves against the spring fingers of the pressure plate, forcing the pressure plate to disengage from the driven disc.

TIE ROD: A rod connecting the steering arms. Tie rods have threaded ends that are used to adjust toe-in.

TIE-UP: Condition where two opposing clutches are attempting to apply at same time, causing engine to labor with noticeable loss of engine rpm.

TIMING BELT: A square-toothed, reinforced rubber belt that is driven by the crankshaft and operates the camshaft.

TIMING CHAIN: A roller chain that is driven by the crankshaft and operates the camshaft.

TIRE ROTATION: Moving the tires from one position to another to make the tires wear evenly.

TOE-IN (OUT): A term comparing the extreme front and rear of the front tires. Closer together at the front is toe-in; farther apart at the front is toe-out.

TOP DEAD CENTER (TDC): The point at which the piston reaches the top of its travel on the compression stroke.

TORQUE: Measurement of turning or twisting force, expressed as foot-pounds or inch-pounds.

TORQUE CONVERTER: A turbine used to transmit power from a driving member to a driven member via hydraulic action, providing changes in drive ratio and torque. In automotive use, it links the driveplate at the rear of the engine to the automatic transmission.

TORQUE CONVERTER CLUTCH: The apply plate (lockup plate) assembly used for mechanical power flow through the converter.

TORQUE PHASE: Sometimes referred to as slip phase or stall phase, torque multiplication occurs when the turbine is turning at a slower speed than the impeller, and the stator is reactionary (stationary). This sequence generates a boost in output torque.

TORQUE RATING (STALL TORQUE): The maximum torque multiplication that occurs during stall conditions, with the engine at wide open throttle (WOT) and zero turbine speed.

TORQUE RATIO: An expression of the gear ratio factor on torque effect. A 3:1 gear ratio or 3:1 torque ratio increases the torque input by the ratio factor of 3. Input torque (100 ft. lbs.) x 3 = output torque (300 ft. lbs.)

TRACTION: The amount of usable tractive effort before the drive wheels slip on the road contact surface.

TORSION BAR SUSPENSION: Long rods of spring steel which take the place of springs. One end of the bar is anchored and the other arm (attached to the suspension) is free to twist. The bars' resistance to twisting causes springing action.

TRACK: Distance between the centers of the tires where they contact the ground.

TRACTION CONTROL: A control system that prevents the spinning of a vehicle's drive wheels when excess power is applied.

TRACTIVE EFFORT: The amount of force available to the drive wheels, to move the vehicle.

TRANSAXLE: A single housing containing the transmission and differential. Transaxles are usually found on front engine/front wheel drive or rear engine/rear wheel drive cars.

TRANSDUCER: A device that changes energy from one form to another. For example, a transducer in a microphone changes sound energy to electrical energy. In automotive air-conditioning controls used in automatic temperature systems, a transducer changes an electrical signal to a vacuum signal, which operates mechanical doors.

TRANSMISSION: A powertrain component designed to modify torque and speed developed by the engine; also provides direct drive, reverse, and neutral.

TRANSMISSION CONTROL MODULE (TCM): Manages transmission functions. These vary according to the manufacturer's product design but may include converter clutch operation, electronic shift scheduling, and mainline pressure.

TRANSMISSION FLUID TEMPERATURE (TFT) SENSOR: Originally called a transmission oil temperature (TOT) sensor, this input device to the ECM/PCM senses the fluid temperature and provides a resistance value. It operates on the thermistor principle.

TRANSMISSION INPUT SPEED (TIS) SENSOR: Measures turbine shaft (input shaft) rpm's and compares to engine rpm's to determine torque converter slip. When compared to the transmission output speed sensor or VSS, gear ratio and clutch engagement timing can be determined.

TRANSMISSION OIL TEMPERATURE (TOT) SENSOR: (See transmission fluid temperature (TFT) sensor.)

TRANSMISSION RANGE SELECTOR (TRS) SWITCH: Tells the module which gear shift position the driver has chosen.

TRANSFER CASE: A gearbox driven from the transmission that delivers power to both front and rear driveshafts in a four-wheel drive system. Transfer cases usually have a high and low range set of gears, used depending on how much pulling power is needed.

TRANSISTOR: A semi-conductor component which can be actuated by a small voltage to perform an electrical switching function.

TREAD WEAR INDICATOR: Bars molded into the tire at right angles to the tread that appear as horizontal bars when 1/16 in. of tread remains.

TREAD WEAR PATTERN: The pattern of wear on tires which can be "read" to diagnose problems in the front suspension.

TUNE-UP: A regular maintenance function, usually associated with the replacement and adjustment of parts and components in the electrical and fuel systems of a vehicle for the purpose of attaining optimum performance.

TURBINE: The output (driven) member of a fluid coupling or fluid torque converter. It is splined to the input (turbine) shaft of the transmission.

TURBOCHARGER: An exhaust driven pump which compresses intake air and forces it into the combustion chambers at higher than atmospheric pressures. The increased air pressure allows more fuel to be burned and results in increased horsepower being produced.

TURBULENCE: The interference of molecules of a fluid (or vapor) with each other in a fluid flow.

TYPE F: Transmission fluid developed and used by Ford Motor Company up to 1982. This fluid type provides a high coefficient of friction.

TYPE 7176: The preferred choice of transmission fluid for Chrysler automatic transmissions and transaxles. Developed in 1986, it closely resembles Dexron and Mercon. Type 7176 is the recommended service fill fluid for all Chrysler products utilizing a lockup torque converter dating back to 1978.

U-JOINT (UNIVERSAL JOINT): A flexible coupling in the drive train that allows the driveshafts or axle shafts to operate at different angles and still transmit rotary power.

UNDERSTEER: The tendency of a car to continue straight ahead while negotiating a turn.

UNIT BODY: Design in which the car body acts as the frame.

UNLEADED FUEL: Fuel which contains no lead (a common gasoline additive). The presence of lead in fuel will destroy the functioning elements of a catalytic converter, making it useless.

UNSPRUNG WEIGHT: The weight of car components not supported by the springs (wheels, tires, brakes, rear axle, control arms, etc.).

UPSHIFT: A shift that results in a decrease in torque ratio and an increase in speed.

VACUUM: A negative pressure; any pressure less than atmospheric pressure.

VACUUM ADVANCE: A device which advances the ignition timing in response to increased engine vacuum.

VACUUM GAUGE: An instrument used for measuring the existing vacuum in a vacuum circuit or chamber. The unit of measure is inches (of mercury in a barometer).

VACUUM MODULATOR: Generates a hydraulic oil pressure in response to the amount of engine vacuum.

VALVES: Devices that can open or close fluid passages in a hydraulic system and are used for directing fluid flow and controlling pressure.

VALVE BODY ASSEMBLY: The main hydraulic control assembly of the transmission/transaxle that contains numerous valves, check balls, and other components to control the distribution of pressurized oil throughout the transmission.

VALVE CLEARANCE: The measured gap between the end of the valve stem and the rocker arm, cam lobe or follower that activates the valve.

VALVE GUIDES: The guide through which the stem of the valve passes.

The guide is designed to keep the valve in proper alignment.

VALVE LASH (clearance): The operating clearance in the valve train.

VALVE TRAIN: The system that operates intake and exhaust valves, consisting of camshaft, valves and springs, lifters, pushrods and rocker arms.

VAPOR LOCK: Boiling of the fuel in the fuel lines due to excess heat. This will interfere with the flow of fuel in the lines and can completely stop the flow. Vapor lock normally only occurs in hot weather.

VARIABLE DISPLACEMENT (VARIABLE CAPACITY) VANE PUMP: Slipper-type vanes, mounted in a revolving rotor and contained within the bore of a movable slide, capture and then force fluid to flow. Movement of the slide to various positions changes the size of the vane chambers and the amount of fluid flow. **Note:** GM refers to this pump design as variable displacement, and Ford terms it variable capacity.

VARIABLE FORCE SOLENOID (VFS): Commonly referred to as the electronic pressure control (EPC) solenoid, it replaces the cable/linkage style of TV system control and is integrated with a spool valve and spring assembly to control pressure. A variable computer-controlled current flow varies the internal force of the solenoid on the spool valve and resulting control pressure.

VARIABLE ORIFICE THERMAL VALVE: Temperature-sensitive hydraulic oil control device that adjusts the size of a circuit path opening. By altering the size of the opening, the oil flow rate is adapted for cold to hot oil viscosity changes.

VARNISH: Term applied to the residue formed when gasoline gets old and stale.

VCM: See Electronic Control Unit (ECU).

VEHICLE SPEED SENSOR (VSS): Provides an electrical signal to the computer module, measuring vehicle speed, and affects the torque converter clutch engagement and release.

VESPEL SEALING RINGS: Hard plastic material that produces excellent sealing in dynamic settings. These rings are found in late versions of the 4T60 and in all 4T60-E and 4T80-E transaxles.

VISCOSITY: The ability of a fluid to flow. The lower the viscosity rating, the easier the fluid will flow. 10 weight motor oil will flow much easier than 40 weight motor oil.

VISCOSITY INDEX IMPROVERS: Keeps the viscosity nearly constant with changes in temperature. This is especially important at low temperatures, when the oil needs to be thin to aid in shifting and for cold-weather starting. Yet it must not be so thin that at high temperatures it will cause excessive hydraulic leakage so that pumps are unable to maintain the proper pressures.

VISCOUS CLUTCH: A specially designed torque converter clutch apply plate that, through the use of a silicon fluid, clamps smoothly and absorbs torsional vibrations.

VOLT: Unit used to measure the force or pressure of electricity. It is defined as the pressure needed to move one amp through the resistance of one ohm.

VOLTAGE: The electrical pressure that causes current to flow. Voltage is measured in volts (V).

VOLTAGE, APPLIED: The actual voltage read at a given point in a circuit. It equals the available voltage of the power supply minus the losses in the circuit up to that point.

VOLTAGE DROP: The voltage lost or used in a circuit by normal loads such as a motor or lamp or by abnormal loads such as a poor (high-resistance) lead or terminal connection.

VOLTAGE REGULATOR: A device that controls the current output of the alternator or generator.

VOLTMETER: An instrument used for measuring electrical force in units called volts. Voltmeters are always connected parallel with the circuit being tested.

VORTEX FLOW: The crosswise or circulatory flow of oil between the blades of the members caused by the centrifugal pumping action of the impeller.

WANKEL ENGINE: An engine which uses no pistons. In place of pistons, triangular-shaped rotors revolve in specially shaped housings.

WATER PUMP: A belt driven component of the cooling system that mounts on the engine, circulating the coolant under pressure.

WATT: The unit for measuring electrical power. One watt is the product of one ampere and one volt (watts equals amps times volts). Wattage is the horsepower of electricity (746 watts equal one horsepower).

WHEEL ALIGNMENT: Inclusive term to describe the front end geometry (caster, camber, toe-in/out).

WHEEL CYLINDER: Found in the automotive drum brake assembly, it is a device, actuated by hydraulic pressure, which, through internal pistons, pushes the brake shoes outward against the drums.

WHEEL WEIGHT: Small weights attached to the wheel to balance the wheel and tire assembly. Out-of-balance tires quickly wear out and also give erratic handling when installed on the front.

WHEELBASE: Distance between the center of front wheels and the center of rear wheels.

WIDE OPEN THROTTLE (WOT): Full travel of accelerator pedal.

WORK: The force exerted to move a mass or object. Work involves motion; if a force is exerted and no motion takes place, no work is done. Work per unit of time is called power. Work = force x distance = ft. lbs. 33,000 ft. lbs. in one minute = 1 horsepower

ZERO-THROTTLE COAST DOWN: A full release of accelerator pedal while vehicle is in motion and in drive range.

Commonly Used Abbreviations

2
2WD	Two Wheel Drive

4
4WD	Four Wheel Drive

A
A/C	Air Conditioning
ABDC	After Bottom Dead Center
ABS	Anti-lock Brakes
AC	Alternating Current
ACL	Air cleaner
ACT	Air Charge Temperature
AIR	Secondary Air Injection
ALCL	Assembly Line Communications Link
ALDL	Assembly Line Diagnostic Link
AT	Automatic Transaxle/Transmission
ATDC	After Top Dead Center
ATF	Automatic Transmission Fluid
ATS	Air Temperature Sensor
AWD	All Wheel Drive

B
BAP	Barometric Absolute Pressure
BARO	Barometric Pressure
BBDC	Before Bottom Dead Center
BCM	Body Control Module
BDC	Bottom Dead Center
BPT	Backpressure Transducer
BTDC	Before Top Dead Center
BVSV	Bimetallic Vacuum Switching Valve

C
CAC	Charge Air Cooler
CARB	California Air Resources Board
CAT	Catalytic Converter
CCC	Computer Command Control
CCCC	Computer Controlled Catalytic Converter
CCCI	Computer Controlled Coil Ignition
CCD	Computer Controlled Dwell
CDI	Capacitor Discharge Ignition
CEC	Computerized Engine Control
CFI	Continuous Fuel Injection
CIS	Continuous Injection System
CIS-E	Continuous Injection System - Electronic
CKP	Crankshaft Position
CL	Closed Loop
CMP	Camshaft Position
CPP	Clutch Pedal Position
CTOX	Continuous Trap Oxidizer System
CTP	Closed Throttle Position
CVC	Constant Vacuum Control
CYL	Cylinder

D
DBC	Dual Bed Catalyst
DC	Direct Current
DFI	Direct Fuel Injection
DIS	Distributorless Ignition System
DLC	Data Link Connector
DMM	Digital Multimeter
DOHC	Double Overhead Camshaft
DRB	Diagnostic Readout Box
DTC	Diagnostic Trouble Code
DTM	Diagnostic Test Mode
DVOM	Digital Volt/Ohmmeter

E
EBCM	Electronic Brake Control Module
ECM	Engine Control Module
ECT	Engine Coolant Temperature
ECU	Engine Control Unit or Electronic Control Unit
EDIS	Electronic Distributorless Ignition System
EEC	Electronic Engine Control
EEPROM	Electrically Erasable Programmable Read Only Memory
EFE	Early Fuel Evaporation
EGR	Exhaust Gas Recirculation
EGRT	Exhaust Gas Recirculation Temperature
EGRVC	EGR Valve Control
EPROM	Erasable Programmable Read Only Memory
EVAP	Evaporative Emissions
EVP	EGR Valve Position

F
FBC	Feedback Carburetor
FEEPROM	Flash Electrically Erasable Programmable Read Only Memory
FF	Flexible Fuel
FI	Fuel Injection
FT	Fuel Trim
FWD	Front Wheel Drive

G
GND	Ground

H
HAC	High Altitude Compensation
HEGO	Heated Exhaust Gas Oxygen sensor
HEI	High Energy Ignition
HO2 Sensor	Heated Oxygen Sensor

I
IAC	Idle Air Control
IAT	Intake Air Temperature
ICM	Ignition Control Module
IFI	Indirect Fuel Injection
IFS	Inertia Fuel Shutoff
ISC	Idle Speed Control
IVSV	Idle Vacuum Switching Valve

Commonly Used Abbreviations

K

KOEO	Key On, Engine Off
KOER	Key ON, Engine Running
KS	Knock Sensor

M

MAF	Mass Air Flow
MAP	Manifold Absolute Pressure
MAT	Manifold Air Temperature
MC	Mixture Control
MDP	Manifold Differential Pressure
MFI	Multiport Fuel Injection
MIL	Malfunction Indicator Lamp or Maintenance
MST	Manifold Surface Temperature
MVZ	Manifold Vacuum Zone

N

NVRAM	Nonvolatile Random Access Memory

O

O2 Sensor	Oxygen Sensor
OBD	On-Board Diagnostic
OC	Oxidation Catalyst
OHC	Overhead Camshaft
OL	Open Loop

P

P/S	Power Steering
PAIR	Pulsed Secondary Air Injection
PCM	Powertrain Control Module
PCS	Purge Control Solenoid
PCV	Positive Crankcase Ventilation
PIP	Profile Ignition Pick-up
PNP	Park/Neutral Position
PROM	Programmable Read Only Memory
PSP	Power Steering Pressure
PTO	Power Take-Off
PTOX	Periodic Trap Oxidizer System

R

RABS	Rear Anti-lock Brake System
RAM	Random Access Memory
ROM	Read Only Memory
RPM	Revolutions Per Minute
RWAL	Rear Wheel Anti-lock Brakes
RWD	Rear Wheel Drive

S

SBC	Single Bed Converter
SBEC	Single Board Engine Controller
SC	Supercharger
SCB	Supercharger Bypass
SFI	Sequential Multiport Fuel Injection
SIR	Supplemental Inflatable Restraint
SOHC	Single Overhead Camshaft
SPL	Smoke Puff Limiter
SPOUT	Spark Output
SRI	Service Reminder Indicator
SRS	Supplemental Restraint System
SRT	System Readiness Test
SSI	Solid State Ignition
ST	Scan Tool
STO	Self-Test Output

T

TAC	Thermostatic Air Cleaner
TBI	Throttle Body Fuel Injection
TC	Turbocharger
TCC	Torque Converter Clutch
TCM	Transmission Control Module
TDC	Top Dead Center
TFI	Thick Film Ignition
TP	Throttle Position
TR Sensor	Transaxle/Transmission Range Sensor
TVV	Thermal Vacuum Valve
TWC	Three-way Catalytic Converter

V

VAF	Volume Air Flow, or Vane Air Flow
VAPS	Variable Assist Power Steering
VRV	Vacuum Regulator Valve
VSS	Vehicle Speed Sensor
VSV	Vacuum Switching Valve

W

WOT	Wide Open Throttle
WU-TWC	Warm Up Three-way Catalytic Converter

ENGLISH TO METRIC CONVERSION: TORQUE

To convert foot-pounds (ft. lbs.) to Newton-meters (Nm), multiply the number of ft. lbs. by 1.36
To convert Newton-meters (Nm) to foot-pounds (ft. lbs.), multiply the number of Nm by 0.7376

ft. lbs.	Nm	ft. lbs.	Nm	ft. lbs.	Nm	ft. lbs.	Nm
0.1	0.1	34	46.2	76	103.4	118	160.5
0.2	0.3	35	47.6	77	104.7	119	161.8
0.3	0.4	36	49.0	78	106.1	120	163.2
0.4	0.5	37	50.3	79	107.4	121	164.6
0.5	0.7	38	51.7	80	108.8	122	165.9
0.6	0.8	39	53.0	81	110.2	123	167.3
0.7	1.0	40	54.4	82	111.5	124	168.6
0.8	1.1	41	55.8	83	112.9	125	170.0
0.9	1.2	42	57.1	84	114.2	126	171.4
1	1.4	43	58.5	85	115.6	127	172.7
2	2.7	44	59.8	86	117.0	128	174.1
3	4.1	45	61.2	87	118.3	129	175.4
4	5.4	46	62.6	88	119.7	130	176.8
5	6.8	47	63.9	89	121.0	131	178.2
6	8.2	48	65.3	90	122.4	132	179.5
7	9.5	49	66.6	91	123.8	133	180.9
8	10.9	50	68.0	92	125.1	134	182.2
9	12.2	51	69.4	93	126.5	135	183.6
10	13.6	52	70.7	94	127.8	136	185.0
11	15.0	53	72.1	95	129.2	137	186.3
12	16.3	54	73.4	96	130.6	138	187.7
13	17.7	55	74.8	97	131.9	139	189.0
14	19.0	56	76.2	98	133.3	140	190.4
15	20.4	57	77.5	99	134.6	141	191.8
16	21.8	58	78.9	100	136.0	142	193.1
17	23.1	59	80.2	101	137.4	143	194.5
18	24.5	60	81.6	102	138.7	144	195.8
19	25.8	61	83.0	103	140.1	145	197.2
20	27.2	62	84.3	104	141.4	146	198.6
21	28.6	63	85.7	105	142.8	147	199.9
22	29.9	64	87.0	106	144.2	148	201.3
23	31.3	65	88.4	107	145.5	149	202.6
24	32.6	66	89.8	108	146.9	150	204.0
25	34.0	67	91.1	109	148.2	151	205.4
26	35.4	68	92.5	110	149.6	152	206.7
27	36.7	69	93.8	111	151.0	153	208.1
28	38.1	70	95.2	112	152.3	154	209.4
29	39.4	71	96.6	113	153.7	155	210.8
30	40.8	72	97.9	114	155.0	156	212.2
31	42.2	73	99.3	115	156.4	157	213.5
32	43.5	74	100.6	116	157.8	158	214.9
33	44.9	75	102.0	117	159.1	159	216.2

METRIC TO ENGLISH CONVERSION: TORQUE

To convert foot-pounds (ft. lbs.) to Newton-meters (Nm), multiply the number of ft. lbs. by 1.36
To convert Newton-meters (Nm) to foot-pounds (ft. lbs.), multiply the number of Nm by 0.7376

Nm	ft. lbs.	Nm	ft. lbs.	Nm	ft. lbs.	Nm	ft. lbs.	Nm	ft. lbs.
0.1	0.1	34	25.0	76	55.9	118	86.8	160	117.6
0.2	0.1	35	25.7	77	56.6	119	87.5	161	118.4
0.3	0.2	36	26.5	78	57.4	120	88.2	162	119.1
0.4	0.3	37	27.2	79	58.1	121	89.0	163	119.9
0.5	0.4	38	27.9	80	58.8	122	89.7	164	120.6
0.6	0.4	39	28.7	81	59.6	123	90.4	165	121.3
0.7	0.5	40	29.4	82	60.3	124	91.2	166	122.1
0.8	0.6	41	30.1	83	61.0	125	91.9	167	122.8
0.9	0.7	42	30.9	84	61.8	126	92.6	168	123.5
1	0.7	43	31.6	85	62.5	127	93.4	169	124.3
2	1.5	44	32.4	86	63.2	128	94.1	170	125.0
3	2.2	45	33.1	87	64.0	129	94.9	171	125.7
4	2.9	46	33.8	88	64.7	130	95.6	172	126.5
5	3.7	47	34.6	89	65.4	131	96.3	173	127.2
6	4.4	48	35.3	90	66.2	132	97.1	174	127.9
7	5.1	49	36.0	91	66.9	133	97.8	175	128.7
8	5.9	50	36.8	92	67.6	134	98.5	176	129.4
9	6.6	51	37.5	93	68.4	135	99.3	177	130.1
10	7.4	52	38.2	94	69.1	136	100.0	178	130.9
11	8.1	53	39.0	95	69.9	137	100.7	179	131.6
12	8.8	54	39.7	96	70.6	138	101.5	180	132.4
13	9.6	55	40.4	97	71.3	139	102.2	181	133.1
14	10.3	56	41.2	98	72.1	140	102.9	182	133.8
15	11.0	57	41.9	99	72.8	141	103.7	183	134.6
16	11.8	58	42.6	100	73.5	142	104.4	184	135.3
17	12.5	59	43.4	101	74.3	143	105.1	185	136.0
18	13.2	60	44.1	102	75.0	144	105.9	186	136.8
19	14.0	61	44.9	103	75.7	145	106.6	187	137.5
20	14.7	62	45.6	104	76.5	146	107.4	188	138.2
21	15.4	63	46.3	105	77.2	147	108.1	189	139.0
22	16.2	64	47.1	106	77.9	148	108.8	190	139.7
23	16.9	65	47.8	107	78.7	149	109.6	191	140.4
24	17.6	66	48.5	108	79.4	150	110.3	192	141.2
25	18.4	67	49.3	109	80.1	151	111.0	193	141.9
26	19.1	68	50.0	110	80.9	152	111.8	194	142.6
27	19.9	69	50.7	111	81.6	153	112.5	195	143.4
28	20.6	70	51.5	112	82.4	154	113.2	196	144.1
29	21.3	71	52.2	113	83.1	155	114.0	197	144.9
30	22.1	72	52.9	114	83.8	156	114.7	198	145.6
31	22.8	73	53.7	115	84.6	157	115.4	199	146.3
32	23.5	74	54.4	116	85.3	158	116.2	200	147.1
33	24.3	75	55.1	117	86.0	159	116.9	201	147.8

ENGLISH/METRIC CONVERSION: TEMPERATURE

To convert Fahrenheit (F°) to Celsius (C°), take F° temperature and subtract 32, multiply the result by 5 and divide the result by 9
To convert Celsius (C°) to Fahrenheit (F°), take C° temperature and multiply it by 9, divide the result by 5 and add 32

F°	C°	F°	C°	C°	F°	C°	F°
-40	-40.0	150	65.6	-38	-36.4	46	114.8
-35	-37.2	155	68.3	-36	-32.8	48	118.4
-30	-34.4	160	71.1	-34	-29.2	50	122
-25	-31.7	165	73.9	-32	-25.6	52	125.6
-20	-28.9	170	76.7	-30	-22	54	129.2
-15	-26.1	175	79.4	-28	-18.4	56	132.8
-10	-23.3	180	82.2	-26	-14.8	58	136.4
-5	-20.6	185	85.0	-24	-11.2	60	140
0	-17.8	190	87.8	-22	-7.6	62	143.6
1	-17.2	195	90.6	-20	-4	64	147.2
2	-16.7	200	93.3	-18	-0.4	66	150.8
3	-16.1	205	96.1	-16	3.2	68	154.4
4	-15.6	210	98.9	-14	6.8	70	158
5	-15.0	212	100.0	-12	10.4	72	161.6
10	-12.2	215	101.7	-10	14	74	165.2
15	-9.4	220	104.4	-8	17.6	76	168.8
20	-6.7	225	107.2	-6	21.2	78	172.4
25	-3.9	230	110.0	-4	24.8	80	176
30	-1.1	235	112.8	-2	28.4	82	179.6
35	1.7	240	115.6	0	32	84	183.2
40	4.4	245	118.3	2	35.6	86	186.8
45	7.2	250	121.1	4	39.2	88	190.4
50	10.0	255	123.9	6	42.8	90	194
55	12.8	260	126.7	8	46.4	92	197.6
60	15.6	265	129.4	10	50	94	201.2
65	18.3	270	132.2	12	53.6	96	204.8
70	21.1	275	135.0	14	57.2	98	208.4
75	23.9	280	137.8	16	60.8	100	212
80	26.7	285	140.6	18	64.4	102	215.6
85	29.4	290	143.3	20	68	104	219.2
90	32.2	295	146.1	22	71.6	106	222.8
95	35.0	300	148.9	24	75.2	108	226.4
100	37.8	305	151.7	26	78.8	110	230
105	40.6	310	154.4	28	82.4	112	233.6
110	43.3	315	157.2	30	86	114	237.2
115	46.1	320	160.0	32	89.6	116	240.8
120	48.9	325	162.8	34	93.2	118	244.4
125	51.7	330	165.6	36	96.8	120	248
130	54.4	335	168.3	38	100.4	122	251.6
135	57.2	340	171.1	40	104	124	255.2
140	60.0	345	173.9	42	107.6	126	258.8
145	62.8	350	176.7	44	111.2	128	262.4

LENGTH CONVERSION

To convert inches (in.) to millimeters (mm), multiply the number of inches by 25.4
To convert millimeters (mm) to inches (in.), multiply the number of millimeters by 0.04

Inches	Millimeters	Inches	Millimeters	Inches	Millimeters	Inches	Millimeters
0.0001	0.00254	0.005	0.1270	0.09	2.286	4	101.6
0.0002	0.00508	0.006	0.1524	0.1	2.54	5	127.0
0.0003	0.00762	0.007	0.1778	0.2	5.08	6	152.4
0.0004	0.01016	0.008	0.2032	0.3	7.62	7	177.8
0.0005	0.01270	0.009	0.2286	0.4	10.16	8	203.2
0.0006	0.01524	0.01	0.254	0.5	12.70	9	228.6
0.0007	0.01778	0.02	0.508	0.6	15.24	10	254.0
0.0008	0.02032	0.03	0.762	0.7	17.78	11	279.4
0.0009	0.02286	0.04	1.016	0.8	20.32	12	304.8
0.001	0.0254	0.05	1.270	0.9	22.86	13	330.2
0.002	0.0508	0.06	1.524	1	25.4	14	355.6
0.003	0.0762	0.07	1.778	2	50.8	15	381.0
0.004	0.1016	0.08	2.032	3	76.2	16	406.4

ENGLISH/METRIC CONVERSION: LENGTH

To convert inches (in.) to millimeters (mm), multiply the number of inches by 25.4
To convert millimeters (mm) to inches (in.), multiply the number of millimeters by 0.04

Inches		Millimeters	Inches		Millimeters	Inches		Millimeters
Fraction	Decimal	Decimal	Fraction	Decimal	Decimal	Fraction	Decimal	Decimal
1/64	0.016	0.397	11/32	0.344	8.731	11/16	0.688	17.463
1/32	0.031	0.794	23/64	0.359	9.128	45/64	0.703	17.859
3/64	0.047	1.191	3/8	0.375	9.525	23/32	0.719	18.256
1/16	0.063	1.588	25/64	0.391	9.922	47/64	0.734	18.653
5/64	0.078	1.984	13/32	0.406	10.319	3/4	0.750	19.050
3/32	0.094	2.381	27/64	0.422	10.716	49/64	0.766	19.447
7/64	0.109	2.778	7/16	0.438	11.113	25/32	0.781	19.844
1/8	0.125	3.175	29/64	0.453	11.509	51/64	0.797	20.241
9/64	0.141	3.572	15/32	0.469	11.906	13/16	0.813	20.638
5/32	0.156	3.969	31/64	0.484	12.303	53/64	0.828	21.034
11/64	0.172	4.366	1/2	0.500	12.700	27/32	0.844	21.431
3/16	0.188	4.763	33/64	0.516	13.097	55/64	0.859	21.828
13/64	0.203	5.159	17/32	0.531	13.494	7/8	0.875	22.225
7/32	0.219	5.556	35/64	0.547	13.891	57/64	0.891	22.622
15/64	0.234	5.953	9/16	0.563	14.288	29/32	0.906	23.019
1/4	0.250	6.350	37/64	0.578	14.684	59/64	0.922	23.416
17/64	0.266	6.747	19/32	0.594	15.081	15/16	0.938	23.813
9/32	0.281	7.144	39/64	0.609	15.478	61/64	0.953	24.209
19/64	0.297	7.541	5/8	0.625	15.875	31/32	0.969	24.606
5/16	0.313	7.938	41/64	0.641	16.272	63/64	0.984	25.003
21/64	0.328	8.334	21/32	0.656	16.669	1/1	1.000	25.400
			43/64	0.672	17.066			